lonely planet

Greece

David Willett
Brigitte Barta
Rosemary Hall
Paul Hellander
Jeanne Oliver

LONELY PLANET PUBLICATIONS
Melbourne • Oakland • London • Paris

GREECE

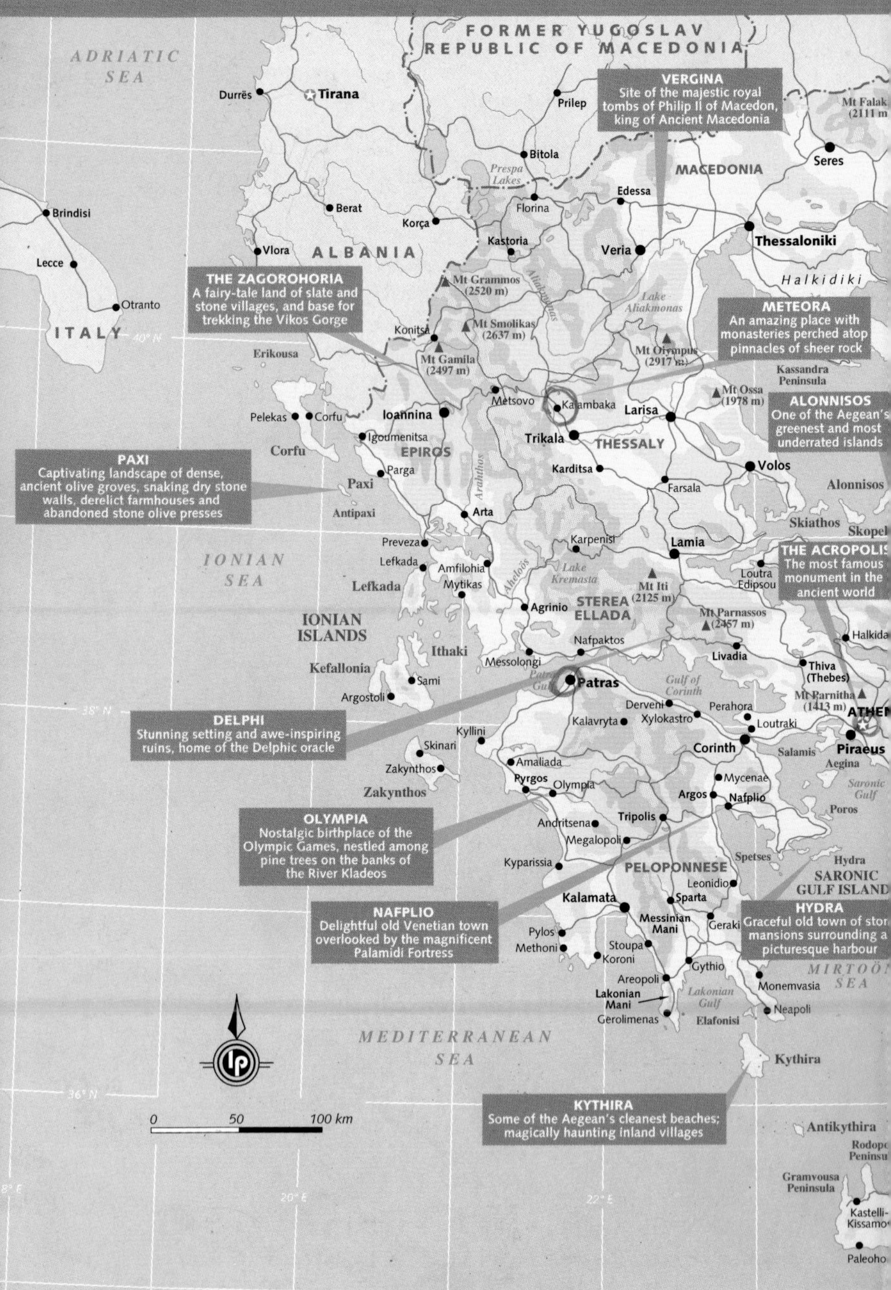
FORMER YUGOSLAV REPUBLIC OF MACEDONIA
ADRIATIC SEA
VERGINA
Site of the majestic royal tombs of Philip II of Macedon, king of Ancient Macedonia
THE ZAGOROHORIA
A fairy-tale land of slate and stone villages, and base for trekking the Vikos Gorge
METEORA
An amazing place with monasteries perched atop pinnacles of sheer rock
ALONNISOS
One of the Aegean's greenest and most underrated islands
PAXI
Captivating landscape of dense, ancient olive groves, snaking dry stone walls, derelict farmhouses and abandoned stone olive presses
THE ACROPOLIS
The most famous monument in the ancient world
DELPHI
Stunning setting and awe-inspiring ruins, home of the Delphic oracle
OLYMPIA
Nostalgic birthplace of the Olympic Games, nestled among pine trees on the banks of the River Kladeos
NAFPLIO
Delightful old Venetian town overlooked by the magnificent Palamidi Fortress
HYDRA
KYTHIRA
Some of the Aegean's cleanest beaches; magically haunting inland villages
Durrës
Tirana
Prilep
Bitola
Prespa Lakes
Florina
Edessa
MACEDONIA
Seres
Brindisi
Berat
Korça
Kastoria
Veria
Thessaloniki
Lecce
Vlora
ALBANIA
Halkidiki
Otranto
ITALY
Mt Grammos (2520 m)
Mt Smolikas (2637 m)
Aliakmonas
Lake Aliakmonas
Konitsa
Mt Gamila (2497 m)
Mt Olympus (2917 m)
Kassandra Peninsula
Erikousa
Metsovo
Kalambaka
Larisa
Mt Ossa (1978 m)
Pelekas
Corfu
Ioannina
Igoumenitsa
Trikala
THESSALY
Corfu
EPIROS
Parga
Karditsa
Volos
Paxi
Arahthos
Farsala
Alonnisos
Antipaxi
Arta
Skiathos
Preveza
Karpenisi
Lamia
IONIAN SEA
Lefkada
Amfilohia
Lake Kremasta
Mt Iti (2125 m)
Loutra Edipsou
Lefkada
Mytikas
Aheloös
STEREA ELLADA
Agrinio
IONIAN ISLANDS
Mt Parnassos (2457 m)
Halkida
Ithaki
Nafpaktos
Livadia
Kefallonia
Messolongi
Thiva (Thebes)
Sami
Patras
Gulf of Corinth
Argostoli
Mt Parnitha (1413 m)
Derveni
Perahora
Kalavryta
Xylokastro
Loutraki
Kyllini
Skinari
Corinth
Salamis
Piraeus
Zakynthos
Amaliada
Aegina
Pyrgos
Olympia
Mycenae
Saronic Gulf
Zakynthos
Argos
Nafplio
Poros
Andritsena
Tripolis
Megalopoli
Kyparissia
Spetses
PELOPONNESE
Hydra
SARONIC
Leonidio
Kalamata
Sparta
Messinian Mani
Geraki
Pylos
Methoni
Stoupa
Koroni
Gythio
Areopoli
Monemvasia
Lakonian Mani
Lakonian Gulf
Neapoli
Gerolimenas
Elafonisi
MEDITERRANEAN SEA
Kythira
Antikythira
Gramvousa Peninsula
Kastelli-Kissamos
Paleohora
0
50
100 km
40° N
38° N
36° N
18° E
20° E
22° E

BULGARIA
Smolyan
Edirne
TURKEY
BLACK SEA
Didymotiho
Evros
İstanbul
Xanthi
Komotini
THRACE
Kavala
Alexandroupolis
DADIA FOREST RESERVE
Wilderness home of some of Europe's last remaining vultures and other large raptors
İzmit
SEA OF MARMARA
THRACIAN SEA
Thasos
Gallipoli
Bandırma
Bursa
Samothraki
Gökçeada
Karyes
Mt Athos (2033 m)
Çanakkale
Athos Peninsula
Myrina
Limnos
Balıkesir
NORTH-EASTERN AEGEAN ISLANDS
Agios Efstratios
Lesvos
Ayvalık
Piperi
Mytilini
Skyros
CHIOS
The extraordinary medieval mastic villages of the south should be on every visitor's itinerary
Uşak
Manisa
Psara
Inousses
EVIA
AEGEAN SEA
Chios
İzmir
Çeşme
TURKEY
Nea Styra
Karystos
ANCIENT DELOS
The most important archaeological site in the Cyclades with many superb mosaics as well as the famous marble lions of Naxos
Aydin
Kuşadası
Denizli
Gavrio
Andros
Samos
IKARIA
Quirky, laid-back villages; great beaches around Armenistis
Kea
Gyaros
Tinos
Ikaria
Agathonisi
Mykonos
Fourni Islands
Arki
Syros
Milas
Renia
Delos
Lipsi
Farmako
Kythnos
Patmos
Naxos
Leros
Serifos
Paros
Donoussa
Bodrum
Sifnos
Kalymnos
Kos
Marmaris
Kimolos
Antiparos
Amorgos
Kos
Datça
RHODES
The splendid fortress city built by the Knights of St John is the largest inhabited medieval town in Europe
Iraklia
Sikinos
Astypalea
Ios
Milos
Folegandros
Santorini (Thira)
Nisyros
Symi
Rhodes
CYCLADES
Thirasia
Anafi
Sirna
Tilos
Alimia
Rhodes
Halki
Kastellorizo
NISYROS
One of the strangest and most beautiful of all Greek islands - an unusual mixture of lush vegetation and barren volcanic moonscapes
DODECANESE
Lindos
SANTORINI
The sheer walls of its volcanic caldera rate among the most spectacular sights in Greece
Katavia
Saria
Karpathos
ELEVATION
3000 m
2000 m
1000 m
500 m
0
SEA OF CRETE
Pigadia
26° E
28° E
30° E
CRETE
Kassos
HANIA
The city's old quarter is a delightful tangle of narrow streets and small squares surrounding the bustling, cafe-lined Venetian harbour
Rethymno
Iraklio
Mt Ida (2456 m)
Agios Nikolaos
Sitia
Matala
Ierapetra
Gavdos

Greece
4th edition – February 2000
First published – February 1994

Published by
Lonely Planet Publications Pty Ltd A.C.N. 005 607 983
192 Burwood Rd, Hawthorn, Victoria 3122, Australia

Lonely Planet Offices
Australia PO Box 617, Hawthorn, Victoria 3122
USA 150 Linden St, Oakland, CA 94607
UK 10a Spring Place, London NW5 3BH
France 1 rue du Dahomey, 75011 Paris

Photographs
Many of the images in this guide are available for licensing from Lonely Planet Images.
email: lpi@lonelyplanet.com.au

Front cover photograph
View of the Acropolis against the Athens skyline (Neil Setchfield)

ISBN 0 86442 682 8

Printed by SNP Offset (M) Sdn Bhd
Printed in Malaysia

Contents – Text

PELOPONNESE 223

CENTRAL GREECE 288

NORTHERN GREECE 328

Contents – Maps

DODECANESE

NORTH-EASTERN AEGEAN ISLANDS

IONIAN ISLANDS

EVIA & THE SPORADES

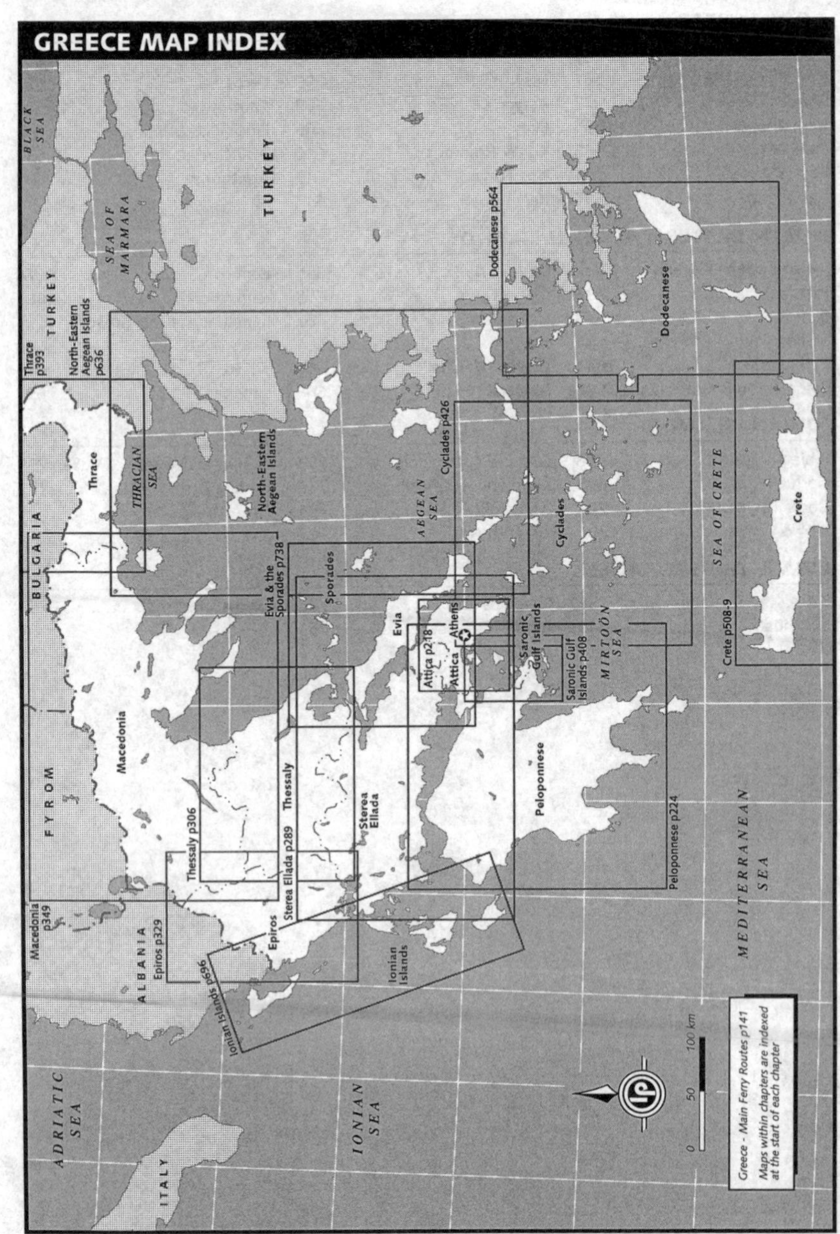
GREECE MAP INDEX
BLACK SEA
SEA OF MARMARA
TURKEY
TURKEY
BULGARIA
FYROM
ALBANIA
ITALY
ADRIATIC SEA
IONIAN SEA
THRACIAN SEA
AEGEAN SEA
MIRTOÖN SEA
SEA OF CRETE
MEDITERRANEAN SEA
Thrace p393
North-Eastern Aegean Islands p636
Macedonia p349
Epiros p329
Ionian Islands p696
Thessaly p306
Sterea Ellada p289
Evia & the Sporades p738
Attica p218
Saronic Gulf Islands p408
Peloponnese p224
Cyclades p426
Dodecanese p564
Crete p508-9
Thrace
North-Eastern Aegean Islands
Macedonia
Epiros
Ionian Islands
Thessaly
Sterea Ellada
Sporades
Evia
Attica
Athens
Saronic Gulf Islands
Peloponnese
Cyclades
Dodecanese
Crete
0
50
100 km
Greece - Main Ferry Routes p141
Maps within chapters are indexed at the start of each chapter

The Authors

David Willett

David is a freelance journalist based near Bellingen on the north coast of New South Wales, Australia. He grew up in Hampshire, England, and wound up in Australia in 1980 after stints working on newspapers in Iran (1975-78) and Bahrain. He spent two years working as a subeditor on the Melbourne *Sun* before trading a steady job for a warmer climate. Between jobs, David has travelled extensively in Europe, the Middle East and Asia.

He is also the author of Lonely Planet's *Tunisia* guide, and has contributed to various other guides, including *Africa, Australia, New South Wales, Indonesia, South-East Asia, Mediterranean Europe* and *Western Europe*. He is the coordinating author of the 1st edition of *Greek Islands*.

Brigitte Barta

Brigitte was born in Wellington, New Zealand. At the age of six months her parents took her to live in Berlin, via Naples, and she first visited Greece when she was three. She grew up mostly in Melbourne, Australia, and later, while roaming Europe, lived for a year on the Greek island of Santorini, where she worked as a cocktail waitress, architectural draftsperson and everything in between. These days she resides in San Francisco and is a senior editor at Lonely Planet's Oakland office.

Rosemary Hall

Rosemary was born in Sunderland, England. She graduated in fine art, but fame and fortune as an artist eluded her, so she spent a few months bumming around Europe and India. After teaching in northern England, she decided to find something more exotic, finally landing a job in Iraq. When, after two years, the Iraqi government refused to renew her work permit, she settled in London, tried to make it again as a painter, did supply teaching, and then travelled in India, South-East Asia and Africa.

Rosemary researched Iraq for Lonely Planet's *West Asia on a shoestring* and wrote the 1st edition of *Greece*. She is the co-author of four walking guides to London.

Paul Hellander

Paul has never really stopped travelling since he was born in England to a Norwegian father and English mother. He graduated with a degree in Ancient, Byzantine and Modern Greek before arriving in Australia in 1977, via Greece and 30 other countries. He subsequently taught Modern Greek and trained interpreters and translators for 13 years before throwing it all away for a life as a travel writer. Paul wrote LP's *Greek phrasebook* before being assigned to *Greece* and *Eastern Europe* where he covers Albania, Bulgaria, the Former Yugoslav Republic of Macedonia and Yugoslavia. Paul has also updated *Singapore* and covered Singapore in the *Malaysia, Singapore & Brunei* and *South-East Asia* guides. He has also worked on *Israel & the Palestinian Territories*, *Jerusalem* and *Middle East*, and wrote the 1st edition of *Cyprus*.

He can usually be found in cyberspace at paul@planetmail.net. When not travelling, he resides in Adelaide, South Australia, where he enjoys cooking Asian food and growing hot chillies.

Jeanne Oliver

Born in New Jersey, USA, Jeanne spent her childhood mulling over the *New York Times* travel section and plotting her future voyages. She received a BA in English and then a law degree but her legal practice was interrupted by ever-more-frequent trips to Central and South America, Europe, the Middle East, Africa and Asia. She finally settled in France to work as a travel writer. Jeanne has contributed to Lonely Planet's *Mediterranean Europe* and *Eastern Europe* guides and wrote the 1st edition of *Croatia*. She can be found in cyberspace at j-oliver@worldnet.fr.

FROM THE AUTHORS

David Willett My thanks go first to my partner, Rowan, and our son, Tom, for holding the fort at home during another extended stay in Greece.

I had a great time in Greece, with a lot of help from friends old and new along the way. Five weeks in Athens flew by, aided and abetted by Maria Economou and Theodoros Nikolaidis from the Greek National Tourism Office; the mysterious Mr Poutsos; Paul and the long-lunch team – Dimitris, Angelos and Angeliki; Matt Barrett and family; Dimitris Agrafiotis; Ana Kamai; Vassilis and Lilika Nastos; and Yiannis and Katerina. I look forward to revisiting my friends in the Peloponnese, particularly Yiannis Dimitreas in Kardamyli and Yiannis and Katerina in Sparta. Thanks also to the many travellers I met on the road, especially Peggy Ives, Janine, Daniel Marlin and Canadian Cathy.

Brigitte Barta Warm thanks to my old friends Sophia, Maria and Andreas Brakoulias and Kyria Giota Bakouli for their generous hospitality every time I visit Athens. Many thanks also to Dimitrios Tsavdaridis for the *mezedes* tours, for the jokes and for the true stories, especially the one about the genie in the bottle at Akrotiri. One thousand thank yous go to the following lovely people: Francesco from Francesco's, and all at Acteon Travel (Ios); Despina Kitini and Stavros Panagopoulos at Naxos Tourist Information Centre, Dimitris Lianos, and Tassos at Vallindras (Naxos); Anna Dakoutros at Dakoutros Travel (Santorini); Giorgos and Rena from the Paros Rooms Association, Zacharias Roussos at Praxis Tours and Cathy Gavalas at Nissiotissa Tours (Paros); Flavio Focciolo at Sottovento Tourism Office (Folegandros); house-fixer Mihalis Venieris, and Ioannis Koundouris (Sikinos); master potter Antonis Kalogirou and master photographer Evangelos Pantazoglou (Sifnos); and Nikitas Simos at Villa Ostria (Koufonisia). Staff at the Sifnos municipal tourist office (Sifnos), Jeyzed Travel (Anafi), TeamWork (Syros), Andros Travel and Greek Sun Holidays (Andros), Sea & Sky (Mykonos) and Aegialis Tours (Amorgos) were also very helpful. Thanks also to editor Shelley Muir and designer Ann Jeffree for patience and support.

Finally, biggest, most special thanks to my man Rob for letting me go. If there's a next time, I hope you can come along.

Rosemary Hall I am grateful to Andrew Stoddart at the Hellenic Book Service in London for his assistance. I also wish to thank the staff of the Greek National Tourism Offices (EOT) and municipal tourist offices I visited in Greece, particularly in Karpenisi, Volos and Rhodes. A special thanks to Tolis in Athens for his hospitality; Nektaria (Arki) for the impromptu Greek lessons; Rena (Lipsi) for assistance and friendship, and for sending a boat to Arki for me when both the inter-island ferry and taxi boat broke down; Alexis from Pension Alexis for the enlightening and entertaining tour of Kos, and Marilena, Maria, Valia and Maro at the Kitsos Makris Folk Art Centre, and Virginia at Il Posto Di Caffe, for filling me in on the hot spots of Volos. Thanks also to Nikos from Hotel Romantzo on Nisyros, Wayne (Patmos), George and Sabine (Agathonisi), and David and Manos (Tilos) for advice and assistance. A big thank you as well to Effie Antonaras and her family on Rhodes for their hospitality, friendship and advice. Finally, thanks to David Willett for his supportive and humorous emails and thanks to all the staff involved with the production of the book.

Paul Hellander During what one person in Greece called the 'largest fly-drive program ever devised', I enlisted and was offered the assistance of many people. I would like to thank a few of them: my wife and photographic assistant Stella for travelling with me and supporting me; the British community of Hora, Alonnisos, for insights into expat life; Andreas & Konstantina Sarmonikas (Limnos) for showing us the good life; Dimitra Kaplanelli (Mytilini) for hospitality and practical assistance; Theo Kosmetos and Melinda McRostie (Mythimna) for more insights and great food; George and Barbara Ballis (Vatera) for welcome hospitality; Demetres Dounas (Athens) for putting up with us yet again; Vasilis Dionysos (Ikaria) for helping us to wrap it all up; Lesvos Shipping Company (NEL) and Strintzis Lines for their excellent service and transport assistance; and especially Geoff Harvey of Driveaway in Sydney for enabling the best fly-drive program ever thought up. Byron and Marcus – another one bites the dust for you.

Jeanne Oliver I would like to thank Toula Chryssanthopoulou of the Greek National Tourism Office (EOT) in Athens for her valuable assistance. Haris Kakoulakis of the EOT office in Iraklion provided an extraordinary amount of advice and assistance that greatly aided the research of this chapter. In Iraklion, Motor Club and Prince Travel helped with my transportation arrangements. A special thanks to Nikos Petrakis and Georgia Stavrakaki of Sitia for their warm welcome and Antonia Karandinou of Sitia for her patience and good humour. Thanks also to David Willett and everyone at LP involved with the production of this book.

This Book

This is the 4th edition of LP's *Greece* guide. The 1st edition was written by Rosemary Hall. The 2nd edition was updated by David Willett, Paul Hellander, Rosemary Hall and Kerry Kenihan, and the 3rd edition by David Willett, Paul Hellander, Rosemary Hall and Corinne Simcock, with David Willett coordinating both editions.

For this 4th edition, the coordinating author was again David Willett, who also updated the introductory chapters and the chapters on Athens, the Peloponnese and the Saronic Gulf Islands. Paul Hellander updated the Northern Greece, North-Eastern Aegean Islands, Ionian Islands and Evia & the Sporades chapters. Rosemary Hall was responsible for the chapters on Central Greece and the Dodecanese, Jeanne Oliver looked after the Crete chapter, and Brigitte Barta updated the Cyclades chapter.

From the Publisher

Production of this edition of *Greece* was coordinated by Shelley Muir (editorial) and Ann Jeffree (mapping and design). Susannah Farfor, Fiona Meiers, Ada Cheung, Kalya Ryan and Susie Ashworth assisted with editing and proofing; Jacqui Saunders, Csanád Csutoros, Joelene Kowalski, Celia Wood, Sarah Sloane and Trudi Canavan assisted with mapping; and Kerrie Williams helped with indexing. New illustrations were provided by Martin Harris, Quentin Frayne prepared the Language section, and the cover was designed by Maria Vallianos. The Philosophy boxed text was written by Rowan McKinnon, and the Art & Architecture section, originally written by Ann Moffat of the Australian National University, was revised by Virginia Maxwell. Most photographs were supplied by Lonely Planet Images, with the remainder supplied by various museums in Greece.

THANKS
Many thanks to the travellers who used the last edition and wrote to us with helpful hints, advice and interesting anecdotes. Your names appear in the back of this book.

Foreword

ABOUT LONELY PLANET GUIDEBOOKS

The story begins with a classic travel adventure: Tony and Maureen Wheeler's 1972 journey across Europe and Asia to Australia. Useful information about the overland trail did not exist at that time, so Tony and Maureen published the first Lonely Planet guidebook to meet a growing need.

From a kitchen table, then from a tiny office in Melbourne (Australia), Lonely Planet has become the largest independent travel publisher in the world, an international company with offices in Melbourne, Oakland (USA), London (UK) and Paris (France).

Today Lonely Planet guidebooks cover the globe. There is an ever-growing list of books and there's information in a variety of forms and media. Some things haven't changed. The main aim is still to help make it possible for adventurous travellers to get out there – to explore and better understand the world.

At Lonely Planet we believe travellers can make a positive contribution to the countries they visit – if they respect their host communities and spend their money wisely. Since 1986 a percentage of the income from each book has been donated to aid projects and human rights campaigns.

Updates Lonely Planet thoroughly updates each guidebook as often as possible. This usually means there are around two years between editions, although for more unusual or more stable destinations the gap can be longer. Check the imprint page (following the colour map at the beginning of the book) for publication dates.

Between editions up-to-date information is available in two free newsletters – the paper *Planet Talk* and email *Comet* (to subscribe, contact any Lonely Planet office) – and on our Web site at www.lonelyplanet.com. The *Upgrades* section of the Web site covers a number of important and volatile destinations and is regularly updated by Lonely Planet authors. *Scoop* covers news and current affairs relevant to travellers. And, lastly, the *Thorn Tree* bulletin board and *Postcards* section of the site carry unverified, but fascinating, reports from travellers.

Correspondence The process of creating new editions begins with the letters, postcards and emails received from travellers. This correspondence often includes suggestions, criticisms and comments about the current editions. Interesting excerpts are immediately passed on via newsletters and the Web site, and everything goes to our authors to be verified when they're researching on the road. We're keen to get more feedback from organisations or individuals who represent communities visited by travellers.

Lonely Planet gathers information for everyone who's curious about the planet – and especially for those who explore it first-hand. Through guidebooks, phrasebooks, activity guides, maps, literature, newsletters, image library, TV series and Web site we act as an information exchange for a worldwide community of travellers.

Research Authors aim to gather sufficient practical information to enable travellers to make informed choices and to make the mechanics of a journey run smoothly. They also research historical and cultural background to help enrich the travel experience and allow travellers to understand and respond appropriately to cultural and environmental issues.

Authors don't stay in every hotel because that would mean spending a couple of months in each medium-sized city and, no, they don't eat at every restaurant because that would mean stretching belts beyond capacity. They do visit hotels and restaurants to check standards and prices, but feedback based on readers' direct experiences can be very helpful.

Many of our authors work undercover, others aren't so secretive. None of them accept freebies in exchange for positive write-ups. And none of our guidebooks contain any advertising.

Production Authors submit their raw manuscripts and maps to offices in Australia, USA, UK or France. Editors and cartographers – all experienced travellers themselves – then begin the process of assembling the pieces. When the book finally hits the shops, some things are already out of date, we start getting feedback from readers and the process begins again ...

WARNING & REQUEST

Things change – prices go up, schedules change, good places go bad and bad places go bankrupt – nothing stays the same. So, if you find things better or worse, recently opened or long since closed, please tell us and help make the next edition even more accurate and useful. We genuinely value all the feedback we receive. Julie Young coordinates a well travelled team that reads and acknowledges every letter, postcard and email and ensures that every morsel of information finds its way to the appropriate authors, editors and cartographers for verification.

Everyone who writes to us will find their name in the next edition of the appropriate guidebook. They will also receive the latest issue of *Planet Talk*, our quarterly printed newsletter, or *Comet*, our monthly email newsletter. Subscriptions to both newsletters are free. The very best contributions will be rewarded with a free guidebook.

Excerpts from your correspondence may appear in new editions of Lonely Planet guidebooks, the Lonely Planet Web site, *Planet Talk* or *Comet*, so please let us know if you *don't* want your letter published or your name acknowledged.

Send all correspondence to the Lonely Planet office closest to you:

Australia: PO Box 617, Hawthorn, Victoria 3122
USA: 150 Linden St, Oakland, CA 94607
UK: 10A Spring Place, London NW5 3BH
France: 1 rue du Dahomey, 75011 Paris

Or email us at: talk2us@lonelyplanet.com.au

For news, views and updates see our Web site: www.lonelyplanet.com

HOW TO USE A LONELY PLANET GUIDEBOOK

The best way to use a Lonely Planet guidebook is any way you choose. At Lonely Planet we believe the most memorable travel experiences are often those that are unexpected, and the finest discoveries are those you make yourself. Guidebooks are not intended to be used as if they provide a detailed set of infallible instructions!

Contents All Lonely Planet guidebooks follow roughly the same format. The Facts about the Destination chapters or sections give background information ranging from history to weather. Facts for the Visitor gives practical information on issues like visas and health. Getting There & Away gives a brief starting point for researching travel to and from the destination. Getting Around gives an overview of the transport options when you arrive.

The peculiar demands of each destination determine how subsequent chapters are broken up, but some things remain constant. We always start with background, then proceed to sights, places to stay, places to eat, entertainment, getting there and away, and getting around information – in that order.

Heading Hierarchy Lonely Planet headings are used in a strict hierarchical structure that can be visualised as a set of Russian dolls. Each heading (and its following text) is encompassed by any preceding heading that is higher on the hierarchical ladder.

Entry Points We do not assume guidebooks will be read from beginning to end, but that people will dip into them. The traditional entry points are the list of contents and the index. In addition, however, some books have a complete list of maps and an index map illustrating map coverage.

There may also be a colour map that shows highlights. These highlights are dealt with in greater detail in the Facts for the Visitor chapter, along with planning questions and suggested itineraries. Each chapter covering a geographical region usually begins with a locator map and another list of highlights. Once you find something of interest in a list of highlights, turn to the index.

Maps Maps play a crucial role in Lonely Planet guidebooks and include a huge amount of information. A legend is printed on the back page. We seek to have complete consistency between maps and text, and to have every important place in the text captured on a map. Map key numbers usually start in the top left corner.

Although inclusion in a guidebook usually implies a recommendation we cannot list every good place. Exclusion does not necessarily imply criticism. In fact there are a number of reasons why we might exclude a place – sometimes it is simply inappropriate to encourage an influx of travellers.

Introduction

Greece has always attracted travellers, drawn by the fascination of some of Europe's earliest civilisations. Philosophers muse that to journey to Greece is to return home, for the legacy of ancient Greece pervades the consciousness of all western nations. Greek Doric, Ionic and Corinthian columns adorn many of our buildings, and much of our greatest early literature drew on the Greek myths for inspiration. Some of our most evocative words are Greek – chaos, drama, tragedy and democracy, to name a few. Perhaps the greatest legacy is democracy itself.

While it was this underlying awareness of Greek culture that drew the wealthy young aristocrats of the 19th century to the country, the majority of today's visitors are drawn by Greece's beaches and sunshine. Island-hopping has become something of an initiation rite for the international singles set. Their numbers are dwarfed, however, by the millions of package holiday-makers who come to Greece every year in search of two weeks of sunshine by the sea.

Package tourism took off with the advent of cheaper airfares in the 1960s and gathered pace through the 70s and 80s. By the early 1990s, almost nine million visitors a year were pouring through the turnstiles, making tourism easily the most important industry in the country.

The ancient sites are an enduring attraction. The Acropolis needs no introduction as the most remarkable legacy of the classical period. At Knossos on Crete, you can wander around the ancient capital of one of Europe's oldest civilisations: the Minoan. The many Minoan, Mycenaean and classical Greek sites, and elaborate Byzantine churches, stand alongside the legacies left by foreign occupiers: towering Venetian, Frankish and Turkish castles, and crumbling, forgotten mosques.

Reminders of the past are everywhere. The Greek landscape is littered with broken columns and crumbling fragments of ancient walls. Moreover, there is hardly a meadow, river or mountaintop which is not sacred because of its association with some deity, and the spectres of the past linger still.

Greece has clung to its traditions more tenaciously than most European countries. Through hundreds of years of foreign occupation by Franks, Venetians, Turks and others, tradition and religion were the factors that kept the notion of Greek nationhood alive. Greeks today remain only too well aware of the hardships their forebears endured, and even hip young people carry on these traditions with enthusiasm.

The traditions manifest themselves in a variety of ways, including regional costumes, such as the baggy pantaloons and high boots worn by elderly Cretan men, and in the embroidered dresses and floral headscarves worn by the women of Olymbos, on Karpathos. Many traditions take the form of festivals, where Greeks express their *joie de vivre* through dancing, singing and feasting.

Festival time or not, the Greek capacity for enjoyment of life is immediately evident. If you arrive in a Greek town in the early evening in summer, you could be forgiven for thinking you've arrived mid-festival. This is the time of the *volta*, when everyone takes to the streets, refreshed from their siesta, dressed up and raring to go. All this adds up to Greece being one of Europe's most relaxed and friendliest countries. But Greece is no European backwater locked in a time warp. In towns and cities you will find discos as lively as any in Italy, France or Britain, and boutiques as trendy.

If you're a beach-lover, Greece, with its 1400 islands, has more coastline than any other country in Europe. You can choose between rocky outcrops, pebbled coves or long swathes of golden sand.

Greece's scenery is as varied as its beaches. There is the semitropical lushness of the Ionian and North-Eastern Aegean Islands and southern Crete; the bare sunbaked rocks of the Cyclades; and the forested mountains, icy lakes and tumbling rivers of northern Greece. Much of this breathtaking landscape is mantled with vibrant wild flowers.

There is yet another phenomenon which even people cynical about anything vaguely supernatural comment upon. It takes the form of inexplicable happenings, coincidences, or fortuitous occurrences. It could be meeting up with a long-lost friend, or bumping into the same person again and again on your travels; or missing the ferry and being offered a lift on a private yacht; or being hot, hungry, thirsty and miles from anywhere, then stumbling upon a house whose occupants offer hospitality.

Perhaps these serendipitous occurrences can be explained as the work of the gods of ancient Greece, who, some claim, have not entirely relinquished their power, and to prove it, occasionally come down to earth to intervene in the lives of mortals.

Facts about Greece

HISTORY

From ancient Minoan palaces and classical Greek temples to spectacular Byzantine churches and remote Frankish castles, the legacy of Greece's long and colourful history is everywhere.

Stone Age

The discovery of a Neanderthal skull in a cave on the Halkidiki peninsula of Macedonia has confirmed the presence of humans in Greece 700,000 years ago. Bones and tools from Palaeolithic times have been found in the Pindos mountains.

The move to a pastoral existence came during Neolithic times (7000-3000 BC). The fertile area that is now Thessaly was the first area to be settled. The people grew barley and wheat, and bred sheep and goats. They used clay to produce pots, vases and simple statuettes of the Great Mother (the earth goddess), whom they worshipped.

By 3000 BC, people were living in settlements complete with streets, squares and mud-brick houses. The villages were centred on a large palace-like structure which belonged to the tribal leader. The most complete Neolithic settlements in Greece are Dimini (inhabited from 4000 to 1200 BC) and Sesklo, both near the city of Volos.

Bronze Age

Around 3000 BC, Indo-European migrants introduced the processing of bronze (an alloy of copper and tin) into Greece – so began three remarkable civilisations: the Cycladic, Minoan and Mycenaean.

Cycladic Civilisation The Cycladic civilisation, centred on the Cyclades islands, is divided into three periods: Early (3000-2000 BC), Middle (2000-1500 BC) and Late (1500-1100 BC). The most impressive legacy of this civilisation is the statuettes carved from Parian marble – the famous Cycladic figurines. Like statuettes from Neolithic times, they depicted images of the Great Mother. Other remains include bronze and obsidian tools and weapons, gold jewellery, and stone and clay vases and pots.

The peoples of the Cycladic civilisation were accomplished sailors who developed prosperous maritime trade links. They exported their wares to Asia Minor (the west of present-day Turkey), Europe and north Africa, as well as to Crete and continental Greece. The Cyclades islands were influenced by both the Minoan and Mycenaean civilisations.

Minoan Civilisation Crete's Minoan civilisation of Crete was the first advanced civilisation to emerge in Europe, drawing its inspiration from two great Middle Eastern civilisations: the Mesopotamian and the Egyptian. Archaeologists divide the Minoan civilisation, like the Cycladic, into three phases: Early (3000-2100 BC), Middle (2100-1500 BC) and Late (1500-1100 BC).

Many aspects of Neolithic life endured during the Early period, but by 2500 BC most people on the island had been assimilated into a new and distinct culture which we now call the Minoan, after the mythical King Minos. The Minoan civilisation reached its peak during the Middle period, producing pottery and metalwork of remarkable beauty and a high degree of imagination and skill.

The Late period saw the civilisation decline both commercially and militarily against Mycenaean competition from the mainland, until its abrupt end around 1100 BC, when Dorian invaders and natural disasters ravaged the island.

Like the Cycladic civilisation, the Minoan was a great maritime power which exported goods throughout the Mediterranean. The polychrome Kamares pottery, which flourished during the Middle period, was highly prized by the Egyptians.

Major Historical Events

Cycladic & Minoan Civilisations 3000-1100 BC

2800 BC Marble figurines carved in Cyclades
2000 BC First palaces built on Crete
1700 BC Minoan palaces (Knossos, Phaestos, Malia & Zakros) rebuilt after earthquake

Mycenaean Age 1900-1100 BC

c1450 BC Massive volcanic eruption on Thira

Dark Age 1200-800 BC

1200 BC Dorians conquer Greece, introducing Iron Age technology
1000 BC First appearance of pottery with geometric patterns (the Geometric Age)
c850 BC The *Iliad* and the *Odyssey* composed, possibly by Homer

Archaic (Middle) Age 800-480 BC

800 BC Emergence of the independent city-states
776 BC First Olympic Games held
600 BC Greek coinage
490 BC Persians defeated at the Battle of Marathon

Classical Age 480-338 BC

461-429 BC Pericles presides over golden age of Athens; plays by Sophocles and Euripides written
438 BC Parthenon completed
431-404 BC Peloponnesian Wars
399 BC Socrates sentenced to death
384 BC Birth of Aristotle

Hellenistic Period 338-146 BC

338 BC Philip of Macedon conquers Greece
323 BC Death of Alexander the Great
168 BC Romans defeat Macedon at the Battle of Pydnaa

The first calamity to strike the Minoans was a violent earthquake in about 1700 BC, which destroyed the palaces at Knossos, Phaestos, Malia and Zakros. The Minoans rebuilt them to a more complex, almost labyrinthine design with multiple storeys, sumptuous royal apartments, reception halls, storerooms, workshops, living quarters for staff and an advanced drainage system. The interiors were decorated with the celebrated Minoan frescoes, now on display in the archaeological museum at Iraklio.

The Minoans were also literate. Their first script resembled Egyptian hieroglyphics, the most famous example of which is the inscription on the Phaestos disc (1700 BC). They progressed to a syllable-based script which 20th century archaeologists have dubbed Linear A, because it consists of linear symbols. Like the earlier hieroglyphics, it has not yet been deciphered, but archaeologists believe that it was used to document trade transactions and the contents of royal storerooms, rather than to express abstract concepts.

Some historians have suggested that the civilisation's decline after 1500 BC was accelerated by the effects of the massive volcanic explosion on the Cycladic island of Santorini (Thira), an eruption vulcanologists believe was more cataclysmic than any on record. They theorise that the fallout of volcanic ash from the blast caused a succession of crop failures – with resulting social upheaval.

Mycenaean Civilisation The decline of the Minoan civilisation in the Late Minoan period coincided with the rise of the first great civilisation on the Greek mainland, the Mycenaean (1900-1100 BC), which reached its peak between 1500 and 1200 BC. Named after the ancient city of Mycenae, where the German archaeologist Heinrich Schliemann made his celebrated finds in 1876, it is also known as the Achaean civilisation after the Indo-European branch of migrants who had settled on mainland Greece and absorbed many aspects of Minoan culture.

Unlike Minoan society, where the lack of city walls seems to indicate relative peace under some form of central authority, Mycenaean civilisation was characterised by independent city-states such as Corinth, Pylos, Tiryns and, the most powerful of them all, Mycenae. These were ruled by kings who inhabited palaces enclosed within massive walls on easily defensible hilltops.

The Mycenaeans' most impressive legacy is their magnificent gold jewellery and ornaments, the best of which can be seen in the National Archaeological Museum in Athens. The Mycenaeans wrote in what is called Linear B (an early form of Greek unrelated to the Linear A of Crete), which has been deciphered. They also worshipped gods who were precursors of the later Greek gods.

Examples of Linear B have also been found on Crete, suggesting that Mycenaean invaders may have conquered the island, perhaps around 1500 BC, when many Minoan palaces were destroyed. Mycenaean influence stretched farther than Crete: the Mycenaean city-states banded together to defeat Troy (Ilium) and thus to protect their trade routes to the Black Sea, and archaeological research has unearthed Mycenaean artefacts as far away as Egypt, Mesopotamia and Italy.

The Mycenaean civilisation came to an end during the 12th century BC when it was overrun by the Dorians.

Geometric Age

The origins of the Dorians remain uncertain. They are generally thought to have come from Epiros or northern Macedonia, but some historians argue that they only arrived from there because they had been driven out of Doris, in central Greece, by the Mycenaeans.

The warrior-like Dorians settled first in the Peloponnese, but soon fanned out over much of the mainland, razing the city-states and enslaving the inhabitants. They later conquered Crete and the south-west coast of Asia Minor. Other Indo-European tribes

Major Historical Events

Roman Rule 146 BC to 324 AD

67 AD Nero starts work on the Corinth Canal
132 Temple of Olympian Zeus completed in Athens

Byzantine Age 324-1453

384 Christianity becomes the official religion of Greece
529 Emperor Justinian closes schools of philosophy in Athens
1204 Crusaders sack Constantinople
1210 Venetians occupy Crete

Ottoman Rule 1453-1829

1453 Ottoman Turks capture Constantinople
1669 Iraklio, Crete, surrenders to Turks after a 21 year siege
1821 Bishop Germanos raises the Greek flag at Patras, starting the War of Independence
1829 Turks accept Greek independence by the Treaty of Adrianople

Modern Greece 1829-Present

1893 Corinth Canal completed
1896 First modern Olympics in Athens
1923 Compulsory population exchange with Turkey agreed at the Treaty of Lausanne; republic proclaimed
1935 Monarchy restored
1946-49 Greek civil war
1967-74 Military rule
1974 Democracy restored under Konstantinos Karamanlis
1981 Andreas Papandreou becomes Greece's first socialist leader when PASOK wins elections; Greece joins EC
1990 Konstantinos Mitsotakis' conservative ND party wins the general election
1993 Papandreou's socialist PASOK party back in power
1996 Costas Simitis elected to lead PASOK

known as the Thessalians settled in what is now Thessaly. Of the original Greek tribal groups, the Aeolians fled to the north-west coast of Asia Minor; the Ionians sought refuge on the central coast and the islands of Lesvos, Samos and Chios, although they also held out in mainland Greece – in Attica and the well fortified city of Athens.

The Dorians brought a traumatic break with the past, and the next 400 years are often referred to as Greece's 'dark age'. But it would be unfair to dismiss the Dorians completely; they brought iron with them and developed a new style of pottery, decorated with striking geometrical designs – although art historians are still out to lunch as to whether the Dorians merely copied the designs perfected by Ionians in Attica. The Dorians worshipped male gods instead of fertility goddesses and adopted the Mycenaean gods of Poseidon, Zeus and Apollo, paving the way for the later Greek religious pantheon.

Perhaps most importantly, the Dorian warriors developed into a class of landholding aristocrats. This worsened the lot of the average farmer but also brought about the demise of the monarchy as a system of government, along with a resurgence of the Mycenaean pattern of independent city-states, this time led by wealthy aristocrats instead of absolute monarchs – the beginnings of 'democratic' government.

Archaic Age

By about 800 BC, local agriculture and animal husbandry had become productive enough to trigger a resumption of maritime trading. New Greek colonies were established in north Africa, Italy, Sicily, southern France and southern Spain to fill the vacuum left by the decline of those other great Mediterranean traders, the Phoenicians.

The people of the various city-states were unified by the development of a Greek alphabet (of Phoenician origin, though the Greeks introduced vowels), the verses of Homer (which created a sense of a shared Mycenaean past), the establishment of the Olympic Games (which brought all the city-states together), and the setting up of central sanctuaries such as Delphi (a neutral meeting ground for lively negotiations), giving Greeks, for the first time, a sense of national identity. This period is known as the Archaic, or Middle, Age.

LOUISE KLEP

Geometric detail from an urn, 750 BC

Most city-states were built to a similar plan, with a fortified acropolis (highest point of a city). The acropolis contained the cities' temples and treasury and also served as a refuge during invasions. Outside the acropolis was the *agora* (market), a bustling commercial quarter, and beyond it the residential areas.

The city-states were autonomous, free to pursue their own interests as they saw fit. Most city-states abolished monarchic rule in favour of an aristocratic form of government, usually headed by an *arhon* (chief magistrate). Aristocrats were often disliked by the population because of their inherited privileges, and some city-states fell to the rule of tyrants after Kypselos started the practice in Corinth around 650 BC. Tyrants seized their position rather than inheriting it. These days they've got an image problem, but in ancient times they were often seen as being on the side of ordinary citizens.

Athens & Solon The seafaring city-state of Athens, meanwhile, was still in the hands of aristocrats, and a failed coup attempt by a would-be tyrant led the legislator Draco to draw up his infamous laws in 620 BC (hence the word 'draconian'). These were so harsh that even the theft of a cabbage was punishable by death.

Solon was appointed arhon in 594 BC with a far-reaching mandate to defuse the mounting tensions between the haves and the have-nots. He cancelled all debts and freed those who had become enslaved because of their debts. Declaring all free Athenians equal by law, he abolished inherited privileges and restructured political power along four classes based on wealth. Although only the first two classes were eligible for office, all four were allowed to elect magistrates and vote on legislation in the general assembly, known as the ecclesia. His reforms have led him to be regarded as the harbinger of democracy.

Sparta Sparta, in the Peloponnese, was a very different kind of city-state. The Spartans were descended from the Dorian invaders and used the Helots, the original inhabitants of Lakonia, as their slaves. They ran their society along strict military rules laid down by the 9th century BC legislator Lycurgus.

Newborn babies were inspected and, if found wanting, were left to die on a mountain top. At the age of seven, boys were taken from their homes to start rigorous training that would turn them into crack soldiers. Girls were spared military training but were forced to keep very fit in order to produce healthy sons. Spartan indoctrination was so effective that dissent was unknown and a degree of stability was achieved that other city-states could only dream of.

While Athens became powerful through trade, Sparta became the ultimate military machine. They towered above the other city-states.

The Persian Wars The Persian drive to destroy Athens was sparked by the city's support for a rebellion in the Persian colonies on the coast of Asia Minor. Emperor Darius spent five years suppressing the revolt, and emerged hellbent on revenge. He appealed to Sparta to attack Athens from behind, but the Spartans threw his envoy in a well and Darius was left to do the job alone.

A 25,000-strong Persian army reached Attica in 490 BC, but suffered a humiliating defeat when outmanoeuvred by an Athenian force of 10,000 at the Battle of Marathon.

Darius died in 485 BC before he could mount another assault, so it was left to his son Xerxes to fulfil his father's ambition of conquering Greece. In 480 BC Xerxes gathered men from every nation of his far-flung empire and launched a coordinated invasion by army and navy, the size of which the world had never seen. The historian Herodotus estimated that there were five million Persian soldiers. No doubt this was a gross exaggeration, but it was obvious Xerxes intended to give the Greeks more than a bloody nose.

Some 30 city-states of central and southern Greece met in Corinth to devise a common defence (others, including Delphi, sided with the Persians). They agreed on a combined army and navy under Spartan command, with the Athenian leader Themistocles providing the strategy. The Spartan King Leonidas led the army to the pass at Thermopylae, near present-day Lamia, the main passage into central Greece from the north. This bottleneck was easy to defend, and although the Greeks were greatly outnumbered they held the pass until a traitor showed the Persians a way over the mountains. The Greeks were forced to retreat, but Leonidas, along with 300 of his elite Spartan troops, fought to the death. The fleet, which held off the Persian navy north of Euboea (Evia), had no choice but to retreat as well.

The Spartans and their Peloponnesian allies fell back on their second line of defence (an earthen wall across the Isthmus of Corinth), while the Persians advanced upon Athens. Themistocles ordered his people to flee the city: the women and children to Salamis, and the men to sea with the Athenian fleet. The Persians razed Attica and burned Athens to the ground.

Things did not go so well for the Persian navy. By skilful manoeuvring, the Greek navy trapped the larger Persian ships in the narrow waters off Salamis, where they became easy pickings for the more mobile Greek vessels. Xerxes, who watched the defeat of his mighty fleet from the shore, returned to Persia in disgust, leaving his general Mardonius and the army to subdue Greece. The result was quite the reverse. A year later the Greeks, under the Spartan general Pausanias, obliterated the Persian army at the Battle of Plataea. The Athenian navy then sailed to Asia Minor and destroyed what was left of the Persian fleet at Mykale, freeing the Ionian city-states there from Persian rule.

Classical Age

After defeating the Persians, the disciplined Spartans once again retreated to their Peloponnesian 'fortress', while Athens basked in its role as liberator and embarked on a policy of blatant imperialism. In 477 BC it founded the Delian League, so called because the treasury was kept on the sacred island of Delos. The league consisted of almost every state with a navy, no matter how small, including many of the Aegean islands and some of the Ionian city-states in Asia Minor.

Ostensibly its purpose was twofold: to create a naval force to liberate the city-states that were still occupied by Persia, and to protect against another Persian attack. The swearing of allegiance to Athens and an annual contribution of ships (later just money) were mandatory. The league, in effect, became an Athenian empire.

Indeed, when Pericles became leader of Athens in 461 BC, he moved the treasury from Delos to the Acropolis and used its contents to begin a building program in which no expense was spared. His first objectives were to rebuild the temple complex of the Acropolis which had been destroyed by the Persians, and to link Athens to its lifeline, the port of Piraeus, with fortified walls designed to withstand any future siege.

Under Pericles' leadership (461-429 BC), Athens experienced a golden age of unprecedented cultural, artistic and scientific achievement. With the Aegean Sea safely under its wing, Athens began to look westward for further expansion, bringing it into conflict with the city-states of the mainland. It also encroached on the trade area of Corinth, which belonged to the Sparta-dominated Peloponnesian League. A series of skirmishes and provocations led to the Peloponnesian Wars.

First Peloponnesian War One of the major triggers of the first Peloponnesian War (431-421 BC) was the Corcyra incident, in which Athens supported Corcyra (present-day Kerkyra or Corfu) in a row with its mother city, Corinth. Corinth, now under serious threat, called on Sparta to help. Sparta's power depended to a large extent on Corinth's wealth, so it rallied to the cause.

Athens knew it couldn't defeat Sparta on land, so it abandoned Attica to the Spartans and withdrew behind its mighty walls, opting to rely on its navy to put pressure on Sparta by blockading the Peloponnese. Athens suffered badly during the siege. Plague broke out in the overcrowded city, killing a third of the population – including Pericles – but the defences held firm. The blockade of the Peloponnese eventually began to hurt, and the two reached an uneasy truce.

The Sicilian Adventure Throughout the war Athens had maintained an interest in Sicily and its grain, which the soil in Attica was too poor to produce. The Greek colonies there mirrored the city-states in Greece, the most powerful being Syracuse, which had remained neutral during the war.

In 416 BC, the Sicilian city of Segesta asked Athens to intervene in a squabble it was having with Selinus, an ally of Syracuse. A hot-headed second cousin of Pericles, Alcibiades, convinced the Athenian assembly to send a flotilla to Sicily; it would go on the pretext of helping Segesta, and then attack Syracuse.

The flotilla, under the joint leadership of Alcibiades, Nicias and Lamachos, was ill-fated from the outset. Nicias' health suffered and Lamachos, the most adept of the three, was killed. After laying siege to Syracuse for over three years, Alcibiades was called back to Athens on blasphemy charges arising from a drinking binge in which he knocked the heads off a few sacred statues. Enraged, he travelled not to Athens but to Sparta and persuaded the surprised Spartans to go to the aid of Syracuse. Sparta followed Alcibiades' advice and broke the siege in 413 BC, destroying the Athenian fleet and army.

Second Peloponnesian War Athens was depleted of troops, money and ships; its subject states were ripe for revolt, and Sparta was there to lend them a hand. In 413 BC the Spartans occupied Decelea in northern Attica and used it as a base to harass the region's farmers. Athens, deprived of its Sicilian grain supplies, soon began to feel the pinch. Its prospects grew even bleaker when Darius II of Persia, who had been keeping a close eye on events in Sicily and Greece, offered Sparta money to build a navy in return for a promise to return the Ionian cities of Asia Minor to Persia.

Athens went on the attack and even gained the upper hand for a while under the leadership of the reinstated Alcibiades, but its days were numbered once Persia entered the fray in Asia Minor, and Sparta regained its composure under the outstanding general Lysander. Athens surrendered to Sparta in 404 BC.

Corinth urged the total destruction of Athens but Lysander felt honour-bound to spare the city that had saved Greece from the Persians. Instead he crippled it by confiscating its fleet, abolishing the Delian League and tearing down the walls between the city and Piraeus.

Spartan Rule The Peloponnesian Wars had exhausted the city-states, leaving only Sparta in a position of any strength. During the wars, Sparta had promised to restore liberty to the city-states who had turned against Athens, but Lysander now changed his mind and installed oligarchies (governments run by the super-rich) supervised by Spartan garrisons. Soon there was widespread dissatisfaction.

Sparta found it had bitten off more than it could chew when it began a campaign to reclaim the cities of Asia Minor from Persian rule. This brought the Persians back into Greek affairs, where they found willing clients in Athens and increasingly powerful Thebes. Thebes, which had freed itself from Spartan control and had revived the Boeotian League, soon became the main threat to Sparta. Meanwhile, Athens regained some of its former power at the head of a new league of Aegean states known as the Second Confederacy – this time aimed against Sparta rather than Persia.

The rivalry culminated in the decisive Battle of Leuctra in 371 BC, where Thebes, under the leadership of the remarkable statesman and general Epaminondas, inflicted Sparta's first defeat in a pitched battle. Spartan influence collapsed, and Thebes filled the vacuum.

In a surprise about-turn Athens now allied itself with Sparta, and their combined forces met the Theban army at Mantinea in the Peloponnese in 362 BC. The battle was won by Thebes, but Epaminondas was killed. Without him, Theban power soon crumbled. Athens was unable to take advantage of the situation. The Second Confederacy became embroiled in infighting fomented by the Persians and when it eventually collapsed, Athens lost its final chance of regaining its former glory.

The city-states were now spent forces and a new power was rising in the north: Macedon. This had not gone unnoticed by the inspirational orator Demosthenes in Athens, who urged the city-states to prepare to defend themselves. Only Thebes took heed of his warnings and the two cities formed an alliance.

The Rise of Macedon

While the Greeks engineered their own decline through the Peloponnesian Wars, Macedon (geographically the modern *nome*, or province, of Macedonia) was gathering strength in the north. Macedon had long been regarded as a bit of a backwater, a loose assembly of primitive hill tribes nominally ruled by a king. The Greeks considered the people to be barbarians (those whose speech sounded like 'bar-bar', which meant anyone who didn't speak Greek).

The man who turned them into a force to be reckoned with was Philip II, who came to the throne in 359 BC.

As a boy, Philip had been held hostage in Thebes where Epaminondas had taught him about military strategy. After organising his tribes into an efficient army of cavalry and long-lanced infantry, Philip made several forays south and manipulated his way into membership of the Amphyctionic Council (a group of states whose job it was to protect the oracle at Delphi).

In 339 BC, on the pretext of helping the Amphyctionic Council sort out a sacred war with Amfissa, he marched into Greece. The result was the Battle of Khaironeia in Boeotia (338 BC), in which the Macedonians defeated a combined army of Athenians and Thebans. The following year, Philip called together all the city-states (except Sparta, which remained aloof) at Corinth and persuaded them to form the League of Corinth and swear allegiance to Macedonia by promising to lead a campaign against Persia. The barbarian upstart had become leader of the Greeks.

Philip's ambition to tackle Persia never materialised, for in 336 BC he was assassinated by a Macedonian noble. His son, the 20-year-old Alexander, who had led the decisive cavalry charge at Khaironeia, became king.

Alexander the Great Alexander, highly educated (he had been tutored by Aristotle), fearless and ambitious, was an astute politician and intent upon finishing what his father had begun. Philip II's death had been the signal for rebellions throughout the budding empire, but Alexander wasted no time in crushing them, making an example of Thebes by razing it to the ground. After restoring order, he turned his attention to the Persian Empire and marched his army of 40,000 men into Asia Minor in 334 BC.

After a few bloody battles with the Persians, most notably at Issus (333 BC), Alexander succeeded in conquering Syria, Palestine and Egypt – where he was proclaimed pharaoh and founded the city of Alexandria. Intent on sitting on the Persian throne, he then began hunting down the Persian king, Darius III, defeating his army in Mesopotamia in 331 BC. Darius III fled east while Alexander mopped up his empire behind him, destroying the Persian palace at Persepolis in revenge for the sacking of the Acropolis 150 years earlier, and confiscating the royal treasury. Darius' body was found a year later: he had been stabbed to death by a Bactrian (Afghan) dissident.

Alexander continued east into what is now known as Uzbekistan, Bactria (where he married a local princess, Roxane) and northern India. His ambition was now to conquer the world, which he believed ended at the sea beyond India. But his soldiers grew weary and in 324 BC forced him to

MICK WELDON

Alexander the Great (356-323 BC), one of antiquity's most heroic and visionary figures return to Mesopotamia, where he settled in Babylon and drew up plans for an expedition south into Arabia. The following year, however, he fell ill suddenly and died, heirless, at the age of 33. His generals swooped like vultures on the empire.

When the dust settled, Alexander's empire had fallen apart into three large kingdoms and several smaller states. The three generals with the richest pickings were Ptolemy, founder of the Ptolemaic dynasty in Egypt (capital: Alexandria), which died out when the last of the dynasty, Cleopatra, committed suicide in 30 BC; Seleucus, founder of the Seleucid dynasty which ruled over Persia and Syria (capital: Antiochia); and Antigonus, who ruled over Asia Minor and whose Antigonid successors would win control over Macedonia proper.

Macedonia lost control of the Greek city-states to the south, which banded together into the Aetolian League, centred on Delphi, and the Achaean League, based in the Peloponnese; Athens and Sparta joined neither. One of Alexander's officers established the mini-kingdom of Pergamum in Asia Minor, which reached its height under Attalos I (ruled 241-196 BC) when it rivalled Alexandria as a centre of culture and learning. The island of Rhodes developed into a powerful mini-state by taxing passing ships.

Still, Alexander's formidable achievements during his 13 years on the world stage earned him the epithet 'the Great'. He spread Greek culture throughout a large part of the 'civilised' world, encouraged intermarriage and dismissed the anti-barbarian snobbery of the classical Greeks. In doing so, he ushered in the Hellenistic period of world history, in which Hellenic ('Greek') culture broke out of the narrow confines of the ancient Greek world and merged with the other proud cultures of antiquity to create a new, cosmopolitan tradition.

Roman Rule

While Alexander the Great was forging his vast empire in the east, the Romans had been expanding theirs to their west. Now they were keen to start making inroads into Greece. They found willing allies in Pergamum and Rhodes, who feared Syrian and Macedonian expansionism. The Romans defeated the Seleucid king, Antiochus III, in a three year campaign and in 189 BC gave all of Asia Minor to Pergamum. Several wars were needed to subjugate Macedon, but in 168 BC Macedon lost the decisive Battle of Pydnaa.

The Achaean League was defeated in 146 BC; the Roman consul Mummius made an example of the rebellious Corinthians by completely destroying their beautiful city, massacring the men and selling the women and children into slavery. Attalos III, king of Pergamum, died without an heir in 133 BC, donating Asia Minor to Rome in his will.

In 86 BC, Athens joined an ill-fated rebellion against the Romans in Asia Minor staged by the king of the Black Sea region, Mithridates VI. In retribution, the Roman statesman Sulla invaded Athens, destroyed its walls and took off with its most valuable sculptures.

Greece then became a battleground as Roman generals fought for supremacy. In a decisive naval battle off Cape Actium (31 BC) Octavian was victorious over Mark Antony and Cleopatra and consequently became Rome's first emperor, assuming the title Augustus, meaning the Grand One.

For the next 300 years, Greece, as the Roman province of Achaea, experienced an unprecedented period of peace, the Pax Romana. The Romans had always venerated Greek art, literature and philosophy, and aristocratic Romans sent their offspring to the many schools in Athens. Indeed, the Romans adopted most aspects of Hellenistic culture, spreading its unifying traditions throughout their empire.

The Romans were also the first to refer to the Hellenes as Greeks, derived from the word *graikos* – the name of a prehistoric tribe.

Christianity & the Byzantine Empire

The Pax Romana began to crumble in 250 AD when the Goths invaded Greece, the first of a succession of invaders spurred on by the 'great migrations'. They were followed by the Visigoths in 395, the Vandals in 465, the

Ostrogoths in 480, the Bulgars in 500, the Huns in 540 and the Slavs after 600.

Christianity, meantime, had emerged as the country's new religion. St Paul had made several visits to Greece in the 1st century AD and made converts in many places. The definitive boost to the spread of Christianity in this part of the world came with the conversion of the Roman emperors and the rise of the Byzantine Empire, which blended Hellenistic culture with Christianity.

In 324 Emperor Constantine I (also known as Constantine the Great), a Christian convert, transferred the capital of the empire from Rome to Byzantium, a city on the western shore of the Bosphorus, which was renamed Constantinople (present-day İstanbul). This was as much due to insecurity in Italy itself as to the growing importance of the wealthy eastern regions of the empire. By the end of the 4th century, the Roman Empire was formally divided into a western and eastern half. While Rome went into terminal decline, the eastern capital grew in wealth and strength, long outliving its western counterpart (the Byzantine Empire lasted until the capture of Constantinople by the Turks in 1453).

Emperor Theodosius I made Christianity the official religion in Greece in 394 and outlawed the worship of Greek and Roman gods, now branded as pagan. Athens remained an important cultural centre until 529, when Emperor Justinian forbade the teaching of classical philosophy in favour of Christian theology, then seen as the supreme form of intellectual endeavour. The Hagia Sofia (Church of the Divine Wisdom) was built in Constantinople and some magnificent churches were built in Greece, especially in Thessaloniki, a Christian stronghold much favoured by the Byzantine emperors.

The Crusades

It is one of the ironies of history that the demise of the Byzantine Empire was accelerated not by invasions of infidels from the east, nor barbarians from the north, but by fellow Christians from the west – the Frankish crusaders.

The stated mission of the crusades was to liberate the Holy Land from the Muslims, but in reality they were driven as much by greed as by religious fervour. By the time the First Crusade was launched in 1095, the Franks had already made substantial gains in Italy at the empire's expense and the rulers of Constantinople were understandably nervous about giving the crusaders safe passage on their way to Jerusalem. The first three crusades passed by without incident, but the fourth proved that the fear was justified. The crusaders struck a deal with Venice, which had a score to settle with the Byzantines, and was able to persuade the crusaders that Constantinople presented richer pickings than Jerusalem.

Constantinople was sacked in 1204 and the crusaders installed Baldwin of Flanders as head of the short-lived Latin Empire of Constantinople. Much of the Byzantine Empire was partitioned into feudal states ruled by self-styled 'Latin' (mostly Frankish) princes. Greece now entered one of the most tumultuous periods of its history. The Byzantines fought to regain their lost capital and to keep the areas they had managed to hold on to (the so-called Empire of Nicaea, south of Constantinople in Asia Minor), while the Latin princes fought among themselves to expand their territories.

The Venetians, meanwhile, had secured a foothold in Greece. Over the next few centuries they acquired all the key Greek ports, including the island of Crete, and became the wealthiest and most powerful traders in the Mediterranean.

Despite this disorderly state of affairs, Byzantium was not yet dead. In 1259, the Byzantine emperor Michael VIII Palaeologos recaptured the Peloponnese from the Frankish de Villehardouin family, and made the city of Mystras his headquarters. Many eminent Byzantine artists, architects, intellectuals and philosophers converged on the city for a final burst of Byzantine creativity. Michael VIII managed to reclaim Constantinople in 1261, but by this time Byzantium was a shadow of its former self.

The Ottoman Empire

Constantinople was soon facing a much greater threat from the East. The Seljuk Turks, a tribe from central Asia, had first appeared on the eastern fringes of the empire in the middle of the 11th century. They established themselves on the Anatolian plain by defeating a Byzantine army at Manzikert in 1071. The threat looked to have been contained, especially when the Seljuks were themselves overrun by the Mongols. By the time Mongol power began to wane, the Seljuks had been supplanted as the dominant Turkish tribe by the Ottomans – the followers of Osman, who ruled from 1289 to 1326. The Muslim Ottomans rapidly expanded the areas under their control and by the mid-15th century were harassing the Byzantine Empire on all sides. Western Europe was too embroiled in the Hundred Years' War to come to the rescue, and in 1453 Constantinople fell to the Turks under Mohammed II (the Conqueror). Once more Greece became a battleground, this time fought over by the Turks and Venetians. Eventually, with the exception of the Ionian Islands, Greece became part of the Ottoman Empire.

Much has been made of the horrors of the Turkish occupation in Greece. However, in the early years at any rate, Greeks probably marginally preferred Ottoman to Venetian or Frankish rule. The Venetians in particular treated their subjects little better than slaves. But life was not easy under the Turks, not least because of the high taxation they imposed. One of their most hated practices was the taking of one out of every five male children to become janissaries, personal bodyguards of the sultan. Many janissaries became infantrymen in the Ottoman army, but the cleverest could rise to high office – including grand vizier (chief minister).

Ottoman power reached its zenith under Sultan Süleyman the Magnificent (ruled 1520-66), who expanded the empire through the Balkans and Hungary to the gates of Vienna. His successor, Selim the Sot, added Cyprus to their dominions in 1570, but his death in 1574 marked the end of serious territorial expansion.

Although they captured Crete in 1670 after a 25 year campaign and briefly threatened Vienna once more in 1683, the ineffectual sultans that followed in the late 16th and 17th centuries saw the empire go into steady decline. They suffered a series of reversals on the battlefield, and Venice succeeded in holding onto the Peloponnese after a campaign in 1687 that saw them advance as far as Athens. The Parthenon was destroyed during the fighting when a shell struck a store of Turkish gunpowder.

Chaos and rebellion spread across Greece. Corsairs terrorised coastal dwellers, gangs of *klephts* (anti-Ottoman fugitives and brigands) roamed the mountains, and there was an upsurge of opposition to Turkish rule by freedom fighters – who fought each other when they weren't fighting the Turks.

Russian Involvement

Russia's link with Greece went back to Byzantine times, when the Russians had been converted to Christianity by Byzantine missionaries. The Church hierarchies in Constantinople and Kiev (later in Moscow) soon went their separate ways, but when Constantinople fell to the Turks, the metropolitan (head) of the Russian Church declared Moscow the 'third Rome', the true heir of Christianity, and campaigned for the liberation of its fellow Christians in the south. This fitted in nicely with Russia's efforts to expand southwards and southwestwards into Ottoman territory – perhaps even to turn the Ottoman Empire back into a Byzantine Empire dependent on Russia.

When Catherine the Great became Empress of Russia in 1762, both the Republic of Venice and the Ottoman Empire were weak. She sent Russian agents to foment rebellion, first in the Peloponnese in 1770 and then in Epiros in 1786. Both rebellions were crushed ruthlessly – the latter by Ali Pasha, the governor of Ioannina, who proceeded to set up his own power base in Greece in defiance of the sultan.

Independence Parties In the 1770s and 1780s Catherine booted the Turks from the Black Sea coast and created a number of towns in the region, which she gave Ancient Greek or Byzantine names. She offered Greeks financial incentives and free land to settle the region, and many took up her offer.

One of the new towns was Odessa, and it was there in 1814 that businessmen Athanasios Tsakalof, Emmanuel Xanthos and Nikolaos Skoufas founded the first Greek independence party, the Filiki Eteria (Friendly Society). The message of the society spread quickly and branches opened throughout Greece. The leaders in Odessa believed that armed force was the only effective means of liberation, and made generous monetary contributions to the freedom fighters.

There were also stirrings of dissent among Greeks living in Constantinople. The Ottomans regarded it as beneath them to participate in commerce, and this had left the door open for Greeks to become a powerful economic force in the city. These wealthy Greek families were called Phanariots. Unlike the Filiki Eteria, who strove for liberation through rebellion, the Phanariots believed that they could effect a takeover from within.

The War of Independence

Ali Pasha's private rebellion against the sultan in 1820 gave the Greeks the opportunity they had been waiting for. On 25 March 1821, Bishop Germanos of Patras signalled the beginning of the War of Independence when he hoisted the Greek flag at the monastery of Agias Lavras in the Peloponnese. Fighting broke out almost simultaneously across most of Greece and the occupied islands, with the Greeks making big early gains. The fighting was savage, with atrocities committed on both sides. In the Peloponnese, 12,000 Turkish inhabitants were massacred after the capture of the city of Tripolitsa (present-day Tripolis) and Maniot freedom fighters razed the homes of thousands of Turks. The Turks retaliated with massacres in Asia Minor, most notoriously on the island of Chios, where 25,000 civilians were killed.

The fighting escalated and within a year the Greeks had captured the fortresses of Monemvasia, Navarino (modern Pylos) and Nafplio in the Peloponnese, and Messolongi, Athens and Thiva (Thebes). Greek independence was proclaimed at Epidaurus on 13 January 1822.

The western powers were reluctant to intervene, fearing the consequences of creating a power vacuum in south-eastern Europe, where the Turks still controlled much territory. Help came from the philhellenes (literally, lovers of Greece and Greek culture)– aristocratic young men, recipients of a classical education, who saw themselves as the inheritors of a glorious civilisation and were willing to fight to liberate its oppressed descendants. The philhellenes included Shelley, Goethe, Schiller, Victor Hugo, Alfred de Musset and Lord Byron. Byron arrived in Messolongi – an important centre of resistance – in January 1824 and died three months later of pneumonia.

The prime movers in the revolution were the klephts Theodoros Kolokotronis (who led the siege on Nafplio) and Markos Botsaris; Georgos Koundouriotis (a ship owner) and Admiral Andreas Miaoulis, both from Hydra; and the Phanariots Alexandros Mavrokordatos and Dimitrios Ypsilantis. Streets all over Greece are named after these heroes.

The cause was not lacking in leaders; what was lacking was unity of objectives and strategy. Internal disagreements twice escalated into civil war, the worst in the Peloponnese in 1824. The sultan took advantage of this and called in Egyptian reinforcements. By 1827 the Turks had captured Modon (Methoni) and Corinth, and recaptured Navarino, Messolongi and Athens.

At last the western powers intervened, and a combined Russian, French and British fleet destroyed the Turkish-Egyptian fleet in the Bay of Navarino in October 1827. Sultan Mahmud II defied the odds and proclaimed a holy war, prompting Russia to send troops into the Balkans to engage the

Ottoman army. Fighting continued until 1829 when, with Russian troops at the gates of Constantinople, the sultan accepted Greek independence by the Treaty of Adrianople.

Birth of the Greek Nation

The Greeks, meanwhile, had been busy organising the independent state they had proclaimed several years earlier. In April 1827 they elected as their first president a Corfiot who had been the foreign minister of Tsar Alexander I, Ioannis Kapodistrias. Nafplio, in the Peloponnese, was chosen as the capital.

With his Russian past, Kapodistrias believed in a strong, centralised government. While he was good at enlisting foreign support, his autocratic manner at home was unacceptable to many of the leaders of the War of Independence, particularly the Maniot chieftains who had always been a law unto themselves, and he was assassinated in 1831.

Amid the ensuing anarchy, Britain, France and Russia once again intervened and declared that Greece should become a monarchy and the throne should be given to a non-Greek so that they wouldn't be seen to favour one Greek faction. A fledgling kingdom was now up for grabs among the offspring of the crowned heads of Europe, but no-one exactly ran to fill the empty throne. Eventually the 17-year-old Prince Otto of Bavaria was chosen, arriving in Nafplio in January 1833. The new kingdom (established by the London Convention of 1832) consisted of the Peloponnese, Sterea Ellada, the Cyclades and the Sporades.

King Otho (as his name became) got up the nose of the Greek people from the moment he set foot on their land. He arrived with a bunch of upper class Bavarian cronies, to whom he gave the most prestigious official posts, and he was just as autocratic as Kapodistrias. Otho moved the capital to Athens in 1834.

Patience with his rule ran out in 1843 when demonstrations in the capital, led by the War of Independence leaders, called for a constitution. Otho mustered a National Assembly which drafted a constitution calling for parliamentary government consisting of a lower house and a senate. Otho's cronies were whisked out of power and replaced by War of Independence freedom fighters, who bullied and bribed the populace into voting for them.

The Great Idea

By the middle of the 19th century the people of the new Greek nation were no better off materially than they had been under the Ottomans, and it was in this climate of despondency that the Megali Idea (Great Idea) of a new Greek Empire was born. This empire was to include all the lands that had once been under Greek influence and have Constantinople as its capital. Otho enthusiastically embraced the idea, which increased his popularity no end. But the Greek politicians did not; they sought ways to increase their own power in the face of Otho's autocratic rule.

By the end of the 1850s, most of the stalwarts from the War of Independence had been replaced by a new breed of university graduates (Athens University had been founded in 1837). In 1862 they staged a bloodless revolution and deposed the king. But they weren't quite able to set their own agenda, because in the same year Britain returned the Ionian Islands (a British protectorate since 1815) to Greece, and in the general euphoria the British were able to push forward young Prince William of Denmark, who became King George I (the Greek monarchy retained its Danish links from that time).

His 50 year reign brought stability to the troubled country, beginning with a new constitution in 1864, which established the power of democratically elected representatives and pushed the king further towards a ceremonial role. An uprising in Crete against Turkish rule was suppressed by the sultan in 1866-68, but in 1881 Greece acquired Thessaly and part of Epiros as the result of another Russo-Turkish war.

When Harilaos Trikoupis became prime minister in 1882, he prudently concentrated his efforts on domestic issues rather than pursuing the Great Idea. The 1880s brought the first signs of economic growth: the country's first railway lines and paved roads were constructed; the Corinth Canal (begun in 62 AD!) was completed – enabling Piraeus to become a major Mediterranean port; and the merchant navy grew rapidly.

However, the Great Idea had not been buried, and reared its head again after Trikoupis' death in 1896. In 1897 there was another uprising in Crete, and the hot-headed prime minister Theodoros Deligiannis responded by declaring war on Turkey and sending help to Crete. A Greek attempt to invade Turkey in the north proved disastrous – it was only through the intervention of the great powers that the Turkish army was prevented from taking Athens.

Crete was placed under international administration. The day-to-day government of the island was gradually handed over to Greeks, and in 1905 the president of the Cretan assembly, Eleftherios Venizelos, announced Crete's union *(enosis)* with Greece, although this was not recognised by international law until 1913. Venizelos went on to become prime minister of Greece in 1910 and was the country's leading politician until his republican sympathies brought about his downfall in 1935.

The Balkan Wars

Although the Ottoman Empire was in its death throes at the beginning of the 20th century, it was still clinging onto Macedonia. It was a prize sought by the newly formed Balkan countries of Serbia and Bulgaria, as well as by Greece, leading to the Balkan Wars. The first, in 1912, pitted all three against the Turks; the second, in 1913, pitted Serbia and Greece against Bulgaria. The outcome was the Treaty of Bucharest (August 1913), which greatly expanded Greek territory by adding the southern part of Macedonia, part of Thrace, another chunk of Epiros, and the North-East Aegean Islands, as well as recognising the union with Crete.

In March 1913, King George was assassinated by a lunatic and his son Constantine became king.

WWI & Smyrna

King Constantine, who was married to the sister of the German emperor, insisted that Greece remain neutral when WWI broke out in August 1914. As the war dragged on, the Allies (Britain, France and Russia) put increasing pressure on Greece to join forces with them against Germany and Turkey. They made promises which they couldn't hope to fulfil, including land in Asia Minor. Venizelos favoured the Allied cause, placing him at loggerheads with the king. Tensions between the two came to a head in 1916, and Venizelos set up a rebel government, first in Crete and then in Thessaloniki, while the pressure from the Allies eventually persuaded Constantine to leave Greece in June 1917. He was replaced by his more amenable second son, Alexander.

Greek troops served with distinction on the Allied side, but when the war ended in 1918 the promised land in Asia Minor was not forthcoming. Venizelos took matters into his own hands and, with Allied acquiescence, landed troops in Smyrna (present-day İzmir) in May 1919 under the guise of protecting the half a million Greeks living in that city (just under half its population). With a firm foothold in Asia Minor, Venizelos now planned to push home his advantage against a war-depleted Ottoman Empire. He ordered his troops to attack in October 1920 (just weeks before he was voted out of office). By September 1921, the Greeks had advanced as far as Ankara.

The Turkish forces were commanded by Mustafa Kemal (later to become Atatürk), a young general who also belonged to the Young Turks, a group of army officers pressing for western-style political reforms. Kemal first halted the Greek advance outside Ankara in September 1921 and then routed them with a massive offensive the following spring. The Greeks were driven out of Smyrna and many of the Greek inhabitants were massacred. Mustafa Kemal was now a national hero, the sultanate was abolished and Turkey became a republic.

The outcome of the failed Greek invasion and the revolution in Turkey was the Treaty of Lausanne of July 1923. This gave eastern Thrace and the islands of Imvros and Tenedos to Turkey, while the Italians kept the Dodecanese (which they had temporarily acquired in 1912 and would hold until 1947).

The treaty also called for a population exchange between Greece and Turkey to prevent any future disputes. The Great Idea, which had been such an enormous drain on the country's finances over the decades, was at last laid to rest. Almost 1.5 million Greeks left Turkey and almost 400,000 Turks left Greece. The exchange put a tremendous strain on the Greek economy and caused great hardship for the individuals concerned. Many Greeks abandoned a privileged life in Asia Minor for one of extreme poverty in shantytowns in Greece.

The Republic of 1924-35

The arrival of the refugees coincided with, ind compounded, a period of political nstability unprecedented even by Greek tandards. In October 1920, King Alexander ied from a monkey bite, resulting in the estoration of his father, King Constantine. onstantine identified himself too closely vith the war against Turkey, and abdicated fter the fall of Smyrna. He was replaced by is first son, George II, but George was no natch for the group of army officers who eized power after the war. A republic was roclaimed in March 1924 amid a series of oups and counter-coups.

A measure of stability was attained with enizelos' return to power in 1928. He pur-ued a policy of economic and educational forms, but progress was inhibited by the reat Depression. His anti-royalist Liberal rty began to face a growing challenge om the monarchist Popular Party, culmin-ing in defeat at the polls in March 1933. e new government was preparing for the storation of the monarchy when Venizelos d his supporters staged an unsuccessful up in March 1935. Venizelos was exiled Paris, where he died a year later. In No-mber 1935 King George II was restored the throne by a rigged plebiscite, and he talled the right-wing General Ioannis Metaxas as prime minister. Nine months later, Metaxas assumed dictatorial powers with the king's consent under the pretext of preventing a communist-inspired republican coup.

WWII

Metaxas' grandiose vision was to create a Third Greek Civilisation based on its glorious ancient and Byzantine past, but what he actually created was more like a Greek version of the Third Reich. He exiled or imprisoned opponents, banned trade unions and the KKE (Kommunistiko Komma Ellados, the Greek Communist Party), imposed press censorship, and created a secret police force and a fascist-style youth movement. Metaxas is best known, however, for his reply of *ohi* (no) to Mussolini's request to allow Italians to traverse Greece at the beginning of WWII, thus maintaining Greece's policy of strict neutrality. The Italians invaded Greece, but were driven back into Albania.

A prerequisite of Hitler's plan to invade the Soviet Union was a secure southern flank in the Balkans. The British, realising this, asked Metaxas if they could land troops in Greece. He gave the same reply as he had given the Italians, but died suddenly in January 1941. The king replaced him with the more timid Alexandros Koryzis, who agreed to British forces landing in Greece and then committed suicide when German troops marched through Yugoslavia and invaded Greece on 6 April 1941. The defending Greek, British, Australian and New Zealand troops were seriously outnumbered, and the whole country was under Nazi occupation within a month. King George II and his government went into exile in Egypt. The civilian population suffered appallingly during the occupation, many dying of starvation. The Nazis rounded up more than half the Jewish population and transported them to death camps.

Numerous resistance movements sprang up. The three dominant ones were ELAS (Ellinikos Laïkos Apeleftherotikos Stratos), EAM (Ethnikon Apeleftherotikon Metopon) and EDES (Ethnikos Dimokratikos Ellinikos Syndesmos). Although ELAS was founded by communists, not all of its members were left-wing, whereas EAM consisted of Stalinist KKE members who had lived in Moscow in the 1930s and harboured ambitions of establishing a postwar communist Greece. EDES (Ethnikos Dimokratikos Ellinikos Syndesmos) consisted of right-wing and monarchist resistance fighters. These groups fought one another with as much venom as they fought the Germans.

By 1943 Britain had begun speculating on the political complexion of postwar Greece. Winston Churchill wanted the king back and was afraid of a communist takeover, especially after ELAS and EAM formed a coalition and declared a provisional government in the summer of 1944. The Germans were pushed out of Greece in October 1944, but the communist and monarchist resistance groups continued to fight one another.

Civil War

On 3 December 1944, the police fired on a communist demonstration in Syntagma Square. The ensuing six weeks of fighting between the left and the right were known as the Dekemvriana (events of December), the first round of the civil war, and only the intervention of British troops prevented an ELAS-EAM victory. An election held in March 1946 and boycotted by the communists was won by the royalists, and a rigged plebiscite put George II back on the throne.

In October, the left-wing Democratic Army of Greece (DAG) was formed to resume the fight against the monarchy and its British supporters. Under the leadership of Markos Vafiadis, the DAG swiftly occupied a large swathe of land along Greece's northern border with Albania and Yugoslavia.

By 1947, the US had replaced Britain as Greece's 'minder' and the civil war had developed into a setting for the new Cold War as the Americans fought to contain the spread of Soviet influence in Europe. Inspired by the Truman Doctrine, the US poured in cash and military hardware to shore up the anti-communist coalition government. Communism was declared illegal and the government introduced its notorious Certificate of Political Reliability (proof that the carrier was not left-wing), which remained valid until 1962 and without which Greeks couldn't vote and found it almost impossible to get work.

US aid did little to improve the situation on the ground. The DAG continued to be supplied through the communist states to the north, and by the end of 1947 large chunks of the mainland were under its control, as well as parts of the islands of Crete, Chios and Lesvos. It was unable, though, to capture the major town it needed as a base for a rival government declared by Vafiades, despite a major assault on the town of Konitsa in northern Epiros on Christmas Day 1947

The tide began to turn the government's way early in 1949 when the DAG was forced out of the Peloponnese, but the fighting dragged on in the mountains of Epiro until October 1949, when Yugoslavia fel out with the Soviet Union and cut th DAG's supply lines. Vafiades was assassinated by a group of his Stalinist underling after the fall of the DAG's last majo stronghold in the Grammos Mountains, an the remnants of his army capitulated.

If this was a victory, there was nothing t celebrate. The country was in an almight mess, both politically and economically More Greeks had been killed in the thre years of bitter civil war than in WWII; quarter of a million people were homeles many thousands more had been taken pri oner or exiled, and the DAG had taken som 30,000 Greek children from northern Greec to Eastern bloc countries for indoctrinatio

The sense of despair left by the civil wa became the trigger for a mass exodu Almost a million Greeks headed off i search of a better life elsewhere, primari to Australia, Canada and the USA. Villag – whole islands even – were abandoned a people gambled on a new start in the su urbs of cities like Melbourne, New Yo and Chicago. While some have drifted ba (including half the restaurant owners in the Peloponnese!), most have stayed away.

Reconstruction & the Cyprus Issue

A general election was held in 1950. The system of proportional representation resulted in a series of unworkable coalitions, and the electoral system was changed to majority voting in 1952 – which excluded the communists from future governments. The next election was a victory for the newly formed right-wing Ellinikos Synagermos (Greek Rally) party led by General Papagos, who had been a field marshal during the civil war. General Papagos remained in power until his death in 1955, when he was replaced by Konstantinos Karamanlis, the minister of public works.

Greece joined NATO in 1951, and in 1953 the US was granted the right to operate sovereign bases. Intent on maintaining a right-wing government, the US gave generous aid and even more generous military support. Living standards improved during the 1950s, but Greece remained poor.

Cyprus occupied centre stage in Greece's foreign affairs, and has remained close to it to this day. Since the 1930s, Greek Cypriots (four-fifths of the island's population) had demanded union with Greece, while Turkey had maintained its claim to the island ever since the British occupied it in 1914 (it became a British crown colony in 1925). After an outbreak of communal violence between Greek and Turkish Cypriots in 1954, Britain stated its intention to make Cyprus an independent state.

The right-wing Greek Cypriot EOKA (National Organisation of Cypriot Freedom Fighters) took up arms against the British, but Greece and Turkey finally accepted independence in 1959. Cyprus duly became a republic the following August with Archbishop Makarios as president and a Turk, Fasal Kükük, as vice president. The changes did little to appease either side. EOKA resolved to keep fighting, while Turkish Cypriots continued to clamour for partition of the island.

Back in Greece, Georgos Papandreou, a former Venizelos supporter, founded the broadly based EK (Centre Union) in 1958, but an election in 1961 returned the ERE (National Radical Union), Karamanlis' new name for Papagos' Greek Rally party, to power for the third time in succession. Papandreou accused the ERE of ballot-rigging – probably true, but the culprits were almost certainly right-wing, military-backed groups (rather than Karamanlis) who feared communist infiltration if the EK came to power. Political turmoil followed, culminating in the murder, in May 1963, of Grigorios Lambrakis, the deputy of the communist EDA (Union of the Democratic Left). All this proved too much for Karamanlis, who resigned and left the country.

Despite the ERE's sometimes desperate measures to stay in power, an election in February 1964 was won by the EK. Papandreou wasted no time in implementing a series of radical changes. He freed political prisoners and allowed exiles to come back to Greece, reduced income tax and the defence budget, and increased spending on social services and education. Papandreou's victory coincided with King Constantine II's accession to the Greek throne, and with a renewed outbreak of violence in Cyprus, which erupted into a full-scale civil war before the UN intervened and installed a peace-keeping force.

The Colonels' Coup

The right in Greece was rattled by Papandreou's tolerance of the left, fearing that this would increase the EDA's influence. The climate was one of mutual suspicion between the left and the right, each claiming that the other was plotting a takeover. Finally, Papandreou decided the armed forces needed a thorough overhaul, which seemed fair enough, as army officers were more often than not the perpetrators of conspiracies. King Constantine refused to cooperate with this, and Papandreou resigned. Two years of ineffectual interim governments followed before a new election was scheduled for May 1967.

The election was never to be. A group of army colonels led by Georgos Papadopoulos and Stylianos Patakos staged a coup on 21 April 1967. King Constantine tried an unsuccessful counter-coup in December, after which he fled the country. A military junta was established with Papadopoulos as prime minister.

The colonels imposed martial law, abolished all political parties, banned trade unions, imposed censorship, and imprisoned, tortured and exiled thousands of Greeks who opposed them. Suspicions of CIA assistance in the coup remain conjecture, but criticism of the coup, and the ensuing regime, was certainly not forthcoming from the CIA or the US government. In June 1972 Papadopoulos declared Greece a republic (confirmed by a rigged referendum in July) and appointed himself president.

In November 1973 students began a sit-in at Athens' Polytechnic college in protest against the junta. On 17 November, tanks stormed the building, injuring many and killing at least 20. On 25 November, Papadopoulos was deposed by the thuggish Brigadier Ioannidis, head of the military security police.

The following July, desperate for a foreign policy success to bolster the regime's standing, Ioannidis decided it was time to play the Cyprus card. He hatched a wild scheme to assassinate President Makarios and unite Cyprus with Greece. The scheme went disastrously wrong after Makarios got wind of the plan and escaped. The junta installed Nikos Sampson, a former EOKA leader, as president, and Turkey reacted by invading the island.

The junta quickly removed Sampson and threw in the towel, but the Turks continued to advance until they occupied the northern third of the island, forcing almost 200,000 Greek Cypriots to flee their homes for the safety of the south.

After the Colonels

The army now called Karamanlis from Paris to clear up the mess in Greece. An election was arranged for November 1974 (won handsomely by Karamanlis' New Democracy party), and the ban on communist parties was lifted. Andreas Papandreou (son of Georgos) formed PASOK (the Panhellenic Socialist Union), and a plebiscite voted 69% against restoration of the monarchy. (Former king Constantine, who now

Urban Guerilla Terror

Greece's deadly November 17 urban guerilla group takes its name from the date in 1973 on which the military junta used tanks to crush a student protest at Athens Polytechnic, killing at least 20 students.

It has proved the most durable of the many left-wing guerilla groups that emerged in Europe in the 1970s. To the acute embarrassment of the police, not one member of the gang has been caught in more than 24 years of activity.

The group claimed the first of its 22 victims on Christmas Eve 1975 when CIA bureau chief Richard Welsh was gunned down in the driveway of his Athens home. It has continued to strike at regular intervals ever since.

Rocket attacks have become the group's trademark, following a raid on a military depot at Larissa in 1987 that netted a haul of antitank missiles. They have been used in a string of attacks over the years, including an assault on the US embassy in Athens in 1998.

The group was busy during the NATO air war against Yugoslavia, firing missiles at the offices of the ruling PASOK party, several banks and at the German ambassador's house.

lives in London, didn't revisit Greece until the summer of 1993. The New Democracy government sent missile boats and a transport plane to follow his yacht. Nonetheless the ex-king said he and his family enjoyed the holiday, and he had no wish to overthrow the Greek constitution.)

Karamanlis' New Democracy (ND) party won the election in 1977, but his personal popularity began to decline. One of his biggest achievements before accepting the largely ceremonial post of president was to engineer Greece's entry into the European Community (now the European Union), which involved jumping the queue ahead of other countries who had waited patiently to be accepted. On 1 January 1981 Greece became the 10th member of the EC.

The Socialist 1980s

Andreas Papandreou's PASOK party won the election of October 1981 with 48% of the vote, giving Greece its first socialist government. PASOK came to power with an ambitious social program and a promise to close US air bases and withdraw from NATO.

After seven years in government, these promises remained unfulfilled (although the US military presence was reduced); unemployment was high and reforms in education and welfare had been limited. Women's issues fared better, though: the dowry system was abolished, abortion legalised, and civil marriage and divorce were implemented. The crunch came in 1988 when Papandreou's love affair with air hostess Dimitra Liani (whom he subsequently married) hit the headlines, and PASOK became embroiled in a financial scandal involving the Bank of Crete.

In July 1989 an unlikely coalition of conservatives and communists took over to implement a *katharsis* (campaign of purification) to investigate the scandal. In September it ruled that Papandreou and four of his ministers be tried for embezzlement, telephone tapping and illegal grain sales. Papandreou's trial ended in January 1992 with his acquittal on all counts.

The 1990s

An election in 1990 brought the ND back to power with a majority of only two seats, and with Konstantinos Mitsotakis as prime minister. Intent on redressing the country's economic problems – high inflation and high government spending – the government imposed austerity measures, including a wage freeze for civil servants and steep increases in public-utility costs and basic services. The government also cracked down on tax evasion – still so rife it's described as the nation's favourite pastime.

The austerity measures sparked off a series of strikes in the public sector in mid-1990, and again in 1991 and 1992. The government's problems were compounded by an influx of Albanian refugees (see the People section later in this chapter), and the dispute over the use of the name Macedonia for the southern republic of former Yugoslavia (see the boxed text 'What's in a Name?' in the Northern Greece chapter).

By late 1992 corruption allegations were being made against the government and it was claimed that Cretan-born Mitsotakis had a large, secret collection of Minoan art, and in mid-1993 there were allegations of government telephone tapping. Former Mitsotakis supporters began to cut their losses: in June 1993 Antonis Samaras, the ND's former foreign minister, founded the Political Spring party and called upon ND members to join him. So many of them joined that the ND lost its parliamentary majority and its capacity to govern.

An early election was held in October, which Andreas Papandreou's PASOK party won with 47% of the vote against 39% for ND and 5% for Political Spring. Through the majority voting system, this translated into a handsome parliamentary majority for PASOK.

Papandreou's final spell at the helm was dominated by speculation about his heart condition and general poor health. Papandreou was rarely sighted outside his villa at Kifissia, where he lived surrounded by his ministerial coterie of family and friends. He was finally forced to step down in early

1996 after another bout of ill-health, and his death on June 26 marked the end of an era in Greek politics.

Papandreou's departure produced a dramatic change of direction for PASOK, with the party abandoning his left-leaning politics and electing economic reformer Costas Simitis as prime minister. The new leader had been an outspoken critic of Papandreou and had been sacked as industry minister four months previously. He surprised many by calling a snap poll in September 1996, and campaigned hard in support of his Mr Clean image. He was rewarded with almost 42% of the vote, enough for a comfortable parliamentary majority.

Simitis belongs to much the same school of politics as Britain's Tony Blair. Since he took power, PASOK policy has shifted right to the extent that it now agrees with the opposition New Democracy on all major policy issues. His government has focused almost exclusively on the push for further integration with Europe, which has meant more tax reform and more austerity measures – as dictated by European Union bosses in Brussels. This hasn't gone down well with the electorate, and it's rare for a day to pass without a protest of some sort. Simitis has stuck to his guns, though, and Greece appears on track to join the euro band in early 2000 – despite the disruption to the economy resulting from the 1999 NATO conflict with Serbia.

Recent Foreign Policy

Greece's foreign policy is dominated by its extremely sensitive relationship with Turkey, its giant Muslim neighbour to the east. These two uneasy NATO allies seem to delight in niggling each other, and are constantly attempting to upstage each other in an ongoing war of one-upmanship. Incidents which might appear trivial to the outsider frequently bring the two to the brink of war – most recently after Turkish journalists symbolically replaced the Greek flag on the tiny rocky outcrop of Imia (Kardak to the Turks) in February 1996. Both sides poured warships into the area before being persuaded to calm down.

The Kurdish rebellion in eastern Turkey has been a constant source of friction. Many Greeks empathise with the Kurds as a fellow people fighting for freedom from Turkish tyranny – much like their own War of Independence fighters. Greece has often been accused of secretly aiding the Kurds, and the Simitis government wound up with egg all over its face when Turkish secret agents captured Kurdish leader Abdullah Ocalan in Kenya in early 1999. The circumstances remain confused, but Ocalan was captured after he was spotted at the Greek embassy in Nairobi.

The massive earthquake which devastated the İzmit area of western Turkey on 17 August 1999 sparked a remarkable turnaround in relations between the warring neighbours. According to geologists, the quake moved Turkey 1.5m closer to Greece. It had the same effect on the Greek people, who urged their government to join the rescue effort. Greek teams were among the first on the scene, where they were greeted as heroes. The Turks were quick to return the favour after the Athens quake which followed on 7 September 1999.

While Turkey remains the top priority, Greece has also had its hands full in recent years coping with events to the north precipitated by the break-up of former Yugoslavia and the collapse of the communist regimes in Albania and Romania.

The first crisis to arise from the break-up of Yugoslavia was sparked by the former Yugoslav republic of Macedonia's attempt to become independent Macedonia. This prompted an emotional outburst from Greece, which argued that the name 'was, is, and always will be' Greek. Greece was able to persuade its EU partners to recognise Macedonia only if it changed its name, which is how the independent acronym of FYROM (Former Yugoslav Republic of Macedonia) came into being.

The wars in Croatia and Bosnia had little political impact on Greece, but the country found itself in an impossible position during the 1999 NATO conflict with Serbia over Kosovo. The Greek public, already strongly sympathetic towards their fellow Orthodox Christian Serbs in the battle against the Muslim Albanian Kosovars, was outraged when the NATO bombing began. The Americans bore the brunt of anti-NATO demonstrations, violent at first, that lasted throughout the war.

Although Thessaloniki was used as a shipment point for NATO equipment, Greece played no active part in the war.

GEOGRAPHY

Greece, at the southern extremity of the Balkan Peninsula, is the only member of the EU without a land frontier with another member. To the north, Greece has land borders with Albania, the Former Yugoslav Republic of Macedonia, and Bulgaria; and to the east with Turkey.

Greece consists of a peninsula and about 1400 islands, of which 169 are inhabited. The land mass is 131,900 sq km and Greek territorial waters occupy 400,000 sq km. The islands are divided into six groups: the Cyclades, the Dodecanese, the islands of the North-Eastern Aegean, the Sporades, the Ionian and the Saronic Gulf Islands. The two largest islands, Crete and Evia, do not belong to any group. In Greece, no area is much more than 100km from the sea. The much indented coastline has a total length of 15,020km.

Roughly four-fifths of Greece is mountainous, with most of the land over 1500m above sea level. The Pindos Mountains, which are an offshoot of the Dinaric Alps, run north to south through the peninsula, and are known as the backbone of Greece. The mountains of the Peloponnese and Crete are part of the same formation. The highest mountain is Mt Olympus (2917m).

Greece does not have many rivers, and none which are navigable. The largest are the Aheloös, Aliakmonas, Aoös and Arahthos, all of which have their source in the Pindos Range in Epiros. The long plains of the river valleys, and those between the mountains and the coast, are the only lowlands. The mountainous terrain, dry climate and poor soil restricts agriculture to less than a quarter of the land. Greece is, however, rich in minerals, with reserves of oil, manganese, bauxite and lignite.

CLIMATE

Greece can be divided into a number of main climatic regions. Northern Macedonia and northern Epiros have a climate similar to the Balkans, with freezing winters and very hot, humid summers; while the Attic Peninsula, the Cyclades, the Dodecanese, Crete, and the central and eastern Peloponnese have a more typically Mediterranean climate with hot, dry summers and milder winters.

Snow is very rare in the Cyclades (it snowed on Paros for the first time in 15 years in 1992), but the high mountains of the Peloponnese and Crete are covered in snow during the winter, and it does occasionally snow in Athens. In July and August, the mercury can soar to 40°C (over 100°F) in the shade just about anywhere in the country. July and August are also the months of the *meltemi*, a strong northerly wind that sweeps the eastern coast of mainland Greece (including Athens) and the Aegean Islands, especially the Cyclades. The wind is caused by air pressure differences between North Africa and the Balkans. The wind is a mixed blessing: it reduces humidity, but plays havoc with ferry schedules and sends everything flying – from beach umbrellas to washing hanging out to dry.

The western Peloponnese, western Sterea Ellada, south-western Epiros and the Ionian Islands escape the meltemi and have less severe winters than northern Greece, but are the areas with the highest rainfall. The North-Eastern Aegean Islands, Halkidiki and the Pelion Peninsula fall somewhere between the Balkan-type climate of northern Greece and the Mediterranean climates. Crete stays warm the longest – you can swim off its southern coast from mid-April to November.

Mid-October is when the rains start in most areas, and the weather stays cold and wet until February – although there are also

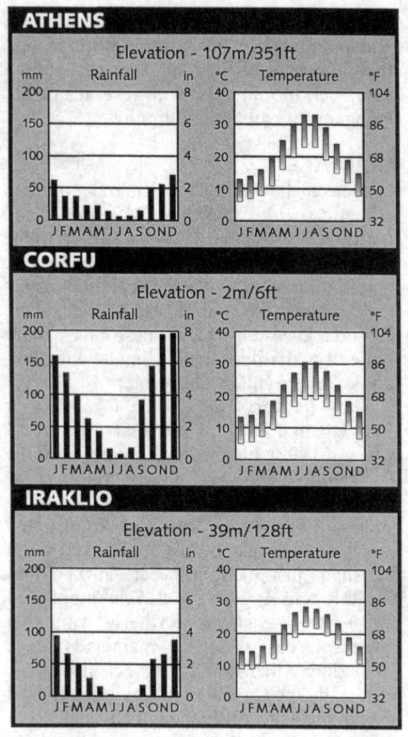

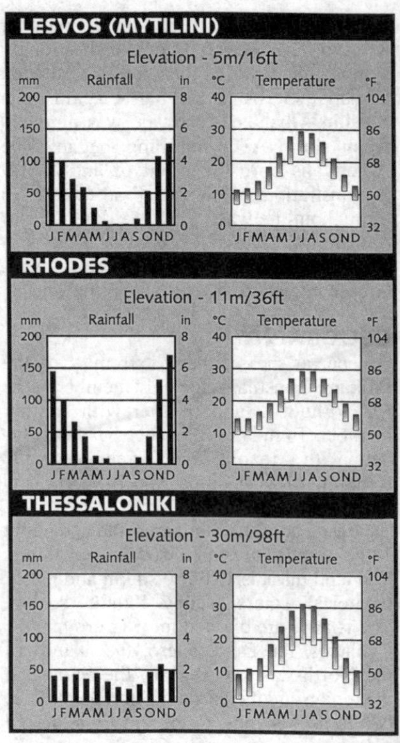

occasional winter days with clear blue skies and sunshine.

ECOLOGY & ENVIRONMENT

Greece is belatedly becoming environmentally conscious; regrettably, it is often a case of closing the gate after the horse has bolted. Deforestation and soil erosion are problems that go back thousands of years. Olive cultivation (see the accompanying boxed text 'The Evil Olive') and goats have been the main culprits, but firewood gathering, shipbuilding, housing and industry have all taken their toll.

Forest fires are also a major problem, with an estimated 25,000 hectares destroyed every year. The 1998 season was one of the worst on record. The worst outbreak destroyed dozens of homes in the hills just north of Athens, and left pine-covered Mt Pendeli so devastated that ecologists fear it may never recover.

The result is that the forests of ancient Greece have all but disappeared. Epiros and Macedonia in northern Greece are now the only places where extensive forests remain. This loss of forest cover has been accompanied by serious soil erosion. The problem is finally being addressed with the start of a long overdue reafforestation program.

General environmental awareness remains at a very low level, especially where litter is concerned. The problem is particularly bad in rural areas, where roadsides are strewn with soft-drink cans and plastic packaging hurled from passing cars. Envir-

The Evil Olive

It is a sad irony that the tree most revered by the Greeks is responsible for the country's worst ecological disaster. The tree is the olive. It was the money tree of the early Mediterranean civilisations, providing an abundance of oil that not only tasted great but could also be used for everything from lighting to lubrication. The ancient Greeks thought it was too good to be true and concluded it must be a gift from the gods.

In their eagerness to make the most of this gift, native forest was cleared on a massive scale to make way for the olive. Landowners were urged on by decrees such as those issued in the 6th century BC by the arhon of Athens, Solon, who banned the export of all agricultural produce other than olive oil and made cutting down an olive tree punishable by death.

Much of the land planted with olives was unsuitable hill country. Without the surface roots of the native forest to bind it, the topsoil of the hills was rapidly washed away. The olive tree could do nothing to help. It has no surface root system, depending entirely on its impressive tap root.

Thus, the lush countryside so cherished by the ancient Greeks was transformed into the harsh, rocky landscape that greets the modern visitor.

onmental education has begun in schools, but it will be some time before community attitudes change.

One area where Greece is aiming to be a leader rather than a follower is in the exploitation of solar energy. Crete looks set to become the site of Europe's first major solar power station, and Athens has announced an ambitious long-term plan to become the first city in the world to operate solar-powered buses.

FLORA & FAUNA

Flora

Greece is endowed with a variety of flora unrivalled in Europe. The wild flowers are spectacular. There are over 6000 species, some of which occur nowhere else, and more than 100 varieties of orchid. They continue to thrive because most of the land is too poor for intensive agriculture and has escaped the ravages of chemical fertilisers.

The regions with the most wild flowers are the mountains of Crete and the Mani area of the Peloponnese. Trees begin to blossom as early as the end of February in warmer areas, and the wild flowers start to appear in March. During spring the hillsides are carpeted with flowers, which seem to sprout even from the rocks. Spring flowers include anemones, white cyclamens, irises, lilies, poppies, gladioli, tulips, countless varieties of daisy and many more. By summer, the flowers have disappeared from all but the northern mountainous regions. Autumn brings flowers too, especially crocuses.

The forests that once covered ancient Greece have been decimated by thousands of years of clearing for agriculture, boat building and housing. Northern Greece is the only region that has retained significant areas of native forest. Here you will find mountain sides covered with dense thickets of hop hornbeam *(Ostrya carpinifolia)*, noted for its lavish display of autumn cover.

Another common species is the Cyprus plane *(Platanus orientalis insularis)*, which thrives wherever there is ample water. It seems as if every village on the mainland has a plane tree shading its central square – and a Taverna Platanos.

Australian eucalypts were widely used in tree-planting programs from the 1920s onwards, particularly in the Peloponnese and Crete.

Wild Flowers

The Greek countryside is the showcase for a spectacular spring display of wild flowers. Autumn is often described as Greece's 'second spring'.

Of Europe's 200 wild orchid species, around half grow in Greece. They flower from late February to early June. Another spring flower is the iris. The word 'iris' is Greek for rainbow – an appropriate name for these multicoloured flowers. Greece's wild irises include the white and yellow *Iris ochreoleuca* and the blue and orange *Iris cretica*. The latter is one of 120 wild flowers unique to Crete. Others include the pink Cretan ebony, the white-flowered symphyandra and the white-flowered *Cyclamen cretic*. Other unique species include the *Rhododendron luteum*, a yellow azalea which grows only on Mytilini, and a peony which is unique to Rhodes.

Spectacular plants include the coastal giant reed. You may get lost among its high, dense groves on your way to a beach. The giant fennel, which grows to 3m, and the tall yellow-horned poppy also grow by the sea. Another showy coastal plant is the magenta-flowered Hottentot fig, which was introduced from Africa. The white-flowered sea squill grows on hills above the coast. Conspicuous thistles include the milk thistle which has green and white variegated leaves and grows in meadows and by roadsides. In rocky terrain you will see the stemless carline thistle, whose silvery-white petalled flowers are used in dried flower displays.

The beautifully perfumed sea daffodil grows along southern coasts, particularly on Crete and Corfu. The conspicuous snake's-head fritillary *(Fritillaria graeca)* has pink flowers shaped like snakes' heads, and the markings on the petals resemble a chequer board – the Latin word *fritillu* means dice box.

Interesting trees include the evergreen carob which grows to 10m. John the Baptist is said to have eaten its pods when he lived in the desert. Mineral-rich carob is sold in some countries as a healthy substitute for chocolate. The flowers of the Judas tree, unusually, appear before the leaves. According to legend they were originally white, but when Judas hanged himself from the tree they turned pink in shame.

Fauna

Greece also has a large range of fauna, but you won't encounter much of interest unless you venture out into the prime habitat areas.

Bird-watchers have more chance of coming across something unusual than animal spotters. Greece has all the usual Mediterranean small birds – wagtails, tits, warblers, bee-eaters, larks, swallows, flycatchers, thrushes and chats – as well as some more distinctive species such as the hoopoe.

A large number of migratory birds, most of which are merely passing by on their way from winter feeding sites in north Africa to summer nesting grounds in Eastern Europe, can also be seen. Out of a total of 408 species of migratory birds in Europe, 240 have been sighted in Greece. One very visible visitor is the stork. Storks arrive in early spring from Africa, and return to the same nest year after year. The nests are built on electricity poles, chimney tops and church towers, and can weigh up to 50kg; look out for them in northern Greece, especially in Thrace.

Lake Mikri Prespa, in Macedonia, has the richest colony of fish-eating birds in Europe, including egrets, herons, cormorants and ibises, as well as the Dalmatian pelican – Turkey and Greece are now the only countries in Europe where this bird is found. The wetlands at the mouth of the Evros River, close to the border with Turkey, are home to two easily identifiable wading birds – the avocet, which has a long upcurved beak, and the black-winged stilt, which has extremely long pink legs.

Upstream on the Evros River in Thrace, the dense forests and rocky outcrops of the 7200 hectare Dadia Forest Reserve play host to the largest range of birds of prey in Europe. Thirty-six of the 38 European species can be seen here, and it is a breeding ground for 23 of them. Permanent residents include the giant black vulture, whose wingspan reaches three metres, the griffon vulture and golden eagles. Europe's last 15 pairs of royal eagles nest on the river delta. The reserve is managed by the Worldwide Fund for Nature Ellas (☎ 01-331 4893, fax 324 7578, email webmaster@wwf.gr), Filellinon 26, Athens 105 58.

About 350 pairs (60% of the world's population) of the rare Eleonora falcon nest on the remote island of Piperi in the Sporades.

The mountains of northern Greece also support a much greater range of wildlife than anywhere else in the country, although

The hoopoe, a member of the kingfisher family, has a prominent black-tipped crest

you're extremely unlikely to spot animals such as the brown bear or the grey wolf (see Endangered Species, following). Wild boar are still found in reasonable numbers in the north and are a favourite target for hunters. Squirrels, rabbits, hares, foxes and weasels are all fairly common on the mainland; less common is the cute European suslik – a small ground squirrel.

Reptiles are well represented. The snakes include several viper species, which are poisonous. For more information on snakes in Greece, see the Health section in the Facts for the Visitor chapter. You're more likely to see lizards, all of which are harmless.

One of the pleasures of island-hopping in Greece is watching the dolphins as they follow the boats. Although there are many dolphins in the Aegean, the striped dolphin has recently been the victim of murbilivirus – a sickness that affects the immune system. Research into the virus is being carried out in the Netherlands. You can get more information about dolphins from the Greek Society for the Protection & Study of Dolphins & Cetaceans (☎ 01-572 6612, fax 265 9917, email delphis@hol.gr), Imitou 50, Peristeri 121 32, Athens.

Endangered Species

The brown bear, Europe's largest land mammal, still survives in very small numbers in the Pindos Mountains, the Peristeri Range that rises above the Prespa Lakes and in the mountains which lie along the Bulgarian border. You can get more information from the Friends of the Greek Bear (☎ 031-554 623) in Thessaloniki.

The same organisation also has information on wolves – another endangered species, but not protected in Greece as in other countries. They survive in small numbers in the forests of the Pindos in Epiros as well as in the Dadia Forest Reserve area.

Europe's rarest mammal, the monk seal, was once very common in the Mediterranean, but is now on the brink of extinction in Europe – it survives in slightly larger numbers in the Hawaiian islands. There are only about 400 left in Europe, half of which live in Greece. There are about 40 in the Ionian Sea and the rest are found in the Aegean. These sensitive creatures are particularly susceptible to human disturbance, and now live only in isolated coastal caves. The majority of reported deaths are the result of accidental trapping, but the main threat to their survival is the continuing destruction of habitat. Tourist boats are major culprits. The Hellenic Society for the Study & Protection of the Monk Seal (☎ 01 522 2888, fax 522 2450), Solomou 53, Athens 104 32, has a seal rescue centre on Alonnisos, and the WWF funds a seal watch project on Zakynthos.

The waters around Zakynthos are also home to the last large sea turtle colony in Europe, that of the loggerhead turtle *(Careta careta)*. The loggerhead also nests in smaller numbers on the Peloponnese and on Crete. The Sea Turtle Protection Society of Greece (☎/fax 01-523 1342, email stps@compulink.gr), Solomou 57, Athens 104 32, runs monitoring programs and is always looking for volunteers. See the Attica section of the Athens chapter for information about the society's rescue centre at Glyfada.

Mediterranean monk seal, once threatened by hunters, is now threatened by tourism

National Parks

Visitors who expect Greek national parks to provide facilities on a par with those in countries like Australia and the US will be very disappointed. Although all have refuges and some have marked hiking trails, Greek national parks have little else by way of facilities.

The most visited parks are Mt Parnitha, just north of Athens, and the Samaria Gorge on Crete. The other national parks are Vikos-Aoös and Prespa in Epiros; Mt Olympus on the border of Thessaly and Macedonia; and Parnassos and Iti in central Greece. Most consist of buffer zones protecting an inner wilderness area. Some activities (including hunting!) are permitted in the buffer areas, but no activities other than walking are allowed in the protected area.

If you want to see wildlife, the place to go is the well organised Dadia Forest Reserve in eastern Thrace (see the Northern Greece chapter for details).

There is also a national marine park off the coast of Alonnisos in the Sporades, with a second due to be declared for Zakynthos in the Ionians.

GOVERNMENT & POLITICS

Since 1975, democratic Greece has been a parliamentary republic with a president as head of state. The president and parliament, which has 300 deputies, have joint legislative power. The PASOK party of Prime Minister Simitis holds 163 seats in the current parliament. Greek governments traditionally name very large cabinets – Simitis fronts a team of 41, with 19 ministries. Papandreou had 52 in his last cabinet!

Greece is divided into regions and island groups. The mainland regions are the Peloponnese, central Greece (officially called Sterea Ellada), Epiros, Thessaly, Macedonia and Thrace. The island groups are the Cyclades, Dodecanese, North-Eastern Aegean, Sporades and Saronic Gulf, all in the Aegean Sea, and the Ionian, which is in the Ionian Sea. The large islands of Evia and

Crete do not belong to any group. For administrative purposes these regions and groups are divided into prefectures or nomes (nomoi in Greek).

ECONOMY

Greece is an agricultural country, but the importance of agriculture to the economy has declined rapidly since WWII. Some 50% of the workforce is now employed in services (contributing 59% of GDP), 22% in agriculture (contributing 15%), and 27% in industry and construction (contributing 26%). Tourism is by far the biggest industry; shipping comes next.

Although Greece has the second-lowest income per capita of all the EU countries (after Portugal), its long-term economic future looks brighter now than it has for some time. Tough austerity measures imposed by successive governments have cut inflation to less than 3%, the Greek stock market has been booming since 1997 and investor confidence appears high.

Despite problems arising from the NATO war against Serbia – the fighting, combined with reports of anti-NATO sentiments in Greece, hit the tourism industry particularly hard – the country appears on track for the second phase of European monetary union in 2000.

POPULATION

A census is taken every 10 years in Greece. The 1991 census recorded a population of 10,264,156 – an increase of 5.4% on the 1981 figure. Women outnumber men by more than 200,000. Greece is now a largely urban society, with 68% of the population living in cities. By far the largest is the capital, Athens, with more than 3.1 million people living in the greater Athens area. The population figures of other major cities are: Thessaloniki (750,000), Piraeus (171,000), Patras (153,000), Iraklio (127,600), Larisa (113,400) and Volos (110,000). Less than 15% of people live on the islands, the most populous of which are Crete (537,000), Evia (209,100) and Corfu (105,000).

PEOPLE

Contemporary Greeks are a mixture of all of the invaders who have occupied the country since ancient times. Additionally, there are a number of distinct ethnic minorities living in the country.

The country's small Roman Catholic popu-lation is of Genoese or Frankish origin. They live mostly in the Cyclades, especially on the island of Syros, where they are 40% of the population. The Franks dominated the island from 1207 AD to Ottoman times.

About 300,000 ethnic Turks who were exempt from the population exchange of 1923 live in western Thrace. There are also small numbers of Turks on Kos and Rhodes which, along with the rest of the Dodecanese, did not become part of Greece until 1947.

There are small Jewish communities in several large towns. In Ioannina, Larisa, Halkidi and Rhodes, they date back to the Roman era, while in Thessaloniki, Kavala and Didymotiho, most are descendants of 15th century exiles from Spain and Portugal. In 1429, 20,000 exiled Jews arrived in Thessaloniki and by the 16th century they constituted the major part of the population. In 1941, the Germans entered Thessaloniki and herded 46,000 Jews off to Auschwitz, most never to return. They comprised 90% of Thessaloniki's Jews and more than half the total number in Greece. The small number of Jews in Athens are mostly German Jews who came over with King Otho in the 1830s. Today there are only about 5000 Jews living in Greece.

Very small numbers of Vlach and Sarakatsani shepherds live a semi-nomadic existence in Epiros. They take their flocks to the high ground in summer and return to the valleys in winter. The Vlachs originate from the region that is now Romania; the origins of the Sarakatsani are uncertain.

You will come across Roma (Gypsies) everywhere in Greece, but especially in Macedonia, Thrace and Thessaly. There are large communities of Roma in the Thracian towns of Alexandroupolis and Didymotiho.

The collapse of the communist regimes in Albania and Romania produced a wave

Three Pillars of Western Philosophy

TAMSIN WILSON

Socrates – 'Know thyself'

Little is certain about Socrates because he committed nothing to paper. Historians and philosophers have constructed a picture of Socrates through the writings of Plato, a one-time pupil.

Socrates was born around 470 BC in Athens and fought in the First Peloponnesian War. Thereafter he gave his life over to teaching in the streets and, particularly, the gymnasia – a mission bestowed on him by his god, the *daimon*.

He was deeply religious but regarded mythology with disdain. The *daimon's* existence was demonstrated by the perfect order of nature, the universality of people's belief in the divine and the revelations that come in dreams.

Socrates' method was dialectic: he sought to illuminate truth by question and answer, responding to a pupil's question with another question, and then another, until the pupil came to answer their own inquiry.

He believed that bodily desires corrupt people's souls, and a person's soul is directly responsible for their happiness. The soul is neither good nor bad, but well or poorly realised. Accordingly, unethical actions are in some sense involuntary – people commit bad actions because they have poor conceptions of themselves. However, those who know the true good will always act in accordance with it.

Believing that a profound understanding of goodness is a prerequisite for those who govern society, Socrates held that democracy was flawed because it left the state in the hands of the unenlightened and valued all opinion as equal.

In 399 BC, at the age of 70, Socrates was indicted for 'impiety'. He was convicted with 'corruption of the young' and 'the practice of religious novelties', and sentenced to death by the drinking of hemlock. The story of Socrates' day of execution is told in Plato's *Phaedo*.

TAMSIN WILSON

Plato – 'Until philosophers are kings ... cities will never cease from ill, nor the human race'

Plato was born around 428 BC in Athens, or perhaps Aegina, in the early years of the First Peloponnesian War into an aristocratic family. He was a student of Socrates, who had a great influence upon him.

Around 387 BC, Plato founded the Academy in Athens as an institute of philosophical and scientific studies.

Plato's prolific writings take the form of dialogues and read like scripts. He never introduced himself as a character in his dialogues, but he did use real people as speakers, including Socrates.

Politically, Plato was an authoritarian. The *Republic* is, in part, given over to his view of the ideal state. He divided people into commoners, soldiers and rulers. Plato declared that all people should live simply and modestly; that women and men should be equal, and given the same education and prospects; that marriages should be arranged by the state and children be removed from their parents at birth. This would minimise personal, possessive emotions, so that public spirit would be the overwhelming emotion that individuals felt.

Three Pillars of Western Philosophy

The notion of divine perfection was a central tenet in his thinking. The problem of class-ideas or 'universals' had long been a conundrum – to define the meaning of nouns like 'woman' or 'house' that can be applied to whole classes of individual instances. 'Woman' in its broadest sense is not this woman or that woman, but is greater, more real and more enduring than any individual woman.

Plato's answer was that objects in the world are merely appearances of perfect 'ideas' or 'forms'. Trees of the material world are merely copies of God's perfect tree, which bears no relation to time or space and which determines the properties of 'treeness'.

Plato held that knowledge cannot be derived from the senses. He argued that we perceive *through* our senses, not *with* them. We have knowledge of concepts that are not derived from experience: perfect symmetry has no manifestation in the material world. Plato believed that knowledge was inside everybody, and claimed that all knowledge is recollection – that it comes as revelation to the intellect.

TAMSIN WILSON

Aristotle – 'He who exercises his reason and cultivates it seems to be both in the best state of mind and most dear to the gods'

Aristotle was born in 384 BC in Stagira, Macedonia. In 367 BC, Aristotle went to Athens to become a pupil of Plato at the Academy. He remained there for nearly 20 years, until Plato's death.

After Plato's death a rift appeared between Aristotle and the Academy. Aristotle left and travelled widely, immersing himself in biological studies. At nearly 50, he returned to Athens and founded a rival institution, the Lyceum, working there for another 12 years and writing prolifically.

After the death of Alexander the Great in 323 BC, the strong anti-Macedonian sentiment that ensued led to Aristotle being indicted for 'impiety', ostensibly over his writings, but the real motives were political. He fled Athens and died a year later of a stomach condition.

He attacked Plato's Theory of Ideas. He regarded class-names as descriptive words, more like adjectives. For Aristotle, a universal derives its meaning from the fact that there are many individual instances of it. If there were no red things in the world, then the notion of 'redness' would be nonsensical.

Central to Aristotle's metaphysic is his distinction between 'form' and 'matter'. The sculptor of a statue confers shape (the form) onto marble (the matter). A thing's form is that which is unified about it – its *essence*. Matter without form is just potentiality, but by acquiring form its actuality increases. God has no matter, but is pure form and absolute actuality. Thus humans, by increasing form in the world, by building houses and bridges, make it more divine.

For Aristotle, the soul is inseparable from the body, but the mind (the rational soul) is divine and impersonal – all people should agree on issues of pure reason, like mathematics. Thus, the immortality of the mind is not a personal immortality. Rather, when exercising pure reason, people partake in the divine – in God's immortality.

Aristotle was the first thinker to look at structures of deductive arguments, or syllogisms, and for 2000 years was unsurpassed in the study of logic, until Gottlob Frege and Bertrand Russell, the 20th century's great symbolic logicians, picked up his thread.

of economic refugees across Greece's poorly guarded northern borders, with an estimated 300,000 arriving from Albania alone. These refugees have been a vital source of cheap labour for the agricultural sector; fruit and vegetable prices have actually gone down as a result of their contribution. Albanians also have a reputation as fine stone masons, and their influence can be seen everywhere.

EDUCATION

Education in Greece is free at all levels of the state system, from kindergarten to tertiary. Primary schooling begins at the age of six, but most children attend a state-run kindergarten from the age of five. Private kindergartens are popular with those who can afford them. Primary school classes tend to be larger than those in most European countries – usually 30 to 35 children. Primary school hours are short (8 am to 1 pm), but children get a lot of homework.

At 12, children enter the *gymnasio*, and at 15 they may leave school, or enter the *lykeio*, from where they take university-entrance examinations. Although there is a high percentage of literacy, many parents and pupils are dissatisfied with the education system, especially beyond primary level. The private sector therefore flourishes, and even relatively poor parents struggle to send their children to one of the country's 5000 *frontistiria* (intensive coaching colleges) to prepare them for the very competitive university-entrance exams. Parents complain that the education system is badly underfunded. The main complaint is about the lack of modern teaching aids in both gymnasio and lykeio.

Grievances reached a peak in 1991, when lykeio students staged a series of sit-ins in schools throughout the country, and organised protest marches. In 1992, gymnasio pupils followed suit, and the government responded by making proposals that called for stricter discipline and a more demanding curriculum. More sit-ins followed, and in the end the government changed its plans and is still reassessing the situation.

ARTS

See the following colour 'Greek Art through the Ages' section for a detailed look at the history of art and architecture in Greece.

Dance

Music and dancing have played an important role in Greek social life since the dawn of Hellenism. You may even think at times that Greeks live solely for the chance to sing and dance. You wouldn't be that wrong. Whether it be at a traditional wedding, a night club, an Athenian *boîte* or a simple village *kafeneio*, a song and a dance are not far from people's minds.

The style of dancing often reflects the climate or disposition of the participants. In Epiros, the stately *tsamiko* is slow and highly emotive, reflecting the often cold and insular nature of mountain life. The Pontian Greeks, on the contrary, have a highly visual, vigorous and warlike form of dancing reflecting years of altercations with their Turkish neighbours. The *kotsari* is one of the best examples of this unique dance form.

The islands with their bright and cheery atmosphere give rise to lilting music and matching dances such as the *ballos* or the *syrtos*, while the graceful *kalamatianos* circle dance, where dancers stand in a row with their hands on one another's shoulders, reflects years of proud Peloponnese tradition. Originally from Kalamata in the Peloponnese, this dance can be seen everywhere, most commonly on festive occasions.

The so-called 'Zorba's dance' or *syrtaki* is a stylised dance for two or three men or women with linked arms on shoulders, while the often spectacular solo male *zeïmbekikos* with its whirling improvisations has its roots in the Greek blues of the hashish dens and prisons of prewar times. The women counterpoint this self-indulgent and showy male display with their own sensuous *tsifteteli*, a svelte, sinewy show of femininity evolved from the Middle Eastern belly dance.

continued on page 65

GREEK ART & ARCHITECTURE

Walk around any capital city in Europe, America or Australasia and the influence of ancient Greek art and architecture is plain to see. It's there in the civic buildings, in the monumental public sculptures, in the plan of the city streets themselves. The product of a truly extraordinary civilisation, the humanism and purity of form of Greek art has inspired artists and architects throughout history. Be it in the paintings and sculptures of the Italian Renaissance or in the playful postmodernist buildings of the late 20th century, the influence of the ancient Greeks cannot be overemphasised.

Ironically, the influence of Greek art has spread throughout the world due to a reality that many travellers (and indeed the Greeks themselves) find unpalatable. This is the fact that many of the greatest works of ancient Greek art haven't had a home in Greece itself for hundreds, sometimes thousands, of years. From the Parthenon frieze taken by Lord Elgin and now displayed in the British Museum to the famous *Nike (Winged Victory of Samothrace)* in Paris' Louvre museum, the work of the Greek masters is held in the collections of the great museums of the world. Many of the great ancient Greek buildings, too, are found in countries other than Greece as they date from the time of the expansive ancient Greek world, which encompassed parts or all of countries such as Italy, Iran, Turkey, Syria and Libya.

Travellers to Greece itself shouldn't despair, however. There's plenty left to see! The buildings, paintings, pots, sculptures and decorative arts of the ancient and Byzantine worlds can be found on the country's streets, cities and islands, as well as in its wonderful museums. They may not be in their original form – it takes a stretch of the imagination to envisage *Hermes of Praxiteles* **with** arms, and magnificent and austere buildings such as the Parthenon overlaid with gaudily coloured paintings and sculptures – but they manage to evoke the history of the Greek nation more powerfully than a library of history books ever could.

Preceding page: Children boxing; fresco from Akrotiri, Santorini (Thira), c1600 BC (National Archaeological Museum, Athens)

Inset & Left: Red-figure kylix, Attic workshop, by the 'Painter of the Paris Gigantomachy', 480 BC (Nicholas P Goulandris Foundation & Musem of Cycladic Art)

ARCHITECTURE

Of all the ancient Greek arts, architecture has perhaps had the greatest influence. Greek temples, seen throughout history as symbols of democracy, have been the inspiration for architectural movements such as the Italian Renaissance and the British Greek Revival.

One of the earliest known architectural sites of ancient Greece is the huge palace and residential complex at Knossos on Crete, built in the Minoan period. Its excavation and reconstruction was begun by Sir Arthur Evans in 1900. Visitors today can see the ruins of the second residential palace built on this site (the first was destroyed by an earthquake in 1700 BC), with its spacious courtyards and grandiose stairways. They can also marvel at the many living rooms, storerooms and bathrooms that give us an idea of day-to-day Minoan life. Similar palaces on Crete, usually of two storeys and built around a large courtyard, have since been excavated at Phaestos, Agia Triada, Malia, Gournia and Zakros.

The Minoan period was followed by the Mycenaean. Instead of the open, labyrinthine palaces of the Minoans, the Mycenaeans used their advanced skills in engineering to build citadels on a compact, orderly plan, fortified by strong walls. Visitors to Greece today can appreciate Mycenaean sites such as those of the ancient city states of Mycenae and Tiryns, excavated by the German archaeologist Heinrich Schliemann in the 1870s. The famous Lion Gate at the palace at Mycenae and the stupendous galleries of the palace at Tiryns both illustrate the engineering expertise of the Mycenaeans.

The next great advance in ancient Greek architecture came with the building of the first monumental stone temples in the Archaic and classical periods. From this time, temples were characterised by the

Doric Ionian Corinthian

famous orders of columns, particularly the Doric, Ionic and Corinthian. These orders were applied to the exteriors of temples, which retained their traditional simple plan of porch and hall but were now regularly surrounded by a colonnade or at least a columnar facade.

Doric columns feature cushion capitals, fluted shafts and no bases. Doric temples still part extant include the Temple of Hera at Olympia, the Temple of Apollo at Corinth and the Temple of Hephaestus in Athens. The most famous Doric temple in Greece is, of course, the Parthenon.

The shaft of the Ionic column has a base in several tiers and has more flutes. Unlike the austere Doric style, its capital has an ornamented necking. In all, the Ionic order is less massive than the Doric, and is generally more graceful. The little temple of Athena Nike by the entrance to the Athenian Acropolis, and the Erechtheion, opposite the Parthenon, are two famous Ionic temples.

The distinct and ornate Corinthian column features a single or

RICK GERHARTER

Left: The Parthenon, showpiece of Athens' Acropolis, built in 447-438 BC

double row of leafy scrolls (usually acanthus). This order was introduced at the end of the classical period and was subsequently used by the Romans in many of their buildings. The Temple of Olympian Zeus in Athens, completed in Hadrian's time, is a good example of a Corinthian temple.

Theatre design was also a hallmark of the classical period. The tragedies of Aeschylus, Sophocles and Euripides and the comedies of Aristophanes were written and first performed in the Theatre of Dionysos, built into the slope of Athens' Acropolis in the 5th century BC. Other theatres dating from this period can be found at Dodoni, Megalopolis, Epidaurus and Argos (the latter seats about 20,000). They all feature excellent acoustics and most are still used for summer festivals.

In the Hellenistic period, private houses and palaces, rather than temples and public buildings, were the main focus. The houses at Delos, built around peristyled (surrounded by columns) courtyards and

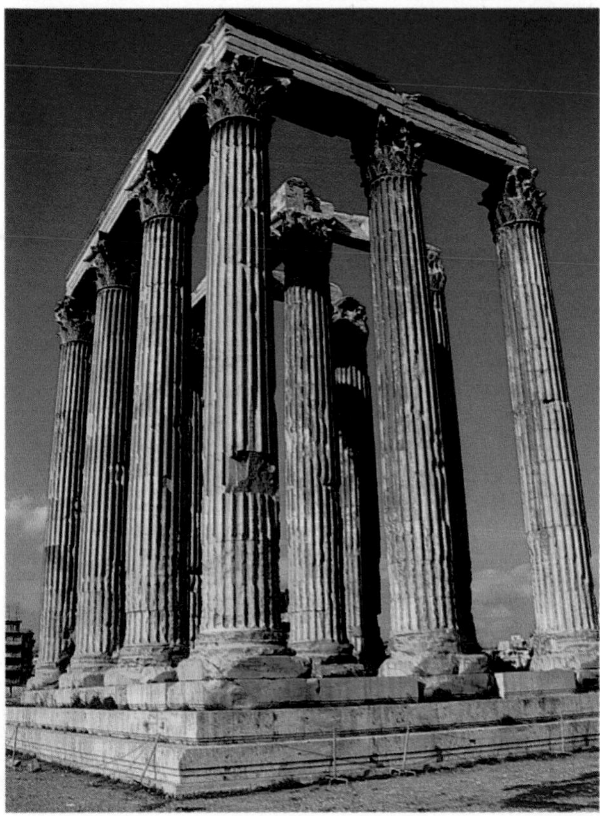
MARK HONAN

Right: The massive Temple of Olympian Zeus, Athens, begun in the 6th century BC, completed in 131 AD

featuring striking mosaics, are perhaps the best examples in existence.

The Roman period saw Corinth become an important Roman city, with recent excavations uncovering fountains, baths and gymnasia. Athens obtained a new commercial agora (now known as the Roman Agora) in the time of Augustus and a century and a half later the emperor Hadrian endowed the city with a library and built an elegant arch that still stands between the old and new parts of the city.

During the Byzantine period the Parthenon in Athens was converted into a church and other churches were built throughout Greece. These usually featured a central dome supported by four arches on piers and flanked by vaults, with smaller domes at the four corners and three apses to the east. The external brickwork, which alternated with stone, was sometimes set in patterns. At Mt Athos and on Patmos, where the first monasteries were built in the 10th century, the monastic buildings as well as the churches survive, though much has changed through centuries of continuous use and a number of fires. At Meteora in central Greece, the monasteries were built high on precipitous rocks and for centuries were almost inaccessible.

GEORGE TSAFOS

Left: A typical Meteora monastery, perched high on a seemingly inaccessible pinnacle

JON DAVISON

Right: The palace at Knossos, Crete, built in the Middle Minoan period (2100-1500 BC)

After the temporary fall of Constantinople to a crusading army in 1204, much of Greece became the fiefdoms of western aristocrats. The most notable of these was the Villehardouin family, who built castles in the Peloponnese at Hlemoutsi, Nafplio, Kalamata and Mystras. At Mystras they also built a palace which was a court of the Byzantine imperial family for two centuries prior to the Turkish conquest.

There is very little architecture of the Ottoman period surviving in Greece. The only examples are found at Kavala, Xanthi and Didymotiho near the Turkish border.

After the War of Independence, Greece continued the neoclassical style that had been dominant in western European architecture and sculpture from 1760 to 1820, thus providing a sense of continuity with its ancient past. This neoclassical style is apparent in Nafplio, initially the capital, and in Athens, notably in the Doric and Ionic ensemble of the National Library and the university. Noteworthy, too, are the old royal palace, the Polytehnio, and the mansions which are now the Byzantine, Benaki and Kanellopoulos museums.

SCULPTURE

Taking pride of place in the collections of the great museums of the world, the sculptures of ancient Greece have extraordinary visual power and beauty.

The prehistoric art of Greece has been discovered only recently, notably in the Cyclades and on Crete. The pared-down sculptures of this period, with their smooth and flattish appearance, were carved from the high-quality marble of Paros and Naxos in the middle of the 3rd millennium BC. Their primitive and powerful forms have inspired many artists since, particularly those of the 20th century.

In the Mycenaean period, small terracottas of women with a circular body or with arms upraised were widely produced. These are known to modern scholars as phi (ϕ) and psi (ψ) figurines from their resemblance to these letters of the Greek alphabet.

Displaying an obvious debt to Egyptian sculpture, the marble sculptures of the Archaic period are the true precursors of the famed Greek sculpture of the classical period. The artists of this period moved away from the examples of their Oriental predecessors and began to represent figures that were true to nature, rather than flat and stylised. For the first time in history a sculptured shape was made to reproduce the complex mechanism of the human body. Seeking to master the depiction of both the naked body and of drapery, sculptors of the period focused on figures of naked youths *(kouroi)*, with their set symmetrical stance and enigmatic smiles. Many great kouros sculptures and draped female kore can be admired at the National Archaeological Museum in Athens.

The sculpture of the classical period shows an obsession with the human figure and with drapery. At first the classical style was rather severe, as can be seen in the bronze charioteer at Delphi and the sculpture from the temple at Olympia. Later, as sculptors sought ideal proportions for the human figure, it became more animated. New poses were explored and the figures became increasingly sinuous, with smaller heads in relation to the body.

Left: Marble statuette of a boy playing with a goose, 3rd century BC

Right: Tanagran figurine; terracotta, Boeotian workshop, 330 BC

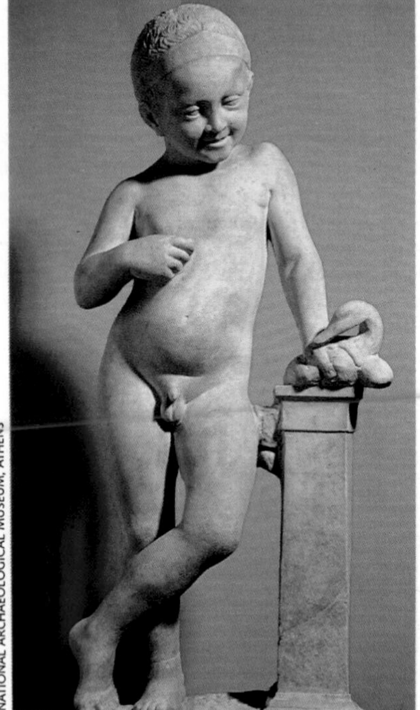

NATIONAL ARCHAEOLOGICAL MUSEUM, ATHENS

NICHOLAS P GOULANDRIS FOUNDATION & MUSEUM OF CYCLADIC ART

Unfortunately, little original work of the classical period survives. Most freestanding classical sculpture described by ancient writers was made of bronze and survives only as marble copies made by the Romans. Looking at these copies is a bittersweet experience. On the one hand, they are marvellous works of art in their own right. On the other, copies of works such as *Diskobolos* (The Discus Thrower) by Myron, *Apoxyomenos* (Scraper) by Lysippos and the various Aphrodites by Praxiteles have made us aware of what an extraordinary body of work has been lost. Fortunately, a few classical bronzes, lost when they were being shipped abroad in antiquity, were recovered from the sea in the 20th century. These include the statue of a youth (c350-330 BC)

NATIONAL ARCHAEOLOGICAL MUSEUM, ATHENS

Right: Grave stele of a woman with her maid; Attica, early 4th century BC

found in the sea off Antikythira, now in the collection of the National Archaeological Museum, Athens. Also on show here is the wonderful *Poseidon of Artemision*, thought to date from 470-450 BC.

The sculpture of the Hellenistic period continued the Greeks' quest to attain total naturalism in their work. Works of this period were animated, almost theatrical, in contrast to their serene Archaic and classical predecessors. The focus was on realism. Just how successful the artists of this period were is shown in the way later artists, such as Michelangelo, revered them. Michelangelo, in fact, was at the forefront of the rediscovery and appreciation of Greek works in the Renaissance. He is said to have been at the site in Rome in 1506 when the famous Roman copy of the *Laocoön* group, one of the iconic sculptural works of the Hellenistic period, was unearthed.

The end of the Hellenistic age signalled the decline of Greek sculpture's pre-eminent position in the history of the artform. The torch was handed to the Romans, who proved worthy successors. Sculpture in Greece itself never again attained any degree of true innovation.

POTTERY

Say the words 'Greek art' and many people immediately visualise a painted terracotta pot. Represented in museums and art galleries throughout the world, the pots of ancient Greece have such a high profile for a number of reasons, chief among these being that there are lots of them around! The excavation of these pots, buried throughout Greece over millennia, has enabled us to appreciate in

Left: Red-figure pelike, Attic workshop, by the 'Painter of the Louvre Centauromachy', 450-440 BC

Right: Black-figure lekythos, Attic workshop, probably by the 'Amasis Painter', 560-550 BC

PHOTOGRAPHS: NICHOLAS P GOULANDRIS FOUNDATION & MUSEUM OF CYCLADIC ART small measure the tradition of ancient pictorial art. Quite simply, in the absence of significant examples of Greek painting, pots are all we've got!

Practised from the Stone Age on, pottery is one of the most ancient arts. At first, vases were built with coils and wads of clay but the art of throwing on the wheel was introduced in about 2000 BC and was then practised with great skill by Minoan and Mycenaean artists.

Minoan pottery is often characterised by a high centre of gravity and beak-like spouts. Painted decoration was applied as a white clay slip (a thin paste of clay and water) or one which fired to a greyish black or dull red. Flowing designs with spiral or marine and plant motifs were used. The Archaeological Museum in Iraklio has a wealth of Minoan pots.

Mycenaean pottery shapes include a long-stemmed goblet and a globular vase with handles resembling a pair of stirrups. Decorative motifs are similar to those on Minoan pottery but are less fluid.

The 10th century BC saw the introduction of the Protogeometric style, with its substantial pots decorated with blackish-brown horizontal lines around the circumference, hatched triangles, and compass-drawn concentric circles. This was followed by the new vase shape and more crowded decoration of the pots of the Geometric period. The decorations on these pots are painted in a lustrous brown glaze on the light surface of the clay, and the same dark glaze is used as a wash to cover the undecorated areas. Occasionally a touch of white is added. By the early 8th century, figures were introduced, marking the introduction of the most fundamental element in the later tradition of classical art – the representation of gods, men and animals.

By the 7th century BC, Corinth was producing pottery with added white and purple-red clay slip. These pots often featured friezes of lions, goats and swans and a background fill of rosettes. In 6th century Athens, artists used red clay with a high iron content. A thick colloidal slip made from this clay produced a glossy black surface that contrasted with the red and was enlivened with added white and purple-red. Attic pots, famed for their high quality, were exported throughout the Greek Empire during this time. Many of these exports are the pots that grace the collections of international museums today.

PAINTING

The lack of any comprehensive archaeological record of ancient Greek painting has forced art historians to largely rely on the painted decoration of terracotta pots as evidence of the development of this Greek artform. There are a few exceptions, such as the Cycladic frescoes in houses on Santorini, excavated in the mid-to-late 20th century. Some of these frescoes are now in the collection of the National Archaeological Museum in Athens. These works were painted in fresco technique using yellow, blue, red and black pigments, with some details added after the plaster had dried. Plants and animals are depicted, as well as men and women. Figures are usually shown in profile or in a combination of profile and frontal views. Stylistically, the frescoes are similar to the paintings of Minoan Crete, which are less well preserved. Reconstructed examples of frescoes from the Minoan period can be seen at the Palace of Knossos, on Crete.

Greek painting came into its own during the Byzantine period. Byzantine churches were usually decorated with frescoes on a dark blue ground with a bust of Christ in the dome, the four Gospel writers in the pendentives supporting the dome and the Virgin and Child in the apse. They also featured scenes from the life of Christ (Annunciation, Nativity, Baptism, Entry into Jerusalem, Crucifixion and Transfiguration) and figures of the saints. In the later centuries of the period, the scenes involved more detailed narratives, including cycles of the life of the Virgin and the miracles of Christ.

Painting after the Byzantine period became more secular in nature, with 19th century Greek painters specialising in portraits, nautical themes and pictorial representation of the War of Independence. Major 19th century painters included Dionysios Tsokos, Andreas Kriezis, Theodoros Vryzakis, Nikiphoros Lytras, Konstantinos Volanakis and

BYZANTINE MUSEUM, ATHENS

Left: The Archangel Michael; icon, 14th century

Opposite Page:
Top Left: Presentation of Christ in the Temple and the Baptism of Christ in the River Jordan by John the Baptist; icon of the Cretan school, 16th century

Top Right: The Virgin Enthroned, with a border of scenes from the life of Christ and portraits of saints; icon of the Cretan school, 16th century

Bottom: Blind Eros and Two Sirens; painting on wood by Agapios Manganaris of Sifnos, 1825

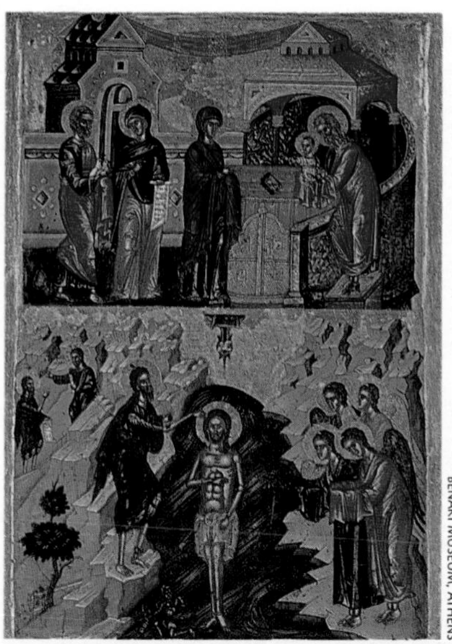

BENAKI MUSEUM, ATHENS

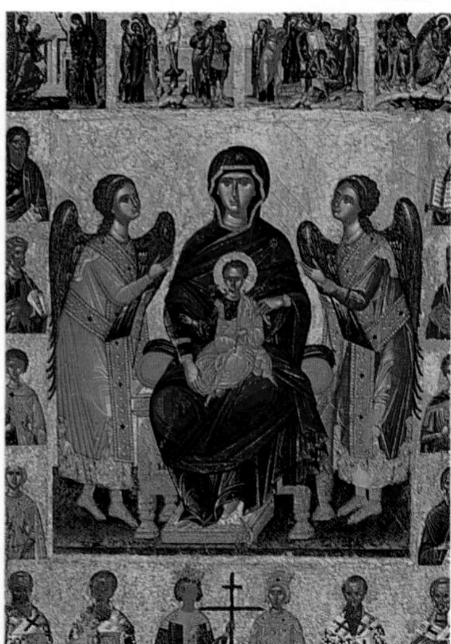

BENAKI MUSEUM, ATHENS

BYZANTINE MUSEUM, ATHENS

NATIONAL ARCHAEOLOGICAL MUSEUM, ATHENS

BENAKI MUSEUM, ATHENS

Nicholas Gyzis. Gyzis' historical paintings, which were painted at the time of the fascination with the 'Great Idea' of a new Greek Empire, feature particularly interesting subject matter.

From the first decades of the 20th century, artists such as Konstantinos Parthenis, Konstantinos Kaleas and, later, George Bouzianis were able to use the heritage of the past and at the same time assimilate various developments in modern art. These paintings are best studied in the National Art Gallery in Athens.

OTHER ARTS

Though we talk predominantly of architecture, sculpture, pottery and painting when discussing Greek art, there are, of course, the many 'minor' arts as well. Examples of many of these artforms can be seen in Greek museums; they are less monumental – in both size and ambition – than the works discussed above but are no less interesting. These arts include:

Weaving and embroidery Often displaying regional characteristics, examples of weaving and embroidery survive in some quantity from the 17th century onwards. Examples can be seen in the folk museum at Thessaloniki.

Decorative arts The Benaki Museum in Athens displays a fine collection of decorative arts from medieval and modern Greece, as well as some from earlier centuries.

Mosaics Mosaic wall decoration with tesserae (tiles) of coloured glass for figures and glass with gold leaf for background can be seen at the 11th century churches at Dafni, at Moni Osiou Louka near Delphi and at Nea Moni on Chios.

Metalwork and jewellery Spectacular Mycenaean gold masks, diadems, cups and dress ornaments occupy the central hall of the Archaeological Museum in Athens.

Opposite page: Fisherman; fresco from Akrotiri, Santorini (Thira), c1600 BC

Right: Cushion embroidered with a fork-tailed Gorgon in the centre; from Crete, 18th to 19th century

Further reading:

Greek Art and Archaeology, JG Pedley, Cassell, London, 1992
The Greek Museums, M Andronicos et al, Athens, 1975
A Handbook of Greek Art, Gisela Richter, Phaidon, London 1974
Greek Art, John Boardman, Thames & Hudson, London 1996

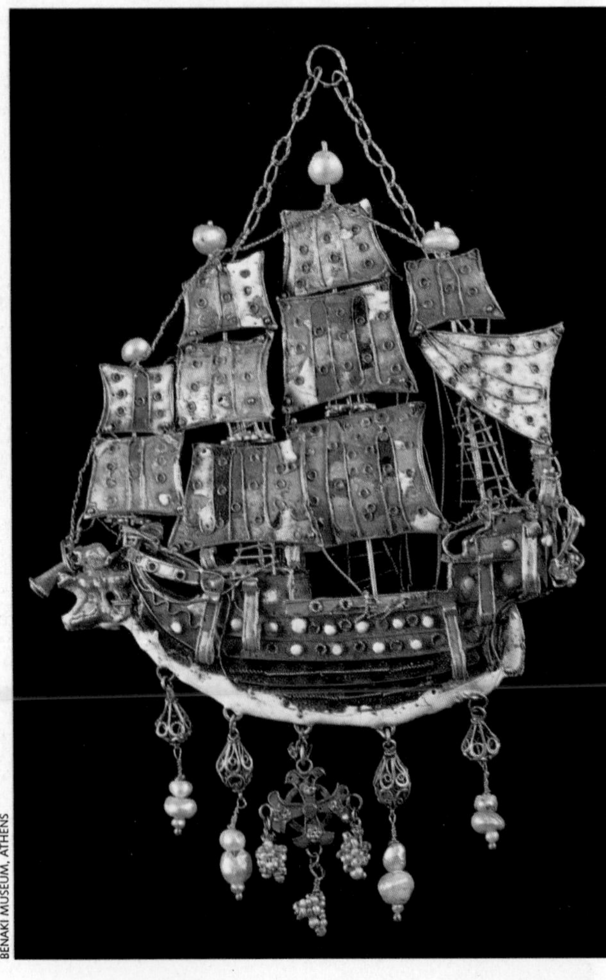

Left: Gold pendant with enamels and pearls; from Patmos, 18th century

continued from page 48

The folk dances of today derive from the ritual dances performed in ancient Greek temples. The syrtos is one of these dances, and is depicted on ancient Greek vases. There are also references to dances in Homer's works. Many Greek folk dances, including the syrtos, are performed in a circular formation; in ancient times, dancers formed a circle in order to seal themselves off from evil influences.

Music

Singing and the playing of musical instruments have also been an integral part of life in Greece since ancient times, and are as widely divergent as Greek dancing. Cycladic figurines holding musical instruments resembling harps and flutes date back to 2000 BC. Musical instruments of ancient Greece included the lyre, lute, *piktis* (pipes), *kroupeza* (a percussion instrument), *kithara* (a stringed instrument), *aulos* (a wind instrument), *barbitos* (similar to a violincello) and the *magadio* (similar to a harp).

If ancient Greeks did not have a musical instrument to accompany their songs, they imitated the sound of one. It is believed that unaccompanied Byzantine choral singing derived from this custom.

The ubiquitous stringed *bouzouki* closely associated with contemporary music, and which you will hear everywhere in Greece, is a relative newcomer to the game. It is a mandolin-like instrument similar to the Turkish *saz* and *baglama*.

The plucked strings of the bulbous *outi* (oud), the strident sound of the Cretan *lyra* (lyre) and the staccato rap of the *toumberleki* (lap drum) bear witness to a rich range of musical instruments that share many common characteristics with instruments all over the Middle East.

The bouzouki is one of the main instruments of *rembetika* music – the Greek equivalent of the American Blues. The name rembetika may come from the Turkish word *rembet* which means outlaw. Opinions differ as to the origins of rembetika, but it is probably a hybrid of several different types of music. One source was the music that emerged in the 1870s in the 'low life' cafes, called *tekedes* (hashish dens), in urban areas and especially around ports. Another source was the Arabo-Persian music played in sophisticated Middle Eastern music cafes *(amanedes)* in the 19th century. Rembetika was popularised in Greece by the refugees from Asia Minor.

The songs which emerged from the tekedes had themes concerning hashish, prison life, gambling, knife fights etc, whereas cafe aman music had themes which centred around erotic love. These all came together in the music of the refugees, from which a subculture of rebels, called *manges*, emerged. The manges wore showy clothes even though they lived in extreme poverty. They worked long hours in menial jobs, and spent their evenings in the tekedes, smoking hashish and singing and dancing. Although hashish was illegal, the law was rarely enforced until Metaxas did his clean-up job in 1936. It was in a tekes in Piraeus that Markos Vamvakaris, now acknowledged as the greatest *rembetis*, was discovered by a recording company in the 1930s.

Metaxas' censorship meant that themes of hashish, gambling and the like disappeared from recordings of rembetika in the late 1930s, but continued clandestinely in

The distinctly Greek bouzouki

some tekedes. This polarised the music, and the recordings, stripped of their 'meaty' themes and language, became insipid and bourgeois; recorded rembetika even adopted another name – *Laïko tragoudi* – to disassociate it from its illegal roots. Although WWII brought a halt to recording, a number of composers emerged at this time. They included Apostolos Kaldaras, Yiannis Papaïoanou, Georgos Mitsakis and Manolis Hiotis; one of the greatest female rembetika singers, Sotiria Bellou, also appeared at this time.

During the 1950s and 1960s rembetika became increasingly popular, but less and less authentic. Much of the music was glitzy and commercialised, although the period also produced two outstanding composers of popular music (including rembetika) in Mikis Theodorakis and Manos Hatzidakis. The best of Theodorakis' work is the music which he set to the poetry of Seferis, Elytis and Ritsos.

During the junta years, many rembetika clubs were closed down, but interest in genuine rembetika revived in the 1980s – particularly among students and intellectuals. There are now a number of rembetika clubs in Athens.

Other musical forms in Greece include *dimotika* – poetry sung and more often than not accompanied by the *klarino* (clarinet) and *defi* (tambourine) – and the widely popular middle-of-the-road *elafrolaïka*, best exemplified by the songs of Giannis Parios. The unaccompanied, polyphonic *pogonisia* songs of northern Epiros and southern Albania are spine-chilling examples of a

Georgos Dalaras

Georgos Dalaras is a musical phenomenon in Greece. With a successful career spanning over 29 years, more than 40 albums of his own and participation in over 50 other albums, he is Greece's undisputed ambassador of song. Largely unknown outside his homeland, Dalaras nonetheless performs regularly to captive audiences in the USA, Australia, Israel and in many countries in Europe. His songs are hummed as much by the youth in Belgrade or Helsinki as by the youth of Greece. Two of his albums have achieved the status of the first gold and platinum records in Greece.

Who is Georgos Dalaras and why is he so popular? His success is due to his remarkable voice and his commitment to the preservation of the popular Greek song in a musical world dominated by disco and techno. Dalaras is a political singer too, and managed to tread that fine line between acceptability and political pariah status during the dark years of the military junta (1967-74). In recent times his musical output has embraced the tragedy of the Turkish occupation of Cyprus with two major concerts in London in 1992 and Paris in 1993. He has participated in cultural and political festivals in Cuba, sung with Mikis Theodorakis in 1981 and alongside Peter Gabriel and Sting for Amnesty International in 1988 in Athens.

More than anyone else, Dalaras was responsible for the reawakened respect for and interest in the *rembetika* genre of music – the Greek blues of the 1920s. His double album *50 Chronia Rembetiko* sold over 100,000 copies. His concerts still pack stadiums and sports halls and his popularity is stronger than ever. If you are in Greece, try and catch one of his concerts. It will be a rare treat. For a retrospective of his vast discography, have a listen to *50 Chronia Rembetiko*. For a live song collection, listen to *Dalaras – Papakonstantinou – Live at the Attikon*, a recent work featuring Vasilis Papakonstantinou, another Greek musical genius. The 1972 album *Mikra Asia*, a nostalgic tribute to the 1921 Asia Minor disaster, is one of the masterpieces of contemporary Greek music.

musical genre that owes its origins to Byzantium. At the lesser end of the scale, the curiously popular *skyladika* or 'dog songs' – presumably because they resemble a whining dog – are hugely popular in night clubs known as *bouzouxidika* where the bouzouki reigns supreme, but where musical taste sometimes takes a back seat.

Since independence, Greece has followed mainstream developments in classical music. The Athens Concert Hall has performances by both national and international musicians.

You'll also find all the main forms of western popular music. Rock, particularly heavy metal, seems to have struck a chord with young urban Greeks, and Athens has a lively local scene as well as playing host to big international names.

Few Greek performers have hit it big on the international scene. The best known are Demis Roussos, the larger than life singer who spent the 1980s strutting the world stage clad in his caftan, and the US-based techno wizard Yanni.

Literature

The first, and greatest, ancient Greek writer was Homer, author of the *Iliad* and *Odyssey*. Nothing is known of Homer's life; where or when he lived, or whether, as it is alleged, he was blind. The historian Herodotus thought Homer lived in the 9th century BC, and no scholar since has proved nor disproved this.

Herodotus (5th century BC) was the author of the first historical work about western civilisation. His highly subjective account of the Persian Wars has, however, led him to be regarded as the 'father of lies' as well as the 'father of history'. The historian Thucydides (5th century BC) was more objective in his approach, but took a high moral stance. He wrote an account of the Peloponnesian Wars, and also the famous *Melian Dialogue*, which chronicles the talks between the Athenians and Melians prior to the Athenian siege of Melos.

Pindar (c518-438 BC) is regarded as the pre-eminent lyric poet of ancient Greece. He was commissioned to recite his odes at the Olympic Games. The greatest writers of love poetry were Sappho (6th century BC) and Alcaeus (5th century BC), both of whom lived on Lesvos. Sappho's poetic descriptions of her affections for other women gave rise to the term 'lesbian'.

In Byzantine times, poetry, like all of the arts, was of a religious nature. During Ottoman rule, poetry was inextricably linked with folk songs, which were not written down but passed on by word of mouth. Many of these songs were composed by the klephts, and told of the harshness of life in the mountains and of their uprisings against the Turks.

Dionysios Solomos (1798-1857) and Andreas Kalvos (1796-1869), who were both born on Zakynthos, are regarded as the first modern Greek poets. Solomos' work was heavily nationalistic and his *Hymn to Freedom* became the Greek national anthem. At this time there were heated debates among writers, politicians and educators about whether the official language should be Demotiki or Katharevousa. Demotic was the spoken language of the people and Katharevousa was an artificial language loosely based on Ancient Greek. Almost all writers favoured Demotic, and from the time of Solomos, most wrote only in that language.

The highly acclaimed poet Constantine Cavafy (1863-1933) was less concerned with nationalism, being a resident of Alexandria in Egypt; his themes ranged from the erotic to the philosophical.

The best known 20th century Greek poets are George Seferis (1900-71), who won the Nobel Prize for literature in 1963, and Odysseus Elytis (1911-96), who won the same prize in 1979. Seferis drew his inspiration from the Greek myths, whereas Elytis' work is surreal. Angelos Sikelianos (1884-1951) was another poet who drew inspiration from ancient Greece, particularly Delphi. His poetry is highly evocative, and includes incantatory verses emulating the Delphic oracle. Yiannis Ritsos is another highly acclaimed Greek poet; his work draws on many aspects of Greece – its landscape, mythology and social issues. The most celebrated 20th century Greek novelist is Nikos Kazantzakis. See the Books section in the Facts for the Visitor chapter for a commentary on his works.

Drama

Drama in Greece can be dated back to the contests staged at the Ancient Theatre of Dionysos in Athens during the 6th century BC for the annual Dionysia festival. During one of these competitions, Thespis left the ensemble and took centre stage for a solo performance regarded as the first true dramatic performance. The term 'thespian' for actor derives from this event.

Aeschylus (525-456 BC) is the so-called 'father of tragedy'; his best-known work is the *Oresteia* trilogy. Sophocles (c496-406 BC) is regarded as the greatest tragedian. He is thought to have written over 100 plays, of which only seven major works survive. These include *Ajax*, *Antigone*, *Electra*, *Trachiniae* and his most famous play, *Oedipus Rex*. His plays dealt mainly with tales from mythology and had complex plots. Sophocles won first prize 18 times at the Dionysia festival, beating Aeschylus in 468 BC, whereupon Aeschylus went off to Sicily in a huff.

Euripides (c485-406 BC) was another famous tragedian, more popular than either Aeschylus or Sophocles because his plots were considered more exciting. He wrote 80 plays of which 19 are extant (although one, *Rhesus*, is disputed). His most famous works are *Medea*, *Andromache*, *Orestias* and *Bacchae*. Aristophanes (c427-387 BC) wrote comedies – often ribald – which dealt with topical issues. His play *The Wasp* ridicules Athenians who resorted to litigation over trivialities; *The Birds* pokes fun at Athenian gullibility; and *Plutus* deals with the unfair distribution of wealth.

You can see plays by the ancient Greek playwrights at the Athens and Epidaurus festivals (see the Athens and Peloponnese chapters), and at various other festivals around the country.

Film

Greeks are avid cinema-goers, although most of the films they watch are North American or British. The Greek film industry has long been in the doldrums, largely due to inadequate funding. The problem is compounded by the type of films the Greeks produce, which are famously slow moving, loaded with symbolism and generally too avant-garde to have mass appeal.

The leader of this school is Theodoros Angelopoulos, winner of the Golden Palm award at the 1998 Cannes Film Festival for *An Eternity and One Day*. It tells the story of a terminally ill writer who spends his last day revisiting his youth in the company of a 10-year-old boy. His other films include *The Beekeeper*, *Alexander the Great* and *The Hesitant Step of the Stork*.

Although Greece produces no action films, there is a lighter side to the Greek cinema. *Orgasmos tis Ageladas* (The Cow's Orgasm) is a comedy by Olga Malea that relates the adventures of two girls from Larissa who are frustrated by the restrictions of small-town society.

SOCIETY & CONDUCT

Traditional Culture

Greece is steeped in traditional customs. Name days (see the accompanying boxed text), weddings and funerals all have great significance. On someone's name day an open-house policy is adopted and refreshments are served to well-wishers who stop by to give gifts. Weddings are highly festive occasions, with dancing, feasting and drinking sometimes continuing for days.

Greeks tend to be more superstitious than other Europeans. Tuesday is considered an unlucky day because on that day the Byzantine Empire fell to the Ottomans. Many Greeks will not sign an important transaction, get married or begin a trip on a Tuesday. Greeks also believe in the 'evil eye', a superstition prevalent in many Middle Eastern countries. If someone is the victim of the evil eye, then bad luck will befall them. The bad luck is the result of someone's envy, so one should avoid being too complimentary

Namedays

Namedays, not birthdays, are celebrated in Greece. Great significance is attached to the name given to a child, and the process of choosing a name follows fairly rigid conventions. The idea of a child being given a name just because the parents like the sound of it is unknown in Greece. Even naming a child after someone as a mark of respect or admiration is unusual. That so many children were named Vyronis (the Greek form of Byron) was a measure of the tremendous gratitude the Greeks felt for the philhellene Lord Byron.

Children are never named after parents, but the eldest son in a family is often called after his paternal grandfather, and the eldest daughter after her paternal grandmother. Names are usually of religious origin. Each island or area in Greece has a patron saint, and people living in that area often name a child after its patron saint. The patron saint of Corfu is Agios Spyridon and it seems as if about half of the men who were born there are called Spyridon. Exceptions to this custom occur if a family is not religious – quite a rarity in Greece. A nonreligious family will often give their offspring a name derived from ancient Greece or mythology. Socrates, Aristotle, Athena and Aphrodite are popular.

Each saint has a special feast day. A person's nameday is the feast day of the saint after which they were named. On someone's nameday, open house is held and a feast is laid on for the friends and neighbours who call. They will give a small gift to the person whose nameday it is, but there is less emphasis on the giving of presents than there is in birthday celebrations.

If you meet someone in Greece on their nameday, the customary greeting is *'chronia polla!'*, which means 'many years'.

about things of beauty, especially newborn babies. To ward off the evil eye, Greeks often wear a piece of blue glass, resembling an eye, on a chain around their necks.

Dos & Don'ts

The Greeks' reputation for hospitality is not a myth, although it's a bit harder to find these days. In rural areas, Greece is probably the only country in Europe where you may be invited into a stranger's home for coffee, a meal or even to spend the night. This can often lead to a feeling of uneasiness in the recipient if the host is poor, but to offer money is considered offensive. The most acceptable way of saying thank you is through a gift, perhaps to a child in the family. A similar situation arises if you go out for a meal with Greeks; the bill is not shared as in northern European countries, but paid by the host.

When drinking wine it is the custom to only half fill the glass. It is bad manners to empty the glass, so it must be constantly replenished. When visiting someone you will be offered coffee; again, it is bad manners to refuse. You will also be given a glass of water and perhaps a small serve of preserves. It is the custom to drink the water, then eat the preserves and then drink the coffee.

Personal questions are not considered rude in Greece, and if you react as if they are you will be the one causing offence. You will be inundated with queries about your age, salary, marital status etc.

If you go into a *kafeneio*, taverna or shop, it is the custom to greet the waiters or assistant with *'kalimera'* (good day) or *'kalispera'* (good evening) – likewise if you meet someone in the street.

You may have come to Greece for sun, sand and sea, but if you want to bare all, other than on a designated nude beach, remember that Greece is a traditional country, so take care not to offend the locals.

Ancient Greek Mythology

RICARDO BUSTOS

Mythology was an integral part of life in ancient times. The myths of ancient Greece are the most familiar to us, for they are deeply entrenched in the consciousness of western civilisation. They are accounts of the lives of the deities whom the Greeks worshipped and of the heroes they idolised.

The myths are all things to all people – a ripping good yarn, expressions of deep psychological insights, words of spine-tingling poetic beauty and food for the imagination. They have inspired great literature, art and music – as well as the odd TV show.

The myths we know are thought to be a blend of Dorian and Mycenaean mythology. Most accounts derive from the works of the poets Hesiod and Homer, produced in about 900 BC. The original myths have been chopped and changed countless times – dramatised, moralised and even adapted for ancient political propaganda, so numerous versions exist.

The Greek Myths by Robert Graves is regarded as being the ultimate book on the subject. It can be heavy going, though. *An Iconoclast's Guide to the Greek Gods* by Maureen O'Sullivan makes more entertaining reading.

The Twelve Deities

The main characters of the myths are the 12 deities, who lived on Mt Olympus.

The supreme deity was **Zeus**, who was also god of the heavens. His job was to make laws and keep his unruly family in order by brandishing his thunderbolt. He was also the possessor of an astonishing libido and vented his lust on just about everyone he came across, including his own mother. Mythology is littered with his offspring.

Zeus was married to his sister **Hera**, the protector of women and the family. Hera was able to renew her virginity each year by bathing in a spring. She was the mother of Ares, Hebe and Hephaestus.

Ares, god of war, was the embodiment of everything warlike. Strong and brave, he was definitely someone to have on your side in a fight – but he was also hot-tempered and violent, liking nothing better than a good massacre. Athenians, who fought only for such noble ideals as liberty, thought that Ares must be a Thracian – whom they regarded as bloodthirsty barbarians.

Hephaestus was worshipped for his matchless skills as a craftsman. When Zeus decided to punish man, he asked Hephaestus to make a woman. So Hephaestus created Pandora from clay and water, and, as everyone knows, she had a box, from which sprang all the evils afflicting humankind.

The next time you have a bowl of corn flakes, give thanks to **Demeter**, the goddess of earth and fertility. The English word 'cereal', for products of corn or edible grain, derives from the goddess' Roman name, Ceres. The Greek word for such products is *demetriaka*.

The goddess of love (and lust) was the beautiful **Aphrodite**. Her *tour de force* was her magic girdle which made everyone fall in love with its wearer. The girdle meant she was constantly pursued by both gods and goddesses – the gods because they wanted to make love to her, the goddesses because they wanted to borrow the girdle. Zeus became so fed up with her promiscuity that he married her off to Hephaestus, the ugliest of the gods.

Athena, the powerful goddess of wisdom and guardian of Athens, is said to have been born (complete with helmet, armour and spear) from Zeus' head, with Hephaestus acting as

Ancient Greek Mythology

midwife. Unlike Ares, she derived no pleasure from fighting, preferring to use her wisdom to settle disputes peacefully. If need be, however, she went valiantly into battle.

Poseidon, the brother of Zeus, was god of the sea and preferred his sumptuous palace in the depths of the Aegean to Mt Olympus. When he was angry (which was often) he would use his trident to create massive waves and floods. His moods could also trigger earthquakes and volcanic eruptions. He was always on the lookout for some real estate on dry land and challenged Dionysos for Naxos, Hera for Argos and Athena for Athens.

Apollo, god of light, was the son of Zeus by the nymph Leto. He was the sort of person everybody wanted to have around. The ancients Greeks associated sunshine with spiritual and intellectual illumination. Apollo was also worshipped as the god of music and song, which the ancients believed were heard only where there was light and security.

Apollo's twin sister, **Artemis**, seems to have been a bit confused by her portfolio. She was worshipped as the goddess of childbirth, yet she asked Zeus to grant her eternal virginity; she was also the protector of suckling animals, but loved hunting!

Hermes, messenger of the gods, was another son of Zeus – this time by Maia, daughter of Atlas. He was a colourful character who smooth-talked his way into the top ranks of the Greek pantheon. Convicted of rustling Apollo's cattle while still in his cradle, he emerged from the case as the guardian of all divine property. Zeus then made Hermes his messenger, and fitted him out with a pair of winged golden sandals to speed him on his way. His job included responsibility for commerce, treaties and the safety of travellers. He remained, however, the patron of thieves.

Hermes completes the first XI – the gods whose position in the pantheon is agreed by everyone. The final berth is normally reserved for **Hestia**, goddess of the hearth. She was as pure as driven snow, a symbol of security, happiness and hospitality. She spurned disputes and wars and swore to be a virgin forever.

She was a bit too virtuous for some, who relegated her to the ranks of the Lesser Gods and promoted the fun-loving **Dionysos**, god of wine, in her place. Dionysos was a son of Zeus by another of the supreme deity's dalliances. He had the job of touring the world with an entourage of fellow revellers spreading the word about the vine and wine.

Lesser Gods

After his brothers Zeus and Poseidon had taken the heavens and seas, **Hades** was left with the underworld (the earth was common ground). This vast and mysterious region was

Ancient Greek Mythology

thought by the Greeks to be as far beneath the earth as the sky was above it. The underworld was divided into three regions: the Elysian Fields for the virtuous, Tartarus for sinners and the Asphodel Meadows for those who fitted neither category. Hades was also the god of wealth, in the form of the precious stones and metals found deep in the earth.

Pan, the son of Hermes, was the god of the shepherds. Born with horns, beard, tail and goat legs, his ugliness so amused the other gods that eventually he fled to Arcadia where he danced, played his famous pipes and watched over the pastures, shepherds and herds.

Other gods included **Asclepius**, the god of healing; **Eros**, the god of love; **Hypnos**, the god of sleep; **Helios**, god of the sun; and **Selene**, goddess of the moon.

Mythical Heroes

Heroes such as **Heracles** and **Theseus** were elevated almost to the ranks of the gods. Heracles, yet another of Zeus' offspring, was performing astonishing feats of strength before he had left the cradle. His 12 labours were performed to atone for the murder of his wife and children in a bout of madness. The deeds of Theseus included the slaying of the Minotaur at Knossos.

Other heroes include **Odysseus**, whose wanderings after the fall of Troy are recorded in Homer's *Odyssey*, and **Jason**, who led his Argonauts to recover the golden fleece from Colchis (in modern Georgia).

Xena, regrettably, does not feature anywhere. The strapping 'warrior princess' of TV fame is a scriptwriter's invention – not a myth!

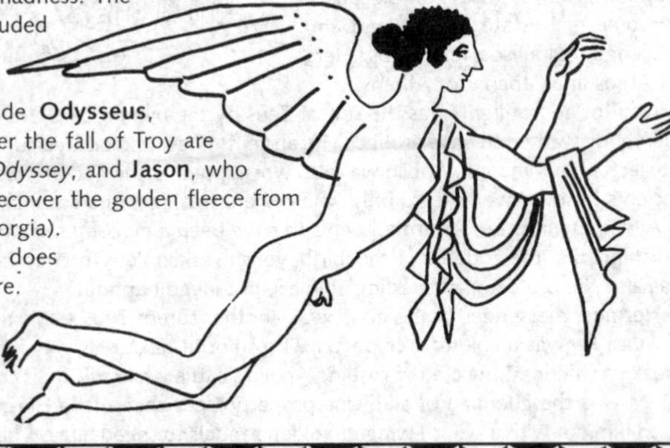

RICARDO BUSTOS

Treatment of Animals

The Greek attitude to animals depends on whether the animal is a cat or not. It's definitely cool to be a cat. Even the mangiest-looking stray can be assured of a warm welcome and a choice titbit on approaching the restaurant table of a Greek. Most other domestic animals are greeted with a certain indifference. You don't see many pet dogs, or pets of any sort for that matter. The various societies for animal protection in Greece are listed in *Atlantis* magazine.

The main threat to animal welfare is hunting. Greek hunters are notorious for blasting anything that moves, and millions of animals are killed during the long 'open' season, from 20 August to 10 March, which encompasses the bird migratory period. The Hellenic Centre for the Rehabilitation of Wild Animals and Birds (☎ 0297-28 367), on the island of Aegina, reports that 80% of the animals it treats have been shot.

RELIGION

About 98% of the Greek population belongs to the Greek Orthodox Church. Most of the remainder are either Roman Catholic, Jewish or Muslim.

Ancient Greek Mythology

Olympian Creation Myth

According to mythology, the world was formed from a great shapeless mass called Chaos. From Chaos came forth Gaea, the earth goddess. She bore a son, Uranus, the Firmament, and their subsequent union produced three 100-handed giants and three one-eyed Cyclopes. Gaea dearly loved her hideous offspring, but not so Uranus, who hurled them into Tartarus (the underworld).

The couple then produced the seven Titans, but Gaea still grieved for her other children. She asked the Titans to take vengeance upon their father, and free the 100-handed giants and the Cyclopes. The Titans did as they were requested, castrating the hapless Uranus, but Cronos (the head Titan), after setting eyes on Gaea's hideous offspring, hurled them back into Tartarus, whereupon Gaea foretold that Cronos would be usurped by one of his own offspring.

Cronos married his sister Rhea, but wary of his mother's warning, he swallowed every child Rhea bore him. When Rhea bore her sixth child, Zeus, she smuggled him to Crete, and gave Cronos a stone in place of the child, which he duly swallowed. Rhea hid the baby Zeus in the Dikteon cave in the care of three nymphs.

On reaching manhood, Zeus, determined to avenge his swallowed siblings, became Cronos' cupbearer and filled his cup with poison. Cronos drank from the cup, then disgorged first the stone and then his children Hestia, Demeter, Hera, Poseidon and Hades, all of whom were none the worse for their ordeal. Zeus, aided by his regurgitated brothers and sisters, deposed Cronos, and went to war against the Titans who wouldn't acknowledge him as chief god. Gaea, who still hadn't forgotten her imprisoned, beloved offspring, told Zeus he would only be victorious with the help of the Cyclopes and the 100-handed giants, so he released them from Tartarus.

The Cyclopes gave Zeus a thunderbolt, and the three 100-handed giants threw rocks at the Titans, who eventually retreated. Zeus banished Cronos, as well as all of the Titans except Atlas (Cronos' deputy), to a far-off land. Atlas was ordered to hold up the sky.

Mt Olympus became home-sweet-home for Zeus and his unruly and incestuous family. Zeus, taking a fancy to Hera, turned himself into a dishevelled cuckoo whom the unsuspecting Hera held to her bosom, whereupon Zeus violated her, and Hera reluctantly agreed to marry him. They had three children: Ares, Hephaestus and Hebe.

Philippi, in Macedonia, is reputedly the first place in Europe where St Paul preached the gospel. This was in 49 AD, and during the next five years he preached also in Athens, Thessaloniki and Corinth.

The Greek Orthodox Church is closely related to the Russian Orthodox Church; together they form the third-largest branch of Christianity. Orthodox, meaning 'right belief', was founded in the 4th century by Constantine the Great, who was converted to Christianity by a vision of the Cross.

By the 8th century, there were a number of differences of opinion, as well as increasing rivalry, between the pope in Rome and the patriarch of Constantinople. One dispute was over the wording of the Creed. The original Creed stated that the Holy Spirit proceeds 'from the Father', which the Orthodox Church adhered to, whereas Rome added 'and the Son'. Another bone of contention concerned the celibacy of the clergy. Rome decreed priests had to be celibate; in the Orthodox Church, a priest could marry before becoming ordained. There were also differences in fasting: in the Orthodox Church, not only was meat forbidden during Lent, but wine and oil also.

By the 11th century these differences had become irreconcilable, and in 1054 the pope and the patriarch excommunicated one another. Ever since, the two have gone their own ways as the (Greek/Russian) Orthodox Church and the Roman Catholic Church.

During Ottoman times membership of the Orthodox Church was one of the most important criteria in defining a Greek, regardless of where he or she lived. The church was the principal upholder of Greek culture and traditions.

Religion is still integral to life in Greece, and the Greek year is centred on the festivals of the church calendar. Most Greeks, when they have a problem, will go into a church and light a candle to the saint they feel is most likely to help them. On the islands you will see hundreds of tiny churches dotted around the countryside. Most have been built by individual families in the name of their selected patron saint as thanksgiving for God's protection.

If you wish to look around a church, you should always dress appropriately. Women should wear skirts that reach below the knees, and men should wear long trousers and have their arms covered. Regrettably, many churches are kept locked nowadays, but it's usually easy enough to locate caretakers, who will be happy to open them up for you.

Facts for the Visitor

The Best & the Worst

The Best

It's tough trying to pick just 10 of the best things about Greece. These are our personal favourites, the places, things and activities the authors of this book would most like to dedicate a lot more of their time to:

1. Late night dinners at village tavernas
2. Swimming at uncrowded island beaches
3. Traditional Cycladic villages
4. Eating fresh seafood by the sea
5. The Peloponnese in spring
6. Dining out beneath the floodlit Acropolis
7. Meteora
8. The Zagoria villages in Epiros
9. Greek hospitality
10. Virgin olive oil

The Worst

We'd be very happy not to experience the following again:

1. The attitude to rubbish
2. Traffic pollution
3. Athens airport
4. Concrete-box *domatia* spoiling island landscapes
5. Smoking
6. Aggressive restaurant touts accosting all passers-by
7. The disappearance of traditional lifestyles as every man, woman, child and dog tries to make a fast buck out of tourism
8. Demon drivers
9. Olympic Airways
10. Greek bureaucracy

SUGGESTED ITINERARIES

One of the most difficult aspects of travel is organising an itinerary. The following list of suggested itineraries provides a choice of one-week and two-week itineraries for each of the major regions and island groups. The one-week itineraries are for people who want no more than a quick tour of the highlights of each region, while the two-week itineraries are for people with a bit more time to spare.

The list can be used to create an individual itinerary of your choice. A month in Greece, for example, could be divided up into a week in the Peloponnese, followed by a couple of weeks in the Cyclades and a week on Crete.

Athens

One week

Combine a walking tour of Plaka with a visit to the Acropolis (one day); National Archaeological Museum (one day); day trip to Cape Sounion (one day); an early morning climb up Lykavittos Hill followed by visits to the Goulandris Museum of Cycladic & Ancient Greek Art and the Byzantine Museum (one day); day trip to Elefsina, stopping at Moni Dafniou on the way (one day); visit the Ancient Agora and the Keramikos (one day); day trip to Moni Kaisarianis (one day). Evening activities to schedule in include the Dora Stratou folk dancers on Filopappos Hill; summer performances of ancient Greek drama at the Theatre of Herodes Atticus; and a visit to a *rembetika* club.

Peloponnese

One week

Head from Athens to Nafplio (two days) and use it as a base for side trips to Epidaurus and Mycenae; go south to Sparta (two days), then visit Mystras; travel across the Taÿgetos Mountains to Kalamata and then up the west coast to Ancient Olympia (one day); visit the site early and continue north around the coast through Patras to Diakofto and ride the rack-and-pinion railway up to Kalavryta (one day); travel back to Diakofto and take the train back to Athens.

Two weeks

Follow the above itinerary as far as Sparta/Mystras, and then head south-east to

Monemvasia (one day). From here, travel west through Gythio to Aeropoli and use it as a base for exploring the Lakonian Mani (two days) before moving up the coast to Kardamyli (two days). Then head west via Kalamata to the old Venetian town of Methoni (one day), and north to Olympia (one day). Visit the site early and then catch the bus to Tripolis (one day), and then take the bus north through the mountains to Kalavryta (one day). From Kalavryta, ride the rack-and-pinion railway to Diakofto via Zahlorou and catch a train to Athens.

Central Greece

One week

Central Greece offers two main sightseeing areas for the short-term visitor: the Meteora and the Pelion Peninsula. Start at Volos and spend two days exploring the Pelion Peninsula. Then head southwards across the mountains via Karditsa, Lamia and Amfissa and visit the oracle of Delphi. Allow two days for this magical place. If time and patience allow, head along the north coast of the Gulf of Corinth from Delphi and visit Messolongi in Etolo-Akarnania. Take along some of Byron's poetry to get in the mood. Otherwise you may prefer going to Galaxidi, a delightful seaside town on the north Gulf of Corinth, 27 km from Delphi.

Two weeks

Start at Volos but allow an extra two to three days to visit the villages of the Pelion Peninsula, overnighting in perhaps Tsangarada and Vyzitsa. From Volos traverse Thessaly – perhaps including a short visit to workaday Larisa – before halting at Meteora. A stay of at least two to three days should be allowed for Meteora, especially if you wish to visit all the monasteries at walking pace. With more time on your hands you might detour slightly to the Monastery of Osiou Loukas in Central Greece before resuming the one week itinerary at Delphi. From Messolongi you might care to loop back to Central Greece via the little-visited mountains of the Agrafa and the capital of Greece's 'little Switzerland', Karpenisi.

Northern Greece

One week

Start in Epiros and use Ioannina as your base to visit Ioannina, Vikos Gorge and the Zagoria villages. Head eastwards to Macedonia via Konitsa and make for Florina via the Prespa Lakes basin. Move on to Thessaloniki via the waterfalls of Edessa. Spend at least two days in Thessaloniki making sure to visit the impressive Archaeological Museum and the splendid Vergina treasures. If you have time (and are male), complete your stay with a couple of nights on Mt Athos. If you are female, perhaps take in the sites of Vergina itself and nearby Pella.

Two weeks

Allow at least four to five days to visit Vikos Gorge and the Zagoria villages, and if walking is your cup of tea then base yourself at Papingo or Konitsa. Include the Vlach village of Metsovo as a side trip from Ioannina then head east via Konitsa to western Macedonia. In addition to the sights listed in the one week itinerary you could perhaps head east to the Dadia Forest Reserve in Thrace, the home of Europe's few remaining birds of prey. From Alexandroupolis you can head to Turkey or take the weekly ferry as far down as Rhodes.

Saronic Gulf Islands

One week

Starting from Athens, head to Aegina (two days), visiting the Temple of Aphaia and exploring the ruins of Paleohora; Poros warrants no more than a brief stopover on the way to tranquil Hydra (three days); continue to Spetses (two days). From Spetses, you can either return to Athens or continue by hydrofoil to one of the ports of the eastern Peloponnese.

Cyclades

One week

Spend two days on Naxos, exploring the hilltop Kastro and the backcountry, visiting old churches, archaeological sites, beaches, the lush Tragaea region, and the villages of Halki, Filoti and Apiranthos. Catch a ferry to Santorini and goggle at the scenery as you pull in. Spend three or four days here, staying in Fira or Oia to view the spectacular sunsets, and visit Ancient Akrotiri and check out Fira's museums. Take a trip out to Thirasia and the volcanic islets. Spend at least one day lazing by the sea, and eating at a beachside taverna. Head to Syros to explore the graceful neoclassical city of Ermoupolis and the hilltop village of Ano Syros, or head to Ios, and dance the night away and then recover on the beach.

Two weeks

Spend a day and night on Syros and explore Ermoupolis and Ano Syros. On Mykonos, sample the nightlife, and take an excursion to Ancient Delos. Then follow the one week itinerary for Naxos and Santorini. Head to Folegandros, and wile away a day or two. Soak up the atmosphere of the lovely Hora, and visit one of the beaches. On the way back to Athens, stop off at Sikinos if you like quiet, or at Ios, if you feel the need to party. Amorgos would make a good alternative to Folegandros, especially if you like walking; in which case make sure you visit Hora and the Moni Hozoviotissis. From Amorgos you can make a side trip to the cute little island of Koufonisia before heading back to Athens.

Crete

One week

Spend two days in Iraklio; visit the archaeological museum, historical museum of Crete and the Minoan site of Knossos. Have two days in Rethymno to visit the fortress and museums and explore the old quarter. If you have time take a day trip to the mountain town of Spili, or the resort of Plakias, if you prefer a beach. Spend three days in Hania to visit the museums, explore the old quarter and hike the Samaria Gorge. Recuperate the following day on the beach at Falasarna. Round off your trip with an evening of music and drinking at Cafe Crete.

Two weeks

Spend two days in Iraklio; visit the archaeological museum, historical museum of Crete and the Minoan site of Knossos. Overnight at one of the Lassithi Plateau villages and explore the Dikteon Cave and the plateau. Spend two nights in Sitia; visit the archaeological museum, walk the gorge to Kato Zakros, visit Ancient Zakros and have a swim. If you have time, visit Ancient Lato. Have two days in Rethymno to visit the fortress and museums and explore the old quarter. Overnight in Agia Galini to visit Phaestos and Agia Triada. Spend two nights in the mountain town of Spili, or the beach resort of Plakias, and visit Moni Preveli. Spend two nights in Hania to explore the old town and visit the museums. Head down to Paleohora for two nights and spend a day hiking the Samaria Gorge. If you have time, unwind on Elafonisi Beach the following day.

Dodecanese

One week

Spend two days on Rhodes, and explore the capital's medieval city. Visit either Lindos or the ancient city of Kamiros, or both if you hire a car and cross Rhodes' unspoilt mountainous interior. Spend the next two days chilling out on the beaches of tranquil Tilos or walking around the island. You may fit in a couple of days on Nisyros, with its extraordinary volcanic landscape, the picturesque villages of Emboreios and Nikea and an impressive ruined kastro on its ancient acropolis. Otherwise, make for Kos, birthplace of Hippocrates, to see its extensive ruins and enjoy its wild nightlife.

Two weeks

Follow the one week itinerary, but spend three days on Rhodes to see more of the interior. Also spend the night on Nisyros and enjoy a drink and dinner on Mandraki's delightful central square – the town undergoes a metamorphosis when the day-trippers leave. To recuperate from the liveliness of Kos, spend three days relaxing on Lipsi's uncrowded beaches, do more walking and take a day trip to remote and traditional Arki. Or, if even Lipsi sounds too touristy for you, go to quieter Agathonisi. Finally, en route to Piraeus, spend a day on Patmos to explore its monasteries.

North-Eastern Aegean Islands

One week

With only seven days, you will be a bit pushed so plan your ferry trips carefully. Fly out to Lesvos (Mytilini) or take the overnight boat. Make sure you visit Mythimna (Molyvos) and maybe Skala Eresou for some beach life. Take a boat to Chios and visit the Mastihohoria (mastic villages) and maybe sit on Homer's stone (Daskalopetra) for some poetic inspiration. Head for Samos if you want a subtropical island, or Ikaria if you want a very laid-back and idiosyncratic visit and a couple of the best beaches in the Aegean. Fly or sail back to the mainland.

Two weeks

Start your itinerary on the underrated but worthwhile island of Limnos. From here, try to make a two day visit to the remote community on Agios Efstratios, one of Greece's most remote islands. Fly to Lesvos (Mytilini) and follow the one week itinerary to Samos. Definitely include Ikaria for three to four days with perhaps a side trip to the Fourni Islands while en route from Samos. Take the overnight boat to Piraeus to finish your trip.

Ionian Islands

One week – Northern Ionian Islands

Spend two days in Corfu Town; explore the narrow streets of the old town and visit the museums. Spend one night in Paleokastritsa or Lakones; walk the path between the two, visit Moni Theotokou and Angelokastro, and have a meal at one of the restaurants on the Lakones-Makrades road. Spend two days at a west coast resort and catch a sunset at Pelekas. Visit Lake Korission and surrounds. Spend one or two nights on Paxi.

One week – Southern Ionian Islands

Spend one day and night on Lefkada, explore the capital and relax on a west coast beach. Overnight on Meganisi. Spend two days on Ithaki, visiting Vathy's museums and the villages of Anogi, Frikes and Kioni. Have two days in Fiskardo on Kefallonia (in the high season stay elsewhere and visit on a day trip), to see Assos village and Myrtos Beach. Spend one day in Sami to visit the nearby caves.

Two weeks

Combine the above itineraries, but allow an extra day for Corfu Town, visiting the Ahillion Palace, and perhaps an extra night on Lefkada. Spending only one day in Fiskardo may enable you to include Kythira – you may find it the greatest surprise in the Ionians.

Evia & the Sporades

One week

Starting in Athens, take the bus to Kymi in Evia and then the ferry to Linaria in Skyros. Give delectable Skyros at least two days of your time. Take a hydrofoil to Alonnisos and work your way towards Volos on the mainland, visiting the islands of Skopelos and Skiathos en route.

Two weeks

Try this adventurous route if you have time at your disposal. From Athens head to Rafina in Attica and take the ferry to Karystos in Evia. Work your way up to Kymi in Evia, perhaps taking in Eretria on Evia's west side and some walking up Mt Dirfys from the inland village of Steni. From Kymi in Evia follow the one week itinerary, allowing two to three days on each island of the Sporades. Finally exit from Skiathos to Thessaloniki (ferry or hydrofoil) and return to Athens by train.

PLANNING

When to Go

Spring and autumn are the best times to visit Greece. Winter is pretty much a dead loss outside the major cities. Most of Greece's tourist infrastructure goes into hibernation from the end of November until the beginning of April – hotels and restaurants are closed and bus and ferry services are either drastically reduced or plain cancelled.

The cobwebs are dusted off in time for Easter, when the first tourists start to arrive. Conditions are perfect between Easter and mid-June, when the weather is pleasantly warm in most places, but not too hot; beaches and ancient sites are relatively uncrowded; public transport operates on close to full schedules; and accommodation is cheaper and easy to find.

Mid-June until the end of August is the high season. It's party time on the islands and everything is in full swing. It's also very hot – in July and August the mercury can soar to 40°C (over 100°F) in the shade just about anywhere in the country; the beaches are crowded, the ancient sites are swarming with tour groups and in many places accommodation is booked solid.

The season starts to wind down after August and conditions are ideal once more until the shutdown at the end of November. Before ruling out a winter holiday entirely, it's worth considering going skiing (see Activities later in this chapter for details).

Maps

Unless you are going to trek or drive, the free maps given out by the EOT (the Greek National Tourist Organization) will probably suffice, although they are not 100% accurate. On islands where there is no EOT office there are usually tourist maps for sale for around 400 dr but, again, these are not very accurate.

The best maps are published by the Greek company Road Editions, in conjunction with the Hellenic Army Geographical Service. There is a wide range of maps to suit various needs, starting with a 1:500,000 map of Greece. Motorists should check out the company's 1:250,000 maroon-cover series covering Thrace, Macedonia, Thessaly and Epiros, Central Greece, the Peloponnese and Crete. Even the smallest roads and villages are clearly marked, and the distance indicators are spot-on – important when negotiating your way around the backblocks. Useful features include symbols to indicate the location of petrol stations and tyre shops.

The company is rapidly expanding its blue-cover Greek island series. At the time of writing, the series featured Corfu, Kea (Tzia), Kos, Milos, Rhodes, Santorini, Syros and Zakynthos; maps of Andros, Kefallonia and Ithaki, Kythira, Lefkada, Mykonos, Naxos, Paros, Paxi and Antipaxi and Samos should be available by the time you read this. The scale of these maps ranges from 1:100,000 for larger islands like Corfu and Rhodes to 1:30,000 for Syros.

Lastly, Road Editions also publishes a 1:50,000 green-cover Greek mountain series, produced with trekkers in mind. The series includes Mt Athos, Mt Iti, Mt Olympia, Mt Parnitha, Mt Parnassos and the Pelion Pensinsula (Pilio).

Freytag & Berndt's 15-map Greece series has good coverage of the islands and the Peloponnese.

What to Bring

Sturdy shoes are essential for clambering around ancient sites and wandering around historic towns and villages, which tend to have lots of steps and cobbled streets. Footwear with ankle support is preferable for trekking, although many visitors get by with trainers.

A day-pack is useful for the beach, and for sightseeing or trekking. A compass is essential if you are going to trek in remote areas, as is a whistle, which you can use should you become lost or disorientated. A torch (flashlight) is not only needed if you intend to explore caves, but comes in handy during occasional power cuts. If you like to fill a washbasin or bathtub (a rarity in Greece), bring a universal plug as Greek bathrooms rarely have plugs.

Many camping grounds have covered areas where tourists without tents can sleep in summer, so you can get by with a lightweight sleeping bag and foam bedroll. Whether or not you are going to self-cater, a plastic food container, plate, cup, cutlery, bottle opener, water container and all-purpose knife are useful, not only for picnics, but for food you take with you on long boat trips.

You will need only light clothing – preferably cotton – during the summer months. But if you're going to climb Mt Olympus (or any other high mountain) you will need a sweater and waterproof jacket, even in July and August. During spring and autumn you'll need a light sweater or jacket in the evening. In winter take a heavy jacket or coat, warm sweaters, winter shoes or boots, and an umbrella.

In summer a sun hat and sunglasses are essential (see the Health section later in this chapter). Sunscreen creams are expensive, as are moisturising and cleansing creams. Film is not expensive, especially in larger towns and tourist areas, but the stock tends to hang around for a while in remoter areas.

If you read a lot, it's a good idea to bring along a few disposable paperbacks to read and swap.

TOURIST OFFICES

Tourist information is handled by the Greek National Tourist Organization, known by the initials GNTO abroad and EOT (Ellinikos Organismos Tourismou) in Greece.

Local Tourist Offices

The EOT's head office is at Amerikis 2, Athens 105 64 (☎ 01-331 0561/0562, fax 325 2895, email gnto@eexi.gr). There are about 25 EOT offices throughout Greece. Most EOT staff speak English, but they vary in their enthusiasm and helpfulness. Some offices, like that in Athens, have loads of useful local information, but most have nothing more than glossy brochures, usually about other parts of the country. Some have absolutely nothing to offer except an apology.

In addition to EOT offices, there are also municipal tourist offices. They are often more helpful.

Tourist Offices Abroad

GNTO offices abroad include:

Australia
(☎ 02-9241 1663/1664/1665)
51 Pitt St, Sydney NSW 2000

Austria
(☎ 1-512 5317/5318) Opernring 8, Vienna A-10105
Belgium
(☎ 2-647 5770) 172 Ave Louise Louizalaan, B-1050 Brussels
Canada
(☎ 416-968 2220) 1300 Bay St, Toronto, Ontario M5R 3K8
Denmark
(☎ 3-325 332) Vester Farimagsgade 1, 1606 Copenhagen
France
(☎ 01-42 60 65 75) 3 Ave de l'Opéra, Paris 75001
Germany
(☎ 69-237 735) Neue Mainzerstrasse 22, 60311 Frankfurt
(☎ 89-222 035/036) Pacellistrasse 5, W 80333 Munich 2
(☎ 40-454 498) Abteistrasse 33, 20149 Hamburg 13
(☎ 30-217 6262) Wittenbergplatz 3A, 10789 Berlin 30
Israel
(☎ 23-517 0501) 5 Shalom Aleichem St, Tel Aviv 61262
Italy
(☎ 06-474 4249) Via L Bissolati 78-80, Rome 00187
(☎ 02-860 470) Piazza Diaz 1, 20123 Milan
Japan
(☎ 03-350 55 911) Fukuda Building West, 5F 2-11-3 Akasaka, Minato-Ku, Tokyo 107
Netherlands
(☎ 020-625 4212/4213/4214) Leidsestraat 13, Amsterdam NS 1017
Norway
(☎ 2-426 501) Ovre Slottsgate 15B, 0157 Oslo 1
Sweden
(☎ 8-679 6480) Birger Jarlsgatan 30, Box 5298 S, 10246 Stockholm
Switzerland
(☎ 01-221 0105) Loewenstrasse 25, CH 8001 Zürich
UK
(☎ 020-7499 4976) 4 Conduit St, London W1R ODJ
USA
(☎ 212-421 5777) Olympic Tower, 645 5th Ave, New York, NY 10022
(☎ 312-782 1084) Suite 600, 168 North Michigan Ave, Chicago, Illinois 60601
(☎ 213-626 6696) Suite 2198, 611 West 6th St, Los Angeles, California 92668

Tourist Police

The tourist police work in cooperation with the regular Greek police and EOT. Each tourist police office has at least one member of staff who speaks English. Hotels, restaurants, travel agencies, tourist shops, tourist guides, waiters, taxi drivers and bus drivers all come under the jurisdiction of the tourist police. If you think that you have been ripped off by any of these, report it to the tourist police and they will investigate. If you need to report a theft or loss of passport, then go to the tourist police first, and they will act as interpreters between you and the regular police. The tourist police also fulfil the same functions as the EOT and municipal tourist offices, dispensing maps and brochures, and giving information on transport. They can often help you to find accommodation.

VISAS & DOCUMENTS

Passport

To enter Greece you need a valid passport or, for EU nationals, travel documents (ID cards). You must produce your passport or EU travel documents when you register in a hotel or pension in Greece. You will find that many accommodation proprietors will want to keep your passport during your stay. This is not a compulsory requirement; they need it only long enough to take down the details.

Visas

The list of countries whose nationals can stay in Greece for up to three months without a visa includes Australia, Canada, all EU countries, Iceland, Israel, Japan, New Zealand, Norway, Switzerland and the USA. Other countries included are Cyprus, Malta, the European principalities of Monaco and San Marino and most South American countries. The list changes – contact Greek embassies for the full list. Those not included can expect to pay about US$20 for a three month visa.

North Cyprus Greece will refuse entry to people whose passport indicates that, since November 1983, they have visited Turkish-occupied North Cyprus. This can be overcome if, upon entering North Cyprus, you ask the immigration officials to stamp a piece of paper (loose-leaf visa) rather than your passport. If you enter North Cyprus from the Greek Republic of Cyprus (only possible for a day visit), an exit stamp is not put into your passport.

Visa Extensions If you wish to stay in Greece for longer than three months, apply at a consulate abroad or at least 20 days in advance to the Aliens Bureau in Athens (☎ 01-770 5711), Leoforos Alexandras 173. Take your passport and four passport photographs along. You may be asked for proof that you can support yourself financially, so keep all your bank exchange slips (or the equivalent from a post office). These slips are not always automatically given – you may have to ask for them. The Aliens Bureau is open 8 am to 1 pm on weekdays. Elsewhere in Greece apply to the local police authority. You will be given a permit which will authorise you to stay in the country for a period of up to six months.

Most travellers get around this by visiting Bulgaria or Turkey briefly and then re-entering Greece.

Travel Permits

You need a special permit to visit the monasteries of the Mt Athos peninsula in Macedonia. The permit can be issued in either Athens or Thessaloniki. See the Mt Athos section of the Northern Greece chapter for details.

Travel Insurance

A travel insurance policy to cover theft, loss and medical problems is a good idea. The policies handled by STA Travel and other student travel organisations are usually good value. There is a wide variety of policies available; check the small print.

Some policies specifically exclude 'dangerous activities' which can include scuba diving, motorcycling, even trekking. A locally acquired motorcycle licence is not valid under some policies.

You may prefer a policy that pays doctors or hospitals direct rather than you having to pay on the spot and claim later. If you have to claim later make sure you keep all documentation. Some policies ask you to call back (reverse charges) to a centre in your home country where an immediate assessment of your problem is made.

Check that the policy covers ambulances or an emergency flight home.

Driving Licence & Permits

Greece recognises all national driving licences, provided the licence has been held for at least one year. It also recognises an International Driving Permit, which should be obtained before you leave home.

Hostel Cards

A Hostelling International (HI) card is of limited use in Greece. The only place you will be able to use it is at the Athens International Youth Hostel.

Student & Youth Cards

The most widely recognised form of student ID is the International Student Identity Card (ISIC). It qualifies you for half-price admission to museums and ancient sites and for discounts at some budget hotels and hostels. Several travel agencies in Athens are licensed to issue cards; see the Information section of the Athens chapter. You must show documents proving you are a student, provide a passport photo and cough up 2500 dr.

There are no student discounts on domestic flights (unless linked to an international flight), and none to be had on buses, ferries or trains. But students will find some good deals on international airfares. See the boxed text 'Student Cards' for more details.

Seniors' Cards

See the Senior Travellers section later in this chapter.

Photocopies

The hassles created by losing your passport, travellers cheques and other important documents can be reduced considerably if you

Student Cards

An ISIC (International Student Identity Card) is a plastic ID-style card displaying your photograph. These cards are widely available from budget travel agencies (take along proof that you are a student). In Athens you can get one from the International Student & Youth Travel Service (ISYTS; ☎ 01-323 3767), 2nd floor, Nikis 11.

Some travel agencies in Greece offer discounts on organised tours to students. However, there are no student discounts for travel within Greece (although Olympic Airways gives a 25% discount on domestic flights which are part of an international flight). Turkish Airlines (THY) gives 55% student discounts on its international flights. THY has flights from Athens to İstanbul and İzmir. Most ferries to Cyprus, Israel and Egypt from Piraeus give a 20% student discount and a few of the services between Greek and Italian ports do so also. If you are under 26 years but not a student, the Federation of International Youth Travel Organisation (FIYTO) card gives similar discounts. Many budget travel agencies issue FIYTO cards including London Explorers Club, 33 Princes Square, Bayswater, London W2 (☎ 020-7792 3770); and SRS Studenten Reise Service, Marienstrasse 23, Berlin (☎ 030-2 83 30 93).

take the precaution of taking photocopies. It is a good idea to have photocopies of the passport pages that cover personal details, issue and expiry date and the current entry stamp or visa. Other items worth photocopying are airline tickets, credit cards, driving licence and insurance details. You should also keep a record of the serial numbers of your travellers cheques, and cross them off as you cash them.

This emergency material should be kept separate from the originals, so that hopefully they won't both get lost (or stolen) at the same time. Leave an extra copy with someone at home just in case.

There is another option for storing details of your vital travel documents before you leave – Lonely Planet's online Travel Vault. Storing details of your important documents in the vault is safer than carrying photocopies. Your password-protected travel vault is accessible at any time. It's the best option if you travel in a country with easy Internet access. You can create your own travel vault for free at www.ekno.lonelyplanet.com.

EMBASSIES & CONSULATES

Greek Embassies & Consulates

The following is a selection of Greek diplomatic missions abroad:

Albania
(☎ 42-34 290/291) Rruga Frederik Shiroka, Tiranë

Australia
(☎ 02-6273 3011) 9 Turrana St, Yarralumla, Canberra ACT 2600

Bulgaria
(☎ 92-946 1027) San Stefano 33, Sofia 1504

Canada
(☎ 613-238 6271) 76-80 Maclaren St, Ottawa, Ontario K2P OK6

Cyprus
(☎ 02-441 880/881) Byron Boulevard 8-10, Nicosia

Denmark
(☎ 33-11 4533) Borgergade 16, 1300 Copenhagen K

Egypt
(☎ 02-355 1074) 18 Aisha el Taymouria, Garden City, Cairo

France
(☎ 01-47 23 72 28) 17 Rue Auguste Vacquerie, 75116 Paris

Germany
(☎ 228-83010) An Der Marienkapelleb 10, 53 179 Bonn

Ireland
(☎ 01-676 7254) 1 Upper Pembroke St, Dublin 2

Israel
(☎ 03-605 5461) 47 Bodenheimer St, Tel Aviv 62008

Italy
(☎ 06-854 9630) Via S Mercadante 36, Rome 00198

Japan
(☎ 03-340 0871/0872) 3-16-30 Nishi Azabu, Minato-ku, Tokyo 106
Netherlands
(☎ 070-363 87 00) Koninginnegracht 37, 2514 AD, The Hague
New Zealand
(☎ 04-473 7775) 5-7 Willeston St, Wellington
Norway
(☎ 22-44 2728) Nobels Gate 45, 0244 Oslo 2
South Africa
(☎ 12-437 351/352) 995, Pretorius Street, Arcadia, Pretoria 0083
Spain
(☎ 01-564 4653) Avenida Doctor Arce 24, Madrid 28002
Sweden
(☎ 08-663 7577) Riddargatan 60, 11457 Stockholm
Switzerland
(☎ 31-951 0814) Postfach, 3000 Berne 6, Kirchenfeld
Turkey
(☎ 312-436 8860) Ziya-ul-Rahman Caddesi 9-11, Gaziosmanpasa 06700, Ankara
UK
(☎ 020-7229 3850) 1A Holland Park, London W11 3TP
USA
(☎ 202-939 5818) 2221 Massachusetts Ave NW, Washington DC 20008

Embassies & Consulates in Greece

All foreign embassies in Greece are in Athens and its suburbs, while there are additional consulates of various countries in Thessaloniki, Patras, Corfu, Rhodes and Iraklio. They include:

Albania
(☎ 01-723 4412) Karahristou 1, Athens 115 21
(☎ 031-547 435, fax 546 656) Odysseos 6, Thessaloniki
Australia
(☎ 01-645 0404) Dimitrou Soutsou 37, Ambelokipi, Athens 115 21
(☎ 031-240 706, fax 260 237) Ionos Dragoumi 20, Thessaloniki (also represents New Zealand)
Bulgaria
(☎ 01-647 8105) Stratigou Kalari 33A, Psyhiko, Athens 154 52
(☎ 031-829 210, fax 854 004) N Manou 12, Thessaloniki
Canada
(☎ 01-727 3400) Genadiou 4, Athens 115 21
(☎ 031-56 350, fax 256 351) Tsimiski 17, Thessaloniki
Cyprus
(☎ 01-723 7883) Irodotou 16, Athens 106 75
Czech Republic
(☎ 031-267 041, fax 266 415) Ploutarhou 8, Thessaloniki
Egypt
(☎ 01-361 8613) Leoforos Vasilissis Sofias 3, Athens 106 71
France
(☎ 01-339 1000) Leoforos Vasilissis Sofias 7, Athens 106 71
(☎ 031-244 030, fax 244 032) McKenzie King 8, Thessaloniki
Germany
(☎ 01-728 5111) Dimitriou 3 & Karaoli, Kolonaki, Athens 106 75
(☎ 031-251 120, fax 240 393) Karolou Dil 4a, Thessaloniki
(☎ 0241-63 730) Parodos Isiodou 12, Rhodes
(☎ 081-22 6288) Zografou 7, Iraklio
Hungary
(☎ 031-547 397, fax 530 988) Danaïdou 4, Thessaloniki
Ireland
(☎ 01-723 2771) Leoforos Vasileos Konstantinou 7, Athens 106 74
Israel
(☎ 01-671 9530) Marathonodromou 1, Psyhiko, Athens 154 52
Italy
(☎ 01-361 7260) Sekeri 2, Athens 106 74
(☎ 031-934 000, fax 902 090) Papanastasiou 90, Thessaloniki
Japan
(☎ 01-775 8101) Athens Tower, Leoforos Mesogion 2-4, Athens 115 27
Netherlands
(☎ 01-723 9701) Vasileos Konstantinou 5-7, Athens 106 74
(☎ 031-227 477, fax 283 794) Komninon 26, Thessaloniki
(☎ 0661-39 900) Idromenon 2, Corfu
(☎ 0241-31 571) Alexandrou Diakou 27, Rhodes
(☎ 081-34 6202) Avgoustou 23, Iraklio
New Zealand (Consulate)
(☎ 01-771 0112) Xenias 24, Athens 115 28
Norway
(☎ 031-234 110, fax 265 026) McKenzie King 12, Thessaloniki
Romania
(☎ 031-225 481, fax 225 428) Leoforos Nikis 13, Thessaloniki
Slovakia
(☎ 031-281 918, fax 230 588) Aristotelous 10, Thessaloniki

South Africa
(☎ 01-680 6645) Kifissias 60, Maroussi, Athens 151 25
(☎ 031-722 519, fax 274 393) Tsimiski 51, Thessaloniki
Sweden
(☎ 031-236 410, fax 283 794) Komninon 26, Thessaloniki
Turkey
(☎ 01-724 5915) Vasilissis Georgiou 8, Athens 106 74
(☎ 031-248 452, fax 204 438) Ag Dimitriou 151, Thessaloniki
(☎ 0241-23 362) Iroön Politechniou 12, Rhodes
UK
(☎ 01-723 6211) Ploutarhou 1, Athens 106 75
(☎ 031-278 006, fax 283 868) El Venizelou 8, Thessaloniki (open 8 am to 1 pm)
(☎ 0661-30 055, 37 995) Menekratous 1, Corfu
(☎ 0241-27 247) Pavlou Mela 3, Rhodes
(☎ 081-22 4012) Apalexandrou 16, Iraklio
USA
(☎ 01-721 2951) Leoforos Vasilissis Sofias 91, Athens 115 21
(☎ 031-242 905, fax 242 915) Tsimiski 3, Thessaloniki (open Tue & Thur, 9 am to 12 pm)
Yugoslavia
(☎ 031-244 266, fax 240 412) Komninon 4, Thessaloniki

Generally speaking, your own country's embassy won't be much help in emergencies if the trouble you're in is remotely your own fault. Remember that you are bound by Greek laws. Your embassy will not be sympathetic if you end up in jail after committing a crime locally, even if such actions are legal in your own country.

In genuine emergencies you might get some assistance, but only if other channels have been exhausted. For example, if you need to get home urgently, a free ticket home is exceedingly unlikely – the embassy would expect you to have insurance. If you have all your money and documents stolen, it might assist with getting a new passport, but a loan for onward travel is out of the question.

CUSTOMS

There are no longer duty-free restrictions within the EU. This does not mean, however, that customs checks have been dispensed with: random searches are still made for drugs.

Upon entering the country from outside the EU, customs inspection is usually cursory for foreign tourists. There may be spot checks, but you probably won't have to open your bags. A verbal declaration is usually all that is required.

You may bring the following into Greece duty-free: 200 cigarettes or 50 cigars; 1L of spirits or 2L of wine; 50g of perfume; 250mL of eau de Cologne; one camera (still or video) and film; a pair of binoculars; a portable musical instrument; a portable radio or tape recorder; a typewriter; sports equipment; and dogs and cats (with a veterinary certificate).

Importation of works of art and antiquities is free, but they must be declared on entry, so that they can be re-exported. Import regulations for medicines are strict; if you are taking medication, make sure you get a statement from your doctor before you leave home. It is illegal, for instance, to take codeine into Greece without an accompanying doctor's certificate.

An unlimited amount of foreign currency and travellers cheques may be brought into Greece. If, however, you intend to leave the country with foreign banknotes in excess of US$1000, you must declare the sum upon entry.

Restrictions apply to the importation of sailboards into Greece. See the Activities section later in this chapter for more details.

It is strictly forbidden to export antiquities (anything over 100 years old) without an export permit. This crime is second only to drug smuggling in the penalties imposed. It is an offence to remove even the smallest article from an archaeological site.

The place to apply for an export permit is the Antique Dealers & Private Collections Section, Archaeological Service, Polygnotou 13, Athens.

Vehicles

Cars can be brought into Greece for four months without a carnet; only a green card (international third party insurance) is required. Your vehicle will be registered in your passport when you enter Greece in order to prevent you leaving the country without it.

MONEY

Currency

The unit of currency in Greece is the drachma (dr). Coins come in denominations of five, 10, 20, 50 and 100 dr. Banknotes come in 100, 200, 500, 1000, 5000 and 10,000 dr.

Exchange Rates

country	unit		drachma
Albania	100 lekë	=	231.20
Australia	A$1	=	195.35
Bulgaria	1000 leva	=	159.30
Canada	C$1	=	203.06
euro	€1	=	329.32
France	1FF	=	50.20
Germany	DM1	=	168.38
Italy	L1000	=	170.10
Japan	¥100	=	288.41
New Zealand	NZ$1	=	154.21
United Kingdom	UK£1	=	506.17
United States	US$1	=	303.15

Warning It's all but impossible to exchange Turkish lira in Greece. The only place you can change them is at the head office of the National Bank of Greece, Panepistimiou 36, Athens – and it'll give only about 75% of the going international rate.

Exchanging Money

Banks will exchange all major currencies in either cash, travellers cheques or Eurocheques. The best-known travellers cheques in Greece are Thomas Cook and American Express. A passport is required to change travellers cheques, but not cash.

Commission charged on the exchange of banknotes and travellers cheques varies not only from bank to bank but from branch to branch. It's less for cash than for travellers cheques. For travellers cheques the commission is 350 dr for up to 20,000 dr; 450 dr for amounts between 20,000 dr and 30,000 dr; and a flat rate of 1.5% on amounts over 30,000 dr.

Post offices can exchange banknotes – but not travellers cheques – and charge less commission than banks. Many travel agencies and hotels will also change money and travellers cheques at bank rates, but their commission charges are higher.

If there is a chance that you may apply for a visa extension, make sure you receive, and keep hold of, a bank exchange slip after each transaction.

Cash Nothing beats cash for convenience – or for risk. If you lose cash, it's gone for good and very few travel insurers will come to your rescue. Those that will, normally limit the amount to about US$300. It's best to carry no more cash than you need for the next few days, which means working out your likely needs whenever you change travellers cheques or withdraw cash from an ATM.

It's also a good idea to set aside a small amount of cash, say US$50, as an emergency stash.

Travellers Cheques The main reason to carry travellers cheques rather than cash is the protection they offer against theft. They are, however, losing popularity as more and more travellers opt to put their money in a bank at home and withdraw it at ATMs as they go along.

American Express, Visa and Thomas Cook cheques are all widely accepted and have efficient replacement policies. Maintaining a record of the cheque numbers and recording when you use them is vital when it comes to replacing lost cheques – keep this separate from the cheques themselves. US dollars are a good currency to use.

ATMs ATMs (automatic teller machines) are to be found in almost every town large enough to support a bank – and certainly in all the tourist areas. If you've got MasterCard or Visa/Access, there are plenty of places to withdraw money. Cirrus and Maestro users can make withdrawals in all major towns and tourist areas.

AFEMs (Automatic Foreign Exchange Machines) are common in major tourist areas. They take all the major European currencies, Australian and US dollars and Japanese yen, and are useful in an emergency. Note that they charge a hefty commission, though.

Credit Cards The great advantage of credit cards is that they allow you to pay for major items without carrying around great wads of cash. Credit cards are now an accepted part of the commercial scene in Greece just about everywhere. They can be used to pay for a wide range of goods and services such as upmarket meals and accommodation, car hire and souvenir shopping.

If you are not familiar with the card options, ask your bank to explain the workings and relative merits of the various schemes: cash cards, charge cards and credit cards. Ask whether the card can be replaced in Greece if it is lost or stolen.

The main credit cards are MasterCard, Visa (Access in the UK) and Eurocard, all of which are widely accepted in Greece. They can also be used as cash cards to draw drachma from the ATMs of affiliated Greek banks in the same way as at home. Daily withdrawal limits are set by the issuing bank. Cash advances are given in local currency only. Credit cards can be used to pay for accommodation in all the smarter hotels. Some C class hotels will accept credit cards, but D and E class hotels rarely do. Most upmarket shops and restaurants accept credit cards.

The main charge cards are American Express and Diner's Club Card, which are widely accepted in tourist areas but unheard of elsewhere.

International Transfers If you run out of money or need more for whatever reason, you can instruct your bank back home to send you a draft. Specify the city and the bank as well as the branch that you want the money sent to. If you have the choice, select a large bank and ask for the international division. Money sent by electronic transfer should reach you within 24 hours.

Security

The safest way of carrying cash and valuables (passport, travellers cheques, credit cards etc) is a favourite topic of travel conversation. The simple answer is that there is no foolproof method. The general principle is to keep things out of sight. The front pouch belt, for example, presents an obvious target for a would-be thief – only marginally less inviting than a fat wallet bulging from your back pocket.

The best place is under your clothes in contact with your skin where, hopefully, you will be aware of an alien hand before it's too late. Most people opt for a money belt, while others prefer a leather pouch hung around the neck. Another possibility is to sew a secret stash pocket into the inside of your clothes. Whichever method you choose, put your valuables in a plastic bag first – otherwise they will get soaked in sweat as you wander around in the heat. After a few soakings, they will end up looking like they've been through the washing machine.

Costs

Greece is still a cheap country by northern European standards, but it is no longer dirt-cheap. A rock-bottom daily budget would be 6000 dr. This would mean hitching, staying in youth hostels or camping, staying away from bars, and only occasionally eating in restaurants or taking ferries. Allow at least 12,000 dr per day if you want your own room and plan to eat out regularly as well as travelling about and seeing the sights. You will still need to do a fair bit of self-catering. If you really want a holiday – comfortable rooms and restaurants all the way – you will need closer to 20,000 dr per day. These budgets are for individuals. Couples sharing a double room can get by on less.

Prices vary quite a lot between islands, particularly for accommodation. Hydra and

Mykonos are the most expensive; the cheapest tend to be the most remote.

Museums & Ancient Sites Most small museums charge up to 500 dr and major sites and museums cost between 1200 dr and 2000 dr. Museums and sites are free on Sunday from 1 November to the end of March, as well as on 6 March, 18 April, 18 May, 5 June and the last weekend in September.

Admission to sites and museums is free all year for anyone under 18, card-carrying EU students and teachers, and journalists. Students from outside the EU qualify for a 50% discount with an International Student Identification Card (ISIC), while pensioners (over 65) from EU countries also pay half price.

Tipping & Bargaining

In restaurants the service charge is included in the bill but it is the custom to leave a small amount. The practice is often just to round off the bill. Likewise for taxis – a small amount is appreciated.

Bargaining is not as widespread in Greece as it is further east. Prices in most shops are clearly marked and non-negotiable. The same applies to restaurants and public transport. It is always worth bargaining over the price of hotel rooms or *domatia* (the Greek equivalent of the British bed and breakfast, minus the breakfast), especially if you are intending to stay a few days. You may get short shrift in peak season, but prices can drop dramatically in the off season. Souvenir shops and market stalls are other places where your negotiating skills will come in handy. If you feel uncomfortable about haggling, walking away can be just as effective – you can always go back.

POST & COMMUNICATIONS

Post offices *(tahydromio)* are easily identifiable by means of the yellow signs outside. Regular post boxes are also yellow. The red boxes are for express mail only.

Postal Rates

The postal rate for postcards and airmail letters to destinations within the EU is 170 dr for up to 20g and 270 dr for up to 50g. To other destinations the rate is 200 dr up to 20g and 300 dr for up to 150g. Post within Europe takes five to eight days and to the USA, Australia and New Zealand, nine to 11 days. Some tourist shops also sell stamps, but with a 10% surcharge.

Express mail costs an extra 400 dr and should ensure delivery in three days within the EU – use the special red post boxes. Valuables should be sent registered post, which costs an extra 350 dr.

Sending Mail

Do not wrap a parcel until it has been inspected at a post office. In Athens, take your parcel to the Parcel Post Office (☎ 01-322 8940) in the arcade at Stadiou 4, and elsewhere to the parcel counter of a regular post office.

Receiving Mail

You can receive mail poste restante (general delivery) at any main post office. The service is free of charge, but you are required to show your passport. Ask senders to write your family name in capital letters and underline it, and to mark the envelope 'poste restante'. It is a good idea to ask the post office clerk to check under your first name as well if letters you are expecting cannot be located. After one month, uncollected mail is returned to the sender. If you are about to leave a town and expected mail hasn't arrived, ask at the post office to have it forwarded to your next destination, c/o poste restante. See the Post section in the Athens chapter for addresses of post offices that hold poste restante mail.

Parcels are not delivered in Greece; they must be collected from the parcel counter of a post office – or, in Athens, from the Parcel Post Office.

Telephone

The Greek telephone service is maintained by the public corporation known as Organismos Tilepikoinonion Ellados, which is always referred to by the acronym OTE (pronounced O-tay). The system is modern and efficient. Public telephones all use phonecards, which cost 1000 dr for 100 units, 1800 dr for 200 units, 4200 dr for 500 units, and 8200 dr for 1000 units. The 100-unit cards are widely available at *periptera* (street kiosks), corner shops and tourist shops; the others can be bought at OTE offices.

The phones are easy to operate and can be used for local, long distance and international calls. The 'i' at the top left of the push-button dialling panel brings up the operating instructions in English. Don't remove your card before you are told to do so or you will wipe out the remaining credit. Local calls cost one unit per minute.

It is possible to use various national card schemes, such as Telstra Australia's Telecard, to make international calls. You will still need a phonecard to dial the scheme's access number, which will cost you one unit, and the time you spend on the phone is also charged at local call rates.

International calls can also be made from OTE offices. A counter clerk directs you to a cubicle equipped with a metered phone, and payment is made afterwards. Villages and remote islands without OTE offices almost always have at least one metered phone for international and long distance calls – usually in a shop, *kafeneio* (cafe) or taverna.

Another option is the periptero. Almost every periptero has a metered telephone which can be used for local, long distance and direct dial international calls. There is a small surcharge, but it is less than that charged by hotels.

Reverse charge (collect) calls can be made from an OTE office. The time you have to wait for a connection can vary considerably, from a few minutes to two hours. If you are using a private phone to make a reverse charge call, dial the operator (domestic ☎ 151, international ☎ 161).

To call overseas direct from Greece, dial the Greek overseas access code (☎ 00), followed by the country code for the country you are calling, then the local area code (dropping the leading zero if there is one) and then the number. The table below lists some country codes and per-minute charges:

Country	Code	Cost per minute
Australia	61	236 dr
France	33	183 dr
Germany	49	183 dr
Ireland	353	183 dr
Italy	39	183 dr
Japan	81	319 dr
Netherlands	31	183 dr
New Zealand	64	319 dr
Turkey	90	183 dr
UK	44	183 dr
USA & Canada	1	236 dr

Off-peak rates are 25% cheaper. They are available to Africa, Europe, the Middle East and India between 10 pm and 6 am; to the Americas between 11 pm and 8 am; and to Asia and Oceania between 8 pm and 5 am.

To call Greece, the international access code is ☎ 30.

Fax & Telegraph

Most post offices have fax machines; telegrams can be sent from any OTE office.

Useful Phone Numbers

Directory inquiries	☎ 131
International dialling instructions in English, French and German	☎ 169
International access code to call Greece	☎ 30
International access code from within Greece	☎ 00

Toll-free 24 hour emergency numbers:

Police	☎ 100
Tourist Police	☎ 171
Ambulance (Athens)	☎ 166
Fire Brigade	☎ 199
Roadside Assistance (ELPA)	☎ 104

Email & Internet Access

Greece was slow to embrace the wonders of the Internet, but is now striving to make up for lost time. There has also been a huge increase in the number of hotels and businesses using email, and these addresses have been listed here where available.

Internet cafes are springing up everywhere, and are listed under the Information section for cities and islands where available. Some hotels catering for travellers also offer Internet access.

INTERNET RESOURCES

Predictably enough, there has recently been a huge increase in the number of Web sites providing information about Greece. A good place to start is the *500 Links to Greece* site at www.viking1.com/corfu/link.htm. It has links to a huge range of sites on everything from accommodation to Zeus.

The address www.greektravel.com takes you to an assortment of interesting and informative sites on Greece by Matt Barrett. The Greek Ministry of Culture has put together an excellent site, www.culture.gr, with loads of information about museums and ancient sites. Other sites include www.gogreece.com/travel and www.aegean.ch. You'll find more specialist Web sites listed through the book.

The Lonely Planet Web site (www.lonelyplanet.com) gives a succinct summary on travelling to Greece, postcards from other travellers and the Thorn Tree bulletin board, where you can ask questions before you go or dispense advice when you get back. The subWWWay section links you to other useful travel resources on the Web.

BOOKS

Most books are published in different editions by different publishers in different countries. As a result, a book might be a hardcover rarity in one country while it's readily available in paperback in another. Fortunately, bookshops and libraries search by title or author, so your local bookshop or library is best placed to advise you on the availability of the following recommendations.

Lonely Planet

The Lonely Planet guides to *Mediterranean Europe* and *Western Europe* also include coverage of Greece, as does *Europe on a shoestring*. The regional titles *Greek Islands*, *Corfu & the Ionian Islands*, *Crete* and *Crete Condensed* will be published in 2000. The handy *Greek phrasebook* will help enrich your visit.

Katherine Kizilos vividly evokes Greece's landscapes, people and politics in her book *The Olive Grove: Travels in Greece*. She explores the islands and borderlands of her father's homeland, and life in her family's village in the Peloponnese mountains. The book is part of the Journeys travel literature series.

These titles are available at major English-language bookshops in Athens, Thessaloniki, Rhodes and Iraklio. See the Bookshop entries in these sections for more details.

Guidebooks

The ancient Greek traveller Pausanias is acclaimed as the world's first travel writer. *The Guide to Greece* was written in the 2nd century AD. Umpteen editions later, it is now available in English in paperback. For archaeology buffs, the *Blue Guides* are hard to beat. They go into tremendous detail about all the major sites, and many of the lesser-known ones. They have separate guides for Greece and Crete.

Travel

During the 19th century many books about Greece were written by philhellenes who went to the country to help in the struggle for self-determination. *Travels in Northern Greece* by William Leake is an account of Greece in the last years of Ottoman rule. Leake was the British consul in Ioannina during Ali Pasha's rule. The English painter and writer Edward Lear, of *The Owl and the Pussy-Cat* fame, spent some time in Greece in the mid-19th century and wrote *Journeys of a Landscape Painter* and *A Cretan Diary*.

Lawrence Durrell, who spent an idyllic childhood on Corfu, is the best known of the 20th century philhellenes. His evocative books *Prospero's Cell* and *Reflections on a Marine Venus* are about Corfu and Rhodes respectively. His coffee-table book *The Greek Islands* is one of the most popular books of its kind. *My Family and Other Animals* by his brother Gerald is a hilarious account of the Durrell family's chaotic and wonderful life on Corfu.

Patrick Leigh Fermor, another ardent philhellene, is well known for his exploits in rallying the Cretan resistance in WWII. He now lives in Kardamyli in the Peloponnese. His highly acclaimed book *The Mani* is an account of his adventures in the Mani peninsula during the 1950s. By the same author, *Roumeli* relates his travels in northern Greece. *Deep into Mani* by Peter Greenhalgh & Edward Eliopoulis details a journey through the Mani some 25 years after Fermor's account.

Travels in the Morea by Nikos Kazantzakis is a highly readable account of the great writer's travels through the Peloponnese in the 1930s.

People & Society

Of the numerous festivals held in Greece, one of the most bizarre and overtly pagan is the carnival held on the island of Skyros, described in *The Goat Dancers of Skyros* by Joy Coulentianou.

The Cyclades, or Life Amongst the Insular Greeks by James Theodore Bent (first published 1885) is still the greatest English-language book about the Greek islands. It relates the experiences of the author and his wife while travelling around the Cyclades in the late 19th century. The book is now out of print, but the Hellenic Book Service may have a second-hand copy; see the Bookshops section later in this chapter.

Time, Religion & Social Experience in Rural Greece by Laurie Kain Hart is a fascinating account of village traditions – many of which are alive and well beneath the tourist veneer.

Portrait of a Greek Mountain Village by Juliet du Boulay is in a similar vein, based on her experiences in an isolated village.

A Traveller's Journey is Done and *An Affair of the Heart*, by Dilys Powell, wife of archaeologist Humfry Payne, are very readable, affectionate insights into Peloponnese village life during the 1920s and 1930s.

Road to Rembetica: Music of a Greek Subculture – Songs of Love, Sorrow and Hashish by Gail Holst explores the intriguing subculture which emerged from the poverty and suffering of the refugees from Asia Minor.

The Colossus of Maroussi by Henry Miller is now regarded as a classic. Miller relates his travels in Greece at the outbreak of WWII with feverish enthusiasm. Another book which will whet your appetite for a holiday in Greece is *Hellas: A Portrait of Greece* by Nicholas Gage.

History & Mythology

A Traveller's History of Greece by Timothy Boatswain & Colin Nicholson gives the layperson a good general reference on the historical background of Greece, from Neolithic times to the present day. *Modern Greece: A Short History* by CM Woodhouse is in a similar vein, although it has a right-wing bent. It covers the period from Constantine the Great to 1990.

Mythology was an intrinsic part of life in ancient Greece, and some knowledge of it will enhance your visit. One of the best publications on the subject is *The Greek Myths* by Robert Graves (two volumes) which relates and interprets the adventures of the main gods and heroes worshipped by the ancient Greeks. Maureen O'Sullivan's *An Iconoclast's Guide to the Greek Gods* presents entertaining and accessible versions of the myths.

There are many translations around of Homer's *Iliad* and *Odyssey*, which tell the story of the Trojan War and the subsequent adventures of Odysseus (known as Ulysses in Latin). The translations by EV Rien are among the best.

Women in Athenian Law and Life by Roger Just is the first in-depth study of the role of women in ancient Greece.

The Argonautica Expedition by Theodor Troev encompasses Greek mythology, archaeology, travel and adventure. It relates the voyage undertaken by the author and his crew in the 1980s following in the footsteps of Jason and the Argonauts.

Mary Renault's novels provide an excellent feel for ancient Greece. *The King Must Die* and *The Bull from the Sea* are vivid tales of Minoan times.

Mistras and Byzantine Style and Civilisation by Sir Steven Runciman and *Fourteen Byzantine Rulers* by Michael Psellus are both good introductions to Greece's Byzantine Age.

Farewell Anatolia and *The Dead are Waiting* by Dido Soteriou are two powerful novels focusing on the population exchange of 1923. Soteriou was born in Asia Minor in 1909 and was herself a refugee.

The Jaguar by Alexander Kotzias is a moving story about the leftist resistance to the Nazi occupation of Greece. Although a novel, it is packed with historical facts. *Greek Women in Resistance* by Eleni Fountouri is a compilation of journals, poems and personal accounts of women in the resistance movement from the 1940s to the 1950s. The book also contains poignant photographs and drawings.

Eleni by Nicholas Gage is an account by the author of his family's struggle to survive the horrors of WWII, the civil war, and his mother's death at the hands of the communists. It was made into a film in 1985.

The third volume of Olivia Manning's Balkan trilogy, *Friends & Heroes*, has Greece as its setting. It is a riveting account of the chaos and confusion among the emigre community fleeing the Nazi invasion of Europe. In another classic, *The Flight of Ikaros*, Kevin Andrews relates his travels in Greece during the 1940s civil war. *Greece in the Dark* by the same author tells of his life in Greece during the junta years.

Poetry

Sappho: A New Translation by Mary Bernard is the best translation of this great ancient poet's works.

Collected Poems by George Seferis, *Selected Poems* by Odysseus Elytis and *Collected Poems* by Constantine Cavafy are all excellent translations of Greece's greatest modern poets.

Novels

The most well known and widely read Greek author is the Cretan writer Nikos Kazantzakis, whose novels are full of drama and larger-than-life characters. His most famous works are *The Last Temptation*, *Zorba the Greek*, *Christ Recrucified* and *Freedom or Death*. The first two have been made into films.

English writer Louis de Bernières has become almost a cult figure following the success of *Captain Corelli's Mandolin*, which tells the emotional story of a young Italian army officer sent to the island of Kefallonia during WWII.

The Australian journalists George Johnston and Charmian Clift wrote several books with Greek themes during their 19 years as expatriates, including Johnston's novel *The Sponge Divers*, set on Kalymnos, and Clift's autobiographical *A Mermaid Singing*, which is about their experiences on Hydra.

Australian writer Gillian Bouras writes of living in Greece in *A Foreign Wife* and *Aphrodite and the Others*. Fellow Australian Beverley Farmer has two collections of beautifully written short stories, *Home Time* and *Milk*, many of which are about foreigners endeavouring to make their home in Greece.

Dinner with Persephone by Patricia Storace has been well reviewed and is of particular interest to women.

The Mermaid Madonna and *The Schoolmistress with the Golden Eyes* are two passionate novels by Stratis Myrivilis, set on two villages on the island of Lesvos.

Museum Guides

Museums and Galleries of Greece and Cyprus by Maria Kontou, of the Ministry of Culture, lists 165 museums in Greek and English with about 1000 photographs to illustrate exhibits that relate to visual arts, natural history, navigation, science, technology and the theatre.

Botanical Field Guides

The Flowers of Greece & the Aegean by William Taylor & Anthony Huxley is the most comprehensive field guide to Greece. The Greek writer, naturalist and mountaineer George Sfikas has written many books on wildlife in Greece. Among them are *Wildflowers of Greece*, *Trees & Shrubs of Greece*, *Medicinal Plants of Greece* and *Wildflowers of Mt Olympos*.

Children's Books

The Greek publisher Malliaris-Paedia puts out a good series of books on the myths, retold in English for young readers by Aristides Kesopoulos. The titles are *The Gods of Olympus and the Lesser Gods*, *The Labours of Hercules*, *Theseus and the Voyage of the Argonauts*, *The Trojan War and the Wanderings of Odysseus* and *Heroes and Mythical Creatures*. Robin Lister's retelling of *The Odyssey* is aimed at slightly older readers (ages 10 to 12), but makes compelling listening for younger ones when read aloud.

Bookshops

There are several specialist English-language bookshops in Athens, as well as shops selling books in French, German and Italian. There are also good foreign-language bookshops in Iraklio, Rhodes, Patras and Thessaloniki (see those sections for details). All other major towns and tourist resorts have bookshops that sell some foreign-language books.

Imported books are expensive – normally two to three times the recommended retail price in the UK and the USA. The Greek publisher Efstathiadis specialises in English translations of books by Greek authors as well as books about Greece by foreign authors. Many hotels have small collections of second-hand books to read or swap.

Abroad, the best bookshop for new and second-hand books on Greece, written in both English and Greek, is the Hellenic Book Service (☎ 020-7267 9499, fax 7267 9498, email hellenicbooks@btinternet.com), 91 Fortress Rd, Kentish Town, London NW5 1AG. It stocks almost all of the books recommended here. Its Web site is www.hellenicbookservice.com.

FILMS

Greece is nothing if not photogenic, and countless films have made the most of the country's range of superb locations. The islands do, of course, figure prominently. Mykonos was the setting for the smash hit *Shirley Valentine*, featuring Pauline Collins in the title role and Tom Conti as her Greek toy boy. *Mediterraneo* (1991) is an Italian movie that achieved cult status worldwide. It was set on Kastellorizo.

James Bond came to Greece too, and *For Your Eyes Only* features some dramatic shots of Roger Moore doing his 007 impersonation around the monasteries of Meteora. Moni Agias Triados features prominently.

Those with longer memories may recall Gregory Peck and David Niven leading the assault on the *Guns of Navarone* back in 1961. It was filmed on the island of Rhodes.

NEWSPAPERS & MAGAZINES

Greeks are great newspaper readers. There are 15 daily newspapers, of which the most widely read are *Ta Nea*, *Kathimerini* and *Eleftheros Typos*.

The main English-language newspapers are the daily (except Monday) *Athens News* (250 dr) which carries Greek and international news, and the weekly *Hellenic Times* (300 dr), with predominantly Greek news. In addition to these, the Athens edition of the *International Herald Tribune* (350 dr) includes an eight page English-language edition of the Greek daily *Kathimerini*. All are widely available in Athens and at major resorts. You'll find the *Athens News* electronic edition, archived from 1995 onwards, on the Web at athensnews.dolnet.gr.

Atlantis (1000 dr) is a glossy monthly magazine with articles on politics, travel and the arts.

Foreign newspapers are also widely available, although only between April and October in smaller resort areas. You'll find all the British and other major European dailies, as well as international magazines such as *Time*, *Newsweek* and the *Economist*. The papers reach Athens (Syntagma) at 3 pm on the day of publication on weekdays, and at 7 pm on weekends. They are not available until the following day in other areas.

RADIO & TV

Greece has two state-owned radio channels, ET 1 and ET 2. ET 1 runs three programs; two are devoted to popular music and news, while the third plays mostly classical music. It has a news update in English at 7.30 am from Monday to Saturday, and at 9 pm from Monday to Friday. It can be heard on 91.6 MHz and 105.8 MHz on the FM band, and 729 KHz on the AM band. ET 2 broadcasts mainly popular music. Local radio stations are proliferating at such a rate that the mountains around Athens have begun to look like pincushions. Western music can be heard on Radio Gold (105 FM), which plays mainly 60s music, or Kiss FM (90.9 FM), which plays a mix of rock and techno.

The best short-wave frequencies for picking up the BBC World Service are:

GMT	Frequency
3 to 7.30 am	9.41 MHz (31m band)
	6.18 MHz (49m band)
	15.07 MHz (19m band)
7.30 am to 6 pm	12.09 MHz (25m band)
	15.07 MHz (19m band)
6.30 to 11.15 pm	12.09 MHz (25m band)
	9.41 MHz (31m band)
	6.18 MHz (49m band)

As far as Greek TV is concerned, quantity rather than quality is the operative word. There are nine TV channels and various pay-TV channels. All the channels show English and US films and soapies with Greek subtitles. A bit of channel-swapping will normally turn up something in English.

VIDEO SYSTEMS

If you want to record or buy video tapes to play back home, you won't get a picture unless the image registration systems are the same. Greece uses PAL, which is incompatible with the North American and Japanese NTSC system. Australia and most of Europe uses PAL.

PHOTOGRAPHY & VIDEO

Film & Equipment

Major brands of film are widely available, although they can be expensive in smaller towns. In Athens, expect to pay about 1500 dr for a 36 exposure roll of Kodak Gold ASA 100; less for other brands. You'll find all the gear you need in the photography shops of Athens and major cities.

In most countries, it is possible to obtain video cartridges easily in large towns and cities, but make sure you buy the correct format. It is usually worth buying at least a few cartridges duty-free to start off your trip.

Photography

Because of the brilliant sunlight in summer, you'll get better results using a polarising lens filter.

As elsewhere in the world, developing film is a competitive business. Most places charge around 80 dr per print, plus a 400 dr service charge.

Video

Properly used, a video camera can give a fascinating record of your holiday. As well as videoing the obvious things – sunsets, spectacular views – remember to record some of the ordinary everyday details of life in the country. Often the most interesting things occur when you're actually intent on filming something else.

Make sure you keep the batteries charged, and have the necessary charger, plugs and transformer for the country you are visiting.

Restrictions & Etiquette

Never photograph a military installation or anything else that has a sign forbidding photography. Flash photography is not allowed inside churches, and it's considered taboo to photograph the main altar.

Greeks usually love having their photos taken but always ask permission first. The same goes for video cameras, probably even more annoying and offensive for locals than a still camera.

TIME

Greece is two hours ahead of GMT/UTC and three hours ahead on daylight-saving time, which begins on the last Sunday in March, when clocks are put forward one hour. Daylight saving ends on the last Sunday in September.

So, when it is noon in Greece it is also noon in İstanbul, 10 am in London, 11 am in Rome, 2 am in San Francisco, 5 am in New York and Toronto, 8 pm in Sydney and 10 pm in Auckland.

ELECTRICITY

Electricity is 220V, 50 cycles. Plugs are the standard continental type with two round pins. All hotel rooms have power points and most camping grounds have supply points.

WEIGHTS & MEASURES

Greece uses the metric system. Liquids – especially barrel wine – are often sold by weight rather than volume: 959g of wine, for example, is equivalent to 1000mL.

Remember that, like other continental Europeans, Greeks indicate decimals with commas and thousands with points.

LAUNDRY

Large towns and some islands have laundrettes. They charge from 2000 dr to 2500 dr to wash and dry a load whether you do it yourself or have it service-washed. Hotel and room owners will usually provide you with a washtub if requested.

TOILETS

Most places in Greece have western-style toilets, especially hotels and restaurants which cater for tourists. You'll occasionally come across Asian-style squat toilets in older houses, kafeneia and public toilets.

Public toilets are a rarity, except at airports, and bus and train stations. Cafes are the best option if you get caught short, but you'll be expected to buy something for the privilege.

One peculiarity of the Greek plumbing system is that it can't handle toilet paper; apparently the pipes are too narrow. Whatever the reason, anything larger than a postage stamp seems to cause a problem; flushing away tampons and sanitary napkins is guaranteed to block the system. Toilet paper etc should be placed in the small bin provided in every toilet.

HEALTH

Travel health depends on your predeparture preparations, your day-to-day health care while travelling and how you handle any medical problem or emergency that does develop. While the list of potential dangers can seem quite frightening, few travellers experience more than upset stomachs.

Predeparture Planning

Health Insurance Refer to Travel Insurance under Visas & Documents earlier in this chapter for information.

Warning Codeine, which is commonly found in headache preparations, is banned in Greece; check labels carefully, or risk prosecution. There are strict regulations applying to the importation of medicines into Greece, so obtain a certificate from your doctor which outlines any medication you may have to carry into the country with you.

Health Preparations Make sure you're healthy before you start travelling. If you are embarking on a long trip make sure your teeth are OK.

If you wear glasses take a spare pair and your prescription.

If you require a particular medication take an adequate supply, as it may not be available locally. Take the prescription or, better still, part of the packaging showing the generic rather than the brand name (which may not be locally available), as it will make getting replacements easier.

Immunisations No jabs are required for travel to Greece but a yellow fever vaccination certificate is required if you are coming from an infected area. There are, however, a few routine vaccinations that are recommended. These should be recorded on an international health certificate, available from your doctor or government health department. Don't leave your vaccinations until the last minute as some require more than one injection. Recommended vaccinations include:

Tetanus & Diphtheria Boosters are needed every 10 years and protection is highly recommended.

Polio A booster of either the oral or injected vaccine is required every 10 years to maintain immunity after childhood vaccination. Polio is still prevalent in many developing countries.

Hepatitis A The most common travel-acquired illness that can be prevented by vaccination. Protection can be provided in two ways – either with the antibody gamma globulin or with the vaccine Havrix 1440. Havrix 1440 provides long-term immunity (possibly more than 10 years) after an initial injection and a booster at six to 12 months. Gamma globulin is a ready-made antibody, which should be given as close as possible to departure because it is at its most effective in the first few weeks after administration; the effectiveness tapers off gradually between three and six months.

Rabies Pretravel rabies vaccination involves having three injections over 21 to 28 days and should be considered by those who will spend a month or longer in a country where rabies is common, especially if they are cycling, handling animals, caving, travelling to remote areas, or for children (who may not report a bite). If someone who has been vaccinated is bitten or scratched by an animal they will require two booster injections of vaccine; those not vaccinated will require more.

Medical Kit Check List

Following is a list of items you should consider including in your medical kit – consult your pharmacist for brands available in your country.

- ☐ **Aspirin** or **paracetamol** (acetaminophen in the USA) – for pain or fever
- ☐ **Antihistamine** – for allergies, eg hay fever; to ease the itch from insect bites or stings; and to prevent motion sickness
- ☐ **Antibiotics** – consider including these if you're travelling well off the beaten track; see your doctor, as they must be prescribed, and carry the prescription with you
- ☐ **Loperamide** or **diphenoxylate** –'blockers' for diarrhoea; **prochlorperazine** or **metaclopramide** for nausea and vomiting
- ☐ **Rehydration mixture** – to prevent dehydration, eg due to severe diarrhoea; particularly important when travelling with children
- ☐ **Insect repellent**, **sunscreen**, **lip balm** and **eye drops**
- ☐ **Calamine lotion**, **sting relief spray** or **aloe vera** – to ease irritation from sunburn and insect bites or stings
- ☐ **Antifungal cream** or **powder** – for fungal skin infections and thrush
- ☐ **Antiseptic** (such as povidone-iodine) – for cuts and grazes
- ☐ **Bandages**, **Band-Aids (plasters)** and other wound dressings
- ☐ **Water purification tablets** or **iodine**
- ☐ **Scissors**, **tweezers** and a **thermometer** (note that mercury thermometers are prohibited by airlines)
- ☐ **Cold** and **flu tablets**, **throat lozenges** and **nasal decongestant**
- ☐ **Multivitamins** – consider for long trips, when dietary vitamin intake may be inadequate

Basic Rules

Care in what you eat and drink is the most important health rule; stomach upsets are the most likely travel health problem (between 30 and 50% of travellers in a two week stay experience this) but the majority of these upsets will be relatively minor. Don't become paranoid; trying the local food is part of the experience of travel, after all.

Avoid climatic extremes: keep out of the sun when it's hot, dress warmly when it's cold. You can avoid insect bites by covering bare skin when insects are around, by screening windows or beds and by using insect repellents.

Seek local advice: if you're told the water is unsafe due to jellyfish, crocodiles or bilharzia, don't go in. In situations where there is no information, discretion is the better part of valour.

Food & Water Tap water is safe to drink in Greece, but mineral water is widely available if you prefer it. You might experience mild intestinal problems if you're not used to copious amounts of olive oil; however, you'll get used to it and current research says it's good for you.

If you don't vary your diet, are travelling hard and fast and missing meals, or simply lose your appetite, you can soon start to lose weight and place your health at risk. Fruit and vegetables are good sources of vitamins and Greece produces a greater variety of these than almost any other European country. Eat plenty of grains (including rice) and bread. If your diet isn't well balanced or if your food intake is insufficient, it's a good idea to take vitamin and iron pills.

In hot weather make sure you drink enough – don't rely on feeling thirsty to indicate when you should drink. Not needing to urinate or very dark yellow urine is a danger sign. Always carry a water bottle with you on long trips. Excessive sweating can lead to loss of salt and therefore muscle cramping. Salt tablets are not a good idea as a preventative, but in places where salt is not used much adding salt to food can help.

Environmental Hazards

Sunburn By far the biggest health risk in Greece comes from the intensity of the sun. You can get sunburnt surprisingly quickly, even through cloud. Use a sunscreen and take extra care to cover areas which don't normally see sun. A hat helps, as does zinc cream or some other barrier cream for your nose and lips. Calamine lotion is good for mild sunburn. Greeks claim that yogurt applied to sunburn is soothing. Protect your eyes with good-quality sunglasses.

Everyday Health

Normal body temperature is up to 37°C (98.6°F); more than 2°C (4°F) higher indicates a high fever. The normal adult pulse rate is 60 to 100 per minute (children 80 to 100, babies 100 to 140). As a general rule the pulse increases about 20 beats per minute for each 1°C (2°F) rise in fever.

Respiration (breathing) rate is also an indicator of illness. Count the number of breaths per minute: between 12 and 20 is normal for adults and older children (up to 30 for younger children, 40 for babies). People with a high fever or serious respiratory illness breathe more quickly than normal. More than 40 shallow breaths a minute may indicate pneumonia.

Prickly Heat Prickly heat is an itchy rash caused by excessive perspiration trapped under the skin. Keeping cool, bathing often, drying the skin and using a mild talcum powder, or resorting to air-conditioning even, may help until you acclimatise.

Heat Exhaustion Dehydration or salt deficiency can cause heat exhaustion. Take time to acclimatise to high temperatures, and drink sufficient liquids. Wear loose clothing and a broad-brimmed hat. Do not do anything too physically demanding.

Salt deficiency is characterised by fatigue, lethargy, headaches, giddiness and muscle cramps and in this case salt tablets may help. Vomiting or diarrhoea can deplete your liquid and salt levels.

Heat Stroke This serious, sometimes fatal, condition can occur if the body's heat-regulating mechanism breaks down and the body temperature rises to dangerous levels. Long, continuous periods of exposure to high temperatures can leave you vulnerable to heat stroke. You should avoid excessive alcohol consumption or strenuous activity when you first arrive in a hot climate.

The symptoms are feeling unwell, not sweating very much or at all and a high body temperature (39 to 41°C or 102 to 106°F). Where sweating has ceased the skin becomes flushed and red. Severe, throbbing headaches and lack of coordination will also occur, and the sufferer may be confused or aggressive. Eventually the victim will become delirious or convulse. Hospitalisation is essential, but in the interim get victims out of the sun, remove their clothing, cover them with a wet sheet or towel and then fan continually. Give fluids, if they are conscious.

Fungal Infections Fungal infections, which are more frequent in hot weather, are most likely to occur on the scalp, between the toes (athlete's foot) or fingers, in the groin and on the body (ringworm). You get ringworm (a fungal infection, not a worm) from infected animals or by walking on damp areas like shower floors.

To prevent fungal infections wear loose, comfortable clothes, avoid artificial fibres, wash frequently and dry carefully. If you do get an infection, wash the infected area daily with a disinfectant or medicated soap and water, and dry well. Apply an antifungal cream or powder (tolnaftate). Expose the infected area to air or sunlight as much as possible and wash all towels and underwear in hot water as well as changing them often.

Hypothermia Too much cold is just as dangerous as too much heat, particularly if it leads to hypothermia. Although everyone associates Greece with heat and sunshine, the high mountainous regions can be cool, even in summer. There is snow on the mountains from November to April. On the highest mountains in the north, snow patches can still be seen in June. Keeping warm while trekking in these regions in spring and autumn can be as much of a problem as keeping cool in the lower regions in summer.

Hypothermia occurs when the body loses heat faster than it can produce it and the core temperature of the body falls. It is surprisingly easy to progress from very cold to dangerously cold due to a combination of wind, wet clothing, fatigue and hunger, even if the air temperature is above freezing. It is best to dress in layers; silk, wool and some of the newer artificial fibres all insulate well. A hat is important, as a lot of heat is lost through the head. A strong, waterproof outer layer is essential, as keeping dry is vital. Carry basic supplies, including food containing simple sugars to generate heat quickly and lots of fluid to drink. A space blanket should always be carried in cold environments.

Symptoms of hypothermia are exhaustion, numb skin (particularly toes and fingers), shivering, slurred speech, irrational or violent behaviour, lethargy, stumbling, dizzy spells, muscle cramps and violent bursts of energy. Irrationality may take the form of sufferers claiming they are warm and trying to take off their clothes.

To treat mild hypothermia, first get the person out of the wind and/or rain, remove their clothing if it's wet and replace it with dry, warm clothing. Give them hot liquids – not alcohol – and some high-kilojoule, easily digestible food. Do not rub victims; instead allow them to slowly warm themselves. This should be enough to treat the early stages of hypothermia. The early recognition and treatment of mild hypothermia is the only way to prevent severe hypothermia, which is a critical condition.

Motion Sickness Sea sickness can be a problem. The Aegean is very unpredictable and gets very rough when the *meltemi* wind blows. If you are prone to motion sickness, eat lightly before and during a trip, and try to find a place that minimises disturbance – near the wing on aircraft, close to midships on boats, near the centre on buses. Fresh air usually helps; reading and cigarette smoke don't. Commercial motion-sickness preparations, which can cause drowsiness, have to be taken before the trip commences; when you're feeling sick it's too late. Ginger (available in capsule form) and peppermint (including mint-flavoured sweets) are natural preventatives.

Infectious Diseases

Diarrhoea Simple things like a change of water, food or climate can all cause a mild bout of diarrhoea, but a few rushed toilet trips with no other symptoms is not indicative of a major problem.

Dehydration is the main danger with any diarrhoea, particularly in children or the elderly as dehydration can occur quite quickly. Under all circumstances *fluid replacement* (at least equal to the volume being lost) is the most important thing to remember. Weak black tea with a little sugar, soda water, or soft drinks allowed to go flat and diluted 50% with clean water are all good.

Hepatitis Hepatitis is a general term for inflammation of the liver. It is a common disease worldwide. The symptoms are fever, chills, headache, fatigue, feelings of weakness and aches and pains, followed by loss of appetite, nausea, vomiting, abdominal pain, dark urine, light-coloured faeces, jaundiced (yellow) skin and the whites of the eyes may turn yellow. **Hepatitis A** is transmitted by contaminated food and drinking water. The disease poses a real threat to the western traveller. You should seek medical advice, but there is not much you can do apart from resting, drinking lots of fluids, eating lightly and avoiding fatty foods. People who have had hepatitis should avoid alcohol for some time after the illness, as the liver needs time to recover.

Hepatitis E is transmitted in the same way, and can be very serious in pregnant women.

There are almost 300 million chronic carriers of **Hepatitis B** in the world. It is spread through contact with infected blood, blood products or body fluids; for example, through sexual contact, unsterilised needles and blood transfusions, or contact with blood via small breaks in the skin. Other risk situations include having a shave, tattoo, or having your body pierced with contaminated equipment. The symptoms of type B may be more severe and may lead to long-term problems. **Hepatitis D** is spread in the same way, but the risk is mainly in shared needles.

Hepatitis C can lead to chronic liver disease. The virus is spread by contact with blood – usually via contaminated transfusions or shared needles.

Tetanus This potentially fatal disease is found worldwide. It is difficult to treat but is preventable with immunisation.

Rabies Rabies is a fatal viral infection and is caused by a bite or scratch by an infected animal. It's rare, but it's found in Greece. Dogs are noted carriers as are monkeys and cats. Any bite, scratch or even lick from a warm-blooded, furry animal should be cleaned immediately and thoroughly. Scrub with soap and running water, and then clean with an alcohol or iodine solution. If there is any possibility that the animal is infected medical help should be sought immediately. Even if the animal is not rabid, all bites should be treated seriously as they can become infected or can result in tetanus. A rabies vaccination is now available and should be considered if you are in a high risk category – eg if you intend to explore caves (bat bites can be dangerous), work with animals, or travel so far off the beaten track that medical help is more than two days away.

Sexually Transmitted Diseases Sexual contact with an infected sexual partner spreads these diseases. While abstinence is the only 100% preventative, using condoms is also effective. Gonorrhoea, herpes and syphilis are among these diseases; sores, blisters or rashes around the genitals, discharges or pain when urinating are common symptoms. In some STDs, such as wart virus or chlamydia, symptoms may be less marked or not observed at all in women. Syphilis symptoms eventually disappear completely but the disease continues and can cause severe problems in later years. The treatment of gonorrhoea and syphilis is with antibiotics.

There are numerous other sexually transmitted diseases, for most of which effective treatment is available. There is currently no cure for herpes.

HIV/AIDS Infection with the human immunodeficiency virus (HIV) may lead to acquired immune deficiency syndrome (AIDS), which is a fatal disease. Any exposure to blood, blood products or body fluids may put the individual at risk. The disease is often transmitted through sexual contact or dirty needles – vaccinations, acupuncture, tattooing and body piercing can be potentially as dangerous as intravenous drug use.

If you do need an injection, ask to see the syringe unwrapped in front of you, or take a needle and syringe pack with you.

Fear of HIV infection should never preclude treatment for serious medical conditions.

Insect-Borne Diseases

Typhus Tick typhus is a problem from April to September in rural areas, particularly areas where animals congregate. Typhus begins with a fever, chills, headache and muscle pains, followed a few days later by a body rash. There is often a large painful sore at the site of the bite and nearby lymph nodes are swollen and painful. There is no vaccine available. The best protection is to check your skin carefully after walking in danger areas such as long grass and scrub. A strong insect repellent can help, and serious walkers in tick areas should consider having their boots and trousers impregnated with benzyl benzoate and dibutylphthalate. (See the Cuts, Bites & Stings section following for information about ticks.)

Lyme Disease Lyme disease is a tick-transmitted infection which may be acquired throughout Europe. The illness usually begins with a spreading rash at the site of the bite and is accompanied by fever, headache, extreme fatigue, aching joints and muscles and mild neck stiffness. If untreated, these symptoms usually resolve over several weeks but over subsequent weeks or months disorders of the nervous system, heart and joints may develop. The response to treatment is best early in the illness. The longer the delay, the longer the recovery period.

Cuts, Bites & Stings

Skin punctures can easily become infected in hot climates and may be difficult to heal. Treat any cut with an antiseptic such as povidone-iodine. Where possible avoid bandages and Band-Aids, which can keep wounds wet.

Although there are a lot of bees and wasps in Greece, their stings are usually painful rather than dangerous. Calamine lotion or sting relief spray will give relief and ice packs will reduce the pain and swelling.

Snakes Always wear boots, socks and long trousers when walking through undergrowth where snakes may be present. Don't put your hands into holes and crevices, and be careful when collecting firewood.

Snake bites do not cause instantaneous death and antivenenes are usually available. Keep the victim calm and still, wrap the bitten limb tightly, as you would for a sprained ankle, and then attach a splint to immobilise it. Then seek medical help, if possible with the dead snake for identification. Don't attempt to catch the snake if there is even a remote possibility of being bitten again. Tourniquets and sucking out the poison are now comprehensively discredited.

Jelly Fish, Sea Urchins & Weever Fish Watch out for sea urchins around rocky beaches; if you get some of their needles embedded in your skin, olive oil will help to loosen them. If they are not removed they will become infected. Be wary also of jelly fish, particularly during the months of September and October. Although they are not lethal in Greece, their stings can be painful. Dousing in vinegar will deactivate any stingers which have not 'fired'. Calamine lotion, antihistamines and analgesics may reduce the reaction and relieve the pain. Much more painful than either of these, but thankfully much rarer, is an encounter with the weever fish. It buries itself in the sand of the tidal zone with only its spines protruding, and injects a painful and powerful toxin if trodden on. Soaking your foot in very hot water (which breaks down the poison) should solve the problem. It can cause permanent local paralysis in the worst instance.

Bedbugs & Lice Bedbugs live in various places, but particularly in dirty mattresses and bedding. Spots of blood on bedclothes or on the wall around the bed can be read as a suggestion to find another hotel. Bedbugs leave itchy bites in neat rows. Calamine lotion or sting relief spray may help.

All lice cause itching and discomfort. They make themselves at home in your hair, your clothing or in your pubic hair. You catch lice through direct contact with infected people or by sharing combs, clothing and the like. Powder or shampoo treatment will kill the lice and infected clothing should then be washed in very hot water.

Leeches & Ticks Leeches may be present in damp conditions. They attach themselves to your skin to suck your blood. Trekkers often get them on their legs or in their boots. Salt or a lighted cigarette end will make them fall off. Do not pull them off, as the bite is then more likely to become infected. An insect repellent may keep them away. You should always check your body if you have been walking through a potentially tick-infested area as ticks can cause skin infections and other more serious diseases.

Sheepdogs In Greece these dogs are trained to guard penned sheep from bears, wolves and thieves. They are often underfed and sometimes ill-treated by their owners. They are almost always all bark and no bite, but if you are going to trek into remote areas, you should consider having rabies injections (see Rabies). You are most likely to encounter these dogs in the mountainous regions of Epiros and Crete. Wandering through a flock of sheep over which one of these dogs is vigilantly (and possibly discreetly) watching is simply asking for trouble.

Women's Health

Antibiotic use, synthetic underwear, sweating and contraceptive pills can lead to fungal vaginal infections, especially when travelling in hot climates. Fungal infections are characterised by a rash, itch and discharge and can be treated with a vinegar or lemon-juice douche, or with yogurt. Nystatin, miconazole or clotrimazole pessaries or vaginal cream are the usual treatment. Maintaining good personal hygiene and wearing loose-fitting clothes and cotton underwear may help prevent these infections.

Sexually transmitted diseases are a major cause of vaginal problems. Symptoms include a smelly discharge, painful intercourse and sometimes a burning sensation when urinating. Medical attention should be sought and male sexual partners must also be treated. For more details see the earlier section on Sexually Transmitted Diseases. Besides abstinence, the best thing is to practise safer sex using condoms.

Hospital Treatment

Citizens of EU countries are covered for free treatment in public hospitals within Greece on presentation of an E111 form. Inquire at your national health service or travel agent in advance. Emergency treatment is free to all nationalities in public hospitals. In an emergency, dial ☎ 166. There is at least one doctor on every island in Greece and larger islands have hospitals. Pharmacies can dispense medicines which are available only on prescription in most European countries, so you can consult a pharmacist for minor ailments.

All this sounds fine, but although medical training is of a high standard in Greece, the health service is badly underfunded and one of the worst in Europe. Hospitals are overcrowded, hygiene is not always what it should be and relatives are expected to bring in food for the patient – which could be a problem for a tourist. Conditions and treatment are better in private hospitals, which are expensive. All this means that a good health-insurance policy is essential.

WOMEN TRAVELLERS

Many women travel alone in Greece. The crime rate remains relatively low, and solo travel is probably safer than in most

European countries. This does not mean that you should be lulled into complacency; bag snatching and rapes do occur, although violent offences are rare.

The biggest nuisance to foreign women travelling alone are the guys the Greeks have nicknamed *kamaki*. The word means 'fishing trident' and refers to the kamaki's favourite pastime, 'fishing' for foreign women. You'll find them everywhere there are lots of tourists; young (for the most part), smooth-talking guys who aren't in the least bashful about sidling up to foreign women in the street. They can be very persistent, but they are a hassle rather than a threat.

The majority of Greek men treat foreign women with respect, and are genuinely helpful.

GAY & LESBIAN TRAVELLERS

In a country where the church still plays a prominent role in shaping society's views on issues such as sexuality, it should come as no surprise that homosexuality is generally frowned upon – especially outside the major cities. While there is no legislation against homosexual activity, it pays to be discreet and to avoid open displays of togetherness.

This has not prevented Greece from becoming an extremely popular destination for gay travellers. Athens has a busy gay scene, as does Thessaloniki – but most gay travellers head for the islands. Mykonos has long been famous for its bars, beaches and general hedonism, while Paros (and Antiparos), Rhodes, Santorini and Skiathos all have their share of gay hang-outs.

The town of Eressos on the island of Lesvos (Mytilini), birthplace of the lesbian poet Sappho, has become something of a place of pilgrimage for lesbians.

Information The *Spartacus International Gay Guide*, published by Bruno Gmünder (Berlin), is widely regarded as the leading authority on the gay travel scene. The Greek section has been given a thorough overhaul for the 1998/99 edition, and it contains a wealth of information on gay venues everywhere from Alexandroupolis to Xanthi.

There's also stacks of information on the Internet. *Roz Mov*, at www.geocities.com/WestHollywood/2225/index.html, is a good place to start. It has pages on travel info, gay health, the gay press, organisations, events and legal issues – and links to lots more sites.

Gayscape has a useful site at www.jwpublishing.com/gayscape.gre.html with lots of links.

Organisations The main gay rights organisation in Greece is the Elladas Omofilofilon Kommunitas (☎ 01-341 0755, fax 883 6942, email eok@nyx.gr), upstairs at Apostolou Pavlou 31 in the Athens suburb of Thisio.

DISABLED TRAVELLERS

If mobility is a problem and you wish to visit Greece, the hard fact is that most hotels, museums and ancient sites in Greece are not wheelchair accessible. This is partly due to the uneven terrain of much of the country, which, with its abundance of stones, rocks and marble, presents a challenge even for able-bodied people.

If you are determined, then take heart in the knowledge that disabled people do come to Greece for holidays. But the trip needs careful planning, so get as much information as you can before you go. The British-based Royal Association for Disability and Rehabilitation (RADAR) publishes a useful guide called *Holidays & Travel Abroad: A Guide for Disabled People*, which gives a good overview of facilities available to disabled travellers in Europe. Contact RADAR (☎ 020-7250 3222, fax 7250 0212, email radar@radar.org.uk) at 12 City Forum, 250 City Road, London EC1V 8AF.

Lavinia Tours (☎ 031-23 2828, fax 21 9714), at Egnatia 101 (PO Box 111 06), Thessaloniki 541 10, specialises in arranging tours for disabled travellers. Managing director Eugenia Stravropoulou has travelled widely both in Greece and abroad in her wheelchair.

SENIOR TRAVELLERS

Card-carrying EU pensioners can claim a range of benefits such as reduced admission charges at museums and ancient sites and discounts on trains.

TRAVEL WITH CHILDREN

Greece is a safe and relatively easy place to travel with children. It's especially easy if you're staying by the beach or at a resort hotel. If you're travelling around, the main problem is a shortage of decent playgrounds and other recreational facilities.

Don't be afraid to take children to the ancient sites. Many parents are surprised by how much their children enjoy them. Young imaginations go into overdrive when let loose somewhere like the 'labyrinth' at Knossos.

Hotels and restaurants are very accommodating when it comes to meeting the needs of children, although highchairs are a rarity outside resorts. Service in restaurants is normally very quick, which is great when you've got hungry children on your hands.

Fresh milk is readily available in large towns and tourist areas, but hard to find on the smaller islands. Supermarkets are the best place to look. Formula is available everywhere, as is condensed and heat-treated milk.

Mobility is an issue for parents with very small children. Strollers (pushchairs) aren't much use in Greece unless you're going to spend all your time in one of the few flat spots. They are hopeless on rough stone paths and up steps, and a curse when getting on/off buses and ferries. Backpacks or front pouches are best.

Travel on ferries and buses is free for children under four. They pay half fare up to the age of 10 (ferries) and 12 (buses). Full fares apply otherwise. On domestic flights, you'll pay 10% of the fare to have a child under two sitting on your knee. Kids aged two to 12 pay half fare.

USEFUL ORGANISATIONS

Mountaineering Clubs

Ellinikos Orivatikos Syndesmos (EOS – Greek Alpine Club; ☎ 01-321 2429/2355) is the largest and oldest Greek mountaineering and trekking organisation. Its headquarters are at Plateia Kapnikareas 2, Athens – on Ermou, 500m west of Syntagma. The place is staffed by volunteers with day-time jobs, but if you call or visit between 7 and 9 pm on a weekday, there should be someone there.

Automobile Associations

ELPA (☎ 01-779 1615), the Greek automobile club, has its headquarters on the ground floor of Athens Tower, Messogion 2-4, Athens 115 27. The ELPA offers reciprocal services to members of national automobile associations on production of a valid membership card. If your vehicle breaks down, dial ☎ 104.

DANGERS & ANNOYANCES

Theft

Crime, especially theft, is low in Greece, but unfortunately it is on the increase. The worst area is around Omonia in central Athens – keep track of your valuables here, on the metro and at the Sunday flea market. The vast majority of thefts from tourists are still committed by other tourists; the biggest danger of theft is probably in dormitory rooms in hostels and at camp sites. So make sure you do not leave valuables unattended in such places. If you are staying in a hotel room, and the windows and door do not lock securely, ask for your valuables to be locked in the hotel safe – hotel proprietors are happy to do this.

Bar Scams

Bar scams continue to be an unfortunate fact of life in Athens, particularly in the Syntagma area. The basic scam is always some variation on the following theme: solo male traveller is lured into bar on some pretext (not always sex); strikes up conversation with friendly locals; charming girls appear and ask for what turn out to be ludicrously overpriced drinks; traveller is eventually handed an enormous bill.

Fortunately, this practice appears confined to Athens at this stage. See under Information in the Athens chapter for the full run-down on this scam and other problems.

LEGAL MATTERS

Consumer Advice

The Tourist Assistance Programme exists to help people who are having trouble with any tourism-related service. Free legal advice is available in English, French and German from July 1 to September 30. The main office (☎ 01-330 0673, fax 330 0591) is at Valtetsiou 43-45 in Athens. It's open 10 am to 2 pm Monday to Friday. Free advice is also available from the following regional offices:

Iraklio
 Consumers' Association of Crete
 (☎ 081-240 666) Milatou 1 and Agiou Titou
Kavala
 Consumers' Association of Kavala
 (☎ 051-221 159) Ydras 3
Patras
 Consumers' Association of Patras
 (☎ 061-272 481) Korinthou 213B
Volos
 Consumers' Association of Volos
 (☎ 0421-39 266) Haziagari 51

Drugs

Greek drug laws are the strictest in Europe. Greek courts make no distinction between possession and pushing. Possession of even a small amount of marijuana is likely to land you in jail.

BUSINESS HOURS

Banks are open 8 am to 2 pm Monday to Thursday, and 8 am to 1.30 pm Friday. Some banks in large towns and cities open between 3.30 and 6.30 pm in the afternoon and on Saturday morning.

Post offices are open 7.30 am to 2 pm Monday to Friday. In the major cities they stay open until 8 pm, and open on 7.30 am to 2 pm Saturday.

The opening hours of OTE offices (for long distance and overseas telephone calls) vary according to the size of the town. In smaller towns they are usually open 7.30 am to 3 pm daily, 6 am to 11 pm in larger towns, and 24 hours in major cities like Athens and Thessaloniki.

In summer, the usual opening hours for shops are 8 am to 1.30 pm and 5.30 to 8.30 pm on Tuesday, Thursday and Friday, and 8 am to 2.30 pm on Monday, Wednesday and Saturday. Shops open 30 minutes later in winter. These times are not always strictly adhered to. Many shops in tourist resorts are open seven days a week.

Department stores and supermarkets are open 8 am to 8 pm Monday to Friday, 8 am to at least 3 pm on Saturday and closed Sunday.

Periptera are open from early morning until late at night. They sell everything from bus tickets and cigarettes to hard-core pornography.

Museums and Ancient Sites

The bigger the attraction, the longer it stays open. Places like the Acropolis and the National Archaeological Museum in Athens, Delphi, Knossos and Olympia are open 8 am to 7 pm daily during summer (1 April to 31 October). They close at 5 pm during the rest of the year.

Most other sites and museums open at 8 or 8.30 am, and close at around 2.30 and 3 pm. It's no coincidence that these are the standard Greek public service hours! It means that you need to get out and about early if you want to visit more than one site a day. Most places are closed on Monday.

Lots of minor sites are unenclosed – and therefore always open to the public.

PUBLIC HOLIDAYS

All banks and shops and most museums and ancient sites close on public holidays. National public holidays in Greece are:

New Year's Day	1 January
Epiphany	6 January
First Sunday in Lent	February
Greek Independence Day	25 March
Good Friday	March/April
(Orthodox) Easter Sunday	March/April
Spring Festival/Labour Day	1 May
Feast of the Assumption	15 August
Ohi Day	28 October
Christmas Day	25 December
St Stephen's Day	26 December

SPECIAL EVENTS

The Greek year is a succession of festivals and events, some of which are religious, some cultural, others an excuse for a good knees-up, and some a combination of all three. The following is by no means an exhaustive list, but it covers the most important events, both national and regional. If you're in the right place at the right time, you'll certainly be invited to join the revelry.

January

Feast of Agios Vasilios (St Basil)

The year kicks off with this festival on 1 January. A church ceremony is followed by the exchanging of gifts, singing, dancing and feasting; the New Year pie *(vasilopitta)* is sliced and the person who gets the slice containing a coin will supposedly have a lucky year.

Epiphany (the Blessing of the Waters)

On 6 January, Christ's baptism by St John is celebrated throughout Greece. Seas, lakes and rivers are blessed and crosses immersed in them. The largest ceremony occurs at Piraeus.

Gynaikratia

On 8 January a day of role reversal occurs in villages in the prefectures of Rodopi, Kilkis and Seres in northern Greece. Women spend the day in kafeneia (cafes) and other social centres where men usually congregate, while the men stay at home to do the housework.

February-March

Carnival

The Greek carnival season is the three weeks before the beginning of Lent (the 40 day period before Easter, which is traditionally a period of fasting). The carnivals are ostensibly Christian pre-Lenten celebrations, but many derive from pagan festivals. There are many regional variations, but fancy dress, feasting, traditional dancing and general merrymaking prevail. The Patras carnival is the largest and most exuberant, with elaborately decorated chariots parading through the streets. The most bizarre carnival takes place on the island of Skyros where the men transform themselves into grotesque 'half man, half beast' creatures by donning goat-skin masks and hairy jackets. Other carnivals worth catching are those at Athens, Veria, Zakynthos, Kefallonia, and at Naoussa in Macedonia.

Shrove Monday (Clean Monday)

On the Monday before Ash Wednesday (the first day of Lent), people take to the hills throughout Greece to have picnics and fly kites.

March

Independence Day

The anniversary of the hoisting of the Greek flag by Bishop Germanos at Moni Agias Lavras is celebrated on 25 March with parades and dancing. Germanos' act of revolt marked the start of the War of Independence. Independence Day coincides with the **Feast of the Annunciation**, so it is also a religious festival.

March-April

Easter

Easter is the most important festival in the Greek Orthodox religion. Emphasis is placed on the Resurrection rather than on the Crucifixion, so it is a joyous occasion. The festival commences on the evening of Good Friday with the *perifora epitavios*, when a shrouded bier (representing Christ's funeral bier) is carried through the streets to the local church. This moving candlelit procession can be seen in towns and villages throughout the country. From a spectator's viewpoint, the most impressive of these processions climbs Lykavittos Hill in Athens to the Chapel of Agios Georgos.

The Resurrection Mass starts at 11 pm on Saturday night. At midnight, packed churches are plunged into darkness to symbolise Christ's passing through the underworld.

The ceremony of the lighting of candles which follows is the most significant moment in the Orthodox year, for it symbolises the Resurrection. Its poignancy and beauty are spellbinding. If you are in Greece at Easter you should endeavour to attend this ceremony, which ends with the setting off of fireworks and candlelit processions through the streets. The Lenten fast ends on Easter Sunday with the cracking of red-dyed Easter eggs and an outdoor feast of roast lamb followed by Greek dancing. The day's greeting is *Hristos anesti* (Christ is risen), to which the reply is *Alithos anesti* (Truly He is risen). On both Palm Sunday (the Sunday before Easter) and Easter Sunday, St Spyridon (the mummified patron saint of Corfu) is taken out for an airing and joyously paraded through Corfu Town. He is paraded again on 11 August.

Feast of Agios Georgos (St George)

The feast day of St George, Greece's patron saint, and patron saint of shepherds, takes place on 23 April or the Tuesday following Easter (whichever comes first). It is celebrated at several places, but with particular exuberance in Arahova, near Delphi.

May

May Day

On the first day of May there is a mass exodus from towns to the country. During picnics, wild flowers are gathered and made into wreaths to decorate houses.

Anastenaria

This fire-walking ritual takes place on 21 May in the village of Langadas, near Thessaloniki. Villagers clutching icons dance barefoot on burning charcoal. See the Northern Greece chapter for more details.

June

Navy Week

The festival celebrates the long relationship between the Greek and the sea with events in fishing villages and ports throughout the country. Volos and Hydra have unique versions of these celebrations. Volos re-enacts the departure of the *Argo*, for legend has it that Iolkos (from where Jason and the Argonauts set off in search of the Golden Fleece) was near the city. Hydra commemorates Admiral Andreas Miaoulis, who was born on the island and was a hero of the War of Independence, with a re-enactment of one of his naval victories, accompanied by feasting and fireworks.

Feast of St John the Baptist

This feast day on 24 June is widely celebrated around Greece. Wreaths made on May Day are kept until this day, when they are burned on bonfires.

July

Feast of Agia Marina (St Marina)

This feast day is celebrated on 17 July in many parts of Greece, and is a particularly important event on the Dodecanese island of Kassos.

Feast of Profitis Ilias

This feast day is celebrated on 20 July at hilltop churches and monasteries dedicated to the prophet, especially in the Cyclades.

August

Assumption

Greeks celebrate Assumption Day (15 August) with family reunions. The whole population seems to be on the move either side of the big day, so it's a good time to avoid public transport. The island of Tinos gets particularly busy because of its miracle-working icon of Panagia Evangelistria. It becomes a place of pilgrimage for thousands, who come to be blessed, healed or baptised, or just for the excitement of being there. Many are unable to find hotels and sleep out on the streets.

September

Genesis tis Panagias (the Virgin's Birthday)

This day is celebrated on 8 September throughout Greece with religious services and feasting.

Exaltation of the Cross

This is celebrated on 14 September throughout Greece with processions and hymns.

October

Feast of Agios Dimitrios (St Dimitri)

This feast day is celebrated in Thessaloniki on 26 October with wine drinking and revelry.

Ohi (No) Day

Metaxas' refusal to allow Mussolini's troops free passage through Greece in WWII is commemorated on 28 October with remembrance services, military parades, folk dancing and feasting.

December

Christmas Day

Although not as important as Easter, Christmas is still celebrated with religious services and feasting. Nowadays much 'western' influence is apparent, including Christmas trees, decorations and presents.

Summer Festivals & Performances

There are cultural festivals throughout Greece in summer. The most important are the Athens Festival (June-September), with drama and music performances in the Theatre of Herodes Atticus, and the Epidaurus Festival (July-September), with drama performances in the ancient theatre at Epidaurus. Others include the Philippi and Thasos Festival (July and August); the Renaissance Festival in Rethymno (July and August); the Dodoni Festival in Epiros (August); the Olympus Festival at Katerini and Litohoro (August); the Hippocratia Festival on Kos (August); and the Patras Arts Festival (August and September).

Thessaloniki hosts a string of festivals and events during September and October, including the International Trade Fair and the Feast of Agios Dimitrios (details on the latter in the preceding list).

The nightly son et lumière in Athens and Rhodes runs from April to October.

Greek folk dances are performed in Athens from mid-May to September and in Rhodes from May to October.

ACTIVITIES

Windsurfing

Windsurfing is the most popular water sport in Greece. Hsrysi Akti on Paros, and Vasiliki on Lefkada vie for the position of the best windsurfing beach. According to some, Vasiliki is one of the best places in the world to learn the sport.

You'll find sailboards for hire almost everywhere. Hire charges range from 2000 dr to 3000 dr an hour, depending on the gear. If you are a novice, most places that rent equipment also give lessons.

Sailboards may only be brought into Greece if a Greek national residing in Greece guarantees that it will be taken out again. To find out how to arrange this, contact the Hellenic Windsurfing Association (☎ 01-323 0330), Filellinon 7, Athens.

Water-Skiing

Islands with water-ski centres are Chios, Corfu, Crete, Kythira, Lesvos, Paros, Skiathos and Rhodes.

Snorkelling & Diving

Snorkelling is enjoyable just about anywhere along the coast off Greece. Especially good places are Monastiri on Paros, Velanio on Skopelos, Paleokastritsa on Corfu, Telendos Islet (near Kalymnos) and anywhere off the coast of Kastellorizo.

Diving is another matter. Any kind of underwater activity using breathing apparatus is strictly forbidden other than under the supervision of a diving school. This is to protect the many antiquities in the depths of the Aegean. There are diving schools on the islands of Corfu, Crete (at Rethymno), Evia, Mykonos and Rhodes, and Halkidiki and Glyfada (near Athens) on the mainland.

Trekking

More than half of Greece is mountainous. It would be a trekkers' paradise but for one drawback – many of the paths in Greece are overgrown and inadequately marked. Like all organisations in Greece, the EOS (Ellinikos Orivatikos Syndesmos), the Greek Alpine Club, is grossly underfunded (see Useful Organisations earlier for details of the club). But don't be put off by this, as the most popular routes are well walked and maintained. You'll find information on maps in the Planning section at the beginning of this chapter.

On small islands it's fun to discover pathways for yourself. You are unlikely to get into danger as settlements or roads are never far away. You will encounter a variety of paths: *kalderimi* are cobbled or flagstone paths which link settlements and date back to Byzantine times. Sadly, many have been bulldozed to make way for roads.

A number of companies run organised treks. One of the biggest is Trekking Hellas (☎ 01-323 4548, fax 325 1474, email trekking@compulink.gr), Filellinon 7, Athens 105 57. You'll find more information at its Web site, www.trekking.gr.

Skiing

Greece provides some of the cheapest skiing in Europe. There are 16 resorts dotted around the mountains of mainland Greece, mainly in the north. The main skiing areas are Mt Parnassos, 195km north-west of Athens, and Mt Vermio, 110km west of Thessaloniki. There are no foreign package holidays to these resorts; they are used mainly by Greeks. Most have all the basic facilities and are a pleasant alternative to the glitzy resorts of northern Europe.

The season depends on snow conditions but runs approximately from January to the end of April. For further information pick up a copy of *Greece: Mountain Refuges & Ski Centres* from an EOT office. Information may also be obtained from the Hellenic Skiing Federation (☎ 01-524 0057, fax 524 8821), PO Box 8037, Omonia, Athens 100 10.

COURSES

Language

If you are serious about learning the language, an intensive course at the start of your stay is a good way to go about it. Most of the courses are in Athens (see the Athens chapter), but there are also special courses on the islands in summer.

The Hellenic Culture Centre (☎/fax 01-360 3379, 0275-61 482, email hccmike@netor) runs courses on the island of Ikaria from June to October. Two-week intensive courses for beginners cost 130,000 dr and involve 40 classroom hours. The centre can also arrange accommodation. You'll find details on the Internet at www.hcc.gr.

The Athens Centre (☎ 01-701 2268, fax 701 8603, email athenscr@compulink.gr), Arhimidous 48 in the suburb of Mets, runs courses on the island of Spetses in June and July. It also has a Web site, www.athenscentre.gr.

Corfu's Ionian University Courses runs courses in Modern Greek and Greek Civilisation in July and August. Details are available at Deligiorgi 55-59 (☎ 01-522 9770) in Athens, or from the Secretariat of the Ionian University (☎ 0661-22 993/994) at Megaron Kapodistria 49, Corfu Town.

Dance

The Dora Stratou Dance Company (☎ 01-324 4395) in Athens holds folk dancing workshops for amateurs during July and August. The *Hellenic Times* carries information about this and other workshops.

WORK

Permits

EU nationals don't need a work permit, but they need a residency permit if they intend to stay longer than three months. Nationals of other countries are supposed to have a work permit.

English Tutoring

If you're looking for a permanent job, the most widely available option is to teach English. A TEFL (Teaching English as a Foreign Language) certificate or a university degree is an advantage but not essential. In the UK, look through the *Times Educational Supplement* or Tuesday's edition of the *Guardian* newspaper for opportunities – in other countries, contact the Greek embassy.

Another possibility is to find a job teaching English once you are in Greece. You will see language schools everywhere. Strictly speaking, you need a licence to teach in these schools, but many will employ teachers without one. The best time to look around for such a job is late summer.

The notice board at the Compendium bookshop in Athens sometimes has advertisements looking for private English lessons.

Bar & Hostel Work

The bars of the Greek islands could not survive without foreign workers and there are thousands of summer jobs up for grabs every year. The pay is not fantastic, but you get to spend a summer in the islands. April/May is the time to go looking. Hostels and travellers' hotels are other places that regularly employ foreign workers.

Volunteer Work

The Hellenic Society for the Study & Protection of the Monk Seal (☎ 01-522 2888, fax 522 2450), Solomou 53, Athens 104 32, and the Sea Turtle Protection Society of Greece (☎/fax 01-523 1342, email stps@compulink.gr), Solomou 57, Athens 104 32, use volunteers for their monitoring programs on the Ionian Islands and the Peloponnese.

Street Performers

The richest pickings are to be found on the islands, particularly Mykonos, Paros and Santorini. Plaka is the place to go in Athens; the area outside the church on Kydathineon is the most popular spot.

Other Work

There are often jobs advertised in the classifieds of the English-language newspapers, or you can place an advertisement yourself. EU nationals can also make use of the OAED (Organismos Apasholiseos Ergatikou Dynamikou), the Greek National Employment Service, in their search for a job. The OAED has offices throughout Greece.

Seasonal harvest work seems to be monopolised by migrant workers from Albania, and is no longer a viable option for travellers.

ACCOMMODATION

There is a range of accommodation available in Greece to suit every taste and pocket. All places to stay are subject to strict price controls set by the tourist police. By law, a notice must be displayed in every room, which states the category of the room and the price charged in each season. The price includes a 4.5% community tax and 8% VAT.

Accommodation owners may add a 10% surcharge for a stay of less than three nights, but this is not mandatory. A mandatory charge of 20% is levied if an extra bed is put into a room. During July and August, accommodation owners will charge the maximum price, but in spring and autumn, prices will drop by up to 20%, and perhaps by even more in winter. These are the times to bring your bargaining skills into action.

Rip-offs rarely occur, but if you suspect you have been exploited by an accommodation owner, report it to either the tourist police or regular police and they will act swiftly.

Mountain Refuges

There are 55 mountain refuges dotted around the Greek mainland, Crete and Evia. They range from small huts with outdoor toilets and no cooking facilities to comfortable modern lodges. They are run by the country's various mountaineering and skiing clubs. Prices range from 1500 dr to 2000 dr per person, depending on the facilities. The EOT publication *Greece: Mountain Refuges & Ski Centres* has details about each refuge.

Camping

There are almost 350 camping grounds in Greece. A few are operated by the EOT, but most are privately run. Very few are open outside the high season (April-October). The Panhellenic Camping Association (☎/fax 01-362 1560), Solonos 102, Athens 106 80, publishes an annual booklet listing all the camp sites and their facilities.

Camping fees are highest from 15 June to the end of August. Most camping grounds charge from 1200 dr to 1400 dr per adult and 600 dr to 800 dr for children aged four to 12. There's no charge for children aged under four. Tent sites cost from 900 dr per night for small tents, and from 1200 dr per night for large tents. Caravan sites start at around 2500 dr.

Between May and mid-September it is warm enough to sleep out under the stars, although you will still need a lightweight sleeping bag to counter the pre-dawn chill. It's a good idea to have a foam pad to lie on and a waterproof cover for your sleeping bag.

Freelance (wild) camping is illegal, but the law is not always strictly enforced. If you do decide to take a chance on this, make sure you are not camping on private land, and clear up all rubbish when you leave. If you are told to move by the police, do so without protest, as the law is occasionally enforced. Freelance camping is more likely to be tolerated on islands that don't have camp sites. It's wise to ask around before freelance camping anywhere in Greece.

Apartments

Self-contained family apartments are available in some hotels and domatia. There are also a number of purpose-built apartments, particularly on the islands, available for either long or short term rental. Prices vary considerably according to the amenities offered. The classified sections of the *Athens News* and *Hellenic Times* both advertise apartments, mostly in Athens. The tourist police may be able to help in other major towns. In rural areas and islands, ask in a kafeneio.

Domatia

Domatia are the Greek equivalent of the British bed and breakfast, minus the breakfast. Once upon a time domatia comprised little more than spare rooms in the family home which could be rented out to travellers in summer; nowadays, many are purpose-built appendages to the family house. Some come complete with fully equipped kitchens. Standards of cleanliness are generally high. The decor runs the gamut from cool grey marble floors, coordinated pine furniture, pretty lace curtains and tasteful pictures on the walls, to so much kitsch, you are almost afraid to move in case you break an ornament.

Domatia remain a popular option for budget travellers. They are classified A, B or C. Expect to pay from 4000 dr to 9000 dr for a single, and 6000 dr to 15,000 dr for a double, depending on the class, whether bathrooms are shared or private, the season and how long you plan to stay. Domatia are found throughout the mainland (except in large cities) and on almost every island which has a permanent population. Many are open only between April and October.

From June to September domatia owners are out in force, touting for customers. They meet buses and boats, shouting 'Room, room!' and often carrying photographs of their rooms. In peak season, it can prove a mistake not to take up an offer – but be wary of owners who are vague about the location of their accommodation. 'Close to town' can turn out to be way out in the sticks. If you are at all dubious, insist they show you the location on a map.

Hostels

There is only one youth hostel in Greece affiliated to the International Youth Hostel Federation (IYHF), the excellent Athens International Youth Hostel (☎ 01-523 4170). You don't need a membership card to stay there; temporary membership costs 600 dr per day.

Most other youth hostels in Greece are run by the Greek Youth Hostel Organisation (☎ 01-751 9530, fax 751 0616, email y-hostels@otenet.gr), Damareos 75, 116 33 Athens. There are affiliated hostels in Athens, Olympia, Patras and Thessaloniki on the mainland, and on the islands of Crete and Santorini.

Hostel rates vary from 1600 dr to 2000 dr and you don't have to be a member to stay in any of them. Few have curfews.

There is a XEN (YWCA) hostel for women in Athens.

Traditional Settlements

Traditional settlements are old buildings of architectural merit that have been renovated and converted into tourist accommodation. You'll find them all over the country, including the islands. There are some terrific places among them, but they are expensive – most are equivalent in price to an A or B class hotel. Some of the best examples are in the Papingo villages of northern Epiros and in the old Byzantine town of Monemvasia in the Peloponnese. Hania (Crete) and Rhodes Town also have a good range of possibilities.

Pensions

Pensions in Greece are virtually indistinguishable from hotels. They are classed A, B or C. An A class pension is equivalent in amenities and price to a B class hotel, a B class pension is equivalent to a C class hotel and a C class pension is equivalent to a D or E class hotel.

Hotels

Hotels in Greece are divided into six categories: deluxe, A, B, C, D and E. Hotels are categorised according to the size of the room, whether or not they have a bar, and the ratio of bathrooms to beds, rather than standards of cleanliness, comfort of the beds and friendliness of staff – all elements which may be of greater relevance to guests.

As one would expect, deluxe, A and B class hotels have many amenities, private bathrooms and constant hot water. C class hotels have a snack bar, rooms have private bathrooms, but hot water may only be available at certain times of the day. D class hotels may or may not have snack bars, most rooms will share bathrooms, but there may be some with private bathrooms, and they may have solar-heated water, which means hot water is not guaranteed. E classes do not have a snack bar, bathrooms are shared and you may have to pay extra for hot water – if it exists at all.

Prices are controlled by the tourist police and the maximum rate that can be charged for a room must be displayed on a board behind the door of each room. The classification is not often much of a guide to price. Rates in D and E class hotels are generally comparable with domatia. You can pay from 10,000 dr to 20,000 dr for a single in high season in C class and 15,000 dr to 25,000 dr for a double. Prices in B class range from 15,000 dr to 25,000 dr for singles, and from 25,000 dr to 35,000 dr for doubles. A class prices are not much higher.

FOOD

Greek food does not enjoy a reputation as one of the world's great cuisines. Maybe that's because many travellers have experienced Greek cooking only in tourist resorts. The old joke about the Greek woman who, on summer days, shouted to her husband 'Come and eat your lunch before it gets hot' is based on truth. Until recently, food was invariably served lukewarm – which is how Greeks prefer it. Most restaurants that cater to tourists have now cottoned on to the fact that foreigners expect cooked dishes to be served hot, and improved methods of warming meals (including the dreaded microwave) have made this easier. If your meal is not hot, ask that it be served *zesto*, or order grills, which have to be cooked to order. Greeks are fussy about fresh ingredients, and frozen food is rare.

Greeks eat out regularly, regardless of socioeconomic status. Enjoying life is paramount to them and a large part of this enjoyment comes from eating and drinking with friends.

By law, every eating establishment must display a written menu including prices. Bread will automatically be put on your table and usually costs between 100 dr and 200 dr, depending on the restaurant's category.

Where to Eat

Tavernas The taverna is usually a traditional place with a rough-and-ready ambience, although some are more upmarket, particularly in Athens, resorts and big towns. In simple tavernas, a menu is usually displayed in the window or on the door, but you may instead be invited into the kitchen to peer into the pots and point to what you want. This is not merely a privilege for tourists; Greeks also do it because they want to see the taverna's version of the dishes on offer. Some tavernas don't open until 8 pm, and then stay open until the early hours. Some are closed on Sunday.

Greek men are football (soccer) and basketball mad. If you happen to be eating in a taverna on a night when a big match is being televised, expect indifferent service.

Psistaria These places specialise in spit roasts and charcoal-grilled food – usually lamb, pork or chicken.

Restaurants A restaurant *(estiatorio)* is normally more sophisticated than a taverna or psistaria – damask tablecloths, smartly attired waiters and printed menus at each table with an English translation. Ready-made food is usually displayed in a *bain-marie* and there may also be a charcoal grill.

Ouzeria An *ouzeri* serves ouzo. Greeks believe it is essential to eat when drinking alcohol so, in traditional establishments, your drink will come with a small plate of titbits or *mezedes* (appetisers) – perhaps olives, a slice of feta and some pickled octopus. Ouzeria are becoming trendy and many now offer menus with both appetisers and main courses.

Galaktopoleia A *galaktopoleio* (literally 'milk shop') sells dairy produce including milk, butter, yogurt, rice pudding, cornflour pudding, custard, eggs, honey and bread. It may also sell home-made ice cream in several flavours. Look for the sign '*pagoto politiko*' displayed outside. Most have seating and serve coffee and tea. They are inexpensive for breakfast and usually open from very early in the morning until evening.

Zaharoplasteia A *zaharoplasteio* (patisserie) sells cakes (both traditional and western), chocolates, biscuits, sweets, coffee, soft drinks and, possibly, bottled alcoholic drinks. They usually have some seating.

Kafeneia Kafeneia are often regarded by foreigners as the last bastion of male chauvinism in Europe. With bare light bulbs, nicotine-stained walls, smoke-laden air, rickety wooden tables and raffia chairs, they are frequented by middle-aged and elderly Greek men in cloth caps who while away their time fiddling with worry beads, playing cards or backgammon, or engaged in heated political discussion.

It was once unheard of for women to enter a kafeneio but in large cities this situation is changing. In rural areas, Greek women are rarely seen inside kafeneia. When a female traveller enters one, she is inevitably treated courteously and with friendship if she manages a few Greek words of greeting. If you feel inhibited about going into a kafeneio, opt for outside seating. You'll feel less intrusive.

Kafeneia originally only served Greek coffee but now most also serve soft drinks, Nescafe and beer. They are generally fairly cheap, with Greek coffee costing about 150 dr and Nescafe with milk 250 dr or less. Most kafeneia are open all day every day, but some close during siesta time (roughly from 3 to 5 pm).

Other Eateries You'll find plenty of pizzerias, creperies and *gelaterias* (which sell Italian-style ice cream in various flavours), but international restaurants are rare outside Athens – and expensive.

Meals

Breakfast Most Greeks have Greek coffee and perhaps a cake or pastry for breakfast. Budget hotels and pensions offering breakfast provide it continental-style (rolls or bread with jam, and tea or coffee) and upmarket hotels serve breakfast buffets (western and continental-style). Otherwise, restaurants and galaktopoleia serve bread with butter, jam or honey; eggs; and the budget travellers' favourite, yogurt *(yiaourti)* with honey. In tourist areas, many menus offer an 'English' breakfast – which means bacon and eggs.

Lunch This is eaten late – between 1 and 3 pm – and may be either a snack or a complete meal. The main meal can be lunch or dinner – or both. Greeks enjoy eating and often have two large meals a day.

Dinner Greeks also eat dinner late. Many people don't start to think about food until about 9 pm, which is why some restaurants don't bother to open their doors until after 8 pm. In tourist areas dinner is often served earlier.

A full dinner in Greece begins with appetisers and/or soup, followed by a main course of either ready-made food, grilled meat, or fish. Only very posh restaurants or those pandering to tourists include western-style desserts on the menu. Greeks usually eat cakes separately in a galaktopoleio or zaharoplasteio.

Greek Specialities

Snacks Favourite Greek snacks include pretzel rings sold by street vendors, *tyropitta* (cheese pie), *bougatsa* (custard-filled pastry), *spanakopitta* (spinach pie) and *sandouits* (sandwiches). Street vendors sell various nuts and dried seeds such as pumpkin for 200 dr to 400 dr a bag. Chestnuts are roasted on the roadsides in winter.

Mezedes In a simple taverna, possibly only three or four mezedes (appetisers) will be offered – perhaps taramasalata (fish-roe dip), tzatziki (yogurt, cucumber and garlic dip), olives and feta (sheep or goat's milk) cheese. Ouzeria and restaurants usually offer wider selections.

Mezedes include *ohtapodi* (octopus), *garides* (shrimps), *kalamaria* (squid), dolmades (stuffed vine leaves), *melitzanosalata* (aubergine or eggplant dip) and *mavromatika* (black-eyed beans). Hot mezedes include *keftedes* (meatballs), *fasolia* (white haricot beans), *gigantes* (lima beans), *loukanika* (little sausages), tyropitta, spanakopitta, *bourekaki* (tiny meat pie), *kolokythakia* (deep-fried zucchini), *melitzana* (deep-fried aubergine) and *saganaki* (fried cheese).

It is quite acceptable to make a full meal of these instead of a main course. Three plates of mezedes are about equivalent in price and quantity to one main course. You can also order a *pikilia* (mixed plate).

Soups Soup is a satisfying starter or, indeed, an economical meal in itself with bread and a salad. *Psarosoupa* is a filling fish soup with vegetables, while *kakavia* (Greek bouillabaisse) is laden with seafood and more expensive. *Fasolada* (bean soup) is also a meal in itself. *Avgolemano soupa* (egg and lemon soup) is usually prepared from a chicken stock. If you're into offal, don't miss the traditional Easter soup *mayiritsa* at this festive time.

Salads The ubiquitous (and no longer inexpensive) Greek or village salad, *horiatiki salata*, is a side dish for Greeks, but many drachma-conscious tourists make it a main

A Greek Feast

Greek dishes are easy to prepare at home. Here's a simple lunch or dinner to share with friends. Recipes serve four people.

Tzatziki (Cucumber and Yoghurt Dip) Peel and grate a medium cucumber. Add a cup of yoghurt, a tablespoon of olive oil, a pinch of salt, a teaspoon of vinegar, a teaspoon of freshly chopped dill and a minced garlic clove and refrigerate for two hours. Garnish with an olive and serve with fresh crusty bread or as an accompaniment to vegetables or fried fish.

Soupa Avgolemono (Egg and Lemon Soup) Add six tablespoons of uncooked rice to six cups of boiling chicken, fish or beef stock, then cover and simmer until the rice is tender. Beat two eggs, adding a pinch of salt and the juice of a large lemon. Add the stock to this mixture slowly, so that it doesn't curdle, then pour the mixture into a pot for reheating. Stir and ensure it does not boil.

Soutzoukakia (Sausages from Smyrna) This hearty dish originated in Smyrna (İzmir) in the days of Greek occupation and has subsequently been adopted by the cooks of Thessaloniki. Soak two slices of white bread in half a cup of water, mash and add three garlic cloves finely chopped, half a teaspoon of pepper and a dessertspoon of cumin.

Add 500g (1lb) of minced lamb or beef and a beaten egg, mix well and form into small sausages. Place in an oiled roasting pan and bake in a medium to hot oven until the sausages brown on the base side. Turn the sausages and add 500g (1lb) of tomatoes, a dollop of butter and teaspoon of sugar and return to the oven for about 15 minutes – or until the tomatoes are soft and the *soutzoukakia* are brown on the other side. Serve with fried potatoes or rice, and salad.

Halvas tou Fournou (Baked Halva) Here's a delightful dessert that is simple to make. Sift half a cup of flour with two teaspoons of baking powder and a pinch of salt. Add two cups of semolina and a cup of finely chopped nuts. Cream ¾ of a cup of butter or margarine with a cup of sugar and add three beaten eggs and grated lemon peel. Combine the mixtures well, then pour into a greased 25cm (10 inch) square pan. Bake in a medium oven until golden.

Boil three cups of water with three cups of sugar, add four cloves and a half stick of cinnamon, then pour over the rest of the dessert. Leave it to stand until the cinnamon and clove mixture has been absorbed, then serve with or without cream, warm or cold. It's filling and keeps for days.

dish. It consists of peppers, onions, olives, tomatoes and feta cheese, sprinkled with oregano and dressed with olive oil and lemon juice. A tomato salad often comes with onions, cucumber and olives, and, with bread, makes a satisfying lunch. In winter, try the cheaper *radikia salata* (dandelion salad).

Main Dishes The most common main courses are *moussaka* (layers of eggplant or zucchini, minced meat and potatoes topped with cheese sauce and baked), *pastitsio* (baked cheese-topped macaroni and bechamel, with or without minced meat), dolmades and *yemista* (stuffed tomatoes or green peppers). Other main courses include *giouvetsi* (casserole of lamb or veal and pasta), *stifado* (meat stewed with onions), *soutzoukakia* (spicy meatballs in tomato sauce, also known as Smyrna sausages) and *salingaria* (snails in oil with herbs). *Melizanes papoutsakia* is baked eggplant stuffed with meat and tomatoes and topped with cheese, which looks, as its Greek name suggests, like a little shoe. Spicy loukanika (sausage) is a good budget choice and comes with potatoes or rice. Lamb fricassee, cooked with lettuce, *arni fricassée me maroulia*, is usually filling enough for two to share.

Fish is usually sold by weight in restaurants, but is not as cheap nor as widely available as it used to be. Calamari (squid), deep-fried in batter, remains a tasty option for the budget traveller at 1000 dr to 1400 dr for a generous serve. Other reasonably priced fish (about 1000 dr a portion) are *marides* (whitebait), sometimes cloaked in onion, pepper and tomato sauce, and *gopes*, which are similar to sardines. More expensive are *ohtapodi* (octopus), *bakaliaros* (cod), *xifias* (swordfish) and *glossa* (sole). Ascending the price scale further are *synagrida* (snapper) and *barbounia* (red mullet). *Astakos* (lobster) and *karabida* (crayfish) are top of the range at about 10,000 dr per kilo.

Fish is mostly grilled or fried. More imaginative fish dishes include shrimp casserole and mussel or octopus saganaki (fried with tomato and cheese). Greece has few rivers and lakes, so freshwater fish are not widely available, although reasonably priced *pestrofa* (trout) can be found in parts of northern Greece – Lake Pamvotis in Ioannina, the Aoös River in Zagoria, and also from the Prespa Lakes.

Desserts Greek cakes and puddings include *baklava* (layers of filo pastry filled with honey and nuts), *loukoumades* (puffs or fritters with honey or syrup), *kataïfi* (chopped nuts inside shredded wheat pastry or filo soaked in honey), *rizogalo* (rice pudding), *loukoumi* (Turkish delight), *halva* (made from semolina or sesame seeds) and *pagoto* (ice cream). Tavernas and restaurants usually only have a few of these on the menu. The best places to go for these delights are galaktopoleia or zaharoplasteia.

Regional Dishes

Greek food is not all moussaka and souvlaki. Every region has its own specialities and it need not be an expensive culinary adventure to discover some of these. Corfu, for example, which was never occupied by the Turks, retains traditional recipes of Italian, Spanish and ancient Greek derivations. Corfiot food is served in several restaurants and includes *sofrito* (lamb or veal with garlic, vinegar and parsley), *pastitsada*, (beef with macaroni, cloves, garlic, tomatoes and cheese) and *burdeto* (fish with paprika and cayenne). Look for poultry and rabbit in the Peloponnese; game is inevitably on the menu in Thessaly and Macedonia.

Santorini's baby tomatoes flavour distinctive dishes, not least a rich soup as thick and dark as blood. The *myzithra* (soft ewe's-milk cheese) of Ios is unique, and the lamb pies of Kefallonia and Crete are worth searching for. Andros' speciality, *froutalia* (spearmint-flavoured potato and sausage omelette), is good value. Rhodes turns out a baked omelette loaded with meat and zucchini.

Vegetarian Food

Greece has few vegetarian restaurants. Unfortunately, many vegetable soups and stews are based on meat stocks. Fried vegetables are safe bets as olive oil is always used – never lard. The Greeks do wonderful things with artichokes *(aginares)*, which thrive in Greece. Stuffed, served as a salad, as a meze, (particularly with *raki* in Crete) and as the basis of a vegetarian stew, the artichoke warrants greater discovery by visitors. Vegetarians who eat eggs can rest assured that an economical omelette can be whipped up anywhere. Salads are cheap, fresh, substantial and nourishing. Other options are yogurt, rice pudding, cheese and spinach pies, and nuts. Creperies also offer tasty vegetarian selections.

Lent, incidentally, is a good time for vegetarians because the meat is missing from many dishes.

Fast Food

Western-style fast food has arrived in Greece in a big way. 'Mac' fans will find their favourite burger at a number of locations in Athens and other major towns, but McDonald's has found Greece a hard market to conquer. Patriotic Greeks seem to prefer the local chain Goody's, which has a better salad bar than most of its rivals. The big international chicken and pizza chains are also around.

It's hard, though, to beat eat-on-the-street Greek offerings. Foremost among them are the *gyros* and the souvlaki. The gyros is a giant skewer laden with slabs of seasoned meat which grills slowly as it rotates and the meat is trimmed steadily from the outside; souvlaki are small individual kebab sticks. Both are served wrapped in pitta bread, with salad and lashings of tzatziki.

Another favourite is *tost*, which is a bread roll cut in half, stuffed with the filling(s) of your choice, buttered on the outside and then flattened in a heavy griddle iron. It's the speciality of the Everest fast-food chain, which has outlets nationwide.

Fruit

Greece grows many varieties of fruit. Most visitors will be familiar with *syka* (figs), *rodakina* (peaches), *stafylia* (grapes), *karpouzi* (watermelon), *milo* (apples), *portokalia* (oranges) and *kerasia* (cherries).

Many will not, however, have encountered the *frangosyko* (prickly pear). Also known as the Barbary fig, it is the fruit of the opuntia cactus, recognisable by the thick green spiny pads that form its trunk. The fruit are borne around the edge of the pads in late summer and autumn and vary in colour from pale orange to deep red. They are delicious but need to be approached with extreme caution because of the thousands of tiny prickles (invisible to the naked eye) that cover their skin. Never pick one up with your bare hands. They must be peeled before you can eat them. The simplest way to do this is to trim the ends off with a knife and then slit the skin from end to end.

Another fruit that will be new to many people is the *mousmoula* (loquat). These small orange fruit are among the first of summer, reaching the market in mid-May. The flesh is juicy and pleasantly acidic.

Self-Catering

Eating out in Greece is as much an entertainment as a gastronomic experience, so to self-cater is to sacrifice a lot. But if you are on a low budget you will need to make the sacrifice – for breakfast and lunch at any rate. All towns and villages of any size have supermarkets, fruit and vegetable stalls and bakeries.

Only in isolated villages and on remote islands is food choice limited. There may only be one all-purpose shop – a *pantopoleio* which will stock meat, vegetables, fruit, bread and tinned foods.

Markets Most larger towns have huge indoor *agora* (food markets) which feature fruit and vegetable stalls, butchers, dairies and delicatessens, all under one roof. They are lively places that are worth visiting for the atmosphere as much as for the shopping. The markets at Hania (Crete) and Kalamata are good examples.

Smaller towns have a weekly *laïki agora* (street market) with stalls selling local produce.

DRINKS

Nonalcoholic Drinks

Coffee & Tea Greek coffee is the national drink. It is a legacy of Ottoman rule and, until the Turkish invasion of Cyprus in 1974, the Greeks called it Turkish coffee. It is served with the grounds, without milk, in a small cup. Connoisseurs claim there are at least 30 variations of Greek coffee, but most people know only three – *glyko* (sweet), *metrio* (medium) and *sketo* (without sugar).

The next most popular coffee is instant, called Nescafe (which it usually is). Ask for Nescafe *me ghala* (pronounced 'me GA-la') if you want it with milk. In summer, Greeks drink Nescafe chilled, with or without milk and sugar – this version is called *frappé*.

Espresso and filtered coffee, once sold only in trendy cafes, are now also widely available.

Tea is inevitably made with a tea bag.

Fruit Juice & Soft Drinks Packaged fruit juices are available everywhere. Fresh orange juice is also widely available, but doesn't come cheap. The products of all the major soft-drink multinationals are available everywhere in cans and bottles, along with local brands.

Milk Fresh milk can be hard to find on the islands and in remote areas. Elsewhere, you'll have no problem. A litre costs about 350 dr. UHT milk is available almost everywhere, as is condensed milk.

Water Tap water is safe to drink in Greece, although sometimes it doesn't taste too good – particularly on some of the islands. Many tourists prefer to drink bottled spring water, sold widely in 500mL and 1.5L plastic bottles. If you're happy with tap water, fill a container with it before embarking on ferries or you'll wind up paying through the nose for bottled water. Sparkling mineral water is rare.

Alcoholic Drinks

Beer Beer lovers will find the market dominated by the major northern European breweries. The most popular beers are Amstel and Heineken, both brewed locally under licence. Other beers brewed locally are Henniger, Kaiser, Kronenbourg and Tuborg.

The only local beer is *Mythos*, launched in 1997 and widely available. It has proved popular with drinkers who find the northern European beers a bit sweet.

Imported lagers, stouts and beers are found in tourist spots such as music bars and discos. You might even spot Newcastle Brown, Carlsberg, Castlemaine XXXX and Guinness.

Supermarkets are the cheapest place to buy beer, and bottles are cheaper than cans. A 500mL bottle of Amstel or Mythos costs about 200 dr (including 25 dr deposit on the bottle), while a 500mL can costs about 260 dr. Amstel also produces a low-alcohol beer and a bock, which is dark, sweet and strong.

Wine According to mythology, the Greeks invented or discovered wine and it has been produced in Greece on a large scale for more than 3000 years.

The modern wine industry, though, is still very much in its infancy. Until the 1950s, most Greek wines were sold in bulk and were seldom distributed any farther afield than the nearest town. It wasn't until industrialisation (and the resulting rapid urban growth) that there was much call for bottled wine. Quality control was unheard of until 1969, when appellation laws were introduced as a precursor to applying for membership of the European Community. Wines have improved significantly since then.

Don't expect Greek wines to taste like French wines. The varieties grown in Greece are quite different. Some of the most popular and reasonably priced labels include Rotonda, Kambas, Boutari, Calliga and Lac des Roches. Boutari's Naoussa is worth looking out for. It's a dry red wine from the Naoussa area of north-west Macedonia.

More expensive, but of good quality, are the Achaïa-Clauss wines from Patras. The most expensive wines are the Kefallonian Robola de Cephalonie, a superb dry white, and those produced by the Porto

Wine + Pine = Retsina

A holiday in Greece would not be the same without a jar or three of retsina, the famous – some might say notorious – resinated wine that is the speciality of Attica and neighbouring areas of central Greece.

Your first taste of retsina may well leave you wondering whether the waiter has mixed up the wine and the paint stripper, but stick with it – it's a taste that's worth acquiring. Soon you will be savouring the delicate pine aroma, and the initial astringency mellows to become very moreish. Retsina is very refreshing consumed chilled at the end of a hot day, when it goes particularly well with tzatziki.

Greeks have been resinating wine, both white and rosé, for millennia. The ancient Greeks dedicated the pine tree to Dionysos, also the god of wine, and held that land that grew good pine would also grow good wine.

No-one seems quite sure how wine and pine first got together. The consensus is that it was an inevitable accident in a country with so much wine and so much pine. The theory that resin entered the wine-making process because the wine was stored in pine barrels does not hold water, since the ancients used clay amphora rather than barrels. It's more likely that it was through pine implements and vessels used elsewhere in the process. Producers discovered that wine treated with resin kept for longer, and consumers discovered that they liked it.

Resination was once a fairly haphazard process, achieved by various methods such as adding crushed pine cones to the brew and coating the insides of storage vessels. The amount of resin also varied enormously. One 19th century traveller wrote that he had tasted a wine 'so impregnated with resin that it almost took the skin from my lips'. His reaction was hardly surprising; he was probably drinking a wine with a resin content as high as 7.5%, common at the time. A more sophisticated product awaits the modern traveller, with a resin content no higher than 1% – as specified by good old EU regulations. That's still enough to give the wine its trademark astringency and pine aroma.

The bulk of retsina is made from two grape varieties, the white *savatiano* and the red *roditis*. These two constitute the vast majority of vine plantings in Attica, central Greece and Evia. Not just any old resin will do; the main source is the Aleppo pine *(Pinus halepensis)*, which produces a resin known for its delicate fragrance.

Retsina is generally cheap and it's available everywhere. Supermarkets stock retsina in a variety of containers ranging from 500mL bottles to 5L casks and flagons. Kourtaki and Cambas are both very good, but the best (and worst) still flows from the barrel in traditional tavernas. Ask for *heema*, which means 'loose'.

Carras estate in Halkidiki. Good wines are produced on Rhodes (famous in Greece for its champagne) and Crete. Other island wines worth sampling are those from Samos (immortalised by Lord Byron), Santorini, Kefallonia and Paros. *Aspro* is white, *mavro* is red and *kokkinelli* is rosé.

Spirits Ouzo is the most popular aperitif in Greece. Distilled from grape stems and flavoured with anise, it is similar to the Middle Eastern *arak*, Turkish *raki* and French Pernod. Clear and colourless, it turns white when water is added. A 700mL bottle of a popular brand like Ouzo 12, Olympic or Sans Rival costs about 1200 dr in supermarkets. In an ouzeri, a glass costs from 250 dr to 500 dr. It will be served neat, with a separate glass of water to be used for dilution.

The second-most popular spirit is Greek brandy, which is dominated by the Metaxa label. Metaxa comes in a wide choice of grades, starting with three star – a high-octane product without much finesse. You can pick up a bottle in a supermarket for about 1500 dr. The quality improves as you go through the grades: five star, seven star, VSOP, Golden Age and finally the top-shelf Grand Olympian Reserve (5600 dr). Other reputable brands include Cambas and Votrys. The Cretan speciality is raki, a fiery clear spirit that is served as a greeting (regardless of the time of day).

If you're travelling off the beaten track, you may come across *chipura*. Like ouzo, it's made from grape stems but without the anise. It's an acquired taste, much like Irish poteen – and packing a similar punch. You'll most likely encounter chipura in village kafeneia or private homes.

ENTERTAINMENT

Cinemas

Greeks are keen movie-goers and almost every town of consequence has a cinema. English-language films are shown in English with Greek subtitles. Admission ranges from 1000 dr in small-town movie houses to 1800 dr at plush big-city cinemas.

Discos & Music Bars

Discos can be found in big cities and resort areas, though not in the numbers of a decade ago.

Most young Greeks prefer to head for the music bars that have proliferated to fill the void. These bars normally specialise in a particular style of music – Greek, modern rock, 60s rock, techno and, very occasionally, jazz.

Ballet, Classical Music & Opera

Unless you're going to be spending a bit of time in Athens or Thessaloniki, you're best off forgetting about ballet, classical music and opera while in Greece. See the Entertainment section of the Athens chapter for information on venues.

Theatre

The highlight of the Greek dramatic year is the staging of ancient Greek dramas at the Theatre of Herodes Atticus in Athens during the Athens Festival from late June to early September. Performances are also staged at the amazing Theatre of Epidaurus. See the Special Events section of the Athens chapter and the Epidaurus section of the Peloponnese chapter for more information.

Rock

Western rock music continues to grow in popularity, but live music remains a rarity outside Athens and Thessaloniki.

Traditional Music

Most of the live music you hear around the resorts is tame stuff laid on for the tourists. If you want to hear music played with a bit of passion, the *rembetika* clubs in Athens are strongly recommended.

Folk Dancing

The pre-eminent folk dancers in Greece are the ones who perform at the Dora Stratou Theatre on Filopappos Hill in Athens, where performances take place nightly in summer. Another highly commendable place is the Old City Theatre, Rhodes City, where the Nelly Dimoglou Dance Company performs during the summer months. Folk dancing is an integral part of all festival celebrations and there is often impromptu folk dancing in tavernas.

SPECTATOR SPORTS

Soccer (football) remains the most popular spectator sport, although basketball is catching up fast following the successes of Greek sides in European club competition in recent years. Greek soccer teams, in contrast, have seldom had much impact on European club competition, and the national team is the source of constant hair-wrenching. The side's only appearance in the World Cup finals, in the USA in 1994, brought a string of heavy defeats. The two glamour clubs of Greek soccer are Olympiakos of Piraeus and Panathinaikos of Athens. The capital supplies a third of the clubs in the first division (see Spectator Sports in the Athens chapter for more information).

The season lasts from September to mid-May; cup matches are played on Wednesday night and first division games on Sunday afternoon. Games are often televised. Entry to a match costs around 1500 dr for the cheapest terrace tickets, or 3000 dr for a decent seat. Fixtures and results are given in the *Athens News*.

Olympiakos and Panathinaikos are also the glamour clubs of Greek basketball. Panathinaikos was European champion in 1996, and Olympiakos followed suit in 1997.

SHOPPING

Greece produces a vast array of handicrafts. The Centre of Hellenic Tradition, at Pandrossou 36, Plaka, Athens, has a good range.

Antiques

It is illegal to buy, sell, possess or export any antiquity in Greece (see Customs earlier in this chapter). However, there are antiques and 'antiques'; a lot of items only a century or two old are regarded as junk, rather than part of the national heritage. These items include handmade furniture and odds and ends from rural areas in Greece, ecclesiastical ornaments from churches and items brought back from far-flung lands. Good hunting grounds for this 'junk' are Monastiraki and the flea market in Athens, and the Piraeus market held on Sunday morning.

Ceramics

You will see ceramic objects of every shape and size – functional and ornamental – for sale throughout Greece. The best places for high-quality handmade ceramics are Athens, Rhodes and the islands of Sifnos and Skyros.

There are a lot of places selling plaster copies of statues, busts, grave stelae and the like.

Leather Work

There are leather goods for sale throughout Greece; most are made from leather imported from Spain. The best place for buying leather goods is Hania on Crete. Bear in mind that the goods are not as high quality nor as good value as those available in Turkey.

Jewellery

You could join the wealthy North Americans who spill off the cruise ships onto Mykonos to indulge themselves in the high-class gold jewellery shops there. But although gold is good value in Greece, and designs are of a high quality, it is priced beyond the capacity of most tourists' pockets. If you prefer something more reasonably priced, go for filigree silver jewellery. Ioannina is the filigree jewellery centre of Greece.

Bags

Tagari bags are woven wool bags – often brightly coloured – which hang from the shoulder by a rope. Minus the rope, they make attractive cushion covers.

Getting There & Away

AIR

Most travellers arrive in Greece by air, the cheapest and quickest way to get there.

Airports & Airlines

Greece has 16 international airports, but only those in Athens, Thessaloniki and Iraklio (Crete) take scheduled flights.

Athens handles the vast majority of flights, including all intercontinental traffic. Thessaloniki has direct flights to Berlin, Brussels, Copenhagen, Dusseldorf, Frankfurt, İstanbul, Cyprus, London, Milan, Moscow, Munich, Paris, Stuttgart, Tirana, Vienna and Zürich. Most of these flights are with Greece's national airline, Olympic Airways, or the flag carrier of the country concerned. Iraklio's sole scheduled connection is to Amsterdam with Transavia.

Greece's other international airports are at Mykonos, Santorini (Thira), Hania (Crete), Kos, Karpathos, Samos, Skiathos, Hrysoupolis (for Kavala), Preveza (for Lefkada), Kefallonia and Zakynthos. These airports are used exclusively for charter flights, mostly from the UK, Germany and Scandinavia. Charter flights also fly to all of Greece's other international airports.

Olympic Airways is no longer Greece's only international airline. Cronus Airlines flies direct from Athens to London and Paris, and via Thessaloniki to Cologne, Dusseldorf, Frankfurt and Stuttgart. Air Manos operates cheap charter flights to London and Manchester, and Air Greece flies to the Italian port of Bari.

BA or Bust for Olympic

Travellers can expect a major shake-up at Olympic Airways following the Greek government's decision to call in British Airways' management in a last-ditch attempt to revive the fortunes of the ailing national carrier.

Under the agreement, announced in June 1999, BA managers will have two years to pull Olympic out of its nose dive. If they succeed, BA stands to win a 20% stake in the airline; if they fail, it's the end of the line. The government has made it clear it will pull the plug if the airline does not recover.

It's a sorry state of affairs for Olympic, founded by shipping tycoon Aristotle Onassis in the 1950s and once the nation's pride and joy. The decline set in after it was taken over by the Greek government in the 1970s. By the 1990s it had become a national liability, dogged by debt, delays, labour problems and a reputation for all-round indifference. Nobody in the airline business was surprised when the decision to call in foreign management was announced.

Buying Tickets

If you are flying to Greece from outside Europe, the plane ticket will probably be the most expensive item in your travel budget, and buying it can be an intimidating business. There will be a multitude of airlines and travel agents hoping to separate you from your money, so take time to research the options. Start early – some of the cheapest tickets must be bought months in advance, and popular flights tend to sell out early.

Discounted tickets fall into two categories – official and unofficial. Official discount schemes include advance-purchase tickets, budget fares, Apex, Super-Apex and a few other variations on the theme. These tickets can be bought from travel agents or direct from the airline. They often have restrictions – advance purchase being the usual one. There might also be restrictions on the period you must be away, such as a minimum of 14 days and a maximum of one year.

Air Travel Glossary

Baggage Allowance This will be written on your ticket and usually includes one 20kg item to go in the hold, plus one item of hand luggage.

Bucket Shops These are unbonded travel agencies specialising in discounted airline tickets.

Bumped Just because you have a confirmed seat doesn't mean you're going to get on the plane (see Overbooking).

Cancellation Penalties If you have to cancel or change a discounted ticket, there are often heavy penalties involved; insurance can sometimes be taken out against these penalties. Some airlines impose penalties on regular tickets as well, particularly against 'no-show' passengers.

Check-In Airlines ask you to check in a certain time ahead of the flight departure (usually one to two hours on international flights). If you fail to check in on time and the flight is overbooked, the airline can cancel your booking and give your seat to somebody else.

Confirmation Having a ticket written out with the flight and date you want doesn't mean you have a seat until the agent has checked with the airline that your status is 'OK' or confirmed. Meanwhile you could just be 'on request'.

Courier Fares Businesses often need to send urgent documents or freight securely and quickly. Courier companies hire people to accompany the package through customs and, in return, offer a discount ticket which is sometimes a phenomenal bargain. In effect, what the companies do is ship their freight as your luggage on regular commercial flights. This is a legitimate operation, but there are two shortcomings – the short turnaround time of the ticket (usually not longer than a month) and the limitation on your luggage allowance. You may have to surrender all your allowance and take only carry-on luggage.

Full Fares Airlines traditionally offer 1st class (coded F), business class (coded J) and economy class (coded Y) tickets. These days there are so many promotional and discounted fares available that few passengers pay full economy fare.

ITX An ITX, or 'independent inclusive tour excursion', is often available on tickets to popular holiday destinations. Officially it's a package deal combined with hotel accommodation, but many agents will sell you one of these for the flight only and give you phoney hotel vouchers in the unlikely event that you're challenged at the airport.

Lost Tickets If you lose your airline ticket an airline will usually treat it like a travellers cheque and, after inquiries, issue you with another one. Legally, however, an airline is entitled to treat it like cash and if you lose it then it's gone forever. Take good care of your tickets.

MCO An MCO, or 'miscellaneous charge order', is a voucher that looks like an airline ticket but carries no destination or date. It can be exchanged through any International Association of Travel Agents (IATA) airline for a ticket on a specific flight. It's a useful alternative to an onward ticket in those countries that demand one, and is more flexible than an ordinary ticket if you're unsure of your route.

No-Shows No-shows are passengers who fail to show up for their flight. Full-fare passengers who fail to turn up are sometimes entitled to travel on a later flight. The rest are penalised (see Cancellation Penalties).

Air Travel Glossary

On Request This is an unconfirmed booking for a flight.

Onward Tickets An entry requirement for many countries is that you have a ticket out of the country. If you're unsure of your next move, the easiest solution is to buy the cheapest onward ticket to a neighbouring country or a ticket from a reliable airline which can later be refunded if you do not use it.

Open Jaw Tickets These are return tickets where you fly out to one place but return from another. If available, this can save you backtracking to your arrival point.

Overbooking Airlines hate to fly empty seats and since every flight has some passengers who fail to show up, airlines often book more passengers than they have seats. Usually excess passengers make up for the no-shows, but occasionally somebody gets 'bumped' onto the next available flight. Guess who it is most likely to be? The passengers who check in late.

Point-to-Point Tickets These are discount tickets that can be bought on some routes in return for passengers waiving their rights to a stopover.

Promotional Fares These are officially discounted fares, available from travel agencies or direct from the airline.

Reconfirmation If you don't reconfirm your flight at least 72 hours prior to departure, the airline may delete your name from the passenger list. Ring to find out if your airline requires reconfirmation.

Restrictions Discounted tickets often have various restrictions on them – such as needing to be paid for in advance and incurring a penalty to be altered. Others are restrictions on the minimum and maximum period you must be away, such as a minimum of 14 days or a maximum of one year.

Round-the-World Tickets RTW tickets give you a limited period (usually a year) in which to circumnavigate the globe. You can go anywhere the carrying airlines go, as long as you don't backtrack. The number of stopovers or total number of separate flights is decided before you set off and they usually cost a bit more than a basic return flight.

Stand-by This is a discounted ticket where you only fly if there is a seat free at the last moment. Stand-by fares are usually available only on domestic routes.

Transferred Tickets Airline tickets cannot be transferred from one person to another. Travellers sometimes try to sell the return half of their ticket, but officials can ask you to prove that you are the person named on the ticket. This is less likely to happen on domestic flights, but on an international flight tickets are compared with passports.

Travel Agencies Travel agencies vary widely and you should choose one that suits your needs. Some simply handle tours, while full-service agencies handle everything from tours and tickets to car rental and hotel bookings. If all you want is a ticket at the lowest possible price, then go to an agency specialising in discounted fares.

Travel Periods Ticket prices vary with the time of year. There is a low (off-peak) season and a high (peak) season, and often a low-shoulder season and a high-shoulder season as well. Usually the fare depends on your outward flight – if you depart in the high season and return in the low season, you pay the high-season fare.

Unofficial tickets are simply discounted tickets the airlines release through selected travel agents.

Return tickets can often be cheaper than a one way ticket. Generally, you can find discounted tickets at prices as low as, or even lower than, Apex or budget tickets. Phone around travel agents for bargains.

If you are buying a ticket to fly out of Greece, Athens is one of the major centres in Europe for budget airfares.

In Greece, as everywhere else, always remember to reconfirm your onward or return bookings by the specified time – usually 72 hours before departure on international flights. If you don't, there's a risk you'll turn up at the airport only to find you've missed your flight because it was rescheduled, or that the airline has given the seat to someone else.

Charter Flights

Charter flight tickets are for seats left vacant on flights which have been block-booked by package companies. Tickets are cheap but conditions apply on charter flights to Greece. A ticket must be accompanied by an accommodation booking. This is normally circumvented by travel agents issuing accommodation vouchers which are not meant to be used – even if the hotel named on the voucher actually exists. The law requiring accommodation bookings was introduced in the 1980s to prevent budget travellers flying to Greece on cheap charter flights and sleeping rough on beaches or in parks. It hasn't worked.

The main catch for travellers taking charter flights involves visits to Turkey. If you fly to Greece with a return ticket on a charter flight, you will forfeit the return portion if you visit Turkey. Greece is one of several popular charter destination countries which have banded together to discourage tourists from leaving the destination country during the duration of the ticket. The countries involved want to ensure people don't flit off somewhere else to spend their tourist cash. The result is that if you front up at the airport for your return charter flight with a Turkish stamp in your passport, you will be forced to buy another ticket.

This does not apply if you take a day excursion into Turkey, because the Turkish immigration officials will not stamp your passport. Neither does it apply to regular or excursion-fare flights.

Charter flight tickets are valid for up to four weeks, and usually have a minimum-stay requirement of at least three days. Sometimes it's worth buying a charter return even if you think you want to stay for longer than four weeks. The tickets can be so cheap that you can afford to throw away the return portion.

The travel section of major newspapers is the place to look for cheap charter deals. More information on charter flights is given later in this chapter under specific point-of-origin headings.

Courier Flights

Another budget option (sometimes even cheaper than a charter flight) is a courier flight. This deal entails accompanying freight or a parcel that will be collected at the destination. The drawbacks are that your time away may be limited to one or two weeks, your luggage is usually restricted to hand luggage (the parcel or freight you carry comes out of your luggage allowance), and you may have to be a resident of the country that operates the courier service and apply for an interview before they'll take you on.

Travel Agents

Many of the larger travel agents use the travel pages of national newspapers and magazines to promote their special deals. Before you make a decision, there are a number of questions you need to ask about the ticket. Find out the airline, the route, the duration of the journey, the stopovers allowed, any restrictions on the ticket and – above all – the price. Ask whether the fare quoted includes all taxes and other possible inclusions.

You may discover when you start ringing around that those impossibly cheap flights, charter or otherwise, are not available, but the agency just happens to know of another one that 'costs a bit more'. Or the agent may claim to have the last two seats available for Greece for the whole of July, which they will hold for a maximum of two hours only. Don't panic – keep ringing around.

If you are flying to Greece from the USA, South-East Asia or the UK, you will probably find the cheapest flights are being advertised by obscure agencies whose names haven't yet reached the telephone directory – the proverbial bucket shops. Many such firms are honest and solvent, but there are a few rogues who will take your money and disappear, only to reopen elsewhere a month or two later under a new name. If you feel suspicious about a firm, don't give them all the money at once – leave a small deposit and pay the balance when you get the ticket. If they insist on cash in advance, go somewhere else or be prepared to take a big risk. Once you have booked the flight with the agency, ring the airline to check you have a confirmed booking.

It can be easier on the nerves to pay a bit more for the security of a better-known travel agent. Firms such as STA Travel, with offices worldwide, Council Travel in the USA or Travel CUTS in Canada offer good prices to Europe (including Greece), and are unlikely to disappear overnight.

The fares quoted in this book are intended as a guide only. They are approximate and are based on the rates advertised by travel agents at the time of writing.

Travel Insurance

The kind of cover you get depends on your insurance and type of ticket, so ask both your insurer and your ticket-issuing agency to explain where you stand. Ticket loss is usually covered.

Buy travel insurance as early as possible. If you buy it just before you fly, you may find you're not covered for such problems as delays caused by industrial action. Make sure you have a separate record of all your ticket details – preferably a photocopy.

Paying for your ticket with a credit card sometimes provides limited travel insurance, and you may be able to reclaim the payment if the operator doesn't deliver. In the UK, for instance, credit card providers are required by law to reimburse consumers if a company goes into liquidation and the amount in contention is more than UK£100.

Travellers with Special Needs

If you've broken a leg, require a special diet, are travelling in a wheelchair, are taking a baby, or whatever, let the airline staff know as soon as possible – preferably when booking your ticket. Check that your request has been registered when you reconfirm your booking (at least 72 hours before departure) and again when you check in at the airport.

Children under two years of age travel for 10% of the standard fare (or free on some airlines) as long as they don't occupy a seat. But they do not get a baggage allowance. 'Skycots' should be provided by the airline if requested in advance. These will take a child weighing up to about 10kg. Olympic Airways charges half-fare for accompanied children aged between two and 12 years, while most other airlines charge two-thirds.

Departure Tax

There is an airport tax of 6800 dr on all international departures from Greece. This is paid when you buy your ticket, not at the airport.

The USA

The North Atlantic is the world's busiest long-haul air corridor, and the flight options to Europe – including Greece – are bewildering. Microsoft's popular Expedia.com Web site at www.expedia.msn.com gives a good overview of the possibilities. Other sites worth checking out are the ITN site (www.itn.net) and the Travelocity site (www.travelocity.com).

The *New York Times*, *LA Times*, *Chicago Tribune* and *San Francisco Chronicle Examiner* all publish weekly travel sections in which you'll find any number of travel agents' advertisements. Council Travel (www.counciltravel.com) and STA Travel (www.sta-travel.com) have offices in major cities nationwide.

New York has the most number of direct flights to Athens. Olympic Airways has at least one flight a day, and Delta Airlines has three a week. Apex fares range from US$960 to US$1600, depending on the season and how long you want to stay away.

Boston is the only other east coast city with direct flights to Athens – on Saturday with Olympic Airways. Fares are the same as for flights from New York.

There are no direct flights to Athens from the west coast. There are, however, connecting flights to Athens from many US cities, either linking with Olympic Airways in New York or flying with one of the European national airlines to their home country, and then on to Athens. These connections usually involve a stopover of three or four hours.

One-way fares can work out very cheap on a stand-by basis. Airhitch (☎ 212-864 2000) specialises in this. It can get you to Europe one-way for US$159 from the east coast and US$239 from the west coast, plus tax. Its Web site is www.airhitch.org.

Courier flights are another possibility. The International Association of Air Travel Couriers (☎ 561-582 8320, fax 582 1581) has flights from six US cities to a range of European capitals – but not Athens. Check out its Web site at www.courier.org.

If you're travelling from Athens to the USA, the travel agents around Syntagma offer the following one-way fares (prices do not include airport tax): Atlanta 110,000 dr, Chicago 110,000 dr, Los Angeles 125,000 dr and New York 85,000 dr.

Canada

Olympic Airways has two flights weekly from Toronto to Athens via Montreal. There are no direct flights from Vancouver, but there are connecting flights via Toronto, Amsterdam, Frankfurt and London on Canadian Airlines, KLM, Lufthansa and British Airways.

Travel CUTS (☎ 1-888-838 CUTS) has offices in all major cities and is a good place to ask about cheap deals. You should be able to get to Athens from Toronto and Montreal for about C$1150 or from Vancouver for C$1500. The *Toronto Globe & Mail*, the *Toronto Star*, the *Montreal Gazette* and the *Vancouver Sun* all carry advertisements for cheap tickets.

For courier flights originating in Canada, contact FB On Board Courier Services in Montreal (☎ 514-631 2677). They can get you to London for C$575 return.

At the time of writing, budget travel agencies in Athens were advertising flights to Toronto for 105,000 dr and to Montreal for 100,000 dr, plus airport tax.

Australia

Olympic Airways has two flights weekly from Sydney and Melbourne to Athens. Return fares normally cost from about A$1799 in low season to A$2199 in high season.

Thai International and Singapore Airlines also have convenient connections to Athens, as well as a reputation for good service. If you're planning on doing a bit of flying around Europe, it's worth checking around for special deals from the major European airlines. Alitalia, KLM and Lufthansa are three likely candidates with good European networks.

STA Travel and Flight Centres International are two of Australia's major dealers in cheap fares. The Sunday tabloid newspapers advertise cheap flights, as well as the travel sections of the *Sydney Morning Herald* and Melbourne's *Age*.

If you're travelling from Athens to Australia, a one way ticket to Sydney or Melbourne costs about 180,000 dr, plus airport tax.

New Zealand

There are no direct flights from New Zealand to Athens. There are connecting flights via Sydney, Melbourne, Bangkok and Singapore on Olympic Airways, United Airlines, Qantas Airways, Thai Airways and Singapore Airlines.

The UK

British Airways, Olympic Airways and Virgin Atlantic operate daily flights between London and Athens. Pricing is very competitive, with all three offering return tickets for around UK£200 in high season, plus tax. These prices are for midweek departures; you will pay about UK£40 more for weekend departures.

There are connecting flights to Athens from Edinburgh, Glasgow and Manchester. Greek newcomer Cronus Airlines (☎ 020-7580 3500) flies the London-Athens route five times weekly for £210, and offers connections to Thessaloniki on the same fare. Olympic Airways has four direct London-Thessaloniki flights weekly. Most scheduled flights from London leave from Heathrow.

The cheapest scheduled flights are with EasyJet (☎ 0870 6 000 000), the no-frills specialist, which has two Luton-Athens flights daily. One-way fares range from UK£89 to UK£139 in high season, and from a bargain UK£39 to UK£69 at other times. Its Web site is www.easyjet.com.

There are numerous charter flights between the UK and Greece. Typical London-Athens charter fares are UK£79/129 one way/return in the low season and UK£99/189 in the high season. These prices are for advance bookings, but even in high season it's possible to pick up last-minute deals for as little as UK£59/99. Many travel agencies offer charter flights to the islands as well as to Athens. Most island destinations cost about UK£109/209 in high season. Charter flights to Greece also fly from Birmingham, Cardiff, Glasgow, Luton, Manchester and Newcastle. Contact the Air Travel Advisory Bureau (☎ 020-7636 5000) for information about current charter flight bargains; try its Web site www.atab.co.uk.

London is Europe's major centre for discounted fares. Some of the most reputable agencies selling discount tickets are:

Usit Campus
(☎ 020-7730 3402, www.usitcampus.co.uk)
52 Grosvenor Gardens, London SW1

Council Travel
(☎ 020-7287 3337, www.counciltravel.com)
28A Poland St, London W1V 3DB

STA Travel
(☎ 020-7361 6161, www.statravel.co.uk)
86 Old Brompton Rd, London SW7

Trailfinders
(☎ 020-7937 5400)
215 Kensington High St, London W8

Listings publications such as *Time Out*, the Sunday papers, the *Evening Standard* and *Exchange & Mart* carry advertisements for cheap fares. The *Yellow Pages* is worth scanning for travel agents' ads, and look out for the free magazines and newspapers widely available in London, especially *TNT*, *Footloose*, *Southern Cross* and *LAM* – you can pick them up outside the main train and tube stations.

Some travel agents specialise in flights for students aged under 30 and travellers aged under 26 (you need an ISIC card or an official youth card). Whatever your age, you should be able to find something to suit your budget.

Most British travel agents are registered with ABTA (Association of British Travel Agents). If you have paid for your flight through an ABTA-registered agent who then goes out of business, ABTA will guarantee a refund or an alternative. If an agency is registered with ABTA, its advertisements will usually say so.

If you're flying from Athens to the UK, budget fares start at 25,000 dr to London or 30,000 dr to Manchester, plus airport tax.

Continental Europe

Athens is linked to every major city in Europe by either Olympic Airways or the flag carrier of each country.

London is the discount capital of Europe, but Amsterdam, Frankfurt, Berlin and Paris are also major centres for cheap airfares.

Albania Olympic Airways has at least one flight a day from Tirana to Athens (US$224/407 one way/return), going via Thessaloniki (US$171/311) twice weekly. Student discounts of 25% are available.

France Air France (☎ 0802 802 802) and Olympic Airways (☎ 01 42 65 92 42) have at least four Paris-Athens flights daily between them. Expect to pay from 2950FF to 3300FF in high season, dropping to about 2100FF at other times. Four times weekly Cronus Airlines (☎ 01 47 42 56 77) flies the same route. Olympic Airways also has three flights weekly to Athens from Marseille.

Charter flights are much cheaper. You'll pay around 2000FF in high season for a return flight from Paris to Athens, and 2050FF to Rhodes or Santorini. The fare to Athens drops to 1500FF in low season. Reliable travel agents include:

Air Sud
(☎ 01 40 41 66 66) 18 Rue du Pont-Neuf, 75001 Paris
Atsaro
(☎ 01 42 60 98 98) 9 Rue de l'Echelle, 75001 Paris
Bleu Blanc
(☎ 01 40 21 31 31) 53 Avenue de la République, 75011 Paris
Héliades
(☎ 01 53 27 28 21) 24-27 Rue Basfroi, 75011 Paris
La Grèce Autrement
(☎ 01 44 41 69 95) 72 Boulevard Saint Michel, 75006 Paris
Nouvelles Frontières
(☎ 08 03 33 33) 87 Boulevard de Grenelle, 75015 Paris
Planète Havas
(☎ 01 53 29 40 00) 26 Avenue de l'Opéra, 75001 Paris

Germany Atlas Reisewelt has offices throughout Germany and is a good place to start checking prices.

Alternativ Tours (☎ 030-8 81 20 89), Wilmersdorfer Strasse 94, Berlin, has discounted fares to just about anywhere in the world. SRS Studenten Reise Service (☎ 030-28 59 82 64), at Marienstrasse 23 near Friedrichstrasse station, offers special student (under 35) and youth (under 26) fares. Travel agents offering unpublished cheap flights advertise in *Zitty*, Berlin's fortnightly entertainment magazine.

In Frankfurt, you might try SRID Reisen (☎ 069-43 01 91), Berger Strasse 118.

The Netherlands Reliable travel agents in Amsterdam include:

Budget Air
(☎ 020-627 12 51) Rokin 34
Malibu Travel
(☎ 020-626 32 20) Prinsengracht 230
NBBS Reizen
(☎ 020-624 09 89) Rokin 66

If you're travelling from Athens to Europe, budget fares to a host of European cities are widely advertised by the travel agents around Syntagma. Following are some typical one-way fares (not including airport tax):

Destination	One Way Fare
Amsterdam	57,500 dr
Copenhagen	59,500 dr
Frankfurt	55,000 dr
Geneva	54,000 dr
Hamburg	52,000 dr
Madrid	73,000 dr
Milan	48,000 dr
Munich	55,000 dr
Paris	55,500 dr
Rome	42,000 dr
Zürich	53,500 dr

Turkey

Olympic Airways and Turkish Airlines share the İstanbul-Athens route, with at least one flight a day each. The full fare is US$250 one way. Olympic Airways also flies twice weekly between İstanbul and Thessaloniki (US$190). Students qualify for a 50% discount on both routes.

There are no direct flights from Ankara to Athens; all flights go via İstanbul.

Cyprus

Olympic Airways and Cyprus Airways share the Cyprus-Greece routes. Both airlines have three flights daily from Larnaca to Athens, and there are five flights weekly to Thessaloniki. Cyprus Airways also flies from Paphos to Athens once a week in winter, and twice a week in summer.

Travel agents in Athens charge 50,000 dr one way to Larnaca and Paphos, or 83,000 dr return.

LAND

Turkey

Bus The Hellenic Railways Organisation (OSE) operates Athens-İstanbul buses (22 hours) daily except Wednesday, leaving the Peloponnese train station in Athens at 7 pm and travelling via Thessaloniki and Alexandroupolis. One-way fares are 21,800 dr from Athens, 14,300 dr from Thessaloniki and 5600 dr from Alexandroupolis. Students qualify for a 15% discount and children under 12 travel for half-fare. See the Getting There & Away sections for each city for information on where to buy tickets.

Buses from İstanbul to Athens leave the Anadolu Terminal (Anatolia Terminal) at the Topkapı *otogar* (bus station) at 10 am daily except Sunday.

See the Alexandroupolis Getting There & Away section for alternative public transport options to Turkey.

Train There are daily trains between Athens and İstanbul (19,000 dr) via Thessaloniki (13,000 dr) and Alexandroupolis (6350 dr). The service is incredibly slow and the train gets uncomfortably crowded. There are often delays at the border and the journey can take much longer than the supposed 22 hours. You'd be well advised to take the bus. Inter-Rail Passes are valid in Turkey, but Eurail passes are not.

Car & Motorcycle If you're travelling between Greece and Turkey by private vehicle, the crossing points are at Kipi, 43km north-east of Alexandroupolis, and at Kastanies, 139km north-east of Alexandroupolis. Kipi is more convenient if you're heading for İstanbul, but the route through Kastanies goes via the fascinating towns of Soufli and Didymotiho, in Greece, and Edirne (ancient Adrianople) in Turkey.

Bulgaria

Bus The OSE operates two Athens-Sofia buses (15 hours, 13,400 dr) daily except Monday, leaving at 7 am and 5 pm. It also operates Thessaloniki-Sofia buses (7½ hours, 5600 dr, three daily). There is a private bus service to Plovdiv (9000 dr) and Sofia (10,000 dr) from Alexandroupolis on Wednesday and Sunday at 8.30 am.

Train There is an Athens-Sofia train daily (18 hours, 10,330 dr) via Thessaloniki (nine hours, 6700 dr).

Car & Motorcycle The Bulgarian border crossing is at Promahonas, 145km north-east of Thessaloniki and 50km from Serres.

Albania

Bus There is a daily OSE bus between Athens and Tirana (12,600 dr) via Ioannina and Gjirokastër. The bus departs Athens (Larisis train station) at 7 pm arriving in Tirana the following day at 5 pm. It leaves Ioannina at 7.30 am and passes through Gjirokastër at 10.30 am. On the return trip, the bus departs Tirana at 7 am. There are buses from Thessaloniki to Korça (Korytsa in Greek) daily at 8 am. The fare is 6600 dr.

Car & Motorcycle If travelling by car or motorcycle, there are two crossing points between Greece and Albania. The main one is 60km north-west of Ioannina. Take the main Ioannina-Konitsa road and turn left at Kalpaki. This road leads to the border town of Kakavia. The other border crossing is at Krystallopigi, 14km west of Kotas on the Florina-Kastoria road. Kapshtica is the closest town on the Albanian side. It is possible to take a private vehicle into Albania, although it's not a great idea, because of security concerns and problems with obtaining spare parts. Always carry your passport in areas near the Albanian border.

Former Yugoslav Republic of Macedonia

Train There are Thessaloniki-Skopje trains (three hours, 4200 dr, two daily), which cross the border between Idomeni and Gevgelija. They leave Thessaloniki at 6 am and 5.30 pm. Both trains continue to the Serbian capital of Belgrade (12 hours, 11,500 dr). The 5.30 pm service goes all the way to Budapest (21 hours, 20,000 dr).

There are no trains between Florina and FYROM, although there may be trains to Skopje from the FYROM side of the border.

Car & Motorcycle There are two border crossings between Greece and FYROM. One is at Evzoni, 68km north of Thessaloniki. This is the main highway to Skopje which continues to Belgrade. The other border crossing is at Niki, 16km north of Florina. This road leads to Bitola, and continues to Ohrid, once a popular tourist resort on the shores of Lake Ohrid.

Western Europe

Overland travel between western Europe and Greece is almost a thing of the past. Airfares are so cheap that land transport cannot compete. Travelling from the UK to Greece through Europe means crossing various borders, so check whether any visas are required before setting out.

Bus There are no bus services to Greece from the UK, nor from anywhere else in northern Europe. Bus companies can no longer compete with cheap airfares.

Train Unless you have a Eurail pass or are aged under 26 and eligible for a discounted fare, travelling to Greece by train is prohibitively expensive. For example, the full one way/return fare from London to Athens is UK£265/521, including the Eurostar service from London to Paris.

Greece is part of the Eurail network. Eurail passes can only be bought by residents of non-European countries and are supposed to be purchased before arriving in Europe. They can, however, be bought in Europe as long as your passport proves that you've been there for less than six months. In London, head for the Rail Europe Travel Centre (☎ 08705 848 848), 179 Piccadilly, W1. Sample fares include UK£461 for an adult Eurail Flexipass, which permits 10 days 1st class travel in two months, and UK£323 for the equivalent youth pass.

If you are starting your European travels in Greece, you can buy your Eurail pass from the Hellenic Railways Organisation offices at Karolou 1 and Filellinon 17 in Athens, and at the station in Patras and Thessaloniki.

Greece is also part of the Inter-Rail Pass system, but the pass for those aged over 26 is not valid in France, Italy and Switzerland – rendering it useless if you want to use the pass to get to Greece. Inter-Rail Youth Passes for those under 26 are divided into zones. A Global Pass (all zones) costs UK£259 and is valid for a month. You need to be under 26 on the first day of travel and to have lived in Europe for at least six months.

Car & Motorcycle Before the troubles in the former Yugoslavia began, most motorists driving from the UK to Greece opted for the direct route: Ostend, Brussels, Salzburg and then down the Yugoslav highway through Zagreb, Belgrade and Skopje and crossing the border to Evzoni.

These days most people drive to an Italian port and get a ferry to Greece. Coming from the UK, this means driving through France, where petrol costs and road tolls are exorbitant.

SEA

Turkey

There are five regular ferry services between Turkey's Aegean coast and the Greek islands. Tickets for all ferries to Turkey must be bought a day in advance. You will almost certainly be asked to turn in your passport the night before the trip but don't worry, you'll get it back the next day before you board the boat. Port tax for departures to Turkey is 3000 dr.

See the relevant sections under individual island entries for more information about the following services.

Rhodes to Marmaris There are three ferries daily from Rhodes to Marmaris between April and October and less frequent services in winter. Prices vary, so shop around. There are also daily hydrofoils to Marmaris (weather permitting) from April to October for 10,000/14,000 dr one way/return plus Turkish port tax.

Chios to Çeşme There are daily Chios-Çeşme boats from July to September, dropping steadily back to one boat a week in winter. Tickets cost 15,000/20,000 dr one way/return, including port taxes.

Kos to Bodrum There are daily ferries in summer from Kos to Bodrum (ancient Halicarnassus) in Turkey. Boats leave at 8.30 am and return at 4 pm. The one hour journey costs 13,000 dr return, including port taxes.

Lesvos to Ayvalık There are up to five boats weekly on this route in high season. Tickets cost 16,000/21,000 dr one way/return.

Samos to Kuşadası There are two boats daily to Kuşadası (for Ephesus) from Samos in summer, dropping to one or two boats weekly in winter. Tickets cost 5000/9000 dr one way/return plus 5000 dr Greek port tax and US$10 Turkish port tax.

Italy

There are ferries to Greece from the Italian ports of Ancona, Bari, Brindisi, Trieste and Venice. For more information about these services, see the Patras, Igoumenitsa, Corfu and Kefallonia sections.

The ferries can get very crowded in summer. If you want to take a vehicle across it's a good idea to make a reservation. In the UK, reservations can be made on almost all of these ferries at Viamare Travel Ltd (☎ 020-7431 4560, fax 7431 5456, email ferries@viamare.com), 2 Sumatra Rd, London NW6 IPU.

You'll find all the latest information about ferry routes, schedules and services on the Internet. For a good overview try www.ferries.gr. Most of the ferry companies have their own Web sites, including:

Adriatica: www.adriatica.it
ANEK Lines: www.anek.gr
Hellenic Mediterranean Lines: www.hml.it
Minoan Lines: www.minoan.gr
Strintzis: www.strintzis.gr
Superfast: www.superfast.com
Ventouris: www.ventouris.gr

The following ferry services are for high season (July and August), and prices are for one way deck class. Deck class on these services means exactly that. If you want a reclining, aircraft-type seat, you'll be up for another 10 to 15% on top of the listed fares. Most companies offer discounts for return travel. Prices are about 30% less in the low season.

Ancona to Patras This route has become increasingly popular in recent years. There can be up to three boats daily in summer, and at least one a day year-round.

Superfast Ferries (☎ 071-20 28 05) provides the fastest and most convenient service, but it's also the most expensive. It has boats daily (20 hours, L148,000). Minoan Lines (☎ 071-20 17 08) has ferries to Patras (20 hours, L124,000) via Igoumenitsa (15 hours) daily except Tuesday. ANEK Lines (☎ 071-20 59 99) runs two direct boats weekly (24 hours, L115,000) and three via Igoumenitsa (34 hours). Strintzis (☎ 071-20 10 68) sails direct to Patras (23 hours, L96,000) three times weekly, twice via Igoumenitsa and Corfu.

All ferry operators in Ancona have booths at the *stazione marittima* (ferry terminal) off Piazza Candy, where you can pick up timetables and price lists and make bookings.

Bari to Corfu, Igoumenitsa & Patras Superfast Ferries (☎ 080-52 11 416) operates daily to Patras (15 hours, L88,000) via Igoumenitsa (9½ hours). Marlines (☎ 080-52 31 824) has daily boats to Igoumenitsa (12 hours, L70,000), while Ventouris (☎ 080-521 7118) goes to Igoumenitsa (13½ hours, L65,000) via Corfu.

Brindisi to Corfu, Igoumenitsa & Patras The route from Brindisi to Patras (18 hours) via Corfu (nine hours) and Igoumenitsa (10 hours) is the cheapest and most popular of the various Adriatic crossings. There can be up to five boats daily in high season.

Companies operating ferries from Brindisi to Greece are: Adriatica di Navigazione

(☎ 0831-52 38 25), Corso Garibaldi 85-87, and on the 1st floor of the stazione marittima, where you must go to check in; Five Star Lines (☎ 0831-52 48 69), represented by Angela Gioia Agenzia Marittima, Via F Consiglio 55; Fragline (☎ 0831-59 01 96), Corso Garibaldi 88; Hellenic Mediterranean Lines (☎ 0831-52 85 31), Corso Garibaldi 8; and Med Link Lines (☎ 0831-52 76 67), represented by Discovery Shipping, Corso Garibaldi 49.

Adriatica and Hellenic Mediterranean are the most expensive at around L100,000 for deck class passage to Corfu (7½ hours), Igoumenitsa (nine hours) or Patras (15½ hours), but they are the best. They are also the only lines which accept Eurail passes. You will still have to pay port tax and a high-season loading in summer – usually about L15,000. If you want to use your Eurail pass, it is important to reserve some weeks in advance, particularly in summer. Even with a booking, you must still go to the Adriatica or Hellenic Mediterranean embarkation office in the stazione marittima to have your ticket checked.

The cheapest crossing is with Five Star Lines, which charges L46,000 to either Igoumenitsa (7½ hours) or Patras (15½ hours). Med Link charges L62,000 to Igoumenitsa and L65,000 to Patras, while Fragline charges L68,000 to Corfu and Igoumenitsa. Fares for cars range from L65,500 to L120,000 in the high season, depending on the line.

From 1 July to 19 September, Italian Ferries (☎ 0831-59 03 05), Corso Garibaldi 96, operates a daily high-speed catamaran to Corfu (3¼ hours, L154,000) leaving Brindisi at 2 pm. The service continues to Paxi (4¾ hours, L190,000 dr).

Brindisi to Kefallonia & Zakynthos Hellenic Mediterranean Lines has daily services to the port of Sami on Kefallonia from late June to early September. The trip takes 15 hours and costs L110,000 for deck class. Med Link also stops occasionally at Sami on its Brindisi-Patras run during July and August.

Warning

The information in this chapter is particularly vulnerable to change: prices for international travel are volatile, routes are introduced and cancelled, schedules change, special deals come and go, and rules and visa requirements are amended. Airlines and governments seem to take a perverse pleasure in making price structures and regulations as complicated as possible. You should check directly with the airline or a travel agent to make sure you understand how a fare (and ticket you may buy) works. In addition, the travel industry is highly competitive and there are many lurks and perks.

The upshot of this is that you should get opinions, quotes and advice from as many airlines and travel agents as possible before you part with your hard-earned cash. The details given in this chapter should be regarded as pointers and are not a substitute for your own careful, up-to-date research.

Hellenic Mediterranean Lines stops at Zakynthos (17 hours, L110,000) two or three times weekly in July and August.

Trieste to Patras ANEK Lines (☎ 040-30 28 88), Stazione Marittima di Trieste, has three boats weekly to Patras travelling via Igoumenitsa. The trip takes 37 hours and costs L106,000 for deck class.

Venice to Patras Minoan Lines (☎ 041-27 12 345), Magazzino 17, Santa Marta, has boats from Venice to Patras (40 hours, L132,000). All services go via Corfu and Igoumenitsa, and from mid-May until late September two a week call in at Kefallonia.

Cyprus & Israel

Two companies ply the route between Piraeus and the Israeli port of Haifa, via Lemesos (Limassol) on Cyprus. These boats also stop at Rhodes and various other Greek islands.

During July and August, Salamis Lines leaves Haifa at 8 pm on Sunday and Lemesos at 4 pm on Monday, reaching Rhodes at noon on Tuesday, Tinos at 6 am on Wednesday, and Piraeus at 3 pm. The return service departs Piraeus at 7 pm on Thursday, and stops at Patmos on the way to Rhodes, Lemesos and Haifa. For the rest of the year, the boat leaves Haifa at 8 pm on Monday and skips Tinos. Bookings in Haifa are handled by Rosenfeld Shipping (☎ 04-861 3670), 104 Ha'Atzmaut St, and in Lemesos by Salamis Tours (☎ 05-355 555), Salamis House, 28 October Ave.

Poseidon Lines operates a similar service. In July and August, it sails from Haifa at 8 pm on Thursday and Lemesos at 1 pm on Friday, and then calls at Rhodes, Santorini and Tinos on the way to Piraeus. It leaves Piraeus at 7 pm on Monday, stopping at Santorini and Patmos on the way to Rhodes, Lemesos and Cyprus. It operates virtually the same timetable for the rest of the year, but stops only at Rhodes and Lemesos. Bookings in Haifa are handled by Caspi Travel (☎ 04-867 4444), 76 Ha'Atzmaut St, and in Lemesos by Poseidon Lines Cyprus (☎ 05-745 666), 124 Franklin Roosevelt St.

Both Salamis and Poseidon lines charge the same. Deck-class fares from Haifa are US$101 to Rhodes and US$106 to Piraeus. Fares from Lemesos are US$68 to Rhodes and US$72 to Piraeus. If you want a seat you'll be up for an extra US$10 more, while the cheapest shared cabins cost an extra US$30.

You'll find the latest information on these services on the Internet: www.ferries.gr for Poseidon Lines, and www.viamare.com/Salamis for Salamis Lines.

ORGANISED TOURS

If a package holiday of sun, sand and sea doesn't appeal to you, but you would like to holiday with a group, there are several companies that organise special-interest holidays.

The UK-based Explore Worldwide (☎ 0125-234 4161) organises reasonably priced, small-group holidays which include visits to many of Greece's ancient sites – its Web site is www.explore.co.uk. Island Holidays (☎ 0176-477 0107) specialises in cultural holidays on Crete.

There are lots of UK companies specialising in package holidays to unspoilt areas of Greece, including Laskarina (☎ 01629-824 881) – Web site www.laskarina.co.uk; Greek Islands Club (☎ 020-8232 9780); Greek Options (☎ 020-7233 5233); and Simply Ionian (☎ 020-8995 9323).

Getting Around

Greece is an easy place to travel around thanks to a comprehensive public transport system.

Buses are the mainstay of land transport, with a network that reaches out to the smallest villages. Trains are a good alternative, where available. To most visitors, though, travelling in Greece means island-hopping on the multitude of ferries that criss-cross the Adriatic and the Aegean. If you're in a hurry, Greece also has an extensive domestic air network.

The information in this chapter was for the 1999 high season. You'll find lots of travel information on the Internet also. The Web site ellada.com is a useful general site with lots of links, including airline timetables.

AIR

Domestic Air Services

Olympic Airways The vast majority of domestic flights are handled by the country's much-maligned national carrier, Olympic Airways, together with its offshoot, Olympic Aviation.

Olympic Airways has offices wherever there are flights, as well as in other major towns. The head office (☎ 01-966 6666) is at Leoforos Syngrou 96 in Athens, and it's at www.olympic-airways.gr on the Web.

The free-baggage allowance on domestic flights is 15kg. However, this does not apply when the domestic flight is part of an international journey. The international free-baggage allowance of 20kg is then extended to the domestic sector. This allowance applies to all tickets for domestic travel sold and issued outside Greece. Olympic offers a 25% student discount on domestic flights, but only if the flight is part of an international journey.

Olympic lost its monopoly on domestic routes in 1993. It took a while for any serious opposition to emerge, but there are now three established competitors on the scene and newcomers appearing all the time.

Air Greece This Crete-based airline was the first newcomer to show any sign of permanence. It has been around since 1995, offering a cheaper alternative to Olympic on some of the major routes. It flies the Athens-Iraklio route four times daily; Athens-Thessaloniki, Athens-Rhodes and Iraklio-Thessaloniki twice daily; Athens-Hania once a day; Rhodes-Thessaloniki four times weekly; and Iraklio-Rhodes three times weekly. It also offers youth discounts (under 26).

Air Manos Discount and package specialist Air Manos flies from Athens to Chios, Hania, Mykonos, Samos, Santorini, Syros and Thessaloniki. It also flies from Thessaloniki to Mykonos, Samos and Santorini. It offers some very cheap flight and accommodation packages, and has a reputation for good service.

Cronus Airlines Another traveller-friendly company, Cronus has quickly established itself on the local scene. It flies Athens-Thessaloniki return four times daily; Athens-Iraklio twice daily; and Athens-Rhodes, Iraklio-Thessaloniki and Rhodes-Thessaloniki daily. The Saturday flight from Rhodes to Thessaloniki goes via Kavala.

Cronus offers discounts for students and for travellers aged over 60, and special rates for advance purchase. Its Web site www.cronus.gr, has information on routes and fares.

Aegean Air Aegean is the latest addition to the line-up. It flies between Athens, Hania, Iraklio and Rhodes.

Mainland Flights

Athens is far and away the busiest of the nine airports on the Greek mainland. The only mainland route that doesn't involve Athens is the daily Olympic Airways Thessaloniki-Ioannina service (50 minutes

Air Services Within Greece

Flights from Athens to the Greek Islands (High Season)

Destination	Flights/ Week	Duration	Price (dr)
Astypalea	4	65 mins	20,100
Chios	34	50 mins	15,800
Corfu	26	50 mins	20,700
Crete (Hania)	25	50 mins	19,900
Crete (Iraklio)	42	60 mins	21,900
Crete (Sitia)	3	85 mins	23,100
Ikaria	4	50 mins	17,100
Karpathos	3	120 mins	26,000
Kassos	1	130 mins	24,700
Kefallonia	10	60 mins	17,900
Kos	21	55 mins	21,400
Kythira	6	45 mins	14,400
Leros	7	65 mins	21,200
Lesvos	35	50 mins	17,100
Limnos	16	60 mins	15,000
Milos	7	45 mins	14,900
Mykonos	37	45 mins	19,100
Naxos	10	45 mins	20,100
Paros	41	45 mins	18,900
Rhodes	43	60 mins	24,900
Samos	31	60 mins	17,000
Santorini	44	50 mins	22,200
Skiathos	8	40 mins	16,700
Skyros	2	50 mins	14,200
Syros	9	35 mins	15,200
Zakynthos	7	35 mins	17,400

Flights from Thessaloniki to the Greek Islands (High Season)

Destination	Flights/ Week	Duration	Price (dr)
Chios	2	50 mins	22,400
Corfu	3	50 mins	20,900
Crete (Hania)	2	75 mins	29,900
Crete (Iraklio)	3	110 mins	29,900
Lesvos	6	60 mins	20,900
Limnos	4	50 mins	15,200
Mykonos	3	75 mins	27,900
Rhodes	2	115 mins	31,900
Samos	2	80 mins	25,400

Mainland Flights from Athens

Destination	Flights/ Week	Duration	Price (dr)
Alexandroupolis	14	65 mins	18,600
Ioannina	14	70 mins	18,400
Kalamata	4	50 mins	13,400
Kastoria	4	75 mins	19,200
Kavala	13	60 mins	18,300
Kozani	3	70 mins	17,400
Preveza	5	60 mins	13,900
Thessaloniki	70	55 mins	22,000

Inter-Island Flights

Route	Flights/ Week	Duration	Price (dr)
Chios – Lesvos	2	30 mins	10,900
Iraklio – Rhodes	4	45 mins	21,900
Iraklio – Santorini	2	40 mins	15,400
Karpathos – Rhodes	14	40 mins	12,800
Kassos – Rhodes	3	40 mins	13,400
Kastellorizo – Rhodes	7	45 mins	10,900
Lesvos – Limnos	1	35 mins	13,400
Mykonos – Rhodes	2	60 mins	22,900
Mykonos – Santorini	5	30 mins	15,400
Rhodes – Santorini	5	60 mins	22,900

12,100 dr). See the accompanying table for details of all Olympic flights to mainland cities from Athens (fares are one-way).

Olympic faces stiff competition from its domestic rivals on the Athens-Thessaloniki route. Both Air Greece and Cronus offer substantial student discounts.

Mainland to Island Flights

Olympic Airways operates a busy schedule to the islands, particularly in summer. Athens has flights to 22 islands, with services to all the island groups as well as to three destinations on Crete – Hania, Iraklio and Sitia. Thessaloniki also has flights to all the island groups except the Sporades. See the tables of summer flights (between 14 June and 26 September) from Athens and Thessaloniki to the Greek islands for details (fares given are one-way). Olympic's competitors offer cheaper fares on some of the more popular routes, so check around.

In spite of the number of flights, it can be hard to find a seat during July and August. Early bookings are recommended. Flight schedules are greatly reduced in winter, especially to Mykonos, Paros, Skiathos and Santorini.

Inter-Island Flights

Olympic and Air Greece both fly the Iraklio-Rhodes route; all other flights are operated by Olympic. See the accompanying table for details.

Domestic Departure Tax

The airport tax for domestic flights is 3400 dr, paid as part of the ticket. All prices quoted in this book include this tax.

BUS

All long-distance buses, on both the mainland and the islands, are operated by regional collectives known as KTEL (Koino Tamio Eispraxeon Leoforion). Every prefecture on the mainland has its own KTEL, which operates local services within the prefecture and services to the main towns of other prefectures. Fares are fixed by the government.

The network is comprehensive. With the exception of towns in Thrace, which are serviced by Thessaloniki, all the major towns on the mainland have frequent connections to Athens. The islands of Corfu, Kefallonia and Zakynthos can also be reached directly from Athens by bus – the fares include the price of the ferry ticket.

Villages in remote areas are often served by only one or two buses daily. They operate for the benefit of school children and people going to town to shop, rather than for tourists. They normally leave the villages very early in the morning and return early in the afternoon.

On islands where the capital is inland rather than a port, buses normally meet the boats. Some of the more remote islands have not yet acquired a bus, but most have some sort of motorised transport – even if it is only a bone-shaking, three-wheeled truck.

Larger towns usually have a central, covered bus station with seating, waiting rooms, toilets, and a snack bar selling pies, cakes and coffee. Big cities like Athens, Iraklio, Patras and Thessaloniki have several bus stations, each serving different regions.

In small towns and villages the 'bus station' may be no more than a bus stop outside a *kafeneio* or taverna which doubles as a booking office. In remote areas, the timetable may be in Greek only, but most booking offices have timetables in both Greek and Roman script. The timetables give both the departure and return times – useful if you are making a day trip. Times are listed using the 24 hour clock system.

When you buy a ticket you will be allotted a seat number, noted on the ticket. The seat number is indicated on the back of each seat of the bus, not on the back of the seat in front; this causes confusion among Greeks and tourists alike. You can board a bus without a ticket and pay on board, but on a popular route, or during the high season, this may mean that you have to stand. Keep your ticket for the duration of the journey; it will be checked several times en route.

It's best to turn up at least 20 minutes before departure to make sure you get a seat.

Buses have been known to leave a few minutes before their scheduled departure time – another reason to give yourself plenty of time. Check the destination with the driver before you board the bus, and ensure your luggage has been placed in the hold.

Buses do not have toilets on board and they don't have refreshments available, so make sure you are prepared on both counts. Buses stop about every three hours on long journeys. Smoking is prohibited on all buses in Greece; only the chain-smoking drivers dare to ignore the no-smoking signs.

Bus fares are reasonably priced, with a journey costing approximately 1000 dr per 100km. Fares and journey times on some of the major routes are: Athens-Thessaloniki, 7½ hours, 8200 dr; Athens-Patras, three hours, 3650 dr; Athens-Volos, five hours, 5250 dr; and Athens-Corfu, 11 hours, 8150 dr (including ferry).

TRAIN

The Greek Railways Organisation, OSE (Organismos Sidirodromon Ellados), is gradually getting its act together and modernising its creaky rolling stock; but train travel in Greece is still viewed by most people as a poor alternative to road travel.

For starters, the rail system is not huge. There are essentially two main, standard-gauge lines: Athens to Thessaloniki and Thessaloniki to Alexandroupolis. The Peloponnese system uses a narrow-gauge track.

There are also two very distinct levels of service: the slow, stopping-all-stations services that crawl around the countryside, and the faster, modern intercity trains that link most major cities.

The slow trains represent the country's cheapest form of public transport. The fares haven't changed for years; 2nd class fares are absurdly cheap, and even 1st class is cheaper than bus travel. The downside is that the trains are painfully slow, uncomfortable and unreliable. There seems to be no effort to upgrade the dilapidated rolling stock on these services. Unless you are travelling on a very tight budget, they are best left alone – except on shorter runs. Sample journey times and fares on these trains include Athens-Thessaloniki, 7½ hours, 5580/3720 dr (1st/2nd class); Athens-Patras, five hours, 2370/1580 dr; and Thessaloniki-Alexandroupolis, seven hours, 4490/2990 dr.

The intercity trains which link the major cities are a much better way to travel. The services are not necessarily express – the Greek terrain is too mountainous for that – but the trains are modern and comfortable. There are 1st and 2nd class smoking/non-smoking seats and there is a cafe-bar on board. On some services, meals can be ordered and delivered to your seat.

Ticket prices for intercity services are subject to a distance loading on top of the normal fares. Seat reservations should be made as far in advance as possible, especially in summer. Sample journey times and fares include Athens-Thessaloniki, six hours, 10,480/8250 dr (1st/2nd class); Thessaloniki-Alexandroupolis, 5½ hours, 6770/4970 dr; and Athens-Patras, 3½ hours, 3970/2980 dr.

A comfortable night service runs between Athens and Thessaloniki, with a choice of couchettes (from 1750 dr) and sleeping cars (from 3000 dr).

Eurail and Inter-Rail cards are valid in Greece, but it's not worth buying one if Greece is the only place you plan to use it. The passes can be used on intercity services without paying the loading.

Another option if you're planning on using the trains a lot is to buy a tourist rail pass, which are available for individual passengers, as well as for families and groups of up to five people. They are valid for 10, 20 or 30 days and entitle the holder to make an unlimited number of journeys on all the rail routes. An individual pass costs 14,850 dr for 10 days, 22,300 dr for 20 days and 29,750 dr for 30 days. Whatever pass you have, you must have a reservation. You cannot board a train without one.

Senior cards are available to passengers over 60 years of age on presentation of their IDs or passports. They cost 25,500 dr for 1st class travel and 17,000 dr for 2nd class, and are valid for one year from the date of issue. Cardholders get a 50% reduction on train travel, plus five free journeys per year.

Tickets can be bought from OSE booking offices in a few major towns, otherwise from train stations. There is a 20% discount on return tickets, and a 30% discount for groups of 10 or more.

You'll find information on fares and schedules on the Hellenic Railways Organisation Web site, www.ose.gr.

CAR & MOTORCYCLE

No-one who has travelled on Greece's roads will be surprised to hear that the country's road fatality rate is the highest in Europe. More than 2000 people die on the roads every year, with overtaking listed as the greatest cause of accidents. Ever-stricter traffic laws have had little impact on the toll; Greek roads remain a good place to practise your defensive-driving techniques.

Heart-stopping moments aside, your own car is a great way to explore off the beaten track. The road network has improved enormously in recent years; many roads marked as dirt tracks on older maps have now been asphalted – particularly in remoter parts of Epiros and the Peloponnese. It's important to get a good road map (see the Maps section in the Facts for the Visitor chapter).

Greece is not the best place to initiate yourself into motorcycling. There are still a lot of gravel roads – particularly on the islands. Novices should be particularly careful; dozens of tourists have accidents every year.

There are seven stretches of highway in Greece where tolls are levied. They are Athens-Corinth, Corinth-Patras, Corinth-Tripolis, Athens-Lamia, Lamia-Larisa, Larisa-Thessaloniki and Thessaloniki-Evzoni. The rates depend on how far you're going. It costs, for example, 500 dr from Athens to Corinth and 600 dr from Corinth to Patras for a car.

Almost all islands are served by car ferries, but they are expensive. Sample prices for small vehicles include Piraeus-Mykonos, 18,570 dr; Piraeus-Crete (Hania and Iraklio), 19,610 dr; Piraeus-Rhodes, 23,960 dr; and Piraeus-Lesvos, 22,230 dr. The charge for a large motorbike is about the same as the price of a 3rd class passenger ticket.

Petrol in Greece is expensive, and the farther you get from a major city the more it costs. Prices vary from petrol station to petrol station. Super can be found as cheaply as 199 dr per litre at big city discount places, but 225 dr to 235 dr is the normal range. You may pay closer to 245 dr per litre in remote areas. The price range for unleaded – available everywhere – is from 200 dr to 225 dr per litre. Diesel costs about 170 dr per litre.

See the Documents section in the Facts for the Visitor chapter for information on licence requirements.

See the Useful Organisations section in the Facts for the Visitor chapter for information about the Greek automobile club (ELPA).

Warning If you are planning to use a motorcycle or moped, check that your travel insurance covers you for injury resulting from a motorbike accident. Many insurance companies don't offer this cover, so check the fine print!

Road Rules

In Greece, as throughout Continental Europe, you drive on the right and overtake on the left. Outside built-up areas, traffic on a main road has right of way at intersections. In towns, vehicles coming from the right have right of way. Seat belts must be worn in front seats, and in back seats if the car is fitted with them. Children under 12 years of age are not allowed in the front seat. It is compulsory to carry a first-aid kit, fire extinguisher and warning triangle, and it is forbidden to carry cans of petrol. Helmets are compulsory for motorcyclists if the motorbike is 50cc or more.

Outside residential areas the speed limit is 120km/h on highways, 90km/h on other roads and 50km/h in built-up areas. The speed limit for motorbikes up to 100cc is 70km/h and for larger motorbikes, 90km/h.

Road Distances (km)

	Alexandroupolis	Athens	Corinth	Edessa	Florina	Igoumenitsa	Ioannina	Kalamata	Kastoria	Kavala	Lamia	Larisa	Monemvasia	Nafplio	Patra	Pyrgos	Sparta	Thessaloniki	Trikala	Tripolis	Volos
Alexandroupolis	---																				
Athens	464	---																			
Corinth	884	84	---																		
Edessa	441	569	596	---																	
Florina	497	592	251	353	---																
Igoumenitsa	816	473	393	380	353	---															
Ioannina	716	447	364	298	320	96	---														
Kalamata	1064	284	175	767	763	501	467	---													
Kastoria	535	489	519	108	67	286	204	690	---												
Kavala	177	682	655	250	320	615	525	878	358	---											
Lamia	643	214	244	355	360	353	263	415	274	466	---										
Larisa	503	361	389	218	231	309	209	561	239	323	151	---									
Monemvasia	1156	350	266	869	855	613	579	156	756	976	505	655	---								
Nafplio	947	165	63	659	664	482	427	163	582	770	307	455	215	---							
Patra	844	220	138	567	513	281	247	220	483	664	193	341	332	201	---						
Pyrgos	944	320	234	636	643	367	347	119	542	747	284	432	275	208	96	---					
Sparta	1060	225	145	737	759	517	483	60	660	848	385	533	96	119	236	180	---				
Thessaloniki	349	513	544	89	159	452	362	715	220	169	303	154	807	610	488	584	711	---			
Trikala	346	330	356	227	233	247	148	520	159	377	115	62	597	419	310	400	501	216	---		
Tripolis	964	194	110	713	681	457	430	90	639	820	324	472	157	81	176	155	61	624	466	---	
Volos	556	326	355	278	293	371	271	518	301	383	115	62	620	417	308	408	524	214	124	435	---

Drivers exceeding the speed limit by 20% are liable for a fine of 20,000 dr; and by 40%, 50,000 dr. Other offences and fines include:

illegal overtaking – 100,000 dr
going through a red light – 100,000 dr
driving without a seat belt – 50,000 dr
motorcyclist not wearing a helmet – 50,000 dr
wrong way down one way street – 50,000 dr
illegal parking – 10,000 dr

The police have also cracked down on drink-driving laws – at last. A blood-alcohol content of 0.05% is liable to incur a fine of 50,000 dr, and over 0.08% is a criminal offence.

The police can issue traffic fines, but payment cannot be made on the spot – you will be told where to pay.

If you are involved in an accident and no-one is hurt, the police will not be required to write a report, but it is advisable to go to a nearby police station and explain what happened. A police report may be required for insurance purposes. If an accident involves injury, a driver who does not stop and does not inform the police may face a prison sentence.

Rental

Car If the deadly driving has not put you off getting behind a wheel in Greece, then perhaps the price of hiring a car will. Rental cars are widely available, but they are more expensive than in most other European countries. Most of the big multinational car hire companies are represented in Athens and large towns, on large islands and at international airports. The smaller islands often have only one car hire outlet.

The multinationals are, however, the most expensive places to hire a car. High season weekly rates with unlimited mileage start at about 110,000 dr for the smallest models, such as a 900cc Fiat Panda. The rate drops to about 90,000 dr per week in winter. To these prices must be added VAT of 18%, or 13% on the islands of the Dodecanese, the North-Eastern Aegean and the Sporades. Then there are the optional extras, such as a collision damage waiver of 3300 dr per day (more for larger models), without which you will be liable for the first 1,500,000 dr of the repair bill (much more for larger models). Other costs include a theft waiver of at least 1000 dr per day and personal accident insurance. It all adds up to an expensive exercise. The major companies offer much cheaper prebooked and prepaid rates.

Local companies offer some good deals for those prepared to shop around. They are normally more open to negotiation, especially if business is slow. Their advertised rates are about 25% cheaper than those offered by the multinationals.

If you want to take a hire car to another country or onto a ferry, you will need advance written authorisation from the hire company. Unless you pay with a credit card, most hire companies will require a minimum deposit of 20,000 dr per day. See the Getting Around sections of cities and islands for details of places to rent cars.

The minimum driving age in Greece is 18 years, but most car hire firms require you to be at least 23, although a few will rent vehicles to 21-year-olds.

Motorcycle Mopeds and motorcycles are available for hire wherever there are tourists to rent them. In many cases their maintenance has been minimal, so check the machine thoroughly before you hire it – especially the brakes: you'll need them!

Motorbikes are a cheap way to travel around. Rates range from 2500 dr to 4000 dr per day for a moped or 50cc motorbike to 6000 dr per day for a 250cc motorbike. Out of season these prices drop considerably, so use your bargaining skills. By October it is sometimes possible to hire a moped for as little as 1500 dr per day. Most motorcycle hirers include third party insurance in the price, but it's wise to check this. This insurance will not include medical expenses.

BICYCLE

Cycling has not caught on in Greece, which isn't surprising considering the hilly terrain. Tourists are beginning to cycle in Greece, but you'll need strong leg muscles. You can hire bicycles in most tourist places, but they are not as widely available as cars and motorbikes. Prices range from 1000 dr to 3000 dr per day, depending on the type and age of the bike. Bicycles are carried free on ferries.

HITCHING

Hitching is never entirely safe in any country in the world, and we don't recommend it. Travellers who decide to hitch should understand that they are taking a small but potentially serious risk. People who do choose to hitch will be safer if they travel in pairs and should let someone know where they are planning to go. Greece has a reputation for being a relatively safe place for women to hitch, but it is still unwise to do it alone. It's better for a woman to hitch with a companion, preferably a male one.

Some parts of Greece are much better for hitching than others. Getting out of major cities tends to be hard work, and Athens is notoriously difficult. Hitching is much easier in remote areas and on islands with poor public transport. On country roads, it is not unknown for someone to stop and ask if you want a lift even if you haven't stuck a thumb out. You can't afford to be fussy about the mode of transport – it may be a tractor or a spluttering old truck.

WALKING

Unless you have come to Greece just to lie on a beach, the chances are you will do quite a bit of walking. You don't have to be a trekker to start clocking up the kilometres. The narrow, stepped streets of many towns and villages can only be explored on foot, and visiting the archaeological sites involves a fair amount of legwork. See the What to Bring, Health and Trekking sections in the Facts for the Visitor chapter for more information about walking.

BOAT

Ferry

For most people, travel in Greece means island-hopping. Every island has a ferry service of some sort, although in winter services to some of the smaller islands are fairly skeletal. Services start to pick up again from April onwards, and by July and August there are countless services criss-crossing the Aegean. Ferries come in all shapes and sizes, from the giant 'superferries' that work the major routes to the small, ageing open ferries that chug around the backwaters.

Routes The hub of Greece's ferry network is Piraeus, the port of Athens. Ferries leave here for the Cyclades, Dodecanese, the North-Eastern Aegean Islands, Saronic Gulf Islands and Crete. Athens' second port is Rafina, 70km east of the city and connected by an hourly bus service. It has ferries to the northern Cyclades, Evia, Lesvos and Limnos. The port of Lavrio, in southern Attica, is the main port for ferries to the Cycladic island of Kea. There are regular buses from Athens to Lavrio.

Ferries for the Ionian Islands leave from the Peloponnese ports of Patras (for Kefallonia, Ithaki, Paxi and Corfu) and Kyllini (for Kefallonia and Zakynthos); from Astakos (for Ithaki and Kefallonia) and Mytikas (for Lefkada and Meganisi), both in Sterea Ellada; and from Igoumenitsa in Epiros (for Corfu).

Ferries for the Sporades leave from Volos, Thessaloniki, Agios Konstantinos, and Kymi on Evia. The latter two ports are easily reached by bus from Athens.

Some of the North-Eastern Aegean Islands have connections with Thessaloniki as well as Piraeus. The odd ones out are Thasos, which is reached from Kavala, and Samothraki, which can be reached from Alexandroupolis year-round and also from Kavala in summer.

Schedules Ferry timetables change from year to year and season to season, and ferries are subject to delays and cancellations at short notice due to bad weather, strikes or boats simply conking out. No timetable is infallible, but the comprehensive weekly list of departures from Piraeus put out by the EOT in Athens is as accurate as humanly possible. The people to go to for the most up-to-date ferry information are the local port police *(limenarheio)*, whose offices are usually on or near the quay side.

There's lots of information about ferry services on the Internet. Try www.ferries.gr, which has a useful search program and links. Many of the larger ferry companies now have their own sites, including:

Agapitos Lines: www.agapitos-ferries.gr
ANEK: www.anek.gr
Minoan Lines: www.minoan.gr
Strintzis: www.strintzis.gr
Superfast: www.superfast.com
Ventouris: www.ventouris.gr

Throughout the year there is at least one ferry a day from a mainland port to the major island in each group, and during the high season (from June to mid-September) there are considerably more. Ferries sailing from one island group to another are not so frequent, and if you're going to travel in this way you'll need to plan carefully, otherwise you may end up having to backtrack to Piraeus.

Travelling time can vary considerably from one ferry to another, depending on how many islands are called in at on the way to your destination. For example, the Piraeus-Rhodes trip can take between 14 and 18 hours depending on the route. Before buying your ticket, check how many stops the boat is going to make, and its estimated arrival time.

Costs Prices are fixed by the government, and are determined by the distance travelled rather than by the facilities of a particular boat. There can be big differences in the size, comfort and facilities of boats offering

Meeting the Ferry

At a few remote islands, the arrival of a ferry boat is a once or twice-weekly occurrence which provides a lifeline for the inhabitants. Witnessing the arrival of a ferry at such an island is an interesting spectacle, as it is one of the most exciting events of the week. It seems as if the whole population – including at least one tail-wagging dog – turns out to meet the ferry. Arriving and departing relations are warmly embraced, sacks of vegetables and crates of drinks are unloaded quickly and haphazardly, and high-tech and industrial appliances are carried off with the utmost care. All this takes place amid frantic arm waving, shouting and general pandemonium in the rush to ensure that the ferry arrives on time at the next island – which invariably it does not. It serves to remember on such occasions that chaos is a Greek word and that the Greeks invented drama. Eventually, the task completed, the ferry departs and the island slips back into its customary tranquillity.

rival services on a given route, but the fares will be the same.

The small differences in price you may find at ticket agencies are the results of some agents sacrificing part of their designated commission to qualify as a 'discount service'. The discount is seldom more than 50 dr. Ticket prices include embarkation tax, a contribution to NAT (the seaman's union) and 8% VAT.

Classes The large ferries usually have four classes: 1st class has air-con cabins and a posh lounge and restaurant; 2nd class has smaller cabins and sometimes a separate lounge; tourist class gives you a berth in a shared four-berth cabin; and 3rd (deck) class gives you access to a room with 'airline' seats, a restaurant, a lounge/bar and, of course, the deck.

Deck class remains an economical way to travel, while a 1st class ticket can cost almost as much as flying on some routes. Children under four travel for free, while children between four and 10 pay half-fare. Full fares apply for children over 10. Unless you state otherwise, when purchasing a ticket, you will automatically be given deck class. As deck class is what most tourists opt for, it is those prices which are quoted in this book.

Ticket Purchase Given that ferries are prone to delays and cancellations, it's best not to purchase a ticket until it has been confirmed that the ferry is leaving. If you need to reserve a car space, however, you may need to pay in advance. If the service is then cancelled you can transfer your ticket to the next available service with that company.

Agencies selling tickets line the waterfront of most ports, but rarely is there one that sells tickets for every boat, and often an agency is reluctant to give you information about a boat they do not sell tickets for. This means you have to check the timetables displayed outside each agency to find out which ferry is next to depart – or ask the port police.

In high season, a number of boats may be due at a port at around the same time, so it is not beyond the realms of possibility that you might get on the wrong boat. The crucial thing to look out for is the name of the boat; this will be printed on your ticket, and in large English letters on the side of the vessel.

If for some reason you haven't purchased a ticket from an agency, makeshift ticket tables are put up beside a ferry about an hour before departure. Tickets can also be purchased on board the ship after it has sailed. If you are waiting at the quay side for a delayed ferry, don't lose patience and wander off. Ferry boats, once they turn up, can demonstrate amazing alacrity – blink and you may miss the boat.

Ferry Travel Once on board, the fun really begins. It can be absolute chaos in high sea-

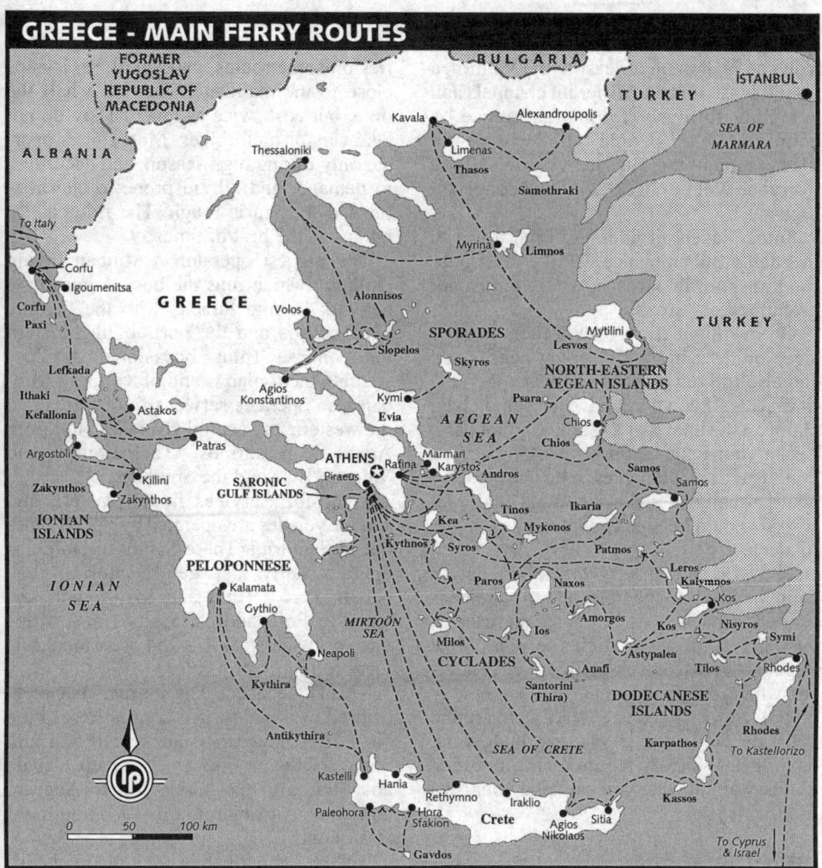

son. No matter how many passengers are already on the ferry, more will be crammed on. Bewildered, black-shrouded grannies are steered through the crowd by teenage grandchildren, children get separated from parents, people stumble over backpacks, dogs get excited and bark – and everyone rushes to grab a seat. As well as birds in cages and cats in baskets there is almost always at least one truck of livestock on board – usually sheep, goats or cattle, vociferously making their presence known.

Greeks travelling deck class usually make a beeline for the indoor lounge/snack bar, while tourists make for the deck where they can sunbathe. Some ferry companies have allegedly attempted to capitalise on this natural division by telling backpackers and non-Greeks that they are barred from the deck-class saloon and indoor-seating area, directing them instead to the sun deck. There is no such thing as 'deck only' class on domestic ferries, although there is on international ferries.

You'll need strong nerves and lungs to withstand the lounge/snack bar, though. You can reckon on at least two TVs turned up full blast, tuned to different channels and crackling furiously from interference. A couple of other people will have ghetto blasters pumping out heavy metal, and everyone will be engaged in loud conversation.

Smoke-laden air adds the final touch to this delightful ambience. Unlike other public transport in Greece, smoking is not prohibited on ferries.

On overnight trips, backpackers usually sleep on deck in their sleeping bags – you can also roll out your bag between the 'airline' seats. If you don't have a sleeping bag, claim an 'airline' seat as soon as you board. Leave your luggage on it – as long as you don't leave any valuables in it. The noise on board usually dies down around midnight so you should be able to snatch a few hours of sleep.

The food sold at ferry snack bars ranges from mediocre to inedible, and the choice is limited to packets of biscuits, sandwiches, very greasy pizzas and cheese pies. Most large ferries also have a self-service restaurant where the food is OK and reasonably priced, with main courses starting at around 1500 dr. However, if you are budgeting, have special dietary requirements, or are at all fussy about what you eat, take your own food with you.

Inter-Island Boat

In addition to the large ferries which ply between the large mainland ports and island groups, there are smaller boats which link islands within a group, and occasionally, an island in one group with an island in another.

In the past these boats were always caïques – sturdy old fishing boats – but gradually these are being replaced by new purpose-built boats, which are usually called express or excursion boats. Tickets tend to cost more than tickets for the large ferries, but the boats are very useful if you're island-hopping.

Hydrofoil

Hydrofoils offer a faster alternative to ferries on some routes, particularly to islands close to the mainland. They take half the time, but cost twice as much. They do not take cars or motorbikes. Most routes operate only during high season, and according to demand, and all are prone to cancellations if the sea is rough. The ride can be bumpy at the best of times.

The biggest operator is Minoan Flying Dolphin, which runs the busy Argosaronic network linking Piraeus with the Saronic Gulf Islands and the ports of the eastern Peloponnese (plus occasional services south to the Ionian island of Kythira). Minoan also operates services from Piraeus to the western and central Cyclades, and from Agios Konstantinos, Thessaloniki and Volos to Evia and the Sporades.

Hydrofoil services in the eastern and south Cyclades are operated by Speed Lines out of Santorini. These Santorini Dolphins operate daily between Santorini, Ios, Naxos, Paros, Tinos and Syros, with services to Folegandros, Sikinos and Milos once or twice weekly – and occasional services to Iraklio on Crete.

The Dodecanese has its own network, centred on Rhodes, and connections to the North-East Aegean islands of Ikaria and Samos. Other routes are between Kavala and Thasos in the North-Eastern Aegean, and from Alexandroupolis to Samothraki and Limnos.

Tickets cannot be bought on board hydrofoils – you must buy them in advance from an agent. You will be allocated a seat number.

Catamaran

High-speed catamarans have rapidly become an important part of the island travel scene. They are just as fast as the hydrofoils – if not faster – and much more comfortable. They are also much less prone to cancellation in rough weather.

Minoan Flying Dolphin again is the major player. Its giant *Highspeed 1* runs daily between Piraeus, Syros, Mykonos,

Paros and Naxos, and it uses smaller cats on many of the routes around the Saronic Gulf.

Catamarans have now taken over from hydrofoils on the routes from Rafina to the central and northern Cyclades. Strintzis Lines uses the *Seajet 1* for the daily run to Syros, Paros, Naxos, Ios and Santorini, and the *Seajet 2* to Tinos and Mykonos, stopping once a week at Andros, Syros, Paros, Naxos and Amorgos. Goutos Lines operates its *Athina 2004* on a similar schedule.

These services are very popular; book as far in advance as possible, especially if you want to travel on weekends.

Taxi Boat

Most islands have taxi boats – small speedboats which operate like taxis, transporting people to places that are difficult to get to by land. Some owners charge a set price for each person, others charge a flat rate for the boat, and this cost is divided by the number of passengers. Either way, prices are usually quite reasonable.

Yacht

Despite the disparaging remarks among backpackers, yachting is *the* way to see the Greek islands. Nothing beats the peace and serenity of sailing the open sea, and the freedom of being able to visit remote and uninhabited islands.

The free EOT booklet *Sailing the Greek Seas*, although long overdue for an update, contains lots of information about weather conditions, weather bulletins, entry and exit regulations, entry and exit ports and guidebooks for yachties. You can pick up the booklet at any GNTO/EOT office either abroad or in Greece.

If your budget won't cover buying a yacht, there are several other options open to you. You can hire a bare boat (a yacht without a crew) if two crew members have a sailing certificate. Prices start at US$1300 per week for a 28-footer that will sleep six. It will cost an extra US$800 per week to hire a skipper. Some yacht charter companies operating in and around Athens and Piraeus are listed here (contact the EOT for others).

Aegean Tourism
(☎ 01-346 6229, fax 342 2121)
Kadmias 8, Athens
www.aegeantours.gr
Alpha Yachting
(☎ 01-968 0486, fax 968 0488,
email mano@otenet.gr)
Poseidonos 67, Glyfada
Ghiolman Yachts & Travel
(☎ 01-323 3696, fax 322 3251,
email ghiolman@travelling.gr)
Filellinon 7, Athens
Hellenic Charters
(☎/fax 01-988 5592,
email hctsa@ath.forthnet.gr)
Poseidonos 66, Alimos
Kostis Yachting
(☎ 01-895 0657, fax 895 0995)
Epaminonda 61, Glyfada
www.kostis-yachting.com

LOCAL TRANSPORT

To/From the Airports

Olympic Airways operates buses to a few domestic airports (see individual entries in the appropriate chapters). Where the service exists, buses leave the airline office about 1½ hours before departure. In many places, the only way to get to the airport is by taxi. Check-in is an hour before departure for domestic flights. Transport to international airports in Greece is covered in the Getting Around section of the relevant city.

Bus

Most Greek towns are small enough to get around on foot. The only places where you may need to use local buses are Athens, Piraeus and Thessaloniki. The procedure for buying tickets for local buses is covered in the Getting Around section for each city.

Metro

Athens is the only city in Greece large enough to warrant an underground system. See the Athens chapter for news on the metro extension program: at the time of writing, two new lines were scheduled to start operations in late 1999.

Taxi

Taxis are widely available in Greece except on very small or remote islands. They are reasonably priced by European standards, especially if three or four people share costs.

Yellow city cabs are metered. Flagfall is 200 dr, followed by 62 dr per kilometre (120 dr per kilometre outside town). These rates double between midnight and 5 am. Costs additional to the per-kilometre rate are 300 dr from an airport, 150 dr from a bus, port or train station and 55 dr for each piece of luggage. Grey rural taxis do not have meters, so you should always settle on a price before you get in.

The taxi drivers of Athens are legendary for their ability to part locals and tourists alike from their drachma – see the 'Dangers & Annoyances' boxed text in the Athens chapter. If you have a complaint about a taxi driver, take the cab number and report your complaint to the tourist police. Taxi drivers in other towns in Greece are, on the whole, friendly, helpful and honest.

ORGANISED TOURS

Tours are worth considering only if your time is very limited, in which case there are countless companies vying for your money. The major players are CHAT, GO Tours and Key Tours, all based in Athens and offering almost identical tours. They include day trips to Delphi (16,300 dr) and Mycenae and Epidaurus (16,300 dr). They also offer longer trips such as a four day tour calling at Mycenae, Nafplio, Epidaurus, Olympia and Delphi (from 89,000 dr). These prices include twin share accommodation and half-board. See Organised Tours in the Athens chapter.

Organised Treks

Trekking Hellas (☎ 01-325 0853, fax 323 4548, email trekking@compulink.gr), at Filellinon 7, Athens 105 57, is a well established company which specialises in treks and other adventure activities for small groups. It offers a wide range of treks lasting from four to nine days and graded from introductory to challenging. It has fairly easy introductory walks in the foothills of the Taÿgetos Mountains in the Peloponnese, on the Ionian island of Ithaki and on the Cycladic islands of Andros and Tinos.

The treks around Meteora and the Pelion Peninsula are a bit more demanding, while only fit, experienced walkers should attempt the challenging treks in the Pindos Ranges and to the summits of Mt Olympus. Other activities include canoeing, river-rafting (January-April), canyoning and cycling. You'll find more information about activities and prices on the Trekking Hellas Web site, www.trekking.gr.

MAINLAND GREECE

DIANA MAYFIELD

Athens Αθήνα

☎ 01 • postcode 102 00 (Omonia), 103 00 (Syntagma) • pop 3.7 million

The perpetual 'high' which novelist Henry Miller experienced during his travels in Greece did not flag when he came to the capital. In *The Colossus of Maroussi*, Miller waxed lyrical about the extraordinary quality of the city's light and rhythm. Few visitors today, however, share his bubbling enthusiasm. Most beat a hasty retreat after the obligatory visit to the Acropolis and the National Archaeological Museum. Despite its glorious past and its influence on western civilisation, it is a city which few fall in love with. Modern Athens is a vast concrete urban sprawl that suffers badly from the curse of the modern age: pollution.

To appreciate Athens (in Greek, Athina), it's important to be aware of the city's traumatic history. Unlike most capital cities, Athens does not have a history of continuous expansion; it is one characterised by glory, followed by decline and near annihilation, and then resurgence in the 19th century – when it became the capital of independent Greece.

The historical event which, more than any other, shaped the Athens of today was the compulsory population exchange between Greece and Turkey that followed the signing of the Treaty of Lausanne in July 1923. The population of Athens virtually doubled overnight, necessitating the hasty erection of concrete apartment blocks to house the newcomers.

The expansion of Athens in all directions began at this time, and accelerated during the 1950s and 60s when the country began the transition from an agricultural to an industrial nation. Young people began to flock to the city from the islands and rural areas, and this trend has continued ever since.

Athens has many redeeming qualities. The city is bounded on three sides by Mt Parnitha (1413m), Mt Pendeli (1109m) and Mt Hymettos (1026m). The latter was once famed for its violet sunsets – these days normally obliterated by the city's appalling pollution. At least one of these mountains can be glimpsed from almost every street in Athens.

Within the city there are no less than eight hills, of which the most prominent are Lykavittos (277m) and the Acropolis (156m). These hills are a pleasant place to escape from the traffic-congested streets. Athens improves considerably when viewed from a height, and there are stunning views over the city to the glistening waters of the Saronic Gulf – its boundary on the fourth side.

HIGHLIGHTS

- The inspirational Acropolis (and outdoor dining below it)
- The treasures of the National Archaeological Museum
- The panoramic view from Lykavittos Hill
- The lively *rembetika* clubs
- Sunset over the sea at Cape Sounion

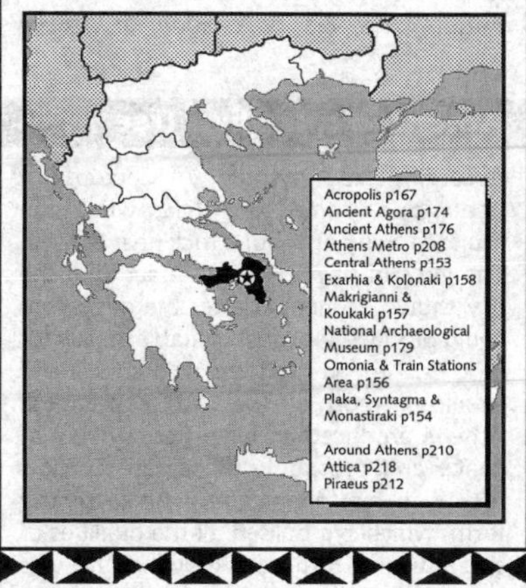

Perhaps most significant of all is the fact that wherever you are in the centre of the city, the Acropolis, with its transcendent and compelling aura, stands proudly on the skyline. It serves as a constant reminder that whatever trials and tribulations might have befallen the city, its status as the birthplace of western civilisation is beyond doubt.

HISTORY

Early History

The early history of Athens is inextricably interwoven with mythology, making it impossible to disentangle fact from fiction. What is known, though, is that the hilltop site of the Acropolis, endowed with two bounteous springs, drew some of Greece's earliest Neolithic settlers. When a peaceful agricultural existence gave way to the war-orientated city-states, the Acropolis provided an ideal defensive position: its steep slopes formed natural defences on three sides and it was an excellent vantage point from which to spot danger approaching from land or sea.

By 1400 BC, the Acropolis had become a powerful Mycenaean city. Unlike the cities of Mycenae, Pylos and Tiryns, it survived the Dorian assault on Greece in 1200 BC. It couldn't, however, escape the dark age that enveloped Greece for the next 400 years, and very little is known of this period.

After its emergence from the dark age in the 8th century BC, a period of peace followed, both for Athens and the surrounding united towns. During this time the city became the artistic centre of Greece, excelling in ceramics. The geometric designs of vases from the dark ages evolved into a narrative style, depicting scenes from everyday life and mythology. This pottery subsequently became known as the Proto-Attic style.

By the 6th century BC, Athens was ruled by aristocrats, generals and the *arhon* (chief magistrate). A person's position in the hierarchy depended on their wealth, which was gained either from commerce or agriculture. Labourers and peasants had no say at all in the functioning of the city – until the reform-oriented Solon became arhon in 594 BC.

Solon did much to improve the lot of the poor and is regarded as the harbinger of Athenian democracy. His most significant reforms were the annulment of all debts and the implementation of trial by jury. Continuing unrest over the reforms created the pretext for the tyrant Peisistratos, formerly head of the military, to seize power in 560 BC.

Peisistratos built up a formidable navy, much to the consternation of other city-states, and extended the boundaries of Athenian influence on land. He was a patron of the arts as well as a general, inaugurating the Festival of the Great Dionysia, which was the precursor of Attic drama, and commissioning many splendid sacred and secular buildings – most of which were

Athena & the Olive Tree

According to mythology, Cecrops, a Phoenician, came to Attica, where he founded a city on a huge rock near the sea. The gods of Olympus proclaimed that the city should be named after the deity who could produce the most valuable legacy for mortals. Athena (goddess of wisdom) and Poseidon (god of the sea) contended. Athena produced an olive tree, symbol of peace and prosperity. Poseidon struck a rock with his trident and a horse sprang forth, which symbolised all the qualities of strength and fortitude for which he was renowned. Athena was the victor, for the gods proclaimed that her gift would better serve the citizens of Athens than the arts of war personified by Poseidon's gift.

destroyed by the Persians on the eve of the Battle of Salamis in 480 BC.

Peisistratos was succeeded by his son Hippias, who was very much a tyrant. Athens managed to rid itself of this oppressor in 510 BC only by swallowing its pride and accepting the help of Sparta. Hippias wasn't finished, however, heading off to Persia to stir up trouble and returning with Darius 20 years later to be defeated at the Battle of Marathon.

Athens' Golden Age

After Athens had finally repulsed the challenge of the Persian Empire at the battles of Salamis and Plataea (again, with the help of Sparta), its power knew no bounds.

In 477 BC Athens established a confederacy on the sacred island of Delos and demanded tributes from the surrounding islands to protect them from the Persians. It was little more than a standover racket because the Persians were no longer much of a threat. The treasury was moved to Athens in 461 BC and Pericles (ruler from 461 to 429 BC) used the money to transform the city. The period has become known as Athens' golden age, the pinnacle of the classical era.

Most of the monuments on the Acropolis today date from this time. Drama and literature flourished in the form of the tragedies written by Aeschylus, Sophocles and Euripides. The sculptors Pheidias and Myron and the historians Herodotus, Thucydides and Xenophon also lived at this time.

Rivalry with Sparta

Arch rival Sparta wasn't prepared to sit back and allow Athens to revel in its newfound glory. The increasing jockeying for power between the two led to the outbreak of the Peloponnesian Wars in 431 BC. The warring dragged on until 404 BC, when Sparta gained the upper hand. Athens was never to return to its former glory. The 4th century BC did, however, produce three of the west's greatest orators and philosophers: Socrates, Plato and Aristotle. The degeneracy into which Athens had fallen was perhaps epitomised by the ignominious death sentence passed on Socrates for the crime of corrupting the young with his speeches.

Athens' days of glory were now numbered. In 338 BC, along with the other city-states of Greece, Athens was conquered by Philip II of Macedon. After Philip's assassination, his son Alexander the Great, a cultured young man, favoured Athens over other city-states. After his untimely death, Athens passed in quick succession through the hands of several of his generals.

Roman & Byzantine Rule

Athens continued to be a major seat of learning under Roman rule, and many wealthy young Romans attended Athens'

The Olympics Come Home

While much of central Athens has disappeared behind construction hoardings amid a frenzy of renovation and reconstruction in the lead-up to the 2004 Olympics, most of the facilities for the games themselves are already completed and operational.

The centrepiece is the 80,000-seat Olympic Stadium, in the northern suburb of Maroussi, which will stage the athletic events as well as the opening and closing ceremonies. The stadium has doubled as the city's No 1 soccer venue since it was completed in 1996.

The stadium is part of the Athens Olympic Sports Complex, next to Irini metro station, which also includes an indoor sports hall for gymnastics and basketball, a swimming complex and diving pool, a velodrome and a tennis centre.

The other major area of Olympic activity is in the coastal suburb of Faliro. Karaïskaki Stadium, home ground of the Olympiakos soccer club, will host the hockey competition, while the nearby Peace and Friendship Stadium will be used for volleyball and handball as well as wrestling and judo. The yachting will be held in Faliro Bay.

schools. Anybody who was anybody in Rome at the time spoke Greek. The Roman emperors, particularly Hadrian, graced Athens with many grand buildings.

After the subdivision of the Roman Empire into east and west, Athens remained an important cultural and intellectual centre until Emperor Justinian closed its schools of philosophy in 529 AD. The city then declined into nothing more than an outpost of the Byzantine Empire.

Between 1200 and 1450, Athens was continually invaded – by Franks, Catalans, Florentines and Venetians, all opportunists preoccupied only with grabbing for themselves principalities from the crumbling Byzantine Empire.

Ottoman Rule & Independence

Athens was captured by the Turks in 1456, and nearly 400 years of Ottoman rule followed. The Acropolis became the home of the Turkish governor, the Parthenon was converted into a mosque and the Erechtheion was used as a harem.

In the early stages of the War of Independence (1821-27), fierce fighting broke out in the streets of Athens, with the city changing hands several times between Turks and Greek liberators. In 1834 Athens superseded Nafplio as the capital of independent Greece and King Otho set about transforming the sparsely populated, war-scarred town into something worthy of a capital. Bavarian architects created a city of imposing neoclassical buildings, tree-lined boulevards, flower gardens and squares. Sadly, many of these buildings have been demolished. The best surviving examples are on Vasilissis Sofias.

The 20th Century

Athens grew steadily throughout the latter half of the 19th and early 20th centuries, and enjoyed a brief heyday as the 'Paris of the eastern Mediterranean'. This came to an abrupt end in 1923 with the Treaty of Lausanne. The treaty resulted in nearly a million refugees from Turkey descending on Athens – an event which marked the beginning of its much-maligned concrete sprawl.

Athens, along with the rest of Greece, suffered appallingly during the German occupation of WWII. During this time more Athenians were killed by starvation than by the enemy. This suffering was perpetuated in the civil war that followed.

The industrialisation program that was launched during the 1950s, with the help of US aid, brought another population boom as people from the islands and mainland villages headed to Athens in search of work.

The colonels' junta (1967-74), with characteristic insensitivity, tore down many of the crumbling old Turkish houses of Plaka and the imposing neoclassical buildings of King Otho's time. The junta failed, however, to take any action on the chronic infrastructural problems resulting from such rapid and unplanned growth. The elected governments that followed in the

Earthquake!

On 7 September 1999, the Greek capital was struck by the most powerful earthquake to hit the region for almost 200 years. It killed 120 people and left 70,000 homeless.

The quake, measuring 5.9 on the Richter scale, was centred some 40km north of the city centre at Menidi, near Mt Parnitha. The jolt flattened many buildings in Menidi and the surrounding areas of Aharnes, Ano Liosia and Metamorphosi, where dozens died in a factory collapse. Buildings throughout the capital and Piraeus were damaged, including the National Archaeological Museum. The tremor left minor cracks in the building, and large cracks in the 2nd floor pottery collection, which is expected to remain closed for some time. The Parthenon, which has survived many quakes in its 2500 year history, suffered minor damage to one of its columns.

late 70s and 80s didn't do much better, and by the end of the 80s the city had developed a sorry reputation as one of the most traffic-clogged and polluted in Europe.

The 1990s appear to have been a turning point in the city's development, with politicians finally accepting the need for radical solutions. Inspired initially by the failed bid to stage the 1996 Olympics, authorities embarked on an ambitious program to prepare the city for the 21st century. Two key elements in this program have been a major expansion of the metro network, and the construction of a new international airport at Spata, east of Athens.

These projects played an important role in the city's successful bid to stage the 2004 Olympics. The Olympics have now created a momentum of their own; confidence is riding high and billions are being poured into city centre redevelopment. The city will look very different by the time the construction hoardings finally disappear. See the earlier boxed text 'The Olympics Come Home' for more information.

ORIENTATION

City Centre (Map 1)

Although Athens is a huge, sprawling city, nearly everything of interest to travellers is located within a small area surrounding Plateia Syntagmatos (Syntagma Square). This area is bounded by the districts of Plaka to the south, Monastiraki to the west, Kolonaki to the east and Omonia to the north.

The city's two major landmarks, the Acropolis and Lykavittos Hill, can be seen from just about everywhere and are useful for getting one's bearings. The streets are clearly signposted in Greek and English.

Here's a brief introduction to the main suburbs:

Syntagma This is the central business district surrounding Syntagma Square, heart of the modern city of Athens. The square is flanked by luxury hotels, banks, airline offices and expensive coffee shops, and is dominated by the old royal palace. It was from the palace balcony that the constitution *(syntagma)* was declared on 3 September

CHRISTINE COSTE

View across Athens from Plaka towards Lykavittos Hill, the highest point in Athens

1843. The building has housed the Greek parliament since 1935.

Syntagma is a pleasant introduction to the city, despite the manic speed at which the traffic zooms around it. At its centre is a large, paved square, planted with orange, oleander and cypress trees.

Amalias is the main street heading south from the eastern side of Syntagma Square. Next to it are the National Gardens, with subtropical trees and ornamental ponds, and the more formal Zappeio Gardens. Amalias skirts the Arch of Hadrian and the Temple of Olympian Zeus and leads into Syngrou, which runs all the way to the coast at Faliro. Buses from the airport and Piraeus approach Syntagma along Amalias.

If you're arriving by bus and want to stay in Plaka, get off at Syntagma. The stop is opposite the National Gardens, just before the square.

Plaka Plaka, south of Syntagma, is the old Turkish quarter of Athens and virtually all that existed when Athens was declared the capital of independent Greece. Its narrow, labyrinthine streets nestle into the north-eastern slope of the Acropolis, and most of the city's ancient sites are close by. Plaka is touristy in the extreme. Its main streets, Kydathineon and Adrianou, are packed solid with restaurants and souvenir shops. It is the most attractive and interesting part of Athens and most visitors make it their base. The most convenient trolleybus stop is on Filellinon, near the junction with Kydathineon.

Monastiraki Monastiraki, centred on busy Plateia Monastirakiou, lies just west of Syntagma and is the city's market district. The famous Athens flea market is south-west of the square on Ifestou, while the central meat and fish market is to the north on Athinas, opposite the fruit and vegetable market. Shops along the streets bordering the markets sell cheeses, nuts, herbs, honey, dried fruits and cold meats. On Eolou most shops sell cut-price clothing and street vendors offer items such as sheets, towels, tablecloths and underwear.

Kolonaki Chic is the best way to describe the smart residential district of Kolonaki, east of Syntagma. Tucked beneath Lykavittos Hill, it has long been the favoured address of Athenian socialites; its streets are full of trendy boutiques and private art galleries, as well as dozens of trendy cafes and international restaurants.

Vasilissis Sofias, on its southern flank, was laid out by the Bavarian architects brought in by King Otho and is one of Athens' most imposing streets. Its neoclassical buildings now house museums, embassies and government offices.

Omonia Chic is not a word that springs readily to mind when describing the district of Omonia, north of Syntagma. Once one of the city's smarter areas, Omonia has gone to the dogs in recent years and is better known for its pickpockets and prostitutes than its architecture.

This can be expected to change though, with a number of high-profile projects scheduled in the lead-up to the 2004 Olympics. The main square, Plateia Omonias, long hidden behind metro construction hoardings, is due to be transformed into a giant glass dome, and big investors have been pouring money into the area. They are unlikely to tolerate the present ragbag population for long.

On a practical level, Plateia Omonias is an important transport hub. All the major streets of central Athens meet here: the two most important are El Venizelou and Stadiou, which run parallel to Syntagma, 1km to the south-east. Athens University is halfway along El Venizelou, which is more commonly known as Panepistimiou (university). Athinas heads south from Omonia to Plateia Monastirakiou; Pireos runs south-west to Piraeus; Agiou Konstantinou goes west towards the train stations; and 3 Septemvriou heads north – although the major street heading north is 28 Oktovriou-Patission, which starts 50m along Panepistimiou from the square.

continued on page 159

continued from page 152

Beyond the City Centre (Map 1)

To get a glimpse of how today's Athenians live, it's well worth exploring the streets beyond the city centre.

South of the Acropolis Plaka dwellers who want to escape the hurly burly of souvenir shops and tourist restaurants need walk no more than a few hundred metres to find relief in the quiet suburbs south of the Acropolis.

The first area you come to is Makrigianni, a trendy residential suburb occupying the southern slope of the Acropolis between Filopappos Hill and Syngrou. It has a smattering of upmarket hotels and restaurants, and is also home to the city's main gay area – occupying the belt between Makrigianni (the street) and Syngrou.

South of Makrigianni is the less risque residential district of Koukaki. To the east, on the other side of Syngrou, is the district of Mets, which has some delightful old Turkish houses. North-east of Mets is Pangrati, another pleasant residential neighbourhood.

West of Monastiraki The suburbs west of Monastiraki have undergone a remarkable transformation during the 1990s.

Thisio, to the south-west, led the way in the early 90s when young professionals started buying up the run-down area's cheap housing. It's now a thriving area full of music bars and cafes, particularly around the junction of Apostolou Pavlou and Iraklidon. Places like Stavlos, at Iraklidon 8, were pioneers of the Athens retro style of renovation – ripping out modern finishings to expose and highlight old stonework and chunky timber beams.

This style is now being taken a step further in nearby Psiri, north-west of Monastiraki. As recently as 1997, Psiri rated as 'Athens at its most clapped-out'; it still looks that way from the outside, but the maze of narrow streets within are now brimming with dozens of stylish restaurants and bars. Some sit incongruously alongside old-style shops with their bizarre arrays of bric-a-brac overflowing onto the pavements.

A new Asian quarter has emerged just north of Psiri, in the blocks west of Plateia Eleftherias. There are several Bangladeshi shops as well as cheap Asian restaurants.

North of Omonia The area to the north-west of Plateia Omonias probably rates as the sleaziest part of Athens, particularly the streets around Plateia Vathis – notorious for prostitutes. The city's main red-light area is actually farther north on Filis, near Plateia Viktorias.

Generally, though, the seediness gradually recedes as you head north from Plateia Vathis, giving way to a respectable, if characterless, neighbourhood. Athens' two train stations are at the western edge of this area, on Deligianni. The National Archaeological Museum is on the eastern side, on 28 Oktovriou-Patission.

Just south of the National Archaeological Museum is the Athens Polytehnio. This establishment has university status, with faculties of fine arts and engineering. It also has a long tradition of radical thinking and alternative culture, and led the student sit-in of 1973 in opposition to the junta.

Squashed between the Polytehnio and Strefi Hill is the student residential area of Exarhia. It's a lively area with graffiti-covered walls and lots of cheap restaurants catering for Bohemian-looking professors and crowds of rebellious-looking students.

Maps

The free map handed out by the tourist office is fine for central Athens, which is all that most visitors get to see. If you want to get serious about exploring Athens beyond the city centre, buy yourself a copy of the Athens-Piraeus *Proasteia* (street directory).

INFORMATION

Tourist Offices

Athens' main EOT tourist office (☎ 331 0561/0562, fax 325 2895, email gnto@eexi.gr) is close to Syntagma at Amerikis 2. It has information sheets and brochures on just about every topic you care to mention, including a very useful timetable of the week's ferry departures from Piraeus and information about public transport prices and schedules from Athens. It also has a useful free map of Athens, which has most of the places of interest, and the main trolleybus routes, clearly marked. The office is open 9 am to 7 pm Monday to Friday and 9.30 am to 2 pm Saturday.

The EOT office at the East Terminal of the airport (☎ 969 4500) is open 9 am to 7 pm Monday to Friday and 11 am to 5 pm Saturday.

Tourist Police

The tourist police's head office (☎ 924 2700) is at Dimitrakopoulou 77, in Koukaki. It is open 24 hours a day, but it's quite a trek from the city centre – take trolleybus No 1, 5 or 9 from Syntagma. The tourist police also have a 24 hour information service (☎ 171), for general tourist information or for emergency help – someone who speaks English is always available.

They will also act as interpreters for any dealings you might have with the crime police (☎ 770 5711/5717), Leoforos Alexandras 173, or the traffic police (☎ 524 4600), Agiou Konstantinou 28, near Omonia.

Money

Most of the major banks have branches around Plateia Syntagmatos, open Monday to Thursday 8 am to 2 pm and Friday 8 am to 1.30 pm. The National Bank of Greece on Karageorgi Servias, Syntagma, is open extended hours for foreign exchange dealings only: 3.30 to 6.30 pm Monday to Thursday; 3 to 6.30 pm on Friday; 9 am to 3 pm Saturday; and 9 am to 1 pm Sunday. It also has a 24 hour automatic exchange machine outside on Stadiou.

American Express (☎ 324 4975/4979), Ermou 2, Syntagma, is open between May and September, 8.30 am to 7 pm Monday to Friday, 8.30 am to 6 pm Saturday and 8.30 am to 1.30 pm Sunday. For the rest of the year, it's open 8.30 am to 4 pm Monday to Friday and 8.30 am to 1.30 pm Saturday.

Eurochange (☎ 322 0155) has an office at Karageorgi Servias 4, Syntagma, open 8 am to 8 pm Monday to Friday and 9 am to 8 pm weekends. Eurochange changes Thomas Cook Travellers cheques without commission.

In Plaka, Acropole Foreign Exchange, Kydathineon 23, is open 9 am to midnight daily. But it charges a hefty 2.5% commission. Ergobank, at the junction of Adrianou and Kydathineon, has a convenient ATM.

The banks at both the East and West airport terminals are open 7 am to 9 pm. The Acropole Foreign Exchange office at the East Terminal is open 24 hours.

Visa (☎ 328 3950) has an office at Lykourgou 1, Omonia.

Post

Athens' central post office (☎ 321 6023) is at Eolou 100, Omonia (postcode 102 00), just east of Plateia Omonias. Unless specified otherwise, poste restante will be sent here.

If you're staying in Plaka, it's far more convenient to get your mail sent poste restante to the large post office on Plateia Syntagmatos (postcode 103 00), on the corner of Mitropoleos.

Both are open 7.30 am to 8 pm Monday to Friday and 7.30 am to 2 pm Saturday.

Parcels for abroad that weigh over 2kg must be taken to the parcel post office (☎ 322 8940), Stadiou 4, Syntagma. The office is in the arcade that runs between Amerikis and Voukourestiou. Parcels should be taken along unwrapped for inspection.

Business communications specialist Mail Boxes Etc (☎ 324 5060, fax 324 5070 email mbeathens@interfranchise.gr), Leka 14, Syntagma, hires out private mail boxes.

Telephone

The OTE office at 28 Oktovriou-Patission 85, Omonia, is open 24 hours a day. There are also offices at Stadiou 15, Syntagma and at Athinas 50, south of Omonia, next to Klaoudatos department store; both of these offices are open 7 am to 11.30 pm daily. There is also an office at Athinas 50. Some useful telephone numbers include:

STELLA HELLANDER

Vild flowers transform Greece's hillsides in spring.

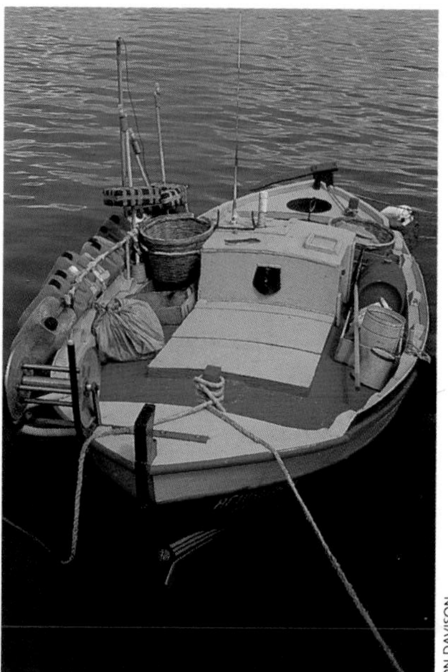
JON DAVISON

Fishing boat in Sitia, Crete

MARK DAFFEY

f that bus doesn't come soon, we'll just have to hitch a ride ...'

JM BRETTELL

The popular northern Greece resort of Parga

JON DAVISON

Catching the sun's last rays, Amorgos (Cyclades)

general telephone information	☎ 134
numbers in Athens and Attica	☎ 131
numbers elsewhere in Greece	☎ 132
international telephone information	☎ 161 or 162
international telegrams	☎ 165
domestic operator	☎ 151 or 152
domestic telegrams	☎ 155
wake-up service	☎ 182

If you simply cannot live without a mobile phone, they can be rented from Trimtel Mobile Communications (☎ 729 1964), Menandrou 9, Omonia.

Fax

You can send faxes from the post office, but you'll find better service and better prices at Mail Boxes Etc, just west of Syntagma at Leka 14. A fax to the UK costs 800 dr for the first page and 500 dr for each subsequent page. To the US it's 1100/700 dr and to Australia and New Zealand 1700/1200 dr.

Email & Internet Access

Internet cafes are popping up like mushrooms all over Athens. Most charge from 1000 dr to 1500 dr per hour of computer time, whether you're on the Net or not. The following is a list of places around the city centre:

Enydreion Net Cafe
: Syngrou 13, Makrigianni; open 7 am to midnight daily

Skynet Internet Centre
: Corner Voulis & Apollonos, Plaka; open 9.30 am to 8.30 pm Monday to Friday, 10 am to 8.30 pm Saturday

Sofokleous.com Internet Café
: Stadiou 5, Syntagma, behind Flocafé; open 10 am to 10 pm Monday to Saturday, 1 to 9 pm Sunday

Student Inn Internet Café
: Kydathineon 16, Plaka, at the Student & Travellers' Inn; open 8 am to 3 pm and 5 to 11 pm daily from June 1 to October 31. Opens at 11 am for the rest of the year.

Astor Internet Café
: Oktovriou-Patission 27, Omonia; open 10 am to 10 pm daily

The Web Café
: George 10, off Plateia Kaningos, Exarhia; open 10 am to 2 am daily

Info Café
: Ippokratous 31, Exarhia; open 8 am to 12.30 am Monday to Saturday

Museum Internet Café
: Oktovriou-Patission 46, Omonia, next to National Archaeological Museum; open 9 am to 2.30 am daily

Travel Agencies

The bulk of the city's travel agencies are around Syntagma Square, particularly just south of it on Filellinon, Nikis and Voulis. Many of these agencies employ touts to roam the area looking for custom. Give them a miss – these places are responsible for most of the rip-offs described under Travel Agents in the 'Dangers and Annoyances' boxed text later in this chapter.

Reputable agencies include STA Travel (☎ 321 1188, 321 1194, email robissa@spark.net.gr), Voulis 43, and ETOS Travel (☎ 324 1884, fax 322 8447, email usit@usitetos.gr), Filellinon 1, which is the Athens representative of the international group USIT. Both these places also issue International Student Identity Cards (ISIC), as does the International Student & Youth Travel Service (ISYTS; ☎ 323 3767), 1st floor, Nikis 11.

Magic Bus (☎ 323 7471), Filellinon 20, has some very good last-minute deals on charter flights.

North of Omonia, try Paloma Tours (☎ 823 3744, fax 822 0732), opposite the National Archaeological Museum at Marni 4. It handles international and domestic flights, and also sells cheap 30-day ferry passes for the Cycladic islands of Paros, Naxos, Ios and Santorini.

Bookshops

Athens has three good English-language bookshops. Compendium (☎ 322 1248), upstairs at Nikis 28, Plaka, has a second-hand section as well as a good selection overall. The place is also child-friendly, and holds a children's story hour at 11 am on the second and fourth Saturday of every month. The English-language notice board outside has information about jobs, accommodation and courses in Athens.

Dangers & Annoyances

Athens is a big city, and it has its fair share of the problems found in all major cities. Fortunately, violent street crime remains very rare, but travellers should be alert to the following traps:

Pickpockets

Pickpockets have become a major problem in Athens. Their favourite hunting grounds are the metro system and the crowded streets around Omonia, particularly Athinas. The Sunday market on Ermou is another place where it pays to take extra care of your valuables. There have been numerous reports of thefts from day-packs and bags.

Taxi Drivers

Many Athens residents will tell you that their taxi drivers are the biggest bunch of bastards in the world. It seems that they have as much trouble getting a fair deal as tourists do.

Most (but not all) rip-off stories involve cabs picked up late at night from the taxi ranks at the city's main arrival and departure points: the airport, the train stations, the two bus terminals – particularly Terminal A at Kifissou, and the port of Piraeus. Paying by the meter, the fare from any of the above places to the city centre shouldn't be more than 2500 dr at any time of day.

The trouble is that the cabbies who work these ranks don't like to bother with the meter, especially after midnight when most public transport stops. They prefer to demand whatever they think they can get away with. If you insist on using the meter, many will simply refuse to take you. You can either negotiate a set fare, or attempt to find a taxi elsewhere.

Every now and again, the police conduct well publicised clamp-downs. One such purge turned up an airport cabby who was well prepared for tourists who want to see the meter working – he was equipped with a handy remote-controlled device that could make the meter spin round at 2000 dr per minute!

A more common trick is to set the meter on night rate (tariff 2) during the day. Between 6 am and midnight the day rate (tariff 1) should be charged.

If there is a dispute over the fare, take the driver's number and report them to the tourist police.

Taxi Touts

Taxi drivers working in league with some of the overpriced C class hotels around Omonia are another problem. The scam involves taxi drivers picking up late night arrivals, particularly at the airport and Bus Terminal A, and persuading them that the hotel they want to go to is full – even if they have a booking. The taxi driver will pretend to phone the hotel of your choice,

You'll find the largest selection of books at Eleftheroudakis (☎ 331 4180), Panepistimiou 17, Syntagma. Eleftheroudakis has a chain of stores around Athens, including a Syntagma branch at Nikis 4 and an Omonia branch in the Minion department store. Pantelides Books (☎ 362 3673), Amerikis 11, Syntagma, stocks a range of feminist books as well as paperbacks, travel guides, maps etc. All these shops stock Lonely Planet guides.

Ippokratous, in the student suburb of Exarhia, is packed solid with bookshops. The map specialists Road Editions (☎ 361 3242) have a shop at No 39. You'll find a wide range of travel literature as well as their complete selection of maps. The

Dangers & Annoyances

announce that it's full and suggest an alternative. You can ask to speak to your chosen hotel yourself, or simply insist on going where you want.

Taxi drivers frequently attempt to claim commissions from hotel owners even if they have just gone where they were told. If the taxi driver comes into the hotel, make it clear to hotel staff that there is no reason to pay a commission.

Bar Scams

Lonely Planet continues to hear from readers who have been taken in by one of the various bar scams that operate around central Athens, particularly around Syntagma.

The basic scam runs something like this: friendly Greek approaches solo male traveller and discovers that the traveller knows little about Athens; friendly Greek then reveals that he, too, is from out of town. Why don't they go to this great little bar that he's just discovered and have a beer? They order a drink, and the equally friendly owner then offers another drink. Women appear, more drinks are provided and the visitor relaxes as he realises that the women are not prostitutes, just friendly Greeks. The crunch comes at the end of the evening when the traveller is presented with an exorbitant bill and the smiles disappear. The con men who cruise the streets playing the role of the friendly Greek can be very convincing: some people have been taken in more than once.

Other bars (see under Bars in the Entertainment section) don't bother with the acting. They target intoxicated males with talk of sex and present them with outrageous bills.

Travel Agents

Several travel agents in the Plaka/Syntagma area employ touts to patrol the streets promoting 'cheap' packages to the islands. These touts like to hang out at the bus stops on Amalias, hoping to find naive new arrivals who have no idea of prices in Greece.

Potential customers are then taken back to the agency, where slick salespeople then pressure them into buying outrageously overpriced packages. Lonely Planet regularly hears complaints from victims of this scam.

There is no need to buy a package; you will always be able to negotiate a better deal yourself when you get to the island of your choice. If you are worried that everywhere will be full, select a place from the pages of this guide and make a booking.

Slippery Surfaces

Many of Athens' pavements and other surfaces underfoot are made of marble and become incredibly slippery when wet, so if you are caught in the rain, be very careful how you tread.

foreign-language bookshop *(xenoglosso vivliopoleio)* at No 10-12 stocks books in English, French, Italian and German.

French, German, English, Italian and Spanish books are available at Kauffmann (☎ 322 2160), Stadiou 28, Syntagma, and The Booknest (☎ 323 1703), Panepistimiou 25-29, Syntagma.

International newspapers reach the *periptera* (kiosks) on Syntagma on the same day as they are published at 3 pm on weekdays and 7 pm on weekends.

Cultural Centres

Following is a list of international cultural centres located in Athens:

British Council
(☎ 363 3215) Plateia Kolonakiou 17, Kolonaki
French Institute of Athens
(☎ 362 4301) Sina 31, Pefkakia
Goethe Institute
(☎ 360 8114) Omirou 14-16, Pefkakia
Hellenic-American Union
(☎ 362 9886) Massalias 22, Pefkakia

These cultural centres hold concerts, film shows and exhibitions from time to time. Major events are listed in various English-language newspapers and magazines.

Laundry

Plaka has a convenient laundrette at Angelou Geronta 10, just off Kydathineon near the outdoor restaurants. It is also the cheapest, charging 2000 dr to wash and dry 5kg. Others are at Psaron 9 near Plateia Karaïskaki (2500 dr), at Kolokinthous 41 on the corner of Leonidou (both in Omonia) and at Erehthiou 9 in Koukaki (2500 dr).

Toilets

Public toilets are a rarity in Athens – and those that do exist are so primitive that they are best avoided except in an absolute emergency. Fortunately there are fast-food outlets everywhere in Central Athens: very handy in an emergency. Failing that, head to a cafe, although you'll be expected to buy something for the privilege of using the facilities.

Left Luggage

Many of Athens' hotels will store luggage free for guests, although a lot of them do no more than pile the bags in a hallway. Pacific Travel (☎ 324 1007), Nikis 26, Plaka, charges 500 dr per day, 1500 dr per week and 3000 dr per month. Opening hours are 8 am to 8 pm Monday to Saturday, 8 am to 2 pm Sunday and holidays.

Emergency

The police emergency number is ☎ 100. For the fire brigade ring ☎ 199. For emergency medical treatment ring the tourist police (☎ 171) and they will tell you the location of the nearest hospital. Hospitals give free emergency treatment to tourists. For hospitals with outpatient departments on duty, call ☎ 106; for the telephone number of an on-call doctor, ring ☎ 105 (2 pm to 7 am); for a pharmacy open 24 hours call ☎ 107; and for first-aid advice phone ☎ 166. US citizens can ring ☎ 721 2951 for emergency medical aid.

Some travellers have recommended SOS Doctors (☎ 322 0046/0015), a 24 hour call-out service employing doctors who speak English and a range of other languages. They charge about 20,000 dr for a call.

WALKING TOUR

This walk takes in most of Plaka's main sites. It involves about 45 minutes' walking, but can take up to four hours if you linger and allow yourself to be lured into a few detours. Plaka is a fascinating place to explore, full of surprises tucked away in the labyrinthine streets that weave over the undulating terrain. The route is marked on Map 2.

The walk begins at **Plateia Syntagmatos**. This square has been a favourite place for protests and rallies ever since the rally that led to the granting of a constitution on 3 September 1843, declared by King Otho from the balcony of the royal palace. In 1944 the first round of the civil war began here after police opened fire on a rally organised by the communists. Known as the Dekembriana (events of December), it was followed by a month of fierce fighting between the communist resistance and the British forces. In 1954 the first demonstration demanding the *enosis* (union) of Cyprus with Greece took place here. At election time, political parties stage their rallies in the square and most protest marches end up here.

Flanking the eastern side of Syntagma Square is the former royal palace, now the **parliament building**. The palace, designed by the Bavarian architect Von Gartner, was built in 1836-42. The building remained the royal palace until 1935, when it became the seat of the Greek parliament. (The royal family moved to a new palace on the corner of Vasileos Konstantinou and Herod Atticus, which became the presidential palace upon the abolition of the monarchy in 1974.)

The parliament building is guarded by the much-photographed *evzones* (guards traditionally from the village of Evzoni in Macedonia). Their somewhat incongruous uniform of short kilts and pom-pom shoes is the butt of much mickey-taking by sightseers. Their uniform is based on the attire worn by the *klephts*, the mountain fighters who battled so ferociously in the War of Independence. Every Sunday at 11 am the evzones perform a full changing-of-the-guard ceremony.

Standing with your back to the parliament building you will see ahead of you, to the right, the **Hotel Grande Bretagne**. This, the grandest of Athens' hotels, was built in 1862 as a 60-room mansion to accommodate visiting dignitaries. In 1872 it was converted into a hotel and became the place where the crowned heads of Europe and eminent politicians stayed. The Nazis made it their headquarters during WWII. The hotel was the scene of an attempt to blow up the British prime minister Winston Churchill on Christmas Eve 1944 while he was in Athens to discuss the Dekembriana fighting. A bomb was discovered in the hotel sewer.

At the time of writing, it was not possible to cross over Amalias and walk through the middle of the square because of the metro works. Instead, cross Amalias and follow Othonos, on the southern flank of the square, down to Mitropoleos, which starts at the post office. Take the first turn left into Nikis, and walk southwards to the crossroads with Kydathineon, a pedestrian walkway and one of Plaka's main thoroughfares.

Turn right and a little way along you will come to the **Church of Metamorphosis** on Plateia Satiros; opposite is the **Museum of Greek Folk Art**. Continue along here, and after Plateia Filomousou Eterias (usually known as Plateia Plakas), the square with the outdoor tavernas, turn left into Adrianou, another of Plaka's main thoroughfares. At the end, turn right, and this will bring you to the square with the **Choregic Monument of Lysicrates**. (The name *choregos* was given to the wealthy citizens who financed choral and dramatic performances.) This monument was built in 334 BC to commemorate a win in a choral festival. An inscription on the architrave states:

> Lysicrates of Kykyna, son of Lysitheides, was choregos; the tribe of Akamantis won the victory with a chorus of boys; Theon played the flute; Lysiades of Athens trained the chorus; Euainetos was arhon.

The reliefs on the monument depict the battle between Dionysos and the Tyrrhenian pirates, whom the god had transformed into dolphins. It is the earliest known monument using Corinthian capitals externally. It stands in a cordoned-off archaeological site which is part of the **Street of Tripods**. It was here that winners of ancient dramatic and choral contests dedicated their tripod trophies to Dionysos.

In the 19th century, the monument was incorporated into the library of a French Capuchin convent, in which Lord Byron stayed in 1810-11 and wrote *Childe Harold*. The convent was destroyed by fire in 1890. Recent excavations around the monument have revealed the foundations of other choragic monuments.

Facing the monument, turn left and then right into Epimenidou. At the top of the steps, turn right into Stratonos, which skirts the Acropolis. A left fork after 150m leads to the highest part of Plaka, an area called **Anafiotika**. The little whitewashed cube houses are the legacy of the people from the small Cycladic island of Anafi who were used as cheap labour in the building of Athens after Independence. It's a beautiful spot, with brightly painted olive-oil cans brimming with flowers bedecking the walls of the tiny gardens in summer.

The path winds between the houses and comes to some steps on the right, at the bottom of which is a curving pathway leading downhill to Pratiniou. Turn left at Pratiniou and veer right after 50m into Tholou. The yellow-ochre building with brown shutters at No 5 is the old university, built by the Venetians. The Turks used it as public offices and it was Athens University from 1837 to 1841. It is now the **Museum of the University**, and its displays include some wonderful, old anatomical drawings and gruesome-looking surgical instruments. It is open 2.30 to 7 pm Monday and Wednesday, and 9.30 am to 2.30 pm Tuesday, Thursday and Friday. Admission is free.

At the end of Tholou, turn left into Panos. At the top of the steps on the left is a restored 19th century mansion which is now the **Paul & Alexandra Kanellopoulos Museum**. It houses the family's eclectic private collection and is open 8 am to 2.30 pm Tuesday to Sunday; admission is 500 dr.

Retracing your steps, go down Panos to the ruins of the **Roman Agora**, then turn left into Polygnotou and walk to the crossroads. Opposite, Polygnotou continues to the **Ancient Agora.** (Further details of these agora, or markets, are given later in this chapter.)

At the crossroads, turn right and then left into Peikilis, then immediately right into Areos. On the right are the remains of the **Library of Hadrian** and next to it is the **Museum of Traditional Greek Ceramics**, open 10 am to 2 pm Wednesday to Monday. Admission is 500 dr. The museum is housed in the Mosque of Tzistarakis, built in 1759. After Independence it lost its minaret and was used as a prison.

Ahead is **Plateia Monastirakiou**, named after the small church. To the left is the metro station and the **flea market**. Plateia Monastirakiou is Athens at its noisiest, most colourful and chaotic. It teems with street vendors selling nuts, coconut sticks and fruit.

Turn right just beyond the mosque into Pandrossou. This street is a relic of the old Turkish bazaar. Today it is full of souvenir shops, selling everything from cheap kitsch to high-class jewellery and clothes. The street is named after King Cecrops' daughter, Pandrosos, who was the first priestess of Athens. At No 89 is Stavros Melissinos, the 'poet sandal-maker' of Athens who names the Beatles, Rudolph Nureyev and Jackie Onassis among his customers. Fame and fortune have not gone to his head, however – he still makes the best-value sandals in Athens, costing 3000 dr to 5000 dr per pair.

Pandrossou leads to **Plateia Mitropoleos** and the **Athens Cathedral**. The cathedral has little architectural merit, which isn't surprising considering that it was constructed from the masonry of over 50 razed churches and from the designs of several architects. Next to it stands the much smaller, and far more appealing, **Church of Agios Eleftherios**, which was once the cathedral. Turn left after the cathedral, and then right into Mitropoleos and follow it back to Syntagma.

THE ACROPOLIS (MAP 6)

Athens exists because of the Acropolis, the most important ancient monument in the western world. Crowned by the Parthenon, it stands sentinel over Athens, visible from almost everywhere within the city. Its monuments of Pentelic marble gleam white in the midday sun and gradually take on a honey hue as the sun sinks. At night they are floodlit and seem to hover above the city. No matter how harassed you may become in Athens, a sudden unexpected glimpse of this magnificent sight cannot fail to lift your spirits.

Inspiring as these monuments are, they are but faded remnants of Pericles' city, and it takes a great leap of the imagination to begin to comprehend the splendour of his creations. Pericles spared no expense – only the best materials, architects, sculptors and artists were good enough for a city dedicated to the cult of Athena, tutelary goddess of Athens. The city was a showcase of colossal buildings, lavishly coloured and gilded, and of gargantuan statues, some of bronze, others of marble plated with gold and encrusted with precious stones.

Visiting the Site

From 1 April to 31 October, the Acropolis archaeological site (☎ 321 0219) is open 8 am to 7 pm daily. The Acropolis **museum** opens the same hours except on Monday, when it opens at noon. For the rest of the year, both site and museum are open 8 am to 2.30 pm daily. The combined admission fee is 2000 dr, or 1000 dr for students.

There is only one entrance to the Acropolis, but there are several approaches to this entrance. The main approach from the north is along the path that is a continuation of Dioskouron in the south-west corner of Plaka. From the south, you can either walk or take bus No 230 along Dionysiou Areopagitou to just beyond the Theatre of Herodes Atticus, where a path leads to the entrance.

The crowds that swarm over the Acropolis need to be seen to be believed. It's best to get there as early in the day as possible. You need to wear shoes with good soles because the paths around the site are uneven and very slippery.

History

The Acropolis (high city) was first inhabited in Neolithic times. The first temples were built during the Mycenaean era in homage to the goddess Athena. People lived on the Acropolis until the late 6th century BC, but in 510 BC the Delphic oracle declared that it should be the province of the gods.

After all the buildings on the Acropolis were reduced to ashes by the Persians on the eve of the Battle of Salamis (480 BC), Pericles set about his ambitious rebuilding program. He transformed the Acropolis into a city of temples which has come to be regarded as the zenith of classical Greek achievement.

All four of the surviving monuments of the Acropolis have received their fair share of battering through the ages. Ravages inflicted upon them during the years of foreign occupation, pilfering by foreign

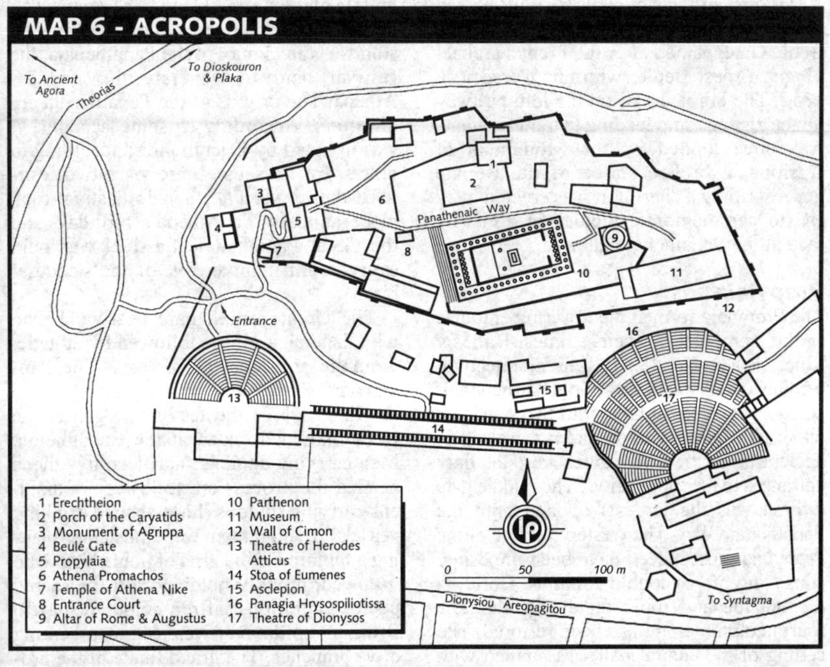

archaeologists, inept renovation following independence, visitors' footsteps and earthquakes have all taken their toll. The year 1687 was a particularly bad one. The Venetians attacked the Turks and opened fire on the Acropolis, causing an explosion in the Parthenon, where the Turks were storing gunpowder. The resulting fire blazed for two days, damaging all the buildings.

However, the most recent menace, acid rain, caused by industrial pollution and traffic fumes, is proving to be the most irreversibly destructive. It is dissolving the very marble of which the monuments are built. Major renovation work is taking place in an effort to save the monuments for future generations, and the site now boasts a World Heritage Site listing.

Beulé Gate & Monument of Agrippa

Once you've bought your ticket for the Acropolis and have walked a little way along the path, you will see on your left the Beulé Gate, named after the French archaeologist Ernest Beulé, who uncovered it in 1852. The 8m pedestal on the left, halfway up the zigzag ramp leading to the Propylaia, was once topped by the Monument of Agrippa, a bronze statue of the Roman general riding a chariot. It was erected in 27 BC to commemorate victory in a chariot race at the Panathenaic games.

Propylaia

The Propylaia formed the towering entrance to the Acropolis in ancient times. Built by Mnesicles in 437-432 BC, its architectural brilliance ranks with that of the Parthenon. It consists of a central hall, with two wings on either side. Each section had a gate, and in ancient times these five gates were the only entrances to the 'upper city'. The middle gate (which was the largest) opened onto the Panathenaic Way. The western portico of the Propylaia must indeed have been imposing, consisting of six double columns, Doric on the outside and Ionic on the inside. The fourth column along has been restored. The ceiling of the central hall was painted with gold stars on a dark blue background. The northern wing was used as a picture gallery *(pinakotheke)* and the south wing was the antechamber to the Temple of Athena Nike.

The Propylaia is aligned with the Parthenon – the earliest example of a building designed in relation to another. It remained intact until the 13th century when various occupiers started adding to it. It was badly damaged in the 17th century when a lightning strike set off an explosion in a Turkish gunpowder store. Heinrich Schliemann paid for the removal of one of its appendages – a Frankish tower – in the 19th century. Reconstruction took place between 1909 and 1917 and there was further restoration after WWII. Once you're through the Propylaia, there is a stunning view of the Parthenon ahead.

Panathenaic Way

The Panathenaic Way, which cuts across the middle of the Acropolis, was the route taken by the Panathenaic procession. The procession was the climax of the Panathenaia, the festival held to venerate the goddess Athena. The origins of the Panathenaia are uncertain. According to some accounts it was initiated by Erichthonius; according to others, by Theseus. There were two festivals: the Lesser Panathenaic Festival took place annually on Athena's birthday, and the Great Panathenaic Festival was held every fourth anniversary of the goddess' birth.

The Great Panathenaic Festival began with dancing and was followed by athletic, dramatic and musical contests. The Panathenaic procession, which took place on the final day of the festival, began at the Keramikos and ended at the Erechtheion. Men carrying animals sacrificed to Athena headed the procession, followed by maidens carrying rhytons (horn-shaped drinking vessels). Behind them were musicians playing a fanfare for the girls of noble birth who followed, proudly holding aloft the sacred peplos (a glorious saffron-coloured shawl). Bringing up the rear were old men bearing olive branches. The grand finale of the procession was the placing of the peplos on the statue of Athena Polias in the Erechtheion.

Temple of Athena Nike

On the right after leaving the Propylaia, there is a good view back to the exquisitely proportioned little Temple of Athena Nike (closed to visitors). It stands on a platform perched atop the steep south-west edge of the Acropolis, overlooking the Saronic Gulf. The temple, designed by Callicrates, was built of Pentelic marble in 427-424 BC.

The building is almost square, with four graceful Ionic columns at either end. Its frieze, of which only fragments remain, consisted of scenes from mythology on the east and south sides, and scenes from the Battle of Plataea (479 BC) and Athenians fighting Boeotians and Persians on the other sides. Parts of the frieze are in the Acropolis Museum. The platform was surrounded by a marble parapet of relief sculptures; some of these are also in the museum, including the beautiful sculpture of Athena Nike fastening her sandal.

The temple housed a statue of the goddess Athena. In her right hand was a pomegranate (symbol of fertility) and in her left, a helmet (symbol of war). The temple was dismantled in 1686 by the Turks, who positioned a huge cannon on the platform. It was carefully reconstructed between 1836 and 1842, but was taken to pieces again in 1936 because the platform was crumbling. The platform was reinforced and the temple rebuilt.

Statue of Athena Promachos

In ancient times, only the pediment of the Parthenon was visible from the Propylaia; the rest was obscured by numerous statues and two sacred buildings.

Continuing ahead along the Panathenaic Way you will see, to your left, the foundations of pedestals for the statues which once lined the path. One of them, about 15m beyond the Propylaia, is the foundation of the gigantic statue of Athena Promachos (*promachos* means 'champion'). The 9m-high statue was the work of Pheidias, and symbolised Athenian invincibility against the Persians. The helmeted goddess held a shield in her left hand and a spear in her right. The statue was carted off to Constantinople by Emperor Theodosius in 426 AD. By 1204 it had lost its spear, so the hand appeared to be gesturing. This led the inhabitants to believe that the statue had beckoned the crusaders to the city, so they smashed it to pieces.

Parthenon

You have now reached the Parthenon, the monument which more than any other epitomises the glory of ancient Greece. The name Parthenon means 'virgin's apartment'. It is the largest Doric temple ever completed in Greece, and the only one to be built completely (apart from its wooden roof) of Pentelic marble. It is built on the highest part of the Acropolis, halfway between the eastern and western boundaries.

The Parthenon had a dual purpose – to house the great statue of Athena commissioned by Pericles, and to serve as a treasury for the tribute money which had been moved from Delos. It was built on the site of at least four earlier temples, all dedicated to the worship of Athena. It was designed by Ictinus and Callicrates, under the surveillance of Pheidias, to be the pre-eminent monument of the Acropolis. Building began in 447 BC and was completed in time for the Great Panathenaic Festival of 438 BC.

The temple consisted of eight fluted Doric columns at either end and 17 on each side. To achieve perfect form, its lines were ingeniously curved in order to counteract inharmonious optical illusions. As a result the foundations are slightly concave and the columns slightly convex, to make both look straight. Supervised by Pheidias, the sculptors Agoracritos and Alcamenes worked on the pediments and the sculpted sections of the frieze (metopes). All of the sculptures they created were brightly coloured and gilded. There were 92 metopes, 44 statues and a frieze which went all the way around.

The metopes on the eastern side depicted Athenians fighting giants *(gigantions)*, and on the western side Theseus leading the Athenians into battle against the Amazons.

Those on the southern side represented the contest of the Lapiths and Centaurs at the marriage feast of Pierithoös. An Ionic frieze 159.5m long ran all around the Parthenon. Much of it was damaged in the explosion of 1687, but the greatest existing part (over 75m) consists of the much publicised Elgin Marbles, now in the British Museum in London. The British Government continues to scorn Greek requests for their return.

The ceiling of the Parthenon, like that of the Propylaia, was painted blue and gilded with stars. At the eastern end was the cella (inner room of a temple), the holy of holies, into which only a few privileged initiates could enter.

Here stood the statue for which the temple was built – the **Athena Polias** (Athena of the City), which was considered one of the wonders of the ancient world. The statue was designed by Pheidias and completed in 432 BC. It was made of gold plate over an inner wooden frame, and stood almost 12m high on its pedestal. The face, hands and feet were made of ivory, and the eyes were fashioned from jewels. The goddess was clad in a long dress of gold with the head of Medusa carved in ivory on the breast. In her right hand, she held a statuette of Nike – the goddess of victory – and in her left a spear; at the base of the spear was a serpent. On her head she wore a helmet, on top of which was a sphinx with griffins in relief at either side.

In 426 BC the statue was taken to Constantinople, where it disappeared. There is a Roman copy (the Athena Varvakeion) in the National Archaeological Museum.

Erechtheion

Although the Parthenon was the most impressive monument of the Acropolis, it was more of a showpiece than a sanctuary. That role fell to the Erechtheion, built on the part of the Acropolis that was held most sacred. It was here that Poseidon struck the ground with his trident and that Athena produced the olive tree. The temple is named after Erichthonius, a mythical king of

TAMSIN WILSON

The Parthenon, epitomising all that was ancient Greece, rises above Athens

Athens. It housed the cults of Athena, Poseidon and Erichthonius.

If you follow the Panathenaic Way around the northern portico of the Parthenon, you will see the Erechtheion to your left. It is immediately recognisable by the six larger-than-life maidens who take the place of columns to support its southern portico, its much-photographed **Caryatids**. They are so called because the models for them were women from Karyai (modern-day Karyes) in Lakonia.

The Erechtheion was part of Pericles' plan for the Acropolis, but the project was postponed after the outbreak of the Peloponnesian Wars, and work did not start until 421 BC, eight years after his death. It is thought to have been completed in 406 BC.

The Erechtheion is architecturally the most unusual monument of the Acropolis. Whereas the Parthenon is considered the supreme example of Doric architecture, the Erechtheion is considered the supreme example of Ionic. Ingeniously built on several levels to counteract the unevenness of the ground, it consists of three basic parts – the main temple, northern porch and southern porch – all with different dimensions.

CHRISTINE COSTE

The graceful Caryatids look out over Athens from the Erechtheion's southern portico

The main temple is of the Ionic order and is divided into two cellae, one dedicated to Athena, the other to Poseidon. Thus the temple represents a reconciliation of the two deities after their contest. In Athena's cella stood an olive-wood statue of Athena Polias holding a shield on which was a gorgon's head. The statue was illuminated by a golden lantern placed at its feet. It was this statue on which the sacred peplos was placed at the culmination of the Panathenaic Festival.

The northern porch consists of six graceful Ionic columns; on the floor are the fissures supposedly cleft by Poseidon's trident. This porch leads into the **Temenos of Pandrossos**, where, according to mythology, the sacred olive brought forth by Athena grew. To the south of here was the **Cecropion** – King Cecrops' burial place.

The southern porch is that of the Caryatids, which prop up a heavy roof of Pentelic marble. The ones you see are plaster casts – the originals (except for one removed by Lord Elgin) are in the site's museum.

Acropolis Museum

The museum at the south-east corner of the Acropolis houses a collection of sculptures and reliefs from the site. The rooms are organised in chronological order, starting with finds from the temples that predated the Parthenon and were destroyed by the Persians. They include the pedimental sculptures of Heracles slaying the Lernaian Hydra and of a lioness devouring a bull, both in Room I.

The Kora (maiden) statues in Room IV are regarded as the museum's prize exhibits. Most date from the 6th century BC and were uncovered from a pit on the Acropolis, where the Athenians buried them after the Battle of Salamis. The statues were votives dedicated to Athena, each once holding an offering to the goddess. The earliest of these Kora statues are quite stiff and formal in comparison with the later ones, which have flowing robes and elaborate headdresses.

Room VIII contains the few pieces of the Parthenon's frieze that escaped the clutches of Lord Elgin. They depict the Olympians at the Panathenaic procession. It also holds the relief of Athena Nike adjusting her sandal. Room IX is home to four of the five surviving Caryatids, safe behind a perspex screen. The fifth is in the British Museum.

SOUTHERN SLOPE OF THE ACROPOLIS (MAP 6)

The entrance to the southern slope of the Acropolis is on Dionysiou Areopagitou. The site (☎ 322 4625) is open 8.30 am to 2.30 pm daily. Admission is 500 dr.

Theatre of Dionysos

The importance of theatre in the life of the Athenian city-state can be gauged from the dimensions of the enormous Theatre of Dionysos on the south-eastern slope of the Acropolis.

The first theatre on this site was a timber structure erected sometime during the 6th century BC, after the tyrant Peisistratos had introduced the Festival of the Great Dionysia to Athens. This festival, which took place in March or April, consisted of contests where men clad in goatskins sang and performed dances. Everyone attended, and the watching of performances was punctuated by feasting, revelry and generally letting rip.

During the golden age in the 5th century BC, the annual festival had become one of the major events on the calendar. Politicians would sponsor the production of dramas by writers such as Aeschylus, Sophocles and Euripides, with some light relief provided by the bawdy comedies of Aristophanes. People came from all over Attica, their expenses met by the state – if only present-day governments were as generous to the arts!

The theatre was reconstructed in stone and marble by Lycurgus between 342 and 326 BC. The auditorium had a seating capacity of 17,000, spread over 64 tiers of seats, of which about 20 survive. Apart from the front row, the seats were built of Piraeus limestone and were occupied by ordinary citizens, although women were confined to the back rows. The front row consisted of 67 thrones built of Pentelic marble, which were reserved for festival officials and important priests. The grandest was in the centre and reserved for the Priest of Dionysos, who sat shaded from the sun under a canopy. The seat can be identified by well preserved lion-claw feet at either side. In Roman times, the theatre was also used for state events and ceremonies as well as for performances.

The reliefs at the rear of the stage, mostly of headless figures, depict the exploits of Dionysos and date from the 2nd century BC. The two hefty, hunched-up guys who have managed to keep their heads are *selini*. Selini were worshippers of the mythical Selinos, the debauched father of the satyrs, whose chief attribute seems to have been an outsized phallus. His favourite pastime was charging up mountains in lecherous pursuit of nymphs. He was also Dionysos' mentor.

Asclepion & Stoa of Eumenes

Directly above the Theatre of Dionysos, wooden steps lead up to a pathway. On the left at the top of the steps is the Asclepion, which was built around a sacred spring. The worship of Asclepius, the physician son of Apollo, began in Epidaurus and was introduced to Athens in 429 BC at a time when plague was sweeping the city.

Beneath the Asclepion is the Stoa of Eumenes, a long colonnade built by Eumenes II, King of Pergamum (197-159 BC), as a shelter and promenade for theatre audiences.

Theatre of Herodes Atticus

The path continues west from the Asclepion to the Theatre of Herodes Atticus, built in 161 AD. Herodes Atticus was a wealthy Roman who built the theatre in memory of his wife Regilla. It was excavated in 1857-58 and completely restored in 1950-61. There are performances of drama, music and dance here during the Athens Festival. The theatre is open to the public only during performances.

Panagia Hrysospiliotissa

If you retrace your steps back to the Theatre of Dionysos, you will see an indistinct rock-strewn path leading to a grotto in the cliff face. In 320 BC, Thrasyllos turned the grotto into a temple dedicated to Dionysos. Now it is the tiny Panagia Hrysospiliotissa (Chapel of our Lady of the Cavern). It is a poignant little place with old pictures and icons on the walls. Above the chapel are two Ionic columns, the remains of Thrasyllos' temple.

ANCIENT AGORA (MAP 7)

The Agora (market) was Athens' meeting place in ancient times. It was the focal point of administrative, commercial and political life, not to mention social activity. All roads led to the Agora, and it was a lively, crowded place. Socrates spent a lot of time here expounding his philosophy, and in 49 AD St Paul disputed daily in the Agora, intent upon winning converts to Christianity.

The site was first developed in the 6th century BC. It was devastated by the Persians in 480 BC, but a new agora was built in its place almost immediately. It was flourishing by Pericles' time and continued to do so until 267 AD, when it was destroyed by the Herulians, a Gothic tribe from Scandinavia. The Turks built a residential quarter on the site, but this was demolished by archaeologists after Independence. If they'd had their way the archaeologists would have also knocked down the whole of Plaka, which was also Turkish. The area has been excavated to classical and, in parts, Neolithic levels.

The main monuments are the Temple of Hephaestus, the Stoa of Attalos and the Church of the Holy Apostles.

The site is bounded by Areopagus Hill in the south, the Athens-Piraeus metro line to the north, Plaka to the east and Leoforos Apostolou Pavlou to the west. There are several entrances, but the most convenient is the southern entrance at the western end of Polygnotou (see the Walking Tour section earlier). The Ancient Agora (☎ 321 0185) is open 8.30 am to 3 pm Tuesday to Sunday; admission costs 1200 dr.

Stoa of Attalos

The Agora Museum in the reconstructed Stoa of Attalos is a good place to start if you want to make any sense of the site. The museum has a model of the Agora upstairs as well as a collection of finds from the site.

The original stoa was built by King Attalos II of Pergamum (159-138 BC). It was two storeys high with two aisles, and housed expensive shops. A popular stamping ground for wealthy Athenians, people also gathered here to watch the Panathenaic procession, which crossed in front of the stoa.

It was authentically reconstructed in 1953-56 by the American School of Archaeology. The reconstruction deviates from the original in only one detail: the facade has been left in natural Pentelic marble, but it was originally painted red and blue. The stoa has a series of 45 columns which are Doric on the ground floor and Ionic on the upper gallery.

Temple of Hephaestus

This temple on the western edge of the Agora was surrounded by foundries and metalwork shops, and was dedicated to Hephaestus, god of the forge. It was one of the first buildings of Pericles' rebuilding program and is the best preserved Doric temple in Greece. Built in 449 BC by Ictinus, one of the architects of the Parthenon, it has 34 columns and a frieze on the eastern side depicting nine of the Twelve Labours of Heracles. In 1300 AD it was converted into the **Church of Agios Georgios**. The last service held here was on 13 December 1834 in honour of King Otho's arrival in Athens.

Unlike the Parthenon, the monument does not evoke a sense of wonder, but it's nevertheless a pleasant place to wander around. The garden that surrounds the temple has been reconstructed to resemble the Roman garden that existed there in antiquity.

To the north-east of the temple are the foundations of the **Stoa of Zeus Eleutherios**, one of the places where Socrates expounded his philosophy. Farther north are the foundations of the **Stoa of Basileios** and the **Stoa Poikile** (Painted Stoa), both

MAP 7 - ANCIENT AGORA

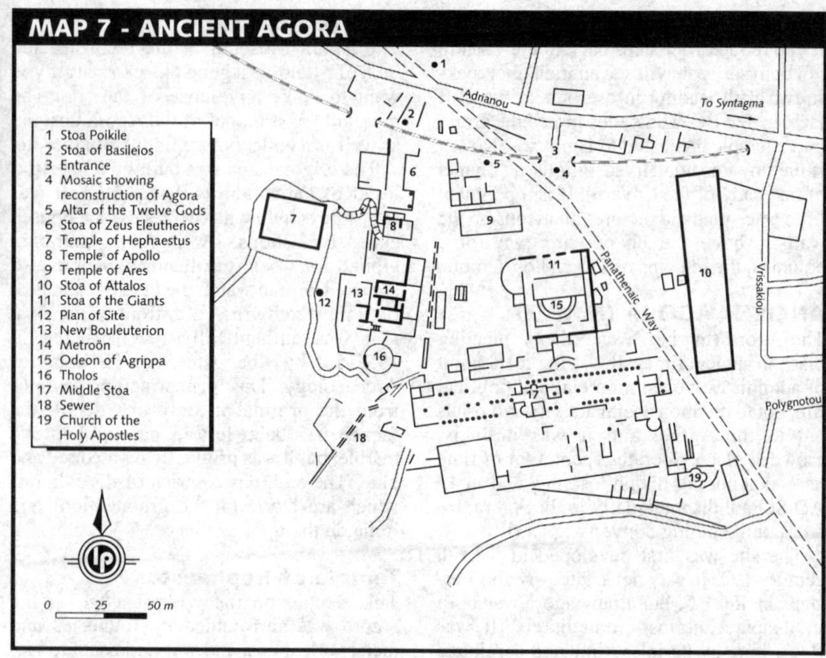

currently inaccessible to the public. The Stoa Poikile was so called because of its murals, painted by the leading artists of the day and depicting mythological and historical battles. At the end of the 4th century BC, Zeno taught his Stoic philosophy here.

To the south-east of the Temple of Hephaestus was the **New Bouleuterion**, or council house, where the Senate (originally created by Solon) met. To the south of here was the circular **Tholos** where the heads of government met.

Church of the Holy Apostles

This charming little church, which stands near the southern entrance, was built in the early 11th century to commemorate St Paul's teaching in the Agora. In 1954-57 it was stripped of its 19th century additions and restored to its original form. It contains some fine Byzantine frescoes.

THE KERAMIKOS (MAP 1)

The Keramikos was the city's cemetery from the 12th century BC to Roman times. It was discovered in 1861 during the construction of Pireos, the street which leads to Piraeus. Despite its location on the seedier part of Ermou, beyond Monastiraki, it is one of the most green and tranquil of Athens' ancient sites. The entrance to the site (☎ 346 3552) is at Ermou 148. It is open 8 am to 2.30 pm Tuesday to Sunday, and entry is 500 dr.

Sacred & Dipylon Gates

Once you have entered the site, head for the small knoll ahead and to the right, to find a plan of the site. A path leads down to the right from the knoll to the remains of the city wall, which was built by Themistocles in 479 BC, and rebuilt by Konon in 394 BC. The wall is broken by the foundations of two gates (see Map 8 – Ancient Athens).

The first, the Sacred Gate, spanned the Sacred Way and was the one by which pilgrims from Eleusis entered the city during the annual Eleusian procession. The second, the Dipylon Gate, to the north-east of the Sacred Gate, was the city's main entrance and was where the Panathenaic procession began. It was also the stamping ground of the city's prostitutes, who gathered there to offer their services to jaded travellers.

From a platform outside the Dipylon Gate, Pericles gave his famous speech extolling the virtues of Athens and honouring those who died in the first year of the Peloponnesian Wars. The speech stirred many more to battle – and to their deaths.

Between the Sacred and the Dipylon gates are the foundations of the **Pompeion**. This building was used as a dressing room for participants in the Panathenaic procession.

Street of Tombs

The Street of Tombs leads off the Sacred Way to the left as you head away from the city. This avenue was reserved for the tombs of Athens' most prominent citizens. The surviving stelae are now in the National Archaeological Museum, and what you see are replicas. They consist of an astonishing array of funerary monuments, and their bas-reliefs warrant more than a cursory examination.

Ordinary citizens were buried in the areas bordering the Street of Tombs. One very well preserved stele shows a little girl with her pet dog. You will find it by going up the stone steps on the northern side of the Street of Tombs. The site's largest stele, that of sisters Demetria and Pamphile, is on the path running from the south-east corner of the Street of Tombs. Pamphile is seated beside a standing Demetria.

Oberlaender Museum

The site's Oberlaender Museum is named after its benefactor, Gustav Oberlaender, a German-American stocking manufacturer. It contains stelae and sculpture from the site, as well as an impressive collection of vases and terracotta figurines. The museum is to the left of the site entrance.

ROMAN ATHENS

All the sites covered in this section appear on Map 8 (Ancient Athens), as well as on individual maps as indicated here.

Tower of the Winds & Roman Agora (Map 2)

These are next to one another to the east of the Ancient Agora and north of the Acropolis.

The well preserved Tower of the Winds was built in the 1st century BC by a Syrian astronomer named Andronicus. The octagonal monument of Pentelic marble is an ingenious construction which functioned as a sundial, weather vane, water clock and compass. Each side represents a point of the compass, and has a relief of a figure floating through the air, which depicts the wind associated with that particular point. Beneath each of the reliefs are the faint markings of sundials. The weather vane, which disappeared long ago, was a bronze Triton that revolved on top of the tower. The Turks, not ones to let a good building go to waste, allowed dervishes to use the tower.

The entrance to the Roman Agora is through the well preserved **Gate of Athena Archegetis**, which is flanked by four Doric columns. It was erected sometime in the 1st century AD and financed by Julius Caesar.

The rest of the Roman Agora appears to the layperson as little more than a heap of rubble. To the right of the entrance are the foundations of a 1st century public latrine. In the south-east area are the foundations of a propylon and a row of shops.

The site (☎ 324 5220) is open 8.30 am to 2.30 pm Tuesday to Sunday. Admission is 500 dr.

Arch of Hadrian (Map 4)

The Roman emperor Hadrian had a great affection for Athens. Although, like all Roman emperors, he did his fair share of spiriting its classical artwork to Rome, he also embellished the city with many monuments influenced by classical architecture. Grandiose as these monuments are, they lack the refinement and artistic flair of their classical predecessors.

The Arch of Hadrian is a lofty monument of Pentelic marble, now blackened by the effluent of exhausts, which stands where traffic-clogged Vasilissis Olgas and Amalias meet. It was erected by Hadrian in 132 AD, probably to commemorate the consecration of the Temple of Olympian Zeus (see the following section). The inscriptions show

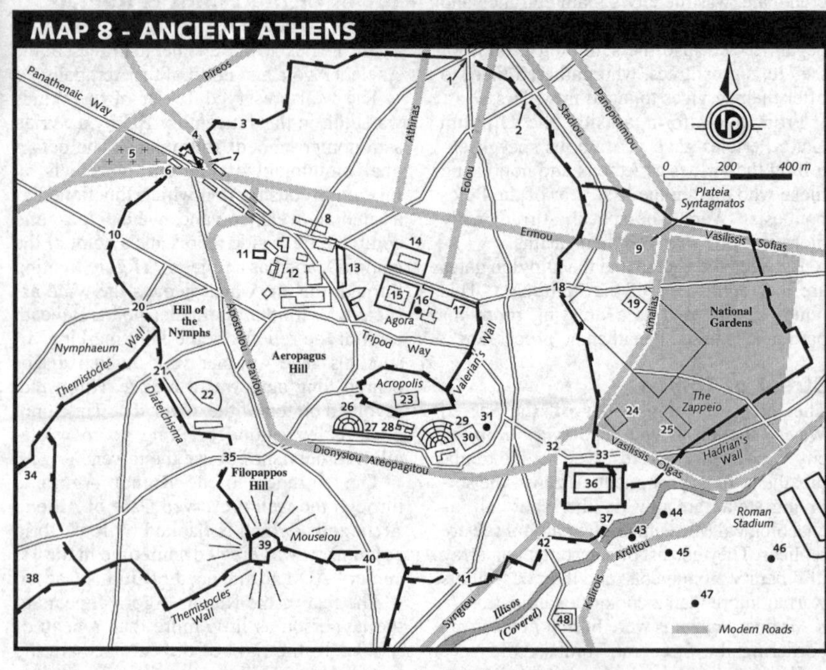

ANCIENT ATHENS

1 Acharnian Gate
2 North-East Gate
3 Eriai Gate
4 Dipylon Gate
5 Keramikos
6 Sacred Gate
7 Pompeion
8 Stoa Poikile
9 Garden of Theophrastos
10 Peiraic Gate
11 Temple of Hephaestus
12 Metroön
13 Stoa of Attalos
14 Library of Hadrian
15 Roman Agora
16 Tower of the Winds
17 Pantheon
18 Diochares Gate
19 Lyceum
20 Demian Gate
21 Melitides Gate
22 Pnyx
23 Parthenon
24 Gymnasium
25 Baths
26 Theatre of Herodes Atticus
27 Stoa of Eumenes
28 Asclepion
29 Theatre of Dionysos
30 Odeon of Pericles
31 Monument of Lysicrates
32 Arch of Hadrian
33 Hippades Gate
34 Northern Long Wall to Piraeus
35 Dipylon above Gate
36 Temple of Olympian Zeus
37 Diomeian Gate
38 Southern Long Wall
39 Monument of Filopappos
40 South Gate
41 Halade Gate
42 Itonian Gate
43 Kallirhoë Fountain
44 Agrai Metroön
45 Artemis Agrotera
46 Ardettos Hill
47 Poseidon Heliconios
48 Hadrian's Gymnasium

that it was also intended as a dividing point between the ancient city and the Roman city. The north-west frieze bears the inscription 'This is Athens, the Ancient city of Theseus'; while the south-east frieze states 'This is the city of Hadrian, and not of Theseus'.

Temple of Olympian Zeus (Map 4)

This is the largest temple in Greece and took over 700 years to build. It was begun in the 6th century BC by Peisistratos, but was abandoned for lack of funds. Various other leaders had stabs at completing the temple, but it was left to Hadrian to complete the work in 131 AD.

The temple is impressive for the sheer size of its 104 Corinthian columns (17m high with a base diameter of 1.7m), of which 15 remain – the fallen column was blown down in a gale in 1852. Hadrian put a colossal statue of Zeus in the cella and, in typically immodest fashion, placed an equally large one of himself next to it. The site (☎ 922 6330) is open 8.30 am to 2.30 pm Tuesday to Sunday. Admission is 500 dr.

Library of Hadrian (Map 2)

This library is to the north of the Roman Agora. The building, which was of vast dimensions, was erected in the 2nd century AD and included a cloistered courtyard bordered by 100 columns. As well as books, the building housed music and lecture rooms and a theatre. The library is at present inaccessible to visitors.

Roman Stadium (Map 1)

The last Athenian monument with Roman connections is the Roman Stadium, which lies in a fold between two pine-covered hills between the neighbourhoods of Mets and Pangrati. The stadium was originally built in the 4th century BC as a venue for the Panathenaic athletic contests. A thousand wild animals are said to have been slaughtered in the arena at Hadrian's inauguration in 120 AD. Shortly after this, the seats were rebuilt in Pentelic marble by Herodes Atticus.

After hundreds of years of disuse the stadium was completely restored in 1895 by wealthy Greek benefactor Georgios Averof. The following year the first Olympic Games of modern times were held here. It is a faithful replica of the Roman Stadium, comprising seats of Pentelic marble for 70,000 spectators, a running track and a central area for field events.

BYZANTINE ATHENS

Byzantine architecture in Athens is fairly thin on the ground. By the time of the split in the Roman Empire, Athens had shrunk to little more than a provincial town and

MARK HONAN

Fallen glory: one of the massive columns in the Temple of Olympian Zeus

Thessaloniki had become the major city. The most important Byzantine building is the **monastery** at Dafni, 10km west of the city, which is covered in the Around Athens section later in this chapter.

Central Athens has a number of churches, of which the 11th century **Church of Agios Eleftherios** (Map 2) on Plateia Mitropoleos, Plaka, is considered the finest. It is built partly of Pentelic marble and decorated with an external frieze of symbolic beasts in bas-relief. It was once the city's cathedral, but now stands in the shadows of the much larger new cathedral.

The **Church of Kapnikarea** (Map 2), halfway down Ermou, in Monastiraki, is another small 11th century church. Its dome is supported by four large Roman columns. The **Church of Agii Theodori** (Map 2), just off Plateia Klafthmonos on Stadiou, has a tiled dome and walls decorated with a terracotta frieze of animals and plants.

Other churches worth peering into are the **Church of the Holy Apostles** (see Ancient Agora, earlier) and the **Church of Agios Dimitrios** (see the Hills of Athens section, later).

NATIONAL ARCHAEOLOGICAL MUSEUM (MAP 9)

This museum (☎ 821 7717), opened in 1874, stands supreme among the nation's finest. Despite all the pilfering by foreign archaeologists in the 19th century, it still has the world's finest collection of Greek antiquities – in particular, the magnificent Hall of Mycenaean Antiquities and the Thira Exhibition, which contains the celebrated collection of Minoan frescoes unearthed at Akrotiri on the island of Santorini (Thira).

The museum highlights are described here, and there are comprehensive explanations in English in each room. Guidebooks on sale in the foyer give more information.

The museum is at 28 Oktovriou-Patission 44, north of Omonia, and is open 8 am to 7 pm Tuesday to Friday; 8.30 am to 3 pm Saturday, Sunday and public holidays; and 12.30 to 7 pm Monday. It closes at 5 pm instead of 7 pm between November and March. Admission is 2000 dr. To reach the museum from Plaka, catch trolleybus No 5 or 15 from outside the National Gardens on Amalias. The walk takes about 30 minutes.

Map 9 features a floor plan of the museum; see Maps 1 and 3 for the museum's location.

Mycenean Antiquities: Rooms 3 & 4

The museum's *tour de force* is the Hall of Mycenaean Antiquities, straight ahead from the entrance foyer. Gold gleams at you from everywhere. The chief exhibits are finds from the six shaft graves of Grave Circle A at Mycenae. Graves one to five were excavated by Heinrich Schliemann in 1874-76 and the sixth by Panagiotes Stamatakis in 1886-1902. The star attraction is the golden **Mask of Agamemnon**, housed in case 3. (It has subsequently been proven to belong to a king who died three centuries before Agamemnon.)

In the centre of the hall, cases 28 and 29 contain gold sheets that covered the bodies of two royal babies. On the left, cases 5 and 6 contain finds from Grave Circle B (from 1650 to 1550 BC), which was outside the citadel at Mycenae. Case 5 has an unusual rock-crystal vase in the shape of a duck: its head and neck are gracefully turned back to form a handle. Case 30, also in the centre, contains miscellaneous finds from Mycenae, including a delightful ivory carving of two voluptuous women and a child, who may represent Demeter, Persephone and Iacchus.

On the right, just beyond here, is the famous **Warrior Vase** which, along with the Mask of Agamemnon, Schliemann rated as one of his greatest finds. It depicts men leaving for war and a woman waving them goodbye.

The rest of the hall is devoted to other Mycenaean sites. Case 9 features tablets with inscriptions in Cretan Linear B script, while case 15 contains objects from Tiryns, including the famous **Tiryns Treasure**. The treasure is believed to have been looted by a tomb robber, who then reburied it and failed to retrieve it. Back in the centre, case 32 contains the famous gold cups from the beehive-shaped tomb at Vaphio, which

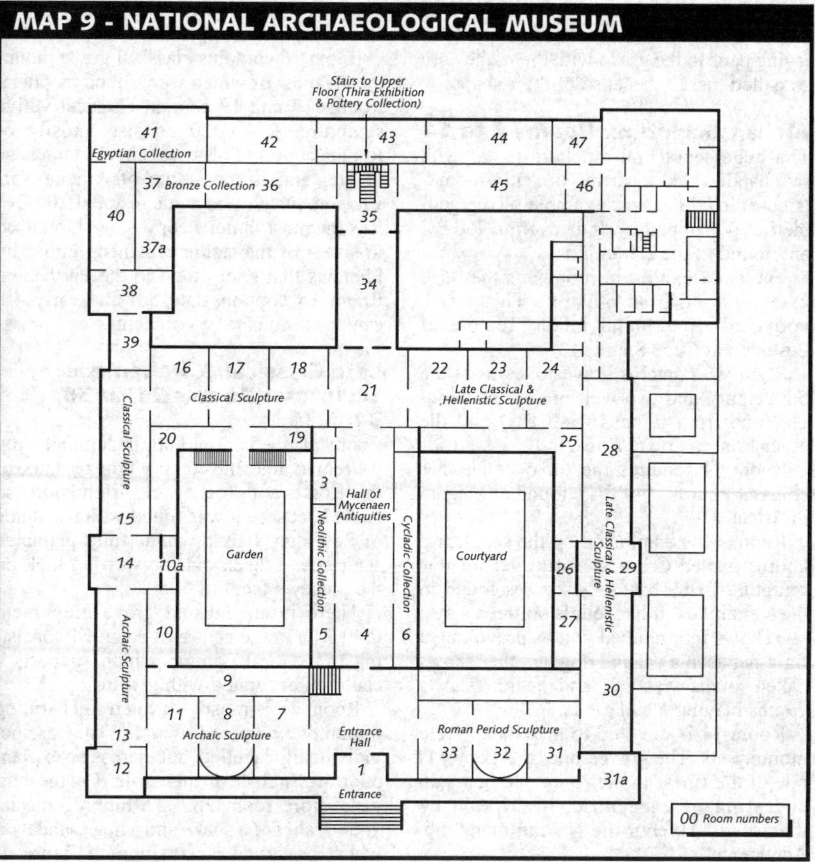

depict the taming of wild bulls. These magnificent cups are regarded as among the finest examples of Mycenaean art.

Room 3 contains Mycenaean finds from Central Greece, Thessaly and the island of Skopelos.

Neolithic Collection: Room 5

To the left of the Hall of Mycenaean Antiquities, Room 5 contains Neolithic finds – mainly from Thessaly. There is also a case of pottery, figurines and jewellery from Troy, including a beautiful necklace of delicate gold beads. These finds were presented to the museum by Sophie Schliemann, wife of Heinrich.

Cycladic Collection: Room 6

The collection includes the largest Cycladic figurine ever found. It is almost life-size and was discovered on the island of Amorgos.

Cases 56, 57 and 58 contain ceramic 'frying pans' from early Cycladic cemeteries on Syros. They are black with intricate inlaid patterns in white. In case you're wondering why on earth these people took frying pans to the grave with them, they are so called merely because of their shape.

Archaic Sculpture: Rooms 7 to 14

The huge sepulchral amphora (a jar with two handles and a narrow neck) in room 7 is considered the best example of the geometric style of pottery. It dates from 760 BC and found in the Keramikos.

The chief exhibit in room 8 is the huge *kouros* dating from 600 BC. This was a votive offering found in the Temple of Poseidon at Cape Sounion.

Room 10 contains gravestones from the 6th century and two well preserved sphinxes, one from Piraeus (540 BC) and the other from Sparta (570 BC).

Room 11 features the torso of another colossal kouros (540 BC), found at Megara in Attica.

Room 13 is dominated by the sepulchral kouros named Croesus. To the left of this sculpture is the base of a kouros found in the Keramikos. It has reliefs on three sides: one shows four clothed youths provoking a fight between a cat and dog; another shows naked youths wrestling; and the third shows youths playing a ball game.

Room 14 is devoted to provincial stele monuments. The gravestone by Alxenor is one of the finest in the room and bears an endearing, if egocentric, inscription by the artist: 'Alxenor the Naxian made me. Admire me'.

Classical Sculpture: Rooms 15 to 20

The bronze statue of **Poseidon of Artemision** (450 BC) in room 15 is another of the highlights of the museum. The statue was hauled out of the sea off Cape Artemision in 1928, and shows Poseidon poised to hurl his trident (now missing). More than any other statue of Poseidon, it conveys the god's strength and unlimited power.

Just within the door of this room is a beautiful relief from Eleusis (440 BC). It depicts Demeter, accompanied by her daughter Persephone, giving Triptolemos an ear of wheat to sprout.

Room 16 contains classical grave monuments, most of which were found in Attica. Rooms 17 and 19 contain classical votive sculpture. Room 20 consists mostly of Roman copies of classical Greek statues. At the far end is the statue of Athena Varvakeion, which was made in about 200 BC. It is the most famous copy – much reduced in size – of the statue of Athena Polias by Pheidias that once stood in the Parthenon. Room 18 contains late 5th and early 4th century sepulchral monuments.

Late Classical & Hellenistic Sculpture: Rooms 21 to 30, 34 & 35

Room 21, the central hall, is dominated by the remarkable 2nd century bronze statue of the **Horse and Jockey of Artemision**, so named because it was found with the statue of Poseidon. It is a wonderfully animated sculpture – check out the worried look on the jockey's face.

There is an unusual grave monument (540 BC) in the centre of room 24 consisting of a floral column which supports a cauldron decorated with griffins.

Room 25 is mostly devoted to charming diminutive reliefs of nymphs. They are not individually labelled, but there is an explanation in English of their role. On the left, just before room 26, is a highly unusual votive relief of a snake and a huge sandal on which is carved a worshipping figure. It dates from 360 BC and is believed to depict the Hero of the Slipper, who was worshipped near the Theatre of Dionysos.

Room 28 contains some extremely realistic funerary monuments, particularly the Grave Monument of Aristonautes (330 BC), found in the Keramikos. The large sepulchral relief of a boy attempting to restrain a frisky horse is a powerful and unprecedented piece of realist sculpture, especially the leg muscles of both the horse and boy, and the magnificent drapery. It was found near Larisis Station in 1948, and dates from the second half of the 3rd century.

The famous **Ephebos of Antikythira** (340 BC) stands in the centre of the room. The amazingly lifelike eyes are almost hypnotic. Behind this statue, to the right, is the head of a bronze statue – probably of the Elean boxer Satyros. He certainly looks a nasty piece of work in contrast to the calm 'other world' expressions on the faces surrounding him.

Room 29 is dominated by the statue of Themis (the goddess of justice). Behind her is a head of Alexander the Great with graffitied cheeks (added later), and a head of the orator Demosthenes looking very perplexed.

The comic masks on the right in room 30 provide some light relief, although some of their expressions are as menacing as they are funny. A little way down, in the middle of the room, is a delightful and sensitive sculpture of a naked boy with his hand on a goose – note his gentle smile and the apparent softness of his skin.

Dominating the room is yet another statue of the sea god, Poseidon (140 BC), which was found on Milos in 1877. Behind this statue is the bronze head of a melancholic-looking guy; it was found on Delos. To the right is an amusing sculpture of Pan making amorous advances towards Aphrodite, who is about to clobber him with her sandal.

Room 34 is built to simulate an open-air sanctuary and displays objects from the **Sanctuary of Aphrodite** which existed near Dafni.

Roman Period Sculpture: Rooms 31 to 33

These rooms house sculptures produced in Greece during the period of the Roman occupation from the 1st to the 5th centuries AD.

Bronze Collection: Rooms 36 & 37

The highlight of these rooms is the **Karapanos Collection** of bronzes (room 36) found at the celebrated Sanctuary of Zeus at Dodoni in Epiros. It includes a chariot from the Roman period. Room 37 was the first bronze room to be opened. A case on the left shows casting techniques; another shows burial offerings. In the middle is a bronze statue of a youth (337 BC), which was found in the Bay of Marathon.

Egyptian Collection: Rooms 40 & 41

The main point of interest is the collection of elaborately decorated mummy cases in room 40.

Prehistoric Jewellery: Room 45

At the time of writing, room 45 was the temporary home to a collection of prehistoric jewellery discovered at a number of sites in Central Greece and around the Black Sea.

Thira Exhibition: Room 48a

The rear section of the hall at the top of the stairs houses the celebrated frescoes unearthed by Spyridon Marinatos at the Minoan settlement of Akrotiri on Santorini (Thira) in the late 1960s.

The frescoes are more varied and better preserved than the Minoan frescoes found on Crete. Extremely beautiful and harmonious in both colour and form, they give a comprehensive insight into the everyday life of the Minoans. Scenes depicted in the frescoes include two boxing youths, a youth holding two strings of fish, and women performing religious rites. The most unusual is the one which shows a flotilla of ships sailing from one coastal town to another. The frescoes will remain here until a suitable museum has been built on Santorini.

Pottery Collection: Rooms 48 to 56

These rooms house the world's most comprehensive collection of ancient Greek pottery. The collection traces the development from the Bronze Age (room 48), through the Protogeometric and Geometric periods, to the beginning of simple decorative motifs.

Flora, fauna and human figures first featured on pottery in the 8th century BC, and mythical scenes appeared a century later. The 6th century BC saw the emergence of the famous Attic black-figured pottery. By the middle of the 5th century BC, the pots with black figures had been superseded by red-figured pottery, which reached the peak of perfection during Pericles' rule.

OTHER MUSEUMS

The National Archaeological Museum might steal the show, but Athens has lots more in store for keen museum-goers with time on their hands. The following selection has been drawn from a list of 28 (available from the tourist office), covering everything from Byzantine art to old theatre props. See the following What's Free in Athens section for more information on museums.

Benaki Museum (Map 5)

This museum contains the sumptuous and eclectic collection of Antoine Benaki, accumulated during Antoine's 35 years of avid collecting in Europe and Asia. In 1931 he turned the family house into a museum and presented it to the Greek nation. The collection includes Bronze Age finds from Mycenae and Thessaly; two early works by El Greco; ecclesiastical furniture brought from Asia Minor by refugees; pottery, copper, silver and woodwork from Egypt, Asia Minor and Mesopotamia; and a stunning collection of Greek regional costumes.

The museum is on the corner of Vasilissis Sofias and Koumbari, in Kolonaki. At the time of writing, it was closed for a complete refit and was not scheduled to reopen until mid-2000. The museum shop (☎ 362 7367) remains open 8.30 am to 3 pm Monday to Friday, selling books, cards and replicas.

Goulandris Museum of Cycladic & Ancient Greek Art (Map 5)

This private museum (☎ 801 5870) houses a collection of Cycladic art, second in importance only to that displayed at the National Archaeological Museum. The museum was custom-built for the collection and the finds are beautifully displayed, lit and labelled. Although the exhibits cover all periods from Cycladic to Roman times, the emphasis is on the Cycladic from 3000 to 2000 BC. The 230 exhibits include the marble figurines with folded arms which inspired many 20th century artists with their simplicity and purity of form.

The museum has now taken over the 19th century mansion next door, which it uses for temporary exhibitions. The entrance to the museum is at Neofytou Douka 4, Kolonaki, just around the corner from Vasilissis Sofias. It is open on 10 am to 4 pm Monday, Wednesday, Thursday and Friday, and 10 am to 3 pm Saturday. Admission is 1000 dr.

Byzantine Museum (Map 1)

This museum (☎ 723 1570) has a large collection of Christian art from the 4th to the 19th century, housed in the Villa Ilissia, an attractive, mock-Florentine mansion at Vasilissis Sofias 22, Kolonaki.

Unfortunately, the museum will be operating at half-capacity until at least 2001, as the wing to the right of the courtyard is being completely rebuilt. This wing housed many of the finest frescoes and icons; some are in storage, others have been moved temporarily to Thessaloniki.

The downstairs rooms in the surviving wing are given over to re-creations of churches, starting with a very solemn basilica from the 5th to the 7th century. The reconstruction of an 11th century Byzantine church is beautiful in its simplicity, in contrast to the elaborate decorations of the post-Byzantine church next door. The bishop's throne in this room was brought to Athens by refugees from Asia Minor. The upstairs rooms contain icons and frescoes.

The museum is open 8.30 am to 3 pm Tuesday to Sunday. Admission is 500 dr.

Numismatic Museum (Map 2)

Housed in a magnificent neoclassical mansion at Panepistimiou 12 in Syntagma (☎ 821 7769), this collection comprises 400,000 coins from ancient Greek, Hellenic, Roman and Byzantine times. The building was once the home of celebrated archaeologist Heinrich Schliemann. It's open 8 am to 2.30 pm Tuesday to Sunday; admission is 800 dr.

Museum of Greek Folk Art (Map 2)

This museum (☎ 322 9031) houses a superb collection of secular and religious folk art, mainly from the 18th and 19th centuries. On the 1st floor is embroidery, pottery, weaving and puppets. On the 2nd floor is a reconstructed traditional village house with paintings by the primitive artist Theophilos of Lesvos (Mytilini). Greek traditional costumes are displayed on the 3rd and 4th floors.

The museum is at Kydathineon 17, Plaka, and is open 10 am to 2 pm Tuesday to Sunday. Admission is 500 dr.

National Art Gallery (off Map 1)

The emphasis in this gallery (☎ 721 1010) is on Greek painting and sculpture from the 19th and 20th centuries. There are also 16th century works and a few works by European masters, including paintings by Picasso, Marquet and Utrillo and Magritte's sculpture *The Therapist*.

Paintings by the primitive painter Theophilos are displayed on the mezzanine floor and 20th century works are on the 1st floor. The 2nd floor has mostly 19th century paintings, with one room of earlier works. It has four El Greco paintings, including *The Crucifixion* and *Symphony of the Angels*.

Greek sculpture of the 19th and 20th centuries is effectively displayed in the sculpture garden and sculpture hall, reached from the lower floor. There are several works by Giannolis Halepas (1851-1937), one of Greece's foremost sculptors.

The gallery is at Vasileos Konstantinou 50 (opposite the Hilton Hotel) and is open 9 am to 3 pm Wednesday to Saturday and 10 am to 2 pm Monday and Sunday. Admission is 1000 dr.

National Historical Museum (Map 2)

This museum (☎ 323 7617) specialises in memorabilia from the War of Independence, including Byron's helmet and sword. There is also a series of paintings depicting events leading up to the war, Byzantine and medieval exhibits and a collection of photographs and royal portraits.

The museum is housed in the old parliament building at Plateia Kolokotroni, Stadiou, in Syntagma. Theodoros Deligiannis, who succeeded Trikoupis as prime minister of Greece, was assassinated on the steps of the building in 1905. It's open 9 am to 1.30 pm Tuesday to Sunday, and admission is 500 dr.

City of Athens Museum (Map 2)

This museum (☎ 324 6164) occupies the palace where King Otho and his consort Amalia lived for a few years during the 1830s. It contains some of the royal couple's furniture, costumes and personal mementoes, as well as paintings, prints and models of Athens in the 19th century.

The museum is at Paparigopoulou 7, Syntagma, and is open on 9 am to 1.30 pm Monday, Wednesday, Friday and Saturday. Admission is 500 dr.

Jewish Museum (Map 2)

This museum (☎ 322 5882) traces the history of the Jewish community in Greece back to the 3rd century BC through an impressive collection of religious and folk art and documents. It includes a reconstruction of a synagogue.

The museum is housed in a 19th century mansion at Nikis 39, Plaka. It's open 9 am to 2.30 pm Monday to Friday and 10 am to 2 pm Sunday. Entry is 300 dr.

Theatre Museum (Map 5)

Aspiring thespians may be interested in visiting this museum (☎ 362 9430), which contains theatre memorabilia from the 19th and 20th centuries. Exhibits include photographs, costumes, props and reconstructions of the dressing rooms of Greece's most celebrated 20th century actors.

The museum is at Akadimias 50. Opening times are 9 am to 2.30 pm Monday to Friday. Admission is 500 dr.

Free Museums

Athens also has some interesting free museums. A favourite is the **Museum of Greek Popular Instruments** (Map 2), near the Tower of the Winds at Diogenous 1-3, Plaka. It has displays and recordings of a wide selection of traditional instruments. It's open 10 am to 2 pm Tuesday to Sunday, except on Wednesday (noon to 6 pm).

The **Centre of Folk Arts & Traditions** (Map 2), Angelika Hatzimihali 6, Plaka, has a good display of costumes, embroideries, pottery and musical instruments. It's open 9 am to 1 pm and 5 to 9 pm Tuesday to Friday, and 9 am to 1 pm weekends.

The **Museum of the History of Greek Costume** (Map 5), Dimokritou 7, Kolonaki, changes its display every year. The 1999 display featured costumes from Evia.

The **War Museum** (Map 1), next to the Byzantine Museum in Kolonaki, is a relic of the colonels' junta, and is also an architectural statement of the times. Greece seems to have been at war since time immemorial, and a look around helps to get the country's history in perspective. All periods from the Mycenaean to the present day are covered, and displays include weapons, maps, armour and models of battles. It's open 9 am to 2 pm Tuesday to Friday, and 9.30 am to 2 pm on Saturday and Sunday.

HILLS OF ATHENS

Lykavittos Hill (Map 5)

The name Lykavittos means 'hill of wolves' and derives from ancient times when the hill was surrounded by countryside and its pine-covered slopes were inhabited by wolves. Today, it is no longer surrounded by countryside nor inhabited by wolves, but rises out of a sea of concrete to offer the finest views in Athens. Pollution permitting, there are panoramic views of the city, the Attic basin, the surrounding mountains and the islands of Salamis and Aegina. A path leads to the summit from the top of Loukianou. Alternatively, you can take the funicular railway from the top of Ploutarhou (500 dr one way).

There is a cafe halfway up the path and another at the top, as well as a restaurant with a spectacular view over the Acropolis. Also on the summit is the little **Chapel of Agios Giorgios**. The chapel is floodlit at night and from the streets below looks like a vision from a fairy tale. The open-air **Lykavittos Theatre** (Map 1), to the north-east of the summit, is used for performances of jazz and rock during the Athens Festival.

West of the Acropolis (Map 1)

The low **Areopagus Hill** (Map 2) lies between the Acropolis and the Ancient Agora. According to mythology, it was here that Ares was tried by the council of the gods for the murder of Halirrhothios, son of Poseidon. The council accepted his defence of justifiable deicide on the grounds that he was protecting his daughter, Alcippe, from unwanted advances.

The hill became the place where murder trials were heard before the Council of the Areopagus, whose jurisdiction by the 4th century had been extended to cover treason and corruption. In 51 AD, St Paul delivered his famous 'Sermon to an Unknown God' from Areopagus Hill and gained his first Athenian convert, Dionysos, who became patron saint of the city.

Areopagus Hill is linked to the Acropolis by a saddle and can be climbed by steps cut into the rock. There are good views of the Ancient Agora from the summit. The rock is very slippery, so wear suitable shoes.

Filopappos Hill (Map 4), also called the Hill of the Muses, is clearly identifiable to the south-west of the Acropolis by virtue of the **Monument of Filopappos** at its summit. The monument was built in 114-16 AD in honour of Julius Antiochus Filopappos, who was a prominent Roman consul and administrator.

There are small paths all over the hill, but the paved path to the top starts next to the Dionysos Taverna on Dionysiou Areopagitou. The pine-clad slopes are a pleasant place for a stroll and offer good views of the plain and mountains of Attica and of the Saronic Gulf. After 250m, the path passes the **Church of Agios Dimitrios**, which contains some fine frescoes. It was sensitively restored in 1951-57.

North of here is the rocky **Hill of the Pnyx** (Map 2). This was the meeting place of the Democratic Assembly in the 5th century BC. Among the great orators who addressed assemblies here were Aristides, Demosthenes, Pericles and Themistocles.

To the north-west of the Hill of the Pnyx is the **Hill of the Nymphs**, on which stands an observatory built in 1842. It is open to visitors on the last Friday of each month.

PARKS

Athens is sadly lacking in parks. Only three are large enough to be worth a mention.

National Gardens (Map 2)

These gardens are a delightful shady refuge during the summer months and are the favourite haunt of Athens' many stray cats. They were formerly the royal gardens and were designed by Queen Amalia.

The gardens contain subtropical trees, ornamental ponds with waterfowl, and a **botanical museum**, which houses interesting drawings, paintings and photographs. There are entrances to the gardens from Vasilissis Sofias and Amalias.

Zappeio Gardens (Map 2)

These gardens are laid out in a network of wide walkways around the Zappeio, which was built in the 1870s with money donated by the wealthy Greek-Romanian benefactor Konstantinos Zappas. Until the 1970s, the Zappeio was used mainly as an exhibition hall. It was used for Council of Europe meetings during Greece's presidency of the EC.

Areos Park (Map 1)

This pleasant park is north of the National Archaeological Museum on Leoforos Alexandras. It is a large park with wide, tree-lined avenues, one of which has a long line of statues of War of Independence heroes.

Athens' First Cemetery (Map 1)

Athens' First Cemetery (Proto Nekrotafeion Athinon) is not strictly a park, but it bears more than a passing resemblance to one. In the absence of real parks, any patch of greenery is welcome. Athenian families who come to attend the graves of loved ones certainly seem to take this attitude, turning duty into an outing by bringing along a picnic. It's a peaceful place to stroll around and is the resting place of many famous Greeks and philhellenes.

The cemetery is well kept and most of the tombstones and mausoleums are lavish in the extreme. Some are kitsch and sentimental, others are works of art created by the foremost Greek sculptors of the 19th century, such as the *Sleeping Maiden* by Halepas, which is the tomb of a young girl. Someone places a red rose in her hand every day.

Among the cemetery's famous residents are the writers Rangavis (1810-92) and Soutsos (1800-68); the politician Harilaos Trikoupis (1832-96); the archaeologists Heinrich Schliemann (1822-90) and Adolph Furtwängler (1853-1907); the benefactors Antoine Benaki, Georgios Averof and Theodoros Syngros; and War of Independence heroes Sir Richard Church (1784-1873), Kolokotronis (1770-1843), Makrygiannis and Androutsos. Schliemann's mausoleum is decorated with scenes from the Trojan War. Located near the entrance is a memorial – poignant in its simplicity – to the 40,000 citizens who died of starvation during WWII.

The cemetery is 600m south-east of the Temple of Olympian Zeus at the end of Anapafseos in Mets. You'll know you're getting close when you see all the stone-masons and flower shops. Other shops sell cemetery paraphernalia, ranging from life-size figures of Christ to miniature picture frames – used to put photographs of the deceased on the gravestones.

ACTIVITIES

Skiing

The nearest ski fields to Athens are at Mt Parnassos, three hours north-west, where the season lasts from mid-December to March or April. The ski department (☎ 324 1915, fax 513 3265) at Klaoudatos, the big department store on Athinas, in Omonia, organises excursions to the resort of Kelaria. Its buses leave from the stadium in Athens every morning at 5.40 am and get to Kelaria at 8.30 am. They leave the resort at 4 pm. Tickets are 8000 dr (10,000 dr at weekends), including a lift pass. An extra 3000 dr gets you all the gear – skis, bindings, boots and poles.

Tennis

Visitors are welcome to use the courts at the Glyfada Golf Club (see following) for 3000 dr per hour. Otherwise, getting a game involves wangling your way into one of the exclusive clubs, such as the Athens Tennis Club (☎ 923 2872), next to the Temple of Olympian Zeus, at Vasilissis Olgas 2.

Golf

The Glyfada Golf Club (☎ 894 6820), near the airport, is Athens' only course. Green fees are 12,000 dr on weekdays, 16,000 dr on weekends and public holidays. You'll be up for another 3000 dr for a bag of clubs, and 800 dr for a buggy.

Tenpin Bowling

The Athens Bowling Centre (☎ 867 3645), 100m north of Plateia Amerikis at Oktovriou-Patission 177, is open 10 am to 2 am daily. On weekdays, it charges 1000 dr per game between 10 am and 5 pm, and 1200 dr per game after 5 pm. At weekends, the rates go up to 1200/1500 dr.

LANGUAGE COURSES

If you are serious about learning Greek, an intensive course at the start of your stay is a good way to go about it.

The Athens Centre (☎ 701 2268, fax 701 8603, email athenscr@compulink.gr), Arhimidous 48, in the quiet residential suburb of Mets, has a very good reputation. Its courses cover five levels of proficiency from beginners to advanced. There are eight immersion courses a year for beginners, packing approximately 60 hours of class time into three weeks for 150,000 dr. The centre occupies a fine neoclassical building. You can find more information on its Web site, www.athenscentre.gr.

Another place offering courses is the Hellenic American Union (☎ 362 9886, fax 363 3174, email dtolias@hau.gr), Massalias 22, Pefkakia. It has courses lasting between one and three months covering all levels of proficiency for 90,000 dr.

Long-term visitors can check out the courses offered by Athens University at its Zografou campus (☎ 727 7672). It has a course lasting from February to May for 110,000 dr, and a longer course from October to June for 150,000 dr.

Private lessons are sometimes advertised on the notice board outside the Compendium Bookshop, Nikis 28, Plaka.

Language courses on the islands are covered under Courses in the Facts for the Visitor chapter.

CHILDREN'S ACTIVITIES

The Children's Museum in Plaka (Map 2; ☎ 331 2995), Kydathineon 14, is more of a play group than a museum. It has a games room and a number of 'exhibits', such as a mock-up of a metro tunnel, for children to explore. It's open 9.30 am to 1.30 pm Monday and Wednesday, 9.30 am to 1.30 pm and 5 to 8 pm Friday, and 10 am to 1 pm weekends. Entry is free. Parents have to stay and supervise their children.

The Museum of Children's Art (Map 2; ☎ 331 2621), nearby at Kodrou 9, Plaka, has a room set aside where children can let loose their creative energy. Admission is free and crayons and paper are supplied. It's open 10 am to 2 pm Tuesday to Saturday and 11 am to 2 pm Sunday. The 200 dr fee applies only to children attending special programs.

ORGANISED TOURS

The three main companies running organised tours around Athens are CHAT (☎ 322 3137), Stadiou 4, GO Tours (☎ 921 9555), Athanassiou 20, and Key Tours (☎ 923 3166/3266), Kaliroïs 4. You will find their brochures everywhere, all offering similar tours and prices. They include a half-day sightseeing tour of Athens (10,000 dr), which does nothing more than point out all the major sights, and Athens by Night (13,600 dr), which takes in the son et lumière (sound-and-light show) before a taverna dinner with folk dancing.

The companies also have one-day tours to Cape Sounion (7600 dr); Delphi (18,000 dr, 21,000 dr with lunch); the Corinth Canal, Mycenae, Nafplio and Epidaurus (same prices); and one-day cruises to

Aegina, Poros and Hydra (19,000 dr including lunch).

ATHENS FESTIVAL

The Athens Festival is the city's most important cultural event, running from mid-June to the end of August. It includes classical music concerts and dance performances by national and international orchestras and dance companies.

The main attraction is the performance of ancient Greek drama at the Theatre of Herodes Atticus. The plays are performed in modern Greek, but somehow it doesn't matter if you don't understand. The setting is superb, backed by the floodlit Acropolis, and the atmosphere is electric.

There are also performances at the nearby Stoa of Eumenes, the Hill of the Pynx, the Lykavittos Theatre and at a new theatre in Piraeus near the junction of Pireos and Kifissou streets.

Tickets sell out quickly, so try to buy yours as soon as possible. They can be bought at the festival box office (Map 2; ☎ 322 1459, fax 323 5172), in the arcade at Stadiou 4, Syntagma. Opening times are 8 am to 5 pm Monday to Friday.

Tickets may also be bought on the day of the performance at the theatre box offices, but queues can be very long. There are student discounts for most performances on production of an ISIC.

PLACES TO STAY

Athens is a noisy city and Athenians keep late hours, so an effort has been made to select hotels in quiet areas, pedestrian precincts or side streets. Except where specified, the prices quoted here were for the 1999 high season. Most places offer considerable discounts in the off season.

The enormous influx of refugees from the troubles in neighbouring Albania (in particular) and other Balkan nations has had a major impact on the budget accommodation scene. Many cheap hotels and hostels that once were popular with travellers have now become little more than refugee camps. The budget places recommended in this section all attempt to ensure a secure environment for their guests.

Plaka is the most popular place to stay. Most of the sights are close by and it's convenient for every transport connection other than the train station. It has a choice of accommodation right across the price spectrum, from travellers' hostels to smart mid-range hotels and pensions. Not surprisingly, rooms fill up quickly in July and August, so it's wise to make a reservation. If you haven't booked, a telephone call can save a fruitless walk.

The other main hotel area is around Plateia Omonias, but the options are not very attractive. They all seem to be either cheap bordellos, where you won't get a wink of sleep, or characterless modern C class places. An added drawback to the Omonia region is the general seediness, although this can be expected to change in the lead-up to the Olympics.

There are also some good pensions and mid-range hotels in the suburbs south of the Acropolis.

If you arrive in the city late and cannot find anywhere to stay, don't be tempted to sleep out. It is illegal and could be dangerous.

Hotel Touts

Many of the budget hotels and hostels in Athens employ touts to meet tourists who arrive by train, particularly the late train from Patras. Some of the hostels recommended in this chapter do this, and it often saves a lot of hassle to take up an offer. Before doing so, however, ask to see the hostel leaflet. This will have a picture of the hostel, information about the facilities offered and (very importantly) a map showing its location. Be very suspicious of a tout who cannot show you a leaflet.

PLACES TO STAY – BUDGET

Camping

There are no camp sites in central Athens. The EOT's *Camping in Greece* brochure lists all 17 sites in Attica. The nearest to the city centre is ***Athens Camping*** *(☎ 581 4114, Leoforos Athinon 198)*, 7km west of the centre (see the Around Athens map later in this chapter). It has hot water, a minimarket and snack bar and is open year-round. To get there, take bus No A16 to Elefsina from Plateia Eleftherias. From Piraeus, take bus No 802 or 845. If you prefer to be by the sea, there are several camp sites on the coast road to Cape Sounion (see the Attica section later in this chapter).

Hostels

There are a few places around Athens making a pitch for the hostelling market by tagging 'youth hostel' onto their names. There are some real dumps among them.

There are only a couple of youth hostels worth knowing about. They include the excellent HI-affiliated ***Athens International Youth Hostel*** *(Map 3; ☎ 523 4170, fax 523 4015, Victor Hugo 16)* in Omonia. The location isn't overly salubrious, but otherwise the place is almost too good to be true. It occupies the former C class Hotel Victor Ougo, which has been completely renovated – it even has double-glazed windows. The spotless rooms, with bathroom, sleep two to four people and include sheets and pillow cases. Rates are 1620 dr per person for those with an HI card. If you don't have a card, you can either pay 4200 dr to join or 700 dr for a daily stamp. Facilities include a guest kitchen, laundry and free safety deposit boxes. There is no curfew and the reception staff speak English.

Another possibility is ***Youth Hostel No 5*** *(off Map 1; ☎ 751 9530, email y-hostel@otenet.gr, Damareos 75)* in the suburb of Pangrati – about 1.5km east of Syntagma. The rooms are very basic, but it's a cheery place. Owner Yiannis is something of a philosopher, and visitors are encouraged to add their jokes or words of wisdom to the hostel noticeboard. It charges 1800 dr per night for dorm beds, or 1500 dr for stays of a week or longer. Facilities include coin-operated hot showers, a communal kitchen, washing machine and a TV room. To get there, take trolleybus No 2 or 11 from Syntagma to the Filolaou stop on Frinis, just past Damareos.

Hotels – Plaka & Syntagma (Map 2)

The ***Student & Travellers' Inn*** *(☎ 324 4808, fax 321 0065, email students-inn@ath.forthnet.gr, Kydathineon 16)* is hard to go past. It's a well run place with spotless rooms. The dormitories are particularly good value, with beds in four/three-person rooms for 3500/4000 dr. Rooms with bunk beds are 3000 dr, and singles/doubles are 7000/9000 dr. All rooms share communal bathrooms. The place stays open all year, and rooms are heated in winter. Student card-holders qualify for a 10% discount on singles and doubles, but not on dorm beds.

There's a big-screen TV in the courtyard where you can watch satellite coverage of international sporting events. Other facilities include Internet access, ferry ticketing and long term luggage storage. Breakfast is available 7.30 to 11 am.

Festos Youth & Student Guesthouse *(☎ 323 2455, email consolas@hol.gr, Filellinon 18)* has long been a popular place with travellers despite being on one of the noisiest streets in Athens. It has dorm beds priced from 3000 dr to 3500 dr, but tends to cram beds into the rooms in summer. There are a couple of doubles for 7500 dr. A popular feature is the bar on the 1st floor, which also serves meals, including several vegetarian items.

Hotel Kouros *(☎ 322 7431, Kodrou 11)* looks extremely promising, but guests appear to be regarded as a bloody nuisance. It's a shame, because it's an old house with beautiful moulded ceilings and loads of character. It charges 7500/10,000 dr for single/double rooms.

The huge timber spiral staircase at ***George's Guest House*** *(☎ 322 6474, Nikis 46)* speaks of grander times. Rooms cost 6000/8000 dr. It closes in winter.

XEN *(YWCA; ☎ 362 4291, Amerikis 11)* is for women only. Rooms cost 6000/9000 dr, or with bathroom 7500/9500 dr. There are laundry facilities and a snack bar which charges 800 dr for continental breakfast. Annual membership costs 600 dr. ***John's Place*** *(☎ 322 9719, Patröou 5)* is a small family-run place just west of Syntagma. The rooms here are basic but clean, and cost 7000/10,000/13,000 dr for singles/doubles/triples.

At the D class ***Hotel Dioskouros*** *(☎ 324 8165, email consolas@hol.gr, Pittakou 6)*, large doubles go for 9000 dr. A shady courtyard at the back has a snack bar that serves breakfast and light meals.

Hotels – Monastiraki (Map 2)

There are a couple of good budget hotels around Plateia Monastirakiou. The D class ***Hotel Tempi*** *(☎ 321 3175, fax 321 4179, Eolou 29)* is a friendly family-run place on the pedestrian precinct part of Eolou. Yiannis and Katerina keep the place spotless and the rooms at the front have balconies overlooking a little square with a church and a flower market. Rates are 5500/8000/9500 dr for singles/doubles/triples, or with bathroom 10,000/11,500 dr for doubles/triples. Credit cards are accepted – unusually for a budget hotel. A washing machine is an added attraction.

At the nearby ***Hotel Carolina*** *(☎ 324 3551/2, fax 324 3550, Kolokotroni 55)*, single/double rooms with outside private bathroom are 6000/9000 dr, or 9000/11,000 dr with inside bathroom. All rooms have air-con.

Hotels – Koukaki (Map 4)

This isn't exactly backpacker territory, but ***Marble House Pension*** *(☎ 923 4058, 922 6461, Zini 35A)*, on a quiet cul-de-sac off Zini, is one of Athens' better budget hotels. Rates are 5500/9500 dr, or with bathroom 6500/10,800 dr. All rooms have a bar fridge, ceiling fans and safety boxes for valuables. There's a book exchange in the reception area. To get there, catch trolleybus No 1, 5, 9 or 18 from Syntagma to the Zini stop on Veïkou.

Hotels – Omonia & Surrounds (Map 3)

This section includes the area around the train stations as well as Omonia. There are dozens of hotels around Omonia, but most of them are either bordellos masquerading as cheap hotels or uninspiring, overpriced C class hotels. There are very few places worthy of a mention.

One place that's definitely worth checking out is the excellent ***Hostel Aphrodite*** *(☎ 881 0589, fax 881 6574, email hostel-aphrodite@ath.forthnet.gr, Einardou 12)*, 10 minutes walk from the train stations. It is very clean, with good-sized rooms – many with balconies. It has dorm beds for 2500 dr, single/double/triple rooms for 5000/7000/9000 dr, and with bathroom 6000/8000/10,000 dr. It seems to be party time every night at the downstairs bar. In the morning, the bar becomes the breakfast room. The hostel also has Internet access.

You can get there on trolleybus No 1, which travels north up Mihail Voda, although the route is not shown on the EOT map. Get off at the Proussis stop, just south of Einardou. The nearest metro station is Viktorias, five minutes walk south-east at Plateia Viktorias.

Zorba's Hotel *(☎ 823 4239, fax 823 4239, Gilfordiou 10)* occupies a quaint old building 100m west of Plateia Viktorias. There are dorms for 2500 dr and singles/doubles for 5000/7000 dr. Breakfast is available in the 1st floor bar.

Hotels – Exarhia (Map 5)

Exarhia is off the beaten track as far as hotels go, but there are a couple of good places to be found tucked away at the base of Strefi Hill.

Hotel Orian and ***Hotel Dryades*** *(☎ 382 7362, fax 380 5193 for both)* are 50m apart on Anehartisias, which skirts the western side of the hill. They are managed by a friendly guy who speaks English. The Orian is clean and well kept with rooms for 6000/7500 dr, while the Dryades charges 8000/10,500 dr for rooms with bathroom. The hotels are to the left at the top of the steps leading off Emmanual Benaki at the junction with Kalidromiou. You can save yourself a long uphill trek by catching bus No 230 from Amalias to the Kalidromiou stop on Harilaou Trikoupi.

Museum Hotel *(☎ 380 5611, fax 380 0507, Bouboulinas 16)* is a long-established hotel behind the National Archaeological Museum. The rooms are plain but comfortable, and reasonably priced at 7000/10,5000 dr with bathroom.

PLACES TO STAY – MID-RANGE

Plaka & Syntagma (Map 2)

Acropolis House Pension *(☎ 322 2344, fax 324 4143, Kodrou 6-8)* is a beautifully preserved 19th century house which retains many original features. The price structure is incredibly complicated owing to the huge choice of rooms. Among the options are singles/doubles for 12,800/15,300 dr or with bathroom for 15,000/18,000 dr, and air-con doubles with bathroom for 22,600 dr. All the rooms are heated in winter. Breakfast costs 1680 dr per person.

Hotel Adonis *(☎ 324 9737, fax 323 1602, Kodrou 3)*, opposite, is a comfortable modern hotel with air-con rooms from 12,000/17,000 dr. It has good views of the Acropolis from the 4th floor rooms, and from the rooftop bar.

The nearby ***Hotel Nefeli*** *(☎ 322 8044, fax 322 5800, Iperidou 16)* has air-con rooms for 16,000/20,500 dr, including breakfast. To get there from Syntagma, head south down Voulis and turn right into Iperidou.

Hotel Athos *(☎ 322 1977, fax 321 0548, Patröou 3)* deserves much better than its D classification handed out by the tourist authorities, The place has undergone a complete refit and offers good rooms with bathroom, air-con as well as TV for 12,000/17,000 dr.

Hotel Achilleas *(☎ 323 3197, fax 322 2412, email rofos@compulink.gr, Leka 21)*, just west of Syntagma, is another possibility. The rooms are large and airy – and those on the top floor open onto garden terraces. It charges 16,000/21,000 dr for rooms with breakfast.

Hotel Adrian *(☎ 322 1553, fax 325 0461, email douros@otenet.gr, Adrianou 74)* is smart and modern with well appointed rooms priced from 18,800/25,000 dr.

Monastiraki (Map 2)

Hotel Attalos *(☎ 321 2801, fax 324 3124, email atthot@hol.gr, Athinas 29)* is a comfortable (if characterless) modern hotel with air-con rooms for 12,500/17,000 dr, including breakfast.

New managers have given a complete facelift to ***Hotel Cecil*** *(☎ 321 8005, fax 321 9606, Athinas 39)*. It's an old building with beautiful high, moulded ceilings that has been sensitively restored – even if the lift is more cute than practical. Rooms with bathroom are 10,000/14,000 dr.

Thisio (Map 2)

Hotel Erechthion *(☎ 345 9606, fax 346 2756, Flammarion 8)* has spotless singles/doubles with TV and bathroom for 8000/ 13,000 dr. Breakfast costs an extra 1000 dr per person. The rooms at the front have superb views of the Acropolis.

Makrigianni (Map 4)

Located just south of the Acropolis, the trendy suburb of Makrigianni has several possibilities, starting with ***Hotel Hera*** *(☎ 923 6682, fax 924 7334, email hhera@hol.gr, Falirou 9)*. It has comfortable air-con rooms with TV and bathroom for 16,500/24,000 dr. Prices include a generous buffet breakfast.

There are indeed views of the Acropolis from many of the rooms at ***Acropolis View Hotel*** *(☎ 921 7303/3035, fax 923 0705, Webster 10)*, just south of the Theatre of Herodes Atticus. The best views are from the roof terrace. Some of the rooms look out over Filopappos Hill. Rates are 20,500/28,500 dr for air-con rooms with buffet breakfast.

Hotel Austria *(☎ 923 5151, fax 924 7350, Mouson 7)* is in a quiet spot on the slopes of Filopappos Hill, with good views over the city from its roof garden. Rooms here are 15,000/19,000 dr, including breakfast.

Koukaki (Map 4)

Art Gallery Pension *(☎ 923 8376, fax 923 3025, email ecotec@otenet.gr, Erehthiou 5)* is a small, friendly place that's always brimming with fresh flowers. It's run by the brother-and-sister team of Ada and Yannis Assimakopoulos, who are full of information about the city. Comfortable singles/ doubles/triples with balcony and bathroom cost 12,000/15,200/18,000 dr. A generous breakfast costs 1500 dr.

Tony's Hotel *(☎ 923 0561, fax 923 6370, Zaharitsa 26)* is another clean, well maintained pension. It offers rooms for 10,800/ 12,000/14,800 dr with bathroom. There is a small communal kitchen downstairs for making tea/coffee and breakfast. Tony also has well equipped two-person studio apartments nearby for long or short term rental. Short term prices are the same as for rooms at the pension.

Around Omonia (Map 3)

Omonia is not really the place to be looking for upmarket accommodation – you can do much better for your money elsewhere.

There are a couple of exceptions. ***Titania Hotel*** *(☎ 330 0111, fax 330 0700, email titania@netplan.gr, Panepistimiou 52)*, with its imposing facade, is a comfortable modern hotel with large rooms for 21,900/26,800 dr, including breakfast. All the rooms have satellite TV. There are great views over the city from the rooftop bar at night.

Novotel Athens *(☎ 825 0422, fax 883 7816, email novotel@hol.gr, Mihail Voda 4-6)*, 150m north-west of Plateia Vathis, has jumped the gun a bit in anticipating the desleazing of this area. The hotel itself, though, is a typical representative of this international chain. There are views over the city to the Acropolis from the rooftop pool and bar area. Rooms cost 36,000/40,000 dr.

Kolonaki (Map 5)

This posh area has the B class ***Athenian Inn*** *(☎ 723 8097/9552, fax 721 5614, Haritos 22)*. It's a small but distinguished place on a quiet street in the heart of Kolonaki that was reputably a favourite of writer Lawrence Durrell. It has a cosy intimacy which is often lacking in hotels of this category. The rooms are unpretentious but comfortable with air-con and pretty pictures of island scenes on the walls. They cost 19,700/29,400 dr, including breakfast.

PLACES TO STAY – TOP END

If you are wealthy, *the* place to stay in Athens is – and always has been – the deluxe ***Hotel Grande Bretagne*** *(Map 2; ☎ 331 4444, fax 322 8034, email gbhotel@otenet.gr)* on Plateia Syntagmatos. Built in 1862 to accommodate visiting heads of state, it ranks among the grand hotels of the world. No other hotel in Athens can boast such a rich history (see the Walking Tour section earlier). It has undergone much expansion since it first became a hotel in 1872, but still has an old-world grandeur. The elegantly furnished rooms have air-con, minibar, satellite TV and video. Singles/double rooms are priced from US$295, and suites start at US$630.

Athens Plaza *(Map 2; ☎ 325 5301, fax 323 5856, email vasil-njv@grecotel.gr)*, next door to the Grande Bretagne, isn't far behind in the luxury stakes following a complete refit and a change of name – it was formerly the Meridien. It has rooms priced from US$260/290 and suites from US$550.

St George Lycabettus Hotel *(Map 5; ☎ 729 0711/0719, fax 729 0439, email info@sglycabettus.gr, Kleomenous 2, Kolonaki)* has a prime position at the foot of Lykavittos Hill. No hotel in Athens offers better views, and the rooms are priced accordingly – from 68,600/78,600 dr for rooms overlooking the Acropolis to 45,300/55,200 dr for no view.

Hilton-hoppers will find their favourite *(off Map 1; ☎ 725 0201, fax 725 3110, email fom_athens@hilton.com, Vasilissis Sofias 46, Ilissia)*, opposite the National Art Gallery. The Athens version is a vast concrete edifice. From the outside, it looks more like a 1950s housing project than a luxury hotel, but inside, no expense has been spared. It has lashings of marble and bronze, public areas with enormous chandeliers and carpets which were especially designed by eminent Greek artists. Rooms cost US$285/315, plus tax, while suites start from US$550.

Plaka's smartest hotel is the A class ***Electra Palace*** *(Map 2; ☎ 337 0000, fax 324 1875, Nikodimou 18)*. The best feature is the roof-top pool with views over to the Acropolis. The official rates start at 36,800/44,800 dr, but there are often special deals.

The posh leafy northern suburb of Kifissia also has a number of luxury hotels. The pick of them is the deluxe ***Pentelikon Hotel*** *(☎ 808 0311, fax 801 0314, Deligianni 66)*. It's an exquisite place built in traditional style with a swimming pool and a lovely garden. All of the beautifully furnished rooms have minibar and satellite TV. Rates are 68,000/80,000 dr, with suites starting at 98,000 dr.

PLACES TO EAT

Plaka is the part of town where most visitors wind up eating. The streets are lined with countless restaurants, tavernas, cafes, patisseries and souvlaki stalls.

There's more to Athens eating than Plaka, though. Every neighbourhood in Athens has its own good eating places, often small unpretentious tavernas tucked away on side streets. Monastiraki is great for souvlaki and cheap eats, and Exarhia also has lots of places with prices in tune with the average student's pocket. The waiters may not speak any English, but you'll find tasty food and reasonable prices.

International cuisine is much harder to find, as is vegetarian food. Both categories are listed separately at the end of this section.

PLACES TO EAT – BUDGET

Plaka (Map 2)

For most people, Plaka is the place to be. It's hard to beat the atmosphere of dining out beneath the floodlit Acropolis. You do, however, pay for the privilege – particularly at the outdoor restaurants around the square on Kydathineon.

The best of this lot is ***Taverna Vizantino*** *(Kydathineon 18)*, which prices its menu more realistically and is popular with locals year-round. Their daily specials are good value, with dishes like stuffed tomatoes (1450 dr), pastitsio (1000 dr) and baked fish (1900 dr).

Plaka Psistaria *(Kydathineon 28)* has a range of gyros and souvlaki to eat there or take away.

One place worth seeking out is ***Ouzeri Kouklis*** *(Tripodon 14)*, an old-style ouzeri with an oak-beamed ceiling, marble tables and wicker chairs. It serves only *mezedes*, which are brought round on a large tray so you can take your pick. They include flaming sausages (ignited at your table) and cuttlefish for 1200 dr, as well as the usual dips for 600 dr. The whole selection, enough for four hungry people, costs 9800 dr. A litre of draught red wine costs 1000 dr and ouzo is 1000 dr for 250ml. The ouzeri is open for lunch and dinner. It gets very busy later in the evening.

With such an emphasis on outdoor eating in summer, it's no great surprise that the three cellar restaurants on Kydathineon are closed from mid-May until October. They are also three of Plaka's cheapest places, where you can expect to pay about 2000 dr per person for a main dish washed down with half a litre of draught retsina. They include ***Taverna Damigos*** *(Kydathineon 41)*, which claims to be the oldest taverna in Plaka and was opened in 1865 by the Damigos family. The others are ***The Cellar*** *(Kydathineon 10)*, downstairs, and ***Saita*** *(Kydathineon 21)*.

Peristeria Taverna *(Patröou 5)*, next to John's Place, is a no-frills place serving all the usual taverna staples at non-Plaka prices. You can tuck into a large plate of *gigantes* beans (900 dr), moussaka (1200 dr) or baked veal and potatoes (1600 dr). It's open all year. Patröou is the fourth street on the left down Mitropoleos from Syntagma.

Most hotels serve breakfast, but if you're not happy with what's on offer you'll find breakfast advertised at many of the Plaka restaurants. Prices start at around 800 dr for continental breakfast.

hurch window, Amorgos (Cyclades)

JON DAVISON

Sadly, neither flying nor fashion was Icarus' forte.

PAUL HELLANDER

olk dancers in Xanthi (Northern Greece)

GEORGE TSAFOS

Handicrafts for sale, Hania, Crete

DIANA MAYFIELD

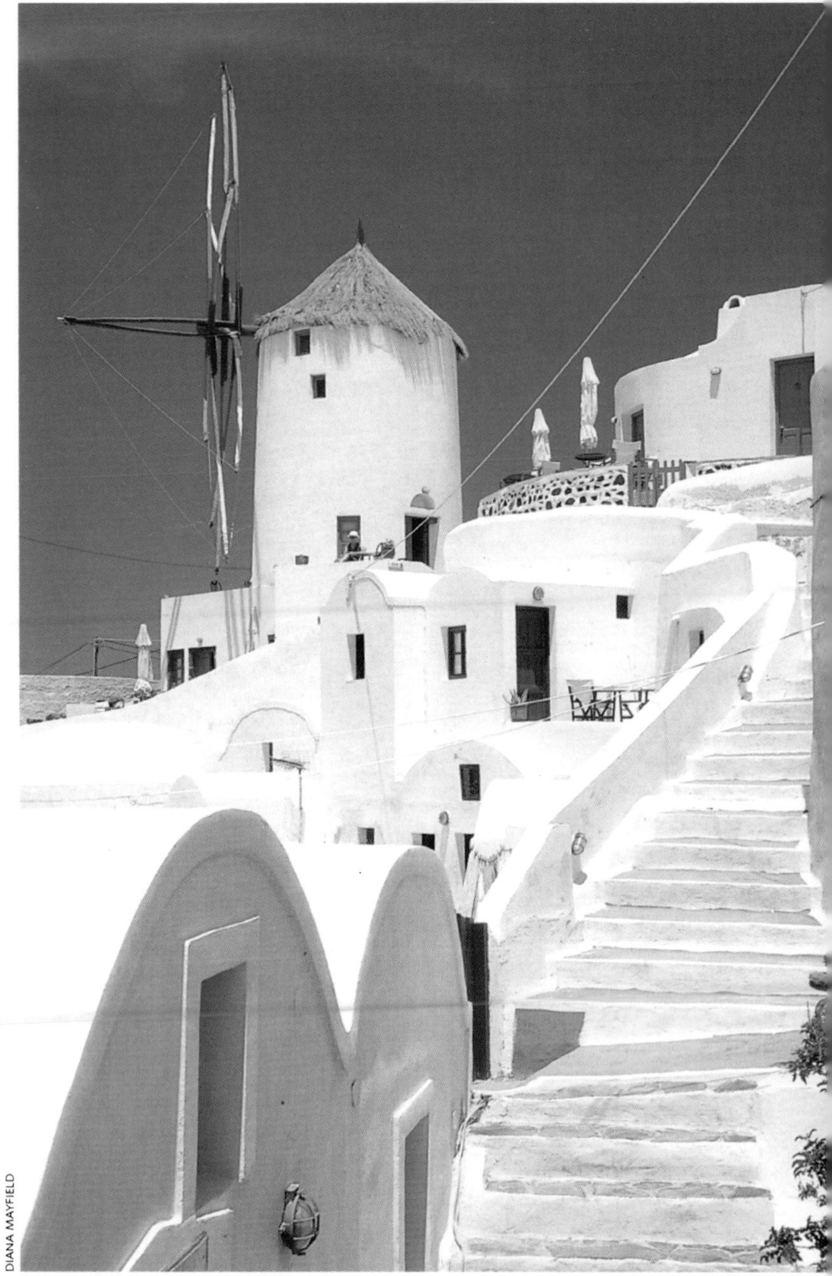
DIANA MAYFIELD

Dazzlingly white streetscape of Oia, Santorini (Cyclades)

Syntagma (Map 2)

Fast food is the order of the day at busy Syntagma. ***Neon Café***, on the south-western corner of Plateia Syntagmatos, is a stylish self-service cafeteria. It has spaghetti or fettucine napolitana for 1000 dr, or bolognese/carbonara for 1350 dr. Main dishes range from moussaka (1450 dr) to roast beef (1550 dr).

Fast Food Heleni *(Perikleos 30-32)* has fast-food favourites like toasted sandwiches and souvlaki as well as a daily selection of taverna dishes. In season, you'll find tasty artichoke stew (900 dr). There's nothing on the menu over 1200 dr.

Meat is the only item on the menu at the tiny ***Souvlaki tou Hasepi*** *(The Butcher's Souvlaki; Apollonos 3)*. Pork souvlakis are 200 dr and come with a slice of bread. A large cold beer costs 270 dr.

It's very hard to ignore the delicious aromas emanating from ***Brazil Coffee Shop*** on Voukourestiou (between Panepistimiou and Stadiou). It does a great cappuccino (600 dr) as well as filter coffee (also 600 dr), plus cakes and croissants priced from 350 dr.

Monastiraki (Map 2)

There are some excellent cheap eats around Plateia Monastirakiou, particularly for gyros and souvlaki fans. ***Thanasis***, at the bottom end of Mitropoleos, is famous among Athenians for its special souvlaki. It uses a traditional house recipe that combines minced lamb, minced beef and seasonings. You'll pay 300 dr for the takeaway version wrapped in a small pitta, or 1300 dr to sit down to a plate of four souvlaki and a large pitta. The place is always packed out and the service is pure theatre – the waiters have to run to keep up with the demand.

Opposite Thanasis is ***Savas*** *(Mitropoleos 86)*, which specialises in gyros. It has a

A Taste of Ancient Greece

Retro is all the rage in Greece these days, with the owners of old buildings everywhere busily stripping back modern finishings to reveal the stonework and timber beams of yesteryear.

No-one, however, has taken things to quite the lengths of the owners of Restaurant Archeon Gefsis, situated west of Omonia in the suburb of Metaxourgio. They have turned the clock back 2500 years to the days of ancient Greece – to a time before the advent of potatoes, rice, tomatoes and many other staples of the modern Greek diet.

Diners will notice a few other differences, too, as they are seated at their solid wooden tables by waiting staff dressed in flowing red robes. There are no glasses – the ancients used earthernware cups, and spoons instead of forks.

Small portions must also be a modern idea, because the servings here are huge. The Cyclopean salad (3000 dr), chosen from a range of salads loaded with herbs, fruit and berries, is a mountain of fresh rocket mixed with crumbled goat's cheese, oil and vinegar that is easily enough for two.

Main courses are equally substantial. Not surprisingly, roast meats and fish dominate the menu, served with purees of peas or chick peas and vegetable. Try the pork stuffed with plums (4200 dr), served with a sweet plum sauce, pea puree and artichoke hearts.

Wine, from the barrel, is 2300 dr for a litre. There is also draught organic beer. Reckon on paying around 20,000 dr for two people, including drinks. The restaurant is open for dinner every day except Sunday. Bookings are essential.

Restaurant Archeon Gefsis *(Map 8; ☎ 523 9661, fax 520 0372, email adamis@arxaion.gr, Kodratou 22, Metaxourgio)*

takeaway stall with a choice of chicken (360 dr), pork or minced beef (both 300 dr), and a restaurant (there's a shop in between) with seating in the square opposite.

The best taverna food in this part of town is at the ***meat market***, 400m along Athinas from Plateia Monastirakiou, on the right. The place must resemble a vegetarian's vision of hell, but the food is great and the tavernas are open 24 hours a day, except Sunday. They serve traditional meat dishes such as *patsas* (tripe soup) and *podarakia* (pig-trotter soup), as well as less exotic dishes such as *stifado* (meat stewed with onions) and meatballs. Soups start at 800 dr, and main dishes at 1350 dr.

There are a few places to eat in the flea market. ***Ipiros Taverna*** *(Filippou 16)* has cheap, tasty food. The outdoor tables are great in summer for watching the market's hustle and bustle.

Psiri (Map 2)

The busy ***O Telis*** psistaria, at the junction of Evripidou and Epikourou near Plateia Eleftherias, is famous for its only dish – pork chops and chips. A huge pile of chips topped by three or four chops costs 1600 dr.

Makrigianni (Map 4)

To 24 Hours is something of an institution among Athenian night owls. The place never closes, except on Easter Sunday, and seems to be at its busiest in the wee small hours. The customers are as much of an attraction as the food: you'll be rubbing shoulders with an assortment of hungry cabbies, middle-aged couples dressed for the opera, and leather-clad gays from the area's many bars – all tucking into steaming bowls of the house speciality, *patsas* (tripe soup). It also has a constantly changing choice of other popular taverna dishes, most priced under 1500 dr.

Socrates Prison *(Mitseon 20)* is a delightful taverna with an Art Nouveau interior and 19th century Parisian posters on the walls. It also has garden seating in summer. The restaurant is not named after the philosopher, but after the owner (also called Socrates), who reckons the restaurant is his prison. It has an imaginative range of mezedes from 850 dr and main dishes from 1500 dr.

Koukaki (Map 4)

Gardenia Restaurant *(Zini 31)*, at the junction with Dimitrakopoulou, claims to be the cheapest taverna in Athens. I wouldn't doubt it. A plate of gigantes beans is 650 dr, chicken and potatoes 650 dr, and moussaka is 700 dr. A large Amstel beer costs 350 dr, and a litre of draught retsina is 450 dr. What's more, the food is good and the service is friendly. The owner is an effervescent woman called Gogo who speaks English.

On the opposite side of the road is ***Meltemi Ouzeri*** *(Zini 26)*, a pleasant spot with white stucco walls, marble-topped tables and blue-painted wooden chairs – all of which give a Cycladic island feel. In summer, an outside eating area is shielded from the traffic by large pot plants. There is a wide choice of delicious mezedes priced from 750 dr and main courses from 1500 dr.

To 38 Taverna *(Veïkou 38)* is another good-value establishment. The restaurant is lively, rough and ready, and very popular. A generous serving of crisp fried cod costs 1500 dr, and a plate of cuttlefish cooked with spinach is 1250 dr. There is no name on the door, only the number. It is open in the evening from 8 pm, but is closed from 1 June to 15 September.

Omonia (Map 3)

The Omonia area is a place where people clutch at their wallets for safety, not a place to relax over a meal. You'll have to run the gauntlet of junkies and pimps if you want to eat at any of the fast-food outlets around Athinas and Pireos on the southern side of Plateia Omonias.

An exception is ***Neon Cafeteria***, an oasis of calm occupying a beautiful neoclassical building on the corner of Dorou, on the opposite side of the square. It is a stable mate of the Neon at Syntagma and serves the same fare.

Flocafé coffee shop *(Oktovriou-Patission 53)* is a good spot to stop for coffee and cakes after visiting the National Archaeological Museum.

Around the Train Stations (Map 3)

Wherever you choose to eat in this area you will find the lack of tourist hype refreshing – it's a million miles from the strategically placed menus and restaurant touts of Plaka.

O Makis Psistaria *(Psaron 48)*, opposite the church, is a lively place serving hunks of freshly grilled pork or beef, plus chips, for 1600 dr. It also does delicious grilled chicken with lemon sauce for 1300 dr.

Dafni Taverna *(Ioulianou 65)*, farther north, offers equally good value with very tasty gigantes beans for 900 dr or baked fish with potatoes for 1500 dr. In summer, there's outdoor seating in the small courtyard.

Exarhia (Map 5)

Exarhia has lots of small ouzeris and tavernas to choose from, and prices are tailored to suit the pockets of the district's student clientele. It's quite a long hike to the area from Syntagma; or you can catch a No 230 bus from Amalias or Panepistimiou to Harilaou Trikoupi and walk across. It is, however, only a short walk from the National Archaeological Museum to lively Plateia Exarhion. The square (triangle actually) is lined with cafes and snack bars, many with seating under shade.

Most of the better eating places are south of Plateia Exarhion. You'll find a string of small ouzeris on Emmanual Benaki, including the excellent ***Ouzeri I Gonia***, at the corner of Emmanual Benaki and Arahovis. It has a good range of tasty mezedes priced between 600 dr and 1800 dr, and has draught wine as well as ouzo.

Ouzeri Amfiliki *(Isavron 29B)*, next to To Taximi rembetika club, is a good place to head if you're feeling peckish at 4 am. It doesn't open until 10 pm and specialises in serving mezedes to night-owl carousers falling out of Exarhia's clubs and bars.

Taverna Barbargiannis *(Emmanual Benaki 94)*, on the corner of Dervenion, is an excellent place with a blackboard list of daily specials. Your best bet is to line up at the counter and ask to have a look. They make a delicious thick chicken soup for 1150 dr that comes with a generous portion of chicken on the side, as well as a tasty bean soup for 800 dr. Most meat dishes are priced around 1500 dr, and draught retsina is 700 dr for a litre.

Kolonaki (Map 5)

Cheap eats are hard to find around Kolonaki, but not impossible. ***Ouzeri Dexameni***, in the middle of shady Plateia Dexameni, is a great spot to stop for a bite. It has a choice of mezedes priced from 600 dr, and a good selection of cold drinks.

PLACES TO EAT – MID-RANGE

Eating out in Athens remains fairly cheap, especially if you're eating Greek. The few places that do charge a bit extra tend to be doing so because of their location rather than the excellence of their cuisine. This is particularly the case in Plaka, where many restaurants charge way over the odds for very average food. A sure way to end up with a large bill is to eat fresh seafood at any of the restaurants on Kydathineon. Psiri is a good place to look if you're happy to pay a bit more for something interesting.

Two people can expect to pay from 10,000 dr to 12,000 dr, plus wine, for a meal at most places in this category.

Plaka (Map 2)

The ***Taverna O Thespis***, at the top end of Thespidos, has a great setting on the lower slopes of the Acropolis with seating under the trees in the small square outside. The speciality here is *bekri meze* (beef in a spicy tomato sauce) for 3000 dr. Thespidos is the south-western extension of Kydathineon, beyond Adrianou, that leads uphill towards the Acropolis.

Restaurant Diogenes *(Plateia Lysikratous 3)* has outdoor seating right next to the Monument of Lysicrates. In winter, it moves indoors to Sellev 3.

Kotsolis *(Adrianou 112)* is a smart pastry shop with a mouth-watering array of goodies. They include such traditional Greek favourites as *galaktoboureko* (900 dr), *baklava* and *kataifi* (both 850 dr).

Syntagma (Map 2)

The air-conditioned ***Estatorio Kentrikon*** *(☎ 323 2482, Kolokotroni 3)*, tucked away in a small arcade, is a cool retreat from the city centre crowds that is very popular with local businessmen. The menu is upmarket taverna with a few international touches. It's open for lunch – noon to 6 pm – Monday to Friday.

Monastiraki (Map 2)

The tiny ***Taverna Abyssinia***, on the western side of Plateia Abyssinias in the Flea Market, is the place to head on Sunday afternoon after the action at the market starts to die down. It serves an array of interesting mezedes priced from 1800 dr at tables spread around the square, and there's live folk music from 3 to 6 pm.

Psiri (Map 2)

The maze of narrow streets that make up the newly trendy district of Psiri are lined with dozens of small restaurants and ouzeris, particularly the central area between Plateia Agion Anargyron and Plateia Iroön. Most places are open 8 pm until late Monday to Saturday, and for Sunday lunch.

If none of the places grabs your attention as you wander around, try ***Embros*** *(Plateia Agion Anargyron 4)*. It's a popular spot with seating in the square, and a choice of about 20 mezedes. They include delicious cheese croquettes (1150 dr) and chicken livers wrapped in bacon (1600 dr).

Frourarheio *(☎ 321 5220, Agion Anargyron 6)* is a stylish restaurant that takes its name from the old army barracks it occupies. It has an interesting Mediterranean menu and courtyard seating.

PLACES TO EAT – TOP END

The following is a selection of Athens' top-end, blow-the-budget restaurants. The prices quoted do not include wine. Reservations are strongly recommended, sometimes essential.

The Hotel Grande Bretagne's ***GB Corner*** *(Map 2; ☎ 331 4444)* restaurant, on Plateia Syntagmatos, Syntagma, has a range of set menus priced from 8900 dr to 11,500 dr for both lunch and dinner. It serves international dishes as well as local specialities such as Athenian tripe soup.

Daphne Restaurant *(Map 2; ☎ 322 7971, Lysikratous 4, Plaka)* is where US First Lady Hillary Clinton and daughter Chelsea dined during their one-night stopover in 1996 on their way to light the Olympic flame at Olympia. It's an exquisitely restored 1830s neoclassical mansion decorated with frescoes from Greek mythology. The menu includes regional specialities like rabbit cooked in mavrodaphne wine. Reckon on about 10,000 dr per person. It's open every night from 7 pm.

Pil Poule *(Map 2; ☎ 342 3665, Apostolou Pavlou 51, Thisio)* is another very stylish place. The menu is modern Mediterranean with a strong French presence. Count on paying upwards of 12,000 dr per person. It's open 8 pm daily except Sunday.

Symposio *(Map 4; ☎ 922 5321, Erehthiou 46, Makrigianni)*, south of the Acropolis, is one of Athens' most elegant restaurants. It occupies a beautifully restored 1920s house, and offers a menu loaded with regional specialities from all over Greece. In season, you'll find such delicacies as wild asparagus, wild mushrooms from Epiros and Lake Ioannina frogs' legs. Symposio's signature dish is fish baked in a salt crust (17,000 dr per kg). The wine list is similarly top of the range. You can reckon on paying at least 12,000 dr per person. It's open 8 pm until late, closed Sunday.

Bajazzo *(Map 1; ☎/fax 921 3013, Tyrteou 1, Mets)*, at the corner of Anapafseos, is widely regarded as being the best restaurant in Athens. It's the only place in town that rates a Michelin star, anyway. The name, which means jester in Greek, is the theme for the decor – with walls adorned with a variety of paintings, puppets, etc. The cuisine is eclectic, with an ever-changing menu of daily specials. Reckon on 20,000 dr per person.

PLACES TO EAT – INTERNATIONAL

International cuisine remains something of a rarity in Athens, although the choice is steadily improving. Most of the non-Greek restaurants that do exist are located in far outer suburbs like Kifissia and Glyfada, but there are a few good places around the city centre. Here are a few suggestions.

American

If you can't get no satisfaction from the burgers at the fast-food places around town, head to ***Jackson Hall*** *(Map 5; Milioni 4, Kolonaki)*. It has a selection of sit-down burgers for 3400 dr, all with chips and salad. It also has huge steaks, priced from 5300 dr. Milioni is the pedestrian precinct on the south-western edge of Plateia Eterias, off Kanari.

Curries

Until very recently, curries were virtually unobtainable in Athens. Suddenly there's a cluster of tiny curry restaurants in the streets between Plateia Eleftherias and Plateia Omonias. It's hardly the most salubrious part of town, but it's the place to go for a good cheap curry. All these place are open 9 am to about 10 pm daily.

The best food is to be found at the tiny ***Restaurant Nargis*** *(Map 3; Sofokleous 60)*, tucked away down a very dodgy-looking alleyway. It specialises in Indian food. There are more than 100 items on the menu. Starters include samosas (250 dr), channa (500 dr) and tandoori chicken wings (1000 dr). For main courses, just tell the chef what you want – biryani, korma, Madras or vindaloo – and he'll prepare it for you. Prices range from 1000 dr for vegetable curry to 1500 dr for beef or chicken. All curry prices include pilau rice.

The nearby ***Kashmeer Mahal*** *(Map 3; Sapfous 16)* is a Pakistani-owned place offering a choice of curries with rice priced from 800 dr. A major attraction here is satellite TV, beaming in cricket from all around the world. For Bangladeshi food, try ***Bengal Garden*** *(Map 2; Korinis 12)*. You'll find its speciality, goat biryani (1400 dr), only on Saturday and Sunday.

Italian

Kolonaki is the area to go to for good Italian food. ***La Pasteria*** *(Map 5; ☎ 363 2032, Tsakalof 18)* is a popular spot, offering a choice of pasta served a dozen different ways. Prices start at 1900 dr. ***Casa di Pasta*** *(Map 5; ☎ 723 3348, Spefsipou 30)* is rated by many as having the city's best Italian food – meaning that bookings are essential. Reckon on 9000 dr per person, plus wine.

Oriental

Far East Restaurant *(Map 2; Stadiou 7, Syntagma)* is a cool, elegant retreat tucked away at the back of the Stadiou 7 arcade. It serves a selection of Korean, Japanese and Chinese food. A good meal for two costs about 12,000 dr, plus drinks.

Furin Kazan Japanese Fast-Food Restaurant *(Map 2; Apollonos 2, Syntagma)* offers a range of yakisoba noodle dishes from 1400 dr and rice dishes from 1250 dr. It's open 11.30 am to 5.30 pm Monday to Friday.

Kiku *(Map 5; ☎ 364 7033, Dimokritou 12, Kolonaki)* is the smart alternative. It's the place to go if you want fresh sushi or sashimi, but you'll pay upwards of 14,000 dr per head (plus drinks) for the privilege. It's open from 7.30 pm Monday to Saturday.

Pizza

Pizza is widely available from a number of restaurants and fast-food outlets, but you'll find the best at ***Brooklyn Pizza*** *(Map 2; Voulis 31-33)*. It was opened by a local guy who wanted pizza like the pizza he'd eaten in New York. A large takeaway slice costs from 450 dr.

PLACES TO EAT – VEGETARIAN

Vegetarian restaurants are very thin on the ground in Athens. The best is ***Eden Vegetarian Restaurant*** *(Map 2; Lyssiou 12, Plaka)*, which has been around for years, substituting soya products for meat in tasty vegetarian versions of moussaka (1600 dr) and other Greek favourites. You'll also find vegie burgers (1800 dr), mushroom stifado (2300 dr) and organically produced beer (1000 dr).

Diavlos Vegetarian Restaurant & Music Bar *(Map 4; ☎ 923 9588, Drakou 9, Koukaki)*, south of the Acropolis, has the most extensive vegetarian menu in town, with more than 50 dishes to choose from. These include home-made pies with chips and salad (from 1250 dr), croquettes and fritters (1250 dr), soya moussaka (1600 dr) and tofu curry with rice (1750 dr). Diavlos is open 8 pm to 3 am Tuesday to Sunday. The place tends to be deserted until the rembetika music starts at 11 pm.

Vegetarian Fast Food *(Map 3; Panepistimiou 55, Omonia)* offers a choice of three dishes from its buffet for 950 dr, as well as portions of wholemeal pizza and pies for 550 dr. You can wash your meal down with a fresh carrot juice for 400 dr. There is also a well stocked health-food shop, which carries a small range of biodynamic produce.

PLACES TO EAT – SELF-CATERING

Markets (Map 2)

You'll find the widest range of whatever's in season and the best prices at the main ***fruit & vegetable market*** on Athinas, opposite the ***meat market***. The stretch of Athinas between the meat market and Plateia Monastirakiou is the place to shop for nuts and nibblies.

Supermarkets

Supermarkets are a bit thin on the ground in central Athens.

There are plenty of shops around Plaka and Syntagma, but no big supermarkets. The closest is ***Marinopoulos*** *(Map 5; Kanari 9, Kolonaki)*. ***Basilopolou*** *(Map 2; Stadiou 18, Syntagma)* is a large, well stocked delicatessen that almost qualifies as a supermarket. It has an excellent selection of cheeses and cold meats, and an imported food section where you'll find such treasured items as Marmite – but not Vegemite!

Omonia (Map 3) is better served than most areas. There is a branch of the ***Marinopoulos*** chain *(Athinas 60)*, with the food section downstairs, while the ***Bazaar Discount Supermarket*** chain has branches at Eolou 104 and another at the Minion department store on Oktovriou-Patission.

The Koukaki area (Map 4) is served by ***Papageorgiou*** *(Dimitrakopoulou 76)* and ***Hellaspar*** *(Parthenos 6)*.

Exarhia (Map 5) has the ***Sklavenitis*** supermarket *(Harilaou Trikoupi 43)*.

ENTERTAINMENT

The best source of entertainment information is the weekly listings magazine *Athenorama*, but you'll need to be able to read some Greek to make much sense of it. It costs 500 dr and is available from periptera all over the city.

English-language listings appear daily in the *Kathimerini* supplement that accompanies the *International Herald Tribune*, while Friday's edition of the *Athens News* carries a 16 page entertainment guide.

Another useful source of information is the quarterly magazine *Welcome to Athens*, available free from the tourist office. It has details of theatre, dance, classical music concerts and art exhibitions.

Bars

Brettos *(Map 2; Kydathineon 41)* is a delightful little place right in the heart of Plaka. Very little has changed here in years except that being old-fashioned has suddenly become very fashionable. It's a family-run business which acts as a shop front for the family distillery and winery in Kalithea. Huge old barrels line one wall and the shelves are stocked with a colourful collection of bottles that is backlit at night. Shots of Brettos brand spirits (ouzo, brandy and many more) cost 500 dr, as does a glass of wine. It's open 10 am to 1 am daily.

Most bars around Syntagma are places to avoid. ***Club 11*** *(Nikis 11)* and ***Athens Club*** *(Nikis 1)* both employ touts to roam Syntagma and Plaka, targeting single male tourists with talk of beautiful girls. The girls then persuade suckers to buy them ludicrously overpriced drinks.

Most bars in Athens have music as a main feature. Thisio is a good place to look, particularly on Iraklidon. ***Stavlos*** *(Map 2; Iraklidon*

10) occupies an amazing old rabbit warren of a building. It has a rock bar playing mainly alternative British music, and more mellow sounds in the cafe/brasserie outside.

Gay Bars

The greatest concentration of gay bars is to be found in Makrigianni (Map 4), south of the Temple of Olympian Zeus. Popular spots include the long-running ***Granazi Bar*** *(Lembesi 20)* and the more risque ***Lamda Club*** *(Lembesi 15)*. Lesbians should check out the lively ***Porta Bar*** *(Falirou 10)*, nearby.

Koukles Club *(☎ 530 4923, San Moreas 32)*, farther south in Koukaki, is the favoured venue of Athens' surprisingly large transsexual community. It stages a drag show on Friday and Saturday nights, starting at about 2 am. Entry is 3000 dr, which includes one free drink.

There are also several gay bars in Kolonaki (Map 5). The popular ***Alexander Club*** *(Anagnostopoulou 44)* is a relaxed, friendly place that draws a mixed crowd of younger gays and lesbians. There's a cruising bar upstairs and a disco downstairs. It's open every night 9 pm to 2 am year-round. ***Alekos Island*** *(Tsakalof 42)* comes highly recommended by no less an authority than *Spartacus*.

Discos

Discos operate in Athens only between October and April. In summer, the action moves to the coastal suburbs of Ellinikon and Glyfada. Many of the big names operate in both locations. They include such places as ***Plus Soda***, which spends winter at Ermou 161 in Thisio and summer at Eurualis 2 in Glyfada, and ***Kingsize***, which moves from inner city Amerikis 3 out to Poseidonos 5 in Ellinikon. Plus Soda plays a mix of techno and disco, while Kingsize is more rock and roll.

Admission at most places ranges from 1000 dr on weekdays to 3000 dr on Friday and Saturday nights. The price often includes one free drink. Subsequently, expect to pay about 800 dr for soft drinks, 1000 dr for a beer and 1500 dr for spirits. Discos don't start to get busy until around midnight.

Live Music

The main rock venue is ***Rodon Club*** *(Map 3; ☎ 524 7427, Marni 24. Omonia)*, north of Plateia Omonias. It has bands most Fridays and Saturdays. Another venue to check out is ***AN Club*** *(Map 5; ☎ 363 9217, Solomou 20, Exarhia)*.

Top-name international acts play at a variety of venues, including the spectacular Lykavittos Theatre on Lykavittos Hill, and the Panathinaïkos football stadium.

Jazz enthusiasts should check out what's happening at ***Half Note Jazz Club*** *(Map 1; ☎ 921 3310, Trivonianou 17, Mets)*, or ***Hi Hat Cafe*** *(☎ 721 8171, Kroussouvou 1)*, west of the Hilton Hotel.

Blues fans should head for ***Blues Hall*** *(Map 1; ☎ 924 7448, Arditou 44, Mets)*.

Traditional Music Tavernas (Map 2)

There is a cluster of tavernas on the upper reaches of Mnissikleos in Plaka that feature live Greek music, occasionally accompanied by folk dancing. The main places are ***Taverna Geros tou Moria*** *(Mnissikleos 27)*, and its neighbour, ***Taverna Alexandros***. Both get packed out with tour groups and the performances are fairly uninspiring. You don't have to eat to watch the shows, but drinks are expensive. If you want to see real Greek music, you're better off going to a rembetika club (see following).

Rembetika Clubs

Athens has a good number of rembetika clubs, but most close down from May to September. Performances in these clubs start at around 11.30 pm; most places do not have a cover charge but drinks are expensive. Clubs open up and close down with great rapidity – telephone to check if a club is still open.

The biggest concentration of clubs is in and around Exarhia (Map 5), including the popular ***Boemissa*** *(☎ 384 3836, Solomou 19)*. It's open 11 pm to 4 am, and it pays to get in early – particularly on Friday and Saturday when it's packed out. ***Rembetika To Taximi*** *(Isavron 29)*, next to the Ouzeri Amfiliki, is smaller and more intimate.

Instant Coffee Culture

You can hardly miss the forest of straws sprouting from glasses of frothy-topped black liquid at countless street cafes throughout Greece. Nes(café) frappé has almost universally overtaken the traditional Greek (or Turkish) coffee as the nation's favourite beverage. But what could possibly be the attraction of a glass of cold water, flavoured with a spoonful of instant coffee and sugar, processed to resemble a glass of Guinness stout and then chilled with ice cubes?

Nes frappé is not a beverage to be taken in a hurry; it is certainly not a beverage to be drunk for the caffeine hit that you might expect from traditional coffee. Its primary role is that of a 'ticket' to sit at a street cafe in order to idly chat and smoke. Its arrival at the table, however, is treated with almost reverential ceremony. Firstly the imbiber will dutifully stir the ice cubes to ensure that every molecule of Nes frappé is equally chilled, and then the first minuscule sip is taken. It is considered extremely bad form to drink the mixture quickly, so never order one if you intend to quench your thirst in Greek company. The next sip may follow between five and 10 minutes later; in fact, the whole drinking procedure may take up to an hour.

The drink's universal popularity throughout the country and at all times of the year may be a puzzle to observers, for its appeal as a beverage is surely limited. The cafe owners, however, are not complaining: at 500 dr a shot, it is a sure-fire money spinner.

Rembetiki Stoa Athanaton *(Map 2; ☎ 321 4362, Sofokleous 19)*, next to the central meat market, is open in the afternoon from 3 to 6 pm and reopens from midnight until 6 am. It's closed Sunday.

Cinema

Athenians are avid cinema-goers. Most cinemas show recent releases from Britain and the USA in English. The two areas with the highest concentration of cinemas are the main streets running between Syntagma and Omonia, and the Oktovriou-Patission and Plateia Amerikis area.

The major cinemas in central Athens are ***Apollon*** *(☎ 323 6811, Stadiou 19)*; ***Astor*** *(☎ 323 1297, Stadiou 28)*; ***Asty*** *(☎ 322 1925, Koraï 4)*; ***Cine Paris*** *(☎ 322 0721)*, on Kydathineon; ***Elly*** *(☎ 363 2789, Akadimias 64)*; ***Ideal*** *(☎ 382 6720, Panepistimiou 46)*; and ***Titania*** *(☎ 381 1147)*, on the corner of Panepistimiou and Themistokleous. The Asty shows mostly avant-garde films; the others show mostly first-run films (usually from Britain or the USA with Greek subtitles).

Admission costs between 1600 dr and 2000 dr.

Theatre

Athens has a dynamic theatre scene, but, as you'd expect, most performances are in Greek. If you're a theatre buff you may enjoy a performance of an old favourite, provided you know the play well enough. The listings mention when a performance is in English – which happens occasionally.

Greek Folk Dancing

In summer, performances of Greek folk dances are given by the ***Dora Stratou Dance Company*** *(☎ 324 4395)* at its own theatre on the western side of Filopappos Hill (Map 1). The company was formed many years ago and has gained an international reputation for authenticity and professionalism.

Performances are held nightly at 10.15 pm from May to October, with additional performances at 8.15 pm on Wednesday and Sunday. Tickets can be bought at the door and cost from 3000 dr. The theatre is signposted from the western end of Dionysiou Areopagitou. The company also runs folk dancing workshops in summer – see Courses in the Facts for the Visitor chapter.

Classical Music, Opera & Ballet

There are frequent classical music concerts, by both international and Greek performers, at the ***Athens Concert Hall*** *(Megaron Mousikis; ☎ 728 2333)*, on Vasilissis Sofias, Ilissia (off Map 1). The ***Pallas Theatre*** *(Map 2; ☎ 322 4434, Voukourestiou 1, Syntagma)* also has performances of classical music.

The ***Olympia Theatre*** *(Map 5; ☎ 361 2461, Akadimias 59, Exarhia)* has performances by the National Opera (Ethniki Lyriki Skini). It also stages ballet.

Son et Lumière

This 'sound and light' spectacle, at the ***Hill of the Pnyx Theatre*** *(Map 2; ☎ 322 1459)*, is not one of the world's best, but it is an enduring and integral part of the Athens tourist scene. There are shows in English every night at 9 pm from the beginning of April until the end of October. There are shows in French at 10 pm every night except Tuesday and Friday, when the show is in German. During the performance, the monuments of the Acropolis are lit up in synchronisation with accompanying music, sound effects and historical narration. The lights are the most exciting part of the performance. Tickets cost 1500 dr. The Hill of the Pnyx is west of the Acropolis off Dionysiou Areopagitou. Bus No 230 from Syntagma will get you there.

SPECTATOR SPORTS

Soccer

Seven of the 18 teams in the Greek first division are from either Athens or Piraeus. They are AEK, Apollon, Ionikos, Olympiakos Piraeus, Panathinaïkos, Panionios and Proödeftiki. Two other clubs, Athinaikos and Ethnikos, fluctuate between the first and second divisions.

Olympiakos is the most popular team, the Greek equivalent of Manchester United. The club's success in the 1998/99 Greek championship was its 28th in 74 years. Its main rival is wealthy Panathinaïkos, which reached the semifinals of the European championship in 1996 – the best result achieved by a Greek team.

Both teams play at the Olympic Stadium in Maroussi, a short walk from Irini station on Metro Line 1 – although Olympiakos is expected to return to Piraeus once renovation work at the Karaïskaki Stadium has been completed. AEK plays at the Nikos Goumas Stadium in Nea Philadelphia; Apollon at Rizoupolis; Panionios at Nea Smyrni; and Proödeftiki at the Korydalos Stadium in Piraeus.

First division matches are played on Sunday and cup matches on Wednesday. They are often televised. Admission charges start at 1500 dr.

The soccer season lasts from September to the middle of May. Fixtures and results are given in the *Athens News*.

Horse Racing

Horse races are held three times a week at the Faliro Ippodromo (☎ 941 7761), at the southern end of Syngrou. Bus No 126 from Syntagma will take you there. Meetings are normally held on Monday, Wednesday and Friday, starting at about 2 pm. Admission prices start at 200 dr

SHOPPING

Flea Market (Map 2)

This market is the first place which springs to most people's minds when they think of buying things in Athens. The flea market is the commercial area which stretches both east and west of Plateia Monastirakiou and consists of shops selling goods running the whole gamut from high quality to trash. However, when most people speak of the Athens flea market, they are referring to the Sunday morning outdoor flea market. This market spills over into Plateia Monastirakiou and onto Ermou.

A visit to Athens isn't complete without a visit to this market. All manner of things – from new to fourth-hand – are on sale. There's everything from clocks to condoms, binoculars to bouzoukis, tyres to telephones, giant evil eyes to jelly babies, and wigs to welding kits. Wandering around the market, you'll soon realise that Greece is top of the league of European countries when it comes to mass-produced kitsch. If you're looking for a plastic jewellery box with a psychedelic picture of the Virgin Mary on the lid, which plays 'Never on a Sunday' when you open it, you might just be in luck at the flea market.

Traditional Handicrafts

The National Welfare Organisation's Hellenic Folk Art Gallery, on the corner of Apollonos and Ipatias, Plaka (Map 2), is a good place for handicrafts. It has top-quality merchandise and the money goes to a good cause – the preservation and promotion of traditional Greek handicrafts. It has a wide range of knotted carpets, kilims, flokatis, needle-point rugs and embroidered cushion covers as well as a small selection of pottery, copper and woodwork. The shop is open 9 am to 8 pm Tuesday to Friday, 9 am to 3 pm Monday and Saturday, and is closed Sunday.

Karamihos Mazarakis Flokati, Voulis 31-33, Plaka, has the largest selection of flokati rugs.

The Centre of Hellenic Tradition, Pandrossou 36, Plaka (Map 2), has a display of traditional and modern handicrafts from each region of Greece. Most of the items are for sale.

Mado, next to the Lysicrates monument on Sellev, Plaka, is a workshop that turns out beautiful, hand-woven wall hangings. Many depict island scenes.

Good-quality leather sandals may be bought from Stavros Melissinos, Pandrossou 89 (see the Walking Tour section earlier in this chapter).

GETTING THERE & AWAY

Air

Athens is served by Ellinikon airport, on the coast 9km south-east of the city. There are two main terminals with separate entrances 1.5km apart: the West Terminal for all Olympic Airways flights (domestic and international) and the East Terminal for all other flights. From April until the end of October, charter flights use the old military terminal 500m south of the East Terminal.

The facilities are primitive at all the terminals, but nothing is likely to change until the swish new Eleftherias Venizelou

Fancy a Flokati?

There are few better souvenirs of a visit to Greece than the luxuriant woollen flokati rugs produced in the mountain areas of central and northern Greece. They make beautiful, cosy floor coverings.

The process by which these rugs are produced has changed little over the centuries. The first step is to weave a loose woollen base. Short lengths of twisted wool are then looped through it, leaving the two ends on top to form the pile – the more loops, the denser the pile.

At this point, the rug looks like a scalp after stage one of a hair transplant – a series of unconvincing little tufts. The twisted threads can easily be pulled through.

A transformation takes place during the next stage, the 'waterfall treatment'. The rugs are immersed in fast-running water for between 24 and 36 hours, unravelling the twisted wool and shrinking the base so that the pile is held fast. They can then be dyed.

The main production areas are the villages of Epiros, around the town of Tripolis in the Peloponnese and around the towns of Trikala and Karditsa in Thessaly. All these villages have plenty of the running water required for the waterfall treatment.

The rugs are sold by weight. A rug measuring 150 x 60cm will cost from 12,000 dr to 45,000 dr, depending on the length and density of the pile.

international airport at Spata (21km east of Athens) opens for business in 2002. Ellinikon will then handle only domestic flights.

For Olympic Airways flight information ring ☎ 936 3363, and for all other airlines ring ☎ 969 4466/4467. The head office of Olympic Airways (☎ 926 7251/4) is at Leoforos Syngrou 96. The most central Olympic Airways branch office (☎ 926 7444, international ☎ 926 7489) is at Filellinon 13, just off Plateia Syntagmatos. For information about domestic flights from Athens see the Getting Around chapter.

There is luggage storage (open 24 hours) at the East Terminal, opposite the domestic arrivals.

Athens is one of Europe's major centres for buying discounted air tickets. There are dozens of travel agents on Filellinon, Nikis and Voulis that sell low-priced air tickets to Europe and the USA. See the Travel Agencies section under Information at the beginning of this chapter for some recommendations.

Airline offices in Athens include:

Aeroflot	☎ 322 0986
Air Canada	☎ 322 3206
Air France	☎ 960 1100
Air India	☎ 360 3584
Alitalia	☎ 995 9200
American Airlines	☎ 325 5061
British Airways	☎ 890 6666
Condor	☎ 925 0390
Continental Airlines	☎ 324 9300
CSA-Czech Airlines	☎ 960 0942
Cyprus Airways	☎ 322 6413/4
Delta Airlines	☎ 331 1660/1
EasyJet	☎ 967 0000
Egypt Air	☎ 921 2818/9
El Al	☎ 363 8681
Garuda Indonesia	☎ 324 5204
Gulf Air	☎ 322 5157
Iberia	☎ 323 4523/6
Japan Airlines	☎ 324 8211
KLM	☎ 964 8865
Lufthansa	☎ 617 5200
Malaysian Airlines	☎ 921 2470
Qantas Airways, see British Airways	
SAS	☎ 361 3910
Singapore Airlines	☎ 323 9111
South African Airways	☎ 361 6305
Thai Airways	☎ 364 7610
Turkish Airlines	☎ 322 1035
TWA	☎ 921 3400
United Airlines	☎ 924 2645
Virgin Atlantic	☎ 924 9100

Bus

Athens has two main intercity bus stations. Terminal A is about 7km north-west of Omonia at Kifissou 100 and has departures to the Peloponnese, the Ionian Islands and western Greece. Terminal B is about 5km north of Omonia off Liossion and has departures to central and northern Greece as well as to Evia. The EOT gives out an intercity bus schedule.

Terminal A Like the infamous airport, Terminal A is not a good introduction to Athens – particularly if you arrive between midnight and 5 am when there is no public transport. See the following Getting Around section for details of fares, and the boxed text 'Dangers & Annoyances' earlier in this chapter for information on avoiding rip-offs. The only public transport to the city centre is bus No 051, which runs between the terminal and the junction of Zinonos and Menandrou, near Omonia. Buses run every 15 minutes from 5 am to midnight. Don't bother visiting the Tourist Information office at the terminal. It's a booking agency. See the accompanying Departures table for more information.

Terminal B Terminal B is much easier to handle than Terminal A, although again there is no public transport from midnight to 5 am. The EOT information sheet misleadingly lists the address of the terminal as being Liossion 260, which turns out to be a small car repair workshop. Liossion 260 is where you should get off the No 024 bus that runs from outside the main gate of the National Gardens on Amalias. From Liossion 260, turn right onto Gousiou and you'll see the terminal at the end of the road on Agiou Dimitriou Oplon. A taxi

Bus & Train Departures from Athens

Bus Terminal A

Destination	Duration	Price (dr)	Frequency
Argos	2 hours	2300	hourly
Astakos	5 hours	5200	3 daily
Corfu	11 hours	8150	2 daily
Corinth	1½ hours	1600	half-hourly
Epidaurus	2½ hours	2100	2 daily
Gythio	4¼ hours	4500	5 daily
Igoumenitsa	8½ hours	8300	4 daily
Ioannina	7½ hours	7250	8 daily
Kalamata	3½ hours	4250	9 daily
Kalavryta	3½ hours	3200	daily
Kavala	10 hours	11,100	3 daily
Kefallonia	8 hours	7500	4 daily
Lefkada	5½ hours	6200	4 daily
Loutraki	1½ hours	1600	9 daily
Monemvasia	5½ hours	5500	4 daily
Nafplio	2½ hours	2550	hourly
Olympia	5½ hours	5650	4 daily
Patras	3 hours	3650	half-hourly
Pyrgos	5 hours	5250	10 daily
Sparta	3¼ hours	3700	11 daily
Thessaloniki	7½ hours	8200	8 daily
Tripolis	2¼ hours	3000	12 daily
Zakynthos	7 hours	6310	8 daily

Bus Terminal B

Destination	Duration	Price (dr)	Frequency
Agios Konstantinos	2½ hours	3000	hourly
Delphi	3 hours	2900	6 daily
Edipsos	3¼ hours	2650	3 daily
Halkida	1 hour	1350	half-hourly
Karpenisi	5 hours	4850	3 daily
Kymi	3½ hours	2950	3 daily
Lamia	3 hours	3700	hourly
Larisa	4½ hours	6000	6 daily
Livadia	2 hours	2350	hourly
Trikala	5½ hours	5400	8 daily
Volos	5 hours	5250	9 daily

Trains for northern Greece, Evia & Europe from Larisis train station

Destination	Duration	Price (dr)	Frequency
Alexandroupolis	15 hours	7310	1 daily
(Intercity)	12¼ hours	11,460	2 daily
Halkida	1½ hours	700	17 daily
(Intercity)	not available		
Larisa	5 hours	2960	8 daily
(Intercity)	4 hours	5660	5 daily
Litohoro	6 hours	3250	3 daily
(Intercity)	not available		
Thessaloniki	7½ hours	4100	4 daily
(Intercity)	6 hours	8250	5 daily
Volos	6 hours	3120	1 daily
(Intercity)	5 hours	5820	2 daily

Trains for the Peloponnese from Sidirodromon

Destination	Duration	Price (dr)	Frequency
Corinth	1¾ hours	780	10 daily
(Intercity)	1½ hours	1530	5 daily
Kalamata	6½ hours	2160	4 daily
(Intercity)	not available		
Nafplio	3½ hours	1400	2 daily
(Intercity)	not available		
Patras	4½ hours	1580	4 daily
(Intercity)	3½ hours	2980	4 daily
Pyrgos	6½ hours	2160	4 daily
(Intercity)	5 hours	4860	2 daily
Tripolis	4 hours	1500	3 daily
(Intercity)	not available		

from the terminal to Syntagma should cost no more than 1500 dr at any time. See the accompanying Departures table for more information.

Buses for nearly all destinations in Attica leave from the Mavromateon terminal at the junction of Alexandras and 28 Oktovriou-Patission, 250m north of the National Archaeological Museum and next to Areos Park. Buses for southern Attica leave from this terminal, while buses to Rafina and Marathon leave from the bus stops 150m north on Mavromateon.

Train

Trains for northern Greece, Evia and Europe leave from Larisis train station, Deligianni, about 1km north-east of Plateia Omonias. Selected destinations, journey times, fares and frequency are listed in the accompanying table.

Four of the trains to Thessaloniki are express intercity services (six hours, 8250 dr 2nd class, 10,500 dr 1st class). The 7 am service from Athens is express right through to Alexandroupolis, arriving at 7 pm. It will get you to Larisa in four hours and to Xanthi in 10½ hours. There are also two express trains daily to Volos, taking five hours. Express services cost about double the standard fare.

Couchettes are available on overnight services to Thessaloniki, priced from 1750 dr in 2nd class and 5800 dr in 1st class.

All trains for the Peloponnese leave from the Peloponnese train station, which is on Sidirodromon.

To reach the stations, which are close together, take trolleybus No 1 from Plateia Syntagmatos. The stop is the same for both stations, but to get to the Peloponnese train station, cross over the metal bridge at the southern end of Larisis train station.

There is baggage storage at Larisis train station, open 6.30 am to 9.30 pm, and the cost is 400 dr per piece. More information on services is available from the following OSE offices: Filellinon 17 (☎ 323 6747) in Plaka; Sina 6 (☎ 362 4402) in Syntagma; and Karolou 1 (☎ 524 0647) in Omonia. These offices also handle advance bookings.

Car & Motorcycle

National Road 1 is the main route north from Athens. It starts at Nea Kifissia. To get there from central Athens, take Vasilissis Sofias from Syntagma. National Road 8, which begins beyond Dafni, is the road to the Peloponnese. Take Agiou Konstantinou from Omonia.

The northern reaches of Syngrou, just south of the Temple of Olympian Zeus, are packed solid with car rental firms. Local companies offer much better deals than international ones. International outlets include:

Avis
(☎ 322 4951) Amalias 48
Budget
(☎ 921 4771) Syngrou 8
Eurodollar Rent a Car
(☎ 923 0548) Syngrou 36-38
Hertz
(☎ 922 0102) Syngrou 12

Hitching

Athens is the most difficult place in Greece to hitchhike from. Your best bet is to ask the truck drivers at the Piraeus cargo wharves for a ride. Otherwise, for the Peloponnese, take bus No 860 or 880 from Panepistimiou to Dafni, where National Road 8 begins. For northern Greece, take the metro to Kifissia, then a bus to Nea Kifissia and walk to National Road 1.

GETTING AROUND

To/From the Airport

Special express buses operate 24 hours a day between central Athens and the East and West terminals, stopping also at the charter terminal when it's in use. The buses are blue and have their destination marked on the front in English.

The 091 service to the airport starts just south of Plateia Omonias on Stadiou (opposite Emmanual Benaki), and stops only at Plateia Syntagmatos, Syntagma (outside the post office). It calls first at the charter terminal, then the East Terminal and finishes at the West Terminal.

The buses run every 20 minutes between 7 am and 10.45 pm, and then (roughly) hourly until 5.40 am. Night buses leave Stadiou at 11.50 pm and at 0.50, 1.50, 2.50, 3.50, 4.50, 5.40, 6.20 and 7 am, and from Plateia Syntagmatos five minutes later. The fare is 250 dr, or 500 dr from 11.50 pm to 5.40 am. Tickets can be bought from booths adjacent to the stops or on the bus. During rush hour the journey can take up to an hour. At other times, it should take about 30 minutes.

The 092 service from the airport starts at the West Terminal and calls at the East and charter terminals before heading for the city. It stops at Stiles, just south of the Temple of Olympian Zeus (for Makrigianni and Koukaki); at Amalias, opposite the National Gardens (for Syntagma); and at the northern end of Stadiou (for Omonia). Night services leave the airport hourly from 11.12 pm to 5.12 am, then half-hourly until 8.42 am and then every 20 minutes.

Olympic Airways passengers also have the option of taking the special buses that leave from the Olympic Airways terminal at Syngrou 96 (every 30 minutes, 6.30 am to 8.20 pm). Bus No 133 from Plateia Syntagmatos, Syntagma, to Agios Kosmas (every 15 minutes, 5.40 am to midnight, 100 dr) and bus No A2 from Stadiou or Plateia Syntagmatos to Voula (every 15 minutes, 5.30 am to 11.30 pm, 100 dr) can drop you outside the West Terminal on Leoforos Poseidonos.

There are also express buses (No 019) between all the airport terminals and Plateia Karaïskaki in Piraeus. Buses leave the East Terminal at 1.45, 3.55, 5.05, 7.05, 8.05, 9.05, 10.05, 10.55 and 11.45 am, and at 12.25, 1.15, 2.05, 2.25, 3.35, 4.35, 5.35, 6.35, 7.45, 8.55, 10.05 and 11.15 pm. They leave Plateia Karaïskaki at 0.20, 2.40, 5, 6, 8, 9.10, 10.10 and 11.10 am, at midday and at 12.50, 1.30, 2.40, 3.10, 3.50, 4.40, 5.40, 6.40, 7.40, 8.50, 10 and 11.10 pm. This timetable is subject to constant change, but gives an idea of how often they run!

Airport Taxis Welcome to Athens! It seems to be virtually impossible to catch a cab from the airport without getting involved in an argument about the fare. See the boxed text 'Dangers & Annoyances' earlier in this chapter for the full run-down on the scams operated by the city's notorious cabbies.

One way of improving your chances of avoiding a dispute is to steer well clear of the taxi ranks at all the terminals. You're better off looking for a passing cab outside the departures terminal. Whatever happens, make sure that the meter is set to the correct tariff (see the following Taxi section for details). You will also have to pay a 300 dr airport surcharge. Fares vary according to the time of day and level of traffic, but you should expect to pay between 1500 dr and 2000 dr to get from the airport to the city centre or to Piraeus during the day, and between 2000 dr and 2500 dr at night. If you have any problems, do not hesitate to threaten to involve the tourist police.

Bus & Trolleybus

Since most of Athens' ancient sites are within easy walking distance of Syntagma, and many of the museums are close by on Vasilissis Sofias near Syntagma, the chances are that you won't have much need for public transport.

The blue-and-white buses that serve Athens and the suburbs operate every 15 minutes from 5 am until midnight. There are also special buses operating 24 hours a day between the city centre and Piraeus – every 20 minutes from 6 am until midnight and then hourly. Bus No 040 runs from Filellinon to Akti Xaveriou in Piraeus, and No 049 runs from the northern end of Athinas to Plateia Themistokleous in Piraeus.

Trolleybuses also operate from 5 am until midnight. The free map handed out by EOT shows most of the routes.

There is a flat fare of 120 dr throughout the city on both buses and trolleybuses. Tickets must be purchased before you board, either at a transport kiosk or at most periptera. They can be bought in blocks of 10, but there is no discount for bulk buying. The same tickets can be used on either buses or trolleybuses and must be validated using the red ticket machine as soon as you board. Monthly travel cards are available and are valid from the first day of each month to the last and cost 6000 dr. Plain-clothed inspectors make spot checks, and the penalty for travelling without a validated ticket is 4800 dr.

Metro

At the time of writing, the first phase of the long-awaited new metro system was scheduled to begin passenger services in November 1999. See the accompanying metro map for details of the network, which adds two new lines and 21 new stations to the old Kifissia-Piraeus line, now known as Line 1.

Line 1 remains unchanged, except that the stations at Attiki, Monastiraki and Omonia have been upgraded to become transfer stations. The most useful stops are Piraeus (for the port), Monastiraki and Omonia (city centre) and Plateia Viktorias (National Archaeological Museum).

Line 2 runs from Agios Antonios in the north-west to Dafni in the south-east. Useful stops include Larissa (for the train stations), Omonia, Panepistimiou and Syntagma (city centre) and Akropoli (Makrigianni).

Line 3 runs north-east from Monastiraki to Ethniki Amyna via Syntagma. Other useful stops are Evangelismos (for the museums on Vasilissis Sofias) and Megaro Musikis (Athens Concert Hall).

Phase two of the metro expansion is already well advanced, with most of the extensions shown on the map due to become operational in time for the Olympics in 2004. The most important of these is the extension of Line 3 to Stavros, connection point for trains to the new international airport at Spata.

Ticket prices for the new system had not been announced at the time of writing. The basic fare can be expected to remain at 120 dr for most journeys, including Monastiraki-Piraeus. There are ticket machines and ticket booths at all stations. The machines for validating tickets are at the platform entrances. As with bus tickets, the penalty for travelling without a validated ticket is 4800 dr.

The trains operate between 5 am and midnight. They run every three minutes during peak periods, dropping to every 10 minutes at other times.

Car & Motorcycle

Appalling traffic, confusing signposting and the one-way system that operates on most streets in the city centre combine to make Athens a nightmarish place to drive in. The traffic jams do at least offer an opportunity to work out where you're going!

Athenian drivers have a cavalier attitude towards driving laws. Contrary to what you will see, parking *is* illegal alongside kerbs marked with yellow lines, where street signs prohibit parking and on pavements and in pedestrian malls.

Athens has numerous small car parks, but these are totally insufficient for the number of cars in the city. There is an underground car park opposite the meat market on Athinas, with entry from Sokratous.

For details of car and motorcycle rental agencies in Athens, see the preceding Getting There & Away section.

Taxi

Athens' taxis are yellow. If you see an Athenian standing in the road bellowing and waving their arms frantically, the chances are they will be trying to get a taxi at rush hour. Despite the large number of taxis careering around the streets of Athens, it can be incredibly difficult to get one.

To hail a taxi, stand on a pavement and shout your destination as they pass. If a taxi is going your way the driver may stop even if there are already passengers inside. This does not mean the fare will be shared: each person will be charged the fare shown on the meter. If you get in one that does not have other passengers, make sure the meter is switched on.

The flag fall is 200 dr, with a 160 dr surcharge from ports and railway and bus stations, and a 300 dr surcharge from the airport. After that, the day rate (tariff 1 on the meter) is 66 dr/km. The rate doubles between midnight and 5 am (tariff 2 on the meter). Baggage is charged at the rate of 55 dr per item over 10kg. The minimum fare is

Athens' New Metro System

The swish new metro system that awaits the visitor to Athens from 2000 began life way back in 1869 as the Athens-Piraeus steam railway. It ran from the port of Piraeus to a northern terminus at Thisio, travelling via the beaches at Faliro Bay – where the railway operators developed a special resort and entertainment complex.

The line was extended to Omonia in 1894, although this section was ripped up again in 1904 when the system was electrified and the Monastiraki-Omonia section went underground – one of the first in Europe to do so. The tunnel continuation north to Plateia Viktorias and Attiki was opened in 1926, followed by the extension to Kifissia in 1957.

It soon became apparent that the single-line system was inadequate for the city's booming population, but further expansion was beyond the means of the cash-strapped government. With public transport unable to cope, Athenians began their love affair with the motor car. From a mere 39,000 private vehicles in 1961, there are now more than a million cars in Athens – making the streets among the most traffic-clogged and polluted in the world. The resulting *nefos* (toxic cloud) began to blot out the city's famous sunsets.

The situation had reached crisis point by the time contracts for the new system were signed in June 1991, with archaeologists warning that vehicle pollution was destroying the Parthenon and other famous monuments.

Now Athenians are pinning their hopes on the metro to reverse this trend. This first phase of expansion, involving 18km of track and 21 new stations, is designed to handle 450,000 passengers a day; planners calculate that this will result in 250,000 fewer vehicle movements – and a dramatic drop in vehicle emissions. Fingers crossed!

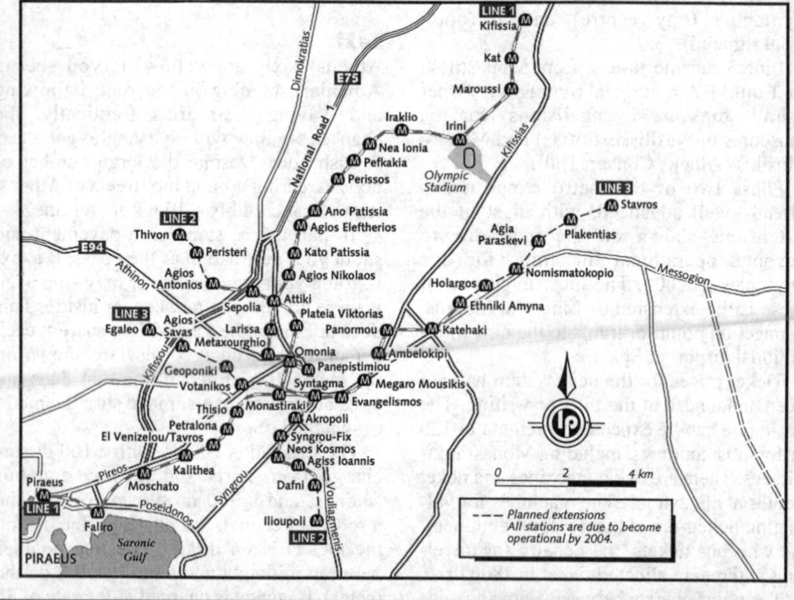

500 dr, which covers most journeys in central Athens. It sometimes helps if you can point out your destination on a map – many taxi drivers in Athens are extremely ignorant of their city.

If it is absolutely imperative that you get somewhere on time (eg to the airport), and you want to go by taxi, it is advisable to book a radio taxi – you will be charged 600 dr extra, but it's worth it. The radio taxis operating out of central Athens include:

Athina 1	☎ 921 7942
Enotita	☎ 645 9000
Ermis	☎ 411 5200
Ikaros	☎ 515 2800
Kosmos	☎ 1300
Parthenon	☎ 532 330

For more information about Athens' taxi drivers, see the boxed text 'Dangers & Annoyances' earlier in this chapter.

Around Athens

PIRAEUS Πειραιάς

☎ 01 • postcode 185 01 • pop 171,000

Piraeus is the port of Athens, the main port of Greece and one of the Mediterranean's major ports. It's the hub of the Aegean ferry network, the centre for Greece's maritime export-import and transit trade and the base for its large merchant navy. Nowadays, Athens has expanded sufficiently to meld imperceptibly into Piraeus. The road linking the two passes through a grey, urban sprawl of factories, warehouses and concrete apartment blocks. Piraeus is as bustling and traffic-congested as Athens. It's not a place in which many visitors want to linger; most come only to catch a ferry.

History

The histories of Athens and Piraeus are inextricably linked. Piraeus has been the port of Athens since classical times, when Themistocles transferred his Athenian fleet from the exposed port of Phaleron (modern Faliro) to the security of Piraeus. After his victory over the Persians at the Battle of Salamis in 480 BC, Themistocles fortified Piraeus' three natural harbours. In 445 BC Pericles extended these fortifying walls to Athens and Phaleron. The Long Walls, as they were known, were destroyed as one of the peace conditions imposed by the Spartans at the end of the Peloponnesian Wars, but were rebuilt in 394 BC.

Piraeus was a flourishing commercial centre during the classical age, but by Roman times it had been overtaken by Rhodes, Delos and Alexandria. During medieval and Turkish times Piraeus diminished to a tiny fishing village, and by the time Greece became independent, it was home to fewer than 20 people.

Its resurgence began in 1834 when Athens became the capital of independent Greece. By the beginning of the 20th century Piraeus had superseded the island of Syros as Greece's principal port. In 1923 its population was swollen by the arrival of 100,000 refugees from Turkey. The Piraeus which evolved from this influx had a seedy but somewhat romantic appeal with its bordellos, hashish dens and rembetika music – all vividly portrayed in the film *Never on a Sunday*.

These places have long since gone and beyond its facade of smart, new shipping offices and banks, much of Piraeus is now just plain seedy. The exception is the eastern quarter around Zea Marina and Mikrolimano, where the seafront is lined with seafood restaurants, bars and discos.

Orientation

Piraeus is 10km south-west of central Athens. The largest of its three harbours is the Great Harbour (Megas Limin), on the western side of the Piraeus peninsula. All ferries leave from here. Zea Marina (Limin Zeas), on the other side of the peninsula, is the port for hydrofoils to the Saronic Gulf Islands (except Aegina) as well as being the place where millionaires moor their yachts. North-east of here is the picturesque Mikrolimano (small harbour), brimming with private yachts.

The metro line from Athens terminates at the north-eastern corner of the Great

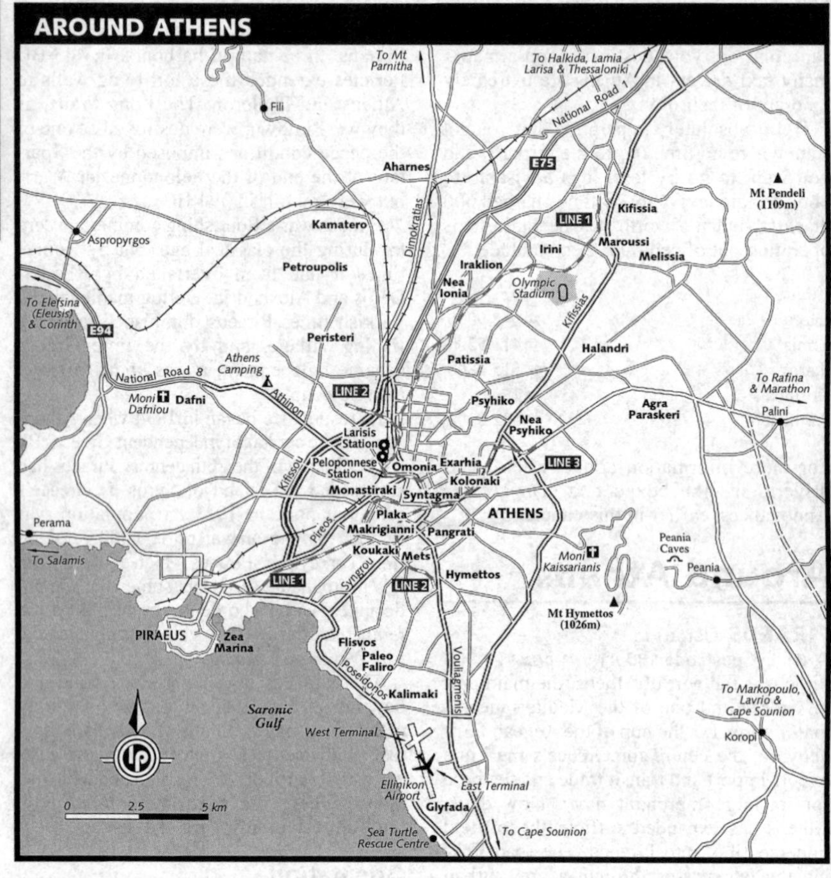

Harbour on Akti Kalimassioti. Most ferry departure points are a short walk from here. A left turn out of the metro station leads after 250m to Plateia Karaïskaki, which is the terminus for buses to the airport. Jutting out into the harbour behind the square is Akti Tzelepi with its mass of ticket agencies.

South of Plateia Karaiskaki, the waterfront becomes Akti Poseidonos, which leads into Vasileos Georgiou beyond Plateia Themistokleous. Vasileos Georgiou is one of the two main streets of Piraeus, running south-east across the peninsula; the other main street is Iroön Polytehniou, which runs south-west along the ridge of the peninsula, meeting Vasileos Georgiou by the main square, Plateia Korai.

Information

Thanks to some kind of bureaucratic bad joke, the Piraeus EOT (☎ 452 2586/2591) is at Zea Marina. Why it should be here and not at the Great Harbour defies imagination. The office is open 8 am to 3 pm

Monday to Friday. The telephone number of Piraeus' port police is ☎ 412 2501.

Money There are lots of places to change money at Great Harbour, including virtually all the ticket and travel agencies. The Emporiki Bank, just north of Plateia Themistokleous on the corner of Antistaseos and Makras Stoas, has a 24 hour automatic exchange machine. The National Bank of Greece has a Great Harbour branch at the corner of Antistaseos and Tsamadou, and another branch above the naval museum at Zea Marina.

Post & Communications The main post office is on the corner of Tsamadou and Filonos, just north of Plateia Themistokleous. It's open 7.30 am to 8 pm Monday to Friday and 7.30 am to 2 pm Saturday. The OTE is just north of here at Karaoli 19 and is open 24 hours.

You can check your email at the Surf Internet Café at Platanos 3, just off Iroön Polytehniou. It's open 8 am to 9 pm Monday to Friday and 8 am to 3 pm Saturday. Another possibility is the Dios Internet Café, Androutsou 170, open 9 am to midnight daily.

Archaeological Museum

If you have time to spare in Piraeus, the archaeological museum (☎ 452 1598) is a good place to spend it. It's well laid out and contains some important finds from classical and Roman times. These include some very fine tomb reliefs dating from the 4th to the 2nd century BC. The star piece of the museum, however, is the magnificent statue of Apollo, the Piraeus Kouros. It is the oldest larger-than-life, hollow bronze statue yet found. It dates from about 520 BC and was discovered, buried in rubble, in 1959. The museum, at Trikoupi 31, is open 8.30 am to 3 pm Tuesday to Sunday. Admission is 500 dr.

Hellenic Maritime Museum

The maritime museum (☎ 451 6822) has a collection spanning the history of the Greek navy from ancient times to the present day, with drawings and plans of battles, models of ships, battle scenes, uniforms and war memorabilia. There are various nautical oddments in the small park outside the museum, including a submarine conning tower which children love to climb. The museum is on Akti Themistokleous at Zea Marina, very close to the hydrofoil quay. It's open 9 am to 2 pm Tuesday to Saturday. Admission is 400 dr.

Places to Stay – Budget

There's no reason to stay at any of the shabby cheap hotels around Great Harbour when Athens is so close.

The cheap hotels are geared more towards accommodating sailors than tourists. ***Hotel Acropole*** *(☎ 417 3313, Gounari 7)* has dorm beds for 3500 dr, and plain singles/doubles for 6000/9000 dr. Gounari is the main thoroughfare running inland from Plateia Karaïskaki.

The C class ***Hotel Delfini*** *(☎ 412 9779, Leoharous 7)* is a bit smarter with rooms for 7000/10,000 dr with bathroom. Make sure you don't get taken there by one of the touts who hang around the port or you will wind up paying the official prices of 14,000/16,000 dr.

Whatever happens, don't attempt to sleep out – Piraeus is the most dangerous place in Greece to do so.

Places to Stay – Mid-Range

The best hotels are to be found around the Mikrolimano. There are three reasonable B class options on Vasilissis Pavlou, which runs around the hillside above the harbour. The pick of them is ***Hotel Castella*** *(☎ 411 4735, fax 417 5716, 75 Vasilissis Pavlou)*, which has rooms with air-con for 20,000/30,000 dr, including breakfast. It has good views of the harbour, as does ***Hotel Mistral*** *(☎ 411 7675, fax 412 2096, 105 Vasilissis Pavlou)*, which charges 20,500/24,000 dr. The third option is ***Hotel Cavo d'Oro*** *(☎ 411 3744, fax 412 2210, 19 Vasilissis Pavlou)*, where air-con rooms cost 15,000/22,000 dr.

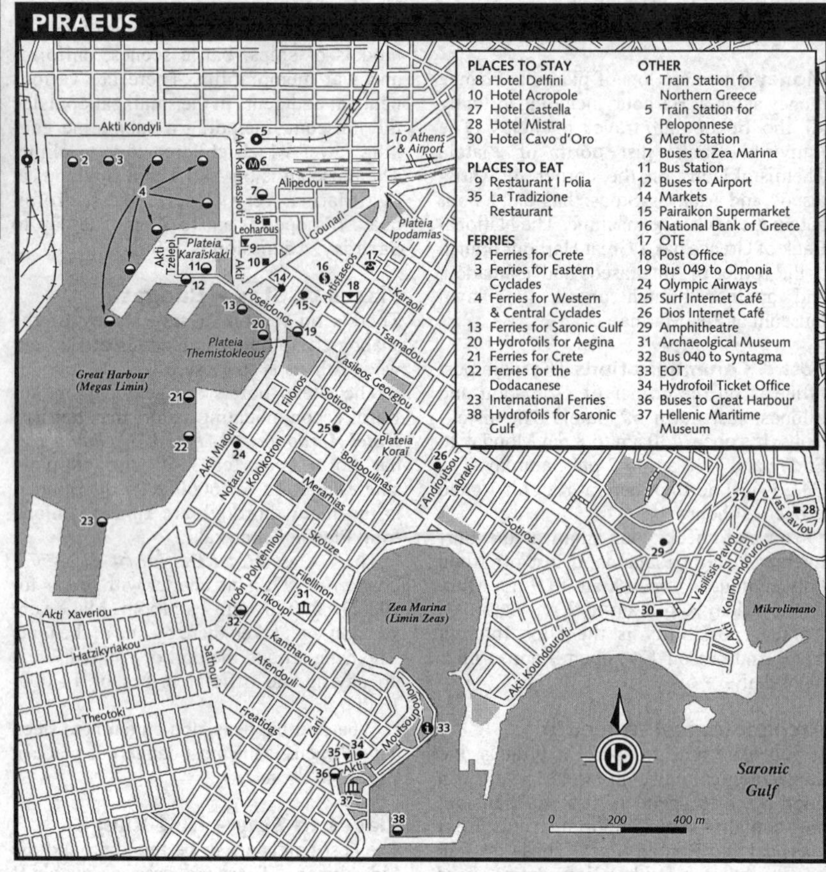

Places to Eat

Great Harbour There are dozens of cafes, restaurants and fast-food places along the waterfront. The tiny ***Restaurant I Folia***, opposite Plateia Karaïskaki on Akti Poseidonos, is a rough and ready place that does a bowl of gigantes beans for 600 dr, calamari for 750 dr and moussaka for 850 dr.

If you want to stock up on supplies before a ferry trip, head for the area just inland from Poseidonos. You'll find fresh fruit and vegetables at the ***markets*** on Demosthenous. Opposite the markets is ***Pairaikon supermarket***, open 8 am to 8 pm Monday to Friday, and 8 am to 4 pm Saturday.

Zea Marina The choice is more limited over at Zea Marina. You'll find pasta dishes priced from 900 dr and pizzas at ***La Tradizione*** Italian restaurant next to the Flying Dolphin office on Akti Moutsoupoulou.

Mikrolimano The setting around the Mikrolimano is rather more relaxed, with a string of seafood restaurants right on the waterfront.

Shopping

Many locals will tell you that the Piraeus flea market is infinitely better than its famous counterpart in Athens. As well as stalls selling junk, there are small shops selling high-quality jewellery, ceramics and antiques. The market is held on Sunday morning on Alipedou and Skilitsi, near Plateia Ippodamias, which is behind the metro station.

Getting There & Away

Air Olympic Airways (☎ 926 7560) has an office at Akti Miaouli 27.

Bus There are no intercity buses to or from Piraeus. There are buses to central Athens, to the airport and to the coastal suburbs of Glyfada and Voula, south of the airport.

Special buses (Nos 040 and 049) operate 24 hours a day between Piraeus and central Athens; they run every 20 minutes from 6 am until midnight and then hourly. No 040 runs between Akti Xaveriou in Piraeus and Filellinon in Athens and is the service that goes closest to Zea Marina; the most convenient stop is outside the Hotel Savoy on Iroön Polytehniou. No 049 runs between Plateia Themistokleous in Piraeus and Plateia Omonias in Athens. The fare is 120 dr on each service.

Buses to the airport leave from the south-western corner of Plateia Karaïskaki. Departure times are listed under To/From the Airport in the Getting Around section earlier in this chapter. The fare is 250 dr, or 500 dr from 11.30 pm to 6 am. Blue bus No 110 runs from Plateia Karaïskaki to Glyfada and Voula every 15 minutes (120 dr). It stops outside the airport's West Terminal.

Metro The metro is the fastest and easiest way of getting from the Great Harbour to central Athens (see the Getting Around section earlier in this chapter). The station is at the northern end of Akti Kalimassioti.

Train Piraeus also has train stations for both northern Greece and the Peloponnese. Piraeus' train station is one block north of the metro. All the railway services to the Peloponnese (see Getting There & Away under Athens) actually start and terminate at Piraeus, although most schedules don't mention it. There are about 15 trains daily to Athens.

The single service from the northern line train station (via Larisis train station) is of purely academic interest, leaving at 1.30 pm and taking more than seven hours to crawl to Volos, stopping all stations. The station for northern Greece is at the western end of Akti Kondyli.

Ferry – Domestic Piraeus is the busiest port in Greece with a bewildering array of departures and destinations, including daily services to all the island groups except the Ionians and the Sporades.

The following table lists all the destinations that can be reached by ferry. The information is for the high season – from mid-June to September.

For the latest departure information, pick up a weekly ferry schedule from the tourist office in Athens. See the Getting There & Away sections for each island for more information, and the Getting Around chapter for general information about ferry travel.

The departure points for the various ferry destinations are shown on the map of Piraeus. Note that there are two departure points for Crete. Ferries for Iraklio leave from the western end of Akti Kondyli, but ferries for other Cretan ports occasionally dock there as well. It's a long way to the other departure point for Crete on Akti Miaouli, so check where to find your boat when you buy your ticket.

Tickets Ferry prices are fixed by the government. All ferries charge the same for any given route, although the facilities on board differ – quite radically at times. The small differences in prices charged by agents are the result of them sacrificing part of their allotted commission to increase sales (allowing them to call themselves 'discount'

Ferries from Piraeus

Destination	Duration	Price (dr)	Frequency	Destination	Duration	Price (dr)	Frequency
Cyclades							
Amorgos	10 hours	4500	daily	Naxos	6 hours	4320	8 daily
Anafi	11 hours	6700	4 weekly	Paros	5 hours	4950	6 daily
Folegandros	9 hours	5150	daily	Santorini	9 hours	6000	5 daily
Ios	7½ hours	5300	4 daily	Serifos	4½ hours	4000	daily
Kimolos	6 hours	4800	daily	Sifnos	5½ hours	4400	daily
Kythnos	2½ hours	2300	daily	Sikinos	8-10 hours	6000	daily
Milos	7 hours	5050	daily	Syros	4 hours	4400	3 daily
Mykonos	5½ hours	5100	daily	Tinos	4½ hours	4700	2 daily
Crete							
Agios Nikolaos	12 hours	7200	3 weekly	Kastelli-Kissamou	18 hours	7000	weekly
Hania	10 hours	5900	daily	Rethymno	10-12 hours	7000	daily
Iraklio	10 hours	7000	2 daily	Sitia	14 hours	7600	3 weekly
Dodecanese							
Astypalea	12 hours	7000	2 weekly	Lipsi	16 hours	7800	weekly
Halki	22 hours	9700	weekly	Nissiros	20 hours	7600	weekly
Kalymnos	16½ hours	7200	2 daily	Patmos	10 hours	7200	daily
Karpathos	19 hours	8000	3 weekly	Rhodes	14-18 hours	9000	daily
Kassos	17½ hours	7800	3 weekly	Symi	22½ hours	8800	weekly
Kos	11-18 hours	7700	2 daily	Tilos	20½ hours	8800	weekly
Leros	11 hours	6500	daily				
North-Eastern Aegean Islands							
Chios	8 hours	5800	daily	Limnos	13 hours	7000	2 weekly
Fournoi	10 hours	5300	weekly	Samos	13 hours	6700	daily
Ikaria	9 hours	5300	daily				
Lesvos (Mytilini)	12 hours	6700	daily				
Saronic Gulf Islands							
Aegina	1½ hours	1400	hourly	Poros	3 hours	2100	3 daily
Hydra	3½ hours	2300	2 daily	Spetses	4½ hours	3200	daily

agencies). These discounts seldom amount to more than 50 dr. Agents cannot charge more than the fixed price.

If you want to book a cabin or take a car on board a ferry, it is advisable to buy a ticket in advance in Athens. Otherwise, you should wait until you get to Piraeus; agents selling ferry tickets are thick on the ground around Plateia Karaïskaki. If you're running short of time, you can buy your ticket at the quay from the tables set up next to each ferry. It costs no more to buy your ticket at the boat, contrary to what some agents might tell you.

Hydrofoils from Piraeus

Destination	Duration	Price (dr)	Frequency	Destination	Duration	Price (dr)	Frequency
Cyclades (*from Zea Marina)							
Kea*	1½ hours	4600	5 weekly	Naxos	3½ hours	9300	daily
Kimolos	3½ hours	8400	1 weekly	Paros	3 hours	9300	daily
Kythnos	1½ hours	6000	daily	Serifos	2½ hours	7400	daily
Milos	4¼ hours	9800	daily	Sifnos	3 hours	8500	daily
Mykonos	3 hours	9500	daily	Syros	2¼ hours	8200	daily
Peloponnese (*from Zea Marina)							
Ermioni	2 hours	5100	3 daily	Methana	1 hour	3500	3 daily
Gerakas*	3¾ hours	7700	6 weekly	Monemvasia*	2½ hours	8500	daily
Kyparissi*	3¼ hours	7200	daily	Porto Heli	2 hours	5600	2 daily
Leonidio*	3 hours	6800	daily				
Saronic Gulf Islands (*most from Zea Marina)							
Aegina	35 mins	2700	hourly	Poros*	1 hour	4000	9 daily
Hydra*	1¼ hours	4600	9 daily	Spetses*	2 hours	6400	9 daily
Ionian Islands (from Zea Marina)				Kythira	4 hours	10,000	4 weekly

Ferry – International There are two ferries weekly in summer to Lemesos (Limassol) in Cyprus and Haifa in Israel, and one a week in winter. Salamis Lines operates the F/B *Nissos Kypros* year-round via Rhodes. It leaves Piraeus at 7 pm on Thursday and Rhodes at 8 pm on Friday, arriving at Lemesos at 2.30 pm on Saturday and Haifa at 6 am on Sunday. In summer, Poseidon Lines operates the F/B *Sea Armony* via Rhodes, leaving Piraeus on Thursday at 8 pm.

Deck-class fares from Piraeus to Lemesos are 16,000/18,000 dr in low/high season, and 24,500/27,500 dr to Haifa. The fares from Crete and Rhodes are virtually the same, although Rhodes is halfway to Cyprus. Both lines offer 20% student (up to 28 years), youth (up to 24 years) and return-ticket discounts.

Hydrofoil Minoan Lines operates its Flying Dolphin hydrofoil services from Piraeus to the Saronic Gulf Islands, the Peloponnese and a growing range of destinations in the Cyclades. Services to the Cyclades leave from Great Harbour, while other departures are split between Great Harbour and Zea Marina – check when you buy your ticket.

The information in the hydrofoil timetable is for the high season, from mid-June to September.

For more information about hydrofoil services, see the Getting Around chapter and the Getting There & Away sections of the island chapters.

Tickets Although it is often possible to buy tickets at Minoan's quayside offices at both Great Harbour and Zea Marina, reservations are strongly recommended – especially at weekends. You can book seats, and pay by credit card, by phoning Minoan's bookings centre (☎ 428 001), or by visiting the Flying Dolphin city centre office at Filellinon 3 in Athens.

Getting Around

Piraeus has its own network of buses and trams, but the only services likely to be of much interest to travellers are the buses (No 904 or 905) which run between Zea Marina and the bus stop next to the metro.

DAFNI Δαφνί

Moni Dafniou

This monastery, 10km north-west of Athens along the busy road to Corinth, is Attica's most important Byzantine monument, and is on UNESCO's World Heritage Sites list. It is built on the route of the Sacred Way and on the site of an ancient Sanctuary of Apollo. Its name derives from the daphne laurels which were sacred to Apollo.

The monastery's 11th century church contains some of Greece's finest **mosaics**. These were created at a time when the artistic and intellectual achievements of Byzantium had reached unprecedented heights. The monastery was sacked in 1205 by the renegades of the Fourth Crusade who had earlier captured Constantinople. It was rebuilt and occupied by monks until the time of the War of Independence, after which it was used as army barracks and as a hospital for the mentally ill. Much restoration has taken place since.

The mosaics on the church walls depict saints and monks, while the ones on the dome depict apostles, prophets and guardian archangels. Exquisite though these mosaics are, they fade into insignificance once the visitor has gazed upon the Christos Pantokrator (Christ in Majesty) which occupies the centre of the dome. Even a confirmed atheist cannot help but be impressed by this masterpiece of Byzantine art. The opening hours of the monastery (☎ 01-581 1558) are 8.30 am to 3 pm daily; admission is 800 dr.

Getting There & Away

Bus No A16 from Plateia Eleftherias, north of Monastiraki, can drop you at the Venzini stop right outside the monastery. The buses run every 20 minutes and take about 30 minutes in reasonable traffic. Don't catch the buses to Dafni from Syntagma, which go to a suburb of the same name to the south-east.

ELEFSINA (ELEUSIS) Ελευσίνα

The ruins of ancient Eleusis lie beside the modern industrial town of Elefsina, 12km farther along the road from Moni Dafniou and on the same bus route.

The ancient city of Eleusis was built around the **Sanctuary of Demeter**. The site dates back to Mycenaean times, when the cult of Demeter began.

The cult became one of the most important in ancient Greece. By classical times it was celebrated with a huge annual festival, which attracted thousands of pilgrims wanting to be initiated into the Eleusian mysteries. They walked in procession from the Acropolis to Eleusis along the Sacred Way, which was lined with statues and votive monuments. Initiates were sworn to secrecy on punishment of death, and during the 1400 years that the sanctuary functioned its secrets were never divulged. The sanctuary was closed by the Roman emperor Theodosius in the 4th century AD.

Although the sanctuary was the most important in ancient Greece after Delphi, the modern site is not particularly inspiring. Most of it is overgrown, and an industrial complex occupies the western edge. A visit to the site's **museum** first will help you to make some sense of the ruins. Both the site and museum are open 8.30 am to 3 pm Tuesday to Sunday. Admission is 500 dr.

MONI KAISSARIANIS

Μονή Καισσαριανής

This 11th century monastery, 5km east of Athens, is set amid pines, plane and cypress trees on the slopes of Mt Hymettos. The air is permeated with the aroma of herbs which grow on the mountain.

The source of the river Ilissos is on the hill above the monastery. Its waters were once believed to cure infertility and were sacred to Aphrodite; a temple dedicated to her stood nearby. The spring feeds a fountain on the eastern wall of the monastery, where the water gushes from a marble ram's head (this is a copy – the 6th century original is in the National Archaeological Museum).

Surrounding the courtyard of the monastery are a mill, bakery, bathhouse and refectory. The church is dedicated to the Presentation of the Virgin and is built to the Greek-cross plan. Four columns taken from a Roman temple support its dome. The 17th century frescoes in the narthex are the work of Ioannis Ipatos. Those in the rest of the church date from the 16th century, and were painted by a monk from Mt Athos.

The monastery (☎ 01-723 6619) is best visited during the week – it's swarming with picnickers at weekends. The grounds are open until sunset and the monastery buildings are open 8 am to 2.30 pm Tuesday to Sunday; admission is 800 dr.

To get to the monastery take bus No 224 from Plateia Kaningos (at the north end of Akadimias), or from the junction of Akadimias and Sina, to the terminus. From here it's a walk of about 30 minutes to the monastery.

MT PARNITHA

Mt Parnitha National Park lies just 20km north of the city centre and is a popular weekend escape for Athenians.

Mt Parnitha itself comprises a number of smaller peaks, the highest of which is Mt Karavola at 1413m – high enough to get snow in winter. The park is criss-crossed by numerous walking trails, marked on the Road Editions trekking map of the area. Most visitors access the park by cable car from the outer Athens suburb of Thrakomakedones. The cable car drops you below ***Casino Mt Parnes*** *(☎ 01-246 9111)* gaming and hotel complex. Room prices here start at 16,000/20,000 dr for singles/doubles.

You can get to the cable car station at the base of Mt Parnes on bus No 714 from the south end of Aharnon, near Plateia Omonias.

Attica Αττική

Attica, a *nomos* of Sterea Ellada, contains more than just the capital and its port of Piraeus. There are several places of interest, most of which can be reached by the orange buses which depart from the Mavromateon bus terminal.

COAST ROAD TO CAPE SOUNION

This road skirts Attica's Apollo coast. It's a beautiful coastline of splendid beaches and stunning sea views which has been spoilt by overdevelopment. Many of the beaches are either EOT pay beaches or belong to hotels. The beaches have boats and water-sports equipment for hire, tennis and volleyball courts and children's playgrounds.

The first place you'll encounter travelling south is **Glyfada**, Attica's largest resort. The place is overrun with package tourists in summer, and they are joined by half the population of Athens at weekends. In addition, Glyfada has a permanent population of wealthy expatriates. Loads of bars and discos and noisy air traffic complete the picture.

One good reason to stop here is to check out the work of the Sea Turtle Rescue Centre (☎/fax 01-898 2600, email stps.rescue@compulink.gr) at Third Marina, about 500m from the bus stops on Glyfada's main square, Plateia Katriki Vasos.

The centre is housed in old freight carriages donated by the Greek railways, and cares for injured turtles found in Greek waters – mainly leatherbacks *(Caretta caretta)*. Some of the injuries are quite heartbreaking. It is open 10 am to 2 pm and 5 to 7 pm daily.

The cheapest rooms in Glyfada are at ***Hotel Ilion*** *(☎ 01-894 6011, Kondyli 4)*, on the corner of the main square, Plateia Vyzaniou, which is where the A2 and E2 buses from Syntagma terminate. It has single/double rooms with bathroom for 6000/7500 dr.

If your budget permits, a much better choice is the quiet ***Hotel Zina*** *(☎ 01-960 3872, fax 960 4004, Evangelistras 6)*, 500m north-east of Plateia Vyzaniou. It has spacious, well equipped apartments with kitchen, lounge and TV priced at a negotiable 28,000 dr for two people – and it's away from the main airport flight path.

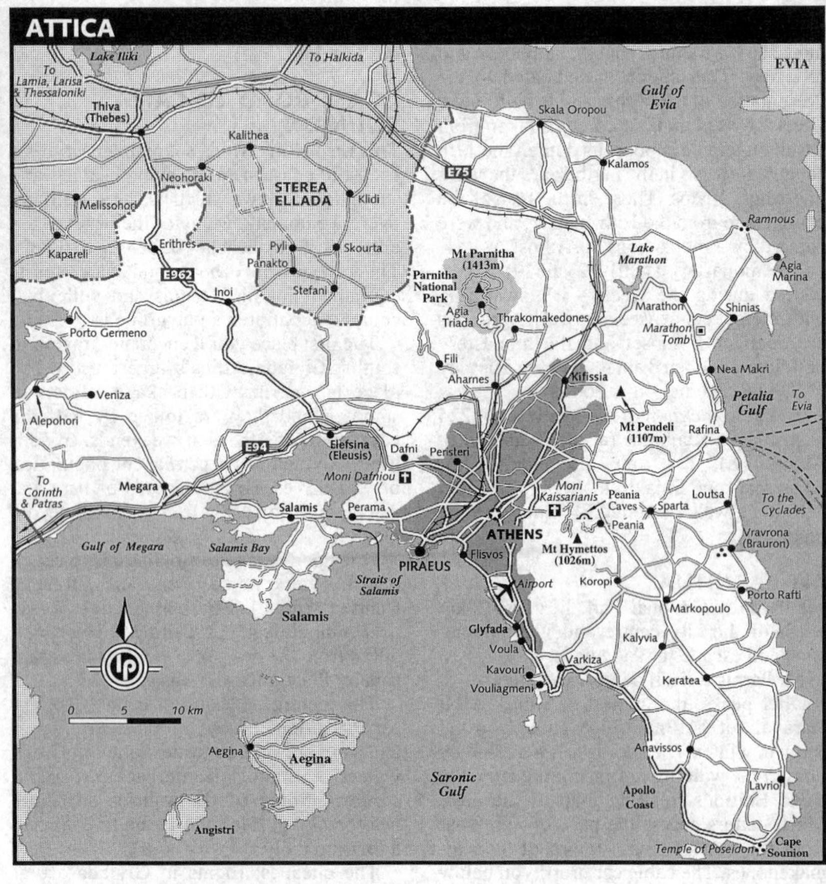

The streets around Glyfada's main square are filled with representatives of every fast-food chain operating in Greece. Konstantinopoleos, which runs inland from the main square, is packed solid with bars and tavernas. ***Tzavelas Taverna***, away from the main pack at the junction of Konstantinopoleos and Lazaridi Sabba, has the best prices. ***JJ's Pub*** *(Maragou 8)* is the favourite haunt of the expatriate community and has a large range of imported British and continental beers.

The beach-resort belt continues south through **Voula**, **Vouliagmeni** and **Varkiza**. There are ***camp sites*** by the beach at both Voula *(☎ 01-895 2712)* and Varkiza *(☎ 01-897 4329)*. The south-eastern beach, known as **Third Beach**, is a popular gay spot.

The coast south of Varkiza to Cape Sounion is dotted with the weekenders of well-to-do Athenians, but it's still possible to find stretches of beach with hardly a soul in sight. Cape Sounion, 70km from Athens, is at the south-eastern tip of Attica.

Getting There & Away

Blue city buses can take you as far south as Varkiza for 120 dr. There are buses from Syntagma in Athens to Glyfada (A3 & E2) and Voula/Vouliagmeni (A2). The A2 buses are much faster and also stop at Glyfada.

If your destination is Sounion, take one of the *paraliako* (coastal) buses which leave Athens hourly, on the half-hour (two hours, 1150 dr), from the Mavromateon bus terminal (see Athens, Getting There & Away for details). These buses also stop on Filellinon, on the corner of Xenofontos, 10 minutes later, but by this time they're usually very crowded.

INLAND ROAD TO CAPE SOUNION

The inland road to Cape Sounion passes through the Mesogeia (middle land) region, renowned for the fine olives and grapes grown on its red soil.

Peania, a village 18km east of Athens in the eastern foothills of Mt Hymettos, was the birthplace of the orator Demosthenes (384-322 BC). Little remains of the ancient town, but visitors come today not for the ruins, but to look around the **Vorres Museum** (☎ 01-664 2520/4771), which houses folkloric items, prints and pictures, and an impressive collection of contemporary Greek paintings. Modern sculptures stand in the courtyard. The museum is a fair hike from the bus stop on Peania's main square, Plateia Vasileos Konstantinou. Walk down Demosthenous (which has the New Democracy building on the corner and the post office next to it) and turn right onto Dimihounta at the bottom. Walk to the top of Dimihounta, and turn left onto Diadohou Konstantinou – where you'll soon find a reassuring sign pointing straight ahead to the museum. The museum is open on weekends only, from 10 am to 2 pm. Admission is 1000 dr.

The **Peania Caves** (☎ 01-664 2108), 4km west of Peania on the slopes of Mt Hymettos, have an impressive array of stalactites and stalagmites that are very effectively lit. The cave is signposted from Peania, but there is no public transport. It is open 9 am to 4.30 pm daily. Admission is 1500 dr.

The largest of the villages of Mesogeia is **Koropi**, a lively market town 7km south of Peania. Its Church of the Transfiguration, on the road to Markopoulo, is one of the oldest churches in Attica and contains the remains of 10th century frescoes.

The road continues to **Markopoulo** – home of the Kourtaki company, producer of Greece's most popular bottled retsina. The road south continues to Lavrio and Cape Sounion.

Getting There & Away

There are Athens suburban blue buses to Peania and Koropi from Eptahalkou, just south of the metro line at Thisio. Bus Nos 125, 307 and 308 all terminate at Koropi.

There are also *mesogiaki* (inland) buses to Cape Sounion (2¼ hours, 1100 dr) from the Mavromateon terminal in Athens. They stop at both Peania and Koropi and continue south via Markopoulo and Lavrio.

CAPE SOUNION Ακρωτήριο Σούνιο

Temple of Poseidon

The ancient Greeks chose their temple sites carefully, with the prime considerations being a site's natural beauty and its appropriateness to the god in question. Nowhere is this more evident than at Cape Sounion, where the Temple of Poseidon stands on a craggy spur that plunges 65m to the sea. The temple was built in 444 BC at the same time as the Parthenon. It is constructed of local marble from Agrilesa and its slender columns – of which 16 remain – are Doric. It is thought that the temple was built by Ictinus, the architect of the Temple of Hephaestus in Athens' Ancient Agora.

The temple looks gleaming white when viewed from the sea and is discernible from a long distance. It gave great comfort to sailors in ancient times; they knew they were nearly home. The views from the temple are equally impressive. On a clear day, you can see Kea, Kythnos and Serifos to the south-east, and Aegina and the Peloponnese to the west. The site also contains scanty remains of a propylon, a fortified tower and, to the north-east, a 6th century temple to Athena.

Visit early in the morning before the tourist buses arrive if you wish to indulge the sentiments of Byron's lines from *Don Juan*:

Place me on Sunium's marbled steep,
Where nothing save the waves and I,
May hear our mutual murmurs sweep ...

Byron was so taken by Sounion that he carved his name on one of the columns – many others have followed suit.

The site is open daily 8 am to sunset in summer, and 10 am to sunset in winter. Admission is 800 dr.

Places to Stay & Eat

There are two camp sites at Cape Sounion, ***Camping Vakchos*** *(☎ 0292-39 571/262)* and ***Sounio Beach Camping*** *(☎ 0292-39 358/718)*. Both are on the road to Lavrio.

The cafe at the cape is expensive, so it's a good idea to bring along something to eat and drink. The nearest tavernas are at Sounio Beach on the way to Lavrio.

Getting There & Away

You can take either the inland or coastal bus to Cape Sounion. See the preceding Coast Road to Sounion and the Inland Road to Sounion sections for more information.

LAVRIO Λαύριο

☎ 0292 • postcode 195 00 • pop 2500

Lavrio is an unattractive industrial town on the east coast of Attica, 10km north of Sounion. It is only worth a mention because it is the departure point for ferries to the islands of Kea and Kythnos. The town has definitely seen better days. In ancient times its silver mines, worked by slaves, helped to finance Pericles' building program.

The island of Makronisos, opposite the port, was used as a place of exile during the civil war. If you have time to spare you could visit the **mineralogical museum** (☎ 26 270), Plateia Iroön Polytehniou. It's open 10 am to noon Wednesday, Saturday and Sunday. Admission is 100 dr.

Getting There & Away

Bus Buses run every 30 minutes to Lavrio from the Mavromateon terminal in Athens (1½ hours, 950 dr).

Ferry Goutos Lines runs the F/B *Myrina Express* from Lavrio to Kea (1600 dr) and Kythnos (2300 dr). From mid-June, there are ferries to Kea every morning and evening from Monday to Friday, and up to six daily at weekends. Three ferries weekly continue to Kythnos. In winter there are ferries to Kea every day except Monday, returning every day except Wednesday. One service a week continues to Kythnos. The EOT in Athens gives out a timetable for this route. The ticket office at Lavrio is opposite the quay.

VRAVRONA (BRAURON)

Βραυρώνα

The ruins of the ancient city of Brauron lie just outside the small village of Vravrona (vrah-**vro**-nah), 40km east of Athens. Brauron belonged to King Cecrops' league of 12 cities (King Cecrops was the mythical founder of Athens). Remains dating back to 1700 BC have been found at the site, but it is best known for the **Sanctuary of Artemis**.

According to mythology, it was to Brauron that Iphigenia and Orestes brought the *xoanon* (sacred image) of Artemis that they removed from Tauris. The site became a sanctuary to Artemis during the time of the tyrant Peisistratos, who made the worship of Artemis the official religion of Athens.

The cult centred around a festival, held every five years, at which girls aged between five and 10 performed a ritual dance that imitated the movements of a bear. The ruins of the dormitories where the girls stayed can be seen at the site.

The sanctuary's Doric temple, of which only a small section still stands, was built in the 5th century BC on the site of an earlier temple that was destroyed by the Persians. The site's **museum** (☎ 0299-27 020) houses finds from the sanctuary and the surrounding area. Both site and museum are open 8 am to 2.30 pm Tuesday to Sunday. Admission is 500 dr.

Getting There & Away

Extremely early risers can follow the tourist office's advice and catch the 5.50 am bus from Mavromateon to Cape Sounion as far as Markopoulo, where you take the 6.50 am bus to Vravrona. A less painful option is to catch a regular A5 bus from the junction of Sina and Akadimias to the ERT (radio and TV) office at Agia Paraskevi on the outskirts of Athens. There are buses to Vravrona (120 dr) from here every 20 minutes.

RAFINA Ραφήνα

☎ 0294 • postcode 190 09 • pop 10,000

Rafina, on Attica's east coast, is Athens' main fishing port and second-most important port for passenger ferries. The port is much smaller than Piraeus and less confusing – and fares are about 20% cheaper, but you have to spend an hour on the bus and 460 dr to get there.

The port police (☎ 22 888) occupy a kiosk near the quay, which is lined with fish restaurants and ticket agents. The main square, Plateia Plastira, is at the top of the ramp leading to the port.

There's no reason to hang about in Rafina and there are frequent bus connections with Athens. If, however, you want to stay the night and catch an early ferry or hydrofoil, there are a couple of reasonable hotels. The D class ***Hotel Koralli*** *(☎ 22 477)*, on Plateia Plastira, has singles/doubles for 5500/8000 dr. The C class ***Hotel Avra*** *(☎ 22 781/ fax 23 320)* overlooks the port just south of the square. It has large rooms with sea views for 13,500/21,000 dr, including breakfast.

Getting There & Away

Bus There are frequent buses from the Mavromateon terminal in Athens to Rafina (one hour, 460 dr) between 5.45 am and 10.30 pm. The first bus leaves Rafina at 5.50 am and the last at 10.15 pm.

Ferry Goutos Lines and Strintzis Lines both operate ferries to the Cycladic islands of Andros (two hours, 2400 dr), Tinos (3½ hours, 3600 dr) and Mykonos (4½ hours, 4100 dr). Strintzis has departures to all three every morning at 8.05 am, and a 7 pm service to Andros only. Goutos has departures to Andros, Tinos and Mykonos at 7.15 am every day except Wednesday. The Tuesday service continues from Mykonos to Syros (5¾ hours, 3400 dr), Paros (7¼ hours, 4100 dr), Naxos (8½ hours, 4200 dr) and Amorgos (11¾ hours, 4700 dr), returning the next day.

The Maritime Company of Lesvos has four boats weekly to Limnos (10 to 13 hours, 5500dr), two of them stopping at Lesvos (8½ hours, 4450 dr).

There are also ferries to the ports of Karystos and Marmari on the island of Evia. There are three services daily to Marmari (1¼ hours, 1230 dr) and two to Karystos (1¾ hours, 1710 dr).

Catamaran High-speed catamarans have now completely taken over from hydrofoils on the routes from Rafina to the western Cyclades. Strintzis Lines' *Seajet I* leaves daily at 8.15 am for Syros (1¾ hours, 6900 dr), Paros (2½ hours, 8200 dr), Naxos (3¼ hours, 8500 dr), Ios (four hours, 8200 dr) and Santorini (4¾ hours, 9600 dr). Strintzis also operates the *Seajet II* to Tinos (1½ hours, 7200 dr) and Mykonos (two hours, 8200 dr) at 7.40 am and 4 pm daily except Tuesday. The Tuesday morning service also calls at Andros (one hour, 4700 dr), and continues from Mykonos to Syros (three hours, 6900 dr), Paros (3¾ hours, 8200 dr), Naxos (4¼ hours, 8500 dr) and finally Amorgos (5½ hours, 9500 dr).

Goutos has departures to Tinos and Mykonos at 8 am and 4.15 pm daily. The Thursday morning service calls at Andros, and continues from Mykonos to Paros, Naxos and Amorgos.

MARATHON REGION

Marathon Μαραθώνας

The plain surrounding the unremarkable small town of Marathon, 42km north-east of Athens, is the site of one of the most celebrated battles in world history. In 490 BC, an army of 9000 Greeks and 1000 Plataeans defeated the 25,000-strong Persian army, proving that the Persians were not invincible. The Greeks were indebted to the ingenious tactics of Miltiades, who altered the conventional battle formation so that there were fewer soldiers in the centre, but more in the wings. This lulled the Persians into thinking that the Greeks were going to be a pushover. They broke through in the centre, but were then ambushed by the soldiers in the wings. At the end of the day, 6000 Persians and only 192 Greeks lay dead. The story goes that after the battle a runner was sent to Athens to announce the victory. After shouting *'Enikesame!'* ('We won!') he collapsed in a heap and never revived. This is the origin of today's marathon foot race.

Marathon Tomb

This burial mound, 4km before the town of Marathon, stands 350m from the Athens-Marathon road. In ancient Greece, the bodies of those who died in battle were returned to their families for private burial, but as a sign of honour the 192 men who fell at Marathon were cremated and buried in this collective tomb. The mound is 10m high and 180m in circumference. The tomb site is signposted from the main road and is open 8.30 am to 3 pm Tuesday to Sunday. The **museum**, nearer to the town, has the same opening hours. The admission fee of 500 dr covers both sites.

Lake Marathon

This huge dam, 8km west of Marathon, was Athens' sole source of water until 1956. The massive dam wall, completed in 1926, is faced with the famous Pentelic marble that was used to build the Parthenon. It's an awesome sight, standing over 50m high and stretching for more than 300m.

Ramnous Ραμνούς

The ruins of the ancient port of Ramnous are 15km north-east of Marathon. It's an evocative, overgrown and secluded little site, standing on a plateau overlooking the sea. Among the ruins are the remains of a Doric **Temple of Nemesis** (435 BC), which once contained a huge statue of the goddess. Nemesis was the goddess of retribution and mother of Helen of Troy. There are also ruins of a smaller 6th century temple dedicated to Themis, goddess of justice. In summer, the site is open 8 am to 5.30 pm daily – to 2:30 pm in winter. Admission is 500 dr.

Shinias Σχοινιάς

The long, sandy, pine-fringed beach at Shinias, south-east of Marathon, is the best in this part of Attica. It's also very popular, particularly at weekends. ***Camping Ramnous*** *(☎ 0294-55 855)* is on the way to the beach.

Getting There & Away

There are hourly buses from Athens' Mavromateon terminal to Marathon (1¼ hours, 700 dr). The tomb, the museum and Shinias Beach are all within short walking distance of bus stops (tell the driver where you want to get out). There are no buses to Lake Marathon or Ramnous; you need your own transport.

Peloponnese Πελοπόννησος

The Peloponnese (pel-o-**pon**-ih-sos in Greek) is the southernmost section of the Balkan Peninsula. The construction of the Corinth Canal through the Isthmus of Corinth in the late 19th century effectively severed it from the mainland, and now the only links are the bridges that span the canal. Indeed, the Peloponnese has every attraction of an island – and better public transport.

It's a region of outstanding natural beauty, with lofty, snow-crested mountains, valleys of citrus groves and cypress trees, cool springs and many fine beaches. The landscape is diverse and dotted with the legacies of the many civilisations which took root in the region: ancient Greek sites, crumbling Byzantine cities, Frankish and Venetian fortresses. The best-known attraction is the ancient site at Olympia. Less well known is that the beaches of the Messinian Mani, south of Kalamata, are some of the finest in Greece. The rugged Mani Peninsula has additional attractions – the remnants of fortified tower houses built from the 17th century onwards.

With your own transport, two weeks is sufficient to visit the major attractions. On public transport, allow at least three weeks, or be selective about your destinations. Ideally, the Peloponnese warrants a month's wandering, such is the variety of its natural and ancient splendours.

Accommodation prices quoted in this section are for high season (July and August). Expect to pay less at other times, and certainly try bargaining at all times.

If you are travelling from Athens to the Peloponnese with your own vehicle, you have the choice of the New National Road (a toll highway) or the slower Old National Road, which hugs the coast and has fine sea views. If you don't have your own transport, travelling by bus is a pleasant way to explore the Peloponnese. Services are adequate to all but the most remote areas.

HIGHLIGHTS

- Ancient Olympia in springtime
- Trekking in the hills above Kardamyli
- Spending a night in the historic tower settlements of the Mani
- The Diakofto to Kalavryta train ride up the spectacular Vouraïkos Gorge
- Kalavryta's splendid Cave of the Lakes
- The charming Venetian town of Nafplio

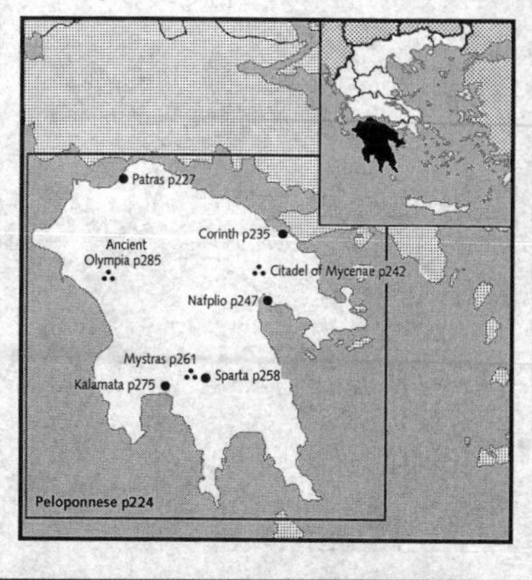

History & Mythology

The name Peloponisos means 'island of Pelops', and derives from the mythological hero Pelops, and from the Greek word for island, *nisos*. The region's medieval name was 'Morea' (*mouria* means mulberry tree), perhaps because mulberry trees grow so well in the area.

The deities may have resided on Mt Olympus, but they made frequent jaunts to the Peloponnese. It is a region rich in myths, and Pelops features in many of them.

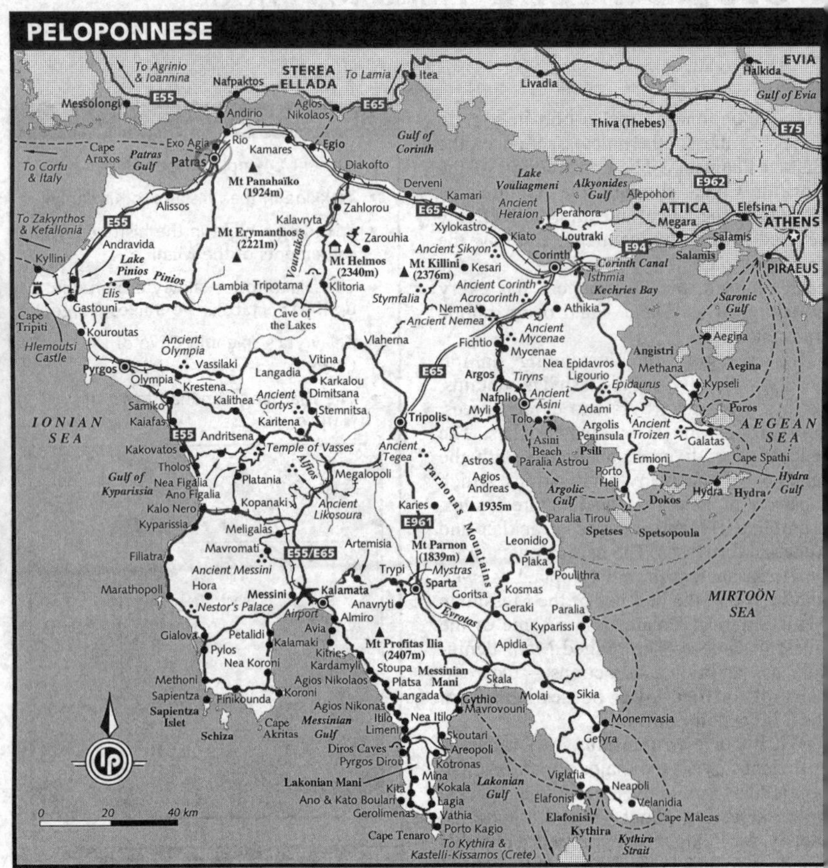

Since ancient times, the Peloponnese has played a major role in Greek history. When the Minoan civilisation declined after 1450 BC, the focus of power in the ancient Aegean world moved from Crete to the hill-fortress palaces of Mycenae and Tiryns in the Peloponnese. As elsewhere in Greece, the 400 years following the Dorian conquests in the 12th century BC are known as the dark age. When the region emerged from it in the 7th century BC, Sparta, Athens' arch rival, had surpassed Mycenae as the most powerful city in the Pelopon nese. The period of peace and prosperit under Roman rule (146 BC to around 25(AD) was shattered by a series of invasion by Goths, Avars and Slavs.

The Byzantines were slow to mak inroads into the Peloponnese, and did no become firmly established until the 9tl century. In 1204, after the fall of Constan tinople to the crusaders, the crusader chief William de Champlitte and Geoffrey d Villehardouin divided the region into 1

The Wily Pelops

Ancient coin depicting a chariot race

TAMSIN WILSON

Pelops was the son of the conniving Tantalos, who invited the gods to a feast and served up the flesh of his son to test their power of omniscience. Of course, the all-knowing gods knew what he had done and refrained from eating the flesh. However, Demeter, who was in a tizz over the abduction of her daughter, Persephone, by Hades, accidentally ate a piece of Pelops' shoulder.

Fortunately, the gods reassembled Pelops, and fashioned another shoulder of ivory. Tantalos was suspended from a fruit tree overhanging a lake, and was punished with eternal tantalising thirst.

Pelops took a fancy to the beautiful Hippodameia, daughter of Oinomaos, king of Elia. Oinomaos, a champion chariot racer, was told by an oracle that his future son-in-law would bring about his death. Oinomaos announced that he would give his daughter in marriage to any suitor who defeated him in a chariot race, but that he would kill those who failed – a fate which befell many suitors. Pelops took up the challenge and bribed the king's charioteer, Myrtilos, to take a spoke out of a wheel of the king's chariot. The chariot crashed during the race and Oinomaos was killed, so Pelops married Hippodameia and became king of Elia. The couple had two children, Atreus and Thyestes. Atreus became king of Mycenae and was the father of that kingdom's greatest king, Agamemnon. Pelops' devious action is blamed for the curse on the Royal House of Atreus, which ultimately brought about its downfall.

fiefs, which they parcelled out to various barons of France, Flanders and Burgundy. These fiefs were overseen by de Villehardouin, the self-appointed Prince of Morea (as the region was called in those days).

The Byzantines gradually won back the Morea. Although the empire as a whole was now in terminal decline, a glorious renaissance took place in the Morea, centred on Mystras, which the Byzantine emperor Michael VIII Paleologus made the region's seat of government.

The Morea fell to the Turks in 1460 and hundreds of years of power struggles between the Turks and Venetians followed. The Venetians had long coveted the Morea and had succeeded in establishing profitable trading ports at Methoni, Pylos, Koroni and Monemvasia.

The War of Independence began in the Peloponnese. Bishop Germanos of Patras raised the flag of revolt near Kalavryta on 25 March 1821. The Egyptian army, under the leadership of Ibrahim Pasha, brutally restored Turkish rule in 1825.

In 1827, the Triple Alliance of Great Britain, France and Russia, moved by Greek suffering and the activities of philhellenes (Byron's death in 1824 was particularly influential), came to the rescue of the Greeks by destroying the Egyptian-Turkish fleet at the Battle of Navarino, ending Turkish domination of the area.

The Peloponnese became part of the independent state of Greece, and Nafplio in Argolis became the first national capital. When Kapodistrias, Greece's first president, was assassinated on the steps of Nafplio's Church of St Spyridon in October 1831, the new king, Otho, moved the capital to Athens in 1834.

Like the rest of Greece, the Peloponnese suffered badly during WWII. The town clock of Kalavryta, in the central north, is forever stopped at 2.34, the time at which, on 13 December 1943, the Germans began a massacre of all the males aged over 15 in reprisal for resistance activity.

The civil war (1944-49) brought widespread destruction and, in the 1950s, many villagers migrated to Athens, Australia, Canada, South Africa and the USA. More recently, the towns of Corinth and Kalamata have suffered devastating earthquakes.

Achaïa Αχαΐα

Achaïa owes its name to the Achaeans, an Indo-European branch of migrants who settled on mainland Greece and established what is more commonly known as the Mycenaean civilisation. When the Dorians arrived, the Achaeans were pushed into this north-western corner of the Peloponnese, displacing the original Ionians. Legend has it that the Achaeans founded 12 cities, which later developed into the powerful Achaean Federation that survived until Roman times. Principal among these cities were the ports of Patras and Egio.

The coast of modern Achaïa consists of a string of resorts more popular with Greeks than with tourists. Inland are the high peaks of Mt Panahaïko, Mt Erymanthos (where Heracles captured the Erymanthian boar) and Mt Helmos.

The village of Diakofto, 55km east of Patras, is the starting point for a ride on the fantastic rack-and-pinion railway to Zahlorou and Kalavryta. Overnight stops at Zahlorou and Kalavryta are highly recommended.

PATRAS Πάτρα

☎ 061 • postcode 260 01 • pop 153,300

Achaïa's capital, Patras (in Greek, Patra), is Greece's third-largest city and the principal port for boats to and from Italy and the Ionian Islands. It is named after King Patreas, who ruled Achaïa in about 1100 BC. Despite a history stretching back 3000 years, Patras is not wildly exciting. Few travellers stay around any longer than it takes to catch the next boat, bus or train.

The city was destroyed by the Turks during the War of Independence and rebuilt on a modern grid plan of wide, arcaded streets, large squares and ornate neoclassical buildings. Some look in dire need of a facelift but many are now being restored. The higher you climb up the steep hill behind the teeming, somewhat seedy waterfront the better Patras gets.

Orientation

Patras' grid system means easy walking. The waterfront is known as Iroön Polytehniou at the north-eastern end, Othonos Amalias in the middle and Akti Dimeon to the south. Customs is at the Iroön Polytehniou end and the main bus and train stations are on Othonos Amalias. Most of the agencies selling ferry tickets are on Iroön Polytehniou and Othonos Amalias. The main thoroughfares of Agiou Dionysiou, Riga Fereou, Mezonos, Korinthou and Kanakari run parallel to the waterfront. The main square is Plateia Vasileos Georgiou, up from the waterfront along Gerokostopoulou.

Information

Tourist Offices The EOT (☎ 620 353) is outside the international arrivals terminal at the port. In theory, it's open 8 am to 10 pm Monday to Friday; in practice, it's invariably closed. The most useful piece of information is an arrow pointing to the helpful tourist police (☎ 451 833), upstairs in the embarkation hall, who are open 7.30 am to 11 pm daily.

Money The National Bank of Greece is on Plateia Trion Symahon, opposite the

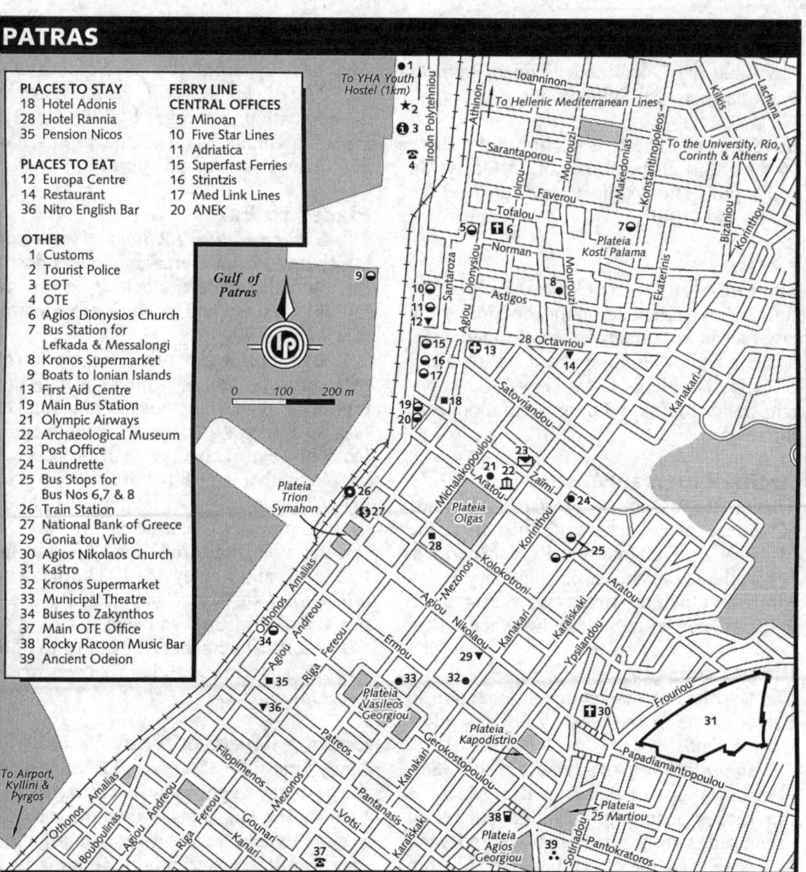

ilway station. Weekday opening times are am to 2 pm (8 am to 1.30 pm on Friday) nd 6 to 8.30 pm. On weekends, in summer nly, it is open 11 am to 1 pm and 6 to 30 pm.

ost & Communications The main post ffice is on the corner of Zaïmi and lezonos. It is open 7.30 am to 8 pm Mon-y to Friday, 7.30 am to 2 pm Saturday, nd 9 am to 1.30 pm Sunday. The main TE office is on the corner of Dimitriou Gounari and Kanakari in the western part of the city. There's another office opposite the tourist office at the port.

For Internet access, head inland to the Rocky Racoon Music Bar, Gerokostopoulou 56. It's open 9 am to 3 am daily.

Bookshops Gonia tou Vivlio, Agiou Nikolaou 32, sells English-language books, newspapers and magazines. You'll find international newspapers at the *periptero* (kiosk) on Plateia Trion Symahon.

Laundry The laundrette on Zaïmi, just uphill from Korinthou, charges 2300 dr to wash and dry a load and is open 9 am to 9 pm daily except Sunday.

Emergency There is a first-aid centre (☎ 277 386) at the corner of 28 Octavriou and Agiou Dionysiou. Patras' port police are on ☎ 341 002.

Kastro

The medieval Venetian kastro, built on the ruins of an ancient acropolis, dominates the city. Set in an attractive pencil-pined park, it is reached by climbing the steps at the end of Agiou Nikolaou. Great views of the Ionian islands of Zakynthos and Kefallonia are the reward.

Archaeological Museum

The small museum (☎ 275 070), Mezonos 42, houses a collection of finds from the Mycenaean, Hellenic and Roman periods. It's well laid out and exhibits are labelled in English. Opening times are 8.30 am to 2.30 pm Tuesday to Sunday. Entrance is free.

Places to Stay

The shortage of budget accommodation in Patras is one of the reasons few travellers stick around.

Camping Rion *(☎ 991 585, fax 993 388)*, 9km north-east of Patras at Rio Beach, is the closest camping ground. This well organised, family-run site is open all year. You can get there on bus No 6 from Kanakari.

It's hard to recommend the ***YHA Youth Hostel*** *(☎ 427 278, Iroön Polytehniou 62)* following a string of complaints from female travellers. It's a fair haul from the city centre, 1.5km north of the customs building. Dorm beds are 2000 dr.

Most travellers head for ***Pension Nicos*** *(☎ 623 757)*, up from the waterfront on the corner of Patreos and Agiou Andreou. It has doubles for 6500 dr, and singles/doubles with bathroom for 4000/7000 dr.

The C class ***Hotel Rannia*** *(☎ 220 114, fax 220 537, Riga Fereou 53)*, facing Plateia Olgas, has comfortable air-con rooms wi TV for 10,000/15,000 dr.

A step up from this is ***Hotel Adon*** *(☎ 224 213, fax 226 971, Zaïmi 9)* behir the bus station. It charges 14,300/16,500 d including breakfast, and the rooms hav good views out over the port.

Places to Eat

The ***Europa Centre*** *(Othonos Amalias 1* is a convenient cafeteria-style place close the international ferry dock. It has taver dishes, spaghetti and a choice of vegetari meals (from 900 dr).

Locals prefer the nameless ***restaura*** *(Michalakopoulou 3)* which specialises traditional dishes like *patsas* (tripe) and *e tosthia arnisia* – translated on the menu lamb bowels! Travellers will probably happier with a large bowl of fish soup (11 dr) or roast chicken with potatoes (700 d

Brits pining for a taste of the Old Da can get stuck into traditional English fa like steak and kidney pie (2500 dr) at t ***Nitro English Bar*** *(Pantanasis 9)*. It al has a choice of English beers.

For self-caterers there are branches of t ***Kronos*** supermarket chain *(Kanakari and Mourouzi 17)*.

Getting There & Away

Many first-time visitors to Greece assur the best way to get from Patras to Athens by bus. The bus is faster than the train, b is more expensive and drops you off a lo way from the city centre at Terminal A Kifissou. This is a real hassle if you' arriving in Athens after midnight, wh there are no connecting buses to the ci centre, leaving newcomers at the mercy the notorious Terminal A taxi drivers.

The train takes you close to the city ce tre, within easy walking distance of go accommodation.

Bus The main bus station on Othon Amalias has buses to Athens (three hou 3650 dr, half-hourly) via Corinth (1½ hou 2400 dr); Pyrgos (two hours, 1800 dr, daily); four daily to Ioannina (four hou

400 dr) and Kalavryta (two hours, 1500 dr); three daily to Thessaloniki (9½ hours, 250 dr) via Amfissa (for Delphi, three hours, 2200 dr); and two daily to both Kalamata (four hours, 4150 dr) and Tripolis four hours, 3100 dr).

There are buses to the Ionian island of Lefkada (3450 dr, two daily) leaving from the bus station on the corner of Faverou and Konstantinopoleos. Buses to Zakynthos 3½ hours, 2900 dr) and Kefallonia leave from the bus station at the corner of Othonos Amalias and Gerokostopoulou. They travel via the port of Kyllini.

Train There are at least eight trains daily to Athens. Half of them are slow trains, which take five hours and cost 1580 dr. They travel via Diakofto (one hour, 510 dr) and Corinth 2½ hours, 1000 dr). The intercity trains to Athens take 3½ hours and cost 2980 dr in nd class. The last intercity train leaves Patras at 6.30 pm. Holders of Eurail passes can travel free, but will need a reservation.

There are also trains to Pyrgos (two hours, 820 dr, seven daily) and Kalamata six hours, 1500 dr, two daily).

Ferry – Domestic There are daily ferries from Patras to the Ionian islands of Kefallonia (four hours, 3200 dr), Ithaki (six hours, 500 dr) and Corfu (10 hours, 5800 dr).

Ferries between Rio, 9km north-east of Patras, and Andirio (for Lefkada) operate every 15 minutes between 7 am and 11 pm, and every 30 minutes through the night (10 minutes, 120 dr/car 1420 dr).

Ferry – International Patras is Greece's main port for ferry services to Italy. The most popular crossing is the 18 hour trip to Brindisi. In summer, there are up to five boats daily on this route. One-way, deck-class fares range from 8000 dr with Five Star Lines, to 12,000 dr with Med Link, and 7,000 dr with the more comfortable Adriatica di Navigazione and Hellenic Mediterranean. Only Adriatica and Hellenic accept Eurail passes, although you will still have to pay the port tax of 1500 dr. From mid-June to the end of September, there is a high-season loading of 3000 dr.

Of the boats to Ancona, Superfast is the fastest, doing the trip in 19 hours for 25,800 dr. Others operating on this route are Minoan (20 hours, 21,800 dr), ANEK Lines (23 hours, 20,100 dr) and Strintzis (26 hours, 16,600 dr).

Superfast has a daily service to Bari (15 hours, 15,800 dr), and Minoan has daily boats to Venice (33 hours, 21,800 dr). ANEK Lines has three boats weekly to Trieste (32 hours, 19,400 dr).

With the exception of the express services to Ancona, most of these ferries stop at Igoumenitsa and Corfu. Some allow a free stopover on Corfu – ask when you buy your ticket. See the Getting There & Away chapter for more details of services.

The contact details and routes of the central offices or representatives of the ferry lines operating out of Patras are:

Adriatica di Navigazione
(☎ 422 138) Othonos Amalias 8: to Brindisi via Igoumenitsa and Corfu

ANEK Lines
(☎ 226 053) Othonos Amalias 25: to Ancona and Trieste via Corfu and Igoumenitsa

Five Star Lines
(☎ 422 102) Othonos Amalias 5: to Brindisi via Igoumenitsa

Hellenic Mediterranean
(☎ 452 521) corner Pente Pigadion and Iroön Polytehniou: to Brindisi via Kefallonia and Corfu

Med Link Lines
(☎ 623 011) Giannatos Travel, Othonos Amalias 15: to Brindisi direct or via Kefallonia and Igoumenitsa

Minoan
(☎ 421 500) corner Norman 1 and Athinon Ancona: to Venice via Igoumenitsa and Corfu

Strintzis
(☎ 622 602) Othonos Amalias 14: to Ancona and Venice via Igoumenitsa and Corfu

Superfast Ferries
(☎ 622 500) Othonos Amalias 12: to Ancona direct

Getting Around

Local buses leave from the bus stops on either side of Aratou. Car rental outlets include

Europcar (☎ 621 360), Agiou Andreou 6; Hertz (☎ 220 990), Karolou 2; and Reliable Rent A Car (☎ 272 764), Othonos Amalias 44.

DIAKOFTO Διακοφτό

☎ 0691 • postcode 251 00 • pop 2250

Diakofto (dih-ah-kof-**to**), 55km east of Patras and 80km north-west of Corinth, is a serene village, tucked between steep mountains and the sea amid lemon and olive groves.

Orientation & Information

Diakofto's layout is easy to figure out. The train station is in the middle of the village. To reach the waterfront, cross the railway track and walk down the road ahead. After 1km you will come to pebbly Egali Beach.

There is no EOT or tourist police. The post office, OTE and the National Bank of Greece are all on the main street that leads inland from the station.

Things to Do

The main reason people come to Diakofto is to ride the rack-and-pinion railway up the Vouraïkos Gorge to Kalavryta (see the boxed text 'Diakofto-Kalavryta Railway').

If you want to relax by the sea, the best section of Egali Beach is on the western side of town; turn right when you reach the seafront on the road from the station.

Places to Stay & Eat

Hotel Lemonies *(☎ 41 229/820)*, halfway down the road towards the sea, has pleasant singles/doubles with bathroom for 5000/8000 dr.

Hotel Helmos *(☎ 41 236)*, 50m from the station on the main street, has very basic rooms for 5500/7500 dr.

Diakofto's best accommodation is at the C class ***Chris Paul Hotel*** *(☎ 41 715/855, fax 42 128)*. The air-con rooms are 8500/16,000 dr. Breakfast costs an extra 1250 dr per person. The hotel has its own swimming pool, bar and restaurant. It's conveniently situated near the train station, and well signposted.

There are several places along the main street heading inland from the station. ***Costas*** is a popular *psistaria* opposite the National Bank. It's run by a friendly Greek-Australian family and has a choice of taverna-style dishes alongside the usual grilled meats. A hearty meal for two with wine costs about 4000 dr. Farther along is ***Soulekas***, another psistaria offering similar fare.

People heading up to Kalavryta on the train can stock up for the trip at the shops opposite the station.

Getting There & Away

Bus There's not much point in catching a bus to/from Diakofto – the trains are much more convenient. Patras-Athens buses bypass the village on the New National Road.

Train Diakofto is on the main Athens-Patras line and there are frequent trains in either direction.

There are trains on the rack-and-pinion line to Kalavryta (one hour, 980 dr 2nd class, 1220 dr 1st class, four daily) via Zahlorou (850/1030 dr) departing 8 am, 10.30 am, 1.15 pm and 3.45 pm Monday to Friday; and 9 am, 11 am, 2.10 pm and 4.4 pm on the weekend. The 1st class compartments at the front and rear of the train have the best views, and are well worth the extra.

ZAHLOROU Ζαχλωρού

☎ 0692 • postcode 250 01 • pop 50

The picturesque and unspoilt settlement of Zahlorou, the halfway stop on the Diakofto-Kalavryta train line, straddles both sides of the river and railway line. Many people take the train to this point and walk back to Diakofto.

Moni Mega Spileou Μονή Μεγάλου Σπήλαιου

A steep path (signposted) leads up from Zahlorou to the Moni Mega Spileou (Monastery of the Great Cavern). The original monastery was destroyed in 1934 when gunpowder stored during the War of Independence exploded. The new

Diakofto-Kalavryta Railway

The railway from Diakofto to Kalavryta takes travellers on an unforgettable ride through the dramatic Vouraïkos Gorge. The train climbs over 700m in 22.5km, using a rack-and-pinion (cog) system for traction on the steep sections. Built by an Italian company between 1885 and 1895, the railway was a remarkable feat of engineering for its time.

The opening section of the journey is fairly sedate, climbing gently through the lush citrus orchards that flank the lower reaches of the Vouraïkos River. The ascent begins in earnest about 5km south of Diakofto, and the section from here to Zahlorou is spectacular as the line switches back and forth across the gorge in search of a foothold. As the gorge narrows, the train disappears into a long curving tunnel and emerges clinging to a narrow ledge that seems to overhang the river. This stretch is quite awesome in spring when the waters are swollen by snowmelt from the surrounding mountains.

South of the charming village of Zahlorou, the line follows the river beneath a leafy canopy of plane trees, before meandering through open country for the final run to Kalavryta.

The journey takes just over an hour, stopping en route at Zahlorou. Second class fares are 850 dr to Zahlorou and 980 dr to Kalavryta, but spending 1030/1220 dr for a 1st class compartment at the front or rear of the train is well worth the extra – they have the best views.

The line was commissioned by Greece's great railway building prime minister, Harilaos Trikoupis, who had the romantic notion of using the new train technology of the time to provide access to the birthplace of the modern Greek nation – Moni Agias Lavras, near Kalavryta. It was at this monastery that Bishop Germanos of Patras raised the flag of revolt that launched the War of Independence on 25 March, 1821.

The original steam engines that first plied the route were replaced in the early 1960s by diesel cars, but the old steam engines can still be seen outside Diakofto and Kalavryta stations.

See the Diakofto Getting There & Away section for information on train departure times.

monastery houses illuminated gospels, relics, silver crosses, jewellery and the miraculous icon of the Virgin Mary which, like numerous icons in Greece, is said to have been painted by St Luke. It was supposedly discovered in the nearby cavern by St Theodore and St Simeon in 362 AD. A monk will show visitors around. Modest dress is required of both sexes – no bare arms or legs. The 3km walk up to the monastery takes about an hour.

Places to Stay & Eat

The quaint D class ***Hotel Romantzo*** *(☎ 0692-22 758)* is one of Greece's more eccentric little hotels. It stands right next to the railway line at the end of the platform and has singles/doubles with bathroom for 5000/10,000 dr. You can almost reach out and touch the trains from the windows of its seven rooms. It's advisable to book at weekends. During the week, the manager uses one triple room as a dorm where hikers can roll out their sleeping bags for 2000 dr. The hotel has a restaurant with outdoor seating on the opposite side of the railway.

Getting There & Away

All Diakofto-Kalavryta trains stop at Zahlorou. You can drive to Zahlorou on a dirt road leading off the Diakofto-Kalavryta road. The turn-off is 7.5km north of Kalavryta.

KALAVRYTA Καλάβρυτα

☎ 0692 • postcode 250 01 • pop 2200

At an elevation of 756m, Kalavryta (kah-**lah**-vrih-tah) is a cool mountain resort with copious springs and shady plane trees. Two relatively recent historical events have assured the town a special place in the hearts of all Greeks. The revolt against the Turks began here on 25 March 1821 when Bishop Germanos of Patras raised the banner of revolt at the monastery of Agia Lavra, 6km from Kalavryta. Also, on 13 December 1943, in one of the worst atrocities of WWII, the Nazis set fire to the town and massacred all its male inhabitants over 15 years old as punishment for resistance activity. The total number killed in the region was 1436. The hands of the old cathedral clock stand eternally at 2.34, the time the massacre began.

Orientation & Information

Most people arrive at the train station, on the northern edge of town. Opposite is a large building that will eventually become the Municipal Museum of the Kalavryta Holocaust. Kalavryta is the founding member of the Union of Martyred Towns. To the right of the museum-to-be is Syngrou, a pedestrian precinct. After one block, it becomes 25 Martiou. To the left of the museum is Konstantinou.

The central square, Plateia Kalavrytou, is between these two streets, two blocks up from the train station.

The bus station is on Kapota. From the train station, walk up Syngrou and turn right at Hotel Maria onto Kapota, cross Ethnikis Antistassis and you'll see the buses parked outside at the bottom of the hill on the left. Kalavryta has neither EOT nor tourist police. The post office is on the main square and the OTE is on Konstantinou. The National Bank of Greece is on 25 Martiou, just before the central square.

Martyrs' Monument

A huge white cross on a cypress-covered hillside just east of the town marks the site of the 1943 massacre. Beneath this imposing monument is a poignant little shrine to the victims. The site is signposted off Konstantinou.

Places to Stay

Kalavryta does not have a lot of accommodation. Peak season here is the ski season, from late November to April. Reservations are essential at this time, and at weekends throughout the year when Athenians come to enjoy the cool mountain air. The prices listed below are slashed by as much as 50% at other times.

There are no budget hotels, but there are several ***domatia*** on the streets behind the train station.

The cheapest hotel is ***Megas Alexandros*** *(☎ 22 221, Kapota 1)*, which has doubles with bathroom for 10,000 dr. The nearby ***Hotel Maria*** *(☎ 22 296, fax 22 686, Syngrou 10)* charges 14,000/18,000 dr for cozy singles/doubles with TV. Breakfast, served in the cafe downstairs, costs 1300 dr.

The best rooms in town are at the brand new ***Hotel Anesis*** *(☎ 23 070)*, behind the church on Plateia Kalavrytou. It has beautifully furnished rooms for 15,000/18,000 dr. The best rooms have their own log fires and cost an extra 2000 dr. Summer rates drop to a bargain 6000/8000 dr!

Hotel Filoxenia *(☎ 22 422, fax 23 009, Ethnikis Antistaseos 10)* has rooms with bathroom, minibar and TV for 16,400/22,000 dr, including breakfast.

Places to Eat

Most places to eat in Kalavryta are on 25 Martiou. ***To Tzaki Taverna***, opposite the church, is large and cheerful, and main meals are reasonably priced. ***Taverna Stani***, opposite the National Bank of Greece, has excellent staples. You can wash down house specialities like roast goat in white sauce (2000 dr) or roast lamb in vine leaves (2250 dr) with a litre of house wine (1200 dr).

Entertainment

The ***Air Music Club***, about 1km north of town on the road to Diakofto, is housed in one of the original Boeing 720-68 planes bought by Aristotle Onassis for the launch of Olympic Airways in the 60s. It was transported here in pieces and reassembled *in situ*.

Getting There & Away

There are buses to Patras (1500 dr, four daily), Athens (3200 dr, two daily) and Tripolis (1600 dr, one daily).

There are trains to Diakofto (via Zahlorou) departing 9.15 am, 11.45 am, 2.30 and 5 pm Monday to Friday, and 10.12 am, 12.45, 3.20 and 6 pm on weekends.

Kalavryta's taxi rank (☎ 22 127) is on the central square.

AROUND KALAVRYTA

Moni Agias Lavras

The original 10th century monastery was burnt by the Nazis. The new monastery has a small museum where the banner standard is displayed along with other monastic memorabilia. Buses heading south from Kalavryta to Klitoria or Tripolis can drop you a short walk from the monastery, or take a taxi.

Cave of the Lakes

The remarkable Cave of the Lakes lies 16.5km south of Kalavryta near the village of Kastria. The cave features in Greek mythology and is mentioned in the writings of the ancient traveller Pausanias, but its whereabouts remained unknown in modern times until 1964, when locals noticed water pouring from the roof of a smaller, lower cave after heavy rain and decided to investigate. They found themselves in a large bat-filled cavern at the start of a winding 2km-long cave carved out by a subterranean river.

The cavern is now reached by an artificial entrance that is the starting point for a 350m raised walkway that snakes up the riverbed. It passes some wonderfully ornate stalactites, but they are mere sideshows alongside the lakes themselves. The lakes are actually a series of 13 stone basins formed by mineral deposits over the millennia. In summer, the waters dry up to reveal a curious lace work of walls, some up to 3m high.

The cave (☎ 0692-31 633) is open 9.30 am to 4.30 pm daily; admission is 1500 dr. Getting there is difficult without your own transport. The daily bus from Kalavryta to Kastria isn't much help. A taxi from Kalavryta will cost about 6000 dr return.

Ski Centre

The ski centre (elevation 1650m to 2100m), with nine pistes and one chairlift, is 14km east of Kalavryta on Mt Helmos. It has a cafeteria and first-aid centre but no overnight accommodation. The ski centre has an office in Kalavryta (☎ 0692-22 661, fax 22 415), at the top of 25 Martiou. Opening times are 7 am to 3 pm Monday to Friday. Several outlets on Konstantinou rent skis for approximately 3000 dr per weekday, 3500 dr on weekends. There is no transport to the centre from Kalavryta, so you will need to organise your own.

Mt Helmos Refuge

The EOS-owned B Leondopoulos Mountain Refuge is situated at 2100m on Mt Helmos. A marked footpath leads to the refuge from the ski centre (one hour's walk). Another leads from the village of Ano Loussi (1½ hours), on the way to Kastria. To stay in the refuge, or for details on walks or climbs on Mt Helmos, talk to the ski-centre staff in Kalavryta.

Corinthia Κορινθία

Corinthia occupies a strategic position adjoining the Isthmus of Corinth. The region was once dominated by the mighty, ancient city of Corinth, now one of the main attractions. Few travellers opt to linger long, although there are several minor sites in the pretty hinterland west of Corinth that are worth a detour if you have your own transport.

CORINTH Κόρινθος

☎ 0741 •postcode 201 00 • pop 27,400

Modern Corinth (in Greek, Korinthos; **ko-rin-thoss**), 6km west of the Corinth Canal, is the dull administrative capital of Corinthia prefecture. It was rebuilt here after the old town was destroyed by an earthquake in

PELOPONNESE

1858. The new town was wrecked by another, equally violent, earthquake in 1928 and badly damaged again in 1981.

The modern town is dominated by concrete buildings built to withstand future earthquakes, but it has a pleasant harbour, friendly people, tasty food and warrants an overnight stay because of its proximity to ancient Corinth and Nemea. Old Corinth is a mere village near the ancient site.

Orientation & Information

It is not difficult to negotiate Corinth, which is laid out on a grid of wide streets stretching back from the waterfront. Social activity centres around the large square by the harbour, Plateia El Venizelou, while transport and administrative activity is based around the small park 200m inland on Ethnikis Antistaseos.

There is no EOT in Corinth. The tourist police (☎ 23 282), located next to the park at Ermou 51, are open 8 am to 2 pm and 5 to 8 pm daily between May and October. The regular police (☎ 22 143) are in the same building. The National Bank of Greece is one of several banks on Ethnikis Antistaseos, the post office is on the edge of the park at Adimantou 33, and the OTE is nearby on the corner of Kolokotroni and Adimantou.

Folk Museum

The Folk Museum, to the south of the wharf, focuses on bridal and festive costumes from the past three centuries. There are costumes from the islands and the mainland, as well as metalwork, embroidery, gold and silver objects, and carvings, both secular and ecclesiastical. The museum is open 8.30 am to 1.30 pm daily, except Monday. Admission is 500 dr.

Ancient Corinth & Acrocorinth

The sprawling ruins of ancient Corinth are 7km south-west of modern Corinth. Towering 575m above them is the massive, fortified bulk of Acrocorinth.

Allow a day to see both ancient Corinth and Acrocorinth. Most people come on day trips from modern Corinth, but there are ***tavernas*** and a few ***domatia*** in the village near the ancient site. Look for the signs.

The site (☎ 0741-31 207) and its museum are open 8 am to 7 pm daily (5 pm in winter). Admission to the site (including the museum) is 1200 dr.

History During the 6th century BC, Corinth was one of ancient Greece's richest cities. It owed its wealth to its strategic position on the Isthmus of Corinth, which meant it was able to build twin ports, one on the Aegean Sea (Kenchreai) and one on the Ionian Sea (Lecheon), and it traded throughout the Mediterranean. It survived the Peloponnesian Wars and flourished under Macedonian rule, but it was sacked by the Roman consul Mummius in 146 BC for rebelling against Roman rule. In 44 BC, Julius Caesar began rebuilding the city and it again became a prosperous port.

During Roman times, when Corinthians weren't clinching business deals, they were paying homage to the goddess of love, Aphrodite, in a temple dedicated to her (which meant they were having a rollicking time with the temple's sacred prostitutes, both male and female). St Paul, perturbed by the Corinthians' wicked ways, spent 18 fruitless months preaching here.

Ancient Corinth Earthquakes and sackings by a series of invaders have left little standing in ancient Corinth. The remains are mostly from Roman times. An exception is the 5th century BC Doric **Temple of Apollo**, the most prominent ruin on the site. To the south of this temple is a huge **agora**, or forum, bounded at its southern side by the foundations of a **stoa**. This was built to accommodate the bigwigs summoned here in 337 BC by Philip II to sign oaths of allegiance to Macedon. In the middle of the central row of shops is the **bema**, a marble podium from which Roman officials addressed the people.

At the eastern end of the forum are the remains of the **Julian Basilica**. To the north

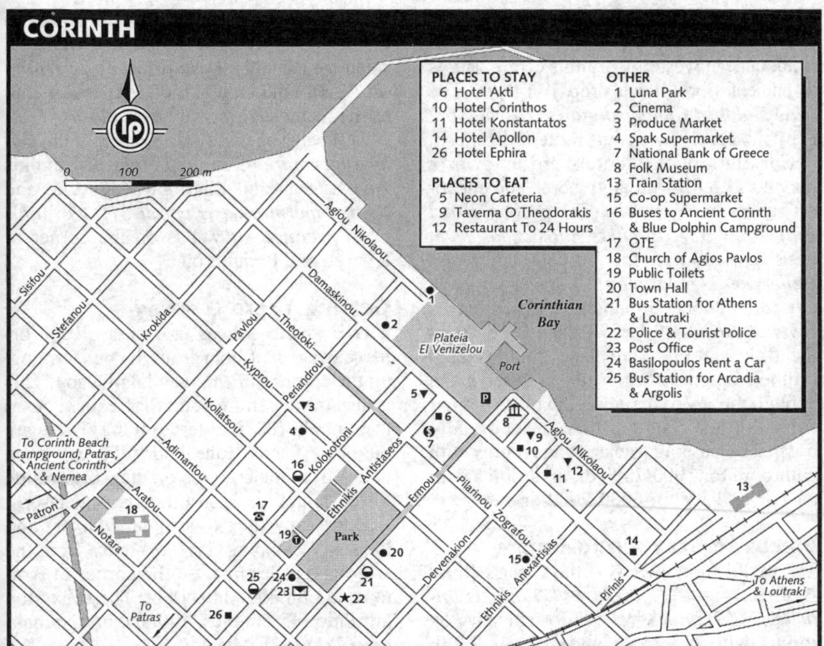

is the **Lower Peirene fountain** – the Upper Peirene fountain is on Acrocorinth. According to mythology, Peirene wept so much when her son Kenchrias was killed by Artemis that the gods, rather than let all the precious water go to waste, turned her into a fountain. In reality, it's a natural spring which has been used since ancient times and still supplies old Corinth with water. The water tanks are concealed in a fountain house with a six-arched facade. Through the arches can be seen the remains of frescoes.

West of the fountain, steps lead to the **Lecheon road**, once the main thoroughfare to the port of Lecheon. On the east side of the road is the **Peribolos of Apollo**, a courtyard flanked by Ionic columns, some of which have been restored. Nearby is a **public latrine**. Some seats remain. The site's **museum** houses statues, mosaics, figurines, reliefs and friezes.

Acrocorinth Earthquakes and invasions compelled the Corinthians to retreat to Acrocorinth (Ακροκόρινθος), a sheer bulk of limestone which was one of the finest natural fortifications in Greece. The original fortress was built in ancient times, but it has been modified many times over the years by a string of invaders. The ruins are a medley of imposing Roman, Byzantine, Frankish, Venetian and Turkish ramparts, harbouring remains of Byzantine chapels, Turkish houses and mosques.

On the higher of Acrocorinth's two summits is the **Temple of Aphrodite** where the sacred courtesans, who so raised the ire of St Paul, catered to the desires of the insatiable Corinthians. Little remains of the temple, but the views are tremendous. The site is open 8 am to 7 pm Tuesday to Sunday (2.30 pm in winter); admission is free.

Places to Stay – Budget

Corinth Beach Campground *(☎ 27 967/968)* is about 3km west of Corinth's centre. Buses to ancient Corinth can drop you there. The ***Blue Dolphin Campground*** *(☎ 25 766/767)* is by the beach on the bus route to Lecheon.

Corinth's budget hotels are as grim a bunch as you'll find anywhere. The cheapest rooms in town are at the grubby ***Hotel Akti*** *(☎ 23 337, Ethnikis Antistaseos 1)*. It has singles/doubles for 4000/8000 dr. ***Hotel Belle Vue*** *(Damaskinou 41)* appears to have closed its doors permanently, which leaves ***Hotel Apollon*** *(☎ 22 587, Pirinis 18)*, near the train station. The place doubles as a brothel, but the owners do at least make enough money to maintain the place – apart from the hotel sign which is continually trashed by passing trucks. It has rooms with bathroom for 5000/7000 dr, and rooms with air-con and TV for 6000/9000 dr.

Places to Stay – Mid-Range

The best deal in town is at the C class ***Hotel Ephira*** *(☎ 24 021, fax 24 514, Ethnikis Antistaseos 52)* which has comfortable air-con rooms with bathroom and TV for 9000/14,000 dr. Breakfast is available for 1200 dr.

The other C class places in town are overpriced in comparison. ***Hotel Corinthos*** *(☎ 26 701, fax 23 693, Damaskinou 26)* has pleasant rooms with bathroom and balcony for 12,500/18,000 dr. ***Hotel Konstantatos*** *(☎ 22 120, fax 85 634)*, also on Damaskinou, has singles for 12,000 dr and singles/doubles with private facilities for 14,500/16,000 dr. Air-con doubles are 20,000 dr.

Places to Eat

Taverna O Theodorakis, just back from the waterfront near the Folk Museum, is a lively place specialising in fresh grilled fish, priced from 7000 dr per kilogram. You can have a plate of sardines for 1000 dr, a large Greek salad for 1000 dr and a litre of retsina for 800 dr. It's open all year, with outdoor seating in summer.

Neon Cafeteria, at the corner of Damaskinou and Ethnikis Antistaseos, is a popular cafeteria with a good range of daily specials like macaroni with octopus (1450 dr) or veal with rice (1650 dr) as well as a salad bar (950 dr). ***Restaurant To 24 Hours*** on Agiou Nikolaou is more expensive but, as the name suggests, it never closes.

Self-caterers will find a branch of the ***Co-op supermarket***, on the corner of Ethnikis Anexartisias and Pilarinou Zografou, and ***Spak supermarket*** *(Kyprou 61)*. Corinth's main ***produce market*** is on the corner of Kyprou and Periandrou.

Getting There & Away

Bus Buses to Athens (1½ hours, 1600 dr) leave every half-hour from the bus terminal on the corner of Ermou and Koliatsou. This is also the departure point for frequent buses to Loutraki (20 minutes, 300 dr). There are buses to Nemea (one hour, 850 dr, seven daily) from the bus stop on the western side of the central park on Ethnikis Antistaseos.

Buses to Argos (one hour, 900 dr) and Nafplio (1¼ hours, 1150 dr) leave from the Argolis bus terminal on the corner of Aratou and Ethnikis Antistaseos. They also stop at Fihtio (45 minutes, 700 dr), on the main road 2km from Mycenae.

Catching a bus to other parts of the Peloponnese is a hassle. Buses south to Tripolis (1½ hours, 1450 dr), Sparta (three hours, 2250 dr) and Kalamata (four hours, 2800 dr) use a new bus station on the southern outskirts of town, 1000 dr by taxi from the centre. Buses to Patras can be picked up from the bus stop on the Athens side of the Corinth Canal – which means you'll have to get there on one of the frequent buses to Loutraki. You're better off catching the train.

Train There are 15 trains daily to Athens (1¾ hours, 780 dr). Four of them are intercity services, but they are only 15 minutes faster. The Peloponnese rail network divides at Corinth, with eight trains daily heading along the north coast to Diakofto and Patras. It's worth checking the timetable before you set out – journey times to Patras range from under two hours on intercity trains to 3½ hours on the slowest slow train. Six trains continue down the west coast from Patras to Pyrgos, five go to Kyparissia and one takes 8½ hours to crawl all the way to Kalamata.

If Kalamata is your destination, you're better off taking the inland line. It has trains to Kalamata (5½ hours, 1650 dr, four daily), via Argos (one hour, 510 dr) and Tripolis (2½ hours, 900 dr). There are also trains on the branch line to Nafplio (1¼ hours, 810 dr, three daily).

Getting Around

Bus Buses to ancient Corinth (20 minutes, 240 dr) leave Corinth hourly on the hour, returning on the half-hour. They leave from the bus stop north-west of the central park on Koliatsou. This is also the place to catch a bus to Lecheon (for the Blue Dolphin Campground). There is no public transport between ancient Corinth and Acrocorinth. You can drive or take a taxi; otherwise it's a strenuous 1½ hour walk.

Car There are several car rental outlets around the city centre, including Basilopoulos Rent a Car (☎ 25 573), Adimantou 39.

CORINTH CANAL

The concept of cutting a canal through the Isthmus of Corinth to link the Ionian and Aegean seas was first proposed by the tyrant Periander, founder of ancient Corinth. The magnitude of the task defeated him, so he opted instead to build a paved slipway across which sailors dragged small ships on rollers – a method used until the 13th century.

In the intervening years, many leaders, including Alexander the Great and Caligula, toyed with the canal idea, but it was Nero who actually began digging in 67 AD. In true megalomaniac fashion, he struck the first blow himself using a golden pickaxe. He then left it to 6000 Jewish prisoners to do the hard work. The project was soon halted by invasions by the Gauls. Finally, in the 19th century (1883-93), a French engineering company completed the canal.

The Corinth Canal, cut through solid rock, is over 6km long and 23m wide. The vertical sides rise 90m above the water. The canal did much to elevate Piraeus' status as a major Mediterranean port. It's an impressive sight, particularly when a ship is passing through it.

Getting There & Away

The canal can be reached on a Loutraki bus from modern Corinth to the canal bridge. Any bus or train between Corinth and Athens will also pass over the canal. Heraion Tours (☎ 0744-21 062) in Loutraki is one of several companies offering cruises through the canal.

ISTHMIA Ισθμία

At the south-eastern end of the canal is the site of ancient Isthmia. The remains of the **Sanctuary of Poseidon**, a defensive wall, and **Roman theatre** are mainly of interest to archaeology buffs. As with Nemea, Delphi and Olympia, ancient Isthmia was one of the sites of the Panhellenic Games, and the site's **museum** (open daily except Tuesday) contains various ancient athletic exhibits. The modern village of Isthmia lies a short distance to the east of the ancient site.

The Old National Road to Athens crosses the canal at Isthmia by a submersible bridge, which is lowered to allow ships to pass over it.

LOUTRAKI Λουτράκι

Loutraki (population 7000), 6km north of the Corinth Canal, lounges between a pebbled beach and the tall cliffs of the Gerania Mountains. Once a traditional spa town patronised by elderly and frail Greeks, it remains a major producer of bottled mineral water. The town was devastated by the 1981 earthquake, and subsequent reconstruction has resulted in its reincarnation as a tacky resort with dozens of modern, characterless hotels along the seafront. Loutraki hardly warrants an overnight stay.

Getting There & Away

Buses run from Corinth to Loutraki (20 minutes, 300 dr) every half-hour, and there are nine buses daily from Athens (1½ hours, 1600 dr).

LAKE VOULIAGMENI

Λιμνι Βουλιαμενισ

Tranquil Lake Vouliagmeni, 23km north-west of Loutraki, is a lovely little lagoon linked to the sea by a narrow channel. It's a popular spot at weekends and there are half a dozen small fish tavernas dotted around the shore.

The road continues beyond the lake to the ruins of **ancient Heraion**, surrounding a tiny natural harbour below Cape Melanhavi. The site was excavated by Humfry Payne from 1930 to 1933. Payne was accompanied by his wife, Dilys Powell, who describes her stay in the area in her book *An Affair of the Heart*. At the site are the ruins of an agora, a stoa and an 8th century BC temple in a **Sanctuary to Hera**. The site is not enclosed and entry is free.

Getting There & Away

There is no public transport to Lake Vouliagmeni, so you will have to find your own way there. There are several places to rent motorcycles in Loutraki.

WEST OF CORINTH

The coastline stretching west from Corinth towards Patras is dotted with a series of fishing villages and small resorts. Places such as **Derveni** (which has a sandy beach), **Kamari, Xylokastro** and **Kiato** are popular mainly with Greek holiday-makers and groups from northern Europe. Beach buffs will be unimpressed. There are several interesting minor sites inland that are worth a detour if you have the time.

Ancient Sikyon Σικυőν

Ancient Sikyon, known as the City of Pumpkins because of the plump terracotta pottery once produced here, is 6km south of Kiato. Founded in the 2nd millennium BC by the Ionians and later conquered by the Dorians, it became an important cultural centre focusing on wax painting, sculpture and pottery. It suffered at the hands of numerous invaders before it was finally destroyed by an earthquake in 23 AD. The only obvious remains are those of a partially preserved **gymnasium** from Hellenistic and Roman times and the ruins of the **Temple of Artemis**.

The site's **museum** (☎ 0742-28 900), housed in restored Roman baths, contains vases from various periods, terracotta statuettes from Archaic to Roman times, and a Praxiteles-styled marble head of Apollo. It was closed for renovations at the time of writing, so check the latest situation with Corinth's tourist police. The site is opposite the museum. It's not enclosed and admission is free.

Getting There & Away There's no public transport to the site, which is 1.5km west of the village of Vasiliko. If you're driving, you'll find signs to Vasiliko from Kiato; otherwise, a taxi from Kiato costs about 1500 dr. There are regular trains to Kiato from Corinth and Patras.

Stymfalia Στυμφαλία

If you've got your own transport, the 36km drive from Kiato to Stymfalia is worth the effort for the scenery as much as anything else. Little remains of the ancient site apart from the ruins of three temples. The site is next to a marshy lake of the same name, which was the home of the mythical man-eating Stymfalian birds that Heracles was ordered to shoo away as the sixth of his 12 labours. The birds were depicted in sculptures on the Temple of Artemis Stymfalia.

Nemea Νεμύα

Ancient Nemea, 31km south-west of Corinth, lies 4km north-east of the modern village of the same name. According to mythology, it was here that Heracles carried out the first of his labours – the slaying of the lion that had been sent by Hera to destroy Nemea. The lion became the constellation Leo (each of the 12 labours is related to a sign of the zodiac).

Like Olympia, Nemea was not a city but a sanctuary and venue for the biennial Nemean Games, held in honour of Zeus. These games became one of the great Panhellenic festivals. Remarkably, three columns of the

4th century BC Doric **Temple of Zeus** remain. Other ruins include a bathhouse and hostelry. The site's **museum** has a model of the site and explanations in English.

At the **stadium**, 500m back along the road, you can see the athletes' starting line and distance markers. The site and museum (☎ 0746-22 739) are open 8.30 am to 3 pm Tuesday to Sunday; it's 500 dr for each.

Getting There & Away There are buses to Nemea (one hour, 850 dr, seven daily) from Corinth that travel past the site. There are also buses to Nemea from Argos (600 dr).

Argolis Αργολίδα

The Argolis Peninsula, which separates the Saronic and Argolic gulfs in the north-east, is a veritable treasure trove for archaeology buffs. The town of Argos, from which the region takes its name, is thought to be the longest continually inhabited town in Greece. Argolis was the seat of power of the Mycenaean Empire that ruled Greece from 1600 to 1200 BC. The ancient cities of Mycenae, Tiryns, Argos and Epidaurus are the region's major attractions.

ARGOS Αργος

☎ 0751 • postcode 212 00 • pop 22,300

Argos may well be the oldest continuously inhabited town in Greece, but most vestiges of its past glory lie buried beneath the uninspiring modern town. Although the town itself is of minor interest, it is a convenient base from which to explore the sites of Argolis and has a refreshing lack of tourist hype. It is also a major transport hub for buses.

Orientation & Information

Argos' showpiece and focal point is the magnificent central square, Plateia Agiou Petrou, with its Art Nouveau street lights, citrus and palm trees and the impressive Church of Agios Petros. Beyond, Argos deteriorates into an unremarkable working town.

The bus station is just south of the central square on Kapodistriou, while the train station is on the south-eastern edge of town by the road to Nafplio.

There is no tourist office or tourist police. The post office and OTE are both close to Plateia Agiou Petrou. The post office is clearly signposted on Kapodistriou, and the OTE office is on Nikitara, which leads off the square next to the National Bank of Greece. The regular police can be contacted on ☎ 100.

PELOPONNESE

Archaeological Museum

Even if you're only passing through Argos, try to pause long enough to visit the archaeological museum, on the edge of the central square. The collection includes some outstanding Roman mosaics and sculptures; Neolithic, Mycenaean and Geometric pottery; and bronze objects from the Mycenaean tombs. The museum (☎ 68 819) is open 8 am to 2.30 pm Tuesday to Sunday. Admission is 500 dr.

Roman Ruins

There are Roman ruins on both sides of Tripolis, the main Argos-Tripolis road. To get there from the central square, head south along Danaou for about 500m and then turn right onto Theatron. Theatron joins Tripolis opposite the star attraction, the enormous **theatre**, which could seat up to 20,000 people (more than at Epidaurus). It dates from classical times but was greatly altered by the Romans. Nearby are the remains of a 1st century AD **odeum** (indoor theatre) and **Roman baths**. The site is open 8.30 am to 3 pm daily. Admission is free.

It is a 45 minute hard slog by footpath from the theatre up to the **Fortress of Larissa**, a conglomeration of Byzantine, Frankish, Venetian and Turkish architecture, standing on the foundations of the city's principal ancient citadel.

The **Sanctuary of Apollo & Athena** and the nearby remains of a **Mycenaean necropolis**, where some chamber tombs and shaft graves have been excavated, lie to the north of the Roman ruins. The hill to the north-east of these ruins is the site of a small ancient citadel and an early Bronze Age settlement, now crowned by the chapel of Agios Elias. To reach these ruins from the Roman ruins, walk north along Tripolis and turn left at the intersection with Tsokri. From the central square, walk up Vasileos Konstantinou, which becomes Tsokri.

Places to Stay & Eat

All five hotels in town are close to the central square. The best budget choice is ***Hotel Apollon*** *(☎ 68 065, Papaflessa 13)* behind the National Bank of Greece. It has singles/doubles for 4500/6000 dr, or 5500/8000 dr with bathroom.

The C class ***Hotel Mycenae*** *(☎ 68 754, fax 68 332)*, on the central square, has large, comfortable rooms for 10,000/13,000 dr, and a four-bed 'apartment' is 22,000 dr. Breakfast costs 2000 dr per person.

The ***restaurants*** on the central square are either relatively expensive or serve fast food. Head for the backstreets for traditional, cheap fare. You'll find a few simple ***ouzeria*** between the main square and the train station. Argos' ***food market*** is in the neoclassical agora on Tsokri.

Getting There & Away

Bus Local services include buses to Nafplio (20 minutes, 250 dr, every half-hour), Mycenae (30 minutes, 360 dr, six daily) and Nemea (one hour, 600 dr, two daily). There are also buses to Athens (two hours, 2300 dr, hourly) via Corinth (900 dr); Tripolis (1¼ hours, 1050 dr, eight daily); and Leonidio (2¼ hours, 1500 dr, three daily).

Train There are seven trains daily to Athens (three hours, 1040 dr), also stopping at Nemea (45 minutes, 310 dr) and Corinth (one hour, 510 dr). There are four trains daily to Kalamata (3½ hours, 1280 dr) via Tripolis (one hour, 590 dr).

KEFALARI

About 7km from Argos off the main road to Tripolis is the pretty village of Kefalari. It is surrounded by vineyards which sprawl out either side of the 2km dirt road that climbs up to the **Pyramid of Helenekion** (or Pyramid of Kenchreai). It was built in 4 BC to commemorate a victory over Sparta and evolved into a fort. It stands – fenced, crude and crumbling – on a hilltop by a church. It's hardly worth the walk, but the deviation to Kefalari is. The village centrepiece is the substantial and beautiful **Church of the Virgin & Child Life-Giving Spring**. Framed by trees and bougainvillea, below grottoes sacred to Dionysos and Pan on the slope of Mt Haon, it spans a gushing mountain stream. You can soak up the tranquillity at open-air summer tavernas. Buses to Kefalari leave from the Arcadia-Lakonia bus station.

MYCENAE Μυκήνες

☎ 0751 • postcode 212 00 • pop 450

The modern village of Mycenae (in Greek, Mikines; mih-**kee**-ness) is 12km north of Argos, just east of the main Argos-Corinth road. The village is geared towards the hordes of package tourists visiting ancient Mycenae, and has little to recommend it other than its proximity to the ancient site, 2km to the north. There is accommodation along its single street. There's no bank, but there is a mobile post office with a currency exchange service at the ancient site.

Ancient Mycenae

In the barren foothills of Mt Agios Ilias (750m) and Mt Zara (600m) stand the sombre and mighty ruins of ancient Mycenae, vestiges of a kingdom which, for 400 years (1600-1200 BC), was the most powerful in Greece, holding sway over the Argolid (the modern-day prefecture of Argolis) and influencing the other Mycenaean kingdoms.

The site (☎ 76 585) is open 8 am to 7 pm daily (5 pm in winter). Admission to the citadel and the Treasury of Atreus is 1500 dr. After exploring, revive yourself with freshly squeezed Argolis orange juice, sold from a van opposite the mobile post office.

History & Mythology Mycenae is synonymous with Homer and Schliemann. In

PELOPONNESE

The Life of Heinrich Schliemann

Heinrich Schliemann is often dismissed as being too eccentric and monomaniacal to be taken seriously in the dry, academic world of archaeology – someone who was driven more by impulse than carefully correlated facts. Despite his inaccurate dating of his finds, Schliemann must be acknowledged as the archaeologist who proved that the kingdom of Mycenae had existed and was not merely a product of Homer's imagination.

The life of Heinrich Schliemann was as dramatic, fantastic and eventful as any of Homer's tales. He was born in the Baltic German state of Mecklenburg in 1822. His father was a feckless womaniser and drunkard whose long-suffering wife died when Schliemann was only nine years old. Schliemann was forced to leave school at 14.

Five years later, he'd had enough of his menial job, and set off to seek his fortune. He worked as a ship's boy on a Hamburg vessel bound for Venezuela. The ship was wrecked off the Dutch coast, but against all odds Schliemann survived and wandered into Amsterdam half-dead and destitute.

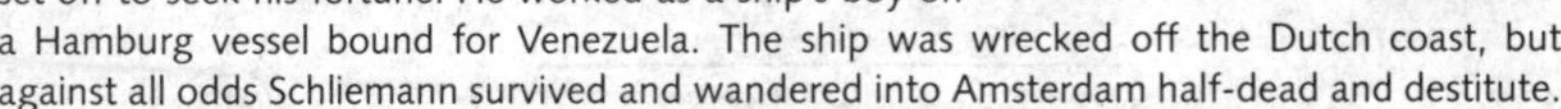

With a thirst for both knowledge and money, he worked for various trading companies in Holland and studied obsessively. Languages were one of his passions; he learnt modern European languages in six weeks, but Ancient Greek took him a while longer. By 24 he was working for an international Dutch trading company, and became their representative in St Petersburg. Already fluent in English, Portuguese, French, Dutch, Spanish and Italian, he now added Russian to his repertoire.

By the age of 40, Schliemann had made a considerable amount of money in various business ventures, and decided to indulge a fantasy that had long obsessed him. Steeped in Greek mythology, he was convinced that Homer's epics were based, albeit loosely, on fact.

In 1868 he decided to prove this, but wanted a sympathetic partner to help him. He wrote to a friend, a bishop in Athens, asking him to find him a suitable wife. Among the likely candidates the bishop suggested was 17-year-old Sophia Engastromenos. When they met, Schliemann asked her a number of questions, the two crucial ones being: Could she recite some of Homer by heart? And would she like to travel? She passed the test, they were married and she was whisked off to Hissartik (ancient Ilium, alias Troy) in Asia Minor to assist Schliemann in his excavations.

In his overenthusiasm Schliemann dug too deep and uncovered treasures which belonged to a pre-Homeric period, not that of King Priam as he believed. The same happened in Mycenae, the site of his next excavation. The gold mask he unearthed and excitedly proclaimed as the death mask of Agamemnon actually belonged to a king who lived three centuries earlier.

Sophia accompanied him on all his expeditions, ever-supportive, hard-working and enthusiastic. Marriage did not, however, diminish Schliemann's eccentricities and obsessions – their house, on El Venizelou in Athens (built by the esteemed German architect Ernst Ziller) was named Iliou Melathron (Palace of Troy) and their son and daughter were called Agamemnon and Andromache. Appropriately, his mausoleum in Athens' First Cemetery, designed by Ziller, is adorned with scenes from the Trojan War.

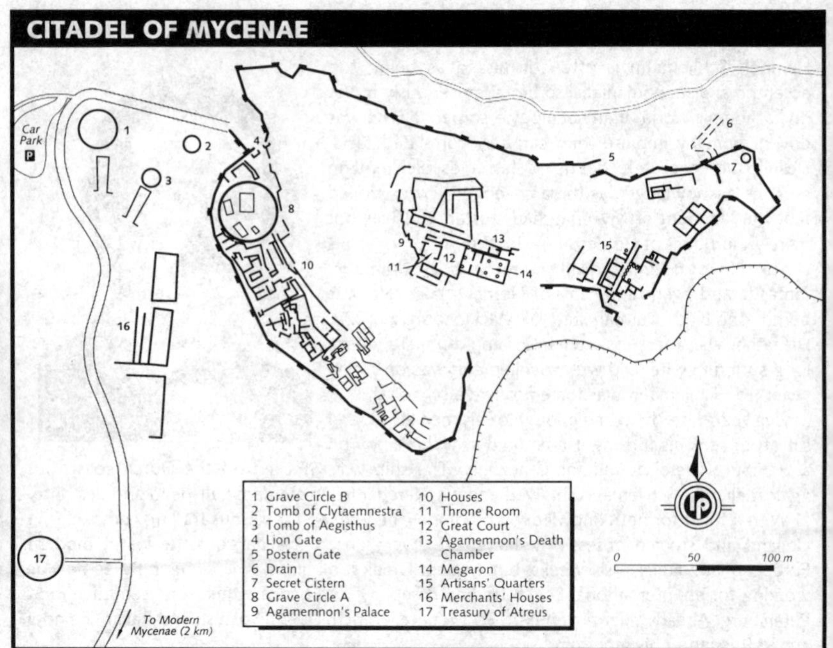

the 9th century BC, Homer told in his epic poems, the *Iliad* and the *Odyssey*, of 'well-built Mycenae, rich in gold'. These poems were, until the 19th century, regarded as no more than gripping and beautiful legends. But in the 1870s, the amateur archaeologist Heinrich Schliemann (1822-90), despite derision from professional archaeologists, struck gold, first at Troy then at Mycenae.

In Mycenae, myth and history are inextricably linked. According to Homer, the city of Mycenae was founded by Perseus, the son of Danaë and Zeus. Perseus' greatest heroic deed was the killing of the hideous snake-haired Medusa, whose looks literally petrified the beholder. Eventually, the dynasty of Perseus was overthrown by Pelops, a son of Tantalus. The Mycenaean Royal House of Atreus was probably descended from Pelops, although myth and history are so intertwined, and the genealogical line so complex, that no-one really knows. Whatever the bloodlines, by Agamemnon's time the House of Atreus was the most powerful of the Achaeans (Homer's name for the Greeks). It eventually came to a sticky end, fulfilling the curse which had been cast because of Pelops' misdeeds.

The historical facts are that Mycenae was first settled by Neolithic people in the 6th millennium BC. Between 2100 and 1900 BC, during the Old Bronze Age, Greece was invaded by people of Indo-European stock who had crossed Anatolia via Troy to Greece. The invaders brought an advanced culture to the then-primitive Mycenae and other mainland settlements. This new civilisation is now referred to as the Mycenaean, named after Mycenae, its most powerful kingdom. The other kingdoms included Pylos, Tiryns, Corinth and Argos in the

Peloponnese. Evidence of Mycenaean civilisation has also been found at Thiva (Thebes) and Athens.

The city of Mycenae consisted of a fortified citadel and surrounding settlement. Due to the sheer size of the walls of the citadel (13m high and 7m thick), the ancient Greeks believed they must have been built by a Cyclops, one of the giants described by Homer in the *Odyssey*.

Archaeological evidence indicates that the palaces of the Mycenaean kingdoms were destroyed around 1200 BC. It was long thought that the destruction was the work of the Dorians, but later evidence indicates that the decline of the Mycenaean civilisation was symptomatic of the general turmoil around the Mediterranean at the time. The great Hittite Empire in Anatolia, which had reached its height between 1450 and 1200 BC, was now in decline, as was the Egyptian civilisation.

The Mycenaeans, Hittites and Egyptians had all prospered through their trade with each other, but this had ceased by the end of the 1200s. Many of the great palaces of the Mycenaean kingdoms were destroyed 150 years before the Dorians arrived.

Whether the destruction was the work of outsiders or due to internal division between the various Mycenaean kingdoms remains unresolved.

Exploring the Site The **Citadel of Mycenae** is entered through the **Lion Gate**, so called because of the relief above the lintel of two lionesses supporting a pillar. This motif is believed to have been the insignia of the Royal House of Atreus.

Inside the citadel, you will find **Grave Circle A** on the right as you enter. This was the royal cemetery and contained six grave shafts. Five were excavated by Schliemann in 1874-76 and the magnificent gold treasures he uncovered are in the National Archaeological Museum in Athens. In the last grave shaft, Schliemann found a well preserved gold death mask with flesh still clinging to it. Fervently, he sent a telegram to the Greek king stating, 'I have gazed upon the face of Agamemnon'. The mask turned out to be that of an unknown king who had died some 300 years before Agamemnon.

To the south of Grave Circle A are the remains of a group of houses. In one was found the famous **Warrior Vase** which Schliemann regarded as one of his greatest discoveries.

The main path leads up to **Agamemnon's palace**, centred around the **Great Court**. The rooms to the north were the private royal apartments. One of these rooms is believed to be the chamber in which Agamemnon was murdered. Access to the **throne room**, west of the Great Court, would originally have been via a large staircase. On the south-eastern side of the palace is the **megaron** (reception hall).

On the northern boundary of the citadel is the **Postern Gate** through which, it is said, Orestes escaped after murdering his mother. In the far north-eastern corner of the citadel is the **secret cistern**. It can be explored by torchlight, but take care – the steps are slippery.

Until the late 15th century BC, the Mycenaeans put their royal dead into shaft graves. They then devised a new form of burial – the tholos tomb, shaped like a beehive. The approach road to Mycenae passes to the right of the best preserved of these, the **Treasury of Atreus** or tomb of Agamemnon. A 40m-long passage leads to this immense beehive-shaped chamber. It is built with stone blocks that get steadily smaller as the structure tapers to its central point. Farther along the road on the right is **Grave Circle B**, and nearby are the **tholos tombs of Aegisthus and Clytaemnestra**.

Places to Stay & Eat

Mycenae's two camping grounds are ***Camping Mycenae*** *(☎ 76 247)* near the bus stop in Mycenae village, and ***Camping Atreus*** *(☎ 62 221)*, near the Corinth-Argos road.

You'll find some good deals at the hotels along the main road. The C class ***Belle Helene Hotel*** *(☎ 76 255, fax 76 179)* has singles/doubles for 5000/7500 dr. The

The Trojan War & the Fall of the House of Atreus

In his epic poems, the *Iliad* and the *Odyssey*, Homer related the events of a crucial period in Mycenaean history – the Trojan War and its aftermath. Homer called Troy 'Ilium' (hence the epic's title, the *Iliad*). The 10 year war, between the Achaeans and the Trojans, took place around 1250 BC during the reign of Mycenae's King Agamemnon and Troy's King Priam.

The Trojan horse: the Greek trick that brought Troy's downfall

Agamemnon's brother, Menelaus, king of Sparta, had suffered great humiliation when his beautiful wife, Helen, was abducted by Paris, the son of King Priam. Menelaus sought the advice of Nestor, king of Pylos, the oldest and wisest of the Mycenaean kings, who told him that nothing less than a combined force of all the armies of Greece would be sufficient to get Helen back. So, accompanied by Agamemnon, Menelaus visited all the princes and heroes in the land to ask for their assistance. Amongst them were Odysseus, king of Ithaca (Ithaki), Patroclus, Achilles and Nestor. Agamemnon, as the most powerful and richest king in Greece, headed the Greek expedition to Troy. Fighting on the Trojan side were Paris, his brother Hector and Priam. The war dragged on for 10 years, during which time Hector killed Patroclus, Achilles killed Hector and Paris killed Achilles, and still there was no end in sight. Finally, Odysseus came up with the idea of deceiving the Trojans by introducing into Troy, in the guise of a religious offering, a wooden horse filled with Greek soldiers who, once inside the city walls, would emerge and seize the city.

While all this was going on in Troy, back in Mycenae, Agamemnon's wife, Clytaemnestra, had taken a lover, Aegisthus. On his return to Mycenae, Agamemnon was greeted lovingly by his wife (despite his being accompanied by his Trojan concubine, Cassandra). However, later while he was taking a bath, Clytaemnestra, assisted by her lover, stabbed him to death. Orestes, her son, then avenged the murder of his father by murdering her, and so the Mycenaean Royal House of Atreus came to its dramatic end.

renowned archaeologist Heinrich Schliemann stayed here while excavating at ancient Mycenae. Other famous guests have included Claude Debussy and Virginia Woolf.

The B class ***La Petit Planete*** *(☎ 76 240, fax 76 610)*, between the village and ancient site, has smart rooms for 14,000/19,000 dr. It also has a swimming pool, a restaurant and bar.

Mycenae's restaurants cater for day-trippers. The best value is to be found at ***Hotel Klitemnistra Restaurant*** *(☎ 76 451)*, which serves good three-course meals for between 2000 and 2500 dr.

Getting There & Away

There are buses to Mycenae from Nafplio (one hour, 600 dr, three daily) and Argos (30 minutes, 360 dr, six daily). Most buses stop at the village and the ancient site.

Other bus services, such as Athens-Nafplio, advertise a stop at Mycenae but they actually go no closer than the village of Fihtio on the main road, leaving you with a 3km uphill walk to the site.

NAFPLIO Ναύπλιο

☎ 0752 • postcode 211 00 • pop 11,900

Nafplio, 12km south-east of Argos on the Argolic gulf, is one of Greece's prettiest towns. The narrow streets of the old town are filled with elegant Venetian houses and gracious neoclassical mansions. The setting is dominated by the towering Palamidi Fortress.

Nafplio was the first capital of Greece after independence and has been a major port since the Bronze Age. So strategic was its position that it had three fortresses – the massive principal fortress of Palamidi, the smaller Akronafplia and the diminutive Bourtzi on an islet west of the old town.

Removed from the spotlight as capital of Greece after Kapodistrias' assassination by the Maniot chieftains Konstantinos and Georgos Mavromihalis, Nafplio has settled into a more comfortable role as a peaceful seaside resort. With good bus connections, the city is an absorbing base from which to explore many ancient sites.

Orientation

The old town occupies a narrow promontory with the Akronafplia fortress on the southern side and the promenades of Bouboulinas and Akti Miaouli on the north side. The principal streets of the old town are Amalias, Vasileos Konstantinou, Staïkopoulou and Kapodistriou. The old town's central square is Plateia Syntagmatos (Syntagma Square), at the western end of Vasileos Konstantinou.

The bus station is on Syngrou, the street separating the old town from the new. The main street of the new town, known to locals as Neapolis, is 25 Martiou – an easterly continuation of Staïkopoulou.

Information

Nafplio's municipal tourist office (☎ 24 444) is on 25 Martiou. It's open 9 am to 1 pm and 4 to 8 pm daily. The tourist police (☎ 28 131) can be found at the western end of 25 Martiou, sharing an office with the regular police (☎ 22 100). The post office is on Syngrou, and the OTE is on 25 Martiou opposite the tourist office. All the major banks have branches in town, including the National Bank of Greece on Plateia Syntagmatos and the Ionian Bank at the western end of Amalias.

There is a laundrette at 22 Papanikolaou. It's open 9.30 am to 1.30 pm and 5.30 to 8.30 pm Monday to Saturday. It charges 2800 dr to wash and dry a 6kg load.

For Internet access head to the Magic Centre Internet Cafe, Bouboulinas 43, or Angelo's, Ethnikis Antistasis 5. Both are open 8 am until late.

Palamidi Fortress

This vast citadel stands on a 216m-high outcrop of rock. Within its walls stand three separate Venetian fortresses, built between 1711 and 1714, but seized by the Turks only a year after completion. Above each of the gates of the citadel is the Venetian emblem of the Lion of St Mark. During the War of Independence, the Greeks, under the leadership of the venerable *klepht* (mountain fighter) chief, Theodoros Kolokotronis, besieged the citadel for 15 months before the Turks surrendered.

In the new town, north of the OTE, stands a splendid equestrian statue of Kolokotronis, who was known as the Grand Old Man of the Morea.

The fortress affords marvellous views. The energetic can tackle the seemingly endless 999 steps that begin south-east of the bus station. Climb early and take water. There's also a road to the fortress. A taxi costs about 1000 dr one way. The fortress (☎ 28 036) is open 8 am to 6.45 pm daily (2.30 pm in winter). Admission is 800 dr.

Akronafplia Fortress

The Akronafplia fortress, which rises above the old part of town, is the oldest of Nafplio's three castles. The lower sections of the walls date back to the Bronze Age. Up until the arrival of the Venetians, the town was restricted to within its walls. The Turks called it İç Kale (meaning 'inner castle'). It was used as a political prison from 1936-56.

It now houses a hotel complex built by the government-run Xenia group.

There's a lift up to the fortress from Plateia Poliko Nosokomiou at the western edge of town – look for the flags at the entrance of the tunnel leading to the lift. The old gateway to the fortress, crowned with a fine Venetian lion emblem, is at the top of Potamianou, the stepped street that heads uphill off Plateia Agios Spridonos.

Bourtzi

This small island fortress lies about 600m west of the port. Most of the existing structure was built by the Venetians. Boats to the island leave from the north-eastern end of Akti Miaouli, provided there are at least four passengers. The trip costs 500 dr.

Museums

Nafplio's **Popular Art Museum** (☎ 28 379) won the European Museum of the Year award in 1981 for its displays of traditional textile-producing techniques (with in-depth explanations in English) and folk costumes. The museum is in the old town at Ypsilandou 1.

It was closed for repairs at the time of writing and was scheduled to reopen in September 1999, when it should return to its previous opening hours of 9 am to 2.30 pm Tuesday to Sunday. The museum shop has been temporarily relocated to the corner of Vasilissis Olgas and Riga Fereou, opposite Hotel Tiryns.

The **archaeological museum** (☎ 27 502) on Plateia Syntagmatos is in an 18th century Venetian building. The collection includes pottery from Neolithic to classical times, and finds from Mycenae and Tiryns. The prize piece is a suit of bronze Mycenaean armour from Tiryns that is virtually intact. The museum is open 8.30 am to 3 pm Tuesday to Sunday. Admission is 500 dr.

The **military museum** on Amalias traces Greece's military history from the War of Independence onwards through a collection of photographs, paintings, uniforms and assorted weaponry. It's open 9 am to 2 pm Tuesday to Sunday. Admission is free.

Beaches

Aravanitia Beach is a small pebble beach just 10 minutes walk south of town, tucked beneath the Palamidi Fortress.

If you're feeling energetic, you can follow a path east around the coast to sandy **Karathona Beach**, at the far side of the Palamidi Fortress. The walk takes about an hour.

It's also possible to walk around the base of the Akronafplia Fortress.

Organised Tours

Staikos Tours (☎ 27 950, fax 28 000), Bouboulinas 50, offers a range of tours around the Peloponnese, including Epidaurus and Mycenae (11,500 dr).

Special Events

Nafplio hosts a classical music festival in late May and early June featuring both Greek and international performers. Venues include the Palamidi Fortress and the Bourtzi.

The town is also a good base for visits to Epidaurus for performances of ancient Greek dramas at the famous theatre during the Epidaurus festival between late June and August. The local bus syndicate operates special buses to the festival, leaving Nafplio at 7.30 pm. Theatre tickets are no longer sold in Nafplio; buy them at the theatre.

Places to Stay – Budget

The closest camping grounds are at the beach resorts, including Tolo, east of Nafplio (see Beaches in the Around Nafplio section).

Nafplio's youth hostel, still mentioned in some guides, closed down years ago due to lack of funding – but all is not lost. George Economou, who opened the original hostel some 25 years ago, offers special deals for backpackers at the D class ***Hotel Economou*** *(☎ 23 955)*, opposite the ex-hostel on Argonafton – about 20 minutes walk from the bus station. He offers beds in a shared room for 2000 dr, or 4000/7000 dr for singles/doubles. To get there, head east from the bus station along Sidiras Merarhias for about 600m, and turn left at Leoforos Argous – the main road north to

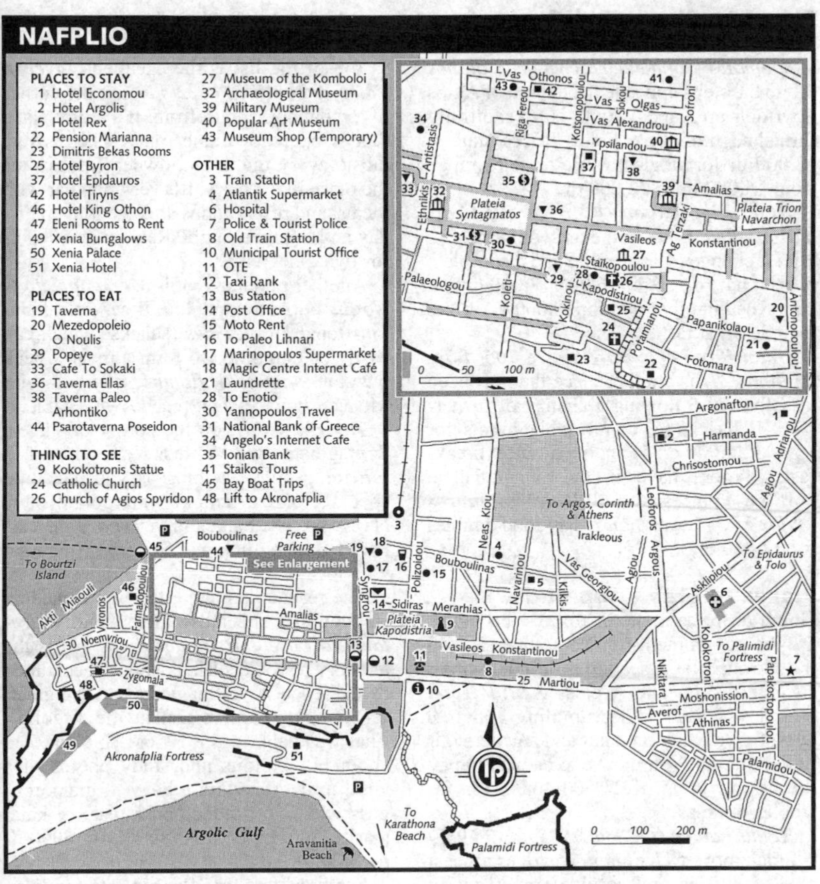

Argos. Keep going for another 400m; Argonafton is the second street on the right after Hotel Argolis.

Most people head for the old town, which is the most interesting place to be. There are no cheap hotels, but there are plenty of domatia dotted around the maze of narrow, stepped streets between Staïkopoulou and the Akronafplia.

Dimitris Bekas *(☎ 24 594, Efthimiopoulou 26)* has a great location just above the Catholic church and charges 4200/6000 dr. ***Eleni Rooms to Rent*** *(☎ 27 036, Zygomala 17)* has rooms with private facilities for 5000/8000 dr.

For a room with a view, head for ***Pension Marianna*** *(☎ 24 256, fax 21 783, Potamianou 9)*, perched high above the town. It's a family business run by brothers Panos, Petros and Takis. They offer large rooms for 10,000/12,000 dr. Breakfast costs an extra 1000 dr – in season you can look forward to free-range eggs and fresh orange or lemon juice from the family farm.

Places to Stay – Mid-Range

The stylish ***Hotel Byron*** *(☎ 22 351, fax 26 338, email byronhotel@otenet.gr, Platanos 2)*, up the steps opposite the church of Agios Spyridon on Kapodistriou, is a beautifully furnished traditional hotel. Prices start at 13,000 dr for singles, while doubles range from 15,000 dr to 22,000 dr.

Hotel King Othon *(☎/fax 27 595, Farmakopoulou 4)* has come up looking a treat after a change of ownership and a complete refit. It has rooms for 16,000/17,000 dr and a four-bed family room for 20,000 dr. Prices include breakfast.

Hotel Rex *(☎ 26 907, fax 28 106, Bouboulinas 21)* is another place that has been transformed following a change of ownership. It has large, comfortable rooms for 14,500/21,500 dr, including a buffet breakfast. All rooms have air-con, TV and fridge.

If these places are full, ***Hotel Epidauros*** *(☎/fax 27 541, Kokinou 2)* has good doubles for 12,000 dr.

Places to Stay – Top End

Going on price alone, Nafplio's top hotels are the government-run Xenia that sit atop the Akronafplia. Location is definitely their strongest suit. The A class ***Xenia Hotel*** *(☎ 28 991/992)* is a crumbling concrete eyesore with flaking paint and a general air of dereliction. You'd have to be mad to pay the asking price of 21,500/36,000 dr for singles/doubles.

Xenia Palace *(☎ 28 981/985, fax 28 987)* is much more welcoming, and does at least have facilities and service somewhat in tune with the asking prices of 33,000/51,000 dr – or 30,000/46,000 dr in the adjoining bungalows.

At the time of writing, the whole set-up was due to be transferred to private ownership and a long-awaited rise in standards.

Places to Eat

The streets of the old town are filled with dozens of restaurants. Staïkopoulou, in particular, is one long chain of restaurants; it would take weeks to eat at all of them. Most of these places close down in winter, and the choice shrinks to a few long-standing favourites.

Top of the list is the excellent ***Taverna Paleo Arhontiko*** *(☎ 22 449)* on the corner of Ypsilandou and Sofroni. It's a tiny place that is open for dinner only. There's live music every night, and owner Tassos runs the place like a party. It's very popular with locals, and reservations are essential on Friday and Saturday night. Reckon on 6000 dr for two, plus wine.

Another popular spot is ***Mezedopoleio O Noulis*** on Antonopoulou. It serves a fabulous range of *mezedes* (snacks) which can easily be combined to form a meal. Check out the *saganaki flambé*, ignited with Metaxa (brandy) as it reaches your table.

Taverna Ellas, on the corner of Plateia Syntagmatos and Vasileos Konstantinou, is fun for people-watching as you tuck into specials like artichoke and potato stew (1100 dr). The nameless ***taverna*** at the corner of Bouboulinas and Syngrou is popular with locals.

The restaurants along the promenade on Bouboulinas specialise in seafood. ***Psarotaverna Poseidon*** *(Bouboulinas 77)* is the territory of Kostas Bikakis, once acclaimed by a French travel magazine as 'the greatest *kamaki* (womaniser) in the Argolid'. That was back in the 1950s. You can read about his exploits and study photos of a youthful Kostas with a bevy of glamorous girls while you munch on a plate of kalamari (1500 dr) or fresh fish from 6000 dr per kilo.

For breakfast, try ***Popeye*** *(Staïkopoulou 32)* or ***Cafe To Sokaki*** *(Ethnikis Antistasis 8)*.

Self-caterers will find a choice of supermarkets in the new town.

Entertainment

Nafplio seems to have almost as many nightclubs and bars as it has restaurants. Most of them are on Bouboulinas – just cruise along until you find a sound that you like at a volume you can handle.

You'll find live Greek music at ***To Paleo Lihnari*** *(Bouboulinas 39)* on Saturday night.

Shopping

The Museum of the Komboloi (worry bead), Staïkopoulou 25, is really more of a shop than a museum. It sells a wide range of worry beads, evil eye charms and amulets. The upstairs museum has a collection of ancient beads assembled by owner Aris Evangelinos. Admission is 500 dr.

To Enotio, Staïkopoulou 40, produces and sells Greek shadow puppets, traditional and modern. Prices start at 2000 dr.

Getting There & Away

Bus There are buses from Nafplio to Athens (2½ hours, 2550 dr, hourly), Argos (30 minutes, 250 dr, half-hourly), Tolo (30 minutes, 250 dr, hourly), Porto Heli (two hours, 1400 dr, three daily); and three daily to Mycenae (one hour, 600 dr), Epidaurus (40 minutes, 600 dr) and Galatas (two hours, 1450 dr). Other destinations include Tripolis (1¼ hours, 1050 dr) and Corinth (1¼ hours, 1150 dr).

Train Train services from Nafplio are of little more than academic interest. There are trains to Athens (three hours, 1400 dr) leaving at 6.10 am and 6.30 pm daily. The station is by the port on Bouboulinas. An old train has been converted into the ticket office and *kafeneio*.

Hydrofoil Hydrofoil services from Nafplio had been suspended at the time of writing. Check at Yannopoulos Travel (☎ 27 454) on Plateia Syntagmatos.

Getting Around

Moto Rent (☎ 21 407, fax 25 642), Polizoidou 8, has a wide range of motorcycles, starting with 50cc models for 3500 dr per day. It also hires cars, as does Staikos Tours (☎ 27 950, fax 28 000), Bouboulinas 50.

AROUND NAFPLIO

Beaches

There's a string of good sandy beaches along the coast to the east of Nafplio. They start with **Asini**, 9km from Nafplio, followed in quick succession by **Tolo**, **Drepano**, **Plaka**, **Kadia** and **Iria**. Tolo, 11km from Nafplio, is the most developed.

Most hotels along this coast are block-booked by package holiday companies, but there are plenty of camping grounds. There's ***Kastraki Camping*** *(☎ 59 386/387)* near Asini Beach; ***Lido II*** *(☎ 59 369)*, ***Sunset Camping*** *(☎ 59 566)* and ***Xeni*** *(☎ 59 338)* at Tolo; ***Plaka Beach*** *(☎ 92 194/195)* at Plaka; and ***Argolic Strand*** *(☎ 92 376)* and ***Triton*** *(☎ 92 228)* at Drepano. The telephone code for all these sites is ☎ 0752.

There are hourly buses from Nafplio to Tolo (30 minutes, 240 dr) via Asini.

Ancient Asini Ασίνη

The ruins of ancient Asini, on a rocky headland 1km inland from Asini Beach, offer a diversion from sun-seeking. There are the remains of an acropolis, Mycenaean tombs, Roman baths and Venetian fortifications.

Tiryns Τίρυνθα

The ruins of Homer's 'wall-girt Tiryns' are 4km north-west of Nafplio. The walls of Tiryns are the apogee of Mycenaean architectural achievement (or paranoia), being even more substantial than those at Mycenae. In parts, they are 20m thick. The largest stones are estimated to weigh 14 tons. Within the walls there are vaulted galleries, secret stairways, and storage chambers. Frescoes from the palace are in Athens' National Archaeological Museum. Tiryns' setting is less awe-inspiring than Mycenae's and much less visited. The site (☎ 0752-22 657) is open 8 am to 8 pm daily (to 2.30 pm in winter). Admission is 500 dr. The ruins stand to the right of the Nafplio-Argos road. Any Nafplio-Argos bus can drop you outside the site.

EPIDAURUS Επίδαυρος

Epidaurus (eh-**pee**-dahv-ross), 30km east of Nafplio, is one of the most renowned of Greece's ancient sites, as reflected by its listing as a World Heritage Site. Epidaurus was a sanctuary of Asclepius, the god of medicine. The difference in the atmosphere here, compared with that of the war-orientated

Mycenaean cities, is immediately obvious. Henry Miller wrote in *The Colossus of Maroussi* that Mycenae 'folds in on itself', but Epidaurus is 'open, exposed … devoted to the spirit'. Epidaurus seems to emanate joy, optimism and celebration.

History & Mythology

Legend has it that Asclepius was the son of Apollo and Coronis. While giving birth to Asclepius, Coronis was struck by a thunder bolt and killed. Apollo took his son to Mt Pelion where the physician Chiron instructed the boy in the healing arts.

Apollo was worshipped at Epidaurus in Mycenaean and Archaic times but, by the 4th century BC, he had been superseded by his son. Epidaurus became acknowledged as the birthplace of Asclepius. Although there were sanctuaries to Asclepius throughout Greece, the two most important were at Epidaurus and on the island of Kos. The fame of the sanctuary spread, and when a plague was raging in Rome, Livy and Ovid came to Epidaurus to seek help.

It is believed that licks from snakes were one of the curative practices at the sanctuary. Asclepius is normally shown with a serpent, which – by renewing its skin – symbolises rejuvenation. Other treatments provided at the sanctuary involved diet instruction, herbal medicines and occasionally even surgery. The sanctuary also served as an entertainment venue. Every four years the Festival of Asclepieia took place at Epidaurus. Dramas were staged and athletic competitions were held.

Theatre

Today, the 3rd century theatre, not the sanctuary, pulls the crowds to Epidaurus. It is one of the best preserved classical Greek buildings, renowned for its amazing acoustics. A coin dropped in the centre can be heard from the highest seat. Built of limestone, the theatre seats up to 14,000 people. Its entrance is flanked by restored Corinthian pilasters. The Festival of Epidaurus takes place each year in July and August (see the Entertainment section).

Museum

The museum, between the sanctuary and the theatre, houses statues, stone inscriptions recording miraculous cures, surgical instruments, votive offerings and partial reconstructions of the sanctuary's once-elaborate tholos. After the theatre, the tholos is considered to have been the site's most impressive building and fragments of beautiful, intricately carved reliefs from its ceiling are also displayed.

Sanctuary

The vast ruins of the sanctuary are less crowded than the theatre. In the south is the huge **katagogeion**, a hostelry for pilgrims and patients. To the west is the large **banquet hall** in which the Romans built an **odeum**. It was here that the Festival of Asclepieia took place. Opposite is the **stadium**, venue for the festival's athletic competitions.

To the north are the foundations of the **Temple of Asclepius** and next to them is the **abaton**. The therapies practised here seemed to have depended on the influence of the mind upon the body. It is believed that patients were given a pep talk by a priest on the powers of Asclepius then put to sleep in the abaton to dream of a visitation by the god. The dream would hold the key to the healing process.

East is the **Sanctuary of Egyptian Gods**, which indicates that the cult of Asclepius was an adaptation of the cult of Imhotep, worshipped in Egypt for his healing powers. To the west of the Temple of Asclepius are the remains of the **tholos**, built in 360-320 BC; the function of which is unknown.

Set among the green foothills of Mt Arahneo, the air redolent with herbs and pine trees, it's easy to see how the sanctuary would have had a beneficial effect upon the ailing. Considering the state of Greece's current health system, perhaps the centre should be resurrected.

Places to Stay & Eat

There was no accommodation at the site at the time of research following the closure of Xenia Hotel.

PELOPONNESE

The closest hotels are at the village of Ligourio, 4km north of Epidaurus. ***Hotel Koronis*** *(☎ 0753-22 450, fax 22 267)*, in the middle of town on the Nafplio-Epidaurus road, has clean singles/doubles with bathroom for 8000/9000 dr.

There are several ***restaurants*** on the main road through Ligourio.

Entertainment

The theatre at Epidaurus is used to stage performances of ancient Greek dramas during the Festival of Epidaurus, from 26 July to 30 August each year. Performances are held on Friday and Saturday night, starting at 9 pm. Tickets can be bought in Epidaurus at the site office (☎ 0753-22 006) at 9.30 am to 1 pm and 6 to 9 pm on Thursday, Friday and Saturday. They can also be bought from the Athens Festival box office (see the Entertainment section in the Athens chapter). Prices vary according to seating. Student discounts are available. There are special buses from Athens and Nafplio.

Getting There & Away

There are buses from Nafplio to Epidaurus (40 minutes, 600 dr, four daily) via Ligourio (also 600 dr), and two buses daily to Athens (2½ hours, 2100 dr).

ANCIENT TROIZEN Τροιζήν

Troizen (also known as Trizin), 49km south-east of Ligourio, was an Ionian colony, the birthplace of Theseus and a refuge for Athenian women and children during the Persian invasion beginning in 480 BC. It shared many traditions and cults with Athens. The site is a few minutes walk from the picturesque hillside village of **Trizin**.

The **Sanctuary of Hippolytos** is the first ruin you come across, followed by the remains of the city wall with an Hellenic tower. Small stones in the upper construction indicate Frankish rebuilding. A further 10 minutes climbing brings you to the **Devil's Bridge**, a natural extension across the deep Gefyron Gorge.

Buses from Nafplio to the seaside village of **Galatas** (two hours, 1450 dr) can drop you at the turn-off to Trizin, from where it's a steep climb to the site. The alternative is to continue to Galatas and take a bus (230 dr) or taxi back to Trizin. Galatas and Trizin can also be visited from the island of Poros (see the Saronic Gulf Islands chapter).

Arcadia Αρκαδία

The picturesque rural prefecture of Arcadia occupies much of the central Peloponnese. Its name evokes images of grassy meadows, forested mountains, gurgling streams and shady grottoes. It was a favourite haunt of Pan, who played his pipes, guarded herds and frolicked with nymphs in this sunny, bucolic idyll.

Almost encircled by high mountains, Arcadia was remote enough in ancient times to remain largely untouched by the battles and intrigues of the rest of Greece. It was the only region of the Peloponnese not conquered by the Dorians. It remains a backwater, dotted with crumbling medieval villages, remote monasteries and Frankish castles, visited only by determined tourists. It also has 100-odd kilometres of unspoilt coastline on the Argolic Gulf, running south from the pretty town of Myli to Leonidio.

TRIPOLIS Τρίπολη

☎ 071 • postcode 221 00 • pop 22,500

The violent recent history of Arcadia's capital, Tripolis (**tree**-po-lee), is in stark contrast with the surrounding rural idyll. In 1821, during the War of Independence, the town was captured by Kolokotronis and its 10,000 Turkish inhabitants massacred. The Turks retook the town three years later, and burnt it to the ground before withdrawing in 1828.

Tripolis itself is not a place to linger long, but it's a major transport hub for the Peloponnese. It also has some impressive neoclassical buildings and Byzantine churches.

Orientation

Tripolis can be a bit confusing at first. The streets radiate out from the central square, Plateia Vasileos Georgiou, like an erratic spider's web. The main streets are Washington, which runs south from Plateia Georgiou to Kalamata; Ethnikis Antistaseos, which runs north from the square and becomes the road to Kalavryta; and Vasileos Georgiou, which runs east from the square to Plateia Kolokotroni. El Venizelou runs east from Plateia Kolokotroni, leading to the road to Corinth.

The main Arkadias bus station is conveniently central on Plateia Kolokotroni. The city's other bus station is opposite the train station, about a 10 minute walk away, at the south-eastern end of Lagopati – the street that runs behind the Arkadias terminal.

Information

There's a tourist information office (☎ 231 844) in the town hall, about 250m north of Plateia Vasileos Georgiou at Ethnikis Antistaseos 43. It's open 7 am to 2 pm Monday to Friday. The tourist police (☎ 222 265) cohabit with the regular police at Plateia Petrinou, which is the square between Plateia Georgiou and the town hall. The police station is next to the ornate Malliaropoulio Theatre.

The post office is just off Plateia Vasileos Georgiou, behind Hotel Galaxy at the junction of Athanasiadou and Nikitara. The OTE is nearby on 28 Oktovriou. Internet access is available at the Pacman Net Cafe, Deligianni 3 – the cafe-packed pedestrian precinct near Hotel Anactoricon. It's open 10 am until late every day.

Tripolis has branches of all the major banks. The National Bank of Greece is on the corner of 28 Oktovriou and Ethnikis Antistaseos. The bookshop on the northern side of Plateia Vasileos Georgiou sells English-language newspapers.

Archaeological Museum

The city's archaeological museum occupies a neoclassical mansion on Evagistrias, and is clearly signposted off Vasileos Georgiou next to Hotel Alex. The museum houses finds from the surrounding ancient sites of Megalopoli, Gortys, Lykosoura and Mantinea. It is open 8.30 am to 3 pm Tuesday to Sunday. Admission is 500 dr.

Places to Stay & Eat

Hotel Alex *(☎ 223 465, Vasileos Georgiou 26)* has the cheapest rooms in town. It charges 7000/11,000 dr for singles/doubles with bathroom, but traffic noise is a problem. You'll be better off at the friendly ***Hotel Anactoricon*** *(☎ 222 545, fax 222 021, Ethnikis Antistaseos 48)*, beyond the town hall. It has comfortable rooms with TV and bathroom for 10,000/12,000 dr. Ask for a room away from the street. Both these places are quick to offer discounts.

Not so the ***Galaxy Hotel*** *(☎ 225 195)*, on the main square, which has rooms with bathroom for 9500/14,000 dr.

There are lots of cafes and restaurants on and around Plateia Vasileos Georgiou, including the budget ***Estiatorio Ioniko***. It's a good place to head for breakfast, where you'll find bacon and eggs for 800 dr.

For something more upmarket, try the popular ***Taverna Piterou*** *(Kalavrytou 11A)*. Kalavrytou is the northern extension of Ethnikis Antistaseos beyond the park with the old steam train.

Getting There & Away

Bus The Arkadias bus station on Plateia Kolokotroni is the city's main terminal. There are 12 buses daily to Athens (2¼ hours, 3000 dr), via Corinth (one hour, 1600 dr). There are also at least two buses daily to Olympia (2½ hours, 2350 dr) and Pyrgos (three hours, 2700 dr).

Regional services include buses to Megalopoli (40 minutes, 700 dr, eight daily) and Stemnitsa (one hour,1150 dr, three daily). There are also two daily to Dimitsana (1½ hours, 1400 dr), Andritsena (1½ hours, 1600 dr) via Karitena (1000 dr), and Leonidio (2½ hours, 1750 dr).

Buses to Tegea (20 minutes, 230 dr, hourly) leave from the stop outside Hotel Arkadia on Plateia Kolokotroni.

The bus station on Lagopati handles departures to Achaïa, Argolis, Lakonia and Messinia. They include buses to Argos (one hour, 1050 dr, nine daily), Sparta (one hour, 1000 dr, nine daily), Kalamata (two hours, 1550 dr, six daily), Nafplio (1¼ hours, 1150 dr, three daily) and Kalavryta (2½ hours, 1600 dr, one daily).

Train Tripolis is on the main Athens-Kalamata line. There are four trains daily to Athens (four hours, 1500 dr), via Argos (1½ hours, 950 dr) and Corinth (2½ hours, 1000 dr). There are also trains to Kalamata (three hours, 840 dr, four daily).

ANCIENT TEGEA Αρχαία Τεγέα

Ancient Tegea, 8km south-east of Tripolis, was the most important city in Arcadia in classical and Roman times. Tegea was constantly bickering with its arch rival, Mantinea, and fought a long war with Sparta, to whom it finally capitulated and became allied in the Peloponnesian Wars. It was laid waste in the 5th century AD but was rebuilt by the Byzantines, who called it Nikli. The ruins of the city lie scattered around the modern village of Tegea (also called Alea).

The bus from Tripolis stops outside Tegea's **museum** (☎ 071-556 540), which houses thrones, statues and reliefs from the site, including fragments of the pediment from the 4th century BC Doric **Temple of Athena Alea**. The temple's pediment was regarded as one of the greatest artworks of its time. The museum is open 8.30 am to 3 pm Tuesday to Sunday. Admission is 500 dr.

Standing on the site of an ancient theatre, the **Church of Episkopi** in Tegea, once a forum for matchmaking, has a festival on Assumption Day, 15 August.

MEGALOPOLI Μεγαλόπολη

☎ 0791 • postcode 222 00 • pop 4700

Despite its name, there's little left of Megalopoli (great city) that reflects its former grandeur. It was founded in 371 BC as the capital of a united Arcadia nestled in a leafy valley on the banks of the Elisson river. The modern town is dominated by a large power station, but it is surrounded by rolling orchard country with mountain backdrops. Megalopoli is an important transport hub on the main route from Tripolis to Kalamata and Pyrgos.

Places to Stay & Eat

There are six modest hotels to choose from, all located on the streets leading off the large central square, Plateia Polyvriou. ***Hotel Paris*** *(☎ 22 410, Agiou Nikolaou 9)*, close to the bus station, has tidy singles/doubles with bathroom for 6500/10,000 dr, while ***Hotel Leto*** *(☎ 22 302, P Kefala 9)* is a bit cheaper at 5000/7500 dr.

There are several restaurants around Plateia Polyvriou, but the best place is the very popular ***Psistaria O Meraklis***, just off the square on Papanastasiou – the road to Tripolis. It has a range of grilled food, starting with souvlaki sticks for 120 dr, as well as salads and vegetable dishes. It's run by an extended Greek-Canadian family.

Getting There & Away

There are bus services to Athens (three hours, 3550 dr, eight daily), via Tripolis (40 minutes, 700 dr); Kalamata (one hour, 1050 dr, eight daily); and Andritsena (1¼ hours, 950 dr, two daily).

AROUND MEGALOPOLI

Poetically described as the first city which saw the sun, **Ancient Lykosoura**, the holy city of the Arcadians, is regarded as Greece's oldest ruin. A small **museum** has copies of statues from the nearby **Sanctuary of Despina and Demeter**. The originals are housed in the National Archaeological Museum in Athens. The site is 10km west of Megalopoli, just past the village of **Lykeo** where the museum caretaker lives. The route passes through oak woods, and there are beautiful mountain views.

CENTRAL ARCADIA

The area to the west of Tripolis is a tangle of medieval villages, precipitous ravines and narrow winding roads, woven into valleys of dense vegetation beneath the slopes of the Menalon Mountains. This is the heart of the Arcadia prefecture, an area with some of the most breathtaking scenery in the Peloponnese. The region is high above sea level and nights are chilly, even in summer. Snow is common in winter.

You need your own transport to do the area justice, but the three most important villages – Karitena, Stemnitsa and Dimitsana – are within reach of Tripolis by public transport. Stemnitsa and Dimitsana are on the 37km stretch of road that cuts through the mountains from the Pyrgos-Tripolis road in the north to the Megalopoli-Andritsena road in the south.

Karitena Καρίταινα

• pop 320

High above the Megalopoli-Andritsena road is the splendid medieval village of Karitena (kar-**eet**-eh-nah), aptly called the 'Toledo of Greece'. A stepped path leads from the central square to the village's 13th century **Frankish castle** atop a massive rock.

Karitena's 13th century **Church of Agios Nikolaos** has well preserved frescoes. The church is locked but if you ask around someone will direct you to the caretaker. From the church, a path leads down to the **Frankish bridge** which spans the River Lousios (a tributary of the Alfios). The bridge features on the 5000 dr note. Karitena has some ***domatia***.

North of Karitena, the road runs to the east of the Lousios Gorge. After 10km, south of the small village of Elliniko, a dirt track to the left leads in 1½ hours of walking to the site of **ancient Gortys**, which can also be reached by hardy vehicle. It's on the west side of the gorge, approached via a bridge. Gortys was an important city from the 4th century BC. Most ruins date from Hellenistic times, but to the north are the remains of a **Sanctuary to Asclepius**.

Getting There & Away Most buses from Megalopoli and Tripolis to Andritsena call at Karitena. A few will leave you on the main road, from where it's an arduous uphill walk to the village. The staff at the bus station you leave from will be able to tell you where the bus will stop.

Stemnitsa Στεμνίτσα

☎ 0795 • postcode 220 24 • pop 550

Stemnitsa, 15km north of Karitena, is a spectacular village of stone houses and Byzantine churches. North of the village, signposts point the way to **Moni Agiou Ioannitou Prodromou**. The monastery is about 20 minutes walk beyond the carpark. A monk will show visitors the chapel's splendid 14th and 15th century frescoes. From here, paths lead to the deserted monasteries of **Paleou** and **Neou Philosophou**, and also south along the riverbank to the site of ancient Gortys. The monks at Prodromou can direct you.

Stemnitsa's only hotel, ***Hotel Triokolonion*** *(☎ 81 297)*, has singles/doubles with bathroom for 8000/11,000 dr. It also has a good restaurant.

Getting There & Away There are three buses daily between Stemnitsa and Tripolis (one hour, 1000 dr).

Dimitsana Διμιτσάνα

☎ 0795 • postcode 220 07 • pop 650

Built amphitheatrically on two hills at the beginning of the Lousios Gorge, Dimitsana (dih-mit-**sah**-nah), 11km north of Stemnitsa, is a lovely medieval village. Despite its remoteness, Dimitsana played a significant role in the country's struggle for self-determination. Its Greek school, founded in 1764, was an important spawning ground for the ideas leading to the uprisings against the Turks. Its students included Bishop Germanos of Patras and Patriarch Gregory V, who was hanged by the Turks in retaliation for the massacre in Tripolis. The village also had a number of gunpowder factories and a branch of the secret Filiki Eteria (friendly society) where Greeks met to discuss the revolution (see History in the Facts about the Country chapter for more details on the Filiki Eteria).

From the heady days before independence, Dimitsana has become a sleepy village where the most exciting event is the arrival of the daily bus from Tripolis. Apart from the beauty of the village and its surroundings, tourists will appreciate the **folk museum** and **library**, on Nikolaou Makri (open 8 am to 2 pm daily, free admission) and the **Moni Aimialon**, 3km south on the road to Stemnitsa (open 9 am to 2 pm daily).

Places to Stay You'll see signs for a couple of ***domatia*** in the middle of town (Plateia Agia Kyriaki), as well as a sign pointing the way to ***Xenonas Kazakou*** *(☎ 31 660)*. The place seemed to be perpetually closed during its time as an EOT-run traditional settlement. This may change following its transfer to private management.

Dimitsana's one hotel, the C class ***Hotel Dimitsana*** *(☎ 31 518)*, is south of the village on the road to Stemnitsa. It has doubles with bathroom for 14,000 dr, including breakfast.

Getting There & Away There are buses from Tripolis to Dimitsana (1½ hours, 1400 dr, two daily).

ANDRITSENA Ανδρίτσαινα

☎ 0626 • postcode 270 61 • pop 900

The village of Andritsena, 81km west of Tripolis, is perched on a hillside overlooking the valley of the River Alfios. Crumbling stone houses with rickety wooden balconies flank its narrow cobbled streets and a stream gushes through its central square.

The post office, OTE and bank are near the central square. The village's only concession to tourism is its small **folk museum**, which is usually open 11 am to 1 pm and 5 to 6 pm daily. Admission is free. Most people come to Andritsena to visit the World Heritage-listed Temple of Vasses, 14km away.

Temple of Vasses

The Temple of Vasses, 14km south of Andritsena, stands at an altitude of 1200m on a hill overlooked by Mt Paliavlakitsa. The road from Andritsena climbs steadily along a mountain ridge, through increasingly dramatic scenery, to Greece's most isolated temple.

Well preserved, it was built in 420 BC by the people of nearby Figalia, who dedicated it to Apollo Epicurus (the Helper) for delivering them from pestilence. Designed by Ictinus, the architect of the Parthenon, it combines Doric and Ionic columns and a single Corinthian column – the earliest example of this order.

At the time of research, the temple was enclosed by a giant tent and was undergoing a much-needed restoration program. The site is open 8 am to 5 pm Tuesday to Sunday. Admission is 500 dr.

There are no buses to Vasses. In summer, it's usually possible to find people in the square to share a taxi for about 5000 dr return.

From Vasses, a dirt road continues for 11km to the village of **Perivolia**, from where a 2km track leads to the village of **Ano Figalia**, which is built on the site of ancient Figalia (see the Elia section later in this chapter for more details). This Fagalia is not to be confused with the village of Nea Fagalia, 19km west of Perivolia on the road to Tholos.

Places to Stay & Eat

Andritsena's only hotel is the grim ***Theoxenia*** *(☎ 22 219)*. Singles/doubles are 9000/12,000 dr.

Andritsena's few eateries are on the central square. Meals are also served at Theoxenia Hotel.

Getting There & Away

There are two buses daily to Andritsena from Athens Bus Terminal A (four hours, 4250 dr). There are also services from Megalopoli (1¼ hours, 900 dr), Pyrgos (1½ hours, 1600 dr) and Tripolis (two hours, 1600 dr).

MYLI TO LEONIDIO

There are lots of opportunities to explore on the scenic coast road that runs south from the pretty town of Myli, 46km east of Tripolis, to Leonidio.

The opening 34km leg from Myli to **Astros** is a delight. Astros, notable for its dahlias and roses, is perched above Paralia Astrou, which has a kastro and camping by the beach. From Astros, a good road hugs the coast, curving above tiny pebble-beached villages. Along the way there are some shady camping grounds, domatia, studios and tavernas. The first settlement of any consequence is the isolated seaside village of **Paralia Tyrou**, also known as **Tyros-apounakia**, which has several hotels and tavernas.

LEONIDIO

☎ 0757 • postcode 223 00 • pop 3800

The small town of Leonidio, 20km south of Paralia Tyrou, has a dramatic setting at the mouth of the Badron Gorge. Its tiny Plateia 25 Martiou is an archetypal, unspoilt, whitewashed Greek village square, surrounded by shady trees. The OTE is visible from the square, and the police (☎ 22 222) are close at hand on Kiloso. Many of the older people around here still speak *chakonika*, the language of ancient Sparta, in preference to Greek.

There are excellent, unspoilt beaches at the nearby seaside villages of **Lakos**, **Plaka** and **Poulithra**. The fertile alluvial river flats between Leonidio and the coast are intensively farmed.

Places to Stay & Eat

There are apartments for rent in town, but most people head for the beach at Plaka. There are several ***domatia***, as well as the D class ***Hotel Dionysos*** *(☎ 23 455)* on the small square by the port. It has doubles for 13,000 dr.

You'll find cold beer and great taverna food at the nearby ***Taverna Michel & Margaret***. It also has fresh seafood.

In Poulithra, 7km south of Plaka, is ***Hotel Kentauros*** *(☎ 51 214)* and more ***domatia***.

Getting There & Away

Bus There are buses down the coast from Argos (2¼ hours, 1500 dr, three daily) and Tripolis (2½ hours, 1750 dr, two daily).

Hydrofoil Leonidio's port of Plaka is part of the Flying Dolphin circuit around the Saronic Gulf and the eastern Peloponnese. In summer, there is a daily service to Zea Marina at Piraeus (2¾ hours, 6800 dr), travelling via Spetses (45 minutes, 2400 dr), and Hydra (80 minutes, 3600 dr). There are also daily services south to Monemvasia (80 minutes, 3800 dr).

SOUTH OF LEONIDIO

The road south from Leonidio over the rugged Parnon Mountains to the town of Geraki in Lakonia, 48km away, is one of the most scenic in the Peloponnese. For the first 12km, the road snakes west up the Badron Gorge, climbing slowly away from the river until at times it is no more than a speck of silver far below. The road then leaves the Badron and climbs rapidly through a series of dramatic hairpin bends towards Kosmas.

Just before the top of the climb, there's a dirt road to the left leading to **Moni Profitas Ilonas**, an amazing little monastery perched precariously on the mountainside. Visitors are welcome providing they are suitably dressed. Almost as amazing as the monastery is the cardphone outside.

It's another 14km from the monastery to the peaceful, beautiful mountain village of **Kosmas**. There are no hotels, but there are several domatia. ***Maleatis Apollo*** *(☎ 0757-31 494)*, on the main square, has comfortable studio rooms for 9000 dr, and a cosy taverna downstairs. Even if you don't stay overnight, it's worth pausing for a cold drink beneath the huge plane trees in the square.

The final 15km is no more than a gentle coast down to Geraki. From here you can head 40km west to Sparta, or continue south through **Vlahiotis**, **Molai** and **Sikia** to Monemvasia.

Lakonia Λακωνία

The modern region of Lakonia occupies almost identical boundaries to the powerful kingdom ruled by King Menelaus in Mycenaean times. Menelaus ruled from his capital at Sparta, which was later to achieve much greater fame as the arch rival of Athens in classical times. The Spartans who fought Athens were the descendants of the Dorians, who had arrived in about 1100 BC after the decline of the Mycenaean empire.

Little remains of ancient Sparta, but the disappointment is more than compensated for by the glorious Byzantine churches and monasteries at Mystras, just to the west. Another place not to be missed is the evocative medieval town of Monemvasia, in the south-east.

English-speakers can thank the Lakonians for the word 'laconic' – brief of speech – which many Lakonians still are.

SPARTA Σπάρτη

☎ 0731 • postcode 231 00 • pop 14,100

Modern Sparta (in Greek, Sparti) is an easy-going town of wide, tree-lined streets that is very much in contrast with the ancient image of discipline and deprivation. The town lies at the heart of the Evrotas Valley, an important citrus and olive growing region. The Taÿgetos Mountains, snow-capped until early June, provide a stunning backdrop to the west.

Orientation

You won't get lost in Sparta. It was constructed in 1834 on a grid system, and has two main thoroughfares. Palaeologou runs north-south through the town, and Lykourgou runs east-west. They intersect in the middle of town. The central square, Plateia Kentriki, is one block west of the intersection. The bus station is at the eastern end of Lykourgou.

Information

The tourist information office (☎ 24 852) in Sparta is on the 1st floor of the town hall on the main square. It's open 8 am to 2.30 pm Monday to Friday. The tourist police (☎ 20 492) are at Hilonos 8, one block east of the museum.

The post office is signposted off Lykourgou on Archidamou, and the OTE is between Lykourgou and Kleomvrotou, one block east of Palaeologou. For Internet access, try the Cosmos Club Internet Cafe, Palaeolgou 34. It's open 8.30 am to 11 pm daily.

The National Bank of Greece is one of many banks on Palaeologou.

Exploring Ancient Sparta

If the city of the Lacedaemonians were destroyed, and only its temples and the foundations of its buildings left, remote posterity would greatly doubt whether their power were ever equal to their renown.

Thucydides

A wander around ancient Sparta's meagre ruins bears testimony to the accuracy of Thucydides' prophecy. Head north along Palaeologou to the statue of a belligerent King Leonidas, standing in front of a soccer stadium. West of the stadium, signs point the way to the southern gate of the **acropolis**.

A dirt path leads off to the left (west) through olive groves to the 2nd or 3rd century BC **ancient theatre**, the site's most discernible ruin. You'll find a reconstructed plan of the theatre on the wall at the Restaurant Elysse (see Places to Eat).

The main cobbled path leads north to the acropolis, passing the ruins of the **Byzantine Church of Christ the Saviour** on the way to the hilltop **Sanctuary of Athena Halkioitou**. Some of the most important finds in the town's archaeological museum were unearthed here.

The history of **Sanctuary of Artemis Orthia**, on the north-eastern side of town, is more interesting than the site itself. Like most of the deities in Greek mythology, the goddess Artemis had many aspects, one of which was Artemis Orthia. In earliest times, this aspect of the goddess was honoured through human sacrifice. The Spartans gave this activity away for the slightly less gruesome business of flogging young boys in honour of the goddess. The museum houses a collection of clay masks used during ritual dances at the sanctuary. The sanctuary is signposted at the junction of Odos Ton 118 and Orthias Artemidos.

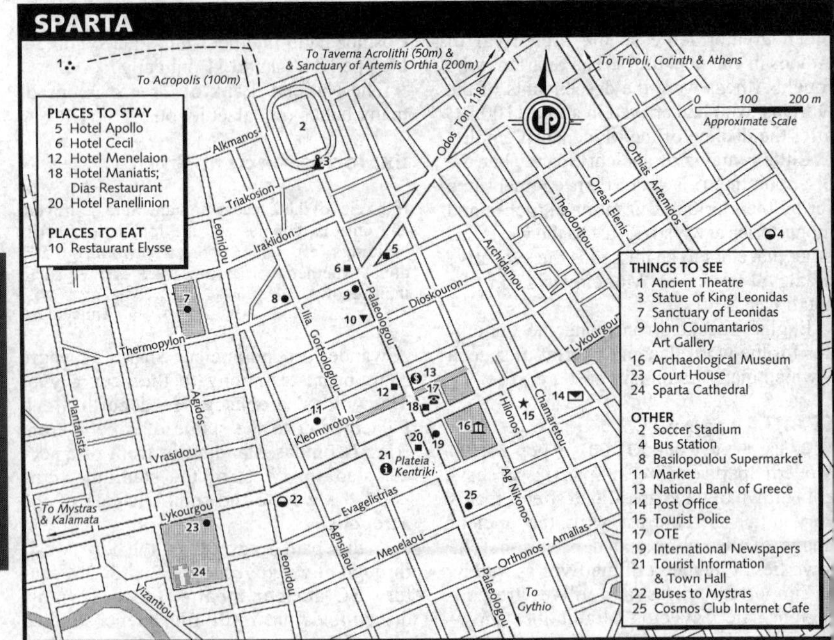

Museum & Gallery

Sparta's **archaeological museum** (☎ 28 575), just east of the town centre on Lykourgou, includes votive sickles which Spartan boys dedicated to Artemis Orthia, heads and torsos of various deities, a statue of Leonidas, masks and a stele. The museum is open 8.30 am to 3 pm Tuesday to Saturday and 8.30 am to 2.30 pm Sunday. Admission is 500 dr.

The **John Coumantarios Art Gallery**, Palaeologou 123, has a collection of 19th and 20th century French and Dutch paintings and also displays changing exhibitions of works by contemporary Greek painters. It's open 9 am to 3 pm Tuesday to Saturday and 10 am to 2 pm Sunday. Admission is free.

Places to Stay

Camping Paleologou Mystras *(☎ 22 724)*, 2km west of Sparta on the road to Mystras, is a friendly, well organised site with good facilities – including a swimming pool. It's open all year. Buses to Mystras can drop you off there.

There's a good choice of hotels back in town. The cheapest rooms are at the crumbling ***Hotel Panellinion*** *(☎ 28 031, Palaeologou 65)*, which has singles/doubles for 4000/6000 dr.

Most travellers head to the family-run ***Hotel Cecil*** *(☎ 24 980, fax 81 318, Palaeologou 125)*. It is top value at 8000/10,000 dr for clean, comfortable rooms with bathroom and TV.

Hotel Apollo *(☎ 22 491, Thermopylon 84)* is not as expensive as its marble-filled foyer might suggest. It charges 7000/10,000 dr for large rooms with bathroom and balcony.

There's very little to choose between the C class ***Hotel Maniatis*** *(☎ 22 665, fax 29 994, Palaeologou 72)* and the B class

Hotel Menelaion *(☎ 22 161, fax 26 332, Palaeologou 91)*. Hotel Maniatis charges 13,500/ 17,000 dr for spotless rooms, while the Menelaion charges 1000 dr more for the luxury of a swimming pool.

Places to Eat

There are lots of restaurants along Palaeologou. ***Restaurant Elysse***, Palaeologou 113, is a popular place run by a helpful Greek-Canadian family. The menu features a couple of Lakonian specialities: *chicken bardouniotiko* (1300 dr) – chicken cooked with onions and feta cheese, and *arni horiatiki* (1400 dr) – lamb baked with bay leaves and cinnamon.

Prices at the elegant ***Dias Restaurant***, next to Hotel Maniatis, are much more reasonable than the decor suggests. The air-conditioning is welcome on a hot day.

Taverna Acrolithi, at the north-eastern end of Odos Ton 118, has live Greek music from 10 pm Wednesday to Sunday. It also has some of the best prices in town.

Self-caterers will find a super-abundance of supermarkets in Sparta. ***Basilopoulou***, opposite the Sparta Inn on Thermopylon, is bigger and better stocked than most.

Getting There & Away

Sparta's well organised modern bus station is at the east end of Lykourgou. Departures are displayed in English on a large information board above the entrance outside. They include 10 buses daily to Athens (3¼ hours, 3700 dr) via Corinth (two hours, 2400 dr), five daily to Gythio (one hour, 800 dr), four to Neapoli (four hours, 2550 dr) and Tripolis (1¼ hours, 1000 dr), and three to Geraki (45 minutes, 750 dr) and Monemvasia (2½ hours, 1850 dr).

There is a service to Kalamata (2½ hours, 1100 dr, two daily), which involves changing buses at Artemisia (600 dr) on the Messinian side of the Langada Pass.

Departures to the Mani Peninsula include buses to Gerolimenas (three hours, 1850 dr, two daily) via Areopoli (two hours, 120 dr) and a 9 am service to the caves at Pyrgos Dirou.

A Spartan Existence

The bellicose Spartans sacrificed many things in life for military expertise. Male children were examined at birth by the city council and those deemed too weak to become good soldiers were left to die of exposure. Those fortunate enough to survive infancy were taken from their mothers at the age of seven to undergo rigorous military training.

Training seems to have consisted mainly of beatings and appalling deprivations. Would-be soldiers were forced to go barefoot, even in winter, and were starved so that they would have to steal food for survival. If discovered, they were punished not for the crime, but for allowing themselves to be caught.

Although girls were allowed to stay with their mothers, they also underwent tough physical training so they would give birth to healthy sons.

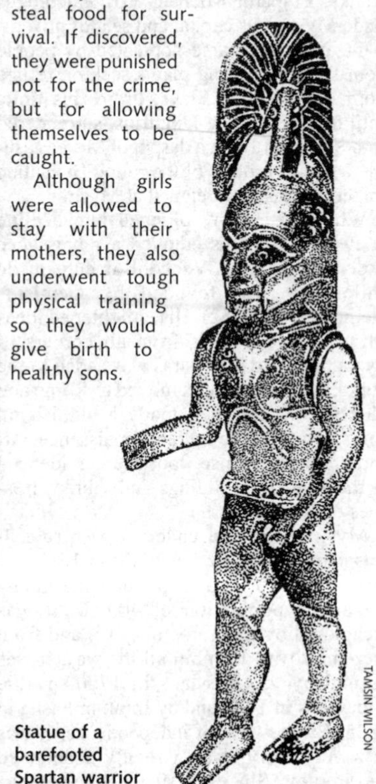

Statue of a barefooted Spartan warrior

PELOPONNESE

There are also 12 buses daily to Mystras (30 minutes, 230 dr). You can catch these on their way out to Mystras, at the bus stop on Leonidou.

MYSTRAS Μυστράς

The captivating ruins of the once-awesome town of Mystras (miss-**trahss**), crowned by an imposing fortress, spill from a spur of Mt Taÿgetos.

History

The fortress of Mystras was built by Guillaume de Villehardouin in 1249. When the Byzantines won back the Morea from the Franks, Emperor Michael VIII Paleologus made Mystras its capital and seat of government. It soon became populated by people from the surrounding plains seeking refuge from the invading Slavs. From this time, until the last despot, Dimitrios, surrendered to the Turks in 1460, a despot of Morea (usually a son or brother of the ruling Byzantine emperor) lived and reigned at Mystras.

While the empire plunged into decline elsewhere, Mystras enjoyed a renaissance under the despots. A school of humanistic philosophy was founded by Gemistos Plethon (1355-1452). His enlightened ideas attracted intellectuals from all corners of Byzantium. After Mystras was ceded to the Turks, Plethon's pupils moved to Rome and Florence where they made a significant contribution to the Italian Renaissance. Art and architecture also flourished, evidenced in the splendid buildings and vibrant frescoes of Mystras.

Mystras declined under Turkish rule. It was captured by the Venetians in 1687 and thrived again with a flourishing silk industry and a population of 40,000. It was recaptured by the Turks in 1715, and from then on it was downhill all the way. It was burned by the Russians in 1770, by the Albanians in 1780 and by Ibrahim Pasha in 1825. By the time of independence, it was in a very sorry state, virtually abandoned and in ruins. Since the 1950s, much restoration has taken place, and it is now listed as a World Heritage Site.

Exploring the Site

A day is needed to do Mystras justice. Wear sensible shoes, bring plenty of water and begin at the upper entrance to the site to walk down, rather than uphill. The site is divided into three sections – the **kastro** (the fortress on the summit), the **upper town** (hora) and the **lower town** (kato hora).

Kastro & Upper Town From opposite the upper entrance ticket office, a path (signposted 'kastro') leads up to the fortress. The fortress was built by the Franks and extended by the Turks. The path descending from the ticket office leads to **Agia Sofia**, which served as the palace church – some frescoes survive. Steps descend from here to a T-junction. A left turn leads to the **Nafplio Gate**, which was the main entrance to the town. Near the gate is the huge **Palace of the Despots**, a complex of several buildings constructed at different times. The vaulted audience room, the largest of the palace's buildings, was added in the 14th century. Its facade is painted, and its window frames are very ornate, but hundreds of years of neglect have robbed it of its former opulence.

From the palace, a winding, cobbled path leads down to the **Monemvasia Gate**, the entrance to the lower town.

Lower Town Through the Monemvasia gate, turn right for the well preserved 14th century **Convent of Pantanassa**. The nuns who live here are Mystras' only inhabitants. The building has beautiful stone-carved ornamentation on its facade and the capitals of its columns. It's an elaborate, perfectly proportioned building – never overstated. Exquisite, richly coloured 15th century frescoes are among the finest examples of late Byzantine art. There is a wonderful view of the pancake-flat and densely cultivated plain of Lakonia from the columned terrace on the northern facade.

The path continues down to the **Monastery of Perivleptos**, built into a rock. Inside, the 14th century frescoes equal those of Pantanassa and have been preserved virtually intact. Each scene is an entity,

MYSTRAS

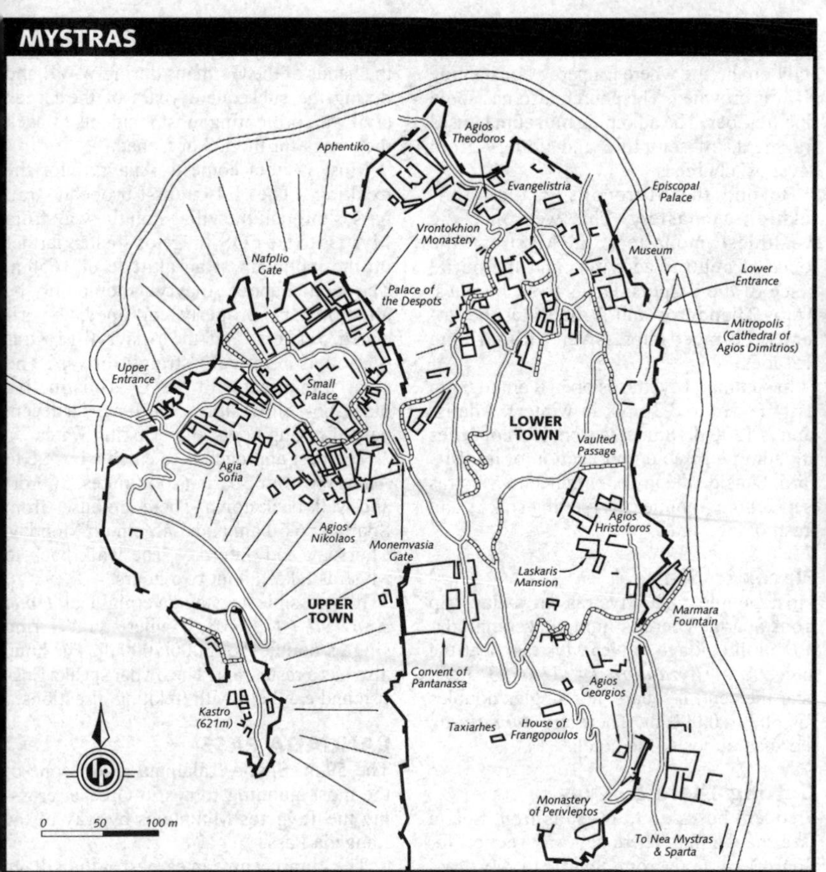

enclosed in a simple symmetrical shape. The overall effect is of numerous icons, placed next to one another, relating a visual narrative. The church has a very high dome. In the centre is the Pantokrator, surrounded by the apostles, and the Virgin flanked by two angels.

As you continue down towards the Mitropolis, you will pass **Agios Georgios**, one of Mystras' many private chapels. Farther down and above the path on the left is the **Laskaris Mansion**, a typical Byzantine house where the ground floor was used as stables and the upper floor was the residence.

The **Mitropolis** (Cathedral of Agios Dimitrios) consists of a complex of buildings enclosed by a high wall. The original church was built in the 13th century but was greatly altered in the 15th century. The church stands in an attractive courtyard surrounded by stoas and balconies. Its impressive ecclesiastical ornaments and furniture include a carved marble iconostasis, an intricately carved wooden throne and a marble slab in the floor in which is carved a two-headed eagle (symbol of Byzantium) – located exactly on the site where Emperor Constantine XI was crowned. The church also has some fine frescoes. The adjoining **museum** houses fragments of sculpture and pottery from Mystras' churches.

Beyond the Mitropolis is the **Vrontokhion Monastery**. This was once the wealthiest monastery of Mystras, the focus of cultural activities and the burial place of the despots. Of its two churches, **Agios Theodoros** and **Aphentiko**, the latter is the most impressive, with striking frescoes.

In summer, Mystras is open 8 am to 6 pm daily (8 am to 3.30 pm in winter). Admission is 1200 dr. Students from EU countries are admitted free on production of an ISIC card. Outside the lower entrance to Mystras is a *kantina* (mobile cafe) selling snacks and fresh orange juice.

Places to Stay

Most people visit Mystras on a day trip from Sparta. There is limited accommodation in the village of Nea Mystras, near the site. ***Hotel Byzantion*** *(☎ 0731-93 309)*, near the central square, has singles/doubles for 6000/10,000 dr. There are ***domatia*** on the road opposite the hotel.

Getting There & Away

Frequent buses go to Mystras from Sparta (see the Getting There & Away section for Sparta). A taxi from Sparta to Mystras' lower entrance costs 1000 dr, or 1500 dr to the upper entrance.

ANAVRYTI Ανάβρυτι

☎ 0731 • postcode 231 00 • pop 300

The pretty little mountain village of Anavryti, 12km south-west of Sparta, stands in magnificent isolation on a small plateau hidden away in the foothills of the Taÿgetos Range. At an altitude of more than 900m, the air is delightfully cool and fresh, and the high peaks of the surrounding mountains are so close that you can almost reach out and touch them.

It was once a substantial town of more than 3000 people, but it suffered badly at the hands of the Germans during WWII and during the subsequent years of the Greek civil war, prompting most residents to pack their bags for the US or Canada.

Most visitors come to Anavryti for the trekking. The E4 trans-European trail passes through the village on the way from Mystras to the EOS Taÿgetos shelter, farther up the mountain at an altitude of 1650m. The section above Anavryti should only be attempted by properly equipped, experienced trekkers. But the Anavryti-Mystras section is relatively straightforward and clearly marked with the E4's distinctive black-on-yellow signs. You'll need a decent pair of hiking boots and drinking water.

The best approach is to catch a bus up to Anavryti from Sparta (40 minutes, 360 dr) and walk back down. There are buses from Sparta at 6.50 am and 1.45 pm on Monday, Thursday and Saturday. The walk back to Mystras takes about two hours.

It's possible to stay overnight at ***Hotel Anavryti*** *(☎ 21 788)*, where you'll find singles/doubles for 5000/7000 dr. The hotel also has a restaurant. The owner speaks English and can help with trekking directions.

LANGADA PASS

The 59km Sparta-Kalamata road is one of the most stunning routes in Greece, crossing the Taÿgetos Mountains by way of the Langada Pass.

The climb begins in earnest at the village of **Trypi**, 9km west of Sparta, where the road enters the dramatic **Langada Gorge**. To the north of this gorge is the site where the ancient Spartans threw babies too weak or deformed to become good soldiers. ***Hotel Keadas*** *(☎ 0731-98 222)* in Trypi has singles/doubles for 4500/7500 dr.

From Trypi, the road follows the course of the Langada River for a while before climbing sharply through a series of hairpin bends to emerge in a sheltered valley. This is a good spot to stop for a stroll among the plane trees along the river bank. The road then climbs steeply once more to the high point of 1524m – crossing the boundary from Lakonia into Messinia on the way. You can stop overnight here at the new ***Hotel Taygetos*** (*☎ 0721-76 236)*. It has rooms for 6000/8000 dr, a restaurant and fantastic views.

The descent to Kalamata is equally dramatic, although the area will take a long time to recover from the devastating forest fires of 1998.

Travelling this route by bus involves changing buses at Artemisia, the closest Messinian settlement to the summit.

GERAKI Γεράκι

Geraki (yeh-**rah**-kih), 40km east of Sparta, is an unsung Mystras. While the latter is on almost everyone's list of 'must sees' in the Peloponnese, the medieval city of Geraki crumbles in obscurity on a remote hillside. The modern village of Geraki was built over the site of ancient Geronthrai, which dates back to Mycenaean times. Fragments of the walls remain to the north and east of the village.

The ruins of the medieval city lie on a hilltop 4km to the east of the modern village. It was one of the 12 Frankish fiefs of the Peloponnese. The fortress was built by Jean de Nivelet in 1245 but was ceded to the Byzantines in 1262. It has breathtaking views of the surrounding plain and mountains. Below the fortress are 15 small churches spread around the hillside.

The local authorities obviously have big plans for the site, judging by the brand new sealed road leading to the entrance. At the time of research, it was locked and deserted – though the site was due to open officially in late 1999. If it's still locked, it's possible to get the key from the caretaker, Mr Tsipouras (☎ 0731-71 393), in modern Geraki. It's best to phone the night before.

There are no hotels in Geraki, but locals in the village square can suggest ***domatia***.

Getting There & Away

If you are driving, the road to Geraki is signposted to the right a little way out of Sparta along the Tripolis road. There are buses from Sparta to the modern village (45 minutes, 750 dr, two daily).

GEFYRA & MONEMVASIA

Γέφυρα & Μονεμβασία

☎ 0732 • postcode 230 70 • pop 900

Monemvasia (mo-nem-vah-**see**-ah), 99km south-east of Sparta, is the Gibraltar of Greece – a massive rock rising dramatically from the sea just off the east coast. It is reached by a causeway from the mainland village of Gefyra (also called Nea Monemvasia). In summer, Gefyra and Monemvasia brim with tourists, but the extraordinary impact of the first encounter with the medieval town of Monemvasia – and the delights of exploring it – override the effects of mass tourism. The poet Yiannis Ritsos, who was born and lived for many years in Monemvasia, wrote of it: 'This scenery is as harsh as silence'.

From Gefyra, Monemvasia is a huge rock topped by a fortress with a few buildings scattered at sea level. But cross the causeway and follow the road that curves around the side of the rock and you will come to a narrow tunnel in a massive fortifying wall. The tunnel is L-shaped so you cannot see the other side until you emerge, blinking, into the magical town of Monemvasia, concealed until that moment. Unlike Mystras, Monemvasia's houses are inhabited, mostly by weekenders from Athens.

History

The island of Monemvasia was part of the mainland until it was separated by a devastating earthquake in 375 AD. Its name means 'single entry' (*moni* – single, *emvasia* – entry), as there is only one way to the medieval town.

During the 6th century, barbarian incursions forced the inhabitants of the surrounding area to retreat to this natural rock fortress. By the 13th century, it had become the principal commercial centre of Byzantine Morea – complementary to Mystras, the spiritual centre. It was famous throughout Europe for its highly praised Malvasia (also called Malmsey) wine.

Later came a succession of invasions from Franks, Venetians and Turks. During the War of Independence, its Turkish inhabitants were massacred on their surrender following a three month siege.

Orientation & Information

All the practicalities are located in Gefyra. The main street is 23 Iouliou, which runs south around the coast from the causeway, while Spartis runs north up the coast and becomes the road to Molai. Malvasia Travel, just up from the causeway on Spartis, acts as the bus stop. The post office and the National Bank of Greece are opposite. The OTE is at the top of 28 Oktovriou, which runs inland off 23 Iouliou.

Medieval Town

The narrow, cobbled main street is lined with souvenir shops and tavernas, flanked by winding stairways that weave between a complex network of stone houses with walled gardens and courtyards. The main street leads to the central square and the **Cathedral of Christ in Chains**, dating from the 13th century. Opposite is the **Church of Agios Pavlos**, built in 956. A new **museum** was under construction next door at the time of research. Farther along the main street is the **Church of Mirtidiotissa**, virtually in ruins, but still with a small altar and a defiantly flickering candle. Overlooking the sea is the recently restored, whitewashed 16th century **Church of Panagia Hrysaphitissa**.

The path to the **fortress** and the upper town is signposted up the steps to the left near the entrance to the old town. The upper town is now a vast and fascinating jumbled ruin, except for the **Church of Agia Sophia**, which perches on the edge of a sheer cliff.

Places to Stay – Budget

***Camping Paradise** (☎ 61 123)*, on the coast 3.5km south of Gefyra, is a pleasant, well shaded camping ground. It's right next to a beach and it has its own minimarket, bar and disco.

There is no budget accommodation in Monemvasia, so if your budget is tight you'll have to stay in Gefyra. The basic ***Hotel Akrogiali** (☎ 61 360)*, facing the National Bank of Greece on Spartis, has the cheapest rooms – singles/doubles with shower for 6000/9000 dr. ***Hotel Aktaion** (☎ 61 234)*, next to the causeway to Monemvasia, is a small step up with rooms for 9000/11,000 dr. There are plenty more hotels in Gefyra, but the best places are in Monemvasia.

Places to Stay – Mid-Range & Top End

If you've got money to spend, Monemvasia is the place to spend it. There's a range of impeccably restored traditional settlements to choose from. They include the excellent ***Malvasia Hotel** (☎ 61 113/323, fax 61 722)*, which has beautifully furnished rooms spread around several locations in the old town. Singles are 9000 dr, doubles cost from 11,000 dr to 15,000 dr and there are apartments from 25,000 dr. All prices include a generous breakfast.

***Byzantino** (☎ 61 254, fax 61 331)* has doubles from 14,000 dr, but you'll be up for at least 20,000 dr for a room with a view.

Bookings are recommended for both these places, especially at weekends.

The EOT-run traditional settlement ***Kellia** (☎ 61 520)*, is above the sea next to the Panagia Hrysaphitissa. Former monastery cells have been converted into delightful doubles/triples, but 19,100/24,600 dr is a bit steep – even with breakfast included.

Places to Eat

Taverna O Botsalo and ***T' Agnantio Taverna*** are a couple of places on 23 Iouliou in Gefyra that serve tasty, reasonably priced dishes.

As with the accommodation, the restaurants in Monemvasia are markedly more upmarket. ***To Kanoni***, on the right of the main street, has an imaginative and extensive menu, while ***Matoula*** has a great setting with a terrace overlooking the sea.

Getting There & Away

Bus Buses leave from Malvasia Travel (☎ 61 752), which also sells tickets. There are four buses daily to Athens (5½ hours, 5500 dr) via Sparta (two hours, 1850 dr), Tripolis and Corinth. The 4.10 am departure is an express service (4½ hours, 4200 dr).

Hydrofoil In summer, there is at least one Flying Dolphin service daily to Zea Marina at Piraeus (8500 dr). Direct services take 2½ hours; other services travel via Leonidio (80 minutes, 3800 dr) and Spetses (2½ hours, 4200 dr) and take four hours. There are also five services weekly to Hydra (three hours, 5200 dr). Buy tickets from Angelakos Travel (☎ 61 219), by the petrol station on the Monemvasia side of the causeway.

Getting Around

A free shuttle bus operates between the causeway and old Monemvasia from June to September between 7.30 am and 10 pm.

Cars and motorcycles can be hired from Christos Rent Car & Moto (☎ 61 581) on 23 Iouliou.

The medieval town of Monemvasia is inaccessible to cars and motorcycles, and cars are not allowed across the causeway between June and September. Parking is available outside the old town as other times.

NEAPOLI Νεάπολη

☎ 0734 • postcode 230 70 • pop 2500

Neapoli (neh-**ah**-po-lih, population 2500), 42km south of Monemvasia, lies close to the southern tip of the eastern prong of the Peloponnese. It's a fairly uninspiring town, in spite of its location on a huge horseshoe bay. The western flank of the bay is formed by the small island of Elafonisi (see later). Few travellers make it down this far, but the town is popular enough with local holidaymakers to have three seafront hotels and several domatia.

Getting There & Away

Bus There are buses to Neapoli from Sparta (three hours, 2550 dr, four daily).

Ferry There are ferries from Neapoli to Agia Pelagia on Kythira (one hour, 1500 dr) on Tuesday, Thursday and Sunday. Tickets are sold at Vatika Bay Travel (☎/fax 22 660), Agios Traidos 3, opposite the ferry quay. Ferries to Elafonisi (30 minutes, 550 dr) leave from the small quay opposite Hotel Aivali.

Hydrofoil In July and August there is a hydrofoil service to Zea Marina (five hours, 9400 dr, four weekly) via Monemvasia, and a Sunday service to Kythira (20 minutes, 3000 dr).

ELAFONISI Ελαφονήσι

Like Neapoli, Elafonisi sees few foreign tourists, but it's popular with Greeks who pop over from the mainland for fish lunches in summer, particularly on Sunday. Locals insist that the *barbounia* (red mullet) from the waters around here are the best you'll find. The island's main attractions, apart from the seafood, are its superb beaches – which the Greeks liken to those of the South Seas. They're not exaggerating.

As well as fish tavernas, there are two pensions and a few domatia. There is no official camping ground.

Getting There & Away

From July to September, there are frequent caïques to Elafonisi (10 minutes, 240 dr) from the village of Viglafia, about 14km west of Neapoli. They shuttle to and fro constantly from 9.30 am to 10 pm. At other times, there are infrequent boats from both Neapoli and Viglafia.

GYTHIO Γύθειο

☎ 0733 • postcode 232 00 • pop 4900

Once the port of ancient Sparta, Gythio (**yee**-thih-o) is the gateway to the Lakonian Mani. It's an attractive fishing town with a bustling waterfront of pastel coloured 19th century buildings, behind which crumbling old Turkish houses clamber up a steep, wooded hill.

Orientation

Gythio is not too hard to figure out. Most things of importance to travellers are along the seafront on Akti Vasileos Pavlou. The bus station is at the northern end, next to the small triangular park known as the Perivolaki – meaning 'tree-filled'.

Vasileos Georgiou runs inland from here past the main square, Plateia Panagiotou Venetzanaki, and becomes the road to Sparta.

The square at the southern end of Akti Vasileos Pavlou is Plateia Mavromihali, hub of the old quarter of Marathonisi. The ferry quay is opposite this square. Beyond it, the waterfront road becomes Kranais, which leads south to the road to Areopoli. A causeway leads out to Marathonisi Islet at the southern edge of town.

Information

The EOT tourist office (☎/fax 24 484) is about 500m north of the waterfront at Vasileos Georgiou 20. Apart from a couple of brochures, it's remarkably information-free, even by EOT's own lamentable standards. For the record, it's open 11 am to 3 pm Monday to Friday. The tourist police (☎ 22 271) and regular police (☎ 22 100) share offices on the waterfront between the bus station and Plateia Mavromihali.

The post office is on Ermou, two blocks north of the bus station, and the OTE office is between the two at the corner of Herakles and Kapsali.

The Sea Turtle Protection Society runs an information tent next to the ferry quay from mid-June until the end of September. It has films and displays about turtle nesting sites on the beaches of the Lakonian Gulf east of Gythio.

Marathonisi Islet

According to mythology, tranquil pine-shaded Marathonisi is ancient Cranae where Paris (prince of Troy) and Helen (wife of Menelaus) consummated the affair that sparked the Trojan Wars. The 18th century Tzanetakis Grigorakis tower at the centre of the island houses a small **museum** which relates Maniot history through the eyes of European travellers who visited the region between the 15th and 19th centuries. The top floor has a fascinating collection of plans of Maniot towers and castles. The museum is open 9 am to 7 pm daily. Admission is 500 dr.

Ancient Theatre

Gythio's small but well preserved ancient theatre is next to an army camp on the northern edge of town. It's signposted off Plateia Panagiotou Venetzanaki along Arheou Theatrou. You can scramble up the hill behind the theatre to the **ancient acropolis**, now heavily overgrown. Most of ancient Gythio lies beneath the nearby Lakonian Gulf.

Beaches

There's safe swimming off the 6km of sandy beaches which extend from the village of **Mavrovouni**, 2km south of Gythio.

Places to Stay

There are three camping grounds near Gythio, all on the coast south of Mavrovouni on the road to Areopoli and easily accessible by bus. They are ***Meltemi*** *(☎ 22 833)*, ***Gythion Beach*** *(☎ 23 441)* and ***Mani Beach*** *(☎ 23 450)*. The pick of them is Meltemi, a very well organised place right behind the beach with sites set among 3000 olive trees. It's open all year.

You'll find plenty of domatia signs around town, both on Akti Vasileos Pavlou and on the streets running inland from Plateia Mavromihali. They include ***Koutsouris Rooms to Rent*** *(☎ 22 321)*, a small old-style place with cosy singles/doubles for 5000/7000 dr and a family room for 8000 dr. To get there, walk up Tzannibi Gregoraki from Plateia Mavromihali, turn right at the church with the clock tower and the rooms are on the left. ***Kontogiannis Rooms to Rent*** *(☎ 22 518)*, up the steps next to the police station, is a new place with spotless rooms with bathroom for 7000/10,000 dr.

The French-run ***Saga Pension*** *(☎ 23 220, fax 24 370)*, on the seafront south of Plateia Mavromihali, is an excellent place with rooms with bathroom and TV for 7000/10,000 dr.

There are several mid-range hotels along Akti Vasileos Pavlou, but nothing worth recommending. ***Hotel Pantheon*** *(☎ 22 166, fax 22 284, Akti Vasileos Pavlou 33)* has rooms with air-con, colour TV and sea views for 15,000/16,000 dr.

Places to Eat

The waterfront is lined with countless fish tavernas with very similar menus. Try ***Psarotaverna I Kostis***, between Rozakis Travel and Hotel Kranai, which offers a big plate of calamari for 1200 dr, and fresh fish by the kilogram. Fish, together with traditional taverna food, also features prominently on the menu at the excellent ***Saga Pension Restaurant*** (see Places to Stay).

For something completely different, head inland to the tiny restaurant run by the Greek-Canadian Thomakos family at the ***General Store & Wine Bar*** *(☎ 24 113, Vasileos Georgiou 67)*. You'll find an unusually varied and imaginative menu featuring dishes like orange and pumpkin soup (600 dr), chicken breast with brie (1500 dr) and fillet of pork with black pepper and ouzo (2800 dr).

Self-caterers can stock up at the ***Kourtakis supermarket***, around the corner from the bus station on Heracles. There is a ***laïki agora*** (street market) on Ermou on Tuesday and Friday morning.

Getting There & Away

Bus There are buses south to Areopoli (30 minutes, 500 dr, five daily), Athens (4¼ hours, 4500 dr, five daily) via Sparta (one hour, 750 dr), Gerolimenas (two hours, 1100 dr, two daily) and the Diros Caves (one hour, 700 dr, one daily). Getting to Kalamata is hard work, and involves changing buses at Itilo (one hour, 700 dr). There are only two buses daily (6 am and 1 pm) to Itilo. You'll find better connections from Areopoli.

Ferry In summer, the F/B *Maria* operates a daily service to Kythira (two hours, 1600 dr). At other times there are four boats weekly. From June to September, the *Maria* continues to Kastelli-Kissamos on Crete (seven hours, 5100 dr) on Monday and Thursday. Tickets are sold at Golden Ferries (☎ 22 996, fax 22 410) opposite the tourist office on Vasileos Pavlou.

ANEK Lines services from Gythio had been suspended at the time of writing. Check with Rozakis Travel (☎ 22 207, fax 22 229, email rosakigy@otenet.gr), on the waterfront near Plateia Mavromihali.

Getting Around

Rozakis Travel (see Ferry) hires cars. Mopeds and scooters are available from Rent-a-Moped on Kranais.

The Mani Η Μάνη

The region referred to as the Mani covers the central peninsula in the south of the Peloponnese. For centuries, the Maniots were a law unto themselves, renowned for their fierce independence and resentment of any attempt to govern them.

Today, the Maniots are regarded by other Greeks as independent, royalist and right-wing. But don't be deterred from visiting the region by descriptions of the Maniots as hostile, wild and hard people. Contact with the outside world and lack of feuding have mellowed them. The Maniots are as friendly and hospitable as Greeks elsewhere, despite the fierce appearance of some older people who dress like the Cretans and offer fiery *raki* (a spirit) as a gesture of hospitality. But the music and dance of the two differ.

The Mani is generally divided into the Messinian Mani (also called the outer Mani) and the Lakonian (or inner) Mani. The Messinian Mani starts south-east of Kalamata and runs south between the coast and the Taÿgetos Mountains, while the Lakonian Mani covers the rest of the peninsula south of Itilo. Such was the formidable reputation of the inhabitants of the remote inner Mani that foreign occupiers thought they were best left alone.

The Mani has no significant ancient sites, but it well compensates with medieval and later remains, bizarre tower settlements – particularly in the inner Mani – built as refuges from clan wars from the 17th century onwards, and magnificent churches, all enhanced by the distant presence of the towering peaks of the Taÿgetos Mountains. The Diros Caves in the south are also a major attraction.

History

The people of the Mani regard themselves as direct descendants of the Spartans. After the decline of Sparta, citizens loyal to the principles of Lycurgus, founder of Sparta's constitution, chose to withdraw to the mountains rather than serve under foreign masters. Later, refugees from occupying powers joined these people who became known as Maniots, from the Greek word *mania*.

The Maniots claim they are the only Greeks not to have succumbed to foreign invasions. This may be somewhat exaggerated but the Maniots have always enjoyed a certain autonomy and a distinctive lifestyle. Until independence, the Maniots lived in clans led by chieftains. Fertile land was so scarce that it was fiercely fought over. Blood feuds were a way of life and families constructed towers as refuges.

The Turks failed to subdue the Maniots, who eagerly participated in the War of Independence. But, after 1834, although reluctant to relinquish their independence, they became part of the new kingdom.

For background reading, try *Mani* by Patrick Leigh Fermor, *Deep into Mani* by Eliopoulis & Greenhold and *The Architecture of Mani* by Ioannis Saïtis.

The Mani by long-time Stoupa resident Bob Barrow is worth seeking out in local shops if you're planning on doing any exploring. Bob manages Thomeas Travel in Stoupa, and spends all his spare time exploring the Mani. His self-published guide is full of little gems of information about the region's villages, towers and churches.

LAKONIAN MANI

Grey rock, mottled with defiant clumps of green scrub, and the occasional stunted olive or cypress tree characterise the bleak mountains of inner Mani. The lower slopes are terraced wherever this unyielding soil has been cultivated. A curious anomaly is the profusion of wild flowers which mantle the valleys in spring, exhibiting nature's resilience by sprouting from the rocks.

The indented coast's sheer cliffs plunge into the sea and rocky outcrops shelter pebbled beaches. This wild and barren landscape is broken only by austere and imposing stone towers, mostly abandoned, but still standing sentinel over the region. Restoration of Maniot buildings is increasing and many refugee Albanians, who are fine stonemasons, have been engaged on these projects.

To explore the Lakonian Mani, head from Gythio to Areopoli and then south to Gerolimenas, loop round and return to Areopoli via Kotronas. You can then continue north from Areopoli to Itilo and continue to the Messinian Mani.

Areopoli Αρεόπολη

☎ 0733 • postcode 230 62 • pop 980

Areopoli (ah-reh-**o**-po-lih), capital of the Mani, is aptly named after Ares, the god of war. Dominating the central square is a statue of Petrobey Mavromihalis, who proclaimed the Maniot insurrection against the Turks. Konstantinos and Georgos Mavromihalis, who assassinated Kapodistrias, belonged to the same family. The town retains many other reminders of its rumbustious past.

In the narrow, cobbled streets of the old town, grim tower houses stand proudly vigilant. Stroll around during siesta time when the heat and silence make it especially evocative.

Also have a look at the unusual reliefs above the doors of the Church of Taxiarhes, on Kapetan Matapan, which depict feuding archangels and signs of the zodiac.

Orientation & Information The bus stop is in front of the Europa Grill on Plateia Athinaton, the central square. There is no tourist office or tourist police. The post office and OTE are on the corner of the square and Kapetan Matapan, the main thoroughfare through the old town that leads downhill from the square. The National Bank of Greece is on P Mavromihali – turn right at the first church on Kapetan Matapan and the bank is on the left after 150m. It's open normal banking hours in July and August, and 9 am to noon on Tuesday and Thursday for the rest of the year. There's an ATM outside.

Places to Stay – Budget The cheapest rooms in Areopoli belong to ***Petros Bathrellos*** *(☎ 51 205)*, who rents out three rooms above his taverna, Barbar Petros, 70m down Kapetan Matapan from the square. He charges 4000/6000/8000 dr for basic singles/doubles/triples.

Keep going down Kapetan Matapan and you'll see a sign at the Church of Taxiarhes pointing to ***Tsimova Rooms*** *(☎ 51 301)*, housed in a beautiful old renovated tower behind the church. Owner George Versakos has cosy rooms, filled with ornaments, family photos and icons, for 7000/12,000 dr, and a two room apartment with kitchen for 15,000 dr. George will show you his private collection of daggers, pistols, a stele and ancient coins.

Hotel Kouris *(☎ 51 340)*, on the main square, has spotless rooms with bathroom for 7500/9500 dr.

Places to Stay – Mid-Range & Top End ***Pyrgos Kapetanakas*** *(☎ 51 233)*, signposted to the right at the bottom of Kapetan Matapan, is a traditional tower settlement that's worth checking out. It's austerely authentic, in keeping with the spirit of the Mani. It was closed for renovation at the time of research following a transfer to private management.

The most stylish rooms are at ***Londas Pension*** *(☎ 51 360, fax 51 012, email londas@otenet.gr)*, a 200-year-old tower signposted to the right off Kapetan Matapan at the Church of Taxiarhes. The rooms have whitewashed stone walls and beamed ceilings. Doubles/triples are 22,000/24,000 dr, including breakfast.

Places to Eat The most popular place is ***Nicola's Corner Taverna***, open all day on the central square. It has a good choice of tasty taverna staples, with most main meals priced around 1500 dr. ***Barbar Petros*** (see Places to Stay) is primarily a psistaria serving grilled steak and chops, but it also has daily specials like eggplant and potato pie – 1200 dr for an enormous serving.

There's a small ***supermarket*** near the square on Kapetan Matapan.

Getting There & Away The bus office (☎ 51 229) is inside the Europa Grill on Plateia Athinaton. There are five buses daily to Gythio (30 minutes, 500 dr); three to Itilo (20 minutes, 230 dr) via Limeni; two to Gerolimenas (45 minutes, 600 dr) and the Diros Caves (15 minutes, 230 dr); one daily to Lagia (40 minutes, 700 dr) via Kotronas; and three weekly (Monday, Wednesday and Friday) to Vathia (one hour, 750 dr).

Diros Caves Σπήλαιο Διρού

These extraordinary caves are 11km south of Areopoli, near the village of Pyrgos Dirou – notable for its towers (signposted to the left off the road down to the caves).

The natural entrance to the caves is on the beach, and locals like to believe the legend that they extend as far north as Sparta (speleologists have so far traced the caves inland for 5km). They were inhabited in Neolithic times, but were abandoned after an earthquake and weren't rediscovered until 1895. Systematic exploration began in 1949. The caves are famous for their stalactites and stalagmites, which have fittingly poetic names such as the Palm Forest, Crystal Lily and the Three Wise Men.

Unfortunately, the guided tour through the caves is disappointingly brief. It covers only the lake section, and bypasses the dry section that features the most spectacular formations. The 20 minute tour isn't good enough to justify the charge of 3500 dr.

The caves are open 8 am to 5.30 pm daily from June to September, and 8 am to 2.30 pm from October to May.

Places to Stay Most people visit the caves on day trips from Areopoli or Gythio, but there is accommodation closer to the caves. The nearest hotel is the D class ***To Panorama*** *(☎ 0733-52 280)*, 1km from the caves on the right coming from Pyrgos Dirou. Comfortable air-con singles/doubles with bathroom and TV are 7000/9000 dr.

Pyrgos Dirou to Gerolimenas

Πύργος Διρού to Γερολιμένας

Journeying south down Mani's west coast from Pyrgos Dirou to Gerolimenas, the barren mountain landscape is broken only by deserted settlements with mighty towers. From one of these settlements, Stavri, reached by turning right (west) from the main road, you can trek in 40 to 50 minutes over rough terrain to the **Castle of Mina**, on the Tigani Promontory. This Frankish castle was built by William II de Villehardouin in 1248. Back on the main road, **Kita**, with a plethora of towers, is worth a stroll.

Although 17km separates Pyrgos Dirou and Gerolimenas, there is only one place to stay in between: the ***Tsitsiris Castle Guest House*** *(☎ 0733-56 297, fax 56 296)* at Stavri. The 'castle' is a wonderfully restored tower house on the edge of the village. It has air-con singles/doubles with bathroom for 14,000/18,700 dr, which includes a generous buffet breakfast. At night, you'll find delicious home-cooked meals in the restaurant at standard taverna prices. The guesthouse is signposted off the main road 4km north of Gerolimenas.

Gerolimenas Γερολιμένας

☎ 0733 • postcode 230 71 • pop 250

Gerolimenas (yeh-ro-lih-**meh**-nahss) is a tranquil fishing village built around a small, sheltered bay at the south-western tip of the peninsula. The village has a post office with a currency exchange service (open 8 am to 2 pm Monday to Friday), but no bank.

Walk to Ano Boulari & Kato Boulari

From the village, walk back along the road towards Pyrgos Dirou. About 100m beyond Hotel Akrogiali, a road off to the right (Mantoivaloi) leads 2km to the almost deserted village of Ano (upper) Boulari. The **Church of Agios Stratigos** has some well preserved frescoes, most dating from the 12th century. Farther on at the village of Kato (lower) Boulari, the **Anemodoura Tower**, built around 1600, is thought to be one of the earliest Maniot towers.

Places to Stay & Eat The cheapest rooms in Gerolimenas are at ***Hotel Akrotenaritis*** *(☎ 54 205)*, by the bus stop, which has air-con singles/doubles with bathroom for 5000/10,000 dr.

You'll find the best rooms at ***Akrogiali*** *(☎ 54 204, fax 54 272)*, overlooking the beach on the way into town. It charges 8500/12,000 dr for air-con rooms with bathroom. The owners also rent out four-person apartments nearby for 16,000 dr.

Both hotels have restaurants. There is a so-called ***supermarket*** on the road behind Hotel Akrogiali.

Getting There & Away There are buses from Gerolimenas to Sparta (2¼ hours, 1850 dr), Gythio (1¼ hours, 1100 dr) and Areopoli (45 minutes, 500 dr).

Gerolimenas to Porto Kagio

Γερολιμένας to Πόρτο Κάγιο

South of Gerolimenas, the road continues 4km to the small village of Alika, where it divides. One road leads east to Lagio and the other goes south to Vathia and Porto Kagio. The southern road follows the coast, passing pebbly beaches. It then climbs steeply inland to **Vathia**, the most dramatic of the traditional Mani villages, comprising a cluster of closely packed tower houses perched on a rocky spur.

A turn-off to the right 9km south of Alika leads to two sandy beaches at Marmari, while the main road cuts across the peninsula to the tiny east coast fishing village of **Porto Kagio**, set on a perfect horseshoe bay.

Places to Stay & Eat The only accommodation in Vathia is at the traditional settlement of ***Vathia Towers*** *(☎ 0733-55 244)*, but it was closed for renovation at the time of research, with no indication of when it might reopen.

Porto Kagio has one place to stay, ***Akroteri Domatia*** *(☎/fax 0733-52 013)*. It has large doubles with balcony and bathroom from 10,000 dr to 13,000 dr. The three ***tavernas*** all specialise in fish dishes.

Lagio to Kotronas

Λάγια to Κότρωνας

Lagio was once the chief town of the south-eastern Mani. Perched 400m above sea level, it's a formidable looking place, especially when approached from Alika.

From Lagio, the road winds down with spectacular views of the little fishing harbour of **Agios Kyprianos** – a short diversion from the main road. The next village is **Kokala**, busy, friendly and with two pebbled beaches. The bus stop is in front of Synantisi Taverna.

Once through Kokala, the road climbs again. After 4km, there are more beaches at the sprawling village of **Nyfi**. A turn-off to the right leads to the sheltered beach of **Alipa**. Continuing north, a turn-off beyond Flomohori descends to Kotronas.

Places to Stay & Eat Lagio has no accommodation but there are several possibilities in Kokala. ***Pension Kokala*** *(☎ 0733-21 107)*, on the main street, has doubles with bathroom for 6000 dr.

You'll see signs promoting ***To Kastro Pension*** *(☎ 0733-21 090)*, formerly ***Papa's Rooms***, all the way down the east coast. The place is perched high above the village, reached by a steep concrete road leading up the hill next to ***Hotel Soleteri***. The rooms are owned by jovial Papageorgis, the local priest. He has doubles priced from 10,000 dr, but Papa, like most Greek owners, is not averse to bargaining.

Marathos Taverna, on the beach, has good food and a great setting.

Kotronas Κοτρώνας

☎ 0733 • pop 600

Around Kotronas the barrenness of the Mani gradually gives way to relative lushness, with olive groves and cypress trees. Kotronas bustles compared with the Mani's half-deserted tower villages. Its main thoroughfare leads to the waterfront where the bus turns around. To the left is a bay with a small, sandy beach. The post office is on the right of the main thoroughfare as you face the sea. The islet off the coast is linked by a causeway. Walk inland along the main thoroughfare and turn left at the fork. Take the first left and walk to a narrow road, which soon degenerates into a path, leading to the causeway. On the island are ruins surrounding a small, well kept church.

Places to Stay & Eat ***Adelfia Pension*** *(☎ 21 209)*, on the right of the main road as you head towards the sea, has singles/doubles for 5000/6000 dr.

Kotronas Bay Bungalows *(☎ 21 340, fax 21 402)* are 500m east of the village on the road that skirts the bay. They can accommodate up to four people and cost 30,000 dr a day. They come with fully equipped kitchens, but there is also the ***To Timoniera*** restaurant.

There are two ***minimarkets*** and a ***bakery*** on the main street.

Kotronas to Skoutari

The upgrading of the coast road from Kotronas to Skoutari, 14km to the north-east, means that it's now possible to complete a circuit of the Mani without doubling back to Areopoli.

Skoutari is a quiet little village overlooking pretty Skoutari Bay, which terminates in a long sandy beach with a small summer ***psarotaverna***. There are ***domatia*** in the village as well as the modern ***Hotel Skoutari Beach*** *(☎ 93 684, fax 93 685)*. It charges 15,000 dr for large studio rooms that cater for up to three people, and 20,000 dr for two-room studios for four people.

There's a good sealed road from Skoutari to the Gythio-Areopoli road, about 5km to the north.

Limeni Λιμένι

The tiny village of Limeni is 3km north of Areopoli on the southern flank of beautiful

Limeni Bay. There are spectacular views over the bay to Itilo from ***Limeni Village Bungalows*** *(☎ 0733-51 111)*, a complex of replica Maniot towers on the cliff top overlooking the village. Singles/doubles are 17,000/21,000 dr and the facilities include a pool, bar and restaurant. The village proper has ***domatia*** and a ***taverna***.

Itilo & Nea Itilo Οίτυλο & Νέο Οίτυλο

☎ 0733 • postcode 230 62 • pop 550

Itilo (**eet-ih-lo**), 11km north of Areopoli, was the medieval capital of the Mani. To travel between Lakonian and Messinian Mani, you must change buses at Itilo.

The village is now a crumbling and tranquil backwater, perched on the northern edge of a deep ravine traditionally regarded as the border between outer and inner Mani. Above the ravine is the massive 17th century **Castle of Kelefa** from which the Turks attempted to constrain the Maniots. You can't miss it on a hill above the road from Nea Itilo. Nearby, the **Monastery of Dekoulou** has colourful frescoes in its church. Nea Itilo, 4km before, lies at the back of secluded Limeni Bay.

Places to Stay Apart from a few ***domatia*** down by Limeni Bay in Nea Itilo, there is no budget accommodation.

The plush C class ***Hotel Itilo*** *(☎ 59 222, fax 59 234)*, right by the beach in Nea Itilo, has single/double rooms for 12,000/16,000 dr including breakfast. ***Alevra's Tower*** *(☎ 59 388)*, on the main road just south of Itilo, has superb views from its well equipped studio rooms. Doubles/triples with bathroom and breakfast facilities are 15,000/17,000 dr.

Getting There & Away There are three buses daily to Areopoli (20 minutes, 230 dr) and Kalamata (two hours, 1250 dr). Areopoli-Itilo buses go via Nea Itilo and Limeni.

MESSINIAN MANI

The Messinian Mani, or outer Mani, lies to the north of its Lakonian counterpart, sandwiched between the Taÿgetos Mountains and the west coast of the Mani Peninsula. Kalamata lies at the northern end of the peninsula. The rugged coast is scattered with numerous small coves and beaches backed by mountains that remain snow-capped until late May. There are glorious views along the way, particularly on the descent from Stavropigi to Kardamyli and farther south around the small village of Agios Nikon.

Stoupa Στούπα

☎ 0721 • postcode 240 54 • pop 730

Stoupa, 10km south of Kardamyli, has undergone a rapid transformation from fishing village to upmarket resort. Tourist development remains fairly low-key; it's billed as a resort for discriminating package tourists intent on discovering the unspoilt Greece. Although not as picturesque as Kardamyli, it does have two lovely beaches.

Celebrated author Nikos Kazantzakis lived here for a while and based the protagonist of his novel *Zorba the Greek* on Alexis Zorbas, a coal mine supervisor in Pastrova, near Stoupa.

Orientation & Information Stoupa is 1km west of the main Areopoli-Kalamata road, connected by link roads both north and south of town. Both roads lead to the larger of Stoupa's two main beaches – a glorious crescent of golden sand.

Stoupa's development has been so rapid that its amenities have yet to catch up. Katerina's supermarket, on the coast road behind the main beach, doubles as both the post office and the OTE. It sells stamps, accepts mail for delivery, changes money and sells phonecards.

There is no tourist office, but most tourists treat Thomeas Travel (☎ 77 689, fax 77 571, email antthom@otenet.gr) as if it were one. Manager Bob Barrow is a keen student of Mani history and a mine of information about local attractions. He can also change money, organise hire cars and advise on accommodation.

Places to Stay & Eat ***Camping Kalogria*** *(☎ 54 319)*, above Stoupa's small beach, is well kept, with shady sites, a children's playground, minimarket and bar. If you want to escape the crowds, try ***Camping Delfinia*** *(☎ 77 318)*, near Kaminia Beach, 2km away on the Kardamyli side of Stoupa.

Stoupa's growing band of pensions and custom-built domatia all seem to be block-booked by package tour operators. Thomeas Travel may know of vacancies.

The C class ***Stoupa Hotel*** *(☎ 54 308)* has doubles with bathroom and balcony for 10,500 dr. The hotel is on the southern approach road to Stoupa. The nearby ***Hotel Lefktron*** *(☎ 77 322, fax 77 700)* has air-con singles/doubles with fridge for 9000/14,000 dr.

Stoupa has lots of restaurants and tavernas, none particularly cheap. ***Taverna Akrogiali*** has a top location at the southern end of the beach, and good food.

Getting There & Away Stoupa is on the main Itilo-Kalamata bus route. There are bus stops at the junctions of both the southern and northern approach roads, but the buses don't go into town.

Kardamyli Καρδαμύλη

☎ 0721 • postcode 240 22 • pop 350

The tiny village of Kardamyli (kah-dah-**mee**-lih) has one of the prettiest settings in the Peloponnese, nestled between the calm waters of the Messinian Gulf and the Taÿgetos Mountains. The deep Vyros Gorge, which emerges just north of town, runs straight up to the foot of Mt Profitas Ilias, (2407m), the highest peak of the Taÿgetos. The gorge and surrounding areas are very popular with trekkers.

Kardamyli was one of the seven cities offered to Achilles by Agamemnon.

Orientation & Information Kardamyli is on the main Areopoli-Kalamata road. The bus stops at the central square, Plateia 25 Martiou 1821, at the northern end of the main thoroughfare. The post office is back towards Stoupa on the main street.

Kardamyli's main pebble-and-stone beach is off the road to Kalamata; turn left beyond the bridge on the northern edge of town. The road up to Old (or Upper) Kardamyli is on the right before the bridge.

Trekking Trekking has become Kardamyli's biggest drawcard. The hills behind the village are crisscrossed with an amazing network of colour-coded trails. All the accommodation places in the village will be able to supply you with a map that explains the routes. Most of the treks are strenuous. Strong footwear is essential to support your ankles on the rough ground, particularly if you venture into the boulder-strewn gorge itself. You will also need to carry plenty of drinking water.

Many treks pass through the mountain village of **Exohorio**, perched on the edge of the Vyros Gorge at an altitude of 450m. The village is also accessible by road, and it's a good place for non-trekkers to do a spot of more gentle exploration. The turn-off to Exohorio is 3km south of Kardamyli.

Places to Stay & Eat ***Melitsina Camping*** *(☎ 73 461)*, by the beach on the northern side of town, has good shady sites among the olive trees.

There are plenty of domatia signs along the main road. The street down to the sea opposite the post office is the place to look. ***Olivia Koumounakou*** *(☎ 73 623)*, on the left after 150m, has double rooms with bathroom for 8000 dr and a communal kitchen. ***Statis Bravacos*** *(☎ 73 326)*, opposite, has spotless studio apartments with kitchen facilities for 12,000 dr.

If you keep going down this street and turn right, you'll come to ***Lela's Taverna & Rooms*** *(☎ 73 541)*. It has doubles with bathroom for 11,000 dr, but the real attraction is the restaurant with terrace seating overlooking the sea. Lela, who runs the kitchen, is the former housekeeper of author Patrick Leigh Fermor, who still lives in the village.

Anniska Apartments *(☎ 73 600, fax 73 000)*, by the sea 200m north of Lela's, has a range of spacious, well appointed studios and apartments, all with kitchen facilities. The studios cost 17,000 dr for two people, while larger apartments cost 25,000 dr for up to four people.

There are nine tavernas in the village, so there's no shortage of eating options. Locals give their vote to ***Taverna Perivolis***, run by a friendly Greek-Australian family. It's on the left as you head towards Anniska Apartments from the main road.

Self-caterers will find all they need at one of the two ***supermarkets*** on the northern edge of the village.

Getting There & Around Kardamyli is on the main bus route from Itilo to Kalamata (one hour, 700 dr).

The Pandora souvenir shop (☎ 73 415) hires mopeds. Early birds can catch the sole bus to Exohorio at 6.15 am; most prefer to take a cab (1200 dr).

Messinia Μεσσηνία

Messinia occupies the south-western corner of the Peloponnese. Its boundaries were established in 371 BC following the defeat of Sparta by the Thebans at the Battle of Leuctra. The defeat ended more than 350 years of Spartan domination of the Peloponnese – during which Messinian exiles founded the city of Messinia in Sicily – and the Messinians were left free to develop their kingdom in the region stretching west from the Taÿgetos Mountains. Their capital was ancient Messini, about 25km north-west of Kalamata on the slopes of Mt Ithomi.

Few travellers make it to Messinia, which is a shame. Finikounda has one of the best beaches in the country, and the old Venetian towns of Koroni and Methoni are delightful little hideaways that have yet to feel the weight of package tourism.

KALAMATA Καλαμάτα

☎ 0721 • postcode 241 00 • pop 44,000

Kalamata is Messinia's capital and the second-largest city in the Peloponnese. 'Calamitous Kalamata' aptly sums up this hapless city. The old town was almost totally destroyed by the Turks during the War of Independence and rebuilt unimaginatively by French engineers in the 1830s. On 14 September 1986, Kalamata was devastated by an earthquake measuring 6.2 on the Richter scale. Twenty people died, hundreds were injured and more than 10,000 homes were destroyed.

Orientation

The old town around the kastro is picturesque, and the waterfront along Navarinou is lively – but it's a long, hot walk between the two. The main streets linking the old town with the waterfront are Faron and Aristomenous. The city centre is around Plateia Georgiou on Aristomenous.

The main bus station is on the north-western edge of town on Artemidos, while local buses leave from Plateia 25 Martiou – the No 1 goes to the waterfront. The train station is on Frantzi, near Plateia Georgiou.

Information

Tourist Offices The town is dotted with arrowed 'tourist information' signs. Most of them are directing people to the unusually helpful tourist police (☎ 95 555), close to the port on Miaouli opposite the Lambos supermarket. They are open 8 am until after midnight Monday to Friday. Other signs point to the old EOT tourist office (now closed) by the yachting marina. None of them point to the new EOT office (☎ 21 700) at Polyvriou 5 in the town centre.

Post & Communications The post office is near the train station at Iatropoulou 4, and the OTE is on the north-western side of Plateia Georgiou. Web-heads can log on at the Diktyo Internet Café, Nedontos 75, or the Lemon Café, Iatropoulou 12B.

Money There are branches of all the major banks, including the National Bank of Greece, opposite the OTE on Aristomenous. There's another branch on the waterfront on the corner of Ariti and Navarinou.

Laundry The laundrette near the waterfront at Methonis 3 charges 1500 dr to wash

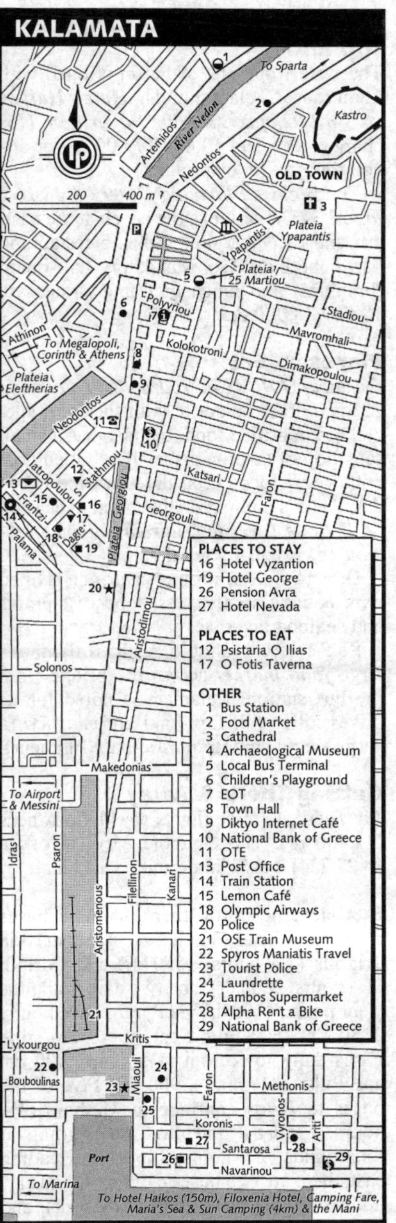

and dry 6kg. It's open 9 am to 1 pm and 5.30 to 9 pm daily.

Kastro

Looming over the town is the 13th century kastro. Remarkably, it survived the 1986 earthquake. There are excellent views from the battlements. The kastro is the setting for an annual summer festival, which includes cultural events such as contemporary musical performances and plays. It was closed at the time of research – in defiance of the sign announcing it's open 10 am to 1.30 pm Monday to Friday.

Archaeological Museum

The Archaeological Museum of Kalamata is just north of Plateia 25 Martiou on Papazoglou. It's signposted off Ypapantis. The museum is slowly being reopened after being badly damaged in the earthquake. It's open 8 am to 2.30 pm Tuesday to Saturday and 8.30 am to 3 pm on Sunday. Admission is 500 dr.

OSE Park

The park at the southern end of Aristomenous is home to a collection of old steam locomotives and carriages, parked next to the city's quaint old station.

Places to Stay – Budget

Camping Fare *(☎ 29 250)* is on the waterfront east of town, and can be reached by bus No 1 from Plateia 25 Martiou. ***Maria's Sea and Sun Camping*** *(☎ 41 314)* is a much better site, but it's 4km east of town. It has a minimarket, bar, restaurant and two-person bungalows. Buses to Avias from the main bus station can drop you close by.

The best budget place in the northern part of town is the spotless D class ***Hotel George*** *(☎ 27 225)*, close to the train station at the corner of Frantzi and Dagre. Singles/doubles with bathroom and TV are listed at 8000/10,000 dr, but normally go for 5000/6600 dr. Ask for a room away from the street.

If the George is full, try the nearby ***Hotel Vyzantion*** *(☎ 86 824/825)*, nearby at the

Kalamata Olives

Kalamata is the capital of Messinia, the region occupying the south-western corner of the Peloponnese and famous as the home of the prized Kalamata olive.

While not all olives grown around here are the Kalamata variety, it is this plump, purple-black variety that is found in delicatessens around the world. They are also grown extensively in neighbouring Lakonia and on the islands of Crete and Lesvos.

Locals insist, though, that the finest olives are grown on Messinian soil, particularly in the Pamisos Valley, north of Messini. The region's reliable winter rains and hot summers make for perfect olive-growing conditions.

The Kalamata tree can be distinguished from the common olive, grown for oil, by the size of its leaves. Like its fruit, the leaves of the Kalamata are twice the size of other varieties – and greener. Another important difference is that the Kalamata is alternate bearing – which means a heavy crop one year followed by a light crop.

Unlike other varieties, Kalamata olives cannot be picked green. They ripen in late November, and must be hand-picked to avoid bruising. The olives are then graded according to size and brine-cured.

You can check out a selection of these famous olives at the markets in Kalamata.

corner of Sidirodromikou Stathmou and Iatropoulou. It charges marginally more.

There are a couple of good places down by the seafront on Santarosa, which runs parallel to Navarinou one block back from the sea. ***Hotel Nevada*** *(☎ 82 429, Santa Rosa 9)* has clean singles/doubles/triples for 4500/6500/9000 dr. Almost opposite is ***Pension Avra*** *(☎ 82 759)*, charging 5000/7000 dr. There is a communal kitchen upstairs. Both these places are on the section of Santarosa between Faron and Kanari.

Places to Stay – Mid-Range & Top End

The waterfront east of Faron is lined with numerous C class hotels. ***Hotel Haikos*** *(☎ 88 902, fax 23 800, Navarinou 115)* charges a typical 13,000/17,000 dr for air-con rooms with bathroom.

The B class ***Filoxenia Hotel*** *(☎ 23 166, fax 23 343)* overlooks the beach at the eastern end of Navarinou. It has a restaurant, bar, pool and disco. Mandatory half-board (breakfast and lunch or dinner) rates are 18,500/28,000 dr.

Places to Eat

Psistaria O Ilias *(Sidirodromikou Stathmou 22)* is a great favourite with locals. It specialises in grilled food, but also has a small selection of taverna dishes like boiled goat with vegetables (1200 dr) and tripe (1100 dr). There's nothing on the menu over 1500 dr. ***O Fotis Taverna*** *(Sidirodromikou Stathmou 15)* is equally good value.

Down by the seafront, Navarinou is lined with countless cafes, fast-food restaurants and seafood tavernas.

Self-caterers should visit Kalamata's large ***food market*** across the bridge from the bus station. Kalamata is noted for its olives, olive oil, figs, raki and *mastica* (a surprisingly smooth mastic-based liqueur).

Getting There & Away

Air There are three flights weekly to Athens (13,400 dr). The Olympic Airways office (☎ 22 724) is at Sidirodromikou Stathmou 17.

Bus Heading north, there are nine buses daily to Athens (3½ hours, 4250 dr) via Tripolis (1¼ hours, 1550 dr) and Corinth (2½ hours, 2800 dr); and two daily to Patras (four hours, 4100 dr) via Pyrgos (two hours, 2350 dr). Heading west, there are nine buses daily to Koroni (1½ hours, 900 dr) and Pylos (1¼ hours, 900 dr). Five of the buses to Pylos continue to Methoni (1¾ hours, 1250 dr) and three keep going to Finikounda (2¼ hours, 1450 dr). Heading east, there are two buses daily to Sparta (1½ hours, 950 dr) via Artemisia (450 dr), and two daily to Itilo (2¼ hours, 1250 dr) via Kardamyli and Stoupa.

Train Kalamata is the end of the line for both branches of the Peloponnese railway. There are four trains daily to Athens (seven hours, 2160 dr) on the inland line via Tripolis (2½ hours, 840 dr); Argos (four hours, 1260 dr) and Corinth (5¼ hours, 1650 dr). There are two trains daily to Patras (six hours, 1500 dr) on the west-coast line via Kyparissia (two hours, 590 dr) and Pyrgos (3¼ hours, 860 dr). One train keeps going to Athens (11 hours, 2860 dr).

Ferry ANEK Lines ferry services from Kalamata to Kastelli-Kissamos on Crete had been suspended at the time of writing. Contact Spyros Maniatis Travel (☎ 20 704), by the port on Psaron, for the latest information.

Getting Around

To/From the Airport Kalamata's airport is 10.5km west of the city near Messini. There is no airport shuttle bus. A taxi costs about 2000 dr.

Bus Local buses leave from Plateia 25 Martiou. The most useful service is bus No 1, which goes south along Aristomenous to the seafront, and then east along Navarinou to Filoxenia Hotel. The flat fare is 170 dr. Buy tickets from the blue kiosk on Ypapantis, just north of Plateia 25 Martiou.

Car & Motorcycle Kalamata is a good place to hire a car thanks to the hot competition between the many agencies at the waterfront end of Faron. Alpha Rent a Bike (☎ 93 423), Vyronos 156, hires a range of bikes from 50 to 400cc.

MAVROMATI (ANCIENT MESSINI)

☎ 0724 • postcode 240 04 • pop 350

The ruins of ancient Messini surround the picturesque village of Mavromati, 25km north-west of Kalamata on the south-western slope of Mt Ithomi. The village takes its name from the fountain in the main square; the water gushes from a hole in the rock that looks like a black eye – *mavro mati* in Greek.

History

Ancient Messini was founded in 371BC after the Theban general Epaminondas defeated Sparta at the Battle of Leuctra, freeing Messinians from almost 350 years of Spartan rule.

Built on the site of an earlier stronghold, the new Messinian capital was one of a string of defensive positions designed to keep watch over Sparta. Epaminondas himself helped to plan the fortifications, which were based on a massive wall that stretched 9km around the surrounding ridges and completely enclosed the town.

Apart from its defensive potential, the site was also favoured by the gods. According to local myth, Zeus was born here – not Crete – and raised by the nymphs Neda and Ithomi, who bathed him in the same spring that gives the modern village its name.

Exploring the Site

The site covers a wide area, but fortunately the main attractions are within reasonable walking distance of Mavromati's main square.

The mighty defensive wall built by Epaminondas remains impressive today, particularly the section surrounding the **Arcadian Gate**, which guarded the ancient route to Megalopoli – now the modern road north-west to Zerbisia. It's well worth the 1km uphill walk from the village. You can see the whole site from the village, making it a good place to start.

The bulk of the ruins are spread out across a small valley immediately below the village, and accessed by steps from the main square. This area remained unexplored until very recent times, and is slowly emerging from the valley floor. Excavations here have so far revealed a large **theatre**, **asklepion**, **stadium** and **gymnasium**, as well as a variety of Roman ruins.

There is a small **museum** housing finds from the site – but not the splendid statue of

Hermes unearthed in the gymnasium. The museum is on the northern edge of the village, on the right as you head out to the Arcadian Gate.

Places to Stay & Eat

There are several domatia in Mavromati, including ***Rooms to Rent Zeus*** *(☎ 51 025)*. It has comfortable doubles for 10,000 dr. Right next door is ***Taverna Ithomi***, where you find grilled food and a small selection of taverna dishes.

Getting There & Away

It's best to visit with your own car – or be prepared to do a lot of walking. There are two buses daily to Mavromati (one hour, 750 dr) from Kalamata, leaving at 5.40 am and 2 pm.

KORONI Κορώνη

☎ 0725 • postcode 240 04 • pop 1420

Koroni (ko-**ro**-nih) is a delightful old Venetian town on the coast 43km southwest of Kalamata. Its narrow streets lead up to the old castle, most of which is occupied by the **Timios Prodromos Convent**. The small promontory beyond the castle is a tranquil place for a stroll with lovely views over the Messinian Gulf to the Taÿgetos Mountains. Koroni's main attraction is **Zaga Beach**, a long sweep of golden sand just south of the town.

Orientation & Information

Buses will drop you in the main square outside the Church of Agios Dimitrios, one block back from the harbour. There is no tourist office, but you'll find all the information you need on the large map of town on the church wall. It shows the location of the post office, OTE and both banks, all of which are nearby. There are no tourist police. The main street runs east from the square, one block back from the sea. Most locals appear unaware that it has a name, Perikli Ralli.

It takes about 20 minutes to walk to Zaga Beach. To get there, take the road that leads up to the castle from above the square; turn right at the top of the hill and follow the road that curves uphill around the castle. You'll see a sign to the beach on the left after 500m.

Places to Stay & Eat

Camping Koroni *(☎ 22 119)* is a good camping ground with a restaurant, bar, shop, pool, kitchen and wash room. It's 500m north of town on the road from Kalamata. Buses stop outside.

Koroni does not have a lot of accommodation. Most of the rooms are spread around a cluster of ***domatia*** by the sea at the eastern end of the main street. Expect to pay around 7000/9000 dr for singles/doubles. There are more domatia overlooking Zaga Beach, but they are often block-booked in summer.

Hotel Diana *(☎/fax 22 312)*, north of town on the road to Kalamata, charges 12,000 dr for good doubles with sea views.

Symposium Restaurant *(☎ 22 385)*, on the main street, is about as traveller-friendly as you could ever want a restaurant to be. Years of New York living have taught George, the amiable Greek-American owner, all about keeping the customer satisfied. He has seafood and grills as well as a daily selection of taverna staples for around 1200 dr. Vegetarians will find at least six dishes to choose from.

There are a couple of seafood restaurants on the seafront. ***Anestasia*** also does pizzas (from 1300 dr), while ***Flisvos*** advertises rabbit (1500 dr) as its speciality.

Self-caterers will find everything they need at the shops around the main square.

Getting There & Away

There are nine buses daily to Kalamata (1½ hours, 900 dr) and two to Finikounda.

FINIKOUNDA Φοινικούντα

☎ 0723 • postcode 240 06 • pop 650

The fishing village of Finikounda, midway between Koroni and Methoni, is a popular place for backpackers to hang out. The attraction is the string of fine beaches that stretch either side of the village. The area has a reputation for good windsurfing.

There are plenty of places hiring out windsurfers and offering lessons.

Finikounda has spread steadily along the beach over the years. All the shops and facilities are in the old village around the port. The bus stop is outside Hotel Finikountas, 100m from the port on the way to Methoni.

Places to Stay

Most young travellers head to either ***Camping Ammos*** *(☎ 71 262)*, 3km west of Finikounda off the road to Methoni, or ***Camping Loutsa Beach*** *(☎ 71 169)*, 2km east of town off the road to Koroni. Both are by the beach and have windsurfers and water sports equipment as well as the usual facilities.

There are a few ***domatia*** in the village and a growing band of mid-range hotels, including ***Hotel Finikountas*** *(☎ 71 308, fax 71 400)*. It has singles/doubles for 11,500/14,500 dr with breakfast.

Getting There & Away

Three buses daily go to Kalamata (2¼ hours, 1450 dr) via Methoni (30 minutes, 400 dr) and Pylos – two go via Koroni. If the lousy bus service tempts you to take a taxi, reckon on about 2000 dr to Methoni and 2500 dr to Koroni.

METHONI Μεθώνη

☎ 0723 • postcode 240 06 • pop 1200

Methoni (meh-**tho**-nih), 12km south of Pylos, was another of the seven cities offered to Achilles by Agamemnon. Homer described it as 'rich in vines'. Today, it's a pretty seaside town, with a sandy beach that's crowded in summer, and a magnificent 15th century Venetian fortress.

This vast fortification is built on a promontory south of the modern town, surrounded on three sides by the sea and separated from the mainland by a moat. The medieval port town, which stood within the fortress walls, was the Venetians' first and longest-held possession in the Peloponnese, and a stopover point for pilgrims en route to the Holy Land. In medieval times, the twin fortresses of Methoni and Koroni were known as 'the Eyes of the Serene Republic'.

Orientation & Information

The road from Pylos forks on the edge of town to create Methoni's two main streets, which then run parallel through town apart to the fortress. As you come from Pylos, the fork to the right is the main shopping street. It has shops, a supermarket and a National Bank of Greece. The left fork leads directly to the fortress car park, passing the post office on the way. Turn left at the fortress end of either street onto Miaouli, which leads to Methoni Beach. The small square by the beach is surrounded by fairly characterless C class hotels and several seafood restaurants.

There is no tourist office and no tourist police. The regular police (☎ 31 203) are signposted near the post office.

Fortress

This splendid fortress, a supreme example of military architecture, is vast and romantic. It's easy to spend half a day wandering around. Within the walls are a Turkish bath, a cathedral, houses, a cistern, parapets and underground passages. See how many Lion of St Mark insignias you can spot. A short causeway leads from the fortress to the diminutive octagonal Bourtzi castle on an adjacent islet. Bring a torch to explore the interior. The site is open 8 am to 7 pm Monday to Saturday and 9 am to 7 pm on Sunday. Admission is free.

Boat Trips

From June to September, the managers of Hotel Albatros (see Places to Stay) operate daily trips around the islands south of Methoni on the cruiser *Alexandros*. The trips last from 9 am to 5 pm and cost 3000 dr.

Places to Stay & Eat

Camping Methoni *(☎ 31 228)* has a good location right behind the beach, but could use a few shade trees. You'll see several signs for domatia in the streets near the fortress, including those of ***Dimitrios Tsonis*** *(☎ 31 640/588)*, above Cafeteria George at the fortress end of the main shopping street. He has doubles/triples for 6000/7000 dr.

The best mid-range place to stay is the friendly ***Hotel Albatros*** *(☎ 31 160, fax 31 114)*, next to the post office. Comfortable air-con singles/doubles with bathroom, refrigerator and balcony cost 12,000/14,500 dr. Breakfast costs an extra 1000 dr a head. The C class ***Hotel Castello*** *(☎ 31 300/280)*, facing the fortress, has beautifully furnished rooms with breakfast for 13,000/15,000 dr.

You'll find the best value eateries away from the restaurants on the beachside square. ***Taverna Nikos***, halfway along Miaouli, is a good choice. It's always full of locals and stays open all year. In town, ***Restaurant Kali Karthia***, on the shopping street, has an interesting menu with main courses from 1200 dr to 2000 dr.

PELOPONNESE

Getting There & Away

Buses leave from the fork at the Pylos end of town where the two main streets meet. You'll find a timetable pinned to the door of the adjacent Assimakis Food Market. There are seven buses daily to Kalamata (1¼ hours, 900 dr) and Pylos (15 minutes, 230 dr), and three to Finikounda (30 minutes, 400 dr). There are no direct buses to Koroni – change at Finikounda and keep your fingers crossed.

PYLOS Πύλος

☎ 0723 • postcode 240 01 • pop 2500

Pylos (**pee**-loss), on the coast 51km southwest of Kalamata, presides over the southern end of an immense bay. On this bay on 20 October 1827, the British, French and Russian fleets, under the command of Admiral Codrington, fired at point-blank range on Ibrahim Pasha's combined Turkish, Egyptian and Tunisian fleet, sinking 53 ships and killing 6000 men, with negligible losses on the Allies' side.

It was known as the Battle of Navarino (the town's former name) and was decisive in the War of Independence, but it was not meant to have been a battle at all. The Allied fleet wanted to achieve no more than to persuade Ibrahim Pasha and his fleet to leave, but things got out of hand. George IV, on hearing the news, described it as a 'deplorable misunderstanding'.

With its huge natural harbour almost enclosed by the Sfaktiria Islet, a delightful tree-shaded central square, two castles and surrounding pine-covered hills, Pylos is one of the most picturesque towns in the Peloponnese.

Orientation & Information

Everything of importance is within a few minutes walk of the central square, Plateia Trion Navarhon, down by the seafront. The bus station is on the inland side of the square. There is no tourist office. The post office is on Nileos, which runs uphill from the bus station towards Arviniti Hotel. The police station (☎ 22 316) and the National Bank of Greece are on the square, while the main Kalamata-Methoni road runs around it.

Castles

There are castles on each side of Navarino Bay. The more accessible of them is the **Neo Kastro**, on the hilltop at the southern edge of town off the road to Methoni. It was built by the Turks in 1573 and was later used as a launching pad for the invasion of Crete. Its remains in good condition, especially the formidable surrounding walls. Within its walls are a citadel, a mosque converted into a church and a courtyard surrounded by dungeons (it was used as a prison until the 1900s). The castle is open 8.30 am to 3 pm daily except Monday. Admission is 800 dr. The road to Methoni from the central square goes past the castle.

The ancient **Paleokastro**, 6km north of Pylos, is covered in the following Around Pylos section.

Boat Tours

You can ask around the waterfront for fishing boats to take you around the Bay of Navarino and the island of Sfaktiria. The price will depend on the number of passengers, but reckon on about 3000 dr each for a group of four or more. On the trip around the island, stops can be made at memorials to admirals of the Allied ships. Boats may pause so you can see wrecks of sunken Turkish ships, discernible in the clear waters.

Places to Stay & Eat

The nearest camping ground is ***Navarino Beach Camping** (☎ 22 761)*, 8km north of Pylos on Gialova Beach. Take a Kyparissia bus from Pylos.

There are no cheap hotels in town, but there are plenty of domatia on the road to Kalamata. The pick of them is the excellent ***12 Gods** (dodeka theoi; ☎ 22 179)*, where the rooms are named after the gods of the ancient Greek pantheon. Appropriately enough, Poseidon has superb views over the Navarino Bay. All the rooms are doubles with bathroom and cost 6500 dr. The place is about 1km from the main square. Bus travellers can ask to be dropped off at the *dodeka theoi*.

***Arvaniti Hotel** (☎ 23 050, fax 22 934)*, above the post office on Nileos, has large air-con singles/doubles for 9000/11,900 dr with breakfast.

***Psarotaverna 4 Epohes** (☎ 22 739)*, on the seafront beyond Hotel Miramare, is a popular family-run place with taverna favourites like stuffed tomatoes (900 dr) and moussaka (1000 dr) as well as fresh seafood by the kilogram.

There are ***supermarkets***, ***fruit and vegetable stalls***, a ***baker*** and ***psistaria*** on lively Ipiskoupou, which is up the steps leading off the northern side of the square.

Getting There & Away

There are buses to Kalamata (1¼ hours, 900 dr, nine daily); Kyparissia (two hours, 1100 dr, five daily) via Nestor's Palace (30 minutes, 450 dr) and Hora (35 minutes); Methoni (20 minutes, 230 dr, five daily); Finikounda (45 minutes, three daily); and Athens (five hours, 5150 dr, two daily) via Tripolis (three hours, 2400 dr).

AROUND PYLOS

Paleokastro

The ruins of this ancient castle lie on Koryphasio Hill at the northern side of Navarino Bay. It was built at the end of the 13th century, and occupies the site of the acropolis of ancient Pylos. It was captured in 1361 by Spanish invaders from Navarra, after whom the bay is named.

The site is best approached by the track leading south from the village of Petrohori, about 12km north of modern Pylos off the road to Hora. The track ends at **Voidokilias Beach**, a beautiful, sandy horseshoe bay presumed to be Homer's 'sandy Pylos' where Telemachus was warmly welcomed when he came to ask wise old King Nestor the whereabouts of his long-lost father, Odysseus, King of Ithaca.

The path up to the castle passes **Nestor's Cave**. According to mythology, this is the cave where Hermes hid the cattle he stole from Apollo. It boasts some impressive stalactites.

Nestor's Palace

The palace, originally a two storey building, is the best preserved of all Mycenaean palaces. Its walls stand 1m high, giving a good idea of the layout of a Mycenaean palace complex. The main palace, in the middle, was a vast building of many rooms. The largest, the **throne room**, was where the king dealt with state business. In the centre was a large, circular hearth surrounded by four ornate columns which supported a 1st floor balcony. Some of the fine frescoes discovered here are in the museum in the nearby village of Hora (see following). Rooms surrounding the throne room include the sentry box, pantry, waiting room, a vestibule and, most fascinating, a bathroom with a terracotta tub still in place.

The most important finds were about 1200 Linear B script tablets, the first discovered on the mainland. Some are in Hora's museum. The site was excavated later than the other Mycenaean sites, between 1952 and 1965. An excellent guidebook by Carl Blegen, who led the excavations, is sold at the site.

Nestor's Palace is 17km north of modern Pylos. It is open 8.30 am to 3 pm Tuesday to Sunday (8 am to 2.30 pm in winter). Admission is 500 dr.

Hora Χώρα

Hora's fascinating little **archaeological museum**, 3km north-east of Nestor's Palace, houses finds from the site and other Mycenaean artefacts from Messinia. The prize pieces are the frescoes from the throne rooms at Nestor's Palace. Opening times and admission fees are the same as for Nestor's Palace.

Getting There & Away

Buses from Pylos to Kyparissia stop at Nestor's Palace and Hora.

Elia Ηλία

The western prefecture of Elia is home to some of the best farming country in Greece. The main agricultural areas are along the broad valley of the River Alfios, the 'Sacred Alph' of Samuel Taylor Coleridge's *Kubla Khan*, and in the north-west around Gastouni and Andravida. The rich alluvial flats around here are watered by the River Pinios, which has been dammed upstream to create Lake Pinios, the largest water storage facility in the Peloponnese.

Ancient Elia took its name from the mythical King Helios. Its capital was the city of Elis, now a forgotten ruin on the road from Gastouni to Lake Pinios. When the Franks arrived, they made Andravida the capital of their principate of Morea. Pyrgos is the dull modern capital. Most people come to Elia for one reason: to visit ancient Olympia.

THOLOS TO PYRGOS

Heading north into Elia from Messinia, the mountains to the east give way to interrupted plains fringed by golden sand beaches. Interspersed by pebbled shores and rocky outcrops, these beaches stretch right around Elia's coastline. The best beaches in the south are at **Tholos**, where there's a camping ground, and at **Kakovatos** and **Kouroutas**. There's seaside accommodation in each village, but most of it is in uninspiring concrete buildings.

A sign outside Tholos points to the mountain village of **Nea Figalia**, 14km inland. From here, it's a further 21km to the tranquil site of **ancient Figalia**, set high above the River Nedron almost at its source. Laurels, cypresses and citrus trees are clustered around the ruins of this ancient Arcadian marketplace, with towers, a small acropolis, an agora, and a temple to Dionysos, the wine pourer. A rough road leads east from Nea Figalia to Andritsena (see the Arcadia section earlier).

PYRGOS Πύργος

☎ 0621 • postcode 271 00 • pop 28,700

Pyrgos, 98km south-west of Patras and 24km from Olympia, is an agricultural service town with little of interest except its municipal theatre and market. It is, however, the capital of Elia prefecture and all forms of public transport pass through here, including buses and trains to Olympia. The bus and train stations are about 400m apart, the former in the town centre on Manolopoulou and the latter at the northern edge of town on Ypsilantou.

If you need to stay overnight there are several hotels on the streets leading into town off Ypsilantou. ***Hotel Olympos*** *(☎ 23 650)* is on the corner of Vasileos Pavlou and Karkavitsa, and ***Hotel Pantheon*** *(☎ 29 746)* is at Themistokleous 7; both charge around 9000 dr a double.

Getting There & Away

Bus There are 16 buses daily to Olympia (30 minutes, 400 dr) on weekdays, 14 on Saturday, and nine on Sunday. There are ten buses daily to Athens (five hours, 5250 dr) and Patras (two hours, 1800 dr); and three daily to Kyllini (50 minutes, 1050 dr), Kyparissia (1¼ hours, 1450 dr), Tripolis (3½ hours, 2650 dr), Kalamata (two hours, 2350 dr) and Andritsena (1½ hours, 1600 dr).

Train Heading north, there are eight trains daily to Patras (two hours, 820 dr) and four to Athens (seven hours, 2160 dr). Three of these trains are intercity, which take five hours to Athens. Heading south, there are four trains daily to Kalamata (3¼ hours, 860 dr) via Kyparissia (1¼ hours). There are also five trains daily on the branch line to Olympia (35 minutes, 210 dr).

OLYMPIA Ολυμπία

☎ 0624 • postcode 270 65 • pop 1000

The modern village of Olympia (o-lim-**bee**-ah) panders unashamedly to the hundreds of thousands of tourists who pour through here each year on their way to ancient Olympia, 500m south on the road to Tripolis. The main street is lined with countless overpriced souvenir shops, coffee shops and restaurants.

Orientation

The modern village lies along the main Pyrgos-Tripolis road, known as Praxitelous Kondyli, through town. The bus stops for Pyrgos and Tripolis are opposite one another by the tourist office towards the southern end of Praxitelous Kondyli, and the train station is close to the centre on Douka.

Information

Olympia's helpful municipal tourist office (☎ 23 100/173) on Praxitelous Kondyli comes as a pleasant surprise after dealing with government-run EOT offices elsewhere. The friendly staff offer a good map of the village, have comprehensive information on bus, train and ferry schedules (from Kyllini and Patras) and can change currency. The office is open 9 am to 9 pm daily June to September. The rest of the year it opens 8 am to 2.45 pm Monday to Saturday. The tourist police (☎ 22 550) are behind the tourist office on Spiliopoulou, which runs parallel to Praxitelous Kondyli one block up the hill.

The post office is up the first street to the right as you walk along Praxitelous Kondyli towards ancient Olympia from the tourist office. The OTE is on Praxitelous Kondyli, beyond the turn-off for the post office. The National Bank of Greece is on the corner of Praxitelous Kondyli and Stefanopoulou.

Historical Museum of the Olympic Games

This museum, two blocks west of Praxitelous Kondyli, is open Monday to Saturday 8.30 am to 3.30 pm, and on Sunday 9 am to 4 pm. Although most of the labelling is in French, the collection of commemorative stamps and literature needs little explanation. Admission is 500 dr.

Ancient Olympia

Ancient Olympia was a complex of temples, priests' dwellings and public buildings. It was also the venue of the Olympic Games, which took place every four years. During the games the city-states were bound by *ekeheiria* (a sacred truce) to stop beating the hell out of one another, and compete in races and sports instead.

The site, now World Heritage-listed, is open 8 am to 7 pm daily. Admission is 1200 dr (free on Sunday and public holidays).

History & Mythology The origins of Olympia date back to Mycenaean times. The Great Goddess, identified with Rea, was worshipped here in the 1st millennium BC. By the classical era, Rea had been superseded by her son Zeus. A small regional festival, which probably included athletic events, was begun in the 11th century BC.

The first official quadrennial Olympic Games were declared in 776 BC by King Iphitos of Elis. By 676 BC, they were open to all male Greeks, reaching their height of prestige in 576 BC. The games were held in honour of Zeus, popularly acclaimed as their founder. They took place at the time of the first full moon in August.

The athletic festival lasted five days and included wrestling, chariot and horse racing, the pentathlon (wrestling, discus and javelin throwing, long jump and running), and the pancratium (a vicious form of fisticuffs).

Originally only Greek-born males were allowed to participate, but later Romans were permitted. Slaves and women were not allowed to enter the sanctuary as participants or spectators. Women trying to sneak in were thrown from a nearby rock.

The event served purposes besides athletic competition. Writers, poets and historians read their works to a large audience, and the citizens of various city-states got together. Traders clinched business deals and city-state leaders talked in an atmosphere of festivity that was conducive to resolving differences through discussion, rather than battle.

The games continued during the first years of Roman rule. By this time, however, their importance had declined and, thanks to Nero, they had become less edifying. In 67 AD, Nero entered the chariot race with 10 horses, ordering that other competitors could have no more than four. Despite this advantage, he fell and abandoned the race. He was still declared the winner by the judges.

The games were held for the last time in 394, before they were banned by Emperor Theodosius I as part of a purge of pagan festivals. In 426, Theodosius II decreed that the temples of Olympia be destroyed.

The modern Olympic Games were instituted in 1896 and, other than during WWI and WWII, have been held every four years in different cities around the world ever since. The Olympic flame is lit at the ancient site and carried by runners to the city where the games are held.

Exploring the Site Ancient Olympia is signposted from the modern village. The entrance is beyond the bridge over the River Kladeos (a tributary of the Alfios). Thanks to Theodosius II and various earthquakes, little remains of the magnificent buildings of ancient Olympia, but enough remains to sustain an absorbing visit in an idyllic, leafy setting. The first ruin encountered is the **gymnasium**, which dates from the 2nd century BC. South of here is the partly restored **palaestra**, or wrestling school, where contestants practised and trained. The next building was the **theokoleon** (the priests' house). Behind it was the **workshop** where Pheidias sculpted the gargantuan ivory-and-gold Statue of Zeus, one of the Seven Wonders of the Ancient World. The workshop was identified by archaeologists after the discovery of tools and moulds. Beyond the theokoleon is the **leonidaion**, an elaborate structure which accommodated dignitaries.

The **altis**, or **Sacred Precinct of Zeus**, lies to the left of the path. Its most important building was the immense 5th century Doric **Temple of Zeus** in which stood Pheidias' statue. The 12m-high statue was later removed to Constantinople by Theodosius II, where it was destroyed by a fire in 475 BC. The temple consisted of 13 lateral columns and six at either end. None is still standing.

The **stadium** lies to the east of the altis and is entered through an archway. The start and finish lines of the 120m sprint track and the judges' seats still survive. There are normally plenty of athletic types weaving through the tourists as they time themselves over the distance. The stadium could seat at least 30,000 spectators. Slaves and women spectators had to be content to watch from the Hill of Cronos. South of the stadium was the **hippodrome**, where the chariot contests thrilled the crowds.

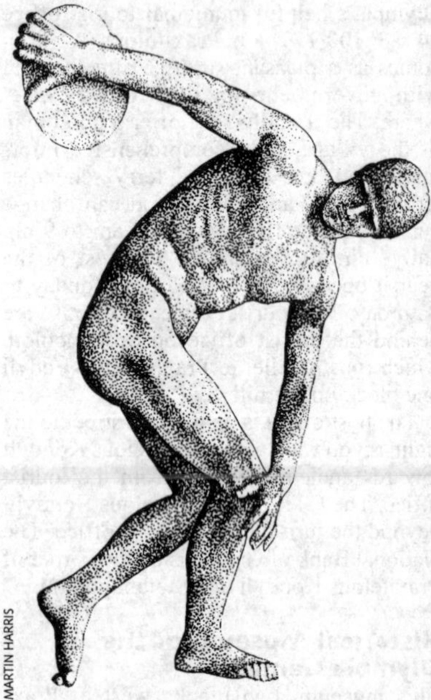

The ancient Greeks used circular stones or plates for discus throwing

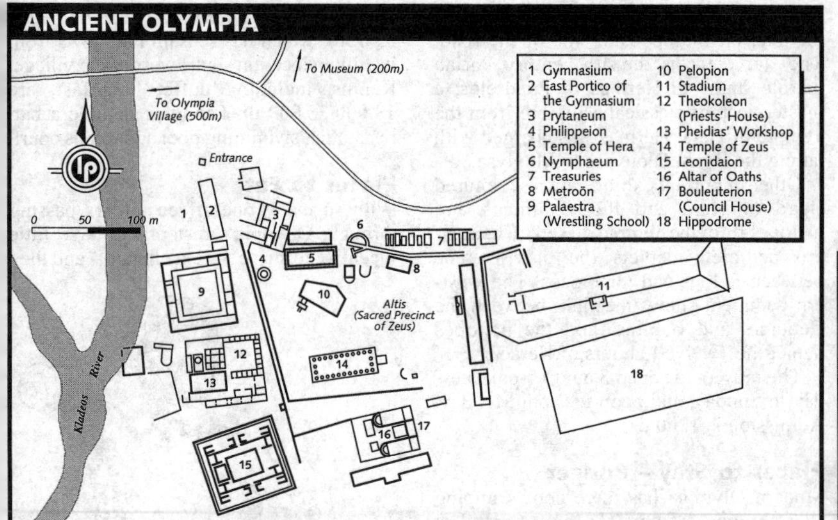

To the north of the Temple of Zeus was the **pelopion**, a small, wooded hillock with an altar to Pelops. It was surrounded by a wall and the remains of its Doric portico can be seen. Many artefacts, now displayed in the museum, were found buried on the hillock.

North is the 6th century Doric **Temple of Hera**, the site's most intact structure. Hera was worshipped along with Rea until the two were superseded by Zeus.

To the east of this temple is the **nymphaeum**, erected by the wealthy Roman banker Herodes Atticus from 156 to 160 AD. Typical of buildings financed by Roman benefactors, it was grandiose, consisting of a semicircular building with Doric columns flanked at each side by a circular temple. The building contained statues of Herodes Atticus and his family. Despite its elaborate appearance, the nymphaeum had a practical purpose: it was a fountain house supplying Olympia with fresh spring water.

From the nymphaeum, a row of 12 **treasuries** stretched to the stadium. These looked like miniature temples. Each was erected by a city-state for use as a storehouse. These buildings marked the northern boundaries of the altis. The remains are reached by ascending a flight of stone steps.

At the bottom of these steps are the scant remains of the 5th century BC **metroön**, a temple dedicated to Rea, the mother of the gods. Apparently the ancients worshipped Rea in this temple with orgies.

To the west of the Temple of Hera are the foundations of the **philippeion**, a circular construction with Ionic columns built by Philip of Macedon to commemorate the Battle of Khaironeia (338 BC), where he defeated a combined army of Athenians and Thebans. The building contained statues of Philip and his family.

North of the philippeion was the **prytaneum**, the magistrate's residence. Here, winning athletes were entertained and feasted.

South of the Temple of Zeus is the **bouleuterion** (council house), where competitors swore to obey the rules decreed by the Olympic Senate.

Museum The museum is 200m north of the site, on the opposite side of the road. The star piece is the 4th century Parian marble statue of **Hermes of Praxiteles**, a masterpiece of classical sculpture from the Temple of Hera. Hermes was charged with taking the infant Dionysos to Mt Nysa.

Other important exhibits are a sculptured **Head of Hera** and the pediments and metopes from the Temple of Zeus. The eastern pediment depicts the chariot race between Pelops and Oinomaos. The western pediment shows the fight between the Centaurs and Lapiths, and the metopes depict the Twelve Labours of Heracles.

The museum is open 8 am to 7 pm Tuesday to Sunday, and noon to 7 pm Monday. Admission is 1200 dr.

Places to Stay – Budget

Modern Olympia has three good camping sites to choose from. The most central is ***Camping Diana*** *(☎ 22 314)*, 250m west of the village. A sign by the National Bank of Greece points the way. ***Camping Olympia*** *(☎ 22 745)* is opposite the BP service station 1km north of town on the road to Pyrgos, and ***Camping Alphios*** *(☎ 22 951)* shares a million-dollar view with the neighbouring Hotel Europa in the hills 1km south-west of town. Camping Alphios is open only from April to the end of October; the others are open all year. All have swimming pools.

The ***Youth Hostel*** *(☎ 22 580, Praxitelous Kondyli 18)* has dorm beds for 1700 dr, including free hot showers and no curfew. Breakfast is available for 600 dr.

Pension Achilleys *(☎ 22 562, Stefanopoulou 4)* has singles/doubles for 4000/7000 dr. The pension is just uphill from the National Bank of Greece. Farther up the hill is ***Pension Posidon*** *(☎ 22 567, Stefanopoulou 9)*, offering spotless rooms for 6000/7500 dr.

Place to Stay – Top End

Olympia's collection of mid-range hotels are invariably block-booked by tour groups. If you want a bit of style, the place to go is the excellent A class ***Best Western Hotel Europa International*** *(☎ 22 650, fax 23 166)*, which has sensational views from its hilltop location south-west of the village. Rooms, including buffet breakfast, are 18,000/28,000 dr. Facilities include a bar, restaurant, swimming pool and tennis court.

Places to Eat

With so many one-off customers passing through, Olympia's restaurants have little incentive to strive for excellence – and they

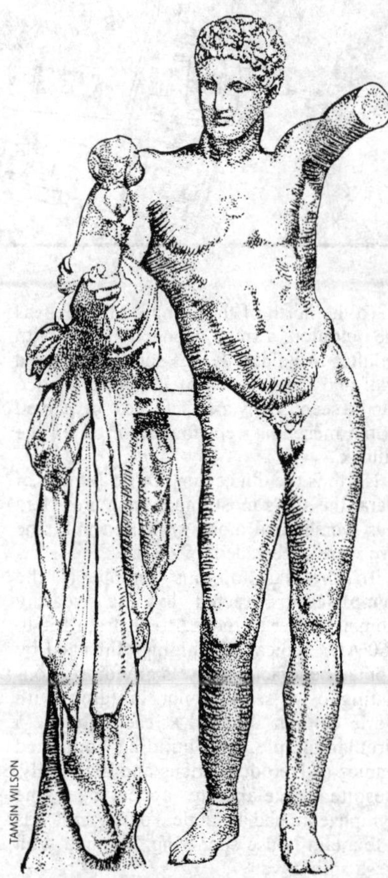

The 4th century BC statue *Hermes of Praxiteles* resides in the museum at Olympia

don't. One exception is ***Fast Food Vassilakis***, a popular psistaria on the corner of Spiliopoulou and Karamanli. It has a range of grilled meats for 1500 dr, pizzas from 1100 dr and pasta from 1000 dr.

Travellers have recommended ***Taverna O Kladeos***, signposted beyond the train station on Douka. It was closed at the time of research, but it's got a great setting overlooking the Kladeos River.

Self-caterers will find ***supermarkets*** along Praxitelous Kondyli.

Entertainment

The ***Touris Club*** puts on displays of folk dancing for tour groups every evening at 9.30 pm between February and October. Admission is 4000 dr. Individual travellers don't fit in very well with the policy of providing one free bottle of cheap plonk and a bowl of peanuts for every four people.

Getting There & Away

There are four buses daily to Athens (5½ hours, 5650 dr), via Pyrgos and the coast, as well as numerous services to Pyrgos (30 minutes, 400 dr). Three buses daily also go east to Tripolis (3½ hours, 2350 dr).

There are five trains daily to Pyrgos (36 minutes, 210 dr).

KYLLINI Κυλλήνη

The tiny port of Kyllini (kih-**lee**-nih), 78km south-west of Patras, warrants a mention only as the jumping-off point for ferries to Kefallonia and Zakynthos. Most people pass through Kyllini on buses from Patras that board the ferries. If you get stuck in Kyllini, the tourist/port police (☎ 0623-92 211) at the quay can suggest accommodation.

Stretching south from Kyllini is a succession of excellent beaches.

Getting There & Away

Bus There are between three and seven buses daily to Kyllini (1¼ hours, 1500 dr) from the Zakynthos bus station in Patras, as well as at least three buses daily from Pyrgos (50 minutes, 1050 dr).

Ferry There are boats to Zakynthos (1½ hours, 1160 dr, up to five daily), Poros (1¼ hours, 1620 dr, four daily) and Argostoli (2¼ hours, 2310 dr, two daily) on Kefallonia.

HLEMOUTSI CASTLE

The castle is 6km south of Kyllini near the appropriately named village of Kastro. It stands on the only hill for miles, and dominates the surrounding agricultural plain.

Hlemoutsi was built by the Franks in 1223 AD. Destroyed in 1430, it was later rebuilt by the Turks to withstand artillery fire.

The castle's battlement walls, hexagonal keep, vaulted galleries and rock location make it one of Morea's most impressive medieval constructions, with a round tower by the entry gate and a western bastion dating from its Turkish period.

The castle can be reached in a roundabout way from **Gastouni**, but it's easier to visit direct from Kyllini.

Central Greece Κεντρική Ελλάδα

Steeped in history, central Greece is a land of contrasts. From the rugged mountains of the South Pindos to densely populated Attica, from the sleepy wetlands of the south-west to the verdant Pelion, central Greece covers a wide range of varied landscapes and two major regions: Thessaly and Sterea Ellada.

Three major attractions draw travellers to this ancient land – the oracle of Delphi, the amazing rock forest of Meteora and its monasteries, and the lush Pelion Peninsula with its traditional stone houses.

HIGHLIGHTS

- The spectacular rock-pillar monasteries of Meteora
- The ancient oracle of Delphi and Sanctuary of Apollo
- The lush, green mountain villages of the Pelion Peninsula
- The superb Byzantine monastery of Osiou Louka

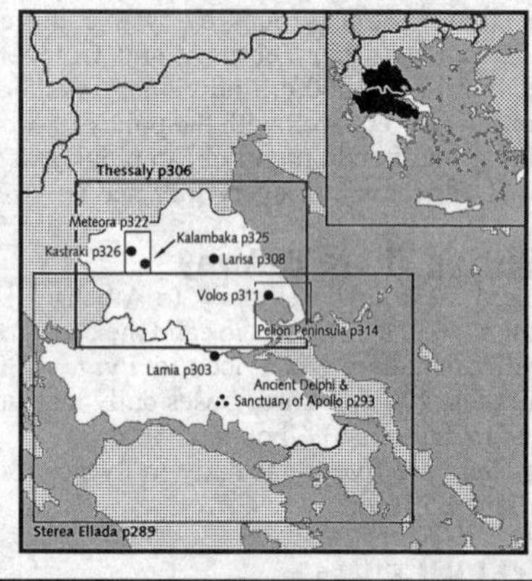

Sterea Ellada Στερεά Ελλάδα

Sterea Ellada is bordered by Thessaly and Epiros to the north and the narrow gulfs of Corinth and Patras in the south. The region acquired the name Sterea Ellada (mainland Greece) in 1827, because it was the only continental portion of the newly formed Greek state – the Peloponnese was classed as an island. To the west is the prefecture of Etolo-Akarnania where England's most famous philhellene bard, Lord Byron, died at Messolongi while assisting in the Greek War of Independence.

To the east is the large island of Evia, which is separated from the mainland by a narrow gulf, and is a jumping-off point for the Sporades islands. Evia is covered in the Sporades chapter.

ATHENS TO THIVA

If you intend travelling from Athens to Delphi you have a choice of two routes: the main highway or the old mountain road to Thiva; the latter is a turn inland just west of Elefsina (Eleusis), and buses run twice daily along this route. Along the way you can take a turn-off left to the well preserved 4th century BC **Fortress of Aigosthena**, and have a swim at nearby **Porto Germeno**, a low-key resort on the north coast of the Gulf of Corinth. There is no public transport to Port Germeno.

Back on the Thiva road, 2km beyond the turn-off for the Fortress of Aigosthena, you will see the less impressive **Fortress of Eleutherai** to the right, standing at the entrance to the pass over Mt Kythairon. According to mythology, baby Oedipus was left to perish on this mountain.

If you are a battle buff you may like to make the 5km detour to the remains of **Plataea**, which once overlooked the plain where the famous Battle of Plataea (479 BC) took place. The ruins are reached by turning left at Erythres.

DIANA MAYFIELD

/hat's for lunch? Cafe menu, Loutro, Crete

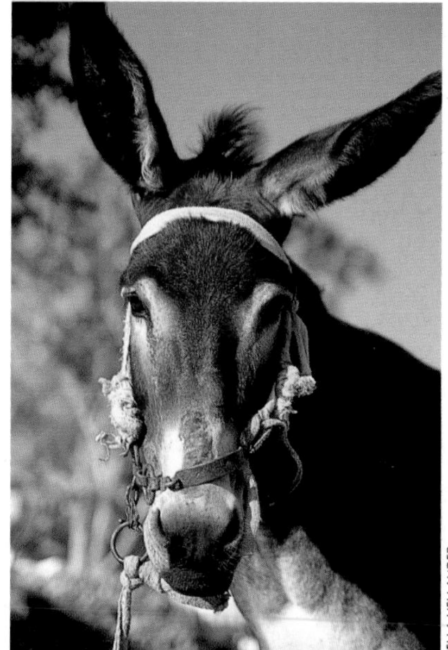

STELLA HELLANDER

A friendly local, Patmos (Dodecanese)

MARK DAFFEY

llen columns, Temple of Zeus, Ancient Olympia

PAUL HELLANDER

Time out; Mesahti Beach, Ikaria (Ionian Islands)

ROD HYETT

A quiet word, Hydra (Saronic Gulf)

DIANA MAYFIELD

Decorative wedding bread, Hania, Crete

CHRIS MELLOR

Athens' outdoor cafes and restaurants line the squares and streets.

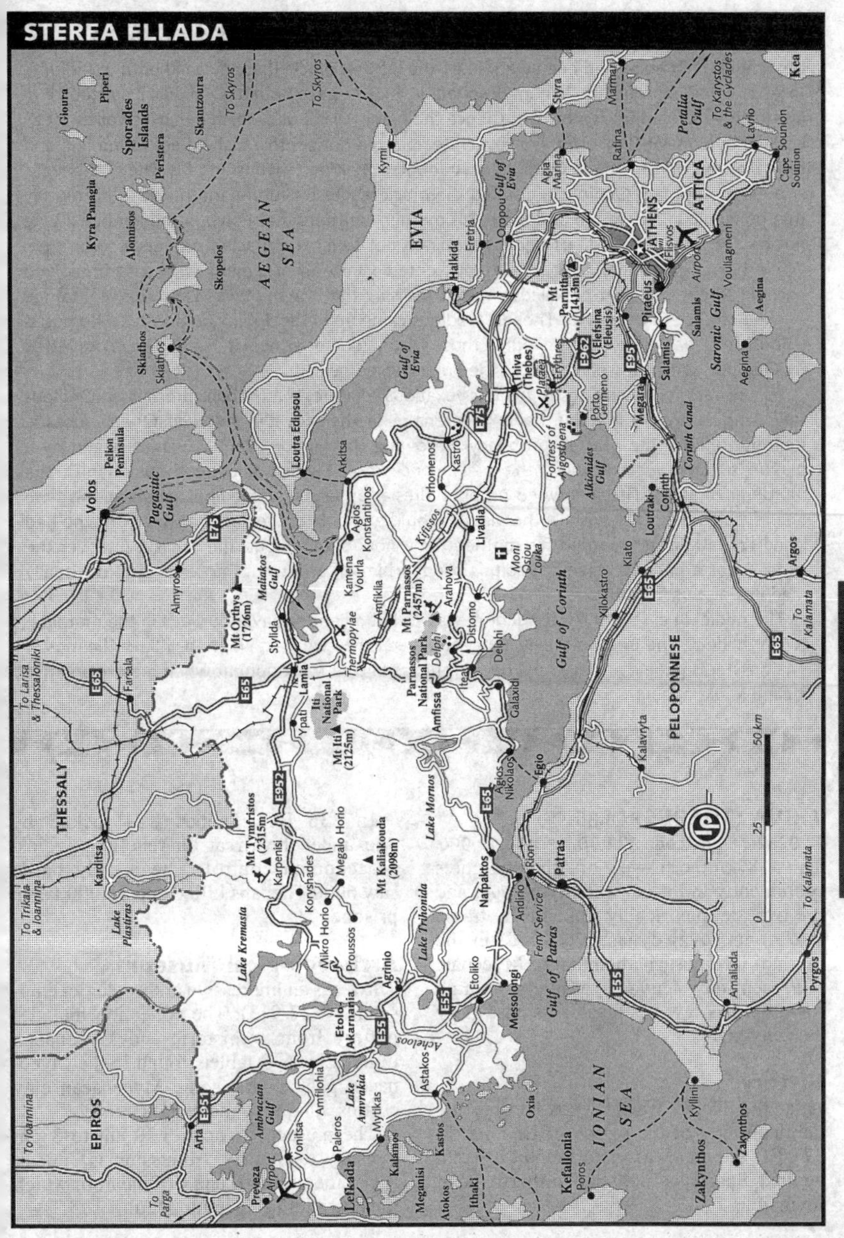

CENTRAL GREECE

Oedipus Rex

Laius, ruler of Thebes, had been warned by the Delphic oracle that any child born to his wife, Jocasta, would murder him. When, despite this, Jocasta gave birth to Oedipus, Laius took him away, drove a nail through his feet (hence the name 'Oedipus', which means 'swollen foot') and left him on Mt Cithaeron. However, Oedipus did not perish – a shepherd found him and took him to Corinth, where Oedipus was adopted by King Polybus and his wife, Periboea.

As a young man, Oedipus consulted the oracle about his future and heard to his dismay that he would kill his father and marry his mother. Unaware that Polybus and Periboea were not his real parents, Oedipus fled, determined not to let the oracle's prophecy come true. While heading towards Thebes, Oedipus entered into an argument with a stranger and became so enraged that he killed him, not realising that the man was Laius, his real father. At the entrance to the city of Thebes, Oedipus came upon the Sphinx, a monster who posed a riddle to all passers-by and devoured those who could not answer it. Having been outwitted by Oedipus, who guessed correctly, the Sphinx killed herself.

As a reward for having destroyed this vexatious creature, the Thebans proclaimed Oedipus their king and gave him the hand in marriage of the recently widowed Queen Jocasta, thereby fulfilling the oracle's prophecy. Following their union, Thebes was besieged by a plague so Oedipus consulted the oracle once more, which said he should banish the murderer of Laius. The renowned prophet Tiresias appeared at Oedipus' court at this time and revealed the gods' wishes: the plague would end only at the death of the man who had killed his father and married his mother. Only now did Oedipus and Jocasta discover the truth. Jocasta hanged herself; Oedipus blinded himself and went into exile and eventually died in Colonus in Attica.

The riddle, in case you're wondering, was 'What creatures have four legs in the morning, two at midday, and three in the evening, and are at their weakest when they have the most?' The answer is people – they crawl on all fours as babies, walk upright when mature and use a cane in old age.

THIVA (THEBES) Θήβα

☎ 0262 • postcode 322 00 • pop 19,000

Thiva, 87km north-west of Athens, figures prominently in history and mythology, and the two are inextricably linked. The tragic fate of its royal dynasty, centred on the myth of Oedipus, rivalled that of Mycenae.

Present-day Thiva is a lively enough town but has few vestiges of its past glory as a city-state.

History

After the Trojan War, Thebes became the dominant city of the region of Boeotia. In 371 BC the city was victorious in a battle against Sparta, which had hitherto been invincible.

In 336 BC, Thebes was sacked by Alexander the Great for rebelling against Macedonian control. The bloody battle saw 6000 Thebans killed and 30,000 taken prisoner.

Archaeological Museum

Thiva has an impressive archaeological museum (☎ 27 913). The collection includes pottery from prehistoric and Mycenaean times, Linear B tablets found in the Mycenaean palaces and some Mycenaean clay coffins, unique to mainland Greece.

The museum is open 8.30 am to 3 pm Tuesday to Sunday. Admission is 500 dr. It's at the northern end of Pindarou, which runs parallel to Epaminondou.

There are many restaurants and cafes lining Delphon. ***To Agnantio***, next to the town hall, is one of the best and has good views. ***I Liakoura***, on Plateia Xenias specialises in soups and other local dishes. The larger ***Restaurant Parnassos***, nearby, serves tasty grills.

Getting There & Away

The five buses daily which run between Athens and Delphi stop at Arahova. In addition there are some local buses to Delphi (20 minutes, 230 dr). A taxi from Arahova to Delphi will cost 2000 dr.

AROUND ARAHOVA

Moni Osiou Louka

Μονή Οσίου Λουκά

The Moni Osiou Louka (Monastery of St Luke Stiris) is 8km east of the village of Distomo, which lies just south of the Athens-Delphi road. Its principal church contains some of Greece's finest Byzantine frescoes.

The monastery is dedicated to a local hermit who was canonised for his healing and prophetic powers. The monastic complex includes two churches. The interior of **Agios Loukas**, the main one, is a glorious symphony of marble and mosaics. There are also icons by Michael Damaskinos, the 16th century Cretan painter.

In the main body of the church the light is partially blocked by the ornate marble window decorations. This creates striking contrasts of light and shade, which greatly enhance the atmosphere. The crypt where St Luke is buried also contains fine frescoes. Bring a torch, since there is little lighting.

The other church, **Theotokos** (Church of St Mary), built in the 10th century, has a less impressive interior.

Listed as a World Heritage Site, the monastery is in an idyllic setting, with breathtaking vistas from its leafy terrace. There is a small cafe in the monastery grounds. The monastery is open 8 am to 7 pm daily but closes from 2 to 4 pm, May to September. Admission is 800 dr, and modest dress is required (no shorts).

Distomo Διίστομο

☎ 0267 • postcode 320 05 • pop 2156

The only thing worth seeking out in Distomo is the **war memorial** which commemorates the slaying of over 200 Distomo villagers by the Nazis in 1944 in reprisal for a guerrilla attack. The large, white marble slab on the memorial wall with an inscription in both Greek and German is an official German government apology for the atrocity. Look for the 'mausoleum' sign.

Places to Stay Moni Osiou Louka is a hassle to get to by public transport, so if you get stuck, Distomo has two hotels: the D class ***Hotel America*** *(☎ 22 079, I Kastriti 1)* where singles/doubles are 4600/8000 dr with bathroom, and the D class ***Hotel Koutriaris*** *(☎ 22 268, Plateia Ethnikis Antistasis 6)*, with rooms for 7500/9700 dr.

Getting There & Away You can take the Delphi bus from Athens and ask the driver to stop at the turn-off for Distomo, from where you should be able to flag down a taxi for the 12km to the monastery (2000 dr). Otherwise it's a 3km walk to the taxi stand at Distomo. From Livadia there are 11 buses daily to Distomo (45 minutes, 750 dr) and one to the monastery at 1 pm (one hour, 1000 dr). There are hourly buses to Athens from Livadia (two hours, 2350 dr).

GALAXIDI Γαλαξίδι

☎ 0265 • postcode 330 52 • pop 1200

With its mountain backdrop, Galaxidi is the prettiest of a string of low key resorts along the north coast of the Gulf of Corinth. If you have your own transport it makes a pleasant base from which to visit Delphi.

Galaxidi's most prosperous period was between 1830 and 1910 when it was a major caïque-building centre. Some fine stone mansions survive from this time.

Galaxidi is more popular as a holiday destination with Greeks than with foreign tourists. At weekends and in high season its narrow streets become choked with car loads of Athenians, but at other times it's fairly tranquil.

Orientation & Information

The approach road to Galaxidi is Nikolaos Giorgiori which is dissected by the main street of Nikolou Mama; turn left here to reach the central square of Plateia Iroon Manoisakia, or right for the waterfront of the larger of Galaxidi's two harbours – the smaller harbour is farther around. The post office is on Nikolou Mama; there is no OTE but there are several cardphones.

A forested headland, opposite the main waterfront, is fringed by a series of pebbled coves.

Things to See

Galaxidi's **naval museum** houses models of ships, marine paintings and paraphernalia from the War of Independence. Opening times are 9.30 am to 1 pm Monday to Friday and 9.30 am to 2 pm Saturday and Sunday. Admission is 500 dr. The **ethnographical museum** has displays of embroidery and costumes and is open 9.30 am to 1.30 pm daily. Admission is 500 dr.

The wood-carved iconostasis in the **Church of Agios Nicholaos** is one of Greece's finest. Signs point to the museums and church from the central square.

The charming little 13th century **Moni Metamorfosis** stands amid olive groves and cypresses, 7km inland from Galaxidi. To reach it go under the flyover and take the road opposite, called Ieromonahoi Eithimioi. The monastery's lone nun may show you around.

Places to Stay

Apart from weekends and in high season, finding accommodation in Galaxidi is fairly easy. All Galaxidi's hotels offer discounts out of high season. Most accommodation is on the large harbour. ***Katherine Theodoroulou Domatia*** (*☎ 42 430*) has nicely furnished singles/doubles with bathroom for 7000/10,000 dr. There is a well equipped communal kitchen. Inquire at To Steki Restaurant on the waterfront.

Pension Votsalo (*☎ 41 788*), on the small harbour, has doubles with bathroom for 12,000 dr. The well maintained ***Filoxenia Studios*** (*☎ 42 230*), just off Nikolaos Giorgiori, has rooms for 10,000/13,000 dr. ***Hotel Koukonas*** (*☎ 41 179*) has clean, simply furnished rooms with bathroom for 11,000/15,000 dr. To reach the hotel walk down Agiou Mamas and turn right onto Georgiou Kouparoili.

Galaxidi Hotel (*☎ 41 850, fax 41 026*) has attractively furnished rooms for 12,000/18,000 dr. Turn right onto the waterfront from Agiou Mamas to reach the hotel. ***Hotel Argo*** (*☎ 41 996, fax 41 878*) on the small harbour has immaculate rooms with pretty pastel decor for 15,000/20,000 dr. The rooms at both these places have air-con, TV and refrigerator.

Places to Eat

One of the nicest tavernas is the modest little ***Albatross***, near the Church of Agios Nicholaos, which serves tasty, low-priced food – look for the signpost on Agiou Mamas. ***Dervenis Taverna***, on Nikolaos Giorgiori, is also good value and has a pleasant bamboo-shaded terrace.

Down on the waterfront, ***To Steki Restaurant*** and ***To Porto***, along with others, specialise in seafood. Farther along, the ***OK Café*** is popular with locals. Look out for the amiable Captain Morgan, the owner's collie.

At ***Liotrivi Ouzeri***, the small harbour's only eatery, snacks and drinks are served in a lovely stone-walled interior with two traditional olive presses.

Getting There & Away

The bus station is on Plateia Iroon Manoisakia. There are at least three buses to Patras and Athens. Travelling to Athens you may have to change buses at Itea. You can also take the Thessaloniki bus from Agrino (2700 dr). This bus will drop you off on the highway from where it's a short walk to Galaxidi.

AROUND GALAXIDI

From the market town of **Itea**, 19km northeast of Galaxidi and 10km from Delphi, a road branches left for 2km to **Kira**. This was ancient Kirrha, the port of Delphi, which was destroyed by the Amphyctionic Council in the First Sacred War (595-586 BC). Kira has a good beach and two camp sites, ***Kaparelis Camping*** *(☎ 0265-32 330)* and ***Ayannis Camping*** *(☎ 0265-32 555)*.

West of Galaxidi the coastal highway passes a number of seaside towns and villages before meeting the important ferryboat link at **Andirio**. Boats here run every 15 minutes between 6.45 am and 10.45 pm to Rion. **Nafpaktos**, 9km east of Andirio, has an attractive harbour, a good beach and a well preserved Venetian castle. Nafpaktos was known as Lepanto in medieval times and it was here in 1571 that the famous naval battle of Lepanto took place.

Between Nafpaktos and Andirio there are several hotels as well as two camp sites; ***Platanitis Beach*** *(☎ 0634-31 555)* and ***Dounis Beach*** *(☎ 0634-31 565)*. There is another camp site, ***Doric Camping*** *(☎ 0266-31 722)*, farther east along the coast at **Agios Nikolaos**.

Getting There & Away

The Delphi-Patras bus goes along this stretch of coast. There are five buses daily from Itea to Nafpaktos and vice versa, stopping at the coastal towns along the way, and six buses daily from Delphi to Itea and vice versa. The ferry between Egio and Agios Nikolaos runs five times daily in high season and three times daily at other times.

MESSOLONGI Μεσολόγγι

☎ 0631 • postcode 302 00 • pop 10,916

Most people come to Messolongi for historical or sentimental reasons, rather than to seek a lively holiday spot. Its location is rather melancholy, as it lies between the outlets of the rivers Aheloös and Evinos, on the shores of a bleak lagoon. It is Messolongi's connection with the War of Independence and the role played by Britain's philhellene bard Lord Byron that gives the town its historic reputation.

History

During the War of Independence, the strategically important town of Messolongi was chosen by the Phanariot Mavrordatos to be the western centre of resistance, in order to inhibit Turkish communications with the Peloponnese. Lord Byron arrived in Messolongi in 1824, already a famous international philhellene, with the intention of lending his weight, reputation and money to the independence cause. After months of vainly attempting to organise the motley Greek forces, who spent much time squabbling among themselves, Byron's efforts came to naught. He contracted a fever, no doubt hastened on by the unsanitary conditions of what was, at the time, a miserable outpost, and died, his immediate aims unfulfilled, on 19 April 1824.

Ironically, Byron's death spurred on internationalist forces to precipitate the end of the War of Independence and he became a Greek national hero. One hundred years after his death, many male children, now in their seventies, were christened with the name Byron (Vyronas in Greek), and most Greek towns have a street named after him.

Messolongi was captured by the Turks in April 1826, after their year-long siege of the city drove 9000 men, women and children to escape on the night of 22-23 April 1826 through what is now called the Gate of Exodus. Most took refuge on Mt Zygos, only to be caught and killed by a nearby Albanian mercenary force. This self-sacrificial exodus is recognised as one of the most heroic deeds of the war and was immortalised in Dionysios Solomos' epic poem *I Eleftheri Poliorkimeni* (The Free Besieged).

Orientation & Information

Messolongi is the capital of the prefecture of Etolo-Akarnania. The town is laid out in a roughly rectangular grid and the two main streets, running more or less parallel along its length, are Eleftheron Poliorkimenon and Spyrou Moustakli. Both bring you to the main square, Plateia Markou Botsari. The OTE and post office are both near the square.

Things to See

All arrivals to Messolongi enter via the aforementioned **Gate of Exodus**. The gate is narrow and dangerous for traffic, so beware if you are entering by car.

Just beyond the gate, to the right, is the **Garden of the Heroes**, translated incorrectly as Heroes' Tombs on the road sign. This memorial garden was established on the orders of the then governor of Greece, Yiannis Kapodistrias, who in May 1829 issued the following decree:

> … within these walls of the city of Messolongi lie the bones of those brave men, who fell bravely while defending the city … it is our duty to gather together, with reverence, the holy remains of these men and to lay them to rest in a memorial where our country may, each year, repay its debt of gratitude.

You will find the Greek text of this decree on the marble slab to the right as you enter the garden. Within the leafy grounds of the garden you will find memorials to many other philhellenes as well. Beneath the statue of **Lord Byron**, which features prominently in the garden, is buried the heart of the poet. A much larger and more modern bronze statue of Byron outside the garden now overshadows the smaller sculpted one inside. The garden is open 9 am to 8 pm (it closes earlier in winter).

On the main square and housed in the town hall is a **museum** dedicated to the revolution. There is also a collection of Byron memorabilia. Bone up on your War of Independence history beforehand in order to get a full feel for the importance of these historic events. Museum opening times are 9 am to 1.30 pm and 4 to 8 pm in summer (mornings only in winter). Entry is free.

Places to Stay & Eat

There isn't a huge choice of hotels here. The D class ***Avra*** *(☎ 22 284, Harilaou Trikoupi 5)*, close to the central square, has singles/doubles for 8000/10,000 dr. The B class ***Theoxenia*** *(☎ 22 683, fax 22 230)*, out of town by the lagoon, has rates in the 10,000/13,000 dr price bracket. The B class ***Liberty*** *(☎ 24 831, fax 24 832)*, close to the Garden of the Heroes, has rates of 13,000/17,000 dr.

Most eateries are on Harilaou Trikoupi and Athanasiou Razikotsika close to the main square.

Getting There & Away

The bus station is on Mavrokordatou 5. This street forms one side of the main square. From here buses go to Athens, Patras and most destinations north, though you may need to change at Agrinio.

SOUTH-WEST COASTAL RESORTS

Amfilohia Αμφιλοχία

This attractive little place at the south-eastern corner of the Gulf of Ambracia attracts a small holiday crowd. Most visitors are merely passing through, since it is on the main highway between Epiros and the south. It is a lively town and is an amenable enough stopover point. Swimming is touch and go, despite the town touting an official beach, as the water is stagnant. You might want to try a bit farther north up the gulf towards Menidi. There is a long, curving promenade with many restaurants and cafes to relax in. If you are here in August or September, look out for the strange luminescence of the water at night.

There are five hotels to choose from, of which ***Oscar*** *(0642-22 155, fax 22 867)* is probably the pick; singles/doubles here are 11,000/12,000 dr. There is also a small camp site, ***Stratis Beach Park***, at Katafourko Beach, north of Amfilohia.

Vonitsa Βόνιτσα

The town of Vonitsa is popular with local holiday-makers, but doesn't have any real beach scene to speak of, since it is on the still waters of the Gulf of Ambracia. It is quiet and pleasant, and conveniently located for the town of Preveza and the Aktio airport. Its waterfront is being developed and there are a number of modern cafes and restaurants. The route through Vonitsa from Preveza is a quicker way through to the main north-south highway to the Peloponnese. There is one D class and four C class hotels to choose from.

Mytikas Μύτικας

The small village of Mytikas is built on the gulf of the same name. This place has yet to feel the effect of mass tourism. It's an oddly pleasant kind of place, though, with its palm trees and houses built right up to the water's edge. The beach is pebbly and uncommercialised, but is being gradually developed. There are only a couple of hotels, a few domatia and a scattering of tavernas. You can take a local caïque to the isolated islands of Kalamos, looming over Mytikas, or Kastos tucked away on the other side.

Astakos Αστακός

Slightly more upmarket and bigger than Mytikas, Astakos is another place for a quiet holiday, though it lacks Mytikas' cosiness. It can be used as a more convenient stepping stone for access to the Ionian Islands, via the daily ferry to and from Ithaki in summer. There is one C class establishment, ***Hotel Stratos*** *(☎ 0646-41 096)*, and some ***domatia*** in summer.

Getting There & Away

Public transport to these locations is by bus from either Agrinio or Vonitsa.

KARPENISI Καρπενήσι

☎ 0237 • postcode 361 00 • pop 10,000

Karpenisi (altitude 960m) is in the foothills of Mt Tymfristos (2315m), 82km west of Lamia. The town itself is not especially attractive but lies in a beautiful, well wooded region the EOT brochures tout as the 'Switzerland of Greece'. There are many opportunities for trekking and, if you have your own transport, you can explore some delightful mountain villages. Karpenisi sees tourists all year round and the skiing centre, 17km away, is popular with Greeks in winter.

Orientation & Information

The central square is in the north-west of the town. The thoroughfares of Zinopoulou, Athanasion Karpenisidi and Spyridon Georgiou Tsitsara run downhill from this square and Ethnikis Antistaseos runs north-west from it. Karpenisi's tourist office (☎/fax 21 016) is on the central square – look for the folksy sign in Greek. The friendly English-speaking staff can help you find accommodation and inform you on the adventure sports popular in the area. It's open 10 am to 2 pm and 5 to 9 pm daily.

The Commercial Bank at Athanasou Karpenisidi 24 has an ATM. The post office is on Agiou Nikolaou Kaprienisiotou. To get there walk 150m down Athanasou Karpenisidi and turn left. The OTE is just off the central square on Ethnikis Antistaseos.

Activities

If you are keen to participate in some kind of organised adventure sport activity, contact Trekking Hellas (☎/fax 25 940, mobile 094 206 308) at Spyridon Georgiou Tsitsara 3. It organises group activities in trekking, kayaking, canyoning and rafting.

Places to Stay

The most convenient option if you arrive by bus are the ***domatia*** of Konstantinos Koutsikos *(☎ 21 400)*. His domatia are high up (51 steps) overlooking the main square, close to the bus station. Beautiful singles/doubles go for 8000/10,000 dr with bathroom.

The C class ***Hotel Galini*** *(☎ 22 914, fax 25 623, Riga Fereou 3)* has rooms with bathroom for 8000/14,000 dr. To reach the hotel, walk down Spyridon Georgiou Tsitsara and take the first right. The C class ***Hotel Helvetia*** *(☎ 22 465, Zinopoulou 33)* has very comfortable rooms for 15,000/17,000 dr.

The beautifully renovated B class but expensive ***Anesis Hotel*** *(☎ 22 840, fax 22 305, Zinopoulou 50)* has rates of 25,000/30,000 dr including breakfast. The luxurious ***Hotel Montana*** *(☎ 80 400, fax 80 409)*, 1.5km from Karpenisi on the road to the ski centre, has indoor and outdoor swimming pools, tennis courts and a gym. The rates are 28,000/37,000 dr.

The Mt Tymfristos refuge of ***Takis Flengas*** *(☎ 22 002)*, at 1840m, can be reached along a 12km road from Karpenisi, or is a 2½ hour walk along a path. To stay there, contact the Karpenisi EOS (☎ 23 506), Spyridon Georgiou Tsitsara 2.

Places to Eat

The cheapest eatery in Karpenisi is the American-style ***Three Stars Restaurant*** *(Athanasiou Karpenisioti 35)*, where a meal costs less than 2000 dr – choose from pasta dishes, pizzas or grills. ***Restaurant Triandafylli***, opposite the OTE, is also good value, offering a range of casserole dishes. The English and Italian-speaking ***Klimataria*** restaurant *(Kosma Etolou 25)* includes hare in oregano and rooster in red-wine sauce among its specialities and has occasional live music. To get there, walk 50m down Athanasiou Karpenisioti and turn right onto Kosmo Etolou.

Greeks prefer the family ambience of ***Panorama*** with its outdoor eating area – somewhat marred by a ghastly unfinished hotel complex overlooking the garden. It is 100m past Hotel Galini on the right. The homy ***Esy Oti Pis*** *(Apodimon Evritanou 13)* with its folksy wooden sign in Greek is also popular with locals. Walk along Ethnikis Antistaseos, turn left after the police station and it is 50m along on your left.

Entertainment

You might want to try and catch some late-night, authentic live Greek music at ***Mousikes Epafe Club*** *(Kosma Etolou 17)*. It is only open on Friday, Saturday and public holidays, and things don't get going until after midnight.

Getting There & Away

Karpenisi's bus station is just beyond the central square. There are three buses daily to Athens (five hours, 4850 dr) and four to Lamia (1¾ hours, 1400 dr). There are also two buses daily to and from Agrinio in Etolo-Akarnania (3½ hours, 2050 dr). For Mikro and Megalo Horio there are three buses daily (20 minutes, 250 dr) and for Proussos, two weekly on Monday and Friday (45 minutes, 650 dr).

AROUND KARPENISI

From Karpenisi a scenic mountain road leads south for 37km to the village of **Proussos**. Along the way you'll pass several picturesque villages. The charming village of **Koryshades** has well preserved mansions and is 5km south-west of Karpenisi, reached by a right turn-off along the Proussos road. **Mikro Horio** and **Megalo Horio** are 12km farther along the road. Megalo Horio, the more attractive of the two, has many traditional stone houses. One of these is the **folklore museum**. It is open 10.30 am to 3 pm on Friday, Saturday and Sunday, October to May, and 10 am to 3 pm and 6 to 8 pm daily, June to October.

In Megalo Horio you can take a pleasant stroll along the banks of the River Karpenisotis along a footpath which begins opposite the bus terminal.

The **Monastery of the Virgin of Proussiotissa** (☎ 0237-80 705), just before the village of Proussos, has a miracle-working icon. There are more icons, wood-carvings and ecclesiastical ornaments in the monastery's 18th century church. A small number of monks live at the monastery and pilgrims flock there in August for the Feast of the Assumption.

Places to Stay

The D class ***Hotel Antigone*** *(☎ 0237-41 395)*, at Megalo Horio, has single/double rooms with bathroom for 12,000/20,000 dr. Nearby, ***Domatia Agnanti*** *(☎ 0237-41 303)* has immaculate and stylish rooms with bathrooms for 8000/10,000 dr. All the rooms have balconies with stunning views of Mt Kalikouva.

Agathidis Pension *(☎ 0237-80 813)*, at Proussos, has rooms with bathroom for 8000/14,000 dr. The A class ***Pension Dryas*** *(☎ 0237-41 131)*, on the Proussos road near Megalo Horio, has double rooms for 19,000 dr.

KARPENISI TO AGRINIO

Two buses daily ply this tortuous (but sealed) road across the mountains and villages of the Agrafa to Agrinio in Etolo-Akarnania. During the Tourkokratia (the period of Turkish occupation of Greece), the villages of this region were considered too remote to be recorded for taxation purposes, so they were classified as *agrafa* (unrecorded). The bus covers the distance in a slow 3½ hours and it is quite a spectacular drive.

The beauty of this trip is the emptiness of the countryside. The road climbs and twists downwards as far as the first main centre of habitation, the twin villages of **Anatoliki** and **Dytiki Frangista**, just before which is the modern taverna ***Sotira*** with a children's play park and a swimming pool. The road then crosses the long bridge over the artificial Lake Kremasta into Etolo-Akarnania, climbs high over the last ridge and eventually winds down through small farm holdings into Agrinio. If you suffer from motion sickness, think twice before making this trip.

LAMIA Λαμία

☎ 0231 • postcode 351 00 • pop 44,000

Lamia is the capital of the prefecture of Fthiotida and is an attractive town at the western end of the Maliakos Gulf, built in the form of an amphitheatre along the foothills of Mt Orthys. Lamia rarely figures

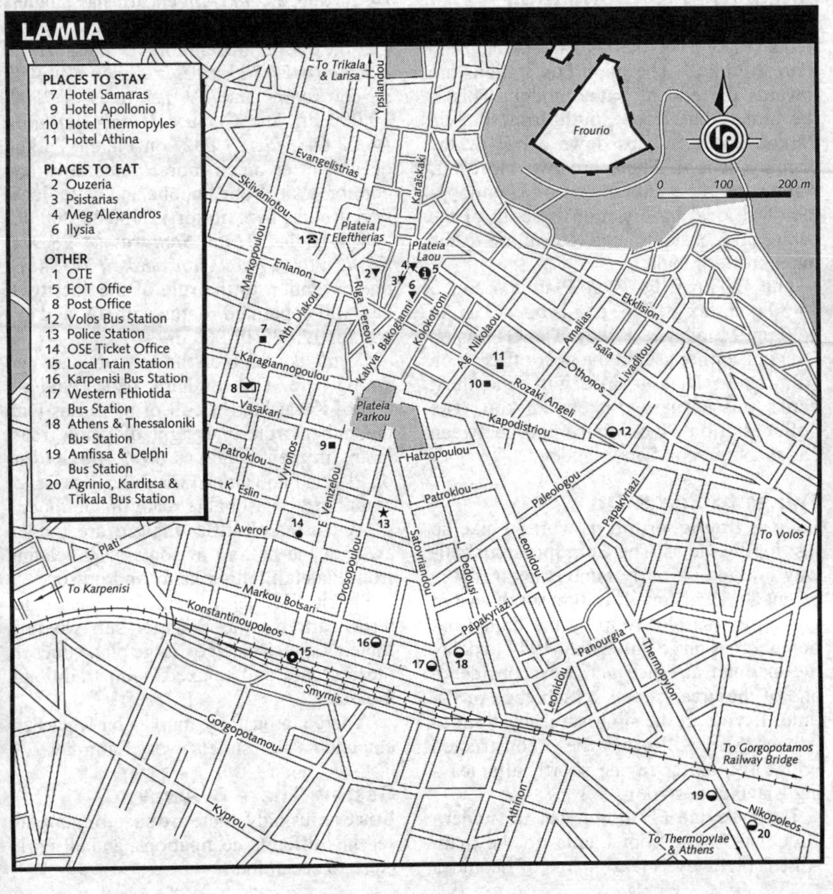

on people's itineraries, but it deserves a look-in. Like most towns that are not dependent on tourism for their livelihood, Lamia is a vibrant and lively place year-round. It is famous for its lamb on the spit, its *kourabiedes* (almond shortcake) and its *xynogala* (sour milk).

To the east of Lamia is the narrow pass of Thermopylae, where, in 480 BC, Leonidas and 300 Spartans managed to temporarily halt the Persian advance of Xerxes and his 30,000-strong army.

Orientation & Information

The main cluster of activity in Lamia is centred on Plateia Eleftherias, Plateia Laou and Plateia Parkou. The main bus stations are towards the end of Satovriandou. This is the street that leads south from Plateia Parkou and then dips down a hill by the primary school. There are two more bus stations on the southern end of Thermopylon. The local train station is south of the centre on Konstantinoupoleos, close to the main bus terminals.

The EOT office is at Plateia Laou 3 (☎ 30 065, fax 30 066) and is open 7 am to 2.30 pm Monday to Friday. The OTE is on Plateia Eleftherias and the post office is on Athanasiou Diakou. You will find most banks on, or near, Plateia Parkou. The police station is on Patroklou, between Drosopoulou and Satovriandou.

Things to See & Do

Lamia's **frourio**, or fort, is worth a hike up just for the views. The **Gorgopotamos railway bridge** is a fairly famous landmark in recent Greek history. It is 7km south-east of Lamia. It was blown up by the united national forces on 25 November 1944 to delay the German advance and was considered one of the greatest acts of sabotage of the time. If you are heading south by train to Athens, you will cross the reconstructed bridge over a deep ravine, shortly after leaving Lianokladi station.

Thermopylae (Thermopyles in modern Greek) is 18km from Lamia on the main Athens highway. A large statue of Leonidas marks the spot where the Persian army was delayed on its way to Thessaly, but where Leonidas and his brave Spartans ultimately perished.

Today the pass is much wider than it was in antiquity because of a gradual silting up of the land on the sea side.

Places to Stay & Eat

The hotel scene in Lamia does not allow for much choice or great quality. Most hotels will offer lower rates than the prices quoted here. The D class ***Hotel Thermopyles*** *(☎ 21 366, Rozaki Angeli 36)* has singles/doubles for 9000/12,000 dr. Directly opposite, the more presentable D class ***Hotel Athina*** *(☎ 27 700, Rozaki Angeli 47)*, with air-con rooms and TV, has rates of 7500/10,000 dr. The C class ***Hotel Apollonio*** *(☎ 22 668, fax 23 032)* on Plateia Parkou doesn't offer much more in facilities and comfort apart from a phone and better location. Rooms here go for 12,000/15,000 dr.

The B class ***Hotel Samaras*** *(☎ 28 971, fax 42 704, Athanasiou Diakou 14)* is the one exception to the rule of mediocrity. It has well appointed rooms with TV and air-con for 12,600/17,000 dr.

If you like lamb on the spit, you can't go wrong here. The southern, pedestrianised, end of Karaïskaki is full of psistarias with the rather grotesque sight of whole roast lambs in their windows. ***Meg Alexandros*** on Plateia Laou and ***Ilysia*** on Kalyva Bakogianni offer reasonable ready-made food.

A cluster of little ***ouzeria*** are hidden away at the bottom of some steps leading from Plateia Eleftherias to Androutsou.

Plateia Eleftherias, with its swish cafeterias, attracts the younger set, whereas Plateia Laou, shaded by large plane trees, is more sedate and relaxed, with traditional ***kafeneia***.

There's a bustling market on Riga Fereou and its side streets every Saturday.

Getting There & Away

Bus Confusingly, there are six terminals, all serving different destinations, and all fairly close to each other.

The terminal for Athens and Thessaloniki buses is on Papakyriazi, which runs off Satovriandou. There are almost hourly buses for Athens (three hours, 3700 dr) and two daily (three on weekends) for Thessaloniki (four hours, 5000 dr). There is a bus for Patras on Friday and Sunday (3½ hours, 4700 dr).

Farther down the hill and on the corner of Konstantinoupoleos is the bus station for western Fthiotida, which includes the village of Ypati in its route.

The terminal for Karpenisi is at Markou Botsari 3. There are four buses daily to Karpenisi (1¾ hours, 1400 dr). There are another two sub-stations on Thermopylon, 100m south of the railway line: one for Agrinio, Karditsa and Trikala (1850 dr) and the other for Amfissa and Delphi. Finally, buses for Volos leave from a small station at the end of Rozaki Angeli.

Train Lamia has a very inconveniently located main train station 7km west of the town centre at Lianokladi. Most intercity trains stop at Lianokladi. Train tickets can be prepurchased from the OSE office at Averof 28. The No 6 bus (to Stavros) links the Lianokladi station with the Lamia town centre and passes the OSE ticket office.

The small train station in town has only two trains daily linking Lamia with Lianokladi from the branch line terminus at Stylida (14km east of Lamia) – hardly a reliable transport option, though the train does go on to Athens.

ITI NATIONAL PARK

If you have the time, an exploration of the area west of the city of Lamia is worthwhile. The attractive village of **Ypati**, 25km past Lamia and 8km south of the Karpenisi-Lamia road, has the remains of a fortress and is the starting point for treks on Mt Iti (2152m).

This mountain is the focus of the Iti National Park. It's a verdant region with forests of fir and black pine. According to mythology, Mt Iti was the place where the dying Hercules built his own funeral pyre and was burned to death. While the mortal elements in Hercules perished, the immortal Hercules joined his divine peers on Mt Olympus.

From Ypati it's a four hour walk along a marked path to the mountain's ***Trapeza Refuge*** (1850m). For information about this refuge contact the Lamia EOS (☎ 0231-26 786), Ipsilandou 20, Lamia.

Ypati has two hotels. The D class ***Hotel Panellinion*** *(☎ 0231-98 340)* is open in July and August only and has rooms for 4500/6500 dr. The D class ***Hotel Panorama*** *(☎ 0231-98 222)* has rooms for 4500/5500 dr, and doubles with bathroom for 6000 dr. This hotel operates from April to October only. Ypati is served by frequent buses from Lamia.

From the Ypati turn-off the road is relatively flat and runs along the valley of the River Sperhios. After Makri, the road begins to climb through forested hills and really climbs at the village of Tymfristos, winding slowly upwards to a pass at the summit of which you enter the prefecture of Evrytania. This road gets quite a bit of snow in winter. A new road then winds down fairly quickly to Karpenisi, bypassing the village of Agios Nikolaos.

AGIOS KONSTANTINOS

Αγιος Κωνσταντίνος

☎ 0235 • postcode 350 06 • pop 2360

Agios Konstantinos, on the main Athens-Thessaloniki route, is one of the three mainland ports that serve the Sporades islands (the others are Thessaloniki and Volos).

With judicious use of buses from Athens to the port, you will probably not need to stay overnight before catching a Sporades-bound ferry or hydrofoil. If you get stuck try ***Hotel Poulia*** *(☎ 31 663)* with rates of 6000/8000 dr for singles/doubles. A more comfortable option is the A class ***Motel Levendi*** *(☎ 32 251, fax 32 255)* where rates are 16,000/20,000 dr.

Getting There & Away

Bus Buses depart hourly for Agios Konstantinos from Athens Terminal B bus station (2½ hours, 3000 dr).

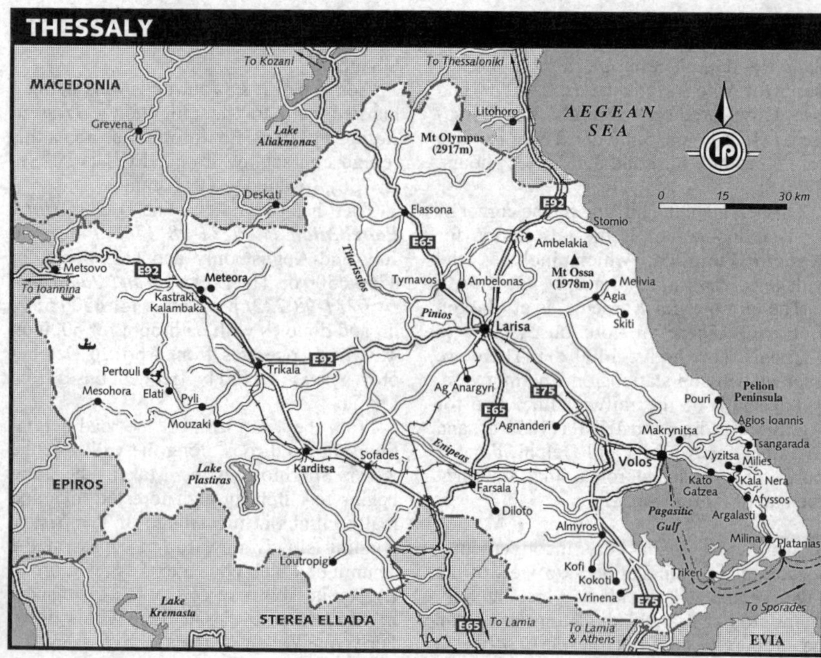

Ferry There are one or two daily ferries from Agios Konstantinos to Skiathos (3½ hours, 3200 dr) and one or two to Skopelos Town (4½ hours, 4000 dr) and Alonnisos (six hours, 4300 dr).

Hydrofoil Hydrofoils depart up to four times daily for Skiathos (1½ hours, 6500 dr), and four times daily for Skopelos Town (2½ hours, 7600 dr) and Alonnisos (three hours, 8200 dr).

Thessaly Θεσσαλία

Thessaly is the proud possessor of two of Greece's most extraordinary natural phenomena: the giant rock pinnacles of Meteora and the riotously fertile Pelion Peninsula. On a more modest scale it also has the beautiful Vale of Tembi. Travelling north from Thessaly to Macedonia, whether by road or train, you will pass through this 12km-long valley, which is a narrow passageway between Mt Olympus and Mt Ossa. The road and railway line share the valley with a river, whose richly verdant banks contrast dramatically with the sheer cliffs on either side. If you have your own transport there are viewpoints at the most scenic spots.

The valley has also been a favoured place for invaders of Greece. The Persian king Xerxes gained access to central Greece via Tembi in 480 BC, as did the Germans in 1941.

LARISA Λάρισα

☎ 041 • postcode 410 00 • pop 112,777

Larisa is the kind of place you would normally bypass on your travels through Greece, but it is worth more than a fleeting glance. Larisa is an important transport hub and it is likely that you will find yourself at least passing through here, if only fleetingly, on the train heading either north or south.

Despite its initial lack of promise, Larisa is nonetheless a lively and sophisticated town, almost bereft of tourists, and is a very important service centre for the whole of the vast agricultural plain of Thessaly. It is a vibrant student town, as the bustling cafeterias around the central area testify, and has a military and air-force base.

Larisa has been inhabited for over 8000 years and its multifarious and fascinating past is only gradually being uncovered, since in recent years fast-growing residential development has tended to disguise what historical remains lie beneath the modern city.

Orientation

Larisa occupies the east bank of the River Pinios, which eventually flows through the Vale of Tembi to the sea. Its main square is called Plateia Laou. The train station is on the southern side of town and the main bus station on the northern side. To get to the town centre from the train station, bear left onto Paleologou outside the station, this runs towards a busy intersection, turn to the right from the intersection, along Alex Panagouli. This street leads directly north to Plateia Laou.

Kyprou and Nikitara run across the south end of this square and Eleftheriou Venizelou and 31 Avgoustou across the north end. Plateia Ethnarhou Makariou (more commonly known as Plateia Tahydromiou) and Plateia Mihail Sapka are the other two squares around which most of the social life revolves. The streets around these squares are mainly pedestrianised.

To get to Plateia Laou from the main bus station, walk directly south along Olympou for about 300m.

Information

The Larisa EOT office is at Koumoundourou 18 (☎ 250 919) near the prefecture office *(nomarhia)* building. Opening hours are 7 am to 2.30 pm Monday to Friday. The post office is on the corner of A Papanastasiou and Athanasiou Diakou. The OTE office is on Filellinon, which is 200m to the west of Plateia Laou. There are ATMs at the train station and the National Bank of Greece on Platiea Mihail Sapra. The police station is at the southern end of A Papanastasiou, just past the church of Agios Nikolaos.

Greece's first Internet cafe, the Planet Café, opened in Larisa in 1996. It is on Skarlatou Soutsou 20, and is open 10 am to 3 am every day.

Things to See

The **Acropolis** on Agios Ahillios Hill has archaeological evidence that indicates this area had been settled since the Neolithic Age (6000 BC), but was used as the ancient settlement's Acropolis during classical times, when the temple of **Polias Athina** once existed. The Acropolis is now the site of the **kastro**. Nearby are the excavations of a newly discovered **ancient theatre** which, when fully excavated, could rival that at

Earthenware tragic mask from 3rd century BC, as used in ancient theatre of Larisa

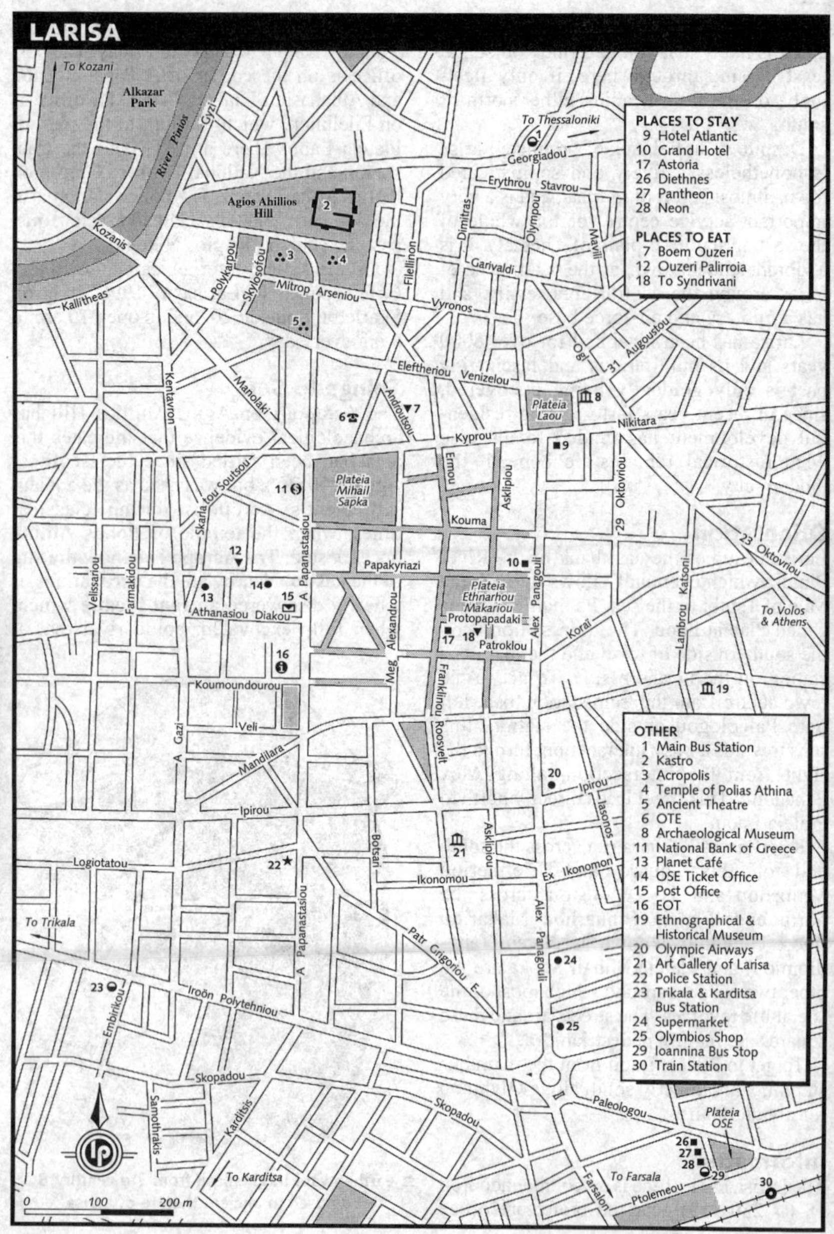
LARISA
PLACES TO STAY
9 Hotel Atlantic
10 Grand Hotel
17 Astoria
26 Diethnes
27 Pantheon
28 Neon
PLACES TO EAT
7 Boem Ouzeri
12 Ouzeri Palirroia
18 To Syndrivani
OTHER
1 Main Bus Station
2 Kastro
3 Acropolis
4 Temple of Polias Athina
5 Ancient Theatre
6 OTE
8 Archaeological Museum
11 National Bank of Greece
13 Planet Café
14 OSE Ticket Office
15 Post Office
16 EOT
19 Ethnographical & Historical Museum
20 Olympic Airways
21 Art Gallery of Larisa
22 Police Station
23 Trikala & Karditsa Bus Station
24 Supermarket
25 Olymbios Shop
29 Ioannina Bus Stop
30 Train Station
To Kozani
Alkazar Park
River Pinios
Agios Ahillios Hill
To Thessaloniki
Plateia Laou
Plateia Mihail Sapka
Plateia Ethnarhou Makariou
To Volos & Athens
To Trikala
To Karditsa
To Farsala
Plateia OSE
0 100 200 m

Epidaurus. The excavation site is on the corner of A Papanastasiou and Eleftheriou Venizelou. It is not particularly impressive at the moment and to fully uncover it will mean demolishing a good section of the neighbouring streets.

The **archaeological museum** (☎ 28 8515), housed in a former mosque at 31 Augoustou, contains Neolithic finds and grave stelae from the region. It is open 8 am to 2.30 pm Tuesday to Sunday. Admission is free.

The **ethnographical and historical museum** (☎ 239 446) at Mandilara 74 has an interesting collection of tools and utensils from the pre-industrial age. There are Greek traditional costumes, displays about nomads and semi-nomads and some samples of weaving and bronze ware from Tyrnavos, a nearby town. Opening hours are 10 am to 2 pm Monday to Saturday. Admission is free. The museum is scheduled to move to larger premises within the next two years.

The **art gallery of Larisa** (☎ 62 120), Franklinou Roosvelt 59, has an impressive collection of contemporary Greek art. It is open 10.30 am to 2.30 pm and 5 to 8.30 pm Tuesday to Thursday, and 10.30 am to 2.30 pm Saturday and Sunday. Entry is free.

Alkazar Park, just across the river on the right at the end of Eleftheriou Venizelou, is a nice place to relax and cool down. Larisa, along with Agrinio in Etolo-Akarnania, shares the unenviable record of being the hottest place in Greece. The grandly titled **sculpted river** is a set of marble sculptures on Plateia Ethnarhou Makariou, with gushing, running water. If nothing else, it is a refreshing sight on a hot day.

Activities

For adventure sports fans, the Olymbios Shop, at Alex Panagouli 99, is very good and able to supply your hiking, climbing, windsurfing and skiing needs. There is also a good mountain bike shop next door.

Places to Stay

There are three D class hotels opposite the train station that are convenient, if not inspiring, for travellers in transit. ***Neon*** doesn't make much of an effort to operate as a hotel, but you might get a room if you're desperate. ***Pantheon*** *(☎ 236 726)* has singles/doubles for 5500/7200 dr, or with bathroom for 7200/8800 dr. ***Diethnes*** *(☎ 234 210)*, next door, has functional rooms for 5500/7200 dr.

The C class ***Hotel Atlantic*** *(☎ 287 711, fax 230 022, Alex Panagouli 1)* is reasonable enough and has rooms for 8000/11,000 dr.

Larisa has a couple of overpriced B class hotels where you will probably get up to 30% discount. ***Astoria*** *(☎ 252 941, fax 229 097, Protopapadaki 4)* is as central as you can get and there's lively nightlife in the immediate area. Rooms here go for 18,500/25,420 dr. The ***Grand Hotel*** *(☎ 257 111, fax 557 888, Papakyriazi 16)* has rooms for 20,000/28,000 dr.

Places to Eat

On Plateia Ethnarhou Makariou is ***To Syndrivani***, which spills out onto the square when the going gets busy. Food here is well prepared and good value. The no-nonsense ***Boem Ouzeri*** on Androutsou is a long-established place serving generous portions of grilled meat. ***Ouzeri Palirroia*** *(Papakyriazi 50)*, with bright blue and yellow decor, specialises in fish dishes.

A large, well stocked supermarket is at the southern end of Alex Panagouli.

Getting There & Away

Bus Buses leave from Larisa's main bus station, on Georgiadou, for many destinations including the following: six daily to Athens (4½ hours, 6000 dr), 13 to Thessaloniki (two hours, 3200 dr) and 12 to Volos (one hour, 1100 dr). Buses run regularly to and from Karditsa and Trikala from a separate bus station south of the city centre on Iroön Polytehniou, near the junction with Embirikou.

There is a third bus station below Neon Hotel opposite the train station. Buses for Ioannina, towns in western Macedonia, Evia, central Greece, the Peloponnese and even Crete leave from here. For this last destination you buy your ferry ticket when you arrive in Piraeus.

Train Larisa is on the main train line to and from Thessaloniki (two hours, 3000 dr) and Athens (five hours, 5650 dr), so there are a number of trains daily between both cities passing through Larisa. In addition to the five intercity services between both cities, there are also two extra intercity services to Athens that originate in Volos and another intercity service to and from Kozani. These better-appointed trains attract a supplementary charge. There are also 15 local trains to Volos (one hour, 600 dr). There are presently no trains to Kalambaka as the line is being upgraded. You can buy train tickets and make reservations at the OSE office in town at Papakyriazi 41. Luggage storage is available at the train station.

VOLOS Βόλος

☎ 0421 • postcode 380 01 • pop 110,000

Volos is a large and bustling city on the northern shores of the Pagasitic Gulf. According to mythology, Volos was the ancient Iolkos from where Jason and the Argonauts set sail on their quest for the Golden Fleece. The name Volos is believed to be a corruption of the original Iolkos.

Volos is not a holiday destination in its own right: the lure of the Pelion Peninsula or the Sporades islands draws people to the city while they are in transit. It is nonetheless a pleasant place to spend a night or two, or even as a base for touring the Pelion villages. Much of Volos was rebuilt after the disastrous 1955 earthquake.

Volos is home to the University of Thessaly and its students give the city a vibrant and youthful feel.

Orientation

The waterfront street of Argonafton is, for half its length, a pedestrian area; running parallel to it are the city's main thoroughfares of Iasonos, Dimitriados and Ermou. The central section of Ermou and its side streets is, in fact, a very lively pedestrian precinct. Heading north-east out of the town centre towards the hills and at right angles to the main thoroughfares are K Kartali and Eleftheriou Venizelou: this latter street is known to the locals as Iolkou. The central square of Plateia Riga Fereou is at the north-western end of the main waterfront. To the west of this square is the train station. The bus station is 500m farther along Grigoriou Lambraki.

Information

The EOT (☎ 23 500, fax 24 750) is on the northern side of Plateia Riga Fereou. The helpful and multilingual staff give out town maps, information on bus, ferry and hydrofoil schedules, and have a list of hotels in all categories for all of Thessaly. Opening hours are 7.30 am to 2.30 pm and 6 to 8.30 pm Monday to Friday and 9.30 am to 1.30 pm weekends and public holidays. In the low season (September to June), opening hours are 7.30 am to 2.30 pm Monday to Friday. The tourist police (☎ 72 421) are in the same building as the regular police at 28 Oktovriou 179.

The post office is at Pavlou Mela 45. The OTE is at Eleftheriou Venizelou 22 and is open 6 am to midnight every day.

The National Bank of Greece, in the middle of the waterfront, on Argonafton, has an ATM. Volos' General Hospital (☎ 24 531) is in the eastern part of town near the archaeological museum.

Archaeological Museum

This excellent museum, on the waterfront at Athanasaki 1, in the south-east of town, has a comprehensive collection of finds from the area. Especially impressive is the large collection of painted grave stelae from the nearby Hellenistic site of Dimitrias. The museum is open 8.30 am to 3 pm Tuesday to Saturday and 9.30 am to 2.30 pm Sunday and public holidays. Admission is 500 dr.

Kitsos Makris Folk Art Centre

This outstanding museum (☎ 30 421) at Kitsos Makris 38 houses the superb collec-

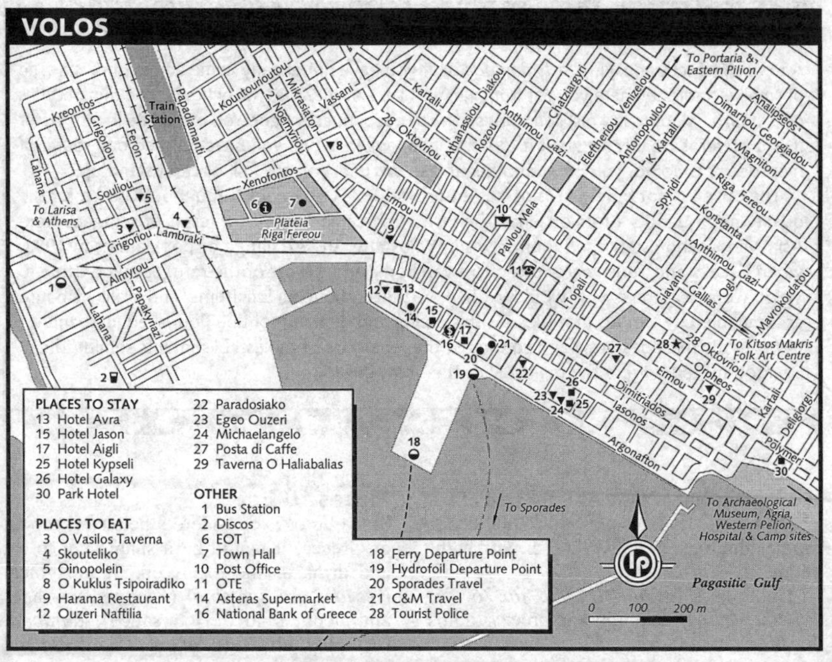

tion of the late Kitsos Makris, a folk art historian. A professional from 1955 till his death in 1988, Kitsos lived here with his wife, Kyveli. The centre now belongs to the university. The items, collected from the Pelion, include 25 paintings by Theophilos Hatzimichael, and some beautiful paper icons from Mt Athos printed from copperplate engravings. Other highlights are the Makris' study, and their living room, which has a beautiful 18th century carved-wood ceiling and a delightful frieze of the Pelion painted by Kitsos Makris.

You will be given a guided tour by one of the knowledgeable and enthusiastic staff. The museum is open 8.30 am to 2 pm, Monday to Friday. Admission is free.

Places to Stay – Budget

The nearest camp sites to Volos are at Kato Gatzea, 20km away, on the west coast of the Pelion Peninsula. They are ***Camping Marina*** *(☎ 0423-22 167)*, an adequate camping place, but there is no beach to speak of.

Farther along, and the best of the bunch, is ***Camping Hellas*** *(☎ 0423-22 267, fax 22 492)* with restaurant, minimarket and beachside bar. Book if you plan to come in July or August. Not far behind is ***Sikia Fig Tree Camping*** *(☎ 0423-22 279)*, with restaurant and bar and all the usual good camping facilities. This place is next to Camping Hellas and shares the same beach. There are also some ***domatia*** at Sikia Camping. The buses to Milies and Platanias pass all three sites.

Volos has many hotels so you will not miss out on a bed too easily. Listed below are some of the more central ones. You can get a full list from the EOT office. The D class ***Hotel Avra*** *(☎ 25 370, Solonos 5)* at

The Ouzeri

An *ouzeri* (strictly speaking, a *tsipouradiko*), if you have not already come across one, is a type of small restaurant where you eat from various plates of *mezedes* (tasty titbits) and drink bottles of *tsipouro*. Tsipouro is a distilled spirit similar to ouzo, but stronger. You can dilute it with water if you prefer it weaker, or want it to last a little longer. When you have finished one round of mezedes or tsipouro, you order another and so on, until you are full, or can't stand up.

The ouzeri is not purely a Volos institution, but Volos is famous throughout Greece for the quality and quantity of its ouzeria. The institution came about as a result of refugees from Asia Minor who established themselves in Volos after the exchange of populations in 1923, when Greeks and Turks were forced to swap homelands. Most of the refugees who came to Volos were seafarers who would gather on the harbour at lunchtime and drink tsipouro accompanied by various mezedes. As this eating and drinking routine flourished, demand for more exotic mezedes grew and so too did the repertoire of the establishments serving them. Seafood mezedes were the mainstay of the Volos ouzeri.

the western end of Iasonos is the best of the cheap hotels. Its rates are 5000/7000 dr for singles/doubles, or 6500/9000 dr with bathroom.

The C class ***Jason*** *(☎ 26 075, fax 26 975, Pavlou Mela 1)* has light and breezy rooms for 6500/10,000 dr.

Places to Stay – Mid-Range & Top End

The C class ***Hotel Kypseli*** *(☎ 24 420, Agiou Nikolaou 1)* has a rather dingy interior, despite its prime location on the waterfront. The clean and functional rooms with aircon are 10,000/14,000 dr.

The C class ***Hotel Galaxy*** *(☎ 20 750, fax 31 444, Agiou Nikolaou 3)* is a modern-looking and very clean hotel with rooms for 11,000/15,500 dr.

The B class ***Park Hotel*** *(☎ 36 511, fax 28 645, Deligiorgi 2)* has recently undergone a major renovation. The stylish rooms have all the expected amenities and rates of 13,800/21,300 dr including breakfast.

The B class ***Aigli*** *(☎ 24 471, fax 33 006, Argonafton 24)* is a long-established hostelry with an impressive neoclassical facade and a warm interior. Rooms here are an equally impressive 15,000/23,000 dr including breakfast.

Places to Eat

Since Volos is considered the ouzeri capital of Greece, it would be a shame not to eat and drink as the locals do. Some typical *mezedes* are *spetsofaï* (chopped sausages and peppers in a rich sauce), *ohtapodi* (octopus), *htypiti* (a mixed feta cheese and hot pepper dip) and fried calamari.

There is a cluster of ouzeria along the Argonafton waterfront of which the most popular seem to be ***Naftilia***, at the western end, and ***Egeo*** towards the middle. The atmospheric ***O Kuklus Tsipoiradiko*** *(Mikrasiaton 85)* offers a range of mezedes, and potatoes baked in a traditional wood-fired oven. There are, of course, many other ouzeria along the waterfront and throughout the city itself, so half the fun may well be in seeking out your own favourite place.

O Vasilos Taverna *(Grigoriou Lambraki 30)* serves reasonably priced casserole dishes and is popular with local garage workers at lunchtime. ***Harama Restaurant*** *(Dimitriados 49)* has similar fare and prices.

O Haliabalias *(Orpheos 8)* is a charming place with welcoming waiters and a range of tasty, well prepared casseroles and grills. Orpheos is also called Kontaratou. ***Michaelangelo*** *(Argonafton 45)* specialises in well prepared pasta dishes, if you fancy a change from Greek food.

At ***Paradosiako*** *(K Kartali 8)* you can listen to live *rembetika* music while you dine. The taverna is open all day, but the live music doesn't start till 10.30 pm. The food is traditional Greek and low-priced.

Volos' trendy young set make for the chic cafes at the eastern end of Orpheos, but ***Posta di Caffe*** *(Ermou 206)*, close by, is a relaxing place that offers superior cappuccino at a lower price.

Skouteliko, on Melounias, behind Grigoriou Lambraki, and ***Oinopolein*** *(Feron 7)* are both sophisticated places and ideal for romantic evenings. Both offer an imaginative menu of well prepared dishes. Of the string of fish tavernas along Nik Plastira, near the archaeological museum, ***Rotunda*** is rated most highly by locals.

Alternatively, the well stocked ***Asteras supermarket*** on Argonafton will supply you with all you need for a picnic lunch.

Entertainment

For a wild night of dancing head for Lahana – a street lined with discos. Most cater for heavy metal fans, but at ***Refrigerator*** some Greek music is played. These are winter-only discos; in summer things get even wilder, with dancing on the tables, at the outdoor discos at Alikes, a beach suburb 1.5km from the city centre. At ***Letdos*** the DJ spins only Greek music, while at the more upmarket ***Fengaria*** you can hear live Greek music.

Getting There & Away

Bus From the bus station there are nine buses daily to Athens (five hours, 5250 dr), 12 daily to Larisa (one hour, 1100 dr), five to Thessaloniki (three hours, 3500 dr), and four to Kalambaka (three hours, 3050 dr) and Ioannina (six hours, 4400 dr). The Ioannina bus continues to Igoumenitsa.

Buses to the major villages of the Pelion Peninsula are as follows: 11 daily to Kala Nera and five daily to Afyssos, 10 daily to Makrynitsa (via Portaria), seven to Vyzitsa (via Milies), six to Milina (via Argalasti and Horto), and three daily to Platanias, Zagora (via Hania) and Agios Ioannis (via Tsangarada). Buses also run to many of the smaller villages, but often only two or three times daily. Check the board at the bus station and bear in mind possible seasonal changes.

Train There are 15 trains daily to Larisa (1¼ hours, 620 dr). Two direct intercity trains daily go to Athens (the *Trikoupis* at 6.25 am and the *Thessalia* at 7 pm, 5820 dr) and three local trains go to Thessaloniki, with a connection at Larisa. However, there are many connections daily to both Thessaloniki and Athens from Larisa. You can make reservations for these connections and the Athens or Thessaloniki intercity trains from the online booking office at the station. There are presently no trains to Kalambaka because of upgrading of the line.

Ferry There are one to two ferries daily from Volos to Skiathos (three hours, 2750 dr), Glossa (Skopelos, 3½ hours, 2750 dr), Skopelos Town (4½ hours, 3400 dr) and Alonnisos (five hours, 3750 dr). Buy tickets from Sporades Travel (☎/fax 35 846), Argonafton 33.

Hydrofoil In summer, there are five or six daily hydrofoils to Skiathos (1½ hours, 5500 dr), Glossa (1¾ hours, 6200 dr), Skopelos Town (two hours, 6800 dr) and Alonnisos (three hours, 7500 dr). Additional services operate to Evia and some of the Sporades services stop at Trikeri Island, Agia Kyriaki and Platanias. Tickets are available from C&M travel (☎ 39 786, fax 24 388), Antonopoulou 11.

Getting Around

Cars can be rented from European Car Rental (☎ 24 381, fax 24 192), at Iasonos 79, and from Avis (☎ 20 849, fax 32 360), at Argonafton 41.

PELION PENINSULA Πήλιον Ορος

The well watered Pelion Peninsula lies to the east and south of Volos. It consists of a mountain range, of which the highest peak

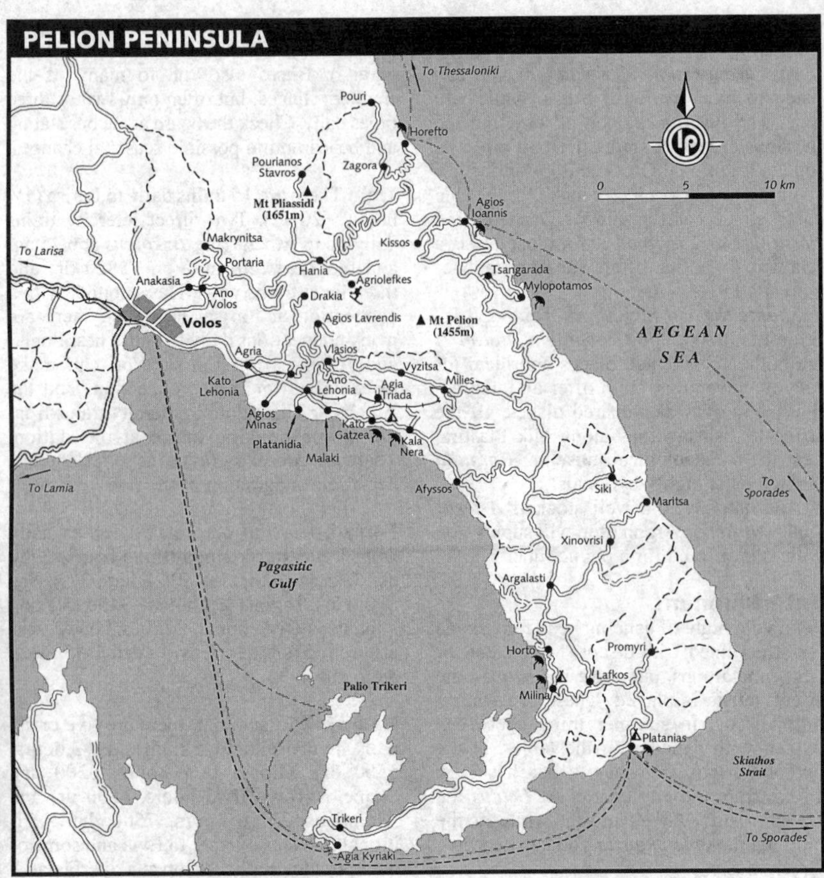

is Mt Pliassidi (1651m). The inaccessible eastern flank consists of high cliffs which plunge dramatically into the sea. The gentler western flank coils around the calm sea of the Pagasitic Gulf. The interior is a green wonderland where trees heavy with fruit vie with wild olive groves, forests of horse chestnut, oak, walnut, eucalyptus and beech trees to reach the light of day.

The villages tucked away in this profuse foliage are characterised by whitewashed, half-timbered houses with overhanging balconies and grey slate roofs, and cobbled mule paths winding around their vibrant gardens. Flagstone squares harbouring little Byzantine churches and sculpted fountains shaded by enormous gnarled plane trees are another feature of these settlements.

If you have your own transport you can see a great deal of the peninsula in one day, but bear in mind that driving here is a tortuous affair with so many bends and turns. If you're travelling by bus, allow for two or three days: no single bus route goes around the whole peninsula, so it isn't possible to tour the coast and inland villages in a single day.

Many of the places to stay in the Pelion are traditional mansions tastefully converted into pensions. They are wonderful places to spend a night or two, but they don't necessarily come cheap.

The Pelion has an enduring tradition of regional cooking. Be sure to try some of the local specialities, such as *fasolada* (bean soup), *kouneli stifado* (rabbit stew), spetsofaï and *tyropsomo* (cheese bread).

History & Mythology

In mythology the Pelion was inhabited by centaurs – reprobate creatures who took delight in deflowering virgins.

The Turkish occupation did not extend into the inaccessible central and eastern parts of the Pelion, and as a result the western coastal towns were abandoned in favour of mountain villages. In these remote settlements, culture and the economy flourished; silk and wool were exported to many places in Europe. Like other remote areas in Greece the Pelion became a spawning ground for ideas that culminated in the War of Independence.

Getting There & Away

Buses to the villages of the Pelion leave from the Volos bus station (see the Volos Getting There & Away section).

Volos to Makrynitsa

Taking the north-eastern route from Volos, the road climbs to the villages of **Anakasia** and **Ano Volos**. The former is 4km north-east of Volos. In its central square is the **Theophilos Museum**, housed in an 18th century mansion. The museum features the works of the primitive painter Theophilos (1866-1934), who lived for many years in Volos. It's open 8 am to 2 pm Monday to Friday. Admission is free.

Portaria, the next village, is 13km north-east of Volos. True to form, its plateia has a splendid old plane tree, and the little 13th century **Church of Panagia of Portaria** has fine frescoes. A fork to the left in the village leads to Makrynitsa, 17km north-east of Volos.

Makrynitsa Μακρυνίτσα

☎ 0428 • postcode 370 11 • pop 650

Makrynitsa, clinging to a mountainside at an elevation of 750m, is aptly called the Balcony of Pelion. The traditional houses were built with three storeys at the front and only one at the back, giving the impression they are stacked on top of one another. It is one of the loveliest of the Pelion villages, but is also the most touristy. However, as it is closed to traffic, it remains tranquil. There's a car park at the entrance to the village; if you've come by bus you will alight a little farther back along the road. To get to the central square walk straight ahead along the cobbled main street. The square has an old hollow plane tree, a sculpted marble fountain and the little church of Agios Ioannis.

Places to Stay & Eat ***Leonidas Domatia*** *(☎ 99 071)* is one of the cheapest places to stay in Makrynitsa. The simply furnished, clean doubles/triples are 7000/10,000 dr. The domatia is on the right between the bus terminus and the car park.

Archontiko Diomidi *(☎ 99 430, fax 99 114)* is a traditional mansion featuring lots of wall hangings, brass and ceramic ornaments and carved-wood furniture. Rooms cost 12,000/16,000 dr. To get there, go up the stone path behind Taverna Galini.

Archontiko Karamarli *(☎ 99 570)* is a beautiful old stone mansion, with exquisitely furnished singles/doubles for 24,000/34,000 dr and four-person suites for 55,000 dr. Look for the pension sign pointing left on the main street. ***Kentavros Xenonas*** *(☎ 99 075)* is a spotless place near the main square and has lovely double rooms for 18,000 dr, dropping to 8000 dr in the summer. ***Hotel Achilles*** *(☎ 99 177, fax 99 140)* on the main square has single/double rooms for 10,000/16,000 dr.

Try the reasonably priced ***Restaurant Galini*** on the central square for excellent spetsofaï, fasolada and kouneli stifado. ***Pantheon*** nearby on the square offers much the same fare, but has a much better view.

Makrynitsa to Tsangarada

Back on the main Volos-Zagora route the road continues to the modern village of **Hania**. Some 16km uphill from here is the ski resort of **Agriolefkes**, where the ski centre (☎ 0428-39 136) has three downhill runs and one cross-country run. Information can be obtained either from the EOT in Volos or the Volos EOS (Greek Alpine Club; ☎ 0421-25 696) at Dimitriados 92.

From Hania the road zigzags down through chestnut trees to a road junction. The left turn leads to **Zagora** (population 3000), the largest of the Pelion villages and a major fruit-growing centre. Zagora is a long, strung-out village, as the approach along the main road will testify, and is not as dependent on tourism as other villages in the area. The very successful Zagora agricultural cooperative was founded in 1916 and has been instrumental in promoting the growing and export of fruit (mainly apples) as a means of sustaining growth in the village region. The cooperative has its own restaurant, cafeteria and minimarket complex in town called ***Milon tis Eridos*** (Apple of Discord). Just down past the turn-off to Horefto, you will pass, on the left, the **Ellinomousio**, a museum dedicated to Rigas Fereos, one of the intellectual instigators of the War of Independence. The museum is open 9.30 am to 1.30 pm and 5.30 to 8.30 pm daily, and admission costs 300 dr.

Horefto, 8km downhill from Zagora, is a popular resort with a long sandy beach. The main beach is OK, but there are a couple of better beaches, within walking distance, north and south of the main village. There is a reasonable camp site here. At the moment, Horefto takes some getting to by road because of the terrain, but you can always jump off a hydrofoil from the Sporades or Thessaloniki if the mood takes you.

North of Zagora, **Pouri**, another charming village, spills down a steep mountainside and is worth the detour from Zagora.

Back at the road junction, the right turn-off takes you through a series of villages to Tsangarada. This route is one of the most scenically spectacular in the Pelion.

The most delightful of the villages is **Kissos**, built on steep terraces. Its 18th century Church of Agia Marina has fine frescoes. From Kissos, a 6km road leads down to the coastal resort of **Agios Ioannis**, which is popular enough, though it would not rank among the best. It is connected to Thessaloniki and the Sporades by a summer hydrofoil service.

Tsangarada Τσαγκαράδα

☎ 0426 • postcode 370 12 • pop 4950

Tsangarada (tsang-ah-**rah**-dah), nestling in oak and plane forests, is an extremely spread-out village comprising the four separate communities of Agii Taxiarhes, Agia Paraskevi, Agios Stefanos and Agia Kyriaki. The largest is Agia Paraskevi, which is just north of the main Volos-Milies-Tsangarada road. The bus stops near the central square of Plateia Paraskevis. The plane tree on this square is reputedly the largest and oldest in Greece – locals claim it is 1500 years old. No doubt this is an exaggeration, but whatever its age it's a magnificent specimen with a girth of 14m.

The small seaside resort of **Mylopotamos** is 8km down the road from Tsangarada. The beach here has earned an EU Blue Flag for cleanliness, so enjoy and respect it.

Places to Stay & Eat There are several domatia on the main road near Plateia Paraskevis. ***Paradisos Pension*** *(☎ 49 209, fax 49 551)* is a lovely place run by the friendly and enthusiastic Rigakis brothers. The pension's immaculate and cosy single/double rooms are 16,000/20,000 dr. It's on the right, travelling south, between the two turn-offs for Mylopotamos.

Konaki Pension *(☎ 49 481)*, just before the second turn-off for Mylopotamos, is a traditional mansion with doubles for 12,000 dr. There are several ***domatia*** along the southernmost turn-off for Mylopotamos. ***Paradisos Restaurant*** (at the pension of the

CENTRAL GREECE

same name) is excellent. Its roast kid and local retsina is top-notch and its home-made preserves are ambrosia to anyone with a sweet tooth.

There are plenty of other restaurants to choose from and in summer there's a small ***taverna*** at Mylopotamos.

Volos to Milies & Vyzitsa

After leaving Volos, the west-coast road passes through the touristy villages of **Agria**, **Kato Lehonia** and **Ano Lehonia**. Several roads off to the left lead to one of the most beautiful areas of Pelion; the road from Ano Lehonia to **Vlasios** is particularly lovely. A right turn leads to the seaside resorts of **Platanidia**, **Malaki** and **Kato Gatzea**. After the tortuous and narrow roads of the eastern Pelion villages, this stretch of road is a blessing.

Farther along the coast road just past Kala Nera, 22km from Volos, there is a turn-off to the left for Tsangarada. A little way along here, another turn-off to the left leads through apple orchards to the photogenic villages of Milies and Vyzitsa.

Milies Μηλιές

☎ 0423 • postcode 370 10 • pop 952

Established in the late 16th century, Milies (mih-lih-**ess**) was a rich agricultural centre, prospering on olive oil, fruit and silk production. Like most of the Pelion it enjoyed semi-autonomy and, largely due to its excellent school, it played a major role in the intellectual and cultural awakening that led to Greek independence.

Milies was the birthplace of Anthinos Gazis (1761-1828), the man who raised the Thessalian revolt in 1821. Shortly after independence a railway line was built between Volos and Milies and the town became a prosperous centre of commerce. **To Trenaki**, the steam train which used to chug along this route, retired formally long ago, but has recently been revived as a weekend tourist attraction (2000 dr). It currently runs a limited route from Milies to Ano Lehonia, though whether its route would ever be extended to Volos is debatable, since it would mean some serious realignment of the old track, which is clearly visible under the surface of the main Volos-Gatzea road. The train stations at Milies and Ano Lehonia have been renovated and you can take a delightful walk along the track between the two stations.

To reach the station from Milies' central square, descend the cobbled path by the post office. If you are approaching under your own steam from Kala Nera, look for the left turn-off to the station just before you reach the main village turn-off. Close to the station is a memorial to the 29 residents of Milies who were executed by the Germans in 1942.

The **Milies folk museum**, which houses a display of local crafts, is on the right beyond the central square.

Places to Stay & Eat The A class ***Palios Stathmos*** *(☎ 86 425)*, by the station in Milies, is an old stone house with traditional furnishings. Doubles go for 14,300 dr, including breakfast.

The setting of ***Palios Stathmos Restaurant*** is idyllic and the food is tasty and reasonably priced. Just up the road from the station is ***Hryso Milo Restaurant*** and beyond the central square, on the road to Vyzitsa, ***Panorama Psistaria*** offers a range of local foods.

However, the gastronomic highlight of Milies is the scrumptious *tyropsomo* (cheese pie). You can buy it at the ***Tournos Bakery*** on the main Volos-Tsangarada road, just before the Milies turn-off.

Vyzitsa Βυζίτσα

☎ 0423 • postcode 370 10 • pop 295

Just 2km beyond Milies is the peaceful little village of Vyzitsa (altitude 555m). Proclaimed a state heritage village by EOT, this is a model Pelion community. It is less touristy than Makrynitsa and in many ways is more attractive. Cobbled pathways wind between its traditional slate-roof houses. To reach Vyzitsa's shady central square walk 50m up a cobbled path to your right from the main parking area.

Places to Stay & Eat Vyzitsa has several domatia where doubles average 10,000 dr – have a look for the signs. ***Thetis Xenonas*** *(☎ 86 111)*, with its accompanying cafe, at the foot of the path to the central square, has doubles for 13,000 dr.

Karagiannopoulos Mansion *(☎ 86 373)*, on the road coming from Milies, is a lovely place – the lounge has a carved-wood ceiling and stained-glass windows. Rates are 20,000 dr for a double with breakfast.

The beautiful ***Kontos Mansion*** *(☎ 86 030, fax 86 793)* is the village's largest mansion. Rates here are 13,000/19,000 dr for singles/doubles. ***Mansion Vafiadis*** *(☎ 86 765)* is equally splendid and has doubles/triples for 19,000/24,000 dr. Signs on the central square point to these two mansions.

Thetis Café, just beyond the parking area, is a serene place with a shady patio. On the main square, nestled in between two enormous plane trees, you have a choice of three establishments, ***Drosia***, ***H Plateia*** and ***Balkonaki***. ***Georgaras*** restaurant on the road leading back to Milies has the views, but not the village intimacy.

CENTRAL GREECE

South to Platanias Πλατανιάς

Continuing south from Kala Nera the bus goes as far as Platanias. Although not as fertile as the northern part of the peninsula, the southern part of the Pelion is still attractive, with pine-forested hills and olive groves. Before heading inland once more, the road skirts the little coastal village of Afyssos, winds upwards through to the large, unexceptional inland farming community of Argalasti, and then forks – the left fork continues inland, the right goes to the coastal resorts of Horto and Milina. From Milina the road heads inland and then south to Platanias. If you are really keen, you can take a twice-daily bus from Volos, all the way to the end of the desolate-looking peninsula to Trikeri and finally to Agia Kyriaki.

Afyssos (Αφψσσος) This upmarket resort features an attractive promenade, but it gets busy in summer. There is one A class hotel, ***Maïstrali*** *(☎ 0423-33 472)*, with doubles in the 16,000 dr range, and several ***domatia/pensions***, if you do really prefer the hustle and bustle of the place.

Horto & Milina (Χόρτο & Μηλίνα) These are the next two villages down that you will meet, if you take the right fork after Argalasti at Metohi. Horto is very low-key and small, while Milina is larger and probably offers a better balance of amenities. Both are on a quiet part of the peninsula with clean water but no spectacular beaches. There are two camp sites at Milina, the very pleasant ***Olizon*** *(☎ 0423-65 236)* and ***Kentauros***, a little farther on.

Just beyond Milina at **Mavri Petra** is an appealing roadside taverna called ***Flavios***. Set on a wide bay with fishing boats at anchor, it is a welcoming culinary oasis.

Trikeri (Τρικέρι) The road from Milina to Trikeri now becomes more and more desolate and the vegetation more stunted as rock takes over. Apart from one or two small sections, the road is sealed all the way and is wide and fast, with little to distract your attention other than the odd house-cum-taverna or goat pen. There is an end-of-the-world feel about this part of the Pelion and Trikeri may come as a surprise when you discover this lively and historically important little community perched on the hilltop, keeping guard over the straits that separate the mainland from Evia.

Donkeys outnumber cars here and the residents pride themselves on their tradition as seafarers, fighters against the Turks in the War of Independence and as upholders of traditional customs and dress. The week following Easter is one of continual revelry as dancing takes place every day and women try to outdo each other in their local costume finery.

Agia Kyriaki (Αγία Κψριακή) This is the last stop on the Pelion Peninsula, a winding 5km drive down the hill, or a fast 15 minute walk down a stone path. This is a fishing village without the tourist trappings and most people only see it during a five minute stopover on the Flying Dolphin from, or to, the Sporades. Here you will find bright, orange-coloured fishing boats put to good use by a lively, hard-working community (population 285).

Rooms are available at ***Lambis Domatia*** *(☎ 0423-91 587)*, just out of Agia Kyriaki at **Mylos**. Follow a dirt road for about 500m and look for the Greek sign. Walk down the path and then look for the EOT sign on the wall, on your left. Haralambos Karapetis, an expat Australian-Greek, should be able to accommodate you as well. Ask around Mylos to be directed to Haralambos.

There are a couple of reasonable-looking places to eat on the waterfront.

Palio Trikeri (Παλιό Τρικέρι) If you really must go that one step farther to get away from it all, then head for this little island (population 91) just off the coast and inside the Pagasitic Gulf. The hydrofoil is supposed to stop here four times weekly, but you may have to ask to make sure. Alternatively, you can twist someone's arm at Agia Kyriaki to take you down a farm track to the end of the headland, where they will whistle or shout to get someone to come from the island to take you over on a caïque.

Palio Trikeri domatia-cum-restaurant *(☎ 0423-91 432)* can probably offer you accommodation and food, as can ***Hariklia Brouzou-Roumbakia*** *(☎ 91 031)*.

Platanias Πλατανιάς

☎ 0423 • postcode 370 06 • pop 171

Platanias (plah-tah-nih-**ahs**) is a popular resort with a good sand and pebble beach. It's a fun place to spend a day or two, although it's quite developed. Les Hirondelles Travel Agency (☎ 71 231) rents various water sports equipment. Turn left at the sea to find them.

Places to Stay & Eat ***Kastri Beach Camping*** *(☎ 71 209)* is at Kastri Beach, 5km east of Platanias. Look for the left turn-off to Kastri on the approach road to Platanias. ***Louisa Camping*** *(☎ 71 260)* is just 500m before Platanias on the left.

The D class ***Hotel Platanias*** *(☎ 65 565)* is good value with pleasant singles/doubles for 6000/9000 dr with bathroom. Turn left at the waterfront and you will see the hotel above the co-owned To Steki Restaurant. Another agreeable option is the D class ***Hotel des Roses*** *(☎ 65 568)* by the bus stop. The owner, Madame Tulla, may show you her collection of guestbooks which date back to the 1950s when she opened her first hotel in Egypt. Doubles/triples are 7500/9500 dr; doubles with bathroom are 10,000 dr.

Archontiko Apartments *(☎ 71 292)* has doubles for 10,000 dr and four-person apartments for 15,000. The C class ***Hotel Drosero Akrogati*** *(☎ 71 210, fax 71 211)* has doubles/triples for 10,000/12,000 dr with bathroom. Turn right at the waterfront to reach these two places.

There are no less than six eating places in Platanias among which ***To Steki Restaurant*** has a large choice of well prepared dishes. Turn left at the waterfront to reach this restaurant.

Getting There & Away See the Getting There & Away section under Volos for bus services to Platanias.

There is a daily caïque running to Skiathos in the Sporades and a whispered rumour of a future car ferry link as well. Don't bank on it yet; though it would be a great service, given the distance and high cost of shipping a vehicle from Volos to the Sporades.

At least two hydrofoils call by Platanias from 1 June onwards on their way to Skiathos (2500 dr), Skopelos Town (3900 dr) and Alonnisos (4000 dr), and there are five weekly to Volos. Tickets can be purchased from Les Hirondelles Travel Agency.

Getting Around Les Hirondelles Travel Agency rents motorbikes. There are ad hoc excursion boats to Skiathos in addition to the regular caïque service. Other caïques run daily to local, but less accessible, beaches.

TRIKALA Τρίκαλα

☎ 0431 • postcode 421 00 • pop 48,000

Trikala (**tree**-kah-lah) is ancient Trikki, the reputed birthplace of Asclepius, the god of healing. It's a bustling agricultural town, through which flows the River Litheos, and is a major hub for buses. While Trikala's attractions hardly warrant a special trip, the chances are if you're exploring central Greece you'll eventually pass through here en route to somewhere else.

Orientation & Information

Trikala's main thoroughfare is Asklipiou, the northern end of which is a pedestrian precinct. Facing the river, turn left from the bus station to reach Plateia Riga Fereou at the northern end of Asklipiou. The train station is at the opposite end of Asklipiou, 600m from Plateia Riga Fereou.

To reach the central square of Plateia Iroön Polytehniou cross the bridge over the river, opposite Plateia Riga Fereou.

Trikala does not have an EOT or tourist police; the regular police (☎ 32 777) are 1km from the town centre on Sidiras Merarchias, a left turn off the road to Larisa. The National Bank of Greece is on the central square. The post office is at Saraphi 13; turn left at the central square and it's a little way along on the left. To reach the OTE walk along the left side of the central square and turn left onto 25 Martiou; it's a little way along here on the right at the far side of a small square.

Things to See

The **River Litheos** which bisects the town is crossed by 10 bridges. The **Fortress of Trikala** is currently closed for restoration, but it's worth a wander up to the gardens which surround it for the views. Walk 400m up Saraphi from the central square and look for the sign pointing right. To get to the old **Turkish quarter** of Varousi, take a sharp right at the sign for the fortress. It's a fascinating area of peaceful narrow streets and fine old houses with overhanging balconies. If you keep on walking through Varousi and up the hill, you will come to the chapel of **Profitis Ilias**. It is a pleasant, tree-lined walk, and you will eventually reach a **zoo** with a collection of sad-looking animals. Entry is free.

At the other side of town is the **Koursoum Tzami**, a Turkish mosque built in the 16th century by Sinan Pasha, the same architect who built the Blue Mosque in İstanbul. This mosque has been the subject of an EU-funded restoration project and has now been restored to its former glory – minus the top of the minaret. From the bus station, turn right, follow the river and you'll reach the mosque after 300m.

Places to Stay

Trikala isn't a tourist centre so hotels are unlikely to be full. The decrepit ***Hotel Panellinio*** on Plateia Riga Fereou is currently receiving a long-overdue refurbishment. This leaves ***Hotel Palladion*** *(☎ 28 091, Vyronos 4)* as Trikala's only budget option. It has well maintained singles/doubles for 6000/8000 dr. The hotel is behind Hotel Achillion.

The brightly painted C class ***Litheon*** *(☎ 20 690, fax 37 390)* next to the bus station has agreeable rooms for 12,500/16,000 dr.

The C class ***Hotel Dina*** *(☎ 74 777, fax 29 490, Karanasiou 1)* has immaculate rooms with air-con, telephone and balconies for 10,000/15,000 dr. The hotel is 100m along Asklipiou from Plateia Riga Fereou.

The palatial B class ***Hotel Achillion*** *(☎ 28 291, fax 74 858, Asklipiou 2, Plateia Riga Fereou)* has rooms for 19,500/29,000 dr. The B class ***Hotel Divani*** *(☎ 27 286, fax 20 519, Dionysiou 13)*, overlooking the river, is Trikala's best hotel with rates of 18,600/24,000 dr.

Places to Eat

Trikala's cafe life is centred on the northern end of Askipilon and traditional kafeneia and ouzeria are mostly in the little streets to the north of 25 Martiou. Recently some trendy tavernas have opened up here. ***Taverna Archontissa*** on Patriarhoi is one of the nicest, with quaint decor and well

JON DAVISON

uayside vendor, Syros (Cyclades)

DIANA MAYFIELD

Turkish tombstones, Rhodes (Dodecanese)

DIANA MAYFIELD

iew from Imerovigli, Santorini, of Nea Kameni, an island of lava born in a 1707 eruption (Cyclades)

DIANA MAYFIELD

Typical brightly painted house, Santorini (Cyclades)

DAVID TIPLING

Spring-flowering tamarisk, Lesbos (NE Aegean)

GEORGE TSAFOS

Actors in an ancient comedy.

prepared mezedes and grills. ***Pliatsikas Restaurant***, on Ioulietas, is a charming place which serves similar fare, and is popular with local families. Ioulietas Adam runs at right angles to Karanasiou.

For ready-made food try ***O Kostaras*** on Plateia Kitrilaki. There are other eateries on this square in the warm months. ***Taverna o Babis***, near Hotel Dina on Karanasiou, is a pleasant restaurant with ready-made dishes and grills.

There is a lively market on the streets north of Trikalon, between the two squares, every Friday.

Getting There & Away

Bus From Trikala's bus station there are 20 buses daily to Kalambaka (30 minutes, 450 dr), almost half-hourly buses to Larisa (one hour, 1200 dr), eight daily to Athens (5½ hours, 5400 dr), six to Thessaloniki (5½ hours, 3600 dr), four to Volos (2½ hours, 2400 dr) and two to Ioannina (3½ hours, 2550 dr).

Train At present trains are not running from Trikala because of upgrading of the narrow-gauge line to standard-gauge.

AROUND TRIKALA

About 18km from Trikala is the village of **Pyli**, which means 'gate' – and rightly so, for just beyond Pyli is a spectacular gorge leading into one of Greece's more attractive wilderness areas and one that is currently embroiled in a vigorous ecological debate. Industrial progressives, despite the protests of the ecological lobby and the local inhabitants, have been building a large, 135m-high dam near Mesohora village on the upper Aheloös River. Once completed, the area behind the dam, which includes two villages and three settlements, will be flooded, thereby destroying the area's native flora and fauna. If that isn't bad enough, the dam builders also want to divert part of the flow of the Aheloös River to the plain of Thessaly, thus radically reducing the natural water flow of the river to the wetlands of Messolongi in Etolo-Akarnania. This, it is claimed, would result in the destruction of the natural habitat of the bird life in the region. The issue is still under heated debate.

At the entrance to the gorge, 1.5km from Pyli, is the 13th century **Church of Porto Panayia**. It has an impressive mosaic and marble iconostasis. To reach the church, cross the footbridge over the river and turn left.

The 16th century **Mono Agios Vissariou** stands on a slope of Mt Koziakis, 5km from Pyli. To get there cross the road bridge over the river and follow the sign.

Pyli's one hotel, the comfortable ***Hotel Babanara*** *(☎ 0434-22 325, fax 22 242)*, has doubles with bathroom for 8000 dr.

The area beyond Pyli is gradually being opened up to tourism. If you have your own transport, you can drive on a very scenic, almost completely sealed road from Pyli to Arta (three hours), via Stournareïka and Mesohora and the disputed upper Aheloös dam. Buses do not currently cover this route.

There is a small, but locally popular skiing centre near **Pertouli**, 30km beyond Pyli, amid alpine scenery. Skis can be hired and the centre has a cosy, family atmosphere. Buses for Pertouli leave from the bus station in Trikala.

For some time now, kayaking enthusiasts have been coming to the **Tria Potamia** area, 15km north of Mesohora, to ride the waters of the Aheloös River. The sport is not as organised as in Konitsa in northern Epiros, but nonetheless attracts a growing number of white-water jockeys. How long this activity will last, once the dam is built, is anyone's guess.

METEORA Μετέωρα

Meteora (meh-**teh**-o-rah) is an extraordinary place. The massive pinnacles of smooth rocks with holes in them like Emmenthal cheese are ancient and yet, paradoxically, could be a setting for a science fiction story. The monasteries atop them are the icing on the cake in this already strange and beautiful landscape, which boasts a World Heritage Site listing.

Each monastery is built around a central courtyard surrounded by monks' cells, chapels and a refectory. In the centre of each courtyard stands the *katholikon* (main church).

History

The name Meteora derives from the adjective *meteoros*, which means suspended in the air. The word 'meteor' is from the same root. Many theories have been put forward as to the origins of this 'rock forest', but it remains a geological enigma.

From the 11th century, solitary hermit monks lived in the caverns of Meteora. By the 14th century, Byzantine power was on the wane and incursions into Greece were on the increase, so monks began to seek peaceful havens away from the bloodshed. The inaccessibility of the rocks of Meteora made them an ideal retreat, and the less safe the monks became, the higher they climbed until eventually they were living on top of the rocks.

The earliest monasteries were reached by climbing articulated, removable ladders. Later, windlasses were used so monks could be hauled up in nets, and this method was used until the 1920s. A story goes that when apprehensive visitors enquired how frequently the ropes were replaced, the monks' stock reply was 'When the Lord lets them break'. These days access to the monasteries is by steps hewn into the rocks. Some windlasses can still be seen (you can have a good look at one at Agia Triada), but they are now used for hauling up provisions.

Monasteries

The monasteries are linked by asphalt roads, but the area is best explored on foot on the old paths, where they still exist. You could walk around all the monasteries in one day, but you would need an early start and plan at least a two hour break from 1 to 3 pm when most monasteries close. In any case, they are only all open at the same time on weekends. Opening times and closure days do vary from season to season. Walking and climbing around the rocks can be thirsty work, but there are mobile canteens selling drinks and snacks at most monastery car parks.

Entry to all monasteries is currently 500 dr unless you are Greek, or can convince the ticket seller that you are, in which case entry is free. Strict dress codes are enforced. Women must wear skirts below their knees, men must wear long trousers and arms must be covered. Skirts, which you can wear over your trousers, are often provided for women upon entering the monastery.

The **Moni Agiou Nikolaou Anapafsa** is a 15 minute walk from Kastraki (see later in this chapter). Beyond Kastraki's central square walk straight ahead, passing Villa San Giorgio. This road peters out to a dirt track. After about 10 minutes the track crosses a stream (which may be dry in summer). Almost immediately after the stream, scramble up a steep slope towards the monastery which you will see perched on a rock high up on your left. You will come out on the main road just to the right of the path leading to the monastery. A slightly longer but more straightforward route is to follow the main road from Kastraki.

The Monastery of Agiou Nikolaou Anapafsa was built in the 15th century. The superlative frescoes in its katholikon were painted by the monk Theophanes Strelizas from Crete. Especially beautiful is the fresco of Adam naming the animals. The monastery is open 9 am to 5 pm every day.

On leaving the monastery, turn left onto the road and five minutes along, just before it begins to wind, take a path off to the left. The start of the path is not marked, so look out for a white chevron road sign on the bend, indicating the start. After about five minutes turn left onto a cobbled path. Soon you will come to a fork at the base of the rocks. Take the right fork (keeping on the cobbled path) and after about 20 minutes of steep, zigzag climbing you will reach the **Moni Megalou Meteorou** (Grand Meteora), the best-known of the monasteries.

The majestic and imposing Megalo Meteoro monastery is built on the highest rock at 613m above sea level. Founded by St Athanasios in the 14th century, it became the richest and most powerful of the monasteries, thanks to the Serbian emperor Symeon Uros, who turned all his wealth over to the monastery and became a monk. Its katholikon has a magnificent 12 sided central dome. Its striking, although gory, series of frescoes entitled *Martyrdom of Saints* depicts the persecution of Christians by the Romans. The monastery is open 9 am to 1 pm and 3 to 6 pm. It is closed on Tuesday.

From Megalo Meteoro turn sharp right on the road to reach the nearby **Moni Varlaam**. It has fine late Byzantine frescoes by Frangos Kastellanos. Varlaam is open 9 am to 1 pm and 3.30 to 6 pm. It is closed on Friday.

On leaving Varlaam walk back to the main road and veer right. In about 15 minutes you will come to a fork: the right fork has a signpost to Rousanou and the left to the Agiou Stefanous Nannery (sic). The best approach is to take the left fork and in about 10 minutes you will come to a signpost pointing right to the Rousanou monastery. A 10 minute walk along a path will lead to **Moni Agias Varvaras Rousanou**; access is across a vertiginous bridge. The katholikon features more gory frescoes. Rousanou is open 9 am to 1 pm and 3.30 to 5 pm in winter and 9 am to 6 pm in summer. It is closed on Wednesday.

After Rousanou you can either take a short walk down the steps to the Agios Nikolaos-Metamorphosis road or go back along the path and continue along the road to Moni Agias Triados. If you do the latter you will reach the Agia Triada monastery in about 45 minutes (you may be able to hitch a lift on this stretch). A path leads down to Kalambaka from this monastery. If you want to take this path then it is better to visit the Agiou Stefanou monastery first and then backtrack to Agia Triada.

Of all the monasteries, **Moni Agias Triados** (Holy Trinity) has the most primitive and remote feel about it. It gained meteoric, though temporal fame, when it featured in the James Bond film *For Your Eyes Only*. The monastery is open 9 am to 12.30 pm and 3 to 5 pm in winter and 9 am to 5 pm in summer. It is closed on Thursday.

Moni Agiou Stefanou is another 10 minute walk farther along the road. After Agia Triados it feels like returning to civilisation, with business-like nuns selling souvenirs and even videotapes of Meteora. Among the exhibits in the monastery's **museum** is an exquisite embroidered Epitaphios (a picture on cloth of Christ on his bier). Agiou Stefanou is open 9 am to 1 pm and 3 to 5 pm.

To find the path to Kalambaka from Agias Triados, walk straight ahead when you leave the monastery; the path is off to the left. The first part is a dirt path but it soon becomes paved. The monks will tell you this walk takes 10 minutes, but unless you're James Bond or have the agility of a mountain goat, it'll take you around 30 minutes. On the walk there are tremendous views of the rocks at close quarters, where you see not only their dramatic contours but the details of their strata, too. The path ends near the Koka Roka Taverna.

For your lunch break try to picnic on the **Psaropetra** lookout, with some great photo opportunities. It is along the road to the Agios Triados and Agiou Stefanou monasteries close to the point where the track down to the Rousanou monastery begins.

Be wary of walking along the paths in high winds as walkers have reported being hit by falling rocks at such times.

Activities

Trekking Hellas (☎ 0432-75 214, fax 23 134, mobile 094-313 898), Rodou 11, Kalambaka (see later in this chapter), runs a rock-climbing school for beginners, and rock-climbing packages in the Meteora region for both beginners and advanced climbers. Meteora is a mecca for rock climbers and if you are one of those people whose feet are firmly planted on terra firma, you won't cease to be amazed at the daily spectacle of fly-like climbers inching their way up almost vertical pillars of rock.

If that wasn't enough for you, Trekking Hellas also organises ultralite flights over Meteora as well as paragliding and parachuting. Trekking Hellas can also be contacted via Vrachos Camping in Kastraki.

KALAMBAKA Καλαμπάκα

☎ 0432 • postcode 422 00 • pop 12,000

Kalambaka is almost entirely modern, having been devastated by the Nazis in WWII. Its chief claim to fame is its proximity to Meteora. It takes a whole day to see all of the monasteries of Meteora, so you'll need to spend the night either in Kalambaka or the village of Kastraki, which is closer to the rocks. First-time visitors to Kalambaka will be amazed at the vertical rocks that guard the northern flank of the town.

Orientation & Information

The central square is the hub of the town and the main thoroughfares of Rodou, Trikalon, Ioanninon, Kastrakiou and Vlahavas radiate from it. Kalambaka's other large square is Plateia Riga Fereou – Trikalon connects the two. The bus station is on Ikonomou (a continuation of Rodou). Most incoming buses stop on the central square to let passengers alight.

There is no EOT in Kalambaka but the Tourist Services Office (☎ 75 306, fax 25 343) on the central square has a wide range of information on all aspects of local tourism. The tourist police (☎ 22 109) are at the junction of Ipirou and Pindou.

The National Bank of Greece, on Plateia Riga Fereou, has both an ATM and an automatic exchange machine. The post office is on Trikalon and the OTE is on Ioanninon.

Places to Stay – Budget

There are several camp sites in the area. ***Theopetra Camping*** *(☎ 81 405)* is the first site you come across if you're coming from Trikala. ***Camping Philoxenia*** *(☎ 24 446)*, with good shade and a children's play area – including a water slide – is next on the right and ***Rizos International*** *(☎ 22 239)* is last. ***Camping Kalambaka*** *(☎ 22 309)* is on a road off to the right just before Kalambaka.

Rooms are plentiful in Kalambaka and you may well be approached as you arrive by bus. Choose with care. Look for the EOT-approved sign, wherever possible, and avoid rooms offered by a Mr Tottis, as they are overpriced. ***Koka Roka Rooms*** *(☎ 24 554)*, at the beginning of the path to Agia Triada monastery, is a bit of an institution among travellers. The few rooms are clean and nicely furnished and cost 8000 dr for doubles with bathroom. The host, Sakis, is an affable Greek-Australian who will proudly show you his impressive guestbooks. From the central square, walk 700m to the top of Vlahavas, and you'll come to the rooms on the left.

Kalambaka's cheapest hotel is the D class ***Hotel Astoria*** *(☎ 22 213, G Kondili 93)*. The clean, pine-furnished single/double rooms cost 5000/7000 dr, or 9000/10,000 dr with bathroom. The C class ***Hotel Meteora*** *(☎ 22 367, fax 75 550, Ploutarhou 14)* is a charming and cosy place with immaculate rooms with air-con and bathroom for

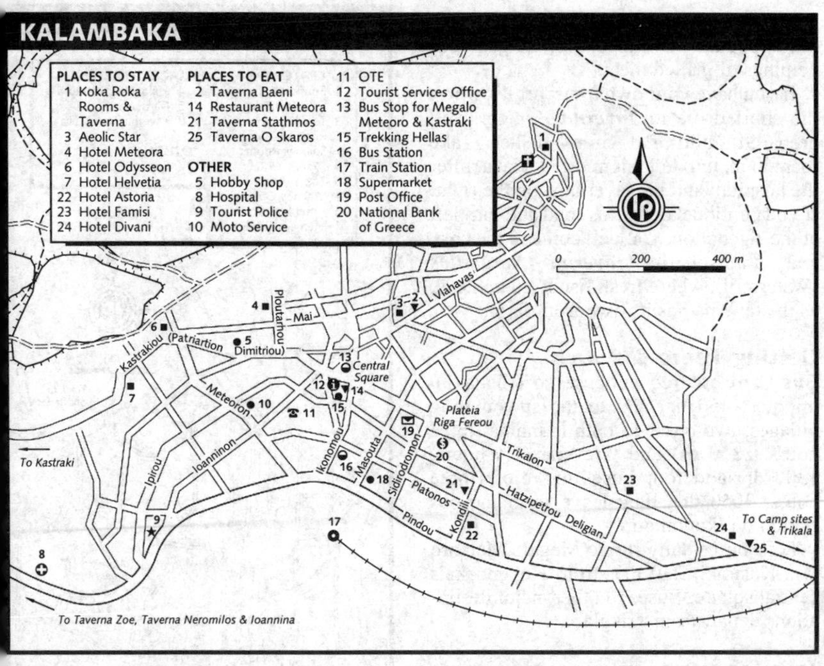

5000/7000 dr including breakfast. From the central square, walk along Kastrakiou, and Ploutarhou is the second turn right.

The C class ***Aeolic Star*** *(☎ 22 325, fax 22 444, Athanasiou Diakou 4)*, just north of the main square, has clean, compact rooms costing 6000/8500 dr. The C class ***Hotel Odysseon*** *(☎ 22 320, fax 75 307, Kastrakiou 54)*, heading out to Kastraki, has light, spacious rooms; rates are 8500/12,000 dr including breakfast.

Places to Stay – Mid-Range & Top End

Hotel Helvetia *(☎ 23 041, fax 25 241, Kastrakiou 45)* has very pleasant rooms for 12,000/15,000 dr. The B class ***Hotel Famisi*** *(☎ 24 117, fax 24 615, Trikalon 103)* has rooms for 13,500/20,600 dr.

The A class ***Hotel Divani*** *(☎ 22 584, fax 23 638)* is the first hotel you come to on the left as you enter Kalambaka from Trikala. Rooms here are 25,000/30,000 dr and include breakfast.

Places to Eat

Restaurant Meteora, on the central square, has a good range of reasonably priced look-and-point fare.

Koka Roka Taverna, below Koka Roka Rooms, serves tasty, low-priced food in a warm and homy environment. Grills prepared on the open hearth are their speciality. Its splendid rosé wine is, however, wicked when overindulged in. ***Taverna Stathmos*** *(Kondili 56)* operates as an ouzeri at lunchtime and at night it is a good psistaria serving spit-roast dishes.

Taverna Baeni *(Vlahavas 53)* is an unpretentious place serving tasty charcoal grilled meats. ***Tavern O Skaros***, just beyond Hotel Divani, has so far escaped the coach-loads of monastery-bound tourists, but is popular with locals for its generous helpings of grilled meat.

If you have your own transport it's worth the short drive to ***Taverna Zoe*** for well prepared traditional Greek dishes. Take Ioanninon, turn left (signposted Diava) after the hospital, and the taverna is on the right. If you continue along this road and turn left at the T-junction, you will come to the cosy and atmospheric ***Taverna Neromilos*** (Watermill), where fresh fish is guaranteed, as the taverna has its own trout farm.

Getting There & Away

Bus There are frequent buses to Trikala (30 minutes, 450 dr) and to the surrounding villages, two buses to both Ioannina (three hours, 2350 dr) and Grevena (1¼ hours, 1300 dr) and four buses to Volos (three hours, 3050 dr); they leave from the bus station on Ikonomou.

Four buses daily run to Megalo Meteoro (via Kastraki, 230 dr), from Kalambaka's central square. Buses to other major destinations depart from Trikala.

Train At present trains are not running from Trikala because of line upgrading.

Getting Around

Motorbikes can be hired from the Hobby Shop (☎/fax 25 262), Patriarhou Dimitriou 28. The shop also offers a full motorbike service and bicycle rental. There is another rental shop called Moto Service (☎ 23 526), on Meteoron.

KASTRAKI Καστράκι

☎ 0432 • postcode 422 00 • pop 1500

The small village of Kastraki is 2km from Kalambaka. Its location right under the rocks is most impressive and the view all around the village has an other-world feel about it. Despite its small size, more than a million people pass through here each year, so it can feel a bit crowded at times. As a base for exploring the Meteora monasteries, or climbing the rocks themselves, Kastraki is a better choice than Kalambaka.

There is a nice walk from Kastraki to Kalambaka along the base of the rocks. From the children's playground by the main square, descend the steps and follow the road opposite up the hill. Turn right at the top and follow the road until you join up with the main road, from where Kalambaka is a 15 minute walk away.

Places to Stay

Vrachos Camping *(☎ 22 293, fax 23 134)*, has excellent facilities and a swimming pool. The sites are reasonably level and many are powered. There is a covered, communal eating area, and in summer there is a restaurant and free use of gas and barbecue for self-caterers. Kastraki also has a couple of other camp sites: ***Meteora Garden*** and ***Boufidis Camping***.

Zozas Pallas *(☎ 24 408, fax 25 344)*, next to Vrachos Camping, has very comfortable singles/doubles for 4000/8000 dr with bathroom. Farther up towards the village are ***Spanias Rooms*** *(☎ 75 966)*, with ample car parking and a relaxed and spacious environment. Rooms here go for 6000/8000 dr. Both Zozas and Spanias have a bar and cafeteria. Between these two is the C class ***Sydney Hotel*** *(☎ 23 079, fax 77 861)* run by a welcoming Greek-Australian. Pleasant rooms go for 8000/9000 dr including breakfast. The C class ***Hotel France*** *(☎ 24 186, fax 75 186)*, opposite Vrachos Camping, is run by a French-speaking Greek man and his wife who can fill you in on some 'hidden' walks around the rocks. Good rooms here go for 6000/8000 dr. The hotel also has a restaurant and bar.

Rooms Batalogianni *(☎ 23 253)* has rates of 8000/10,000 dr with bathroom. The rooms are on the right as you go up the hill towards the main square. Beyond the square, ***Villa San Giorgio*** *(☎ 22 289)* has well furnished doubles for 12,000 dr. The immaculate ***Tsileli Rooms*** *(☎ 22 438)* has rooms with bathroom for 10,000/15,000 dr. Take the main road to Meteora and look for the sign for the rooms on the left.

Places to Eat

There is no shortage of eating places in Kastraki. The best meals can be had at ***Gardenia*** near the main square. ***Taverna Triantafilia*** next to Spanias Rooms serves generous portions of grilled meat.

At ***Philoxenia Restaurant***, on the main road to Meteora, the speciality is moussaka but grills are also served.

Northern Greece Βόρεια Ελλάδα

Northern Greece comprises the regions of Epiros, Macedonia and Thrace. With thickly forested mountains and tumbling rivers, these areas resemble the Balkans more than other parts of Greece. Northern Greece offers great opportunities for trekking, but it is an area where you don't have to go into the wilds to get off well worn tourist tracks, because its towns are little visited by foreign holiday-makers. Unlike the unglamorous and noisy towns of the Peloponnese and central Greece, many of which serve as transport hubs to get out of quickly, most towns in northern Greece have considerable appeal, with atmospheric old quarters of narrow streets and wood-framed houses.

HIGHLIGHTS

- The fairy-tale slate and stone villages of the Zagorohoria
- Greece's natural wonder, the Vikos Gorge
- The solitude and spiritual peace in the monastic community of Mt Athos
- Thessaloniki, the dynamic, bustling capital of northern Greece
- Vergina, site of the majestic royal tombs of Philip II of ancient Macedonia
- The lonely beauty of the Prespa Lakes
- Climbing Mt Olympus, and being at one with the gods of ancient Greece
- The lush forest and bird life of the Dadia Forest Reserve

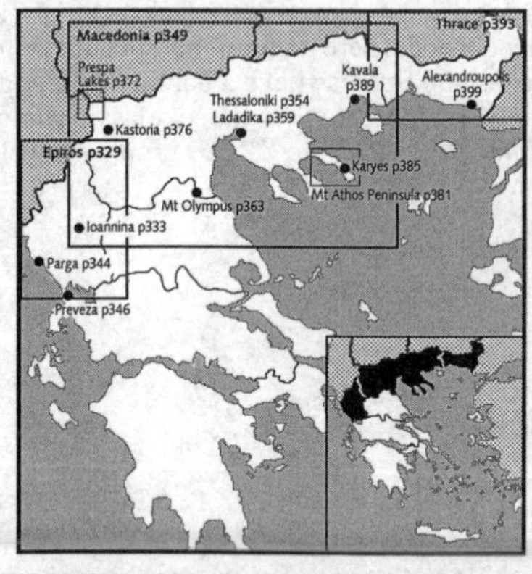

Epiros Ηπειρος

Epiros occupies the north-west corner of the Greek mainland. To the north is Albania, to the west is the Ionian Sea and Corfu. Its port of Igoumenitsa is a jumping-off point for ferries to Corfu and Italy. The high Pindos Mountains form the region's eastern boundary, separating it from Macedonia and Thessaly.

The road from Ioannina to Kalambaka cuts through the Pindos Mountains and is one of the most scenically spectacular in Greece, particularly the section between Metsovo and Kalambaka, called the Katara Pass. In northern Epiros the Vikos-Aoös National Park is a wilderness of lofty mountains, cascading waterfalls, precipitous gorges, fast-flowing rivers and dense forests harbouring villages of slate-stone houses. These settlements, in the Zagoria region, are known as the Zagorohoria.

The beaches on the Ionian Sea are very popular with Greeks, and also with visiting Italians and Germans, while the ancient site of Dodoni is known for its oracle which predates the more illustrious oracle of Delphi.

History

In early times Epiros' remote mountainous terrain was inhabited by tribes unaffected by, and oblivious to, what was happening in the rest of the country. Eventually one tribe, the Molossi, became so powerful that it

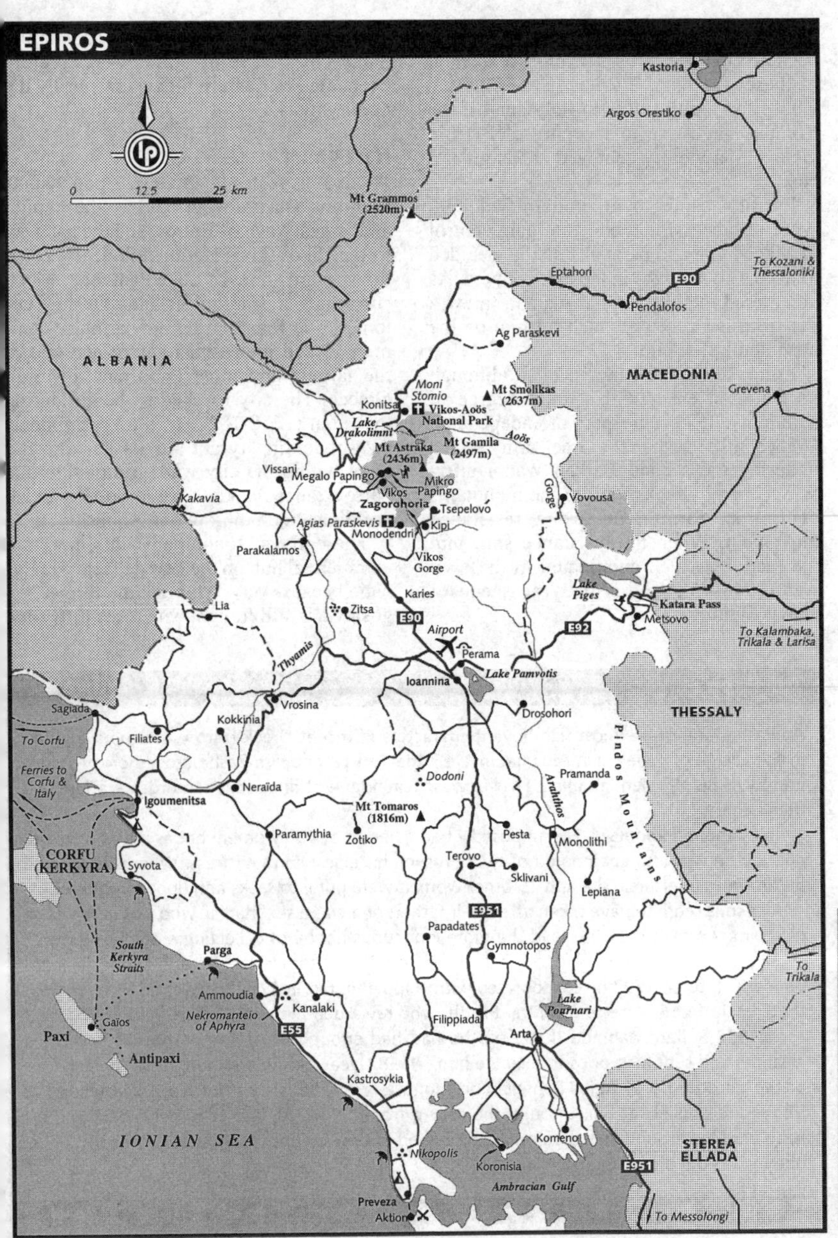

NORTHERN GREECE

dominated the whole region, and its leader became king of Epiros. The most renowned of these was King Pyrrhus (319-272 BC), whose foolhardy fracas in Italy against the Romans gave rise to the phrase 'Pyrrhic victory' – a victory achieved at too great a cost.

Pyrrhus came to an undignified end. After unsuccessful attempts to gain control of Macedonia and parts of Italy, he decided to have a go at Argos in the Peloponnese. As he entered the city, an old woman threw a tile from her rooftop which hit him on the head and killed him.

Epiros fell to the Turks in 1431, although its isolation ensured it a great degree of autonomy. It became part of independent Greece in 1913 when the Greek army seized it during the second Balkan War. During WWII many Greeks took to the mountains of Epiros, forming a strong resistance movement. When the resistance split into the factions which culminated in the civil war (1944-45), Epiros was the scene of heavy fighting.

During this time, as in Macedonia, many children from Epiros were forcibly evacuated to Eastern bloc countries by the communists.

IOANNINA Ιωάννινα

☎ 0651 • postcode 450 00 • pop 90,000

Ioannina (ih-o-**ah**-nih-nah) is the capital and largest town of Epiros, and the gateway to the Vikos-Aoös National Park. It lies on the western shore of Lake Pamvotis, which surrounds a tranquil island. During Ottoman rule Ioannina became a major commercial and intellectual centre and one of the largest and most important towns in Greece. The city reached its height during the reign (1788-1822) of the ignominious, swashbuckling tyrant Ali Pasha. The old town within the city walls has picturesque narrow lanes flanked by traditional Turkish buildings, including two mosques.

These days, Ioannina is an important commercial hub on the new de facto Via Egnatia because travel through the former Yugoslavia is still fraught with some difficulty.

Ali Pasha

Ali Pasha, one of the most flamboyant characters of recent Greek history, was born in 1741 in the village of Tepeleni in Albania. In 1787 the Turks made him Pasha (governor) of Trikala and by 1788 he ruled Ioannina. His life was a catalogue of brigandage, murder, warfare and debauchery.

Tales abound about Ali. He supposedly had a harem of 400 women, but as if that were not enough he was also enamoured of Kyra Frosyni, his eldest son's mistress. When she rejected his amorous overtures, she and 15 other women were put into sacks and tipped into the lake.

Ali's sons seem to have taken after their father: one was a sex maniac who was in the habit of raping women; the other had the more innocuous hobby of collecting erotic literature.

Ali's lifelong ambition was to break away from the Ottoman Empire and create an independent state. In 1797 he collaborated with Napoleon, but in 1798 he wrested Preveza from the French. In 1817 he courted the British, who rewarded him with Parga.

In 1822 Sultan Mahmud II decided he had had enough of Ali's opportunistic and fickle alliances and sent his troops to execute him. The 82-year-old Ali took refuge on the 1st floor of the guesthouse of Agios Panteleimon monastery on the island, but was killed when the troops fired bullets at him through the ceiling from below. Ali was then beheaded, and his head paraded around Epiros before being buried in Constantinople (İstanbul) – the rest of his body was buried in Ioannina.

Orientation

Ioannina's main bus station is on the corner of Sina and Zosimadon (the northern extension of Markou Botsari). To get to the town centre, find the pharmacy outside the bus station, walk left along Markou Botsari opposite, turn right at the Hotel Egnatia and then left into 28 Oktovriou, which is the first main road you come to. Continue along 28 Oktovriou to the major road junction; this is Ioannina's main street – to the left it is called Averof and to the right, Dodonis.

To reach the old town, turn left into Averof and continue to Plateia Georgiou; on the right is the gateway into the old town. To reach the quay from where boats leave for the island, walk across Plateia Georgiou and follow the kastro walls along Karamanli, which leads towards the lakefront. The ferry quay is on the right.

Ioannina's other bus station is at Vizaniou 28, the southerly continuation of 28 Oktovriou.

Information

Most people come to Epiros to trek in the mountains, and Ioannina is a good place for information or arrange an organised trek. The EOT (☎ 25 086, fax 72 148) is on Napoleonda Zerva 2. Turn right from 28 Oktovriou into Dodonis and it's on the right, set back on a square. It has information on the Vikos Gorge trek and is open year-round 7.30 am to 2.30 pm and 5.30 to 8.30 pm Monday to Friday, and 9 am to 1 pm Saturday.

The tourist police (☎ 25 673) are opposite the post office on 28 Oktovriou.

The OTE and post office are on 28 Oktovriou. There is a new post office on Georgiou Papandreou, about a 10 minute walk from Limnopoula Camping in the direction of the kastro and just past the Big Atlantik supermarket.

There are two Internet cafes, close to each other. The Giannena Club (☎ 35 312) at Stoa Saka 30-32, close to Plateia Pargis, is the newer and sports nine terminals. Kourdisto Portokali ('Clockwork Orange'; ☎ 72 176) is harder to find, at Pyrsinella 5, downstairs off a dark arcade. Both are open from 10 am onwards.

Museums

Archaeological Museum This excellent museum is spacious and well laid out. The first room on the right has a collection of Palaeolithic tools, including a hand axe from Kokkinopolis, near Preveza, dated to 200,000 BC. Also in this room are finds from Dodoni, including two charming bronze statuettes of children; one is throwing a ball and the other is holding a dove. Another delightful piece is a tortoise-shaped terracotta rattle.

The far room on the left houses a permanent exhibition of 19th and 20th century paintings, sculptures and prints, including some mildly risque nudes among the stuffy portraits of local dignitaries. Don't miss the beautiful little terracotta sculpture entitled *Two Friends*, by Theodoros Hrisohoïdou.

The museum (☎ 25 490) is in a small park set back from the east side of Averof. It is open 8 am to 6 pm Tuesday to Friday and 8.30 am to 3 pm on weekends, year-round. Admission is 500 dr; students free.

Byzantine Museum It's worth visiting this museum (☎ 25 989), in the kastro, for its collection of Byzantine art. It's open 8.30 am to 3 pm Tuesday to Sunday. Entry is 500 dr.

Popular Art Museum Known also as the Municipal Museum (☎ 26 356), this museum is housed in the Aslan Pasha mosque in the old town. Its eclectic collection includes local costumes and photographs of old Ioannina. It's open 8 am to 3 pm Monday to Friday and 9 am to 3 pm on weekends. Admission is 700 dr; students 400 dr.

Folkloric Museum This museum (☎ 20 515), at Mihail Angelou 42, has a small display of local costumes, embroidery and cooking utensils. It is open 5.30 to 8 pm Monday and 10 am to 1 pm Wednesday. Admission is 100 dr.

Vrellis Wax Museum This museum (☎ 92 128) is a mini Madame Tussaud's, but with an emphasis on modern Greek history. The museum is at Bizani, 14km out of Ioannina on the road to Athens. It is open 10 am to 5 pm daily. Admission is 1000 dr; 500 dr for students.

Trekking

If you wish to trek in more remote areas than the Vikos Gorge, then talk to someone at the EOS (Greek Alpine Club; ☎ 22 138), Despotatou Ipirou 2. The office is open 7 to 9 pm Monday to Friday.

Robinson Travel (☎ 29 402, fax 27 071), 8 Merarhias Grammou 10, specialises in treks to remote areas of Epiros. Treks are usually block-booked by groups. Call or fax to see if you can join a group as a 'blow-in'.

Every Sunday between October and June the EOS organises a one day trek in the Pindos Mountains. Anyone is welcome and the cost is approximately 2000 dr per person.

Special Events

During July and August the Festival of Ancient Drama takes place at the restored theatre at the nearby site of Dodoni. Information is available from the EOT.

Places to Stay – Budget

Limnopoula Camping *(☎ 25 265, fax 38 060)* is on the edge of the lake, 2km north-west of town. The site has a restaurant and bar and should be open all year. Take a Perama-bound bus from Plateia Dimokratias and alight at the roundabout with the two petrol stations.

Near the main bus station, the rather dingy but functional D class ***Hotel Paris*** *(☎ 20 541, Tsirigoti 6)* has clean singles/doubles for 6000/9000 dr. In the same alleyway is the cheap E class pension ***Agapi Inn*** (same management and telephone) which has doubles/triples for 6000/8000 dr.

Places to Stay – Mid-Range

All hotels in this category have TV and private bathroom. The C class ***Hotel Egnatia*** *(☎ 25 667, fax 75 060)* on the corner of Dangli and Aravantinou, near the main bus station, has somewhat spartan rooms for 12,000/17,000 dr for singles/doubles. The C class ***King Pyrros Hotel*** *(☎ 27 652, fax 29 980, Gounari 3)* charges 12,000/18,000 dr. Gounari is opposite the clock tower on Averof.

Near Agapi Inn, the comfortable and family-oriented C class ***Dioni*** *(☎ 27 864, fax 27 032, Tsirigoti 10)* has rooms for 12,000/17,000 dr. On the south side of the main square (Plateia Pyrrou) is the decidedly pleasant and modern C class ***Galaxy Hotel*** *(☎ 25 432, fax 30 724, email galaxy@hol.gr)*, with rooms for 12,000/17,000 dr; some have fine views over the lake.

Places to Stay – Top End

The long-standing B class ***Xenia*** *(☎ 47 301, fax 47 189, Dodonis 33)* is a decent, upper market hotel handy to the city centre. Singles/doubles cost 15,250/22,100 dr, with breakfast. The hotel has a bar and restaurant. The B class ***Palladion*** *(☎ 25 856, fax 74 034, email palladion@otenet.gr, Noti Botsari 1)* is 100m up the pedestrian street from Hotel Egnatia. This modern hotel has very well appointed rooms for 15,500/18,800 dr.

The newest, poshest and best is the sumptuous ***Hotel du Lac*** *(☎ 59 100, fax 59 200)* on the corner of A. Miaouli and Ikkou. It's a custom-built complex, complete with congress hall, on the lakefront on the south side of town. Superb rooms with special phone jacks for Internet access go for 24,000/33,000 dr, including a large buffet breakfast.

Places to Eat

For a wide choice of teas, coffee and liqueurs, visit the small but very atmospheric ***Filistro Cafe*** *(Andronikou Paleologou 20)* inside the kastro. This is also a good place for breakfast on weekends.

On the main square is the oldest established eatery, still going strong. ***Oasi*** on Plateia Pyrrou serves up a wide variety of ready-made dishes ranging in price from 1000 dr to 1700 dr.

There are a couple of joints opposite the main kastro entrance worth checking out. The first is ***To Manteio Taverna***, where a

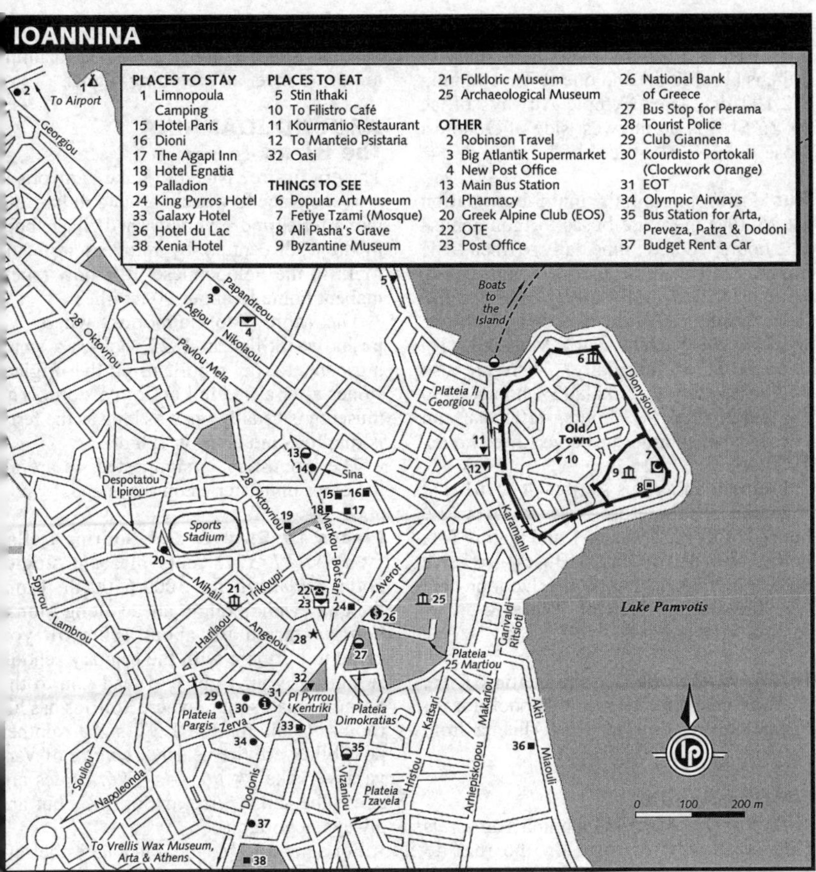

good feed will cost about 2200 dr. To the right is the more intimate and slightly cheaper ***Kourmanio*** with excellent home cooking as well as the usual grills.

Gourmands and gastronomes alike will do well to head over to the restaurant strip on the western side of the kastro. By the lake is ***Stin Ithaki*** (☎ *73 012, Str Papagou 20a)*, the pick of the bunch. Its imaginative menu includes *aïvaliotiko*, a Lesvos speciality made from aubergines and pork, and *bekri mezes Thrakiotikos*, a tasty dish of beef cubes in a spicy sauce. Prices are very reasonable.

Shopping

For a long time Ioannina has been a centre for the manufacture of filigree silver. Shops selling this type of jewellery line Averof and Karamanli. Prices start at around 3000 dr for rings and earrings.

You can also buy woodcarvings and other souvenirs in the same area. Epiros is famous for its flokati rugs, also known as *velenzes*.

Getting There & Away

Air There are usually two flights daily to Athens (18,400 dr) and one to Thessaloniki (12,100 dr). The Olympic Airways office (☎ 26 518) is on the west side of Dodonis, close to the EOT office.

Bus From Ioannina's main bus station (☎ 26 404) there are buses to Igoumenitsa (2½ hours, 1800 dr, nine daily), Athens (7½ hours, 7250 dr, nine daily), Konitsa (two hours, 1150 dr, 11 daily), Thessaloniki (seven hours, 6050 dr, five daily with one weekly via Kozani) and Metsovo (1½ hours, 1050 dr, four daily). There are also two buses daily to Trikala (3½ hours, 2750 dr) and Kozani (4½ hours, 4100 dr), and one daily in summer to Parga (three hours, 1900 dr).

From the other bus station (☎ 25 014) at Vizaniou 28, there are buses to Arta (2½ hours, 1400 dr, 10 daily) and Patras (4½ hours, 4400 dr, two daily). Buses also leave here for Preveza, Parga and Dodoni here (see the Dodoni Getting There & Away section for details).

To/From Albania See the Getting There & Away chapter earlier in this book for information on going to/from Albania from Ioannina.

Getting Around

To/From the Airport Ioannina's airport is 5km north-west of town on the road to Perama. Take bus No 7, which runs every 20 minutes from the bus stop just south of Averof near the clock tower. Bus Nos 1 and 2 run less frequently, but they also go past the airport.

Bus & Taxi The local bus service covers most parts of Ioannina. Buses from the lakefront usually take you up to the main square. Buy your ticket before you board the bus; there is a kiosk near the Olympic Airways office. Within the central area a single-trip ticket costs 150 dr.

Taxis (☎ 46 777) can be found around the main square and by the lake.

Car Budget Rent a Car (☎/fax 43 901) is at Dodonis 109, and it has a booth at Ioannina airport to meet all incoming flights.

AROUND IOANNINA

The Island To Νησί

This traffic-free island in Lake Pamvotis is a serene place to wander around. It has four monasteries and a whitewashed village built in the 17th century by refugees from the Mani in the Peloponnese. It is now a permanent home to about 90 families.

The **Moni Panteleïmonos**, where Ali Pasha was killed in 1822, houses a small museum. It was rebuilt using the original stones after a tree fell on it in a storm. The museum is usually open as long as the ferry is running, and entry is 100 dr.

The monastery is signposted, as are all the other monasteries on the island.

Places to Stay & Eat Sotirios Dellas *(☎ 0651-81 894)* rents pleasant single/double ***domatia*** for 5000/6500 dr. From the quay walk straight ahead along Monahon Nektariou for about 100m till you come to a square with the primary school. A sign on your right will lead you to the Saraï, a small square where Sotirios has his rooms. Look for the EOT sign. Another possibility are the nearby ***domatia*** of Varvara Varvaka *(☎ 0651-81 596)*. Rates are about the same price as Sotirios', but are always negotiable.

For a memorable meal in a lakeside setting, head for ***Gripos*** restaurant, to the right as you disembark from the ferry. The grilled trout is exquisite. ***Pamvotis*** restaurant, to the left of the quay, is owned by the same proprietor. It is equally good, and more likely to be open in the low season. A trout meal here will cost about 3000 dr.

Getting There & Away There are regular boats to the island (10 minutes, 200 dr). They usually run every hour in winter and every half-hour in summer, leaving from near the gate to the fortress, 50m west of Plateia Mavili.

Perama Cave Σπήλαιο Περάματος
This cave (☎ 0651-81 521), 4km north of Ioannina, is one of the largest in Greece. It was discovered in 1940 by locals searching for a hiding place from the Nazis, and explored by speleologists Ioannis and Anna Petrohilos, who also explored the Diros Caves in the Peloponnese. The cave at Perama is second in Greece only to the Diros Caves in its astonishing array of stalactites and stalagmites. It consists of many chambers and passageways and is 1100m long.

It's open 8 am to 8 pm daily. Admission is 1000 dr; 500 dr for students.

Bus No 8 runs every 20 minutes from near the clock tower to the village of Perama, 250m south of the cave.

Dodoni Δωδώνη

Dodoni, lying in a fertile valley at the foot of Mt Tomaros, 21km south-west of Ioannina, is Epiros' most important ancient site.

History An earth goddess was worshipped here as long ago as 2000 BC. She spoke through an oracle, reputedly the oldest in Greece. By the 13th century BC Zeus had taken over and it was believed he spoke through the rustling of leaves from a sacred oak tree. Around 500 BC a temple to Zeus was built, but only the foundations and a few columns of this and other smaller temples remain. The oracle was the most important in Greece until superseded by the Delphic oracle in the 6th century BC.

Exploring the Site The site's colossal 3rd century BC **theatre**, an ambitious project overseen by King Pyrrhus, has been restored, and is now the site of the Festival of Ancient Drama (see Special Events in the Ioannina section for details). To the north of the theatre a gate leads to the **acropolis**; part of its once-substantial walls are still standing. To the east of the theatre are the foundations of the **bouleuterion** (council house) and a small temple dedicated to Aphrodite. Close by are the scant remains of the **Sanctuary of Zeus**. This sacred precinct was the site of the oracle of Zeus and the sacred oak.

Christianity also left its mark on Dodoni, as evident from the remains of a 6th century Byzantine basilica, which was built over the remains of a sanctuary dedicated to Hercules.

The site is open 8 am to 5 pm daily. Admission is 500 dr; 400 dr for students.

Places to Stay & Eat ***Pension Andromahi*** *(☎ 0651-82 296)* is in the village of Dodoni, near the site. Double rooms cost 15,000 dr. ***Restaurant Andromachi*** (same owners and telephone) is open all year and does great pot-roast lamb which goes down well with a drop of Zitsa wine.

Getting There & Away The bus service to Dodoni is pretty abysmal considering it's Epiros' major ancient site. Buses leave from the bus station on Vizaniou in Ioannina on Monday, Tuesday, Wednesday, Friday and Saturday at 6.30 am and 4.30 pm. There are no buses on Thursday and only one on Sunday at 6 pm, which returns at 6.45 pm.

Buses return to Ioannina at 7.30 am and 5.30 pm. An alternative is to get a Zotiko bus, which stops 1.5km from the site. This bus leaves the Vizaniou station on Monday, Wednesday and Friday at 5.30 am and 2 pm, and returns at 7.15 am and 4.30 pm.

If your interest in archaeology is not enough to get you out of bed at dawn, then a taxi will cost around 5000 dr return plus 600 dr per hour of waiting time.

ZAGORIA Ζαγόρια

☎ 0653

The region of Zagoria, north of Ioannina, offers some breathtaking vistas and is drawing more and more visitors. The 44 villages in the area are collectively known as the Zagorohoria. As with many inaccessible mountainous areas in Greece, the Zagorohoria maintained a high degree of autonomy in Turkish times, so the economy and culture flourished.

An outstanding feature of the villages is the architecture. The houses are built entirely of slate from the surrounding mountains – a perfect blending of nature and architecture. With winding, cobbled and stepped streets, the villages could have leapt straight out of a Grimm fairy tale. Some are sadly depopulated, with only a few elderly inhabitants, while others, like Papingo, Monodendri and Tsepelovo, are beginning to thrive on the new-found tourism in the area.

There are three main destinations in the Zagorohoria of interest to travellers: the Papingo villages to the north; central Monodendri; and Tsepelovo farther east. Good roads connect most of the villages, and with a car you can see many of them in one day.

The **Vikos-Aoös National Park** encompasses much of the area. Within the park is the Tymfi Massif, part of the north Pindos Range which comprises Mt Astraka (2436m), Mt Gamila (2497m) and Mt Smolikas (2637m), the Vikos Gorge and the Aoös River Gorge. It's an area of outstanding natural beauty which is becoming popular with trekkers.

The area is thickly forested; hornbeam, maple, willow and oak predominate, but there are also fir, pine and cedar trees. Bears, wolves, wild boars, wild cats, wild goats and the rare Rissos quadruped roam the mountains. Vlach and Sarakatsani shepherds still live a semi-nomadic existence, taking their flocks up to high grazing ground in the summer and returning to the valleys in the autumn.

Monodendri is 38km north of Ioannina, and is reached by turning right off the main Ioannina-Konitsa road near the village of Karyes.

Farther north are the twin villages of **Megalo Papingo** and **Mikro Papingo**. The view is awe-inspiring as you approach these villages by road from the bed of the **Voïdomatis River**, after you have passed through **Aristi**, the last village before Papingo. There are no fewer than 15 hairpin bends that switchback in rapid succession up to the ledge where the Papingo villages nestle under the looming hulk of Mt Astraka. As you wind your way up, there are spectacular views into the Vikos Gorge on your right.

Papingo is popular with wealthy Greeks, so be prepared to pay for services accordingly. Trekkers of less lavish means can buy some food items, though it might be a good idea to stock up on provisions in Ioannina, since there are limited supplies in the Papingo villages.

After a strenuous hike to Papingo you might want to cool off in the natural **rock pools**, which are exquisitely refreshing on a hot day. The 300m path to the pools starts at a bend in the road between Megalo and Mikro Papingo. Look out for the EU logo with the word 'Life' in the middle of the telltale stone gateway.

The village of **Vikos**, 5km beyond Aristi, is a good starting point for the gorge trek and it is a shorter hike to Monodendri or vice versa than from the Papingo villages. The view from the panoramic platform in Vikos is stunning.

Tsepelovo is a delightful Zagoria village 51km north of Ioannina. There are many opportunities for scenic day walks from here. There is a post office and public phone.

Vikos Gorge Χαράδρα του Βίκου

The focal point of the region is the 10km-long Vikos Gorge, which begins at the village of **Monodendri** (1090m), situated at the southern end of the gorge.

The Vikos Gorge is the most trekked gorge in Greece after the Samaria Gorge on Crete. It doesn't require any special expertise, but it is a strenuous walk of around 7½ hours, ending at either of the twin villages of **Megalo Papingo** or **Mikro Papingo**. Stout walking boots are recommended. You can tackle the gorge from either end, but if you have come by car, you will have to arrange a lift back to your vehicle via the long road route.

Before you come to Monodendri, visit the Ioannina EOT or the EOS. The staff there will give you a map of the gorge, and answer any questions. Whatever you do, come prepared for serious walking; this is no Sunday afternoon stroll in the park.

At the far end of Monodendri there is a spectacular view down into the gorge from the 15th century **Moni Agias Paraskevis**. The descent into the gorge is a steep marked path between the village and the monastery. Once in the gorge, it's a four hour walk to the end, from where a trail up to the right leads to the settlement of Mikro Papingo (2½ hours). The larger settlement of Megalo Papingo is a farther 2km west, but the track splits into two at the base of the climb. You can also terminate your trek at the village of **Vikos**.

Klima Spring, about halfway along the gorge, is the only source of water, so take plenty along with you. Probably the most breathtaking view of the gorge for the less energetic is from the **Oxya Lookout**, 5km beyond Monodendri. You will have to hitch or walk since there is no public transport.

Mt Gamila to Tsepelovo

From Mikro Papingo there is a good marked path to the ***Gamila Refuge*** (also called Rodovoli Refuge) at 1950m, owned by the EOS (☎ 41 115) in Megalo Papingo, which you must contact for bookings (2500 dr per person per night). Cooked meals, soft drinks, beer and wine are all available from the refuge at somewhat inflated prices. If it is fully booked you should be able to camp by the dry lake *(xiroloutsa)* on the next valley floor.

From this refuge there are marked trails to Drakolimni, or 'dragon lake' (one hour), and to the village of Tsepelovo (six to seven hours). For rock climbers there are over 20 routes up Mt Astraka. The EOS in Ioannina has a leaflet detailing these.

Activities

So far the region is untouched by mass tourism, but several companies organise treks in the Zagoria region, including the British-based Exodus Expeditions and Robinson Travel Agency in Ioannina.

The latter also runs an Activity Centre (☎ 71 041, email robinson@compulink.gr) in the village of Kipi. It is open from May to October. The staff organise a whole range of activities in the area, including walking, rock climbing, paragliding, canyoning and mountain biking.

Places to Stay & Eat

Monodendri The choicest accommodation here is the lovely, traditional ***Monodendri Pension & Restaurant*** *(☎ 71 300)* where doubles are 9000 dr. The restaurant serves reasonably priced, well prepared food, specialising in *pittes* – oven-baked pies made from filo pastry with various delicious fillings – the regional speciality. The pension is on the upper square on the main road. Another pleasant place is ***Vikos Hotel*** *(☎ 71 232)* with doubles for 8750 dr. There are also rooms available in private houses – look for signs. ***Haradra tou Vikou*** *(☎ 71 559)*, close by Monodendri Pension on the main road, is another taverna that also does great pittes and other local dishes.

Megalo Papingo There are domatia and a couple of hostelries here. ***Xenonas tou Kouli*** *(☎/fax 41 115)* has six rooms in various combinations from 12,000 dr to 15,000 dr for doubles/triples. There is a minimarket and cafe-bar as well. It is best to book in advance. The owners also serve as official EOS tour guides. ***Xenonas Kalliopi*** *(☎/fax 41 081)*, on the southern side of the village (look out for the purple and blue gate), has eight rooms, again in various combinations ranging from 10,000/15,000 dr for singles/triples. There is also a small restaurant-bar here serving home cooking and pittes.

Mikro Papingo There is one pleasant place to stay here: ***Xenonas Dias*** *(☎ 41 257, fax 41 892)* with 12 doubles/triples for 11,000/12,500 dr. There is also a little restaurant for breakfast and excellent meals, and the place is open year-round.

O Nikos *(☎ 41 893)* serves good food. It offers local pittes along with other regular fare, and has a good wine selection. Expect to pay between 3000 dr and 4000 dr. Nearby, ***Ioannides*** *(☎ 41 125)* is a little stone cottage-cum-restaurant and serves tasty, if a little pricey, home-cooked meals.

Vikos The ***domatia*** of Sotiris Karpouzas *(☎ 41 176)* have modern doubles/triples with bathroom for 12,000/15,000 dr. Food is also available.

Tsepelovo The immaculate ***Gouris Pension*** *(☎ 094-789 909)* has doubles for 12,000 dr, including breakfast and an evening meal. There are a few domatia in the village. Try ***Erasmia Deligianni Domatia*** *(☎ 81 232)*, on the main (upper) square, with doubles/triples for 10,000/12,000 dr. ***Hagiati Hotel*** *(☎/fax 81 301)*, just back from the same square, charges 12,000 dr for double studios with a 20% loading for each extra person. A buffet breakfast is included. Winter prices are higher.

Kitas Taverna is on the main square and there is another taverna on the right of the main road as you approach from Ioannina.

Getting There & Away

There are buses from Ioannina to Megalo and Mikro Papingo (two hours, 1100 dr, Monday, Wednesday and Friday at 6 am and 2.30 pm with the Wednesday bus calling in at Vikos in summer), Tsepelovo (1½ hours, 900 dr, Monday, Wednesday and Friday at 6 am and 3.15 pm) and Monodendri (one hour, 700 dr, daily at 6 am and 4.15 pm).

All buses return to Ioannina almost immediately upon arrival in the villages.

KONITSA Κόνιτσα

☎ 0655 • postcode 441 00 • pop 4000

Konitsa (**ko**-nit-sah), 64km north of Ioannina, is the largest settlement in the area. It's a lively market town and a good base from which to explore the northern Zagorohoria. In recent times it has become a centre of sorts for kayaking and trekking in the Vikos-Aoös National Park.

Konitsa is built amphitheatrically on a hillside, and the view over the Voïdomatis Valley as the sun sets over the mountains in Albania is quite a sight. A serpentine road leads to the town centre from the main Ioannina-Kozani road.

Information

The bus station is on the central square, where you will also find the post office and a Commercial Bank with an ATM. There is no EOT or tourist police.

Activities

The scenic walk to **Stomio Monastery** along the Aoös River Gorge takes about 1½ hours. Cross the stone bridge at the beginning of the town (coming from Ioannina), turn left and follow the Aoös River to the waterfall. Cross the bridge and follow the path up to the monastery. Occasionally there is a lone monk in residence here who shows visitors around, but even if you find the monastery locked, the walk is worthwhile for the tremendous views.

Paddler (☎ 23 102, fax 23 101), Averof 16, organises kayaking, rafting, canyoning, paragliding and trekking expeditions. Ask for Nikos Kyritsis.

Places to Stay & Eat

There is a swathe of domatia along the winding road leading up to Konitsa from the main road, but ***To Dentro Guesthouse*** *(☎/fax 22 055)*, 500m before the town centre on the Ioannina road, is the best deal. Look for the bright orange exterior on the last bend of the road to the main square. This guesthouse has beautifully furnished, spotless doubles/triples for 9500/14,000 dr with bath. The English-speaking owner, Ioannis, can advise on local walks. To Dentro also has the best restaurant in town. Pot-roast goat or lamb is a good bet and trout is equally satisfying, or try the speciality of grilled feta with chilli and tomato.

A newcomer is the very tastefully furbished ***Kougias Hotel*** *(☎ 23 830, fax 23 960)* on Kentriki Plateia, which offers exquisite rooms, each decorated with a different floral colour scheme. There is a bar and cafeteria, and favoured guests get to taste the owner's award-winning cabernet sauvignon wine. Singles/doubles are 9000/12,000 dr.

The main square has a fast-food joint, and the reasonable ***Zourloukas Psistaria*** *(☎ 22 915)*. There is also a small supermarket behind the post office.

Getting There & Away

On weekdays there are eight buses to Ioannina (two hours, 1150 dr); there are five on weekends. Two daily Ioannina-Kozani buses (four hours, 3000 dr) pass through Konitsa. If you want to go farther, go to Kozani first, then take an onward bus. There are also buses from Ioannina to Thessaloniki that pass through Konitsa on Monday in winter (six hours, 5100 dr) and on Monday and Friday in summer.

METSOVO Μέτσοβο

☎ 0656 • postcode 442 00 • pop 2900

The village of Metsovo (**met**-so-vo, 1160m), 58km from Ioannina and 90km from Trikala, sprawls down a mountainside just south of the Katara Pass, at the junction of Epiros, Thessaly and Macedonia. The inhabitants are descendants of Vlach shepherds, most of whom have hung up their crooks to make a living in the tourist trade.

Metsovo has much tourist appeal: locals dressed in traditional costumes, local handicrafts, regional cuisine, stone mansions, invigorating air, a superb mountain setting and good skiing. Some find the village twee and artificial while others are enamoured of its considerable charm.

Despite its peasant origins, Metsovo attracts an urban set and there is a wide choice of quality hotels and restaurants. If you are on your way by road across the Pindos Range, stop for a day or two and sample the ambience.

History

Originally a small settlement of shepherds, Metsovo was granted many privileges in Ottoman times as reward for guarding the pass upon which the village stands. This pass was the only route across the Pindos Range, and Metsovite vigilance facilitated the passage of Ottoman troops. These privileges led to Metsovo becoming an important centre of finance, commerce, handicrafts and sheep farming. A school was established in 1659, at a time when Greek-language schools were not allowed in other parts of the country.

Metsovo's privileges were abolished in 1795 by that spoilsport Ali Pasha, and in 1854 it suffered considerable damage from Ottoman troops. But Metsovo was very lucky in its many prosperous benefactors: locals who had gone on to achieve national and international recognition. The most famous of them were Georgios Averof (1815-99) and Mihail Tositsas (1885-1950). Both bequeathed large amounts of money to Metsovo, which was used to restore the town to its former glory and to finance several small industries.

Orientation & Information

From Kalambaka, turn left after the Katara Pass to reach Metsovo. Orientation in Metsovo is easy as there is only one main thoroughfare, which loops down to the central square, passing many restaurants, hotels and souvenir shops. A maze of stone pathways winds between the fine, traditional houses.

The bus stop is on the central square, in front of Café Diethnes. There is no EOT or tourist police. The regular police (☎ 41 233) are on the right, along the road opposite the bus stop.

The post office is on the right side of the main thoroughfare as you leave the central square. To reach the OTE, walk along the road opposite the bus station, keep veering right and the OTE is on the right. The building is a bit inconspicuous, so keep your eyes open.

The National Bank of Greece is on the far side of the central square, and there are another two banks as well.

Things to See

The **Tositsas mansion** has been restored as a folk museum, and is a faithful reconstruction of a wealthy 19th century Metsovite household, with exquisitely handcrafted furniture, artefacts and utensils. It's about halfway up the main street – look for the wooden sign. It's open 8.30 am to 1 pm and 4 to 6 pm daily except Thursday. Wait at the door until the guide lets you in (every half-hour). Admission is 500 dr.

The 14th century **Moni Agiou Nikolaou** stands in a gorge below Metsovo. Its chapel has post-Byzantine frescoes and a beautiful carved wooden iconostasis. The monastery is a 30 minute walk from Metsovo and is signposted to the left, just before Hotel Athens.

The **Averof Gallery** was financed by Georgios Averof's three children. It houses a permanent collection of 19th and 20th century works by Greek painters and sculptors. Turn left at the far side of the central square – the gallery is on the right. It's open 9 am to 1.30 pm and 5 to 7.30 pm daily except Tuesday. Admission is 500 dr; 300 dr for students.

Skiing

As you come from Kalambaka, Metsovo's ski centre (☎ 41 211) is on the right-hand side of the main Kalambaka-Ioannina highway, just before the turn-off for the town. There is a taverna and an 82 seat ski lift, two downhill runs and a 5km cross-country run. Ski hire is available in Metsovo.

Places to Stay – Budget

There is no shortage of accommodation, with no fewer than 14 hotels and abundant domatia. The hotels, predictably, have a folksy ambience, right down to the only E class establishment, ***Hotel Athens*** *(☎ 41 332, fax 42 009)*. Just off the central square, it's old but clean, and the woven rugs on the floors add a homy touch; doubles/triples cost 8000/10,000 dr with bathroom. Allied to the Athens are the ***Filoxenia*** domatia *(☎ 41 021, fax 42 009)* just behind the central park area, close to the art gallery. Singles/doubles cost 8000/10,000 dr, while 15,000 dr will get you a four-person suite with one of the most spectacular views in town.

The D class ***Hotel Acropolis*** *(☎ 41 672)* has traditional furniture, wooden floors and ceilings, and colourful wall hangings. Doubles/triples with bathroom are 10,000/14,000 dr. Look out for it on the right at the beginning of the road to Metsovo.

Places to Stay – Mid-Range & Top End

Hotel Galaxias *(☎ 41 202, fax 41 124)* is the closest hotel to the bus stop. Very comfortable singles/doubles cost 12,000/16,000 dr. The C class ***Hotel Egnatia*** *(☎ 41 263, fax 41 485)* has cosy rooms with balcony and wood-panelled walls for 11,000/13,200 dr. It's on the right side of the main road as you approach the central square.

Opposite, farther up the hill, the C class ***Hotel Bitouni*** *(☎ 41 217, fax 41 545)* has immaculate rooms and a charming lounge with a flagstone floor, brass plates, embroidered cushions and carved wooden coffee tables. Singles/doubles/suites are 10,830/13,000/18,000 dr.

Hotel Apollon *(☎ 41 844, fax 42 110)* is Metsovo's best hotel. The gorgeous, carpeted rooms cost 14,500/18,000/28,500 dr. Walk along the road opposite the bus station and look for the sign pointing right.

Places to Eat

The restaurant at ***Hotel Athens*** has tasty, reasonably priced food with many local specialities. Expect to pay under 2000 dr for an average meal. ***Restaurant Galaxias***, next to its associated hotel, is a very good choice. Try the local pittes and *hilopittes* (pasta) with veal, accompanied by fine rosé, for around 2350 dr.

The 1st-floor ***Taverna Metsovitiko Saloni*** is a largish establishment just up from the post office, with a beautiful interior of traditional carved wooden furniture and colourful wall hangings. A meal here costs about 2600 dr.

Shopping

Craft shops selling both quality stuff and kitsch are ubiquitous. The old-fashioned food shop opposite the bus stop sells the famous local cheeses.

Getting There & Away

There are six direct buses to Ioannina (1000 dr) and two or three to Trikala (1500 dr). In summer there is also a direct bus to Athens (7000 dr). To catch a Thessaloniki bus you will have to walk up to the main road and wave the bus down – these buses normally come from Ioannina.

The new Pindos vehicle tunnel from Metsovo to Malakasi (in Thessaly) has been finished, but bureaucracy continues to prevent the completion of the new Via Egnatia road which will traverse the tunnel, so the Katara Pass is still the only option to cross the Pindos Range. The latest plan seems to be to build huge suspension bridges at either side of the tunnel to solve the access problem.

IGOUMENITSA Ηγουμενίτσα

☎ 0665 • postcode 461 00 • pop 6800

Once a sleepy little outpost, the west coast port of Igoumenitsa (ih-goo-meh-**nit**-sah), 100km from Ioannina, is where you get ferries to Corfu and Italy. It is growing quickly thanks to its strategic position as an important port to Western Europe from the southern Balkans and Middle East. There is little of interest, but if you are travelling by ferry and using Igoumenitsa as your Greek entry or exit point, then you are likely to be spending some time here, if only to have a meal or wait for a boat or bus. Ferries leave in the morning and evening, so you may not have to stay overnight.

There is a very pleasant beach and taverna at **Drepanos**, about 6km north of town, if you feel like a relaxing swim and a meal.

Orientation

Ferries for Italy and Corfu leave from three separate quays quite close to one another on the waterfront of Ethnikis Antistasis. Ferries to Ancona and Venice (in Italy) depart from the new port on the south side of town; those for Brindisi and Bari (in Italy) use the old port in front of the main shipping offices; and ferries for Kerkyra (Corfu) and Paxi depart from just north of the new port.

For the bus station, turn left from the ferry quays, walk along Ethnikis Antistasis, turn right into 23 Fevrouariou – look out for the sign – and turn left into Kyprou two blocks inland. The bus station is a little way on the left.

Information

The main EOT office (☎ 22 227), in the old port area, is open 7 am to 2.30 pm daily. There is also an EOT booth just outside the arrivals area of the new port. The post office and OTE are next to each other on Evangelistrias. Currency exchange machines and ATMs are available at the Commercial and National banks. The tourist police and regular police (☎ 22 222) are together on the main road near the port entrance. The port police are beside the ferry quays.

Places to Stay & Eat

Campers might head for ***Il Sole Mare*** on the south side of town, or if you have independent transport, there is a quiet camp site at ***Drepanos Beach***, 6km north of town. There are also ***domatia*** around the new port. Look for signs.

Budget hotels are in short supply. The D class ***Egnatia*** *(☎ 23 648, fax 23 63, Eleftherias 2)* has comfortable singles/doubles for 8500/11,500 dr with bathroom. Turn right from the bus station and walk 100m. You will see it across the square on your left. The C class ***Hotel Oscar*** *(☎ 23 338, fax 23 557, Agion Apostolon 149)*, opposite the new port arrivals area, has reasonable rooms for 8000/10,000 dr. The C class ***Hotel Aktaion*** *(☎/fax 22 330, Agion Apostolon 27)*, on the waterfront between the Corfu ferry quay and the old port, costs 12,000/16,000 dr.

Bilis *(☎ 26 214, Agion Apostolon 15)*, opposite the Corfu ferry quay, is pretty handy for a quick meal. ***Restaurant Martinis-Bakalis*** *(☎ 24 357)*, on the corner of Fevrouariou and Grigoriou Lambraki, serves reasonably priced, tasty food. Locals eat here, so you can be assured of good value. Plan on about 2500 dr for a meal at both places.

Getting There & Away

Bus From the bus station (☎ 22 309) there buses to Ioannina (two hours, 1800 dr, nine daily), Parga (one hour, 1150 dr, five daily), Athens (eight hours, 8300 dr, three daily), Preveza (2½ hours, 2100 dr, two daily) and Thessaloniki (eight hours, 7800 dr, one daily).

Ferry – Corfu There are ferries to Corfu Town hourly between 5 am and 10 pm (1½ hours, 1300 dr). Ferries also go to Lefkimmi in southern Corfu (one hour, 750 dr, six daily), and Paxi (1½ hours, 1600 dr, three weekly). Agency booths opposite the quay sell tickets. Boats are now a mixture of closed hull ferries and smaller landing craft type ferries.

Most of the ferries to/from Italy also stop at Corfu (Kerkyra). There are also weekly passenger and car ferries to Kerkyra from Sagiada (45 minutes, 1100 dr), 20km north of Igoumenitsa (see the Sagiada section later in this chapter).

Ferry – Italy There is a veritable plethora of options for getting to Italy from Igoumenitsa. You can usually just turn up and buy an onward ticket, although demand is high in summer and securing a vehicle spot may be trickier. Phoning and booking ahead is always advisable at these times. There are different prices for low, middle and high seasons, and return tickets are 30% cheaper than two one-way tickets.

There are ferries to Brindisi (11 hours, six to eight daily), Bari (13 hours, two to four daily), Ancona (24 hours, two or three daily), Venice (33 hours, nine weekly) and Trieste (28 hours, six weekly). Some go to Italy direct, but most go via Corfu (two hours), where some lines allow you to stop over free of charge. Boats leave between 6 and 8 am, and between 6 and 9 pm, but timetables are subject to change. You should turn up at the port at least two hours before departure and check in at the shipping agent's office.

Travellers with campervans should note that on board 'camping' is allowable on a number of service – check with the individual ferry lines.

The following table shows one-way passenger fares, based on high season deck rates.

Destination	Company	Price
Ancona	ANEK Lines	20,100 dr
Ancona	Minoan Lines	21,800 dr
Ancona	Strintzis Lines	9600 dr
Bari	Marlines	12,500 dr
Bari	Superfast Ferries	15,800 dr
Bari	Ventouris Ferries	12,600 dr
Brindisi	Adriatica	18,000 dr
Brindisi	Fragline	12,500 dr
Brindisi	Strintzis Lines	7000 dr
Brindisi	Hellenic Mediterranean	17,000 dr
Brindisi	Ventouris Ferries	11,700 dr
Trieste	ANEK Lines	19,400 dr
Venice	Minoan Lines	21,800 dr
Venice	Strintzis	16,600 dr

The quality of service varies from company to company, but it should be noted that Superfast Ferries' prices are higher because the transit times are appreciably faster and the fleet is noticeably more modern and streamlined. Strintzis Lines has smaller but comfortable and well appointed boats and offers the best overall deals. For a comprehensive brochure of ferry options, go to Chris Travel (☎ 25 351, fax 25 350) at Ethnikis Antistasis 60. You can also book most ferry companies at Alfa Travel (☎ 22 797, fax 26 330) at Agion Apostolon 167 opposite the new port.

There are quite a number of shipping offices on Ethnikis Antistasis and another brace over on Agion Apostolon opposite the new port.

The main ferry offices are:

Adriatica
(☎ 26 410, fax 26 712) Oscar Travel, Agion Apostolon 149

ANEK Lines
(☎ 22 104, fax 25 421) Revis Travel Tourism & Shipping, Ethnikis Antistasis 34

Fragline
(☎ 22 158, fax 25 421) Revis Travel Tourism & Shipping, Ethnikis Antistasis 34

Hellenic Mediterranean
(☎ 22 180, 25 682, email hml@otenet.gr) Ethnikis Antistasis 30

Marlines
(☎ 23 301, fax 25 428) Ethnikis Antistasis 42

Minoan Lines
(☎ 22 952, fax 22 101, email minoanig@compulink.gr) Ethnikis Antistasis 58a

Strintzis Lines
(☎ 28 259, fax 25 492, email sales@strintzis.gr) Yioyiakas Travel, Ethnikis Antistasis 44

Superfast Ferries
(☎ 28 150, fax 28 156, email sfast@compulink.gr) Pitoulis & SIA, Agion Apostolon, New Harbour
Ventouris Ferries
(☎ 23 565, fax 24 880) Milano Travel, Agion Apostolon 11b

SAGIADA Σαγιάδα

Sagiada (sah-**yiah**-dah) is a sleepy fishing village 20km north of Igoumenitsa favoured by the day-tripping yachtie set from Corfu, as well as the passengers on the weekly ferry service to/from Corfu. Aside from the five tavernas and five bars that crowd its waterfront, there is not much activity.

If all eventually goes to plan, this will become Greece's last waterside settlement before a border crossing to Konispol in Albania. The crossing was due to open in 1999, but remained firmly closed at the time of writing.

There are a few rooms to be had, and the village is linked by two daily buses to both Igoumenitsa and Filiates farther inland.

PARGA Πάργα

☎ 0684 • postcode 480 60 • pop 1700

Parga, 48km south of Igoumenitsa and 77km north of Preveza, spills down to a rocky bay flanked by coves and islets. Add a Venetian kastro and the long pebble and sand Valtos Beach, and you have somewhere truly alluring. So it will come as no surprise that it's overrun with tourists in midsummer and that hotels, domatia and travel agents have swamped this once-serene fishing village.

Despite this, it is still a very attractive place to spend a day or two and is Epiros' number one tourist resort. Try to visit in early or late summer; if you're travelling along this coast, it would be a shame to miss this gem.

Orientation & Information

There is no EOT, but there is now a tourist police office in the same building as the regular police (☎ 31 222), which is shared with the post office and the bus station, at Alexandrou Baga 18. Walk south from the bus station, past the crossroads, into Vasila where you'll find the OTE and the National Bank of Greece; continue along this street to reach the waterfront.

There are ATMs at the National Bank of Greece and the Commercial Bank.

Nekromanteio of Aphyra

Just about every travel agent in Parga advertises trips to the Nekromanteio of Aphyra. This involves a boat ride down the coast to the Aheron River and then up the navigable river as far as the Nekromanteio itself, which you approach on foot. The day trip costs about 2500 dr. If you have your own transport, take the Preveza road as far as the village of Mesopotamos and look out for the sign to the Nekromanteio, 1km off the main road.

The Nekromanteio is a truly fascinating place if you have time to ponder the mysteries and the ancient rituals of the dead and the underworld.

According to mythology, the Aheron River was the River Styx across which the ferryman of the dead, Charon, rowed departed souls to the underworld. Until the departed had taken this journey they could not enter Hades (the world of the dead) and so were in a state of limbo.

The Nekromanteio was the ancients' venue for the equivalent of a modern seance. They believed this to be the gate of Hades, god of the underworld, and so it became an oracle of the dead and a sanctuary to Hades and Persephone. Pilgrims made offerings of milk, honey and the blood of sacrificed animals in the hope that the spirits of the departed would communicate with them.

The labyrinth of buildings was only discovered in 1958, revealing not only the Nekromanteio itself, but also the monastery of Agios Ioannis Prodromos and a graveyard. The eerie underground vault, the purpose of which is still not known, could easily have been the meeting place for the dead and the living.

The site is open 8.30 am to 4.30 pm on weekdays and 8.30 am to 3 pm on weekends.

Entrance is 500 dr; 300 dr for students. There is a good, colour guidebook written in English by Professor Sotiris Dakaris of the University of Ioannina. It's available at the sanctuary entrance for 1500 dr.

The Kastro

The kastro dominates the town and separates Valtos Beach from Parga proper. A reminder of 400 years of Venetian presence in Epiros, the kastro is a bit overgrown, but its ramparts provide some lovely rambling, as well as superb views of the coastline.

Activities

If you like scuba diving, contact International Travel Services (see the following section) who will put you in touch with the diving school. A one day beginner's course costs around 12,000 dr. ITS also organises Aheron River cruises for about 2500 dr; cruises with a beach barbecue and unlimited drinks cost 7000 dr.

Places to Stay – Budget

There is a veritable plethora of accommodation available during the tourist season, from top hotels to camping grounds, from domatia to studios. Avoid mid-July to the end of August if you are not planning to stay for more than a week. Take your pick during the low season.

For help with accommodation, try International Travel Services (☎ 31 833, fax 31 834, email zigourisco@otenet.gr), Anexartisias 37-39 on the main waterfront, or at its other office on Kryoneri Beach.

There are three camp sites: ***Lihnos Beach Camping** (☎ 31 161)*, ***Elia Camping** (☎ 31 130)* and, probably the best choice, ***Valtos Camping** (☎ 31 287)* at Valtos Beach.

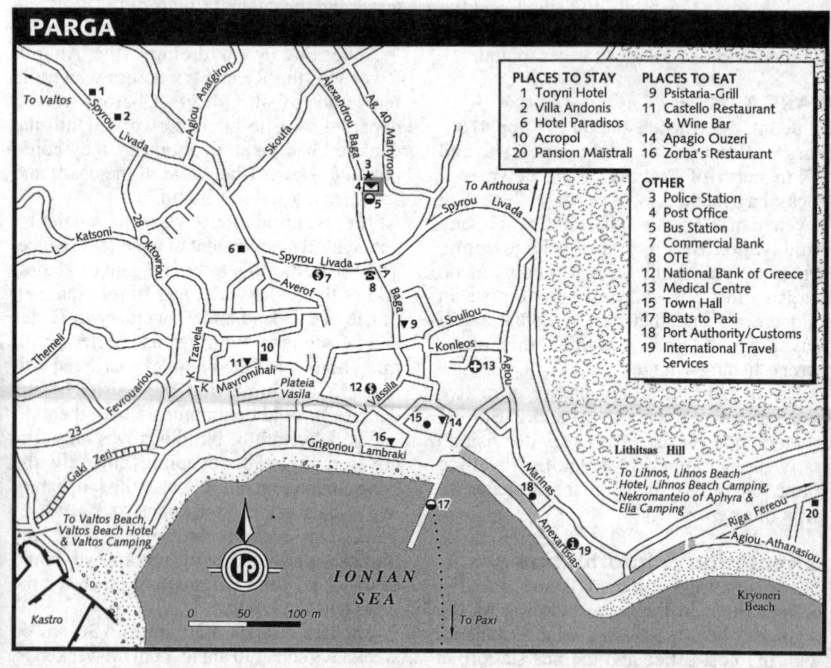

Domatia are best found by heading up towards the kastro and looking along the streets to your right near the top. Chances are that you'll be stopped and asked if you need a room.

Places to Stay – Mid-Range

Villa Andonis *(☎ 31 540, fax 31 340)* on Spyrou Livada is a neat set of domatia which deals with package groups as well as individuals, and offers modern doubles/triples for 12,000/15,000 dr. Also worth mentioning is the C class ***Acropol*** *(☎ 31 239, fax 31 236, Agion Apostolon 6),* a small but cosy hotel with singles/doubles for 15,000/19,000. At the C class ***Hotel Paradisos*** *(☎ 31 229, fax 31 266, Spyrou Livada 23)* rooms go for 11,500/16,000 dr. The C class ***Toryni*** *(☎ 31 219, fax 32 376)*, also on Spyrou Livada, is another good choice with rooms for about 11,000/13,000 dr.

Pansion Maïstrali *(☎/fax 31 275, Riga Fereou 4)* on the south side of town, up from Kryoneri Beach, is very clean and convenient. Doubles/triples cost 15,000/18,000 dr.

Places to Stay – Top End

The B class ***Valtos Beach Hotel*** *(☎ 31 610, fax 31 904)* on the beach at Valtos has singles/doubles for 15,000/18,500 dr, with breakfast; the hotel also has a cafe. ***Lihnos Beach Hotel*** *(☎ 31 257, fax 31 157)* charges 15,500/19,000 dr. Both places also have a bar, restaurant and tennis court. Valtos Beach is just north of Parga and Lihnos Beach is just to the south.

Places to Eat

Not surprisingly, there are plenty of places to eat, many of them touting tourist menus and English breakfasts. In high season, tourist prices are all the rage.

For cheap and tasty food, try ***Psistaria-Grill*** *(Alexandrou Baga 4)*, 100m from the bus station. ***Zorba's Restaurant*** is open all year and caters for locals as well as visitors, offering good food, draught wine and the most picturesque location. It is on the waterfront by the statue of Ioannis Dimoulitsas, 50m to the right as you face the pier.

Try the homy ***Apagio Ouzeri*** in a little alley just off the promenade; it's one of the few places that deals mainly with a Greek clientele. *Spetsofaï* (peppers, onions and sausage in tomato sauce) with salad and draught wine will cost about 2300 dr.

Castello Restaurant & Wine Bar *(☎ 32 239)*, part of the Hotel Acropol, is an upmarket joint with professionally prepared food served in an enticing outdoor garden. It's worth trying for a special night out.

Getting There & Away

Bus From the bus station (☎ 31 218) there are buses to Igoumenitsa (one hour, 1150 dr, four daily), Preveza (two hours, 1350 dr, five daily), Ioannina (three hours, 1900 dr, one daily in summer) and Athens (seven hours, 7900 dr, three daily).

Excursion Boat The small Ionian islands of Paxi and Antipaxi lie just 20km off the coast. In summer there are daily excursion boats to Paxi (4500 dr); the excursions are widely advertised by Parga's travel agents.

PREVEZA Πρέβεζα

☎ 0682 • postcode 481 00 • pop 13,340

Preveza (**preh**-veh-zah), built on a peninsula between the Ionian Sea and the Ambracian Gulf, is primarily a port from which ferries cross the narrow strait to Aktion, but it is also a popular holiday destination for Greeks as well as German and Austrian tour groups. Most people coming to Preveza are either heading out to the resorts at Parga, or to the beach resorts north of the town. Preveza is a pleasant town in its own right and a leisurely stroll through its narrow, pedestrian-only central streets is a great pleasure.

Orientation & Information

If you arrive by bus, you will alight at the bus station on Irinis, the main commercial thoroughfare. Turn left along Irinis and walk about 500m, bearing left until you reach the harbour. The EOT, post office and National Bank of Greece are in a row on the waterfront, to the left as you reach the quay.

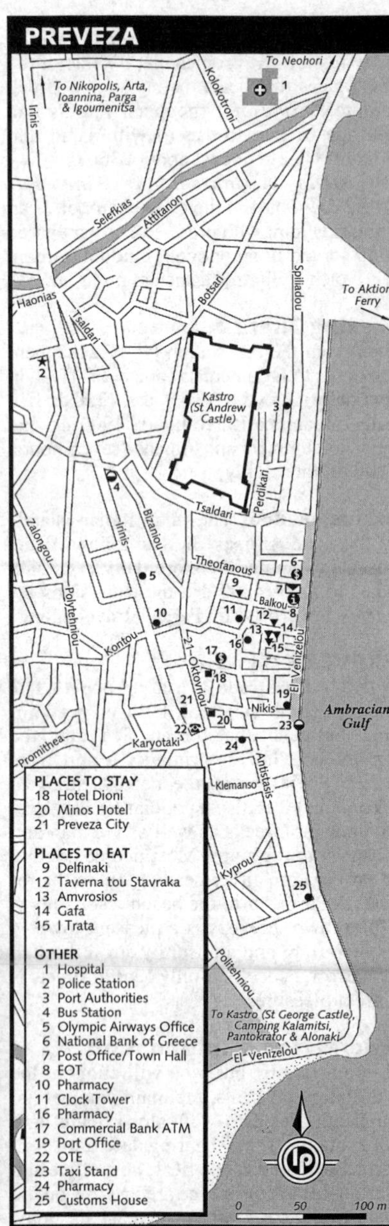

There are a couple of Commercial Bank ATMs around town.

Special Events

In July each year there is an International Choral Festival with up to 20 or more choirs taking part – Preveza's own choir has won considerable international acclaim. For detailed information, check with the municipal tourist office (☎ 28 120, fax 27 553), housed in the town hall.

At the beginning of August you may come across a mildly whimsical sardine festival. The Nikopolia Festival is an umbrella event for various musical and theatrical presentations held in August at Nikopolis to the north-west of town. Again, check with the municipal tourist office for details.

Places to Stay

The best of four camping grounds is ***Camping Kalamitsi*** *(☎ 22 192, fax 28 660)*, which has 116 grassed sites with ample shade, a large pool, restaurant, laundry facilities, communal fridges and a minimarket. It's 4km along the main Preveza-Igoumenitsa road.

The C class ***Preveza City*** *(☎ 27 370, fax 23 872, Irinis 61-63)* is 200m on the left from the bus station, in the direction of the waterfront, and has clean singles/doubles for 9000/12,000 dr. The spartan C class ***Minos Hotel*** *(☎ 28 424, 21 Oktovriou 11)* charges 11,350/15,000 dr. Within the town precinct, the C class ***Hotel Dioni*** *(☎ 27 381, fax 27 384)* on the quiet Plateia Theofilou Papageorgiouis is a good but somewhat pricey choice for 13,750/18,150 dr; the bar has a pool table.

Places to Eat

The main road along the waterfront has a large number of drink and snack places, but there is a clutch of fish tavernas along the street leading from the waterfront to the clock tower of the St Haralambos church.

For a no-nonsense, unadorned meal in a low-ceilinged room lined with functioning wine barrels, head for ***Amvrosios*** *(Grigoriou*

E 9). Sardines, salad and draught wine will cost less than 2000 dr. Next door, ***Gafa*** *(Tsakalof 2)* offers similar fare, but you can sit outside. Nearby are the similar ***Taverna tou Stavraka*** and ***I Trata***.

Delfinaki *(Sapountzaki 4)* is a tastefully modern but touristy taverna. It serves some excellent home-made specialities, such as baked peppers stuffed with cheese.

Getting There & Away

Air Preveza airport, 7km south of the town, is sometimes called Lefkada or Aktion. The Olympic Airways bus to the airport costs 500 dr, plus the ferry fare.

There are at least five flights weekly to Athens in the low season and daily flights in the high season (20 minutes, 13,900 dr). The Olympic Airways office (☎ 28 343) is on Irinis.

Bus From the intercity bus station (☎ 22 213) there are buses to Ioannina (two hours, 1950 dr, 10 daily), Parga (two hours, 1350 dr, five daily), Arta (one hour, 1000 dr, five daily), Igoumenitsa (2½ hours, 2100 dr, two daily), Athens (six hours, 7300 dr, four daily) and Thessaloniki (eight hours, 7800 dr, one daily).

Ferry The Preveza-Aktion ferry departs every half-hour (90 dr per person; 850 dr per car) from the new harbour, to the north of town.

AROUND PREVEZA

Nikopolis Νικόπολη

In 31 BC, Octavian (later the Roman emperor Augustus) defeated the allies Mark Antony and Cleopatra in the famous naval Battle of Actium (present-day Aktion). To celebrate, Octavian built Nikopolis, the 'city of victory', and populated it by forcible resettlement of people from surrounding towns and villages. It was plundered by Vandals and Goths in the 5th and 6th centuries AD, but was rebuilt by Justinian. It was sacked again by the Bulgars in the 11th century, after which nobody bothered to rebuild it.

Little is left of the Roman walls, but the Byzantine walls and a theatre survive, and there are remains of temples to Mars and Poseidon (an appropriate choice of gods for the warmongering Octavian), an aqueduct, Roman baths and a restored Roman odeum. The immense site sprawls over both sides of the Preveza-Arta road.

There is an **archaeological museum** at the site (☎ 0682-41 336). It has exhibits from the ancient citadel and is open 8.30 am to 3 pm daily except Monday. Admission to the museum and site is 500 dr or 300 dr for students. Other exhibits from Nikopolis are displayed in Ioannina's Archaeological Museum.

Preveza-Arta buses stop at Nikopolis.

Beaches

Just north of Preveza, beaches are strung out for some 30km along the **Bay of Nikopolis**. Those at **Monolithi**, 10km from Preveza, and **Kastrosykia**, 15km away, are particularly popular. They are accessible on Parga-bound buses.

ARTA Αρτα

☎ 0681 • postcode 471 00 • pop 18,000

Arta, the second-largest town of Epiros, is 76km south of Ioannina and 50km north-east of Preveza. It's easy to miss if you're speeding to Athens or locations farther south, which is a pity, because it's worth a visit. After the barren agricultural scenery of Ioannina and the north, it's refreshing to come across groves of citrus plantations as you leave the Louros Valley and reach the open plains and wetlands of the north Ambracian Gulf.

The town is built over ancient Ambracia, which King Pyrrhus of Epiros made his capital in the 4th century BC. In the 14th century AD the Frankish despot of Epiros made it his seat of government. The town has a wealth of Byzantine monuments of which the locals are justifiably proud.

Today, Arta is a bustling supply centre for the north Ambracia region and is a pleasant place to stroll around.

Orientation & Information

The main bus station is on the Ioannina-Athens road on the eastern side of town, just outside the town walls. From the bus station, walk about 200m to your right and look for Krystalli, which will lead to Nikiforou Skoufa, the main street. Half of this street is for pedestrians only.

The OTE is on the main square, Plateia Ethnikis Antistasis, which is halfway along Skoufa. The post office is on Amvrakias, about five minutes from the OTE in the general direction of the fortress walls.

Things to See

The most distinguished feature is its fine 18th century **Bridge of Arta**, which spans the Arahthos River. This bridge, made famous by Greek Demotic poetry, is probably Arta's most photographed monument. Legend has it that the master builder had difficulty in preventing the bridge from being washed away every time he tried to complete it, and was advised to entomb his wife in the stonework of the central arch. The bridge is still standing, although it has had a facelift or two in recent times and is now used by pedestrians.

Arta also has several churches of note. The 13th century **Church of Panagia Parigoritisa**, overlooking Plateia Skoufa just south of Plateia Kilkis, is a well preserved and striking building. The churches of **Agios Vasilios** and **Agia Theodora** have attractive ceramic decorations on their exterior walls. Both of these churches are just west of Pyrrou, the main thoroughfare which runs south from the fortress to Plateia Kilkis.

Places to Stay & Eat

There are two C class hotels. ***Hotel Cronos*** *(☎ 22 211, fax 73 795)* on Plateia Kilkis has singles/doubles for 10,500/14,000 dr with bathroom. ***Hotel Amvrakia*** *(☎ 28 311, fax 78 544, Priovolou 13)*, one block east of Pyrrou, has rooms for 8500/12,000 dr with bathroom.

There are several ***restaurants*** on Plateia Kilkis, and you can always get a snack at the ***cafeterias*** on Plateia Ethnikis Antistasis. Hotel Amvrakia has an associated restaurant next to it called ***Skaraveos***, where you can get some genuine, tasty home-cooking for around 2000 dr.

On either side of the bridge are two pricier establishments: ***Mylos*** on the Ioannina side and ***Protomastoras*** on the Arta side.

Getting There & Away

There are buses to Ioannina (2½ hours, 1400 dr, 10 daily), Arta (one hour, 1000 dr, five daily), Athens (five hours, 6500 dr, four daily) and Thessaloniki (7½ hours, 7550 dr, one daily).

Macedonia
Μακεδονία

Macedonia (mah-keh-do-**nee**-ah) is the largest prefecture in Greece, and its capital, Thessaloniki, is the country's second city. With abundant and varied attractions, it's surprising that more travellers don't find their way here. Tucked in the north-western corner are the beautiful Prespa Lakes, home to one of Europe's most important bird sanctuaries. To the south, Mt Olympus, Greece's highest peak at 2917m, rises from a plain just 6km from the sea.

The unsung towns of Veria, Edessa and Florina unfold their charms to only the occasional visitor. For archaeology buffs there is Alexander the Great's birthplace of Pella; the sanctuary of Dion, where he sacrificed to the gods; Vergina, where the Macedonian kings (apart from Alexander) were buried; and Philippi, where the battle which set the seal on the future of the western world was fought. Macedonia is also the site of the Monastic Republic of Athos.

THESSALONIKI Θεσσαλονίκη

☎ 031 • postcode 541 00 • pop 750,000

Thessaloniki (thess-ah-lo-**nee**-kih) was the second city of Byzantium and is the second city of modern Greece. However, being second does not mean that Thessaloniki lies in the shadow of, or tries to emulate, the capital.

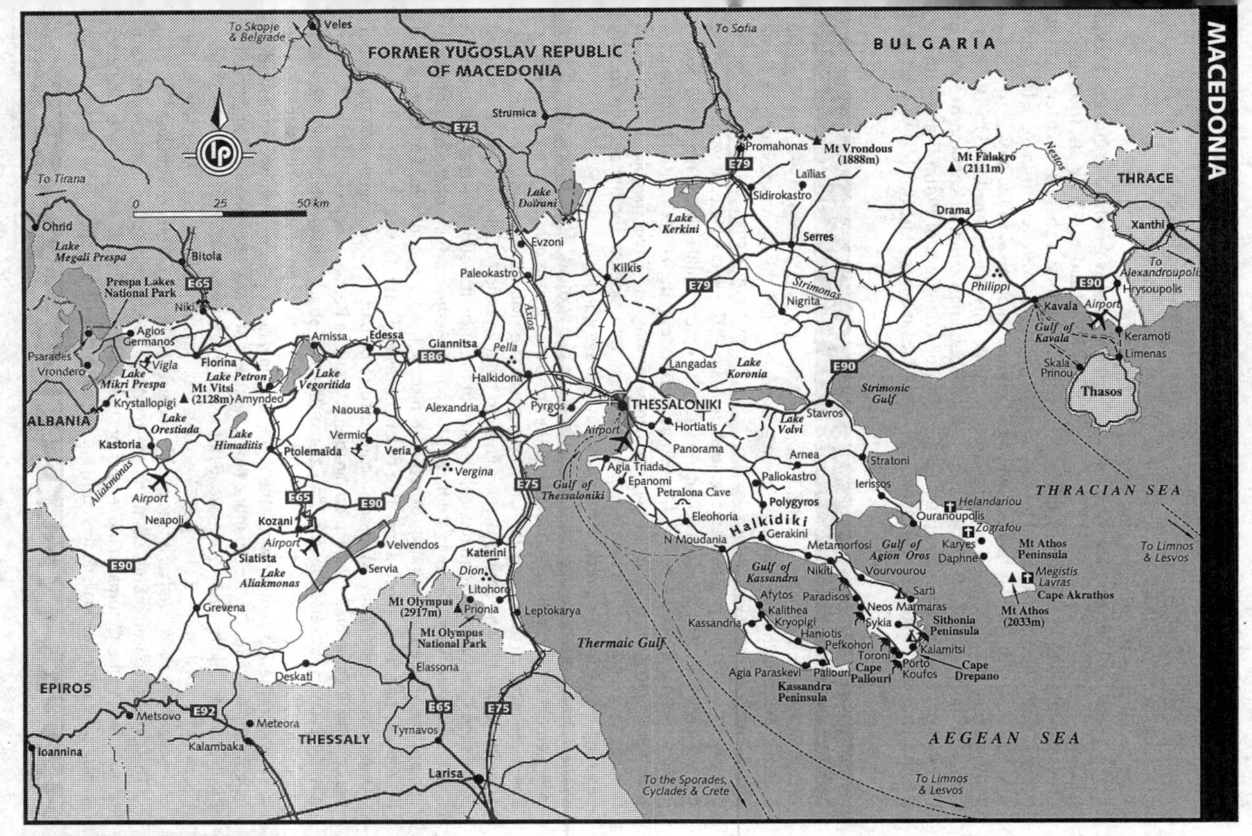
MACEDONIA
BULGARIA
FORMER YUGOSLAV REPUBLIC OF MACEDONIA
ALBANIA
THRACE
THESSALY
EPIROS
THRACIAN SEA
AEGEAN SEA
To Sofia
To Skopje & Belgrade
To Tirana
To Alexandroupoli
To Limnos & Lesvos
To Limnos & Lesvos
To the Sporades, Cyclades & Crete
0
25
50 km
Veles
Strumica
Bitola
Ohrid
Lake Megali Prespa
Prespa Lakes National Park
Lake Mikri Prespa
Psarades
Vrondero
Agios Germanos
Vigla
Niki
Florina
Lake Petron
Mt Vitsi (2128m)
Krystallopigi
Lake Orestiada
Kastoria
Amyndeo
Lake Himaditis
Ptolemaïda
Lake Vegoritida
Arnissa
Edessa
Kozani
Lake Aliakmonas
Siatista
Airport
Aliakmonas
Neapoli
Grevena
Deskati
Meteora
Kalambaka
Metsovo
Ioannina
Naousa
Vermio
Veria
Vergina
Alexandria
Giannitsa
Pella
Halkidona
Paleokastro
Evzoni
Lake Doirani
Axios
Pyrgos
Kilkis
Lake Kerkini
Sidirokastro
Promahonas
Mt Vrondous (1888m)
Laïlias
Serres
Strimonas
Nigrita
Drama
Mt Falakro (2111m)
Philippi
Nestos
Kavala
Xanthi
Hrysoupolis
Keramoti
Limenas
Thasos
Skala Prinou
Gulf of Kavala
Strimonic Gulf
Lake Koronia
Lake Volvi
Langadas
Stavros
Stratoni
Ierissos
Arnea
Paliokastro
Polygyros
Gerakini
Halkidiki
THESSALONIKI
Hortiatis
Panorama
Agia Triada
Epanomi
Petralona Cave
Eleohoria
N Moudania
Gulf of Thessaloniki
Thermaic Gulf
Leptokarya
Katerini
Litohoro
Prionia
Dion
Mt Olympus (2917m)
Mt Olympus National Park
Elassona
Tyrnavos
Larisa
Velvendos
Servia
Gulf of Kassandra
Kassandria
Afytos
Kalithea
Kryopigi
Haniotis
Pefkohori
Paliouri
Agia Paraskevi
Kassandra Peninsula
Cape Paliouri
Nikiti
Metamorfosi
Paradisos
Neos Marmaras
Sykia
Toroni
Porto Koufos
Kalamitsi
Sarti
Vourvourou
Sithonia Peninsula
Cape Drepano
Gulf of Agion Oros
Ouranoupolis
Helandariou
Zografou
Karyes
Daphne
Mt Athos Peninsula
Megistis Lavras
Cape Akrathos
Mt Athos (2033m)
E90
E79
E75
E86
E65
E92

It is a sophisticated city with its own distinct character. It has a lively nightlife, good restaurants and, although without the impressive ancient monuments of the capital, it has several good museums, a scattering of Roman ruins and superlative Byzantine churches.

Thessaloniki sits at the top of the wide Thermaic Gulf. The oldest part of the city is the kastro, the old Turkish quarter, whose narrow streets huddle around a Byzantine fortress on the slopes of Mt Hortiatis.

Thessaloniki is best avoided during festival time (September-October), as accommodation is almost impossible to find and rates are at a premium. Finding a room at other times should not be a problem.

History

Like almost everywhere in Greece, Thessaloniki has had not only its triumphs but more than its fair share of disasters. As with Athens, an awareness of these helps greatly in one's appraisal of the city.

The city was named in 316 BC by the Macedonian general Kassandros, after his wife, a daughter of Philip II and half-sister of Alexander the Great, who was born when

What's in a Name?

An awful lot if you are Greek and the name is Macedonia. In January 1992, the Yugoslav Republic of Macedonia declared its full independence. After this pronouncement the Greek government protested vociferously, insisting that the new country change its name before the European Community granted it recognition. In May 1992, Greece stated it would recognise the republic's independence and cooperate with it to ensure stability in the region, so long as its name did not include the word Macedonia. In response, the EC recognised Macedonia in June 1992, provided it adopted another name. Among the Greek people, the issue has resulted in a surge of unprecedented nationalism with slogans throughout the country declaring 'Macedonia is Greek, always was, and always will be'.

The Greeks' objections to the name Macedonia are twofold. They believe that it is an infringement of their cultural heritage, and they read into it undercurrents of territorial claims. The 'Greekness' of Alexander the Great, the greatest of Macedonian kings, is indisputable. After all, it was he who spread Greek culture to India and the Middle East, and in so doing established Greek as the international language of the ancient world. Whether Alexander the Great's ancestors were Greek is a different matter. The ethnic origins of the ancient Macedonians has, since the beginning of recorded history, been a conundrum, for it seems that Macedonia has always been a melange of languages and nationalities.

After Alexander's death, Macedonia continued to be part of Greece until, with the rest of the country, it came under Roman domination. When the Roman Empire split in the 4th century, Macedonia, traversed by the Via Egnatia (the long straight road which linked Rome to Byzantium), became a powerful region with a relatively stable population. This stability came to an end in the 7th century when the region was invaded by Serbs, who were followed by Bulgars and Muslims. During Byzantine times, Samuel, a Slav Macedonian king, fought against the Byzantines, and his army made inroads into Macedonia. In the 14th century the Serb Stefan Dusan (who ruled from 1331 to 1355) occupied all of Macedonia, except Thessaloniki. This occupation was short-lived as it was quickly superseded by the Ottoman conquest.

The Greeks' concern about claims on the territory of Macedonia stem from the late 19th century, when the Ottoman Empire was on the point of collapse. At this time, countries welling over with nationalistic fervour were poised to pick up the spoils. The Serbs made no

Philip was successfully expanding his territory in Thessaly. When he arrived home, Philip announced that the child would be called Thessaloniki, 'Victory in Thessaly'.

After the Roman conquest in 168 BC, Thessaloniki became capital of the province of Macedonia. Thessaloniki's location on the Thermaic Gulf and its position on the Via Egnatia helped to promote its development. It was also an important staging post on the trade route to the Balkans.

The Roman emperor Galerius made it the eastern imperial capital, and after the empire officially divided it became the second city of Byzantium, flourishing as both a spiritual and economic centre. Inevitably, its strategic position brought attacks and plundering by Goths, Slavs, Muslims, Franks and Epirots. In 1185 it was sacked by the Normans, and in 1204 was made a feudal kingdom under Marquis Boniface of Montferrat, but was reincorporated into the Byzantine Empire in 1246. After several sieges it finally capitulated to Ottoman rule when Murad II staged a successful invasion in 1430.

Along with the rest of Macedonia, Thessaloniki became part of Greece in 1913. In August 1917 a fire broke out in the city and,

What's in a Name?

secret of the fact that they coveted Macedonia, but a much greater threat came from King Ferdinand of Bulgaria.

This volatile situation culminated in the two Balkan Wars (1912-13). In the first Balkan War, the Serbs, Bulgarians and Greeks fought the Turks, and in the second round the Serbs and Greeks fought the Bulgarians. The second Balkan War was ended by the Treaty of Bucharest, which ceded more than half of Macedonia to Greece and divided the rest between Serbia and Bulgaria. In both World Wars Bulgaria fought against Greece and in WWII parts of Macedonia were occupied by Bulgaria, which implemented a policy of enforced 'Bulgarianisation'. After the victory of the Allies in WWII, the threat from Bulgaria was replaced by one from Yugoslavia.

In April 1945, Tito proclaimed the Socialist Republic of Macedonia. Greece is convinced that Tito did this to strengthen the southern flank of his territory and that his ultimate ambition was to create an independent Macedonian state which would include the Greek province of Macedonia, and the Bulgarian region of Macedonia known as Pirin. Greece says it was too busy fighting the civil war to protest at the time, a situation Tito was only too aware of. In 1952 a Macedonian grammar was published in Tito's republic and in 1968 the republic acquired the autocephalous Macedonian church. To Greece, these factors added credence to its suspicions.

Greece continued to protest against the name Macedonia throughout 1992 and into 1993. Then in April 1993, Macedonia was admitted to the UN under the temporary name of the Former Yugoslav Republic of Macedonia (FYROM), which doesn't exactly trip off the tongue. By the end of 1999 the issue of the name was no closer to being resolved, though the war in Yugoslavia played a great role in distracting both sides from the issue while forcing them to focus on more serious issues that threatened the stability of both their homelands.

To this day there are people in Greek villages on the borders of Bulgaria and the new republic who speak Macedonian. This is one of the south Slavonic group of languages, which is a dialect of Bulgarian, with some Turkish, Greek, Albanian and Vlach words. An offshoot of the present nationalistic fervour is that a minority of these people are demanding greater autonomy for Macedonian-speaking Greeks within Greece. The country is not without other ethnic minorities. Could it be that Greece, in its much ado about Macedonia, has inadvertently opened a Pandora's box?

as there was no fire brigade, the flames spread quickly, destroying 9500 houses and rendering 70,000 inhabitants homeless. The problem of homelessness was exacerbated by the influx of refugees from Asia Minor after the 1923 population exchange. During the late 1920s the city was carefully replanned and built on a grid system with wide streets and large squares.

In 1978 Thessaloniki experienced a severe earthquake. Most of the modern buildings were not seriously damaged, but the Byzantine churches suffered greatly and most are still in the process of being restored. Thessaloniki was chosen as Europe's 'Cultural Capital' in 1997.

Orientation

Thessaloniki's waterfront of Leoforos Nikis stretches from the port in the west to the White Tower (Lefkos Pyrgos) in the east. North of the White Tower are the exhibition grounds where the annual International Trade Fair is held. The university campus is to the north.

The other principal streets of Mitropoleos, Tsimiski and Ermou run parallel to Nikis. Egnatia, the next street up, is the main thoroughfare and most of the Roman remains are between here and Agiou Dimitriou. The two main squares, both abutting the waterfront, are Plateia Eleftherias, which is one of the local bus terminals, and Plateia Aristotelous. Kastra, the old Turkish quarter, is north of Athinas and just within the ramparts.

The central food market is between Egnatia, Irakliou, Aristotelous and Dragoumi. The train station is on Monastiriou, a westerly continuation of Egnatia. The main bus terminal is at Plateia Dikastirion. The city does not have one general intercity bus station, but several terminals for different destinations (see Getting There & Away).

Information

Tourist Offices The EOT (☎ 271 888, 263 112), Plateia Aristotelous 8, is open 8.30 am to 8 pm Monday to Friday and 8.30 am to 2 pm Saturday.

The tourist police (☎ 554 871), at Dodekanisou 4, 5th floor, are open 7.30 am to 11 pm daily all year.

Money Most banks around town are equipped with credit card-friendly ATMs. You will find most banks along central Tsimiski. The National Bank of Greece at Tsimiski 11 opens on weekends for the benefit of people wishing to change currency. There is an exchange machine and an ATM at the train station. American Express (☎ 269 521) is at Tsimiski 19 and is open 8 am to 2 pm Monday to Thursday and 8 am to 1.30 pm Friday.

Midas Exchange, at the western end of Tsimiski close to the Ladadika district, is a reasonably efficient exchange bureau open 8.30 am to 8.30 pm Monday to Friday, 8.30 am to 2 pm Saturday and 9 am to 1.30 pm Sunday. It's handy for people using the ferry terminal.

Post & Communications The main post office is at Aristotelous 26 and is open 7.30 am to 8 pm Monday to Friday, 7.30 am to 2.15 pm Saturday and 9 am to 1.30 pm Sunday. The OTE, open 24 hours, is at Karolou Dil 27.

The most central Internet cafe is Globus Internet Cafe (☎ 232 901) at Amynta 12, open 10 am until late daily. But it is closed for one month (mid-July to mid-August) during summer. Netcafé (☎ 943 939) is less conveniently located at Agiou Spyridona, Triandria. It is open 11 am to 1 am daily. Triandria is the suburb immediately to the east of the Kaftanzoglio stadium on the east side of the university. Take the No 32 bus and alight at the Church of Agios Spyridon.

Bookshops Molho, at Tsimiski 10, has a comprehensive stock of English-language books, magazines and newspapers. Malliaris Kaisia, at Aristotelous 9, also has many English-language publications.

Foreign-language newspapers and magazines can be most conveniently obtained from a kiosk on the corner of Polytehniou and Aristotelous.

Laundry Wash & Go, just north-east of the university at Nestoros Telloglou 15, is a trendy, airy place. Follow Agiou Dimitriou from the city until just past the university – it's set back on your left, off a small grassy square, opposite the dental school. It's open 9 am to 8.30 pm Monday to Saturday, and closed Sunday. A wash and dry will cost you 1900 dr. Bianca Laundrette, on Antoniadou, has a more utilitarian ambience. Walk up D Gournari from the Arch of Galerius and Antoniadou is off to the right. It's open 8 am to 8.30 pm Monday to Friday, and charges 1500 dr.

Mt Athos Permits Permits for the monastic region of Mt Athos may be obtained from the Pilgrims' Office (☎/fax 861 811), Leoforos Karamanli 14. For further information, see under Mt Athos in the Halkidiki section later in this chapter.

Emergency There is a first-aid centre (☎ 530 530) at Navarhou Koundourioti 6, near the port. The largest public hospital is the Ippokration (☎ 837 921), Papanastasiou 50, 2km east of the city centre.

Archaeological Museum

In 1977 one of Greece's most eminent archaeologists, Professor Manolis Andronikos, was excavating at Vergina near Thessaloniki when he found an unlooted tomb which turned out to be that of King Philip II of Macedon. The spectacular contents of this tomb, now on display in this museum, are comparable to the grave treasures of Mycenae.

Among the exhibits are exquisite gold jewellery; bronze and terracotta vases; tiny, intricately detailed ivory reliefs; and a solid gold casket with lion's feet, embossed with the sunburst symbol of the royal house of Macedonia, which contained the bones of Philip II. The most mind-boggling exhibit is the bones themselves, which are carefully laid out to reconstruct an almost complete skeleton. There is something very strange about looking at someone who has been just a name in a history book.

The opening hours of the museum (☎ 830 538) are 12.30 to 7 pm Monday; 8 am to 7 pm Tuesday to Sunday. Admission costs 1500 dr. The museum is opposite the entrance to the exhibition grounds; either walk east along Tsimiski or take bus No 3.

White Tower

This 15th century tower is both the city's symbol and most prominent landmark. During the 18th century it was used as a prison for insubordinate janissaries, the elite troops of forcibly converted Christian boys who became servants of the sultan. In 1826, at the order of Mahmud II, many of the janissaries were massacred in the tower and thereafter it was known as the 'bloody tower'. After independence it was whitewashed as a symbolic gesture to expunge its Turkish function. The whitewash has now been removed and it has been turned into a very fine **Byzantine Museum** (☎ 267 832), with splendid frescoes and icons.

In the pleasant museum cafe a 30 minute audiovisual is shown every hour between 10 am and 2 pm. The museum is open 8 am to 2.30 pm Tuesday to Sunday; entry is free.

Other Museums

The **Museum of the Macedonian Struggle** (☎ 229 778) outlines the story of the liberation of Macedonia from the Ottomans and the threat of Bulgarian nationalism. The museum is at Proxenou Koromila 23, in what was the Greek consular building when Macedonia was still part of the Ottoman Empire. Proxenou Koromila runs parallel to, and between, Mitropoleos and Nikis. Opening times are 9 am to 2 pm Tuesday to Friday; also 6 to 8 pm Wednesday; and 11 am to 2 pm on weekends (closed Monday). Admission is free.

Kemal Atatürk, the founder of the Republic of Turkey, was born in Thessaloniki in 1881. The Turkish timber-framed house at Apostolou Pavlou 17 where he was born and spent his childhood has been faithfully restored and is now a museum called **Atatürk's House**. Visiting is a bit of a cloak-and-dagger affair, but is worth the effort: you

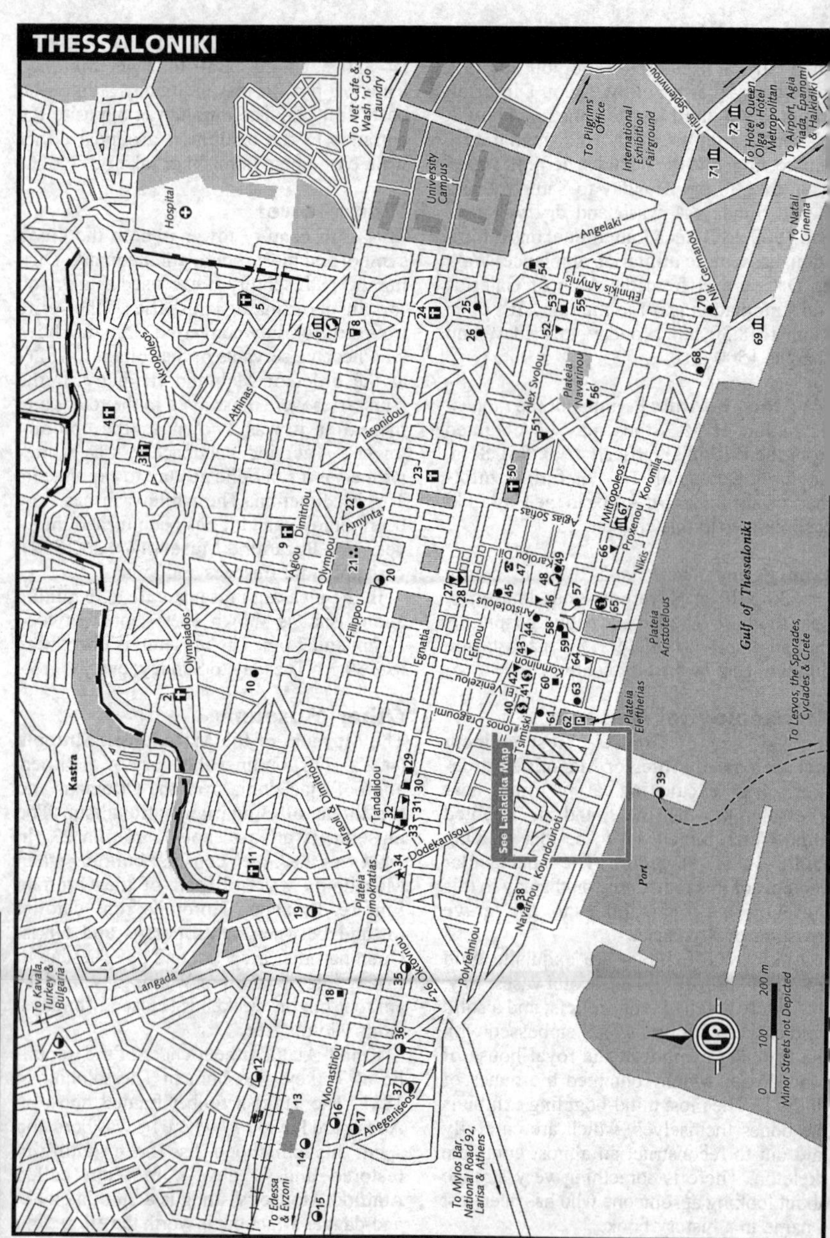

NORTHERN GREECE

THESSALONIKI

PLACES TO STAY
18 Capsis Hotel
29 Hotel Atlas
30 Hotel Averof
32 Hotel Atlantis
33 Hotel Acropol
53 GYHA Hostel
54 ABC Hotel
59 Electra Palace Hotel
60 Hotel Tourist

PLACES TO EAT
27 Ta Spata Psistaria
31 Ta Nea Ilysia
42 O Loutros Fish Taverna
43 Babel Snack Bar
46 Ouzeri Aristotelous
52 Hryso Pagoni
56 Taverna Ta Aderfia tis Pyxarias
64 Ouzeri Toumbourlika
66 Ta Nisia Restaurant

THINGS TO SEE
2 Church of Agia Ekaterini
3 Church of Osios David
4 Monastery of Vlatadon
5 Church of Nikolaos Orfanos
6 Atatürk's House
9 Church of Agios Dimitrios
11 Church of the Dodeka Apostoli
21 Roman Agora
23 Church of Panagia Ahiropiitos
24 Rotonda
26 Arch of Galerius
50 Church of Agia Sofia
67 Museum of the Macedonian Struggle
69 White Tower
71 Archaeological Museum

OTHER
1 Kavala Bus Station
7 Turkish Consulate
8 Show Avantaz
10 Ministry of Macedonia & Thrace
12 Alexandroupolis Bus Station
13 Train Station
14 Airport Bus Terminal
15 Ioannina Bus Station
16 Athens & Trikala Bus Station
17 Florina Bus Station
19 Langadas Bus Station
20 Local Bus Station
22 Globus Internet Cafe
25 Bianca Laundrette
28 Main Post Office
34 Tourist Police
35 Veria Bus Station
36 Katerini Bus Station
37 Pella, Kastoria, Volos & Edessa Bus Station
38 Olympic Airways Office
39 Ferry Departure Point
40 National Bank of Greece
41 American Express
44 Malliaris Kaisia Bookshop
45 Train Tickets Office (OSE)
47 OTE
48 US Consulate
49 EOS (Alpine Club)
51 Rivoli Nightclub
55 En Chordais
57 Olympian Cinema
58 Foreign Newspapers Kiosk
61 Molho Bookshop
62 Car Parking
63 Doucas Tours; UK Consulate
65 EOT
68 Cinema Pallas
70 Aristotelion Cinema
72 Museum of Byzantine Culture

ring the bell of the Turkish Consulate building (around the corner on Agiou Dimitriou), produce your passport, and then someone will show you around. The museum opens 2 to 6 pm daily; admission is free.

The **Museum of Byzantine Culture** (☎ 868 570) opened in 1994 and currently houses three permanent exhibitions: 'Early Christian Churches', 'Early Christian Cities and Dwellings' and another entitled 'From the Elysian Fields to the Christian Paradise'. Located at Leoforos Stratou 12, the museum is open 8.30 am to 2 pm and entry costs 1000 dr.

Roman & Byzantine Thessaloniki

Thessaloniki has few remaining Roman ruins, but its churches represent every period of Byzantine art and architecture, once the city's foremost glory, and enjoy World Heritage Site status. Notwithstanding the extensive damage from fire and earthquakes and conversion to mosques, a visit to the most renowned ones is still worthwhile. The circular walk described here takes you around the Roman ruins and the major churches.

The **Roman agora**, in the upper part of Plateia Dikastirion, is reached by crossing Egnatia from Aristotelous. Excavations began in the 1970s and are still in progress, so the site is cordoned off from the public. So far, the odeum and two stoas have come to light.

From the north-east corner of this site, walk up Agnostou Stratioti, cross Olympou, and straight ahead you will see the 5th century **Church of Agios Dimitrios** across the road. Dimitrios was born in the city in the 3rd century and became an eminent scholar and Christian convert. He was martyred on the orders of Galerius, not a Christian and ruthless in persecuting those who were.

There are several claims that Dimitrios' ghost appeared in warrior-like guise at apposite moments during sieges, causing the enemy to flee in terror. This, coupled with claims of miraculous cures at the site of his martyrdom, gained him sainthood.

The church is Greece's largest and was built on the site where he was martyred. It was converted into a mosque by the Turks who plastered over the interior walls. When it was restored to the Christians, it was discovered to have the finest mosaics of all the city's churches. The frescoes and the buildings were extensively damaged in the 1917 fire. However, five 8th century mosaics have survived and can be seen on either side of the altar. The church is open to the public 7.30 am to noon and 5 to 8.30 pm daily. Entry is free.

Turn left from Agios Dimitrios and walk along Agiou Dimitriou till you come to Dragoumi, which leads off to the right. Here you'll reach Filippou, with the 3rd century AD **Rotonda**, the oldest of Thessaloniki's churches, ahead. The Roman brick rotunda was originally intended as a mausoleum for Galerius, but never fulfilled this function; Constantine the Great transformed it into a church. The minaret, erected during its days as a mosque, remains. The church is closed for eventual restoration, opening only for occasional services.

Walk a little way around the church and turn right into D Gounari, where you'll see the imposing **Arch of Galerius**, erected in 303 AD to celebrate the emperor's victories over the Persians in 297. Its eroded bas-reliefs depict battle scenes with the Persians. Turn right into Egnatia, and then left to reach the 8th century **Church of Agia Sofia** on Agias Sofias, which emulates its renowned namesake in İstanbul. The dome has a striking mosaic of the Ascension.

On leaving the Church of Agia Sofia, retrace your steps back to Egnatia, cross the road, and continue a little way up Agias Sofias to the **Church of the Panagia Ahiropiitos**, on the right. This 5th century church is an early example of basilica form; some mosaics and frescoes remain. The name means 'made without hands' and derives from the 12th century, when an icon miraculously appeared in the church.

Several of the smaller churches are also worth a look, including the 13th century **Church of Agia Ekaterini**, the **Church of the Dodeka Apostoloi** (Twelve Apostles) and the 4th century **Church of Nikolaos Orfanos**, which has exquisite frescoes. The little 5th century **Church of Osios David** in Kastra was allegedly built to commemorate Galerius' daughter, Theodora, who was clandestinely baptised while her father was on one of his campaigns.

Kastra & the Ramparts

The Turkish quarter of Kastra is all that is left of 19th century Thessaloniki. The original ramparts of Kastra were built by Theodosius (379-475), but were rebuilt in the 14th century.

Kastra's streets are narrow and steep, with lots of steps, flanked by timber-framed houses with overhanging upper storeys and tiny, whitewashed dwellings with shutters. From Kastra there are stunning views of modern Thessaloniki and the Thermaic Gulf. Take either bus No 22 or 23 from Plateia Eleftherias, or walk north along Agias Sofias, which becomes Dimadou Vlatadou after Athinas, and turn right into Eptapyrgiou at the top.

Organised Tours

Doucas Tours (☎ 269 984, fax 286 610, email info@doucas.gr), at El Venizelou 8, organises a wide range of half and full-day tours around Thessaloniki and Halkidiki. Prices range from 8000 dr for a half-day Thessaloniki City tour to 14,000 dr for a full-day eco-trekking tour of the Sithonian Peninsula in Halkidiki.

Special Events

Thessaloniki hosts a string of festivals in the exhibition grounds during September and October. The first is the International Trade Fair, followed by a cultural festival, which includes film shows and Greek song performances and culminates in the celebration of St Dimitrios' Day on 26 October. This is followed by military parades on Ohi Day on 28 October. Ask the EOT what is currently on.

Places to Stay – Budget

There are no close camp sites; the nearest ones are the EOT camps on the crowded beach at ***Agia Triada*** *(☎ 0392-51 360)* which opens on June 1 and is 27km away, and at ***Epanomi*** *(☎ 0392-41 358)* which opens April 1 and is 33km out of town. Both close by the start of October, and charge about 1200 dr per person and 650 dr per tent. Take bus No 69 for Epanomi; for Agia Triada take either bus No 67 or 72 from Plateia Dikastirion.

GYHA hostel *(☎ 225 946, fax 262 208, Alex Svolou 44)* has dorm beds for 2000 dr. The dormitories are open all day. It's not part of the HI organisation, but an HI, VIP Backpacker or ISIC card will get you a 10% discount.

The E class ***Hotel Atlantis*** *(☎ 540 131, Egnatia 14)* has pokey but clean doubles/triples for 5400/8640 dr. The D class ***Hotel Acropol*** *(☎ 536 170, Tandalidou 4)*, just beyond the central police station, is Thessaloniki's best budget hotel. It's clean, quiet and owned by a friendly English-speaking family. Singles/doubles are 6000/9000 dr.

Another quiet option is the D class ***Hotel Averof*** *(☎ 538 498, fax 543 194, Leontos Sofou 24)* where the attractive pine-furnished rooms cost 6000/9000 dr. The D class ***Hotel Atlas*** *(☎/fax 537 046, Egnatia 40)* has clean, carpeted rooms for 8000/11,000 dr; doubles with bathroom are 14,000 dr. The hotel is reasonable, but the rooms at the front get a lot of traffic noise.

The D class ***Hotel Tourist*** *(☎ 270 501, fax 226 865, Mitropoleos 21)* has a spacious lounge with comfortable armchairs and a TV; pleasant rooms go for a hefty (for its category) 14,000/20,000 dr.

Places to Stay – Mid-Range

The B class ***ABC Hotel*** *(☎ 265 421, fax 276 542, Angelaki 41)*, at the eastern end of Egnatia, has 102 rooms, all with bathroom, telephone and balcony, for 25,900/33,900 dr. Farther east, the modern B class ***Hotel Queen Olga*** *(☎ 824 621, fax 868 581, Vasilissis Olgas 44)* has cosy rooms with a warm, mellow decor and bathroom, radio, colour TV, minibar and air-con for 24,000/30,300 dr. This hotel also has a car park; if you're travelling east, it's on the right. A little farther along is the B class ***Hotel Metropolitan*** *(☎ 824 221, fax 849 762, Vasilissis Olgas 65)*, where attractively furnished rooms with bathroom, telephone and radio cost 24,900/35,400 dr. All of these hotels have bars and restaurants, and include breakfast in the room rate.

Places to Stay – Top End

Close to the train station is the well appointed A class ***Capsis Hotel*** *(☎ 521 321, fax 510 555, email capsis@spark.net.gr, Monastiriou 18)*. Mainly a business hotel, this may be one of the few places where you can get your laptop to talk to the phone lines, since many older hotels still have ancient phone plugs. Comfortable doubles cost between 29,000 dr and 40,000 dr depending on season and demand.

The A class ***Electra Palace Hotel*** *(☎ 232 221, fax 235 947, email electrapalace@the.forthnet.gr, Plateia Aristotelous 5a)* has an impressive facade in the style of a Byzantine palace and costs 29,000/32,000 dr in July and August and 39,000/48,000 dr at other times. It also has two restaurants and a bar.

Places to Eat

You'll never go hungry in Thessaloniki since you're spoiled with a very good selection of eating places. There are lots of fast-food places and snack bars where you can get gyros, pizza or a cheese pie for around 500 dr. ***Babel Snack Bar*** *(Komninon 20)* is a good place for a snack or breakfast with reasonably priced crepes, pies, toasted sandwiches and filter coffee.

A popular place near the west end hotel strip with reasonably priced Greek staples is ***Ta Nea Ilysia*** on Leontos Sofou, opposite Hotel Averof. ***Hryso Pagoni*** *(Alex Svolou*

40) opposite the youth hostel is simple, clean, green (in colour) and popular with locals. Preprepared food goes for around 1100 dr a serve, though the restaurant is best known for its roast chicken.

For a lively evening out you could try the venerable ***O Loutros Fish Taverna*** *(Komninon 15)*, in an old Turkish hammam (bathhouse) near the flower market. Don't be misled by the rough-and-ready ambience – this taverna has a cult following and you'll be rubbing shoulders with politicians, professors and actors. Excellent fish costs around 2000 to 3000 dr. The taverna is always crowded and there are often spontaneous renderings of *rembetika* music.

At the popular ***Ta Spata Psistaria*** *(Aristotelous 28)* you choose from the dishes on display – a simple meal of beans, feta cheese and half a litre of retsina will cost about 2250 dr. Service is smart and business-like. ***Taverna Ta Aderfia tis Pyxarias*** *(Plateia Navarinou 7)* is another popular place. It has a pleasing ambience, with enlarged pictures of old Thessaloniki on the walls; the very tasty kebabs cost around 1350 dr.

Apparently little more than a hole in the wall but with tables aplenty inside is ***Ouzeri Toumbourlika*** *(Kalapothaki 11)*, on a pedestrian street off Plateia Eleftherias. It has tasty *mezedes* to be washed down with ouzo or draught wine. Prices are low to mid-range.

Ouzeri Aristotelous *(Aristotelous 8)* has first-rate mezedes including cuttlefish stuffed with cheese, grilled eggplant with garlic and prawns in red sauce. In the Vosporion Megaron arcade off Aristotelous, the restaurant has a Parisian ambience with marble-topped tables, and is open all day until late Monday to Saturday, but closes at 6 pm on Sunday.

Ta Nisia Restaurant *(Koromila 13)* is another wonderful place with white stucco walls, a wood-beamed ceiling, lots of plants, and pretty plates on the walls. The unusual, imaginative mezedes include cuttlefish and spinach in wine, and little triangles of pastry filled with eggplant. It's on the slightly expensive side.

Ta Ladadika This is a small area consisting of a few blocks of formerly derelict warehouses and small shops close to the ferry terminal. Over the last few years the area has been gradually restored and is now the focus of a number of tavernas, music bars and pubs.

Psarotaverna Istira *(Egyptou 5)* is a cosy, traditional taverna. Meat dishes start from 1200 dr; fish, however, is fairly expensive. Farther up the same street is ***Kokoretsina*** *(Egyptou 17)*, offering *kokoretsi* (spit-grilled offal) for around 1500 dr – and, naturally, retsina. Around the corner is the small ***Iatros tis Pinas*** *(Katouni 7)* which doubles as a snack bar and ouzeri.

On Fasianou, a short street leading to the seafront, two unassuming fish and chip joints do a reasonable job of this staple Anglo dish. ***Ta Bakaliarakia sto Limani*** and ***Ta Bakaliarakia tou Aristou*** *(Fasianou 1)* are as popular with locals as they are with visitors from northern Europe. They both close at about 6 pm, though.

Zithos on Plateia Katouni does an admirable pint of Murphy's stout for 1350 dr and offers an imaginative lunch and dinner menu, albeit on the pricey side. On Plateia Morihovou, ***Sirines*** doubles as a restaurant and funky music bar. Should you be hankering after an oriental banquet, ***Kali Orexi*** *(Oplopiou 3)* on the eastern side of the Ladadika is a rather expensive Chinese restaurant.

Entertainment

Discos & Music Bars *Mylos (☎ 525 968, Andreou Georgiou 56)* is a huge old mill which has been converted into an entertainment complex with an art gallery, restaurant, bar and live music club (classical and rock). Walk down 26 Oktovriou from Plateia Vardari to Andreou Georgiou, which is off to the right, next to the petrol station at 26 Oktovriou 36. Mylos is a spruce cream and terracotta building, 250m on the right.

Music bars abound in the Ladadika area, with the main emphasis on music and all kinds of draught and bottled beer. ***Very***

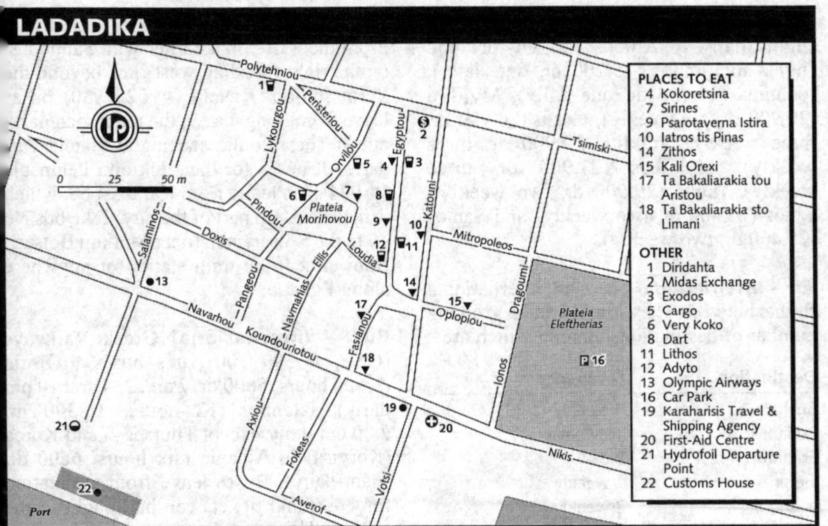

Koko (a pun on the Greek for 'apricot') on Plateia Morihovou is big, bouncy and loud. On Orvilou nearby is the classy ***Cargo***. Egyptou hosts a cluster of bars, among which ***Adyto*** offers live music, and ***Lithos***, ***Dart*** and ***Exodos*** compete for the patronage of the young and hip. If all that weren't enough, ***Diridahta*** on Polytehniou offers Greek dance music and a 'Ladies' Night' three times a week. Spirits at these bars cost between 1800 dr and 2500 dr.

Live bouzouki and Greek folk music are played at ***Show Avantaz*** *(Agiou Dimitriou 156)*. The club is open 11 pm to 4 am nightly, but closes June to September; there's no cover charge, but spirits cost 1800 dr. Also in the town centre, ***Rivoli*** *(Pavlou Mela 40)* is a popular bouzouki nightclub for die-hard fans of this instrument.

Cinema Cinemas showing first-run English-language films include the revamped ***Olympian*** on Plateia Aristotelous, ***Aristotelion*** opposite the White Tower and ***Cinema Pallas*** *(Nikis 69)*. ***Natali*** is an open-air summer cinema on Megalou Alexandrou.

Shopping

Thessaloniki's women have a reputation for being the most chic in Greece so, to supply the demand, there are many shops selling ultra-fashionable clothes and shoes. Bargains can be found along Egnatia and the shops around the indoor food market, and there's high quality, expensive stuff on Tsimiski. Also on Tsimiski, look out for trendy hand-made jewellery at reasonable prices.

If you are seriously interested in Greek or Middle Eastern music, you can buy some genuine traditional instruments at En Chordais (☎ 282 248), which is hidden away somewhat at L Margariti at the back of the same block as the GYHA hostel. Kyriakos Kalaïtzidis, the owner, is also an accomplished musician and runs a music school, should you have a burning desire to learn the *oud*, the *toumberleki* (lap drum) or Byzantine choral music.

Getting There & Away

Air The airport (☎ 473 720) is 16km south-east of the city. The Olympic Airways office (☎ 230 240) is at Navarhou Koundourioti 3.

Air – Domestic Olympic has at least seven flights daily to Athens (22,000 dr) and flights to Limnos (15,200 dr, one daily), Ioannina (12,100 dr, one daily), Mytilini (20,900 dr, six weekly), Corfu (20,900 dr, three weekly), Iraklio (29,900 dr, three weekly), Mykonos (27,900 dr, three weekly), Hania (29,900 dr, two weekly), Chios (22,400 dr, two weekly) and Samos (25,400 dr, two weekly).

Air – International There are international flights between Thessaloniki and a growing number of destinations, among which are:

Destination	Frequency
Bucharest	4 weekly
Budapest	10 weekly
Frankfurt	2 daily
Helsinki	1 weekly
İstanbul	2 weekly
Larnaca	2 weekly
London	11 weekly
Milan	2 daily
Moscow	4 weekly
Munich	2 daily
Paris	3 weekly
Tirana	2 weekly
Vienna	9 weekly
Zürich	7 weekly

For full details see Thessaloniki's Makedonia Airport Web page: users.otenet.gr/~cpnchris/skgd.html.

Bus – Domestic Most of Thessaloniki's bus terminals are close to the train station.

Destination	Terminal
Alexandroupolis	Koloniari 17 (☎ 514 111)
Athens	Monastiriou 65 (☎ 510 834)
Edessa	Anageniseos 22 (☎ 525 100)
Florina	Anageniseos 42 (☎ 522 161)
Ioannina	Giannitson 19 (☎ 512 444, enter via Hristou Pipsou)
Kastoria	Anageniseos 22 (☎ 522 162)
Pella	Anageniseos 22
Trikala	Monastiriou 67 (☎ 517 188)
Veria	26 Oktovriou 10 (☎ 522 160)
Volos	Anageniseos 22 (☎ 534 087)

The Katerini bus station (☎ 519 101) is at Promitheos 10, on a corner with Sapphous, on the right (heading west) just beyond the Veria station. Kavala (☎ 525 530) buses leave from Langada 59, the main road north out of Thessaloniki starting at Plateia Vardari. All buses for the Halkidiki Peninsula (☎ 924 445) leave from Karakasi 68, which is in the eastern part of the city. Take bus No 10 to the Botsari stop (near Markou Botsari) from either the train station or anywhere along Egnatia.

Bus – International Greek Railways (OSE; ☎ 599 100) runs buses to Sofia (seven hours, 5600 dr, 7 am, 2, 4 and 10 pm daily), İstanbul (12 hours, 14,300 dr, 2.30 am daily except Thursday) and Korça (Korytsa) in Albania (six hours, 6600 dr, 8 am daily). Buses leave from the station forecourt and tickets can be bought in the station. These services, however, are subject to change, so check beforehand.

Train – Domestic All domestic trains leave from the station on Monastiriou (☎ 517 517/518). There are four regular trains daily to Athens (7½ hours, 4100 dr) and Kozani (four hours, 1580 dr) with connections to Florina (3¼ hours, 1370 dr), and three daily to Alexandroupolis (8 hours, 2990 dr) and Larisa with connections to Volos (4½ hours, 2020 dr).

There are five additional express intercity services to Athens (six hours, 8250 dr) – one is nonstop with a meal included in the ticket price; two to Alexandroupolis (5½ hours, 4990 dr) and one to Kozani (3¼ hours, 2580 dr). Note that tickets to all destinations and intermediate stations using the intercity services attract a supplement which is worked out on a sliding scale, determined by the distance travelled. There are also a couple of overnight sleepers to Athens.

Tickets are available from the train station or the OSE office (☎ 598 120, 517 114), Aristotelous 18.

The station also has a National Bank of Greece, a post office, a couple of ATMs, an OTE and a restaurant which is open 6 am to

10 pm. Luggage storage is 1000 dr per item per day, or 500 dr if you have a train ticket.

Train – International There are currently four international services operating out of Thessaloniki. There are trains to Belgrade (11,500 dr, two daily) – one departs at 6 am, and the other, at 7.30 pm, continues on to Budapest (20,000 dr) and beyond; İstanbul (13,000 dr, one daily at 7.25 am); and Sofia (6700 dr, one daily at 8.25 am), with a connection for Bucharest. These times are subject to seasonal changes, so do check before making plans.

Ferry A ferry to Chios (18 hours, 8300 dr) via Limnos (eight hours, 5300 dr) and Lesvos (13 hours, 8300 dr) sails on Sunday throughout the year. In summer there are three to six boats weekly to Iraklio on Crete (12,000 dr), via Paros and Santorini; one also stops at Tinos and Mykonos.

There are also boats to the Sporades islands of Skiathos, Skopelos and Alonnisos three times weekly (5½ to seven hours, 3800 dr) in July and August, and one weekly to Rhodes (21 hours, 14,800 dr) via Samos and Kos throughout the year.

Ferry tickets are available from Karaharisis Travel & Shipping Agency (☎ 524 544, fax 532 289), Koundourioti 8. The telephone number of Thessaloniki's port police is ☎ 531 504.

Hydrofoil In summer there are more or less daily hydrofoils to the Sporades islands of Skiathos (3¼ hours, 8500 dr), Skopelos (four hours, 9300 dr) and Alonnisos (4½ hours, 11,700 dr), via Nea Moudania, Horefto and Agios Ioannis on the Pelion Peninsula. Tickets can be purchased from Karaharisis Travel & Shipping Agency (see Ferry).

Getting Around

To/From the Airport There is no Olympic Airways shuttle, but bus No 78 plies the airport route; it leaves from in front of the train station and stops in front of the ferry terminal (140 dr). A one way taxi costs around 2000 dr.

Bus Orange articulated buses operate within the city, and blue and orange buses operate both within the city and out to the suburbs. The local bus station is on Filippou.

On the articulated buses you buy a ticket from the conductor who sits next to the door; driver-only buses have ticket machines. Make sure you have change before you board. There are three different ticket zones: 100 dr within the city, 135 dr for the suburbs and 150 dr for outlying villages.

Taxi Thessaloniki's taxis are blue and white, and the procedure for hailing one is the same as in Athens: stand on the edge of the pavement and bellow your destination as they pass. There are five taxi companies:

Alfa – Lefkos Pyrgos
(☎ 249 100) Omirou 12, Sykies
Makedonia
(☎ 550 500) Karyofylli 4
Megas Alexandros
(☎ 866 866)
Omega
(☎ 546 522) Terma Giannitson
Thessaloniki
(☎ 551 525) Giannitson 140

Car The ELPA (Greek Automobile Club; ☎ 426 319) is at Vasilissis Olgas 228 in Kalamaria. Cars can be hired from Budget Rent a Car (☎ 229 519), Angelaki 15; and Euro Rent (☎ 826 333), G Papandreou 5, among others.

Drivers arriving in Thessaloniki would be best advised to head for Plateia Eleftherias, where there is a decent-sized pay car park.

AROUND THESSALONIKI

Langadas Λαγκαδάς

The village of Langadas, 12km north-east of Thessaloniki, is famous for the *anastenaria* fire walking ritual which takes place on 21 May, the feast day of St Constantine and his mother, St Helena.

The fire walkers, or *anastenarides* (groaners), believe that the ritual originated in the village of Kosti (an abbreviation of

Konstantinos) in eastern Thrace. The story is that in 1250 AD the Church of St Constantine caught fire and the villagers, hearing the icons groan, entered the church, rescued them, and escaped unscathed.

The icons were kept by the families concerned, and their descendants and other devotees honoured the saint each year by performing the ritual. In 1913, when the village was occupied by Bulgarians, the families fled to the villages of Serres, Drama and Langadas, taking the icons with them.

The anastenarides step barefoot onto burning charcoal. Holding the icons and waving coloured handkerchiefs, they dance while emitting strange cries, accompanied by drums and lyres. They believe they will not be burned because God's spirit enters into them. New fire walkers are initiated each year.

The Church condemns the ritual as pagan, and indeed the celebration seems to have elements of the pagan worship of Dionysos. If you would like to see this overtly commercial but intriguing spectacle, it begins at 7 pm – turn up early to get a ringside seat. Frequent buses leave for Langadas from the Thessaloniki terminal at Irinis 17, near Langada.

PELLA Πέλλα

Pella, most famous as the birthplace of Alexander the Great, lies on the Macedonian plain astride the Thessaloniki-Edessa road. Its star attraction is its marvellous mosaics. King Archelaos (who ruled from 413-399 BC) moved the Macedonian capital from Aigai (Vergina) to Pella, although Aigai remained the royal cemetery.

The mosaics, which mainly depict mythological scenes, are made from naturally coloured stones; the effect is one of subtle and harmonious blends and contrasts. They were discovered in the remains of houses and public buildings, on the northern side of the road. Some are *in situ* and others are housed in the museum. Also on this side is a courtyard laid out with a black and white geometric mosaic and six re-erected columns.

The **museum**, which is on the southern side, is one of Greece's best site museums. Room 1 has a reconstruction of a wall from a house at Pella, and a splendid circular table inlaid with intricate floral and abstract designs, thought to have belonged to Philip II. Room 2 houses the mosaics which have been removed from the site.

The site (☎ 0382-31 160) is open 8 am to 7 pm daily; admission is 500 dr. The museum is open 8 am to 7 pm Tuesday to Friday, 8.30 am to 3 pm Saturday and Sunday and 12.30 to 7 pm Monday. Entry is a further 500 dr. There is a drinking fountain outside the museum, and a ***kafeneio*** near the northern side of the site.

Getting There & Away

There are frequent buses from Thessaloniki (40 minutes, 650 dr). If you wish to visit Pella and Vergina by bus in one day, first see Pella, then take a Thessaloniki bus back along the main road and get off at Halkidona, where you can pick up a bus to Vergina.

MT OLYMPUS Ολυμπος Ορος

Mt Olympus, chosen by the ancients as the abode of their gods, is Greece's highest and most awe-inspiring mountain. It has around 1700 plant species, some of which are rare and endemic. The lower slopes are covered with forests of holm oak, arbutus, cedar and conifers; the higher ones with oak, beech, black and Balkan pine. The mountain also maintains varied bird life. In 1937 it became Greece's first national park.

In August 1913, Christos Kakalos, a native of Litohoro, and the Swiss climbers Frederic Boissonas and Daniel Baud-Bovy, were the first mortals to reach the summit of Mytikas (2918m), Olympus' highest peak.

Litohoro Λιτόχωρο

☎ 0352 • postcode 602 00 • pop 6600

The village of Litohoro (lih-**to**-ho-ro, 305m) is the place to go if you wish to climb Olympus. The village was developed in the 1920s as a sanatorium for the tubercular; later it settled comfortably into its

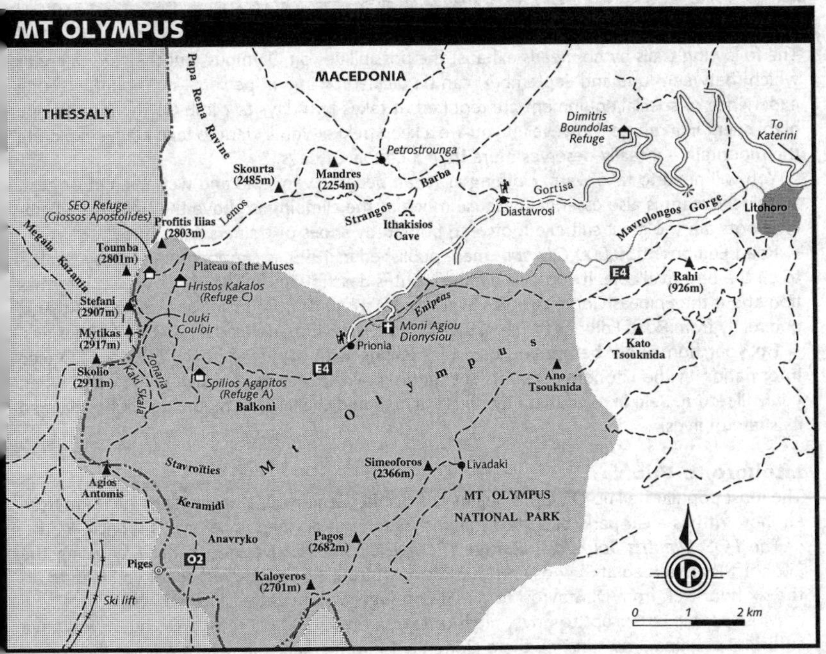

role as 'base camp' for climbers. The approach to Litohoro along the main road is picture-postcard stuff on a fine day. Directly in front as you make the final approach to the village, the gorge of the Enipeas River parts to reveal the towering peaks of Olympus. The ancients sure knew how to choose an abode for their gods.

In recent years Litohoro has once again begun to promote its health resort image. This has resulted in difficulties in finding a hotel room in July and August, particularly at weekends.

Orientation The main road is Agiou Nikolaou, which, from Thessaloniki or Katerini, is the road by which you enter the village; it leads up to Plateia Kentriki, the central square. On the right side of this road is a large army camp. The road to Prionia, where the main trail up Olympus begins, is on the right, just before the central square. Uphill to the left of the main square is 28 Oktovriou, where most of the provision stores are.

The bus terminal is on Plateia Kentriki, on the right as you face the sea.

Information The EOT information booth is in a little white building with wooden eaves on Agiou Nikolaou, just before the Prionia turn-off.

The EOS's (☎ 84 544) helpful, English-speaking staff give out information about Olympus and a free pamphlet which details some of the treks. Face inland on Agiou Nikolaou, turn left opposite Myrto Hotel and follow the signs. The office is open 9 am to 1 pm and 6 to 8.30 pm Monday to Friday, and 9 am to 1 pm Saturday (closed Sunday). The EOS runs three refuges on Olympus.

Mt Olympus Trails

The following trails by no means exhaust the possibilities on Olympus, but they are the ones which (between June and September) can be tackled by any fit person – no mountaineering experience or special equipment are required. It takes two days to climb Olympus, with one night spent in a refuge. However, if you are a keen trekker you'll want to take longer exploring the mountain – it really deserves more than a couple of days.

You will need to take warm clothing as it can become very cold and wet, even in August. Sunblock cream is also essential because much of the climbing is above the tree line. Climbing boots are the most suitable footwear, but sturdy shoes or trainers will suffice.

Road Editions' 1:50,000 *Olympus* map, published in 1999, is considered – even by locals – to be the best available. It contains detailed routes descriptions in English, as well as information about the Enipeas Gorge trek. It's available for 1830 dr from major bookstores in Athens, or directly from Road Editions (☎ 01-929 6541, fax 929 6492), Ilia Iliou 41, GR-117 43 Athens.

Do your homework before you begin by talking with someone at the EOS or SEO (see Information in the Litohoro section). Let them know how long you plan to trek and when you will return. Bear in mind that Olympus is a high and challenging mountain – it has claimed its share of lives.

Litohoro to Prionia

The most popular trail up Olympus begins at **Prionia** (Πριόνια), a tiny settlement 18km from Litohoro. It has a car park, basic taverna and water, but no telephone or bus service.

The EOS ***Dimitris Boundolas Refuge*** *(Refuge D; ☎ 0352-84 519)* is halfway along the Litohoro-Prionia road at Stavros (940m). It is open from April to November. If you plan to do the six hour trek from Diastavrosi to the SEO refuge, you might wish to stay here.

Most people either opt to drive, hitch or take a taxi (5500 dr) to Prionia, but if you have sufficient stamina, you can trek there along an 11km marked trail, which follows the course of the Enipeas River. The strenuous 4½ hour trek is over sharply undulating terrain but offers glorious views. It begins beyond the cemetery in Litohoro and ends just before the taverna at Prionia. One kilometre before Prionia is the ruined **Moni Agiou Dionysiou**, built at the beginning of the 16th century and blown up by the Turks in 1828. It was rebuilt, only to be blown up again in 1943 by the Nazis who believed that resistance fighters were using it as a hide-out.

Prionia to Spilios Agapitos

The trail begins just beyond the taverna in Prionia. You'll have to fill up with water here as it is the last source before Refuge A at **Spilios Agapitos** (Σπήλαιος Αγαπητός). The trail is well maintained and well used – there is no chance of getting lost and you will meet other trekkers along the way. The steep trail passes first through thick deciduous forests, then conifers. It takes around 2½ hours to reach the refuge.

Refuge A *(☎ 0352-81 800)* can accommodate up to 140 people. It has cold showers and serves very good meals from 6 to 9 am, lunch to order, and from 6 to 8 pm both to guests and to people just popping in. Lights out and bed for all is at 10 pm. The warden, Kostas Zolotas, speaks fluent English, and is an experienced mountaineer who will be able to answer any questions. The refuge is open from May to October, and costs 3000 dr a night (2500 dr for Alpine Club members). During July and August it is advisable to make a reservation either through the EOS in Litohoro or Thessaloniki, or by telephoning the refuge.

Mt Olympus Trails

Spilios Agapitos to Mytikas (via Kaki Skala)

The path to **Mytikas** (Μύτικας) begins just behind Refuge A. Fill up your water bottles because there is no water beyond here. The last of the trees thin out rapidly; the path is still marked by red slashes and once again it is easy to follow. After one to 1½ hours you will come to a sign pointing right towards the SEO refuge. Continue straight ahead for Mytikas. The path now zigzags over the scree for another hour before reaching the summit ridge. From the ridge there is a 500m drop into the chasm of **Kazania** (the cauldron).

Just before the drop, in an opening to the right, is the beginning of **Kaki Skala** (Κακή Σκάλα, meaning bad stairway), which leads, after 40 minutes of rock scrambling, to the summit of Mytikas. The route is marked by red slashes on the rocks. It is perhaps surprising that no-one has yet coined the nickname 'the original Stairway to (Olympian) Heaven', given the divine destination of the Kaki Skala. The route keeps just below the drop into Kazania, although at a couple of places you can look down into the cauldron – a dramatic sight.

If you have never done rock scrambling before, look at Kaki Skala and decide then and there whether you want to tackle it. Many turn back here, but just as many novices tackle Kaki Skala. If you decide against it, all is not lost, for if you turn left at the summit ridge, an easy path leads in 15 to 20 minutes to **Skolio** (Σκολιό, 2911m), Mt Olympus' second-highest peak.

Mytikas to Giossos Apostolides (SEO Refuge)

After you've admired the breathtaking views from Mytikas, signed the summit book and said a prayer of thanks to the gods for helping you up (and another asking them to help you down), you face the choice of returning to Refuge A via Kaki Skala, or continuing on to the SEO ***Refuge of Giossos Apostolides*** (Γιόσος Αποστολίδης). At 2720m, this is the highest refuge in the Balkans, with a stunning panorama of the major peaks of Olympus. The refuge has 90 beds and serves meals. It has no showers or natural drinking water, but bottled water is sold. The EOS ***Refuge C Hristos Kakalos*** (Χρήστος Κάκαλος) is nearby with 18 beds, but is open only during July and August. Both refuges are more exposed to the weather than Refuge A and are not as popular.

Neither of these refuges has a telephone. To reach them you can return via Kaki Skala to the Zonaria (Ζωνάρια) path signposted to the SEO Refuge; this leads to the refuge in one hour. Alternatively, you can descend Mytikas via **Louki Couloir**, which begins just north of the summit and is another 45 minute rock scramble. A few experienced climbers claim that Louki Couloir is easier than Kaki Skala, but the general consensus is that it's more difficult. It is certainly more sheer and prone to rock falls – more of a danger to those climbing up than to those descending. At the bottom of Louki Couloir you meet the Zonaria path. Turn left and the SEO lodge is 20 minutes away.

SEO Refuge to Diastavrosi

The refuge is on the edge of the Plateau of the Muses and from here a well maintained path leads, in 4½ hours, to **Diastavrosi** (Διασταύρωση), on the Prionia-Litohoro road. From the plateau the path goes along a ridge called **Lemos** (Λαιμός, meaning neck) with the Enipeas Ravine on the right and the Papa Rema Ravine on the left. After one hour you arrive at **Skourta** summit (2485m), from which it is 1½ hours to **Petrostrounga** (stony sheepfold). The next stretch of path leads through woodland to a small meadow known as **Barba**; from here it is 40 minutes to Diastavrosi, 14km from Litohoro.

The SEO (Association of Greek Climbers; ☎ 84 200) also gives information, but you are more likely to find someone who speaks English at the EOS. To reach the SEO, walk along the road to Prionia and take the first turn left and first left again. The office is open 6 to 10 pm daily, and runs one refuge on Olympus.

The modern post office is on 28 Oktovriou. The OTE is on Agiou Nikolaou, diagonally opposite the EOT booth.

The National Bank of Greece is on Plateia Kentriki; both this and the nearby Commercial Bank sport ATMs.

The police station (☎ 81 100) is on the corner of the road to Prionia. There is a health centre (☎ 22 222) 5km away, at the Litohoro turn-off from the main coastal highway.

Places to Stay There's a plethora of camp sites along the coast around the Litohoro turn-off. They include ***Olympios Zeus*** *(☎ 22 115)*, ***Olympos Beach*** *(☎ 22 112)* and ***Minerva*** *(☎ 22 177)*. All of these sites have good facilities and a taverna, snack bar and minimarket.

There are some rooms to rent around town – look for signs – but the supply is not great.

The cheapest hotel is the clean, well kept D class ***Hotel Markesia*** *(☎ 81 831)* which costs 6500/7500 dr for singles/doubles with bathroom. However, this place only opens from June to the start of October. Face inland from Plateia Kentriki, turn left into 28 Oktovriou, and the hotel is on the left.

On the corner of the main square is the bright, breezy and spotlessly clean ***Hotel Enipeas*** *(☎/fax 81 328)* with doubles/triples for 9000/12,000 dr and balconies with probably the best views of Olympus in town. Directly opposite is the C class ***Hotel Aphrodite*** *(☎ 81 415, fax 22 123)* with tidy, colour-coded rooms for 12,000/17,000 dr with bathroom.

Litohoro's poshest hotel is the C class ***Myrto Hotel*** *(☎ 81 398, fax 82 298)*, near the central square, where singles/doubles cost 11,00/13,000 dr, all with air-con, telephone and TV.

Places to Eat There is a selection of places to eat on both the main square and the approach road from the army barracks, with the choice ranging from fast to traditional. On the main square itself, ***Olympus Taverna*** serves tasty mezedes and ready-made food. Make a point of trying the unusual red retsina. Owner Christos Kakalos is the grandson of one of the first three men to climb Mt Olympus.

To Pazari, just down from Hotel Markesia on 28 Oktovriou, specialises in fish. Not 50m away is the locally popular ***Damaskinia***, with a garden at the back. Next to the OTE, ***Deas Psistaria*** has reasonably priced, generous portions of charcoal-grilled chicken.

Getting There & Away From the bus station (☎ 81 271), there buses to Katerini (25 minutes, 450 dr, 16 daily), Thessaloniki (1½ hours, 1700 dr, 10 daily) and Athens (5½ hours, 7250 dr, three daily via Katerini). Buses from Thessaloniki to Athens or Volos will drop you off on the main highway, where you can catch the Katerini-Litohoro bus.

Litohoro is on the Athens-Volos-Thessaloniki line (10 trains daily), but the station is 9km from town.

Ancient Dion Δίον

Recently rediscovered, Ancient Dion is an extensive, well watered site at the foot of Mt Olympus, just north of Litohoro and 16km south of Katerini. It was the sacred city of the Macedonians, who worshipped the Olympian gods here. Alexander the Great sacrificed here before setting off to conquer the world.

Dion's origins are unknown, but there is evidence that an earth goddess of fertility was first worshipped here. Later, other gods were worshipped, including Asclepius, the god of medicine. The most interesting discovery so far is the evocative **Sanctuary to Isis**, the Egyptian goddess, in a lush, low-lying part of the site.

Its votive statues were found virtually intact with traces of colour remaining. Copies have been placed in the positions of the originals, which are now in the site museum. Also worth seeking out is the magnificent, well preserved **mosaic floor**, dating from 200 AD, which depicts the Dionysos Triumphal Epiphany.

The site, known as the **Dion Archaeological Park**, is open 8 am to 7 pm daily, but closes at 6 pm in winter. Admission is 800 dr; students 400 dr. During the Olympus Festival, which takes place during August, plays are performed at the site's reconstructed theatre.

The site **museum** (☎ 0351-53 206) is well laid out with a large collection of statues and offerings from Ancient Dion, labelled in English and Greek. It is open 8 am to 7 pm Tuesday to Friday, and 12.30 to 7 pm Monday. Admission is 800 dr; 400 dr for students.

Places to Stay Because it is a bit of a hassle to get to Dion, you may wish to stay overnight in the modern village. The pleasant C class ***Dion Hotel*** *(☎ 0351-53 222, fax 31 202)* is on the main road in (modern) Dion, near the bus stop. Singles/doubles with bathroom are 7500/8000 dr.

Getting There & Away There are no buses from Litohoro, but there is a direct road and taking a cab is the best way to get there. It shouldn't cost more than 2000 dr. There are also regular buses from Katerini.

VERIA Βέροια

☎ 0331 • postcode 591 00 • pop 37,000

Most people merely pass through Veria, 75km west of Thessaloniki, en route to the ancient site of Vergina. But Veria, capital of the prefecture of Imathia, is a fascinating town with over 70 churches – some call it 'Little Jerusalem'. There are many rather dilapidated houses from the Turkish era, but a government preservation order is in force and most of them are now undergoing gradual restoration. Mineral springs are located all over the town and the local tap water is said to be very good. Veria is also the centre of a vast peach-growing industry, and wines made from grapes grown on the escarpment from Veria to Edessa are among Greece's most famous exports.

Orientation & Information

The town's two main squares, Plateia Antoniou and Plateia Raktivan (more commonly known as Plateia Orologiou), are 1km apart, linked by the town's two main thoroughfares: the modern Venizelou which becomes Mitropoleos halfway along, and the traditional Vasileos Konstantinou (also called Kentrikis). To reach Plateia Antoniou from the intercity bus station, exit from the rear of the station onto Iras, turn right and immediately left into Malakousi – the square is a little way along, with both Venizelou and Vasileos Konstantinou running off to the left. The train station is 3km from the town centre on the old road to Thessaloniki.

There is no tourist office or tourist police. The National Bank of Greece is on the corner of Mitropoleos and Ippokratous. The post office and the OTE are both on Mitropoleos, at 33 and 45 respectively. The police (☎ 22 391) are on Mitropoleos, next to the post office.

Things to See

The most interesting part of Veria is the old Turkish quarter. For a short tour around this area, begin by walking down Vasileos Konstantinou from Plateia Antoniou. The narrow, winding Vasileos Konstantinou is the commercial street of old Veria, flanked by old-fashioned tailor shops, bookbinders, kafeneia and antique shops.

Halfway along on the right is a huge, ancient plane tree where in 1430 the Turks, after taking Veria, hanged Archbishop Arsenios. Directly opposite is the dilapidated **old cathedral**, which dates from the 12th century. A rather incongruous and now decapitated minaret bears testament to the cathedral's conversion to a mosque during the Turkish era. To reach the residential part of the old Turkish quarter, turn right at the plane tree into Goudi and wander among the old streets with their many abandoned houses.

The **archaeological museum** is in this part of town on Leoforos Anixeos, which snakes its way to the left across the escarpment from the end of Elias. It contains some finds from the tombs of Vergina and Levkadia, and is open 8.30 am to 3 pm Tuesday to Sunday. Admission is 500 dr. Any of the roads running east from Venizelou will lead to Leoforos Anixeos.

St Paul the Apostle visited Veria twice on his second and third voyages (49-52 and 53-58 AD). Veria was referred to as Beroea in the New Testament, and there is now a **shrine** at Mavromihali 1 where Paul is believed to have preached. Mavromihali runs off Plateia Orologiou and leads to the Papakia district.

Places to Stay

The best value among the few hotels is ***Hotel Veroi*** *(☎ 22 866, fax 23 566)* on Plateia Orologiou. Very clean, large, comfortably furnished singles/doubles with balcony and bathroom are 9800/13,500 dr.

At ***Hotel Villa Elia*** *(☎ 26 800, fax 21 880, Elias 16)* rates are 13,000/16,000 dr with bathroom. Both Elias and Megalou Alexandrou are left turns off Venizelou from Plateia Antoniou.

The best hotel is the B class ***Hotel Macedonia*** *(☎ 66 902, fax 66 902, Kontogiorgaki 50)*. The spacious, tastefully furnished rooms are 15,900/18,500 dr with bathroom. Walk along Venizelou, turn left into Elias and then right into Paster at the Top Café. Kontogiorgaki is the continuation of Paster. The hotel is at the end of this street on the right.

Places to Eat

Veria is famous for its *revani*, a sweet syrupy cake found throughout most of the town. It's also known for the infamous bean concoction, *fasolada*, usually cooked in an oven.

The long-established ***Estiatorion-Kosmas Sarafopoulos*** *(☎ 22 118)*, on Vasileos Konstantinou, 100m around the corner and down the hill from Hotel Veroi, is popular with locals. There is a similar but slightly more modern place called ***Menou*** *(Plateia Orologiou 14)* next to the Kozani bus terminal on Plateia Orologiou.

For more relaxed eating, head for the Papakia district. Follow Mavromihali, near the Kozani bus station, uphill for about 200m. Here is a pleasant square with waterfalls, little streams and a couple of pleasant places to eat. ***Saroglou*** is slightly pretentious, but very popular. Next door is the traditional ***Kostalar***, in business since 1939.

Getting There & Away

Bus Frequent buses leave from the intercity bus station for Thessaloniki (1¼ hours, 1300 dr), Athens (seven hours, 8500 dr), Edessa (one hour, 900 dr) and Vergina (20 minutes, 280 dr). Buses for Kozani (1¼ hours, 1100 dr) depart from a separate bus station on Plateia Orologiou; buses from Ioannina (six hours, 4000 dr) also stop on this square.

Train There are eight trains daily in both directions on the Thessaloniki-Kozani-Florina line. Additional intercity services to/from Kozani pass through Veria twice daily – one goes to Athens and the other to Thessaloniki.

VERGINA Βεργίνα

☎ 0331 • postcode 590 31 • pop 1255

The ancient site of Vergina (ver-**yee**-nah), 11km south-east of Veria, is ancient Aigai, the first capital of Macedon. The capital was later transferred to Pella, but Aigai continued to be the royal cemetery. Philip II was assassinated here in 336 BC at the wedding of his daughter Cleopatra.

To fully appreciate the significance of the discoveries, you need to visit Thessaloniki's archaeological museum, where the magnificent finds of Philip II's tomb are displayed, along with Philip II himself! Unfortunately, the actual tomb is off limits to visitors as it is still being excavated.

The ruins are spread out, but well signposted from the modern village of the same name. The **Macedonian tomb**, 500m uphill from the village, has a facade of four Ionic half-columns and a marble throne inside. Continue 400m farther up the road to reach the ruins of an extensive **palatial complex**, built as a summer residence for Antigonos Gonatas (king from 283-240 BC). The focal point is a large Doric peristyle which was surrounded by pebble mosaic floors. One of the mosaics, with a beautiful floral design, is well preserved *in situ*. A large oak tree on the highest point of the site affords some welcome shade.

Both the site (☎ 92 347) and the Macedonian tomb are open 8 am to 7 pm Tuesday to Sunday and 12.30 to 7 pm Monday. Entrance to this World Heritage-listed site is 1200 dr.

There is a ***cafe*** opposite the Macedonian tomb and for those who wish to stay overnight, there is a choice of ***Pansion Vergina*** *(☎ 92 510, fax 92 511)* with singles/doubles for 12,000/14,000 dr, or the slightly cheaper ***Ikos*** *(☎ 92 366)* domatia, both on the same road as the tombs.

EDESSA Εδεσσα

☎ 0381 • postcode 582 00 • pop 16,000

Edessa (**ed**-eh-sah) is the capital of the prefecture of Pella. Extolled by Greeks for its many waterfalls, it is little-visited by foreign tourists. Edessa is a truly delightful town which has water and greenery, unlike the majority of Greek towns. Little streams and bridges, and cool and shady parks, dot the whole of Edessa which, being a small town, is very easy and pleasant to explore on foot. The town is perched precariously on a ledge overlooking the seemingly endless agricultural plain, and is the most northern of the Mt Vermion escarpment centres.

Until the discovery of the royal tombs at Vergina, Edessa was believed to be the ancient Macedonian city of Aigai.

Orientation

The intercity bus station is on the corner of Filippou and Pavlou Mela. To reach the town centre, cross over Filippou and walk straight ahead along Pavlou Mela to the T-junction, and turn right into Egnatia where the road forks almost immediately. The left branch continues as Egnatia, and the right is Dimokratias. These two streets, along with Filippou, are the main thoroughfares.

The train station is opposite the end of 18 Oktovriou. To reach the town centre, walk up 18 Oktovriou for 400m to a major junction; the biggest waterfall is signposted sharp left, or veer right for Dimokratias.

Information

There is a helpful and well stocked Tourist Information Office (☎ 20 300) in a kiosk at the falls themselves, with a handy map of Edessa and surrounding tourist attractions.

The National Bank of Greece is at Dimokratias 1 and has an ATM. The post office is at Dimokratias 26. The OTE is on Agiou Dimitriou – turn right from Pavlou Mela (by Hotel Pella) and it's off to the left.

There is no tourist police; the regular police is on Iroön Polytehniou, which runs between Filippou and Dimokratias.

Things to See

Edessa's main attraction is its **waterfalls**. There are a number of little ones (usually artificial) dotted around the town, but the biggest waterfall, called *katarraktes* (waterfalls), plunges dramatically down a cliff to the agricultural plain below. There are actually two falls: one drops more or less vertically, and another, a little way to the left, tumbles and twirls, zigzagging down the cliff face.

The whole setup is actually very becoming, if you discount the tacky tourist stalls on the street. The cliff is mantled with abundant vegetation and there are wonderful views of the vast plain which extends all the way to Thessaloniki.

Places to Stay

The D class ***Hotel Elena*** *(☎ 23 218, fax 23 951)* on Plateia Timenidon has light and airy singles/doubles for 8200/11,800 dr with bathroom and TV. From the bus station turn right at Filippou, walk three blocks to the junction signposted to the waterfalls and Florina, turn right into Arch Panteleimonos, and the hotel is a little way along on the left.

The D class ***Hotel Pella*** *(☎ 23 541, Egnatia 26)* has rooms for 8000/9500 dr with bathroom.

The C class ***Hotel Alfa*** *(☎ 22 221, fax 24 777, Egnatia 28)* has double-glazed and soundproofed rooms with air-con for 7250/11,000 dr. It is much better than Hotel Pella, its immediate neighbour.

Edessa's best hotel is the B class ***Hotel Katarraktes*** *(☎ 22 300, fax 27 237, Karanou 18)* where comfortable, traditionally furnished rooms with bathroom and balcony are 12,400/17,280 dr. Follow the signposts for the cataracts, and look for the hotel on the left, just before the waterfalls.

Places to Eat

Close to the bus station on the same street as Hotel Pella and Hotel Alfa is ***Estiatorion Omonia*** *(Egnatia 20)*. The food at this long-established eating place is cheap and good, with preprepared dishes to choose from. A meal with draught wine costs about 2000 dr. Diagonally opposite the bus station, ***Taverna-Psistaria*** *(Filippou 26)* is convenient, though a little uninspiring.

You'll pay more to eat at the waterfalls, where there are at least five restaurants. ***Katarraktes Edessas*** *(Kapetan Gareti-Perdika 1)* is a publicly owned institution with the prime spot next to the falls. Try the specialities of *tsoblek kebab* or *kleftiko*; both are delicious dishes made with veal and various vegetables, and go for around 1700 dr.

The younger set's bar and cafe life is centred on the little brick-paved Angeli Gatsou, which starts just opposite the post office by the little bridge.

Getting There & Away

Bus From the main bus station (☎ 23 511) there are buses to Thessaloniki (one hour 40 minutes, 1600 dr, hourly), Veria (one hour, 900 dr, six daily) and Athens (eight hours, 8850 dr, three daily). Four buses daily go to Florina and Kastoria from a second bus station, marked by a sign on the corner of Egnatia and Pavlou Mela.

Train There are eight trains daily both ways on the Thessaloniki-Kozani/Florina line, plus an additional two intercity services. The stretch between Edessa and Amyndeo skirts the western shore of Lake Vegoritida and is particularly beautiful. For further information call ☎ 23 510.

FLORINA Φλώρινα

☎ 0385 • postcode 531 00 • pop 12,500

The mountain town of Florina (**flo**-rih-nah) is the capital of the prefecture of the same name. Tourists used to come to Florina only because it was the last Greek town before the border with the former Yugoslavia. Now its economy is seriously compromised by the continuing political troubles in its northern neighbour. Despite this, it's a lively town, and a pleasant place for an overnight stopover if you are touring the area.

If you enjoy your stay you're in good company. Greece's most famous film director, Theodoros Angelopoulos, loves Florina (although it is not his birthplace). Two of his films, *Alexander the Great* and *The Hesitant Step of the Stork*, were made on location here.

Florina is the only place from which you can take a bus to the Prespa Lakes and there is also a low-key ski resort at Vigla, just west of Florina on the Prespa Lakes road.

Orientation & Information

Florina is laid out in a long curve, much like a boomerang, and is divided by the river that flows along the length of the town. The main street is Pavlou Mela, which leads to Plateia Georgiou Modi, the central square. Half of Pavlou Mela is a pedestrian mall. From the train station, walk straight ahead, keeping the archaeological museum to your left. Bear left and you are on Pavlou Mela.

From Plateia Georgiou Modi, turn right into Stefanou Dragoumi for the intercity bus station, 250m up the street. Bear right at the end of the street, cross the road and look for the KTEL office. Turn left from Plateia Georgiou Modi into 25 Martiou for the river. Megalou Alexandrou is the continuation of Pavlou Mela on the other side of the square.

There is no EOT or tourist police. The gaudy National Bank of Greece is about 50m up Megalou Alexandrou on the right, and the Commercial Bank is just behind it. Both banks provide ATM facilities. The post office is at Kalergi 22; walk along Stefanou Dragoumi towards the bus station and Kalergi is off to the left. The OTE is at

Tyrnovou 5. As you walk along Pavlou Mela from the train station, Tyrnovou is a turn-off to the left.

The telephone number of the police is ☎ 22 100.

Things to See & Do

The **archaeological museum** is housed in a modern building near the train station. It is well laid out, though the downstairs section feels a little bare. Only the downstairs labels are in English. The curator will show you around, but his English is limited. Downstairs there is pottery from the Neolithic, early Iron and Bronze Ages, and Roman grave stelae and statues. Upstairs there are some Byzantine reliefs and fragments of frescoes, and finds from an as yet unidentified town built by Philip II, discovered on the nearby hill of Agios Panteleimonas. The museum is open 8.30 am to 3 pm daily except Monday. Admission is free.

Close to the archaeological museum and easily mistaken for a railway building is the **Florina Artists' Gallery**, which houses a collection of local artists' works. It is open 5 to 8 pm Wednesday to Saturday and 10 am to 1 pm Sunday and public holidays.

Old Florina occupied both river banks, and many Turkish houses and neoclassical mansions survive. The town has a thriving artistic community, and the Society for the Friends of Art of Florina has restored one of the neoclassical mansions on the river bank, now the **Museum of Modern Art** at Leoforos Eleftherias 103. The museum houses a permanent collection of works by contemporary Greek artists and hosts frequent exhibitions. It is open 5 to 8 pm Monday to Saturday and 10 am to 1 pm Sunday. Admission is free. Walk down 25 Martiou, cross the bridge over the river and turn right; walk for about 200m. Even if you are not interested in art, this is a pleasant walk along the river bank.

If you feel energetic, there is a pleasant walk up to the old Tottis hotel where there's an unparalleled view of Florina. From the little **Church of Koimisis Theotokou** there is an established path that snakes up the hill. The blue and white church is on the southern side of the river, just above Plateia Sholion. Walk down 25 Martiou, cross the river and turn left; after about 200m you will come across the square – the church is above it.

Places to Stay

The nearest hotel to the train station is the C class ***Hotel Ellenis*** *(☎ 22 671, fax 22 815, Pavlou Mela 39)*. The pleasantly clean if somewhat basic singles/doubles cost 9000/12,000 dr with bathroom. As you come from the train station, it's on the left.

Up a notch, the C class ***Hotel Antigone*** *(☎ 23 180, fax 45 620, Arianou 1)* has slightly jaded but pleasant rooms for a pricey 15,000/20,000 dr. Turn right into Stefanou Dragoumi from Plateia Georgiou Modi, and the hotel is 200m along on the left, close to the bus station.

The B class ***Hotel Lingos*** *(☎ 28 322, fax 29 643, Tagmatarhou Naoum 1)*, just north of Plateia Georgiou Modi, has comfortable, refurbished rooms for 15,000/24,000 dr.

The B class ***King Alexander*** *(☎ 23 501, fax 29 643, Leoforos Nikis 68)*, a little out of town along the road to Prespa, has passé rooms stuck in a 70s timewarp for 14,000/20,500 dr. The views over Florina from the front rooms are millennial stuff, though.

Places to Eat

There's an array of eating places, from fastfood to traditional, centred on the Pavlou Mela/Plateia Modi area; while the choice is not huge, you won't go hungry. Florina is famous for its *piperies Florinis* – large, sweet red peppers served pickled. Make sure you try them.

Pavlou Mela hosts a swathe of fast-food joints. However, since the arrival of yet another ***Goody's*** on the scene, local hamburger fans now prefer the chain product.

Restaurant Olympos *(Megalou Alexandrou 22)*, close to Plateia Modi, has a good choice of well prepared, low priced, preprepared food. It's only open at lunchtime, but is a very good budget choice – lunch with wine costs about 2000 dr.

Tria Adherfia, 70m to the left as you exit the bus station ticket office, is unpretentious, clean and convenient. Back in the centre, ***High*** *(Plateia Modi 5)* does pizzas and grills. The filling baked spaghetti with cheese and mushrooms and a large Dab beer will cost you under 2000 dr.

To Steki tou Pavlara *(25 Martiou 18)* is one of the few traditional restaurants left in town. This places does good roast chicken; a hearty meal with salad and wine is about 2400 dr.

Getting There & Away

Bus – Domestic From the main bus station buses go to Athens (nine hours, 9000 dr, daily at 8.30 am), Thessaloniki (three hours, 2800 dr, six daily), Kozani (1¾ hours, 1500 dr, seven daily) and, for the Prespa Lakes, to Agios Germanos (1½ hours, 800 dr, two daily at 6.45 am and 2.30 pm). For Kastoria, you have to take a bus to Amyndeo and change there.

Bus – International If you are planning to enter the Former Yugoslav Republic of Macedonia from Florina, there are three buses daily to the border town of Niki (30 minutes, 320 dr).

For Albania, there are two buses daily to the border post near Krystallopigi (1½ hours, 1000 dr). There's also a Greek Railways (OSE) bus to Korça (Korytsa) in Albania; it operates on Monday, Tuesday, Wednesday, Friday and Saturday. The bus, which originates in Thessaloniki, leaves Florina train station between 11.30 am and 12.30 pm (three hours, 3250 dr). See also the Getting There & Away chapter earlier in this book for details on travel to Albania.

Train – Domestic Florina is at the end of the Thessaloniki-Edessa-Amyndeo line. There are five to seven trains daily (depending on the season) in both directions. The approximate journey time from Thessaloniki is 3½ hours and the ticket costs 1370 dr. You can also take the train to Kozani (1¾ hours, 810 dr), via Amyndeo. There is a surcharge for the intercity service from Amyndeo to Athens or Thessaloniki.

Train – International There is currently no through service to Bitola, or beyond, in the Former Yugoslav Republic of Macedonia. See the Getting There & Away chapter for details on getting there from Florina.

PRESPA LAKES Λίμνες Πρεσπών

In the mountainous north-west corner of Greece at an altitude of 850m are the two lakes of Megali Prespa and Mikri Prespa, separated by a narrow strip of land. The area is one of outstanding natural beauty and is little-visited by foreign tourists. The road from Florina crosses the Pisoderi Pass and winds its way through thick forests and lush meadows with grazing cattle; if you have your own transport, there are lots of picnic tables.

Mikri (little) Prespa has an area of 43 sq km and is located almost entirely in Greece, except for the south-western tip, which is in Albania. Megali Prespa is the largest lake in the Balkans; the majority

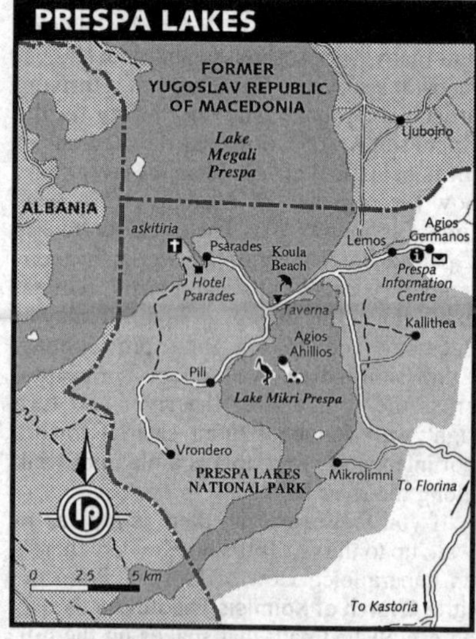

(1000 sq km) is in the Former Yugoslav Republic of Macedonia – 38 sq km is in Greece and a small south-western part is in Albania. Much of the Megali Prespa shore is precipitous rock which rises dramatically from the chilly blue water. The Prespa area became a national park in 1977. There is an excellent information centre in Agios Germanos.

Mikri Prespa is a wildlife refuge of considerable interest to ornithologists. It is surrounded by thick reed beds where numerous species of birds, including cormorants, pelicans, egrets, herons and ibis, nest.

The islet of **Agios Ahillios** has Byzantine remains. The boat operator will take you across and back for about 2000 dr for a boatload of four people. Call the ferryman on ☎ 0385-46 112.

Incidentally, one of the best places for viewing the lake's wildlife is the top of the sizable hillock harbouring the little jetty for Agios Ahillios – but it is often swarming with school groups on field trips.

Agios Germanos Αγιος Γερμανός

☎ 0385 • postcode 530 77 • pop 267

This little village serves as the main transport hub to the Prespa region and, although it is a little way from the lakes themselves, it is an attractive and convenient base. There are some good walks to be made from the village, and there is always a taxi (☎ 51 207) handy should you need to move farther afield.

The village is primarily an agricultural settlement renowned for its bean crops. The mounds of cut cane you will see in springtime as you enter the village are used for supporting the beanstalks.

Orientation & Information Agios Germanos has a bus terminus and the only post office in the Prespa basin. There are no banking facilities, but you can change money at the post office. The Prespa Information Centre (☎/fax 51 452) is on the right just before you enter the village proper. The phone number of the local police is ☎ 51 203.

The Dalmatian pelican can be seen around Lake Mikri Prespa

Things to See There are two churches that may be of interest to fans of Byzantium: **Agios Athanasios** and **Agios Germanos**, named after the village's patron saint.

For friends of nature, the Information Centre is a very well presented display and resource centre for the Prespa National Park. There is some excellent material in Greek, but not too much in English. Nonetheless, the photos, maps and diagrams are pretty self-explanatory. It is open 9.30 am to 2.30 pm daily.

Places to Stay & Eat The well run and comfortable ***Agios Germanos Hostel*** *(☎ 51 320)*, managed by the local Women's Cooperative, is at the top end of the village – follow the signs. Doubles/triples cost 9000/10,800 dr. ***Les Pelicans*** *(☎ 51 442)* has EOT-approved domatia at 8500/9500 dr for singles/doubles, and is just below the main square.

Lefteris Taverna *(☎ 51 418)*, opposite the hostel, is the best place for a meal. Bank on about 3000 dr for a good feed. The Women's Cooperative also runs a ***taverna*** *(☎ 51 320)* serving pittes, *trahanas* and fasolada that can be washed down with local wine. A meal will cost no more than 1700 dr.

Getting There & Away Florina is the only town with a direct bus link to the lakes. There are two buses on weekdays to Agios Germanos, 16km east of Psarades; they leave Florina at 7.45 am and 2.30 pm. Buses for Florina leave Agios Germanos at 6.45 am and 3 pm on weekdays and 7.45 am on Saturday (none on Sunday).

Psarades Ψαράδες

☎ 0385 • postcode 530 77 • pop 143

The village of Psarades, 70km from Florina, is a revelation. It's positioned within a small inlet of Megali Prespa and is the last Greek village before the tri-national border on Megali Prespa Lake. Psarades is a delectable little village with traditional stone houses which are subject to a National Trust preservation order, old fishing boats made of cedar and oak, and some of the most unusual miniature cows in Greece.

According to the last census, only 143 permanent residents remain from a prewar population of 770. Many emigrated to the USA and Australia – 600 people from Psarades live in Perth, Western Australia. A large lakefront marble memorial from the Macedonian Association of Chicago attests to the strong bonds between Psarades and its emigrants.

Orientation & Information Psarades village consists of an attractive, landscaped lakefront lined with numerous modern restaurants and fish tavernas.

There is no bank or post office, but Philippos Papadopoulos, the owner of the grocery shop on the village square, will exchange cash, as will Lazaros Hristianopoulos at Syntrofia taverna. There is no OTE, but Syntrofia taverna has metered telephones, as do the grocery store and Hotel Psarades on the other side of the bay.

Things to See & Do It will be hard to resist a **boat trip** out onto Megali Prespa, since Psarades is the only Greek village with anchorage on this lake. More specifically, you should strive to be taken to the three *askitiria* (places of solitary worship) that can only be visited by boat.

All three are out past the Roti headland to the left. The first one, **Metamorphosi**, dates from the 13th century. There are only a few remnants of the rich painting that once decorated this site and two sections from the woodcarved *temblon* (votive screen), the rest of which is in the Florina museum. The second is called **Mikri Analipsi** and is from the 14th or 15th century. Access to this one is a little difficult. The third and probably the best is **Panagia Eleousa**.

A typical trip will cost you about 800 dr for a short tour to the rock paintings and one of the askitiria, or 1350 dr for the full tour to all of them, assuming there are at least four people per boatload.

More or less opposite the village are rock paintings of **Panagia Vlahernitisa** (1455-56) and of **Panagia Dexiokratousa** (1373), along with some inscriptions. These are included in the boat tours mentioned above.

The church of **Kimisis Theotokou** in the village itself dates from 1893 and is decorated on the outside with the double-headed eagle of the Byzantine Empire. There is also an inscription that refers to the old name of the village, Nivitsa.

Places to Stay If you plan on arriving in July or August without a reservation, think twice, as the region is becoming very popular and accommodation is limited.

There is no official camp site, but you can camp freelance at Koula Beach on the southern shore of Megali Prespa, 5km east of Psarades.

Psarades' only official, EOT-approved ***domatia*** are the clean, comfortable rooms of Lazaros and Eleni Hristianopoulos *(☎ 46 107)*, where a double with bathroom costs 7500 dr. The domatia are above Syntrofia, the family taverna at the far end of the village. Several other families rent rooms unofficially.

Hotel Psarades *(☎ 46 015)* is right opposite the village. It has excellent singles/

doubles for 9600/12,000 dr, all with views over Psarades, as well as a bar and restaurant.

Places to Eat Five tavernas line the waterfront at Psarades. They all dish up excellent fish, straight from the lake. ***Paradosi*** is probably the best and is possibly the only one open out of season. The fasolada is very filling. ***Syntrofia*** taverna is also pretty reasonable. Try the trout and house wine.

Getting There & Away You will need your own transport to get to Psarades, or you can take a taxi from either Lemos or Agios Germanos.

Buses from Florina to Agios Germanos stop at the road junction between the two lakes. The left fork leads to Koula Beach and Psarades, and the right fork leads to the villages of Lemos and Agios Germanos. The Pyli bus meets the second bus on Tuesday and Thursday at the junction and takes passengers on to Pyli. Ask the Pyli bus driver to let you off at Koula Beach, 5km from Psarades.

From here you have the choice of either hitching the long uphill then downhill walk to Psarades, or asking someone at the taverna at Koula Beach to telephone for a taxi (☎ 0385-51 247) – they will willingly do this.

Approximate taxi fares from Psarades are 2000 dr to Lemos (to pick up the bus to Florina), 7000 dr to Florina and 8000 dr to Kastoria.

KASTORIA Καστοριά

☎ 0467 • postcode 521 00 • pop 17,000

Kastoria (kah-sto-rih-**ah**) lies between Mt Grammos and Mt Vitsi in western Macedonia, 200km west of Thessaloniki. It is regarded by many Greeks as their most beautiful town. Indeed, its setting is exemplary, occupying the isthmus of a promontory which projects into the tree-fringed Lake Orestiada, surrounded by mountains.

Its architecture is also outstanding, featuring many Byzantine and post-Byzantine churches and many 17th and 18th century mansions, known as *arhontika* because they were the homes of the *arhons* – the town's leading citizens. In Kastoria the arhontika were the dwellings of rich fur merchants.

The town has a long tradition of fur production. Jewish furriers (refugees from Europe) came to Kastoria because of the large numbers of beavers around the lake. They carried out their trade with such zeal that by the 19th century the beaver was extinct in the area. The furriers then began to import scraps of fur. Whatever your feelings are about the fur trade, you are not going to escape it in Kastoria – every street has some kind of associated office or business.

Orientation

The main bus station is one block inland from the southern lakeside, on 3 Septemvriou. To reach the town centre, face away from the station office and head left, bearing right just past the soccer stadium, to Plateia Davaki, one of the main squares. Mitropoleos, the main commercial thoroughfare, runs southeast to Plateia Omonias, the other main square.

Information

The EOT (☎ 24 484) is in the town hall on Ioustinianou, which runs north-east from Plateia Davaki. The staff are helpful and give out lots of brochures, maps and information.

The National Bank of Greece is on 11 Noemvriou, just north of Plateia Davaki and has an ATM. The post office is at the northern end of Leoforos Megalou Alexandrou, which skirts the lake. The OTE is on Agiou Athanasiou, which runs off Plateia Davaki, just north of Mitropoleos. The police (☎ 83 333) are near the bus station.

Things to See

Many of the numerous **Byzantine churches** in Kastoria were originally private chapels attached to arhontika. Almost all of the churches are locked, and gaining access to them is something of a Byzantine experience in itself. The key man (literally) for the ones around Plateia Omonias is Hristos Philikas. If you can track him down he will

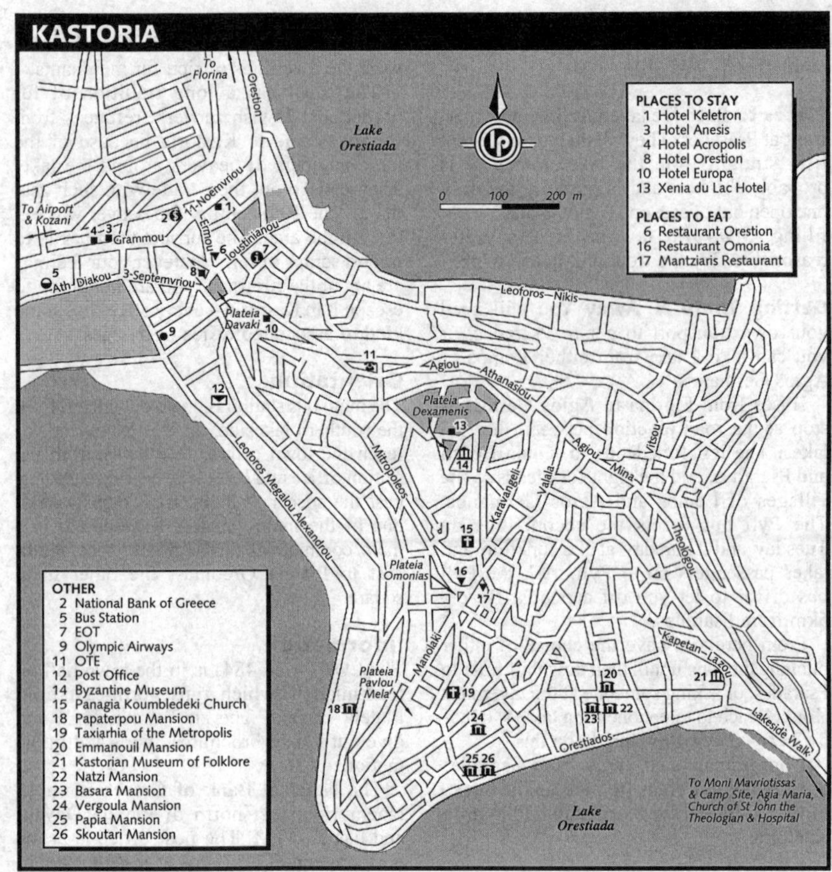

be happy to open them up for you – ask around the kafeneia on the square. Another possibility is the Byzantine Museum's curator, who may be able to contact someone who can show you some of the churches.

Even if you don't manage to get a look inside any churches, all is not lost, for some of them have external frescoes. One such church is the **Taxiarhia of the Metropolis**, on Plateia Pavlou Mela, south of Plateia Omonias, which has a 13th century fresco of the Madonna and Child above the entrance. Inside is the tomb of Pavlos Melas, a Macedonian hero killed by Bulgar terrorists during the struggles that culminated in the 1912-13 Balkan Wars. Melas' life is documented in Thessaloniki's Museum of the Macedonian Struggle. Many Macedonian streets are named Pavlou Mela in his memory.

The **Byzantine Museum** houses outstanding icons from many of the town's churches. Visiting this museum first will help you to appreciate the churches. It is adjacent to

Xenia du Lac Hotel on Plateia Dexamenis. The museum is open 8.30 am to 5 pm daily except Monday. Admission is free.

Most of the surviving **arhontika** are in the southern part of the town in the area called Doltso. The most important are the Emmanouil, Basara, Natzi, Skoutari, Papia, Vergoula and Papaterpou mansions – named after the families who once lived in them. These are closed to the public.

One of the arhontika has been converted into the **Kastorian Museum of Folklore**, a visit to which should be considered a must. The 530-year-old house belonged to the wealthy Neranzis Alvazis family. It is sumptuously furnished and has displays of ornaments, kitchen utensils and tools. The museum is open 10 am to noon and 3 to 5 pm daily. Admission is 300 dr.

Lakeside Walk

A pretty, shaded 9km road skirts the promontory. The lake is fringed with reeds, the habitat of frogs and turtles and many species of birds. On the lake are many species of water fowl and the great crested grebe.

Just under halfway is the **Moni Mavriotissas**. The resident monk will give you a guided tour. Next to the monastery are the 11th century **Agia Maria** and the 16th century **Church of St John the Theologian**. Both churches are liberally festooned with frescoes and icons, and are usually open. Beside the monastery there is a reasonably priced restaurant, the only source of refreshment on the walk. To begin the walk, take the road to the hospital.

Places to Stay

There is a free ***camp site*** in the grounds of the Moni Mavriotissas.

The vaguely seedy C class ***Hotel Keletron*** *(☎ 22 676, 11 Noemvriou 52)* has reasonable singles/doubles for 6300/7800 dr with bathroom. The C class ***Hotel Acropolis*** *(☎ 83 737, Grammou 14)* has tidy rooms for 8000/9600 dr, with bathroom.

The neat C class ***Hotel Anesis*** *(☎ 83 908, fax 83 768, Grammou 10)* has clean and comfortable rooms for 10,00/13,000 dr with bathroom. From the bus station, face the lake and turn left, take the first left into Filikis Eterias, then turn right at the T-junction – the hotel is on the left.

Hotel Orestion *(☎ 22 257, fax 22 258, Plateia Davaki 1)* is a superior C class with very pleasant rooms for 12,000/14,500 dr with bathroom. In a similar vein is ***Hotel Europa*** *(☎ 23 826, fax 25 154, Agiou Athanasiou 12)*, just up from Plateia Davaki, with rooms for 10,000/14,000 dr.

Kastoria's A class ***Xenia du Lac Hotel*** *(☎ 22 565, fax 26 391, Plateia Dexamenis 11)* is a quaintly old-fashioned place despite its A rating. It's in a quiet part of town and rooms are good value at 9,000/14,500 dr with bathroom.

Places to Eat

One of the best restaurants is the bright and modern ***Restaurant Omonia*** on Plateia Omonias, with meals for under 2000 dr. Nearby, ***Mantziaris Restaurant*** *(Valala 8)* is also good and reasonably cheap, with meals for about 1800 dr.

Restaurant Orestion *(Ermou 37)* is an unpretentious little place which dishes up tasty, low-priced, preprepared food. It is closed Saturday evening and Sunday. A meal will cost around 1900 dr.

Getting There & Away

Air The airport is 10km south of Kastoria. Between May and October, there are flights to Athens (19,200 dr) on Sunday, Tuesday, Wednesday and Friday. The Olympic Airways office (☎ 22 275) is at Leoforos Megalou Alexandrou 15.

Bus From Kastoria's main bus station (☎ 83 455) there are buses to Thessaloniki (four hours, 3700 dr, six daily), Kozani (two hours, 1750 dr, five daily) and Athens (nine hours, 9700 dr, two daily). The 6.30 am and 3.30 pm Thessaloniki buses go via Kozani and Veria. There are more buses in summer.

HALKIDIKI Χαλκιδική

The Halkidiki Peninsula is a large blob to the south-east of Thessaloniki, from which three long 'fingers' extend into the Aegean. The two large lakes of Koronia and Volvi separate the peninsula from the rest of Macedonia.

Halkidiki boasts 500km of coastline, with superb sandy beaches surrounded by calm, aquamarine sea. Unfortunately, these assets have been ruthlessly exploited and the two 'fingers' of Kassandra and Sithonia consist either of luxurious holiday complexes for the rich and famous, or package tourist ghettos. The easternmost promontory of Halkidiki is the Monastic Republic of Mt Athos (Agion Oros).

Halkidiki is not a place for budget or independent travellers as virtually all accommodation is booked solid throughout summer. If you are camping, however, a visit is more practicable: Halkidiki has many camp sites which, even if they are bursting at the seams, are unlikely to turn you away.

Northern Halkidiki

The **Petralona Cave**, 56km south-east of Thessaloniki in northern Halkidiki, has stalactites and stalagmites and is where a 700,000-year-old Neanderthal skull (evidence of one of Europe's earliest inhabitants) was found. The cave is open 9 am to 7 pm daily (until 5 pm in winter). Admission is 1500 dr; students 800 dr. There is a booklet about the cave in English for 700 dr. Doucas Tours (see Organised Tours in the Thessaloniki section earlier in this chapter) sometimes takes tours to the caves.

The **archaeological museum** at Polygyros, the capital of Halkidiki, houses finds from the peninsula's ancient sites, including the Sanctuary of Zeus at Aphytis and the ancient city of Acanthos. The museum is open 8.30 am to 3 pm Tuesday to Sunday. Admission is 500 dr.

Getting There & Away A bus from Thessaloniki goes to Petralona Cave (one hour, 1000 dr) at 1.15 pm every day except Sunday and public holidays, and continues on to the village of Krini from where it immediately heads back for Thessaloniki. This hardly leaves time to see the cave, so to get back to Thessaloniki you must walk or hitch 5km south to the village of Eleohoria, where you can pick up a regular Nea Moudania bus to Thessaloniki.

A number of buses to the Sithonia 'finger' stop at Polygyros.

Kassandra Peninsula

The Kassandra Peninsula is less beautiful than the Sithonian Peninsula. Its commercialism is horrendous and even if you're not averse to package tourists, roaring motorbikes, fast-food joints and discos, you're unlikely to easily find independent accommodation. However, if you have a tent, there are lots of well advertised camp sites. Freelance camping is prohibited and there are large signs alerting you to that fact.

For what it's worth, the western side of the 'finger' is somewhat quieter, with a couple of almost get-away-from-it-all camp sites at Posidi and Nea Skioni. The little resort of Siviri, also on this side, has a sandy beach, but has been taken over by the luxurious private apartments of Thessaloniki's elite.

Getting There & Away There are 13 buses daily from Thessaloniki to Kallithea (1½ hours, 1600 dr) on the east coast; 11 to Pefkohori (two hours, 2100 dr), also on the east coast, via Kryopigi and Haniotis; seven to Paliouri (two hours, 2300 dr) and three to Agia Paraskevi (2½ hours, 2350 dr), both on the southern tip. All the buses leave from the terminal at Karakasi 68 in Thessaloniki.

Sithonian Peninsula

Sithonia is an improvement on Kassandra. The landscape en route is quite spectacular with sweeping vistas of thickly forested hills.

An undulating road makes a loop around Sithonia, skirting wide bays, climbing into the pine-forested hills and dipping down to the resorts. Down the west coast are good stretches of sandy beach between **Nikiti** and **Paradisos**. Beyond, **Neos Marmaras** is Sithonia's largest resort, with a very crowded beach but lots of domatia. Look out for the big information boards on both waterfronts. The gigantic monstrosity of

Porto Carras sits at one side of the bay. This is a luxury holiday complex for 3000 guests built by the wine magnate John G Carras and modelled on Spanish Marbella – ugh.

Beyond Neos Marmaras the road climbs into the hills where dirt roads lead down to several beaches and camp sites. **Toroni** and **Porto Koufos** are small resorts at the south-western tip. The latter is a picturesque little place with a good beach. The southern tip of Sithonia is still relatively isolated and is the most spectacular region of Halkidiki (excluding the Athos Peninsula) – rocky, rugged and dramatic. As the road rounds the south-eastern tip, Mt Athos comes into view across the gulf, further adding to the spectacular vistas.

Kalamitsi The resort of Kalamitsi is the most delightful corner of the Sithonian Peninsula. This little enclave has a gorgeous sandy beach, a couple of tavernas, some domatia, two camp sites – ***Porto Camping*** on the main beach and ***Camping Kalamitsi*** around the headland – and boat hire facilities. Not yet commercialised, it's one of the Sithonian Peninsula's hidden delights.

O Giorgakis *(☎ 0375-41 338, fax 41 013)*, just above the restaurant of the same name, is a stone's throw from the beach. Fully equipped studios here cost around 15,000 dr for five persons. On the main road, set back in a spacious garden with fruit and olive trees are the nine self-contained apartments of ***Ennea Mouses*** *(☎ 0375-41 704)*. These very comfortable and well equipped apartments cost between 10,000 dr and 13,000 for four persons.

Continuing up the east coast, the bus does a little 2km detour inland to the pleasant village of **Sykia**, which has less tourist hype than the coastal resorts. Back on the coast, the resort of Sarti is next along the route.

Sarti Sarti has not succumbed entirely to the package tourist industry and has a good, laid-back atmosphere. From its excellent, long, sandy beach there are splendid views of the startling, pyramid-like hulk of Mt Athos. The town is compact and pleasant enough and tends to cater for local tourism and Eastern Europeans, though it used to be popular with Germans and Austrians.

Sarti consists of two streets: one is along the waterfront and the other is parallel, one block inland. The bus terminal is on the latter – a timetable is pinned to a nearby tree. There is no tourist office, but the staff of Koutras Travel (☎ 0375-94 017, fax 94 387), near the bus terminal, are helpful and speak English. The agency organises half-day mule treks in the mountains for 5000 dr, and Mt Athos cruises for 5000 dr.

Places to Stay & Eat ***Sarti Beach Camping*** *(☎ 0375-94 450, fax 94 211)* is not only a camp site, but a holiday complex with a variety of accommodation. The camp site itself is well shaded, but offers little greenery. From the south it's on the right side of the main approach road – buses stop outside.

In Sarti itself, ***Hotel Three Stars*** *(☎ 0375-94 370)* has smallish but modern apartments for 12,000 dr for three persons and 15,000 dr for four. Ask at the cigarette kiosk next to the bus stop for directions. There are many ***domatia***, too. Ask Koutras Travel for advice if you are stuck.

Pergola Café Restaurant *(☎ 0375-94 005)* in Sarti is a great place to have a drink, a snack or a full meal; it's open all day till late evening. The 'pergola plate' has a bit of everything – meatballs, calamari, souvlaki – and is generally good value. From the bus stop turn left opposite Koutras Travel and you'll see the restaurant on the right; it's painted purple, grey and orange.

Getting There & Away Buses leave from the bus terminal at Karakasi 68 in Thessaloniki for Neos Marmaras (2½ hours, 2400 dr, four daily) and Sarti (3½ hours, 3350 dr, three daily). Most of the Sarti buses loop around the Sithonian Peninsula, enabling you to see its magnificent southern tip. Call ☎ 0371-22 309 for bus information.

Athos Peninsula (Secular Athos)

Most of the easternmost portion of the three prongs of the Halkidiki Peninsula is occupied by the Athonite monasteries. You will probably only want to pass through secular Athos on your way to see the monasteries. The beaches are admittedly very fine in parts, but they have long been developed for the package tour industry. Soulless resorts based on large hotels with neither interest in nor of interest to independent travellers are dotted along the coast.

Ierissos is one of the few real towns, notable mainly as the terminus for the irregular boat serving the east coast monasteries.

The **canal** dug across the peninsula by the Persian king Xerxes in the 5th century BC for his invading fleet is featured proudly on most maps, but was filled in centuries ago so there's precious little for the untrained eye to see.

Ouranoupolis The village of Ouranoupolis (Ουρανούπολη) is at the northern end of secular Athos. The most prominent feature is the 14th century tower built to guard what was then a dependency of Vatopediou monastery. A building housing a pharmacy in a side street, one block back from the waterfront, is, despite appearances, actually early 20th century. It once housed a monastic copper works. Most of the rest of the village was founded in 1922-23 by refugees from Asia Minor.

As well as the ferry for pilgrims to Athos, boats run tourist trips along the coast of Mt Athos for those unwilling or unable (because of their gender) to set foot there.

Places to Stay & Eat The reasonable ***camp site*** is on the north side of the village. There are ***domatia*** and a few hotels, including the D class ***Hotel Galini*** *(☎ 0377-71 217)*, one block back from the coast road. It has single/double rooms for 7000/9000 dr. The D class ***Hotel Akrogiali*** *(☎ 0377-71 201, fax 71 395)* on the waterfront charges 8000/10,000 dr.

If you want to splurge before plunging into the rigours of Athonite monastic life, the waterfront A class ***Xenia*** *(☎ 0377-71 202, fax 71 362)* has rooms for 24,300/36,000 dr, but this includes most daily meals. There are a number of restaurants on the beach facing the sea; the best would have to be ***Paralia*** *(☎ 0377-71 355)* with its fetching blue and white decor, where a substantial meal with wine will cost around 3000 dr.

Mt Athos (Agion Oros)

☎ 0337

This semiautonomous monastic area, known in Greek as the 'Holy Mountain', occupies most of the Athos Peninsula, and is listed as a World Heritage Site. To enter is to step back in time – literally by 13 days because the Athonite community still uses the Julian calendar, and metaphorically by 500 years as this is a remnant of the Byzantine Empire, which otherwise ended with the fall of Constantinople in 1453.

Setting foot here, however, is not straightforward. Foreign men are allowed to stay in the monasteries for four nights (extendible to six) after completing some formalities – see Obtaining a Permit. Visitors walk from monastery to monastery, enjoying the landscape (Athos is also called the Garden of the Virgin Mary), experiencing a little of the ascetic life of the monks. Despite the rigours associated with a visit to the Holy Mountain, this unique experience can be a very enriching one.

Women may not enter the area at all, unfortunately. The closest they may approach the monasteries is to view them from one of the round-trip cruises from Ouranoupolis. Boats carrying women must stay at least 500m offshore.

History Hermits gravitated to Mt Athos from the very early years of the Byzantine Empire. The first monastery on Athos, Megistis Lavras, was founded between 961 and 963 by St Athanasios with support from Emperor Nikephoros II Phokas. The next emperor, Ioannis Tsimiskis, gave Athos its first charter.

The Athonite community flourished under the continuing support of the Byzantine emperors, whose decrees reinforced its status. The most notorious was that made under Constantine IX Monomahos barring access to women, beardless persons and female

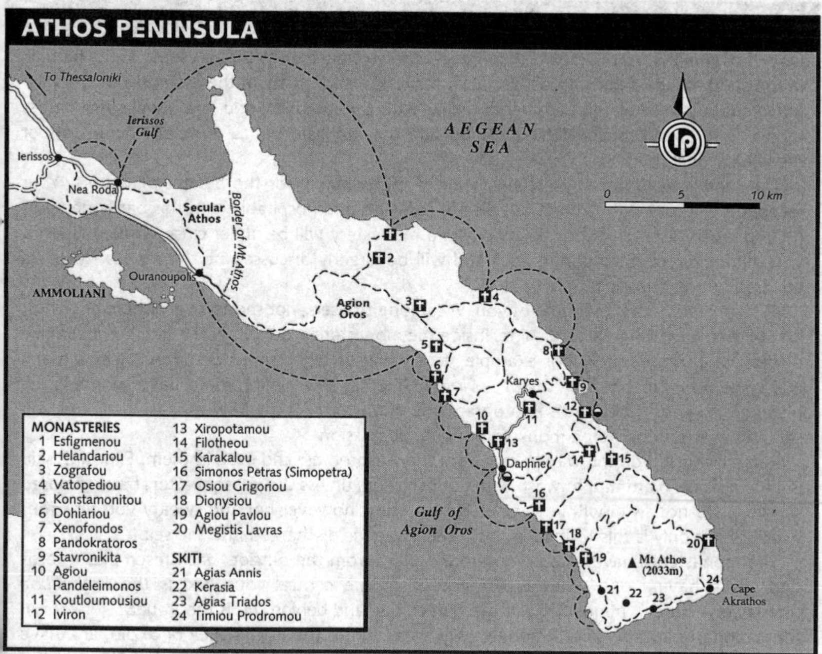

domestic animals. This is still in force, except that beards are no longer mandatory. Hens (for eggs) are tolerated; other birds are apparently too lowly to be included in the ban.

Monasteries continued to be founded, particularly when Christians from outside the area came in during the first crusades. By 1400 there were said to be 40 monasteries, including foundations by Bulgarian, Russian and Serbian princes. The Athos community submitted to Turkish rule after the fall of Constantinople, but managed to retain its semi-independent status. The last monastery to be founded was Stavronikita, in 1542. The community declined over the centuries and today there are 20 ruling monasteries.

In the Greek War of Independence (1821-29) many monasteries were plundered and entire libraries burned by Turkish troops. The present constitution of Athos dates from 1924. It was guaranteed by the 1975 Greek Constitution, and recognises Athos as a part of Greece (all the monks, regardless of their origin, must become Greek nationals), with the Iera Synaxis (holy council, composed of one representative from each of the 20 monasteries) responsible for all the internal administration.

Obtaining a Permit Only 10 foreign adult males may enter Mt Athos per day, but unrestricted numbers of Orthodox men may enter. Start the procedure early, particularly for summer visits, when you may have to wait weeks for a place – make a reservation. Athos can get quite crowded at weekends.

You can start the process from outside Thessaloniki, but you'll have to pass through Thessaloniki anyway in order to pick up your written reservation confirmation.

Mixing with the Monks

Don't imagine that all the monks are simple, otherworldly men. Although some of the hermits in the south of the peninsula are, to put it politely, weird, many of the monks in the monasteries are highly educated men very familiar with the outside world – you will come across monks who spend much of their life outside the monasteries, as university professors or missionary doctors.

The monks have not chosen their way of life primarily for the benefit of visitors. Your reception will vary from correct but distant to warm and hospitable, and this partly depends on you. Every aspect of your behaviour in a monastery will be under close scrutiny (even if you think everyone is ignoring you) and will be eagerly discussed by the monks (who are apparently great gossips).

Certain behaviour is expected of you. Wear long trousers, not shorts, everywhere on Athos; it's polite to wear long-sleeved shirts. Inside the monasteries, do not wear a hat, do not smoke or behave inconsiderately (for example, by singing or whistling). When you meet a monk along the way, greet him by saying '*evloyite*' (literally 'bless me'); the usual response is the blessing *'o kyrios'* (the Lord). Photography is often forbidden within monasteries, and you should never photograph a monk without his permission.

Remain dressed on the way to and from the washrooms, and even in them. Exposing skin is a big no-no, so attempt to wash with your shirt on, unless the guest quarters have enclosed showers. Do not swim within sight of a monastery, however hot and sweaty you feel after walking; not only is this forbidden, but raw sewage is discharged into the sea.

The monasteries have a common ground plan; from the outside, each resembles a fortified castle having one gateway for access. In the central courtyard is the *katholikon* (monastery church), frequently blood-red in colour, and behind this is the *trapeza* (refectory). Most monasteries now accommodate only a fraction of the monks they once did, and have abandoned derelict sections; some of these are being renovated with the aid of EU funds for heritage protection.

The monastic day begins at sunset, which is midnight in the Byzantine time kept in the monasteries (distrust the clocks, which must be adjusted every day). This is when the outer gate is shut, and it is not reopened until daybreak. When you reach a monastery, head for the guest quarters, *arhontariki* (usually signposted), and find the guest master. The monks traditionally welcome visitors by offering them home-distilled *tsipouro* and *loukoumi*, or coffee. The guest master will show you to a two to 10-bed guest room.

Visitors are not expected to participate completely in the monastic religious life, and some monasteries do not permit the non-Orthodox within the church; however, you should, if permitted, attend the morning and evening services which usually precede the meal times (it's bad form to sneak straight into the refectory for the food).

Services are indicated by a monk walking round the monastery striking a *simandro*, a large wooden plank, with a mallet in a distinctive rhythm. The only music permitted is that of the human voice (heavenly in some monasteries, diabolical in others), and the liturgical language used is an archaic form of Greek. The apparently endless repetition of some sections has a hypnotic effect.

Religious practice on Athos derives from the 14th century Hesychast movement, according to which the divine light radiated at the Transfiguration can be perceived by certain practices of meditation and repetitive chanting.

Mixing with the Monks

If the non-Orthodox are permitted in the church, they will usually be confined to the *exonarthex*, the outer porch (the double narthex is a peculiarity of the Athos churches). When there is no service in progress some monasteries make a point of showing non-Orthodox visitors the church interior – most of them are stuffed with more relics and icons than you can shake a censer at.

The monks dine twice a day, or only once on the frequent fasting days. The simple vegetarian meals rely heavily on produce from the monastery gardens, but are occasionally supplemented by fish. Common accompaniments to the cooked vegetables include home-baked bread, olives, eggs and cheese. Some monasteries serve very palatable wine with the meals, an uncharacteristic epicurean touch.

In some monasteries, non-Orthodox visitors eat separately from the monks, at others they eat with them, in which case you must stop eating as soon as the monks rise and leave, no matter how much food remains. On fasting days the monks normally provide some light refreshment for their guests.

Older books classify the monasteries into coenobite or idiorhythmic type, depending on whether communal life is centrally or more loosely organised. This distinction is now obsolete: the last idiorhythmic monastery, Pandokratoros, became coenobite on 8 June 1992 (Byzantine calendar), along with much feasting and celebration.

The lives of monks who live in *skites* – clusters of houses around a church – are not as strict as those of the monks who reside in the monasteries. Monks in the skites have more free time, and produce most of the Athos artefacts sold in Daphne and Karyes. One of the houses acts as the guest quarters, and visitors are received hospitably. Some *kelloi* – literally cells, but more like small farmhouses, and usually accommodating two to four monks – also receive guests.

The accommodation offered by the monasteries can be spartan, the food frugal and you won't meet any women, but you will have been in exalted company. The Byzantine emperor John VI Cantacuzenus, on his enforced abdication in 1354, became a monk on Athos for the rest of his life. Rasputin, the Mad Monk (an unfair name, as technically speaking he wasn't a monk) walked here in 1891 from Siberia, a journey of 2000 miles.

David Hall

LIZ THOMPSON

NORTHERN GREECE

Ordained clergymen should have an introduction from their bishop, and need permission to visit Athos from the Ecumenical Patriarchate of Constantinople – apply at the Metropolis of Thessaloniki (☎ 031-227 677), Vogatsikou 5.

You must first book a date for your visit. This is now handled by the Mount Athos Pilgrims' Office (☎ 031-861 611, fax 861 811) at Leoforos Karamanli 14, just east of the Thessaloniki Exhibition Site. This office is open 8.30 am to 1.30 pm and 6 to 8 pm weekdays, excluding Wednesday. Make a telephone booking first. The phone number given above is for English speakers; Greek speakers may phone ☎ 031-833 733.

The Ecclesiastic Authorities require that you declare your intention to be a pilgrim. Letters of recommendation are no longer required, but you will be asked to mail a photocopy of your passport details and, if you are Orthodox, a photocopied certificate showing your religion (a baptismal certificate will suffice). You must then call in to the Pilgrims' Office to collect your booking confirmation.

Once you have secured a reservation and written confirmation from the Pilgrims' Office, you may now proceed to Ouranoupolis to obtain your *diamonitirion* (permit).

Entering Athos When you arrive in Ouranoupolis, you must first call in at the Pilgrims' Office (☎ 0377-71 422), on a street to the right, just before a Jet Oil petrol station, as you enter the village. Look for the Byzantine flag. The Pilgrims' Office is open 8.10 am to 2 pm daily.

Officials will check your passport and booking confirmation and issue a diamonitirion for 8000 dr (4000 dr for students) to actually enter Athos. Both diamonitirion and passport will be checked as you board the ferry for Athos. Make sure you get to Ouranoupolis early as there may be queues, especially on weekends. Leave video cameras behind – they're prohibited on Athos.

The boat, usually the small car ferry *Axion Esti*, leaves Ouranoupolis at 9.45 am for the small port of Daphne (850 dr). The journey takes about two hours; some intermediate stops are made for monks and other residents, and if you are not heading directly to Karyes you may alight earlier. Once you arrive in Daphne, a clapped-out bus takes you to Karyes for 550 dr.

Alternatively, you can depart from Ierissos at 8 am or from Nea Roda at about 8.30 am. This service operates daily between 1 July and 12 September, and on Monday, Thursday and Saturday during the rest of the year. This ferry drops you off at Iviron. There is no land access from secular Greece.

Once in the main square of Karyes you are free to start walking to the monastery of your choice for the first night. The monasteries will not expect any further donations for accommodating you, but technically you're supposed to spend only one night in each. You might get two nights if you ask politely. The diamonitirion can be extended for another two days in Karyes at the end of the initial four days.

Orientation & Information Daphne, the small port of Athos, has a port authority building, police and customs, a post office, a couple of general stores selling food and religious artefacts made on Athos, and a cafe. There is no OTE office, but one of the shops has a metered telephone.

The only other town is Karyes, the administrative capital, which includes the headquarters of the Holy Epistasia (council), an inn, post office, OTE, doctor and a couple of shops. The remaining settlements are the 20 monasteries plus 12 scattered *skiti* – the isolated dwellings of hermits. The total population of monks and resident laymen is about 1600.

There are no tourist police, but there is a regular police station in Karyes. In addition to Karyes and Daphne, there are police at Agiou Pandeleimonos, Megistis Lavras, Agias Annis, Zografou and Helandariou.

The landscape is dominated in the south by the white peak of Mt Athos itself; the northern part is densely wooded. Wildlife abounds; the small population and absence of industry (apart from some logging) have virtually turned the area into a nature reserve.

Exploring Athos With a diamonitirion, you are free to roam. There are few proper roads, and not many vehicles – you get around on foot, following the old paths, or by boat.

A caïque leaves Agias Annis every day at 9.45 am for Daphne, serving intermediate west-coast monasteries or their *arsanas* (landing stage for inland monasteries) and returning from Daphne every afternoon. A less regular caïque serves the east coast (theoretically three times weekly, weather permitting) between Ierissos and Mandraki, the harbour for Megistis Lavras. Another service around the south connects Mandraki and Agias Annis. The caïques are inexpensive; for example, at the time of writing, the trip from Daphne to Dionysiou cost 250 dr.

Unless you travel exclusively by boat, you need to be reasonably fit and prepared to walk for several hours daily in the heat. Carry water and, as food often becomes an obsession among visitors, extra supplies such as biscuits and dried fruit. You will need a map; the best is the Reinhold & Klaus Zwerger 1:50,000 *Athos* contour map available through Stanfords of London (☎ 020-7836 1321) or directly from the cartographers at Wohlmutstrasse 8, A-1020 Vienna, Austria.

Other useful things to take include a torch (flashlight), compass, whistle (in case you get lost), small shaving mirror (not all monastic washrooms have mirrors) and mosquito coils. Take extra food since monastic meal times may not always coincide with your activities.

You can only spend one night in each monastery. Some of the heavily visited ones near Karyes request that you telephone in advance to be sure of a place (the numbers are displayed in the Holy Epistasia), but this can be a frustrating experience as the telephone is not answered for many hours during daily periods of rest and meditation. You must reach the monastery before sunset, as the gate is then shut, and not opened for anyone.

In **Karyes** you should see the 10th century **Protaton**, the basilican church opposite the Holy Epistasia, which contains a number of treasures including paintings by Panselinos, the master of the Macedonian School. Karyes itself is a strange place – a ghost town with many derelict buildings testifying to a former, grander era. If you've had a long day, you may decide to stay at the monastery of **Koutloumousiou** (☎ 23 226) in Karyes. Otherwise, you should decide on your itinerary now.

A popular route is to head for one of the east coast monasteries, and then to continue to Megistis Lavras, returning to Daphne on the west coast. This can involve some lengthy walks unless you use the caïques, but these can be unreliable.

From Karyes, you can walk to either **Stavronikita** (☎ 23 255) or **Iviron** (☎ 23 248) on the coast, to continue by caïque or coastal paths (easier to follow than the inland paths). Alternatively, you can walk to **Filotheou** (☎ 23 256, fax 23 674) along a pleasant shady path (spring water available) in about 3½ hours. About 30 minutes farther

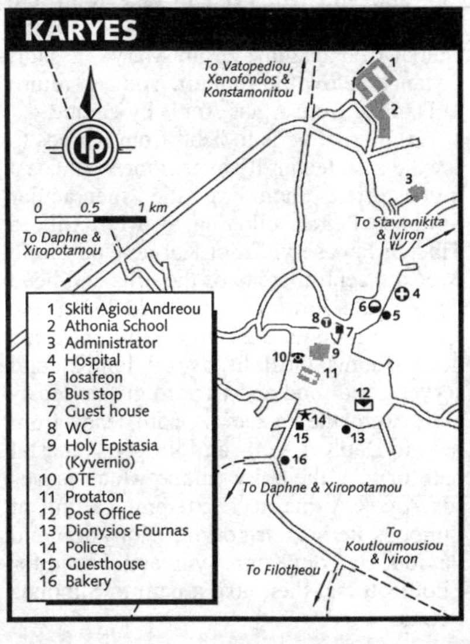

on is **Karakalou** (☎ 23 225). Beyond, the old Byzantine path has been converted into a road, and you face a 5½ hour walk (unless a monastic vehicle gives you a lift) to **Megistis Lavras** (☎ 23 758).

Not only is this the oldest monastery on Athos, it is also the only one to remain undamaged by fire. Its 10th century structure protects a number of treasures, including frescoes by Theophanes of Crete and the tomb of St Athanasios, the founder.

A caïque leaves Megistis Lavras at about 3 pm for the skiti of **Agias Annis**. Alternatively, you can follow the path around the wilderness of the southern end of the peninsula. You first approach the skiti of **Timiou Prodromou**, then **Agias Triados** on the coast (off the main track), then **Kerasia**, and subsequently Agias Annis, either of which can be used as a base for climbing Mt Athos, although Agias Annis has a better reputation for hospitality.

The climb up **Mt Athos** (2033m) should not be undertaken lightly, and it is wise not to attempt it alone. It also wouldn't hurt to inform someone of your plans before setting off. Remember that it will be cold at the top, and you will need to take food and water. Water is available from a well at the chapel of Panagia (Virgin Mary), a short distance below the summit. You can return to Daphne from Agias Annis by caïque.

An alternative is to head from Karyes to see the architecturally interesting west coast monasteries, including the spectacular Simonos Petras, clinging to a cliff like a Tibetan lamasery. From Karyes you climb over the central spine of the hills and head down again. **Xiropotamou** (☎ 23 251) is the first you'll come to, with newly renovated guest rooms (still lit by oil lamps) and serves good food and wine to guests separately from the monks. A path leads from here to Daphne; you can follow the coastal path or take the daily caïque which leaves for Agias Annis at 12.30 pm, calling at Simonos Petras, Grigoriou, Dionysiou and Pavlou. Or from Karyes you could head for Filotheou and then take a path to Simonos Petras.

Simonos Petras (☎ 23 254, fax 23 707), also called Simopetra, is an awesome sight from its arsanas, from which it's a stiff climb to the monastery. The monastery's outside walls are surrounded by wooden balconies – as you walk along these from the guest rooms to the washroom, you can see the sheer drop beneath your feet. Swallows nest in the eaves and delight in taking vertiginous swoops to the sea. You can't normally get outside the monasteries to experience Athos at night – standing on these balconies in the dark, listening to the swallows and staring down towards the light of a solitary fishing boat is a magical experience.

From Simonos Petras you can descend to a coastal path which branches off the path to the arsanas at a small shrine. The path brings you to **Osiou Grigoriou** (☎ 23 218, fax 23 671), which has a very pleasant position by the sea, and a comfortable guesthouse by the harbour outside the main monastery building. This has electric light and the rare luxury of showers.

The coastal path from here onwards is quite strenuous as it climbs and descends three times before reaching **Dionysiou** (☎ 23 687, fax 23 686), another cliff-hanger monastery resembling Simonos Petras. One of the treasures of its *katholikon* (main church) is an age-blackened icon claimed as the oldest in Athos, housed in a separate chapel. It is said to have been carried round the walls of Constantinople to inspire its successful defence against a combined Persian and Avar siege in 626. The coastal path continues to **Agiou Pavlou** and Agias Annis.

A road less travelled covers the monasteries north of Karyes. Your first stop could be the slightly out of the way **Pandokratoros** (☎ 23 253) monastery with its own pretty harbour, or you can keep going to **Vatopediou** (☎ 23 219), also on the coast. This picturesque monastery is an oddity in that it keeps to the Gregorian (western) calendar. When Athos was at its height, Vatopediou had a celebrated school, now in ruins. A coastal path leads to **Esfigmenou** (☎ 23 796); farther on, little-visited because of its isolation, is **Helandariou** (☎ 23 797), a Serbian foundation still inhabited by Serbs and noted for its hospitality.

The somewhat hard to get to and humble **Konstamonitou** (☎ 23 228) monastery might be worth a visit if you are really keen, but farther north between the east and west coasts is the Bulgarian monastery, **Zografou** (☎ 23 247). Its name, meaning 'Painter', comes from a miraculous icon not painted by human hands. The northernmost west coast monastery is **Dohiariou** (☎ 23 245), considered to have some of the best architecture on Athos.

Coming south on the coastal path you reach **Xenofondos** (☎ 23 249) and then **Agiou Pandeleimonos** (☎ 23 252), the Russian monastery which welcomes visitors with tea. This enormous building used to accommodate over 1000 monks, who came from Russia in droves in the 19th century. Most of the distinctive Russian-style buildings date from that period and many are now derelict. The monastery was once renowned for the quality of its singing, which has been through a low point in the recent past, but is happily picking up again. Note that accommodation may not be available here. These west coast monasteries are served by the Ouranoupolis-Daphne ferry.

Many alternative routes are possible using the network of old Byzantine paths – most of which have been recently marked by the Thessaloniki Mountaineering Club, but unmarked logging tracks make it amazingly easy to get lost in the woods. Monks' paths, which cross vehicle tracks and lead directly to and from monasteries, are marked by small roadside crosses.

Getting There & Away Entry to Athos is usually by boat from Ouranoupolis, which is accessible by bus from Thessaloniki's Halkidiki terminal at Karakasi 68 (☎ 031-924 445). There are seven buses daily (2½ hours, 2080 dr). The first bus (6 am) from Thessaloniki arrives just in time for the boat, but leaves you little time to organise your diamonitirion; otherwise, you need to stay overnight in Ouranoupolis. This gives you a chance to buy easily carried food, and find somewhere to store unwanted gear (probably for a fee). Take only the bare minimum to Athos, as you'll have to lug it round all the time.

You may prefer to store unneeded baggage in Thessaloniki – when you return from Athos to Ouranoupolis, the Thessaloniki bus will be waiting, and you may miss it while recovering luggage. Also, you might want to leave Athos via the east coast boat to Ierissos – no good if all your worldly goods are in Ouranoupolis.

The daily boat from Athos to Ouranoupolis leaves Daphne at noon – there is a fairly rigorous customs check to ensure that you're not taking off with any antiquities (even visiting clerics have been known to snaffle valuable relics).

The morning caïque from Agias Annis arrives in Daphne in ample time for the Ouranoupolis boat. The irregular east-coast caïque provides an alternative exit to Ierissos.

KAVALA Καβάλα

☎ 051 • postcode 655 00 • pop 57,000

Kavala, 163km east of Thessaloniki, is one of the most attractive of Greece's large cities. It spills gently down the foothills of Mt Symvolon to a commodious harbour. The old quarter of Panagia nestles under a massive Byzantine fortress.

Modern Kavala is built over ancient Neopolis, which was the port of Philippi. Mehmet Ali (1769-1849), who became Pasha of Egypt and founder of its last royal dynasty, was born in Kavala. Like Athens and Thessaloniki, its population was almost doubled by the 1923 population exchange with Asia Minor.

Orientation

Kavala's focal point is Plateia Eleftherias. The two main thoroughfares, Eleftheriou Venizelou and Erythrou Stavrou, run west from here parallel with the waterfront Ethnikis Antistasis. The old quarter of Panagia occupies a promontory to the south-east of Plateia Eleftherias. Walk east along Eleftheriou Venizelou from Plateia Eleftherias, turn left at the T-junction and take the first right (signposted to Panagia and the Castle).

The intercity bus station is on the corner of Hrysostomou Kavalas and Filikis Eterias, near the Thasos ferry quay.

One of the town's most prominent landmarks is an imposing aqueduct built during the reign of Süleyman the Magnificent (1520-66).

Information

Tourist Offices The EOT (☎ 222 425) is on the western side of Plateia Eleftherias. The helpful staff give out a map of the town, provide transport information and have a list of the town's hotels with prices. They also have information on the summer drama festivals at Philippi and Thasos.

Opening times are 8 am to 2 pm Monday to Friday. If staffing allows, the office is also open 5 to 8 pm and 8 am to 1 pm Saturday (closed Sunday).

The tourist police (☎ 222 905) are in the same building as the regular police at Omonias 119.

Money The National Bank of Greece is on the corner of Megalou Alexandrou and Dragoumi and has an exchange machine and ATM. There is a 24 hour Ionian Bank exchange machine and ATM on the harbour front, and the Midas Exchange office next to the EOT is open 8.30 am to 8 pm Monday to Friday and 9 am to 8 pm Saturday (closed Sunday).

Post & Communications The main post office is on the corner of Hrysostomou Kavalas and Erythrou Stavrou. The OTE is at the intersection of Antistasis and Averof.

Bookshops The Papadogiannis Bookshop, Omonias 46 (on the corner with Amynta), stocks a wide range of international newspapers and magazines. It also has a few English-language paperbacks.

Things to See

The **archaeological museum** (☎ 222 335) houses well displayed finds from ancient Amphipolis, between Thessaloniki and Kavala. Amphipolis was an Athenian colony, and a gold-rush town with mines on Mt Pangaeum. The finds include sculpture, jewellery, grave stelae, terracotta figurines and vases. The museum entrance is at the western end of Ethnikis Antistasis. It's open 8.30 am to 6 pm Tuesday to Sunday. Admission is 500 dr, but free on Sunday and public holidays.

The **Municipal Museum of Kavala**, at Filippou 4, is also worth a visit. On the ground floor are pictures and sculptures by contemporary Greek artists, including a large collection of works by Polygnotos Vagis (1894-1965), who was born in Potamia on Thasos, and emigrated to the US where he gained an international reputation. On the upper floor is a superb folk art collection with costumes, jewellery, handcrafts, household items and tools. The museum is open 9 am to 5 pm; admission is 500 dr.

Panagia The pastel houses in the narrow, tangled streets of the Panagia (Παναγία) quarter are less dilapidated than those of Thessaloniki's Kastra and the area is less commercialised than Athens' Plaka.

The most conspicuous building is the **Imaret**, a huge structure with 18 domes, which overlooks the harbour from Poulidou. In Turkish times the Imaret was a hostel for theology students. It has been restored and is now a pleasant cafe and restaurant (see Places to Eat). Within the cafe are some cabinets displaying memorabilia from Mehmet Ali's time. The carefully restored **Turkish house** where Mehmet Ali was born is now open to the public. Ring the bell and the caretaker will show you around; along with other rooms, you will see Ali's harem. The house is at the southern end of Poulidou, near an equestrian statue of Ali.

Places to Stay – Budget

Irini Camping *(☎ 229 785)* is the military-looking EOT camp site 2km east of Kavala on the coast road. ***Alexandros Camping*** *(☎ 316 347)* is another 8km out of town, by

NORTHERN GREECE

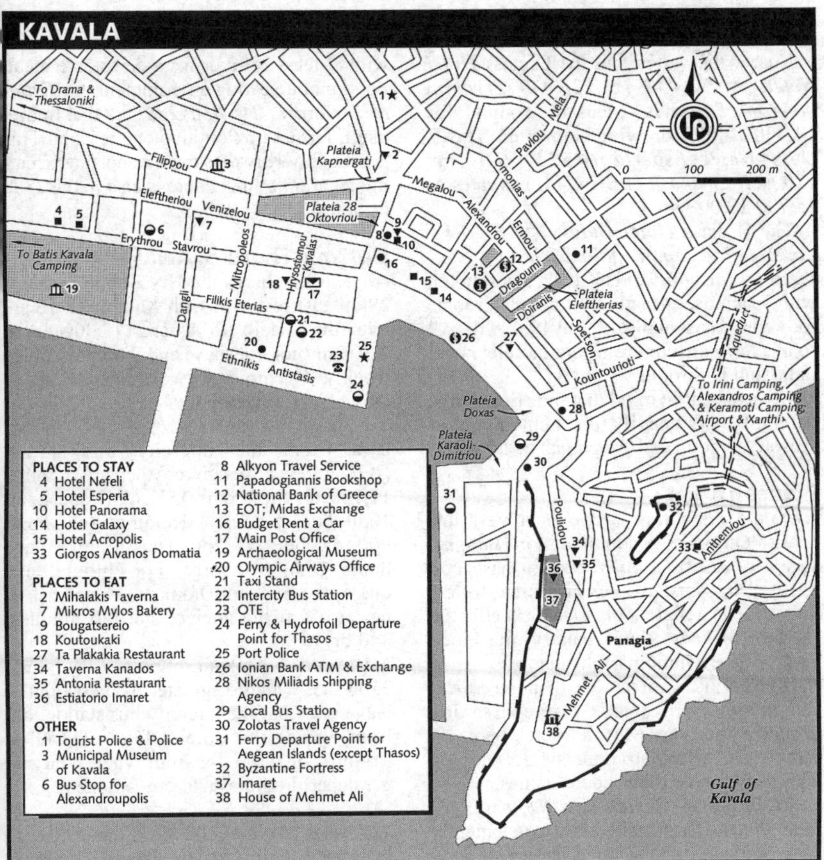

the beach at Nea Karvali. ***Batis Kavala Camping*** (*☎ 243 051)* is 3km west of Kavala at Batis Beach. Finally, 37km from Kavala at Keramoti, there is ***Keramoti Camping*** (*☎ 0591-51 279)*. They all charge around of 1200 dr per person and 850 dr per tent per night.

The best deal for budget travellers and perhaps the cosiest environment in Kavala are the homy ***domatia*** in the beautiful 300-year-old house rented by Giorgos Alvanos (*☎ 228 412, Anthemiou 35)* in Panagia. Singles/doubles are 5000/7000 dr. The C class ***Hotel Acropolis*** (*☎ 223 543, fax 830 752, Eleftheriou Venizelou 29)* is the closest thing to a budget hotel, and has singles for 7500 dr and doubles with bathroom for 14,000 dr. Take the lift to reception as you enter the building.

Places to Stay – Mid-Range & Top End

The C class ***Hotel Panorama*** (*☎ 224 205, fax 224 685, Eleftheriou Venizelou 26 C)* has reasonable rooms for 9000/12,500 dr, or 12,000/16,000 dr with bathroom.

Nearer the waterfront the C class ***Hotel Nefeli*** *(☎ 227 441, fax 227 440, Erythrou Stavrou 50)* has pleasant rooms for 14,000/18,000 dr with bathroom. The B class ***Hotel Esperia*** *(☎ 229 621, fax 220 621, Erythrou Stavrou 44)* has rates of 15,700/18,000 dr.

The B class ***Hotel Galaxy*** *(☎ 224 812, fax 226 754, email galaxy@hol.gr, Eleftheriou Venizelou 27)* is Kavala's best hotel, with spacious, attractively furnished rooms for a very reasonable 13,200/19,400 dr. All rooms have air-con, refrigerator, telephone, radio and bathroom.

Always bear in mind that the prices listed here may be heavily discounted out of season, sometimes by as much as 50%.

Places to Eat

Kavala's restaurant scene is a vast improvement on its accommodation. ***Bougatsereio*** on Eleftheriou Venizelou has good cheese pies, custard pies and filter coffee, and you can get great bread and cakes at the modern ***Mikros Mylos*** bakery one block south of the Municipal Museum.

If you don't want a meal, then the ***cafe*** in the Imaret is in a lovely serene setting around a courtyard of fruit trees, where you can while away an hour or so playing backgammon or other board games.

Ta Plakakia Restaurant *(Doïranis 4)*, near Plateia Eleftherias, is a conveniently located place with a huge choice of low-priced dishes. ***Mihalakis Taverna*** *(Kassandrou 3)*, on Plateia Kapnergati, is more upmarket. Don't be put off by the tacky murals and folksy wall hangings – the food is good. Prices at these two places go from 2000 dr to 2600 dr for a generous meal.

There are at least three popular restaurants on Poulidou, opposite the Imaret. The first is ***Taverna Kanados*** which has a wide-ranging fish menu and other seafood specialities – try the mussels in tomato sauce. ***Antonia Restaurant***, next door, is also recommended by locals and is equally well patronised, while farther along, ***Koutoukaki*** pulls in its own clientele. All have similar fare and prices; expect to part with at least 2800 dr for a delectable meal. For a unique eating environment, try ***Estiatorio Imaret*** *(☎ 836 286)* in the Imaret itself, farther up Poulidou on the right. This is probably Kavala's most atmospheric eating location. A meal here is also in the 2800 dr bracket.

Getting There & Away

Air Kavala shares the Hrysoupolis airport, 29km east of town, with Xanthi. There are two flights daily to Athens (18,300 dr) at 7.30 pm (not Tuesday) and 9.05 pm. Twice weekly Olympic Airways also flies to Düsseldorf in Germany.

Bus From the intercity bus station (☎ 223 593) buses go to Athens (9½ hours, 11,100 dr, three daily), Xanthi (one hour, 1050 dr, half-hourly), Keramoti (one hour, 900 dr, hourly) and Thessaloniki (two hours, 2850 dr, hourly). For Philippi, take one of the frequent Drama buses and ask to be let off at the ancient site (20 minutes, 340 dr).

Buses for Alexandroupolis (2½ hours, 3100 dr), which originate in Thessaloniki, leave not from the intercity bus station, but from outside the Dore Café (☎ 227 601), Erythrou Stavrou 34, from where you can get departure times and buy a ticket.

To/From Turkey OSE buses that originate in Thessaloniki depart from Kavala at 4.30 am daily except Thursday (9450/16,100 dr single/return). Student and youth discounts apply to student card-holders.

The buses depart from Alkyon Travel Service (☎ 231 096, fax 836 251) at Eleftheriou Venizelou 26d, next door to Hotel Panorama, and this is also where you buy tickets.

Train The nearest train station to Kavala is at Drama, 30km away. Drama is on the Thessaloniki-Alexandroupolis line and there are eight trains daily in either direction. There is a frequent bus service between Kavala and Drama. Train tickets can be bought in advance from Alkyon Travel Service on Eleftheriou Venizelou, which also acts as an OSE agency.

Ferry There are ferries to Skala Prinou on Thasos (1¼ hours, 850 dr, 4400 dr for a car, hourly). There is also a service every hour or so in summer from the small port of Keramoti, 46km east of Kavala, to Limenas (35 minutes, 330 dr, 2700 for a car).

In summer there are ferries to Samothraki (four hours, 3000 dr). Times and frequency vary month by month. Buy tickets and check the latest schedule at Zolotas Travel Agency (☎ 835 671) near the entrance to the Aegean Islands ferry departure point.

There are ferries to Limnos (4½ hours, 3100 dr), Agios Efstratios (six hours, 3700 dr) and Lesvos (11½ hours, 5200 dr). Some services also go through to Rafina (in Attica) and Piraeus via Chios and Samos. Tickets and the latest schedules are available from Nikos Miliadis Shipping Agency (☎ 226 147, fax 838 767), Karaoli-Dimitriou 36.

Hydrofoil There are about nine hydrofoils daily to Limenas (30 minutes, 1500 dr) and two to Potos (2500 dr) via Kallirahi, Maries and Limenaria. Purchase tickets at the departure point at the port.

Both hydrofoil and ferry schedules are posted in the window of the port police near the hydrofoil departure point.

Getting Around

To/From the Airport There is no Olympic Airways bus to the airport, but KTEL buses leave from the intercity bus station at 6 and 11.30 am and 7.30 pm (850 dr, 30 minutes), connecting with departing and incoming flights.

Car Budget Rent a Car (☎ 228 785) is on the 1st floor of Eleftheriou Venizelou 35, opposite Hotel Panorama. You can also rent a car from the Europcar agency at Alkyon Travel Service.

Taxi Kavala's bright orange taxis congregate outside the main bus station and can be ordered on ☎ 831 600. A taxi to the airport will cost around 4500 dr.

PHILIPPI Φίλιπποι

The ancient site of Philippi (**fee**-lih-pih) lies 15km inland from Kavala astride the Kavala-Drama road. The original city was called Krenides. Philip II seized it from the Thasians in 356 BC because it was in the foothills of Mt Pangaion, and there was 'gold in them thar hills', which he needed to finance his battles to gain control of Greece.

During July and August the Philippi Festival is held at the site's theatre. Information can be obtained from the EOT in Kavala.

History

A visit to Philippi is worthwhile more for the significance of the events that happened there than for what can actually be seen, so some knowledge of its history is essential. Philippi is famous for two reasons: it was the scene of one of the most decisive battles in history, and it was the first European city to accept Christianity.

By mid-1st century BC, Greece had become the battleground of the Roman Republic, and Philippi was coveted for its strategic position on the Via Egnatia. After Julius Caesar's assassination in 44 BC, the assassins (or Liberators, as they called themselves), led by Brutus and Cassius, assumed command of the armies stationed in Macedonia and the surrounding provinces. In 42 BC they were confronted at Philippi by the combined forces of Mark Antony, Caesar's experienced lieutenant, and the 19-year-old Octavian, the dead dictator's great-nephew and heir.

In fact, two battles were fought at Philippi in the space of three weeks. Initially, Cassius was defeated by Antony (and committed suicide in a fit of despair) while Brutus was victorious over Octavian's wing. Later, Brutus himself was defeated by Antony, and also chose suicide over surrender. The rest of the Republican forces capitulated. This set the stage for the inevitable conflict between Antony and Octavian, which ended 11 years later with Antony's defeat at Actium and subsequent suicide in Egypt, leaving Octavian the undisputed ruler of Rome.

Neopolis (modern Kavala), the port of Philippi, was the European landing stage for travellers from the Orient. And so it was here that St Paul came in 49 AD to embark on his conversion of the pagan Europeans. His overzealous preaching landed him in prison – a misadventure which would be repeated many times in the future.

Exploring the Site

Despite Philippi being the first Christian city in Europe, its people didn't have much luck in their church-building endeavours. The 5th century **Basilica A** was the first church built in the city, but it was wrecked by an earthquake shortly after completion. The remains can be seen on the northern side of the site (on the right coming from Kavala), near the road, to the west of the theatre.

Their next attempt was the 6th century **Basilica B**, on the southern side of the site, next to the large and conspicuous forum. This was an ambitious attempt to build a church with a dome, but the structure was top-heavy and collapsed before it was dedicated. In the 10th century its sole remaining part, the narthex, was made into a church – several of its Corinthian columns can be seen.

Philippi's best preserved building is the **theatre**, which isn't Roman but was built by Philip II. Also in good nick are 50 marble latrines at the southern end of the forum. The site's **museum**, on the north side, houses both Roman and Christian finds, and also Neolithic finds from the nearby site of Dikili Tach. It was closed for renovation in 1997, but hopefully should be up and running again now.

The site (☎ 051-516 470) is open 8.30 am to 6 pm Tuesday to Sunday. Entry to the site and museum is 800 dr; 400 dr for students.

Getting There & Away

Kavala-Drama buses will let passengers off at Philippi (20 minutes, 340 dr).

Thrace Θράκη

Thrace (**thrah**-kih) is the north-eastern region of Greece and the backwater of the mainland. If you ask Greeks from elsewhere what it has to offer, chances are most will reply 'nothing', and some will add words to the tune of 'and Turks live there'. The Turkish population of Thrace, along with the Greek population of Constantinople and the former Greek islands of Imvros (Gökçeada) and Tenedos (Bozcaada), were exempt from the 1923 population exchange. This phenomenon alone sets Thrace apart.

The landscape is dotted with the slender minarets of mosques and villages of Turkish-style red-roofed houses. There is also a more pronounced Turkish influence in the food, and a greater proliferation of eastern-style bazaars and street vendors.

Besides being of ethnographical interest, the region has some picturesque towns and a varied landscape. It has a long coastline interspersed with wetlands and a hinterland of mountains (the Rodopi Range) covered in thick forest and undergrowth. The mountains are punctuated by valleys through which flow several rivers. The most important is the Evros River, which marks the boundary with Turkey.

Between the coast and the mountains is a fertile plain where sunflowers, grown for oil, create a pretty foreground to the mountainous backdrop. Tobacco is also grown, to supply a thriving industry – although the rest of Europe is giving up the noxious weed, smoking among Greeks is increasing at an alarming rate. Another feature of the area is the large number of storks. Look out for their huge, untidy nests on high extremities of buildings.

History

The earliest Thracian tribes were of Indo-European extraction, and the ethnic and

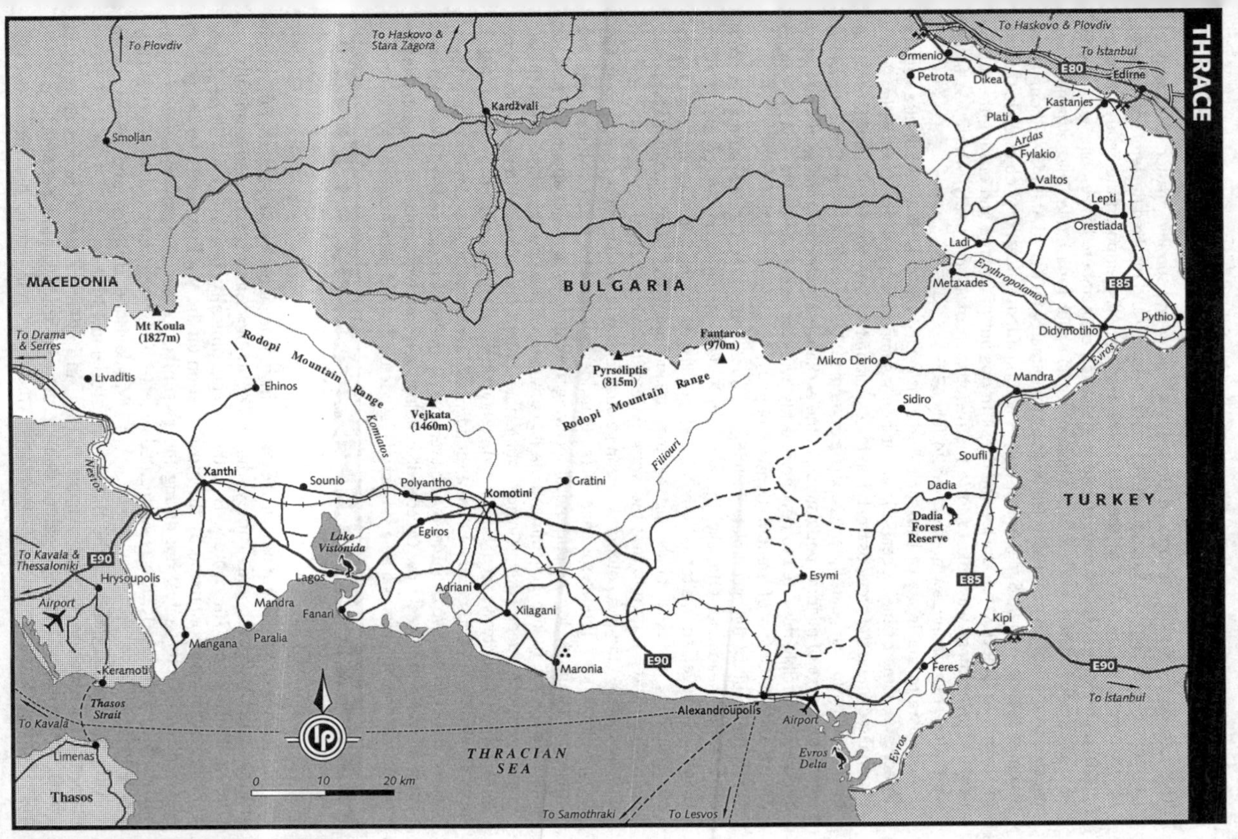

NORTHERN GREECE

The Turkish Minority Question

The issue of the Turkish minority in Greece is a touchy and sensitive matter. The Treaty of Lausanne (1923) settled the boundaries of modern Turkey and resolved the territorial disputes raised in Anatolia by WWI. At the end of the war the Allies imposed the Treaty of Sèvres (1920) on the defeated Ottoman Empire; it effectively dismembered the empire, leaving only Anatolia (minus a Greek enclave at Smyrna, or İzmir) under Turkish rule. This settlement was rejected by the Turkish nationalists led by Mustafa Kemal (later Kemal Atatürk). Although they accepted the loss of Iraq, Syria, Arabia, and other non-Turkish areas, they objected to the loss of Smyrna to Greece. After driving the Greek troops out of Smyrna and ousting the sultan, Kemal's government was able to force the negotiation of a new treaty, which was finally concluded at Lausanne, Switzerland, on 24 July 1923.

According to the Treaty of Lausanne, Turkey regained not only Smyrna but also eastern Thrace and some of the Aegean islands. It also resumed control of the Dardanelles (internationalised under the previous treaty) on the condition that they were kept demilitarised and open to all nations in peacetime. A separate agreement between Turkey and Greece provided for the exchange of minority populations. In the exchange, whole communities of Greeks and Turks were forcibly relocated to new homelands, with the exception of the Turks of central Thrace and the Greeks of İstanbul (Constantinople).

It is the result of this incomplete exchange of populations that is today causing Greece a considerable headache. Officially, there are no Turkish minorities in Greece, but 'Muslim Greeks'. However, any visitor to Komotini and the villages around this town in central Thrace could easily be mistaken in believing that they are in Turkey. The Turkish language is spoken everywhere and it is hard to miss the women dressed in Muslim attire.

Paradoxically, and in a country where individual television satellite dishes cost a small fortune, there is not a Turkish-speaking village that does not sprout a forest of these expensive antennae, ostensibly for the purpose of receiving Turkish television and apparently paid for indirectly by the Turkish government, via its consulate in Thessaloniki. This 'Turkish Trojan Horse' positioned deep within Greece's vulnerable eastern flank causes jitters whenever the term 'Turkish minority' is raised. Events in Yugoslavia in early 1999 though not involving Greece and Turkey directly caused more than a shudder in Athenian political circles. Occasional skirmishes between the two countries over barren rocks in the Aegean claimed by Turkey also raise the brinkmanship stakes. How Greece will handle its relations with Turkey in a region already beset by ethnic conflicts will be a subject of close scrutiny by all Balkan-watchers.

cultural origins of the region have a greater affinity with Bulgaria and Turkey than Greece. During the 7th century BC, the Thracian coast was conquered by the most powerful Greek city-states, but during the 6th and 5th centuries BC it was subjugated by the Persians.

After the Persian defeat at the Battle of Plataea, Thrace was governed by Athens. In 346 BC, Philip II of Macedon gained control. During Roman times it was an insignificant backwater, but after the empire split, the region developed culturally and economically, because of its strategic position on the Via Egnatia. Later, its fate was similar to that of pretty much everywhere else in Greece: invaded by Goths, Huns, Vandals and Bulgars, and finally by the Turks in 1361.

In 1920 the Treaty of Sèvres decreed that all of Thrace should become part of the modern Greek state, but after the 1923 population exchange, eastern Thrace was ceded to Turkey.

XANTHI Ξάνθη

☎ 0541 • postcode 671 00 • pop 31,000

If you're travelling east from Thessaloniki or Kavala, Xanthi is the first Thracian town you will encounter. The old town has many beautiful, well maintained 19th century Turkish dwellings. Xanthi is a lively and flourishing town where Turks make up 10% of the population, and live amicably with Greeks. The town is the centre of Thrace's tobacco-growing industry. The areas to the north, though you technically can visit them, are subject to military control and a pass is required.

Orientation & Information

The main thoroughfare is 28 Oktovriou, which runs north-south. Halfway along is Plateia Eleftherias, just west of which on Iroön is a huge, fascinating indoor food market. The main bus station is at the northern end of this market and the bus station for Kavala is opposite the southern end, on Eklission. The train station is 2km from town, just off the main Kavala-Xanthi road.

If you continue up 28 Oktovriou from Plateia Eleftherias, you will come to the central square of Plateia Kentriki, with a prominent clock tower on the western side. To reach the old town, continue north along Vasileos Konstantinou, a picturesque cobbled street.

Walk one block up Vasileos Konstantinou, turn right and you'll see the National Bank of Greece on the left. The post office is at A Giorgiou 16, and the OTE is at Michael Vogdou 2; both streets lead west from Plateia Kentriki.

There is no tourist office or tourist police, but the regular police (☎ 22 100), at 28 Oktovriou 223, will do what they can to help, bringing in an English speaker off the street if necessary.

Old Xanthi

Old Xanthi was built on a hillside overlooking the modern town. The narrow winding streets have some lovely neoclassical mansions which once belonged to wealthy tobacco merchants. The more modest dwellings also have considerable charm; most are pastel, with overhanging timber-framed floors.

Two of the old town's adjoining mansions have been converted into a **museum**. They were built for the Koumtzogli brothers, who were tobacco magnates. The well laid out exhibits include traditional agricultural and household implements, carpets, embroidery and jewellery. While you're in the museum cast your eyes upwards to the amazing ceilings. Some are made of carved wood, others are painted with intricate designs. Also, don't miss the antique toilet upstairs (no longer usable). The bowl is decorated with elaborate floral designs.

Exhibits are labelled in Greek, but the curator will do his best to explain things, although his English is limited. The museum is at Antika 7 and is open 11 am to 1 pm daily. Admission is 300 dr.

Places to Stay

The rather sleazy D class ***Lux Hotel*** *(☎ 22 341, Georgiou Stavriou 18)* near Plateia Kentriki has singles/doubles for 4000/5000 dr. If you're coming from Vasileos Konstantinou, turn right at the National Bank of Greece.

The two clean and comfortable C class hotels are much better options. ***Hotel Dimokritos*** *(☎ 25 111, fax 25 537, 28 Oktovriou 41)* near Plateia Kentriki has rates of 8000/10,450 dr with bathroom.

Hotel Xanthippion *(☎ 77 061, fax 77 076, 28 Oktovriou 212)* has rooms for around 13,000/16,000 dr with bathroom. This hotel has a car park, and is at the southern end of town. Prices at both these places are usually negotiable.

Xanthi's best hotel is the modern B class ***Hotel Nestos*** *(☎ 27 531, fax 27 535)* on Terma 28 Oktovriou, which charges 14,000/17,500 dr, including bathroom. The hotel is 1km south of the town centre. Coming from Kavala by road, it's on the right as you enter the town. This hotel also has a car park.

Places to Eat

Locals rate ***Klimataria Restaurant*** on Plateia Kentriki as the town's best eating place. It has a large selection of ready-made food – a healthy lunch of beans, Greek salad and retsina will set you back around 2500 dr.

Students hang out at ***Haradra Taverna*** which has outdoor eating in a walled garden, but only opens in the summer. At the top of Vasileos Konstantinou you will see a sign on a wall pointing to the taverna. Turn left and the restaurant is immediately, though not obviously, to your left. A decent meal will cost about 2700 dr.

Close by, where Paleologou begins to climb to old Xanthi, are two ouzeria, ***Kivotos*** and ***Arhontissa***. Give them a try if you can manage to order one or two mezedes in Greek, but keep track of what you are eating and drinking or the bill might be higher than you'd anticipated. Expect to pay a minimum of about 3000 dr.

Getting There & Away

Air Xanthi shares the Hrysoupolis airport, 47km away, with Kavala in Macedonia (see the Kavala section for flight details). The Olympic Airways office (☎ 22 944) is at Michael Vogdou 4, near the OTE.

Bus From the main bus terminal (☎ 22 684) buses go to Komotini (45 minutes, 950 dr, eight daily), Thessaloniki (four hours, 3400 dr, seven daily) and Athens (10 hours, 11,350 dr, two daily). Thessaloniki buses go via Kavala (one hour, 1100 dr). There are no direct buses to Alexandroupolis; you must change at Komotini.

Train Trains go to Alexandroupolis (1½ hours, 860 dr, six daily) and Thessaloniki (four hours, 2160 dr, six daily). Thessaloniki-bound intercity services leave Xanthi at 8.49 am and 6.51 pm. The equivalent services to Alexandroupolis depart at 11.32 am and 5.52 pm. The 11.32 am intercity service connects at Pythio with a train to İstanbul. These intercity trains attract a ticket supplement. Tickets may be purchased either at the station (☎ 22 581) or from the OSE agent, Tarpidis Tours (☎/fax 22 277) at Tsaldari 5, which is in the Agora Nousa (an indoor shopping precinct) just east of Plateia Kentriki. A taxi to the train station will cost about 700 dr.

Getting Around

There are no Olympic Airways buses to Hrysoupolis; a taxi costs 6000 dr. Alternatively, take a Kavala-bound bus to Hrysoupolis, then a taxi 12km to the airport.

KOMOTINI Κομοτηνή

☎ 0531 • postcode 691 00 • pop 37,000

Komotini (ko-mo-tih-**nee**), 57km east of Xanthi, is the capital of the prefecture of Rodopi. Its population is half Greek and half Turkish. It lacks the character of Xanthi and is an unremarkable place except for its outstanding **archaeological museum** (☎ 22 411) at Simeonidi 4, which houses well displayed finds from little-known ancient sites in Thrace, most notably Abdera and Maronia.

The latter was Homer's Ismaros, where Odysseus obtained the wine which he used to intoxicate the Cyclops Polyphemus who had imprisoned him. While in this drunken state, Polyphemus was blinded by Odysseus and his men, enabling their escape. (The scant remains of the ancient site are near the modern village of Maronia, 31km southeast of Komotini.) The museum is well signposted and is open 9 am to 5 pm daily. Admission is free.

Have a look in the **Museum of Folk Life & History** (☎ 25 975, fax 37 145), at Agiou Georgiou 13. It's worth a visit if you're between buses. Housed in the Peïdi Mansion, the display has samples of home wares, manuscripts and costumes. The more important displays are also labelled in English. A useful book on the history of Komotini and the Rodopi prefecture is available for 1000 dr. The museum is open 10 am to 1 pm only (closed on Sunday); entrance is free. Turn right from the bus station, walk 100m along Agiou Georgiou Mameli, turn left onto Agiou Georgiou and after another 100m you'll find it on your right.

Places to Stay

The nearest camp site to Komotini is ***Fanari Komotinis Camping*** *(☎ 0535-31 217)*. The site is by the sea near the village of Fanari, about 26km south-east of Komotini.

If you get stuck in Komotini, finding a place to stay shouldn't be too much of a problem. Among the possibilities are the E class ***Hotel Hellas*** *(☎ 22 055, Dimokritou 31)* where singles/doubles are 5000/7000 dr. ***Pension Olympos*** *(☎ 37 690, fax 37 693, Orfeos 37)* has rooms costing 13,000/17,000 dr with bathroom. ***Democritos Hotel*** *(☎ 22 579, fax 23 396, Plateia Vizynou 8)* charges 12,800/17,000 dr, including bathroom. The snazzy ***Hotel Astoria*** *(☎ 35 054, fax 22 707)* on Plateia Irinis has neat, modern rooms with air-con for 14,000/19,000 dr. Most hotel prices are negotiable.

Getting There & Away

Bus There are frequent departures from Komotini's bus station (☎ 22 912) to Xanthi (45 minutes, 950 dr) and Alexandroupolis (70 minutes, 1150 dr). There are also buses to Thessaloniki (4½ hours, 4450 dr, eight daily), stopping at Kavala (1½ hours, 1900 dr), and to Athens (11 hours, 12,800 dr, one daily).

Train There are six trains daily to both Alexandroupolis (one hour, 600 dr) and Thessaloniki (4½ hours, 2500 dr). The Thessaloniki-bound intercity trains leave Komotini in the morning and early evening. The equivalent services to Alexandroupolis depart at about midday and mid-evening. These trains attract a ticket supplement. The midday eastbound intercity train connects at Pythio with a service to İstanbul.

For further information call the train station on ☎ 22 650. The station is at the end of Pangi Tsaldari in an oddly unmarked cream building.

ALEXANDROUPOLIS

Αλεξανδρούπολη

☎ 0551 • postcode 681 00 • pop 37,000

Alexandroupolis (ah-lex-an-**droo**-po-lih), the capital of the prefecture of Evros, is a modern and prosaic town with a lively student atmosphere supplemented by a considerable population of young soldiers. Most travellers come here simply in transit heading east to Turkey, or to catch ferries to Samothraki or even to the Dodecanese Islands. The maritime ambience of this

The blinding of the Cyclops Polyphemus by Odysseus

town, and its year-round liveliness, make it a pleasant stopover.

Alexandroupolis' hotels get surprisingly full, since Greek holiday-makers from northern Evros flock here in July and August. Their numbers are swelled by overlanders who descend upon the town en route to Turkey. During these months try to continue your journey to Samothraki, other islands farther south, or Turkey; otherwise, reserve accommodation in advance.

Orientation

The town is laid out roughly on a grid system, with the main streets running east-west, parallel with the waterfront, where the lively evening *volta* (promenade) takes place. Karaoli Dimitriou is at the eastern end of the waterfront, with Megalou Alexandrou at the western end.

The town's most prominent landmark is the large 19th century lighthouse on the middle of the waterfront. The two main squares are Plateia Eleftherias and Plateia Polytehniou, both just one block north of Karaoli Dimitriou.

The train station is on the waterfront just south of Plateia Eleftherias and east of the port where boats leave for Samothraki. The intercity bus station is at Eleftheriou Venizelou 36, five blocks inland. The local bus terminal is on Plateia Eleftherias, just outside the train station.

Information

Tourist information is now handled by the EOT office at Alexandroupolis' camp site (see Places to Stay). The tourist police (☎ 37 424) are at Karaïskaki 6.

The main post office is on the waterfront on the corner of Nikiforou Foka and Megalou Alexandrou. The OTE is on the corner of Mitropolitou Kaviri and Eleftheriou Venizelou.

The National Bank of Greece is at Dimokratias 246 and has an ATM. There is another ATM-equipped branch diagonally opposite.

There are three Internet cafes in Alexandroupolis. The Internet Cafe (☎ 81 811) is at Koletti 4, close to the Olympic Airways office. There are 10 terminals and it's open all day. There is another branch at Apolloniados 11 with 20 terminals. Cafe Del Mar (☎ 81 187) at Psarron 1 has only three terminals and is open all day.

Foreign newspapers and magazines can be purchased at the tobacconist on Dimokratias diagonally opposite the Folkloric and Historical Museum.

The phone number for the port police is ☎ 26 468.

Things to See

The outstanding **Ecclesiastical Art Museum of Alexandroupolis** is one of the best in the country. It contains a priceless collection of icons and ecclesiastical ornaments brought to Greek Thrace by refugees from Asia Minor. Unfortunately, due to a cutback in government funding, the museum is unable to keep regular opening hours, but if you ring the bell of the offices next door, someone will show you around. Entrance is free. The museum is in the grounds of the St Nicholas Cathedral.

The **Folkloric and Historical Museum** (☎ 28 926), on the corner of Dimokratias and Kanari in a brand new, swish building, is organised by the Society of the Friends of Antiquities of the Evros Prefecture. The displays offer an insight into the life and culture of Eastern Thrace. Opening hours are 10.30 am to 1.30 pm and 6.30 to 9.30 pm Tuesday to Saturday; by appointment only Sunday and holidays. Entry to the museum is free.

Children will be pleased to learn that there is a lively funfair just off the promenade in front of the lighthouse.

Places to Stay

The EOT-run ***Camping Alexandroupolis*** *(☎ 28 735)* is on the beach 2km west of the town. It's a clean, well run site with good facilities. Take a local bus from Plateia Eleftherias to reach the site.

Hotel Lido *(☎ 28 808, Paleologou 15)* is an outstanding D class hotel with comfortable singles/doubles for 4000/5000 dr, and

5500/6500 dr for doubles/triples with bathroom. The hotel is one block north of the bus station. ***Hotel Erika*** *(☎ 34 115, fax 34 117, Karaoli Dimitriou 110)* is a very superior D class where rates are a rather high 14,000/16,000 dr for singles/doubles. All rooms have bathroom, telephone, TV and balcony.

The C class ***Hotel Okeanis*** *(☎ 28 830, fax 34 118, Paleologou 20)*, almost opposite the Lido, has very comfortable rooms for 12,500/15,500 dr. You can successfully connect your laptop to the Internet from the rooms. The C class ***Hera Hotel*** *(☎ 23 941, fax 34 222, Leoforos Dimokratias 179)*, closer to the train station, has pricey, but smaller rooms for 14,500/18,000 dr.

One other excellent option for groups of two or more is ***Apartment Hotel Athina*** *(☎ 34 492, fax 37 301, Paleologou 53)*. Rooms are self-contained with air-con and modern kitchen facilities. Doubles are 26,400 dr and suites for three to five people cost 35,500 dr. Prices are negotiable and are usually considerably lower than these published rates.

Places to Eat

Neraïda Restaurant, on Plateia Polytehniou where Kyprou widens to form a small square, is a good choice and has a range of standard fare and some local specialities for 1600 dr to 2200 dr. In a similar vein and with similar prices, but with a creative English-language menu, is ***Klimataria*** also on Plateia Polytehniou, diagonally opposite Neraïda.

Opposite the fish market and where freshness is guaranteed is ***Psarotaverna Anestis*** *(Athanasiou Diakou 5)*, one street east of Kyprou. This place looks very unassuming, but has a fine choice of mezedes, especially those with fish. *Mydia saganaki* (chilli mussels) are highly recommended. Prices are reasonable for a fish taverna.

Also not far away is the newish ***To Nisiotiko*** *(Bouboulinas 2)* with its tasteful blue and white decor and selection of very tasty and reasonably priced mezedes.

Getting There & Away

Air Alexandroupolis' domestic Dimokritos airport, 7km east of town and near the village of Loutra, does receive occasional international charter flights. The airport has a morning and evening flight to Athens (18,600 dr) and usually extra flights in summer. The Olympic Airlines office (☎ 26 361) is at Ellis 6.

Bus From Alexandroupolis' bus station (☎ 26 479) there are frequent buses to Soufli (1½ hours, 1500 dr), Didymotiho (1¾ hours, 1700 dr), Orestiada (two hours, 1950 dr) and Komotini (70 minutes, 1150 dr). There are buses to Thessaloniki (six hours, 6000 dr, six daily) via Xanthi and Kavala.

For what it's worth, there is one bus daily to Athens (12 hours, 14,000 dr) though it's cheaper and probably more fun to take the boat to Rafina, near Athens.

To/From Turkey There is a daily OSE bus to İstanbul, leaving at 8.30 am (five to seven hours, 5600 dr). There are currently no private buses running to Turkey. Otherwise, you can take a bus from the intercity bus station to the border town of Kipi (three daily, 750 dr), 43km from Alexandroupolis. You cannot walk across the border but it is easy enough to hitch across – you may be lucky and get a lift all the way to İstanbul. Otherwise, take a bus to Ipsala (5km beyond the border) or Kesan (30km beyond the border) from where there are many buses to İstanbul.

To/From Bulgaria There is a private bus service to Plovdiv (six hours, 9000 dr) and Sofia (seven hours, 10,000 dr) which departs from Alexandroupolis on Wednesday and Sunday at 8.30 am. Return dates and times from Bulgaria are the same. Contact Kikon Travel Agency (☎ 25 455, fax 34 755), Eleftheriou Venizelou 68 for details.

Train There trains to Thessaloniki (seven hours, 3000 dr, five daily), including one which continues on to Athens and intermediate stations (14 hours, 7100 dr). Two of these trains are intercity services; the *Alexandros* terminates in Thessaloniki and the *Vergina* terminates in Athens – both attract a ticket supplement. There are also seven trains daily to Dikea via Pythio, Didymotiho, Orestiada (2½ hours, 1250 dr) and Kastanies for the Turkish border crossing. However, only the 5.18, 6.32 and 9.49 am services will get you to Kastanies in time to cross before the border closes at 1 pm. For further information call the train station on ☎ 26 395.

To/From Turkey There is one train daily to İstanbul, which currently leaves Alexandroupolis at 1 pm. This is the IC90 intercity service with a connection to Üzunköpru in Turkey at Pythio. This time is subject to frequent changes, so check with OSE. Tickets cost 6350 dr and the journey can take 10 hours. The train is hot and crowded in summer – the OSE bus is a marginally better choice.

To/From Bulgaria There is one service daily to Svilengrad (four hours, 3000 dr) with an ongoing connection to Plovdiv and Sofia. The train currently leaves Alexandroupolis at 5.15 am. Double-check with OSE in case of any changes.

Ferry In July and August there are two to three sailings daily to Samothraki. In spring and autumn there are two and in winter, one. Tickets for the *Saos* ferry and the latest departure details may be obtained from Vatitsis Shipping Agency (☎ 26 721, fax 32 007, email saos@orfeasnet.gr), Kyprou 5 (opposite the port). Tickets cost 2300 dr, a car costs an exorbitant 10,500 dr and the trip takes two hours.

There is a weekly ferry to Rhodes, via five other islands en route. Sample base prices are: Limnos (five hours, 3300 dr), Lesvos (11½ hours, 5000 dr) and Rhodes (18 hours, 11,500 dr). This currently leaves on Tuesday. On Friday there is a ferry to Limnos, Agios Efstratios and Rafina (17¼ hours, 7500 dr). Contact Kikon Travel Agency (see Bus) for tickets and reservations.

Hydrofoil The Flying Dolphin services operate mainly during the summer months, linking Alexandroupolis with Samothraki (one hour, 4700 dr), Limnos (1¾ hours, 5400 dr) and mainland ports to the west. Contact Kaga Marina Agents (☎/fax 81 700) at Emboriou 70 for current timetables and tickets.

Getting Around

There is no airport shuttle bus. Take a Loutra-bound bus from Plateia Eleftherias. A taxi (☎ 28 358) to the airport will cost about 1200 dr.

EVROS DELTA Δέλτα Εβρου

The Evros Delta, 20km south-east of Alexandroupolis, is ecologically one of Europe's most important wetlands. Three hundred species of birds have been recorded, including the last 15 surviving pairs of royal eagles, and more than 200,000 migrating waterfowl spend part of their winter here. Unfortunately, the wetlands are in a highly sensitive area due to their proximity to Turkey, and permission from the security police in Alexandroupolis is technically required in order to visit.

Contact Kikon Travel Agency (☎ 0551-25 455) or the tourist police (☎ 0551-37 424) in Alexandroupolis, or the Feres municipal tourist office (☎ 0555-22 211) for further information on organised tours.

ALEXANDROUPOLIS TO DIDYMOTIHO

North-east of Alexandroupolis the road, railway line and Evrosrun River close together, skirting the Turkish border. This is a highly sensitive area with many signs prohibiting photography. It's also a lush and attractive region with fields of wheat and sunflowers, and forests of pine trees.

Feres, 29km north-east of Alexandroupolis, has the interesting 12th century Byzantine Church of Panagia Kosmosotira. It is signposted from the main road.

Soufli

Farther north, the little town of Soufli, 67km north-east of Alexandroupolis and 31km south of Didymotiho, has lots of character. It has retained a number of its Turkish wattle-and-daub houses and is renowned in Greece for its production of silk. This is because the mulberry tree, upon which the silkworms feed, used to thrive in the region.

Unfortunately, most of the mulberry trees have been chopped down to make way for crops, but the town still has one silk factory.

Soufli has an interesting **silk museum** (☎ 23 700) with a display of silk-producing equipment. Opening times are 8 am to 3.30 pm Monday to Friday, and 9 am to 2 pm Saturday (300 dr). The yellow and brown museum is 400m back from the town's main through road and is clearly signposted. There's also a bank in Soufli with an ATM.

If you decide to spend the night, the D class ***Egnatia Hotel*** *(☎ 0554-22 124, Vasileos Georgiou 225)* has singles/doubles for 5000/8000 dr. The only other place is the C class ***Hotel Orpheas*** *(☎ 0554-22 922, fax 22 305, Tsimiski 1)* on a corner with

The grey wolf still survives in small numbers in the mountains of northern Greece and in the Dadia Forest area

Vasileos Georgiou. Rates are 10,500/15,700 dr with bathroom.

Soufli is on the Alexandroupolis-Orestiada bus and train routes.

Dadia Forest Reserve

Some 8km off the main Alexandroupolis-Orestiada highway is the little-known but highly recommendable Dadia Lefkimmi Soufli Forest, to use its full title. Created in 1980, it consists of a protected zone of some 7290 hectares and a buffer zone of 35,170 hectares. Here are some of Europe's last remaining breeding and feeding grounds of rare raptors (birds of prey). Of the 38 known species of European raptors, 36 are found here, making the site unique.

There is an informative **Ecotourist Centre** (☎ 0554-32 209, email ecodadia@otenet.gr) with detailed bilingual wall displays and free slide shows. Visitors can take a minibus to a well constructed bird hide (500 dr), hire a mountain bike (1000 dr an hour) and ride up, or opt to take the free walking track and hike up. The track is marked orange for the upward leg and yellow for the (different) downward leg. It takes about an hour to walk up. Binoculars are usually provided at the hide and there is a tripod available for photographers. But you will need at least a 500mm telephoto lens to get any serious joy out of photographing the vultures or other raptors commonly visible at the feeding grounds across the wooded valley.

The centre is open daily 10 am to 4 pm in December and January; 9 am to 7 pm from March to May and September to November; 8.30 am to 8.30 pm from June to August.

You can stay the night in the very smart ***Ecotourist Hostel of Dadia*** *(☎ 0554-32 263, fax 32 463)*. Well appointed, raptor-coded rooms cost 6000/8000 dr for singles/doubles. Meals can be had in the restaurant next door, or in the village of Dadia itself, a 1km walk from the Ecotourist Centre.

There are three buses daily from Soufli to Dadia, leaving at 7.45 and 11.30 am and 2 pm, and returning from Dadia some 15 or 20 minutes later (300 dr).

DIDYMOTIHO Διδυμότειχο

☎ 0553 • postcode 683 00 • pop 8500

Didymotiho (dih-dih-**mo**-tih-ho) is the most interesting of the towns north of Alexandroupolis, although few tourists venture here. The town's name derives from the double walls that once enclosed it (*didymo* 'twin', *tihos* 'wall').

In Byzantine times it was an important town. When it fell to the Turks in 1361, Murad I made it the capital. In 1365 he transferred the capital to Adrianople (modern Edirne). The town's most prominent landmark is a large mosque, with a pyramid-shaped roof, on Plateia Kentriki.

Turks comprise 15% of the town's population, and there are also Roma (Gypsies).

Orientation & Information

Almost everything you need is on or near Plateia Kentriki, the central square, which you can't miss because of the mosque.

To get to Plateia Kentriki from the bus station, walk along the road straight ahead, and turn right into Venizelou, the town's main thoroughfare – the square is at the end. From the rather inconveniently located train station turn left, keep walking to 25 Maïou, and continue along here to Venizelou.

There is no tourist office or tourist police. The OTE and the National Bank of Greece are on Plateia Kentriki and the post office is just north of here. Walk along Vasileos Alexandrou, and take the first left into Kolokotroni, and it's on the right.

Things to See

Didymotiho is yet another place to wander in. With the mosque on your left, walk straight ahead from Plateia Kentriki to the picturesque, tree-shaded Plateia Vatrahou (Frog Square), so named because of its frog-shaped fountain. Continue straight ahead up Metaxa. In this area there are many Turkish timber-framed houses. Continue uphill to the **Cathedral of Agios Athanasios**. Next to the cathedral are some well preserved sections of the town's Byzantine walls.

If you walk back down Metaxa, and turn left into Vatatzi, you will come to the **folk museum** on the right. This outstanding museum has displays of Thracian costumes; 19th and early 20th century agricultural equipment and household implements; and a reconstructed 1920s kitchen. The museum is open 5 to 8 pm Wednesday and Thursday and 10 am to 2 pm weekends (300 dr). Call ☎ 22 154 if you wish to visit out of hours.

Construction of the **mosque** on Plateia Kentriki was started by Murad I and finished by his son, Bayazıt, in 1368. It is the oldest and largest mosque in Europe. Its minaret, which has two intricate ornate balconies, has lost its top, all the windows are smashed and the walls are crumbling, but it is still obvious that it must once have been a fine building.

Places to Stay & Eat

Didymotiho has two hotels. The tidy D class ***Hotel Anesis*** *(☎ 24 850, Vasileos Alexandrou 55)* has singles/doubles for 9000/12,000 dr with bathroom. Vasileos Alexandrou runs off Plateia Kentriki.

The other option is the rather tatty B class ***Hotel Plotini*** (*☎ 23 400, fax 22 251, Agias Paraskevis 1*), 1km south of town on the road to Alexandroupolis. If you're coming from Alexandroupolis, it's on the left. Rooms go for 10,000/16,000 dr.

There are fast-food and cheap souvlaki places on Venizelou. ***Zythestiatorio Kypselaki*** *(Ypsilantou 8)*, opposite the OTE, is about the only place resembling a traditional eatery within the central area. Lunch will cost you about 2100 dr with wine, but it's only open until 5 pm.

Didymotiho has some fine old ***kafeneia***. The one at the top of Kolokotroni looks as if it's jumped straight out of the museum opposite. The one on Plateia Vatrahou has tables set under shady plane trees.

Getting There & Away

There are many buses daily from Alexandroupolis (two hours, 1100 dr). There are also trains from Alexandroupolis (three hours, 800 dr, seven daily).

NORTH OF DIDYMOTIHO

From Didymotiho the road continues for another 20km to **Orestiada** (population 13,000). This town was built in the 1920s to house refugees who came from Turkey during the population exchange. It's a modern town with little character. Despite its apparent backwater status, Orestiada has been given a magnificent train station, better than most in Greece and one that hardly justifies the eight trains daily that it services. However, it is now the terminus for one of the intercity trains from Thessaloniki.

If you get stuck, there are a couple of budget hotels. The cheapest one is the D class ***Hotel Acropolis*** *(☎ 0552-22 277, Vasileos Konstantinou 48)* where singles/doubles are 4000/6500 dr with bathroom. The C class ***Hotel Vienna*** *(☎ 0552-22 578, fax 22 258, Orestou 64)* has rates of 8500/12,500 dr with bathroom. The best hotel in this area is the gaudy ***Hotel Electra*** *(☎ 0552-23 540, fax 23 133, A Pantazinou 50)*. Rooms here, with air-con and TV cost 9500/10,000 dr.

On the same street as Hotel Electra, some 300m north on the right, is ***Koutoukaki*** *(☎ 0552-29 692)* grill and restaurant. The chicken and draught retsina are recommended and are very good value. A big chicken meal with retsina and salad will cost no more than 2200 dr.

It's another 19km to **Kastanies**, Greece's northern road border point into Turkey. Unless you're planning to continue to Turkey, there's little point coming here.

If you cross the Turkish border, the first town you'll arrive at is the eastern Thracian town of **Edirne** (Adrianoupolis in Greek), 9km from Kastanies. The town is overlooked by most tourists and retains much of its traditional character.

If you want to cross the border here, bear in mind that the crossing is only open from 9 am to 1 pm, so time your arrival accordingly. However, the only reason anyone would want to cross here is to visit Edirne, since it's way off the Alexandroupolis-İstanbul axis. Three morning trains will get you to the border in time for the crossing (see the Alexandroupolis section earlier in this chapter).

THE ISLANDS

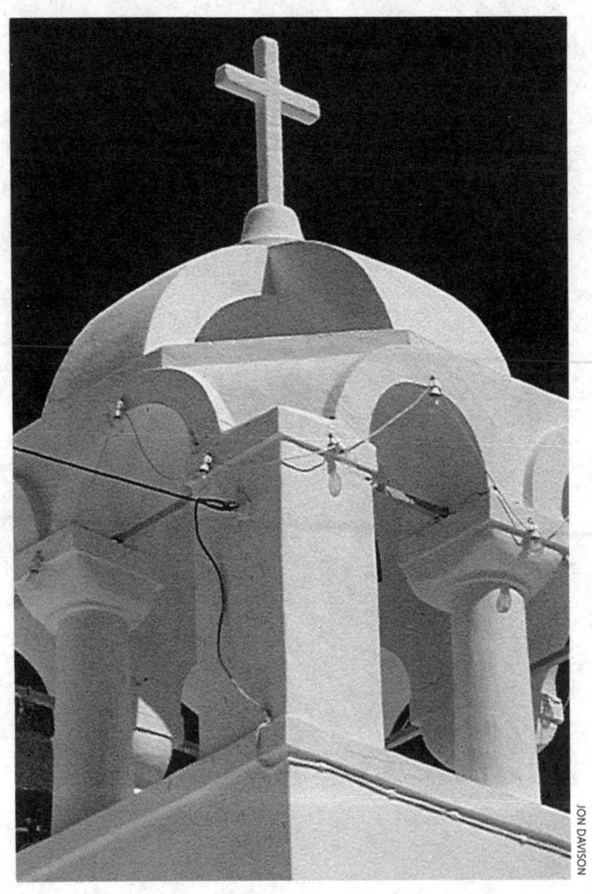

JON DAVISON

Saronic Gulf Islands
(Νησιά του Σαρωνικού)

The five Saronic Gulf Islands are the closest group to Athens. The closest, Salamis, is little more than a suburb of the sprawling capital. Aegina is also close enough to Athens for people to commute to work. Along with Poros, the next island south, it is a popular package-holiday destination. Hydra, once famous as the rendezvous of artists, writers and beautiful people, manages to retain an air of superiority and grandeur. Spetses, the most southerly island in the group, receives an inordinate number of British package tourists.

Spetses has the best beaches, but these islands are not the place to be if long stretches of golden sand are what you want. And with the exception of the Temple of Aphaia, on Aegina, the islands have no significant archaeological remains.

Nevertheless, the islands are a very popular escape for Athenians. Accommodation can be nigh on impossible to find between mid-June and mid-September, and weekends are busy all year round. If you plan to go at these times, it's a good idea to reserve a room in advance.

The islands have a reputation for high prices, which is a bit misleading. What is true is that there are very few places for budget travellers to stay – no camp sites and only a couple of cheap hotels. There is plenty of good accommodation available if you are happy to pay 10,000 dr or more for a double. Midweek visitors can get some good deals. Food is no more expensive than anywhere else.

The Saronic Gulf is named after the mythical King Saron of Argos, a keen hunter who drowned while pursuing a deer that had swum into the gulf to escape.

HIGHLIGHTS

- The rambling ruins of the old town of Paleohora on Aegina
- Views over the Saronic Gulf from the Temple of Aphaia on Aegina
- Staying in Hydra's gracious old stone mansions
- Exploring the back roads of Spetses by motorcycle

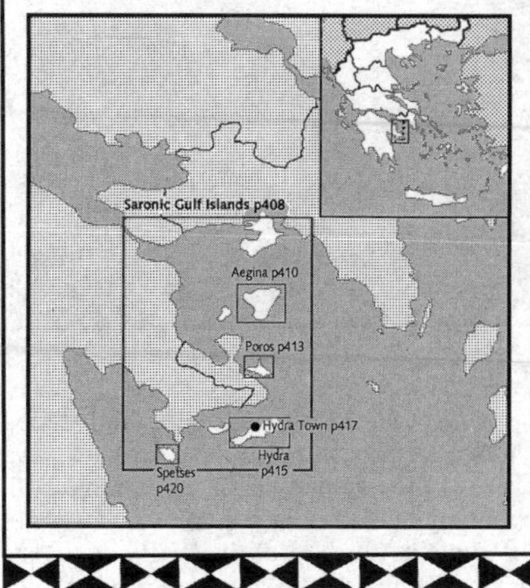

Getting There & Away

Ferry At least 10 ferries daily sail from Piraeus' Great Harbour to Aegina Town (1½ hours, 1400 dr). Three continue to Poros (three hours, 2100 dr), two keep going to Hydra (3½ hours, 2300 dr), and one goes all the way to Spetses (4½ hours, 3200 dr).

Hydrofoil & Catamaran Minoan Lines operates a busy schedule to the islands and nearby Peloponnesian ports with its Flying Dolphin hydrofoils. Services to Aegina leave from Piraeus' Great Harbour, while services to Hydra, Poros and Spetses leave from both the Great Harbour and Zea Marina – be sure to note the departure point.

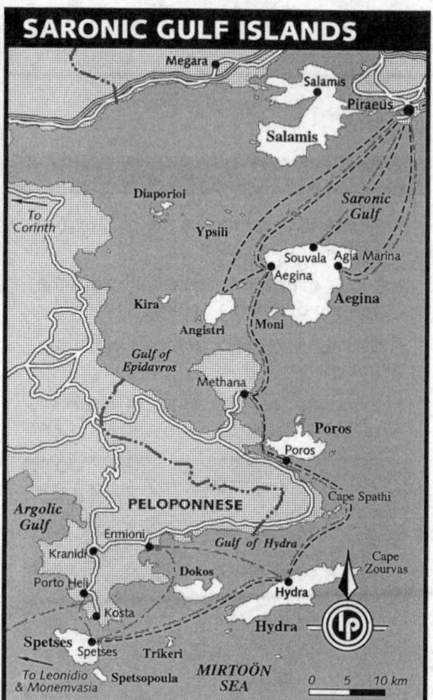

Minoan Lines also operates high-speed catamarans on some routes. These Flying Cats, as the company calls them, have both economy and VIP class. Economy fares are the same as for hydrofoils; VIP class costs twice as much – and gets you a plush red-leather seat, free drinks and headphone music.

Getting Around

There is a comprehensive network of ferries and hydrofoils linking the Saronic Gulf Islands. See individual island entries for details.

Organised Tours The *Aegean Glory* offers a daily cruise from Piraeus to the islands of Aegina, Poros and Hydra. Passengers get to spend about an hour on shore at each island – long enough to buy a souvenir and take the obligatory 'been there, done that photo'. You'll see the cruise advertised all over Athens for 19,000 dr, which includes a buffet lunch. The cruises operate all year.

Aegina Αίγινα

☎ 0297 • postcode 180 10 • pop 11,000

Unassuming Aegina (**eh**-yee-nah) was once a major player in the Hellenic world, thanks largely to its strategic position at the mouth of the Saronic Gulf. It began to emerge as a commercial centre in about 1000 BC. By the 7th century BC, it was the premier maritime power in the region and amassed great wealth through its trade with Egypt and Phoenicia. The silver 'turtle' coins minted on the island at this time are thought to be the first coins produced in Europe. The Aeginian fleet made a major contribution on the Greek side at the Battle of Salamis.

Athens, uneasy about Aegina's maritime prowess, attacked the island in 459 BC. Defeated, Aegina was forced to pull down its city walls and surrender its fleet. It did not recover.

The island's other brief moment in the spotlight came during 1827 to 1829, when it was declared the temporary capital of partly liberated Greece. The first coins of the modern Greek nation were minted here.

Aegina has since slipped into a more humble role as Greece's premier producer of pistachio nuts. The writer Nikos Kazantzakis was fond of the island and wrote *Zorba the Greek* while living in a house in Livadi, just north of Aegina Town.

Aegina was named after the daughter of the river god, Asopus. According to mythology, Aegina was abducted by Zeus and taken to the island. Her son by Zeus, Aeacus, was the grandfather of Achilles of Trojan War fame.

Getting There & Away

Ferry In summer there are at least 10 ferries daily from Aegina Town to Piraeus (1½ hours, 1400 dr) as well as services from Agia Marina (1000 dr) and Souvala (950 dr). There are at least three boats daily to Poros (1½ hours, 1100 dr) via Methana (40 minutes, 1000 dr), two daily to Hydra (two hours, 1600 dr), and one to Spetses (three hours, 2400 dr). The ferry companies have ticket offices at the quay, where you'll find a full list of the day's sailings.

Hydrofoil Hydrofoils operate almost hourly from 7 am to 8 pm between Aegina Town and the Great Harbour at Piraeus (35 minutes, 2700 dr). Services south are restricted to two daily to Poros (40 minutes, 2400 dr) via Methana (20 minutes, 1900 dr). Tickets are sold at the quay in Aegina Town.

Services from Piraeus to Agia Marina (30 minutes) and Souvala (25 minutes) are operated by Sea Falcon Lines. Both trips cost 2200 dr one way, 3600 dr return.

Getting Around

There are frequent buses from Aegina Town to Agia Marina (30 minutes, 400 dr), via Paleohora and the Temple of Aphaia. Other buses go to Perdika (15 minutes, 230 dr) and Souvala (20 minutes, 300 dr). Departure times are displayed outside the ticket office in Plateia Ethnegersias.

There are numerous places to hire motorcycles.

AEGINA TOWN

Aegina Town, on the west coast, is the island's capital and main port. The town is a charming and bustling, if slightly ramshackle, place; its harbour is lined with colourful caïques. Several of the town's crumbling neoclassical buildings survive from its days as the Greek capital.

Orientation & Information

The ferry dock and nearby small quay used by hydrofoils are on the western edge of town. A left turn at the end of the quay leads to Plateia Ethnegersias, where you'll find the bus terminal and post office. The town beach is 200m farther along. A right turn at the end of the quay leads to the main harbour.

Aegina doesn't have an official tourist office. The 'tourist offices' you'll see advertised on the waterfront are booking agencies, which will do no more than add a 25% commission to the price of whatever service you care to nominate. The tourist police (☎ 27 777) are on Leonardou Lada, opposite the hydrofoil quay. The port police (☎ 22 328) are next to the hydrofoil ticket office at the entrance to the hydrofoil quay.

The OTE is off Aiakou, which heads inland next to the port authority building. The National Bank of Greece is on the waterfront just past Aiakou, and the Credit Bank is 150m farther around the harbour. You can check your email at the Nesant Internet Cafe, Afeas 13, which is open 10 am to 2 am daily.

Temple of Apollo

'Temple' is a bit of a misnomer for the one Doric column which stands at this site. The column is all that's left of the 5th century Temple of Apollo which once stood on the Hill of Koloni. The hill was the site of the ancient acropolis, and there are remains of a Helladic (early) settlement. The site, on the far side of the town beach, also has a **museum**. Both are open 8.30 am to 3 pm Tuesday to Sunday. Admission is 500 dr.

Places to Stay

The best place to head for is ***Hotel Plaza*** *(☎ 25 600, fax 28 404)*, on the waterfront 100m past Plateia Ethnegersias. It has good singles/doubles overlooking the sea for 4500/7500 dr with bathroom. There are several ***domatia*** at the top of Leonardou Lada offering rooms with bathroom for 6000/9000 dr.

Hotel Artemis *(☎ 25 195, fax 28 466, email pipinis@otenet.gr)*, north of Plateia Ethnegersias, is virtually unrecognisable following a change of management and a complete refit. It has a wide range of rooms and offers good discounts for midweek visitors. Rooms with bathroom cost 7500/8500 dr, with air-con an extra 2000 dr.

The most interesting rooms in town are at ***Eginitiko Arhontiko*** *(☎ 24 968, fax 24 156)*, located 100m from the harbour at the junction of Aiakou and Thomaïdou. This fine 19th century sandstone *arhontiko* has beautifully furnished rooms for 10,000/15,000 dr, and a splendid, ornate two-room suite for 28,000 dr. The drawback here is the constant ringing of the church bells next door.

Xenon Pavlou Guest House *(☎ 22 795)* is popular, even if the prices are a bit steep at 9000/13,000 dr. The guesthouse is on the far side of the harbour from the ferry dock, at the back of the square next to the church.

Places to Eat

The harbourfront is lined with countless cafes and restaurants – good for relaxing and soaking up the atmosphere, but not particularly good value.

Locals prefer to head for the cluster of small *ouzeria* and restaurants around the fish markets at the southern end of the harbour. The tiny ***Restaurant I Agora*** *(Pan Irioti 47)*, behind the fish market, is a good place to start. You'll find the local speciality, barbecued octopus (1000 dr), as well

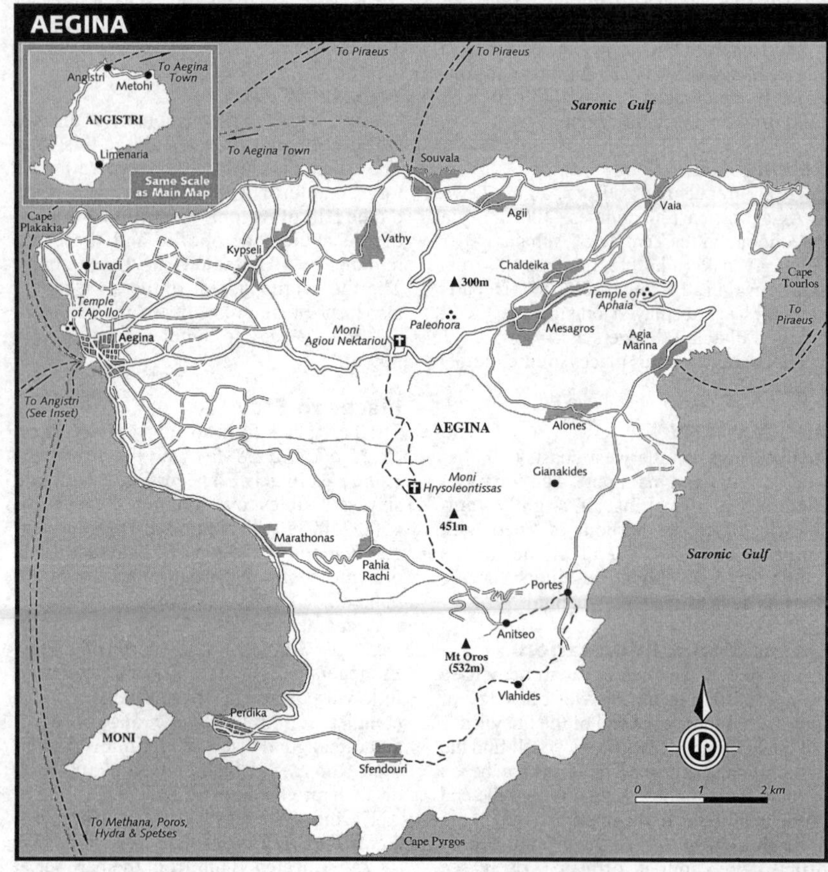

as fresh calamari (1200 dr) and sardines (900 dr).

Taverna I Synantasis *(Afeas 40)* has live music on Friday and Saturday night.

Local pistachio nuts are on sale everywhere, priced from 1000 dr for 500g.

Entertainment

There are dozens of music bars dotted around the maze of small streets behind the waterfront. ***One For The Road*** *(Afeas 3)* plays a mixture of modern Greek and rock and is popular with young people. ***Avli*** *(Pan Irioti 17)* attracts an older audience with a mixture of 60s music and Latin.

AROUND AEGINA

Temple of Aphaia

The splendid, well preserved Doric Temple of Aphaia, a local deity of pre-Hellenic times, is the major ancient site of the Saronic Gulf Islands. It was built in 480 BC when Aegina was at its most powerful.

The temple's pediments were decorated with outstanding Trojan War sculptures, most of which were spirited away in the 19th century and eventually fell into the hands of Ludwig I (father of King Otho). They now have pride of place in Munich's Glyptothek. The temple is impressive even without these sculptures. It stands on a pine-covered hill and commands imposing vistas of the Saronic Gulf and Cape Sounion.

The site (☎ 32 398) is open 8.30 am to 7 pm Monday to Friday and 8.30 am to 3 pm Saturday and Sunday. Admission is 800 dr. Aphaia is 10km east of Aegina Town. Buses to Agia Marina stop at the site. A taxi from Aegina Town costs about 2000 dr.

Paleohora Παλαιοχώρα

The ruins of Paleohora, on a hillside 6.5km east of Aegina Town, are fascinating to explore. The town was the island's capital from the 9th century to 1826, after pirate attacks forced the islanders to flee the coast and settle inland. It didn't do them much good when the notorious pirate Barbarossa arrived in 1537, laid waste to the town and took the inhabitants off into slavery.

The ruins are far more extensive than they first appear. The only buildings left intact are the churches. There are more than two dozen of them, in various states of disrepair, dotted around the hillside. Beautiful frescoes can be seen in some of them.

In the valley below Paleohora is **Moni Agiou Nektariou**, an important place of pilgrimage. The monastery contains the relics of a hermit monk, Anastasios Kefalas, who died in 1920. When his body was exhumed in 1940 it was found to have mummified – a sure sign of sainthood in Greek Orthodoxy, especially after a lifetime of performing miracle cures. Kefalas was canonised in 1961 – the first Orthodox saint of the 20th century. The enormous new church that has been built to honour him is a spectacular sight beside the road to Agia Marina. A track leads south from here to the 16th century **Moni Hrysoleontissas**, in a lovely mountain setting.

The bus from Aegina Town to Agia Marina stops at the turn-off to Paleohora.

Beaches

Beaches are not Aegina's strong point. The east coast town of **Agia Marina** is the island's premier tourist resort, but the beach is not great – if you can see it for package tourists. There are a couple of sandy patches that almost qualify as beaches between Aegina and Perdika, at the southern tip of the west coast.

MONI & ANGISTRI ISLETS

Νήσος Μονή & Νήσος Αγκίστρι

The Moni and Angistri islets lie off the west coast of Aegina, opposite Perdika. Moni, the smaller of the two, is a 10 minute boat ride from Perdika – frequent boats make the trip in summer.

Angistri is much bigger with around 500 inhabitants. There's a sandy beach at the port and other smaller beaches around the coast. Both package-holiday tourists and independent travellers find their way to Angistri, which has ***tavernas***, ***hotels*** and ***domatia***. There are regular boats to Angistri from Aegina Town (600 dr) and from Piraeus (1100 dr).

Poros Πόρος

☎ 0298 • postcode 180 20 • pop 4000

The island of Poros is little more than a stone's throw from the mainland. The slender passage of water that separates it from the Peloponnesian town of Galatas is only 360m wide at its narrowest point.

Poros was once two islands, Kalavria and Sferia. These days they are connected by a narrow isthmus, cut by a canal for small boats and rejoined by a road bridge. The vast majority of the population lives on the small volcanic island of Sferia, which is more than half-covered by the town of Poros. Sferia hangs like an appendix from the southern coast of Kalavria, a large, well forested island that has all the package hotels. The town of Poros is not wildly exciting, but it can be used as a base for exploring the ancient sites of the adjacent Peloponnese.

Getting There & Away

Ferry There are up to eight ferries daily to Piraeus (three hours, 2100 dr), via Methana and Aegina (1½ hours, 1200 dr), two daily to Hydra (one hour, 1000 dr), and one to Spetses (two hours, 1600 dr). Ticket agencies are opposite the ferry dock.

Small boats shuttle constantly between Poros and Galatas (80 dr) on the mainland. They leave from the quay opposite Plateia Iroön in Poros Town. Car ferries to Galatas leave from the dock on the road to Kalavria.

Hydrofoil Services from Poros to Piraeus (one hour, 4000 dr) are evenly split between the Great Harbour and Zea Marina, with up to five daily to each. Two daily travel via Methana and Aegina (40 minutes, 2400 dr). There are also seven hydrofoils south to Hydra (30 minutes, 2000 dr) and five to Spetses (one hour, 3300 dr) and Porto Heli.

The Flying Dolphin agency is on Plateia Iroön, and has a timetable of departures outside.

Getting Around

The Poros bus operates almost constantly along a route that starts near the hydrofoil dock on Plateia Iroön in Poros Town. It crosses to Kalavria and goes east along the south coast as far as Moni Zoödohou Pigis (150 dr), then turns around and heads west as far as Neorion Beach.

Some of the caïques operating between Poros and Galatas switch to ferrying tourists to beaches in summer. Operators stand on the waterfront and call out their destinations.

There are several places on the road to Kalavria offering bikes for hire, both motorised and pedal-powered. They include Kostas Bikes, near Cinema Diane.

POROS TOWN

Poros Town is the island's main settlement. It's a pretty place of white houses with terracotta-tiled roofs, and there are wonderful views over to the mountains of Argolis. It is a popular weekend destination for Athenians as well as for package tourists and cruise ships.

Orientation & Information

The main ferry dock is at the western tip of Poros Town, overlooked by the striking blue-domed clock tower. A left turn from the dock puts you on the waterfront road leading to Kalavria. The OTE building is on the right after 100m. A right turn at the ferry dock leads along the waterfront facing Galatas. The first square (triangle actually) is Plateia Iroön, where the hydrofoils dock. The bus leaves from next to the kiosk at the eastern end of the square.

The next square along is Plateia Karamis, where the post office is located. The National Bank of Greece is 500m farther along the waterfront. There are branches of the Credit Bank and the Bank Emporiki on Plateia Iroön.

Poros does not have a tourist office. The tourist police (☎ 22 462/256) are at Dimosthenous 10 – behind the Poros high school. Dimosthenous runs inland from the road to Kalavria, starting just beyond the small supermarket.

Suzi's Laundrette Service, next to the OTE, charges 2000 dr to wash and dry a 5kg load.

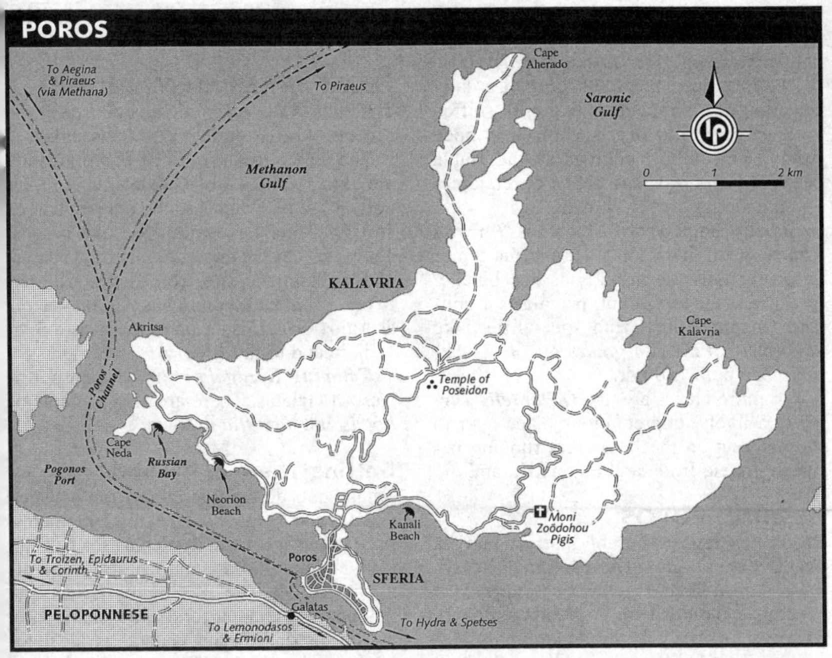

Places to Stay

Poros has very little cheap accommodation. The cheapest rooms are at ***Hotel Aktaion*** *(☎ 22 281)* on Plateia Iroön, which charges 6300/7200 dr for basic singles/doubles.

If things are not too hectic, you may be offered a room by one of the domatia owners when you get off the ferry. Otherwise, head left along the waterfront and turn right after about 400m, beyond the small supermarket. There are lots of ***domatia*** on the streets around here.

The place to be for a room with a view is the charming ***Villa Tryfon*** *(☎ 22 215, 25 854)*, on top of the hill overlooking the port. Double rooms are 11,000 dr, and all have bathroom and kitchen facilities as well as great views over to Kalavria. To get there, turn left from the ferry dock and take the first right up the steps 20m past the Agricultural Bank of Greece. Turn left at the top of the steps on Aikaterinis Hatzopoulou Karra, and you will see the place signposted up the steps to the right after 150m.

The Seven Brothers Hotel *(☎ 23 412)*, on Plateia Iroön, is a smart C class hotel with large, comfortable rooms for 12,000/16,000 dr.

The travel agents opposite the ferry dock also handle accommodation. They include Hellenic Sun Travel (☎ 22 636, fax 25 653, email sungr1@compulink.gr) and Family Tours (☎ 23 743, fax 24 480).

Places to Eat

Poros has a couple of excellent restaurants. It's worth coming to the island just to eat at ***Taverna Karavolos*** *(☎ 26 158)*, behind the Cinema Diana on the road to Kalavria. Karavolos means 'big snail' in Greek and is the nickname of cheerful owner Theodoros. Sure enough, snails (1000 dr) are a speciality of the house – served in a delicious thick tomato sauce. You'll find a range of imaginative *mezedes* like *taramokeftedes* (fish roe balls) priced from 800 dr, and a daily selection of main courses like pork stuffed with garlic (1500 dr). The place is open from 7 pm daily. Bookings are advisable because Theodoros has only a dozen tables – and a strong local following.

Equally popular with locals is ***Taverna Platanos***, on the small square at the top of Dimosthenous. Owner Tassos is a butcher by day and the restaurant specialises in spit-roast meats. You'll find specialities like *kokoretsi* (offal) and *gouronopoulo* (suckling pig), both 1400 dr.

For more basic fare, try ***O Pantelis Taverna***, a lively, unpretentious place next to the markets on the backstreet running between Plateia Iroön and Plateia Karamis.

AROUND POROS

Poros has few places of interest and its beaches are no great shakes. **Kanali Beach**, on Kalavria 1km east of the bridge, is a mediocre pebble beach. **Neorion Beach**, 3km west of the bridge, is marginally better. The best beach is reputedly at **Russian Bay**, 1.5km past Neorion.

The 18th century **Moni Zoödohou Pigis** has a beautiful gilded iconostasis which came from Asia Minor and is decorated with paintings from the gospels. The monastery, on Kalavria, is well signposted and is 4km east of Poros Town.

From the road below the monastery you can strike inland to the 6th century **Temple of Poseidon**. The god of the sea and earthquakes was the principal deity worshipped on Poros. There's very little left of this temple, but the walk is worthwhile for the scenery on the way. From the site there are superb views of the Saronic Gulf and the Peloponnese. The orator Demosthenes, after failing to shake off the Macedonians who were after him for inciting the city-states to rebel, committed suicide here in 322 BC.

From the ruins you can continue along the road, which eventually winds back to the bridge. The road is drivable, but it's also a fine 6km walk that will take around 1½ hours.

PELOPONNESIAN MAINLAND

The Peloponnesian mainland opposite Poros can easily be explored from the island.

The vast citrus groves of **Lemonodasos** are 2km south-east of **Galatas**. About 9km north-west of Galatas is the ancient site of **Troizen**, legendary birthplace of Theseus. Take a bus to Dhamala, 6km from Galatas, and walk to the site from there. Alternatively, a Methana-bound bus will let you off at Agios Georgios, from where it is a 3km walk inland to the site.

Camping Kyragelo is about 1km north-west of Galatas. There are also a couple of ***hotels*** and ***domatia*** in town.

Getting There & Around

Small boats do the five minute run between Galatas and Poros (80 dr) every 10 minutes. A couple of buses daily depart for Nafplio (two hours, 1300 dr) and can drop you off at the ancient site of Epidaurus (see the Peloponnese chapter for details on this site).

The district around Galatas is ideal for exploring by bicycle. These can be hired on the seafront in Galatas.

Hydra Υδρα

☎ 0298 • postcode 180 10 • pop 3000

Hydra (**ee**-drah) is the Saronic Gulf island with the most style. The gracious stone, white and pastel mansions of Hydra Town are stacked up the rocky hillsides that surround the fine natural harbour. Film-makers were the first foreigners to be seduced by the beauty of Hydra. They began arriving in the 1950s when the island was used as a location for the film *Boy on a Dolphin*, among others. The artists and writers moved in next, followed by the celebrities, and nowadays it seems the whole world is welcomed ashore.

If you've been in Greece for some time you may fall in love with Hydra for one reason alone – the absence of kamikaze

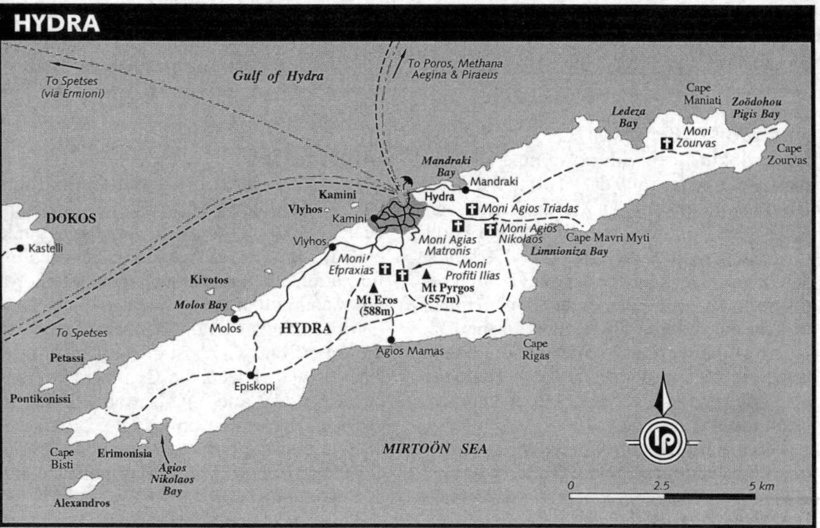

motorcyclists. Hydra has no motorised transport except for sanitation and construction vehicles. Donkeys (hundreds of them) are the only means of transport.

The name Hydra suggests that the island once had plenty of water. Legend has it that the island was once covered with forests, which were destroyed by fire. Whatever the story, these days the island is almost totally barren and imports its water from the Peloponnese.

History

Like many of the Greek islands, Hydra was ignored by the Turks, so many Greeks from the Peloponnese settled on the island to escape Ottoman suppression and taxes. The population was further boosted by an influx of Albanians. Agriculture was impossible, so these new settlers began building boats. By the 19th century, the island had become a great maritime power. The canny Hydriots made a fortune by running the British blockade of French ports during the Napoleonic Wars. The wealthy shipping merchants built most of the town's grand old arhontika from the considerable profits. It became a fashionable resort for Greek socialites, and lavish balls were a regular feature.

Hydra made a major contribution to the War of Independence. Without the 130 ships supplied by the island, the Greeks wouldn't have had much of a fleet with which to blockade the Turks. It also supplied leadership in the form of Georgios Koundouriotis, who was president of the emerging Greek nation's national assembly from 1822 to 1827, and Admiral Andreas Miaoulis, who commanded the Greek fleet. Streets and squares all over Greece are named after these two.

A mock battle is staged in Hydra harbour during the Miaoulia Festival held in honour of Admiral Miaoulis in late June.

Getting There & Away

Ferry There are two ferries daily to Piraeus (3½ hours, 2300 dr), sailing via Poros (1000 dr), Methana (1500 dr) and Aegina (1600 dr). There's also a daily boat to Spetses (one hour, 1200 dr). Departure times are listed on a board at the ferry dock.

You can buy tickets from Idreoniki Travel (☎ 54 007), just off the waterfront on the street leading to the post office and market.

Hydrofoil Hydra is well served by the Flying Dolphin fleet with up to nine services daily to Piraeus (4600 dr) – two to the Great Harbour, the rest to Zea Marina. Direct services take 1¼ hours, but most go via Poros (30 minutes, 2000 dr) and take 1½ hours. There are also frequent services to Spetses (30 minutes, 2300 dr), some of which call at Ermioni, adding 20 minutes to the trip. Many of the services to Spetses continue to Porto Heli (50 minutes, 2500 dr). There are also occasional services to Kyparissi, Leonidio and Monemvasia.

The Flying Dolphin office (☎ 53 814) is on the waterfront opposite the ferry dock.

Getting Around

In summer, there are caïques from Hydra Town to the island's beaches. There are also water taxis (☎ 53 690) which will take you anywhere you like. A water taxi to Kamini costs 1600 dr, and 2500 dr to Mandraki and Vlyhos.

The donkey owners clustered around the port charge around 2500 dr to transport your bags to the hotel of your choice.

HYDRA TOWN

Most of the action in Hydra Town is concentrated around the waterfront cafes and shops, leaving the upper reaches of the narrow, stepped streets virtually deserted – and a joy to explore.

Orientation

Ferries and hydrofoils both dock on the eastern side of the harbour. The town's three main streets all head inland from the waterfront at the back of the harbour. Walking around from the ferry dock, the first street you come to is Tombazi, at the eastern corner. The next main street is Miaouli, on the left before the clock tower, which is the town's main thoroughfare. The third is Lignou, at the western extreme. It heads inland and links up with Kriezi, which runs west over the hills to Kamini. Lignou is best reached by heading up Votsi, on the left after the clock tower, and taking the first turn right.

Information

There is no tourist office, but Saitis Tours (☎ 52 184, fax 53 469), on the waterfront near Tombazi, puts out a useful free guide called *Holidays in Hydra*. You can find information about the island on the Internet at www.compulink.gr/hydranet.

Most things of importance are close to the waterfront. The post office is on a small side street between the Commercial (Emporiki) Bank and the National Bank of Greece. The tourist police (☎ 52 205) can be found at the police station opposite the OTE on Votsi from mid-May until the end of September.

You can check your email at Hydranet, 100m from the waterfront on Lignou. It's open 10.30 to 2.30 pm daily.

There's a laundry service in the small market square just past the post office. It's open 9 am to 9 pm daily (4 to 9 pm on Sunday) and charges 2200 dr to wash and dry a load.

Things to See

The **Historical Archives Museum of Hydra** is close to the ferry dock on the eastern side of the harbour. It houses a collection of portraits and naval oddments, with an emphasis on the island's role in the War of Independence. The museum is open 10 am to 5 pm Tuesday to Sunday. Admission is 500 dr.

The **Byzantine Museum**, upstairs at the Monastery of the Assumption of Virgin Mary, houses a collection of icons and assorted religious paraphernalia. It's open 10 am to 5 pm Tuesday to Sunday. Admission is 500 dr. The entrance is through the archway beneath the clock tower on the waterfront.

The **Georgios Koundouriotis mansion**, overlooking the harbour from the west, is destined to become the town's third museum once renovation work has been

BRIGITTE BARTA

Temple of Apollo, Naxos, with the city behind

DIANA MAYFIELD

Old doorway in Hania's Venetian quarter, Crete

PATRICK HORTON

Ancient acropolis of Lindos, on Rhodes, established 3000 years ago (Dodecanese).

GEORGE TSAFOS

Whitewashed houses of picturesque Skyros Town, Skyros (Sporades)

JON DAVISON

Stark Cycladic architecture on Syros

JON DAVISON

Ancient storage jars, Knossos, Crete

completed. Koundouriotis was a wealthy shipowner as well as a War of Independence leader, and the mansion houses a large portrait collection. It's unlikely to be open to the public before 2001.

Places to Stay

Accommodation in Hydra is generally of a very high standard, and you pay accordingly for it. The prices listed here are for the high season, which in Hydra means every weekend as well as July and August.

Places to Stay – Budget

The cheapest rooms are at ***Hotel Dina*** *(☎ 52 248)* on Stavrou Tsipi. It's a small, cheery place offering singles/doubles with bathroom for 10,000/12,000 dr. The location, high up on Stavrou Tsipi, means great views over the town and harbour.

Another popular place is ***Pension Theresia*** *(☎ 53 984, fax 53 983)*, about 300m from the waterfront on Tombazi. It has clean, comfortable rooms with bathroom for 10,000/15,000 dr.

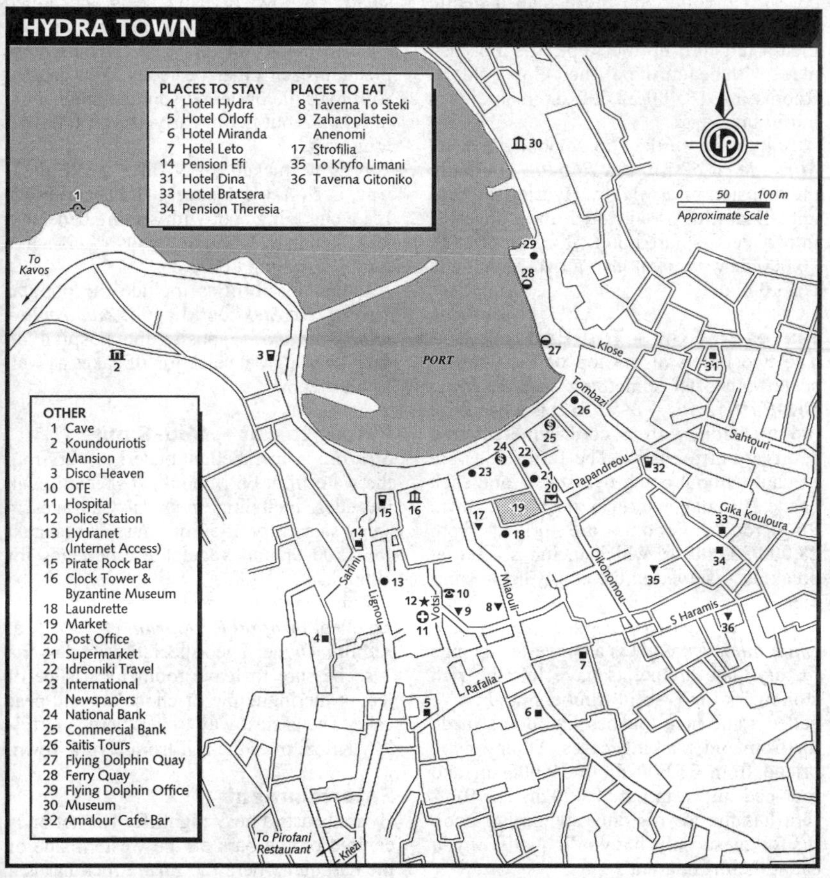

You'll find similar prices at ***Pension Efi*** *(☎ 52 371)*, close to the harbour at the junction of Lignou and Sahini.

Places to Stay – Mid-Range

Hotel Hydra *(☎ 52 102)* has a great setting overlooking the town from the west. It has large, comfortable rooms for 12,000/17,000 dr with bathroom. It's a fair haul to get there – more than 100 steps up Sahini from Lignou – but the views over the town and harbour are worth it.

Finding ***Hotel Leto*** *(☎ 53 385, fax 53 806)* involves no more than a gentle stroll up Miaouli to the first square, and then a left turn up the steps. It's a stylish place with beautiful polished timber floors. Rooms are 16,400/22,000 dr, including a buffet breakfast.

A little bit further up Miaouli is ***Hotel Miranda*** *(☎ 52 230, fax 53 510)*, originally the mansion of a wealthy Hydriot sea captain. Beautifully renovated and converted into a very smart hotel, it costs 16,000/20,000 dr with breakfast; a two-room suite is 33,000 dr.

Places to Stay – Top End

The two hotels at the top of the comfort scale both offer something special. ***Hotel Orloff*** *(☎ 52 564, fax 53 532)* is a beautiful old mansion with a cool, vine-covered courtyard at the back. The furnishings are elegant without being overstated, and each of the 10 rooms has a character of its own. Single/double rooms are priced from 28,000/32,000 dr, which includes a buffet breakfast – served in the courtyard in summer.

Hotel Bratsera *(☎ 53 971, fax 53 626, email tallos@hol.gr)* is a converted sponge factory. The architects have left the rich stonework and solid timbers and have added some nice touches like doors made up from old packing cases. Doubles are priced from 31,000 dr to 39,000 dr, and four-bed suites start at 50,000 dr. The Bratsera has the town's only swimming pool. It's for guests only, but you'll qualify if you eat at their restaurant.

Places to Eat – Budget

Hydra has dozens of tavernas and restaurants. Unlike the hotels, there are plenty of cheap places around – especially if you're prepared to head away from the waterfront.

Taverna Gitoniko, on Spilios Haramis, is better known by the names of its owners, Manolis and Christina. The menu is nothing special, but they have built up an enthusiastic local following through the simple formula of turning out consistently good traditional taverna food. Try their beetroot salad – a bowl of baby beets and boiled greens with a dollop of cold, very garlicky, mashed potato on top. The flavours complement each other perfectly. You can eat well for 2500 dr per person, including a jug of *retsina*, but get in early or you'll have a long wait.

Nearby, tucked away on a small alleyway, is ***To Kryfo Limani*** (The Secret Port). It's a charming spot with seating beneath a large lemon tree, and delicious specials like hearty fish soup (1600 dr).

Other possibilities include the popular ***Taverna To Steki*** on Miaouli. ***Zaharoplasteio Anenomi***, opposite the hospital on Votsi, has a great selection of cakes as well as ice cream.

Places to Eat – Mid-Range

Strofilia is an excellent ouzeri just up from the waterfront on Miaouli. It specialises in mezedes, including *spetsofai* (sausages in spicy sauce) for 1450 dr, mussels saganaki for 1500 dr and vegetable croquettes for 1000 dr.

For something special, head out to the excellent ***Pirofani Restaurant*** *(☎ 53 175)* at Kamini. Owner Theo specialises in desserts – so be sure to leave room for a slice of lemon meringue pie or chocolate and pear cake. The easiest way to get there is to follow Kriezi over the hill from Hydra Town.

Entertainment

Hydra boasts a busy nightlife. The action is centred on the bars on the western side of the harbour, where the ***Pirate*** rock bar is a long-standing favourite. ***Amalour***, 100m up Tombazi, is a more sophisticated cafe-bar that sells a wide range of fresh juices as well as alcohol.

Discos operate only during the summer months. The most popular is ***Disco Heaven***, overlooking the harbour on the western side and accessed from the coastal path to Kamini. ***Kavos***, with its sign made up of nautical oddments, is a popular disco just west of town on the coastal path to Kamini, but there is no point heading out there before 11 pm.

AROUND HYDRA

It's a strenuous but worthwhile one hour walk up to **Moni Profiti Ilias**, starting from Miaouli. Monks still live in the monastery, which has fantastic views down to the town. It's a short walk from here to the convent of **Moni Efpraxias**.

The beaches on Hydra are a dead loss, but the walks to them are enjoyable. **Kamini**, about 20 minutes walk along the coastal path from town, has rocks and a very small pebble beach. **Vlyhos**, 20 minutes farther on, is an attractive village with a slightly larger pebble beach, two tavernas and a ruined 19th century stone bridge. There are ***domatia*** at Vlyhos as well as ***Antigoni's Apartments*** *(☎ 53 228)*, which has self-catering apartments to sleep four/six for 16,000/24,000 dr.

From here, walkaholics can continue to the small bay at **Molos**, or take a left fork before the bay to the inland village of **Episkopi**. There are no facilities at Episkopi or Molos.

An even more ambitious walk is the three hour stint from Hydra Town to **Moni Zourvas**, in the north-east of the island. Along the way you will pass **Moni Agias Triadas** and **Moni Agios Nikolaos**.

A path leads east from Hydra Town to the pebble beach at **Mandraki**. The beach is the exclusive reserve of ***Hotel Miramare*** *(☎ 52 300, fax 52 301)*, which has doubles with breakfast for 28,000 dr. There's a range of water sports equipment for hire, including windsurfers.

Spetses Σπέτσες

☎ 0298 • postcode 180 50 • pop 3700

Pine-covered Spetses, the most distant of the group from Piraeus, has long been a favourite with British holiday makers.

Spetses' history is similar to Hydra's. It became wealthy through shipbuilding, ran the British blockade during the Napoleonic Wars and refitted its ships to join the Greek fleet during the War of Independence. Spetsiot fighters achieved a certain notoriety through their pet tactic of attaching small boats laden with explosives to the enemy's ships, setting them alight and beating a hasty retreat.

The island was known in antiquity as Pityoussa (meaning 'pine-covered'), but the original forest cover disappeared long ago. The pine-covered hills that greet the visitor today are a legacy of the far-sighted and wealthy philanthropist Sotirios Anargyrios.

Anargyrios was born on Spetses in 1848 and emigrated to the USA, returning in 1914 an exceedingly rich man. He bought two-thirds of the then largely barren island and planted the Aleppo pines that stand today. He also financed the island's road system and commissioned many of the town's grand buildings, including the Hotel Possidonion. He was a big fan of the British public (ie private) school system, and established Anargyrios & Korgialenios College, a boarding school for boys from all over Greece. British author John Fowles taught English at the college in 1950-51, and used the island as a setting for his novel *The Magus*.

Getting There & Away

Ferry There is one ferry daily to Piraeus (4½ hours, 3200 dr), via Hydra (1200 dr), Poros (1600 dr) and Aegina (2400 dr). Two companies operate the service on alternate days. You'll find departure times on the waterfront outside Alasia Travel (☎ 74 098), which sells tickets. The port police (☎ 72 245) are opposite the quay.

Between July and September, there are also caïques to Kosta, 25 minutes away on

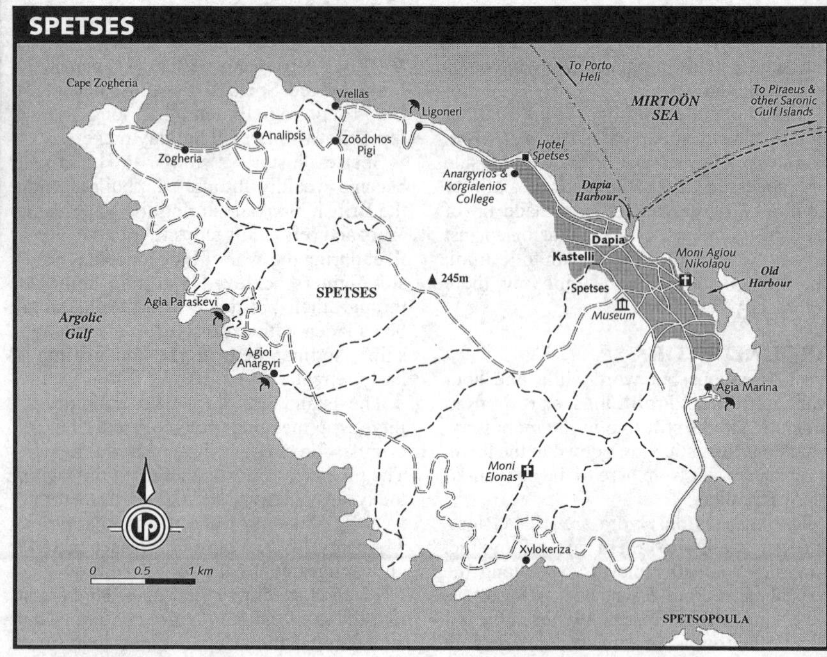

the Peloponnese. The ferries depart at 7.15 and 10 am, and at 1 and 4.30 pm; they return half an hour later. Get your ticket (130 dr) on the boat. Water taxis do the trip in 10 minutes for 3000 dr. There are three buses daily from Kosta to Nafplio (2¼ hours, 1500 dr).

Hydrofoil There are up to nine Flying Dolphins daily to Piraeus (6400 dr). Most services travel via Hydra (30 minutes, 2300 dr) and Poros (70 minutes, 3300 dr) and take about 2½ hours. In high season, there are also daily connections to Leonidio (one hour, 2400 dr) and Monemvasia (1½ hours, 4200 dr).

Getting Around

Spetses has two bus routes. There are three or four buses daily from Plateia Agias Mamas in Spetses Town to Agioi Anargyri (800 dr return), via Agia Marina and Xylokeriza. Departure times are displayed on a board by the bus stop. There are hourly buses to Ligoneri (160 dr) departing from in front of Hotel Possidonion.

No cars are permitted on the island. Unfortunately this ban has not been extended to motorbikes, resulting in there being more of the critters here than just about anywhere else.

The colourful horse-drawn carriages are a pleasant but expensive way of getting around. Prices are displayed on a board where the carriages gather by the port.

Boat Water taxis (☎ 72 072) go anywhere you care to nominate from opposite the Flying Dolphin office at Dapia Harbour. Fares are displayed on a board. Samples include 5000 dr to Agia Marina and 9000 dr to Agioi Anargyri. In summer, there are caïques from the harbour to Agioi Anargyri (1500 dr return) and Zogheria (1000 dr return).

SPETSES TOWN

Spetses Town sprawls along almost half the north-east coast of the island, reflecting the way in which the focal point of settlement has changed over the years.

There's evidence of an early Helladic settlement near the old harbour, about 1.5km east of the modern commercial centre and port of Dapia. Roman and Byzantine remains have been unearthed in the area behind Moni Agios Nikolaos, halfway between the two.

The island is thought to have been uninhabited for almost 600 years before the arrival of Albanian refugees fleeing fighting between the Turks and the Venetians in the 16th century. They settled on the hillside just inland from Dapia, the area now known as Kastelli.

The Dapia district has a few impressive arhontika, but the prettiest part of town is around the old harbour.

Lascarina Bouboulina

Spetses contributed one of the most colourful figures of the War of Independence, the dashing heroine Lascarina Bouboulina. Her exploits on and off the battlefield were the stuff of legend. She was widowed twice by the time the war began – both her ship-owning husbands had been killed by pirates, leaving her a very wealthy woman – and she used her money to commission her own fighting ship, the *Agamemnon*, which she led into battle during the blockade of Nafplio.

Bouboulina was known for her fiery temperament and her countless love affairs, and her death was in keeping with her flamboyant lifestyle – she was shot during a family dispute in her Spetses home. Bouboulina was featured on the old 50 drachma note in a dramatic portrayal of her directing cannon fire.

The Bouboulina mansion is on the western side of the square behind the OTE building. It houses a small museum, which is open 9 am to 5 pm Tuesday to Sunday. Admission is 700 dr.

Orientation & Information

The quay at Dapia Harbour serves both ferries and hydrofoils. A left turn at the end of the quay leads east along the waterfront on Sotirios Anargyris, skirting a small square where the horse-drawn carriages wait. The road is flanked by a string of uninspiring, concrete C class hotels, and emerges after 200m on Plateia Agias Mamas, next to the town beach. The bus stop for Agioi Anargyri is next to the beach. The post office is on the street running behind the hotels; coming from the quay, turn right at Hotel Soleil and then left.

The waterfront to the right of the quay is also called Sotirios Anargyris. It skirts Dapia Harbour, passes the decaying shell of the once-grand Hotel Possidonion and continues west around the bay to Hotel Spetses.

The main road inland from Dapia is N Spetson, which runs off the small square where the horse-drawn carriages wait. It soon becomes Botassi, which continues inland to Kastelli. These two streets are among the very few on Spetses with street signs.

There is no tourist office on Spetses. The tourist police (☎ 73 100) are based in the police station – on the well signposted road to the museum – from mid-May to September.

The OTE is behind Dapia Harbour, opposite the National Bank of Greece. Internet access is available at Cafe Delfinia on Plateia Agias Mamas.

Things to See

The **old harbour** is a delightful place to explore. It is ringed by old Venetian buildings, and filled with boats of every shape and size – from colourful little fishing boats to sleek luxury cruising yachts. The shipbuilders of Spetses still do things the traditional way and the shore is dotted with the hulls of emerging caïques. The walk from

Dapia Harbour takes about 20 minutes. **Moni Agios Nikolaos** straddles a headland at the halfway mark.

The **museum** is housed in the arhontiko of Hadzigiannis Mexis, a shipowner who became the island's first governor. While most of the collection is devoted to folklore items and portraits of the island's founding fathers, there is also a fine collection of ships' figureheads. It's open 8.30 am to 3 pm Tuesday to Sunday. Admission is 500 dr. The museum is clearly signposted from Plateia Orologiou.

Places to Stay – Budget

The best budget option is ***Orloff Apartments*** *(☎ 72 246, fax 74 470)*, above the old harbour on the road leading out to Agioi Anargyri – about 1.5km from the port. Manager Christos has a dozen or so well equipped studio rooms set in the gardens of the family home. Rates for singles/doubles are 8000/12,000 dr, dropping to 6000/8000 dr outside July and August.

The friendly ***Villa Marina*** *(☎ 72 646)*, just off Plateia Agias Mamas beyond the row of restaurants, is another popular place. It has good rooms with bathroom for 10,000/16,000 dr – available most of the year for 7000/10,000 dr. All rooms have refrigerators and there is a well equipped communal kitchen downstairs.

If these two are full try ***Hotel Kamelia*** *(☎ 72 415)*, signposted to the right at the supermarket, 100m past Plateia Agias Mamas on the road that leads inland to Agioi Anargyri. The place is almost hidden beneath a sprawling burgundy bougainvillea. Spotless rooms with bathroom are 10,000/12,000 dr.

Otherwise, you might be forced to fall back on one of the uninspiring C and D class places that line the waterfront between the ferry dock and Plateia Agias Mamas, or seek help from one of the travel agents.

Places to Stay – Top End

If money is no object, there are some good places at the luxury end of the market. ***Zoe's Club*** *(☎ 74 447, fax 72 841)* and ***Nissia*** *(☎ 75 000, fax 75 012, email nissia@otenet.gr)* are a couple of stylish resorts with accommodation spread around large swimming pools. Both charge close to 45,000 dr for doubles with buffet breakfast.

Zoe's is up the steps next to the post office, while Nissia is on the waterfront west of Hotel Possidonion (closed).

Places to Eat

Restaurant Stelios, between Plateia Agias Mamas and the post office, is a popular taverna that pitches for the tourist trade with a series of set menus. Prices start at 2600 dr for three courses.

Getting away from the tourist hype involves a bit of walking. The place to head for is the excellent ***Taverna O Lazaros*** *(☎ 72 600)* in the district of Kastelli, about 600m inland at the top end of Spetson. Treat yourself to a plate of *taramasalata* (800 dr); their home-made version of this popular fish roe dip is unrecognisable from the pink, food colouring-filled muck served at most Greek restaurants. The speciality of the house is baby goat in lemon sauce (1600 dr).

Restaurant Exedra, halfway around the bay on the road to Hotel Spetses, has seating on a small platform built out over the beach. Surprisingly, given its location, fish hardly features on the menu.

Fish fans should keep walking around the bay to ***Restaurant Patralis***. It has a great setting, a good menu and fish supplied by the restaurant's own boat. The fish à la Spetses (2000 dr), a large tuna or swordfish steak baked with vegetables and lots of garlic, goes down perfectly with a cold beer.

If character is what you want, you won't find a better place than ***Byzantino***, halfway to the old harbour on the other side of town. The early 19th century port-authority building has been converted into a stylish restaurant specialising in mezedes. Reckon on about 9000 dr for two, with drinks.

Self-caterers can head to ***Kritikos Supermarket***, next to Hotel Soleil on the waterfront near Plateia Agias Mamas. There is a very well stocked bottle shop across the alleyway behind it.

Entertainment

For a quiet beer and a great selection of music from the 60s and 70s, try ***Bar Spetsa***, 50m beyond Plateia Agias Mamas on the road to Agioi Anargyri. Look out for the sign that announces 'No disco, house, acid, rap or crap in here'. If that's what you're after, though, try one of the discos at the old harbour.

AROUND SPETSES

Spetses' coastline is speckled with numerous coves with small, pine-shaded beaches. A 24km road (part sealed, part dirt) skirts the entire coastline, so a motorcycle is the ideal way to explore the island.

The beach at **Ligoneri**, west of town, has the attraction of being easily accessible by bus. **Agia Marina**, to the south of the old harbour, is a small resort with a crowded beach. **Agia Paraskevi** and **Agioi Anargyri**, on the south-west coast, have good, albeit crowded, beaches; both have water sports of every description. A large mansion between the two beaches was the inspiration for the Villa Bourani in John Fowles' *The Magus*.

The small island of **Spetsopoula** to the south of Spetses is owned by the family of the late shipping magnate Stavros Niarchos.

Cyclades Κυκλάδες

The Cyclades (kih-**klah**-dez) are the quintessential Greek islands – rugged outcrops of rock dotted with brilliant white buildings offset by vividly painted balconies and bright blue church domes, all bathed in dazzling light and fringed with golden beaches lapped by aquamarine seas.

Goats and sheep are raised on the mountainous, barren islands, as well as some pigs and cattle. Naxos is the most fertile island, producing potatoes and other crops for export to Athens and neighbouring islands. Many islanders still fish, but tourism is becoming the dominant source of income.

Some islands, especially Mykonos, Santorini (Thira) and Ios, have eagerly embraced tourism – their shores are spread with sun lounges, umbrellas and water sports equipment. Other islands, such as Andros, Syros, Kea, Serifos and Sifnos, are less visited by foreigners but, thanks to their proximity to the mainland, are popular weekend and summer retreats for Athenians.

Tinos is not a holiday island but the country's premier place of pilgrimage – a Greek Lourdes. Other islands, such as Anafi and the Little Cyclades east of Naxos, are little more than clumps of rock with tiny depopulated villages.

The Cyclades are so named because they form a circle *(kyklos)* around the island of Delos, one of the country's most significant ancient sites.

The islands are small and closely grouped, making them ideal for island-hopping. It's best to avoid them in high season (July and August), when accommodation can be scarce. Most places are open only from April to October. Accommodation prices quoted throughout this chapter are for high season; expect to pay a lot less at other times.

The Cyclades are more exposed to the north-westerly *meltemi* wind than other island groups, but this usually provides a welcome respite from the heat.

HIGHLIGHTS

- Spectacular sunsets over Santorini's submerged volcano
- Walks though the verdant countryside of Naxos and Andros
- Unspoilt whitewashed villages on Amorgos and Folegandros
- Ouzo and freshly grilled fish at beachside tavernas
- Uncrowded island beaches with crystal-clear water
- The island-size archaeological site of ancient Delos
- Nightlife on Mykonos, Santorini and Ios
- Island-hopping by ferry

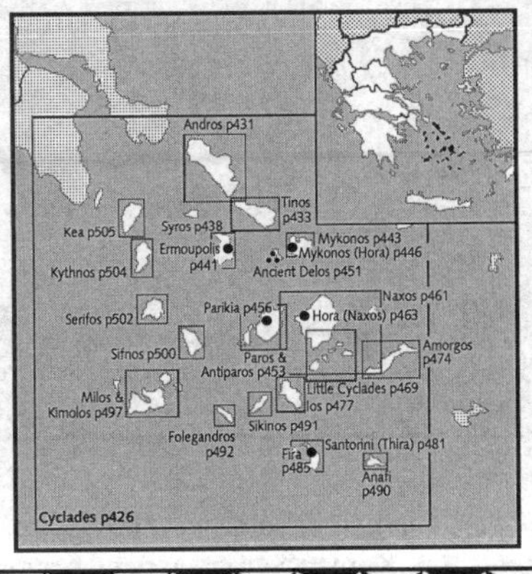

History

The Cyclades have been inhabited since at least 7000 BC, and there is evidence that the obsidian on Milos was exploited as early as 7500 BC. Around 3000 BC, the Cycladic civilisation, a culture famous for its seafarers, appeared. During the Early Cycladic

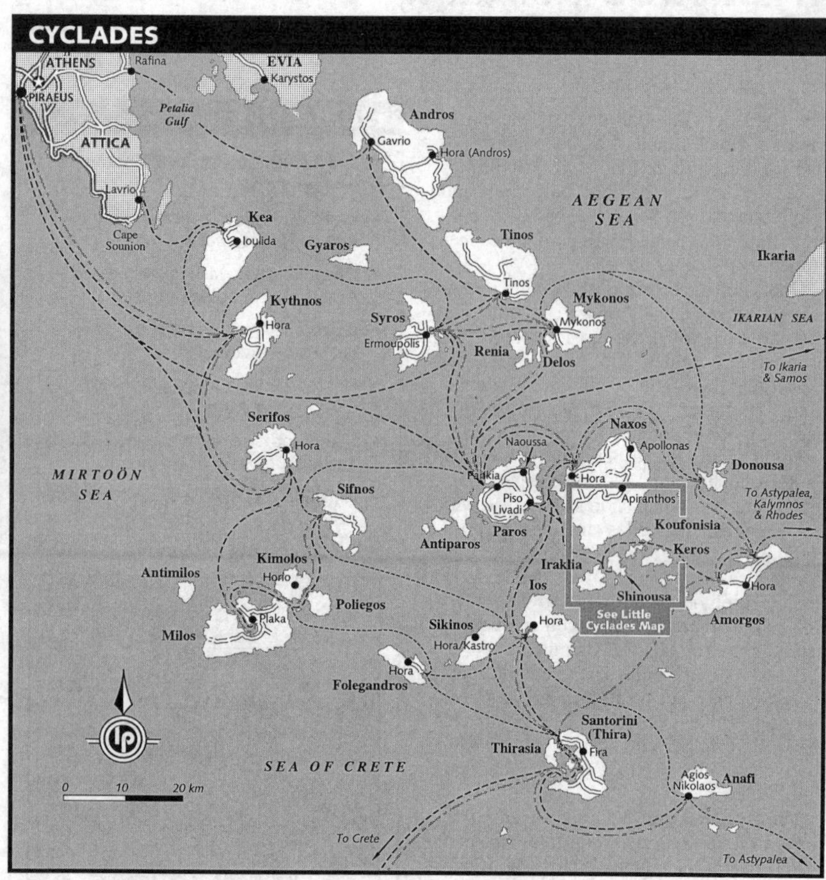

period (3000-2000 BC) there were settlements on Keros, Syros, Milos, Naxos, Milos, Sifnos and Amorgos. It was during this time that the famous Cycladic marble figurines were sculpted.

In the Middle Cycladic period (2000-1500 BC), many of the islands were occupied by the Minoans – at Akrotiri on Santorini, a Minoan town has been excavated. At the beginning of the Late Cycladic period (1500-1100 BC), the Cyclades passed to the Mycenaeans. The Dorians followed in the 8th century BC, bringing their Archaic culture with them.

Most of the Cyclades joined the Delian League in 478 BC, and by the middle of the 5th century the islands were members of a fully fledged Athenian empire. In the Hellenistic era (323-146 BC) the islands fell under the control of Egypt's Ptolemies, and, later, the Macedonians. In 146 BC, the islands became a Roman province and trade links were established with many parts of the Mediterranean, bringing prosperity.

After the division of the Roman Empire into western and eastern entities in 395 AD, the Cyclades were ruled from Byzantium (Constantinople). Following the fall of Byzantium in 1204, the Franks gave the Cyclades to Venice, which parcelled the islands out to opportunistic aristocrats. The most powerful was Marco Sanudo (self-styled Duke of Naxos), who acquired Naxos, Paros, Ios, Santorini, Anafi, Sifnos, Milos, Amorgos and Folegandros.

The islands came under Turkish rule in 1537. Neglected by the Ottomans, they became backwaters prone to pirate raids, hence the labyrinthine, hilltop character of their towns – the mazes of narrow lanes were designed to disorientate invaders. On many islands, people moved inland to escape pirates. Nevertheless, the impact of piracy led to massive depopulation; in 1563 only five out of 16 islands were still inhabited.

In 1771 the Cyclades were annexed by the Russians during the Russian-Turkish War, but were reclaimed by the Ottomans a few years later.

The Cyclades' participation in the Greek War of Independence was minimal but they became havens for people fleeing islands where insurrections against the Turks had led to massacres. During WWII the islands were occupied by the Italians.

The fortunes of the Cycladic islands have been revived by the tourism boom that began in the 1970s. Until then, many islanders lived in abject poverty and many more gave up the battle and headed for the mainland in search of work.

Getting There & Away

For information on travel within the Cyclades, see this chapter's Getting Around section and individual island entries.

Air Olympic Airways links Athens with Naxos, Syros, Santorini, Mykonos, Paros and Milos. Santorini has direct flights to/from Mykonos, Thessaloniki, Iraklio (Crete) and Rhodes, and Mykonos has flights to/from Thessaloniki and Rhodes.

At the time of writing, a few new airlines were also offering flights to the islands; see individual island entries for details.

Ferry – Domestic Ferry routes tend to separate the Cyclades into western, northern, central and eastern subgroups. Most ferries serving the Cyclades connect one of these subgroups with Piraeus, Lavrio or Rafina on the mainland.

The central Cyclades (Paros, Naxos, Ios and Santorini) are the most visited and have the best links with the mainland, usually Piraeus.

The northern Cyclades (Andros, Tinos, Syros and Mykonos) also have very good connections with the mainland. The jumping-off point for Andros is Rafina, but it's possible to access it from Piraeus by catching a ferry to Syros, Tinos or Mykonos and connecting from there.

The western Cyclades (Kea, Kythnos, Milos, Serifos, Sifnos, Folegandros and Sikinos) have less frequent connections with the mainland. Lavrio is the mainland port for ferries serving Kea.

The eastern Cyclades (Anafi, Amorgos, Iraklia, Shinousa, Koufonisia and Donousa) are the least visited and have the fewest links with the mainland. They are best visited from Naxos and Santorini.

Ferries from Paros and Naxos connect the Cyclades with Ikaria and Samos in the North-Eastern Aegean and with Rhodes in the Dodecanese. There are also a couple of boats a week from Santorini to Rhodes and one a week to Astypalea, also in the Dodecanese.

The central and northern Cyclades are linked a few times a week with Thessaloniki and once a week with Volos.

Boats from the Cretan ports of Agios Nikolaos and Sitia depart for Milos three times weekly, while ferries from Rethymno head for Sifnos twice weekly. Iraklio has frequent connections with Santorini and other islands in the central Cyclades.

The following table gives an overview of high-season ferry services to the Cyclades from the mainland and Crete.

Ferry Connections to the Cyclades

Origin	Destination	Duration	Price	Frequency
Agios Nikolaos (Crete)	Milos	7 hours	4850 dr	3 weekly
Iraklio (Crete)	Mykonos	10 hours	7100 dr	2 weekly
Iraklio	Ios	6 hours	4180 dr	1 weekly
Iraklio	Naxos	4¼-7½ hours	5000 dr	4 weekly
Iraklio	Paros	7-8 hours	4950 dr	6 weekly
Iraklio	Santorini	4 hours	3700 dr	7 weekly
Iraklio	Syros	8½ hours	5400 dr	3 weekly
Iraklio	Tinos	9 hours	6100 dr	3 weekly
Lavrio	Kea	1¼ hours	1600 dr	2 daily
Lavrio	Kythnos	3½ hours	2300 dr	2 weekly
Piraeus	Amorgos	10 hours	4500 dr	6 weekly
Piraeus	Anafi	11 hours	6700 dr	4 weekly
Piraeus	Folegandros	6-9 hours	5150 dr	8 weekly
Piraeus	Ios	7 hours	5300 dr	4 daily
Piraeus	Kythnos	2½ hours	2300 dr	1 daily
Piraeus	Milos	5-7 hours	5050 dr	10 weekly
Piraeus	Mykonos	6 hours	5100 dr	1 daily
Piraeus	Naxos	6 hours	5000 dr	8 daily
Piraeus	Paros	5 hours	4950 dr	6 daily
Piraeus	Santorini	9 hours	6100 dr	5 daily
Piraeus	Serifos	4½ hours	4000 dr	1 daily
Piraeus	Sifnos	5 hours	4400 dr	1 daily
Piraeus	Sikinos	10 hours	6000 dr	7 weekly
Piraeus	Syros	4 hours	4400 dr	3 daily
Piraeus	Tinos	5 hours	4700 dr	1 daily
Rafina	Amorgos	10¾ hours	4700 dr	1 weekly
Rafina	Andros	2 hours	2400 dr	4 daily
Rafina	Kea	1¼ hours	1900 dr	1 weekly
Rafina	Mykonos	5 hours	4100 dr	1 daily
Rafina	Paros	7 hours	4150 dr	5 weekly
Rafina	Syros	5¾ hours	3400 dr	3 weekly
Rafina	Tinos	3¾ hours	3600 dr	2 daily
Rethymno (Crete)	Sifnos	5½ hours	5100 dr	2 weekly
Sitia (Crete)	Milos	9 hours	5100 dr	3 weekly
Thessaloniki	Mykonos	18 hours	9100 dr	2 weekly
Thessaloniki	Naxos	14¾ hours	7100 dr	4 weekly
Thessaloniki	Paros	12-15 hours	9350 dr	4 weekly
Thessaloniki	Santorini	17¾ hours	10,100 dr	5 weekly
Thessaloniki	Syros	13 hours	8400 dr	2 weekly
Thessaloniki	Tinos	13 hours	9100 dr	4 weekly
Volos	Paros	8 hours	6950 dr	1 weekly
Volos	Santorini	14 hours	8100 dr	1 weekly
Volos	Tinos	9 hours	6000 dr	1 weekly

From early June to mid-October you can buy a 20-day island pass that offers round-trip travel from Piraeus to Paros, Naxos, Ios and Santorini for 16,500 dr. The passes are issued by Agapitos Express Ferries for use on their ships only, and are available from most Athens travel agents.

Ferry – International Ferries from Piraeus to Cyprus and Israel stop at Santorini and Tinos.

Hydrofoil Although hydrofoils can travel faster than ferries, they often take longer to get to their destination because of their sensitivity to bad weather and the many stops made.

Minoan is the major operator in the Cyclades. In summer, there are daily hydrofoils from the main harbour at Piraeus to Kythnos, Serifos, Sifnos and Milos, and five weekly to Kea from Zea Marina at Piraeus. There are daily hydrofoils from Iraklio (Crete) to Santorini.

Catamaran Large high-speed cats are now major players on Cyclades routes. The travel time is usually half that of regular ferries. Tickets cost about twice as much as deck-class ferry fares. Catamarans are very popular and seats fill fast – it's worth booking your ticket a day or so in advance.

Minoan operates *Highspeed 1*, which travels daily between Piraeus, Syros, Mykonos, Paros and Naxos. Strintzis Lines runs *Seajet 1* daily from Rafina to Syros, Paros, Naxos, Ios and Santorini, and *Seajet 2* daily from Rafina to Tinos and Mykonos. Once a week, *Seajet 2* continues to Syros, Paros, Naxos and Amorgos. Goutos Lines' *Athina 2004* also makes daily runs between Rafina, Tinos and Mykonos, continuing to Andros twice weekly and to Paros, Naxos and Amorgos once a week.

Getting Around

Air Olympic Airways flights between Mykonos and Santorini (15,400 dr) provide the only inter-island link within the Cyclades.

Ferry There are usually relatively good connections within each of the western, northern, central and eastern subgroups, but infrequent connections between the different subgroups. When you plan your island-hopping, it pays to bear this pattern of ferry routes in mind. However, Paros is the ferry hub of the Cyclades, and connections between different groups are usually possible via Paros if not direct.

The central Cyclades (Paros, Naxos, Ios and Santorini) have the best links with the other subgroups and each other. The northern Cyclades (Andros, Tinos, Syros and Mykonos) have very good connections with each other and with the central Cyclades.

The western Cyclades (Kea, Kythnos, Milos, Serifos, Sifnos, Folegandros and Sikinos) have less frequent connections with other Cyclades subgroups. Kea is only liked a few times a week (in high season) to Kythnos and the other islands in the western Cyclades.

The eastern Cyclades (Anafi, Amorgos, Iraklia, Shinous, Koufonisia and Donousa) are the least visited and have the fewest links with other islands. Naxos is the best jumping-off point for the Little Cyclades (Iraklia, Shinousa, Koufonisia and Donousa) and Amorgos, while Santorini has the most ferries to Anafi.

Hydrofoil Minoan is the major operator in the Cyclades. In summer, there are daily hydrofoils between Kythnos, Serifos, Sifnos and Milos, as well as frequent connections between Mykonos, Naxos, Paros and Syros.

Santorini Dolphins runs daily hydrofoils from Santorini to Ios, Naxos, Paros, Tinos and Syros, with services to Folegandros, Sikinos, Amorgos and the Little Cyclades once or twice weekly.

Catamaran There are daily cats between Syros, Mykonos, Tinos, Paros, Naxos, Ios and Santorini. Cats link Andros and Amorgos to other islands in the group twice weekly.

Andros Ανδρος

☎ 0282 • postcode 845 00 • pop 8781

Andros is the northernmost island of the Cyclades and the second largest after Naxos. It is also one of the most fertile, producing citrus fruit and olives, and is unusual in that it has retained its pine forests and mulberry woods. There is plentiful water – indeed, Andros is famous for its water, which is bottled at Sariza.

More distinctive features are its dovecotes (although Tinos has more of them) and elaborate stone walls. Many of the old water mills are now being restored. If you have a sweet tooth, seek out the island's walnut and almond sweets: *kalsounia* and *amygdolota*.

Getting There & Away

Ferry At least four ferries daily leave Andros' main port of Gavrio for Rafina (two hours, 2400 dr), Tinos (1½ hours, 1700 dr) and Mykonos (2½ hours, 2600 dr). There are ferries to Paros (four hours, 2700 dr, three weekly) and Syros (four hours, 1800 dr, weekly).

Catamaran Four catamarans weekly go to Rafina (one hour, 4700 dr), Tinos (30 minutes, 3500 dr), Mykonos (1¼ hours, 5200 dr), Paros (three hours, 5500 dr) and Naxos (3½ hours, 6000 dr.), and three go to Amorgos (4¼ hours, 8100 dr). A catamaran also runs once a week to Syros (two hours, 3700 dr).

Getting Around

Around nine buses daily (fewer on weekends) link Gavrio and Hora (750 dr) via Batsi (250 dr); if there's no schedule posted, call ☎ 22 316 for information. A taxi (☎ 22 171) from Batsi to Hora costs 4000 dr. Caïques from Batsi go to some of the island's nicest beaches.

GAVRIO Γαύριο

Gavrio, on the west coast, is the main port of Andros. Nothing much happens in Gavrio, but there are lovely beaches nearby.

Orientation & Information

The ferry quay is in the middle of the waterfront and the bus stop is next to it. Turn left from the quay and walk along the waterfront for the post office. The tourist office opposite the quay is rarely open. The telephone number of the port police is ☎ 71 213.

Places to Stay & Eat

If you decide to stay in town, look for ***domatia*** signs along the waterfront or try ***Hotel Galaxy*** *(☎ 71 005)* to the left of the quay. It has reasonable singles/doubles for 6000/7000 dr with bathroom. The B class ***Andros Holiday Hotel*** *(☎ 71 384)*, overlooking the beach, has a restaurant, bar, tennis court, sauna, jacuzzi and gym. Aircon singles/doubles/triples cost 22,000/25,000/33,500 dr with breakfast.

Veggera and ***Neraida*** are both nice eateries with tables on a large plateia one block back from the waterfront. Turn left from the quay and take the first right after the Batsi road.

BATSI Μπατσί

Batsi, 8km south of Gavrio, is Andros' major resort. The attractive town encircles a bay with a fishing harbour at one end and a nice sandy beach at the other. There is no EOT, but Greek Sun Holidays (☎ 41 198, fax 41 239) and Andros Travel (☎ 41 252, fax 41 608), near the car park, are very helpful and can handle everything from accommodation to sightseeing and ferry tickets.

The post office is near the large car park. The taxi rank, bus stop and Ionian Bank (with ATM) are all on the main square near the fishing boats. A stepped path leads up from behind the square through lush vegetation sprouting along a watercourse. Car hire is available at Auto Europe (☎ 41 995, fax 41 239).

Organised Tours

Andros Travel (see preceding section) offers an interesting range of walks and an island tour (6000 dr) that takes in Menites, Apikia, Moni Agiou Nikolaou, Korthi and Paleopolis. Guided half and full-day walks

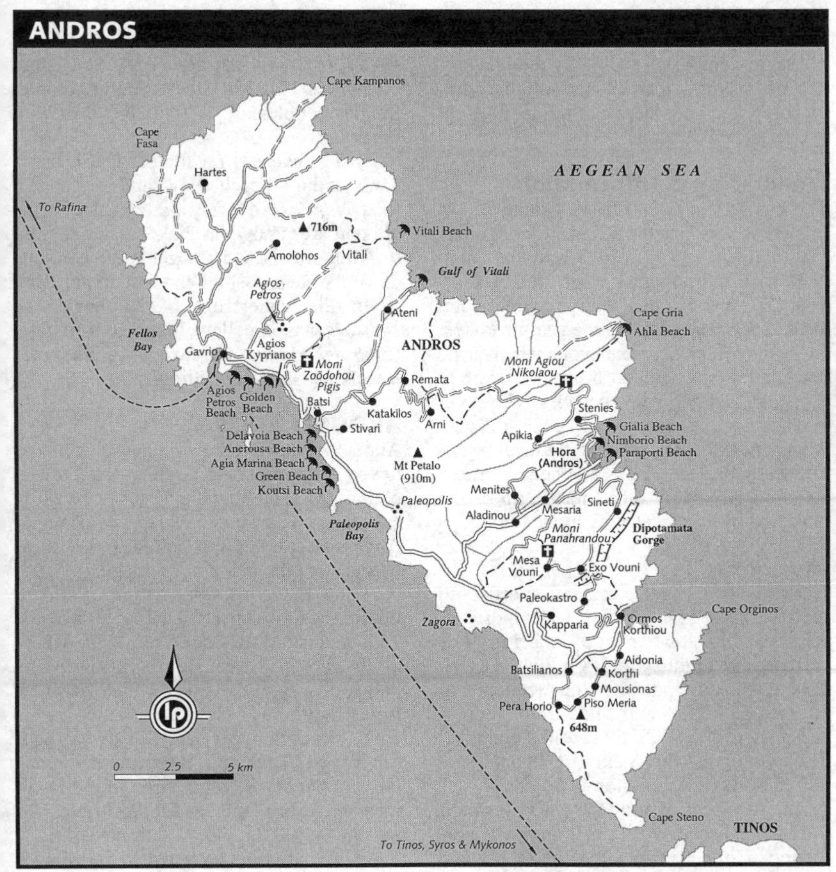

following old paths through beautiful countryside range from 4100 dr to 5200 dr.

Places to Stay & Eat

Scan the waterfront and side streets for domatia signs. ***Cavo d'Oro*** *(☎ 41 776)* at the beach end of the waterfront, above the pizzeria of the same name, has doubles for 10,000 dr with telephone and bathroom. ***Scouna Hotel*** *(☎ 41 165)*, overlooking the beach, has singles/doubles for 7500/10,000 dr with bathroom. ***Karanassos Hotel*** *(☎ 41 480)*, 50m from the beach, has pleasant rooms for 12,000/14,000 dr with bathroom. ***Hotel Chryssi Akti*** *(☎ 41 237)*, right on the beach, has a pool and charges 13,000/15,000 dr for rooms with TV, fridge, phone and balcony. ***Likio Studios*** *(☎ 41 050)* is set back from the beach amid masses of geraniums. Spotless double studios with kitchen, TV, phone and balcony cost 16,500 dr.

There are a few decent tavernas along the waterfront, including ***Oti Kalo***, ***Stamatis*** and ***Esthesis***.

HORA (ANDROS)

Hora (Χώρα) is on the east coast, 35km east of Gavrio, and is set strikingly along a narrow peninsula. It's an enchanting place full of surprises, and there are some fine old neoclassical mansions.

Orientation & Information

The bus station is on Plateia Goulandri. To the left as you face the sea is a tourist information office (☎ 25 162) and the main pedestrian thoroughfare where the post office, OTE and National Bank of Greece are. Walk along here towards the sea for Plateia Kaïri, the central square, beyond which is the headland. Steps descend from the square to Paraporti and Nimborio beaches. The street leading along the promontory ends at Plateia Riva, where there is a bronze statue of an unknown sailor. The ruins of a Venetian fortress stand on an island joined to the tip of the headland by an old, steeply arched bridge.

Museums

Hora has two outstanding museums; both were endowed by Vasili Goulandris, a wealthy ship owner and Andriot. The **archaeological museum** is on Plateia Kaïri. Its contents include the 2nd century BC Hermes of Andros and finds from Andros' two ancient cities of Zagora and Paleopolis. The museum is open 8 am to 2.30 pm Tuesday to Sunday. Admission is 500 dr.

The **museum of modern art** is a small, intimate museum with an impressive collection of 20th century Greek and European paintings and sculpture. It's around the corner immediately left of the archaeological museum and is open 10 am to 2 pm and 6 to 8 pm Saturday to Monday (closed Sunday afternoon). Admission is 200 dr.

There is also a **nautical museum** near the end of the promontory, open 10 am till 1 pm and 6 to 8 pm Saturday to Monday (closed Sunday afternoon).

Places to Stay & Eat

***Hotel Egli** (☎ 22 303)*, between the two squares, off the right side of the main road as you head towards the sea, has doubles for 14,000/18,000 dr with shared/private bathroom, including breakfast. ***Paradise Hotel** (☎ 22 187)* is a partner of the St George Lycabettus Hotel in Athens and has a pool. Singles/doubles are 17,000/28,000 dr with breakfast.

Parea Taverna, on Plateia Kaïri, has a commanding beach view and reasonable food. ***Nonnas*** is a lovely *mezedes* place in the old port area known as Plakoura, on the way to Nimborio Beach; to get there continue down the steps past the modern art museum.

On the waterfront at Nimborio, ***Ta Delfinia*** has excellent home-cooked fare. ***Cabo del Mar***, at the far end of Nimborio Beach, has a lovely setting.

AROUND ANDROS

About 2.5km from Gavrio, the **Agios Petros** tower is an imposing circular watchtower, dating from Hellenistic times – possibly earlier. It's a 30 minute walk from Camping Andros. Look for the signpost for Agios Petros, also the name of a village.

Along the coast road from Gavrio to Batsi is a turn-off left leading 5km to the 12th century **Moni Zoödohou Pigis**, where a few nuns still live. Between Gavrio and Paleopolis Bay are several nice beaches: **Agios Kyprianos** (where a former church is now a beachfront ***taverna***), **Delavoia** (nudist), **Green Beach** and **Anerousa**. ***Anerousa Beach Hotel** (☎ 41 044)*, open from May to October, offers singles/doubles/triples for 15,500/18,500/22,000 dr with breakfast.

An old path running between the villages of **Arni** and **Remata**, both east of Batsi, passes water mills. **Paleopolis**, 9km south of Batsi on the coast road, is the site of Ancient Andros, where the Hermes of Andros was found. There is little to see, but the mountain setting is lovely. **Menites**, southwest of Hora, has springs and a row of drinking fountains with spouts shaped like lions' heads.

From the pretty village of **Mesaria**, it's a strenuous two hour walk to the 12th century **Moni Panahrandou**, the island's largest and most important monastery. **Apikia**, northwest of Hora, is famous for its mineral springs. Near **Sineti**, the wild **Dipotamata Gorge** and its water mills are now EU-protected. An old cobbled path, once the main route from Korthi to Hora, leads along the gorge.

The pretty blue-green bay and holiday hamlet at **Ormos Korthiou**, in the south-east, has a lot of faded charm. ***Hotel Korthion*** *(☎ 61 218)*, on the shore, has singles/doubles for 8000/9000 dr with bath.

Tinos Τήνος

☎ 0283 • postcode 842 00 • pop 7747

Tinos is green and mountainous, like nearby Andros. The island is a Greek Orthodox place of pilgrimage, so it's hardly surprising that churches feature prominently among the attractions. The celebrated Church of Panagia Evangelistria dominates the uninteresting capital, while unspoilt hill villages and ornate whitewashed dovecotes are rural attractions.

Tinos also has a large Roman Catholic population – the result of its long Venetian occupation. The Turks didn't succeed in wresting the island from the Venetians until 1715, long after the rest of the country had surrendered to Ottoman rule.

Getting There & Away

Ferry At least six ferries daily go to Mykonos (30 minutes, 1100 dr), and around two daily go to Rafina (3¾ hours, 3600 dr) and Andros (1½ hours, 1700 dr). There is at least one daily to Syros (45 minutes, 1100 dr) and Piraeus (five hours, 4700 dr).

Four ferries weekly go to Thessaloniki (13 hours, 9100 dr), three weekly go to Paros (1½ to three hours, 1700 dr), Santorini (4¾ hours, 4000 dr), Crete (nine

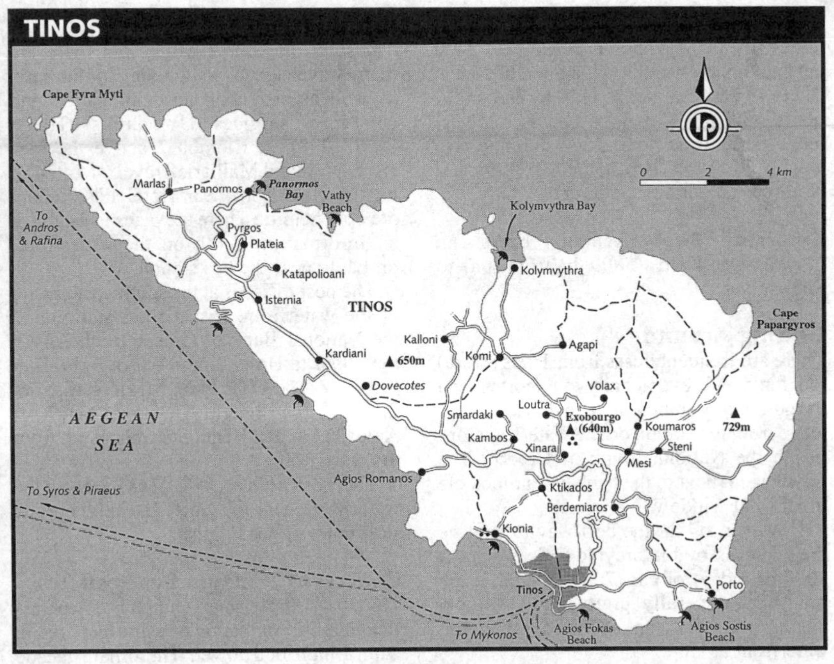

hours, 6100 dr) and Skiathos (7¼ hours, 5300 dr). There are also weekly services to Naxos (4¼ hours, 1900 dr), Iraklia (8¾ hours, 2600 dr), Shinousa (8¼ hours, 2600 dr), Koufonisia (7¾ hours, 2800 dr) and Donousa (2½ hours, 3200 dr), Amorgos (3½ hours, 2600 dr), Ios (6¼ hours, 2900 dr) and Volos (nine hours, 6000 dr).

Twice weekly there are ferries to Lemesos (Limassol) in Cyprus (38 hours) and the port of Haifa in Israel (58 hours).

Hydrofoil There are daily hydrofoils to Syros (15 minutes, 2100 dr), Mykonos (15 minutes, 2400 dr), Paros (1¼ hours, 3500 dr) and Santorini (at least 3¼ hours, 8400 dr). Five hydrofoils weekly go to Ios (3½ hours, 7100 dr) and Naxos (two hours, 3200 dr), and two go to Amorgos (5½ hours, 5100 dr), Folegandros (4½ to six hours, 5700 dr), Milos (3¼ to six hours, 6300 dr) and Sifnos (2½ hours, 6200 dr).

Catamaran There are around four catamarans daily to Mykonos (15 minutes, 2400 dr) and three to Rafina (1½ hours, 6000 dr). There are at least six weekly to Paros (1¼ hours, 3500 dr), Naxos (two hours, 3200 dr) and Andros (one hour, 3500 dr), and two weekly to Syros (two hours, 2100 dr) and Amorgos (2¾ hours, 5100 dr).

Excursion Boat Excursion boats run most days to Delos (5000 dr) from June to September.

Getting Around

There are frequent buses from Tinos (Hora) to Kionia and several daily to Panormos via Pyrgos and Kambos, and to Porto. Buses leave from the station on the waterfront, opposite the National Bank of Greece. The travel agent next to the bank has a timetable in its front window.

However, by far the best way to explore the island is by motorcycle (prices start at 3000 dr a day) or car (7000 dr a day); the roads are generally pretty good. Motorcycles and cars can be hired along the waterfront at Hora.

TINOS (HORA)

Tinos, also known as Hora, is the island's rather shabby capital and port. The waterfront is lined with cafes and hotels, while the little streets behind have shops and stalls catering to pilgrims and tourists. The Church of Panagia Evangelistria is uphill in the centre of town.

Orientation

The new ferry quay is at the north-western end of the waterfront, about 300m from the main harbour, but there are two other, more central, quays where catamarans and smaller ferries dock. When you buy your ticket, check which quay your boat departs from.

Leoforos Megaloharis, straight ahead from the main harbour, is the route pilgrims take to the church. The narrow Evangelistria, to the right facing inland, also leads to the church.

Information

Tinos has no tourist office, but there are many travel agencies supplying information as well as providing accommodation and car hire services. Windmills Travel (☎ 23 398), at Kionion 2 above the new ferry quay, and Malliaris Travel (☎ 24 241), on the waterfront near Hotel Posidonion, are both helpful. There are plans to establish an information booth on the waterfront, probably near the bus station.

The post office is at the south-eastern end of the waterfront, past the bus station and the National Bank of Greece (with ATM), next door to Hotel Tinion – turn right from the quay. The OTE is on Megaloharis, not far from the church. The town beach of Agios Fokas is a 10 minute walk south from the waterfront.

The port police (☎ 22 348) are on the waterfront, near the Hotel Oceanis, but the staff don't speak English.

Church of Panagia Evangelistria

This surprisingly small church is a neoclassical marble confection of white and cream, with a high bell tower. The ornate facade

Beware the Evil Eye

When travelling through Greece – particularly in rural areas – you may notice that some bus drivers keep a chain bearing one or two blue stones dangling over the dashboard. Or you may spot a small, plastic blue eye attached to the cross hanging around someone's neck. Or maybe you'll wonder why there is a string of blue beads hanging from the front fender of a tractor.

Puzzle no longer. The Greeks are not sporting colours in support of their favourite soccer team or to show a particular political leaning. No – they are warding off the evil eye.

The evil eye is associated with envy, and can be cast – apparently unintentionally – upon someone or something which is praised or admired (even secretly). So those most vulnerable to the evil eye include people, creatures or objects of beauty, rarity and value. Babies are particularly vulnerable, and those who admire them will often spit gently on them to repel any ill effects. Adults and older children who are worried about being afflicted by the evil eye will wear blue.

Who then is responsible for casting the evil eye? Well, most culprits are those who are already considered quarrelsome or peculiar in some way by the local community. And folk with blue eyes are regarded with extreme suspicion – no doubt more than partly because being blue-eyed is a trait Greeks associate with Turks. All these quarrelsome, peculiar or blue-eyed folk have to do is be present when someone or something enviable appears on the scene – and then the trouble starts.

If, during your travels, someone casts the evil eye on you, you'll soon know about it. Symptoms include dizziness, headaches, a feeling of 'weight' on the head or of tightening in the chest. Locals will point you in the direction of someone, usually an old woman, who can cure you.

The cure usually involves the curer making the sign of the cross over a glass of water; then praying silently, at the same time dropping oil into the glass. If the oil disappears from the surface, it proves you have the evil eye – but also cures it, for the 'blessed' water will be dabbed on your forehead, stomach and at two points on your chest (at the points of the crucifix).

Apparently, the cure works. But you know the old adage about prevention being better than cure. If you're worried about the evil eye, don't take any chances – wear blue.

has graceful white upper and lower colonnades. The final approach is up carpeted steps, doubtless a relief to pious souls choosing to crawl. Inside, the miracle-working icon is draped with gold, silver, jewels and pearls, and surrounded by gifts from the hopeful.

A lucrative trade in candles, icon copies, incense and evil-eye deterrents is carried out on Evangelistria. The largest candles, which are about 2m long, cost 1000 dr; after an ephemeral existence burning in the church, the wax remains are gathered, melted and resold.

Within the church complex, several **museums** house religious artefacts, icons and secular artworks. Below the church, a crypt marks the spot where the icon was found. Next to it is a memorial to the sailors killed on the *Elli*, a Greek ship torpedoed by an Italian submarine in Tinos' harbour on Assumption Day, 1940. The church and museums are open 8 am to 8 pm daily.

Archaeological Museum

This somewhat disappointing museum (☎ 22 670), below the church on Leoforos Megaloharis, has a small collection that includes impressive clay *pithoi* (large storage jars), a few Roman sculptures, and a 1st century sundial. It's open 8 am to 3 pm Tuesday to Sunday. Admission is 500 dr.

Places to Stay

Avoid Tinos on 25 March (Annunciation), 15 August (Feast of the Assumption) and 15 November (Advent), unless you want to join the huddled masses who sleep on the streets.

Camping Tinos *(☎ 22 344)* is a lovely site with good facilities south of the town, near Agios Fokas. It charges 1500 dr per adult (children 850 dr) and 900 dr to 1100 dr per tent, depending on size. Tents can be rented for 1250 dr. Cute little bungalows are 6000/4500 dr with/without bathroom. A minibus meets ferries. The camp site is signposted from the waterfront.

Look for domatia signs along Evangelistria and other streets leading inland from the waterfront. ***Rooms to Rent Giannis*** *(☎ 22 575)*, on the waterfront next to Hotel Oceanis and five minutes from the beach, is a lovely, clean, homy place run by friendly people. There's a shared kitchen (free Greek coffee) and fridge, and a laundry tub made from the local green marble. Doubles are 10,000/7000 dr with/without bathroom. There are also nice triple apartments for 15,000 dr.

Hotel Posidonion *(☎ 23 123)*, on the waterfront opposite the bus station, has bright doubles for 14,000 dr, with balcony and bathroom. The B class ***Hotel Tinion*** *(☎ 22 261)*, at the southern end of the waterfront near the roundabout, is a grand old place with marble staircase and balconies overlooking the harbour. Spacious doubles with bathroom are 14,500 dr.

Places to Eat

The waterfront is lined with places serving the usual fare – none of them outstanding. ***P Pallada Taverna***, just off the waterfront, behind Hotel Lito, is popular with the locals. It serves hearty, if somewhat oily, traditional dishes; the wine is poured from huge barrels overhead. It's opposite the only bakery on Tinos that still uses wood ovens. ***Mixhalis Taverna***, in the first lane to the right off Evangelistria, is noted for high-quality meat. ***Kypos Taverna***, behind Hotel Posidonion, also has decent food.

AROUND TINOS

Unless you've come solely to visit the church, you'll need to explore the countryside and its villages to make the most of Tinos. Most of the island is still farmed in one way or another, and you should look out for livestock (including piglets, goats and donkeys) wandering onto roads.

Kionia, 3km north-west of Hora, has several small beaches, the nearest overlooked by Tinos Beach Hotel. The site of the **Sanctuary of Poseidon & Amphitrite**, before the hotel, dates from the 4th century BC. Poseidon was worshipped because he banished the snakes that once infested the island.

At **Porto**, 6km east of Hora, there's a sandy, uncrowded beach. **Kolymvythra Bay**, beyond Komi, has two beautiful sandy beaches; a lovely road leads through reed beds and vegetable gardens to the bay.

Farther along the coast there's a small beach at **Panormos** from where distinctive green marble quarried in nearby **Marlas** was once exported. **Pyrgos** is a picturesque village where marble is still carved. There's a sculpture school and several little workshops with traditional items such as lintels and plaques (which both adorn houses around the village) and figurines for sale. About three buses per day run to Pyrgos; from there it's a pleasant 2km walk to Panormos.

The ruins of the Venetian fortress of **Exobourgo**, atop a 640m-high hill, stand sentinel over a cluster of unspoilt villages. At the fortress, built on an ancient acropolis, the Venetians made their last stand against the Turks in 1715. The ascent can be made from several villages; the shortest route is from Xinara. It's a steep climb, but the views are worth it.

The famous basket weavers of Tinos are based in the tiny, traditional village of **Volax**, nestled on a spectacular rocky plain in the centre of the island. You can usually buy direct from the workshops, but if they're shut for siesta, a cafe sells baskets as well. There is a small folkloric museum (free entry) and an attractive Catholic chapel. ***O Rokos*** *(☎ 41 989)* is one of the best tavernas on the

Azolimnos, the next beach along, has a ɛw *fish tavernas*.

Mykonos Μύκονος

☎ 0289 • postcode 846 00 • pop 6170

lykonos is perhaps the most visited and ex-ensive of all Greek islands (although these ays Santorini runs a pretty close second) nd it has the most sophisticated nightlife. Despite its reputation as the gay capital of ireece, this shouldn't – and doesn't – deter thers. The days when Mykonos was the ıvourite rendezvous for the world's rich nd famous may be over, but the island robably still has more poseurs per square ıetre than any other Mediterranean resort.

Depending on your temperament, you'll ither be captivated or take one look and stay n the ferry. Barren, low-lying Mykonos would never win a beauty contest, but it has some decent beaches and is the jumping-off point for the sacred island of Delos.

Getting There & Away

Air There are at least five flights daily to and from Athens (19,100 dr), as well as flights to Santorini (15,400 dr, five weekly), Thessaloniki (27,900 dr, three weekly) and Rhodes (22,900 dr, two weekly).

Ferry Mykonos has daily services to Rafina (five hours, 4100 dr) via Tinos (30 minutes, 1100 dr) and Andros (2½ hours, 2600 dr); to Piraeus (six hours, 5100 dr) via Tinos and Syros (1½ hours, 1500 dr); and to Naxos (three hours, 1900 dr), Paros (two hours, 1800 dr), Ios (five hours, 3100 dr) and Santorini (six hours, 3600 dr).

There are six ferries weekly to Amorgos (six hours, 3100 dr), five to Iraklia (five to

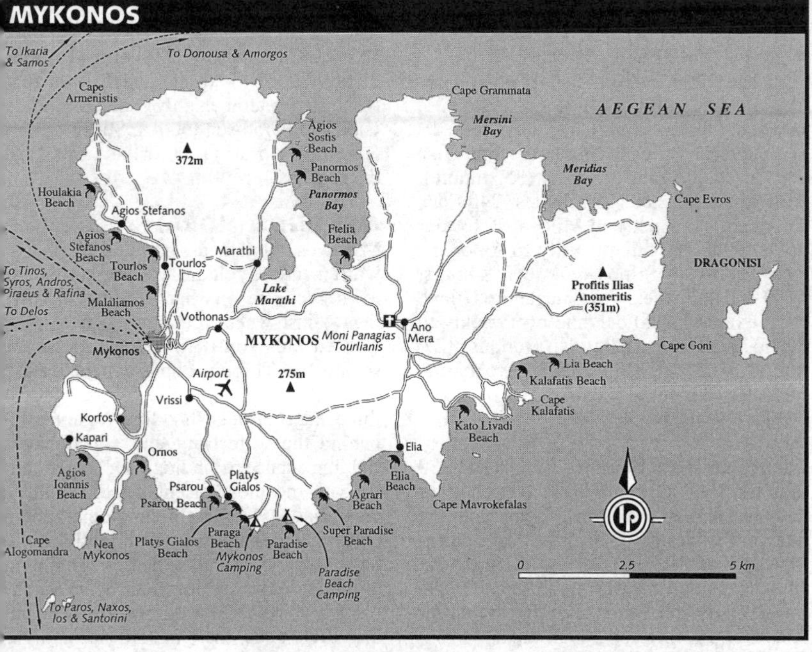

eight hours, 2100 dr), Shinousa (4½ to 7½ hours, 2500 dr) and Koufonisia (5½ to seven hours, 2500 dr), and two to Samos (3½ to 5¾ hours, 5300 dr), Patmos (four to 10 hours, 5000 dr), Lipsi (five to 11 hours, 4900 dr) and Crete (10 hours, 7100 dr). There are two weekly to Skiathos (8½ hours, 5100 dr), Thessaloniki (18 hours, 9100 dr) and Ikaria (2¾ hours, 3100 dr), and one weekly to Fourni (four hours), Leros (6¼ hours, 4300 dr), Kalymnos (seven hours, 5000 dr), Kos (eight hours, 5000 dr), Nisyros (10 hours, 4800 dr), Tilos (11 hours, 5000 dr), Symi (13 hours, 5600 dr), Rhodes (14½ hours, 6700 dr), Megisti (19 hours, 7900 dr) and Donousa (two hours, 2400 dr).

Hydrofoil & Catamaran There are daily catamarans connecting Mykonos with Andros (1¼ hours, 5300 dr), Paros (45 minutes, 3400 dr), Syros (35 minutes, 3100 dr) and Tinos (15 minutes, 2400 dr). Six weekly go to Naxos (1½ hours, 3600 dr), Piraeus (three hours, 10,000 dr) and Rafina (2½ hours, 8300 dr), and two weekly go to Amorgos (three hours, 6200 dr).

At least three hydrofoils daily go to Paros (45 minutes, 3400 dr), two go to Ios (2¾ hours, 6300 dr), Naxos (1½ hours, 3600 dr) and Santorini (three to four hours, 6800 dr), and one daily goes to Syros (35 minutes, 3100 dr) and Tinos (15 minutes, 2400 dr). There are six weekly to Milos (2¾ to four hours, 9900 dr), three weekly to Amorgos, five weekly to Sifnos (2½ to 3½ hours, 6100 dr), four weekly to Folegandros (three to five hours, 5700 dr), and one weekly to Serifos (2½ hours, 6300 dr), Donousa (2½ hours, 5800 dr), Koufonisia (two hours, 5000 dr), Shinousa (1¾ hours, 5000 dr) and Iraklia (1½ hours, 5000 dr).

Excursion Boat Boats for Delos (20 to 30 minutes, 1900 dr return) leave every hour or so between 8.30 am and 1.20 pm, from the quay at the western end of the port, returning between 12.20 and 3 pm daily except Monday (when the site is closed). Of the three, *Hera* and *Delos Express* are faster and safer than the very small boat.

Between May and September, guide[d] tours (8000 dr, including boat fare and sit[e] entrance) are conducted in English, Frenc[h] and German. Tickets are available fro[m] several travel agencies.

A boat also departs for Delos from Platy[s] Gialos at 10.15 am daily.

Getting Around

To/From the Airport Buses no longe[r] serve Mykonos' airport, 3km south-east o[f] the town centre. A taxi is around 1300 dr.

Bus Mykonos (Hora) has two bus station[s]. The northern station has frequent departure[s] to Ornos, Agios Stefanos (via Tourlos), An[o] Mera, Elia, Kato Livadi and Kalafatis. Th[e] southern station serves Agios Ioanni[s] Beach, Paraga, Psarou, Platys Gialos, Para-dise Beach, and, sometimes, Ornos.

Car & Motorcycle Most car and motor-cycle rental firms are around the souther[n] bus station.

Caïque Caïques leave Mykonos (Hora) fo[r] Super Paradise, Agrari and Elia beache[s] (June to September only) and from Platy[s] Gialos to Paradise (800 dr), Super Paradis[e] (1000 dr), Agrari (1200 dr) and Elia (120[0] dr) beaches.

MYKONOS (HORA)

Mykonos, the island's port and capital, is [a] warren-like Cycladic village turned to[y] town. It can be very hard to find your bear-ings – just when you think you've got i[t] worked out, you'll find yourself back a[t] square one. Throngs of pushy people add t[o] the frustration. Familiarise yourself with th[e] three main streets that form a horsesho[e] behind the waterfront and you'll have [a] fighting chance of finding your way aroun[d].

Even the most disenchanted could no[t] deny that Mykonos – a conglomeration o[f] chic boutiques, houses with brightly painte[d] balconies and bougainvillea and geranium[s] growing against whiter than white walls – has a certain charm. And, somehow, agains[t] incredible odds, there are still locals livin[g] here; chances are you'll glimpse an old Greek granny watering the plants on her balcony while the club next door pumps out throbbing disco.

Orientation

The waterfront is to the right of the ferry quay (facing inland), beyond the tiny town beach. The central square is Plateia Manto Mavrogenous (usually called Taxi Square), south along the waterfront.

The northern bus station is near the OTE, while the southern bus station is on the road to Ornos. The quay for boats to Delos is at the western end of the waterfront. South of here is Mykonos' famous row of windmills and the Little Venice quarter, where balconies overhang the sea.

Information

Mykonos has no tourist office. When you get off the ferry, you will see a low building with four numbered offices. No 1 is the Hotel Reservation Department (☎ 24 540), open 8 am to midnight daily; No 2 is the Association of Rooms & Apartments (☎ 26 860), open 10 am to 6 pm daily; No 3 has camping information (☎ 22 852); and No 4 houses the tourist police (☎ 22 482), with variable opening times.

The National Bank of Greece is on the waterfront and has an ATM. Two doors away, Delia Travel (☎ 22 322) represents American Express.

The post office is in the southern part of town, with the police (☎ 22 235) next door. The OTE is beside the northern bus station. The Mykonos Cyber Cafe, on the road between the southern bus station and the windmills, provides email access and connections for laptops; it also rents mobile phones. The Public Medical Center of Mykonos (☎ 23 994, 23 996) is on the road to Ano Mera. The port police (☎ 22 218) are on the waterfront, above the National Bank.

Museums

There are five museums. The **archaeological museum**, near the quay, houses pottery from Delos and some grave stelae and jewellery from the island of Renia (Delos' necropolis). Chief exhibits are a pithos featuring a Trojan War scene in relief, and a statue of Heracles. It's open 8 am to 2.30 pm Tuesday to Sunday. Admission is 500 dr.

The **Aegean Maritime Museum** has a fantastic collection of nautical paraphernalia from all over the Aegean, including fascinating models of ancient vessels. It's open 10.30 am to 1 pm and 6.30 to 9 pm daily. Admission is 500 dr.

Next door, **Lena's House** is a 19th century, middle class Mykonian house with furnishings intact. It's open 6 to 9 pm daily (from 7 pm Sunday). Entrance is free.

The **folklore museum**, housed in an 18th century sea captain's house, features a large collection of memorabilia, a reconstructed 19th century kitchen and a bedroom with a four-poster bed. The museum, near the Delos quay, is open 5.30 to 8.30 pm daily. Entrance is free.

The **windmill museum** is on Agiou Ioannou, near the road to Ano Mera. Entrance is free but opening times are very erratic.

Church of Panagia Paraportiani

The Panagia Paraportiani is the most famous of Mykonos' many churches. It is actually four little churches amalgamated into one beautiful, white, lumpy, asymmetrical building. It could do with some paint, but even so, the interplay of light and shade on the multifaceted structure make it a photographer's delight.

Activities

Dive Adventures (☎ 26 539), on Paradise Beach, offers the full range of scuba diving courses right up to instructor level. The Aphrodite Diving School is owned by Aphrodite Beach Hotel (☎ 71 367) on Kalafatis Beach. Other activities include tennis and horse riding, and there's a gym and aerobics.

Organised Tours

Excursion boats run day trips to Delos. See the Mykonos Getting There & Away section for details.

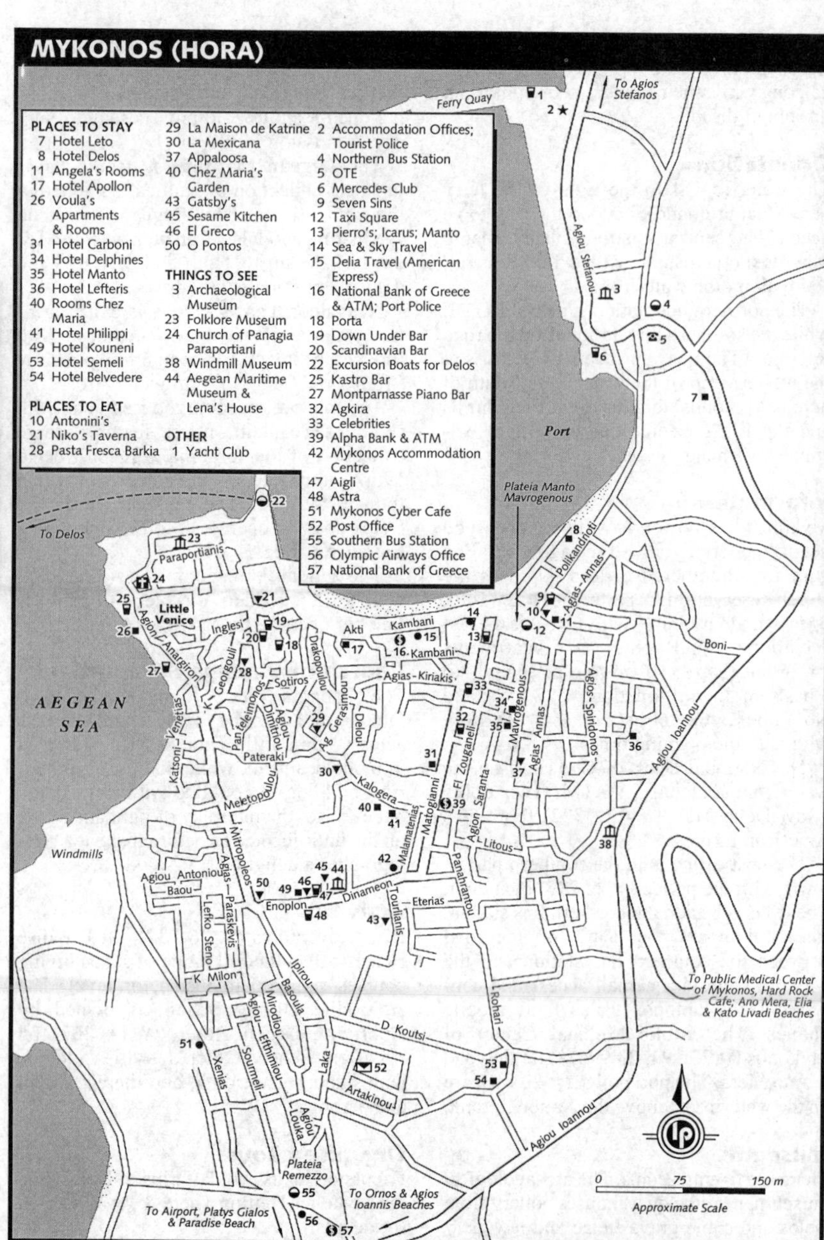
MYKONOS (HORA)
PLACES TO STAY
7 Hotel Leto
8 Hotel Delos
11 Angela's Rooms
17 Hotel Apollon
26 Voula's Apartments & Rooms
31 Hotel Carboni
34 Hotel Delphines
35 Hotel Manto
36 Hotel Lefteris
40 Rooms Chez Maria
41 Hotel Philippi
49 Hotel Kouneni
53 Hotel Semeli
54 Hotel Belvedere
PLACES TO EAT
10 Antonini's
21 Niko's Taverna
28 Pasta Fresca Barkia
29 La Maison de Katrine
30 La Mexicana
37 Appaloosa
40 Chez Maria's Garden
43 Gatsby's
45 Sesame Kitchen
46 El Greco
50 O Pontos
THINGS TO SEE
3 Archaeological Museum
23 Folklore Museum
24 Church of Panagia Paraportiani
38 Windmill Museum
44 Aegean Maritime Museum & Lena's House
OTHER
1 Yacht Club
2 Accommodation Offices; Tourist Police
4 Northern Bus Station
5 OTE
6 Mercedes Club
9 Seven Sins
12 Taxi Square
13 Pierro's; Icarus; Manto
14 Sea & Sky Travel
15 Delia Travel (American Express)
16 National Bank of Greece & ATM; Port Police
18 Porta
19 Down Under Bar
20 Scandinavian Bar
22 Excursion Boats for Delos
25 Kastro Bar
27 Montparnasse Piano Bar
32 Agkira
33 Celebrities
39 Alpha Bank & ATM
42 Mykonos Accommodation Centre
47 Aigli
48 Astra
51 Mykonos Cyber Cafe
52 Post Office
55 Southern Bus Station
56 Olympic Airways Office
57 National Bank of Greece
Ferry Quay
To Agios Stefanos
Agiou Stefanou
Port
Plateia Manto Mavrogenous
To Delos
Paraportianis
Little Venice
AEGEAN SEA
Windmills
Polikandrioti
Agias Annas
Boni
Kambani
Akti
Inglesi
Agion Anargiron
K Georgouli
Sotiros
Drakopoulou
Agias Kiriakis
Mavrogenous
Agios Spiridonos
Agiou Ioannou
Pan teleimonos
Agiou Dimitriou
Ag Gerasimou
Deloui
Fl Zouganeli
Katsoni Venetias
Pateraki
Kalogera
Meletopoulou
Malamatenias
Matogianni
Agion Saranta
Litous
Mitropoleos
Agiou Antoniou
Baou
Agias Paraskevis
Dinameon
Enoplon
Eterias
Tourlianis
Panahrantou
Lefko Steno
K Milon
Ipirou
Basoula
Rohari
D Koutsi
Agiou Efthimiou
Mirodiou
Sourmeli
Xenias
Laka
Artakinou
Agiou Louka
Plateia Remezzo
To Public Medical Center of Mykonos, Hard Rock Cafe; Ano Mera, Elia & Kato Livadi Beaches
To Ornos & Agios Ioannis Beaches
To Airport, Platys Gialos & Paradise Beach
0
75
150 m
Approximate Scale

CYCLADES

'laces to Stay – Budget

f you arrive without a reservation between une and September and manage to find uitably priced accommodation, take it.)therwise seek the assistance of the ccommodation organisations mentioned in ne Information section, or ask John at ne Mykonos Accommodation Centre ☎ 23 408), on the corner of Enoplon)inameon and Malamatenias. If you choose omatia from owners meeting ferries, ask if ney charge for transport – some do.

Angela's Rooms (*☎ 22 967*), on Taxi quare, has doubles with bathroom for 5,000 dr. For a place with a bit of charac-er, try the old-world D class *Hotel Apollon* ☎ *22 223, fax 24 237*), on the waterfront. t's been around since 1930 and most of the urniture looks older, but it is very well kept nd the owner is sweet. Clean and tidy ingles/doubles go for 12,000/15,000 dr. *Iotel Delphines* (*☎ 24 505, fax 27 307*), on Aavrogenous, is also run by friendly people nd charges 13,000/16,500 dr for rooms vith TV, fridge and bathroom.

Hotel Philippi (*☎ 22 294, 24 680*), on Kalogera, has an agrarian feel; the garden ut the back has fruit trees and a motley ssortment of flowers planted in rows as if hey were vegetables. Doubles (one of vhich seems to occupy an old stable) with athroom go for 16,000 dr. Next door, *Rooms Chez Maria* (*☎ 22 480*) is a pretty lace with potted geraniums out the front nd lovely doubles/triples for 15,000/ 0,000 dr with bathroom.

Hotel Lefteris (*☎ 27 117, Apollonos 9*), in he residential backstreets away from the ubbub, also has geraniums on its steps. Singles/doubles, some with balcony, go for 6,000/21,000 dr. Signs point the way from Taxi Square. The D class *Hotel Carboni* *☎ 22 217, fax 23 264*), on Andronikou Mato-gianni, has plain but clean doubles/triples for 7,000/21,000 dr with TV and bathroom.

'laces to Stay – Mid-Range

The C class *Hotel Delos* (*☎ 22 517, fax 22 312*), on the town beach, charges 18,000/ 23,000 dr for doubles/triples, including bathroom. *Hotel Manto* (*☎ 22 330, fax 26 664*), just off Mavrogenous, has singles/ doubles for 18,000/27,000 dr with bathroom.

Little Venice's only seafront accommodation is *Voula's Apartments & Rooms* (*☎ 22 951, 0945-223 026*). Its balconied rooms are above a club and taverna, so bring earplugs if you're not prepared to party. Doubles/triples are 15,000/20,000 dr with bathroom, more with balcony. Voula meets boats and does not charge for transport.

Hotel Kouneni (*☎ 22 301*), on Enoplon Dinameon, has a charming garden; doubles with bathroom cost 28,000 dr.

Places to Stay – Top End

The time-worn *Hotel Leto* (*☎ 22 207, fax 23 985*), facing the town beach, has singles/doubles/triples for a whopping 59,000/70,000/93,000 dr, with breakfast.

Much better value can be found at *Hotel Belvedere* (*☎ 25 122, fax 25 126*) and *Hotel Semeli* (*☎ 27 466, fax 27 467*), next to each other on Rohari, away from the centre of town. The hotels, run by the same family (the Belvedere by a brother, the Semeli by a sister), are built around the old family house that has been converted into a very good traditional restaurant.

Both places are stylish and have made an effort to combine old-world charm with modern comforts. The Belvedere has jacuzzis, steam room, fitness studio, DVD, Internet corner (no access charge) and a large and lovely conference room. Both hotels have a pool, bar and lounge areas and all rooms in both have balconies with a view over town. Semeli charges 55,000 dr a double, including breakfast. Belvedere charges 59,000 dr for a double; suites are also available.

For more top-end listings, see the Beaches and Ano Mera sections.

Places to Eat

The high prices charged in many eating establishments are not always indicative of quality. The fish served in most of the tavernas is cheap frozen stuff imported from Asia which often tastes like warmed up old boots. If you want good fish, try another island.

Antonini's, on Taxi Square, is where the locals go. It serves reliably good Greek food and is reasonably priced – try the moussaka. At ***Niko's Taverna***, up from the Delos quay, waiters take your order on a palmtop, which seems to make service pretty efficient. The food is nothing great, but it's better than what's on offer in a lot of the other 'traditional' places. Avoid ***Restaurant Klimataria***: its food is dreadful.

Pasta Fresca Barkia, on Georgouli, serves pizza and fresh pasta made on the premises; *tagliatelle siciliana* is 2100 dr. ***Gatsby's*** has a slightly refined atmosphere and serves some interesting food, including shrimp with spinach and green apple in a hot black sauce (3300 dr) and *spaghetti alla fornala* (with garlic, walnuts and parmesan; 2500 dr). ***Appaloosa*** is a cute little Mexican-inspired place that has guacamole (1500 dr) and nachos (2000 dr), as well as more substantial burgers (2800 dr) and pasta dishes (from 2700 dr).

El Greco, next to Hotel Kouneni, offers dishes such as stuffed fresh anchovies with white *tarama* and fresh herbs (1650 dr), zucchini stuffed with Mykonos cheese and fennel (1850 dr), *sofrito* (Corfu-style veal with parsley, garlic and vinegar; 2450 dr) and mountain goat (2300 dr). Some of their fish is local. ***Sesame Kitchen***, a few doors up, serves innovative fare, much of it vegetarian, including Delos salad with arugula, fresh asparagus, Mykonos goat's cheese and sesame seeds (3000 dr), and veal fillet with radicchio and balsamic vinegar (6200 dr).

Chez Maria's Garden has a lovely outdoor candlelit setting. It's a bit pricey (set menus are 6000 dr per person – and that's considerably less than a la carte) and a tad pretentious, but the food isn't at all bad. ***La Maison de Katrine*** *(☎ 22 169)*, probably the classiest restaurant, serves Greek food with a French twist. It's been open since 1971 and has diligent service and a relaxed, unfussy atmosphere. The white taramasalata is superb, as is the *coq au vin*, but make sure you leave room for the *tarte tatin* with caramelised calvados cream. Expect to pay at least 15,000 dr per person for a full meal including wine. It's on Gerasimou a[illegible] Nikou.

There's a cluster of cheap fast-food outlets and creperies in the centre of town. ***O Pontos*** serves gyros for 400 dr. There are several supermarkets and fruit stalls, particularly around the southern bus station.

Entertainment

Seven Sins, the oldest bar in Mykonos (established 1965), is a cosy little place with background music by, appropriately enough, the Stones and other 60s outfits. For classy ambience and a mature but not necessarily sedate crowd, try ***Montparnasse Piano Bar*** in Little Venice.

On Enaplon Dinameon is a cluster of large bars playing dance music, including ***Astra*** and ***Aigli***. ***Agkira*** ('anchor') and ***Celebrities*** (pity about the name) on Matogianni are in a similar vein, but rather more chic.

Gay venues include ***Porta***, which has a reputation for being the best pick-up bar in town; ***Kastro Bar*** in Little Venice; and ***Pierro's***, which is the place for late-night dancing. Adjoining it, ***Icarus*** and ***Manto*** are popular haunts.

Mercedes Club, near the archaeological museum, attracts an older clientele. ***Cavo Paradiso*** *(☎ 26 124)*, 300m above Paradise Beach, has all-night raves with international DJs; doors open at 3 am.

The cheap alcohol at ***Down Under Bar*** and ***Scandinavian Bar*** attracts hordes of backpackers and kids on Kontiki Tours; go for it if that's your thing. ***Hard Rock Cafe***, about 4km along the Ano Mera road, has a restaurant, nightclub and pool. If you're roomless or an insomniac, head for the ***Yacht Club***, by the quay, which is open 24 hours. A pink shuttle bus runs from the Yacht Club to the Hard Rock every half-hour between noon and 4 am.

AROUND MYKONOS

Beaches

The nearest beaches to Hora are **Malaliamos** and the tiny, crowded **Tourlos**, 2km to the north. **Agios Stefanos**, 2km beyond, is larger but just as crowded. To the south, beyond

JON DAVISON

usted anchor, Aegina (Saronic Gulf)

DIANA MAYFIELD

Fishing boat, Crete

JON DAVISON

:orinth Canal, begun in Roman days, links the Ionian and Aegean seas (Peloponnese).

JON DAVISON

Ancient statues of Cleopatra and Dioscrides, two of Delos' wealthier citizens (Cyclades)

CHRIS CHRISTO

Hania's waterfront, with the bustling Venetian quarter rising behind, Crete

It's a Cat's Life

Cats are everywhere in Greece: stalking plump pigeons around Athens' parliament house; congregating under restaurant tables in the hope of scavenging scraps; and looking cute on tourist-geared calendars and postcards. Most of the cats are strays, but sometimes you'll see a domestic cat – sporting a collar and bell – out hunting with them.

Greece is swarming with cats because the expense of having them spayed is prohibitive. Owners allow their female cats to produce litter after litter.

Although Greeks recognise that the mighty cat population keeps the rodent numbers down, the cats are still regarded as a major problem. To keep them at bay, some restaurateurs display signs requesting that patrons do not feed the cats. Other restaurant owners will discourage cats from bothering diners by feeding the cats leftovers themselves.

Travellers should take care when feeding the cats – although many of them are friendly, hunger can make them snatch at food with their paws, sometimes scratching or puncturing the skin. And people with a phobia about cats may feel very uneasy in a country which has so many!

Whatever Greeks and tourists feel about the cats, the population is likely to increase until the cost of desexing them comes down.

Ornos, is **Agios Ioannis**, where *Shirley Valentine* was filmed. **Psarou**, east of Ornos, is a pretty little cove. **Platys Gialos**, on the south-west coast, is bumper to bumper sun lounges backed by very ordinary package tour hotels – really not nice at all.

From here, caïques call at the island's best beaches farther around the south coast: **Paradise**, **Super Paradise**, **Agrari** and **Elia**. Nudism is accepted on all these beaches. Elia is the last caïque stop, so is the least crowded. The next beach along, **Kato Livadi**, is also relatively quiet. North-coast beaches are exposed to the meltemi, but **Panormos** and **Agios Sostis** are sheltered and uncrowded.

Places to Stay Mykonos has two camping grounds: ***Paradise Beach Camping*** *(☎ 22 852)* on Paradise Beach and ***Mykonos Camping*** *(☎ 24 578)* on Paraga Beach (10 minutes walk from Platys Gialos). Both have good facilities and charge 1800 dr per person per day, plus 1000 dr per tent per day. Paradise Beach Camping also has two-person bungalows for 10,000 dr. Minibuses from the camping grounds meet ferries.

There are many top end places around the coast. ***Ornos Beach Hotel*** *(☎ 23 216)* has great sea views and a swimming pool; doubles are 36,000 dr. ***Villa Katerina*** *(☎ 23 414)*, a quiet, romantic place, 300m up the hill above Agios Ioannis, has a garden and pool. Double studios cost 24,500 dr. Close by, the A class ***Apollonia Bay*** *(☎ 27 890)* charges 52,000 dr for doubles, including breakfast. At Agios Stefanos, the A class ***Princess of Mykonos*** *(☎ 23 806)* was once a Jane Fonda hang-out. Singles/doubles are 40,000/46,000 dr with breakfast.

On Kalafatis Beach, the A class ***Aphrodite Beach Hotel*** *(☎ 71 367)* has masses of facilities including water sports and scuba diving. Doubles/triples cost 58,000/71,000 dr with breakfast. The deluxe ***Tharroe of Mykonos*** *(☎ 27 370)* in Vrissi has singles/doubles for 60,000/88,000 dr, including breakfast. The A class ***Kivotos*** *(☎ 24 094)* in Ornos has its own private beach, as well as fitness centre, restaurants, bars etc. Rooms are 72,000/79,000 dr; superior rooms go for 86,000/98,000 dr.

Ano Mera Ανω Μέρα

The village of Ano Mera, 7km east of Hora, is the island's only inland settlement. On its central square is the sumptuous 6th century

Moni Panagias Tourlianis, which has a fine carved marble bell tower, an ornate wooden iconostasis carved in Florence in the late 1700s, and 16th century icons painted by members of the Cretan School. Speakers turned up to 11 crank out beautiful Orthodox hymns, which makes for a powerful experience. It's open 9 am to 1 pm and 2 to 7.30 pm daily.

The A class ***Ano Mera Hotel*** *(☎ 71 215, fax 71 276)* has a pool, restaurant and disco. Singles/doubles/triples are 24,300/30,400/40,700 dr with breakfast, but there's no real reason why you should stay up here. The central square is edged with tavernas. ***O Apostolis***, near the bus stop, has decent traditional food.

Delos Δήλος

Despite its diminutive size, Delos is one of the most important archaeological sites in Greece, and certainly the most important in the Cyclades. Lying a few kilometres off the west coast of Mykonos, this sacred island is the mythical birthplace of the twins Apollo and Artemis. The site is World Heritage-listed, and, like most archaeological sites, it is closed on Mondays.

History

Delos was first inhabited in the 3rd millennium BC. In the 8th century BC, a festival in honour of Apollo was established; the oldest temples and shrines on the island (many donated by Naxians) date from this era. For a long time, the Athenians coveted Delos, seeing its strategic position as one from where they could control the Aegean. By the 5th century BC, it had come under their jurisdiction.

Athens' power grew during the Persian Wars, and in 478 BC it established an alliance known as the Delian League that kept its treasury on Delos. Athens carried out a number of 'purifications', decreeing that no-one could be born or could die on Delos, thus strengthening its control over the island by removing the native population.

Delos reached the height of its power in Hellenistic times, becoming one of the three most important religious centres in Greece and a flourishing centre of commerce. It traded throughout the Mediterranean and was populated with wealthy merchants, mariners and bankers from as far away as Egypt and Syria. These inhabitants built temples to the various gods worshipped in their homelands, although Apollo remained the principal deity.

The Romans made Delos a free port in 167 BC, which brought even greater prosperity – due largely to a lucrative slave market that sold up to 10,000 people a day. Later, Delos was prey to pirates and to looters of antiquities.

Getting There & Away

See Excursion Boats in the Mykonos section for schedules and prices of services from Mykonos. Boats also operate to Delos from Tinos and Paros.

ANCIENT DELOS

Orientation & Information

The quay where excursion boats dock is south of the tranquil Sacred Harbour. Many of the most significant finds from Delos are in the National Archaeological Museum in Athens. The site museum has a modest collection.

Overnight stays on Delos are forbidden, and boat schedules allow a maximum of six or seven hours there (depending on which boat you're with). Bring water and food, as the cafeteria is poor value. Wear a hat and sensible shoes. Entrance to the site costs 1200 dr (museum included). If you hire a guide once you get to Delos, you'll need to fork out more cash.

Exploring the Site

Following is an outline of some significant archaeological remains on the site. For further details, buy a guidebook at the ticket office, or – even better – take a guided tour.

If you have the energy, climb Mt Kythnos (113m), which is south-east of the harbour, to see the layout of Delos. There are terrific

ANCIENT DELOS

1 Stadium
2 Gymnasium
3 House of Comedians
4 Sanctuary of Archegetes
5 House of Diadumenos
6 Lake House
7 Hill House
8 Institution of the Poseidoniasts
9 Palaestra
10 Terrace of the Lions
11 Roman Wall
12 Agora of the Italians
13 Stoa of Poseidon
14 Dodekatheon
15 Tourist Pavillion
16 Stoa of Antigonas
17 Sanctuary of Dionysos
18 Museum
19 Temple of Artemis
20 Poros Temple
21 Temple of the Athenians
22 Keraton
23 Temple of Apollo
24 Stoa of the Naxiots
25 House of the Naxiots
26 Monument of the Bulls
27 Agora of the Competialists
28 Stoa of Philip V
29 South Stoa
30 Agora of the Delians
31 Wall of the Triarus
32 House of Cleopatra
33 House of Dionysos
34 House of Hermes
35 Sanctuary of the Syrian Gods
36 House of the Trident
37 Shrine to the Samothracian Great Gods
38 Shrine to the Egyptian Gods
39 Cistern
40 Theatre
41 House of the Dolphins
42 House of the Masks
43 Sacred Cave
44 Warehouses

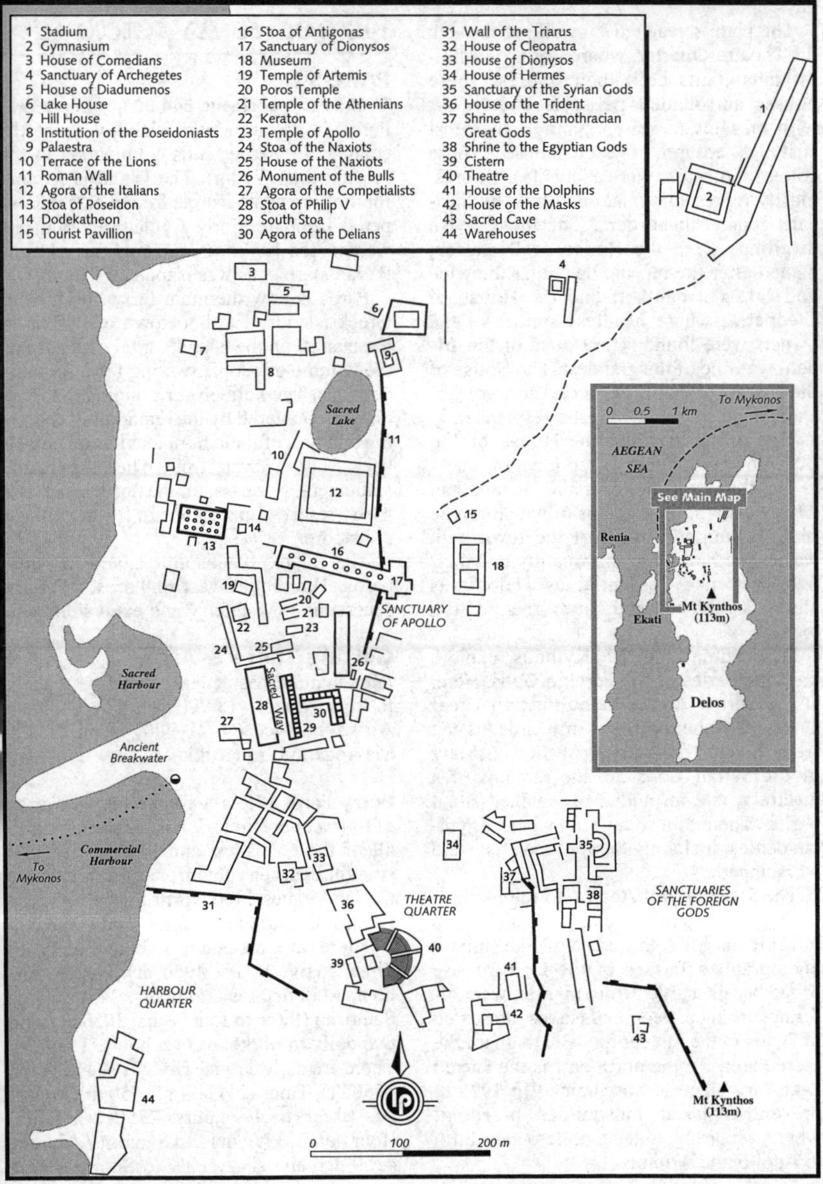

views of the surrounding islands on clear days.

The path is reached by walking through the **Theatre Quarter**, where Delos' wealthiest inhabitants built their houses. These houses surrounded peristyle courtyards, with mosaics (a status symbol) the most striking feature of each house. These colourful mosaics were exquisite art works, mostly representational and offset by intricate geometric borders. The most lavish dwellings were the **House of Dionysos**, named after the mosaic depicting the wine god riding a panther; and the **House of Cleopatra**, where headless statues of the owners were found. The **House of the Trident** was one of the grandest. The **House of the Masks**, probably an actors' hostelry, has another mosaic of Dionysos resplendently astride a panther, and the **House of the Dolphins** has another exceptional mosaic.

The **theatre** dates from 300 BC and had a large cistern, the remains of which can be seen. It supplied much of the town with water. The houses of the wealthy had their own cisterns – essential as Delos was almost as parched and barren then as it is today.

Descending from Mt Kythnos, explore the **Sanctuaries of the Foreign Gods**. Here, at the **Shrine to the Samothracian Great Gods**, the Kabeiroi (the twins Dardanos and Aeton) were worshipped. At the **Sanctuary of the Syrian Gods** are the remains of a theatre where an audience watched ritual orgies. There is also an area where Egyptian deities, including Serapis and Isis, were worshipped.

The **Sanctuary of Apollo**, to the north of the harbour, contains temples dedicated to him. It is also the site of the much-photographed **Terrace of the Lions**. These proud beasts, carved from marble, were offerings from the people of Naxos, presented to Delos in the 7th century BC to guard the sacred area. To the north-east is the **Sacred Lake** (dry since it was drained in 1925 to prevent malarial mosquitoes breeding) where, according to legend, Leto gave birth to Apollo and Artemis.

CYCLADES

Paros & Antiparos
Πάρος & Αντίπαρος

PAROS

☎ 0284 • postcode 844 00 • pop 9591

Paros is an attractive island with softly contoured, terraced hills culminating in Mt Profitis Ilias (770m). The island is famous for the pure white marble from which it prospered from the Early Cycladic period onwards – the *Venus de Milo* was carved from Parian marble, as was Napoleon's tomb.

Paros is now the main ferry hub for the Greek islands. The port town of Parikia is the busiest on the island, largely because of the volume of people waiting for ferry connections. The hubbub surrounding the ferry quay is countered by the remarkably charming and peaceful old hora that lies one block back from the waterfront. The other major settlement, Naoussa, on the north coast, is a pretty resort with a colourful fishing village at its core.

The relatively unspoilt island of Antiparos, 1km south-west of Paros, is easily accessible by car ferry and excursion boat.

Getting There & Away

Air Olympic has at least five flights daily to/from Athens (18,900 dr). The Olympic Airways office (☎ 21 900) is on Plateia Mavrogenous in Parikia.

Ferry Paros offers a comprehensive array of ferry connections. It has frequent links to all of the Cyclades, and is also a regular stop for boats en route from the mainland to the Dodecanese, the North-Eastern Aegean islands of Ikaria and Samos, and Crete.

There are around six boats daily to Piraeus (five hours, 4950 dr), Naxos (one hour, 1350 dr), Ios (2½ hours, 2450 dr) and Santorini (three to four hours, 3050 dr), and two daily to Mykonos (1¾ hours, 1750 dr). There are daily services to Syros (1½ hours, 1550 dr), Tinos (2½ hours, 1750 dr), Amorgos (three to 4½ hours, 2750 dr), Ikaria (four hours, 3350 dr) and Samos (7½ hours, 4250 dr), and six weekly to Sikinos (three to four hours, 1750 dr) and Crete (seven to eight hours, 4950 dr).

There are five ferries weekly to Folegandros (3½ hours, 1950 dr) and Rhodes (12 to 15 hours, 6950 dr), and four to Thessaloniki (12 to 15 hours, 9350 dr), Rafina (seven hours, 4150 dr), Andros (4½ hours, 2750 dr) and Anafi (six hours, 3550 dr). Three weekly go to Astypalea (six hours, 4850 dr) and Koufonisia (4½ hours, 2750 dr).

Two boats weekly serve Skiathos (six hours, 6450 dr), Fourni (five hours, 4050 dr), Kalymnos (6½ hours, 3750 dr), Kos (six to eight hours, 4350 dr), Serifos (three hours, 1000 dr), Sifnos (two hours, 1000 dr), Milos (4½ hours, 2900 dr), Kimolos (four hours, 2250 dr) and Donousa (two to four hours, 2350 dr). Only one weekly connection goes to poor old Patmos (four hours, 3950 dr), Leros (4450 dr), Shinousa (four hours, 2150 dr) and Volos (eight hours, 6950 dr).

There is also a half-hourly car ferry from Pounta on the west coast of Paros to Antiparos (10 minutes, 170 dr – car extra); the first ferry runs to Antiparos at around 7 am, and the last boat back leaves Antiparos at 12.30 am.

Hydrofoil There are at least four hydrofoils daily to Naxos (30 minutes, 2700 dr) and Mykonos (one hour, 3300 dr), and three to Ios (1¼ hours, 4950 dr), Santorini (two hours, 6100 dr), Tinos (1¼ hours, 3500 dr) and Syros (45 minutes, 3100 dr). They run almost daily to Amorgos (1½ hours, 5500 dr), Crete (four hours, 10,000 dr), Folegandros (1½ hours, 3800 dr), Milos (two hours, 5700 dr) and Sifnos (one hour, 1900 dr).

Hydrofoils also serve Andros (three hours, 5500 dr, two weekly), Sikinos (two hours, 3500 dr, two weekly) and Serifos (one hour, 3800 dr, one weekly).

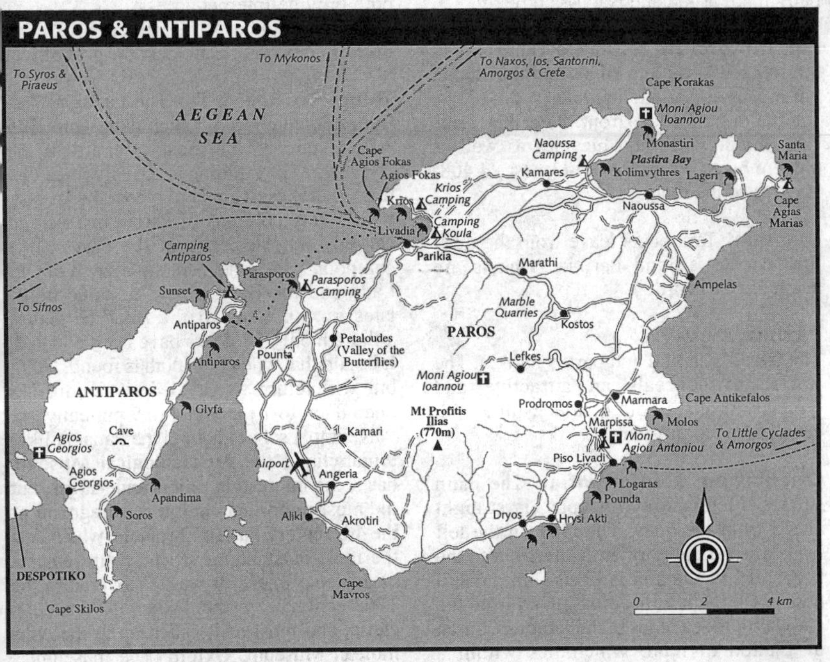

Catamaran There are at least two catamarans daily to Naxos (30 minutes, 2700 dr), one or two daily to Rafina (2½ hours, 8200 dr), and one to Syros (45 minutes, 3100 dr), Ios (1¼ hours, 4950 dr) and Santorini (two hours, 6100 dr). There are six services weekly to Piraeus (three hours, 9700 dr), and two weekly to Mykonos (one hour, 3300 dr), Tinos (1¼ hours, 3500 dr), Andros (three hours, 5500 dr) and Amorgos (1¾ hours, 5500 dr).

Excursion Boat In summer, frequent excursion boats depart for Antiparos from Parikia on Paros (45 minutes, 460 dr one way).

Getting Around

Bus There are around seven buses daily from Parikia to Naoussa via Dryos, Hrysi Akti, Marpissa, Marmara, Prodromo, Kosto, Marathi and Lefkes, and frequent buses to Pounta (for Antiparos), Aliki (for Petaloudes) and the airport. Around 12 buses daily link Parikia and Naoussa directly.

Car, Motorcycle & Bicycle There are numerous rental outlets all around the island. Parai Rent-a-Car-Motorcycle (☎ 21 1771), south along the waterfront in Parikia, rents cars, motorcycles and bicycles as well as tandem bikes. Paros Rent-a-Car (☎ 24 408) is north of the quay.

Taxi Boat Taxi boats leave from the quay for beaches around Parikia. Tickets are available on board.

Parikia Παροικία

The island's capital and port is Parikia. The waterfront conceals an attractive and typically Cycladic old quarter with a 13th century Venetian kastro.

Orientation & Information The main square, Plateia Mavrogenous, is straight ahead from the quay. The road on the left leads around the northern waterfront to the beach at Livadia and is lined with modern hotels. On the left, heading inland from the quay, Prombona leads to the famous Church of Ekatontapyliani, which lies within a walled courtyard. The road to the right follows the cafe-lined south-western waterfront, a pedestrian precinct in high season.

Market St (Agora in Greek, but also known by other names) is the main commercial thoroughfare running south-west from Plateia Mavrogenous through the old town, which is all narrow pedestrian streets.

Kiosks on the quay give out information on domatia and hotels (see Places to Stay). Praxis Tours (☎ 24 415), opposite the quay, can help with accommodation and sells ferry tickets.

The National Bank of Greece, the Commercial Bank of Greece and the police (☎ 23 333) are all on Plateia Mavrogenous. The bus station is 50m left of the quay (looking inland), and the post office is 300m farther along. The OTE is on the waterfront, to the right of the ferry quay (facing inland). The Wired Cafe, on Market St, and Memphis.net, near the bus station, both provide Internet access.

The port police (☎ 21 240) are back from the northern waterfront, near the post office.

Things to See & Do The **Panagia Ekatontapyliani** church, which dates from 326 AD, is one of the most splendid in the Cyclades. The building is actually three distinct churches: Agios Nikolaos, the largest, with lovely columns of Parian marble and carved iconostasis, is in the east of the compound; the others are the Church of Our Lady and the Baptistery. The name translates as Our Lady of the Hundred Gates, although only 99 doors have been counted. It is said that when the 100th is found, İstanbul will return to Greek jurisdiction. It's open 8 am to 1 pm and 4 to 9 pm daily.

Next to a school behind the Panagia Ekatontapyliani, the **Archaeological Museum** has some interesting reliefs and statues, but the most important exhibit is a fragment of the 4th century Parian Chronicle, which lists the most outstanding artistic achievements of ancient Greece. It was discovered in the 17th century by the Duke of Arundel's cleric, and most of it ended up in the Ashmolean Museum, Oxford. The museum is open 9 am to 2.30 pm daily except Monday and public holidays. Admission is 500 dr.

North along the waterfront there is a fenced **ancient cemetery** dating from the 7th century BC; it was excavated in 1983. Roman graves, burial pots and sarcophagi are floodlit at night. Photographs and other finds are exhibited in an attached building, but it's rarely open.

The **Frankish kastro** was built on the remains of a temple to Athena by Marco Sanudo, Venetian Duke of Naxos, in 1260 AD. Not much remains, save an impressively large wall with cross-sectional chunks of columns from the temple embedded in it. To find it, head west along Market St and take the first right.

Eurodivers Club (☎ 92 071), down the coast at Pounta, offers **scuba diving** courses.

Places to Stay All camping grounds have minibuses that meet the ferries. ***Camping Koula*** *(☎ 22 081)*, 1km along the northern waterfront at Livadia, is the most central. It charges 1000 dr per person and 500 dr for tent hire. ***Parasporos Camping*** *(☎ 22 268)*, 2km south of Parikia, charges 1400 dr per person. ***Krios Camping*** *(☎ 21 705)* is on Krios Beach, beyond Livadia Beach. It charges 1200/700 dr per person/tent, and runs a taxi boat across the bay to Parikia every 10 minutes for 400 dr per person (return). It also has a restaurant and minimarket.

The Rooms Association (☎/fax 24 528) on the quay has information on domatia; if it's closed, call Giorgos Epitropakis, the president, on ☎ 22 220. He will collect you from the port at all hours and deliver you safely to a suitable domatio. Alternatively, you can haggle with some of the owners right outside the port. For hotel details, call ☎ 24 555 (Parikia) or ☎ 41 333 (around the island).

Right in the midst of the atmospheric old Kastro, ***Jane's Rooms*** *(☎ 21 338)* have sea views and balconies; doubles cost 13,000 dr. She also has an apartment nearby, as well as some farther out of town. There's no sign identifying the rooms, but Jane will meet you at the port if you book ahead.

Rooms Rena *(☎ 22 220, ☎/fax 21 427)* has spotless singles/doubles/triples for 10,000/13,000/15,000 dr with bath, balcony and fridge. To find it, turn left at the quay and walk 300m along the waterfront, then turn right at the ancient cemetery. Around the corner, ***Mariza Rooms*** *(☎ 22 629)* has similar doubles/triples for 15,000/18,000 dr.

Rooms Mike *(☎ 22 856)* is popular with backpackers; rooms cost 15,000/18,000 dr, with TV, shared kitchen and a roof terrace. To get there, walk 50m left from the quay – it's next to Memphis.net, not far from the bus station. Mike also has self-contained studios for 19,000/21,000 dr around the corner near Ephesus restaurant.

Angie's Studios *(☎ 23 909)*, out in the back blocks but a nice walk from the centre of town, are dripping with bougainvillea and have a pleasant patio and lawn. Rooms cost 21,000/24,000 dr. Close by, ***Asteriou Rooms*** *(☎ 23 584)* has well kept, spacious rooms for 15,000/18,000 dr.

Hotel Dina *(☎ 21 325)*, in the old town on Market St, charges 15,000 dr for doubles with bathroom; some have a balcony. The lovely, central C class ***Hotel Argonauta*** *(☎ 21 440)*, on the main square, has sparkling singles/doubles for 14,000/17,000 dr with bathroom, air-con and balcony.

For something a bit more rural and quiet, ***Denis Apartments*** *(☎ 22 466)*, near Livadia, has spacious doubles/triples for 13,000/15,000 dr with bathroom. Take the first major road on the right after Camping Koula to get there, or telephone in advance to be picked up from the boat. Not far away, ***Maggie's Studios*** *(☎ 24 370)* are nicely designed and have a great view; there's also a pool. Double studios cost 22,000 dr. There are also plenty of run-of-the-mill hotels to choose from along the waterfront at Livadia, near Camping Koula.

The fine A class ***Yria Hotel Bungalows*** *(☎ 24 154)*, 2.5km south of Parikia, open April to October, overlooks pretty Parasporos Beach. It has a restaurant, bar, pool and water sports. Singles/doubles/triples cost 33,000/39,000/50,000 dr. There are also four-person maisonettes for 69,000 dr.

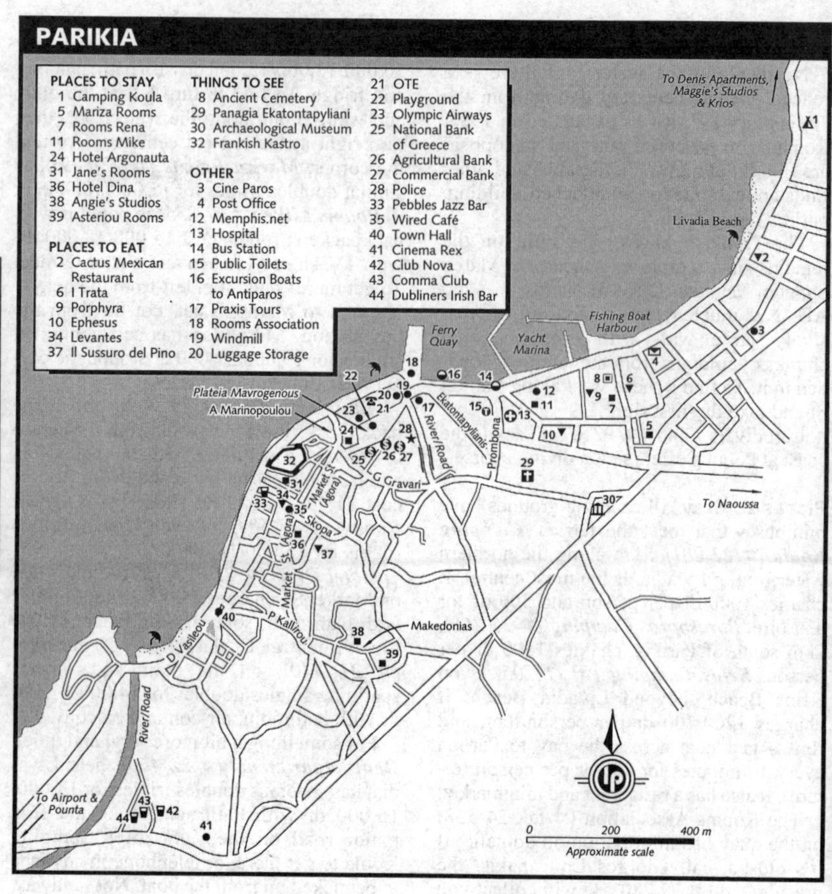

Places to Eat ***I Trata***, next to the ancient cemetery, has very good seafood, not least shrimp saganaki, and a stimulating array of mezedes, fresh fish and salads. On the opposite side of the cemetery, ***Porphyra*** (named after a shellfish famed for its purple dye and ability to drill a hole into its prey) specialises in unusual seafood delicacies, including raw shellfish. Tamer offerings include fresh fish, calamari and prawns cooked to perfection, and various mixed platters (2300 dr). The service is a little chilly but the good food makes up for this. ***Ephesus***, an Anatolian place behind the hospital, has delicious, herb-laden home-made dips and appetisers (500 dr to 700 dr), a large selection of kebabs (around 2000 dr), and bread and stuffed pizzas (around 1700 dr) cooked in a wood-fired oven. Halfway down Market St, ***Levantes*** is an interesting place with creative international cuisine. ***Il Sussuro del Pino***, in a shady garden, has fresh fish and unusual dishes such as artichokes with calamari, and octopus with macaroni (both 1400 dr). Follow the signs from Skopa, which runs off Market St.

Cactus Mexican Restaurant, by the beach at Livadia, has fajitas, tacos and enchiladas for around 2500 dr. It also has a wide variety of Greek and international fare.

Entertainment Most bars are along the south-west waterfront. ***Pebbles Jazz Bar*** is a good place to watch the sunset and sometimes has live music. Farther south, before the bend, is a cluster of rowdy discos – ***Nova***, ***Comma Club*** and ***Dubliners Irish Bar***. Avoid bars offering very cheap cocktails (invariably made from the local hooch).

Parikia's popular open-air cinemas are ***Cine Paros***, in Livadia's backstreets, and ***Cinema Rex***, not far from the discos at the southern end of the waterfront.

Naoussa Νάουσσα

Naoussa, on the north coast, has metamorphosed from pristine fishing village into popular tourist resort. For many visitors, Naoussa *is* Paros; its popularity is due in part to its proximity to nice beaches and to its slightly upmarket, French Riviera feel. It's certainly a lot less hectic than Parikia. Despite an incursion by package tourists, Naoussa remains relaxed.

Naoussa is still a working harbour with piles of yellow fishing nets, bright caïques, and little ouzeria with rickety tables and raffia chairs. Behind the central square (where the bus terminates) is a picturesque village, with narrow alleyways whitewashed with fish and flower motifs.

There is an information booth near the bus station. The post office is a tedious uphill walk from the central square. Nissiotissa Tours has a book exchange.

Naoussa's **Byzantine museum**, open 10 am to noon and 7 to 9 pm Tuesday, Thursday and weekends, and the **folklore museum**, open 7 to 9 pm daily, are both near the post office. Admission to each is 400 dr.

The best beaches are **Kolimvythres**, which has interesting rock formations, and **Monastiri**. **Santa Maria**, on the other side of the eastern headland, is good for windsurfing.

Activities & Organised Tours The Santa Maria Diving Club (☎ 094 385 307) offers scuba diving courses. Kokou Riding Centre offers morning, afternoon and evening horse rides, starting from the central square, for 7000/9000/10,000 dr for one/two/three hours; the one hour ride is recommended for children. Book with Cathy at Nissiotissa Tours (☎ 51 480), left off the main square.

Nissiotissa Tours can also organise caïque fishing trips (2500 dr), boats to nearby beaches, windsurfing and scuba outings, and excursions to Naxos, Delos, Mykonos, Santorini and Amorgos.

Places to Stay There are two camping grounds: ***Naoussa Camping** (☎ 51 595)*, at Kolimvythres, charges 1300/500 dr per person/tent, and ***Surfing Beach** (☎ 51 013)*, at Santa Maria, has a surfing and water-ski school. Minibuses from both meet ferries.

***Anna's Rooms** (☎ 51 538)* has simple, clean doubles with bathroom and patio for 12,000 dr. To get there, turn right off the main road into town at Hotel Atlantis (just before the main square). The E class ***Hotel Madaky** (☎ 51 475)*, off the central square, has doubles/triples for 8000/9000 dr with fridge, and singles/doubles for 13,000/15,000 dr with bathroom.

In the heart of town, ***Pension Stella** (☎ 51 317)* has a shady garden and doubles with bathroom for 15,000 dr. To reach it, turn left from the central square at Café Naoussa, then take the first right; continue past a small church on the left.

There is no shortage of good self-contained accommodation. ***Sunset Apartments** (☎ 51 733)*, has nice double apartments for 18,500 dr and two-bedroom apartments for four costing 24,000 dr. Face inland from the main square, follow the one way street uphill, and turn right at the T-junction – it's on the left. ***Katerina's** (☎ 51 642)* is a stunning place with red shutters and a beautiful patio with views over town and beach; two-person apartments are 14,000 dr. ***Isabella Apartments** (☎ 51 090)* next door and ***Senia Apartments** (☎ 51 971)* charge similar prices. As you come into town, these are all off the main road to the right, behind the OTE. The attractive ***Spiros Apartments*** *(☎ 51 210)*, right on the beach at Kolimvythres, has doubles/triples for 15,000/16,000 dr.

The elegant B class ***Hotel Fotilia*** *(☎ 52 581, fax 52 583)*, near the big church 200m uphill from the town centre, has spacious, traditional doubles for 21,000 dr, including breakfast. There is an old windmill in its courtyard, as well as a jacuzzi and pool. ***Hotel Papadakis*** *(☎ 51 643, fax 51 269)*, also with a pool, has stylish double suites and apartments for 25,000 dr. To get there, turn right off the main road (coming into town) at Hotel Atlantis and continue for about 200m. The B class ***Kondiratos Hotel*** *(☎ 51 693)* at Agia Anagyri Beach is also nice and has doubles for 29,600 dr, with breakfast.

Head for Nissiotissa Tours (☎ 51 480) if you need help with accommodation.

Places to Eat ***Moshonas Ouzeri*** (pronounced 'moskonas'), at the harbour, serves great fish; most dishes cost between 1500 dr and 2000 dr. Don't miss Argyro Barbarigou's ***Papadakis***, on the waterfront near the caïques. The food is traditional but inventive, and prices are very reasonable. The octopus and onion stew is luscious, and there are refreshing salads with fennel, soft local cheese and an assortment of olives and greens. Even the bread, which is rolled in fennel and sesame seeds, is very good. Home-made syrupy fruits are served for dessert.

Barbarossa Ouzeri, also by the port, has great char-grilled octopus and fish. ***Perivolaria*** garden restaurant, on the left, along from the bus stop, and ***Christos Taverna***, on the way to the post office, are both fine, upmarket places.

Around Paros

Marathi (Μαράθι) In antiquity Parian marble was considered the world's finest. The **marble quarries** have been abandoned, but it's exciting to explore the three shafts by torchlight. Take the Lefkes bus and get off at Marathi village, where you'll find a signpost to the quarries.

Lefkes to Moni Agiou Antoniou Lefkes (Λεύκες), 12km south-east of Parikia, is the island's highest and loveliest village, and was its capital during the Middle Ages. It boasts the magnificent **Agias Trias** cathedral, as well as the **Museum of Popular Aegean Civilisation** (open in summer), an amphitheatre and an interesting library.

The only accommodation is ***Hotel Pantheon*** *(☎ 41 646)*, with doubles for 13,500 dr, but there are some ***domatia*** on the road into town.

From the central square, a signpost points to a well preserved Byzantine paved path which leads to the village of **Prodromos**. Just below the village the path takes a sharp left which is easy to miss because there isn't a sign – don't take the wider route straight ahead. The walk through beautiful countryside takes about an hour.

From Prodromos, it's a short walk to either **Marmara** or **Marpissa**. From Marmara, it's a stroll to the sandy beach at **Molos**; from Marpissa you can puff your way up a steep paved path to the 16th century **Moni Agiou Antoniou** atop a 200m-high hill. On this fortified summit, the Turks defeated Paros' Venetian rulers in 1537. Although the monastery and its grounds are generally locked, there are breathtaking views to neighbouring Naxos.

After this exertion, you'll probably feel like having a swim at the nice little beach at **Piso Livadi**. This pretty fishing village is well on the way to becoming a resort and there are plenty of places to stay and eat overlooking the harbour. There's a ***camping ground*** on the outskirts of town.

Petaloudes (Πεταλούδες) In July and August, butterflies almost enshroud the copious foliage at Petaloudes (Valley of the Butterflies), 8km south of Parikia. They're actually tiger moths, but spectacular all the same. Travel agents organise tours from both Parikia and Naoussa; or take the Aliki bus and ask to be let off at the Petaloudes turn-off. Petaloudes is open only in July and August, 9 am to 8 pm Monday to Saturday and 9 am to 1 pm and 4 to 8 pm Sunday.

Beaches Apart from the beaches already mentioned, there is a good beach at **Krios**, accessible by taxi boat (400 dr return) from Parikia. Paros' most talked about beach, **Hrysi Akti** (Golden Beach), on the south-east coast, is nothing spectacular, but it's popular with windsurfers. Equipment for various water sports, including sailing, water-skiing and windsurfing, is available here.

The coast between Piso Livadi and Hrysi Akti has some decent, empty beaches. Some of the attempts to concoct beach resorts along here are heartbreaking – at **New Golden Beach** you can watch the bulldozers create a beach from scratch while builders work overtime to erect the usual box-style accommodation compounds.

ANTIPAROS

☎ 0284 • postcode 840 07 • pop 819

Antiparos was once regarded as the quiet alternative to Paros, but development is increasing. The permanent inhabitants live in an attractive village (also called Antiparos) that is rapidly becoming obscured by tourist accommodation. It's still a very pleasant place and is a popular holiday spot for families with young kids. No cars are allowed in the village, which makes it even nicer.

Getting There & Around

For details on boats from Paros, see Getting There & Away under Paros.

The only bus service on Antiparos runs to the cave in the centre of the island. In summer, this bus continues to Agios Georgios.

Captain Yannis runs caïque day trips (20,000 dr for up to six people) to secluded beaches. Ask for the friendly old captain at Smiles Cafe on the main square in Antiparos village or at the port.

Orientation & Information

To reach the village centre if you've come from Pounta, turn right from the quay, walk along the waterfront and turn left into the main street at Anarghyros restaurant. If you've come by excursion boat, walk straight ahead from the quay.

The post office is a fair way down on the left. The OTE, with currency exchange and ferry information, is just beyond. The central square is left at the top of the main street and then right, behind Smiles Cafe.

To reach the kastro, another Marco Sanudo creation, go under the stone arch that leads north off the central square.

Beach bums will direct you to the decent beaches. Nudism is only permitted on the camp-site beach.

Cave of Antiparos

Despite previous looting of stalactites and stalagmites, this cave is still awe-inspiring. In 1673, the French ambassador, Marquis de Nointel, organised a Christmas Mass (enhanced by a large orchestra) inside the cave for 500 Parians. In summer, the cave is open 10 am to 4 pm daily; admission is 600 dr.

There are buses every half-hour from the village of Antiparos (220 dr one way) or you can take an excursion boat (high season only) from Antiparos village (1200 dr) or Parikia (2500 dr); the price includes the 1.5km bus ride from the landing stage to the cave.

Places to Stay & Eat

The well equipped camp site, ***Camping Antiparos*** *(☎ 61 221)*, is on a beach 1km north of the quay; signs point the way. It charges 1000/300 dr per person/tent.

Domatia are prevalent and there are several hotels. On the waterfront, ***Anarghyros*** *(☎ 61 204)* has doubles with bathroom for 10,000 dr. The newish ***Hotel Mantalena*** *(☎ 61 206)*, farther along to the left, has doubles/triples for 17,000/20,000 dr with bathroom. All rooms have a balcony overlooking the port and there's a nice terrace. Nearby, ***Margarita Studios*** (same telephone) has good doubles for 17,000 dr.

The main street has many cafes. The popular ***Taverna Yorgis***, on the right, serves Greek family staples and specialises in fish. ***O Damis***, about 100m west of the main square (go under the stone archway that leads to the beach – not the one that goes into the kastro), is the oldest taverna on the island. It has a large menu of home-cooked

CYCLADES

traditional food and the service is friendly. Prices are very reasonable. Ask about *tsikoudia*, the local firewater.

Agios Georgios, in the south, has several ***tavernas***.

Naxos Νάξος

☎ 0285 • postcode 843 00 • pop 16,703

According to legend, it was on Naxos that Theseus abandoned Ariadne after she helped him find his way out of the Cretan labyrinth. She didn't pine long – she was soon ensconced in the arms of Dionysos, the god of wine and ecstasy and the island's favourite deity. Ever since, Naxian wine has been considered a fine remedy for a broken heart.

The island is the Cyclades' largest and most fertile, producing olives, grapes, figs, citrus, corn and potatoes. Rugged mountains and lush green valleys also make it one of the most beautiful. Mt Zeus (1004m; also known as Mt Zas or Zefs) is the archipelago's highest peak.

Naxos was an important Byzantine centre and boasts about 500 churches and monasteries, many containing interesting frescoes. Some of the early Christian basilicas were originally ancient temples.

The island is a wonderful place to explore on foot and walking is now a major draw for many visitors, especially Germans. Many old paths linking villages, churches and other sights still survive. For detailed route information, consult Christian Ucke's excellent *Walking Tours on Naxos*, available from local bookshops.

Getting There & Away

Air There is at least one flight daily to Athens (20,100 dr). Olympic Airways is represented by Naxos Tours (☎ 22 095, 23 043).

Ferry Naxos has around eight ferry connections daily with Piraeus (six hours, 5000 dr); seven with Paros (one hour, 1350 dr); six with Ios (1¼ hours, 2100 dr) and Santorini (three hours, 3100 dr); and two with Mykonos (three hours, 1900 dr).

There are daily boats to Iraklia (1¼ to 5¼ hours, 1300 dr), Shinousa (1¾ to five hours, 1400 dr), Koufonisia (2½ to 4¼ hours, 1500 dr) and Amorgos (two to 5½ hours, 2300 dr), and a few every week to Donousa (one to four hours, 1500 dr). Six boats weekly go to Sikinos (three hours, 1600 dr), five go to Folegandros (three hours, 2300 dr), Anafi (four hours, 2800 dr) and Samos (4¾ to 7½ hours, 4000 dr), four go to Syros (three hours, 3000 dr), Thessaloniki (14¾ hours, 7100 dr) and Iraklio on Crete (4¼ to 7½ hours, 5000 dr), and three go to Astypalea (5½ hours, 4000 dr), Rhodes (10 hours, 5000 dr) and Skiathos (8½ hours, 5300 dr).

There are two ferries weekly to Ikaria (2½ hours, 2500 dr) and Tinos (4¼ hours, 1900 dr), and one to Fourni (four hours, 3000 dr) and Kos (15 hours, 4000 dr).

Zas Travel (☎ 23 330) sells tickets for all ferries.

Hydrofoil There are around two hydrofoils daily to Paros (30 minutes, 2700 dr), Santorini (1¾ hours, 6100 dr) and Mykonos (1¼ hours, 3600 dr), one daily to Ios (50 minutes, 4200 dr), six weekly to Sifnos (1½ hours, 5800 dr), five weekly to Milos (three hours, 8200 dr) and Syros (1½ hours, 4100 dr), four weekly to Tinos (two hours, 3200 dr), three weekly to Amorgos (2¼ to 3¼ hours, 4000 dr), two weekly to Folegandros (1½ hours, 4600 dr) and Sikinos (one hour, 3000 dr), and one a week to Serifos (1½ hours, 5700 dr), Iraklia (30 minutes, 2200 dr), Shinousa (50 minutes, 2300 dr), Koufonisia (one hour, 2600 dr) and Donousa (1½ hours, 2500 dr).

The hydrofoil representative is Passenger Tours (☎ 25 329).

Catamaran There are at least two catamarans daily to Paros (30 minutes, 2700 dr) and Rafina (3¼ hours, 7000 dr), one daily to Syros (1½ hours, 4100 dr), Ios (50 minutes, 4200 dr) and Santorini (1½ hours, 6100 dr), six weekly to Piraeus (3¾ hours, 8000 dr), Mykonos (1½ hours, 3600 dr) and Tinos (two hours, 3200 dr), three weekly to Andros (3½ hours, 6000 dr), and two weekly to Amorgos (one to two hours, 3800 dr).

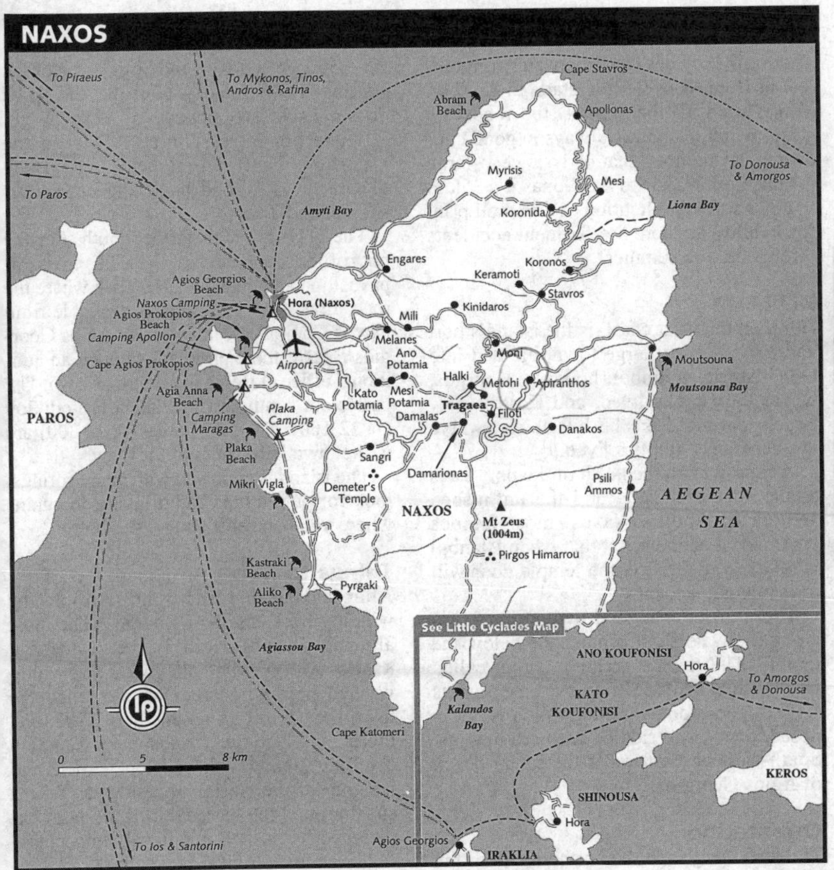

Naxos Tours sells Goutos and Minoan tickets and Kykladikon Travel (☎ 23 830) is the official agent for Strintzis Lines.

Excursion Boat There are daily excursions to Mykonos (9000 dr) and frequent excursions to Delos.

Getting Around

To/From the Airport There is no shuttle bus, but buses to Agios Prokopios and Agia Anna pass close by. A taxi costs 1500 dr.

Bus Frequent buses run to Agia Anna (300 dr) from Hora. Five buses daily serve Filoti (400 dr) via Halki (340 dr), four serve Apiranthos (600 dr) via Filoti and Halki, three serve Apollonas (1100 dr), and two serve Pyrgaki (400 dr) and Melanes (300 dr). There are less frequent departures to other villages.

Buses leave from the end of the wharf; timetables are posted outside the bus station and the Naxos Tourist Information Centre in Hora.

Car, Motorcycle & Bicycle You can hire cars and motorcycles as well as 21-speed all-terrain bicycles from the waterfront outlets in Hora. Bicycle hire starts at 1500 dr. You'll need all the gears – the roads are steep, winding and not always in good condition. Remember that it is a very large island: from Naxos to Apollonas it's 35km.

Pay particular attention to the small print for liability as there are frequent accidents throughout the summer.

HORA

Hora, on the west coast, is the island's port and capital. It's a large town, divided into two historic neighbourhoods – Bourgos, where the Greeks lived, and Kastro (now largely derelict), on the hill above, where the Venetian Catholics lived.

A causeway to the north of the port leads to the islet of Palatia and the unfinished **Temple of Apollo**, Naxos' most famous landmark. Legend has it that when İstanbul is returned to Greece, the temple door will miraculously appear.

There are some good swimming areas along the waterfront promenade below the temple. The town's northern shore, called Grotta – nicknamed Grotty by some tourists – is not good for swimming as it's very exposed, rocky, and riddled with sea urchins. South-west of the town is the sandy beach of Agios Georgios.

Orientation

The ferry quay is at the northern end of the waterfront, with the bus terminal in front. The busy waterfront is lined with cafes and restaurants and is the focus of most of the action. Behind the waterfront, a warren of little laneways and steps leads up to the Kastro.

Information

There is no EOT, but the privately owned Naxos Tourist Information Centre (NTIC; ☎ 25 301, emergency 24 525, fax 25 200), opposite the quay, provides advice on accommodation, excursions and rental cars. Despina Kitini and her staff have an amazing knowledge of the island and are more than willing to share it. Other services include reverse-charge phone calls, laundry for 2500 dr a load, and luggage storage starting at 500 dr a day. Note that the NTIC does not sell ferry tickets.

There are at least three ATMs on the waterfront. Not far from the National Bank of Greece is a good book and newspaper shop called Zoom.

The OTE is 150m farther south. For the post office, continue past the OTE, cross Papavasiliou and take the left branch where the road forks. Internet access is available from Naxos Computers, inland from Agios Georgios Beach; there are plans to open an additional office closer to the centre of town. The police are south-east of Plateia Protodikiou (☎ 22 100). The port police (☎ 23 300) are in the town hall, south of the quay.

The island is endowed with many springs; look for public taps and drinking fountains where you can refill your water bottle.

Things to See

After leaving the waterfront, turn into the winding backstreets of Bourgos. The most alluring part of Hora is the residential **Kastro**, with winding alleyways and whitewashed houses. Marco Sanudo made the town the capital of his duchy in 1207, and there are some handsome Venetian dwellings, many with well kept gardens and insignia of their original residents. Take a stroll around the kastro during siesta to experience its hushed, medieval atmosphere.

The **archaeological museum** (☎ 22 725) is in the Kastro, housed in a former school where author Nikos Kazantzakis was briefly a pupil. The contents include the usual collection of vases, torsos and funerary stelae, as well as Hellenistic and Roman terracotta figurines. There are, more interestingly, also some Early Cycladic figurines. The museum is open 8 am to 2.30 pm Tuesday to Sunday; admission is 1000 dr.

Close by, **Sanudo's Palace**, near the kastro ramparts, and the Roman Catholic **cathedral** (open daily at 6.30 pm) are worth seeing. The nearby **Naxos Cultural Centre** has art exhibits in summer.

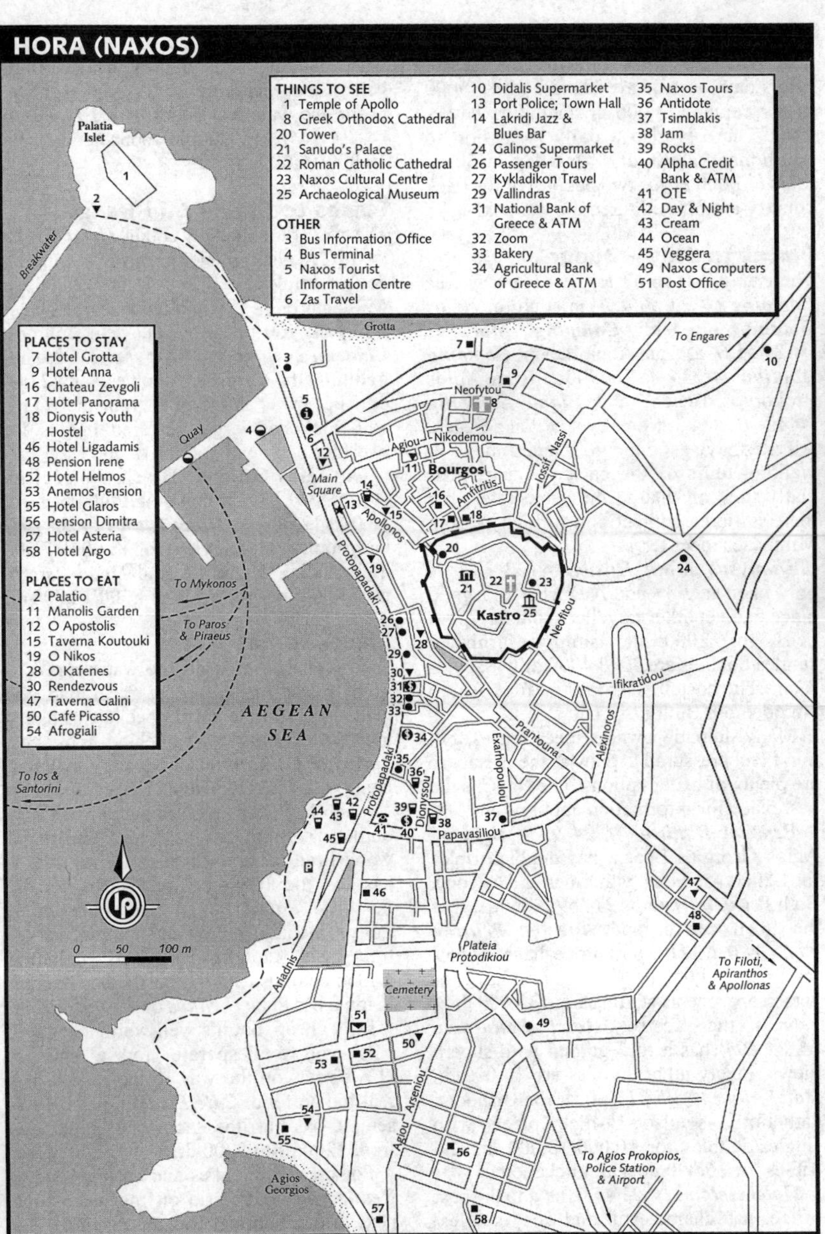
HORA (NAXOS)
THINGS TO SEE
1 Temple of Apollo
8 Greek Orthodox Cathedral
20 Tower
21 Sanudo's Palace
22 Roman Catholic Cathedral
23 Naxos Cultural Centre
25 Archaeological Museum
OTHER
3 Bus Information Office
4 Bus Terminal
5 Naxos Tourist Information Centre
6 Zas Travel
10 Didalis Supermarket
13 Port Police; Town Hall
14 Lakridi Jazz & Blues Bar
24 Galinos Supermarket
26 Passenger Tours
27 Kykladikon Travel
29 Vallindras
31 National Bank of Greece & ATM
32 Zoom
33 Bakery
34 Agricultural Bank of Greece & ATM
35 Naxos Tours
36 Antidote
37 Tsimblakis
38 Jam
39 Rocks
40 Alpha Credit Bank & ATM
41 OTE
42 Day & Night
43 Cream
44 Ocean
45 Veggera
49 Naxos Computers
51 Post Office
PLACES TO STAY
7 Hotel Grotta
9 Hotel Anna
16 Chateau Zevgoli
17 Hotel Panorama
18 Dionysis Youth Hostel
46 Hotel Ligadamis
48 Pension Irene
52 Hotel Helmos
53 Anemos Pension
55 Hotel Glaros
56 Pension Dimitra
57 Hotel Asteria
58 Hotel Argo
PLACES TO EAT
2 Palatio
11 Manolis Garden
12 O Apostolis
15 Taverna Koutouki
19 O Nikos
28 O Kafenes
30 Rendezvous
47 Taverna Galini
50 Café Picasso
54 Afrogiali
Palatia Islet
Breakwater
Grotta
Quay
Main Square
Bourgos
Kastro
Neofytou
Agiou Nikodemou
Amfitritis
Iossif Nassi
Apollonos
Protopapadaki
Neofitou
Ifikratidou
Prantouna
Exarhopoulou
Alexinoros
Dionysou
Papavasiliou
Plateia Protodikiou
Cemetery
Ariadnis
Agiou Arseniou
Agios Georgios
AEGEAN SEA
To Mykonos
To Paros & Piraeus
To Ios & Santorini
To Engares
To Filoti, Apiranthos & Apollonas
To Agios Prokopios, Police Station & Airport
0 50 100 m
CYCLADES

Organised Tours

The Naxos Tourist Information Centre offers day tours of the island by bus (5000 dr) or caïque (13,000 dr, including barbecue). There is also a daily excursion to Apollonas (2000 dr). One-day walking tours (15,000 dr for two people) of the back country are offered three times weekly.

Places to Stay – Budget

There are four camp sites near Hora: ***Naxos Camping*** *(☎ 23 500)*, 1km south of Agios Georgios Beach; ***Camping Maragas*** *(☎ 24 552)*, at Agia Anna Beach; ***Camping Apollon*** *(☎ 24 417)*, 700m from Agios Prokopios Beach; and ***Plaka Camping*** *(☎ 42 700)*, 6km from town at Plaka Beach. All sites have good facilities and some offer walking tours of the back country. Officially they all charge the same rates, but there is fierce competition in high season. Minibuses meet ferries.

Dionysos Youth Hostel *(☎ 22 331)* is only open in July and August. It's a good place to meet other travellers, and has dorm beds for 2000 dr; simply furnished singles/doubles are 3000/4000 dr with bathroom. The hostel is signposted from Agiou Nikodemou, Bourgos' main street.

Many domatia owners meet ferries, but don't feel pressured to go with them as there are plenty of better options. The NTIC is the best place for information about rooms.

Pension Dimitra *(☎ 24 922)*, right on Agios Georgios Beach, has doubles/triples for 12,000/15,000 dr with fridge and balcony. Both ***Pension Irene*** *(☎ 23 169)*, south-east of the town centre, and ***Anemos Pension*** *(☎ 25 098)*, near the post office, have doubles for around 14,000 dr. Anemos also has two-person apartments starting from 12,000 dr.

Near the Kastro, ***Hotel Panorama*** *(☎ 24 404)* has a roof garden with superb views; lovely quiet doubles are 14,000 dr. ***Hotel Anna*** *(☎ 25 213)*, near the Orthodox cathedral, is also a nice place with singles/doubles for 10,000/12,000 dr, and triples for 15,000 dr with kitchenette.

Hotel Helmos *(☎ 22 455)*, next to the post office, has characterful and cosy singles/doubles/triples for 8000/10,000/ 13,000 dr with balcony and bathroom; two/four-person apartments are 12,000/18,000 dr. Opposite the waterfront park, ***Hotel Ligdamis*** *(☎ 23 745)* has double rooms/studios for 10,000/15,000 dr.

Places to Stay – Mid-Range

The well furnished and quiet ***Hotel Grotta*** *(☎ 22 215)* has splendid sea views; singles/doubles/triples are 12,000/16,000/ 20,000 dr with bathroom. If you telephone, the owner will pick you up at the quay. In Bourgos, ***Chateau Zevgoli*** *(☎ 24 525, fax 25 200)* has traditionally furnished doubles for 22,000 dr. The owner is Despina from the NTIC, who also has large, restored homes for two/four people at 16,000/18,000 dr.

On Agios Georgios Beach, ***Hotel Argo*** *(☎ 25 330)* has air-con singles/doubles for 10,000/12,000 dr, ***Hotel Glaros*** *(☎ 23 101)* has rooms with sea view for 13,000/17,500 dr including breakfast, and ***Hotel Asteria*** *(☎ 23 002)* has rooms for 14,000/18,000 dr.

Places to Eat

Lively ***O Apostolis*** on the waterfront is a great place for mezedes, fresh fish and grilled octopus (a local speciality); prices are very reasonable. Just behind Apollonos, ***Taverna Koutouki*** is also very popular. Nearby, ***Manolis Garden*** specialises in chicken in yogurt and wine and has a nice outdoor setting. It's next to a traditional wood-fired bakery. ***Taverna Galini***, south-east of the town centre, is the locals' favourite. ***Palatio***, a bar-cafe at the end of the promenade below the temple, serves light meals and fresh seafood, including grilled octopus. But the best fish restaurant in town has to be ***O Nikos*** on the waterfront. It's not cheap, but it's well worth a splurge.

If you're desperate for a change, ***O Kafenes***, on the way to the Kastro, has real Indian food. ***Café Picasso***, just off Arseniou, has burritos, tacos and quesadillas from 1200 dr to 2300 dr.

For breakfast, cakes and coffee, head to ***Rendezvous*** patisserie on the waterfront, next to the National Bank. ***Afrogiali***, near

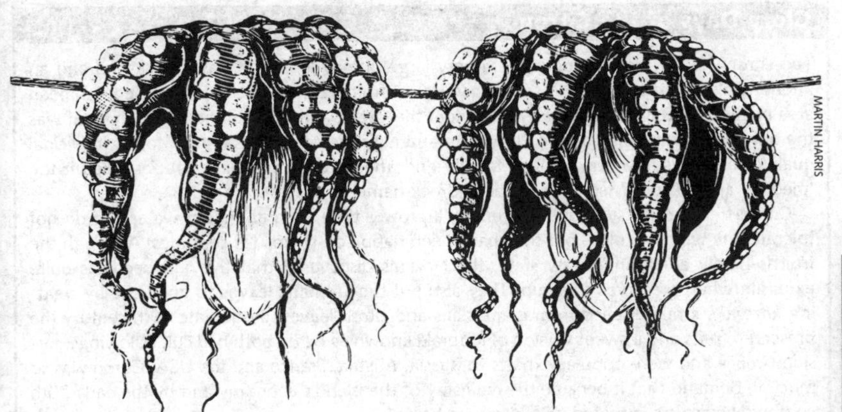

Octopus *(ohtapodi)* drying; seafood features prominently on Greek menus

Agios Georgios Beach, is the best place for gyros (350 dr).

Immediately adjacent to Zoom bookshop is the town's best ***bakery***. The cheapest ***supermarkets*** are Galinos and Didalis, both a little way out of town.

Naxian specialities include *kefalotyri* (hard cheese), honey, *citron* (a liqueur made from the leaves of the citron tree), *raki*, ouzo, and fine white wine. ***Tsimblakis*** olive and cheese shop, on Papavasilou, is a fascinating, cavernous old place selling local produce. You'll see rabbit and partridge on restaurant menus in spring.

Entertainment

One block back from the waterfront, ***Rocks*** and ***Jam*** are popular late-night bars. ***Day & Night***, ***Cream***, ***Ocean*** and ***Veggera***, all at the end of the waterfront near the OTE, are the places to go disco dancing. On the Grotta road, not far from the waterfront, is a collection of ***clubs*** that change name each year.

Antidote bar has at least 55 different types of beer from around the world, ranging from 400 dr to 4500 dr for Belgian Trappist. ***Lakridi Jazz & Blues Bar***, behind the waterfront, on the way to the Kastro, is a nice, laid-back little place.

Shopping

You can find citron liqueur in beautiful French and Italian bottles at the Vallindras shop on the waterfront. The green citron is the sweetest; the yellow is a bit stronger and has more citron aroma, and the clear stuff is reminiscent of Cointreau and quite potent indeed. Vallindras also makes very good ouzo untainted by additives. Samples are available at the shop. The citron fruit itself is bottled in a sugary syrup for 'spoon sweets'; the preserved fruit is a little bit lemony but quite subtle and almost quince-like. Take-home jars are available at Vallindras.

In the streets heading up to the Kastro you can find beautiful embroidery and hand-made silver jewellery. Most of the gold and silver baubles here are the same as those available on Mykonos, but 30% cheaper.

AROUND NAXOS

Beaches

Agios Georgios is just a typical town beach, but you can windsurf here on water so shallow that it seems you could wade to Paros, visible in the distance; the beach becomes so crowded that you may develop an uncontrollable desire to do so. The next beach south is **Agios Prokopios**, a sheltered bay,

Glory Days of the Citron

The citron *(Citrus medica)* looks like a very large, lumpy lemon. It has a thick rind and an interior yielding little juice. This seemingly useless fruit was introduced to the Mediterranean area in about 300 BC, probably by Alexander the Great, and up until the Christian era it was the only citrus fruit cultivated in Europe. In antiquity the citron was known for its medicinal qualities and was also a symbol of fertility and affluence. The ancient Greeks called it the 'median' apple (from Media, the ancient Greek name for Persia).

Citron trees are fussy about where they'll grow – they need abundant water and do not tolerate any wind or cold – but they have been happy on Naxos for centuries. Although the fruit is barely edible in its raw state, the Naxians discovered that the rind becomes quite exquisite when preserved in syrup. They also put the aromatic leaves to good use by creating *kitroraki*, a raki distilled from grape skins and citron leaves. By the late 19th century the preserved fruits and a sweet version of kitroraki known as *citron* both had cult followings outside Greece and were popular exports to Russia, Austria, France and the USA. Citron was so much in demand that it became the mainstay of the island's economy and by the early 20th century Naxos was carpeted with citron orchards.

Alas, citron went out of vogue after WWII; even the islanders abandoned it, seduced by the invasion of exotic alcohols from the outside world. In the 1960s most citron trees were uprooted to make way for more useful, more profitable crops.

This might seem like a sad story, but fear not: the citron is on the rise. On Naxos there are currently two distilleries producing citron liqueur. At Vallindras distillery in Halki they still distil citron the old-fashioned way, using leaves collected from the orchards in the autumn and winter. The harvesting of leaves is an arduous, time-consuming task, due to the trees' thorns, and if too many leaves are taken this can destroy the tree. The leaves are laid out in a dry room, dampened with water, and then placed with alcohol and water in a boiler fuelled by olive wood. The distillate is added to water and sugar, and citron is born.

These days approximately 13,000 to 15,000L of citron are produced each year at Vallindras. Still, this is nowhere near enough to meet current demand, and nothing can be done about this until more citron trees are planted. As the 20th century draws to a close it is nearly impossible to get hold of citron outside Greece, so make sure you track some down while visiting its island home. It comes in three strengths and sweetnesses: the green is the traditional Naxian liqueur and has the most sugar and least alcohol; the yellow has little sugar, more aroma and more alcohol; the white falls somewhere in between and resembles Cointreau. Citron is very good after dinner, especially after fish.

If you want to see citron trees in action, look for orchards around Hora and in Engares, Melanes, Halki and Apollonas.

followed by **Agia Anna** – a lovely long arc of sand. Sandy beaches continue down as far as **Pyrgaki**. There are ***domatia*** and ***tavernas*** aplenty along this stretch, and any of these beaches would make a good spot to stop for a few days. Other worthy beaches are **Plaka**, **Aliko**, **Mikri Vigla** and **Kastraki**. **Abram**, north of Hora, is also a nice spot.

Tragaea Τραγαία

The lovely Tragaea region is a vast plain of olive groves and unspoilt villages harbouring numerous little Byzantine churches. **Filoti**, on the slopes of Mt Zeus, is the region's largest village; the Maharis butcher shop sells all you'll need for a perfect picnic, including fresh cheese and bread, wine and fruit. On the outskirts of the village (coming from Hora), an asphalt road leads off right into the heart of the Tragaea. This road brings you to the isolated hamlets of **Damarionas** and **Damalas**.

The picturesque village of **Halki** has several tower houses built by aristocratic families as refuges and lookouts in the days of pirate raids and feuds between the islanders and the Venetians and Turks. The best preserved is the **Gratsia Pyrgos**; to reach it turn right at **Panagia Protothronis** church, which is itself worth checking out for its fine frescoes. It is on the main road near the bus stop. The **Vallindras distillery**, housed in a lovely old building in the centre of town, offers citron tastings and impromptu tours.

Agii Apostoli (Holy Apostles) church in Metohi is famous for its odd triple storey architecture, while **Agios Mamas**, near Potamia, is known for its early 'cross in a square' layout. The **Panagia Drosiani** at **Moni**, north of Halki, is one of the oldest and most important churches in the Balkans. Successive layers of frescoes have been uncovered, some dating back to the 7th century. If it's locked, seek out the priest's wife and ask for the key.

South-west of the Tragaea, near **Sangri**, an impressive **Temple to Demeter** (also known as Dimitra's Temple) is being restored. The small church next to the temple was originally built from remnants of the temple and was recently demolished and rebuilt so that the temple material could be salvaged. Signs point the way from Sangri.

Melanes Μέλανες

Near the hillside villages of Melanes and Mili, there is a large unfinished 6th century BC **kouros** (male statue), abandoned in a quarry that is now encircled by orchards. The Kondylis family, who own the land, are the official guardians. Near the site, next to a large goldfish pond, they have a little ***cafe*** of sorts where the old lady serves Greek coffee, wine, omelettes and salads. Another, less famous, kouros was found nearby a few years ago; ask at the cafe for directions.

Taverna Xenaki *(☎ 62 374)* in Melanes has rabbit and free-range chicken; if you order an hour in advance, it will prepare a feast. From Melanes you can walk down to **Kato Potamia**, **Mesi Potamia** and **Ano Potamia**, where there are more orchards and lovely tavernas. From there, it's not far to Halki, where you can catch the bus back to town.

Pirgos Himarrou Πύργος Χειμάρρου

South of Filoti, in the island's remote south-east, the Pirgos Himarrou is a well preserved cylindrical marble tower dating from Hellenistic times. It is three storeys high with an internal spiral staircase. One theory holds that it was a lookout post used to warn of approaching pirates, but the position of the tower in a place with limited views discounts this. It was more likely a fortified house on a prosperous farmstead – the marble base of a large olive or wine press lies nearby.

After checking out the tower, continue south for a swim at **Kalandos Bay**. Take food and water as there are no shops or tavernas.

Apiranthos Απείρανθος

Apiranthos is a handsome village of stone houses and marble-paved streets. Its inhabitants are descendants of refugees who fled Crete to escape Turkish repression. The village is known for its communist tendencies – its most famous son is Manolis Glezos, the resistance fighter who during WWII replaced the Nazi flag atop the Acropolis with the Greek one. He later became the parliamentary representative for the Cyclades.

On the right of the village's main thoroughfare (coming from the Hora-Apollonas road) is a **museum of natural history**. Just before the museum a path on your left leads to the centre of town, past the **women's handcrafts co-op**, which has looms and textiles, the **geology museum** and the **archaeology museum**. The museums are open 9 am to 2 pm (sometimes later in summer) Tuesday to Sunday. Admission to the archaeology museum is 1000 dr.

Just before the beautiful main square dominated by a huge plane tree is the famous

Taverna Lefteris, where you can eat in the garden overlooking the valley. Apiranthos has no accommodation.

Moutsouna Μουτσούνα

The road from Apiranthos to Moutsouna winds through spectacular mountain scenery. Formerly a busy port shipping the emery mined in the region, Moutsouna is now something of a ghost town. It feels peaceful rather than spooky and there are some nice beaches with superbly clear water. ***Pension Ostria*** *(☎ 094-148 904)* is a lovely place and has singles/doubles for 12,000/15,000 dr, and there's also a couple of ***tavernas***.

Apollonas Απόλλωνας

Apollonas, on the north coast, was once a tranquil fishing village but is now a popular resort. It has a small sandy beach and a larger pebble one.

Hordes of day-trippers come to see the gargantuan 7th century BC **kouros** which lies in an ancient quarry a short walk from the village. The largest of three on the island (the other two are in the Melanes region), it is signposted to the left as you approach Apollonas on the main inland road from Hora. This 10.5m statue was apparently abandoned unfinished because it cracked. Apollonas has several ***domatia*** and ***tavernas***.

The inland route from Hora to Apollonas winds through spectacular mountains – a worthwhile trip. With your own transport you can return to Hora via the west-coast road, passing through wild and sparsely populated country with awe-inspiring sea views. Several tracks branch down to secluded beaches.

Little Cyclades
Μικρές Κυκλάδες

The chain of small islands between Naxos and Amorgos is variously called the Little Cyclades, Minor Islands, Back Islands and Lesser Islands. Only four – Donousa, Koufonisia, Iraklia and Shinousa – have permanent populations.

All were densely populated in antiquity, as evident from the large number of graves found. In the Middle Ages, the islands were uninhabited except by pirates and goats. After independence, intrepid souls from Naxos and Amorgos re-inhabited them, and now each island has a small population. Until recently, their only visitors were Greeks returning to their roots. These days they receive a few tourists, mostly backpackers looking for splendid beaches and a laid-back lifestyle.

Donousa is the northernmost of the group and farthest from Naxos. The others are clustered near the south-east coast of Naxos. Each has a public telephone and post agency. Money can usually be changed at the general store or post agency, but rates are lousy – bring drachmas with you.

Getting There & Away

Links with the Little Cyclades are regular but tenuous, so make sure you have plenty of time before embarking on a visit – these islands do not make a convenient last stop a few days before you're due to fly home!

At least a few times a week the F/B *Express Skopelitis* provides a lifeline service between Naxos and Amorgos via the Little Cyclades (see the Naxos and Amorgos sections for details of prices and times), but it's small, extremely slow, and susceptible to bad weather. In high season it does a daily run from Amorgos to Koufonisia, Shinousa, Iraklia, Naxos, Paros and Mykonos, returning by the same route.

Twice a week the F/B *Express Hermes* sails from Piraeus to each of the Little Cyclades via Paros and Naxos, continuing to Amorgos and Astypalea. A few other large ferries call at the islands in high season, often at ungodly hours.

Once a week there is a hydrofoil from Naxos to Iraklia (30 minutes, 2200 dr), Shinousa (50 minutes, 2300 dr), Koufonisia (one hour, 2600 dr) and Donousa (1½ hours, 2500 dr).

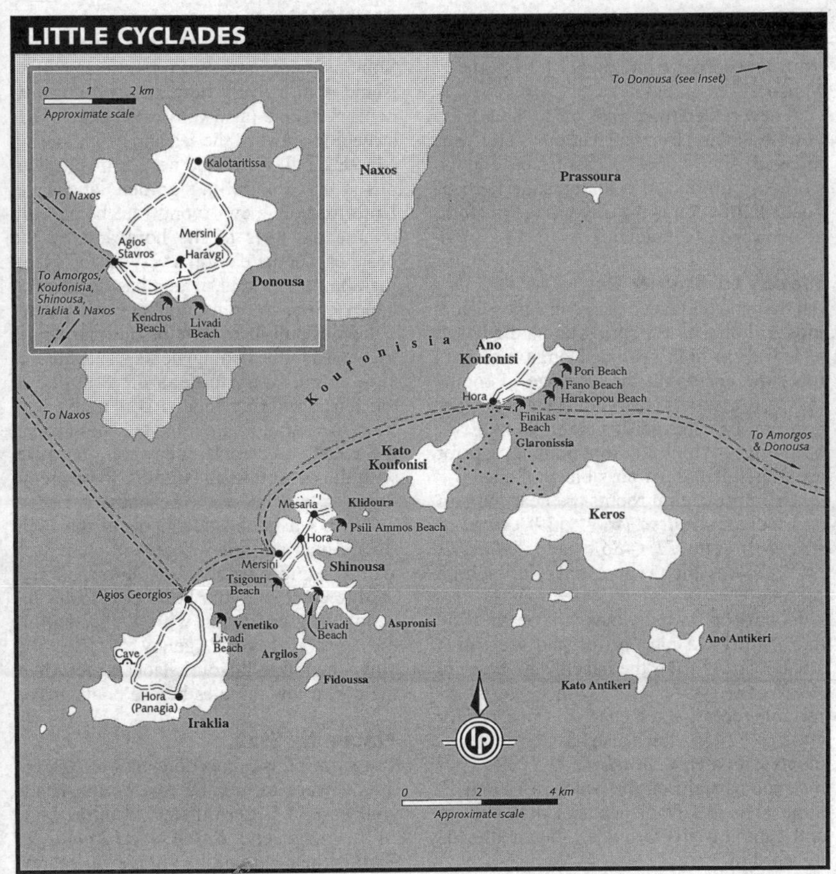

Because of its northerly position, it is sometimes easier to get to Donousa from Mykonos than from Naxos.

IRAKLIA Ηράκλεια

☎ 0285 • postcode 843 00 • pop 110

This rather barren island has a couple of tiny villages, a nice beach and not much else, save a small clique of Germans who return each year. The island's only sight as such is a **cave** with fine stalactites. Tourism is increasing, but amenities (including rooms) are few. The port and main village is **Agios Georgios**. It's very quiet and not particularly scenic, although the deep cove-like harbour is rather pretty. The way into town is to the right, around the port beach, and then left up the hill. From here the town's two main roads fork around a cactus-filled ravine.

The right fork leads to Melissa, the general store that sells ferry tickets. Melissa also has a cardphone, serves as the island's post office and has domatia. The left fork leads past the second minimarket (which is also Perigiali restaurant) and more domatia. You can exchange money at Melissa and at Maistrali bar-cafe.

A new sealed road leads off to the left (as you face inland from the harbour). This runs to **Livadi** – the island's nicest beach, and the stomping ground of a picturesque herd of goats. Farther on is the tiny village of **Hora**, also known as Panagia.

Places to Stay & Eat

All domatia and tavernas are in Agios Georgios, although a few spring up on the beach at Livadi in high season. Domatia owners meet the boats, but the shortage of rooms makes it a sellers' market – take whatever you can get and don't bother looking for bargains. In high season doubles go for around 10,000 dr. If possible, call ahead.

The most central rooms are near the port and include ***Melissa*** *(☎ 71 539)*, ***Anthi & Angelo's*** *(☎ 71 486)*, and ***Manolis*** *(☎ 71 569)*, which is open only during high season.

Rooms up on the windy hill on the way to Livadi have nice patios and are just a stone's throw from the beach. The best are ***Alexandra*** *(☎ 71 482)*, with clean, comfortable rooms, and the swish ***Anna's Place*** *(☎/fax 71 145)*, which also has deluxe apartments with a view. ***Marietta*** *(☎ 71 252)* has nice rooms right on the beach at Livadi. A large sign at Livadi declares that nudism and camping are forbidden, but neither is unheard of.

There are three tavernas in Agios Georgios, all serving fresh fish and the usual fare. ***Perigiali*** is a popular place with a large marble table encircling an old pine tree. ***O Pevkos***, also known as Dimitri's, is more traditional and shaded by an even larger pine. You'll be led into the kitchen to choose your meal; for breakfast try the yogurt served with the local thyme honey. ***Maistrali***, opposite Pevkos, is the local bar; it also sells tickets for Ventouris Sea Lines' *Georgios Express* and Agapitos Lines' *Naias Express*, both of which call about once a week.

SHINOUSA Σχοινούσα

☎ 0285 • postcode 843 00 • pop 120

Shinousa (skih-**noo**-sah) is a little gem of an island with a lively **hora** and smiling residents. The hora (also known as Panagia) has sweeping views of the sea and neighbouring islands on all sides, and nestles inconspicuously into the rolling golden landscape. Unfortunately, new 'rooms' are being built on the outskirts of the hora and by the beaches, but there's still a very pastoral feeling about the island, which has its share of happy cows, chickens, donkeys and goats.

Ferries pull in at **Mersini** Harbour, home to the island's fishing boats. The hora is 1km uphill, so try to get a lift with one of the locals offering rooms. Dirt tracks lead from the hora to numerous beaches around the coast; take food and water, because, with the exception of **Tsigouri**, there are no shops or tavernas at the beaches.

There's a public telephone in the main square and a couple of general stores sell stamps. Unfortunately, ferry information is hard to come by; your best bet is to ask the people you're staying with. Or try calling the Central Travel Agency (☎ 71 950), down the hill at Tsigouri. Tickets are sold at the port a few minutes before boats arrive.

Places to Stay

There are a few rooms down at Mersini, but if you want to see the rest of the island you're much better off staying in the hora. At the budget end, ***Kafe-Ouzeri Rooms for Rent*** in the centre of the village has spartan triples for 5000 dr. ***Kyra Pothiti*** *(☎ 71 184)*, a bit farther along the main street, has nice, cosy doubles for 7000 dr with balcony and bathroom. On the road to Mesaria, ***Anna Domatia*** *(☎ 71 161)* has good, clean singles/doubles for 7000/8000 dr. ***Hotel Sunset*** *(☎ 71 948)* is a brand new, comfortable but impersonal complex with rooms for 8000/12,000 dr; it's run by the folk at Anna Domatia.

Ghrispos Tsigouri Beach Villas *(☎ 71 930, fax 71 176)* is a crazy family affair about 500m away from the hora, down by the beach at Tsigouri. Doubles go for

16,500 dr, including breakfast. It's close to the beach (though the path to the beach is unfinished and access is difficult), but if you want to pop into the hora occasionally, you're faced with a long, dusty walk uphill. Similarly isolated is ***Panorama*** *(☎ 71 160)*, by the beach at Livadi, where doubles with bathroom are 9000 dr, or 13,000 dr with kitchen.

Places to Eat

You're unlikely to have any very uplifting culinary adventures on Shinousa, an island where you might want to do a bit of self-catering. Outside high season the only establishment open for lunch is ***Kyra Pothiti***. All drinks and meals come with obligatory serves of her home-made *myzithra*, which isn't bad the first time. Steer clear of the greasy-spoon *giouvetsi* (meat with macaroni) and stick to fish and baked vegetables. ***Panorama*** has good salads and charcoal grilled fish, and ***tavernas*** at the port serve freshly caught fish and lobster. The ***bakery*** just past Anna Domatia on the road to Mesaria is a good place to have breakfast.

To Kentro kafeneio is the most popular and nicest looking bar, but is pretty much a male-only domain; brave women may wish to transgress its boundaries. The only other bar is the ***Cafe-Pub Margarita*** down the steps just around the corner.

KOUFONISIA (Κουφονήσια)

☎ 0285 • postcode 843 00 • pop 284

Koufonisia is the only one of the Little Cyclades that's anywhere near the tourist trail, and it has a lot to offer. It's really two islands, Ano Koufonisi and Kato Koufonisi, but only the latter is permanently inhabited.

Despite being the smallest of the Little Cyclades, Koufonisia is the most densely populated, which adds quite a bit of life to its hora. Every family is involved with fishing – the island boasts the largest fishing fleet in Greece in proportion to its population. And because it's so attractive, it hasn't suffered from an exodus of young people to the mainland and the consequent ghost-town effect seen on many of the Cyclades; in fact, it's brimming with happy children and teenagers.

The beaches are picture-perfect swathes of golden sand lapped by crystal-clear turquoise waters; the locals are hospitable and friendly; and food and accommodation options are far more plentiful and refined than on neighbouring islands.

A caïque ride away, **Kato Koufonisi** has beautiful beaches and a lovely church. Archaeological digs on **Keros**, the large lump of rock that looms over Koufonisia to the south, have uncovered over 100 Early Cycladic figurines, including the famous harpist and flautist now on display in Athens' archaeological museum. There are no guides at the site.

Orientation & Information

Koufonisia's only settlement extends behind the ferry quay and around the pretty harbour filled with the island's fishing flotilla. The older part of town, the hora, is on the low hill behind the quay.

From the quay head right towards the town beach, and take the first road to the left. Continue to the crossroads, then turn left onto the village's main pedestrian thoroughfare, decorated with flower motifs.

Along here you'll find a small mini-market and an inconspicuous ticket agency (look for the dolphins painted above the door). Also here is the tiny, one-phone OTE, complete with straw ceiling; the old guy standing by obviously doesn't see much action now that the island has cardphones. The post office is on the first road to the left as you come from the ferry quay.

The town beach sees a few swimmers but mostly serves as a football field (fishing nets are strung up on the goal posts) for the local kids. Cars and pedestrians heading to the south coast road also traverse it.

Beaches

Koufonisia is blessed with some outstanding beaches and a wild coastal landscape of low sand dunes punctuated by rocky coves and caves. The dunes are covered in wild flowers and hardy shrubs.

A walk along the south coast road is the nicest way to access the island's beaches. The road extends a couple of kilometres from the eastern end of the town beach to **Finikas**, **Harakopou** and **Fano** beaches.

However, the best beaches and swimming places are farther along the path that follows the coast from Fano to the superb stretch of sand at **Pori**. There are no facilities at Pori, so take food and water. Pori can also be reached by an inland road that heads east from the crossroads in the hora.

Organised Tours

Koufonisia Tours (☎ 71 671, fax 74 091) at Villa Ostria can organise caïque trips to Keros (6000 dr for two people) and Kato Koufonisi (7000 dr for two).

Places to Stay

The ***camping ground*** *(☎ 71 683)* is by the beach at Harakopou; it's a bit shadeless but otherwise adequate.

At the western end of the village, ***Rooms Maria*** *(☎ 71 778)* has cute two-person apartments overlooking the small fishing harbour for 10,000 dr. To get there, walk along the main pedestrian street and take the first left after Scholeio bar. ***Rooms to Let Akrogiali*** *(☎ 71 685)* has nice rooms with sea views at the eastern end of the town beach; doubles with fridge are 10,300 dr. ***Lefteris Rooms*** *(☎ 71 458)*, on the town beach, has doubles/triples/quads for 10,000/12,000/14,000 dr. ***Katerina's*** *(☎ 71 670)*, on the road leading from the port to the hora, has nice clean doubles with balcony and shared kitchen for 12,000 dr.

Villa Ostria *(☎/fax 71 671)* is a cosy little hotel with very comfortable rooms with telephone, fridge and veranda for 18,000/16,000 dr with/without breakfast. To get there, walk along the town beach and take the first left. ***Keros Studios*** *(☎ 71 600)*, near the post office, also has nice rooms for 16,000 dr.

On the beach at Finikas, ***Hotel Finikas*** *(☎ 71 368)* has simple rooms for around 8000 dr and fancier new ones for 13,000 dr. All have a balcony and bathroom.

Places to Eat

Giorgos, at the eastern end of the waterfront on the road to the beaches, has excellent fish and good wines from all over Greece. Everything at ***Capitan Nikolas*** is delicious and beautifully presented, but the grilled fresh fish, which comes hidden under a veil of finely chopped parsley, is hard to beat. The restaurant looks out over the small harbour at the western end of the village; to get there, follow the main pedestrian street to the end and turn left.

Nikitouri, past Keros Studios, also has good fish. ***Lefteris***, below the rooms of the same name, has fine, reasonably priced Greek standards and is one of the few places open for lunch. ***Fanari***, next to the windmills above the quay, has good wood-fired pizzas, *pastitsio* and gyros.

Scholeio is a cosy little bar occupying an old schoolhouse at the far end of the main pedestrian street.

Out of town, there's a ***taverna*** by the beach at Finikas and a good fish ***restaurant*** on Kato Koufonisi.

DONOUSA (Δονούσα)

☎ 0285 • postcode 843 00 • pop 110

Donousa is the least accessible of the Little Cyclades because it's too far north to be a convenient stop for ferries en route to more popular islands. The main attraction here, as on Iraklia, is that there is nothing much to do except lie on the beach.

Agios Stavros is the main settlement and the island's port. It has a reasonably nice beach, which also serves as a thoroughfare for vehicles and foot traffic. Behind the beach there are lush vegetable gardens and vineyards.

Kendros, over the hill to the west, is a sandy and secluded beach. **Livadi**, the next beach along, sees even fewer visitors. As on many of the other small islands, a frenzy of road construction is currently under way on Donousa, making many of the walks, which used to be so pleasurable, a lot less attractive.

There is one public telephone, up the hill two streets back from the waterfront; look for the large satellite dish above the OTE shack. Stamps are sold at the minimarket on the street running behind the beach.

There is a ticket agency on the waterfront, but it is rarely open and the posted schedule is years out of date; buy your ticket on board from the purser if the agency is closed. Be aware that no-one on the island has much of an idea when the next boat is due or where it's going; unless you are happy to be marooned here for weeks on end, it's worth establishing – before you set out for Donousa – how you're going to leave. Some of the boats to Naxos go via Astypalea, a 12 hour detour you may wish to avoid.

Places to Stay & Eat

Camping is tolerated at Kendros, but you'll need to hike into town for food and water.

The following domatia all charge around 9000 dr for a double. ***Spiros Skopelitis Rooms*** (☎ *51 586*), halfway along the town beach, are nice bungalows, decorated with oriental rugs, set in a shady garden. ***Nikitas Markoulis Rooms***, near the kafeneio, and ***To Ilio Vasilema*** (☎ *51 570*), the taverna at the far end of the town beach, also have reasonable rooms.

Aposperitis taverna is next to Spiros Skopelitis and, along with To Ilio Vasilema, serves the usual fare. The hub of village life is the little ***Kafeneio To Kyma*** by the quay. Everyone seems to pass through here at least once a day and in the evenings it gets rather lively.

Amorgos Αμοργός

☎ 0285 • postcode 840 08 • pop 1630

Elongated Amorgos (ah-mor-**goss**) is the most easterly Cycladic island. With rugged mountains and an extraordinary monastery clinging to a cliff, Amorgos is an enticing island for those wishing to venture off the well worn Mykonos-Paros-Santorini route. It also offers excellent walking.

Amorgos has two ports, Katapola and Aegiali; boats from Naxos usually stop at Katapola first. The beautiful, unspoilt capital, Hora (also known as Amorgos), is up high, north-east of Katapola.

Getting There & Away

Ferry Most ferries stop at both Katapola and Aegiali, but check if this is the case with your ferry. There are daily boats to Naxos (two to 5¾ hours, 2300 dr), Koufonisia (one hour, 1500 dr), Shinousa (1½ hours, 2000 dr), Iraklia (two hours, 2100 dr) and Paros (three hours, 2750 dr), but some of these go to the resort of Piso Livadi (three to 4½ hours, 2750 dr) rather than Parikia. There are at least six ferries weekly to Piraeus (10 hours, 4500 dr).

Ferries also serve Mykonos (six hours, 3100 dr, five weekly), Donousa (30 minutes, 1400 dr, four weekly), Astypalea (2½ hours, 2700 dr, three weekly) and Syros (4½ to 9½ hours, 3400 dr, two weekly). There is a weekly boat to Rafina (10¾ hours, 4700 dr) via Tinos and Andros, and to Kalymnos (three hours, 3400 dr), Kos (4¼ hours, 4100 dr) and Rhodes (eight hours, 4600 dr).

Hydrofoil Four hydrofoils weekly go to Naxos (2¼ to 3¼ hours, 4000 dr) and Mykonos (three to five hours, 6200 dr), and three to Syros (6¼ hours, 6800 dr), Santorini (1½ hours, 4620 dr) and Ios (two hours, 4200 dr). Two weekly serve Paros (1½ hours, 5500 dr), Tinos (six hours, 5100 dr), Syros (2¾ to 4¾ hours, 6800 dr), Koufonisia (one hour, 2600 dr), Iraklia (two hours, 3500 dr) and Shinousa (1½ hours, 3300 dr). A weekly service goes to Donousa (one hour, 2400 dr).

Catamaran Goutos Lines and Strintzis both have weekly fast cats from Katapola to Rafina (five to seven hours, 9500 dr), via Naxos (one to two hours, 3800 dr), Paros (1½ to 2½ hours, 5500 dr), Mykonos (2¼ to four hours, 6200 dr), Tinos (2¾ hours, 5100 dr) and Andros (3½ to 6¼ hours, 8100 dr). Strintzis also stops at Aegiali.

Getting Around

Regular buses go from Katapola to Hora (15 minutes, 220 dr), Moni Hozoviotissis

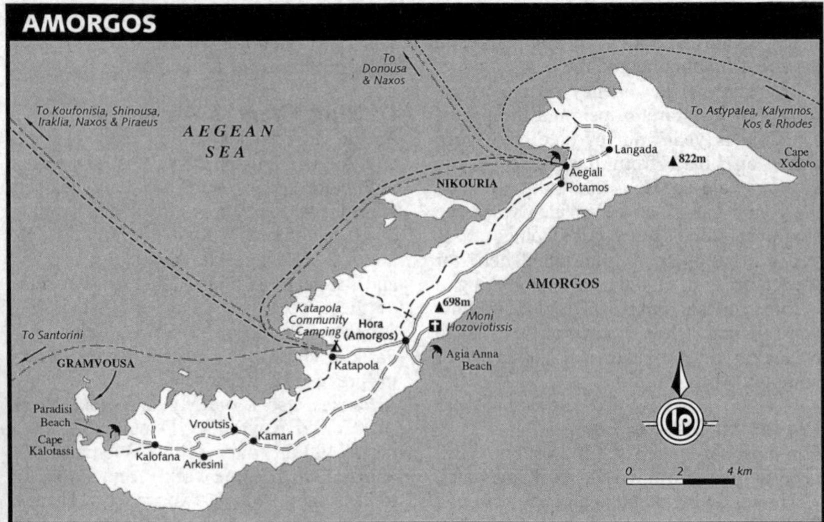

(15 minutes, 220 dr), Agia Anna Beach (20 minutes, 220 dr) and Aegiali (30 minutes, 450 dr), but services are few on weekends. There are also buses from Aegiali to the picturesque village of Langada. Schedules are posted on bus windscreens.

Motorcycles are available for rent in both Katapola and Aegiali. Aegialis Tours (☎ 73 107, fax 73 394), in Aegiali, is the only car hire agency.

KATAPOLA Κατάπολα

Katapola, the principal port, is a pretty town occupying a large, dramatic bay in the most verdant part of the island. A smattering of remains from the ancient Cretan city of Minoa, as well as a Mycenaean cemetery, lie above the port. Amorgos has also yielded many Cycladic finds; the largest figurine in the National Archaeological Museum in Athens was found in the vicinity of Katapola. Boats dock either in front of the central square or to the right (facing inland). The bus station is on the waterfront, near the square.

There is no tourist office or tourist police. Contact Aegialis Tours (see Getting Around) for information. The regular police (☎ 71 210) are on the central square. There is a post office on the square and an ATM on the waterfront nearby.

It can be difficult to extract information about ferries despite the existence of a number of ticket agencies; the old guy at the ouzeri ticket agency (see Places to Stay & Eat) is the most helpful.

Places to Stay & Eat

***Katapola Community Camping** (☎ 71 257)* is back from the northern end of the waterfront. Turn left from the quay (as you face inland).

Domatia owners usually meet the ferries. ***Pension Maroussa** (☎ 71 038)*, just past Katapola Camping, has a beautiful garden; doubles with fridge and bathroom start from 10,000 dr. The C class ***Hotel St George** (☎ 71 228)* is tucked away up the steps behind the northern end of the harbour and charges 14,900 dr. Spotless studios at ***Pension Amorgos** (☎ 71 814)*, on the waterfront near the square, cost 15,000 dr. The C class ***Hotel Minoa** (☎ 71 480)*, on the square, has comfortable doubles for 17,500 dr. ***Vitsentzos***, at the northern end of the waterfront beyond Pension Maroussa, has good, reasonably priced daily specials and serves delicious, freshly squeezed lemon juice. ***Psaropoula***, nearby, is the best for fish. ***Mouragio***, on the waterfront near the square, is a good traditional place. ***Idiston***, around the corner from Hotel Minoa, has local sweets and liqueurs.

The nicest place to have a drink is the laid-back ***Moon Bar***, with tables under a large tree on the waterfront; it's just beyond Pension Maroussa. On the waterfront near the square, ***Naftilia E Preka***, doubling as a ferry ticket agency, is a beautiful old ouzeri with an ornately tiled floor, green ceiling and impressive collection of defunct TVs.

HORA (AMORGOS)

This amazingly well preserved Cycladic village is 400m above sea level, so high that it's often shrouded in clouds when the rest of the island is sunny. It's an impressive sight, all white and capped with a 13th century kastro atop a large lump of rock.

The bus stop is on a square at the edge of town. The post office is on the main square, reached by a pedestrian laneway from the bus stop. The OTE is in a new building on the main road near the high school. There are no hotels, but domatia are available. ***Pension Ilias*** *(☎ 71 277)* and ***Pension Panorama*** are both close to the bus stop.

MONI HOZOVIOTISSIS

A visit to the 11th century Moni Hozoviotissis is unreservedly worthwhile, as much for the spectacular scenery as for the monastery itself. The dazzling white building clings precariously to a cliff face above the east coast. A few monks still live there and, if you're lucky, one will show you around.

The monastery contains a miracle-working icon found in the sea below the monastery, having allegedly arrived unaided from Asia Minor, Cyprus or Jerusalem, depending on which legend you're told. Modest dress is required – long trousers for men, and a long skirt or dress and covered shoulders for women. The monastery is open 8 am to 1 pm and 5 to 7 pm daily.

The walk to the monastery down the steep hillside from Hora is breathtaking; an old stepped path winds down from near the radio tower. There's also a bus; the monastery bus stop is at the Agia Anna road junction, about 500m uphill from the monastery itself.

AEGIALI Αιγιάλη

Aegiali is Amorgos' other port. The atmosphere is much more laid-back than Katapola and there is a good beach stretching left of the quay.

Organised Tours Aegialis Tours organises some interesting outings, including boat trips around the island with stops at remote beaches (8000 dr, including picnic), and bus tours of the island (7000 dr). Afternoon donkey-riding expeditions cost 5000 dr, and guided explorations of the island's wild herbs cost 3500 dr for a relaxed half-day outing or 5000 dr for a more strenuous full day of clambering about.

Places to Stay & Eat As in Katapola, domatia owners meet ferries. Right on the beach, ***Lakki Pension*** *(☎ 73 253)* has immaculate singles/doubles/triples for 12,000/14,000/17,500 dr with bathroom and breakfast; and two/four-person apartments for 17,000/22,000 dr. Luxury two-person apartments with air-con, view and traditional furniture are 20,000 dr, including breakfast. The pension has a delightful garden, a taverna and a bar.

Rooms Irini *(☎ 73 237)*, at the top of the steps after the terrace restaurants, is a pretty place with doubles for 12,500 dr. ***Grispos Hotel*** *(☎ 73 502)*, up the hill behind the waterfront, has spacious studios for two/four people for 15,000/21,000 dr. ***Pension Nostos*** *(☎ 73 528)*, across the road, has triple studios with kitchen for 15,000 dr. ***Aegialis Hotel*** *(☎ 73 393, fax 73 395)* sits above two sandy beaches and is the classiest place around. It has a seawater pool, two bars and a restaurant known for excellent seafood. Singles/doubles cost 23,500/26,500 dr with phone and balcony.

Liminaki, on the waterfront, and ***To Steki***, behind Aegialis Tours, both serve good Greek food, but the best place is ***Restaurant Lakki***, on the beach at the pension of the same name. Home-grown ingredients make all the difference – the food is simple yet fragrant and delicious. The moussaka is surprisingly delicate, and the stuffed vine leaves and zucchini flowers are plump and aromatic. Interesting wines are also available.

AROUND AMORGOS

Pebbled **Agia Anna Beach**, on the east coast south of Moni Hozoviotissis, is the nearest decent beach to both Katapola and Hora. It has no facilities, so take water and food.

Langada is the most picturesque of the villages inland from Aegiali.

Ios Ιος

☎ 0286 • postcode 840 01 • pop 2000

Ios – the apogee of sun, sea and sex – is the *enfant terrible* of the Greek islands. There's no denying that most visitors come to party hard, but for those who are looking for a more relaxing stay, the island also offers plenty to explore: beautiful beaches, a pretty capital and an interesting rocky, Mars-like landscape. Ios also has a tenuous claim to being Homer's burial place; his tomb is supposedly in the island's north, although no-one seems to know exactly where.

Getting There & Away

Ferry There are at least four daily connections with Piraeus (seven hours, 5300 dr), Paros (2½ hours, 2450 dr) and Naxos (1¼ hours, 2100 dr). There are daily boats to Mykonos (four hours, 3100 dr) and Santorini (one hour, 1500 dr), five weekly to Sikinos (20 minutes, 1100 dr) and Folegandros (1½ hours, 1500 dr), four weekly to Anafi (two hours, 1900 dr) and two weekly to Syros (2¾ hours, 3700 dr). There are weekly boats to Crete (six hours, 4180 dr), Amorgos (2½ hours, 2115 dr), Kimolos (2½ hours, 1900 dr), Milos (3½ hours, 2800 dr), Sifnos (five hours, 2600 dr) and Serifos (six hours, 2900 dr).

Hydrofoil There are at least three hydrofoils daily to Santorini (30 minutes, 3100 dr) and Naxos (50 minutes, 4200 dr); two to three daily to Paros (1½ hours, 4900 dr), Mykonos (2¾ hours, 6300 dr) and Tinos (3½ hours, 7100 dr); and one or two to Syros (2¼ hours, 7300 dr).

There are six services weekly to Sikinos (10 minutes, 2200 dr) and Folegandros (45 minutes, 3000 dr), four weekly to Amorgos (two hours, 4200 dr), three to Anafi (one hour, 3900 dr), two to Koufonisia (3½ hours, 3300 dr), Shinousa (three hours, 3300 dr), Iraklia (3½ hours, 4400 dr) and Crete (2¼ hours, 8400 dr), and one weekly to Donousa (2½ hours, 4100 dr). Hydrofoil and catamaran tickets are available from Acteon Travel.

Catamaran There are daily cats to Santorini (30 minutes, 3100 dr), Naxos (50 minutes, 4200 dr), Paros (1½ hours, 4900 dr), Syros (2¼ hours, 7300 dr) and Rafina (four hours, 8200 dr).

Getting Around

In summer, crowded buses run between Ormos, Hora (230 dr) and Milopotas (230 dr) about every 15 minutes. Private excursion buses go to Manganari Beach (2000 dr); inquire at Acteon Travel.

Caïques from Ormos to Manganari cost around 2500 dr per person. Ormos and Hora both have car and motorcycle rental firms.

WARNING

Ios' roads are rough and steep. Don't hire an underpowered motorcycle or attempt to ride on unsealed roads unless you are an experienced rider.

HORA, ORMOS & MILOPOTAS

Ios has three population centres, all very close together on the west coast: the port (Ormos); the capital, Hora (also known as the 'village'), 2km inland from the port; and Milopotas, the beach 1km downhill from Hora. Gialos Beach stretches west of the port.

Orientation

The bus terminal in Ormos is straight ahead from the ferry quay on Plateia Emirou. If you want to walk from the port to Hora, turn left from Plateia Emirou, then immediately right and you'll see the stepped path leading up to the right after about 100m. The walk takes about 30 minutes.

In Hora, the church is the main landmark. It's opposite the bus stop, across the car park. To reach the central square of Plateia Valeta from the church, head in to the village and turn left at the junction. There are public toilets up the hill behind the main square. The road straight ahead from the bus stop leads to Milopotas Beach.

Information

There is no EOT but Acteon Travel (☎ 91 343), on the square near the quay, is very helpful and is also the American Express representative. At the port, travel agents offer free luggage storage, including free safes. There is a hospital (☎ 91 227) 250m north-west of the quay, on the way to Gialos. The port police (☎ 91 264) are at the southern end of the waterfront, just before Ios Camping.

In Hora, the National Bank of Greece, behind the church, and the Commercial Bank nearby both have ATMs. To get to the post office from the church, continue uphill along the edge of the village, past the bakery, and take the second left.

The OTE is in Hora, along the street that leads right (east) from the top of the port steps; a signpost points the way. It's a difficult uphill walk. The office is open 7.30 am to 3.10 pm daily, closed weekends and public holidays. Internet access is available at Plakiotis Travel and Acteon Travel.

Things to See

Hora itself is a very lovely Cycladic village with myriad laneways and cute houses and shops. Its charm is most evident during daylight hours when the bars are shut and the locals come out of the woodwork.

The only real 'cultural' attraction is the new **archaeological museum** in Hora. The building is immaculately decked out, but the exhibits are a tad disappointing. It's in the yellow building by the bus stop and is open 8 am to 2 pm Tuesday to Sunday (free).

The views from the top of the hill in Hora are worth the climb, especially at sunset. On the way, pause at **Panagia Gremiotissa**, the large church next to the palm tree.

Activities

Ios Diving Centre (☎ 0932-638 646) and Meltemi Watersports (☎/fax 91 680) have outlets at both Milopotas and Manganari. A range of diving courses is offered and windsurfing and water-skiing equipment is available for hire. There are also some very strange innovations, including the 'banana' – an inflatable yellow object which thrill-seekers cling to as they are pulled along behind a speedboat.

Places to Stay – Budget

Far Out Camping *(☎ 91 468)* at Milopotas is a slick, somewhat overhyped operation. It has a 24 hour bar, restaurant and two swimming pools, as well as volleyball and basketball courts, and, of course, water sports facilities. All facilities but the accommodation are open to everyone. Charges are 1200/1000 dr per person, with/without tent hire. Basic 'bungalows' that look like dog kennels cost 1500 dr per person; larger ones with double and single beds cost 1800 dr per person. There's little tree cover and roofed areas provide most of the shade. A minibus makes frequent runs to Hora and Ormos.

Purple Pig Camping Stars *(☎ 91 302)*, also at Milopotas, is a smaller, friendlier place shaded by tall trees. It has a swimming pool, disco and restaurant, as well as refreshingly low-key activities such as darts and pool. Internet access is also available. Camping/bungalows cost 1000/2500 dr per person. ***Ios Camping*** *(☎ 91 329)* in Ormos has a pool, restaurant, house doctor, travel agency and minimarket, and it also hosts film nights. It charges 1500 dr per person. Turn right at Plateia Emirou and walk along the waterfront to find it.

Backpackers who aren't camping tend to stay at the friendly ***Francesco's*** *(☎/fax 91 223)* in the village. Dorm beds cost 3000 dr; doubles/triples are 12,000/15,000 dr with bathroom and 6000/9000 dr without. It's a lively meeting place with a bar and terrace and a wonderful view of the bay. Internet access, free safety deposit boxes, and laundry facilities are also offered. Port transfers are free – call from the port if the van is not there. To get there from the church, head for the central square and turn left at the Second Skin boutique; Francesco's is about 50m farther along. ***Pension Panorama*** *(☎ 91 592)*, nearby, offers great views and has doubles/triples for 12,000/15,000 dr with bathroom.

There are lots of domatia signs on the route towards Milopotas Beach from the Hora bus stop. ***Rooms Helena*** *(☎ 91 595)* is an old-style place with a bit of character; it's on the left, halfway between Hora and the beach. Basic rooms are 5000/6000 dr. Over the road, ***Hermes Rooms*** *(☎ 91 471)*, has rooms for 14,000/20,000 dr with bathroom.

Farther along is ***Katerina Rooms to Let*** *(☎ 91 614)*, with a lovely garden full of flowers. Rooms are 15,000/18,000 dr with bathroom. Home-made breakfast is served on its terrace. ***Petradi Rooms*** *(☎ 91 510)*, opposite, offers rooms for 18,000/21,000 dr with balcony and bathroom. There is a bar-restaurant and a nice terrace.

Straight ahead from the quay in Ormos is ***Zorba's Rooms*** *(☎ 91 871)*. Neat singles/doubles/triples are 4000/8000/12,000 dr, or 5000/10,000/15,000 dr with bathroom. ***Irene Rooms*** *(☎ 91 023)*, signposted nearby, has doubles/triples for 14,000/16,000 dr with balcony and bathroom.

There are also some nice options at Gialos Beach, a short walk from the port. Set back a bit from the beach, ***Pension O Kampos*** *(☎ 91 424)* is a great, old-fashioned place with red shutters and green doors. Simple doubles go for 8000/12,000 dr without/with bath. Next door, ***Galini Pension*** *(☎ 91 115)* has a lovely shady garden; rooms cost 12,000 dr with bathroom, some with fridge.

Hotel Glaros *(☎/fax 91 876)* is a relaxed, family-run place on the beach with rooms for 15,000 dr. ***Galaxy Hotel*** *(☎ 91 922)*, near Purple Pig Camping Stars at Milopotas, has rooms with bath and fridge for 15,000 dr.

Places to Stay – Mid-Range & Top End

Hotel Yialos Beach *(☎ 91 421)*, in Gialos, is a friendly new place with nicely designed Cycladic-style units around a pool. Doubles with air-con, phone, bathroom and balcony go for 18,000 dr.

In Ormos, ***Hotel Poseidon*** *(☎ 91 091)* is a nice quiet place with a view over the port and a pool; singles/doubles/triples are 15,000/18,000/22,000 dr with phone. From the waterfront, turn left at Enigma Bar and climb the steps on the left.

Hotel Ios Plage *(☎/fax 91 301)* is a beautiful, French-run place at the far end of Milopotas Beach, with quite a different feel from the other hotels. Rooms are simply decorated, with large mosquito nets over the beds; doubles cost 18,000 dr. There is a lively bar and a French restaurant.

Sun Club *(☎ 92 140)*, on the road to Hora, has immaculate rooms for 24,000 dr, with bath, TV, phone and view. There's also a pool and bar.

The plush B class ***Ios Palace*** *(☎ 91 269)* is a cluster of traditional Cycladic cubes rising up the hill at the Hora end of Milopotas Beach. Singles/doubles/triples are 22,000/27,000/31,000 dr, including breakfast. Four-person suites with private pool go for 70,000 dr. The classy ***Far Out Village Hotel*** *(☎ 92 305)*, right on the beach at Milopotas, is the newest addition to the Far Out empire. Traditional rooms go for 18,100/24,800/35,500 dr, with breakfast.

Places to Eat

Fishermen's Restaurant, in Ormos on the way to Ios Camping, is known for its excellent fish. ***Corner Cafe***, also at the port, serves good breakfasts and coffee.

In Hora, ***Zorba's*** and ***Nest*** are both good value. ***Pithari Taverna***, behind the large church, serves cheap, traditional Greek dishes. Close by, ***Lord Byron*** is a *mezedopolion* with a very cosy atmosphere augmented by rembetika music; different mezedes are served every day.

Pinocchio Pizzeria has good pizza and pasta, and *panna cotta* for dessert. Look for the signs and Pinocchio standing outside. ***La Buca***, next to the bus stop, also has reasonably authentic Italian food, including wood-fired pizza and nice salads. There are also numerous gyros stands where you can get a cheap bite. ***Fiesta***, on the Ormos-Hora road, serves good Greek food.

Restaurant Polydoros on Koumbara Beach is popular, and ***Filippos***, a huge place on the left-hand side of the road as you head to Koumbara, has spectacular seafood. The legendary ***Drakos Taverna*** at Milopotas is not be missed. ***Harmony***, at the village end of Milopotas beyond Ios Palace, has a lovely terrace dotted with deckchairs and hammocks. Aside from the laid-back atmosphere, the Mexican food is the main attraction, although the pizza, pasta, grills and breakfasts are also pretty good.

Entertainment

At night Hora's tiny central square is transformed into a noisy crowded open-air party so packed it can take half an hour to get from one side to the other. The crowd is mostly made up of alcohol-swilling backpackers in their teens and early twenties – if you're older, the fun wears thin quite quickly.

Popular bars and clubs on the square include ***Disco 69***, ***Slammer Bar*** and ***Red Bull***. There is also a gauntlet of Scandinavian bars scattered around town, including ***Blue Note***, ***Scandinavians*** and ***Scandinavian Bar***.

Other famous drinking cultures are also well represented, especially the Irish, who claim ***Dubliner's***, opposite the bus stop, and ***Sweet Irish Dream*** across the road. ***Upside Down*** and ***Scorpion's***, both on the Milopotas road, are also popular.

Ios Club provides sweeping views and is a relaxed, quiet place for a drink. It's signposted from the top of the steps down to the port. ***Orange Bar***, 150m beyond the central square, is a good, laid-back escape hatch.

The nightlife down at Ormos is pretty lame in comparison to Hora's. ***Frog's Club***, on the waterfront, caters mainly to a yachtie

WARNING

There's no such thing as a free cocktail. The cheap local moonshine used in mixed drinks and cocktails is bad news, particularly for the unwary.

clientele and sometimes has a live guitarist. Nearby, ***Enigma*** is also worth a look. ***Marina Bar***, overlooking Gialos Beach, has good Greek music.

AROUND IOS

Apart from the nightlife, the beaches are what lure travellers to Ios. From Ormos, it's a 10 minute walk past the little church of Agia Irini for **Valmas Beach**. **Kolitzani Beach**, south of Hora, down the steps by Scorpion's, is also nice. **Koubara**, a 30 minute walk north-west of Ormos, is the official nudist beach. **Tsamaria**, nearby, is nice and sheltered when it's windy elsewhere.

Vying with Milopotas for best beach is **Manganari**, a long swathe of fine white sand on the south coast, reached by bus or by excursion boat in summer. There are several domatia, including ***Dimitri's*** *(☎ 91 483)*, which has lovely doubles for 10,000 dr. ***Cristos Taverna*** *(☎ 0932-411 547)*, 200m away, has a very good restaurant – they catch their own fish – and doubles for 10,000 dr. ***Hotel Manganari*** *(☎ 91 200)* is accessible only by boat and has villas for two at 32,000 dr, including breakfast and dinner. ***Antonio's Restaurant*** has incredibly fresh fish and calamari, and good grills; make sure you sample the different home-made cheeses made with milk from their goats.

Agia Theodoti, **Psathi** and **Kalamos** beaches, all on the north-east coast, are more remote. **Moni Kalamou**, on the way to Manganari and Kalamos, stages a huge religious festival in late August and a festival of music and dance on 7 September.

Santorini (Thira)

Σαντορίνη (Θήρα)

☎ 0286 • postcode 847 00 • pop 9360

Santorini, officially known as Thira, is regarded by many as the most spectacular of all the Greek islands. Thousands visit annually to gaze in wonder at the submerged caldera (crater), a vestige of what was probably the biggest volcanic eruption in recorded history. Although it gets crowded and is overly commercial, Santorini is unique and should not be missed. The caldera is a real spectacle – it's worth arriving by ferry rather than catamaran or hydrofoil if you want to experience the full dramatic impact. The main port is Athinios. Buses meet all ferries and cart passengers to Fira, the capital, which teeters on the lip of the caldera, high above the sea.

History

Greece is susceptible to eruptions and earthquakes – mostly minor – but on Santorini these have been so violent as to change the shape of the island several times.

Dorians, Venetians and Turks occupied Santorini, as they did all other Cycladic islands, but its most influential early inhabitants were the Minoans. They came from Crete some time between 2000 and 1600 BC, and the settlement at Akrotiri dates from the height of their great civilisation.

The island then was circular and called Strongili (the Round One). Around 1650 BC, a colossal volcanic eruption caused the centre of Strongili to sink, leaving a caldera with high cliffs – one of the world's most dramatic geological sights. Some archaeologists have speculated that this catastrophe destroyed not only Akrotiri but the whole Minoan civilisation as well. Another theory that has fired the imaginations of writers, artists and mystics since ancient times postulates that the island was part of the mythical lost continent of Atlantis. See the following boxed text for more details on the volcano.

Getting There & Away

Air Olympic Airway operates at least six flights daily to Athens (22,200 dr), five weekly to Rhodes (22,900 dr) and Mykonos (15,400 dr), three weekly to Thessaloniki (30,400 dr) and two weekly to Iraklio (15,400 dr). The Olympic Airways office (☎ 22 493) is in Fira, on the road to Kamari, one block east of 25 Martiou. Air Manos flies to Athens (21,200 dr) six days a week, and to Mykonos (14,400 dr), Samos (16,400 dr) and Thessaloniki (18,400 dr) twice weekly. Trans-European flies to Athens (23,400 dr) at least twice weekly. Various travel agencies in Fira sell tickets for these airlines.

Ferry Santorini is the southernmost island of the Cyclades, and as a major tourist destination it has good connections with Piraeus and Thessaloniki on the mainland, as well as with Crete. Santorini also has useful services to Anafi, Folegandros and Sikinos. No travel agent sells tickets for all the ferries, so make sure you check schedules with at least three before you hand over your cash.

There are at least seven boats daily to Naxos (three hours, 3100 dr) and Paros (three to four hours, 3050 dr), six daily to Ios (1¼ hours, 1700 dr), five to Piraeus (nine hours, 6100 dr), two to Mykonos (six hours, 3600 dr), and one to Crete (four hours, 3700 dr), Tinos (five hours, 4200 dr) and Syros (5¼ hours, 4300 dr).

Five boats weekly go to Anafi (one hour, 1900 dr), Thessaloniki (17¾ hours, 10,100 dr) and Folegandros (1½ to 2½ hours, 1900 dr), and four weekly depart for Amorgos (2½ hours, 2350 dr).

There are three ferries weekly to Sikinos (2½ hours, 1700 dr), and two weekly to Milos (four hours, 3650 dr), Kimolos (3½ hours, 3000 dr), Sifnos (six hours, 3060 dr), Serifos (seven hours, 3600 dr), Rhodes (seven to eight hours, 6400 dr) and Skiathos (11¾ hours, 8200 dr).

There are weekly ferries to Volos (14 hours, 8100 dr) and Astypalea (four hours, 3350 dr), and, outside high season, usually two weekly to Karpathos (4900 dr) and Kassos (4100 dr). Once a week there is a ferry to Lemesos (Limassol) in Cyprus (38 hours) and Haifa in Israel (58 hours).

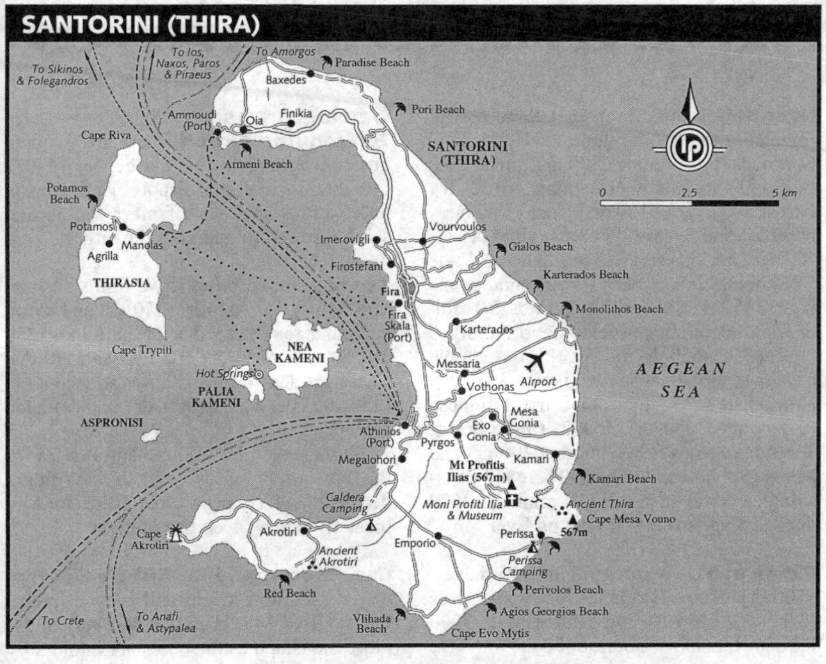

Santorini's Unsettling Past

Santorini's violent upheaved volcanic history is visible everywhere you look – in black sand beaches, in raw lava-layered cliffs that plunge into the sea, in earthquake-damaged dwellings, and in fertile soil that supports coiled-up grape vines. The volcano may be dormant but it's not dead. Santorini's caldera ('cauldron'), which often has a surface as calm and glassy as a backyard fish pond, could start to boil at any moment…

Santorini first appeared when the landmass known as Aegis, which joined the European and Asian continents, was gradually flooded around one million years ago, leaving only the highest peaks above water. Profitis Ilias and Monolithos are both ancient rocks dating back to this time. At some point a complex of submarine, overlapping shield volcanoes began to toil and trouble, eventually erupting and filling in the area between Santorini's mountains with lava. This process continued for thousands of years and over time the island took on a conical shape.

Eventually the volcanoes quieted, and vegetation established itself in the fertile ash. Around 3000 BC the first human settlers arrived and, from evidence found at Akrotiri, it appears that they led very idyllic lives and fashioned a highly evolved culture.

But peace and harmony never last long enough, and around 1650 BC a chain of earthquakes and eruptions culminated in one of the largest explosions in the history of the planet. Thirty cubic kilometres of magma spewed forth and a column of ash 36km high jetted into the atmosphere. So much magma was ejected that the magma chambers of the volcano gave way and the centre of the island collapsed, producing a caldera that the sea quickly filled. It's hard to imagine the magnitude of the explosion, but it is often compared to thousands of

Hydrofoil There are at least three hydrofoils daily to Ios (30 minutes, 3100 dr) and Mykonos (three hours, 6800 dr), and at least two daily to Naxos (1¾ hours, 6100 dr), Paros (two hours, 6100 dr), Tinos (3¼ hours, 8400 dr) and Syros (3½ hours, 9000 dr).

There are also services to Iraklio on Crete (2¾ hours, 7200 dr, daily), Folegandros (one hour, 3350 dr, six weekly), Sikinos (30 minutes, 3400 dr, five weekly) and Amorgos (1½ hours, 4650 dr, four weekly). A couple a week serve Donousa (two hours, 3650 dr), Koufonisia (2½ hours, 3650 dr), Shinousa (2¾ hours, 3650 dr), Iraklia (three hours, 3650 dr), Sifnos (three hours, 6200 dr) and Milos (3½ hours, 7450 dr). There are occasional services to Anafi (30 minutes, 3500 dr) and Karystos (3½ hours) on Evia.

Catamaran Daily cats go to Ios (30 minutes, 3100 dr), Naxos (1½ hours, 6100 dr), Paros (2¼ hours, 6100 dr), Syros (three hours, 9000 dr) and Rafina (4¾ hours, 9600 dr).

Getting Around

To/From the Airport There are frequent bus connections in summer between Fira's bus station and the airport. Enthusiastic hotel and domatia staff meet flights and some also return guests to the airport.

Bus In summer, buses leave Fira's bus station hourly for Akrotiri (370 dr) and every half-hour for Oia (270 dr), Monolithos (250 dr), Kamari (260 dr) and Perissa (390 dr). There are less frequent buses to Exogonia (250 dr), Perivolos (390 dr) and Vlihada (450 dr).

Buses leave Fira, Kamari and Perissa for the port of Athinios (370 dr) 1½ hours before most ferry departures. Buses for Fira meet all ferries, even late at night.

Car, Motorcycle & Bicycle Fira has many car, motorcycle and bicycle rental firms. Hired wheels are the best way to explore the island as the buses are intolerably

Santorini's Unsettling Past

atomic bombs all having their pins pulled simultaneously. The event sent ash all over the Mediterranean, and it also generated huge tsunamis (tidal waves) that travelled with dangerous force all the way to Crete and Israel. Anafi was hit by a wave 250m high. The fall-out from the explosion was more than just dust and pumice – it's widely believed that the catastrophe was responsible for the demise of Crete's Minoan culture, one of the most powerful civilisations in the Aegean at that time. After the Big One, Santorini once again settled down for a time and allowed plants, animals and humans to recolonise it. In 286 BC the rumbles from the deep resumed and volcanic activity separated Thirasia from the main island. Further changes to the landscape continued intermittently. In 197 BC the islet now known as Palia Kameni appeared in the caldera, and in 726 AD there was a major eruption that catapulted pumice all the way to Asia Minor. The south coast of Santorini collapsed in 1570, taking the ancient port of Eleusis with it. In 1650 earthquakes and explosions caused tsunamis and killed and blinded many people on the island. An eruption of lava in 1707 created Nea Kameni islet next to Palia Kameni, and further eruptions in 1866-70, 1925-26, 1928, 1939-41 and 1950 augmented it. A major earthquake measuring 7.8 on the Richter scale savaged the island in 1956, killing scores of people and destroying most of the houses in Fira and Oia.

Volcanic activity has been pretty low-key since 1956, but minor tremors are quite common and the ground shakes, usually imperceptibly, almost every day. A major earthquake is due at any moment, but the locals don't seem worried – they seem to like living on the edge. For lovers of impermanence, precariousness and drama, no other place even comes close.

overcrowded in summer and you'll be lucky to get on one at all.

Taxi Call ☎ 23 951 or 22 555 for a taxi.

Cable Car & Donkey Cable cars shunt passengers from cruise ships and excursion boats up to Fira from the small port below known as Fira Skala. Tickets cost 800 dr one way. Or you can go by donkey, for the same price.

FIRA Φήρα

The commercialism of Fira has not diminished its all-pervasive, dramatic aura. Walk to the edge of the caldera for spectacular views of the cliffs and their multicoloured strata of lava and pumice.

Orientation

The central square is Plateia Theotokopoulou. The main road, 25 Martiou, runs north-south, intersecting the square and is lined with travel agencies. The bus station is on 25 Martiou, 50m south of Plateia Theotokopoulou. West of 25 Martiou the streets are old pedestrian laneways; Erythrou Stavrou, one block west of 25 Martiou, is the main commercial thoroughfare.

Another block west, Ypapantis runs along the crest of the caldera and provides staggering panoramic views. Head north on Nomikou for the cable car station. If you keep walking along the caldera – and it's well worth it – you'll come to the Nomikos Convention Centre and, eventually, the clifftop villages of Firostefani and Imerovigli.

Information

Fira doesn't have an EOT or tourist police. Dozens of travel agencies offer tourist information. The staff at Dakoutros Travel (☎ 22 958, fax 22 686) are particularly helpful and can organise accommodation, ferry tickets and excursions. The National Bank of Greece is between the bus station and Plateia Theotokopoulou, on the caldera side of the road. American Express is represented by Alpha Credit Bank on Plateia Theotokopoulou. Both banks have ATMs. The post office is about 150m south of the bus station. Lava Internet Cafe, just up from the main square, provides Internet access at 600/900/1800 dr for 15/30/60 minutes.

There is a laundrette and dry cleaner 200m north of Plateia Theotokopoulou, underneath Pension Villa Maria, and another laundrette next to Pelican Hotel.

The hospital (☎ 222 37) is on the road to Karterados, near the Olympic Airways office. The police station (☎ 22 649) is south of Plateia Theotokopoulou; the port police (☎ 22 239) are north of the square.

Museums

Megaron Gyzi museum, behind the Catholic cathedral, has local memorabilia, including fascinating photographs of Fira before and immediately after the major 1956 earthquake. Theoretically, it's open 10.30 am to 1.30 pm and 5 until 8 pm Monday to Saturday, 10.30 am to 4.30 pm Sunday (closed holidays). In practice, opening times are erratic. Entrance is 400 dr.

The **archaeological museum**, opposite the cable car station, houses finds from Akrotiri and Ancient Thira, some Cycladic figurines, and Hellenistic and Roman sculpture. It's open 8 am to 2.30 pm Tuesday to Sunday. Admission is 400 dr. At the time of writing, a new archaeological museum (opposite the bus station) was nearing completion.

For the past few years the **Nomikos Convention Centre** (☎ 23 016), also known as the Thera Foundation, has displayed fascinating three-dimensional photographic reproductions of the Akrotiri frescoes, which offer a glimpse of what life was like on the island in the 16th century BC. Saffron had an important religious and symbolic role and many of the paintings show young women collecting it. The exhibit is open 10 am to 9 pm Tuesday to Sunday; admission is 1000 dr, but before you go, call to see if it is still running. To get there, follow the old Byzantine path along the caldera, past the cable car station.

The **Bellonio Cultural Centre & Library**, next to the post office, has a large collection of books about Santorini. It's open 9 am to 2 pm and 6 to 9 pm daily.

Organised Tours

Tour agencies operate trips to Thirasia, the volcanic island of Nea Kameni, Palia Kameni's hot springs and Oia. See the Thirasia & Volcanic Islets section for details.

Places to Stay – Budget

Camping Santorini *(☎ 22 944)* is a nice site with many facilities, including a restaurant and pool. The cost is 1500/800 dr per person/tent. It's 400m east of Plateia Theotokopoulou – look for the sign.

Accommodation owners meeting boats and buses are fairly aggressive but are now confined to 'official' information booths; this doesn't mean that you'll get impartial information or the best accommodation available, so don't jump at the first offer. Some owners of rooms in Karterados (3km south-east of Fira) claim that their rooms are in town; ask to see a map showing the location.

The massive ***Thira Hostel*** *(☎ 23 864)*, 300m north of Plateia Theotokopoulou, is a beautiful old place that was formerly part of the Catholic monastery. Some of the rooms have remnants of antique furniture and there's a lovely secret garden. The hostel has a variety of small dorms with up to 10 beds for 2500 dr per person, plus doubles/triples for 9000/10,000 dr with bath. Beds on the roof cost 2000 dr.

Hotel Keti *(☎ 22 324)* is a real gem with lovely traditional rooms dug into the cliffs; doubles with terrace overlooking the caldera go for 14,000 dr. ***Argonaftis Villas*** *(☎ 22 055)*, near the school , is run by a talented painter who is also a port policeman. His folksy paintings, most with nautical themes, decorate many of the rooms. Doubles with bath are 16,000 dr, and apartments for two/four are 17,000/25,000 dr – one of these is a traditional cave house.

A short walk north-east of the town centre takes you to Kontohori, a peaceful, vaguely rural area with plenty of domatia.

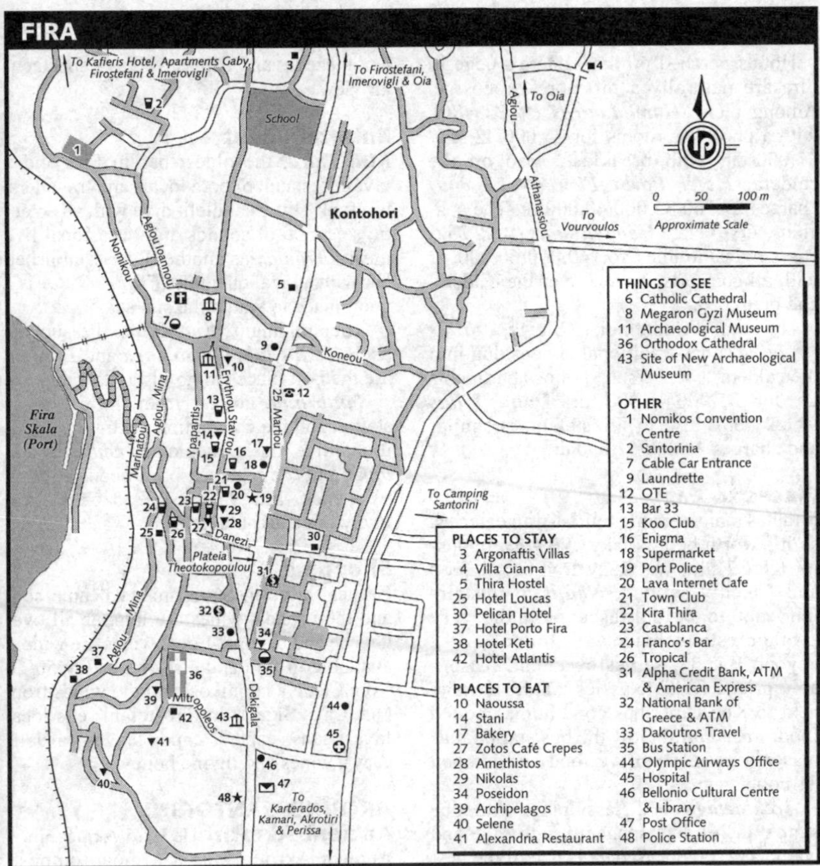

Among these is ***Villa Gianna*** *(☎ 23 367)*, which has a pool and air-con; doubles/triples are 21,000/28,000 dr.

On the path up to Firostefani, not far from the convention centre, ***Kafieris Hotel*** *(☎ 22 189)* has lovely doubles on the caldera for 10,000 dr. Nearby, ***Apartments Gaby*** *(☎ 22 057)* is a great place with doubles for 18,000 dr and four-person apartments for 32,000 dr. Gaby also has some rooms closer to the main road with a view of the eastern side of the island, for 12,000 dr.

Farther up the hill, near Firostefani's main square, ***Hotel Sofia Sigala*** *(☎ 22 802)* has nice doubles for 16,000 dr with bathroom and fridge. ***Hotel Mylos*** *(☎ 23 884)*, opposite, has similar rooms for 15,000 dr. Nearby, ***Ioaniss Roussos Rooms*** *(☎ 22 611)* has doubles for 14,000 dr.

Places to Stay – Mid-Range & Top End

Pelican Hotel *(☎ 23 113)*, right in the centre of town, has comfortable singles/doubles/

triples for 23,000/29,000/36,000 dr, including breakfast.

Hotels perched on the caldera's edge in Fira are naturally a bit more expensive. Among them, ***Hotel Loucas*** *(☎ 22 480)*, with a pool, has rooms for 25,000/32,500/41,000 dr, with breakfast. Also on the caldera, ***Hotel Porto Fira*** *(☎ 22 849)* charges 27,500/35,000/40,000 dr. The spacious, airy A class ***Hotel Atlantis*** *(☎ 22 232)* has singles/doubles for 40,000/60,000 dr with all comforts, a view over the caldera, and breakfast.

Up in Firostefani, ***Eterpi Villas*** *(☎ 22 541)* has traditional abodes dug into the caldera; two-person studios/apartments go for 35,000/48,000 dr. ***Dana Villas*** *(☎ 22 566)*, also in Firostefani, is similar and charges 48,600/51,600 dr.

Places to Eat

Fira has many terrible tourist-trap eateries, so it's worth being picky. ***Nikolas***, opposite Kira Thira, has tasty traditional food and friendly service. ***Naoussa***, upstairs (and not to be confused with the very average establishment at ground level), beyond Bar 33, serves excellent, reasonably priced Greek classics. ***Stani***, upstairs next to Koo Club, has good home-cooked food. ***Poseidon***, below the bus station, has reasonable, inexpensive food and is open 24 hours.

Archipelagos is a classy place with nice simple dishes like spaghetti with sage and walnuts (2200 dr). ***Selene*** is one of the best restaurants and has a lovely romantic atmosphere; creative main courses start at 3700 dr. ***Kukumavlos*** has an innovative menu featuring local and imported exotica, including ostrich fillet with caramelised onions in merlot sauce (5200 dr).

The best places for juices, coffee, cake and crepes are ***Zotos Cafe Crepe*** and ***Amesthistos***, opposite each other on Erythrou Stavrou. The ***bakery*** up from the main square sells pies as well as bread and is open 24 hours.

On the main square in Firostefani, ***To Aktaion*** is a nice little taverna serving traditional food. Farther up the caldera in Imerovigli, ***Skaros Fish Tavern*** has excellent mezedes and fish as well as a spectacular view.

Entertainment

Kira Thira, the oldest bar in Fira and a favourite haunt of both locals and travellers, is a funky little candlelit dive with an eclectic selection of sounds and occasional live music. ***Tropical*** is another long-established bar with a loyal clientele. ***Franco's Bar*** is a good place to watch the sun set.

After midnight, ***Koo Club***, the superkitsch ***Town Club***, ***Casablanca*** and ***Enigma*** are the best places to go disco dancing.

Santorinia, not far from the cable car station and the convention centre, has traditional live music, including *rembetika* and *laïko*; outside high season it opens only on weekends. ***Bar 33***, past Koo Club, is a lively bouzouki place.

Shopping

Grapes thrive in Santorini's volcanic soil, and the island's wines are famous all over Greece and beyond. Local wines are widely available in Fira and elsewhere. Try 50-50 from Canava Nomikos, and the wines from Oia. Cava Sigalas in Firostefani sells local fava beans, capers, caper leaves (a delicacy), wines and thyme honey.

AROUND SANTORINI

Ancient Akrotiri Παλαιό Ακρωτήρι

Ancient Akrotiri was a Minoan outpost; excavations begun in 1967 have uncovered an ancient city beneath the volcanic ash. Buildings, some three storeys high, date to the late 16th century BC. The absence of skeletons and treasures indicates that inhabitants were forewarned of the eruption and escaped.

The most outstanding finds are the stunning frescoes, many of which are now on display at the National Archaeological Museum in Athens. (Very accurate replicas are on display at the Nomikos Convention Centre; see Fira.) The site is open 8 am to 8 pm Tuesday to Sunday. Admission is 1200 dr.

***Caldera View Camping** (☎ 82 010)* near Akrotiri doesn't really have a view over the caldera and it's a long way from any nightlife, but it's a nice enough spot. It charges 1500 dr per person and 600 dr per tent. There are also two-person bungalows from 15,000 dr, including breakfast.

There are some nice little fish ***tavernas*** on the beach below the archaeological site. On the way to Akrotiri, pause at the enchanting traditional settlement of **Megalohori**.

Ancient Thira Αρχαία Θήρα

Ancient Thira, first settled by the Dorians in the 9th century BC, has Hellenistic, Roman and Byzantine ruins. These include temples, houses with mosaics, an agora, a theatre and a gymnasium. The site has splendid views. It's open 9 am to 2.30 pm Tuesday to Sunday (free).

It takes about 30 minutes to walk to the site along the path from Perissa. If you're driving, take the road from Kamari.

Moni Profiti Ilia

Μονή Προφήτη Ηλία

This monastery crowns Santorini's highest peak, Mt Profitis Ilias (567m). Although it now shares the peak with radio and TV pylons and a radar station, it's worth the trek for the stupendous views. The monastery has an interesting **folk museum**. You can walk there from Pyrgos (1½ hours) or from Ancient Thira (one hour).

Oia Οία

The village of Oia (**ee**-ah) was devastated by the 1956 earthquake and has never fully recovered, but it's dramatic, striking and quieter than Fira. Built on a steep slope of the caldera, many of its dwellings nestle in niches hewn into the volcanic rock. Oia is famous for its sunsets and its narrow passageways get crowded in the evenings.

From the bus turnaround, go left (following signs for the youth hostel), turn immediately right, take the first left, ascend the steps and walk across the central square to the main street, Nikolaou Nomikou, which skirts the caldera. You can get information and book hotels through Ecorama (☎ 71 507, fax 71 509), by the bus turnaround, and Kargounas Tours (☎ 71 290) on Nikolaou Nomikou.

The last bus for Fira leaves Oia at 10.20 pm in summer. After that, three to four people can bargain for a shared taxi for about 3000 dr. Six buses daily connect Oia with Baxedes Beach.

The **maritime museum** is open 12.30 to 4 pm and 5 to 8.30 pm daily except Tuesday; admission is 800 dr.

You can swim at **Ammoudi**, the tiny port with tavernas that lies 300 steps below. In summer at least two boats daily go from Ammoudi to Thirasia (1000 dr per person); check the times at Kargounas Tours.

The traditional settlement of **Finikia**, just east of Oia, is a beautiful, quiet place to wander around.

CYCLADES

Places to Stay Oia's exceptional ***youth hostel*** *(☎ 71 465)* has dorm beds for 3500 dr, including breakfast. The hostel has a bar, laundry facilities and a nice terrace, but is open in summer only.

A little farther on there are several domatia with reasonable prices. ***Irini Halari*** *(☎ 71 226)*, on the main road near the pink church, has singles/doubles/triples for 5000/10,000/12,000 dr with bathroom. Next door, ***Antonis*** has similar rooms and prices.

Lauda Traditional Pension *(☎ 71 157)*, on the main pedestrian thoroughfare overlooking the caldera, has singles/doubles for 12,000/15,000 dr and double/triple studios for 18,000/24,000 dr.

If you can afford to splurge, Oia is the place to do it. For lovingly restored traditional cave dwellings, contact ***Chelidonia*** *(☎ 71 287, fax 71 649)*. The office is in the centre of town (the Web address is www.chelidonia.com); apartments for two/four cost 28,000/42,000 dr. ***Restaurant Lotza*** *(☎ 71 357)*, on the same street, has traditional houses at similar prices. ***Zoe-Aegeas*** *(☎ 71 466)* has lovely two-person studios in traditional houses with shared/private courtyard for 25,000/30,000 dr.

Katikies (☎ *71 401*) is one of the most beautiful hotels on the island and has a spectacular pool filled to the brim and balanced on the lip of the caldera. Doubles rooms cost 43,000 dr and apartments for four cost 100,000 dr. Double studios (51,000 dr), two-person apartments (58,000 dr) and a honeymoon suite (79,000 dr) are also available.

Places to Eat *Anemomylos*, at the eastern edge of the town, serves traditional food at reasonable prices. For fish, locals eat at ***Thalami*** in the centre of town, and at ***Dimitri's*** and ***Sunset***, gorgeous little tavernas at the port of Ammoudi. There is no shortage of restaurants with a view; ***Skala***, on the caldera, has excellent lamb, salads and hors d'oeuvres. ***1800***, in a restored sea captain's house complete with original furniture, is an upmarket place serving contemporary Greek cuisine. Expect to pay at least 10,000 dr a head, including wine.

Karterados Καρτεράδος

There's not a lot to see here, and the old village with houses dug into a ravine is very neglected now that new apartments have been built on its periphery. However, accommodation is cheaper than in Fira and it makes a good base, providing you don't mind the 20 minute walk to town.

Agapi & Stavros Filitsis (☎ *22 694, 23 720*), at Taverna Neraïda, have 65 rooms to choose from. Singles/doubles are 8000/15,000 dr with bathroom; two-person apartments at a nearby beach are 24,000 dr. Turn left off the main approach road from Fira, and it's the last in a row of tavernas on the left.

The comfortable ***Pension George*** (☎ *22 351*) has singles/doubles for 12,000/14,000 dr with bathroom. George will collect guests from Fira, the ferry port or the airport if phoned. Otherwise, walk or take a bus to the village turn-off. Follow the road and turn right after a church on your left. The pension is on the left, cloaked in bougainvillea.

Messaria Μεσσαριά

Situated at a shady junction between Karterados and Kamari, Messaria has a few tavernas and domatia. The main attraction is the **Arhontiko Argirou** (☎ 31 669), a sumptuously restored neoclassical mansion that dates from 1888. It's open 10 am to 1 pm and 5 to 7 pm daily. You can also stay here: doubles with bathroom are 14,000 dr, while apartments with kitchen are 24,000 dr.

Wineries

There are five commercial wineries that hold tastings in summer: **Canava Roussos** and **Lava**, both on the way to Kamari; **Santo Wines**, near Pyrgos; and **Antoniou** and **Boutari**, both in Megalohori.

Antoniou winery is an old place with dungeons that descend down the cliffs; wine is no longer made at this site, but it's a fascinating place to visit. Santo Wines is the local vine growers' cooperative and worth supporting.

Beaches

Santorini's black sand beaches become so hot that a mat is essential. The nicest beaches are on the east coast. **Perissa** gets quite busy, but **Perivolos** and **Agios Georgios**, farther south, are more relaxed. The Mediterranean Dive Club (☎ 83 080), based at Perissa, offers diving certification, wreck dives and volcano dives.

Perissa Camping (☎ *81 343*) charges 1500 dr per person and 800 dr per tent. ***Hostel Anna*** (☎ *82 182*), also in Perissa, has a free bus from the port. Dorm beds cost 1800 dr, and nearby double/quad rooms with pool are 10,000/20,000 dr. Plenty of ***domatia*** are available in Perissa and at Perivolos.

Leonidas taverna at Agios Georgios is a nice place to kick back and have a relaxing ouzo or raki and a bite to eat. ***The Nets***, closer to Perissa, serves exquisite, delicate mezedes and seafood and is open year-round. Nearby, ***Perivolos*** also serves superb seafood. ***Taverna Lava***, on the beachfront at Perissa, is a well established, low-key place with deliciously simple mezedes and excellent, unfussy traditional food.

Kamari is a long strand now covered by beach umbrellas and backed by package tour hotels. There are a few ***domatia*** in the backstreets. If you're tired of the bland eateries along the beach, ***Ouzeria Pontios***, which is festooned with Chinese lanterns and other paraphernalia, can provide a bit of local colour. Try the mezedes or the grilled fish. It's up in Kamari village, near the football ground. To get there, turn off the main road at the large church and take the first street on the right.

Kamari Cinema, on the main road coming into Kamari, is a great open-air theatre set in a thicket of trees and showing recent releases; entry is 1800 dr. In July it hosts the Santorini Jazz Festival.

Monolithos Beach, farther along the coast near an abandoned tomato cannery, is less crowded and there are sometimes sizable waves to splash about in. ***Galini Fish Taverna*** *(☎ 32 924)* has good fresh seafood and is set right on the beach. ***Mythos Mezedopoleio*** is another nice place to stop for ouzo and a nibble. North of Monolithos, the beaches are almost deserted.

Red Beach, near Ancient Akrotiri, has some novelty value but is overrated. **Vlihada**, also on the south coast, is much nicer. On the north coast near Oia, **Paradise** and **Pori** are both worth a stop. ***Captain John***, at Pori, is a good spot for lunch. At **Armeni** and **Ammoudi**, down the cliffs below Oia, you can plunge right into the caldera. Contact Atlantis Diving (☎ 0932-778 411) at Ammoudi if you're interested in exploring the depths.

THIRASIA & VOLCANIC ISLETS

Unspoilt Thirasia (Θηρασιά) was separated from Santorini by an eruption in 236 BC. The cliff-top hora, **Manolas**, has ***tavernas*** and ***domatia***. It's a pretty place that gives some idea of what Santorini was like before tourism took over.

The *Nisos Thirasia* leaves Athinios port for Thirasia on Monday and Friday at the inconveniently early hour of 7 am, returning at 2 pm. On Wednesday it leaves Athinios at 1.30 pm but does not return to Santorini. Tickets are available only at the port. There are also morning and afternoon boats to Thirasia from Oia's port of Ammoudi; see the Oia section for details.

The islets of **Palia Kameni** and **Nea Kameni** are still volcanically active and can be visited on half-day excursions from Fira Skala and Athinios for around 3500 dr. A two hour trip to Nea Kameni costs about 2000 dr. A day's excursion taking in Nea Kameni, the hot springs at Palia Kameni, Thirasia and Oia is about 5000 dr. A tour around the caldera by glass-bottomed boat costs 5000 dr. Tours that include Akrotiri as well are 7000 dr. Shop around Fira's travel agencies for the best deals and the nicest boats.

The very bella *Bella Aurora*, an exact copy of an 18th century schooner, scoots around the caldera every afternoon on a sunset tour (8000 dr), stopping for sight-seeing at Nea Kameni and for ouzo at Thirasia.

Anafi Ανάφη

☎ 0286 • postcode 840 09 • pop 250

Unpretentious Anafi is a one hour ferry ride east of Santorini. The main attractions are the beaches, the slow-paced, traditional lifestyle and the lack of commercialism – it's an ideal place to unwind. In mythology, Anafi emerged at Apollo's command when Jason and the Argonauts were in dire need of refuge during a storm. The island's name means 'no snakes'.

Its little port is **Agios Nikolaos**. The main town, the **hora**, is a 10 minute bus ride or steep 30 minute walk from the port. To get to the hora's main pedestrian thoroughfare, head up the hill behind the ouzeri at the first bus stop. This street has most of the domatia, restaurants and minimarkets, and there is also a post office that opens occasionally.

There are several lovely beaches near Agios Nikolaos; palm-lined **Klissidi**, a 10 minute walk east of the port, is the closest and most popular.

Anafi's main sight, **Moni Kalamiotissas**, is a three hour walk from the hora in the extreme east of the island, near the meagre remains of a sanctuary to Apollo. **Monastery Rock** (584m) is the highest rock formation in the Mediterranean Sea. There is also a ruined Venetian kastro at **Kastelli**, east of Klissidi.

Jeyzed Travel (☎ 61 253), down at the port, sells tickets, exchanges money, can help with accommodation and organises Monastery Rock climbs.

Getting There & Away

There are five ferries weekly to Ios (two to 3½ hours, 1900 dr), Naxos (four hours, 2800 dr) and Paros (6½ hours, 3500 dr). Four ferries weekly go to Santorini (one hour, 1700 dr) and Piraeus (11 hours, 6700 dr), and one goes to Syros (eight hours, 4100 dr), Folegandros (five hours, 2450 dr), Sikinos (four hours, 1850 dr) and Astypalea (1½ hours, 2500 dr). Twice weekly there's a post boat to Santorini (3½ hours, 2000 dr). Two hydrofoils weekly serve Ios (1½ hours, 4000 dr) and Santorini (30 minutes, 3500 dr).

Getting Around

An undersized bus carts passengers from the port up to the hora (200 dr). Caïques serve various beaches and nearby islands.

Places to Stay & Eat

Camping is tolerated at Klissidi Beach, but the only facilities are at nearby tavernas.

Rooms in the hora are overpriced and pretty much of a muchness. Shop around if you can, but be careful not to miss out altogether. Domatia owners are looking for long stays – if you're only staying one night you should take whatever you can get. Contact Jeyzed Travel (☎ 61 253) in advance to be sure of a room. ***Rooms Rent Paradise*** *(☎ 61 243)*, on the main street, has clean doubles with a nice view for 8000 dr. ***Panorama*** *(☎ 61 292)*, next door, has similar rooms for the same price. ***Anafi Rooms*** *(☎ 61 271)*, nearby, charges 9000 dr. ***Villa Apollon*** at Klissidi Beach is the nicest and priciest place, charging around 12,000 dr for traditional rooms with a few extra modern comforts such as telephones. ***Rooms to Let Artemis*** *(☎ 61 235)*, also at Klissidi, has rooms for around 10,000 dr. Places at Klissidi fill fast, so book well in advance.

Tavernas in the hora are all reasonably priced and have nice views. These include ***Alexandra's***, ***Astrakan*** and ***To Steki***. ***Taverna Armenaki***, below the main street, past To Steki, has a nice atmosphere and a menu that includes Cretan tacos, local greens and cheeses, and lamb. It also has raki with honey.

Klissidi has a few ***tavernas*** as well.

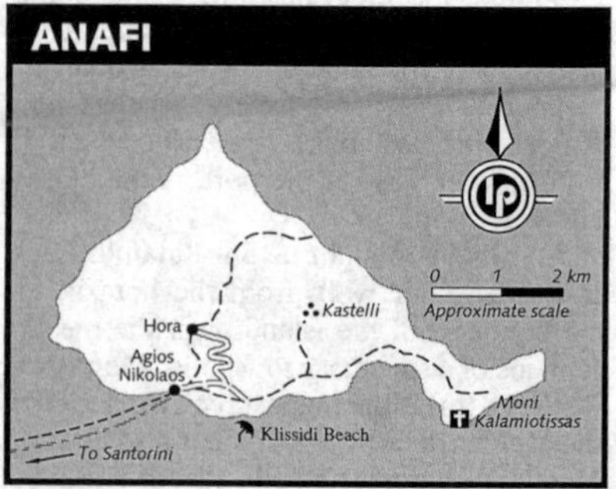

Sikinos Σίκινος

☎ 0286 • postcode 840 10 • pop 287

If a quiet, unspoilt island is what you're looking for, Sikinos fits the bill. It has some nice beaches and a beautiful terraced landscape that drops dramatically down to the sea. The port of Alopronia, and the contiguous villages of Hora and Kastro that together comprise the hilltop capital, are the only settlements. Hora/Kastro has a combined post office and OTE, but no banks. Ferry tickets are sold at Koundouris Travel (☎ 51 168) in Hora/Kastro and at a booth at the port before departures. If you're bringing a car or motorcycle, bring petrol too – there's no petrol station on the island.

Getting There & Around

Ferry Seven ferries weekly go to Piraeus (10 hours, 6000 dr) and Ios (30 minutes, 1100 dr), six to Naxos (three hours, 1600 dr) and Paros (four hours, 1700 dr), five to Folegandros (45 minutes, 1200 dr), four to Santorini (2½ hours, 1700 dr), two to Kimolos (2½ hours, 1700 dr), Milos (three hours, 2800 dr), Sifnos (four hours, 1800 dr), Serifos (five hours, 2700 dr), Kythnos (seven hours,

3100 dr) and Thirasia (2½ hours, 1700 dr), and one weekly to Syros (six hours, 2700 dr).

Hydrofoil Santorini Dolphins go twice weekly to Ios (10 minutes, 2200 dr), Naxos (one hour, 3000 dr), Paros (1¼ hours, 3500 dr), Tinos (three hours, 5500 dr) and Syros (six hours, 5500 dr), and weekly to Folegandros (30 minutes, 2500 dr) and Santorini (30 minutes, 3400 dr).

The local bus meets all ferries and runs between Alopronia and Hora/Kastro every half-hour in August. A timetable is sometimes posted near the minimarket.

Things to See & Do

The **Kastro** is a cute and compact place with some lovely old houses and friendly locals. In the centre there's a pretty square that was created in the 40s by the occupying Italians, who apparently planned to stay. The fortified **Moni Zoödohou Pigis** stands on a hill above the town.

Sikinos' main excursion is a one hour scenic trek (or five minute drive along a rather silly new road) south-west to **Episkopi**. When ruins there were investigated by 19th century archaeologists, the Doric columns and inscriptions led them to believe it had originally been a shrine to Apollo, but the remains are now believed to be those of a 3rd century AD Roman mausoleum. In the 7th century the ruins were transformed into a church, which was extended in the 17th century to become **Moni Episkopis**. The church and monastery are open 6.30 to 8.30 pm daily. From here it's possible to climb up to a little church and ancient ruins perched on a precipice to the south, from where the views are spectacular.

Caïques run to nice beaches at **Agios Georgios**, **Malta** – with ancient ruins on the hill above – and **Karra**. **Katergo**, a swimming place with interesting rocks, and **Agios Nikolaos Beach** are both within easy walking distance of Alopronia.

Places to Stay & Eat

Alopronia has the bulk of accommodation. ***Lucas Rooms to Let*** *(☎ 51 075)*, near the restaurant of the same name, has doubles for 9000 dr with fridge and bathroom, and three to four-person apartments for 13,000 dr. Bougainvillea-covered ***Tasos Rooms*** *(☎ 51 005)*, past the Rock Café, has doubles with bathroom, fridge and balcony for 10,000 dr. The stylish B class ***Porto Sikinos*** *(☎/fax 51 220)*, on the port beach, has doubles with bathroom for 15,000 dr, including breakfast. This traditional Cycladic-style establishment has a bar and restaurant.

In Hora/Kastro, ***To Steki tou Garbi*** is a good grill house. There is also a good ***taverna*** at Agio Georgios. Down at the port, ***Lucas*** serves the best food. In high season a lovely ***bar*** opens over the water at the northern end of Alopronia's bay; at other times the ***Rock Café,*** above the quay, suffices.

Folegandros
Φολέγανδρος

The happiest man on earth is the man with fewest needs. And I also believe that if you have light, such as you have here, all ugliness is obliterated.

Henry Miller

☎ 0286 • postcode 840 11 • pop 650

Folegandros (fo-**leh**-gan-dross) is one of Greece's most enticing islands, bridging the gap between tourist traps and small, underpopulated islands on the brink of total abandonment. The number of visitors is

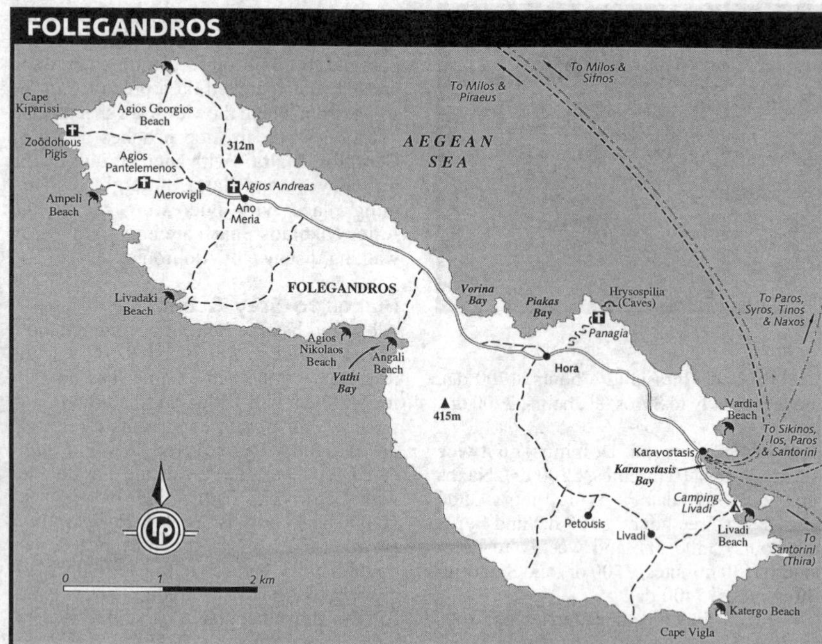

increasing, but most locals still make a living from fishing and farming.

Tourists tend to come in search of unspoilt island life and, except for July and August, the island is uncrowded and blissful. The island has several good beaches – be prepared for strenuous walking to reach some of them – and a striking landscape of cultivated terraces that give way to precipitous cliffs.

The capital is the concealed cliff-top Hora, one of the prettiest capitals in the Cyclades. All boats dock at the small harbour of Karavostasis, on the east coast. The only other settlement is Ano Meria, 4km northwest of Hora.

Getting There & Away

Ferry There are eight services weekly to Piraeus (six to nine hours, 5150 dr), seven to Santorini (1½ to 2½ hours, 1700 dr), and six to Ios (1½ hours, 1500 dr), Paros (four hours, 1900 dr) and Naxos (three hours, 2300 dr). There are also five boats weekly to Sikinos (40 minutes, 1200 dr), three weekly to Milos (2½ hours, 1700 dr), Sifnos (four hours, 1600 dr) and Kythnos (six hours, 2900 dr), and two weekly to Kimolos (1½ hours, 1200 dr) and Serifos (five hours, 1600 dr). Once weekly there are ferries to Thirasia (1½ hours, 1700 dr), Syros (six hours, 2900 dr) and Anafi (five hours, 2450 dr).

Hydrofoil There are four hydrofoils weekly to Paros (one to four hours, 3800 dr), Syros (seven hours, 5700 dr), Mykonos (five hours, 5700 dr) and Tinos (six hours, 5700 dr). There are three services weekly to Santorini (one hour, 3315 dr), two weekly to Naxos (two hours, 4600 dr), Milos (one hour, 3400 dr) and Sifnos (two hours, 3200 dr), and one weekly to Ios (one to two hours, 3000 dr), Sikinos (20 minutes, 2400 dr) and Thirasia (one hour, 3400 dr).

Getting Around

The local bus meets all boats and takes passengers to Hora (240 dr). From Hora there are buses to the port one hour before all ferry departures, even late at night. Buses from Hora run hourly to Ano Meria (300 dr), stopping at the road leading to Angali Beach. The bus stop for Ano Meria is on the western edge of town, next to the Sottovento Tourist Office. There is one overworked taxi (☎ 41 048, 0944-693 957) on the island.

In July and August, excursion boats make separate trips from Karavostasis to Angali and Agios Nikolaos (both 2500 dr return) and from Angali to Livadaki Beach (1000 dr return).

KARAVOSTASIS Καραβοστάσις

This port town lacks charm but makes a convenient base from which to explore the island's beaches.

Places to Stay & Eat

Camping Livadi *(☎ 41 204)* is at Livadi Beach, 1km from Karavostasis. Turn left onto the cement road skirting Karavostasis Beach. It charges 1200 dr per person and 600 dr for tent hire.

Karavostasis has several domatia and hotels – look for the signs when you get off the ferry. The C class ***Aeolos Beach Hotel*** *(☎ 41 205)*, on the beach, has clean singles/doubles/suites for 8000/14,000/20,000 dr with bathroom.

Restaurant Kati Allo, by Poseidon Hotel, has one of the best reputations for top quality traditional food and fresh fish. There are two bars, ***Evangelos*** and ***Sirma***, on the beach, which are good for snacks and mezedes.

HORA Χώρα

The captivating Hora, complete with a medieval kastro filled with little houses draped in bougainvillea, is perhaps the most beautiful capital in the Cyclades.

Orientation & Information

From the bus turnaround, facing away from the port, turn left and follow the curving road. An archway on the right leads into the kastro, the walls of which have been incorporated into dwellings. A left turn leads to a row of three shady squares. The third is the central plateia.

There is no EOT or tourist police. The post office is 200m downhill from the bus turnaround, on the port road. There are cardphones, but no OTE.

There is no bank, but Maraki Travel (☎ 41 273), by the first square, exchanges currency, as does the Sottovento Tourism Office (☎/fax 41 430), by the bus stop for Ano Meria and Angali. Note that, except for a couple of boutiques, credit cards are not usually accepted on Folegandros.

Ferry tickets can be purchased from Maraki Travel; there is no ticket booth at the port.

The police (☎ 41 249) are beyond the third plateia, past Nikos' Restaurant.

Things to See

The Hora is a well preserved Cycladic village with aspirin-white churches, sugar cube houses and shady squares. The medieval **kastro**, a tangle of narrow streets spanned by low archways, dates from when Marco Sanudo ruled the island in the 13th century. The houses' wooden balconies blaze with bougainvillea and hibiscus.

The newer village, outside the kastro, is just as pretty. From the first bus stop, a steep path leads up to the large church of the **Panagia**, which is perched on a cliff top above the town. It's open between 6 and 8 pm daily.

Courses

The Cycladic School (founded on Folegandros in 1984) offers one and two-week courses in drawing, painting, Greek cookery, folk dancing and hatha yoga. Accommodation is included. For details, contact Anne and Fotis Papadopoulos (☎ 41 137).

Organised Tours

Three times weekly in summer, Sottovento Tourism Office (see the Hora Orientation &

Information section) operates day trips by caïque to hidden bays and the little-known **Hrysospilia Caves** on the east coast for 6000 dr, including lunch.

A tour of the island by jeep, departing at 10 am and returning at 3 pm, costs 13,000 dr for up to four people.

Places to Stay

In July and August most domatia and hotels are booked solid; unless you're happy to join the homeless overspill down at Camping Livadi, make sure you book well in advance.

Pavlos' Rooms *(☎ 41 232)* are comfortable, converted stables on the main road, five minutes walk uphill from the village. Doubles are 11,000 dr, or 15,000 dr with bathroom. Rooftop sleeping is available in summer if there are no rooms. A bus meets the boats.

There are reasonably priced domatia near the police station, including ***Spyridoula Rooms*** *(☎ 41 078)*, where doubles with bathroom and fridge are 13,000 dr. ***Nikos Rooms*** *(☎ 41 055)* has clean rooms with kitchen and bathroom for 16,000 dr. Turn right at Piatsa Restaurant on the central square – the rooms are on the right. The atmospheric ***Hotel Castro*** *(☎ 41 414)* has cosy doubles/triples for 17,000/25,000 dr with en suite. Some rooms have incredible views straight down the cliffs to the sea. Walk straight ahead from the entrance to the kastro and you'll find the hotel on the left. Opposite, ***Rooms Margarita*** *(☎ 41 321)* has doubles for 12,000 dr.

The C class ***Folegandros*** *(☎ 41 276)*, where the port bus terminates, has large, well equipped apartments priced from 24,000 dr for two people. Views don't come any better than from the top-of-the-range ***Anemomilos Apartments*** *(☎ 41 309)*, by the bus station. Traditional Cycladic-style apartments are furnished with pottery and antiques and there is one unit for the disabled. Rates for doubles/triples overlooking the sea are 31,000/37,000 dr.

Places to Eat

Pounta, at the port-Hora bus turnaround, has tables in a lovely little garden out the back. Excellent breakfast, *spanakopita*, rabbit *stifado*, lamb and vegetarian dishes are served at very reasonable prices. ***Apanemos***, next to the Sottovento Tourism Office, is run by the same crew and is also worth a visit. ***Melissa***, on the main square, has very good home-cooked food.

The Caper Caper

Capers are the unopened buds of the caper bush *Capparis spinosa*, which grows wild throughout the Mediterranean region. They have a radishy, pungent taste and are usually pickled in vinegar. Capers were known to the ancient Greeks, and carbon dating of fossilised seeds and buds has shown that they were eaten as far back as 6000 BC in Iraq and Turkey.

Folegandros, Santorini and Anafi are all very proud of their capers, and Andros even has a town named after them – Kapparia. The bushes, which are small, fleshy and sprawling, often inhabit the stone walls that line old paths and divide fields. The harvesting of the buds and the leaves (a delicacy) from the low-lying plants is a laborious process that must be done by hand. Spring is caper-collecting season, although you can still find buds in abundance in early summer. Any buds not collected blossom into surprisingly showy pink and white flowers, which are, of course, also edible. The torpedo-shaped fruit is packed in salt or pickled in vinegar and eaten as well.

Capers are experiencing a comeback in Greek cuisine, especially on the islands. Many tavernas, notably those that take pride in serving traditional local food, are spiking salads and mezedes with liberal sprinklings of these tasty buds.

Piatsa Restaurant is one of the best on the island and has interesting daily specials including rabbit with onions (1900 dr) and beef in lemon sauce with green peas (2000 dr), as well as vegetarian dishes. It's on the second square past the kastro. On the third square, ***O Kritikos***, with the rotisserie in front, has succulent grilled meat.

Entertainment

Astarti, on the main square, is a good place to go after dinner for Greek music. In the kastro, ***Kellari*** is a moody little wine bar. ***Anihto*** is the place to go for a late-night drink; it's on the road that leads west off the third square towards the Ano Meria bus stop and the Sottovento office. ***Rakendia Sunset Bar***, signposted from the road to Ano Meria, has a fabulous view over the cliffs and is also open late.

AROUND FOLEGANDROS

Ano Meria Ανω Μεριά

The settlement of Ano Meria stretches for several kilometres because small farms surround most of the dwellings. Agriculture is still very much alive at this end of the island and you'll see haystacks, market gardens, goats and donkeys.

The **folklore museum**, near the eastern end of the village, is open 10 am to noon and 6 to 8 pm daily; admission is 400 dr. Ask the bus driver to drop you off nearby.

There are several excellent tavernas, including ***I Synantisi***, which specialises in fresh swordfish and *matsada* – a type of handmade pasta served with rabbit or rooster; and ***Mimi's***, which has good grilled meat as well as matsada. ***Barbakosta***, a very old and authentic kafeneio frequented by locals, is well worth a stop.

Beaches

Karavostasis has a pebbled beach. For **Livadi Beach**, follow the signs for Camping Livadi. The sandy and pebbled **Angali Beach** has a lovely aspect but gets a bit dirty before its annual clean-up in mid-May. There are a few domatia; try ***Panagiotis Rooms*** (☎ *41 116*).

There are other good beaches at **Agios Nikolaos** and **Livadaki**, both west of Angali. The steep path to the beach at Agios Nikolaos is only for those with strong boots and a head for heights, but it's worth it if you plan to stop for lunch – don't miss the octopus in wine sauce at ***Taverna Papalagi***. **Agios Georgios** is north of Ano Meria. A path from Agios Andreas church in Ano Meria leads to Agios Georgios Beach. The walk takes about an hour.

Most of the beaches have no shops or tavernas, so make sure you take food and water.

Milos & Kimolos

Μήλος & Κίμωλος

MILOS

☎ 0287 • postcode 848 00 • pop 4390

Volcanic Milos (**mee**-loss), the most westerly island of the Cyclades, is overlooked by most foreign tourists. While not as visually dramatic as the volcanic islands of Santorini and Nisyros, it does have some weird rock formations, hot springs and pleasant beaches. A boat trip around the island allows you to visit most of Milos' stunning beaches (many inaccessible by road), coves and geologically interesting places.

Filakopi, the ancient Minoan city in the north-east of the island, was one of the earliest settlements in the Cyclades. During the Peloponnesian Wars, Milos remained neutral and was the only Cycladic island not to join the Athenian alliance. It paid dearly in 416 BC when avenging Athenians massacred the adult males and enslaved the women and children.

The island's most celebrated asset, the beautiful *Venus de Milo* (a 4th century BC statue of Aphrodite) is far away in the Louvre (apparently having lost its arms on the way to Paris in the 19th century).

Since ancient times, the island has been quarried for minerals, resulting in huge gaps and fissures in the landscape. Obsidian (hard, black volcanic glass used for manufacturing sharp blades) was mined on the island and exported throughout the Mediterranean. These days, about a third of the working population is employed in the mining industry.

Getting There & Away

Air There is a daily flight to Athens (14,900 dr). The Olympic Airways office (☎ 22 380) is in Adamas, just past the main square, on the road to Plaka.

Ferry There are at least 10 ferries weekly to Piraeus (five to seven hours, 5050 dr), six weekly to Sifnos (1¼ hours, 1550 dr), five weekly to Serifos (two hours, 1650 dr) and Kythnos (3½ hours, 2550 dr), four weekly to Kimolos (one hour, 1220 dr), three weekly to Folegandros (two hours, 1750 dr) and Santorini (four hours, 3650 dr), two weekly to Sikinos (three hours, 2850 dr), and one weekly to Ios (three hours, 2850 dr). Three times weekly the *Vitsentsos Kornaros* sails to the Cretan ports of Agios Nikolaos (seven hours, 4850 dr) and Sitia (nine hours, 5100 dr), sometimes continuing on to Kassos (11 hours, 5850 dr), Karpathos (12 hours, 7150 dr) and Rhodes (13 hours, 8450 dr).

Hydrofoil Minoan Flying Dolphins and Santorini Dolphins run daily to Piraeus (four hours, 9800 dr), daily except Friday to Sifnos (45 minutes, 3000 dr) and Serifos (one hour, 3300 dr), five times weekly to Paros (two hours, 5200 dr), Mykonos (3½ hours, 9100 dr), Naxos (2½ hours, 8200 dr) and Syros (four hours, 5800 dr), four times weekly to Kythnos (two hours, 5100 dr), twice weekly to Folegandros (one hour, 3400 dr), Santorini (3½ hours, 7900 dr) and Tinos (six hours, 6300 dr), and once weekly to Kimolos (30 minutes, 2400 dr).

A boat that transports mine workers between Pollonia and Kimolos (20 minutes, 600 dr) has a tourist-unfriendly schedule linked to shift times, usually running at 6 or 7 am and returning at 9 pm, after the last bus back to Adamas has departed. If you're staying in Pollonia it might suit.

Getting Around

There are no buses to the airport, so you'll need to take a taxi (1500 dr from Adamas).

Buses leave Adamas for Plaka and Trypiti (both 350 dr) every hour or so. Four buses daily go to Pollonia (250 dr) and Paleohori (350 dr), and three go to Provatas (350 dr). Taxis can be ordered on ☎ 22 219. Cars, motorcycles and mopeds can be hired along the waterfront.

Adamas Αδάμας

Although Plaka is the capital, the rather plain port of Adamas has most of the accommodation.

To get to the town centre from the quay, turn right at the waterfront. The central square, with the bus stop, taxi rank and outdoor cafes, is at the end of this stretch of waterfront. Just past the square is a road to the right that skirts the town beach. Straight ahead is the town's main thoroughfare and the road to Plaka.

There is no EOT; Milos' municipal tourist office (☎ 22 445) is opposite the quay and open only in summer. For the post office, turn right just after the square and take the third street on the left. Note that Adamas has its own postcode: 848 01. There are ATMs on the main square. The police (☎ 21 378) are on the main square, next to the bus stop; the port police (☎ 22 100) are on the waterfront.

Mining Museum This new museum has some interesting geological exhibits and traces the island's long history of mining, which dates back to Neolithic times. It's open 9.30 am to 1 pm and 5 to 8 pm daily and is free. To get there, take the first right after the central square and continue along the waterfront for about 500m.

Organised Tours The *Delphina* tour boat chugs around the island, stopping at beaches and Kleftiko, and pausing at Kimolos for lunch. It leaves Adamas at 9 am, and returns at 6.30 pm; the tour costs 4000 dr and tickets are available from most travel agents.

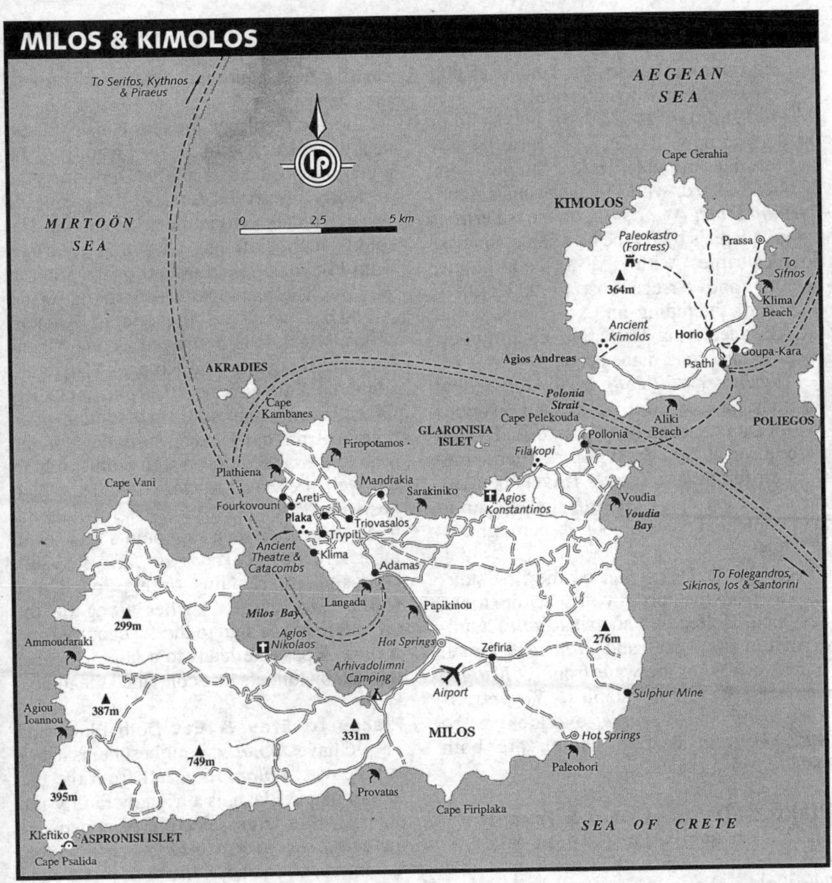

Terry's Travel (☎ 22 640), up the steps from the quay, has a range of tours, including a sailing trip to the island's nicest beaches and coves. It costs 13,000 dr per person and features a seafood lunch caught by the captain.

Places to Stay Adamas' ***camping ground*** *(☎ 31 410)* is 6.5km east of town at Arhivadolimni; to get there, follow the signs along the waterfront from the central square.

In summer, lists of domatia are given out at the tourist office on the quay, but decent accommodation is quite thin on the ground – make sure you call ahead. Options include the excellent ***Ethelvina's Rooms*** *(☎ 22 169)*, uphill from the bakery on the main square, where singles/doubles/triples are 7000/15,000/18,000 dr; most have refrigerator and bathroom. ***Langada Beach Hotel*** *(☎ 23 411)*, left of the ferry quay, behind Langada Beach, is a huge complex with a pool; rooms with fridge cost 12,000/15,000/

18,000 dr. ***Hotel Delfini*** *(☎ 22 001)*, behind Langada Beach Hotel, has friendly owners and nice simple doubles for 10,000/15,000 dr with shared/private bathroom.

Hotel Dionysis *(☎ 23 118)*, just up from the square, opposite Olympic Airways, has comfortable double/triple studios for 20,000/24,000 dr with TV, phone and air-con. ***Portiani Hotel*** *(☎ 22 940)*, on the waterfront at the square, is by far the best value. Singles/doubles/triples with TV, air-con, phone, balcony and terrace cost 20,000/24,000/34,500 dr, including an exceptional buffet breakfast featuring fresh figs, comb honey, cheeses and home-made jams.

Villa Ilios *(☎ 22 258)*, on the hill behind the quay, has beautifully furnished, spacious two-person apartments with phone, TV and air-con for 20,000 dr. If you're after something different, ask Terry's Travel about accommodation in a ***windmill***. It sleeps up to six people and costs 35,000 dr per night.

CYCLADES

Places to Eat ***Vedema***, on the first staircase up from the port as you head into town, has local delicacies such as *peltes* (sun-dried tomato paste) and *pittarakia* (small cheese pies). On the waterfront, ***O Kinigos*** has superb Greek staples. ***Trapetselis Restaurant*** and ***Navagio***, overlooking the water beyond Portiani Hotel, are both excellent fish places.

Plaka & Trypiti Πλάκα & Τρυπητή

Plaka, 5km uphill from Adamas, is a typical Cycladic town with white houses and labyrinthine laneways. It merges with the settlement of Trypiti to the south.

The **Milos Folk & Arts Museum** is located in a 19th century house in Plaka and contains household items, furniture, tools, embroidery and weavings. It's open 10 am to 2 pm and 6 to 8 pm (closing 2 pm Sunday) daily except Monday; admission is 500 dr. It's signposted at the bus turnaround in Plaka.

At the bus turnaround, turn right for the path to the Frankish **kastro** built on the ancient acropolis. The 13th century church, **Thalassitras**, is inside the walls. The final battle between the ancient Melians and Athenians was fought on this hill. The kastro offers panoramic views of most of the island.

The **archaeology museum** is in Plaka, near the junction with the road leading to the much signposted catacombs. Don't miss the perfectly preserved terracotta figurine of Athena (unlabelled) in the middle room. The room on the left has charming figurines from Filakopi. The museum opens 8 am to 2.30 pm, Tuesday to Sunday. Entry is 500 dr.

Plaka is built on the site of Ancient Milos, which was destroyed by the Athenians and rebuilt by the Romans. There are some Roman ruins near Trypiti, including Greece's only Christian **catacombs**, open 8 am to 1 pm daily except Monday. On the road to the catacombs, a sign points right to the well preserved **ancient theatre**, which hosts the Milos Festival every July. On the track to the theatre, a sign points to where a farmer found the *Venus de Milo* in 1820. Opposite are remains of massive Doric walls. Fifty metres farther along on the cement road is a sign to the 1st century catacombs. A passage leads to a large chamber flanked by tunnels that contained the tombs.

Places to Stay & Eat Both Plaka and Trypiti have ***domatia***; your best bet is to ask at tavernas. ***Arhontoula***, left from the bus turnaround in Plaka, is a friendly family-run place, with a large selection of appetisers, including cod with *skordalia* (garlic sauce) and interesting salads. ***Alisahni***, just around the corner, is also very good.

Around Milos

Klima, once the port of ancient Milos, is now a charming, unspoilt fishing village skirting a narrow beach below Trypiti and the catacombs. Whitewashed buildings, with bright blue, green and red doors and balconies, have boat houses on the ground floor and living quarters on the 1st floor. Klima's one hotel, 2km from the village, is ***Hotel Panorama*** *(☎ 21 623)*, where double rooms are 18,000 dr, with breakfast; there's also a restaurant.

Plathiena is a lovely sandy beach below Plaka. On the way to Plathiena you can detour to the tiny fishing villages of **Areti** and **Fourkovouni**. The beaches of **Provatas** and **Paleohori**, on the south coast, are long and sandy, and there are hot springs at Paleohori.

Pollonia, on the north coast, is a fishing village-cum-resort with a small beach and domatia. It serves as the jumping-off point for the boat to Kimolos. **Mandrakia** is a lovely fishing hamlet north-east of Plaka.

The Minoan settlement of **Filakopi** is 2km inland from Pollonia. Three levels of cities have been uncovered here – Early, Middle and Late Cycladic.

The islet of **Glaronisia**, off the north coast, is a rare geological phenomenon composed entirely of hexagonal volcanic stone bars.

KIMOLOS

This small island lies just north-east of Milos. It receives few visitors, although there are ***domatia***, ***tavernas***, and decent beaches.

Those who do make the effort tend to be day-trippers arriving on the boat from Pollonia, on the north-eastern tip of Milos. The boat docks at the port of **Psathi**, from where it's 3km to the pretty capital of **Horio**. There's no petrol station on Kimolos – if you're bringing a car or moped from Milos, make sure you've got enough fuel.

Donkeys are still the principal mode of transport, and there are tracks all around the island. There are thermal springs at the settlement of **Prassa** on the north-east coast. **Beaches** can be reached by caïque from Psathi. At the centre of the island is the 364m-high cliff on which sits the fortress of **Paleokastro**.

Day-trippers should try the local speciality, *ladenia*, a pizza-like pie with tomato, onion and olives.

Getting There & Away

Ferry There are seven ferries weekly to Adamas (one hour, 1220 dr). Twice weekly ferries go to Folegandros (1½ hours, 1200 dr), Sikinos (2½ hours, 1700 dr), Santorini (four hours, 2987 dr), Sifnos (1½ hours, 1460 dr), Serifos (two hours, 1750 dr) and Kythnos (three hours, 2000 dr) and Piraeus (six hours, 4800 dr). One ferry weekly goes to Ios (2½ hours, 1900 dr). Boats go daily to/from Pollonia on Milos (see the Milos Getting There & Away section for details).

Hydrofoil Once a week Minoan Flying Dolphins go to Milos (30 minutes, 2400 dr), Sifnos (25 minutes, 2800 dr), Serifos (one hour, 3500 dr), Kythnos (two hours, 4800 dr) and Piraeus (3½ hours, 8800 dr).

Sifnos Σίφνος

☎ 0284 • postcode 840 03 • pop 2900

Sifnos coyly hides its assets from passing ferry passengers. At first glance it looks barren, but the port is in the island's most arid area. Explore and you'll find an abundantly attractive landscape of terraced olive groves and almond trees, with oleanders in the valleys and hillsides covered in wild juniper, which used to fuel potters' kilns. There are numerous dovecotes, whitewashed houses and chapels. Plenty of old paths link the villages, which makes it an ideal island for walking.

During the Archaic period the island was very wealthy due to its gold and silver resources. To protect their loot the islanders constructed an elaborate communications network of watchtowers that used fire and smoke signals to warn of attack. The ruins of 55 towers have been located to date. By the 5th century BC the mines were exhausted and Sifnos' fortunes were reversed – the island became so poor that it was the butt of endless jokes in Athens and elsewhere.

The island has a long history of producing superior pottery because of the quality of its clay, and many shops sell local ceramics. Some potters' workshops are open to the public – it's quite mesmerising to watch them work.

Sifniot olive oil is highly prized throughout Greece, which might have something to do with the island's reputation for producing some of the country's best chefs. Local specialities include *revithia* (baked chickpeas), *revithokeftedes* (falafel-like vegetable balls), *xynomyzithra* (a sharpish fresh cheese) and almond sweets flavoured with orange flowers.

Getting There & Away

No travel agency sells all ferry and hydrofoil tickets, so you'll probably be shunted from one office to another.

Ferry There are daily ferries to Milos (two hours, 1560 dr), Piraeus (five hours, 4400 dr) via Serifos (one hour, 1460 dr), and Kythnos (2½ hours, 1960 dr). There are three ferries weekly to Kimolos (1½ hours, 1460 dr), Folegandros (four hours, 1660 dr), Sikinos (five hours, 1860 dr) and Santorini (six hours, 3060 dr), two weekly to Paros (three hours, 1000 dr), Syros (5½ hours, 2000 dr) and Rethymno on Crete (5½ hours, 5100 dr), and one weekly to Mykonos (4½ hours, 3100 dr).

Hydrofoil At least one hydrofoil daily serves Piraeus (three hours, 8500 dr), Serifos (25 minutes, 2800 dr), Kythnos (1¼ hours, 3800 dr), Paros (one hour, 1900 dr) and Mykonos (2½ to 3½ hours, 6100 dr), and two daily go to Milos (one hour, 3000 dr). There are five weekly to Naxos (1½ hours, 5800 dr), and two weekly to Santorini (three hours, 6000 dr), Folegandros (1½ hours, 3100 dr), Syros (3½ hours, 4000 dr) and Tinos (2½ hours, 6200 dr).

Getting Around

Frequent buses link Apollonia (stopping at Artemonas) with Kamares (240 dr), Kastro (240 dr), Vathi (290 dr), Faros (240 dr) and Platys Gialos (290 dr); inquire at the municipal tourist office at the port for timetables.

Taxis (☎ 094-761 210) hover around the port and Apollonia's main square. Cars can be hired from Hotel Kamari (☎ 33 383) in Kamares, and from Apollo Rent a Car (☎ 32 237) in Apollonia.

KAMARES Καμάρες

Unlike most villages on the island, the port of Kamares is a newish resort-style town. It has a nice enough 'holiday' feel about it, with lots of waterfront cafes and tavernas, and a reasonable sandy beach. The bus stop is the stand of tamarisk trees outside the municipal tourist office.

Opposite the quay there is a very helpful municipal tourist office (☎ 31 977) with staff who can find you accommodation anywhere on the island. It also offers free luggage storage and has copies of the bus schedule.

Places to Stay & Eat

Camping Makis *(☎ 32 366)* just behind the beach north of the port charges 1600 dr per person, including tent. Domatia owners rarely meet the boats and in high season it's best to book ahead. The C class ***Stavros***

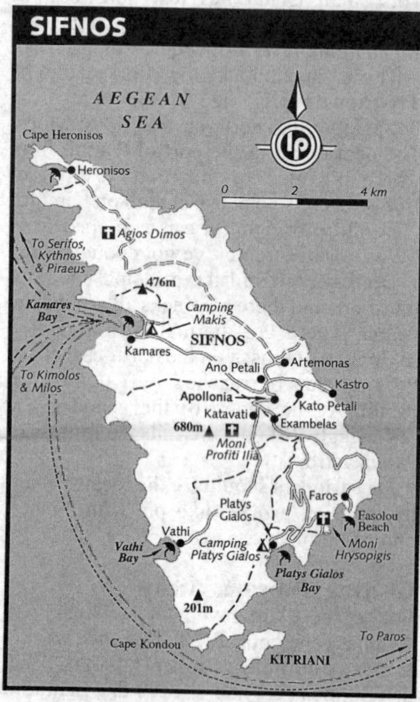

Hotel *(☎ 31 641)*, in the middle of the waterfront, has basic, clean doubles with bathroom for 10,000 dr. ***Hotel Kamari*** *(☎ 33 383)*, 400m up the road to Apollonia, has attractive doubles with bathroom and telephone for 15,000 dr.

Restaurant Simos and ***I Meropi***, next to each other on the waterfront, serve well prepared traditional Greek fare. ***Ouzeri Kamares***, also on the waterfront, has good mezedes. Nearby, ***Captain Andreas*** is the best place for fish.

APOLLONIA Απολλώνια

The capital, situated on a plateau 5km uphill from the port, is a conglomeration of six pretty whitewashed villages: Artemonas, Apollonia, Ano Petali, Kato Petali, Katavati and Exambelas.

The bus stop for Kamares is on the lively central square where the post office and OTE are located; all other buses stop outside Hotel Anthousa. The main pedestrian thoroughfare – with jewellery and clothes shops, restaurants and bars – is to the right behind the museum. The National Bank of Greece, which has an ATM, is a bit farther out on the road to Artemonas, and the police are about 50m beyond.

The interesting little **Museum of Popular Art**, on the central square, contains old costumes, pots and textiles, and is open 9 am to 1.30 pm and 6 to 11 pm daily; admission is 300 dr.

Courses

Greek-language courses take place in Apollonia during the summer. Two weeks' tuition costs around US$700/400 with/without accommodation. For details contact Dr Anna Kyritsi on ☎/fax 01-775 5021.

Places to Stay & Eat

The C class ***Hotel Sofia*** *(☎ 31 238)*, north of the central square, has basic singles/doubles for 8000/11,000 dr with bathroom.

Hotel Anthousa *(☎ 31 431)*, around the corner, has nice rooms for 12,000/15,000 dr with bathroom, TV and telephone. It also has laundry facilities. Downstairs there's a lovely patisserie that sells local produce as well as sweets, coffee and snacks. There are a few bars nearby and it can get a bit noisy at night, especially on weekends.

A better option is the C class ***Hotel Sifnos*** *(☎ 31 629, 33 067)* on the main pedestrian street that leads off to the right behind the museum; it has immaculate singles/doubles/triples for 13,000/16,000/19,000 dr with bathroom. ***Peristeronas Apartments*** *(☎ 71 288)*, downhill from Hotel Anthousa, is a new Sifnos-style house overlooking terraced fields with doubles/triples/quads for 23,000/25,000/27,000 dr. ***Hotel Petali*** *(☎ 33 024)*, about 100m along the footpath to Artemonas, is a newer, more upmarket place with spacious doubles/triples for 30,000/33,000 dr with air-con, TV and telephone.

Apostoli tou Koutouki on the main pedestrian street serves very good meat, while ***Restaurant Sifnos***, a bit farther along, below the hotel of the same name, has excellent vegetable balls and other local fare. In Artemonas, try ***Manganas*** and ***Margarita***.

Shopping

As well as fine ceramics and jewellery, you can also find beautiful hand-woven textiles. On the main pedestrian thoroughfare, Margarita Baki has a tiny workshop where she weaves on a loom and sells tablecloths, cushion covers, curtains, shawls and kilims, all at reasonable prices.

AROUND SIFNOS

The pretty village of **Artemonas** is a short walk or bus ride north of Apollonia. Not to be missed is the walled cliff-top village of **Kastro**, 3km from Apollonia. The former capital, it is a magical place of buttressed alleys and whitewashed houses. Its small archaeological museum is open 8 am to 2.30 pm Tuesday to Sunday (free).

The pretty downhill walk along old paths from Apollonia to Kastro takes under an hour and you can return by bus. The serene village of **Exambelas**, south of Apollonia, is said to be the birthplace of most of Sifnos' accomplished chefs.

The resort of **Platys Gialos**, 10km south of Apollonia, has a long sandy beach. The spectacularly situated **Moni Hrysopigis**, near Platys Gialos, was built to house a miraculous icon of the Virgin found in the sea by two fishermen. A path leads from the monastery to a beach with a ***taverna***. **Vathi**, on the west coast, is a gorgeous sandy bay. **Faros** is a cosy little fishing hamlet with a couple of nice beaches.

Places to Stay & Eat

Platys Gialos has quite a few accommodation options. ***Camping Platys Gialos*** *(☎ 31 786)* is in an olive grove behind the beach. ***Angeliki Rooms*** *(☎ 71 288)*, right on the beach, has doubles/triples for 14,000/16,500 dr with fridge and bathroom. The lodge-like ***Platys Gialos Beach Hotel*** *(☎ 71 324)* has doubles with air-con, TV, minibar and sea view for 40,000 dr. In Faros, ***Fabrika*** *(☎ 71 427)* has rooms in an old flour mill for 13,500 dr.

Dimitri's, at the sweet little beach of Fasolou, up the stairs and over the headland from the bus stop in Faros, has very good home-cooked food. ***Faros***, in Faros, is the place to go for fish.

Serifos Σέριφος

☎ 0281 • postcode 840 05 • pop 1020

Serifos is a barren, rocky island with a few pockets of greenery that are the result of tomato and vine cultivation. Livadi, the port, is on the south-east coast; the whitewashed capital, Hora, clings onto a hillside 2km inland.

Getting There & Away

Ferry There are daily ferries from Serifos to Piraeus (4½ hours, 4000 dr), Sifnos (one hour, 1460 dr), Milos (two hours, 1650 dr) and Kimolos (2½ hours, 1750 dr). Four times weekly the Piraeus ferry stops at Kythnos (1½ hours, 1750 dr), and twice weekly boats go to Paros (two hours, 2000 dr), Mykonos (three hours, 3000 dr), Syros (three to five hours, 2000 dr) and Folegandros (five hours, 1600 dr).

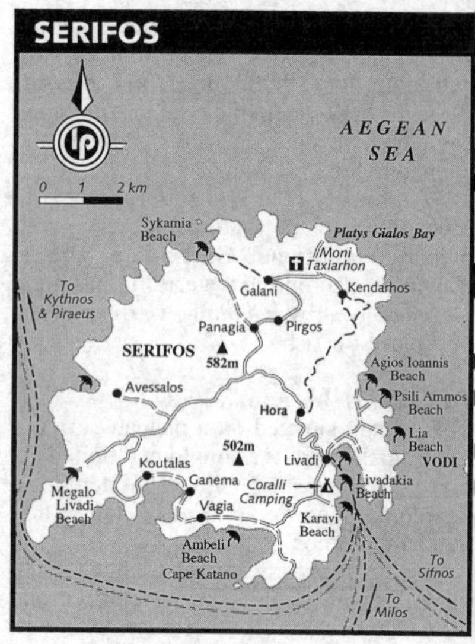

There are weekly boats to Santorini (seven hours, 3587 dr), Ios (six hours, 2900 dr) and Sikinos (five hours, 2700 dr).

Hydrofoil Flying Dolphin hydrofoils travel daily to Piraeus (2½ hours, 7400 dr), Kythnos (45 minutes, 3500 dr), Sifnos (25 minutes, 2800 dr) and Milos (1½ hours, 3300 dr). There is a weekly service to Paros (one hour, 3800 dr), Naxos (1½ hours, 5700 dr), Mykonos (2½ hours, 6300 dr) and Kimolos (one hour, 3500 dr).

Getting Around

There are frequent buses between Livadi and Hora (240 dr); a timetable is posted at the bus stop by the yacht marina. Motorcycles and cars can be hired from Krinas Travel (☎ 51 488, fax 51 073), upstairs next to Captain Hook Bar, 50m from the quay.

LIVADI Λιβάδι

This rather scrappy port is at the top end of an elongated bay. Continue around the bay for the ordinary town beach or climb over the headland that rises from the ferry quay for the pleasant, tamarisk-fringed beach at **Livadakia**. **Karavi Beach**, a walk farther south over the next headland, is the unofficial nudist beach. There is an Ionian Bank, with ATM, on the waterfront. Krinas Travel (see Getting Around) offers a wide range of services. The port police (☎ 51 470) are up steps from the quay.

Places to Stay & Eat

The excellent, shady ***Coralli Camping*** *(☎ 51 500)* at sandy Livadakia Beach charges 1500 dr per person and 700 dr for a tent. The bungalows – probably the nicest accommodation on the island – have bathroom, phone and fridge and cost 15,000/18,000 dr for doubles/triples. There's also a restaurant, bar and minimarket, and a minibus meets all ferries.

Anna Domatia *(☎ 51 263)*, about 500m along the waterfront next to Hotel Asteria, has airy doubles with fridge for 10,000 dr. The light and bright ***Hotel Areti*** *(☎ 51 479)*, on the hill above the ferry quay, has lovely singles/doubles for 11,000/14,000 dr. ***Rooms to Let Marianna*** *(☎ 51 338)* is a nice, secluded, shady place set back a little from the waterfront; doubles go for 15,000 dr with bathroom and fridge. ***Hotel Albatros*** *(☎ 51 148)*, on the waterfront, has singles/doubles for 12,000/14,000 dr. Next door, the C class ***Maistrali Hotel*** *(☎ 51 381, fax 51 298)* has good doubles for 16,800/18,500 dr without/with sea views.

Mokka, near the quay, is a good place specialising in seafood. ***Perseus***, farther along the waterfront, serves the best Greek standards. There are also a couple of reasonable ***tavernas*** on the beach at Livadakia.

Those with a sweet tooth should check out the almond versions of baklava and other pastries that are an island speciality.

AROUND SERIFOS

The dazzling white **Hora**, clinging to a crag above Livadi, is one of the most striking Cycladic capitals. It can be reached either by bus or by walking up the steps from Livadi. More steps lead to a ruined 15th century Venetian fortress above the village.

The post office is by the first bus stop; the OTE is farther uphill, off the central square. There is no bank. For a journey back in time, visit ye olde medieval cobbler near the square. He makes sturdy – occasionally bizarre – leather shoes and sandals to order.

About an hour's walk north of Livadi along a track (negotiable by moped) is **Psili Ammos Beach**. A path from Hora heads north to the pretty village of **Kendarhos** (also called Kallitsos), from where you can continue to the 17th century fortified **Moni Taxiarhon**, which has impressive 18th century frescoes. The walk from the town to the monastery takes about two hours, but you will need to take food and water as there are no facilities in Kendarhos.

CYCLADES

Kythnos Κύθνος

☎ 0281 • postcode 840 06 • pop 1632

Kythnos, the next island north of Serifos, is virtually barren. It is popular mainly with Athenian holiday-makers, and there is little to enthuse about unless you're looking for a cure for rheumatism at the thermal baths.

The main settlements are the port of Merihas and the capital, Hora, also known as Kythnos. Merihas has an OTE, and there is an agency of the National Bank of Greece at Cava Kythnos travel agency and minimarket, which also sells Flying Dolphin tickets, and ferry tickets to Kea and Lavrio. Hora has the island's post office, police station and OTE.

Getting There & Away

There are daily boats to Piraeus (2½ hours, 2300 dr). Most services coming from Piraeus continue to Serifos (1½ hours, 1750 dr), Sifnos (2½ hours, 1750 dr), Kimolos (three hours, 2000 dr) and Milos (3½ hours, 2550 dr). There are four ferries weekly to Kea (1¼ hours, 1500 dr), two weekly to Folegandros (six hours, 2900 dr), Sikinos (seven hours, 3100 dr), Santorini (eight hours, 4000 dr), Syros (two hours, 2000 dr) and Lavrio (3½ hours, 2300 dr), and one weekly to Ios (7½ hours, 3400 dr).

In summer, hydrofoils travel daily to Piraeus (1½ hours, 6000 dr), Serifos (45 minutes, 3500 dr) and Sifnos (1¼ hours, 3800 dr). They continue to Milos (two hours, 5100 dr) six days a week and to Kimolos (two hours, 4800 dr) once a week.

Getting Around

There are regular buses from Merihas to Dryopida (300 dr) and Hora (300 dr), occasionally continuing to Loutra (500 dr). The buses supposedly meet the ferries, but usually they leave from the turn-off to Hora in Merihas.

Taxis are a better bet, except at siesta time. There are two motorcycle rental outlets on the waterfront.

MERIHAS Μέριχας

Merihas does not have a lot going for it other than a small, dirty-brown beach. But it's a reasonable base and has most of the island's accommodation. There are better beaches within walking distance north of the quay (turn left facing inland).

Places to Stay & Eat

Domatia owners usually meet the boats, but if no-one is waiting, wander around the waterfront and backstreets and you'll see plenty of signs advertising rooms.

If you want to stay in the town's one hotel – ***Kythnos Hotel*** *(☎ 32 092)* – you'd best book ahead. It's up the first set of steps on the way into town from the harbour and has decent doubles/triples overlooking the harbour for 8500/10,000 dr.

There are no especially exciting eateries. ***Ostria*** and ***Restaurant Kissos*** provide reasonable standard stuff, while ***Taverna to Kantouni***, near the abandoned Hotel Posidonion, has good grilled meat.

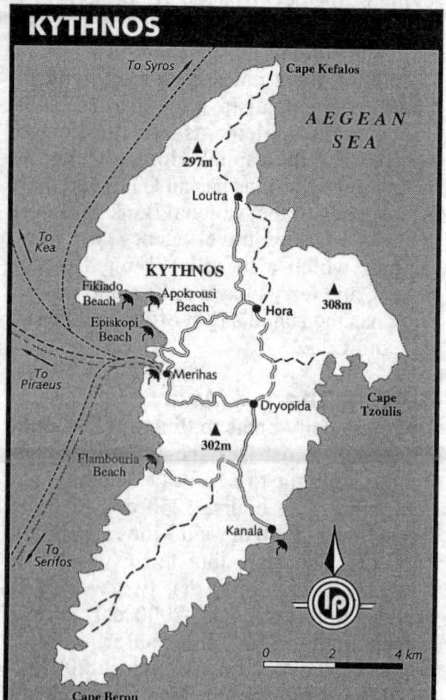

AROUND KYTHNOS

The capital, **Hora** (also known as Kythnos), lacks the charm of other Cycladic capitals. The main reason for visiting is the walk south to **Dryopida**, a picturesque town of red-tiled roofs and winding streets that was the island's capital in the Middle Ages. It takes about 1½ hours to cover the 6km. From Dryopida, you can either walk the 6km back to Merihas or catch a bus or taxi.

Loutra offers the only accommodation outside Merihas. There are several ***domatia*** as well as ***Hotel Porto Klaras*** *(☎/fax 31 276)*, reportedly the best on the island, with doubles/self-contained studios for 13,000/ 16,000 dr.

The **thermal baths** at Loutra in the north-east are reputedly the most potent in the Cyclades. The best **beaches** are on the south-east coast, near the village of Kanala.

Kea Κέα or Τζία

☎ 0288 • postcode 840 02 • pop 1800

Kea, to the north of Kythnos, is the closest of the Cyclades to the mainland. The island is a popular summer weekend escape for

Athenians, but remains relatively untouched by tourism. While it appears largely barren from a distance, there is ample water and the bare hills hide fertile valleys filled with orchards, olive groves, and almond and oak trees (acorns, a raw material used by the tanneries, made the inhabitants rich in the 18th century). The main settlements are the port of Korissia, and the capital, Ioulida, 5km inland.

Getting There & Away

The F/B *Myrina Express* connects Kea with Lavrio (1¼ hours, 1600 dr) on the mainland at least twice daily and also with Kythnos (1¼ hours, 1500 dr) twice weekly. In addition, the F/B *Georgios Express* goes twice weekly to Kythnos and Syros (four hours, 2250 dr).

On Sunday, the supercat *Haroula* goes to the mainland port of Rafina (1¼ hours, 1900 dr). In summer, there are at least five hydrofoils weekly to Zea Marina at Piraeus (1¼ hours, 4800 dr).

Getting Around

In July and August there are, in theory, regular buses from Korissia to Vourkari (150 dr), Otzias (300 dr), Ioulida (300 dr) and Pisses (500 dr). In practice, however, the bus driver operates at his own whim; if there isn't a bus waiting for the boat, you're better off catching one of the taxis (☎ 21 021/228) that hang about near the port. Alternatively, there are three expensive motorcycle rental outlets.

KORISSIA Κορησσία

The port of Korissia is an uninspiring place in spite of its setting on a large bay with a long, sandy beach.

The tourist police (☎ 22 100) can be found one block back from the waterfront between June and September. The fairly useless tourist information office opposite the ferry quay has lists of domatia. Stefanos Lepouras, next door at Stegali bookshop (☎ 21 435, fax 21 012) and Minoan Flying Dolphin agency, is a good source of information. He also changes money.

Places to Stay & Eat

The C class ***Hotel Karthea*** *(☎ 21 222)* is a large concrete box at the corner of the bay with ordinary singles/doubles for 12,000/16,000 dr. There are better places along the road that runs behind the beach, including a couple of ***domatia***. The recently renovated ***Hotel Tzia*** *(☎ 21 305)* has lovely doubles that open right onto the beach for 13,000 dr with bathroom and telephone. ***Hotel Korissia*** *(☎ 21 484)* has large, modern singles/doubles for 11,000/14,000 dr, and double/triple studios for 18,000/21,000 dr. Turn right off the beach road at the creek and the hotel is on the right after about 150m.

Lagoudera, near the tourist office, has good home-cooked local specialities.

IOULIDA Ιουλίδα

Ioulida is a delightful higgledy-piggledy hillside town, full of alleyways and steps that beg to be explored. The architecture here is quite different from other Cycladic capitals – the houses have red-tiled roofs.

The bus turnaround is on a square at the edge of town. An archway leads to Ioulida proper, and Ilia Malavazou, the main thoroughfare, leads uphill to the right. The post office is along here on the right. The pathway continues uphill and crosses a small square, just beyond which, on the right, is an agency of the National Bank of Greece, signposted above a minimarket.

Things to See

The **archaeological museum**, on the main thoroughfare, houses local finds, mostly from Agia Irini. It's open 8.30 am to 3 pm Tuesday to Sunday (free).

The celebrated **Kea Lion**, chiselled from a huge chunk of slate in the 6th century BC, lies on the hillside an easy, pleasant 10 minute walk north-east of town. The path to the lion leads off to the left (the main path goes sharp right) about 150m past the bank agency. Keep walking past the cemetery and you'll find the gate that leads downhill to the lion, which is surrounded by whitewashed rocks.

Places to Stay & Eat

Apart from a couple of ***domatia***, the only option is ***Hotel Filoxenia*** *(☎ 22 057)*, a tiny old place with lots of character. Singles/doubles are 8000/10,000 dr. To get there, head up the stairs straight ahead from the square; it's on the right above the shoe shop.

There are a couple of decent tavernas. ***Estiatorio I Piatsa***, just inside the archway, serves a generous plate of fresh fish for 1500 dr. Carnivores should not dilly-dally: go directly to ***Kalofagadon*** on the main square and order the lamb chops (2000 dr).

AROUND KEA

The beach road from Korissia leads past nice but slightly suburban **Gialiskari Beach** to the trendy resort of **Vourkari**, 2.5km away. Just north of Vourkari is the ancient site of **Agia Irini** (named after a nearby church), where a Minoan palace has been excavated.

The road continues for another 3km to a sandy beach at **Otzias**. A dirt road continues beyond here for another 5km to the 18th century **Moni Panagias Kastriani**, with a commanding position and terrific views.

The island's best beach, 8km south-west of Ioulida, has the unfortunate name of **Pisses**. It is long and sandy and backed by a verdant valley of orchards and olive groves. **Flea**, also with an interesting name, occupies a lush valley and makes a nice walking destination from either Korissia or Ioulida.

Places to Stay

The island's camping ground, ***Kea Camping*** *(☎ 31 302)*, is at Pisses Beach and has a shop, bar and restaurant. It costs 1200 dr per person and 1200 dr per tent, and there are additional charges for cars and motorcycles. There are also ***domatia*** and ***tavernas*** here.

Kea Beach Hotel *(☎ 31 230, fax 31 234)* is on a headland overlooking Koundouros Beach, 2km south of Pisses. The hotel complex has a bar, restaurant, disco and swimming pool. Doubles/triples are 19,000/20,500 dr with breakfast.

Crete Κρήτη

Crete is Greece's largest and most southerly island, and arguably the most beautiful. A spectacular mountain chain runs from east to west across the island, split into three ranges: the Mt Dikti Range in the east, the Mt Ida (or Mt Psiloritis) Range in the centre and the Lefka Ori (white mountains) in the west. The mountains are dotted with agricultural plains and plateaus, and sliced by numerous dramatic gorges. Long, sandy beaches speckle the coastline, and the east coast boasts Europe's only palm-tree forest.

Administratively, the island is divided into four prefectures: Lassithi, Iraklio, Rethymno and Hania. Apart from Lassithi, with its capital of Agios Nikolaos, the prefectures are named after their major cities. The island's capital is Iraklio with a population of 127,600. It's Greece's fifth-largest city. Nearly all Crete's major population centres are on the north coast. Most of the south coast is too precipitous to support large settlements.

Crete is famous for its wildflowers. You'll find *Wild Flowers of Crete* by George Sfikas a comprehensive field guide, but *Flowers of Crete* by Yanoukas Iatrides may be a better bet for the layperson.

Scenery and beaches aside, the island is also the birthplace of Europe's first advanced civilisation, the Minoan. If you intend to spend much time at the many Minoan sites, *Palaces of Minoan Crete* by Gerald Cadogan is an excellent guide.

Crete's size and its distance from the rest of Greece allowed an independent culture to evolve. Vibrant Cretan weavings are sold in many of the island's towns and villages. The traditional Cretan songs differ from those heard elsewhere in Greece. Called *mantinades*, these songs are highly emotive, expressing the age-old concerns of love, death and the yearning for freedom. You will still come across a few old men wearing the traditional dress of breeches tucked into knee-high leather boots, and black-fringed kerchiefs tied tightly around their heads.

HIGHLIGHTS

- Iraklio's archaeological museum and the historical museum of Crete
- The ancient Minoan site of Knossos
- The stunning expanse of the Lassithi Plateau
- Walking the gorge between Zakros and Kato Zakros, site of ancient Zakros
- Hania's beautiful old Venetian quarter
- Trekking the spectacular Samaria Gorge
- The lovely sand beaches and coves at Elafonisi

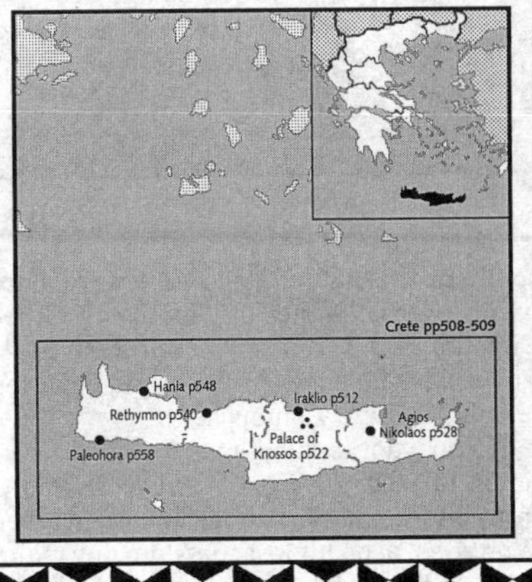

The attractions of Crete have not gone unnoticed by tour operators, and the island has the dubious honour of playing host to almost a quarter of Greece's tourists. The result is that much of the north coast is packed solid with hastily constructed hotels for package tourists, particularly between Iraklio and Agios Nikolaos and west of Hania. The tour operators have also taken over several of the

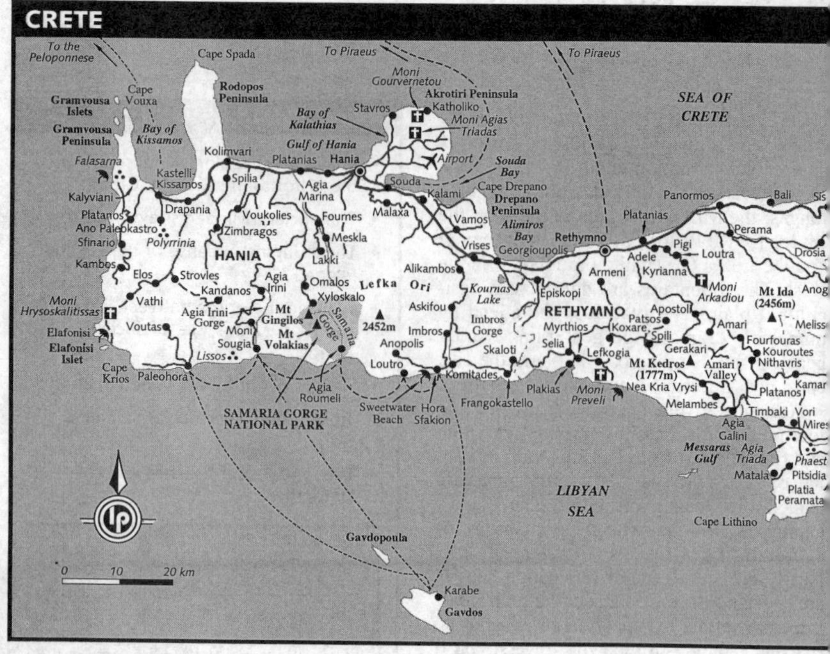

southern coastal villages that were once backpacker favourites. If you haven't visited Crete for a while, brace yourself for a shock. The wild and rugged west coast, however, remains relatively untouched.

If you want to avoid the crowds, the best times to visit are from April to June and from mid-September to the end of October. Winter is a dead loss outside the major population centres, as most hotel owners and restaurateurs choose to shut their establishments and recharge their batteries in preparation for the next tourist onslaught.

History

Although Crete has been inhabited since Neolithic times (7000 to 3000 BC), as far as most people are concerned its history begins with the Minoan civilisation. The glories of Crete's Minoan past remained hidden until British archaeologist Sir Arthur Evans made his dramatic discoveries at Knossos in the early 1900s. The term 'Minoan' was coined by Evans and derived from the King Minos of Greek mythology. Nobody knows what the Minoans called themselves.

Among the ruins unearthed by Evans, were the famous Knossos frescoes. Artistically, the frescoes are superlative; the figures that grace them have a naturalism lacking in contemporary Cycladic figurines, ancient Egyptian artwork (which they resemble in certain respects), and the Archaic sculpture that came later. Compared with candle-smoke-blackened Byzantine frescoes, the Minoan frescoes, with their fresh, bright colours, look as if they were painted yesterday. See the following boxed text 'The Mysterious Minoans' for more details.

But no matter how much speculation the frescoes inspire about the Minoans, all we really know is that early in the 3rd millen-

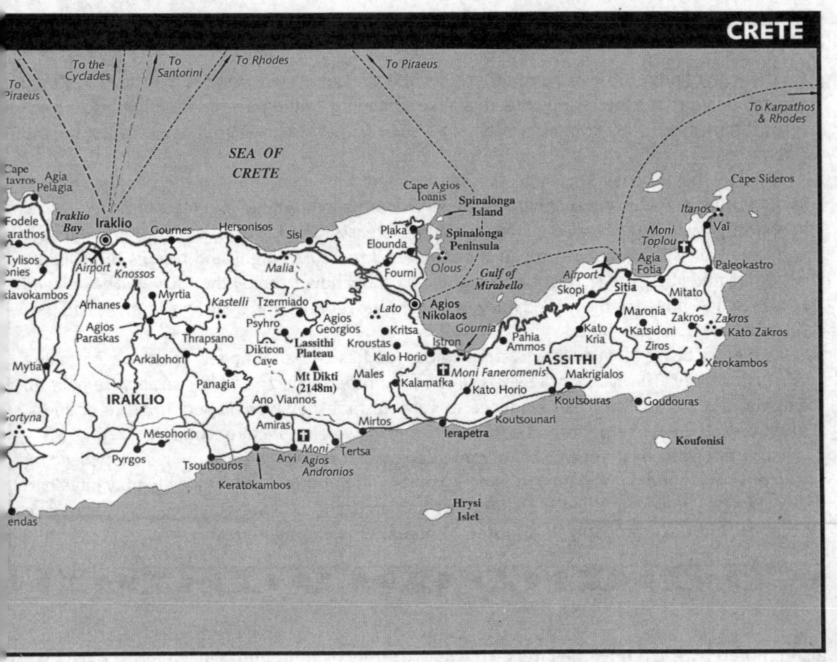

nium BC, an advanced people migrated to Crete and brought with them the art of metallurgy. Many elements of Neolithic culture lived on in the Early Minoan period (3000 to 2100 BC), but the Middle Minoan period (2100 to 1500 BC) saw the emergence of a society with unprecedented artistic, engineering and cultural achievements. It was during this time that the famous palace complexes were built at Knossos, Phaestos, Malia and Zakros.

Also during this time, the Minoans began producing their exquisite Kamares pottery (see Archaeological Museum in the Iraklio section) and silverware, and became a maritime power trading with Egypt and Asia Minor.

Around 1700 BC, all four palace complexes were destroyed by an earthquake. Undeterred, the Minoans built bigger and better palaces on the sites of the originals, as well as new settlements in other parts of the island.

Around 1500 BC, when the Minoan civilisation was at its peak, the palaces were destroyed again, signalling the start of the Late Minoan period (1500 to 1100 BC). This destruction was probably caused by Mycenaean invasions, although the massive volcanic eruption on the island of Santorini (Thira) may also have had something to do with it. The Knossos palace was the only one to be salvaged. It was finally destroyed by fire around 1400 BC.

The Minoan civilisation was a hard act to follow. The war-orientated Dorians, who arrived in 1100 BC, were pedestrian by comparison. The 5th century BC found Crete, like the rest of Greece, divided into city-states. The glorious classical age of mainland Greece had little impact on Crete, and the Persians bypassed the island. It was

The Mysterious Minoans

Of the many finds at Knossos and other sites, it is the celebrated frescoes that have captured the imagination of experts and amateurs alike, shedding light on a civilisation hitherto a mystery. The message they communicate is of a society that was powerful, wealthy, joyful and optimistic.

Gracing the frescoes are white-skinned women with elaborately coiffured glossy black locks. Proud, graceful and uninhibited, these women had hourglass figures and were dressed in stylish gowns that revealed perfectly shaped breasts. The bronze-skinned men were tall, with tiny waists, narrow hips, broad shoulders and muscular thighs and biceps; the children were slim and lithe. The Minoans also seemed to know how to enjoy themselves. They played board games, boxed and wrestled, played leap-frog over bulls and over one another, and performed bold acrobatic feats.

As well as being literate, they were religious, as frescoes and models of people partaking in rituals testify. The Minoans' beliefs, like many other aspects of their society, remain an enigma, but there is sufficient evidence to confirm that they worshipped a nature goddess, often depicted with serpents and lions. Male deities were distinctly secondary.

From the frescoes it appears that women enjoyed a respected position in society, leading religious rituals and participating in games, sports and hunting. Minoan society may have had its dark side, however. There is evidence of human sacrifice being practised on at least one occasion, although probably in response to an extreme external threat.

also ignored by Alexander the Great, so was never part of the Macedonian Empire.

By 67 BC, Crete had fallen to the Romans. The town of Gortyna in the south became the capital of Cyrenaica, a province that included large chunks of North Africa. Crete, along with the rest of Greece, became part of the Byzantine Empire in 395 AD. In 1210 the island was occupied by the Venetians, whose legacy is one of mighty fortresses, ornate public buildings and monuments, and the handsome dwellings of nobles and merchants.

Despite the massive Venetian fortifications, which sprang up all over the island, by 1669 the whole of the Cretan mainland was under Turkish rule. The first uprising against the Turks was led by Ioannis Daskalogiannis in 1770. This set the precedent for many more insurrections, and in 1898 the Great Powers intervened and made the island a British protectorate. It was not until the signing of the Treaty of Bucharest in 1913 that Crete officially became part of Greece, although the island's parliament had declared a de facto union in 1905.

The island saw heavy fighting during WWII. Germany wanted to use the island as an air base in the Mediterranean, and on 20 May 1941 German parachutists landed on Crete. It was the start of 10 days of fierce fighting that became known as the Battle of Crete. For two days the battle hung in the balance until Germany won a bridgehead for its air force at Maleme, near Hania. The Allied forces of Britain, Australia, New Zealand and Greece then fought a valiant rearguard action which enabled the British Navy to evacuate 18,000 of the 32,000 Allied troops trapped on the island. Most were picked up from the rugged southern coast around Hora Sfakion. The German occupation of Crete lasted until the end of WWII.

During the war a large active resistance movement drew heavy reprisals from the Germans. Many mountain villages were temporarily bombed 'off the map' and their occupants were shot. Among the bravest members of the resistance were the 'runners' who relayed messages on foot over the mountains. One of these runners, George Psychoundakis, wrote a book based on his experiences entitled *The Cretan Runner*.

Getting There & Away

The following section provides a brief overview of air and boat options to and from Crete. For more comprehensive information, see the relevant sections under specific town entries.

Air Crete has two international airports. The principal one is at Iraklio and there is a smaller one at Hania. In addition there is a domestic airport at Sitia. All three airports have flights to Athens. Iraklio and Hania have flights to Thessaloniki; Iraklio also has flights to Rhodes and Santorini.

Ferry Crete has ports at Iraklio, Hania, Agios Nikolaos, Sitia, Kastelli-Kissamos and Rethymno. The following are high season schedules; services are reduced by about half during low season.

Direct daily ferries travel to Piraeus from Iraklio, Hania and Rethymno. There are three ferries weekly from Iraklio to Santorini, and from Sitia via Agios Nikolaos to Piraeus, stopping once a week at Milos. Three ferries weekly go from Iraklio to Thessaloniki via Santorini stopping twice a week at Paros, Tinos and Skiathos and once a week at Naxos, Syros and Volos. There's also a weekly boat to Rhodes from Iraklio, and from Agios Nikolaos via Sitia stopping at Karpathos and Halki. Two ferries weekly sail from Kastelli-Kissamos to Antikythira, Kythira and Githio.

Getting Around

A four lane national highway skirts the north coast from Hania in the west to Agios Nikolaos in the east, and is being extended farther west to Kastelli-Kissamos. There are frequent buses linking all the major northern towns from Kastelli-Kissamos to Sitia.

Less frequent buses operate between the north coast towns and resorts and places of interest on the south coast, via the mountain villages of the interior. These routes are Hania to Paleohora, Omalos (for the Samaria Gorge) and Hora Sfakion; Rethymno to Plakias, Agia Galini, Phaestos and Matala; Iraklio to Agia Galini, Phaestos, Matala and the Lassithi Plateau; Agios Nikolaos to Ierapetra; and Sitia to Ierapetra, Vaï, Paleokastro and Kato Zakros.

There is nothing comparable to the national highway on the south coast and parts of this area have no roads at all. There is no road between Paleohora and Hora Sfakion, the most precipitous part of the south coast; a boat (daily from June through August) connects the two resorts via Sougia and Agia Roumeli.

As well as the bus schedules given in each section in this chapter, clapped-out 'village buses' travel to just about every village which has a road to it. These buses usually leave in the early morning and return in the afternoon.

Central Crete

Central Crete is occupied by Iraklio prefecture, named after the island's burgeoning major city and administrative capital. The area's major attractions are the Minoan sites of Knossos, Malia and Phaestos. The north coast east of Iraklio has been heavily exploited by the package tourism industry, particularly around Hersonisos.

IRAKLIO Ηράκλειο

☎ 081 • postcode 710 01 • pop 127,600

The Cretan capital of Iraklio is a bustling modern city and the fifth largest in Greece. It has none of the charm of Hania or Rethymno, but it is a dynamic city boasting the highest average per capita income in Greece. That wealth stems largely from Iraklio's position as the island's trading capital, but also from the year-round flow of visitors who flock to nearby Knossos.

History

The Arabs who ruled Crete from 824 to 961 AD were the first people to govern from the

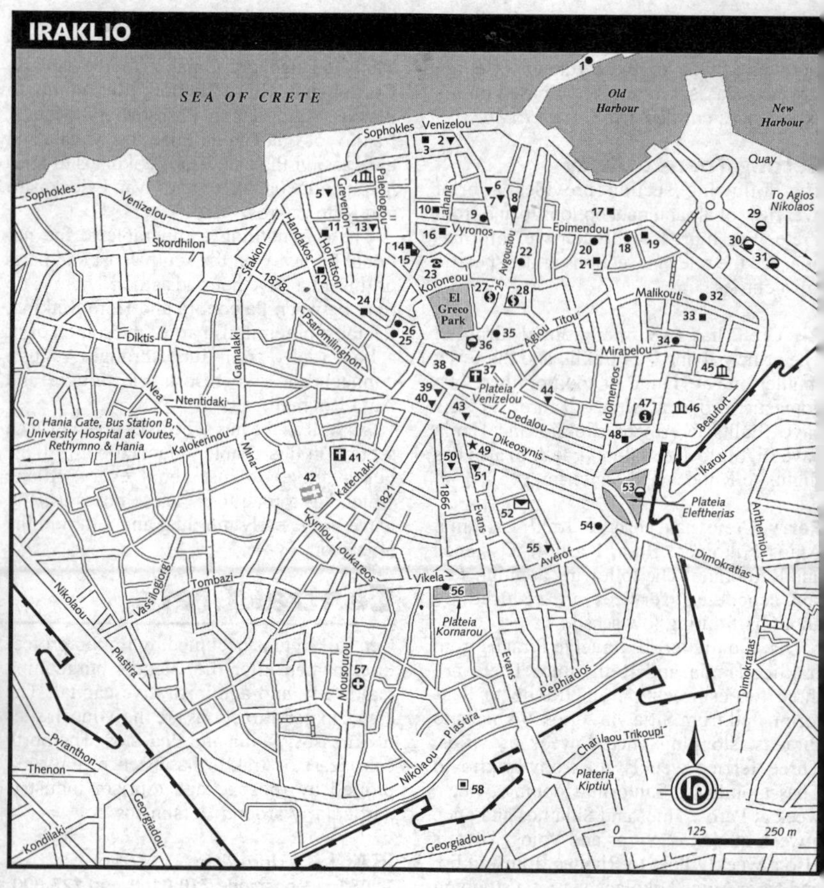

site of modern Iraklio. It was known then as El Khandak, after the moat that surrounded the fortified town, and was reputedly the slave trade capital of the eastern Mediterranean.

El Khandak became Khandakos, after Byzantine troops finally dislodged the Arabs, and then Candia under the Venetians who ruled the island from here for more than 400 years. While the Turks quickly overran the Venetian defences at Hania and Rethymno, Candia's fortifications proved as effective as they looked – an unusual combination. They withstood a siege of 21 years before the garrison finally surrendered in 1669.

Hania became the capital of independent Crete at the end of Turkish rule in 1898, and Candia was renamed Iraklio. Because of its central location, Iraklio became a commercial centre, and resumed its position as the island's administrative centre in 1971.

The city suffered badly in WWII, when most of the old Venetian and Turkish town was destroyed by bombing.

IR

PLACES TO STAY
3 Hotel Kronos
10 Hotel Lena
11 Vergina Rooms
12 Hotel Rea
14 Hotel Mirabello
15 Hotel Kastro
16 Youth Hostel
17 Hotel Lato
19 Hotel Ilaira
21 Hotel Irini
24 Youth Hostel (Rent Rooms Hellas)
33 Atlantis Hotel
48 Astoria Hotel

PLACES TO EAT
2 Ippokampos Ouzeri
5 Garden of Deykaliola Taverna
6 Vareladika Ouzeri
7 Katsina Ouzeri
13 Baxes
39 Ta Leontaria 1922
40 Bougatsa Serraikon
43 Loukoumades Cafe
44 Giovanni Taverna
50 Giakoumis Taverna
51 Restaurant Ionia
55 Bella Casa

THINGS TO SEE
1 Venetian Fortress
4 Historical Museum of Crete
37 Basilica of San Marco
38 Morosini Fountain
41 Church of Agia Ekaterini
42 Agios Minos Cathedral
45 Battle of Crete Museum
46 Archaeological Museum
56 Bembo Fountain

OTHER
8 Prince Travel
9 Grecomar Holidays
18 Crete Travel
20 Summerland Trave
22 Adamis Travel Bure
23 OTE
25 Laundry Washsalon
26 Planet International Bookshop
27 Credit Bank
28 National Bank of Greece
29 Buses to Hania & Rethymno
30 Buses to Knossos & Airport
31 Bus Station A
32 Istos Cyber Cafe
34 Wash-O-Mate
35 Venetian Loggia
36 Buses to Knossos
47 EOT
49 Tourist Police
52 Post Office
53 Buses to Airport
54 Olympic Airways
57 Apollonia Hospital
58 Kazantzakis' Tomb

Orientation

Iraklio's two main squares are Plateia Venizelou and Plateia Eleftherias. Plateia Venizelou, instantly recognisable by its famous Morosini fountain (better known as the Lion fountain), is the heart of Iraklio and the best place from which to familiarise yourself with the layout of the city. The city's major intersection is a few steps south of the square. From here, 25 Avgoustou runs north-east to the harbour; Dikeosynis runs south-east to Plateia Eleftherias; Kalokerinou runs west to the Hania Gate; 1866 (the market street) runs south; and 1821 runs to the south-west. To reach Plateia Venizelou from the New Harbour, turn right, walk along the waterfront and turn left onto 25 Avgoustou.

Iraklio has three intercity bus stations. Station A, on the waterfront between the port and 25 Avgoustou, serves eastern Crete. A special bus station for Hania and Rethymno only is opposite Station A. Station B, just beyond the Hania Gate, serves Phaestos, Agia Galini and Matala. To reach the city centre from Station B walk through the Hania Gate and along Kalokerinou. For details on bus schedules, see the Iraklio Getting There & Away section.

Information

Tourist Offices The EOT (☎ 22 8225/6081/8203, fax 22 6020) is just north of Plateia Eleftherias at Xanthoudidou 1. The staff at the information desk are often work-experience students from a local tourism training college. They can give you photocopied lists of ferry and bus schedules, plus a map of the city. Opening times are 8 am to 2 pm Monday to Friday. In high season they also open on Saturday and Sunday.

The tourist police (☎ 28 3190), at Dikeosynis 10, are open 7 am to 11 pm.

Money Most of the city's banks are on 25 Avgoustou, including the National Bank of Greece at No 35. It has a 24 hour automatic exchange machine, as does the Credit Bank at No 94.

American Express (☎ 24 6202, 22 2303) is represented by Adamis Travel Bureau,

25 Avgoustou 23. Opening hours are 8 am to 2 pm Monday to Saturday. Thomas Cook (☎ 24 1108/1109) is represented by Summerland Travel, Epimenidou 30.

Post & Communications The central post office is on Plateia Daskalogianni. Coming from Plateia Venizelou, turn right off Dikeosynis opposite Hotel Petra, and you will see the post office across the square. Opening hours are 7.30 am to 8 pm Monday to Friday, and 7.30 am to 2 pm Saturday. From June through August there is a mobile post office at El Greco Park, just north of Plateia Venizelou, open 8 am to 6 pm Monday to Friday, and 8 am to 1.30 pm Saturday. The OTE, on Theotokopoulou just north of El Greco Park, opens 7.30 am to 11 pm daily. Istos Cyber Cafe (☎ 22 2120), Malikouti 2, charges 1300 dr an hour for computer access and can also scan, print and fax documents. It's open 9 am to 1 am daily.

Bookshops The huge Planet International Bookshop (☎ 28 1558) on the corner of Hortatson and Kidonias stocks most of the books recommended in this guide and has a large selection of Lonely Planet titles.

Laundry There are two laundrettes: Laundry Washsalon, Handakos 18, and Wash-O-Mate, Merabelou 25, near the archaeological museum. A wash and dry costs 2000 dr.

Left Luggage The left-luggage office at Bus Station A charges 300 dr per day and is open 6.30 am to 8 pm daily. Other options include Prince Travel (☎ 28 2706), 25 Avgoustou 30, which charges 500 dr, Washsalon (see Laundry) which charges 450 dr and the youth hostel at Vyronos 5 which charges 500 dr.

Emergency The new University Hospital (☎ 39 2111) at Voutes, 5km south of Iraklio, is the city's best equipped medical facility. The Apollonia Hospital (☎ 22 9713), inside the old walls on Mousourou, is more convenient.

Archaeological Museum

This outstanding museum (☎ 22 6092) is second in size and importance only to the National Archaeological Museum in Athens. If you are seriously interested in the Minoans you will want more than one visit, but even a fairly superficial perusal of the contents requires half a day.

The exhibits, arranged in chronological order, include pottery, jewellery, figurines and sarcophagi as well as some famous frescoes, mostly from Knossos and Agia Triada. All testify to the remarkable imagination and advanced skills of the Minoans. Unfortunately, the exhibits are not very well explained. If they were, there would be no need to part with 2200 dr for a copy of the glossy illustrated museum guide.

Room 1 of Iraklio's Archaeological Museum is devoted to the Neolithic and Early Minoan periods. Room 2 has a collection from the Middle Minoan period. Among the most fascinating exhibits here are the tiny glazed reliefs of Minoan houses from Knossos.

Room 3 covers the same period with finds from Phaestos, including the famous **Phaestos disc**. The symbols inscribed on the disc have not been deciphered. Here also are the famous **Kamares pottery vases**, named after the sacred cave of Kamares where the pottery was first discovered. The four large vases in case 43 were part of a royal banquet set. They are of exceptional quality and are some of the finest examples of Kamares pottery.

Exhibits in Room 4 are also from the Middle Minoan period. Most striking is the 20cm black stone **Bull's Head**, which was a libation vessel. The bull has a fine head of curls, from which sprout horns of gold. The eyes of painted crystal are extremely lifelike. Also in this room are relics from a shrine at Knossos, including two fine figurines of **snake goddesses**. Snakes symbolised immortality for the Minoans.

Pottery, bronze figurines and seals are some of the exhibits displayed in Room 5. These include vases imported from Egypt and some Linear A and B tablets. The

Mycenaean Linear B script has been deciphered, and the inscriptions on the tablets displayed here have been translated as household or business accounts from the palace at Knossos.

Room 6 is devoted to finds from Minoan cemeteries. Especially intriguing are two small clay models of grouped figures which were found in a *tholos* (Mycenaen tomb shaped like a beehive). One depicts four male dancers in a circle, their arms around each other's shoulders. The dancers may have been participating in a funeral ritual. The other model depicts two groups of three figures in a room flanked by two columns. Each group features two large seated figures being offered libations by a smaller figure. It is not known whether the large figures represent gods or departed mortals. On a more grisly level, there is a display of the bones of a horse sacrificed as part of Minoan worship.

Finds in Room 7 include the beautiful **bee pendant** found at Malia. It's a remarkably fine piece of gold jewellery depicting two bees dropping honey into a comb. Also in this room are the three celebrated vases from Agia Triada. The **Harvester Vase**, of which only the top part remains, depicts a light-hearted scene of young farm workers returning from olive picking. The **Boxer Vase** depicts Minoans indulging in two of their favourite pastimes – wrestling and bull grappling. The **Chieftain Cup** depicts a

Linear B Script

The methodical decipherment of the Linear B script by English architect and part-time linguist Michael Ventris was the first tangible evidence that the Greek language had a recorded history longer than any scholar had previously believed. The decipherment demonstrated that the language disguised by these mysterious scribblings was an archaic form of Greek 500 years older than the Ionic Greek used by Homer.

Linear B was written on clay tablets that lay undisturbed for centuries until they were unearthed at Knossos in Crete. Further clay tablets were unearthed later on the mainland at Mycenae, Tiryns and Pylos on the Peloponnese and at Thebes in Boeotia.

The clay tablets, found to be mainly inventories and records of commercial transactions, consist of about 90 different signs and date from the 14th to the 13th century BC. Little of the social and political life of these times can be deduced from the tablets, though there is enough to give a glimpse of a fairly complex and well organised commercial structure.

For linguists, the script did not provide a detailed image of the actual language spoken, since the symbols were used primarily as syllabic clusters designed to give an approximation of the pronunciation of the underlying language. Typically, the syllabic cluster 'A-re-ka-sa-da-ra' is the woman's name Alexandra, but the exact pronunciation remains unknown.

Importantly, what is clear is that the language is undeniably Greek, thus giving the modern-day Greek language the second-longest recorded written history, after Chinese. The language of an earlier script, Linear A, remains to this day undeciphered. It is believed to be of either Anatolian or Semitic origin, though even this remains pure conjecture.

CRETE

more cryptic scene: a chief holding a staff and three men carrying animal skins.

Room 8 holds finds from the palace at Zakros. Don't miss the gorgeous little crystal vase which was found in over 300 pieces and was painstakingly reconstructed by museum staff. Other exhibits include a beautiful elongated libation vessel decorated with shells and other marine life.

Room 10 covers the postpalatial period (1350 to 1100 BC) when the Minoan civilisation was in decline and being overtaken by the warrior-like Myceaneans. Nevertheless, there are still some fine exhibits, including a child (headless) on a swing.

Room 13 is devoted to Minoan sarcophagi. However, the most famous and spectacular of these, the **sarcophagus from Agia Triada**, is upstairs in Room 14 (the Hall of Frescoes). This stone coffin, painted with floral and abstract designs and ritual scenes, is regarded as one of the supreme examples of Minoan art.

The most famous of the Minoan frescoes are also displayed in Room 14. Frescoes from Knossos include the **Procession Fresco**, the **Griffin Fresco** (from the Throne Room), the **Dolphin Fresco** (from the Queen's Room) and the amazing **Bull-Leaping Fresco**, which depicts a seemingly double-jointed acrobat somersaulting on the back of a charging bull. Other frescoes here include the two lovely **Frescoes of the Lilies** from Amisos and fragments of frescoes from Agia Triada. More frescoes can be

El Greco

One of the geniuses of the Renaissance, El Greco (meaning 'The Greek' in Spanish; his real name was Domeniko Theotokopoulos) was born and educated on Crete but had to travel to Spain to earn recognition.

El Greco was born in the Cretan capital of Candia (present-day Iraklio) in 1541 during a time of great artistic activity in the city. Many of the artists, writers and philosophers who fled Constantinople after it was conquered by the Turks in 1453 had settled on Crete, leading to the emergence of the Cretan school of icon painters. The painters had a formative influence upon the young El Greco, giving him the early grounding in the traditions of late Byzantine fresco painting that was to give such a powerful spiritual element to his later paintings.

Because Candia was a Venetian city it was a logical step for El Greco to head to Venice to further his studies, and he set off when he was in his early twenties to join the studio of Titian. It was not, however, until he moved to Spain in 1577 that he really came into his own as a painter. His highly emotional style struck a chord with the Spanish, and the city of Toledo was to become his home until his death in 1614. To view the most famous of his works like his masterpiece *The Burial of Count Orgaz* (1586), you will have to travel to Toledo. The only El Greco work on display in Crete is *View of Mt Sinai and the Monastery of St Catherine* (1570), painted during his time in Venice. It hangs in Iraklio's Historical Museum of Crete.

A white marble bust of the painter stands in Iraklio's Plateia El Greco, and streets are named after him throughout the island.

seen in Rooms 15 and 16. In Room 16 there is a large wooden model of Knossos.

The museum is on Xanthoudidou, just north of Plateia Eleftherias. Opening times are 8 am to 7 pm Tuesday to Sunday, and 12.30 to 7 pm Monday. The museum closes at 5 pm from late October to early April. Admission is 1500 dr.

Historical Museum of Crete

This museum (☎ 28 3219), just back from the waterfront, houses a fascinating range of bits and pieces from Crete's more recent past. The ground floor covers the period from Byzantine to Turkish rule, with plans, charts, photographs, ceramics and maps. On the 1st floor is the only **El Greco painting** on display in Crete. Other rooms contain fragments of 13th and 14th century frescoes, coins, jewellery, liturgical ornaments and vestments, and medieval pottery.

The 2nd floor has a reconstruction of the **library of author Nikos Kazantzakis**, with displays of his letters, manuscripts and books. Another room is devoted to Emmanual Tsouderos, who was born in Rethymno and who was prime minister in 1941. There are some dramatic photographs of a ruined Iraklio in the **Battle of Crete** section. On the 3rd floor there is an outstanding **folklore collection**.

The museum is open 9 am to 5 pm Monday to Friday, and 9 am to 2 pm Saturday, from June through August. From December through February it opens 9.30 am to 2.30 pm Monday to Saturday. Admission is 1000 dr.

Other Attractions

Iraklio burst out of its **city walls** long ago but these massive fortifications, with seven bastions and four gates, are still very conspicuous, dwarfing the concrete structures of the 20th century. Venetians built the defences between 1462 and 1562. The 16th century **Rocca al Mare**, another Venetian fortress, stands at the end of the Old Harbour's jetty. The fortress (☎ 24 6211) is open 8 am to 6 pm Monday to Saturday, and 10 am to 3 pm Sunday. Admission is 500 dr.

Several other notable vestiges from Venetian times survive in the city. Most famous is the **Morosini fountain** on Plateia Venizelou. The fountain, built in 1628, was commissioned by Francesco Morosini while he was governor of Crete. Opposite is the three-aisled 13th century **Basilica of San Marco**. It has been reconstructed many times and is now an exhibition gallery. A little north of here is the attractively reconstructed 17th century **Venetian loggia**. It was a Venetian version of a gentleman's club where the male aristocracy came to drink and gossip.

The delightful **Bembo fountain**, at the southern end of 1866, is shown on local maps as the Turkish fountain, but it was actually built by the Venetians in the 16th century. It was constructed from a hotchpotch of building materials including an ancient statue. The ornate edifice next to the fountain was added by the Turks, and now functions as a snack bar.

The former Church of Agia Ekaterini, next to Agios Minos Cathedral, is now a **museum** (☎ 28 8825) housing an impressive collection of icons. Most notable are those painted by Mihail Damaskinos, the mentor of El Greco. The museum is open 9 am to 1.30 pm Monday to Saturday. In addition it is open 5 to 8 pm on Tuesday, Thursday and Friday afternoons. Admission is 500 dr.

The **Battle of Crete Museum**, on the corner of Doukos Dofor and Hatzidaki, chronicles this historic battle through photographs, letters, uniforms and weapons. It is open 9 am to 1 pm daily. Admission is free.

You can pay homage to Crete's most acclaimed contemporary writer, Nikos Kazantzakis (1883-1957), by visiting his **tomb** at the Martinenga Bastion (the best preserved bastion) in the southern part of town. The epitaph on his grave, 'I hope for nothing, I fear nothing, I am free', is taken from one of his works.

Trekking

The Iraklio branch of the EOS (☎ 22 7609) is at Dikeosynis 53. It operates the Prinos Refuge on Mt Ida, a 1½ hour walk from the village of Melisses, 25km south-west of Iraklio.

Organised Tours

Iraklio's travel agents run coach tours the length and breadth of Crete. Creta Travel (☎ 22 7002), Epimenidou 20-22, has a good range.

Places to Stay – Budget

The nearest ***camp sites*** are 26km away at Hersonisos.

Iraklio has two youth hostels. Although stripped of its official status, the ***youth hostel*** *(☎ 28 6281, Vyronos 5)* is a clean, well run place, where a bed in a single-sex dorm costs 1500 dr and basic doubles/triples cost 4000/5000 dr. Many prefer the livelier atmosphere at the hostel called ***Rent Rooms Hellas*** *(☎ 28 8851, Handakos 24)* where there's a roof garden and a bar. Rates are 1800 dr for a dorm bed and 5200/6700/8200 dr for doubles/triples/quads.

There are few *domatia* in Iraklio and not enough cheap hotels to cope with the number of budget travellers who arrive in high season. One of the nicest budget places is the spiffy ***Hotel Mirabello*** *(☎ 28 5052, Theotokopoulou 20)* which has clean singles/doubles for 6500/8500 dr, or 8000/10,000 dr with bathroom. ***Hotel Lena*** *(☎ 22 3280, fax 24 2826, Lahana 10)* has basic rooms for 6500/9000 dr, and doubles with bathroom for 11,000 dr.

The pleasant ***Vergina Rooms*** *(☎ 24 2739, Hortatson 32)* is a characterful, century-old house with a small courtyard and spacious high-ceilinged rooms. Doubles/triples/quads are 5000/6500/8500 dr. Bathrooms are on the terrace and hot water is available upon request.

Hotel Rea *(☎ 22 3638)*, at the junction of Hortatson and Kalimeraki, is clean, quiet and friendly. Singles/doubles are 5000/6500 dr, while doubles/triples with bathroom are 7500/8000 dr.

Places to Stay – Mid-Range

One of the cheapest B class hotels is ***Hotel Kastro*** *(☎ 28 4185/5020, Theotokopoulou 22)*, where singles/doubles cost 13,000/16,000 dr. The best value C class hotel is ***Hotel Kronos*** *(☎ 28 2240, fax 28 5853, Venizelou 2)*, which has large rooms in excellent condition for 9,000/12,000 dr. Try to get a room overlooking the sea. You could also try ***Hotel Ilaira*** *(☎ 22 7103/7125, Ariadnis 1)*, which has a roof garden and rooms for 10,000/14,000 dr. Nearby ***Hotel Irini*** *(☎ 22 6561, fax 22 6407, Idomeneos 4)* has large airy rooms with TV and telephone for 13,500/18,000 dr.

Places to Stay – Top End

The best place in town is the A class ***Astoria Hotel*** *(☎ 34 3080, fax 22 9078, Plateia Eleftherias 11)* which has rates of 28,500/36,000 dr. Facilities include a glorious outdoor swimming pool. The A class ***Atlantis Hotel*** *(☎ 22 9103/4023, fax 22 6265, Igias 2)* also offers comfortable rooms with air-conditioning. Rates are 24,000/34,000 dr and facilities include a health studio, sauna and indoor swimming pool. ***Hotel Lato*** *(☎ 22 8103, fax 24 0350, Epimenidou 15)* has rooms with spectacular sea views for 22,700/28,500 dr.

Places to Eat – Budget

Iraklio has some excellent restaurants, and there's something to suit all tastes and budgets.

If you're after traditional taverna food the place to look is Theodasaki, a little street between 1866 and Evans. Choices include ***Giakoumis Taverna***, a popular spot turning out a big bowl of tasty bean stew for 900 dr. ***Restaurant Ionia***, 20m away on the corner of Evans and Giannari, serves similar food in fancier surroundings for a few drachma more.

Ippokampos Ouzeri, on the waterfront just west of 25 Avgoustou, is as good as this style of eating gets. It has a huge range of *mezedes* on offer, priced from 400 dr. The fish dishes are especially recommended. They include grilled octopus (1100 dr), calamari (1000 dr) and sea urchin salad (1500 dr). The place is always busy, so it's a good idea to get in early. It's closed between 3.30 and 7 pm and on Sunday. The stylish ***Vareladika Ouzeri*** on Moni Agarathou has similar fare at about the same price.

The simple little ***Katsina Ouzeri*** *(Marineli 12)* has tasty main dishes from 700 dr to 1200 dr. The cosy ***Baxes*** *(Gianni Chroaki 14)* offers hearty Cretan meat dishes to a mostly local crowd that appreciates lamb and pork roasted in a brick oven as well as excellent stewed goat and rabbit.

In the charming ***Garden of Deykaliola Taverna*** *(Kalokerinou 8)* you'll soon forget you're in Crete's largest and least picturesque city. It offers a wide range of reasonably priced, imaginative mezedes and main dishes. It's open evenings only and really gets rolling around 11 pm when the tourists leave and the Cretans arrive.

If you haven't yet tried *loukoumades* (fritters with syrup), then ***Loukoumades Cafe*** on Dikeosynis is a good place to sample this gooey confection. For a meal on the move, try the tiny ***Bougatsa Serraikon***, on Idis in the city centre. It makes excellent sweet (custard filled) or savoury (cheese filled) *bougatsa* for 380 dr. The more leisurely paced can while away some time people-watching at ***Ta Leontaria 1922***, beside the Morosini fountain. The delicious bougatsa here costs 450 dr.

Whether you're self-catering or not, you'll enjoy a stroll up 1866 (the market street). This narrow street is always packed, and stalls spill over with produce of every description, including ornate Cretan wedding loaves. These loaves (smaller versions of the one on display at the Historical Museum of Crete) are not meant to be eaten; rather, they make an attractive kitchen decoration.

Places to Eat – Top End

Giovanni Taverna *(Korai 12)* is a splendid place with elegant antique furniture. In summer there is outdoor eating on a quiet pedestrian street. The food is a very Mediterranean combination of Greek and Italian specialities. A meal for two people, including a carafe of house red, costs about 12,000 dr.

Bella Casa, on the corner of Zografou and Averof, serves the same style food at more moderate prices. The restaurant is set in a stunning early 20th century villa with a verdant terrace.

Getting There & Away

Air – Domestic Olympic Airways has at least six flights daily to Athens (21,900 dr) from Iraklio's Nikos Kazantzakis airport. It also has flights to Thessaloniki (29,900 dr, three weekly), Rhodes (21,900 dr, four weekly) and Santorini (15,400 dr, two weekly). The Olympic Airways office (☎ 22 9191) is at Plateia Eleftherias 42.

Air Greece has flights to Athens (20,400 dr, four daily), Thessaloniki (28,400 dr, two daily) and, from June through August, Rhodes (21,900 dr, three weekly). The Air Greece office (☎ 33 0729/0739) is at Ethnikis Antistaseos 67.

Aegean Airlines has flights to Athens (18,500 dr, three daily) and Thessaloniki (29,700 dr, one daily). Its office is at the airport (☎ 33 0475).

Air – International The KLM associate Transavia flies direct between Amsterdam and Iraklio on Monday and Friday. Transavia is represented by Sbokos Tours (☎ 22 9712), Dimokratias 51.

Iraklio has lots of charter flights from all over Europe. Prince Travel (☎ 28 2706), 25 Avgoustou 30, advertises cheap last-minute tickets on these flights. Sample fares include London for 28,000 dr and Munich for 41,000 dr.

Bus There are buses every half-hour (hourly from December through February) to Rethymno (1½ hours, 1550 dr) and Hania (three hours, 2900 dr) from the Rethymno/ Hania bus station opposite Bus Station A. Buses from Bus Station A are:

Destination	Duration	Price	Frequency
Agia Pelagia	45 mins	650 dr	5 daily
Agios Nikolaos	1½ hours	1400 dr	half-hourly
Arhanes	30 mins	340 dr	15 daily
Hersonisos/Malia	1 hour	750 dr	half-hourly
Ierapetra	2½ hours	2100 dr	7 daily
Lassithi Plateau	2 hours	1400 dr	2 daily
Milatos	1½ hours	1000 dr	1 daily
Sitia	3½ hours	2850 dr	5 daily

Buses from Bus Station B are:

Destination	Duration	Price	Frequency
Agia Galini	2½ hours	1500 dr	7 daily
Anogia	1 hour	750 dr	6 daily
Matala	2 hours	1500 dr	9 daily
Phaestos	2 hours	1250 dr	8 daily

Taxi Long-distance taxis (☎ 21 0102) leave from Plateia Eleftherias and Bus Station B for all parts of Crete. Sample fares include Agios Nikolaos (9700 dr), Rethymno (12,000 dr) and Hania (20,000 dr).

Ferry Minoan Lines and ANEK Lines operate ferries every evening each way between Iraklio and Piraeus (10 hours). They depart from both Piraeus and Iraklio between 7.45 and 8 pm. Fares are 7000 dr deck class and 14,100 dr for cabins. Minoan Lines' boats are more modern and more comfortable than their ANEK Lines rivals. ANEK Lines, though, is a better bet for deck class travellers. It has dorm beds with plastic-covered mattresses, while Minoan Lines has only seats.

GA Ferries has three boats weekly to Santorini (four hours, 3700 dr), continuing to Paros (8½ hours, 5200 dr) and Piraeus, stopping at Naxos. GA also has three ferries weekly to Rhodes (11 hours, 6400 dr) via Karpathos (3800 dr). Minoan Lines runs three boats weekly to Thessaloniki (12,100 dr) via Santorini, Paros, Volos, Tinos and the Sporades. The travel agencies on 25 Avgoustou are the place to get information and buy tickets. Iraklio's port police can be contacted on ☎ 24 4912.

Getting Around

To/From the Airport Bus No 1 goes to and from the airport every 15 minutes between 6 am and 1 am (170 dr). It leaves the city from outside the Astoria Hotel on Plateia Eleftherias.

Bus Bus No 2 goes to Knossos every 10 minutes from Bus Station A (20 minutes, 240 dr). It also stops on 25 Avgoustou and 1821.

Car, Motorcycle & Bicycle Most of the car and motorcycle rental outlets are on 25 Avgoustou. You'll get the best deal from local companies like Sun Rise (☎ 22 1609) at 25 Avgoustou 46, Loggeta Cars & Bikes (☎ 28 9462) at Plateia Kallergon 6, next to El Greco Park, or Ritz Rent-A-Car at Hotel Rea (see Places to Stay), which offers discounts for hotel guests. There are also many car rental outlets at the airport.

Mountain bicycles can be hired from Porto Club Travel Services (☎ 28 5264), 25 Avgoustou 20.

KNOSSOS Κνωσσός

Knossos (no-**sos**), 5km from Iraklio, was the capital of Minoan Crete. Nowadays it's the island's major tourist attraction.

The ruins of Knossos were uncovered in 1900 by the British archaeologist Sir Arthur Evans. Heinrich Schliemann, who had earlier uncovered the ancient cities of Troy and Mycenae, had had his eye on the spot (a low, flat-topped mound), believing an ancient city was buried there, but was unable to strike a deal with the local landowner.

Evans was so enthralled by his discovery that he spent 35 years and £250,000 of his own money excavating and reconstructing sections of the palace. Some archaeologists have disparaged Evans' reconstruction, believing he sacrificed accuracy to his overly vivid imagination. However, most nonspecialists agree that Sir Arthur did a good job and that Knossos is a knockout. Without these reconstructions it would be impossible to visualise what a Minoan palace looked like.

You will need to spend about four hours at Knossos to explore it thoroughly. The cafe at the site is expensive – you'd do better to bring a picnic along. Between April and October the site (☎ 081-23 1940) is open 8 am to 7 pm daily. In winter it closes at 5 pm. Admission is 1500 dr.

History

The first palace at Knossos was built around 1900 BC. In 1700 BC it was destroyed by an earthquake and rebuilt to a grander and more sophisticated design. It is this palace that Evans reconstructed. It was partially destroyed again sometime between 1500 and 1450 BC. It was inhabited for another 50 years before it was devastated once and for all by fire.

The city of Knossos consisted of an immense palace, residences of officials and priests, the homes of ordinary people, and burial grounds. The palace comprised royal domestic quarters, public reception rooms, shrines, workshops, treasuries and storerooms, all built around a central court. Like all Minoan palaces, it also doubled as a city hall, accommodating all the bureaucracy necessary for the smooth running of a complex society.

Until early 1997 it was possible to enter the royal apartments, but it was decided to cordon this area off before it disappeared altogether under the continual pounding of tourists' feet. Extensive repairs are under way but it is unlikely to open to the public again.

Exploring the Site

Numerous rooms, corridors, dog-leg passages, nooks and crannies, and staircases prohibit a detailed walk-through description of the palace. However, Knossos is not a site where you'll be perplexed by heaps of rubble, trying to fathom whether you're looking at the throne room or a workshop. Thanks to Evans' reconstruction, the most significant parts of the complex are instantly recognisable (if not instantly found). On your wanders you will come across many of Evans' reconstructed columns, most painted deep brown-red with gold-trimmed black capitals. Like all Minoan columns, they taper at the bottom.

It is not only the vibrant frescoes and mighty columns which impress at Knossos; keep your eyes open for the little details which are evidence of a highly sophisticated society. Things to look out for include the drainage system, the placement of light wells, and the relationship of rooms to passages, porches, light wells and verandahs, which kept rooms cool in summer and warm in winter.

The usual entrance to the palace complex is across the Western Court and along the **Corridor of the Procession Fresco**. The fresco depicted a long line of people carrying gifts to present to the king; only fragments remain. A copy of one of these fragments, called the **Priest King Fresco**, can be seen to the south of the Central Court.

If you leave the Corridor of the Procession Fresco and walk straight ahead to enter the site from the northern end, you will come to the **theatral area**, a series of steps, the function of which remains unknown. The area could have been a theatre where spectators watched acrobatic and dance performances, or the place where people gathered to welcome important visitors arriving by the Royal Road.

The **Royal Road** leads off to the west. The road, Europe's first (Knossos has lots of firsts), was flanked by workshops and the houses of ordinary people. The **lustral basin** is also in this area. Evans speculated that this was where the Minoans performed a ritual cleansing with water before religious ceremonies.

Entering the **Central Court** from the north, you pass the relief **Bull Fresco** which depicts a charging bull. Relief frescoes were made by moulding wet plaster, and then painting it while still wet.

Also worth seeking out in the northern section of the palace are the **giant pithoi**. Pithoi were ceramic jars used for storing olive oil, wine and grain. Evans found over 100 of these huge jars at Knossos, some 2m high. The ropes used to move them inspired the raised patterns decorating the jars.

Once you have reached the Central Court, which in Minoan times was surrounded by the high walls of the palace, you can begin exploring the most important rooms of the complex.

From the northern end of the west side of the Central Court, steps lead down to the **throne room**. This room is fenced off but you can still get a good view of it. The centrepiece, the simple, beautifully proportioned throne, is flanked by the **Griffin Fresco**. (Griffins were mythical beasts regarded as

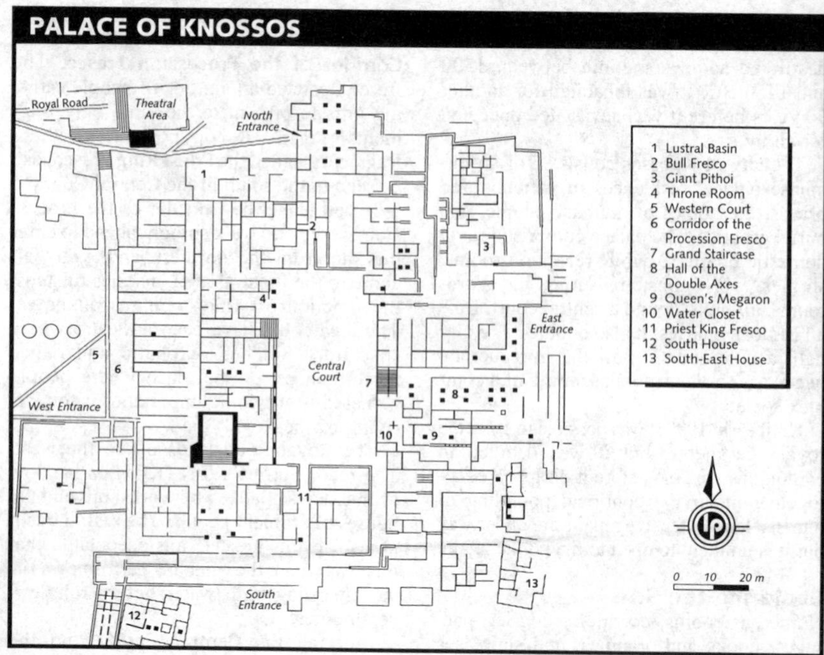

sacred by the Minoans.) The room is thought to have been a shrine, and the throne the seat of a high priestess, rather than a king. Certainly, the room seems to have an aura of mysticism and reverence rather than pomp and ceremony. The Minoans did not worship their deities in great temples but in small shrines, and each palace had several.

On the 1st floor of the west side of the palace is the section Evans called the **Piano Nobile**, for he believed the reception and state rooms were here. A room at the northern end of this floor displays copies of some of the frescoes found at Knossos.

Returning to the Central Court, the impressive **grand staircase** leads from the middle of the eastern side of the palace to the royal apartments, which Evans called the Domestic Quarter. This section of the site is now cordoned off. Within the royal apartments is the **Hall of the Double Axes**. This was the king's *megaron*, a spacious double room in which the ruler both slept and carried out certain court duties. The room had a light well at one end and a balcony at the other to ensure air circulation.

The room takes its name from the double axe marks on its light well. These marks appear in many places at Knossos. The double axe was a sacred symbol to the Minoans. *Labrys* was Minoan for 'double axe' and the origin of our word 'labyrinth'.

A passage leads from the Hall of the Double Axes to the **queen's megaron**. Above the door is a copy of the **Dolphin Fresco**, one of the most exquisite Minoan artworks, and a blue floral design decorates the portal. Next to this room is the queen's bathroom, complete with terracotta bathtub and **water closet**, touted as the first ever to work on the flush principle; water was poured down by hand.

Getting There & Away

Regular buses operate from Iraklio. See Iraklio's Getting Around section for details.

MYRTIA Μυρτιά

Myrtia (mir-tih-**ah**, also called Varvari), 22km south of Iraklio, makes the most of being the village that spawned Crete's favourite literary son, Nikos Kazantzakis. Kazantzakis was born in Iraklio and lived most of his life abroad, but his father was born here – and the writer himself did live here for a time. The **Nikos Kazantzakis Museum**, on the central square of the village, has a collection of the writer's personal mementoes. A video compiled from film clippings of the author's life is shown in Greek, German, French and English.

The museum is open 9 am to 1 pm and 4 to 8 pm Monday, Wednesday and weekends, and 9 am to 1 pm Tuesday and Friday. Admission is free.

The Myth of the Minotaur

King Minos of Crete invoked the wrath of Poseidon when he failed to sacrifice a magnificent white bull sent to him for that purpose. Poseidon's revenge was to cause Pasiphae, King Minos' wife, to fall in love with the animal.

In order to attract the bull, Pasiphae asked Daedalus, chief architect at Knossos and all-round handyman, to make her a hollow, wooden cow structure. When she concealed herself inside it, the bull found her irresistible. The outcome of their bizarre association was the Minotaur: a hideous monster who was half-man and half-bull.

King Minos asked Daedalus to build a labyrinth in which to confine the Minotaur and demanded that Athens pay an annual tribute of seven youths and seven maidens to satisfy the monster's huge appetite.

TAMSIN WILSON

Theseus killing the Minotaur

Minos eventually found out that Daedalus had been instrumental in bringing about the union between his wife and the bull, and threw the architect and his son Icarus into the labyrinth. Daedalus made wings from feathers stuck together with wax, and father and son made their getaway. As everyone knows, Icarus flew too close to the sun, the wax on his wings melted, and he plummeted into the sea off the island of Ikaria.

Athenians, meanwhile, were enraged by the tribute demanded by King Minos. The Athenian hero, Theseus, vowed to kill the Minotaur and sailed off to Crete posing as one of the sacrificial youths. On arrival, he fell in love with Ariadne, the daughter of King Minos, and she promised to help him if he would take her away with him afterwards. She provided him with the ball of twine that he unwound on his way into the labyrinth and used to retrace his steps after slaying the monster. Theseus fled Crete with Ariadne. The two married, but Theseus abandoned Ariadne on the island of Naxos on his way back to Athens.

On his return to Athens, Theseus forgot to unfurl the white sail that he had promised to display to announce that he was still alive. This prompted his distraught father, Aegeus, to hurl himself to his death from the Acropolis. This, incidentally, is how the Aegean sea got its name.

TYLISOS Τύλισος

The minor Minoan site at the village of Tylisos (**til**-is-os), 13km from Iraklio, is only for the insatiable enthusiast. Three villas dating from different periods have been excavated. The site (☎ 081-22 6092) is open 8.30 am to 3 pm daily. Admission is 400 dr. Buses from Iraklio to Anogia go through Tylisos. They also go past another Minoan site at **Sklavokambos**, 8km closer to Anogia. The ruins date from 1500 BC and were probably the villa of a district governor.

ARHANES Αρχάνες

The attractive village of Arhanes, 16km from Iraklio, lies in the heart of Crete's principal grape-producing region. Several Minoan remains have been unearthed in the vineyards surrounding the village. The most noteworthy is the elaborate **Vathypetro Villa**, the home of a prosperous Minoan noble.

The villa complex included storerooms where wine and oil presses, a weaving loom and a kiln were discovered. The villa is 5km from Arhanes, on the road south – look for a signpost to the right. Admission is free.

Getting There & Away

It's a pleasant outing from Iraklio to Arhanes if you have your own transport. Otherwise, there are 15 buses daily (fewer on weekends) from Iraklio's Bus Station A to Arhanes (30 minutes, 340 dr). There are no buses to Vathypetro, but Creta Travel in Iraklio has a tour which includes a visit to the villa.

CRETE

GORTYNA Γόρτυνα

The archaeological site of Gortyna (**gor**-tih-nah, also called Gortys) lies 46km south-west of Iraklio, and 15km from Phaestos, on the plain of Mesara. It's a vast and wonderfully intriguing site with bits and pieces from various ages strewn all over the place. The site was a settlement from Minoan to Christian times. In Roman times, Gortyna was the capital of the province of Cyrenaica.

The most significant find at the site was the massive stone tablets inscribed with the **Laws of Gortyna**, dating from the 5th century BC. The laws deal with just about every imaginable offence. The tablets are on display at the site.

The 6th century **basilica** is dedicated to Agios Titos, a protege of St Paul and the first bishop of Crete.

Other ruins at Gortyna include the 2nd century AD **praetorin**, which was the residence of the governor of the province, a **nymphaeum**, and the **Temple of Pythian Apollo**. The site (☎ 0892-31 144) is open 8 am to 6 pm daily. Admission is 800 dr. The ruins are on both sides of the main Iraklio-Phaestos road.

PHAESTOS Φαιστός

The Minoan site of Phaestos (fes-**tos**), 63km from Iraklio, was the second most important palace city of Minoan Crete. Of all the Minoan sites, Phaestos has the most awe-inspiring location, with all-embracing views of the Mesara Plain and Mt Ida. The layout of the palace is identical to Knossos, with rooms arranged around a central court.

In contrast to Knossos, Phaestos has yielded very few frescoes. It seems the palace walls were mostly covered with a layer of white gypsum. Perhaps, with such inspiring views from the windows, the inhabitants didn't feel any need to decorate their walls. Evans didn't get his hands on the ruins of Phaestos, so there has been no reconstruction. Like the other palatial period complexes, there was an old palace here which was destroyed at the end of the Middle Minoan period. Unlike the other sites, parts of this old palace have been excavated and its ruins are partially superimposed upon the new palace.

The entrance to the new palace is by the 15m-wide **Grand Staircase**. The stairs lead to the west side of the **Central Court**. The best preserved parts of the palace complex are the reception rooms and private apartments to the north of the Central Court; excavations continue here. This section was entered by an imposing portal with half columns at either side, the lower parts of which are still *in situ*. Unlike the Minoan freestanding columns, these do not taper at the base. The celebrated Phaestos disc was found in a building to the north of the palace. The disc is in Iraklio's archaeologic-al museum. The site is open 8 am to 7 pm daily. Admission is 1200 dr.

Getting There & Away

There are buses to Phaestos from Iraklio's Bus Station B (1½ hours, 1250 dr, eight daily). There are also buses from Agia Galini (40 minutes, 400 dr, six daily) and Matala (30 minutes, 300 dr, five daily). Services are halved from December through February.

AGIA TRIADA Αγία Τριάδα

Agia Triada (ah-**yee**-ah trih-**ah**-dah) is a small Minoan site 3km west of Phaestos. Its principal building was smaller than the other royal palaces but built to a similar design. This, and the opulence of the objects found at the site, indicate that it was a royal residence, possibly a summer palace of Phaestos' rulers. To the north of the palace is a small town where remains of a *stoa* (long colonnaded building) have been unearthed.

Finds from the palace, now in Iraklio's archaeological museum, include a sarcophagus, two superlative frescoes and three vases: the Harvester Vase, Boxer Vase and Chieftain Cup.

The site is open 8.30 am to 3 pm daily. Admission is 500 dr. The road to Agia Triada takes off to the right about 500m from Phaestos on the road to Matala. There is no public transport to the site.

MATALA Μάταλα

☎ 0892 • postcode 702 00 • pop 300

Matala (**mah**-tah-lah), on the coast 11km south-west of Phaestos, was once one of Crete's best-known hippie hang-outs.

It was the old Roman caves at the northern end of the beach that made Matala famous in the 1960s. There are dozens of them dotted over the cliff-face. They were originally tombs, cut out of the sandstone rock in the 1st century AD. In the 1960s, they were discovered by hippies, who turned the caves into a modern troglodyte city – moving ever higher up the cliff to avoid sporadic attempts by the local police to evict them. Joni Mitchell was among the visitors, and she sang the praises of life under a Matala moon in *Carey*.

These days, Matala is a decidedly tacky tourist resort packed out in summer and bleak and deserted in winter. The sandy beach below the caves is, however, one of Crete's best, and the resort is a convenient base from which to visit Phaestos and Agia Triada.

Orientation & Information

Matala's layout is easy to fathom. The bus stop is on the central square, one block back from the waterfront. There is a mobile post office near the beach, on the right of the main road as you come into Matala. The OTE is beyond here in the beach car park.

Places to Stay

Matala Community Camping *(☎ 42 340)* is a reasonable site just back from the beach. There is another ***camp site*** near Komos Beach *(☎ 42 596)*, about 4km before Matala on the road from Phaestos.

There are several pleasant options in Matala proper. Walk back along the main road from the bus station and turn right at Zafiria Hotel. This street is lined with budget accommodation. One of the cheapest is ***Fantastic Rooms to Rent*** *(☎ 45 362)*, on the right. The comfortable doubles/triples cost 6000/7000 dr with bathroom. ***Pension Antonios*** *(☎ 45 123/438)*, opposite, has attractively furnished rooms with bathroom for 4000/6000/7000 dr, and double/triple apartments for 8000/9000 dr.

The C class ***Hotel Fragiskos*** *(☎ 45 380/135)*, on the left as you head out of town, charges 8000/14,500 dr for singles/doubles with bathroom, including breakfast. It has a swimming pool.

If you don't like the sound of Matala, **Pitsidia Village**, 4.5km inland and 7km from Phaestos, is a quieter alternative. There are no hotels but plenty of ***domatia***.

Places to Eat

Most of the restaurants in Matala are poor value. An exception is ***Taverna Giannis***, where a huge plate of calamari, chips and salad costs 1200 dr, while a bowl of tasty lentil soup is 800 dr. Walk towards the southern headland and the taverna is on the right.

Restaurant Mystical View, high above Komos Beach about 3km from Matala, has views that live up to its name and serves good food to boot. The restaurant is signposted off the road to Phaestos.

Getting There & Away

There are buses between Iraklio and Matala (two hours, 1500 dr, five daily), and between Matala and Phaestos (30 minutes, 300 dr, five daily).

MALIA Μάλια

The Minoan site of Malia is the only cultural diversion on the stretch of coast east of Iraklio, which otherwise has surrendered lock, stock and barrel to the package tourist industry. Malia is smaller than Knossos and Phaestos, but like them consisted of a palace complex and a town. Unlike Knossos and Phaestos, the palace was built on a flat, fertile plain, not on a hill.

Entrance to the ruins is from the **West Court**. At the extreme southern end of this court there are eight circular pits which archaeologists think were used to store grain. To the east of the pits is the main entrance to the palace which leads to the southern end of the **Central Court**. At the south-west corner of this court you will find the **Kernos Stone**, a disc with 34 holes around its edge. Archae-ologists still don't know what it was used for.

The **central staircase** is at the north end of the west side of the palace. The **loggia**, just north of the staircase, is where religious ceremonies took place.

The site (☎ 0897-31 597), 3km east of the resort of Malia, is open 8.30 am to 3 pm Tuesday to Sunday. Admission is 800 dr.

Any bus going to or from Iraklio along the north coast can drop you at the site.

CRETE

Eastern Crete

The eastern quarter of the island is occupied by the prefecture of Lassithi, named after the quaint plateau tucked high in the Mt Dikti Ranges rather than its uninspiring administrative capital of Agios Nikolaos, which is becoming something of a monument to package tourism. The main attractions, apart from the Lassithi Plateau, are the palm forest and beach at Vaï and the remote Minoan palace site of Zakros.

AGIOS NIKOLAOS Αγιος Νικόλαος

☎ 0841 • postcode 721 00 • pop 9000

The manifestations of package tourism gather momentum as they advance east from Iraklio, reaching their peak at Agios Nikolaos (ah-**yee**-os nih-**ko**-laos). In July and August the town's permanent population is increased by 11,000 tourists. The result is that there is very little to attract the independent traveller. It's pointless trying to squeeze into Agios Nikolaos in the peak season between July and mid-September, and the place just about closes down entirely from December through February.

Orientation

The town centre is Plateia Venizelou, 150m up Sofias Venizelou from the bus station. The most interesting part of town is around the picturesque Voulismeni Lake, which is ringed with tavernas and cafes. The lake is 200m from Plateia Venizelou. Walk north-east along Koundourou and turn left at the bottom and you will come to a bridge that separates the lake from the harbour. The tourist office is at the far side of the bridge.

Once over the bridge, if you turn right and follow the road as it veers left, you will come to the northern stretch of waterfront which is the road to Elounda. A number of large and expensive hotels are along here.

Alternatively, if you turn right at the bottom of Koundourou you will come to a stretch of waterfront with steps leading up to the right. These lead to the streets that have the highest concentration of small hotels and pensions.

Information

The municipal tourist office (☎ 22 357, fax 82 354), by the bridge, is open 8 am to 9.30 pm daily from the start of April to mid-November. The tourist police (☎ 26 900), Kondogianni 34, open between 7.30 am and 2.30 pm daily.

The National Bank of Greece on Nikolau Plastira has a 24 hour automatic exchange machine. The tourist office also changes money. The post office, 28 Oktovriou 9, is open 7.30 am to 2 pm Monday to Friday. The OTE is on the corner of 25 Martiou and K Sfakianaki. It is open 7 am to 11 pm daily.

Internet access is available at the pleasant Polychoros (☎ 24 876), Oktovoriou 28, open 9 am to 2 am daily. There is a well stocked English-language bookshop at Koundourou 5 next to the bank.

The general hospital (☎ 25 221) is between Lassithiou and Paleologou.

Things to See

The **folk museum**, next to the tourist office, has a well displayed collection of traditional handcrafts and costumes. It's open 10 am to 3 pm Sunday to Friday. Admission is 250 dr.

The **archaeological museum** (☎ 22 462), on Paleologou, is a modern building housing a large, well displayed collection from eastern Crete. It's open 8.30 am to 3 pm Tuesday to Sunday. Admission is 500 dr.

The **Local Aquarium of Agios Nikolaos** (☎ 24 953), on Akti Koundourou, has interesting displays of fish and information about diving (including PADI courses) and snorkelling throughout Crete. It is open 10 am to 9 pm Monday to Saturday. Admission is 1300 dr.

Voulismeni Lake (Λίμνη Βουλισμένη) is the subject of many stories about its depth and origins. The locals have given it various names, including Xepatomeni (bottomless), Voulismeni (sunken) and Vromolimni (dirty). The lake isn't bottomless – it is 64m deep. The 'dirty' tag came about because the lake used to be stagnant and gave off quite a pong in summer. This was rectified in 1867 when a canal was built linking it to the sea.

Beaches

The popularity of Agios Nikolaos has nothing to do with its beaches. The town beach, south of the bus station, and Kritoplatia Beach, have more people than pebbles. Ammoudi Beach, on the road to Elounda, is equally uninspiring.

The sandy beach at Almiros about 1km south of town is the best of the lot and tends to be less crowded than the others. There's little shade but you can rent umbrellas for 500 dr a day.

Organised Tours

Travel agencies in Agios Nikolaos offer coach outings to all Crete's top attractions. Nostos Tours (☎ 22 819), Koundourou 30, has boat trips to Spinalonga (4000 dr) as well as guided tours of Phaestos and Matala (7500 dr), the Samaria Gorge (12,500 dr) and the Lassithi Plateau (7000 dr).

Places to Stay – Budget

The nearest camp site to Agios Nikolaos is ***Gournia Moon Camping*** *(☎ 0842-93 243)*, near the Minoan site of Gournia. It has a swimming pool, restaurant, snack bar and minimarket. Buses to Sitia can drop you off outside.

Green House *(☎ 22 025, Modatsou 15)* is a backpacker favourite. It is ramshackle but clean, with a lush garden. Singles/doubles are 3000/4000 dr. Breakfast is an additional 500 dr per person. Walk up Tavla (a continuation of Modatsou) from the bus station, and you'll find it on the right.

Hotel Pergola *(☎ 28 152)*, on Akti Themistokleous, has comfortable rooms with bathroom for 5000/7000 dr. ***Aphrodite Rooms*** *(☎ 28 058, Koritsas 27)* has rooms for 3000/4000 dr and a tiny communal kitchen. At ***Mary Pension*** *(☎ 23 760, Evans 13)*, rooms with bathroom cost 5000/6000 dr.

One of the few places to stay open all year is the charming ***Hotel Doxa*** *(☎ 24 614, Idomeneos 7)* which has rooms for 8000/10,000 dr and a comfortable lounge filled with plants and flowers.

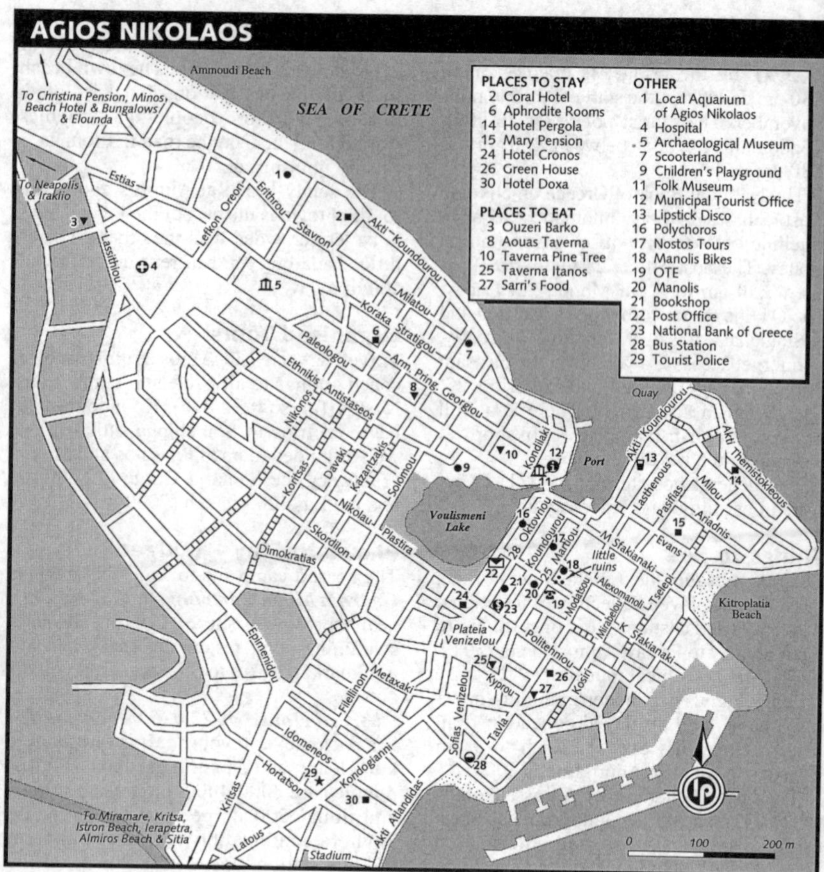

Places to Stay – Mid-Range & Top End

The opulent B class ***Coral Hotel*** *(☎ 28 363/367)* on the northern waterfront is about as upmarket as places get in town. It has rooms for 15,250/19,500 dr. There is a swimming pool.

Most luxury hotels are north of town on the road to Elounda but at ***Miramare*** *(☎ 23 875, fax 24 164)* you're less than 1km out of town near Almiros Beach. Rooms with air-conditioning, private balcony and panoramic views are 21,000/28,000 dr. The most luxurious hotel is the deluxe ***Minos Beach Hotel & Bungalows*** *(☎ 22 345/349, fax 22 548)*, north of town with seaside bungalows for 46,400/61,800 dr. Both places have a swimming pool and tennis courts.

Places to Eat

Agios Nikolaos' waterfront tavernas are expensive – head inland for better value. ***Taverna Itanos*** *(Kyprou 1)* is a lively traditional taverna, with a stuffed eggplant speciality for 1000 dr and *stifado* (beef stew) for 1800 dr.

Ouzeri Barko *(Lassithiou 23)* is a bit out of the way but well worth the effort. It has an excellent selection of mezedes priced from 500 dr to 900 dr. It opens only in the evenings.

Taverna Pine Tree, next to the lake, specialises in charcoal-grilled food, such as a plate of prawns for 1700 dr. ***Aouas Taverna*** *(Paleologou 50)* has traditional decor and a lovely garden. A large plate of mezedes (enough for four people) is 2700 dr. The tiny ***Sarri's Food*** *(Kyprou 15)* has tasty main courses for between 900 dr and 1400 dr.

Entertainment

Bars are everywhere in Agios Nikolaos. The only operating disco is ***Lipstick Disco*** on Akti Koundourou.

Getting There & Away

Bus Buses leave the Agios Nikolaos bus station for Elounda (230 dr, 20 daily), Kritsa (230 dr, 12 daily), Ierapetra (750 dr, eight daily), Iraklio (1400 dr, half-hourly), Istron (280 dr, 11 daily), Lassithi Plateau (1900 dr, one daily) and Sitia (1500 dr, six daily).

Ferry Agios Nikolaos has the same ferry schedule as Sitia (see Getting There & Away in the Sitia section later). Ferry tickets can be bought from Nostos Tours, among others. The port police (☎ 22 312) are in the same building as the tourist office.

Getting Around

You will find many car and motorcycle rental outlets on the northern waterfront. Scooterland (☎ 26 340), Akti Koundourou 10, has a huge range of scooters and motorcycles beginning at 4000 dr a day for a scooter, to 15,000 dr a day for a Kawasaki EN.

You can rent mountain bikes from Manolis (☎ 24 940) down the street from the OTE office on 25 Martiou. Prices begin at 2000 dr a day.

GOURNIA Γουρνιά

The important Minoan site of Gournia (goor-**nyah**) lies just off the coast road, 19km south-east of Agios Nikolaos. The ruins, which date from 1550 to 1450 BC, consist of a town overlooked by a small palace. The palace was far less ostentatious than the ones at Knossos and Phaestos because it was the residence of an overlord rather than a king. The town is a network of streets and stairways flanked by houses with walls up to 2m in height. Trade, domestic and agricultural implements found on the site indicate Gournia was a thriving little community.

The site (☎ 0841-24 943) is open 8.30 am to 3 pm Tuesday to Sunday. Admission is 500 dr. Gournia is on the Sitia and Ierapetra bus routes from Agios Nikolaos and buses can drop you at the site.

MONI FANEROMENIS

Μονή Φανερωμένης

There are stunning views down to the coast from this late-Byzantine monastery, 5km south of the Agios Nikolaos-Sitia road. The turn-off to Moni Faneromenis is 2km west of Gournia.

KRITSA Κριτσά

The village of Kritsa (krit-**sah**), perched 600m up the mountainside 11km from Agios Nikolaos, is on every package itinerary. Tourists come in bus loads to the village every day in summer. The villagers exploit these invasions to the full, and craft shops of every description line the main streets.

The tiny triple-aisled **Church of Panagia Kera** is on the right 1km before Kritsa on the Agios Nikolaos road. The frescoes that cover its interior walls are considered the most outstanding examples of Byzantine art on Crete. Unfortunately the church is usually packed with tourists. It's open 8.30 am to 3 pm Monday to Friday, and 8.30 am to 2 pm Saturday. Admission is 500 dr.

Kritsa doesn't have any hotels, but there are several ***domatia*** – look for the signs.

There are 12 buses daily from Agios Nikolaos to Kritsa (15 minutes, 230 dr).

ANCIENT LATO Λατώ

The ancient city of Lato (lah-**to**), 4km north of Kritsa, is one of Crete's few non-Minoan ancient sites. Lato was founded in the 7th century BC by the Dorians and at its height was one of the most powerful cities on Crete. It sprawls over the slopes of two acropolises in a lonely mountain setting, commanding stunning views down to the Gulf of Mirabello.

The city's name derived from the goddess Leto whose union with Zeus produced Artemis and Apollo, both of whom were worshipped here. Lato is far less visited than Crete's Minoan sites. It's open 8.30 am to 3 pm Tuesday to Sunday. Admission is free.

In the centre of the site is a deep well which is cordoned off. As you face the Gulf of Mirabello, to the left of the well are some steps which are the remains of a **theatre**.

Above the theatre was the **prytaneion**, where the city's governing body met. The circle of stones behind the well was a threshing floor. The columns next to it are the remains of a stoa which stood in the *agora* (commercial area). There are remains of a pebble mosaic nearby. A path to the right leads up to the **Temple of Apollo**.

There are no buses to Lato. The road to the site is signposted to the right on the approach to Kritsa. If you don't have your own transport, it's a pleasant walk through olive groves along this road.

SPINALONGA PENINSULA

Χερσόνησος Σπιναλόγκας

Just before Elounda (coming from Agios Nikolaos), a sign points right to **ancient Olous**, once the port of Lato. The city stood on and around the narrow isthmus (now a causeway) which joined the southern end of the Spinalonga Peninsula to the mainland. Most of the ruins lie beneath the water, and if you go snorkelling near the causeway you will see outlines of buildings and the tops of columns. The water around here appears to be paradise for sea urchins. The peninsula is a pleasant place to stroll and there is an early Christian mosaic near the causeway.

SPINALONGA ISLAND

Νήσος Σπιναλόγκα

Spinalonga Island lies just north of the Spinalonga Peninsula. The island's massive fortress was built by the Venetians in 1579 to protect Elounda Bay and the Gulf of Mirabello. It withstood Turkish sieges for longer than any other Cretan stronghold, finally surrendering in 1715, some 30 years after the rest of Crete. The Turks used the island as a base for smuggling. Following the reunion of Crete with Greece, Spinalonga Island became a leper colony. The last leper died there in 1953 and the island has been uninhabited ever since. It is still known among locals as 'the island of the living dead'.

The island is a fascinating place to explore. It has an aura that is both macabre and poignant. The **cemetery**, with its open graves, is an especially strange place. Dead lepers came in three classes: those who saved up money from their government pension for a place in a concrete box; those whose funeral was paid for by relations and who therefore got a proper grave; and the destitute, whose remains were thrown into a charnel house.

Getting There & Away

There are regular excursion boats to Spinalonga Island from Agios Nikolaos and a boat every half-hour from the port in Elounda (2000 dr). Alternatively, you can negotiate with the fishermen in Elounda and Plaka (a fishing village 5km farther north) to take you across. The boats from Agios Nikolaos pass Bird Island and Kri-Kri Island, one of the last habitats of the *kri-kri*, Crete's wild goat. Both these islands are uninhabited and designated wildlife sanctuaries.

ELOUNDA Ελούντα

☎ 0841 • postcode 720 53 • pop 1800

There are magnificent mountain and sea views along the 11km road from Agios Nikolaos to Elounda. Although formerly a quiet fishing village, Elounda is now bristling with tourists and is only marginally calmer than Agios Nikolaos. But the harbour is attractive, and there's a sheltered lagoon-like stretch of water formed by the Spinalonga Peninsula.

Orientation & Information

Elounda's post office is opposite the bus

CRETE

stop. From the bus stop walk straight ahead to the clock tower and church which are on the central square. There is a small OTE office next to the church. Elounda doesn't have tourist police but a tourist office (☎ 42 464) has recently opened opposite the church.

Places to Stay

There's some good accommodation around, but nothing particularly cheap. ***Hotel Aristea*** *(☎ 41 300)*, in the town centre, has doubles/triples with a sea view for 7000/10,000 dr. ***Hotel Sofia*** *(☎ 41 482)*, on the seafront 100m from the town centre, has pleasantly furnished two-room apartments with kitchen for 12,000 dr among its range of options.

Getting There & Away

There are 20 buses daily from Agios Nikolaos to Elounda (20 minutes, 230 dr).

LASSITHI PLATEAU

Οροπέδιο Λασιθίου

☎ 0844 • postcode 720 52

The first view of the mountain-fringed Lassithi Plateau, laid out like an immense patchwork quilt, is stunning. The plateau, 900m above sea level, is a vast expanse of pear and apple orchards, almond trees and fields of crops, dotted by some 7000 windmills. These are not conventional stone windmills, but slender metal constructions with white canvas sails. They were built in the 17th century to irrigate the rich farmland but few of the original windmills are in service. Most have been replaced by less-attractive mechanical pumps. There are 20 villages dotted around the periphery of the plateau, the largest of which is **Tzermiado**, with 1300 inhabitants, a bank, post office and OTE.

The plateau's rich soil has been cultivated since Minoan times. The inaccessibility of the region made it a hotbed of insurrection during Venetian and Turkish rule. Following an uprising in the 13th century, the Venetians drove out the inhabitants of Lassithi and destroyed their orchards. The plateau lay abandoned for 200 years.

Most people come to Lassithi on coach trips, but it deserves an overnight stay. Once the package tourists have departed clutching their plastic windmill souvenirs, the villages return to pastoral serenity.

Dikteon Cave Δίκταιον Αντρον

Lassithi's major sight is Dikteon Cave, just outside the village of **Psyhro**. Here, according to mythology, Rhea hid the newborn Zeus from Cronos, his offspring-gobbling father. The cave, which has both stalactites and stalagmites, was excavated in 1900 by British archaeologist David Hogarth. He found numerous votive offerings, indicating the cave was a place of cult worship. These finds are housed in the archaeological museum in Iraklio.

The moment you reach the parking area beneath the site, representatives from the Association of Cave Guides & Donkey Owners will be upon you. The cave guides want 2000 dr for a lantern-guided tour, while the donkey owners want the same to save you the 15 minute walk up to the cave. A guide is not essential, but a torch is. So are sensible shoes. The path to the cave is pretty rough, and the cave itself is slippery. Opening times are 8 am to 4 pm daily. Admission is 800 dr.

Walk from Tzermiado to Psyhro

The 90 minute walk from Tzermiado to Psyhro goes through the heart of the plateau. From Tzermiado's central square take the street with the Agricultural Bank and OTE. At the end, turn right, and then take the first left onto a road which becomes a dirt track. Continue ahead for 1km. At the T-junction turn right, and then veer right onto the surfaced road. At the crossroads, turn left onto a rough dirt track. Turn right at the second crossroads and you will see Psyhro in the distance to the left. Continue straight ahead for 1km, and at the T-junction turn left. At the road, turn left to reach Psyhro's central square, or continue straight ahead to reach Dikteon Cave.

Places to Stay & Eat

Psyhro, the village nearest the cave, has only one place to stay – the D class ***Zeus***

Hotel *(☎ 31 284)* where singles/doubles with bathroom cost 6000/8000 dr. On the main street, ***Stavros*** and ***Platanos*** tavernas serve similar fare at similar prices.

Agios Georgios, 5km away, has three accommodation options. At ***Hotel Rea*** *(☎ 31 209)*, opposite the school on the main street, there are cosy rooms for 2500/5000 dr. ***Rent Rooms Maria*** nearby has spacious stucco rooms decorated with weavings for 6000/8500/10,800 dr with bathroom. ***Hotel Dias*** *(☎ 31 207)*, also on the main street, has pleasant rooms for 3000/4000 dr. Both hotels have restaurants.

In Tzermiado, the well signposted ***Hotel Kourites*** *(☎ 22 194)* is the only accommodation. Its comfortable rooms cost 6000/8000 dr with bathroom, breakfast included. There is free use of the hotel's bicycles.

Restaurant Kronio, on Tzermiado's main square, has a pleasant, folksy decor. The food is excellent, but avoid the place when the tour buses call, as the waiters go into frenzy mode. Nearby ***Taverna Kri-Kri*** is a good place to meet locals. The menu is limited but the food is good.

Getting There & Away

Public transport to the Dikteon Cave is problematic if you don't have your own wheels. From Agios Nikolaos there's an afternoon bus to Lassithi on Monday, Wednesday and Friday (1900 dr, 2½ hrs) and a morning bus from Lassithi to Agios Nikolaos also on Monday, Wednesday and Friday. From Iraklio there are two buses on weekdays to Lassithi (two hours, 1400 dr), and three on weekdays returning to Iraklio.

All buses go through Tzermiado and Agios Georgios before terminating at Psyhro at the foot of the road leading to Dikteon Cave.

SITIA Σητεία

☎ 0843 • postcode 723 00 • pop 8000

Back on the north coast road, Sitia (sih-**tee**-ah) is a good deal quieter than Agios Nikolaos. A sandy beach skirts a wide bay to the east of town. The main part of the town is terraced up a hillside, overlooking the port. The buildings are a pleasing mixture of new and fading Venetian architecture.

Orientation & Information

The bus station is at the eastern end of Karamanli, which runs behind the bay. The town's main square, Plateia El Venizelou – recognisable by its palm trees and statue of a dying soldier – is at the western end of Karamanli.

There's no tourist office but Tzortzakis Travel (☎ 25 080), Kornalou 150, is a good source of information. There are plenty of ATMs and places to change money. The National Bank of Greece on the main square has a 24 hour exchange machine.

The harbour near the square is for small boats. Ferries use the large quay farther out, about 500m from Plateia Agnostou.

The post office is on Democritou. To get there from the main square, follow El Venizelou inland and take the first left. The OTE is on Kapetan Sifis, which runs uphill directly off Plateia El Venizelou.

Things to See & Do

Sitia's **archaeological museum** (☎ 23 917) houses a well displayed collection of local finds spanning from Neolithic to Roman times, with emphasis on the Minoan. The museum is on the left side of the road to Ierapetra. It is open 8.30 am to 3 pm Tuesday to Sunday. Admission is 500 dr.

Sitia produces superior sultanas and a **sultana festival** is held in the town in the last week of August, during which wine flows freely and there are performances of Cretan dances.

Places to Stay

Sitia's ***youth hostel*** *(☎ 22 693, Therissou 4)* is on the road to Iraklio. It's a well run hostel with hot showers and a communal kitchen and dining room. Dorm beds cost 1500 dr and double rooms are 3000 dr. Camping in the grounds costs 1000 per person.

The D class ***Hotel Arhontiko*** *(☎ 28 172, 22 993, Kondylaki 16)* is beautifully maintained and spotless. Singles/doubles are 5000/6000 dr. On summer evenings, the

CRETE

friendly owner enjoys sharing a bottle of *raki* with guests on the communal terrace. Kondylaki is two streets uphill from the port. The best way to get there is to walk out towards the ferry dock along El Venizelou, turn left up Filellinon and then right into Kondylaki. The co-owned ***Rooms to Let Apostolis*** *(Kazantzaki 27)*, an upmarket domatio, has doubles with fridge for 7500 dr. Kazantzaki runs uphill from the waterfront, one street north of the OTE.

Another attractive place is ***Kazarma Rooms to Rent*** *(☎ 23 211, Ionias 10)* where doubles with bathroom cost 8000 dr. There is a communal lounge and a well equipped kitchen. The rooms are signposted from Patriarch Metahaki. The well signposted ***El Greco Hotel*** *(☎ 23 133, Arkadou 13)* has more character than the town's other C class hotels. Comfortable rooms with bathroom cost 7000/10,000 dr. The B class ***Itanos Hotel*** *(☎ 22 900, fax 22 915)*, along the harbour, has air-conditioned rooms with balconies for 9000/12,000 dr. Add another 1500 dr per person for breakfast at the hotel but there are plenty of cafes nearby.

Places to Eat

There is a string of tavernas along the quay side on El Venizelou that offer an array of mezedes and fish dishes at comparable prices. Inland, there's ***Mixos Taverna*** *(Kornarou 117)*, which has excellent charcoal-grilled souvlaki. Walk up Patriarch Metahaki from the waterfront, take the first left and the taverna is on the right.

Kali Kardia Taverna *(Foundalidhou 20)* is excellent value and popular with locals. Mezedes cost from 400 dr to 800 dr and main dishes from 1250 dr to 1800 dr. Walk up Kazantzaki from the waterfront, take the second right and the taverna is on the right. ***The Balcony***, on the corner of Kazantzaki and Foundalidou, provides the finest dining in Sitia with an extraordinarily creative menu that combines Greek, Italian and Mexican food. A meal for two with wine will cost about 12,000 dr.

The ***galaktopoleio*** *(Kornarou 33)* specialises in fine sheep's-milk products, including fresh milk, curdled milk, delicious yogurt and cheese.

Getting There & Away

Air Sitia's tiny airport has flights to Athens once weekly for 23,100 dr. The agent for Olympic Airways is Tzortzakis Travel (☎ 25 080/090) at Kornarou 150.

Bus There are buses to Ierapetra (1½ hours, 1200 dr, six daily); Iraklio (3½ hours, 2850 dr, five daily) via Agios Nikolaos (1½ hours, 1500 dr); Vaï (one hour, 600 dr, five daily); and Kato Zakros (one hour, two daily) via Paleokastro and Zakros (one hour, 1000 dr). Buses to Vaï and Kato Zakros run during May to October only. During the rest of the year, the Vaï service terminates at Paleokastro and the Kato Zakros service at Zakros.

Ferry Ferries depart Sitia Tuesday, Thursday and Sunday afternoons for Piraeus (14½ hours, 7600 dr) via Agios Nikolaos. Ferries also leave Sitia on Thursday and Saturday morning for Karpathos (four hours, 3400 dr) and Kassos (six hours, 2600 dr), and Saturday morning for Rhodes (6000 dr). Ferry tickets can be bought at Tzortzakis Travel (☎ 22 631, 28 900), Kor-narou 150.

Getting Around

The airport (signposted) is 1km out of town. There is no airport bus; a taxi costs about 1000 dr. Car and motorcycle rental outlets are mostly on Papandreou on the way to the archaeological museum.

AROUND SITIA

Moni Toplou Μονή Τοπλού

The imposing Moni Toplou, 18km from Sitia on the back road to Vaï, looks more like a fortress than a monastery. It was often treated as such, being ravaged by both the Knights of St John and the Turks. It holds an 18th century icon by Ioannis Kornaros, one of Crete's most celebrated icon painters. The monastery is open 9 am to 1 pm and 2 to 6 pm daily.

It is a 3km walk from the road from Sitia to Paleokastro. Buses can drop you off at the junction.

Vaï Βάι

The beach at Vaï, on Crete's east coast 24km from Sitia, is famous for its palm forest.

There are many stories about the origin of these palms, including the theory that they sprouted from date pits spread by Roman legionaries relaxing on their way back from conquering Egypt. While these palms are closely related to the date, they are a separate species unique to Crete.

You'll need to arrive early to appreciate the setting, because the place gets packed in July and August. It's possible to escape the worst of the ballyhoo – jet skis and all – by clambering over a rocky outcrop (to the right, facing the sea) to a small secluded beach. Alternatively, you can go over the hill in the other direction to a quiet beach frequented by nudists.

There are two tavernas at Vaï but no accommodation. If you're after more secluded beaches, head north for another 3km to the ancient Minoan site of **Itanos**. Below the site are several good swimming spots. There are buses to Vaï from Sitia (one hour, 600 dr, five daily).

ZAKROS & KATO ZAKROS

☎ 0843 • postcode 72 300

The village of Zakros (Ζάκρος), 37km southeast of Sitia, is the nearest permanent settlement to the Minoan site of Zakros, a further 7km away (see Ancient Zakros following).

Kato Zakros, next to the site, is a beautiful little seaside settlement that springs to life between March and October. If the weather is dry, there is a lovely two hour walk from Zakros to Kato Zakros through a gorge known as the Valley of the Dead because of the cave tombs dotted along the cliffs. The gorge emerges close to the Minoan site.

Places to Stay

Zakros has ***domatia*** and one hotel, the bleak C class ***Hotel Zakros*** *(☎ 93 379)*, where doubles with bathroom are 5000 dr.

It's much better to stay at Kato Zakros, where there are three places to choose from. ***Athena Rooms*** *(☎ 93 458/377)* has doubles with bathroom for 8000 dr, and is jointly owned with ***Poseidon Rooms***, which has singles/doubles for 5000/6000 dr with shared bathroom. All these places are at the far end of the beach road.

George's Villas *(☎ 93 201/207)* has spotless, beautifully furnished rooms with bathroom and terrace. Rates are 6000/7000 dr. The villas are in a verdant setting 500m along the old road to Zakros.

Getting There & Away

There are buses to Zakros via Paleokastro from Sitia (one hour, 1000 dr, two daily). They leave Sitia at 11 am and 2.30 pm and return at 12.30 and 4 pm. From June through August, the buses continue to Kato Zakros. Hotel Zakros offers guests free transport to Kato Zakros.

ANCIENT ZAKROS

The smallest of Crete's four palatial complexes, ancient Zakros was a major port in Minoan times, maintaining trade links with Egypt, Syria, Anatolia and Cyprus. The palace comprised royal apartments, storerooms and workshops flanking a central courtyard.

The town occupied a low plain close to the shore. Water levels have risen over the years so that some parts of the palace complex are submerged. The ruins are not well preserved, but a visit to the site is worthwhile for its wild and remote setting. The site is open 8.30 am to 3 pm Tuesday to Sunday. Admission is 500 dr.

XEROKAMBOS Ξερόκαμπος

The tiny village of Xerokambos, on the next bay south of Kato Zakros, is an unspoilt haven near several coves of inviting pale sand. Unlike most domatia in Xerokambos, ***Villa Petrina Rent Rooms*** *(☎ 0843-31 115, fax 31 693)* is open all year. Its beautiful apartments cost 8000 dr per day.

There are no buses to Xerokambos. To get there from Zakros take the Kato Zakros road, and on the outskirts of Zakros turn left at the signpost for Liviko View Restaurant. This 10km dirt road to Xerokambos is only suitable for 4WDs. Otherwise there is a good paved road from Ziros.

IERAPETRA Ιεράπετρα

☎ 0842 • postcode 722 00 • pop 11,000

Ierapetra (yeh-**rah**-pet-rah) is Crete's most southerly major town. It was a major port of call for the Romans in their conquest of Egypt. After the tourist hype of Agios Nikolaos, the unpretentiousness of Ierapetra is refreshing, and the main business continues to be agriculture, not tourism.

Orientation & Information

The bus station is on the eastern side of town on Lasthenous, one street back from the beachfront. From the ticket office, turn right and after about 50m you'll come to a six-road intersection. There are signposts to the beach via Patriarhou Metaxaki, and to the city centre via the pedestrian mall section of Lasthenous.

The mall emerges onto the central square of Plateia Eleftherias. On the left of the square is the National Bank of Greece. Turn right opposite the bank to get to the OTE, one block inland on Koraka.

If you continue straight ahead from Plateia Eleftherias you will come to Plateia Emmanual Kothri, where you'll find the post office at Stylianou Houta 3.

There is no tourist office, but South Crete Tours (☎ 22 892), opposite the bus station, might have maps of Ierapetra. To reach it, turn right from Plateia Emmanual Kothri.

Things to See

The one-room **archaeological museum** is perfect for those with a short concentration span. Pride of place is given to an exquisite statue of Demeter. The museum is open 8.30 am to 3 pm Tuesday to Sunday (free).

If you walk south along the waterfront from the central square you will come to the **fortress**, built in the early years of Venetian rule and strengthened by Francesco Morosini in 1626. It's in a pretty fragile state but you can visit it 8.30 am to 3 pm Tuesday to Sunday. Admission is free.

Inland from the fortress is the labyrinthine old quarter, a delightful place to lose yourself for a while.

Beaches

Ierapetra has two beaches. The main town beach is near the harbour and the other beach stretches east from the bottom of Patriarhou Metaxaki. Both have coarse, grey sand.

The beaches to the east of Ierapetra tend to get crowded. For greater tranquillity, head for **Hrysi Islet**, where there are good, uncrowded sandy beaches. From June through August an excursion boat (5500 dr) leaves for the islet every morning and returns in the afternoon. The islet has three tavernas.

Places to Stay

The nearest camp site is ***Koutsounari Camping*** *(☎ 61 213)*, 7km east of Ierapetra at Koutsounari. It has a restaurant, snack bar and minimarket. Ierapetra-Sitia buses pass the site.

Most places to stay in Ierapetra are either near the bus station or in the old quarter. An exception is ***Katerina Hotel*** *(☎ 28 345)* on the seafront where pleasant doubles with bathroom are 7000 dr. To reach the hotel from the bus station, follow Patriarhou Metaxaki to the waterfront, turn right and you'll see the hotel on the right.

Hotel Coral *(☎ 22 846)* has well kept singles/doubles for 3000/5000 dr with bathroom. The owner also has some rooms for 3000/4000 dr with shared bathroom, and comfortable apartments for 6000 dr. The hotel is signposted just south of the port police building on the waterfront.

Cretan Villa Hotel *(☎ 28 522, Lakerda 16)* is a lovely, well maintained 18th century house with traditionally furnished rooms and a peaceful courtyard. Rooms are 7000/9000 dr with bathroom. From the bus station walk towards the town centre and take the first right from where the hotel is signposted.

The best hotel in town is the B class ***Astron Hotel*** *(☎ 25 114, fax 25 917)* at the beach end of Patriarhou Metaxaki. Rates are 13,000/17,500 dr, including breakfast.

Places to Eat

There are many souvlaki outlets on Kyrba. ***Restaurant Castello*** is one of the better tavernas along the waterfront in the old quarter. When the locals celebrate a special occasion they often head to ***Lambrakis*** about 1km east of the town centre along the beach road. The grilled chicken (1100 dr) is tender and juicy and it would be hard to find better stuffed tomatoes (1000 dr).

Getting There & Away

From June through August, there are buses to Iraklio (2½ hours, 2100 dr, six daily) via Agios Nikolaos (one hour, 750 dr), Gournia and Istron. There are also buses to Makrigialos (30 minutes, 600 dr, eight daily); Sitia (1½ hours, 1200 dr, six daily) via Koutsounari; Mirtos (30 minutes, 320 dr, six daily); and Ano Viannos (one hour, 800 dr, two weekly).

MIRTOS Μυρτός

☎ 0842 • postcode 722 00 • pop 600

Mirtos, on the coast 17km west of Ierapetra, is a sparkling village of whitewashed houses with flower-filled balconies. Mirtos has preserved its charm, despite having become popular with independent travellers. It has a decent dark sand and pebble beach.

You'll soon find your way around Mirtos which is built on a grid system. To get to the waterfront from the bus stop, facing south, take the road to the right passing Mertiza Studios on the right.

There is no post office, bank or OTE, but Aris Travel Agency (☎ 51 017/300) on the main street has currency exchange.

Places to Stay & Eat

Despina Rent Rooms *(☎ 51 343)* has pleasant but noisy doubles/triples with bathroom for 5000/6500 dr. At ***Pandora Domatia*** *(☎ 51 589)*, on the main street, there are prettily furnished singles/doubles for 3500/4000 dr. ***Hotel Panorama*** *(☎ 51 362)*, uphill from the town centre, has studios with bathrooms, kitchenettes and spectacular views for 5000/7000 dr. The superior C class ***Hotel Mirtos*** *(☎ 51 227)* has large, well kept rooms for 5000/7000 dr with bathroom.

Big Blue *(☎ 51 094)*, on the western edge of town, has rooms for 6000/7000 dr with bathroom, and two-room apartments with two bathrooms and a kitchenette for 12,000 dr.

Mirtos Hotel Restaurant is popular with both locals and tourists. The no-frills ***Kostos Taverna*** nearby has good *dolmades* for 800 dr and stifado for 1500 dr. The waterfront ***Karavoslasi Restaurant*** is more stylish, with vegetarian dishes for 1000 dr and meat dishes for 1500 dr to 1800 dr.

Lost Wax

The *cire perdue* (lost wax) method of casting bronze statues was pioneered by the Cretans in preclassical times. A wax original was made, with iron ducts placed at strategic points. These ducts were sufficiently long to stick out of the clay mould which was subsequently put around the wax. A pouring funnel was fitted into the mould at a suitable place. The cast was then heated so that the wax melted and ran out through the ducts. When all the wax had escaped, the ducts were removed and the holes were plugged. Molten bronze was then poured through the funnel. When the bronze had cooled the mould was carefully chipped away.

Advantages of the cire perdue method of casting include the high degree of detail that can be achieved, and the absence of joining lines on the bronze cast. The process is still used today for high-precision work.

The cire perdue method may have given rise to various legends including one which tells of Talos, a man made of bronze, who had one vein running from his neck to his leg. He was a servant of King Minos, and it was his duty to help defend Crete. When the Argonauts arrived, he tried to repel them, but Medea, who had accompanied them, unplugged a pin in his ankle. He was drained of his colourless life-blood and died.

DIANA MAYFIELD

Traditional Cretan dress of breeches tucked into knee-high leather boots, and a black-fringed kerchief on the head, can still be seen.

Getting There & Away

Six buses daily go from Ierapetra to Mirtos (30 minutes, 320 dr). The Ano Viannos-Ierapetra bus passes through Mirtos.

MIRTOS TO ANO VIANNOS

Ano Viannos, 16km west of Mirtos, is a delightful village built on the southern flanks of Mt Dikti. The flower-decked **folklore museum** presents colourful costumes and traditional implements such as an olive press and key-making tools. It is open 10 am to 2 pm daily. Admission is 500 dr.

The village's 14th century **Church of Agios Pelagia** has fine frescoes by Nikoforos Fokas. Follow signs from the main street but first ask in a *kafeneio* for the whereabouts of the key.

From Ano Viannos it's 13km south to the unspoilt village of **Keratokambos**, where there's a pleasant tree-lined beach.

The turn-off for **Arvi** (population 300) is 3km east of Ano Viannos. Arvi is bigger than Keratokambos, but only gets crowded during July and August. Hemmed in by cliffs, Arvi is a sun trap where bananas grow in abundance. The main street skirts a long sand and pebble beach. It's a 15 minute walk inland to Moni Agios Andronios.

Places to Stay & Eat

Ano Viannos has one domatia. ***Taverna & Rooms Lefkas*** *(☎ 0895-22 719)*, opposite the large church, has singles/doubles for 3000/4000 dr with bathroom.

In Keratokambos, a left turn at the coast will lead to ***Taverna & Rooms Thoinikas*** *(☎ 0895-51 401)*, where singles/doubles with bathroom cost 4000/6000 dr. ***Komis Studios*** *(☎ 0895-51 390)* offers stunningly decorated three-level apartments on the sea built from stone, wood and stucco and outfitted with air-conditioning among other amenities. They cost 25,000 dr and are worth every bit of it.

Morning Star Taverna is the best bet for vegetarians with tasty artichoke stew for 1000 dr. ***Taverna Kriti*** offers excellent fish dishes and ***Taverna Thoinikas*** specialises in grilled food.

Arvi's ***Pension Kolibi*** *(☎ 0895-71 250)*, in a quiet setting 1km west of the town, has immaculate doubles/triples with bathroom costing 6000/7000 dr. ***Pension Gorgona*** *(☎ 0895-71 353)*, on Arvi's main street, has pleasant doubles for 7500 dr with bathroom. ***Hotel Ariadne*** *(☎ 0895-71 300)*, farther west, has well kept singles/doubles for 7000/8000 dr with bathroom. At ***Apartments Kyma*** *(☎ 0895-71 344)* at the eastern end of the village luxurious apartments cost 8000 dr.

Kima Restaurant, on the main street, serves hearty Greek fare, and ***Taverna Diktina*** features vegetarian food.

Getting There & Away

Public transport is poor. From Ano Viannos there are two buses weekly to Iraklio (2½ hours, 1900 dr) and Ierapetra (one hour, 800 dr) via Mirtos. There is no bus service to Keratokambos or Arvi, but in term-time it may be possible to use the school buses from Ano Viannos.

With 4WD you can use the 10km coastal dirt road between Keratokambos and Arvi.

Western Crete

The western part of Crete comprises the prefectures of Hania and Rethymno, which take their names from the old Venetian cities which are their capitals. The two towns rank as two of the region's main attractions, although the most famous is the spectacular Samaria Gorge. The south coast towns of Paleohora and Plakias are popular resorts.

RETHYMNO Ρέθυμνο

☎ 0831 • postcode 741 00 • pop 24,000

Rethymno (**reh**-thim-no) is Crete's third-largest town. The main attraction is the old Venetian-Ottoman quarter that occupies the headland beneath the massive Venetian *fortezza* (fortress). The place is a maze of narrow streets, graceful wood-balconied houses and ornate Venetian monuments; several minarets add a touch of the Orient. The architectural similarities invite comparison with Hania, but Rethymno has a character of its own. An added attraction is a beach right in town.

The approaches to the town couldn't be less inviting. The modern town has sprawled out along the coast, dotted with big package hotels attracted by a reasonable beach.

History

The site of modern Rethymno has been occupied since Late Minoan times – the evidence can be found in the city's archaeological museum. In the 3rd and 4th centuries BC, the town was known as Rithymna, an autonomous state of sufficient stature to issue its own coinage. A scarcity of references to the city in Roman and Byzantine periods suggest it was of minor importance at that time.

The town prospered once more under the Venetians, who ruled from 1210 until 1645, when the Turks took over. Turkish forces held the town until 1897, when it was taken by Russia as part of the occupation of Crete by the Great Powers.

Rethymno became an artistic and intellectual centre after the arrival of a large number of refugees from Constantinople in 1923. The city has a campus of the University of Crete, bringing a student population that keeps the town alive outside the tourist season.

Orientation

The city's old quarter occupies the headland north of Dimakopoulou, which runs from Plateia Vardinogianni on the west coast to Plateia Iroön on the east (becoming Gerakari en route).

Most of the good places to eat and sleep are to be found here, while banks and government services are just to the south on the edge of the new three-quarters of town. The beach is on the eastern side of town, curving around from the delightful old Venetian Harbour in the north. El Venizelou is the beachfront street. Curving parallel one block back is Arkadiou, the main commercial street.

A maze of twisting and curving streets make the old quarter an easy place to get lost in, especially since street signs are a rarity. Coming from the south, the best approach is through the Porto Guora (Great Gate) onto Ethnikis Antistaseos. This busy shopping street leads to the Rimondi fountain, the old quarter's best known landmark. The area around here is thick with cafes, restaurants and souvenir shops.

If you arrive in Rethymno by bus, you will be dropped at the new terminal at the western end of Igoumenou Gavriil, about 600m from the Porto Guora. To get there, follow Igoum Gavriil back into the town centre. A left turn at the far end of the park will leave you facing the gate. If you arrive by ferry, the old quarter is as far away as the end of the quay.

If you are driving into town from the expressway, your final approach to the city centre is along Dimitrikaki. The car park opposite the municipal park is a convenient spot to stop and check things out.

Information

Tourist Offices Rethymno's municipal tourist office (☎ 29 148) is on the beach side of El Venizelou, opposite the junction with Varga Kallergi. It's open 8 am to 8 pm Monday to Friday in summer, and 8 am to 3 pm in winter. The tourist police (☎ 28 156) occupy the same building and are open 7 am to 10 pm daily.

Money Banks are concentrated around the junction of Dimokratias and Pavlou Kountouriotou. The National Bank of Greece is on Dimokratias, on the far side of the square opposite the town hall. The Credit Bank, Pavlou Kountouriotou 29, and the National Mortgage Bank, next to the town hall, have 24 hour automatic exchange machines.

Post & Communications The OTE is at Kountouriotou 28, and the post office is a block south at Moatsou 21. From June through August there is a mobile post office about 200m south-east of the tourist office on El Venizelou. You can check your email at Net C@fe (☎ 55 133), Venieri 2, open 10 am to 10 pm daily. Take Papandreou from El Venizelou east of Plateia Iroön and you'll find it behind Elina Hotel.

Bookshops The International Press Bookshop, located at El Venizelou 81, stocks English-language novels, travel guides and history books. The bookshop at Souliou 43 stocks novels in English, books about Greece and tapes of Greek music, and has a small second-hand section.

Laundry The Laundry Mat laundrette at Tombazi 45, next door to the youth hostel, charges 2500 dr for a wash and dry.

Things to See

Rethymno's 16th century **fortress** stands on Paleokastro Hill, the site of the city's ancient acropolis. Within its massive walls once stood a great number of buildings, of which only a church and a mosque survive intact. The ramparts offer good views, while the site has lots of ruins to explore. The fortress is open 8 am to 8 pm daily. Admission is 800 dr.

The **archaeological museum** (☎ 29 975) is opposite the entrance to the fortress. The finds displayed here include an important coin collection. The museum is open 8.30 am to 3 pm Tuesday to Sunday. Admission is 500 dr. Rethymno's excellent **historical & folk art museum**, Vernardou 30, is open 10 am to 2 pm Monday to Saturday. Admission is 500 dr.

Pride of place among the many vestiges of Venetian rule in the old quarter goes to the **Rimondi fountain** with its spouting lion heads, and the 16th century **loggia**.

At the southern end of Ethnikis Antistaseos is the well preserved **Porto Guora**, a remnant of the Venetian defensive wall. Turkish legacies in the old quarter include the **Kara Musa Pasa mosque** near Plateia Iroön and the **Neradjes Mosque**, which was converted from a Franciscan church.

Activities

The Happy Walker (☎ 52 920), Tombazi 56, runs a varied program of mountain walks in the region. Most walks start in the early morning and finish with lunch. Prices start at 6500 dr per person. The EOS (☎ 57 766) is at Dimokratias 12.

Paradise Dive Centre (☎ 53 258), El Venizelou 76, offers activities and a PADI course for all grades of divers.

Special Events

Rethymno's main cultural event is the annual Renaissance Festival that runs during July and August. It features dance, drama and films as well as art exhibitions.

Some years there's a Wine Festival in mid-July held in the municipal park. Ask the tourist office for details.

Places to Stay – Budget

The nearest camp site is ***Elizabeth Camping** (☎ 28 694)*, near Myssiria Beach, 3km

east of Rethymno. The site has a taverna, snack bar and minimarket. An Iraklio-bound bus can drop you at the site.

The ***youth hostel*** *(☎ 22 848, Tombazi 41)* is friendly and well run with beds for 1500 dr and free hot showers. Breakfast is available and there's a bar in the evening. There is no curfew and the place is open all year.

An excellent budget choice is ***Olga's Pension*** *(☎ 28 665, Souliou 57)*, right in the heart of town. There's a wide choice of rooms which are spread about in clusters off a network of terraces – all bursting with greenery. Prices range from basic singles for 6000 dr, to studio rooms with kitchen for 10,000 dr. In between comes a comfortable double with shower for 9000 dr. Owners George and Stella Mihalaki speak good English and run a very friendly show.

At ***Rooms to Rent Barbara Dolomaki*** *(☎ 24 581, Thambergi 14)*, there are comfortable doubles with bathroom for 10,000 dr. Double studios with a fridge and small stove cost 11,000 dr.

If you're after sea views ***Lefteris Papadakis Rooms*** *(☎ 23 803, Plastira 26)* has clean singles/doubles with bathroom for 6500/7500 dr. Alternatively, try ***Rent Rooms Sea Front*** *(☎ 51 062/981, El Venizelou 45)* which has light, airy rooms with bathroom for 5000/7000 dr.

Rooms for Rent Anda *(☎ 23 479, Nikiforou Foka 33)* is on a quiet street and has prettily furnished doubles/triples for 9000/11,000 dr with bathroom.

Places to Stay – Mid-Range

An outstanding domatia is ***Rent Rooms Garden*** *(☎ 26 274, 28 586, Nikiforou Foka 82)* in the heart of the old town. It's an impeccably maintained 600-year-old Venetian house with many original features and a gorgeous grape-arboured garden. Double/triple rooms are 10,000/15,000 dr with bathroom.

Park Hotel *(☎ 29 958, Igoum Gavriil 9)* is good value, offering air-conditioned rooms with TV for 11,000/14,000 dr. ***Astali*** *(☎ 24 721, fax 24 723, Papandreou 1)* is a new hotel that offers spiffy air-conditioned rooms for 11,500/16,000 dr.

The smartest hotel in town is the B class ***Hotel Fortezza*** *(☎ 55 551/552, 23 828, fax 54 073, Melissinou 16)*. It has a snack bar, restaurant and swimming pool. Singles/doubles/triples are 15,000/19,000/23,000 dr.

Places to Eat

The waterfront along El Venizelou is lined with amazingly similar tourist restaurants staffed by fast-talking waiters desperately cajoling passers-by into eating at their establishments. The situation is much the same around the Venetian Harbour, except the setting is better and the prices higher.

To find cheaper food and a more authentic atmosphere, wander inland down the little side streets. ***Taverna Kyria Maria*** *(Diog Mesologiou 20)*, behind the Rimondi fountain, is a cosy, traditional taverna that has outdoor seating under a leafy trellis with twittering birds. They serve a hearty vegetarian plate for 1800 dr and all meals end with a complementary dessert and shot of raki.

Another reasonably priced place is ***Old Town Taverna*** *(Vernardou 31)*. Set menus for two with wine are 4000 dr. ***Taverna Pontios*** *(Melissinou 34)*, near the archaeological museum, is a popular hang-out with locals. The cheese-stuffed calamari at 1400 dr is commendable.

Gounakis Restaurant & Bar *(Koroneou 6)* is worth visiting for its food as much as for its music (see Entertainment). ***Stella's Kitchen*** *(Souliou 55)* serves tasty low-priced snacks and full meals.

If you have your own wheels, head to ***Taverna Zisi***, about 2km out of town on the old road to Iraklio. This is where local families go for an evening out. The speciality is a platter of meaty mezedes for 3000 dr.

Entertainment

If your interests include drinking cheap wine and listening to live Cretan folk music, ***Gounakis Restaurant & Bar*** *(Koroneou 6)* is the place to go. There's music and impromptu dancing most nights.

Rethymno has no shortage of discos, most of them in the streets behind the old harbour. The current favourite is ***Baja Club*** on Salaminos which plays international and Greek music nightly from midnight on. ***Fortezza Disco***, close to the waterfront, plays disco music.

Shopping

Zaharias Theodorakis turns out onyx bowls and goblets on the lathe in his small workshop opposite Pension Anna on Katehaki. Prices start at 5000 dr for a small bowl.

Getting There & Away

Bus There are numerous services to both Hania (one hour, 1350 dr) and Iraklio (1½ hours, 1550 dr) from Rethymno. There's a bus in each direction every half-hour during June to August, every hour during December to February. During June to August there are also buses to Plakias (one hour, 950 dr, four daily), Agia Galini (1½ hours, 1300 dr, four daily), Moni Arkadiou (30 minutes, 500 dr, three daily), Preveli (950 dr, two daily) and Omalos (two hours, 2750 dr, one daily). The morning bus to Plakias continues to Hora Sfakion (two hours, 1450 dr).

Services to these destinations are greatly reduced from December through February.

Ferry Cretan Lines (☎ 29 221) operates a daily ferry between Rethymno and Piraeus (7000 dr) leaving both Rethymno and Piraeus at 7.30 pm.

Tickets are available from the Cretan Lines office at Arkadiou 250.

Getting Around

Most of the car rental firms are near Plateia Iroön. Motor Stavros (☎ 22 858), Paleologou 14, has a wide range of motorcycles and also rents bicycles.

AROUND RETHYMNO

Moni Arkadiou Μονή Αρκαδίου

This 16th century monastery, 23km south-east of Rethymno, is surrounded by attractive hill country. The most impressive of the buildings is the Venetian baroque church. Its striking facade, which features on the 100 dr note, has eight slender Corinthian columns and an ornate triple-belled tower.

In November 1866 the Turks sent massive forces to quell insurrections which were gathering momentum throughout the island. Hundreds of men, women and children who had fled their villages used the monastery as a safe haven. When 2000 Turkish soldiers attacked the building, rather than surrender, the Cretans set light to a store of gunpowder. The explosion killed everyone, Turks included, except one small girl, who lived to a ripe old age in a village nearby. Busts of the woman, and the abbot who lit the gun powder, stand outside the monastery.

The monastery is open 8 am to 1 pm and 3.30 to 8 pm daily. Admission is free. The small **museum** has an admission charge of 700 dr.

There are buses from Rethymno to the monastery (30 minutes, 500 dr) at 6 am, 10.30 am and 2.30 pm, returning at 7 am, noon and 4 pm.

Amari Valley Κοιλάδα Αμαρίου

If you have your own transport you can explore the enchanting Amari Valley, south-east of Rethymno, between Mts Ida and Kedros. The region harbours around 40 well watered, unspoilt villages set amid olive groves and almond and cherry trees.

The valley begins at the picturesque village of **Apostoli**, 25km south-east of Rethymno. The turn-off for Apostoli is on the coast 3km east of Rethymno. The road forks at Apostoli and then joins up again 38km to the south, making it possible to do a circular drive around the valley. Alternatively, you can continue south to Agia Galini.

There is an EOS refuge on **Mt Ida**, a 10km walk from the small village of **Kouroutes**, 5km south of Fourfouras. For information contact the Rethymno EOS (see Activities in the Rethymno section).

RETHYMNO TO SPILI

Heading south from Rethymno, there is a turn-off to the right to the Late Minoan cemetery of **Armeni** 2km before the modern village of Armeni. The main road south continues through woodland, which gradually gives way to a bare and dramatic landscape. After 18km there is a turn-off to the right for **Selia** and **Frangokastello** and, a little beyond, another turn-off for Plakias (this turn-off is referred to on timetables as the Koxare junction or Bale). The main road continues for 9km to Spili.

SPILI ΣΠήΛΙ

☎ 0832 • postcode 740 53 • pop 700

Spili is a gorgeous mountain town with cobbled streets, rustic houses and plane trees. Its centre piece is a unique Venetian fountain which spurts water from 19 lion heads. Tourist buses hurtle through but Spili deserves an overnight stay.

The post office and bank are on the main street. The huge building at the northern end of town is an ecclesiastic conference centre. The OTE is up a side street, north of

CRETE

the central square. The bus stop is just south of the square. Spili is on the Rethymno-Agia Galini bus route.

Places to Stay & Eat

Green Hotel *(☎ 22 225)*, opposite the police station on the main street, is a homy place practically buried under plants and vines that also fill the interior. Attractive singles/doubles with bathroom are 5000/6000 dr. Behind it is ***Heracles Rooms*** *(☎ 22 111, fax 22 411)* where sparkling, beautifully furnished rooms with bathroom cost 5000/8000 dr.

Farther along on the left ***Costos Inn*** *(☎ 22 040/750)* has well kept, ornate rooms which are something of a minimalist's nightmare with TV, radio, even bathrobes – in case you forgot to pack yours. Doubles/triples with bathroom cost 8000/9000 dr. Another good choice is ***Sunset Rooms*** *(☎ 22 3060)*, which has doubles for 5000 dr with bathroom.

Taverna Stratidakis, opposite Costos Inn, serves excellent traditional Greek dishes. The specials of the day are in pots at the back of the room.

AROUND SPILI

Most people come to the alluring little village of **Patsos** to visit the nearby **Church of Agios Antonios** in a cave above a picturesque gorge. You can drive here from Rethymno, or you can walk from Spili along a scenic 10km dirt track.

To reach the track, walk along 28 Oktovriou, passing the lion fountain on your right. Turn right onto Vermopilan and ascend to the Spili-Gerakari road. Turn right here and eventually you will come to a sign for Gerakari. Take the dirt track to the left, and at the fork bear right. At the crossroads turn right, and continue on the main track for about one hour to a T-junction on the outskirts of Patsos. Turn left to get to the cave.

West of Spili, past the village of Koxare on the Plakias road, the road enters the dramatic **Kourtaliotis Gorge**. After the village of Astomatis there is a turn-off for Moni Preveli (see the Around Plakias section later in the chapter). The road continues through Lefkogia, then passes the turn-off for Myrthios (2km) and enters Plakias.

PLAKIAS Πλακιάς

☎ 0832 • postcode 740 60 • pop 100

The south coast town of Plakias was once a tranquil retreat for adventurous backpackers – until the package tour operators discovered the fine beaches and dramatic mountain backdrop. It's still not a bad place to visit outside peak season and there are some good walks. A booklet of walks around Plakias is on sale at the minimarket by the bus stop (1200 dr).

Orientation & Information

It's easy to find your way around Plakias. One street skirts the beach and another runs parallel to it one block back. The bus stop is at the middle of the waterfront. The 30 minute path to Mythos begins just before the youth hostel.

Plakias doesn't have a bank, but Monza Tours (☎ 41 433, 31 923), near the bus stop, offers currency exchange. From June to August a mobile post office is on the waterfront.

Places to Stay

Camping Apollonia *(☎ 31 318)*, on the right of the main approach road to Plakias, has a restaurant, minimarket, bar and swimming pool. Rates are 900 dr per person and 600 dr per tent.

The excellent ***youth hostel*** is tucked away in the olive trees behind the town, 10 minutes walk from the bus stop – follow the yellow signs from the waterfront. Dorm beds are 1200 dr and hot showers are free. The hostel is open from April until the end of October.

Morpheas Rent Rooms *(☎ 31 583)*, next to the bus stop, has light, airy and attractively furnished rooms. Singles/doubles are 7000/10,000 dr with bathroom.

There are some agreeable pensions among the olive trees behind the town. ***Pension Afrodite*** *(☎ 31 266)* has spotless doubles/triples for 10,000/13,000 dr with bathroom. Head inland at Monza Tours,

CRETE

turn left at the T-junction and then take the first right and after 100m the pension is on the left. A right turn at the T-junction leads to *Studio Emilia (☎ 31 302)*, set back in the trees to the left after 100m. It charges 6000/7000 dr for large rooms with bathroom and access to a well equipped communal kitchen. Studios cost 8000 dr.

Pension Paligremnos (☎ 31 003) has a great position at the southern end of Plakias Beach. Pleasant doubles with bathroom cost 6000 dr, and studio doubles are 7000 dr.

Plakias Bay (☎ 31 315) is a C class hotel also on the beach. Sparsely outfitted singles/doubles cost 12,000/15,000 dr with breakfast.

Places to Eat

Restaurant Ariadne, on the street opposite the mobile post office, is popular and reasonably priced. One of the best waterfront tavernas is *Taverna Christos* with a romantic terrace overlooking the sea. It has a good choice of main dishes for around 1450 dr.

Nikos Souvlaki, just inland from Monza Tours, is a good souvlaki place where a monster mixed grill of *gyros*, souvlaki, sausage, hamburger and chips costs 1500 dr.

Getting There & Away

Plakias has good bus connections during June to August, but virtually none from December through February. A timetable is displayed at the bus stop.

Services from June through August include four buses daily to Rethymno (one hour, 950 dr), and one to Hora Sfakion.

From December through February there are three buses daily to Rethymno, two at weekends. It's possible to get to Agia Galini from Plakias by catching a Rethymno bus to the Koxare junction (referred to on timetables as Bale) and waiting for a bus to Agia Galini. This works best with the 11.30 am bus from Plakias, linking with the 12.45 pm service from Rethymno to Agia Galini.

Getting Around

Cars Allianthos (☎ 31 851) is a reliable car rental outlet. Odyssia (☎ 31 596), on the waterfront, has a large range of motorcycle and mountain bikes available for hire.

AROUND PLAKIAS

Myrthios Μύρθιος

This pleasant village is perched on a hillside overlooking Plakias and the surrounding coast. Apart from taking in the views, the main activity is walking, which you'll be doing a lot of unless you have your own transport.

There are a few domatia in the village, including the comfortable *Niki's Studios & Rooms (☎ 0832-31 593)*. Singles/doubles with bathroom cost 3500/6000 dr, and a studio costs 8000 dr for two.

Just above, *Restaurant Panorama* lives up to its name – it has great views. It also does good food, including vegetarian dishes and delicious desserts.

Moni Preveli Μονή Πρέβελη

The well maintained Moni Preveli, 14km east of Plakias, stands in splendid isolation high above the Libyan Sea. Like most of Crete's monasteries, it played a significant role in the islanders' rebellion against Turkish rule. It became a centre of resistance during 1866, causing the Turks to set fire to it and destroy surrounding crops. After the Battle of Crete in 1941, many Allied soldiers were sheltered here by Abbot Agathangelos before their evacuation to Egypt. In retaliation the Germans plundered the monastery. The monastery's **museum** contains a candelabra presented by grateful British soldiers after the war. It's open daily 8 am to 7 pm mid-March through May, and 8 am to 1.30 pm and 3.30 to 8 pm June to October (mornings only, in winter). Admission to the monastery and museum is 700 dr.

The road to Moni Preveli leads past the ruins of the old monastery, a fascinating place to explore. It was a hippie hang-out in the 1970s, and they left a large marijuana leaf on one wall and a few other cosmic decorations. It is now fenced off.

Lefkogia Village has ***domatia*** and ***tavernas***, and is a pleasant base from which to explore the area.

DIANA MAYFIELD

Traditional lace making, Vrises village, Crete

ROSEMARY HALL

Decorated facade, Olymbos village, Karpathos

MARK DAFFEY

Windmill silhouetted at sunset, Oia, Santorini (Cyclades)

MARK DAFFEY

Street performer on Thessaloniki's waterfront

CHRIS MELLOR

Orthodox Church bell

STELLA HELLANDER

A cutout local, Fiskardo, Kefallonia

ROSEMARY HALL

Traditional dress, Olymbos, Karpathos

From June through August there are two buses daily from Rethymno to Moni Preveli.

Beaches

Preveli Beach, at the mouth of the Kourtaliotis Gorge, is one of Crete's most photographed beaches. The River Megalopotamos cuts the beach in half on its way into the Libyan Sea. It's fringed with oleander bushes and palm trees and is popular with freelance campers.

A steep path leads down to it from the road to Moni Preveli. You can get to Preveli Beach from Plakias by boat from June through August for 2500 dr return, or by taxi boat from Agia Galini for 5000 dr return.

Between Plakias and Preveli Beach there are several secluded **coves** popular with freelance campers and nudists. Some are within walking distance of Plakias, via **Damnoni Beach**. To reach them ascend the path behind Plakias Bay Hotel. Just before the track starts to descend turn right into an olive grove. At the first T-junction turn left and at the second turn right. Where six tracks meet, take the one signposted to the beach. Walk to the end of Damnoni Beach and take the track to the right, which passes above the coves. Damnoni Beach itself is pleasant out of high season, despite being dominated by the giant Hapimag tourist complex.

AGIA GALINI Αγία Γαλήνη

☎ 0832 • postcode 740 56 • pop 600

Agia Galini (ah-**yee**-ah gah-**lee**-nih) is another picturesque little town which has gone down the tubes due to an overdose of tourism. Still, it does boast 340 days of sunshine a year, and some places remain open out of season. It's a convenient base from which to visit Phaestos and Agia Triada, and although the town beach is mediocre, there are boats to better beaches.

Orientation & Information

The bus station is at the top of Eleftheriou Venizelou, which is a continuation of the approach road. The central square, overlooking the harbour, is downhill from the bus station. You'll walk past the post office on the way and the OTE is on the square. There is no bank but there are lots of travel agencies with currency exchange.

Places to Stay

Agia Galini Camping *(☎ 91 386/239)* is next to the beach, 2.5km east of the town. It is signposted from the Iraklio-Agia Galini road. The site is well shaded and has a restaurant, snack bar and minimarket.

On the road to town ***Areti*** *(☎ 91 240)* has pleasant singles/doubles with bathroom and balcony for 6000/10,000 dr. In the centre of town ***Angelika*** *(☎ 91 304)* is over a newspaper kiosk and has rooms with bathroom and a balcony for 5000/6000 dr.

The D class ***Hotel Selena*** *(☎ 91 273)* has pleasant rooms for 10,000/12,000 dr with bathroom. It's open all year. To reach the hotel walk downhill from the bus station, turn left after the post office, take the second right and turn left at the steps.

The only accommodation on the beach is ***Stochos Rooms*** *(☎ 91 433)*, where studios for two or three people cost 12,000/13,000 dr.

Places to Eat

Restaurant Megalonissis, near the bus stop, is one of the town's cheapest restaurants if not the friendliest. ***Medousa Taverna*** in the town centre is owned by a German-Greek couple and presents a menu of specialities from both countries. The upmarket ***Acropol Taverna***, on Vasileos Ioannis, has an extensive menu of both Greek and international dishes. A meal for two with wine costs around 6000 dr.

Getting There & Away

Bus The story is the same here as at the other beach resorts – heaps of buses in summer, skeletal services in winter.

In peak season there are buses to Iraklio (2½ hours, 1500 dr, eight daily), Rethymno (1½ hours, 1300 dr, four daily), Matala (45 minutes, 600 dr, six daily) and Phaestos (40 minutes, 420 dr, six daily). You can get to Plakias by taking a Rethymno-bound bus and changing at Koxare (Bale).

Taxi Boat From June through August there are daily taxi boats from the harbour to the beaches of Agios Giorgios and Agios Pavlos. These beaches, west of Agia Galini, are difficult to get to by land, but are less crowded than, and far superior to, Agia Galini Beach.

AROUND AGIA GALINI

The outstanding **Museum of Cretan Ethnology** (☎ 0892-91 394) is in the pleasant, unspoilt village of Vori, 14km from Agia Galini, just north of the main Agia Galini-Iraklio road. It's open 9 am to 3 pm Monday to Friday, from November to March. From June through August it opens 10 am to 6 pm daily. Admission is 500 dr.

HANIA Χανιά

☎ 0821 • postcode 731 00 • pop 65,000

Hania (hahn-**yah**) is Crete's second city and former capital. The beautiful, crumbling Venetian quarter of Hania that surrounds the Old Harbour is one of Crete's best attractions. A lot of money has been spent on restoring the old buildings. Some of them have been converted into very fine accommodation while others now house chic restaurants, bars and shops.

The Hania district gets a lot of package tourists, but most of them stick to the beach developments that stretch out endlessly to the west. Even in a town this size many hotels and restaurants are closed from November to April.

Hania is a main transit point for trekkers going to the Samaria Gorge.

History

Hania is the site of the Minoan settlement of Kydonia, which was centred on the hill to the east of the harbour. Little excavation work has been done, but the finding of clay tablets with Linear B script has led archaeologists to believe that Kydonia was both a palace site and an important town.

Kydonia met the same fiery fate as most other Minoan settlements in 1450 BC, but soon re-emerged as a force. It was a flourishing city-state during Hellenistic times and continued to prosper under Roman and Byzantine rule.

The city became Venetian at the beginning of the 13th century, and the name was changed to La Canea. The Venetians spent a lot of time constructing massive fortifications to protect their city from marauding pirates and invading Turks. This did not prove very effective against the latter, who took Hania in 1645 after a siege lasting two months.

The Great Powers made Hania the island capital in 1898 and it remained so until 1971, when the administration was transferred to Iraklio.

Hania was heavily bombed during WWII, but enough of the old town survives for it to be regarded as Crete's most beautiful city.

Orientation

The town's bus station is on Kydonias, two blocks south-west of Plateia 1866, one of the city's main squares. From Plateia 1866 to the Old Harbour is a short walk north down Halidon.

The main hotel area is to the left as you face the harbour, where Akti Kountourioti leads around to the old fortress on the headland. The headland separates the Venetian port from the crowded town beach in the quarter called Nea Hora.

Zambeliou, which dissects Halidon just before the harbour, was once the town's main thoroughfare. It's a narrow, winding street, lined with craft shops, hotels and tavernas.

Information

Tourist Offices Hania's EOT (☎ 92 943, fax 92 624) is at Kriari 40, close to Plateia 1866. It is well organised and considerably more helpful than most. Opening hours are 7.30 am to 2.30 pm weekdays. The tourist police (☎ 53 333) are on Irakliou 23 and are open 7.30 am to 2.30 pm Monday to Friday. To get there, follow Apokoronou about 500m out of town when it becomes Irakliou.

Money The National Bank of Greece on the corner of Tzanakaki and Gianari and the Credit Bank at the junction of Halidon and

Skalidi have 24 hour automatic exchange machines. There are numerous places to change money outside banking hours. Most are willing to negotiate the amount of commission, so check around.

Post & Communications The central post office is at Tzanakaki 3, open 7.30 am to 8 pm Monday to Friday, and 7.30 am to 2 pm Saturday. The OTE is next door at Tzanakaki 5, open 7.30 am to 10 pm daily. Internet access is available at Vranas Studios (☎ 58 618), on Ag Deka.

Bookshops The George Chaicalis Bookshop, on Plateia Venizelou, sells English-language newspapers, books and maps.

Laundry Both Laundry Fidias, at Sarpaki 6, and the other laundry at Ag Deka 18 charge 1800 dr for a wash and dry.

Left Luggage Luggage can be stored at the bus station for 400 dr per day.

Museums

The **archaeological museum** (☎ 90 334) in Hania, at Halidon 21, is housed in the 16th century Venetian Church of San Francisco. The Turkish fountain in the grounds is a relic from the building's days as a mosque.

The museum houses a well displayed collection of finds from western Crete dating from the Neolithic to the Roman era. Exhibits include statues, pottery, coins, jewellery, three splendid floor mosaics and some impressive painted sarcophagi from the Late Minoan cemetery of Armeni. The museum is open 8 am to 4.30 pm Tuesday to Sunday. Admission is 500 dr.

The **naval museum** (☎ 44 156) has an interesting collection of model ships, naval instruments, paintings and photographs. It is open 10 am to 4 pm daily. Admission is 500 dr. The museum is housed in the fortress on the headland overlooking the Venetian port.

Hania's interesting **folklore museum** (☎ 90 816) is at Halidon 46B. It is open 9 am to 3 pm and 6 pm to 9 pm Monday to Friday. Admission is 500 dr. The new **war museum of Chania**, on Tzanakaki, is open 9 am to 1 pm Tuesday to Saturday. Admission is free.

Other Attractions

The area to the east of the Old Harbour, between Akti Tombazi and Karaoli Dimitriou, is the site of **ancient Kydonia**.

The search for Minoan remains began in the early 1960s and excavation work continues sporadically. The site can be seen at the junction of Kanevaro and Kandanoleu, and many of the finds are on display in the archaeological museum.

Kydonia has been remodelled by a succession of occupiers. After ejecting the Arabs, the Byzantines set about building their *kastelli* (castle) on the same site, on top of the old walls in some places and using the same materials. It was here, too, that the Venetians first settled. Modern Kanevaro was the Corso of their city. It was this part of town that bore the brunt of the bombing in WWII.

The massive **fortifications** built by the Venetians to protect their city remain impressive today. The best preserved section is the western wall, running from the fortezza to **Promahonas Hill**. It was part of a defensive system begun in 1538 by engineer Michele Sanmichele, who also designed Iraklio's defences.

The **lighthouse** at the entrance to the harbour is the most visible of the Venetian monuments. It looks in need of tender loving care these days, but the 30 minute walk around the sea wall to get there is worth it.

You can escape the crowds of the Venetian quarter by taking a stroll around the **Splantzia quarter** – a delightful tangle of narrow streets and little plateias.

Whether you are self-catering or not you should at least feast your eyes on Hania's magnificent covered **food market**. It makes all other food markets look like stalls at a church bazaar. Unfortunately, the central bastion of the city wall had to be demolished to make way for this fine cruciform creation, built in 1911.

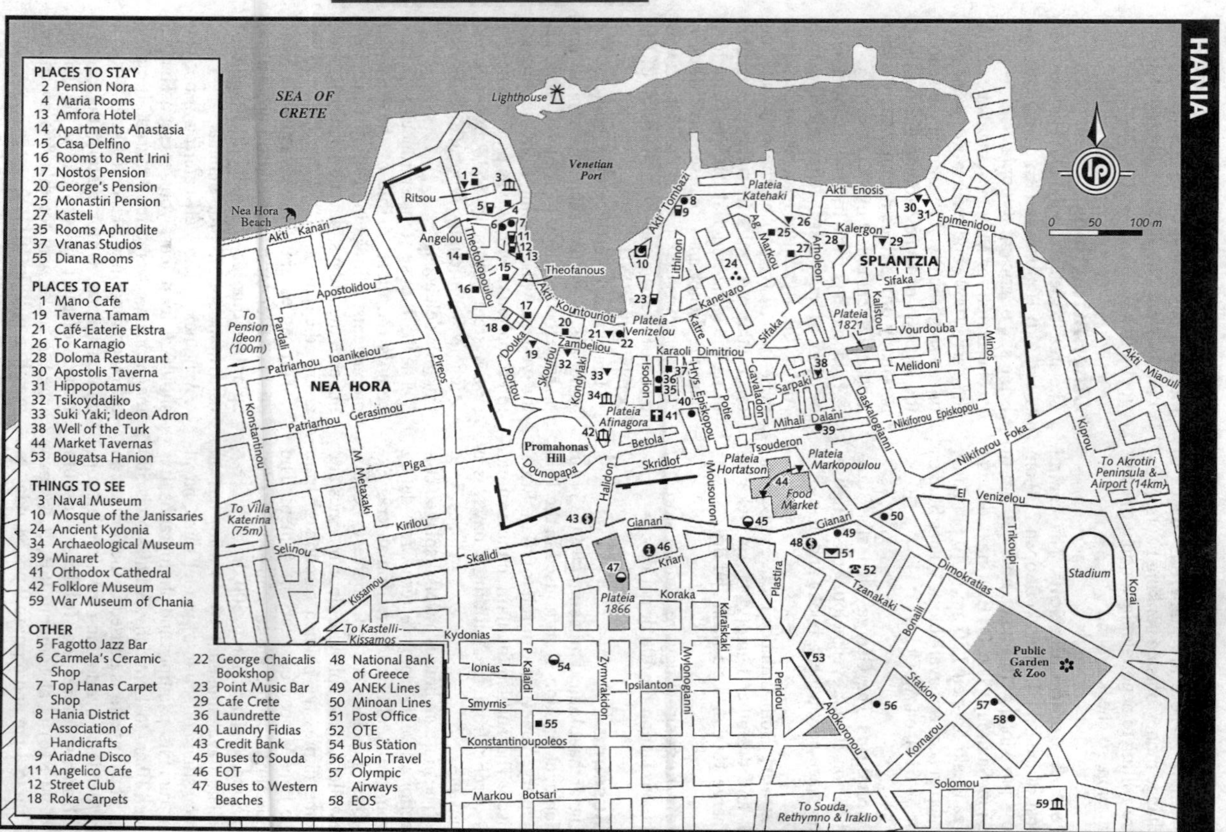
HANIA
SEA OF CRETE
Venetian Port
Lighthouse
Nea Hora Beach
NEA HORA
SPLANTZIA
Promahonas Hill
Stadium
Public Garden & Zoo
Food Market
Plateia 1821
Plateia Venizelou
Plateia Katehaki
Plateia Markopoulou
Plateia Hortatson
Plateia Afinagora
Plateia 1866
To Akrotiri Peninsula & Airport (14km)
To Souda, Rethymno & Iraklio
To Kastelli-Kissamos
To Villa Katerina (75m)
To Pension Ideon (100m)
0 50 100 m
PLACES TO STAY
2 Pension Nora
4 Maria Rooms
13 Amfora Hotel
14 Apartments Anastasia
15 Casa Delfino
16 Rooms to Rent Irini
17 Nostos Pension
20 George's Pension
25 Monastiri Pension
27 Kasteli
35 Rooms Aphrodite
37 Vranas Studios
55 Diana Rooms
PLACES TO EAT
1 Mano Cafe
19 Taverna Tamam
21 Café-Eaterie Ekstra
26 To Karnagio
28 Doloma Restaurant
30 Apostolis Taverna
31 Hippopotamus
32 Tsikoydadiko
33 Suki Yaki; Ideon Adron
38 Well of the Turk
44 Market Tavernas
53 Bougatsa Hanion
THINGS TO SEE
3 Naval Museum
10 Mosque of the Janissaries
24 Ancient Kydonia
34 Archaeological Museum
39 Minaret
41 Orthodox Cathedral
42 Folklore Museum
59 War Museum of Chania
OTHER
5 Fagotto Jazz Bar
6 Carmela's Ceramic Shop
7 Top Hanas Carpet Shop
8 Hania District Association of Handicrafts
9 Ariadne Disco
11 Angelico Cafe
12 Street Club
18 Roka Carpets
22 George Chaicalis Bookshop
23 Point Music Bar
29 Cafe Crete
36 Laundrette
40 Laundry Fidias
43 Credit Bank
45 Buses to Souda
46 EOT
47 Buses to Western Beaches
48 National Bank of Greece
49 ANEK Lines
50 Minoan Lines
51 Post Office
52 OTE
54 Bus Station
56 Alpin Travel
57 Olympic Airways
58 EOS

Activities

Alpin Travel (☎ 53 309), in the complex at Bonaili 11-19, offers many trekking programs. The owner, George Antonakakis, helps run the EOS (☎ 44 647), Tzanakaki 90, and is the guy to talk to about serious climbing in the Lefka Ori. George can provide information on Greece's mountain refuges, the E4 trail, and climbing and trekking in Crete in general. Alpin Travel is open 9 am to 2 pm (and sometimes in the evening after 7 pm) weekdays.

Trekking Plan (☎ 60 861), in Agia Marina on the main road next to Santa Marina Hotel, offers treks to the Agia Irini Gorge and climbs of Mt Gingilosamong and other destinations for about 7000 dr.

It also offers a full program of mountain bike tours at varying levels of difficulty. Prices begin at 8000 dr.

Children's Activities

If your five-year-old has lost interest in Venetian architecture before the end of the first street, head for the public garden between Tzanakaki and Dimokratias. There's plenty to occupy children here, including a playground, a small zoo with a resident krikri (the Cretan wild goat) and a children's resource centre that has a small selection of books in English.

Places to Stay – Budget

The nearest camp site is ***Hania Camping*** *(☎ 31 138)*, 3km west of town on the beach. The site is shaded and has a restaurant, bar and minimarket. Take a Kalamaki Beach bus (every 20 minutes) from the south-east corner of Plateia 1866 and ask to be let off at the camp site.

The most interesting accommodation is around the Venetian port, but bear in mind it's a noisy area with numerous music bars. If you get a room in the back you'll have a better shot at a good night's sleep but you may swelter in the summer heat without the harbour breeze.

If it's character you're after, you can't do better than ***George's Pension*** *(☎ 88 715, Zambeliou 30)*, in a 600-year-old house dotted with antique furniture. Singles/doubles cost 3500/ 6000 dr.

Rooms to Rent Irini *(☎ 93 909, Theotokopoulou 9)* has clean, simply furnished doubles with bathroom for 7000 dr.

Monastiri Pension *(☎ 54 776, Ag Markou 18)* has a great setting next to the ruins of the Santa Maria de Miracolioco monastery in the heart of the old kastelli. Double rooms are fair value at 6000 dr, and there's a communal kitchen.

Vranas Studios *(☎/fax 58 618, Ag Deka 10)* is on a lively pedestrian street and has spacious studios with polished wood floors, balconies, TV and air-conditioning for 11,000 dr, except in August when the price climbs to 17,000 dr. Equally attractive rooms without air-conditioning are 1000 dr less.

If you want to hop straight out of bed and onto an early morning bus, the best rooms in the vicinity of the bus station are at ***Diana Rooms*** *(☎ 97 888, P Kalaïdi 33)*. The light, airy and clean rooms are 5000/7000 dr with bathroom.

Apartments Anastasia *(☎ 46 582, Theotokopoulou 21)* has stylish, well equipped studios for 10,000 dr. ***Rooms Aphrodite*** *(☎ 57 602, Ag Deka 10)* has two-person apartments for 8000 dr, and double rooms with shared facilities for 5000 dr.

The Nea Hora quarter to the west of the old town has some accommodation bargains. The area lacks the charm of the old town but is considerably quieter. ***Villa Katerina*** *(☎ 95 183, 98 940, Selinou 78)* has a range of rooms starting with attractively furnished doubles for 8000 dr.

The well kept, friendly ***Pension Ideon*** *(☎ 70 132/133)* on Patriarhou Ioanikeiou charges 6000/10,000 dr for singles/doubles. Both these places are very near Nea Hora Beach.

Farther out of town, at Kalamaki Beach, ***Akasti Hotel*** *(☎ 31 352)* offers roomy singles/doubles across the street from a small cove for 5000/8000 dr except in August when prices increase 50%. The Kalamaki bus will let you off in front of the hotel.

Places to Stay – Mid-Range

Most places in this category are renovated Venetian houses, and there are some very stylish ones about. One of the best is ***Nostos Pension*** *(☎ 94 740, Zambeliou 42-46)*, a mixture of Venetian style and modern fixtures. The 600-year-old building has been modelled into some very stylish split-level rooms/units, all with kitchen and bathroom. Rates for singles/doubles are 12,000/ 18,500 dr.

Pension Nora *(☎/fax 72 265, Theotokopoulou 60)* has large rooms attractively outfitted with Cretan rugs, iron lamps and wooden furniture. The composer Mikis Theodorikas reputedly lodged in one of them when he was a soldier. Rooms are 6500/10,000 dr with bathroom.

At ***Kasteli*** *(☎ 57 057, fax 45 314, Kanevaro 39)*, immaculate rooms with high ceilings and white walls cost 8000/9000 dr, and very comfortable renovated apartments cost from 16,000 dr to 20,000 dr depending on size.

Places to Stay – Top End

In the A class category is ***Amfora Hotel*** *(☎/fax 93 224/226, Parados Theotokopolou 2)*, an immaculately restored mansion with rooms around a courtyard. Rooms are 16,000/20,000 dr. Although beautifully furnished, front rooms can be noisy in the summer and there's no air-conditioning, only small fans.

Nearby is the old city's smartest accommodation, ***Casa Delfino*** *(☎ 93 098, fax 96 500, Theofanous 7)*, the modernised former mansion of a wealthy merchant. The courtyard at the entrance features patterned cobblestones and the elegant rooms combine traditional furnishings with modern features such as air-conditioning. Doubles are 35,000 dr and a huge palatial split-level apartment, which sleeps up to four people, costs 66,000 dr including breakfast.

Places to Eat – Budget

The two ***restaurants*** in the food market are good places to seek out traditional food. Their prices are almost identical. You can get a solid chunk of swordfish with chips for 1200 dr. More adventurous eaters can tuck into a bowl of garlic-laden snail and potato casserole for 1100 dr.

You'll find very similar fare at ***Doloma Restaurant*** *(Kalergon 8)*. The place is a great favourite with students from the nearby Polytehnio.

For a treat try the excellent *bougatsa tyri* (filo pastry filled with local *myzithra* cheese) at ***Bougatsa Hanion*** *(Apokoronou 37)*. A slice costs 500 dr and comes sprinkled with a little sugar. ***Mano Cafe***, on Theotokopoulou, is a convenient place for juice, breakfast, or a light snack.

Places to Eat – Mid-Range

The port is the place to go for seafood. The prices are not cheap especially considering most of the seafood is frozen, but the setting is great. A favourite with locals is ***Apostolis Taverna*** on Akti Enosis, where swordfish is 1800 dr. Next door, ***Hippopotamus*** provides a change of pace with a menu of Mexican dishes.

There are some chic places in the streets behind the port. An old Turkish *hammam* has been converted into the ***Taverna Tamam*** *(Zambeliou 51)*, where you'll find tasty soups for about 800 dr and a good range of well prepared main dishes from 1700 dr. ***Cafe-Eaterie Ekstra*** *(Zambeliou 8)* offers a choice of Greek and international dishes. There are set menus for 2300 dr and many vegetarian dishes.

Tsikoydadiko *(Zambeliou 31)* offers a good mixed plate of mezedes for 2000 dr in a splendid old plant-filled courtyard. ***Well of the Turk*** *(Sarpaki 1)* is in the heart of the old Turkish residential district of Splantzia and has a wide range of Middle Eastern dishes, as well as occasional live music. ***Suki Yaki*** *(Halidon 26)*, through the archway, is a Chinese restaurant run by a Thai family. The result is a large Chinese menu supported by a small selection of Thai favourites.

The best place in Hania for Cretan specialities is ***To Karnagio*** *(Katehaki 8)*. Its specialties are outstanding, especially the zucchini-cheese pies known as *bourekia*.

Entertainment

***Cafe Crete** (Kalergon 22)* is the best place in Hania to hear live Cretan music. It's a rough-and-ready joint with cheap mezedes and bulk wine, plus a lot of locals who like to reach for the instruments that line the walls once they've had a couple of drinks.

Ideon Adron** (Halidon 26)*, next to Suki Yaki, promotes a more sophisticated atmosphere with discreet music and garden seating. ***Fagotto Jazz Bar** (Angelou 16)* has photographs of jazz greats lining the walls and an excellent selection of CDs. ***Point Music Bar on Plateia Venizelou has great sea views from its 1st floor vantage point.

Angelico Cafe, on the waterfront, plays rock music at a volume that renders conversation possible for lip readers only. For soul and Latin sounds try ***Street Club*** nearby. Angelico Cafe and Street Club charge very similar prices: beer is 800 dr, spirits are 1200 dr and cocktails start at 1300 dr. ***Ariadne Disco***, on Akti Tombazi, is the most central disco.

Shopping

Good quality handmade leather goods are available from shoemakers on Skridlof, off Halidon, where shoes cost from 8500 dr. The old town has many craft shops. Top Hanas carpet shop, Angelou 3, specialises in Cretan kilims that were traditional dowry gifts; prices start at 30,000 dr. Carmela's Ceramic Shop nearby sells beautiful jewellery and ceramics handcrafted by young Cretans. At Roka Carpets, Zambeliou 61, you can watch Mihalis weave his wondrous rugs using methods that have remained essentially unchanged since Minoan times. Prices begin at 8000 dr for a small rug.

The Hania District Association of Handicrafts showroom, on Akti Tombazi, has ceramics, jewellery and embroidery for sale.

Getting There & Away

Air Olympic Airways has flights to Athens (19,900 dr, four daily) and Thessaloniki (29,900 dr, two weekly). The Olympic Airways office (☎ 57 701) is at Tzanakaki 88. Aegean Airlines, Air Greece, Air Manos and Cronus Airlines all offer cheaper competition on the Athens route, while Aegean also offers a daily flight to Thessaloniki (28,100 dr). Aegean's office (☎ 63 366) is at the airport.

The airport is on the Akrotiri Peninsula, 14km from Hania.

Bus Buses depart from the bus station for the following destinations:

Destination	Duration	Price	Frequency
Hora Sfakion	2 hours	1400 dr	3 daily
Iraklio	2½ hours	2900 dr	half-hourly
Kastelli-Kissamos	1 hour	900 dr	15 daily
Lakki	1 hour	600 dr	4 daily
Moni Agias Triadas	30 mins	400 dr	3 daily
Omalos (for Samaria Gorge)	1 hour	1250 dr	4 daily
Paleohora	2 hours	1450 dr	3 daily
Rethymno	1 hour	1500 dr	half-hourly
Sougia	2 hours	1400 dr	1 daily
Stavros	30 mins	300 dr	6 daily

Ferry Ferries for Hania dock at Souda, about 7km east of town. There is at least one ferry daily for the 10 hour trip to and from Piraeus. ANEK Lines has a boat leaving for Piraeus every night at 8.30 pm which costs 5900 dr for deck class. The ANEK Lines office (☎ 27 500) is opposite the food market. Souda's port police can be contacted on ☎ 89 240.

Getting Around

There is no airport bus. A taxi to the airport costs about 3000 dr.

Local buses (blue) for the port of Souda leave from outside the food market. Buses for the western beaches leave from Plateia 1866.

Car rental outlets include Avis (☎ 50 510), Tzanakaki 58; Budget (☎ 92 778), Karïskaki 39; and Europrent (☎ 40 810, 27 810), Halidon 87. Most motorcycle rental outlets are on Halidon.

The Good Oil

DIANA MAYFIELD

The olive has been part of life in the eastern Mediterranean since the beginnings of civilisation. Olive cultivation can be traced back about 6000 years. It was the farmers of the Levant (modern Syria and Lebanon) who first spotted the potential of the wild European olive *(Olea europaea)* – a sparse, thorny tree that was common in the region. These farmers began the process of selection that led to the more compact, thornless, oil-rich varieties that now dominate the Mediterranean.

Whereas most westerners think of olive oil as being just a cooking oil, to the people of the ancient Mediterranean civilisations it was very much more. It was almost inseparable from civilised life itself. As well as being an important foodstuff, it was burned in lamps to provide light, it could be used as a lubricant and it was blended with essences to produce fragrant oils.

The Minoans were among the first to grow wealthy on the olive, and western Crete remains an important olive-growing area, specialising in high-quality salad oils. The region's show piece, Kolymvari cooperative, markets its extra-virgin oil in both the USA (*Athena* brand) and Britain (*Kydonia* brand).

Locals will tell you that the finest oil is produced from trees grown on the rocky soils of the Akrotiri Peninsula, west of Hania. The oil that is prized above all others, however, is *agourelaio*, meaning unripe, which is pressed from green olives.

Few trees outlive the olive. Some of the fantastically gnarled and twisted olive trees that dot the countryside of western Crete are more than 1000 years old. The tree known as *dekaoktoura*, in the mountain village of Anisaraki – near Kandanos on the road from Hania to Paleohora – is claimed to be more than 1500 years old.

Many of these older trees are being cut down to make way for improved varieties. The wood is burnt in potters' kilns and provides woodturners with the raw material to produce the ultimate salad bowl for connoisseurs. The dense yellow-brown timber has a beautiful swirling grain.

AKROTIRI PENINSULA

Χερσόνησος Ακρωτήρι

The Akrotiri (ahk-ro-**tee**-rih) Peninsula, to the east of Hania, has a few places of fairly minor interest, as well as being the site of Hania's airport, port and a military base. There is an immaculate **military cemetery** at Souda, where about 1500 British, Australian and New Zealand soldiers who lost their lives in the Battle of Crete are buried. The buses to Souda port from outside the Hania food market can drop you at the cemetery.

If you haven't yet had your fill of Cretan monasteries, there are three on the Akrotiri Peninsula. The impressive 17th century **Moni Agias Triadas** was founded by the Venetian monks Jeremiah and Laurentio Giancarolo. The brothers were converts to the Orthodox faith. The monastery is open 6 am to 2 pm and from 5 to 7 pm daily. Admission is 300 dr.

The 16th century **Moni Gourvernetou** (Our Lady of the Angels) is 4km north of Moni Agias Triada. The church inside the monastery has an ornate sculptured Venetian facade. It's open 8 am to 12.30 pm and 4.30 to 7.30 pm daily. Both Moni Agias Triadas and Moni Gourvernetou are still in use.

From Moni Gourvernetou, it's a 15 minute walk on the path leading down to the coast to the ruins of **Moni Katholiko**. The monastery is dedicated to St John the Hermit who lived in the cave behind the ruins. It takes another 30 minutes to reach the sea.

There are three buses daily (except Sunday) to Moni Agias Triadas from Hania bus station (400 dr).

HANIA TO XYLOSKALO

The road from Hania to the beginning of the Samaria Gorge is one of the most spectacular routes on Crete. It heads through orange groves to the village of **Fournes** where a left fork leads to **Meskla**. The main road continues to the village of **Lakki**, 24km from Hania. This unspoilt village in the Lefka Ori Mountains affords stunning views wherever you look. The village was a centre of resistance during the uprising against the Turks, and during WWII.

In Lakki ***Kri-Kri Restaurant & Rooms*** *(☎ 0821-67 316)* has comfortable singles/doubles for 3000/5000 dr. The restaurant serves good-value meals.

From Lakki, the road continues to the Omalos Plateau and **Xyloskalo**, the start of the Samaria Gorge. ***Kallergi Refuge*** *(☎ 0821-74 560)*, a one hour walk along a signposted track from the Omalos-Xyloskalo road, is a good base for trekking and climbing in the surrounding mountains. Make a reservation either through the EOS in Hania (☎ 0821-44 647), or by telephoning the refuge.

SAMARIA GORGE

Φαράγγι της Σαμαριάς

It's a wonder the stones and rocks underfoot haven't worn away completely, given the number of people who tramp through the Samaria (sah-mah-rih-**ah**) Gorge. Despite the crowds, a trek through this stupendous gorge is still an experience to remember.

At 18km, the gorge is supposedly the longest in Europe. It begins just below the Omalos Plateau, carved out by the river that flows between the Lefka Ori and Mt Volikas. Its width varies from 150m to 3m and its vertical walls reach 500m at their highest points. The gorge has an incredible number of wildflowers, which are at their best in April and May.

It is also home to a large number of endangered species. They include the Cretan wild goat, the kri-kri, which survives in the wild only here and on the islet of Kri-Kri, off the coast of Agios Nikolaos. The gorge was made a national park in 1962 to save the kri-kri from extinction. You are unlikely to see too many of these shy animals, which show a marked aversion to trekkers.

An early start helps to avoid the worst of the crowds, but during July and August even the early bus from Hania to the top of the gorge can be packed.

The trek from Xyloskalo, the name of the steep wooden staircase that gives access to the gorge, to Agia Roumeli takes around six hours. Early in the season it's sometimes necessary to wade through the stream. Later, as the flow drops, it's possible to use rocks as stepping stones.

The gorge is wide and open for the first 6km, until you reach the abandoned village of Samaria. The inhabitants were relocated when the gorge became a national park. Just south of the village is a small church dedicated to Saint Maria of Egypt, after whom the gorge is named.

The gorge then narrows and becomes more dramatic until, at the 12km mark, the walls are only 3.5m apart – the famous **Iron Gates**.

The gorge ends just north of the almost abandoned village of Old Agia Roumeli. From here the path continues to the small, messy and crowded resort of Agia Roumeli, with a much-appreciated pebble beach and sparkling sea.

The Samaria gorge is open most years from May until mid-October. The opening date depends on the amount of water in the gorge. Visiting hours are 6 am to 4 pm daily, and there's an admission fee of 1200 dr. Spending the night in the gorge is forbidden.

What to Bring

Sensible footwear is essential for walking on the uneven ground covered by sharp stones. Trainers will do but hiking shoes are better. You'll also need a hat and sunscreen. There's no need to take water; while it's inadvisable to drink water from the main stream, there are plenty of springs along the way spurting delicious cool water straight from the rock. There is nowhere to buy food, so bring something to snack on.

Getting There & Away

There are excursions to the Samaria Gorge from every sizable town and resort on Crete. Most travel agents have two excursions: 'Samaria Gorge Long Way' and 'Samaria Gorge Easy Way'. The first comprises the regular trek from the Omalos Plateau to Agia Roumeli; the second starts at Agia Roumeli and takes you as far as the Iron Gates.

Obviously it's cheaper to trek the Samaria Gorge under your own steam, and Hania is the most convenient base. There are buses to Xyloskalo (one hour, 1250 dr) at 6.15, 7.30 and 8.30 am and 1.45 pm. If you intend to stay on the south coast ask for a one way ticket (750 dr), otherwise you'll automatically be sold a return. There's also a direct bus to Xyloskalo from Paleohora (1½ hours, 1400 dr) at 6 am.

AGIA ROUMELI TO HORA SFAKION

Agia Roumeli (Αγία Ρούμελη) has little going for it, but if you have just trekked through the Samaria Gorge and are too exhausted to face a further journey, there is one hotel here, the B class ***Hotel Agia Roumeli*** *(☎ 0825-91 232)*, where singles/doubles are 6000/8000 dr with bathroom. There are also a number of ***domatia*** where you'll pay around 6000 dr for a double.

The small but rapidly expanding fishing village of **Loutro** (Λουτρό) lies between Agia Roumeli and Hora Sfakion. Loutro doesn't have a beach but there are rocks from which you can swim. There is one pension, the comfortable ***Porto Loutro*** *(☎ 0825-91 433)*, which has doubles with bathroom for 9000 dr. There are plenty of ***domatia*** and ***tavernas***.

An extremely steep path leads up from Loutro to the village of **Anopolis**, where there are also ***domatia***. Alternatively, you can save yourself the walk by taking the Hania-Skaloti bus which runs via Anopolis. The bus leaves Hania at 2 pm and returns the following morning, calling in at Anopolis at 7 am.

From Loutro it's a moderate 2½ hour walk along a coastal path to Hora Sfakion. On the way you will pass the celebrated **Sweet Water Beach**, named after freshwater springs which seep from the rocks. Freelance campers spend months at a time here. Even if you don't feel inclined to join them, you won't be able to resist a swim in the translucent sea.

There are three boats daily from Agia Roumeli to Hora Sfakion (one hour, 1500 dr) via Loutro (30 minutes, 850 dr). It connects with the bus back to Hania, leaving you in Hora Sfakion just long enough to spend a few drachma. There's also a boat from Agia Roumeli to Paleohora (2100 dr) at 4.45 pm, calling at Sougia (950 dr).

HORA SFAKION Χώρα Σφακίων

☎ 0825 • postcode 730 01 • pop 340

Hora Sfakion (**ho**-rah sfah-**kee**-on) is a small coastal port where hordes of walkers from the Samaria Gorge spill off the boat and onto the bus. As such, in high season it can seem like Piccadilly Circus at rush hour. Most people pause only long enough to catch the next bus out.

Hora Sfakion played a prominent role during WWII when thousands of Allied troops were evacuated by sea from the town after the Battle of Crete.

Orientation & Information

The ferry quay is at the western side of the harbour. Buses leave from the square on the eastern side. The post office and OTE are on the square, and the police station overlooks it. There is no tourist office or tourist police.

Places to Stay & Eat

If you do end up staying, the options aren't so exciting. The D class ***Hotel Stavros*** *(☎ 91 220)*, up the steps at the western end of the port, has clean singles/doubles with bathroom for 5000/5500 dr. Don't expect a warm welcome though. ***Hotel Samaria*** *(☎ 91 261)*, on the waterfront, has rooms with bathroom for 4000/6000 dr. It also has a good restaurant which turns out a tasty plate of seafood pilaf for 1400 dr.

Hotel Xenia *(☎ 91 202/206)*, close to the ferry dock, has the best rooms around. Hora Sfakion is one of the few places where this government-run chain has come up with the goods. It has spacious rooms overlooking the sea from 9000/12,000 dr including breakfast.

Getting There & Away

Bus There are four buses daily from Hora Sfakion to Hania (two hours, 1400 dr). From June through August there are two daily buses to Plakias (1¼ hours, 1150 dr) via Frangokastello, leaving at 11.30 am and 5.30 pm, and one to Rethymno (two hours, 1700 dr) at 7.30 pm.

Boat From June through August there are daily boats from Hora Sfakion to Paleohora (three hours, 3500 dr) via Loutro, Agia Roumeli and Sougia. The boat leaves at 12.30 pm. There are also three or four boats daily to Agia Roumeli (one hour, 1500 dr) via Loutro (30 minutes, 500 dr).

From June there are boats to Gavdos Island on Saturday and Sunday leaving at 9.30 am and returning at 4 pm (2650 dr).

AROUND HORA SFAKION

The road from Vrises to Hora Sfakion cuts through the heart of the Sfakia region in the eastern Lefka Ori. The inhabitants of this region have long had a reputation for fearlessness and independence – characteristics they retain to this day. Cretans are regarded by other Greeks as being immensely proud and there is none more so than the Sfakiot.

One of Crete's most celebrated heroes, Ioannis Daskalogiannis, was from Sfakia. In 1770, Daskalogiannis led the first Cretan insurrection against Ottoman rule. When help promised by Russia failed to materialise, he gave himself up to the Turks to save his followers. As punishment the Turks skinned him alive in Iraklio. Witnesses related that Daskalogiannis suffered this excruciating death in dignified silence.

The Turks never succeeded in controlling the Sfakiots, and this rugged mountainous region was the scene of fierce fighting. The story of their resistance lives on in the form of folk tales and *rizitika* (local folk songs).

The village of **Imbros**, 23km from Vrises, is at the head of the beautiful 10km Imbros Gorge, which is far less visited than the Samaria Gorge. To get there, take any bus bound for Hora Sfakion from the north coast and get off at Imbros. Walk out of the village towards Hora Sfakion and a path to the left leads down to the gorge. The gorge path ends at the village of **Komitades**, from where it is an easy walk by road to Hora Sfakion. You can of course do the trek in reverse, beginning at Komitades. The Happy Walker organises treks through this gorge (see Organised Tours in the Rethymno section).

Frangokastello Φραγγοκάστελλο

Frangokastello is a magnificent fortress on the coast 15km east of Hora Sfakion. It was built by the Venetians in 1371 as a defence against pirates and rebel Sfakiots, who resented the Venetian occupation as much as they did the Turkish.

It was here in 1770 that Ioannis Daskalogiannis surrendered to the Turks. On 17 May 1828 many Cretan rebels, led by Hadzi Mihalis Dalanis, were killed here by the Turks. Legend has it that at dawn each anniversary the ghosts of Hadzi Mihalis Dalanis and his followers can be seen riding along the beach.

The castle overlooks a gently sloping, sandy beach. Domatia and tavernas are springing up rapidly here, but it's still relatively unspoilt.

Buses between Hora Sfakion and Plakias go via Frangokastello.

SOUGIA Σούγια

☎ 0823 • postcode 730 01 • pop 50

It's surprising that Sougia (**soo**-yiah) hasn't yet been commandeered by the package tour crowd. With a wide curve of sand and pebble beach and a shady, tree-lined coastal road, Sougia's tranquillity has been preserved only because it lies at the foot of a narrow, twisting road that would deter most tour buses.

If you arrive by boat, walk about 150m along the coast to the town centre. If you arrive by bus, the bus will drop you on the coastal road in front of Santa Irene hotel. The only other road intersects the coastal road by Santa Irene Hotel and runs north to the Agia Irini Gorge and Hania.

Sougia doesn't have a post office, OTE or bank, but you can change money at several places, including Polifimos Travel (☎ 51 022) and Roxana's Office (☎ 51 362). Both are just off the coastal road on the road to Hania.

Places to Stay

There's no camp site, but the eastern end of the long pebbled beach is popular with freelance campers.

It seems almost every building in Sougia is a domatia or pension. ***Rooms Maria*** *(☎ 51 337)* has clean, white singles/doubles with bathroom for 5000/7000 dr in August, 1000 dr less during the rest of high season. Next door is the equally attractive ***Rooms Ririka*** *(☎ 51 167)* also with rooms overlooking the sea for about the same price. The smartest accommodation is ***Santa Irene Hotel*** *(☎ 51 342, fax 51 181)*, which has studios for 8000/12,000 dr. Air-conditioning costs 2000 dr extra.

Inland, on the road to Hania, ***Aretouca Rooms to Rent*** *(☎ 51 178)* has lovely rooms with wood-panelled ceilings and balconies for 7000/8000 dr. Next door, ***Pension Galini*** *(☎/fax 51 488)* has beautiful rooms with bathroom for 5000/6000/7000 dr and studios for 8000 dr.

Places to Eat

Restaurants line the waterfront and there are more on the main street. ***Kyma***, on the seafront as you enter town, has a good selection of ready-made food. ***Taverna Rebetiko***, on the road to Hania, has an extensive menu including such Cretan dishes as *boureki* and stuffed zucchini flowers.

Getting There & Away

There's a daily bus from Hania to Sougia (2½ hours, 1400 dr) at 1.30 pm. Buses from Sougia to Hania leave at 7 am. Sougia is on the Paleohora-Hora Sfakion boat route.

AROUND SOUGIA

Sougia is at the mouth of the pretty **Agia Irini Gorge** which may not be as fashionable as the Samaria Gorge but is less crowded and less gruelling to walk. Paleohora travel agents offer guided walks through the gorge for 4500 dr. It's easy enough to organise independently – just catch the Omalos bus from Paleohora or the Hania bus from Sougia, and get off at Agia Irini. There are a couple of beautiful **Byzantine churches** tucked away in the olive groves at the start of the gorge.

The ruins of ancient **Lissos**, once a sanctuary to Asclepius, are 1½ hours away on the coastal path to Paleohora. The path heads inland at the western end of the beach.

PALEOHORA Παλαιοχώρα

☎ 0823 • postcode 730 01 • pop 2150

Paleohora was discovered by hippies back in the 1960s and from then on its days as a tranquil fishing village were numbered. However, the resort operators have not gone way over the top – yet. The place retains a certain laid-back feel. It is also the only beach resort on Crete which does not go into total hibernation in winter.

The little town is set on a narrow peninsula with a long, curving sandy beach exposed to the wind on one side and a sheltered pebbly beach on the other. On summer evenings the main street is closed to traffic and the tavernas move onto the road.

It's worth clambering up the ruins of the 13th century **Venetian castle** for the splendid view of the sea and mountains. The most picturesque part of Paleohora is the narrow streets huddled around the castle.

From Paleohora, a six hour walk along a scenic coastal path leads to Sougia, passing the ancient site of Lissos.

Orientation & Information

Paleohora's main street, El Venizelou, runs north to south, with several streets leading off east to the pebble beach. Boats leave from the old harbour at the southern end of this beach. At the southern end of El Venizelou, a west turn onto Kontekaki leads to the tamarisk-shaded sandy beach.

The municipal tourist office (☎ 41 507) is in the town hall on El Venizelou. It is open 10 am to 1 pm and 6 to 9 pm Wednesday to Monday between May and October.

The post office is on the road that skirts the sandy beach. On El Venizelou are the National Bank of Greece, with ATM, the OTE (on the west side, just north of Kontekaki) and PC Corner (☎ 42 422), where Internet access is available.

Organised Tours

Travel agents around town offer excursions to ancient Lissos (6500 dr) and dolphin-watching trips (3500 dr).

Places to Stay

***Camping Paleohora** (☎ 41 225/120)* is 1.5km north-east of town, near the pebble beach. The camp site has a taverna but no minimarket.

***Homestay Anonymous** (☎ 41 509, 42 098)* is a great place for backpackers, with clean, simply furnished rooms set around a small, beautiful garden. Singles/ doubles/ triples cost 3500/4500/5000 dr, and there is a communal kitchen. The owner, Manolis, is an amiable young guy who speaks good English and is full of useful information for travellers. To get there, walk south along El Venizelou from the bus stop and turn right at the town hall. Follow the road as it veers right, and the rooms are on the left.

***Oriental Bay Rooms** (☎ 41 076)* occupies the large modern building at the northern end of the pebble beach. The owner, Thalia, is a very cheerful woman and the immaculate singles/doubles with bathroom and ceiling fans are good value at 5000/7000 dr. There's also a shaded terrace restaurant overlooking the sea, that serves decent meals.

***Dream Rooms** (☎ 41 112)*, nearer the old quarter, is aptly named for the large, excellently maintained rooms with balconies overlooking the sea. Rooms with bathroom cost 6000/8000 dr. ***Spamandos Rooms** (☎ 41 197)*, in the old quarter, has spotless, nicely furnished doubles/triples with bathroom for 7000/8000 dr. To get there, walk south along Einai Yrela, take the first left after Pelican Taverna and then the first right. After 60m turn left and the rooms are on the right.

Nearby ***Kostas Rooms** (☎/fax 41 248)* offers simple, attractive rooms with ceiling fans, bathroom, fridge and sea views for 3500/5000 dr.

Out of season, try looking for a deal at one of the places offering self-catering apartments along the sandy beach on the other side of town. ***Poseidon Pension***

CRETE

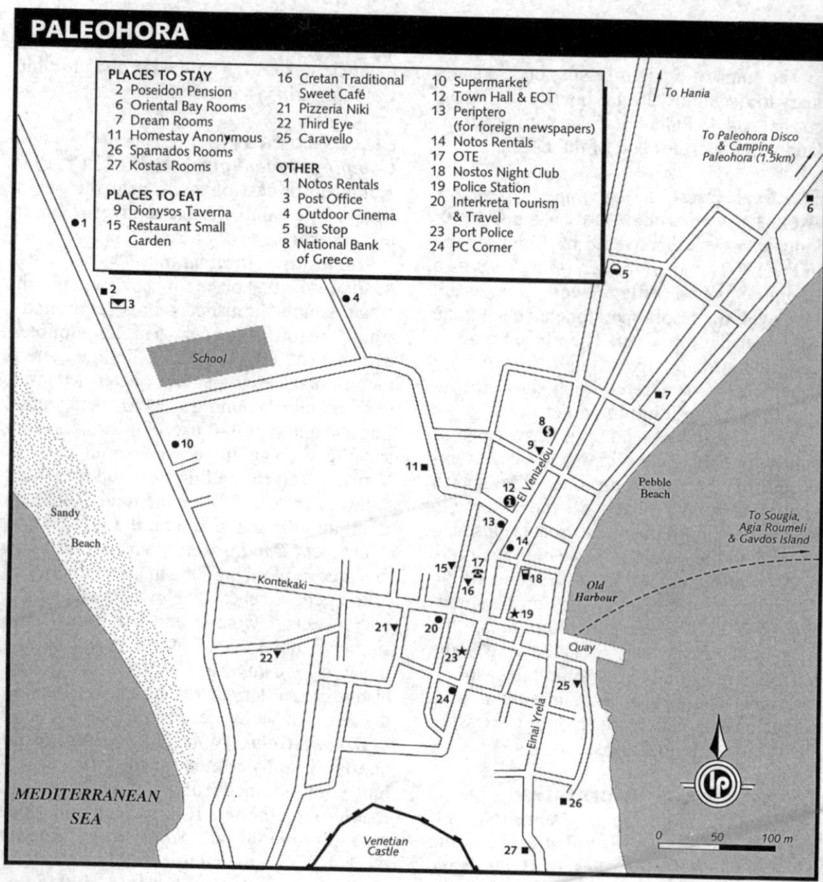

(☎ 41 374/115) has cosy rooms for 5000/6000 dr with bathroom, and studios for 7000/9000 dr.

Places to Eat

You'll find some good eateries in Paleohora. ***Restaurant Small Garden***, behind the OTE, is a fine little taverna and does a good job of old favourites like fried aubergine (800 dr).

The very popular ***Dionysos Taverna***, on El Venizelou, is a bit more expensive but also serves tasty food. ***Pizzeria Niki***, just off Kontekaki, serves superior pizzas cooked in a wood-fired oven.

Vegetarians have a treat in store at the ***Third Eye***, near the sandy beach. The menu includes curries and a range of Asian dishes, all at very reasonable prices. You can eat well and enjoy a beer for less than 2000 dr. Unfortunately the place is closed from December through February.

Caravello Restaurant has a prime position overlooking the old harbour and offers a full array of fresh seafood.

Wherever you dine, round your meal off with a delicious dessert from the ***Cretan Traditional Sweet Cafe*** almost opposite Restaurant Small Garden.

Entertainment

Most visitors to Paleohora spend at least one evening at the well signposted ***outdoor cinema***. Another option for a night out is the ***Paleohora Disco***, next to Camping Paleohora north-east of town. If you've seen the movie and don't fancy the trek to the disco, try ***Nostos Night Club*** right in town, between El Venizelou and the old harbour.

Getting There & Away

Bus From June through August there are three buses daily to Hania (two hours, 1450 dr), going via Omalos (1½ hours, 1250 dr) to cash in on the Samaria Gorge trade. From December through February there are two, direct to Hania.

Ferry From June through August there are daily ferries from Paleohora to Hora Sfakion (three hours, 3700 dr) via Sougia (one hour, 950 dr), Agia Roumeli (two hours, 2100 dr) and Loutro (2½ hours, 2850 dr). The ferry leaves Paleohora at 9.30 am, and returns from Hora Sfakion at 12.30 pm. There's also a boat three times weekly from June through August to Gavdos (four hours, 3000 dr) that leaves Paleohora at 8.30 am.

Tickets for all of these boats can be bought at Interkreta Tourism & Travel (☎ 41 393/888, fax 41 050), Kontekaki 4.

Excursion Boat The excursion boat M/B *Elafonisos* gets cranked into action in mid-April ferrying people to the west coast beach of Elafonisi (one hour, 1300 dr). The service builds up from three times weekly to daily in June through September.

Getting Around

If you'd like to hire a car, motorcycle or bicycle, they are available at Notos Rentals (☎ 42 110), on El Venizelou and by the sandy beach.

AROUND PALEOHORA

Gavdos Island Νήσος Γαύδος

Gavdos Island (population 50), in the Libyan Sea, 65km from Paleohora, is the most southerly place in Europe. It is an excellent choice for those craving isolation and peace. The island has three small villages and pleasant beaches. There is a post office, OTE, police officer and doctor. The best source of information about the island is Interkreta Tourism & Travel in Paleohora.

There are no hotels but several of the locals have ***domatia***, and there are ***tavernas***. There is no official camp site but camping freelance is tolerated. Fishermen from Gavdos can take tourists to the remote, uninhabited island of Gavdopoula.

Getting There & Away A small post boat operates between Paleohora and Gavdos on Monday and Thursday all year, weather permitting. It leaves Paleohora at 8.30 am and takes about four hours (3000 dr). From June through August there's also a Tuesday boat. The boats turn around in Gavdos almost immediately.

There are also two boats weekly from Hora Sfakion to Gavdos (2650 dr) and a weekly boat from Sougia (2300 dr).

Elafonisi Ελαφονήσι

As one of the loveliest sand beaches in Crete it's easy to understand why people enthuse so much about Elafonisi, at the southern extremity of Crete's west coast. The beach is long and wide and is separated from Elafonisi Islet by about 50m of knee-deep water on its northern side. The islet is marked by low dunes and a string of semisecluded coves that attract a sprinkling of naturists.

The beaches are popular with day-trippers but there are two small hotels and a pension on a bluff overlooking the main beach for those who want to luxuriate in the late afternoon quiet that descends on the area: ***Rooms Elafonissi*** *(☎ 0822-61 274)*, ***Rooms Elafonissos*** *(☎ 0822-61 294)* or ***Inahorion*** *(☎ 0822-61 111)*. All three have singles/doubles for 5000/7000 dr with bathroom.

Getting There & Away There are two boats daily from Paleohora to Elafonisi (one hour, 1140 dr) from June through August, as well as daily buses from Hania (2½ hours, 1500 dr) and Kastelli-Kissamos (1½ hours, 900 dr). The buses leave Hania at 7.30 am and Kastelli-Kissamos at 8.30 am, and both depart from Elafonisi at 4 pm. The final section of road from Hrysoskalitissas to the beach is very rugged.

Moni Hrysoskalitissas

Μονή Χρυσοσκαλίτισσας

Moni Hrysoskalitissas (mo-**nee** hris-o-skah-**lee**-tis-as), 5km north of Elafonisi, is inhabited by two nuns. It's a beautiful monastery perched on a rock high above the sea. Hrysoskalitissas means 'golden staircase', from a legend claiming that one of the 90 steps leading from the sea up to the monastery is made of gold. There are ***tavernas*** and ***domatia*** in the vicinity. Buses to Elafonisi drop passengers here.

CRETE

KASTELLI-KISSAMOS

Καστέλλι-Κίσσαμος

☎ 0822 • postcode 734 00 • pop 3000

If you find yourself in the north coast town of Kastelli-Kissamos, you've probably arrived by ferry from the Peloponnese or Kythira. The most remarkable part of Kastelli-Kissamos is its unremarkableness. It's simply a quiet town of mostly elderly residents that neither expects nor attracts much tourism.

In antiquity, its name was Kissamos; it was the main town of the province of the same name. When the Venetians came along and built a castle here, the place became known as Kastelli. The name persisted until 1966 when authorities decided that too many people were confusing this Kastelli with Crete's other Kastelli, 40km south-east of Iraklio. The official name reverted to Kissamos, and that's what appears on bus and shipping schedules. Local people still prefer Kastelli, and many books and maps agree with them. An alternative that is emerging is to combine the two into Kastelli-Kissamos, which leaves no room for misunderstanding.

Orientation & Information

The port is 3km west of town. From June through August a bus meets the boats; otherwise a taxi costs 800 dr. The bus station is just below the square, Plateia Kissamos, and the main street, Skalidi, runs east from Plateia Kissamos.

Kastelli-Kissamos has no tourist office. The post office is on the main road. Signs from the bus station direct you through an alley on the right of Skalidi which takes you to the post office. Turn right at the post office and you'll come to the National Bank of Greece which is on the central square. Turn left at the post office and the OTE office is opposite you about 50m along the main road. There is also a string of pensions and tavernas along the sea below the bus station.

Places to Stay

There are three camp sites to choose from. ***Camping Kissamos*** *(☎ 23 444/322)*, close to the city centre, is convenient for the huge supermarket next door and for the bus station, but not much else. It's got great views of the olive-processing plant next door.

A much better choice is ***Camping Mithimna*** *(☎ 31 444/445)*, 6km west of town. It's an excellent, shady site near the best stretch of beach. Facilities include a restaurant, bar and shop. It charges 900 dr per person and 600 dr per tent. It also has rooms to rent nearby. Getting there involves either a 4km walk along the beach, or a bus trip to the village of Drapanias – from where it's a pleasant 15 minute walk through olive groves to the site.

Camping Nopigia *(☎ 31 111)* is another good site, 2km west of Camping Mithimna. While the beach is no good for swimming, the swimming pool here makes up for that.

Back in town, one of the best deals is ***Koutsounakis Rooms*** *(☎ 23 753, 22 064)*, adjacent to the bus station. Spotless singles/doubles are 4000/5500 dr with bathroom.

The C class ***Hotel Castell*** *(☎ 22 140)* opposite has similar prices.

Argo Rooms for Rent *(☎ 23 563/322)* on Plateia Teloniou has spacious rooms for 5000/7000 dr with bathroom. From the central square, walk down to the seafront, turn left, and you will come to the rooms on the left.

The C class ***Hotel Kissamos*** *(☎ 22 086)*, west of the bus station on the north side of the main road, is in an uninspiring location but has rooms with bathroom for 5500/7700 dr, including breakfast.

Places to Eat

Papadakis Taverna, opposite Argo Rooms for Rent, has a good setting overlooking the beach and serves well prepared food. For a meal with local colour go to the no-frills ***Restaurant Macedonas*** just west of Plateia Kissamos where an excellent meal of crispy fried whitebait and Greek salad costs 1800 dr.

Getting There & Away

Bus There are 13 buses daily to Hania (one hour, 900 dr), where you can change for Rethymno and Iraklio. There are also two buses daily for Falasarna (600 dr) at 10 am and 5.30 pm.

Ferry Golden Ferries Maritime operates the F/B *Maria* on a route that takes in Antikythira (two hours, 2100 dr), Kythira (four hours, 4200 dr) and Gythio (seven hours, 5100 dr). It leaves Kastelli-Kissamos at 2.30 pm Monday and Thursday.

Both the Miras agent Horeftakis Tours (☎ 23 250), and the ANEK Lines office (☎ 22 009, 24 030) are on the right side of Skalidi, east of Plateia Kissamos.

Getting Around

Cars can be hired from Hermes (☎ 22 980) on Skalidi, and motorcycles from Motor Fun (☎ 23 400) on Plateia Kissamos.

AROUND KASTELLI-KISSAMOS

Falasarna Φαλασαρνά

Falasarna, 16km west of Kastelli-Kissamos, was a Cretan city-state in the 4th century BC. There's not much to see, and most people are here for the superb beach, which is long, sandy and interspersed with boulders. There are several ***domatia*** at the beach.

From June through August there are two buses daily from Kastelli-Kissamos to Falasarna (600 dr) as well as buses from Hania (1500 dr).

Gramvousa Peninsula

Χερσόνησος Γραμβούσα

North of Falasarna is the wild and remote Gramvousa Peninsula. There is a wide track, which eventually degenerates into a path, along the east coast side to the sandy beach of **Tigani**, on the west side of the peninsula's narrow tip. The beach is overlooked by the two islets of Agria (wild) and Imeri (tame) Gramvousa. To reach the track, take a west-bound bus from Kastelli-Kissamos and ask to be let off at the turn-off for the village of Kalyviani (5km from Kastelli-Kissamos). Walk the 2km to Kalyviani, then take the path that begins at the far end of the main street. The shadeless walk takes around three hours – wear a hat and take plenty of water.

You don't have to inflict this punishment upon yourself to see the beautiful peninsula. From June through August there are daily cruises around the peninsula in the *Gramvousa Express* (5000 dr). The boat leaves Kastelli-Kissamos at 9 am and returns at 6 pm.

Ennia Horia Εννιά Χωριά

Ennia Horia (nine villages) is the name given to the highly scenic mountainous region south of Kastelli-Kissamos, renowned for its chestnut trees. If you have your own transport you can drive through the region en route to Moni Hrysoskalitissas and Elafonisi or, with a little backtracking, to Paleohora. Alternatively, you can take a circular route, returning via the coast road. The village of **Elos** stages a chestnut festival on the third Sunday of October when sweets made from chestnuts are eaten. The road to the region heads inland 5km east of Kastelli-Kissamos.

Polyrrinia Πολυρρηνία

The ruins of the ancient city of Polyrrinia (po-lih-reh-**nee**-ah) lie 7km south of Kastelli-Kissamos, above the village of Ano Paleokastro (sometimes called Polyrrinia). It's a steep climb to the ruins but the views are stunning.

The city was founded by the Dorians and was continuously inhabited until Venetian times. There are remains of city walls, and an aqueduct built by Hadrian. It's a scenic walk from Kastelli-Kissamos to Polyrrinia, otherwise there is a very infrequent bus service – ask at the Kastelli-Kissamos bus station.

To reach the Polyrrinia road, walk east along Kastelli-Kissamos' main road, and turn right after the OTE.

Ano Paleokastro has one taverna, ***Taverna Odysseos***, but no accommodation.

Dodecanese Δωδεκάνησα

Strung along the coast of western Turkey, the Dodecanese archipelago is much closer to Asia Minor than to mainland Greece. Because of their strategic and vulnerable position, these islands have encountered an even greater catalogue of invasions and occupations than the rest of Greece.

The name means 'Twelve Islands', but a glance at the map confirms that the group includes quite a few more. The name originated in 1908 when 12 of the islands united against the newly formed Young Turk-led Ottoman parliament which had retracted the liberties the Dodecanese had been granted under the sultans. The Dodecanese islanders enjoyed greater autonomy than did the rest of Greece under the sultans, and they paid fewer taxes.

The 12 islands were Rhodes, Kos, Kalymnos, Karpathos, Patmos, Tilos, Symi, Leros, Astypalea, Nisyros, Kassos and Halki. The islands' vicissitudinous history has endowed them with a wealth of diverse archaeological remains, but these are not the islands' only attractions. The highly developed resorts of Rhodes and Kos have beaches and bars galore, while Lipsi and Tilos have appealing beaches, but without the crowds. The far-flung islands of Agathonisi, Arki, Kassos and Kastellorizo await Greek-island aficionados in pursuit of traditional island life, while everyone boggles at the extraordinary landscape that geological turbulence has created on Nisyros.

HIGHLIGHTS

- The fascinating medieval city of Rhodes
- Enjoying the nightlife on Kos
- Nisyros' moon-like volcanic craters
- Trekking around picturesque Tilos

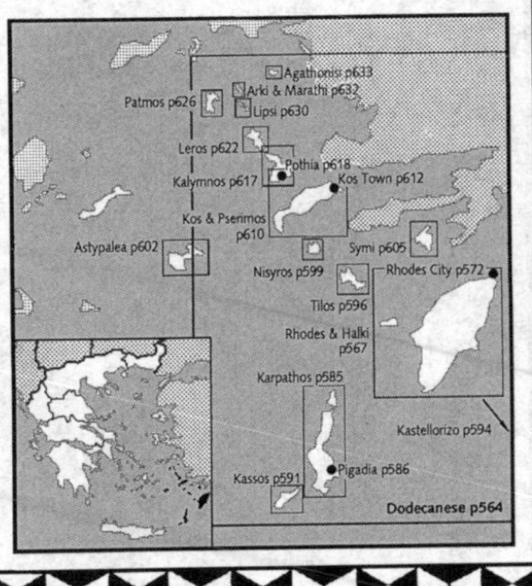

History

The Dodecanese islands have been inhabited since pre-Minoan times; by the Archaic period Rhodes and Kos had emerged as the dominant islands of the group. Distance from Athens gave the Dodecanese considerable autonomy and they were, for the most part, free to prosper unencumbered by subjugation to imperial Athens. Following Alexander the Great's death, Ptolemy I of Egypt ruled the Dodecanese.

The Dodecanese islanders were the first Greeks to become Christians. This was through the tireless efforts of St Paul, who made two journeys to the archipelago, and through St John, who was banished to Patmos – where he had his revelation.

The early Byzantine era saw the islands prosper, but by the 7th century AD they were plundered by a string of invaders. By the early 14th century it was the turn of the crusaders – the Knights of St John of Jerusalem, or Knights Hospitallers. The Knights eventually became rulers of almost all the Dodecanese, building mighty fortifications, but not mighty enough to keep out the Turks in 1522.

The Turks were ousted by the Italians in 1912 during a tussle over possession of Libya. Inspired by Mussolini's vision of a

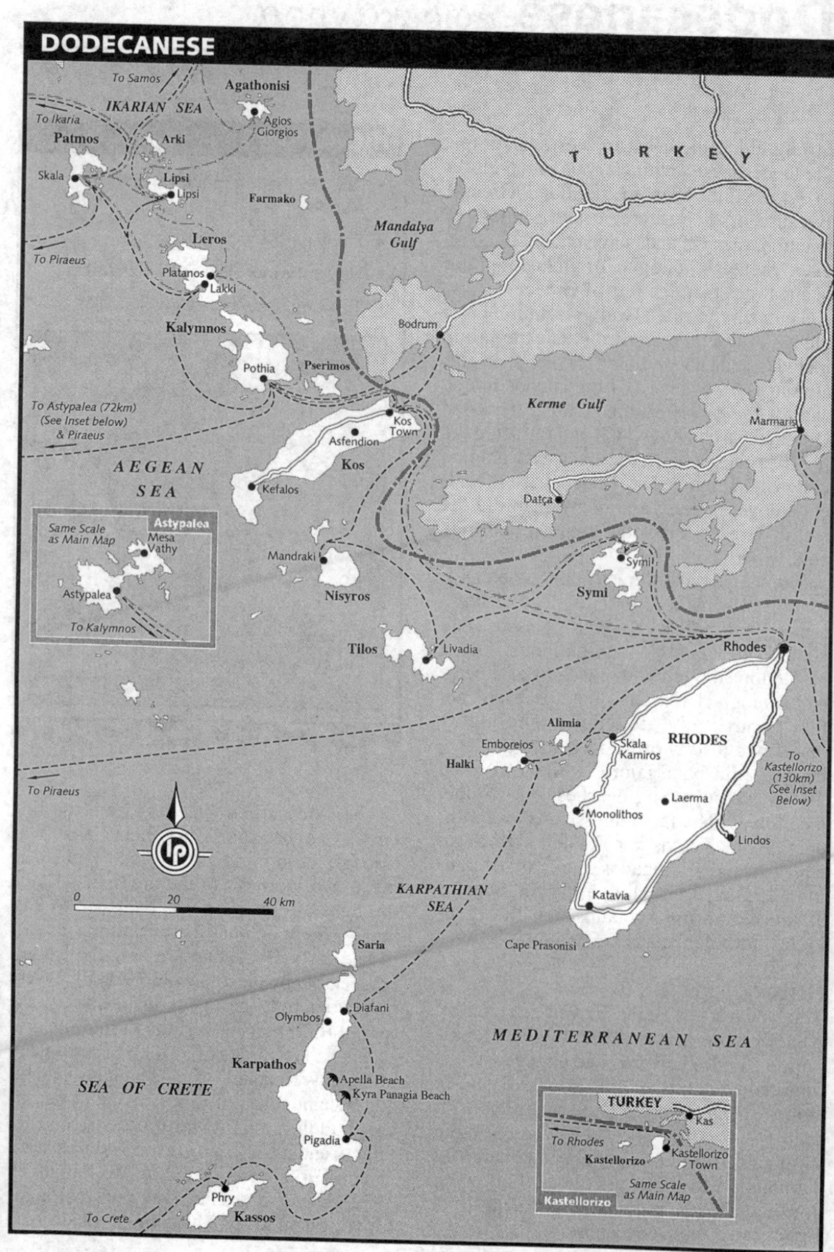
DODECANESE
To Samos
Agathonisi
IKARIAN SEA
To Ikaria
Agios Giorgios
Patmos
Arki
Skala
Lipsi
Lipsi
Farmako
TURKEY
To Piraeus
Leros
Mandalya Gulf
Platanos
Lakki
Bodrum
Kalymnos
Pothia
Pserimos
To Astypalea (72km) (See Inset below) & Piraeus
Kos Town
Kerme Gulf
Marmaris
Asfendion
AEGEAN SEA
Kos
Kefalos
Datça
Astypalea
Same Scale as Main Map
Mesa Vathy
Astypalea
To Kalymnos
Mandraki
Nisyros
Symi
Symi
Tilos
Livadia
Rhodes
Alimia
Emborejos
Halki
Skala Kamiros
RHODES
To Kastellorizo (130km) (See Inset Below)
To Piraeus
Laerma
Monolithos
Lindos
0
20
40 km
KARPATHIAN SEA
Katavia
Saria
Cape Prasonisi
Diafani
Olymbos
MEDITERRANEAN SEA
Karpathos
SEA OF CRETE
Apella Beach
Kyra Panagia Beach
TURKEY
Kas
Pigadia
To Rhodes
Kastellorizo
Kastellorizo Town
Same Scale as Main Map
Kastellorizo
Phry
Kassos
To Crete

vast Mediterranean empire, Italian was made the official language and the practice of Orthodoxy was prohibited. The Italians constructed grandiose public buildings in the Fascist style, which was the antithesis of archetypal Greek architecture. More beneficially, they excavated and restored many archaeological monuments.

After the Italian surrender of 1943, the islands became battle grounds for British and German forces, with much suffering inflicted upon the population. The Dodecanese were formally returned to Greece in 1947.

Getting There & Away

Air Astypalea, Karpathos, Kassos, Kos, Leros and Rhodes have flights to Athens. In addition, Rhodes has flights to Iraklio and Hania on Crete, Thessaloniki, and in summer to Mykonos and Santorini (Thira) in the Cyclades.

Ferry – Domestic Ferry schedules to the Dodecanese are incredibly complicated, mainly because of the distance from the mainland. The shortest round trip from Piraeus to the main port, Rhodes, takes about 28 hours, therefore it is impossible for the ferry companies to operate a simple daily timetable. Departure times in both directions tend to be geared to an early morning arrival at both Piraeus and Rhodes. This means that island-hopping in between can involve some antisocial hours.

The following table gives an overall view of ferry connections to the Dodecanese from the mainland and Crete in high season.

Connecting from the Dodecanese to the Cyclades can be difficult. It is possible to reach Astypalea from the Dodecanese and connect with ferries serving the Cyclades from there, but this is more by luck than by design.

Ferry Connections to the Dodecanese

Origin	Destination	Duration	Price	Frequency
Alexandroupolis	Kos	26 hours	10,800 dr	1 weekly
Alexandroupolis	Rhodes	30 hours	11,500 dr	1 weekly
Iraklio	Karpathos	7¾ hours	3800 dr	3 weekly
Iraklio	Rhodes	11 hours	6400 dr	3 weekly
Piraeus	Astypalea	10½ hours	7000 dr	3 weekly
Piraeus	Halki	25 hours	9700 dr	1 weekly
Piraeus	Kalymnos	12¾ hours	7200 dr	1 daily
Piraeus	Karpathos	21¼ hours	8000 dr	2 weekly
Piraeus	Kassos	17½ hours	7800 dr	2 weekly
Piraeus	Kos	11½ hours	7700 dr	1 daily
Piraeus	Leros	11¾ hours	6500 dr	1 daily
Piraeus	Lipsi	14 hours	7800 dr	1 weekly
Piraeus	Nisyros	19½ hours	7600 dr	1 weekly
Piraeus	Patmos	9½ hours	7200 dr	1 daily
Piraeus	Rhodes	14½ hours	9000 dr	1 daily
Piraeus	Symi	22½ hours	8800 dr	1 weekly
Piraeus	Tilos	20½ hours	8800 dr	1 weekly
Sitia	Karpathos	4 hours	3400 dr	1 weekly
Sitia	Kassos	2½ hours	2600 dr	1 weekly
Sitia	Rhodes	11 hours	6000 dr	1 weekly
Thessaloniki	Kos	18 hours	12,500 dr	1 weekly
Thessaloniki	Rhodes	21 hours	14,800 dr	1 weekly

Ferry – International There are ferries to the Turkish ports of Marmaris and Bodrum from Rhodes and Kos respectively, and day trips to Turkey from Kastellorizo and Symi. Boats en route from Piraeus to Cyprus and Israel call at Rhodes.

Hydrofoil Samos Hydrofoils operates daily services from the North-East Aegean island of Samos to the northern Dodecanese, and occasional services from Ikaria.

Getting Around

Air There are flights between Rhodes and Kastellorizo, Karpathos and Kassos.

Ferry Island-hopping within the Dodecanese is fairly easy as the principal islands in the group have daily connections by either ferries or excursion boats. The more remote islands do not have daily boats and some depend on the F/B *Nissos Kalymnos*, which operates out of Kalymnos and plies up and down the chain, calling in at most of the islands at least twice weekly. Karpathos and Kassos are not included on its route. For more information, see the relevant sections under entries on individual islands.

Hydrofoil The Dodecanese Hydrofoil Company operates hydrofoils from Rhodes to most islands in the group. Samos Hydrofoils provides additional services on its routes from the North-East Aegean to Kos.

Rhodes Ρόδος

Rhodes (**ro**-dos in Greek), the largest by far of the Dodecanese, with a total population of 98,181, is the number one package tour destination of the group. With 300 days of sunshine a year, and an east coast of virtually uninterrupted sandy beaches, it fulfils the two prerequisites of the sun-starved British, Scandinavians and Germans who flock there.

But beaches and sunshine are not its only attributes. Rhodes is a beautiful island with unspoilt villages nestling in the foothills of its mountains. The landscape varies from arid and rocky around the coast to lush and forested in the interior.

The World Heritage-listed old town of Rhodes is the largest inhabited medieval town in Europe, and its mighty fortifications are the finest surviving example of defensive architecture of the time.

History & Mythology

As is the case elsewhere in Greece, the early history of Rhodes is interwoven with mythology. The sun god Helios chose Rhodes as his bride and bestowed upon her light, warmth and vegetation. Their son, Cercafos, had three sons, Camiros, Ialyssos and Lindos, who each founded the cities that were named after them.

The Minoans and Mycenaeans had outposts on the islands, but it was not until the Dorians arrived in 1100 BC that Rhodes began to exert power and influence. The Dorians settled in the cities of Kamiros, Ialyssos and Lindos and made each an autonomous state. They utilised trade routes to the east which had been established during Minoan and Mycenaean times, and the island flourished as an important centre of commerce.

Rhodes continued to prosper until Roman times. It was allied to Athens in the Battle of Marathon (490 BC), in which the Persians were defeated, but had shifted to the Persian side by the time of the Battle of Salamis (480 BC). After the unexpected Athenian victory at Salamis, Rhodes hastily became an ally of Athens again, joining the Delian League in 478 BC. After the disastrous Sicilian Expedition (416-412 BC), Rhodes revolted against Athens and formed an alliance with Sparta, which it aided in the Peloponnesian Wars.

In 408 BC, the cities of Kamiros, Ialyssos and Lindos consolidated their powers for mutual protection and expansion by cofounding the city of Rhodes. The architect Hippodamos, who came to be regarded as the father of town planning, planned the city. The result was one of the most harmonious cities of antiquity, with wide, straight

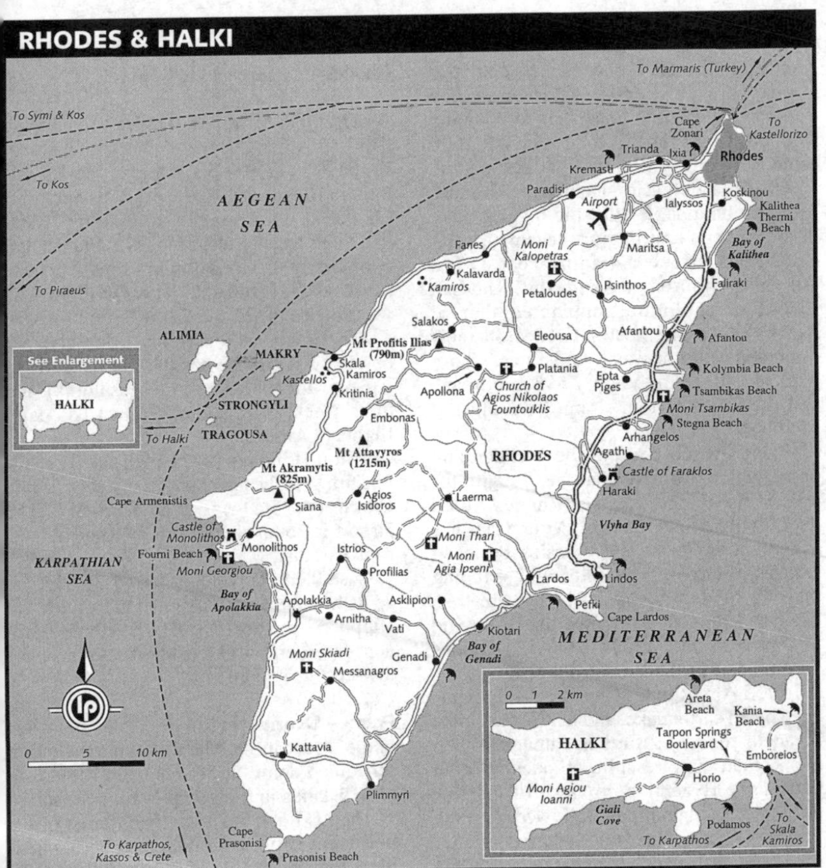

streets connecting its four distinct parts: the acropolis, agora, harbour and residential quarter.

Rhodes now became Athens' ally again, and together they defeated Sparta at the battle of Knidos, in 394 BC. Rhodes then joined forces with Persia in a battle against Alexander the Great. However, when Alexander proved invincible, Rhodes hastily allied itself with him. In the skirmishes following Alexander's death, Rhodes sided with Ptolemy.

In 305 BC, Antigonus, one of Ptolemy's rivals, sent his son, the formidable Demetrius Poliorketes (the Besieger of Cities), to conquer the city. Rhodes managed to repel Demetrius after a long siege. To celebrate this victory, the 32m-high bronze statue of Helios Apollo (Colossus of Rhodes), one of the Seven Wonders of the Ancient World, was built. The statue was traditionally thought to have straddled Mandraki Harbour but this has now been refuted. It only stood for 65 years though, before collapsing during an earthquake. It lay abandoned until 653 AD when it was chopped up by the Saracens, who sold it to a merchant in Edessa (in modern-day Turkey). The story goes that after being shipped to Syria, it took almost 1000 camels to convey it to its final destination.

After the defeat of Demetrius, Rhodes knew no bounds. It built the biggest navy in the Aegean and its port became a principal Mediterranean trading centre. The arts also flourished, and the Rhodian school of sculpture supplanted that of Athens as the foremost in Greece. Its most esteemed sculptor was Pythocretes, whose works included the Victory of Samothrace, and the relief of the trireme (warship) at Lindos.

When Greece became the battleground upon which Roman generals fought for leadership of the empire, Rhodes allied itself with Julius Caesar. After Caesar's assassination in 44 BC, Cassius besieged Rhodes, destroying its ships and stripping the city of its artworks, which were then taken to Rome. This marked the beginning of Rhodes' decline. In 70 AD, Rhodes became part of the Roman Empire.

In 155 AD, Rhodes City was badly damaged by an earthquake, and in 269 the Goths invaded, rendering further damage. When the Roman Empire split, Rhodes became part of the Byzantine province of the Dodecanese. Raid upon raid followed; first the Persians in 620, then the Saracens in 653; the Turks followed. When the crusaders seized Constantinople, Rhodes was given independence. Later the Genoese gained control. The Knights of St John arrived in Rhodes in 1309 and ruled for 213 years until they were ousted by the Ottomans. Rhodes suffered several earthquakes during the 19th century, but greater damage was rendered to the city in 1856 by an explosion of gunpowder which had been stored and forgotten – almost 1000 people were killed and many buildings were wrecked. In 1947, after 35 years of Italian occupation, Rhodes became part of Greece along with the other Dodecanese islands.

Getting There & Away

All the addresses listed in this section are in Rhodes City (area code 0241).

Air Olympic Airways has at least five flights daily to Athens (24,900 dr), two daily to Karpathos (12,800 dr), one daily to Kastellorizo (10,900 dr), five weekly to Santorini (22,900 dr), four weekly to Iraklio (21,900 dr), three weekly to Kassos (13,400 dr) and two weekly to Thessaloniki (31,900 dr) and Mykonos (22,900 dr). The Olympic Airways office (☎ 24 571) is at Ierou Lohou 9.

Air Greece and Cronus offer cheaper options. Air Greece has two flights daily to Athens, four weekly to Thessaloniki and three weekly to Iraklio. Cronus has daily flights to Athens.

Triton Holidays (☎ 21 690, fax 31 625), Plastira 9, is the agent for Air Greece, while Cronus (☎ 25 444) is at 25 Martiou 5. The airport is 16km south-west of Rhodes City, near Paradisi.

Castellania Travel Service (☎ 75 860, fax 75 861, email castell@otenet.gr), on Plateia Hippocrates, specialises in youth and student fares, and is one of the best places for low-cost air tickets.

Ferry – Domestic Rhodes is the main port of the Dodecanese. The following table lists scheduled domestic ferries from Rhodes to other islands in the group in high season.

The EOT and the municipal tourist office in Rhodes City can provide you with schedules. Further details and inter-island links can be found under each island entry.

Destination	Duration	Price	Frequency
Astypalea	10 hours	4940 dr	2 weekly
Halki	1½ hours	2000 dr	1 weekly
Kalymnos	5½ hours	4300 dr	1 daily
Karpathos	3½ hours	4400 dr	2 weekly
Kassos	5 hours	4100 dr	2 weekly
Kastellorizo	3½ hours	4100 dr	2 weekly
Kos	3½ hours	3500 dr	1 daily
Leros	7½ hours	4700 dr	1 daily
Lipsi	9½ hours	5100 dr	1 weekly
Nisyros	3¾ hours	2800 dr	3 weekly
Patmos	8½ hours	5500dr	1 daily

Symi	2 hours	1600 dr	1 daily
Tilos	2½ hours	2800 dr	3 weekly

Ferry – International Poseidon Lines and Salamis Lines both stop at Rhodes en route from Piraeus to Cyprus (Lemesos/Limassol) and Israel (Haifa). From Rhodes to Cyprus takes 15 hours (22,000 dr), with a further 11 hours to Haifa (36,000 dr). The boats leave Rhodes on Tuesday and Friday. See the introductory Getting There & Away chapter and the Piraeus section of the Athens chapter for more information. You can buy tickets from Kydon Agency (☎ 23 000, 75 268) on Ethelondon Dodekanision, between Amerikis and Makariou in the new town, or Kouros Travel (☎ 24 377, 22 400), Karpathou 34.

There are two ferry services daily between Rhodes and Marmaris in Turkey. They leave Rhodes at 8 am and 3 pm, and leave Marmaris at 10 am and 4 pm. The crossing takes one hour. In addition, small Turkish car ferries run between Rhodes and Marmaris daily (except Sunday) between April and October; less frequently in winter. Prices vary, so shop around.

Immigration and customs are on the quay.

Hydrofoil – Domestic The Dodecanese Hydrofoil Company (☎ 24 000), on the quay at Plateia Neoriou 6, operates the following services from Rhodes in high season:

Destination	Duration	Price	Frequency
Astypalea	5½ hours	9880 dr	1 weekly
Kalymnos	3½ hours	8530 dr	1 weekly
Kos	2 hours	6790 dr	2 daily
Leros	3½ hours	9320 dr	3 weekly
Nysiros	2¼ hours	5550 dr	1 weekly
Patmos	3½ hours	10,730 dr	3 weekly
Symi	1 hour	3100 dr	2 weekly
Tilos	1¼ hours	5550 dr	2 weekly

Hydrofoil – International There are daily hydrofoils to Marmaris (weather permitting) from April to October. Fares are currently cheaper than ferries at 10,000/14,000 dr one way/return (plus 3500 dr Turkish port tax). You can buy tickets from Triton Holidays (☎ 21 657, fax 31 625), Plastira 9, to whom you must submit your passport on the day before your journey.

Caïque See the Getting There & Away section for Halki for information about caïques between Rhodes and Halki.

Excursion Boat There are excursion boats to Symi (4000 dr return) every day in summer, leaving Mandraki Harbour at 9 am and returning at 6 pm. You can buy tickets at most travel agencies, but it is better to buy them at the harbour, where you can check out the boats, and bargain. Look for shade and the size and condition of the boat, as these vary greatly. You can buy an open return if you want to stay on Symi.

Getting Around

To/From the Airport Each day 21 buses travel between the airport and Rhodes City's west side bus station (400 dr). The first leaves Rhodes City at 6 am and the last at 11 pm; from the airport, the first leaves at 5.55 am and the last at 11.45 pm.

Bus Rhodes City has two bus stations. From the east side bus station on Plateia Rimini there are 18 buses daily to Faliraki (400 dr), 10 to Lindos (1000 dr), eight to Kolymbia (600 dr), five to Genadi (1200 dr) via Lardos, and three to Psinthos (500 dr).

From the west side station next to the New Market there are 16 buses daily to Kalithea Thermi (400 dr), 11 to Koskinou (400 dr), five to Salakos (800 dr), and one to ancient Kamiros (1000 dr), Monolithos (1400 dr) via Skala Kamiros, and Embonas (1150 dr). The EOT and municipal tourist office give out schedules.

Car & Motorcycle There are numerous car and motorcycle rental outlets in Rhodes City's new town. Shop around and bargain because the competition is fierce.

Taxi Rhodes City's main taxi rank is east of Plateia Rimini. There are two zones on the island for taxi meters: zone one is Rhodes City and zone two (slightly higher) is everywhere else. Rates are a little higher between midnight and 6 am. Sample fares are: the airport (2500 dr), Filerimos (2200 dr), Petaloudes (4000 dr), ancient Kamiros (5500 dr), Lindos (7000 dr) and Monolithos (9000 dr). Taxi company phone numbers include ☎ 64 712, 64 734 and 64 778.

Rip-offs are rare but if you think you have been ripped off take the taxi number and go to the tourist police.

Bicycle The Bicycle Centre (☎ 28 315), Griva 39, Rhodes City, has three-speed bikes for 800 dr and mountain bikes for 1200 dr.

Excursion Boat There are excursion boats to Lindos (4000 dr return) every day in summer, leaving Mandraki Harbour at 9 am and returning at 6 pm. You might like to buy a one way ticket and return by bus or taxi.

RHODES CITY

☎ 0241 • postcode 851 00 • pop 43,500

The heart of Rhodes City is the old town, enclosed within massive walls. Avoid the worst of the tourist hordes by beginning your exploration early in the morning. But at any time of the day, away from the main thoroughfares and squares, you will find many deserted labyrinthine alleyways. Much of the new town to the north is a monument to package tourism, but it does have several places of interest to visitors.

Orientation

The old town is a mesh of Byzantine, Turkish and Latin architecture with quiet, twisting alleyways punctuated by lively squares. Sokratous, which runs east to west, and its easterly continuation Aristotelous, are the old town's bustling main commercial thoroughfares. The old town's two main squares are also along here: Plateia Martyron Evreon, with an attractive fountain, at the eastern end of Aristotelous; and Plateia Hippocrates, with the distinctive Castellania fountain, at the eastern end of Sokratous. Acquainting yourself with these two squares will help with orientation, but getting lost is almost inevitable and part of the fun of exploring the place. Farther north, parallel to Sokratous, is Ippoton (Avenue of the Knights), which was the main medieval thoroughfare.

The commercial harbour, for international ferries and large inter-island ferries, is east of the old town. Excursion boats, small ferries, hydrofoils and private yachts use Mandraki Harbour, farther north. When you buy a ticket check where the ferry is leaving from.

In Mandraki, two bronze deer on stone pillars mark the supposed site of the Colossus of Rhodes. Mandraki's grandiose public buildings are relics of Mussolini's era. The main square of the new town is Plateia Rimini, just north of the old town. The tourist offices, bus stations and main taxi rank are on or near this square.

Most of the old town is off limits to motorists, but there are car parks on the periphery.

Information

Tourist Offices The EOT (☎ 23 255/655, fax 26 955, email eot~rodos@otenet.gr), on the corner of Makariou and Papagou, supplies brochures and maps of the city, and will help in finding accommodation. Opening times are 7.30 am to 3 pm Monday to Friday. In summer the same service is provided by Rhodes' municipal tourist office (☎ 35 945), Plateia Rimini. Opening times are 8 am to 8 pm Monday to Saturday and 8 am to noon on Sunday; closed in winter.

From either of these you can pick up the *Rodos News*, a free English-language newspaper.

The tourist police (☎ 27 423) are next door to the EOT and are open 24 hours daily.

Money The main National Bank of Greece and the Alpha Credit Bank are on Plateia Kyprou. In the old town there is a National Bank of Greece on Plateia Moussiou, and a Commercial Bank of Greece nearby. All have ATMs. Opening times are 8 am to 2 pm Monday to Thursday, 8 am to 1.30 pm Friday.

American Express (☎ 21 010) is represented by Rhodos Tours, Ammohostou 18.

Post & Communications The main post office is on Mandraki. Opening times are 7.30 am to 8 pm Monday to Friday. The old town sub post office is open seven days. The OTE at Amerikis 91 is open 7 am to 11 pm daily.

Rhodes has two Internet cafes: Rock Style, Dimokratias 7, just south of the old town, and Mango Cafe Bar, Plateia Dorieos 3, in the old town.

Bookshops Kostas Tomaras Bookstore, Venizelou Sofi 5, stocks some English-language books including Lonely Planet guides. Second Story Books, Amarantou 24, has a wide selection of second-hand foreign-language books.

Laundry Rhodes has two self-service laundrettes: Lavomatique, 28 Oktovriou 32, and Express Servis, Dilberaki 97 (off Orfanidou). Both charge around 1400 dr a load. Express Laundry, Kosta Palama 5, does service washes for 1000 dr.

Luggage Storage You can store luggage at Planet Holidays (☎ 35 722), Galias 6, for 500 dr for two hours and 1200 dr for up to two days. You can negotiate a price for a longer period.

Emergency Rhodes' general hospital (☎ 25 580) is at Papalouka, just north-west of the old town. For emergency first aid and the ambulance service, call ☎ 25 555 or ☎ 22 222.

Old Town

The town is divided into two parts. In medieval times, the Knights of St John lived in the Knights' Quarter and the other inhabitants lived in the Hora. The 12m-thick city walls are closed to the public, but at 2.45 pm on Tuesday and Saturday you can take a guided walk along them starting at the courtyard of the Palace of the Grand Masters (1200 dr).

Knights' Quarter An appropriate place to begin an exploration of the old town is the imposing cobblestone **Avenue of the Knights** (Ippoton), where the knights lived. The knights were divided into seven 'tongues' or languages, according to their place of origin – England, France, Germany, Italy, Aragon, Auvergne and Provence – each responsible for protecting a section of the bastion. The Grand Master, who was in charge, lived in the palace, and each tongue was under the auspices of a

The Knights of St John

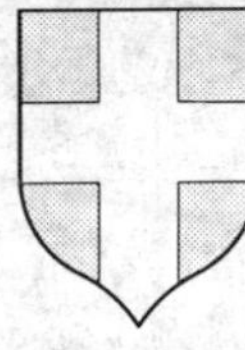

The Knights of St John were a religious order of the church of Rome founded in Amalfi in the 11th century. They went to Jerusalem initially to minister to the pilgrims who arrived there, but soon extended their duties to tending the poor and sick of the Holy Land. Over the years they became increasingly militant, joining forces with the Knights Templars and the Teutonic Knights of St Mary in battles against infidels.

The Knights of St John were expelled from the Holy Land with the fall of Jerusalem. They went first to Cyprus and then, in 1309, to Rhodes. Through some wheeling and dealing with the island's ruling Genoese admiral, Viguolo de Viguoli, they became the possessors of Rhodes, transforming it into a mighty bulwark that stood at the easternmost point of the Christian west, safeguarding it from the Muslim infidels of the east. The knights withstood Muslim offensives in 1444 and 1480, but in 1522 Sultan Süleyman the Magnificent staged a massive attack with 200,000 troops. After a long siege the 600 knights, with 1000 mercenaries and 6000 Rhodians, surrendered – hunger, disease and death having taken their toll.

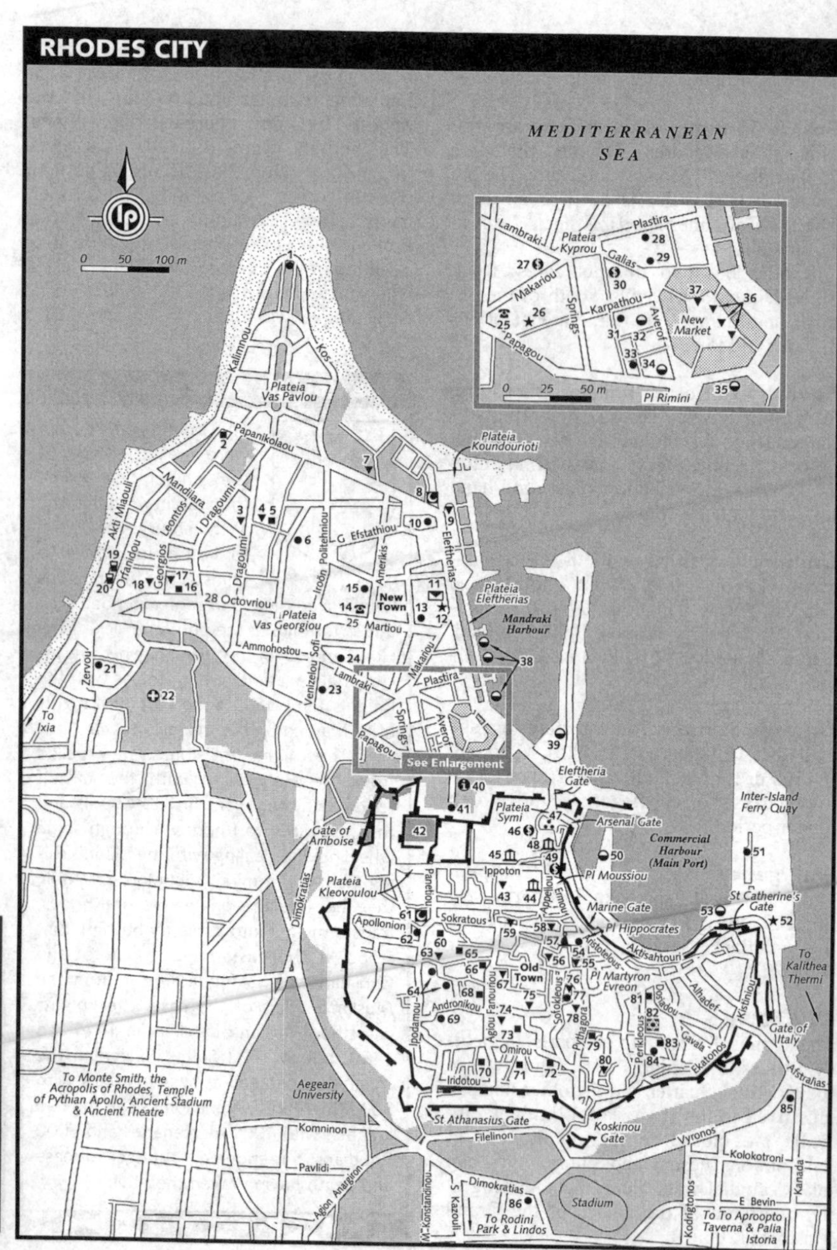
RHODES CITY
MEDITERRANEAN SEA
0 50 100 m
Plateia Vas Pavlou
Kalimnou
Kos
Papanikolaou
Akti Miaouli
Mandilara
Leontos
I Dragoumi
Dragoumi
Orfanidou
Georgios
28 Octovriou
G Efstathiou
Iroon Politehniou
Amerikis
Eleftherias
New Town
Plateia Vas Georgiou
25 Martiou
Ammohostou
Venizelou Sofi
Lambraki
Makariou
Plastira
Springs
Averof
Papagou
See Enlargement
Zervou
To Ixia
Plateia Koundourioti
Plateia Eleftherias
Mandraki Harbour
Eleftheria Gate
Inter-Island Ferry Quay
Plateia Symi
Arsenal Gate
Commercial Harbour (Main Port)
Pl Moussiou
Marine Gate
Pl Hippocrates
St Catherine's Gate
Gate of Amboise
Plateia Kleovoulou
Panetou
Ippoton
Apellou
Ermou
Dimokratias
Apollonion
Sokratous
Aristotelous
Aktisahtouri
Pl Martyron Evreon
Old Town
Andronikou
Agiou Fanouriou
Sofokleous
Pythagora
Ipodamou
Omirou
Iridotou
Perikleous
Dosiadou
Alhadef
Gavala
Ekatonos
Kisthiniou
To Kalithea Thermi
Gate of Italy
Afstralias
To Monte Smith, the Acropolis of Rhodes, Temple of Pythian Apollo, Ancient Stadium & Ancient Theatre
Aegean University
St Athanasius Gate
Koskinou Gate
Komninon
Filelinon
Vyronos
Kolokotroni
Pavlidi
Agion Anargiron
M Konstandinou
S Kazouli
Dimokratias
Stadium
Kodrigtonos
Kanada
E Bevin
To Rodini Park & Lindos
To To Aproopto Taverna & Palia Istoria
Lambraki
Plateia Kyprou
Plastira
Galias
Makariou
Karpathou
New Market
Pl Rimini
0 25 50 m
1 2 3 4 5 6 7 8 9 10 11 12 13 14 15 16 17 18 19 20 21 22 23 24 25 26 27 28 29 30 31 32 33 34 35 36 37 38 39 40 41 42 43 44 45 46 47 48 49 50 51 52 53 54 55 56 57 58 59 60 61 62 63 64 65 66 67 68 69 70 71 72 73 74 75 76 77 78 79 80 81 82 83 84 85 86

RHODES CITY

PLACES TO STAY
2 Grand Hotel Astir Palace
5 New Village Inn
16 Hotel Anastasia
60 Maria's Rooms
65 Mike and Mama's Pension
66 Rodos Youth Hostel
68 Pension Olympos
70 Pink Elephant
71 Pension Andreas
72 Pension Minos
73 Mango Rooms & Café Bar
79 Hotel Via Via
81 Hotel Spot
83 Kamiros Rooms to Let

PLACES TO EAT
3 Kringlans Swedish Bakery
4 India Restaurant
7 Restaurant Ellinikon
9 Neohora Psistaria
17 Thomas & Charlotte's Taverna
18 Belgium Restaurant Rhobel
36 Patisseries
37 Ipiros
43 Entos Ton Teeohon
55 Petite Cafe
56 Pizza da Spillo
58 Alexis Restaurant
59 Cafe
63 Diafani Garden Restaurant
67 Cleo's Italian Restaurant
74 Walk-in Beer Garden
75 Paradosiako Kafeneio Araliki
76 Fisherman's Ouzeria
78 Taverna Kostas
80 Le Bistrot de L'Auberge

THINGS TO SEE
1 Aquarium
8 Mosque of Murad Reis
42 Palace of the Grand Masters
44 Archaeological Museum
45 Museum of Decorative Arts
47 Temple of Aphrodite
48 Byzantine Museum
57 Castellania Fountain
61 Mosque of Süleyman
62 Turkish Library
64 Turkish Bath
82 Synagogue

OTHER
6 Second Story Books
10 National Theatre
11 Post Office
12 Port Police
13 Blue Lagoon; Dracula's Palace; Mega Club Gas Disco
14 OTE
15 Olympic Airways
19 Down Under Bar
20 Red Lion
21 Sticky Fingers
22 Hospital
23 Kostas Tomaras Bookstore
24 Rhodos Tours
25 EOT
26 Tourist Police
27 National Bank of Greece
28 Triton Holidays
29 Planet Holidays
30 Alpha Credit Bank
31 Kouros Travel
32 Bus Station (West Side)
33 Express Laundry
34 Bus Station (East Side)
35 Taxi Rank
38 Departure Points for Hydrofoils, Diving & Excursion Boats
39 Dodecanese Hydrofoil Company
40 Rhodes Municipal Tourist Office
41 Son et Lumière
46 Commercial Bank of Greece
49 National Bank of Greece
50 Departure Point for F/B Nissos Kalymnos
51 Customs Office
52 Port Police
53 Departure Point for Boats to Turkey
54 Castellenia Travel
69 Folk Dance Theatre
77 Kafe Besara
84 Waterhoppers Diving Centre
85 YAR Maritime Centre
86 Rock Style Internet Cafe

bailiff. The knights were divided into soldiers, chaplains and ministers to the sick.

To this day the street exudes a noble and forbidding aura, despite modern offices now occupying most of the inns. Its lofty buildings stretch in a 600m-long unbroken wall of honey-coloured stone blocks, and its flat facade is punctuated by huge doorways and arched windows. The inns reflect the Gothic styles of architecture of the knights' countries of origin. They form a harmonious whole in their bastion-like structure, but on closer inspection each possesses graceful and individual embellishments.

First on the right, at the eastern end of the Avenue of the Knights, is the **Inn of the Order of the Tongue of Italy** (1519); next to it is the **Palace of Villiers de l'Île Adam**. After Sultan Süleyman had taken the city, it was Villiers de l'Île who had the humiliating task of arranging the knights' departure from the island. Next along is the **Inn of France**, the most ornate and distinctive of all the inns. On the opposite side of the street is a wrought-iron gate in front of a Turkish garden.

Back on the right side is the **Chapelle Française** (Chapel of the Tongue of France), embellished with a statue of the Virgin and Child. Next door is the residence of the Chaplain of the Tongue of France. Across the alleyway is the **Inn of Provence**, with four coats of arms forming the shape of a cross, and opposite is the **Inn of Spain**.

On the right is the magnificent 14th century **Palace of the Grand Masters** (☎ 23 359). It was destroyed in the gunpowder explosion of 1856 and the Italians rebuilt it in a grandiose manner, with a lavish interior, intending it as a holiday home for Mussolini and King Emmanuel III. It is now a museum, containing sculpture, mosaics taken from Kos by the Italians, and antique furniture. The palace is open 8.30 am to 3 pm Tuesday to Sunday, and admission is 1200 dr.

The **archaeological museum** (☎ 27 657), Plateia Moussiou, is housed in the 15th century knights' hospital. Its most famous exhibit is the exquisite Parian marble statuette, the *Aphrodite of Rhodes*, a 1st century BC adaptation of a Hellenistic statue.

Less charming, to most people, is the 4th century BC *Aphrodite of Thalassia* in the next room. However, writer Lawrence Durrell was so enamoured of this statue that he named his book *Reflections on a Marine Venus* after it. Also in this room is the 2nd century BC marble *Head of Helios*, found near the Palace of the Grand Masters where a Temple of Helios once stood. The museum is open 8.30 am to 3 pm Tuesday to Sunday. Admission is 800 dr.

Across the square is the 11th century Church of the Virgin of the Castle. It was enlarged by the knights and became their cathedral. It is now the **Byzantine Museum**, with Christian artworks. It is open 8.30 am to 3 pm Tuesday to Sunday. Admission is 500 dr.

Farther north, on the opposite side, the **Museum of the Decorative Arts** houses a collection of artefacts from around the Dodecanese. Opening times are 8.30 am to 3 pm Tuesday to Sunday. Admission is 600 dr.

On Plateia Simi, there are the remains of a 3rd century BC **Temple of Aphrodite**, one of the few ancient ruins in the old town.

Hora The Hora has many Ottoman legacies. During Turkish times, churches were converted to mosques, and many more were built from scratch. Most are now dilapidated. The most important one is the newly renovated, pink-domed **Mosque of Süleyman**, at the top of Sokratous. It was built in

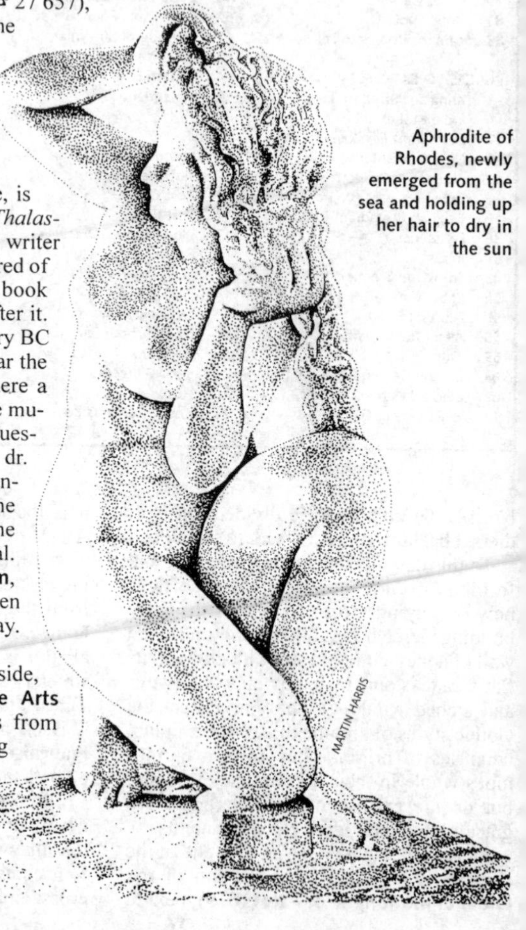

Aphrodite of Rhodes, newly emerged from the sea and holding up her hair to dry in the sun

DODECANESE

1522 to commemorate the Ottoman victory against the knights, then rebuilt in 1808.

Opposite is the 18th century **Turkish library** where many Islamic manuscripts are kept. It is sometimes open to the public – check the times on the notice outside.

The 18th century **Turkish bath**, on Plateia Arionos, offers a rare opportunity to have a Turkish bath in Greece. It is open 1 pm to 7 pm Tuesday, 11 am to 7 pm on Wednesday, Thursday and Friday and 8 am to 6 pm Saturday. Entry is 500 dr.

The **synagogue** on Dosiadou has a commemorative plaque to the many members of Hora's large Jewish population who were sent to Auschwitz during the Nazi occupation. Jews still worship here and it is usually open in the morning. Close by is Plateia Martyron Evreon (Square of the Jewish Martyrs).

New Town

The **Acropolis of Rhodes**, south-west of the old town on Monte Smith, was the site of the ancient Hellenistic city of Rhodes. The hill is named after the English admiral Sir Sydney Smith, who watched for Napoleon's fleet from here in 1802. It has superb views.

The site's restored 2nd century **stadium** once staged competitions in preparation for the Olympic Games. The adjacent **theatre** is a reconstruction of one used for lectures by the Rhodes School of Rhetoric. Steps above here lead to the **Temple of Pythian Apollo**, with four re-erected columns. The unenclosed site can be reached on city bus No 5.

North of Mandraki, at the eastern end of G Papanikolaou, is the graceful **Mosque of Murad Reis**. In its grounds are a Turkish cemetery and the Villa Cleobolus, where Lawrence Durrell lived in the 1940s, writing *Reflections on a Marine Venus*.

The **aquarium** is housed in a red and cream Italianate building at the island's northernmost point. Opening times are 9 am to 9 pm daily. Admission is 600 dr.

The town **beach** begins north of Mandraki and continues around the island's northernmost point and down the west side of the new town. The best spot is on the northernmost point, where it's not quite as crowded.

Rodini Park, 3km south of the town, is a pleasant shady park with deer and peacocks. It's believed to have been the site of the School of Rhetoric. City bus No 3 goes there.

Activities

Scuba Diving Two diving schools operate out of Mandraki: the Waterhoppers Diving Centre (☎/fax 38 146), Perikleous 29, and Dive Med Centre (☎ 33 654). Both offer a range of courses including a One Day Try Dive for 13,500 dr. You can get information from the Waterhoppers boat MV *Kouros*, and Dive Med Centre's boats *Pheonix* and *Free Spirit* at Mandraki. Kalithea Thermi is the only site around Rhodes where diving is permitted.

Yachting You can hire yachts at the YAR Maritime Centre (☎ 22 927, fax 23 393), Vyronos 1. For more yachting information, contact the Rodos Yacht Club (☎ 23 287).

Windsurfing Pro Horizon (☎ 95 819), just west of town at Ialysos Beach, Ixia, rents boards. There are many other rental outlets around the coast. The Fun & Action Windsurfing School at Faliraki offers expert tuition.

Tennis Many of the large hotels have tennis courts open to nonguests. Rhodes Tennis Club (☎ 25 705) is on the waterfront north of Mandraki.

Greek Dancing Lessons The Nelly Dimoglou Dance Company (☎ 20 157, 29 085), at the Folk Dance Theatre on Andronikou, gives lessons.

Organised Tours

Triton Holidays (☎ 21 690, fax 31 625), Plastira 9, Mandraki, has a wide range of tours, and provides specialist advice on any of the islands and Turkey.

Places to Stay – Budget

The old town of Rhodes has lots of cheap accommodation. The unofficial ***Rodos Youth Hostel*** *(☎ 30 491, Ergiou 12)* charges

1500 dr per person. There is a kitchen for self-caterers. The more comfortable ***Mike and Mama's Pension*** *(☎ 25 359, Menekleous 28)* has singles/doubles/triples for 4000/5000/6000 dr. At ***Mango Rooms*** *(☎/fax 24 877, Plateia Dorieos 3)* clean, nicely furnished rooms with bathroom and refrigerator go for 7000/11,000/13,000 dr.

Hotel Via Via *(☎ 27 895, Lisipou 2)*, just off Pythagora, has pristine, tastefully furnished doubles/triples for 7000/9500 dr, or with bathroom for 11,000/11,600 dr.

Pension Minos *(☎ 31 813, Omirou 5)* has spotless, spacious rooms for 8000/10,000 dr and a roof garden with views of the old town.

The exceptionally friendly ***Pension Andreas*** *(☎ 34 156, fax 74 285, email andreasch@otenet.gr, Omirou 28D)* has clean, pleasant doubles for 8000 dr, triples with bathroom for 12,000 dr, and a terrace bar with terrific views. ***Kamiros Rooms to Let*** *(☎ 33 545, Tavriscou 27 and Ikarou 26)* is a characterful place (in two separate buildings) with immaculate doubles/triples for 9000/11,000 dr with bathrooms.

Maria's Rooms *(☎ 20 730, Menekleous 147)*, just off Sokratous, has nicely furnished doubles for 8000/9000 dr with shared/private bathroom. ***Hotel Spot*** *(☎ 34 737, Perikleous 21)* has exceptionally clean, pleasant singles/doubles/triples for 9000/11,000/12,000 dr with bathroom. This long-established hotel was run until recently by a charming elderly couple. It is now run by their English-speaking son who plans to renovate. ***Pink Elephant*** *(☎/fax 22 469, Irodotou 42)* has doubles with bathroom for 9000 dr, doubles/triples for 7000/9000 dr without. Despite the name, the hotel's attractive decor is blue and white.

Pension Olympos *(☎/fax 33 567)*, on Agiou Fanouriou, has pleasant singles/doubles for 8000/14,000 dr with bathroom and television. It has an attractive little courtyard.

Most of the new town's hotels are modern and characterless, but there are some exceptions. ***Hotel Anastasia*** *(☎ 21 815, 28 Octovriou 46)*, in a former Italian mansion, is set back from the road, and is reasonably quiet. The high-ceilinged rooms, with tiled floors, are spotless; singles/doubles are 7000/13,000 dr with breakfast. The hotel has a lovely, shady, flower and tree-filled garden – home to two large tortoises and five cats. The English-speaking owners enjoy helping guests to plan their itineraries.

New Village Inn *(☎ 34 937, Konstantopedos 10)* has tastefully furnished rooms with refrigerator and fan, and a traditional stone-walled courtyard, festooned with plants. Singles/doubles/triples cost 6000/10,000/12,000 dr. The Greek-American owned inn is on a quiet street.

Places to Stay – Top End

The pricey ***Grand Hotel Astir Palace*** *(☎ 26 284)* on Akti Miaouli has a bar, restaurant and swimming pools. Singles/doubles are 25,000/ 35,300 dr, and suites are 62,000 dr.

At Ixis, the A class ***Cosmopolitan Hotel*** *(☎ 35 373)* has singles/doubles/triples for 15,500/25,000/34,375 dr.

The deluxe ***Rodos Palace*** *(☎ 25 222, fax 25 350)*, also at Ixia, is a vast place with loads of amenities. Singles/doubles cost 32,250/44,150 dr.

You can get discounts of up to 30% on the more expensive hotels if you book through Triton Holidays (see Organised Tours).

Places to Eat – Budget

Enthusiastic touting and displays of tacky photographs of food seem to be the order of the day at many restaurants in Rhodes, with the enthusiasm of the touts not reflected in the quality of the food. But if you hunt around you will find good-value places.

Fisherman's Ouzeria on Sofokleous is one of the best-value seafood places around. A huge plateful of *gavros* (small fish) is only 1200 dr. ***Taverna Kostas*** *(Pythagora 62)* is also good value with souvlaki for 1800 dr and swordfish for 2500 dr.

The unpretentious, low-priced ***Neohora Psistaria***, on the corner of Kathopouli and Kazouli in the new town, features tender grilled liver among its well prepared dishes.

Thomas & Charlotte's Taverna, on Georgios Leontos, serves a selection of

JON DAVISON

rete's olive trees provide some of the finest oil available.

JON DAVISON

'he sheer cliffs of Santorini's caldera make a dramatic coastline (Cyclades).

CHRIS CHRISTO

The magnificent Samaria Gorge, Crete

DIANA MAYFIELD

Athens' quaint Panagia Hrysospiliotissa chapel

DIANA MAYFIELD

Greek salad: a delicious meal in itself.

MARK DAFFEY

Agia Triada Monastery, Meteora

Greek and Scandinavian dishes. One tasty dish is *Kleftiko* ('the thieves' dish'), which was originally prepared by *klepht* sheep thieves who skinned their prey, wrapped the meat in the skins with herbs and vegetables, buried it and lit fires above, so hiding all evidence of their crime. The meat, over a couple of days, cooked into a very tasty meal. Thomas' version is served wrapped in greaseproof paper.

Ipiros is the best of the *psistarias* in the New Market. A huge helping of succulent spit-roast lamb, Greek salad and soft drink costs 3000 dr.

To Aproopto Taverna *(Kanada 95)*, half an hour's walk from the old town, serves well prepared, generous portions of ready-made food and grills. The chickpea patties are a delicious starter.

Back in the old town, ***Diafani Garden Restaurant***, opposite the Turkish bath, serves gratifying, reasonably priced dishes, 'cooked from the heart', as the German owner says. The atmospheric ***Paradosiako Kafeneio Araliki*** *(Aristofanois 45)* serves creative dishes which reflect its Italian ownership.

Entos Ton Teeohon *(Lahitos 13)* is a welcome antidote to Rhodes' tacky tourist restaurants. 'Tourists are welcome here, but we do nothing to attract them' says the owner. Nothing, that is, except serve some of the most imaginative and reasonably priced dishes in town. They include chicken stuffed with cheese, cuttlefish stuffed with feta and spicy pork.

If you crave something other than Greek food, ***Le Bistrot de L'Auberge*** *(Praxitelous 21)* serves terrific French dishes, while the Italian chef at ***Pizza da Spillo*** *(Apellou 41)* conjures up a variety of mouthwatering pizzas. In the new town, ***India Restaurant*** *(☎ 38 395, Konstantopedos 16)* has a fantastic selection of Indian food. It's directly opposite the Kringlans Swedish Bakery on I Dragoumi.

If your feet are killing you after hours of walking the old town's pebbled thoroughfares, two pleasant options for a break are ***Petite Cafe*** *(Evripidou 13-15)*, near the Castellania fountain, with a tranquil walled garden, and ***Walk-in Beer Garden***, just off Plateia Dhorias. Both serve coffee and snacks. For the best Greek coffee in town and a game of backgammon or chess, head for the fantastically funky old ***cafe*** *(Sokratous 76)*.

In the new town, ***Kringlans Swedish Bakery*** *(I Dragoumi 14)* serves sandwiches and pastries that are out of this world.

If you're self-catering, there is a small ***supermarket*** on Evripidou. There are many supermarkets in the new town, and fruit and vegetable stalls in the New Market.

Places to Eat – Mid-Range & Top End

Alexis Restaurant, on Sokratous, is a first-rate seafood restaurant. ***Belgium Restaurant Rhobel*** *(George Leontos 13-15)* specialises in steaks but, for something a bit different, the 'rabbit cooked in the traditional way' (with dried fruit) is commendable. ***Restaurant Ellinikon*** *(Papanikolaou 6)* excels in traditional Greek fare. The *stifado* is highly recommended, but leave room for the luscious iced caramel, which often features as dessert of the day. Three-course meals with wine at these places will cost around 9000 dr.

Cleo's Italian Restaurant *(Agiou Fanouriou 17)* is a sophisticated place with a cool, elegant interior and a quiet courtyard. Set menus cost around 4000 dr.

Feverish touting reaches its acme at the people-watching patisseries bordering the New Market. Nevertheless, they're convivial meeting places. Coffee and cake costs around 2000 dr.

Palia Istoria *(☎ 32 421, 108 Mitropoleos)*, south of the old town, is popular with well heeled locals. Its large, imaginative menu includes delicious and unusual *mezedes* such as scallops with mushrooms, and artichokes in nutmeg sauce. Expect to pay 10,000 dr to 12,000 dr for a meal with wine. Reservations are recommended.

Entertainment

The ***son et lumière*** *(☎ 21 922)*, staged in the grounds of the Palace of the Grand Masters, depicts the Turkish siege of Rhodes and is superior to most such efforts. The entrance is on Plateia Rimini and admission is 1200 dr. A noticeboard outside gives the times for performances.

The Nelly Dimoglou Dance Company gives first-rate performances at the ***Folk Dance Theatre*** *(☎ 29 085, 20 157)* on Andronikou. Performances are nightly except Saturday from May to October and begin at 9.20 pm. Admission is 3500 dr. There are classical music recitals at the ***National Theatre*** *(☎ 29 678)*.

Kafe Besara *(Sofokleous 11-12)* is Aussie owned, and one of the old town's liveliest bars. Live music is played three evenings a week. ***Mango Cafe Bar*** *(Dorieos 3)* claims to have the cheapest drinks in the old town as well as Internet access.

The new town has a plethora of discos and bars – over 600 at last count and rising. The two main areas are called Top Street and the Street of Bars. Top Street is Alexandrou Diakou and the Street of Bars is Orfanidou, where a cacophony of western music blares from every establishment. For a wild night of dancing on the bar top, make for ***Down Under Bar*** *(Orfanidou 35)*. If you prefer somewhere more subdued, try ***Red Lion*** *(Orfanidou 9)*, with the relaxed atmosphere of a British pub. Proprietors Ron and Vasilis will gladly answer questions about Rhodes for the price of a drink.

The most amazing of the theme music bars is ***Blue Lagoon*** *(25 Martiou 2)*, where you can indulge your tropical island fantasies amid a shipwreck and lagoon, watched over by a live parrot, three turtles and a waxwork pirate who must have escaped from the adjoining ***Dracula's Palace*** – Rhodes' answer to Madame Tussaud's Chamber of Horrors. Above the bar is ***Mega Club Gas Disco***.

For live rock and roll, try ***Sticky Fingers*** *(Zervou 6)*.

Shopping

Good buys in Rhodes' old town are gold and silver jewellery, leather goods and ceramics. However, leather goods are cheaper in Turkey. Look around and be discriminating – it's quite acceptable to haggle.

Getting Around

Local buses leave from Mandraki. Bus No 2 goes to Analipsi, No 3 to Rodini, No 4 to Agios Dimitrios and No 5 to Monte Smith. You can buy tickets at the kiosk on Mandraki.

EASTERN RHODES

Rhodes' best beaches are on the east coast. There are frequent buses as far as Lindos, but some of the beaches are a bit of a trek from the road. With a bit of leg work, it's possible to find uncrowded stretches of coast even in high season.

Kalithea Thermi, 10km from Rhodes City, is a derelict Italian-built spa. Within the complex are crumbling colonnades, domed ceilings and mosaic floors. Buses from Rhodes City stop opposite the turn-off to the spa. The small beach is used by Rhodes' diving schools (see Activities in the Rhodes City section). To the right there's a small sandy beach (with a snack bar); take the track which veers right from the turn-off to the spa. Kalithea is currently being restored.

Faliraki Beach, 5km farther south, is the island's premier resort and comes complete with high-rise hotels, fast-food joints and bars. Although the main stretch of beach is crowded, the bay at the extreme southern end is uncrowded and popular with nude bathers.

Most accommodation is monopolised by package tour companies, but a pleasant option for independent travellers is the Greek-American owned ***Cannon Bar Pension*** *(☎ 0241-85 596)* where doubles/triples with bathrooms cost 9000/10,000 dr. ***Falaraki Camping*** *(☎ 0241-85 358)* has a restaurant, bar, minimarket and swimming pool. The bus stop is close to the beach.

Afantou, 6km farther on, has a long pebble beach and is the home of the island's only 18 hole golf course (☎ 0241-51 256, 51 451).

At Kolymbia, 4km south of Afantou, a right turn leads in over 4km of pine-fringed road to the **Epta Piges** (Seven Springs), a beautiful spot where a lake fed by springs can be reached either along a path or through a tunnel. There are no buses here, so take a Lindos bus and get off at the turn-off. With your own transport you can continue another 9km to **Eleousa** on the slopes of Profitis Ilias, and then another 3km to the **Church of Agios Nikolaos Fountouklis,** which has fine Byzantine frescoes.

Back on the coast, **Kolymbia** and **Tsambikas** are good but crowded beaches. A steep road (signposted) leads in 1.5km to **Moni Tsambikas**, from where there are terrific views. It is a place of pilgrimage for childless women. On 18 September, the monastery's festival day, they climb up to it on their knees and pray to conceive.

Arhangelos, 4km farther on and inland, is a large agricultural village with a tradition of carpet weaving and handmade goatskin boots production, both of which are being overtaken by tourism as the major money-earner. Just before Arhangelos there is a turn-off to **Stegna Beach**, and just after to the lovely sandy cove of **Agathi**; both are reasonably quiet. The **Castle of Faraklos** above Agathi was a prison for recalcitrant knights and the island's last stronghold to fall to the Turks. The fishing port of **Haraki**, just south of the castle, has a pebbled beach. There are more beaches between here and Vlyha Bay, 2km from Lindos.

Lindos Λίνδος

☎ 0244 • postcode 851 07 • pop 900

Lindos village, 47km from Rhodes, lies below the Acropolis and is a showpiece of dazzling-white 17th century houses, many with courtyards with black and white *hohlakia* (pebble mosaics) floors. Once the dwellings of wealthy admirals, many have been bought and restored by foreign celebrities. The main thoroughfares are lined with tourist shops and cafes, so you need to explore the labyrinthine alleyways to fully appreciate the place.

The 15th century **Church of Agia Panagia** on Acropolis is festooned with 18th century frescoes.

Orientation & Information The town is pedestrianised. All vehicular traffic terminates on the central square of Plateia Eleftherias, from where the main drag, Acropolis, begins. The donkey terminus is a little way along here.

The municipal tourist information office (☎ 31 900/288/227) is on Plateia Eleftherias, open 7.30 am to 10 pm daily. Pallas Travel (☎ 31 494, fax 31 595) and Lindos Sun Tours (☎ 31 333), both on Acropolis, have room-letting services. The latter also rents cars and motorcycles.

The Commercial Bank of Greece, with ATM, is by the donkey terminus. The National Bank of Greece is on the street opposite the Church of Agia Panagia. Turn right at the donkey terminus for the post office. There is no OTE, but there are cardphones on Plateia Eleftherias and the Acropolis. Lindos' Internet cafe is near the post office.

The privately owned Lindos Lending Library, on Acropolis, is well stocked with English books. It also has a laundrette (2500 dr per load).

The Acropolis of Lindos Lindos is the most famous of the Dodecanese's ancient cities, receiving 500,000 visitors a year. It was an important Doric settlement because of its excellent vantage point and good harbour. It was first established around 2000 BC and is overlaid with a conglomeration of Byzantine, Frankish and Turkish remains.

After the founding of the city of Rhodes, Lindos declined in commercial importance, but remained an important place of worship. The ubiquitous St Paul landed here en route to Rome. The Byzantine fortress was strengthened by the knights, and also used by the Turks.

The Acropolis of Lindos is spectacularly perched atop a 116m-high rock. It's about a 10 minute climb to the well signposted entrance gate. Once inside, a flight of steps leads to a large square. On the left (facing the next flight of steps) is a trireme (warship) hewn out of the rock by the sculptor Pythocretes. A statue of Hagesandros, priest of Poseidon, originally stood on the deck of the ship. At the top of the steps ahead, you enter the acropolis by a vaulted corridor. At the other end, turn sharp left through an enclosed room to reach a row of storerooms on the right. The stairway on the right leads to the remains of a 20-columned **Hellenistic stoa** (200 BC). The Byzantine **Church of Agios Ioannis** is to the right of this stairway. The wide stairway behind the stoa leads to a 5th century BC propylaeum, beyond which is the 4th century **Temple to Athena**, the site's most important ancient ruin. Athena was worshipped on Lindos as early as the 10th century BC, so this temple has replaced earlier ones on the site. From its far side there are splendid views of Lindos village and its beach.

Donkey rides to the acropolis cost 1200 dr one way. The site is open 8 am to 6.30 pm Tuesday to Sunday and 12.30 pm to 6.30 pm Monday. Admission is 1200 dr.

Places to Stay & Eat Accommodation is expensive and reservations are essential in summer.

Fedra Rooms to Rent *(☎ 31 286)*, along the street opposite the Church of Agia Panagia, has doubles/triples for 8000/10,000 dr with bathroom.

Pension Electra *(☎ 31 266)* has a roof terrace with superb views and a beautiful shady garden; doubles with shared bathroom cost 9000 dr, and double/triple studios cost 14,000/16,000 dr. ***Pension Katholiki*** *(☎ 31 445)*, next door, has doubles with shared bathroom for 10,000 dr. To get there, follow the signs to the Acropolis but don't turn right at Restaurant Aphrodite – carry on towards the beach.

WESTERN RHODES

Western Rhodes is more green and forested than the east coast, but it's more exposed to winds so the sea tends to be rough, and the beaches are mostly of pebbles or stones. Nevertheless, tourist development is rampant, and consists of the suburb resorts of Ixia, Trianda and Kremasti. Paradisi, despite being next to the airport, has retained some of the feel of a traditional village. If you are on Rhodes between flights or have an early morning flight you may consider staying here. There are several *domatia* and restaurants.

Ialyssos Ιαλυσσός

Like Lindos, Ialyssos, 10km from Rhodes, is a hotchpotch of Doric, Byzantine and medieval remains. The Doric city was built on Filerimos Hill, which was an excellent vantage point, attracting successive invaders. The only ancient remains are the foundations of a 3rd century BC temple and a restored 4th century BC fountain. Also at the site are the restored **Monastery of Our Lady** and the **Chapel of Agios Georgios**.

The ruined fortress was used by Süleyman the Magnificent during his siege of Rhodes City. The site is open 8 am to 5 pm Tuesday to Sunday. Admission is 800 dr.

No buses go to ancient Ialyssos. The airport bus stops at Trianda, on the coast. Ialyssos is 5km inland from here.

Kamiros Κάμειρος

The extensive ruins of the Doric city of Kamiros stand on a hillside above the west coast, 34km from Rhodes City. The ancient city, known for its figs, oil and wine, reached the height of its powers in the 6th century BC. By the 4th century BC, it had been superseded by Rhodes. Most of the city was destroyed by earthquakes in 226 and 142 BC, but the layout is easily discernible.

From the entrance, walk straight ahead and down the steps. The semicircular rostrum on the right is where officials made speeches to the public. Opposite are the remains of a **Doric temple** with one standing column. The area next to it, with a row of intact columns, was probably where the public watched priests performing rites in the temple. Ascend the wide stairway to the ancient city's main street. Opposite the top of the stairs is one of the best preserved of the **Hellenistic houses** which lined the street. Walk along the street, ascend three flights of steps, and continue straight ahead to the ruins of the 3rd century **great stoa**, which had a 206m portico supported by two rows of Doric columns. It was built on top of a huge 6th century cistern which supplied the houses with rainwater through an advanced drainage system. Behind the stoa, at the city's highest point, stood the **Temple to Athena**, with terrific views inland.

The site is open 8 am to 5 pm Tuesday to Sunday. Admission is 800 dr. Buses from Rhodes City to Kamiros stop on the coast road, 1km from the site.

Kamiros to Monolithos Μονόλιθος

Skala Kamiros, 16km south of Kamiros, is touted as an 'authentic fishing village' so it's very much on the tour-bus circuit and only worth a visit to get a caïque to Halki (see the Halki section). The road south from here to Monolithos has some of the island's most impressive scenery. From Skala Kamiros the road winds uphill with great views across to Halki. This is just a taste of what's to come at the ruined 16th century **Castle of Kastellos**, reached along a rough road from the main road, 2km beyond Skala Kamiros. There is a left fork to Embonas (see The Interior, later in this section) 8km farther along. The main road continues for another 9km to **Siana**, a picturesque village below Mt Akramytis (825m), famed for its honey and *souma*, a local firewater.

The village of Monolithos, 5km beyond Siana, has the spectacularly sited **Castle of Monolithos** perched on a sheer 240m rock and reached along a dirt track. Continuing along this track, at the fork bear right for **Moni Georgiou** and left for the very pleasant shingled **Fourni Beach**.

Hotel Thomas *(☎ 0246-61 291)* at Monolithos has doubles for 10,000 dr.

SOUTHERN RHODES

South of Lindos, Rhodes becomes progressively less developed. Although **Pefki**, 2km south of Lindos, does get package tourists, it's still possible to get out of earshot of other tourists, away from the main beach.

Lardos is a pleasant village 6km west of Lindos and 2km inland from Lardos Beach. From the far side of Lardos a turn right leads in 4km to **Moni Agia Ipseni** (Monastery of Our Lady) through hilly, green countryside.

The well watered village of **Laerma** is 12km north-west of Lardos. From here it's another 5km (signposted) to the beautifully sited 9th century **Moni Thari**, which was the island's first monastery and has recently been re-established as a monastic community. It contains some fine 13th century frescoes.

Asklipion, 8km north of Genadi, is an unspoilt village with the ruins of yet another castle and the 11th century **Church of Kimisis Theotokou**.

Genadi Γεννάδι

☎ 0244 • postcode 851 09 • pop 400

Genadi, 13km south of Lardos, is another burgeoning resort. Inland from the main street, however, it's an unspoilt agricultural village, with narrow, winding streets of whitewashed houses, an **olive press museum** and a stone fountain by a huge mulberry tree. At the crossroads turn left to reach the long pebble and sand beach, and right to reach the village. Genadi's main street is to the right (facing inland) of the central square.

Places to Stay & Eat ***Tina's Studios*** *(☎ 43 204)*, off the main street, has modern double studios for 10,000 dr. ***Effie's Dreams Apartments*** *(☎/fax 43 437, email dreams@srh.forthnet.gr)*, right by the mulberry tree, has modern, spotlessly clean studios with lovely rural and sea vistas from the communal balcony. Doubles/triples cost 9200/11,000 dr. The friendly Greek-Australian owners will meet you if you call ahead. The spacious ***Betty Studios & Apartments*** *(☎ 43 020)*, on the main street, has double/triple studios for 8600/10,000 dr and four-person apartments for 11,800 dr.

The nicest restaurant is ***Restaurant Antonis*** at the beach. The new ***Effie's Dream Cafe Bar***, below the apartments, serves drinks and tasty snacks in a tranquil setting.

Greek Weddings

Greek weddings are lavish affairs and if you have ever been lucky enough to attend one and its ensuing lively wedding feast, you have indeed been privileged. While civil weddings in Greece have been legal for over fifteen years, most Greek couples still prefer the ritualistic ceremony of an orthodox church service followed by an afternoon and evening, or even weekend of eating, drinking and dancing.

The church ceremony is redolent of incense and ceremony. The participation of the bride and bridegroom is mainly passive since the main action is conducted by the priest and the *koumbaros* (best man) or *koumbara* (best woman) who literally 'crowns' the couple with a pair of interlinked garlands. The real excitement starts with the 'dance' during which the newly wed couple are led around in a circle by the priest while church participants shower them with rice.

After the ceremony it is customary for everyone in the church to line up and congratulate the couple, their family, the best man or woman and the bridesmaids with wishes such as *na zisete* (may you enjoy long life) to the couple and *na sas zisoun* (may they live for many years) to the parents. If the bridesmaids are single they are greeted with *kai sta dika sou* (your turn next).

Those invited to the wedding feast, which in rural areas often means the whole village, will retire to an evening of revelry and entertainment, part of which sees the bride and groom take the first dance and then literally get covered with money that is pinned to their clothes by guests. The party will often carry on all night and into the next day.

Genadi to Prasonisi Πρασονήσι

From Genadi an almost uninterrupted beach of pebbles, shingle and sand dunes extends down to **Plimmyri**, 11km south. It's easy to find deserted stretches.

From Plimmyri the main road continues to **Kattavia**, Rhodes' most southerly village. The 11km dirt road north to Messanagros winds through terrific scenery. From Kattavia a 10km road leads south to the remote **Prasonisi** (Green Island), the island's southernmost point, joined to Rhodes by a narrow sandy isthmus with rough sea on one side and calm water on the other. It's a popular spot for windsurfing. ***The Lighthouse Taverna*** (☎ *0244-91 030*), one of two tavernas on the access road, has double rooms for 10,000 dr. Many people simply pitch a tent on the surrounding land.

South of Monolithos

On the west coast the beaches south of Monolithos are prone to strong winds. From Apolakkia, 10km south of Monolithos, a road crosses the island to Genadi, passing through the unspoilt villages of Arnitha, Istrios, Profilias and Vati. A turn-off to the left 7km south of Apolakkia leads to the 18th century **Moni Skiadi**. It's a serene place with terrific views down to the coast, and there is free basic accommodation for visitors.

The coast road beyond this turn-off is unsurfaced and runs close to the sea before veering inland for Kattavia.

THE INTERIOR

The east-west roads that cross the island have great scenery and very little traffic. If you have transport they're well worth exploring.

Petaloudes Πεταλούδες

Petaloudes (Valley of the Butterflies), one of the 'must sees' on the package tour itinerary, is reached along a 6km turn-off from the west coast road, 2.5km south of Paradisi.

The butterflies *(Callimorpha quadripunctarea)* are lured to this gorge of rustic footbridges, streams and pools by the scent of the resin exuded by the styrax trees. Regardless of what you may see other tourists doing, do not make any noises to disturb the butterflies; their numbers are declining rapidly, largely due to noise disturbance. Petaloudes is open 8 am to 6 pm daily from 1 May to 30 September. Admission is 600 dr. There are buses to Petaloudes from Rhodes City.

Around Petaloudes

From Petaloudes a 2km dirt track leads to the 18th century **Moni Kalopetras** built by Alexander Ypsilantas, the grandfather of the Greek freedom-fighter. A small snack bar here sells soft drinks and *loukoumades*.

Also from Petaloudes, a 5km road leads to **Psinthos**, a pleasant village where ***Artemidis Restaurant & Rooms*** *(☎ 0246-51 735)* serves tasty traditional Greek fare and has a swimming pool. Double rooms above the restaurant cost 10,000 dr. Psinthos can also be reached from the east coast.

Salakos & Mt Profitis Ilias

Σάλακος & Ορος Προφήτης Ηλίας

Salakos is an attractive village below Mt Profitis Ilias (790m) reached along an 8km turn-off, 30km from Rhodes City along the west coast road. ***Hotel Nimfi*** *(☎ 0246-22 206/346)* has doubles for 10,000 dr.

From the village, a path leads almost to Mt Profitis Ilias' summit. Walk along the main road towards the mountains; at the curve, 60m beyond Hotel Nimfi, turn left, and after 50m take a path to the right signposted 'Profitis Ilias'. It ends near an asphalt road and the defunct Elafos Hotel. The ***cafe*** opposite is often open.

Beyond Salakos

The road forks 6km beyond Salakos. The left fork leads to Elafos Hotel from where a dirt road continues to the Byzantine **Church of Agios Nikolaos Fountouklis**, and Eleousa (see the Eastern Rhodes section). The right fork leads to **Embonas** on the slopes of Mt Attavyros (1215m), the island's highest mountain. Embonas is, unfortunately, touted as a 'traditional mountain village' and visited by many tourist buses. It's also renowned for its wine and is surrounded by vineyards that produce the dry white 'Villare'. It costs around 1800 dr a bottle and is produced at the **Emery Winery** (☎ 0246-29 111), where you can enjoy free wine tasting on weekdays until 3 pm.

Agios Isidoros, 14km south of Embona, is a lovely unspoilt village to which you can detour en route to Siana.

Halki Χάλκη

☎ **0241** • **postcode 851 10** • **pop 281**

Halki is a small island 16km off the west coast of Rhodes (refer to the map at the start of the Rhodes section). It has escaped the tourist development of its large neighbour; but much of the accommodation is monopolised by package tourists who want a holi-day on an untouristy island. It's a barren, rocky island with a severe water shortage. The population has been greatly reduced by emigration. Many islanders moved to Tarpon Springs, Florida, where they have established a sponge-fishing community.

Getting There & Away

Ferry Ferries call at Halki once weekly in summer on the Piraeus-Rhodes run.

Caïque A caïque operates between Halki and Skala Kamiros on Rhodes. From Monday to Saturday, it leaves Halki at 5.30 am (to connect with the 7.30 am bus from Skala Kamiros to Rhodes); the return trip departs Skala Kamiros at 2.30 pm. On Sunday, it leaves Halki at 9 am and Skala Kamiros at 4 pm. The fare is 2000 dr.

To get to Skala Kamiros from Rhodes City, take the 1.15 pm Monolithos bus from the west side bus station. There are no connecting buses on Sunday morning.

Getting Around
Halki has no cars, buses or taxis. There are excursion boats to the island's beaches and to the nearby uninhabited islet of Alimia which has good beaches.

EMBOREIOS Εμπορειός
Halki has only one settlement, the attractive little port town of Emboreios. Many of its imposing mansions are now derelict. The Church of Agios Nikolaos has the tallest belfry in the Dodecanese.

Orientation & Information
The quay is in the middle of the harbour. There is one road out of Emboreios, incongruously named Tarpon Springs Boulevard for the ex-Halkiots in Florida, who financed its construction. It passes Podamos, the island's only sandy beach.

There is a small tourist information kiosk between the post office (opposite the quay) and the war memorial. The staff will help you to find accommodation. There is no OTE, but there are cardphones.

Places to Stay & Eat
The nicest place to stay is ***Captain's House*** *(☎ 45 201)*, a beautiful 19th century mansion with period furniture and a tranquil tree-shaded garden. It is owned by a retired Greek sea captain and his British wife, Christine. Doubles with bathroom are 10,000 dr. ***Pension Cleanthi*** *(☎ 45 334)*, on the road to Podamos Beach, has modern doubles with bathroom for 10,000 dr.

Several ***tavernas*** line the waterfront and there is a good taverna on Podamos Beach.

AROUND HALKI
Horio, a 30 minute walk along Tarpon Springs Boulevard from Emboreios, was the 'pirate-proof' inland town. Once a thriving community of 3000 people, it's now derelict and uninhabited. A path leads from Horio's churchyard to a Knights of St John castle.

Moni Agiou Ioanni is a two hour walk from Horio. There are no monks here now, but the shepherd-cum-caretaker, Dimitris, lives here with his family. Free beds are available for tourists, but you must take your own food and water. Take the right fork of Tarpon Springs Boulevard. There are fine views of many Dodecanese islands and Turkey.

Karpathos Κάρπαθος

☎ 0245 • postcode 857 00 • pop 5323

The elongated island of Karpathos (**kar**-pah-thos), midway between Crete and Rhodes, is traversed by a north-south mountain range. For hundreds of years the north and south parts of the island were isolated from one another and so they developed independently. It is even thought that the northerners and southerners have different ethnic origins. The northern village of Olymbos is of endless fascination to ethnologists for the age-old customs of its inhabitants. Karpathos has rugged mountains, numerous beaches and unspoilt villages, and despite having charter flights from northern Europe, it has not, so far, succumbed to the worst excesses of mass tourism.

Karpathos has a relatively uneventful history. Unlike almost all other Dodecanese islands, it was never under the auspices of the Knights of St John. It is a wealthy island, receiving more money from emigrants living abroad (mostly in the USA) than any other Greek island.

A culinary speciality is *makarounes* (handmade macaroni cooked with onions and cheese).

Getting There & Away
Air There are three flights weekly to Athens (26,000 dr) and two daily to Rhodes (12,800 dr). The Olympic Airways office (☎ 22 150/057) is on the central square in Pigadia. The airport is 18km south-west of Pigadia.

Ferry Karpathos has two ports: Pigadia (Karpathos Port) and Diafani. At 3.45 pm on Wednesday the F/B *Daliana* arrives at Pigadia from Piraeus, Syros, Paros, Naxos, Ios, Santorini, Iraklio and Kassos, and then departs for Diafani and Rhodes. At 7.30 am

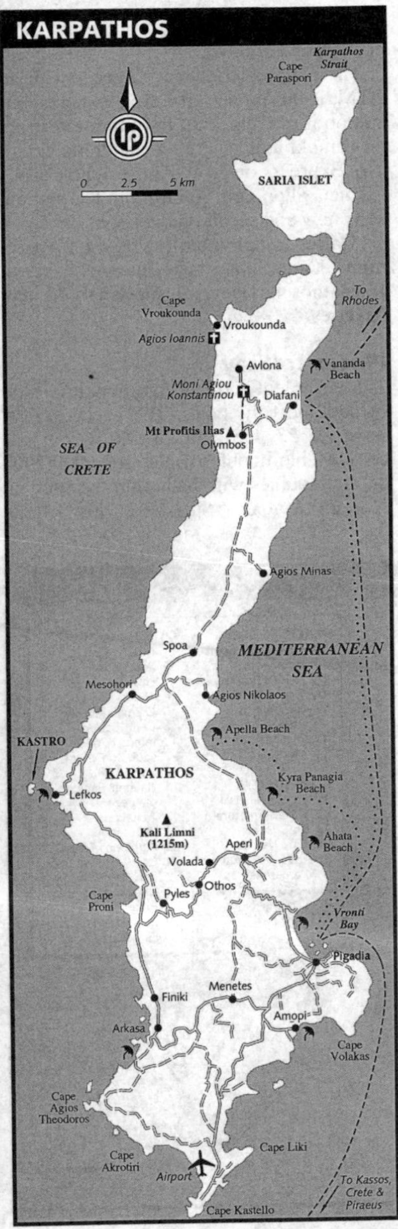

on Wednesday it arrives back at Diafani from Rhodes, and takes the same route back to Piraeus.

At 2.10 pm on Saturday the F/B *Vitsentsos Kornaros* arrives at Pigadia from Piraeus, Milos, Crete and Kassos. From Pigadia it continues to Diafani, Halki and Rhodes. At 8.50 am on Sunday it leaves Pigadia for Piraeus via the same route.

Getting Around

To/From the Airport There was no airport bus at the time of research, but check with the Olympic Airways office.

Bus Pigadia is the transport hub of the island. A schedule is posted at the bus terminal. There are four buses daily to Amopi (300 dr), Pyles (380 dr) via Aperi (300 dr), Volada (300 dr) and Othos (300 dr); two daily to Finiki (380 dr) via Menetes (300 dr) and Arkasa (380 dr); and buses to Lefkos on Monday and Thursday. There is no bus between Pigadia and Olymbos or Diafani.

Car, Motorcycle & Bicycle Gatoulis Car Hire (☎ 22 747, fax 22 814), on the east side of the road to Aperi, hires cars, motorcycles and bicycles.

The 21km stretch of road from Spoa to Olymbos is unsurfaced but driveable. Check on its current condition with the tourist police before setting off, though, and make sure you know where the petrol stations are – they're few and far between.

Taxi Pigadia's taxi rank (☎ 22 705) is on Dimokratias, just around the corner from Apodimon Karpathou. A price list is supposed to be displayed. If this is not the case check the price with the tourist police or a travel agent, as rip-offs do occur. A taxi from Pigadia to Diafani is a steep 25,000 dr.

Excursion Boat In summer there are daily excursion boats from Pigadia to Diafani for 5000 dr return. There are also frequent boats to the beaches of Kyra Panagia and Apella for 3000 dr. Tickets can be bought from Karpathos Travel in Pigadia.

PIGADIA Πηγάδια

• pop 1300

Pigadia is the island's capital and main port. It's a modern town, pleasant enough, but without any eminent buildings or sites. The town is built on the edge of Vronti Bay, a 4km-long sandy beach where you can rent water sports equipment. On the beach are the remains of the early Christian basilica of Agia Fotini.

Orientation & Information

From the quay, turn right and take the left fork onto Apodimon Karpathou, Pigadia's main thoroughfare, which leads to the central square of Plateia 5 Oktovriou.

Pigadia has no EOT. The tourist police (☎ 22 218) are on Ethnikis Anastasis. Also on this street are the post office and OTE. The most helpful of the travel agencies is Karpathos Travel (☎ 22 148/754), on Dimokratias; its guided walks around the island cost around 5000 dr.

The National Bank of Greece, with an ATM, is on Apodimon Karpathou. The bus station is one block up from the waterfront on Dimokratias. There's a laundrette, Laundro Express, on Mitr Apostolou. Carol's Corner Shop, on Apodimon Karpathou, sells new and second-hand books.

Caffe Galileo Internet 2000, on Apodimon Karpathou, has Internet access. Karpathos has several supermarkets and bakeries.

Places to Stay

There's plenty of accommodation and owners meet the boats. The E class ***Hotel Avra*** *(☎ 23 468)*, on 28 Oktovriou, has comfortable doubles/triples for 6000/7000 dr, and doubles with bathroom for 8000 dr. ***Harry's Rooms*** *(☎ 22 188)*, just off 28

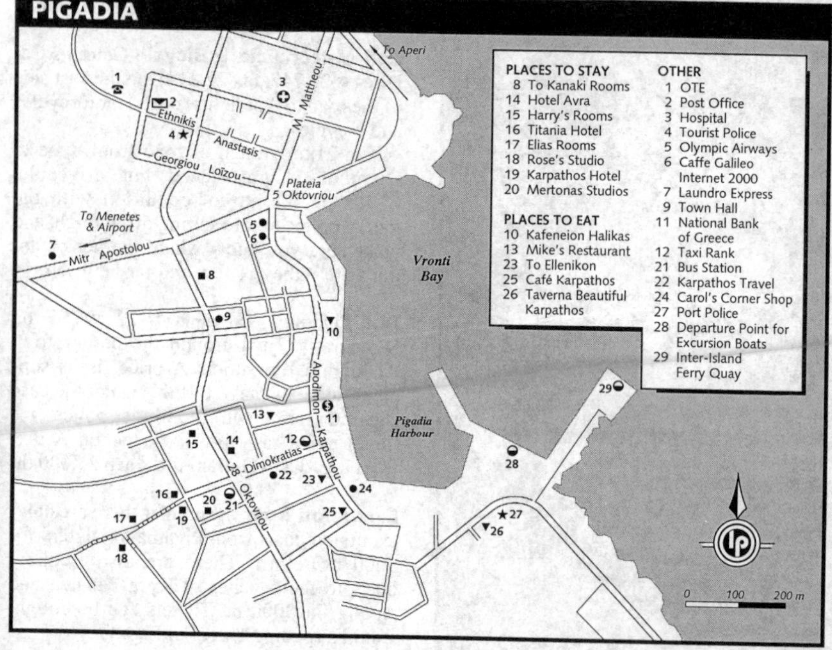

Oktovriou, has spotless singles/doubles for 3500/6000 dr. Farther along 28 Oktovriou, ***To Kanaki Rooms*** *(☎ 22 908)* has very pleasant doubles for 7000 dr with bathroom.

The immaculate, cosy ***Elias Rooms*** *(☎ 22 446)* is in a quiet part of town with great views. Singles/doubles/triples with bathroom are 4000/6000/8000 dr. The owner, Elias Hatzigorgiou, is friendly and helpful. Ascend the steps by the Karpathos Hotel to reach the rooms. Farther up the steps, ***Rose's Studios*** *(☎/fax 22 284)*, has well kept double studios with bathroom and kitchen for 6000 dr. Doubles with large well equipped communal kitchen and bathrooms cost 4000 dr.

The C class ***Karpathos Hotel*** *(☎ 22 347)* has light, airy rooms for 6000/6500 dr with bathroom. Opposite, the C class ***Titania Hotel*** *(☎ 22 144, fax 23 307)* has spacious, pleasant rooms for 8000/10,000/13,000 dr. ***Mertonas Studios*** *(☎ 22 622, 31 396)* has lovely, tastefully furnished studios, managed by the warm and friendly Eva Angelos. Rates for doubles/triples are 8000/9000 dr, and four-person studios are 10,000 dr. Take the first left after Cafe Karpathos, turn right at the T-junction, take the first left, and the studios are on the right.

Places to Eat

Pigadia is well supplied with good restaurants. ***Mike's Restaurant***, just off Apodimon Karpathou, is excellent. A meal of lamb stew, Greek salad and retsina costs 3000 dr.

The popular ***Kafeneion Halikas*** is open all day for drinks, but only serves meals in the evenings. The menu is limited but the food is tasty and live music is played. It's a crumbling white building, just beyond the National Bank of Greece.

Taverna Beautiful Karpathos, near the quay, serves a wide range of traditional Karpathian dishes and reputedly the best makarounes in Pigadia. ***To Ellenikon***, on Apodimou Karpathou, has a pleasant outdoor terrace and a tasteful interior. The Karpathian *stifado* is particularly commendable.

Cafe Karpathos, at the beginning of Apodimou Karpathou, is a great place to meet locals, expats and tourists. If you speak Greek or Italian, Ilias, the owner, can fill you in on some interesting walks on the island. The cafe serves good coffee and tasty sandwiches.

SOUTHERN KARPATHOS

Amopi Αμόπι

The island's premier holiday resort, Amopi, is 8km from Pigadia. It's not especially attractive but has two bays of golden sand, translucent sea and pebbled coves. There are four buses daily from Pigadia.

Places to Stay & Eat Amopi is a scattered place without any centre or easily identifiable landmarks, so ask the bus or taxi driver to drop you off at whichever establishment you decide to check. The cheapest place is ***Amopi Beach Rooms*** *(☎ 22 723)* where spotless, simply furnished doubles cost 3500 dr. The rooms are at the far end of Amopi.

Farther back along the main road, ***Hotel Sophia*** *(☎ 22 078)*, behind the Blue Sea Hotel, has doubles/triples for 9000/15,000 dr. Nearby, ***Votsalakia Rooms & Restaurant*** *(☎ 22 204)*, has attractively furnished doubles for 8000 dr. ***Four Seasons Studios*** *(☎ 22 116)*, farther back along the road, has equally commendable doubles with bathroom for 8000 dr.

Kastelia Bay Hotel *(☎ 22 678)* has light, airy singles/doubles for 12,000/14,000 dr. A little way along the approach road to Amopi a sign points to the hotel.

Four Seasons Restaurant serves delicious Greek dishes and freshly baked brown bread.

Menetes Μενετές

Menetes is perched on a sheer cliff 8km above Pigadia. It's a picturesque, unspoilt village with pastel-coloured neoclassical houses lining its main street. Behind the main street are narrow, stepped alleyways that wind between more modest whitewashed dwellings. The village has a little **museum** on the right as you come from

Pigadia. The owner of Taverna Manolis will open it up for you.

Places to Stay & Eat Menetes has only one place to stay: the ***domatia*** of friendly Greek-American Mike Rigas *(☎ 81 269/255)*, in a traditional Karpathian house with a garden brimming with trees and flowers. Doubles/triples with bathroom are 4700/5500 dr. As you approach from Pigadia, the rooms are 150m down a cement road (signposted 'Lai') veering off to the right. ***Taverna Manolis*** dishes up generous helpings of grilled meat. ***Fiesta Dionysos*** specialises in local dishes, including omelette made with artichokes and Karpathian sausages.

Arkasa & Finiki Αρκάσα & Φοινίκι

Arkasa, 9km farther on, straddles a ravine. It is metamorphosing from traditional village to holiday resort. Turn right at the T-junction to reach the authentic village square.

A turn-off left, just before the ravine, leads after 500m to the remains of the 5th century Basilica of Agia Sophia. Two chapels stand amid mosaic fragments and columns.

The serene fishing village of Finiki is 2km north of Arkasa. The little sculpture at the harbour commemorates the heroism of seven local fishers during WWII – locals will tell you the story.

Places to Stay & Eat ***Pension Philoxenia*** *(☎ 61 341)*, on the left before the T-junction, has clean doubles for 6500 dr. ***Elini Rooms*** *(☎ 61 248)*, on the left along the road to Finiki, has attractive double apartments for 10,000 dr.

Fay's Paradise *(☎ 61 308)*, near Finiki's harbour, has lovely double studios for 10,000 dr. ***Finiki View Hotel*** *(☎ 61 309/400)*, on the right as you come from Arkasa, has spacious doubles for 12,000 dr and a swimming pool and bar.

There is a good taverna on Arkasa's main square and locals come from all over the island to eat the fresh fish at ***Dimitrios Fisherman's Taverna*** in Finiki.

Lefkos Λεύκος

Lefkos, 13km north of Finiki, and 2km from the coast road, is a burgeoning resort centred around a little fishing quay. It is a beach-lover's paradise with five superb sandy beaches. In summer Lefkos gets crowded, but at other times it still has a rugged, off-the-beaten-track feel about it.

Local boat owners sometimes take visitors to the islet of Sokastro where there is a ruined castle. Another diversion from the beaches is the ancient catacombs, reached by walking inland and turning left at Imeri Rooms.

Places to Stay & Eat ***Imeri Rooms*** *(☎ 71 375)*, owned by a friendly elderly couple, is in a peaceful rural setting halfway between the coast road and the beaches. Sparkling doubles/triples cost 7000/8000 dr with bathroom. Inquire at ***Small Paradise Taverna & Rooms*** *(☎ 71 171/184)*, farther down the road, about its Sunset Studios which overlook Golden Beach. Immaculate doubles/triples cost 8000/9000 dr. ***Golden Sands Studios*** *(☎ 71 175, fax 71 219)*, almost on Golden Beach, are bright, new double/triple studios with well equipped kitchens, for 9000/12,000 dr. ***Zorba's Rooms***, near the quay, are equally nice with double studios for 11,000 dr.

Small Paradise Taverna serves tasty local dishes and fresh seafood on a vine-shaded terrace.

Getting There & Around There are two buses weekly to Lefkos and a taxi costs 8000 dr, but telephone the rooms' proprietors and they may be able to arrange a lift from Pigadia, providing you intend staying with them, of course! Hitching is dicey as there is not much traffic.

Lefkos Rent A Car (☎/fax 71 057) is a reliable outlet with very competitive prices. The English-speaking owner will deliver vehicles free of charge to anywhere in southern Karpathos.

East Coast Beaches

The fine beaches of **Ahata**, **Kyra Panagia** and **Apella** can be reached along dirt roads off the east coast road, but are most easily reached by excursion boat from Pigadia. Only Kyra Panagia has accommodation and tavernas.

Mesohori & Spoa Μεσοχώρι & Σπόα

Mesohori, 4km beyond the turn-off for Lefkos, is a pretty village of whitewashed houses and stepped streets. Spoa village, 5km farther on along a dirt road, is at the beginning of the 21km dirt road to Olymbos. It overlooks the east coast and has a track down to **Agios Nikolaos Beach**.

Mountain Villages

Aperi, **Volada**, **Othos** and **Pyles**, the well watered mountain villages to the north of Pigadia, are largely unaffected by tourism. None has any accommodation, but all have tavernas and kafeneia. Aperi was the island's capital from 1700 until 1892. Its ostentatious houses were built by wealthy returning emigrants from the USA. Like Aperi, Volada has an air of prosperity.

Othos (altitude 510m) is the island's highest village. It has a small ethnographic museum. From Othos the road winds downhill to Pyles, a gorgeous village of twisting, stepped streets, pastel houses and citrus groves. It clings to the slopes of Mt Kali Limni (1215m), the Dodecanese's second-highest peak.

NORTHERN KARPATHOS

Diafani & Olymbos

Διαφάνι & Ολυμπος

Diafani is Karpathos' small northern port. There's no post office or bank, but Orfanos Travel Holidays (☎ 51 410), owned by helpful English-speaking Nikos, has currency exchange. There's no OTE but there are cardphones.

Clinging to the ridge of barren Mt Profitis Ilias, 4km above Diafani, Olymbos is a living museum (population 340). Women wear bright, embroidered skirts, waistcoats and headscarves, and goatskin boots. The interiors of the houses are decorated with embroidered cloth and their facades feature brightly painted, ornate plaster reliefs. The inhabitants speak in a vernacular which contains some Doric words, and the houses have wooden locks of a kind described by Homer. Olymbos is a matrilineal society – a family's property passes down from the mother to the first-born daughter. The women still grind corn in windmills and bake bread in outdoor communal ovens.

Olymbos, alas, is no longer a pristine backwater caught in a time warp. Nowadays hordes of tourists come to gape, and tourist shops are appearing everywhere. However, Olymbos is still a fascinating place, and accommodation and food are inexpensive.

Avlona & Vroukounda

Until early this century the inhabitants of Olymbos spent the summer in Avlona, a village lying in a fertile valley to the north of Olymbos. It's an attractive place of pastel coloured *stavlos* (farmhouses) and neat terraces. Nowadays, due to migration and, more recently, the locals' preference for involvement in the tourist industry, Avlona has only a small population of farmers in summer.

Avlona is reached along a dirt road from the Diafani-Olymbos road, or in a two hour walk along a path which begins at the bottom of the steps to the right of the row of windmills in Olymbos. The **Church of Agios Ioannis** at Vroukounda, a deserted village to the north of Avlona, is the scene of a lively four day festival which begins on 29 August.

Places to Stay & Eat There's an unofficial ***camp site*** at Vananda Beach, 30 minutes walk (signposted) north of Diafani. ***Golden Beach Hotel*** *(☎ 51 315)*, opposite the quay in Diafani, has doubles with bathroom for 8000 dr. ***Nikos Hotel*** *(☎ 51 289)*, just back from the waterfront, has comfortable singles/doubles/triples for 5000/7000/85000 dr with bathroom and breakfast included. The hotel is owned by Nikos of Orfanos Travel. The new ***Balaskas Hotel***, close by, has pleasant doubles for 8000 dr with bathroom.

Just off the main street in Olymbos, the clean, simply furnished rooms at ***Pension Olymbos*** *(☎ 51 252)* cost 3000/6000 dr. Just beyond the bus turnaround, ***Mike's Rooms*** *(☎ 51 304)* cost 6000 dr a double.

Hotel Aphrodite *(☎ 51 307/454)*, near the central square, has immaculate doubles/ triples for 7000/9000 dr with bathroom.

In Diafani the ***Golden Beach Taverna*** and ***Taverna Anatoli*** are good.

Makarounes are served at all the restaurants in Olymbos. You'll eat well at ***Olymbos Taverna***, below Pension Olymbos, at ***Mike's Taverna***, directly below his rooms, and also at ***Parthenonas Restaurant***, on the central square.

Getting Around A bus meets the excursion boats from Pigadia at Diafani and transports people up to Olymbos.

From Diafani, excursion boats go to nearby beaches and occasionally to the uninhabited islet of Saria where there are some Byzantine remains.

Kassos Κάσσος

☎ 0245 • postcode 858 00 • pop 1088

Kassos, 11km south of Karpathos, is a rocky little island with prickly pear trees, sparse olive and fig trees, drystone walls, and sheep and goats. One of the least-visited of the Dodecanese, it's the perfect island to see something of traditional Greek life, and is also great for walks.

History

Despite being diminutive and remote, Kassos has an eventful and tragic history. During Turkish rule it flourished, and by 1820 it had 11,000 inhabitants and a large mercantile fleet. Mohammad Ali, the Turkish governor of Egypt, regarded this fleet as an impediment to his plan to establish a base on Crete from which to attack the Peloponnese and quell the uprising there. So, on 7 June 1824, Ali's men landed on Kassos and killed around 7000 inhabitants. This massacre is commemorated annually on the anniversary of the slaughter and Kassiots return from around the world to participate.

During the late 19th century, many Kassiots emigrated to Egypt and around 5000 of them helped build the Suez Canal. In this century many have emigrated to the USA.

Getting There & Away

Air There are three flights weekly to Rhodes (13,400 dr), and one weekly from Athens (24,700 dr). The Olympic Airways office (☎ 41 444) is on Kritis.

Ferry Kassos has the same ferry schedule as Karpathos.

Excursion Boat In summer there are excursion boats from Phry to the uninhabited Armathia Islet (2000 dr return) where there are sandy beaches.

Getting Around

At the time of writing there was no island bus. The airport is only 600m along the coast road from Phry.

There are just two taxis on Kassos. For further details ask Kassos Maritime and Travel Agency (see Information). Motorbikes can be rented from Frangiscos Moto Rentals (☎ 41 746).

PHRY Φρυ

Phry is the island's capital and port. The town's focal point is the picturesque old fishing harbour of Bouka. The suburb of Emboreios is 1km east of Phry.

Orientation & Information

Turn left at the quay to reach Bouka. Veer left, and then right, and continue along the waterfront to the central square of Plateia Iroön Kassou. Turn right here to reach Kritis, Phry's main street. To reach Emboreios, continue along the waterfront passing the turn-off (signposted 'Agia Mamas') for Panagia, Poli and Agia Mamas.

Kassos does not have an EOT or tourist police, but Emmanuel Manousos, at Kassos Maritime and Travel Agency (☎ 41 495,

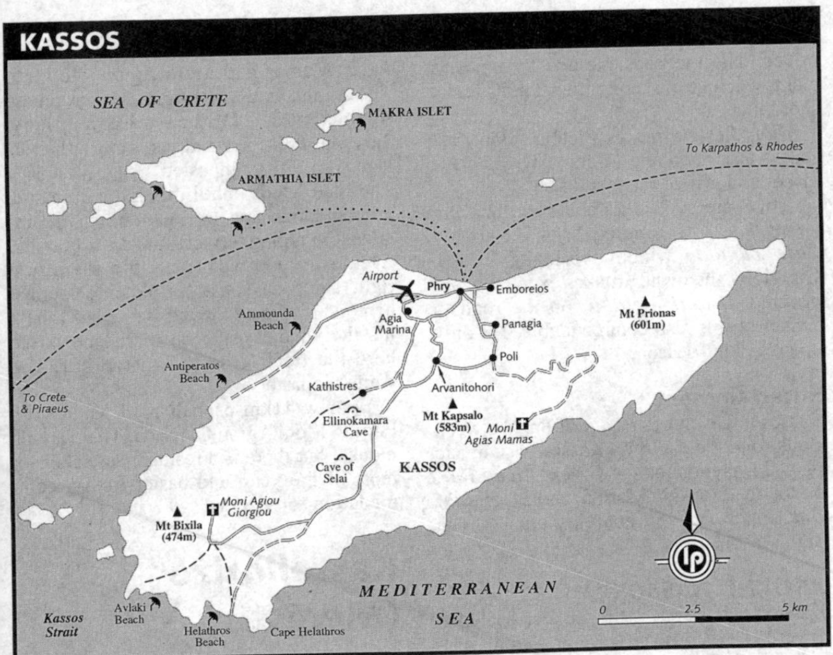

41 323), Plateia Iroön Kassou, is helpful and speaks English.

The National Bank of Greece is represented by the supermarket on Kritis. At the time of writing there was a rumour that Kassos would soon have a bank. From the waterfront, take the first turn left along Kritis to reach the post office. The OTE is behind Plateia Dimokratias – you'll see the huge satellite dishes.

The port police (☎ 41 288) are behind the Church of Agios Spyridon. The police (☎ 41 222) are just beyond the post office, on the opposite side.

Places to Stay

All of the island's accommodation (and there's not that much) is in Phry, except for the rooms at Moni Agiou Giorgiou (see Monasteries in the Around Kassos section). ***Ketty Markous*** *(☎ 41 613/ 498)* rents doubles for 5000 dr, including kitchen. They're on the south side of the road to Emboreios. Farther along this road, on the opposite side, ***Elias Koutlakis Rooms*** *(☎ 41 363)* costs 8000 dr a double with bathroom.

Anessis Hotel *(☎ 41 234/201)*, above the supermarket on Kritis, has singles/doubles for 6000/8000 dr with bathroom. ***Anagennisis Hotel*** *(☎ 41 495, fax 41 036)*, on Plateia Iroön Kassou, has clean and comfortable rooms for 5500/7000 dr, or with bathroom for 7000/9500 dr.

The owner of the Anagennisis Hotel, Emmanuel Manousos, also has well equipped double/triple ***apartments*** for 15,000/18,000 dr. Emmanuel's brother, Georgios Manousos, has apartments for the same price.

Places to Eat

Phry has two restaurants and several snack bars. ***Kassos Restaurant*** on Plateia

Dimokratias is run by a women's cooperative. The food is well prepared and low-priced. The mezedes include *kritamos*, a plant which grows along the island's rocky shore line.

Milos Restaurant, on Plateia Iroön Kassou, is also good and offers tasty casserole dishes and grilled meat and fish.

There are several kafeneia in Phry, but young Kassiots congregate at the trendy ***Cafe Zananta*** which overlooks Bouka. Giorgious, the owner, makes excellent cappuccino. ***Ouzeri Meltimi***, on the road to Emborious, is also commendable, but only opens in high season.

Entertainment

Kassos' night club is ***Perigaili Bar***, between Bouka and Plateia Iroön Kassou. The music played is predominantly Greek. ***Alenti Bar***, on the road to Agia Marina, and ***Marianthi Bar***, on the way to Emboreios, open only in high season.

AROUND KASSOS

Kassos' best beach is the isolated, pebbled cove of **Helathros**, near Moni Agiou Giorgiou. The beach has no facilities. You can get there either along a dirt track which bears left (downhill) from the road to the monastery, or along a slightly longer track from the monastery. Avlaki is another decent beach reached along a path from the monastery.

The mediocre **Ammounda Beach**, beyond the airport, near the blue-domed Church of Agios Konstantinos, is the nearest to Phry. There are slightly better beaches farther along this stretch of coast.

Agia Marina, 1km south-west of Phry, is a pretty village with a gleaming white and blue church. On 17 July the Festival of Agia Marina is celebrated here. From Agia Marina the road continues to verdant **Arvanitohori**, with fig and pomegranate trees.

Poli, 3km south-east of Phry, is the former capital, built on the ancient acropolis. **Panagia**, between Phry and Poli, has fewer than 50 inhabitants. Its once-grand sea captains' and ship owners' mansions are now derelict.

Monasteries

The island has two monasteries: **Moni Agias Mamas** and **Moni Agiou Giorgiou**. The uninhabited Moni Agias Mamas on the south coast is a 1½ hour walk from Phry. Take the Poli road and just before the village turn left (signposted 'Agia Mamas'). The road winds uphill through a dramatic, eroded landscape of rock-strewn mountains, crumbling terraces and soaring cliffs. Eventually you will come to a sharp turn right (signposted again). Hold onto your hat here, as it's known locally as *aeras* (air) – it's the windiest spot on the island. From here the track descends to the blue and white monastery.

A new 11km asphalt road leads from Phry to Moni Agiou Giorgiou. There are no monks, but there is a resident caretaker for most of the year, and basic (free) accommodation for visitors.

Kastellorizo (Megisti)

Καστελλόριζο

☎ 0241 • postcode 851 11 • pop 275

Tiny, rocky Kastellorizo (kah-stel-**o**-rih-zo), a mere speck on the map, is 118km east of Rhodes, its nearest Greek neighbour, and only 2.5km from the southern coast of Turkey. Its official name is Megisti (the biggest), for it is the largest of a group of 14 islets. The island's remoteness has so far ensured that its tourism is low-key. There are no beaches, but there are rocky inlets from where you can swim and snorkel in a crystal-clear sea.

The island featured in the Oscar-winning Italian film *Mediterraneo* (1991) which was based on a book by an Italian army sergeant. The little book *Capture Kastellorizo* by Marina Pitsonis is available on the island. The author is a Greek/Australian whose father came from Kastellorizo. The book features eight island walks.

History

The ghost town you see today is made all the more poignant by an awareness of the island's past greatness. Due to its strategic position, Dorians, Romans, crusaders, Egyptians, Turks, Venetians and pirates have all landed on its shores. The 20th century has been no less traumatic, with French, British and Italian occupiers.

In 1552, Kastellorizo surrendered peacefully to the Turks and so was granted special privileges. It was allowed to preserve its language, religion and traditions. Its cargo fleet became the largest in the Dodecanese and the islanders achieved a high degree of culture and education.

Kastellorizo lost all strategic and economic importance after the 1923 population exchange. In 1928 it was ceded to the Italians, who severely oppressed the islanders; in contrast, Turkish rule must have seemed like the good old days. Many islanders emigrated to Perth, Australia, where today some 10,000 of them live.

During WWII, Kastellorizo suffered severe bombardment, and English commanders ordered the few remaining inhabitants to abandon their island. They fled to Cyprus, Palestine and Egypt, with no belongings. In October 1945, 300 islanders boarded the Australian ship *Empire Control* to return to Kastellorizo. Tragically, the ship caught fire and 35 people lost their lives. Two months later the remaining refugees returned to their island to find that most of their houses had been destroyed by bombing and the remainder ransacked by the occupying troops. Not surprisingly, more islanders emigrated. Most of the houses that escaped the bombing in WWII stand empty. Despite this gloomy picture, Kastellorizo's waterfront is very lively.

Getting There & Away

Air In July and August there are daily flights to and from Rhodes (10,900 dr), dropping to three weekly at other times. You can buy tickets from Dizi Tours & Travel (☎/fax 49 240) in Kastellorizo Town.

The Woman of Ro

The islet of Ro, one of Kastellorizo's 13 satellites, has been immortalised along with its last inhabitant, Despina Achladioti, alias the Woman of Ro, who died in 1982. Despina and her shepherd husband were the only inhabitants of Ro. When her husband died, Despina remained alone on the island, staunchly hoisting the Greek flag every morning, and lowering it in the evening, in full view of the Turkish coast. The Woman of Ro has become a symbol of the Greek spirit of indomitability in the face of adversity. There are excursion boats to the islet; look for signs along the waterfront at Kastellorizo Town. There is a bust of the Woman of Ro on Plateia Horafia.

Ferry The F/B *Nissos Kalymnos* leaves Rhodes at 4 pm on Monday and Friday, arriving in Kastellorizo at 10 pm. At 10.15 pm it heads back for Rhodes. In addition, a ferry on a long indirect route to Piraeus, via the Cyclades and Crete or the northern Dodecanese, calls once a week, but this schedule is subject to frequent changes.

Excursion Boat to Turkey Islanders go on frequent shopping trips to Turkey and day trips (5000 dr) are also offered to tourists. Look for the signs along the waterfront.

Getting Around

There is one bus on the island, which is used solely to transport people to and from the airport (500 dr).

Excursion boats go to the islets of **Ro**, **Agios Georgios** and **Strogyli** and the spectacular **Blue Cave** (Parasta), named for its brilliant blue water, due to refracted sunlight. All of these trips cost around 5000 dr.

KASTELLORIZO TOWN

Kastellorizo Town is the only settlement. Built around a U-shaped bay, its waterfront is skirted with imposing, spruced-up three

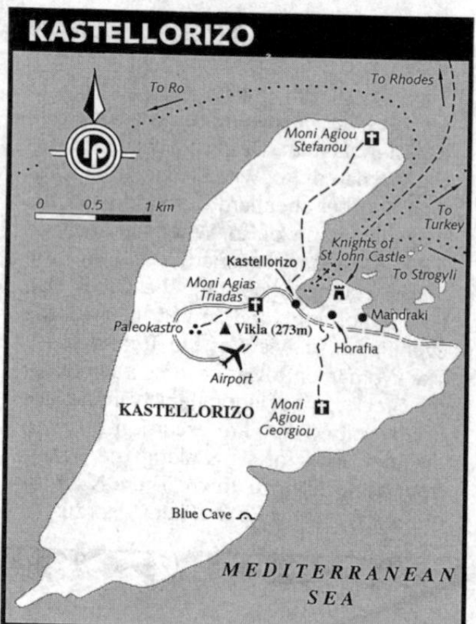

storey mansions with wooden balconies and red-tiled roofs. However, this alluring facade contrasts with backstreets of abandoned houses overgrown with ivy, crumbling stairways and stony pathways winding between them.

Orientation & Information

The quay is at the eastern side of the bay. The central square, Plateia Ethelonton Kastellorizou, abuts the waterfront almost halfway round the bay, next to the yachting jetty. The suburbs of Horafia and Mandraki are reached by ascending the wide steps at the east side of the bay.

On the bay's western side are the post office and police station (☎ 49 333). There is no OTE but there are cardphones. The National Bank of Greece is in the middle of the waterfront, next to the ferry ticket agency (☎ 49 356). The port police (☎ 49 333) are at the eastern tip of the bay.

Things to See

The **Knights of St John Castle** stands above the quay. A metal staircase leads to the top from where there are splendid views of Turkey. The **museum** within the castle houses a well displayed collection. Opening times, in theory, are 7.30 am to 2.30 pm Tuesday to Sunday; entry is free. Beyond the museum, steps lead down to a coastal pathway, from where more steps go up the cliff to a **Lycian tomb** with a Doric facade. There are several along the Anatolian coast, but this is the only known one in Greece.

Moni Agiou Georgiou is the largest of the monasteries which dot the island. Within its church is the subterranean Chapel of Agios Haralambous reached by steep stone steps. Here Greek children were given religious instruction during Turkish times. The church is kept locked; ask around the waterfront for the whereabouts of the caretaker. To reach the monastery ascend the conspicuous zigzag white stone steps behind the town and at the top take the path straight ahead.

Moni Agiou Stefanou, on the north coast, is the setting for one of the island's most important celebrations, Agiou Stefanou Day on 1 August. The path to the little white monastery begins behind the post office. From the monastery a path leads to a bay where you can swim.

Paleokastro was the island's ancient capital. Within its Hellenistic walls are an ancient tower, a water cistern and three churches. Concrete steps, just beyond a soldier's sentry box on the airport road, are the beginning of the steep path to Paleokastro.

Places to Stay – Budget

Accommodation is of a high standard. Most ***domatia*** do not display signs but it's not difficult to find the owners – that is, if they don't find you first when you disembark.

Villa Kaserma *(☎ 49 370, fax 49 365)* is the red and white building standing above the western waterfront. The very pleasant doubles/triples with bathrooms cost 9000/11,000 dr. Inquire about a room here at Lazarakis Restaurant (see Places to Eat).

Pension Palameria *(☎ 49 282)* is a newly converted building on the small square at the north-west corner of the waterfront. Spotless

DODECANESE

doubles cost 10,000 dr with bathroom and kitchen/dining area. Inquire about these rooms at Little Paris Taverna. ***Sydney Rooms*** *(☎ 49 302)*, above the Sydney Restaurant, has rates of 4000/7000 dr for singles/doubles. The owner, Angelo, also has some lovely double rooms with bathroom for 10,000 dr.

Karreta Apartments *(☎/fax 49 028)*, just off Plateia Ethelonton Kastellorizou, are lovely light and airy rooms with blue and white decor. Doubles with bathrooms are 11,000 dr and a family room is 15,000 dr. Inquire about these rooms at the Karreta Art and Crafts shop behind the agora, or at Restaurant Oraia Megisti.

Places to Stay – Mid-Range

Farther around, the island's only hotel, the B class ***Hotel Megisti*** *(☎ 49 272)*, has attractive singles/doubles/triples for 14,500/19,000/26,500 dr. The friendly English-speaking manager, Nektarios Karavelatzis, owns ***Karnayo Apartments*** *(☎/fax 49 266)*, housed in a beautifully restored red and ochre mansion near the top of the harbour's west side. These traditionally furnished double/triple apartments cost 15,000 dr and a five-person apartment is 20,000 dr.

Krystalls Apartments *(☎ 49 363, fax 49 368)*, just beyond the central square, has comfortable, spotless doubles/triples for 16,000/19,000 dr with TV and well equipped kitchen.

Places to Eat

As with the accommodation, restaurants are of a high standard on Kastellorizo. ***Restaurant Oraia Megisti***, on Plateia Ethelonton Kastellorizou, serves a range of well prepared casserole dishes and also spit-roast goat and lamb, both of which are superlative, especially when accompanied with rice cooked with herbs – a local speciality. ***Little Paris Taverna*** farther along the waterfront has been going strong for 30 years. It serves generous helpings of grilled fish and meat. ***Sydney Restaurant***, a little farther around, is also highly commendable and serves similar fare. Beyond the square, ***Lazarakis Restaurant*** on the waterfront opposite the jetty, excels in seafood.

Restaurant Platania, on Plateia Horafian, is a nice unpretentious place which appeared in the film *Mediterraneo*, a fact it proudly proclaims in huge lettering on the outside wall.

There are several traditional kafeniea on the waterfront. The younger set hang out at ***Poseidon Coffee Bar*** next to the old agora. At the time of writing, the finishing touches were being put to ***Kaz Bar***, close by.

Tilos Τήλος

☎ 0241 • postcode 850 02 • pop 279

Tilos lies 65km west of Rhodes. With good, uncrowded beaches, two abandoned, evocative villages, a well kept monastery at the end of a spectacularly scenic road, and its authentic Greek-island image intact, Tilos, is still remarkably little visited. It's a terrific island for walkers, with vistas of high cliffs, rocky inlets and sea, valleys of cypress, walnut and almond trees, and bucolic meadows with well fed cattle.

Tilos' agricultural potential is not utilised, since, rather than work the land for a pittance, young Tiliots prefer to leave for the mainland or emigrate to Australia or the USA.

There are two settlements: the port of Livadia, and Megalo Horio, 8km north.

History

Bones of mastodons – midget elephants that became extinct around 4600 BC – were found in a cave on the island in 1974. The cave, named **Cherkadio**, is signposted from the Livadia-Megala Horio road, but is kept locked. Irini, one of the greatest of ancient Greece's female poets, lived on Tilos in the 4th century BC.

Elephants and poetry apart, Tilos' history shares the same catalogue of invasions and occupations as the rest of the archipelago.

Getting There & Away

Ferry The F/B *Nissos Kalymnos* calls at Tilos on Tuesday and Saturday. Tilos is also

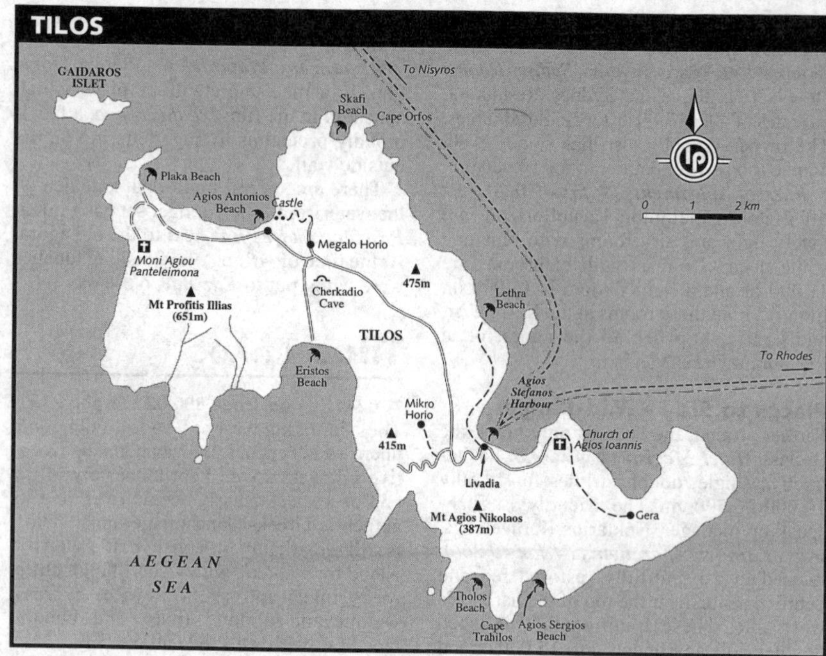

included in the weekly connection between the Dodecanese and Mykonos and Syros.

Hydrofoil On Wednesday a hydrofoil from Kalymnos via Kos and Nisyros arrives at Tilos at 9.40 am and then continues to Rhodes. It follows the same route back, arriving at Tilos at 7.30 pm and continuing to Nisyros and Kos. On Sunday there is a morning hydrofoil from Kos via Rhodes to Tilos, returning late afternoon through Rhodes and Kos to Kalymnos.

Excursion Boat A high-speed inflatable boat goes to numerous small beaches around the island, but it costs a pricey 7500 dr per person. Make inquiries at Taverna Blue Sky.

Getting Around

Tilos' public transport consists of two buses, a minibus and a full-sized bus. They go frequently in summer from Livadia to Megalo Horio (300 dr), Eristos Beach and Agios Antonios Beach (350 dr). There are three motorcycle rental outlets in Livadia.

Tilos has two taxis (☎ 44 066/169).

LIVADIA Λιβάδια

Livadia skirts a large bay with a long pebble beach on the island's east coast. All the tourist facilities, and most of the accommodation, are here.

Orientation & Information

From the quay, turn left, ascend the steps beside Stefanakis Travel, and continue ahead to the central square. If you continue straight ahead, the road curves and turns right, passing the Church of Agios Nikolaos, to skirt the beach.

Tilos has no EOT but the staff at both Stefanakis Travel (☎ 44 310) and Tilos

Travel Agency (☎ 44 259), opposite the quay, are helpful. The post office and OTE are on the central square. The port police (☎ 44 322) share the white Italianate building at the quay with the regular police (☎ 44 222).

Walks

Lethra Beach is a long pebble beach an hour's walk along a path going south from Livadia. Before WWII, Tilos had two villages, Megalo Horio and **Mikro Horio**. No-one lived at the port because it was vulnerable to pirates. After WWII people began to leave Mikro Horio, although one elderly woman remained there alone until her death in 1974. The village, signposted 3km from Livadia, on the Livadia-Megala Horio road, is a lonely, evocative place. Hawks circle overhead and lizards run for cover as you wander along the overgrown pathways.

High above Tilos' east coast, **Gera** was the summer settlement of Mikro Horio. Its wooden-roofed houses are now derelict. You can walk there in about one hour, along a scenic path which begins by Faros Rooms (see Places to Stay).

Two Scottish expatriates, Iain and Lynne, organise group walks around the island. Inquire at Joanna's Cafe Bar.

Places to Stay

The information kiosk at the harbour is open whenever a ferry arrives and has photographs and prices of Livadia's accommodation. Freelance ***camping*** is permitted on the beaches – Plaka Beach is good if you have your own transport, but there are no facilities or drinking water. Eristos Beach is better and has a small facilities block, but charges 500 dr per tent.

Paraskevi Rooms *(☎ 44 280)*, the best of the three domatia on the beach has clean, nicely furnished doubles with bathrooms and well equipped kitchens for 10,000 dr. To get there, walk between the sea and the Italianate building, and continue ahead.

The E class ***Hotel Livadia*** *(☎ 44 202/131)*, behind the central square, has doubles with bathrooms for 7000 dr. ***Casa Italiana Rooms*** *(☎ 44 253/259)*, overlooking the quay, has well kept doubles with bathrooms and refrigerators for 8000 dr, and a four-person apartment for 15,000 dr. ***Stefanakis Studios*** *(☎ 44 310/384)* above Stefanakis Travel is equally commendable and has the same rates for doubles.

Manos Hagifundas Studios *(☎ 44 259)*, past Sophia's Taverna on the beach road, has nice doubles for 12,000 dr. Telephone in advance and Manos will meet the boat; alternatively, you'll find him in Taverna Blue Sky.

Hotel Eleni *(☎ 44 062, fax 44 063)*, 400m along the beach road, has beautiful, tastefully furnished double rooms with bathrooms, refrigerator and telephone. The rate for singles/doubles/triples is 9000/12,000/14,000 dr, including breakfast.

Marina Beach Rooms *(☎/fax 44 169)* on the bay's eastern side, 1km from the quay, has immaculate but small rooms with sea-view balconies. Doubles are 12,000 dr. A little farther along, the new ***Faros Rooms*** *(☎ 44 029)* has spotless, tastefully furnished doubles/triples for 12,000/14,500 dr.

Places to Eat

Sophia's Taverna, 20m along the beach road, serves delicious, low-priced food. ***Taverna Blue Sky***, on the harbour, is good for grilled fish and ***Taverna Michalas,*** beyond the central square, and ***Zorba's Taverna***, beyond the Ereni Hotel, serve tasty grilled meat. The zany owner of Zorbas may break into a song and dance routine while taking your order.

Kafeneion Omonoias, next to the post office, is a favourite place for breakfast. The newer ***Joanna's Cafe Bar*** is equally popular, serving good cappuccino, yogurt and muesli, pizza made by Joanna's Italian husband, Andrea, and delicious home-made cakes.

Beyond the central square there is a ***bakery*** and three ***supermarkets***.

Entertainment

La Luna at the quay and a new place, still unnamed, next to Zorba's Taverna on the waterfront, are the local hot spots. In summer the ***Mikro Horio Music Bar*** belts out music till 4 am.

MEGALO HORIO Μεγάλο Χωριό

Megalo Horio is a serene whitewashed village, crowned by a ruined **knights' castle** which has an intact gateway, and a small chapel with frescoes. Follow the signpost for Kastro at the beginning of the village to reach the castle.

The little **museum** on the main street houses finds from the Cherkadio Cave. It's kept locked, but if you ask at the town hall on the first floor someone will show you around.

Places to Stay & Eat

Megalo Horio has three places to stay. ***Pension Sevasti*** *(☎ 44 237)*, just beyond the Eristos Beach turn-off, has singles/doubles for 3000/4500 dr. ***Milou Rooms and Apartments*** *(☎ 44 204)* and ***Elefantakia Studios*** *(☎ 44 242/213)*, next to one another on the main street, have doubles for 8000 dr. ***Kali Kardia***, next to Pension Sevasti, is Megalo Horio's nicest taverna.

Entertainment

Megalo Horio has two atmospheric bars. ***Ilakati***, on the steep road signposted Kastro, plays rock and blues, and ***Anemona***, at the top of the steps by the Castle Restaurant, plays Greek music.

AROUND MEGALO HORIO

Just before Megalo Horio, a turn-off to the left leads after 2.5km to the pleasant, tamarisk-shaded **Eristos Beach** – a mixture of gritty sand and shingle. A signposted turn-off to the right from this road leads to **Agios Antonios Beach**. **Plaka Beach**, 3km farther west, is dotted with trees.

The 18th century **Moni Agiou Panteleimona** is 5km beyond here along a scenic road. It is uninhabited but well maintained, with fine 18th century frescoes. The island's minibus driver takes groups of visitors here on Sunday. A three day festival takes place at the monastery, beginning on 25 July.

Places to Stay

Tropicana Taverna & Rooms *(☎ 44 223/020)*, on the Eristos road, has doubles/ triples for 5000/6500 dr, and ***Nausika Taverna & Rooms***, to the left of Eristos Beach (signposted), has similar rates. The new ***Eristos Beach Hotel*** *(☎ 44 024)*, right on the beach, has attractive doubles for 10,000 dr.

The immaculate D class ***Hotel Australia*** *(☎ 44 296)* overlooks Agios Antonios Beach. Doubles/triples with bathroom are 7000/8000 dr.

Nisyros Νίσυρος

☎ 0242 • postcode 853 03 • pop 913

Nisyros (**nee**-sih-ros) is one of the strangest and most beautiful of all Greek islands – an unusual mixture of lush vegetation and dramatic, barren moonscapes.

The nucleus of the island is a dormant volcano. This creates a curious anomaly whereby the island, although waterless, is fertile. The mineral-rich earth holds moisture and yields olives, vines, figs, citrus fruit and almonds. Another unusual feature of Nisyros is that it is completely free of mosquitoes.

The island's settlements are Mandraki, the capital; the fishing village of Pali; and the crater-top villages of Emboreios and Nikea.

The island's population has not suffered the drastic depletion of other small islands because some of its men earn a living quarrying pumice.

The island attracts a lot of day-trippers from Kos, but few stop overnight.

Getting There & Away

Nisyros has the same ferry schedule as Tilos. The island is serviced by a weekly hydrofoil from Rhodes. In summer there are daily excursion boats from Kardamena, Kefalos and Kos Town on Kos (3000-5500 dr).

Getting Around

Bus There are at least two buses every day to the volcano (2000 dr), and at least four daily to Pali, Nikea and Emboreios. The bus terminal is at the quay.

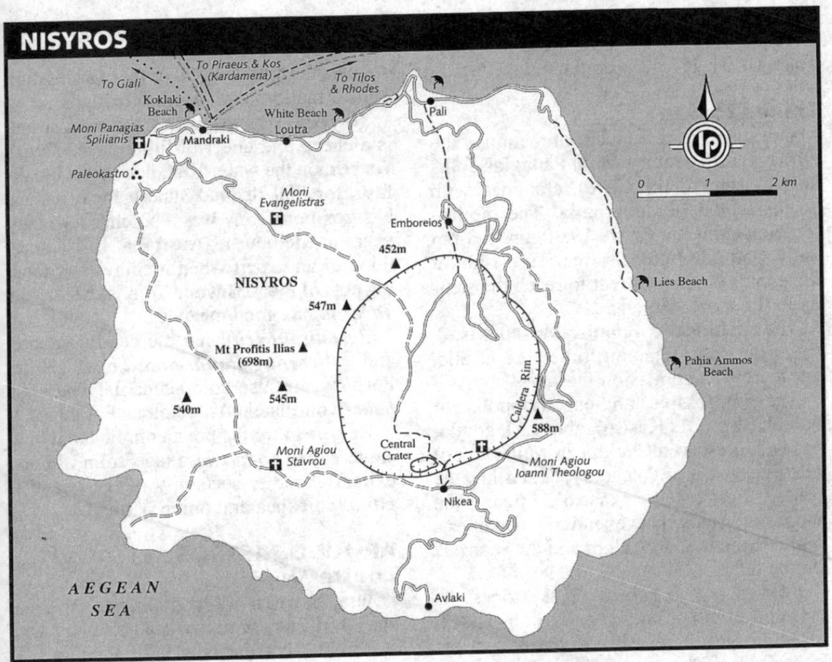

Motorcycle There are three motorcycle-rental outlets on Mandraki's main street.

Taxi There are two taxi companies on Nisyros: Bobby's Taxi (☎ 31 460) and Irene's Taxi (☎ 31 474). A sample of tariffs are: the volcano (5000 dr), Emboreios (4000 dr), Nikea (5000 dr) and Pali (5000 dr).

Excursion Boat From June to September there are excursion boats (2500 dr return) to the pumice-stone islet of **Giali** where there is a good sandy beach.

MANDRAKI Μανδράκι

Mandraki is the attractive port and capital of Nisyros. Its two-storey houses have brightly painted wooden balconies. Some are whitewashed but many are painted in bright colours, predominantly ochre and turquoise. The web of streets huddled below the monastery and the central square are especially charming.

Orientation & Information

To reach Mandraki's centre, walk straight ahead from the quay. At the fork bear right; the left fork leads to Hotel Porfyris. Beyond here a large square adjoins the main street, which proceeds to Plateia Aristotelous Fotiadou, then continues diagonally opposite, passing the town hall. Turn left at the T-junction for the central square of Plateia Elikiomini.

There is a tourist information office (☎ 31 204) at the quay, open 10 am to 1 pm and 6 to 8 pm daily. The staff here, and at Enetikon Travel (☎ 31 180, fax 31 168), on the main street, are helpful. The latter has a good library of used books.

The post office, port police (☎ 31 222) and the regular police share premises opposite the quay. The National Bank of Greece is represented by Diakomihalis Tours (☎ 31 457/527) on the main street.

Things to See

Mandraki's greatest tourist attraction is the cliff-top 14th century **Moni Panagias Spilianis** (Virgin of the Cave), crammed with ecclesiastical paraphernalia. The monastery's opening times are 10.30 am to 3 pm daily, and admission is free. Turn right at the end of the main street to reach the steps up to the monastery.

The **Historical & Popular Museum** is on the waterfront. Opening times are erratic, but there's no admission fee.

The impressive ancient acropolis of **Paleokastro** (Old Kastro), above Mandraki, has well preserved Cyclopean walls built of massive blocks of volcanic rock. Follow the route signposted 'kastro', near the monastery steps. This eventually becomes a path. At the road turn right and the *kastro* is on the left.

Koklaki is a beach of black stones. Its 'Heath Robinson' house was built by a local artist. To get there, walk to the end of the waterfront, go up the steps and turn right onto a path.

Places to Stay & Eat

Mandraki has a fair amount of accommodation but, unusually, owners do not meet the ferries. There is no camp site.

If you turn left from the quay, you will come to ***Hotel Romantzo*** *(☎/fax 31 340)* with clean, well kept singles/doubles/triples for 5000/7000/10,000 dr with bathroom. The rooms are above a snack bar and there is a large communal terrace with a refrigerator, tables and chairs. ***Three Brothers Hotel*** *(☎ 31 344)*, opposite, is another pleasant option, with single/double rooms with bathooms for 5000/8000 dr. Almost next door, ***Xenon Hotel*** *(☎ 31 012)* has rooms for 6500/9000/10,000 dr. Beyond here on the right, ***Mire Mare Apartments*** *(☎ 31 100)* has modern, well equipped rooms for 6000/10,000/14,000 dr. There is a communal washing machine and iron.

The C class ***Hotel Porfyris*** *(☎/fax 31 376)*, with a swimming pool, has singles/doubles for 8000/14,000 dr (see Orientation & Information, earlier, for directions).

Taverna Nisyros, just off the main street, is a cheap and cheerful little place. ***Tony's Tavern***, on the waterfront, does great breakfasts for 800 dr, and superb meat dishes. Nisyros-born Tony was a butcher for many years in Melbourne, Australia, so is something of an expert when it comes to choosing cuts of meat. Beyond Tony's, ***Klearithis Taverna*** has good mezedes.

Restaurant Irini, on the central square, and ***Taverna Panorama***, near Hotel Porfyris, are also commendable. There's a ***bakery*** on Plateia Aristotelous Fotiadou.

Be sure to try the nonalcoholic local beverage called *soumada*, made from almond extract. Another speciality of the island is *pittia* (chickpea and onion patties).

AROUND NISYROS

Loutra Λουτρά

Loutra, 2km east of Mandraki, has a thermal spa (☎ 31 284), with two spa buildings. One is derelict, but the other still functions. If you fancy a curative dip you'll need a quick health check at the clinic (☎ 31 217) near Hotel Porfyris first. The spa's well worn ***Loutra Restaurant*** is surprisingly good.

The Volcano

Nisyros is on a volcanic line which passes through the islands of Aegina, Paros, Milos, Santorini, Nisyros, Giali and Kos. The island originally culminated in a mountain of 850m, but the centre collapsed 30,000-40,000 years ago after three violent eruptions. Their legacy is the white and orange pumice stones which can still be seen on the northern, eastern and southern flanks of the island, and the large lava flow which covers the whole south-west of the island around Nikea village. The first eruption partially blew off the top of the ancestral cone, but the majority of the sinking of the central part of the island came about as a result of the removal of magma from within the reservoir underground.

Another violent eruption occurred in 1422 on the western side of the caldera depression (called Lakki), but this, like all others since, emitted steam, gases and mud, but no lava. The islanders call the volcano Polyvotis, because the Polyvotis crater on the western side of the caldera floor was the site of the eruptions in 1873, 1874 and 1888, and remains the most active of the craters.

There are five craters in the caldera. A path descends into the largest one, Stefanos, where you can examine the multicoloured fumaroles, listen to their hissing and smell their sulphurous vapours. The surface is soft and hot, making sturdy footwear essential.

If you arrive by bus you'll be with hordes of day-trippers, which detracts from the extraordinary sight. Also, the bus does not allow you long enough to wander around and savour a glass of soumada from the cafe. It's a good idea to walk either to or from the crater from Nikea.

Emboreios & Nikea

Εμπορειός & Νίκαια

Emboreios and Nikea perch on the volcano's rim. From each, there are stunning views down into the caldera. Only 20 inhabitants linger on in Emboreios. You may encounter a few elderly women sitting on their doorsteps crocheting, and their husbands at the kafeneio. However, generally, the winding, stepped streets are empty, the silence broken only by the occasional braying of a donkey or the grunting of pigs.

In contrast to Emboreios, picturesque Nikea, with 50 inhabitants, buzzes with life. It has dazzling white houses with vibrant gardens and a central square with a lovely pebble mosaic. The bus terminates on Plateia Nikolaou Hartofili. Nikea's main street links the two squares.

The steep path down to the volcano begins from Plateia Nikolaou Hartofili. It takes about 40 minutes to walk it one way. Near the beginning you can detour to **Moni Agiou Ioanni Theologou**.

Places to Stay & Eat Emboreios has no accommodation for tourists and no tavernas, but the owner of its ***kafeneio*** can rustle up a tasty meal.

Nikea's only accommodation is a ***Community Hostel***, on Plateia Nikolaou Hartofili, managed by Panayiotis Mastromihalis *(☎ 31 285)*, the owner of Nikea's only taverna. Doubles cost 5000 dr.

Pali Πάλοι

The island's best beaches are at Pali, 4km east of Mandraki, and **Lies**, 5km farther on. Pali's C class ***Hotel Hellenis*** *(☎ 31 453)* has comfortable doubles for 8000 dr with bathroom. Paraskevi, the owner, serves up delectable dishes in the adjoining restaurant. Her shepherd husband, the charismatic Manolis, sometimes plays the lyre in the restaurant.

Astypalea
Αστυπάλαια

☎ 0243 • postcode 859 00 • pop 1073

Astypalea (ah-stih-**pah**-lia), the most westerly island of the archipelago, is geographically and architecturally more akin to the Cyclades. The island's two land masses are joined by a narrow isthmus.

With a wonderfully picturesque hilltop Hora, and bare, gently contoured hills, high mountains, green valleys and sheltered coves, it's surprising Astypalea does not get more foreign tourists. It is, however, popular with urban Greeks.

Getting There & Away

Air There are four flights weekly from Astypalea to Athens (20,100 dr). Astypalea Tours, in Astypalea Town, is the agent for Olympic Airways.

Ferry Lying between the Cyclades and the Dodecanese, Astypalea is the most easterly destination of some Cyclades services, and the most westerly of the Dodecanese services.

The F/B *Nissos Kalymnos* does a round trip to Astypalea from Kalymnos on Tuesday and Saturday.

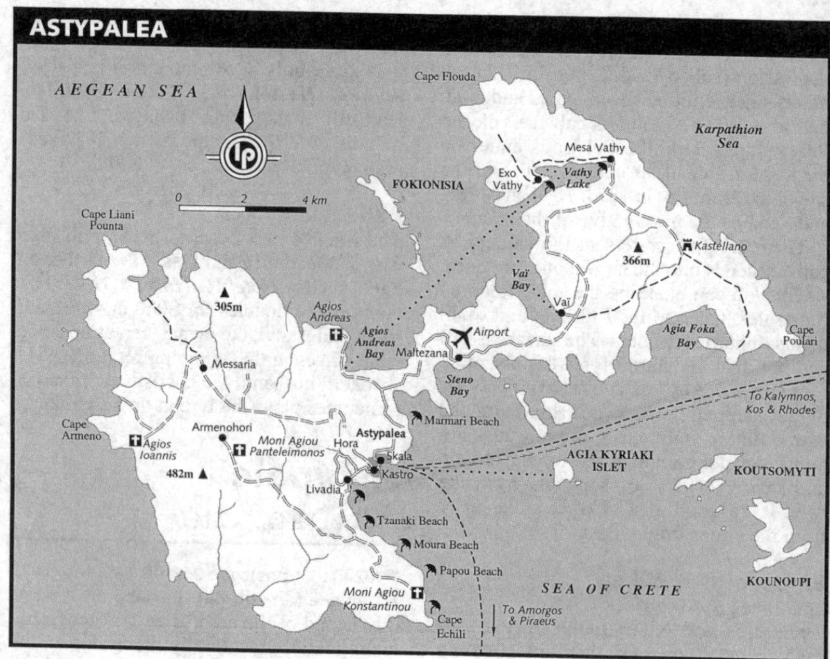

Ferries sail twice weekly to and from Piraeus via the Cyclades Islands (16 hours). One ferry goes via Syros, Paros, Naxos, Donousa, Katapola (Amorgos) and Aegiali (Amorgos) to Astypalea; the other sails via Paros, Naxos, Iraklia, Shinousa, Koufonisia, Donousa, as well as both ports on Amorgos.

Two ferries weekly make a through-connection from Piraeus to the Dodecanese and Rhodes via Astypalea.

Hydrofoil Between June and September there is one hydrofoil a week plying its way on a round trip from Rhodes (5½ hours, 9880 dr) to Astypalea via Symi, Kos and Kalymnos.

Getting Around

Bus From Skala a bus travels fairly frequently to Hora and Livadia (200 dr), and from Hora and Skala to Maltezana (300 dr) via Marmari.

Excursion Boat In summer there are daily excursion boats to the island's less accessible beaches and to Agia Kyriaki Islet (2000 dr). Tickets can be bought from the stalls by the boats.

ASTYPALEA TOWN

Astypalea Town, the capital, consists of the port of Skala and the hilltop district of Hora, crowned by a fortress.

Skala has a friendly pelican, who blew in one windy day. He landed on his feet, it seems, for the local fishers throw him lots of tasty titbits. Hora has narrow streets of dazzling-white cubic houses with brightly painted wooden balconies, doors and banisters. A line of windmills completes the picture.

Orientation & Information

From Skala's quay, turn right to reach the waterfront. The steep road to Hora begins beyond the white Italianate building. In Skala the waterfront road skirts the beach and then veers right to continue along the coast to Marmari and beyond.

A municipal tourist office adjoins the quayside cafe. The owner of Astypalea Tours (☎ 61 571/572, fax 61 328), below Vivamare Apartments, is helpful and is the agent for Olympic Airways and ferry lines.

The post office is at the top of the Skala-Hora road. The OTE is close to the waterfront's Hotel Paradissos. The Commercial Bank, with an ATM, is on the waterfront.

The police (☎ 61 207) and port police (☎ 61 208) are in the Italianate building.

Castle

During the time of the Knights of St John, Astypalea was occupied by the Venetian Quirini family, who built the imposing castle. In the Middle Ages the population lived within its walls, but gradually the settlement outgrew them. The last inhabitants left in 1948 and the stone houses are now in ruins. Above the entrance is the Church of Our Lady of the Castle and within the walls is the Church of Agios Giorgios.

Places to Stay

Camping Astypalea *(☎ 61 338)* is 3km east of Skala.

Hotel and domatia owners meet incoming boats. ***Hotel Australia*** *(☎ 61 338)*, on the waterfront, has well kept doubles/triples for 7500/9000 dr, and a friendly Greek-Australian owner. At the time of writing, some co-owned luxury studios were near completion.

Farther along, ***Karlos Rooms*** *(☎ 61 330)* has rates of 9000/10,000 dr. ***Akth Rooms*** *(☎ 61 281/168, email astrooms@otenet.gr)*, beyond Karlos Rooms, has attractive singles/doubles/triples for 6000/10,000/12,000 dr and good sea views from the communal terrace.

Hotel Aegeon *(☎ 61 236)*, on the Skala-Hora road, has singles/doubles for 5000/8000 dr. The ageing but well maintained ***Hotel Paradissos*** *(☎ 61 224/256)* has comfortable singles/doubles/triples with bathroom for 8000/9500/10,000 dr. ***Vivamare Apartments*** *(☎ 61 571/572)*, a little way up the Skala-Hora road, has double/triple/quad studios for 10,000/12,000/14,500 dr.

Aphrodite Studios *(☎ 61 478/086, fax 61 087)*, between Skala and Hora, has beautiful, well equipped double/triple studios for 12,000/14,000 dr. Take the Hora road, turn left after the shoe shop and it's on the left.

Places to Eat

Restaurant Australia, below Hotel Australia, serves delicious fish; the speciality is lobster and macaroni. ***Restaurant Astropalia*** is also commendable and has wonderful views down to Skala from its terrace. ***Vicki's*** near the quay offers decent, low-priced fare. ***Aitherio Restaurant*** is a trendy place serving a range of imaginative mezedes and main courses.

Up in Hora, ***Kafeneio Apaskoi*** and ***Ouzeri Meltimi***, opposite the windmills, are popular hang-outs with Astypalea's young crowd.

There is a ***supermarket*** on the waterfront and two in Hora, near the post office.

LIVADIA Λιβάδια

The little resort of Livadia lies in a fertile valley 2km from Hora. Its beach is the best on the island, but also the most crowded.

Quieter beaches can be found farther south at **Tzanaki**, the island's unofficial nudist beach, and at **Agios Konstantinos** below the monastery of the same name. You can drive to Moni Agiou Konstantinou, or walk there in about 40 minutes.

Places to Stay & Eat

There's plenty of accommodation in Livadia. Pleasant budget options are ***Gerani Rooms*** *(☎ 61 484/337)*, where doubles/triples go for 9000/9500 dr with bathrooms and refrigerators, and ***Kaloudis Domatia*** *(☎ 61 318/336)*, with doubles for 9000 dr and a communal kitchen. Both are on the dirt road (a dried-up riverbed) that runs inland from the waterfront.

A sign at the end of the beach road points to ***Jim Venetos Studios & Apartments*** *(☎ 61 490/150)*, where attractive double studios cost 12,000 dr and four-person apartments are 17,000 dr. ***H Kalamia***, the first taverna on the waterfront, serves good food. Its speciality is rice-stuffed goat.

OTHER BEACHES

Marmari, 2km north-east of Skala, has three bays with pebble and sand beaches. **Maltezana** is 7km beyond Marmari in a fertile valley on the isthmus. Maltezana is a scattered, pleasantly laid-back settlement, but its two beaches are grubby. There are some remains of Roman baths with mosaics on the settlement's outskirts.

The road from Maltezana is reasonable as far as **Vaï**, but it's atrocious beyond here. **Mesa Vathy** is a fishing hamlet with a beach at the end of a narrow inlet. It takes about 1½ hours to walk here from Vaï. From Mesa Vathy a footpath leads to **Exo Vathy**, another hamlet with a beach.

Places to Stay & Eat

There are plenty of accommodation options in Maltazena but many only operate during the summer. ***Maltezana Rooms*** *(☎ 61 446)*, to the left of the quay, has doubles for 8000 dr.

Hotel Castillo *(☎/fax 61 552/553)*, a complex of self-contained units on both sides of the main road, has beautifully furnished, immaculate studios with a well equipped kitchen area, television and telephone. Doubles cost 10,000 dr and four-person apartments are 13,000 dr. ***Oveli Taverna*** and ***Armera Restaurant*** are recommended; their fish dishes are especially good.

There is a ***domatia*** at Exo Vathy, but check with Astypalea Tours in Astypalea town whether it's operating.

Symi Σύμη

☎ 0241 • postcode 856 00 • pop 2332

Symi lies in the straits of Marmara, 24km north of Rhodes, its nearest Greek neighbour, and only 10km from the Turkish peninsula of Dorakis. The island has a scenic rocky interior, dotted with pine and cypress woods. It has a deeply indented coast with precipitous cliffs, and numerous small bays with pebbled beaches.

The island suffers from a severe water shortage.

Symi gets an inordinate number of day-trippers from Rhodes. Most of them don't venture any farther than the restaurants, bars and tourist shops on the waterfront in Gialos.

History

Symi has a long tradition of both sponge diving and shipbuilding. During Ottoman times it was granted the right to fish for sponges in Turkish waters. In return Symi supplied the sultan with first-class boat builders and top-quality sponges.

These factors, and a lucrative shipbuilding industry, brought prosperity to the island. Gracious mansions were built and culture and education flourished. By the beginning of the 20th century the population was 22,500 and the island was launching some 500 ships a year. But the Italian occupation, the introduction of the steamship and Kalymnos' rise as the Aegean's principal sponge producer put an end to Symi's prosperity.

The treaty surrendering the Dodecanese islands to the Allies was signed on Symi on 8 May 1945.

Getting There & Away

Ferry & Hydrofoil Symi has a similar ferry schedule to Tilos and Nisyros. Every Saturday a hydrofoil departs Rhodes at 8 am, arriving on Symi at 8.50 am before leaving for Kos, Kalymnos and Astypalea. It returns to Symi at 7.30 pm and heads back for Rhodes.

Excursion Boat There are daily excursion boats running between Symi and Rhodes' Mandraki Harbour. The Symi-based *Symi I* and *Symi II* are the cheapest. They are owned cooperatively by the people of Symi, and operate as excursion boats as well as

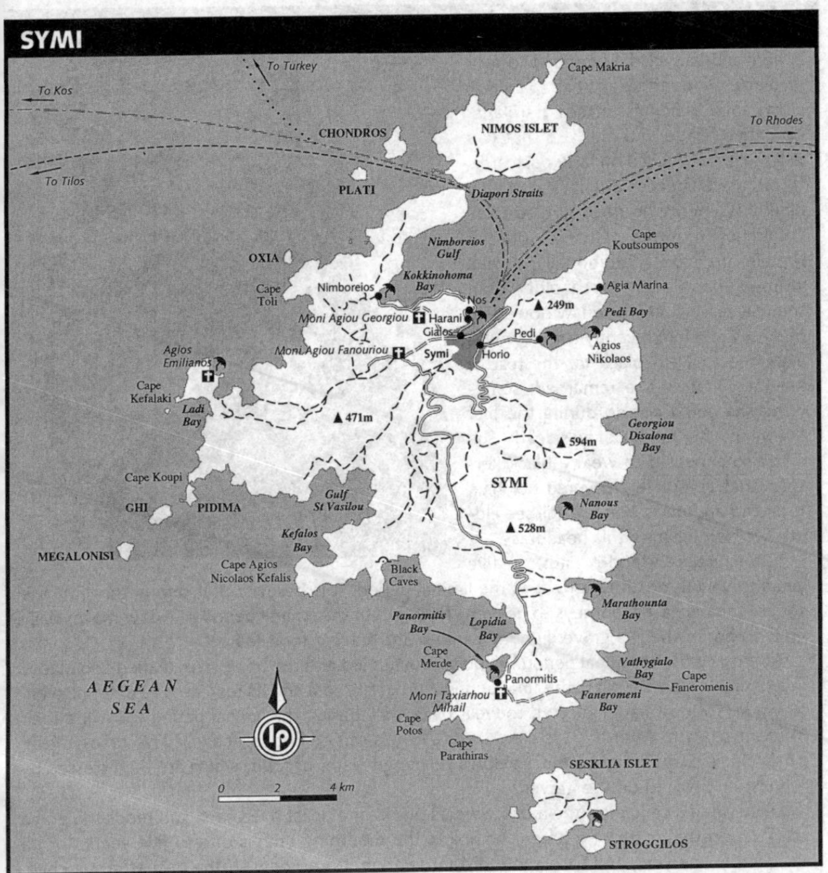

regular passenger boats. Tickets cost 3200 dr return and can be bought on board.

Symi Tours has excursion trips to the town of Datça in Turkey on Saturday, which is market day. The cost is 10,000 dr return (including 4000 dr Turkish port tax). You must hand in your passport the day before.

Getting Around

Bus & Taxi A minibus makes frequent runs between Gialos and Pedi Beach (via Horio). Check the current schedule with Symi Tours. The bus stop and taxi rank (☎ 72 666) are on the east side of the harbour. Sample taxi tariffs are Horio (600 dr), Pedi (700 dr) and Nimboreios (1200 dr).

Excursion Boat Several excursion boats do trips to Moni Taxiarhou Mihail and Sesklia Islet where there's a shady beach. Check the boards for the best value tickets. Symi Tours also has trips to the monastery (10,000 dr).

As Long as It's Black

LIZ THOMPSON

A bent old lady clad from head to foot in black, silhouetted against sparkling, sugar cube buildings, makes a striking, evocative image – so much so that you will see it reproduced on 'arty postcards' throughout Greece. But it is not only elderly women who dress in black, the colour of mourning; many younger people do, too. Traditionally, Greek women marry men much older than themselves, so are often widowed in middle age. Until recently a widow was expected to wear black for the rest of her life, or until she remarried, something she could not do during the first five years after her husband's death. She was also expected to wear a black kerchief that completely covered her hair, forehead and neck. You will still see elderly women wearing this headdress.

In the Greek Orthodox faith, the five years following death is known as the liminal period. It is believed that during this time the soul of the deceased journeys to heaven. Throughout the liminal period a widow makes daily visits to her husband's grave, lighting candles and leaving food there.

At the end of the liminal period the body is exhumed and the bones are cleaned and placed in a casket. This symbolises the final purification of the soul and its readiness to enter heaven. Nowadays widows are expected to wear black only during the liminal period following their husband's death. After this the care of the grave is carried out collectively. Five times a year, on All Souls' Days, neighbouring widows exchange plates of food, which are then blessed by a priest and placed on the graves.

Likewise, if a child dies, the mother wears black for at least five years, and tends the grave daily. Upon the death of a parent or sibling the mourning time is one to five years, for an in-law it is one year, and for a more distant relation it is 40 days. If the deceased is a child, a relation she was close to, or someone who died in tragic circumstances, a woman is expected to wear black for longer. After the period of mourning, a woman is expected to dress in a subdued manner, replacing black with dark blue, then with brown and then gradually adding brighter colours. During the time of mourning a woman is not expected to socialise or entertain.

In comparison, men get off lightly. The only requirement expected of a man is that he wears a black armband and refrains from socialising for the 40 days following a death.

In keeping with the rest of the western world's hip, young Greek women have come to hold the maxim 'any colour as long as it's black' with regard to clothes. However, it is not difficult to spot the difference between a woman wearing black to make a fashion statement and one wearing black because she is in mourning!

Excursion boats also go to some of the island's more remote beaches.

Taxi boats These small boats do trips to many of the island's beaches.

SYMI TOWN

Symi Town is a Greek treasure. Neoclassical mansions in a harmonious medley of colours are heaped up the steep hills which flank its U-shaped harbour. Behind their strikingly beautiful facades, however, many of the buildings are derelict. The town is divided into two parts: Gialos, the harbour, and Horio, above, crowned by the kastro (castle).

Symi Town's beach is the crowded, minuscule Nos Beach. Turn left at the quay's clock tower to get there.

The **Symi Maritime Museum**, behind the central square, is open 10 am to 2 pm Tuesday to Sunday. Admission is 500 dr.

Orientation & Information

Facing inland, the quay front skirts the right side of the harbour. Inter-island ferries dock at the tip of the quay, and excursion boats from Rhodes dock farther in. Excursion boats to Symi's beaches leave from the top of the opposite side. The central square is behind the top of the harbour's right side. The smaller Plateia tis Skalas is near the top of the left side. Kali Strata, a broad stairway, leads from here to Horio.

There is no EOT in Symi Town, but the staff at Symi Tours (☎ 71 307, fax 72 292) are helpful.

The post office, police (☎ 71 111) and port police (☎ 71 205) share the large white building beside the clock tower. The OTE is signposted from the eastern side of the central square. The National Bank of Greece is at the top of the harbour. The Ionian Bank on the waterfront has an ATM.

Symi's Internet cafe is the Vapori Bar, near the beginning of Kali Strata.

Things to See & Do

Horio consists of narrow, labyrinthine streets crossed by crumbling archways. As you approach the kastro, the once-grand 19th century neoclassical mansions give way to small, modest stone dwellings of the 18th century.

The **Museum of Symi**, on the way to the castle, has archaeological and folklore exhibits. Opening times are 10 am to 2 pm Tuesday to Sunday. Admission is 500 dr. The castle incorporates blocks from the ancient acropolis, and the **Church of Megali Panagia** is within its walls.

Symi Tours has multilingual guides who lead **walks** around the island. The publication *Walking on Symi* by Francis Noble (3000 dr) is on sale at Kalodoukas Holidays at the beginning of Kali Strata.

Places to Stay – Budget

There is very little budget accommodation. The cheapest doubles cost around 12,000 dr. Some accommodation owners meet the boats.

Rooms to Let Titika, located behind the Nautical Museum, has clean, nicely furnished air-con double/triple rooms for 12,000/14,000 dr with bathrooms. Make inquiries at Kostos Tourist Shop at the top of the harbour.

Hotel Kokona *(☎ 71 549/451, fax 72 620)* has comfortable rooms with bathroom for 12,000/14,000 dr. The hotel is on the street to the left of the large church.

Nikolitsi Fotini Studios *(☎ 71 780)*, near Nos Beach, are clean, comfortable studios with well equipped kitchen areas. Doubles are 12,000 dr. If you call ahead the owner will pick you up from the harbour.

Pension Katerinettes *(☎/fax 72 698, email marina~epe@rho.forthnet.gre)* is housed in the former town hall where the treaty granting the Dodecanese to the Allies was signed. Some of its rooms have magnificent painted ceilings. Doubles with a sea view are 15,000 dr, and those without are 9500 dr.

Hotel Fiona *(☎/fax 72 088)*, in Horio, has lovely rooms with wood-panelled ceilings. Doubles/triples are 14,000/16,500 dr with bathroom. To reach the hotel turn left at Taverna Georgios.

Places to Stay – Mid-Range

Opera House Hotel *(☎ 72 034, fax 72 035)*, well signposted from the harbour, is an impressive cluster of buildings in a peaceful garden. Spacious double/triple studios are 20,000/25,000 dr.

Hotel Nireus *(☎ 72 400/403, fax 72 404)* has elegant, traditional double/triple rooms for 20,000/30,000 dr and double/triple suites for 29,000/30,200 dr. Turn left at the clock tower (facing the sea) and the hotel is on the left. Farther along, the A class ***Hotel Aliki*** *(☎/fax 71 665)* is another traditional-style hotel. Singles/doubles are 20,000/30,000 dr.

Places to Eat

Many of Gialos' restaurants are mediocre, catering for day-trippers. Some exceptions are ***Vigla Restaurant*** and ***Vassilis Restaurant***, both at the top of the harbour; ***O Meraklis Taverna***, two blocks back; and the excellent, low-priced ***Taverna Neraida***, beyond Hotel Glafkos.

Restaurant Les Katerinettes, below the pension, offers an extensive range of well prepared dishes; the mixed mezedes plate costs 2500 dr.

Taverna Tholos, just before Nos Beach, is excellent. The imaginative dishes include chicken in orange sauce, lamb in egg and lemon sauce, and green beans with feta.

In Horio, there are three good restaurants in a row on Kali Strata. ***To Kima*** and ***Georgios*** serve well prepared traditional Greek dishes, and ***Restaurant Sillogos*** offers imaginative fare such as chicken with prunes and pork with leek.

O'Hylios, at the top of the harbour, is a good vegetarian restaurant serving snacks during the day and three-course meals in the evening. ***White House Cafe***, nearby, serves great coffee and a range of snacks. ***Vapori Bar*** serves good breakfasts and snacks and has free newspapers and magazines as well as Internet access.

Hellenikon, in Gialos, has a cellar of 140 different Greek wines, and is known as the wine restaurant of Symi. The food offered is equally impressive. Unusual mezedes include sea urchin roe, snails with pesto and goat's cheese with mulberries. Desserts include a luscious concoction of ice cream, cream, dried fruits, red wine and rum. Expect to pay around 12,000 dr for a three course meal with wine.

Entertainment

There are several lively bars in the streets behind the south side of the harbour. ***White House Cafe*** and ***Vapori Bar*** are also lively in the evenings, and sometimes feature live music. The expat-owned ***Jean & Tonic*** in Horio is a popular late night bar.

AROUND SYMI

Pedi is a little fishing village and burgeoning holiday resort in a fertile valley 2km downhill from Horio. It has some sandy stretches on its narrow beach. There are domatia, hotels and tavernas.

Nimboreios is a long pebbled beach 2km west of Gialos. It has some natural shade as well as sun-beds and umbrellas. You can walk there from Gialos along a scenic Byzantine path. Take the road by the east side of the central square, and continue straight ahead. At the fork, bear right and go uphill, passing a cemetery and a monastery on either side. When the road curves right, take the narrower cement road to its left, which becomes a paved path passing between stone walls. Continue ahead through two gates. After passing Moni Agiou Georgiou the path drops down to **Kokkinohoma Bay**. Turn left to reach Nimboreios.

Taxi boats go to **Georgiou Disalona Bay** and the more developed **Nanous Beach**, which has sun-beds, umbrellas and a taverna, and **Agia Marina**, which also has a taverna. These are all shingle beaches. Symi's only sandy beach is the tamarisk-shaded **Agios Nikolaos**.

The more remote **Marathounta** and **Agios Emilianos** beaches are best reached by excursion boat.

Moni Taxiarhou Mihail

Μονή Ταξιάρχου Μιχαήλ

Symi's principal sight is the large Moni Taxiarhou Mihail (Monastery of Michael of

DODECANESE

Panormitis) in Panormitis Bay, and it's the stopping-off point for many of the day-trippers from Rhodes. A monastery was first built here in the 5th or 6th century, but the present building dates from the 18th century. The katholikon contains an intricately carved wooden iconostasis, frescoes, and an icon of St Michael which supposedly appeared miraculously where the monastery now stands. St Michael is the patron saint of Symi, and protector of sailors.

The monastery complex comprises a museum, restaurant and basic guest rooms. Beds cost 3000 dr; reservations are necessary in July and August.

Kos Κως

☎ 0242 • postcode 853 00 (Psalidi 852 00) • pop 26,379

Kos is the third-largest island of the Dodecanese and one of its most fertile and well watered. It lies only 5km from the Turkish peninsula of Bodrum. It is second only to Rhodes in both its wealth of archaeological remains and its tourist development, with most of its beautiful beaches wall-to-wall with sun beds and parasols. It's a long, narrow island with a mountainous spine.

Pserimos is a small island between Kos and Kalymnos. It has a good sandy beach, but unfortunately becomes overrun with day-trippers from both of its larger neighbours.

History

Kos' fertile land attracted settlers from the earliest times. So many people lived here by Mycenaean times that it was able to send 30 ships to the Trojan War. During the 7th and 6th centuries BC, Kos flourished as an ally of the powerful Rhodian cities of Ialyssos, Kamiros and Lindos. In 477 BC, after suffering an earthquake and subjugation to the Persians, it joined the Delian League and flourished once more.

Hippocrates (460-377 BC), the father of medicine, was born and lived on the island. After Hippocrates' death, the Sanctuary of Asclepius and a medical school were built, which perpetuated his teachings and made Kos famous throughout the Greek world.

Ptolemy II of Egypt was born on Kos, thus securing it the protection of Egypt, under which it became a prosperous trading centre. In 130 BC, Kos came under Roman domination, and in the 1st century AD it was put under the administration of Rhodes, with which it came to share the same vicissitudes, right up to the tourist deluge of the present day.

Getting There & Away

Air There are three flights daily to Athens (21,400 dr). The Olympic Airways office (☎ 28 330) is at Vasileos Pavlou 22, in Kos Town.

Ferry – Domestic Kos has daily connections to Rhodes and Piraeus. It is also included in the route linking the Dodecanese with Mykonos and Syros and has a link with Thessaloniki via Samos.

Ferry – International There are daily ferries in summer from Kos Town to Bodrum (ancient Halicarnassus) in Turkey (one hour, 13,000 dr return, including Turkish port tax). Boats leave at 8.30 am and return at 4 pm. Many travel agents around Kos Town sell tickets.

Hydrofoil Kos is served by both the Dodecanese Hydrofoil Company and Samos Hydrofoils. In high season there are daily shuttles, morning and evening, to and from Rhodes, (two hours, 6670 dr), with good connections to all the major islands in the group, as well as Samos, Ikaria and Fourni in the North-Eastern Aegean. From Samos you can easily connect with the Cyclades.

Information and tickets are readily available from the many travel agents.

Excursion Boat From Kos Town there are many boat excursions, both around the island and to other islands. Some examples of return fares include: Kalymnos (3000 dr); Pserimos, Kalymnos and Plati (6000 dr);

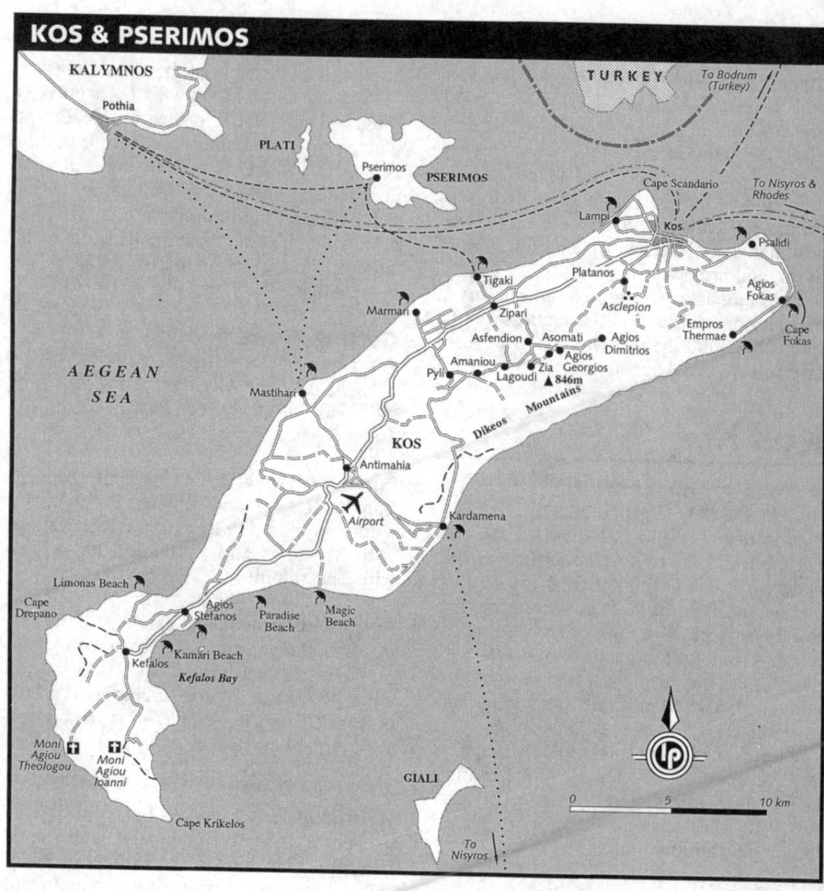

and Nisyros and Giali (5500 dr). There is also a daily excursion boat from Kardamena to Nisyros (3000 dr return) and from Mastihari to Pserimos and Kalymnos.

Getting Around

To/From the Airport An Olympic Airways bus (1000 dr) leaves the airline's office two hours before each flight. The airport is 26km south-west of Kos Town, near the village of Antimahia, and is poorly served by public transport, though buses to and from Kardamena and Kefalos stop at the roundabout nearby.

Many travellers choose to share a taxi into town (4000 dr).

Bus The bus station (☎ 22 292, fax 20 263) is at Kleopatras 7, just west of the Olympic Airways office. There are 10 buses daily to Tigaki (350 dr), five to Mastihari (550 dr), six to Kardamena (600 dr), five to Pyli (350 dr), six to Kefalos (800 dr) via Paradise, Agios Stefanos and Kamari beaches, and three to Zia (350 dr). There are frequent local buses to the Asclepion, Lampi and Agios Fokas from the bus stop on Akti Kountouriotou.

Car, Motorcycle & Bicycle There are numerous car, motorcycle and moped rental outlets.

You'll be tripping over bikes to rent. Prices range from 1000 dr for an old bone-shaker to 3000 dr for a top-notch mountain bike.

Excursion Boat These boats line the southern side of Akti Kountouriotou in Kos Town and make trips around the island.

KOS TOWN

Kos Town, on the north-east coast, is the island's capital and main port. The old town of Kos was destroyed by an earthquake in 1933. The new town, although modern, is picturesque and lush, with palms, pines, oleander and hibiscus everywhere. The Castle of the Knights dominates the port, and Hellenistic and Roman ruins are strewn everywhere.

Orientation

The ferry quay is north of the castle. Excursion boats dock on Akti Kountouriotou to the south-west of the castle. The central square of Plateia Eleftherias is south of Akti Kountouriotou along Vasileos Pavlou. Kos' so-called Old Town is on Ifestou. Its souvenir shops, jewellers and boutiques denude it of any old-world charm, though.

South-east of the castle, the waterfront is called Akti Miaouli. It continues as Vasileos Georgiou and then G Papandreou, which leads to the beaches of Psalidi, Agios Fokas and Empros Thermae.

Information

Kos Town's municipal tourist office (☎ 24 460, fax 21 111) is on Vasileos Georgiou. The staff are efficient and helpful. From May to October the office is open 8 am to 8 pm Monday to Friday and 8 am to 3 pm on weekends. The tourist police (☎ 22 444) and regular police (☎ 22 222) share the yellow building opposite the quay.

The post office is on Vasileos Pavlou and the OTE is at Vyronos 6. Kos Town has two Internet cafes, Del Mare at Megalou Alexandrou 4 and Status at Navarinou 55.

Both the National Bank of Greece, on Antinavarhou Ioannidi, and the Ionian Bank, on El Venizelou, have ATMs. The Alpha Credit Bank on Akti Kountouriotou has a 24 hour automatic exchange machine.

To get to the bus station walk up Vasileos Pavlou and turn right at the Olympic Airways office.

The hospital (☎ 22 300) is at Ippokratous 32. The Happy Wash laundrette is at Mitropolis 20 and the Laundromat Center is at Alikarnassou 124.

The port police (☎ 28 507) are at the corner of Akti Kountouriotou and Megalou Alexandrou.

Archaeological Museum

The archaeological museum (☎ 28 326), on Plateia Eleftherias, has a fine 3rd century AD mosaic in the vestibule and many statues from various periods. The most renowned is the statue of Hippocrates. The museum is open 8.30 am to 3 pm Tuesday to Sunday. Admission is 800 dr.

Archaeological Sites

The **ancient agora** is an open site south of the castle. A massive 3rd century BC stoa, with some reconstructed columns, stands on its western side. On the north side are the ruins of a **Shrine of Aphrodite**, **Temple of Hercules** and a 5th century **Christian basilica**. There is no admission charge.

North of the agora is the lovely cobblestone Plateia Platanou where you can pay your respects to the **Hippocrates Plane Tree**. Under this tree, according to the EOT brochure, Hippocrates taught his pupils. Plane trees don't usually live for more than 200 years – so much for the power of the Hippocratic oath – though in all fairness it is certainly one of Europe's oldest. This once-magnificent tree is held up with scaffolding, and looks to be in its death throes. Beneath it is an old sarcophagus which the Turks converted into a fountain. Opposite the tree is the well preserved 18th century **Mosque of Gazi Hassan Pasha**, its ground floor loggia now converted into souvenir shops.

From Plateia Platanou a bridge leads across Finikon (called the Avenue of Palms) to the **Castle of the Knights**. Along with the castles of Rhodes City and Bodrum, this impregnable fortress was the knights' most stalwart defence against the encroaching Ottomans. The castle, which had massive outer walls and an inner keep, was built in the 14th century. Damaged by an earthquake in 1495, it was restored by the Grand Masters d'Aubusson and d'Amboise (each a master of a 'tongue' of knights) in the 16th century. The keep was originally separated from the town by a moat (now Finikon). Opening times are 8.30 am to 3 pm Tuesday to Sunday. Admission is 800 dr.

The other ruins are mostly in the southern part of the town. Walk along Vasileos Pavlou to Grigoriou and cross over to the

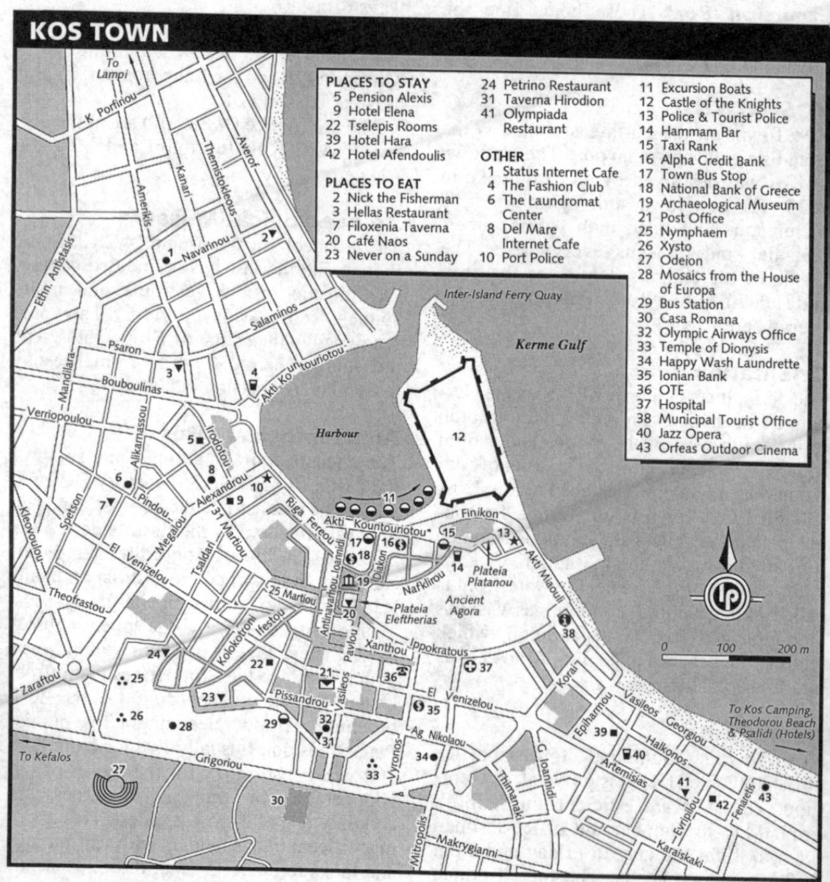

restored **Casa Romana**, an opulent 3rd century Roman villa which was built on the site of a larger 1st century Hellenistic house. It is open 8.30 am to 3 pm Tuesday to Sunday. Admission is 800 dr. Opposite here are the scant ruins of the 3rd century **Temple of Dionysos**.

Facing Grigoriou, turn right to reach the **western excavation** site. Two wooden shelters at the back of the site protect the 3rd century mosaics of the **House of Europa**. The best preserved mosaic depicts Europa's abduction by Zeus in the guise of a bull. In front of here an exposed section of the Dekumanus Maximus (the Roman city's main thoroughfare) runs parallel to the modern road, then turns right towards the **nymphaeum**, which consisted of once-lavish public latrines, and the **xysto**, a large Hellenistic gymnasium, with some restored columns. On the opposite side of Grigoriou is the restored 3rd century **odeion**.

Places to Stay – Budget

Kos' one camp site is ***Kos Camping*** *(☎ 23 910/275)*, 3km along the eastern waterfront. It's a well kept, shaded site with a taverna, snack bar, minimarket, kitchen and laundry. Rates are 1400 dr per person and 700 dr per tent.

The convivial ***Pension Alexis*** *(☎ 28 798, 25 594, Irodotou 9)* is highly recommended. Clean singles/doubles/triples cost 4500/7000/8500 dr. The friendly English-speaking Alexis promises never to turn anyone away, and he's a mine of information. A little farther east, his other hotel, ***Hotel Afendoulis*** *(☎/fax 25 797, Evripilou 1)*, has tastefully furnished rooms with bathroom for 7000/10,000/12,000 dr. Laundry for guests costs 1000 dr a load.

Other commendable budget options include the D class ***Hotel Elena*** *(☎ 22 740, Megalou Alexandrou 7)* with doubles/ triples with bathroom for 7000/8000 dr, and ***Tselepis Rooms*** *(☎ 28 896, Metsovou 8)* where rooms cost 10,000/12,000 dr with bathroom.

At the other end of town the D class ***Hotel Hara*** *(☎ 22 500, Halkonos 6)* is a clean, well maintained hotel, with singles/doubles/triples with bathroom for 6000/8500/10,000 dr.

Places to Stay – Mid-Range & Top End

The B class ***Theodorou Beach*** *(☎ 23 363)*, on G Papandreou, has a cool, spacious interior and nicely furnished rooms. Singles/doubles/triples cost 12,500/16,000/18,800 dr with bathroom.

Most of Kos' top end hotels are on the beaches to either side of town. The luxurious ***Kipriotis Village*** *(☎ 27 640)* at Psalidi, 4km east of town, has singles/doubles for 45,000/55,000 dr and apartments for up to three people for 60,000 dr. The A class ***Platanista Hotel*** *(23 749)*, also at Psalidi, is an architecturally interesting, crenellated building. Singles/doubles are 22,000/27,800 dr.

Places to Eat

The restaurants lining the central waterfront are generally expensive and poor value. ***Taverna Hirodion*** *(Artemisias 27)* serves good food and has a highly entertaining menu, featuring dishes such as Godfish (1700 dr), Humbergers (1400 dr), Gordon Blu (1800 dr) and Jack potato (750 dr). ***Olympiada Restaurant***, behind the Olympic Airways office is an unpretentious place serving reasonably priced, tasty food.

Filoxenia Taverna, on the corner of Pindou and Alikarnassou, has a good reputation for traditional home-cooked food. ***Hellas Restaurant***, on Amerikis, and ***Never on a Sunday***, on Pissandrou, are also highly commendable.

Cafe Aenaos, in a former mosque opposite the market at Plateia Eleftherias, and ***Central Cafe*** *(Vasileos Pavlou 17)* are popular meeting places for locals and tourists alike.

Restaurant Ambavros, on the outskirts of town, serves a delicious array of mezedes. Walk inland along Grigoriou, turn left after the Casa Romana and the taverna is 800m along on the left.

Petrino Restaurant *(Theologou 1)* is a stylish place in a stone mansion, with outdoor eating in a romantic garden setting. It offers a wide range of well prepared food. For a fishy feast head for ***Nick the Fisherman*** on Averof.

Entertainment

Kos Town has two streets of bars, Diakon and Nafklirou, that positively pulsate in high season. Most belt out techno, but ***Hammam Bar*** *(Akti Kountourioti 1)* plays Greek music. ***Jazz Opera*** *(Arseniou 5)* is popular with locals and tourists.

Kos Town has three discos. ***Heaven*** *(Zouroudi 5)* plays mostly house. At ***Calua*** next door the music is more mixed and includes R&B. Both are outdoor and have swimming pools. The indoor ***Fashion Club*** *(Kanari 2)* has three air-con bars. ***Orfeus*** outdoor cinema is on Vasileos Georgiou (open summer only).

AROUND KOS TOWN

Asclepion Ασκληπιείον

The Asclepion (☎ 28 763), built on a pine-covered hill 4km south-west of Kos Town, is the island's most important ancient site. From the top there is a wonderful view of Kos Town and Turkey. The Asclepion consisted of a religious sanctuary to Asclepius, the god of healing, a healing centre, and a school of medicine, where the training followed the teachings of Hippocrates.

Hippocrates was the first doctor to have a rational approach to diagnosing and treating illnesses. Until 554 AD people came from far and wide to be treated here, as well as for medical training.

The ruins occupy three levels. The **propylaea**, the Roman-era public **baths** and the remains of guest rooms are on the first level. On the next level is a 4th century BC **altar of Kyparissios Apollo**. West of this is the **first Temple of Asclepius**, built in the 4th century BC. To the east is the 1st century BC **Temple to Apollo**; seven of its graceful columns have been re-erected. On the third level are the remains of the once-magnificent 2nd century BC **Temple of Asclepius**. The site is open 8.30 am to 3 pm Tuesday to Sunday. Admission is 800 dr.

Frequent buses go to the site, but it is pleasant to cycle or walk there.

Platanos

The village of Platanos, on the way to the Asclepion, has many Turkish inhabitants. The village has a mosque and Turkish and Jewish cemeteries. ***Arup Taverna***, on the central square, serves well prepared traditional Greek/Turkish fare.

AROUND KOS

Kos' main road runs south-west from Kos Town with turn-offs for the mountain villages and the resorts of Tigaki and Marmari. Between the main road and the coast, a quiet road, ideal for cycling, winds through flat agricultural land as far as Marmari.

The nearest decent beach to Kos Town is the crowded **Lampi Beach**, 4km to the north. Farther round the coast, **Tigaki**, 11km from Kos Town, has an excellent, long, pale sand beach. **Marmari Beach**, 4km west of Tigaki, is slightly less crowded.

G Papandreou in Kos Town leads to the three crowded beaches of **Psalidi**, 3km from Kos Town; **Agios Fokas**, 7km away; and **Empros Thermae**, 11km away. The latter has hot mineral springs which warm the sea.

Antimahia (near the airport) is a major crossroads with two large roundabouts. A worthwhile detour is to the **Castle of Antimahia** along a turn-off to the left, 1km before Antimahia. There's a ruined settlement within its well preserved walls.

Kardamena, 27km from Kos Town, and 5km south-east of Antimahia, is an overdeveloped, tacky resort best avoided, unless you want to take an excursion boat to Nisyros (see the Getting There & Away section for Kos).

Mastihari Μαστιχάρι

Mastihari, north of Antimahia and 30km from Kos Town, retains some charm, despite recent development. It has a good sandy beach and secluded spots can be found at its extreme western end. From here there are excursion boats to Kalymnos and the small island of **Pserimos**. The road from

Antimahia terminates at the central square at Mastihari's waterfront.

There's loads of accommodation in Mastihari. ***Fessaras Rooms to Rent*** *(☎ 59 005)* has doubles for 5000 dr. Walk up the road by Kali Kardia Restaurant, take the third turn to the right and the rooms are on the left. Make inquiries at Thomas minimarket. Walk inland along the main road to ***Rooms to Rent Anna*** *(☎ 59 041)*, on the left, where doubles are 6000 dr. Farther up on the right, ***Pension Elena*** *(☎ 59 010)* has doubles for 5500 dr. Next door, ***Rooms to Let David*** *(☎ 59 122)* has doubles for 7000 dr.

Kali Kardia Restaurant, on the central square, is commendable and the fish is particularly good.

Kamari & Kefalos

Καμάρι & Κέφαλος

From Antimahia the main road continues south-west to the huge Kefalos Bay, fringed by a 5km stretch of sand and pebble beaches which, although not isolated, are less crowded than most on Kos. The first is the sandy **Paradise Beach** reached down a track from the main road. The next, **Agios Stefanos**, is taken up by a vast Club Med complex. But the beach, reached along a short turn-off from the main road, is still worth a visit to see the island of Agios Stefanos (named after its church), which is within swimming distance, and the ruins of two 5th century basilicas to the left of the beach as you face the sea. The beach continues to Kamari.

Kefalos, 43km south of Kos Town, is the sprawling village perched high above Kamari Beach. It's a pleasant place with few concessions to tourism. The central square, where the bus terminates, is at the top of the 2km road from the coast.

Between Antimahia and Kefalos a dirt road leads down to the undeveloped **Magic Beach**. Along the same road a turn off leads to **Plaka**, a pleasant forested valley with a network of paths.

Places to Stay Most of the accommodation in Kefalos Bay is monopolised by tour groups. A good option is ***Petros and Maria Rooms*** *(☎ 71 306)*, on the main road 50m from the Agios Stefanos bus stop. It has a beautiful garden and doubles/triples with bathroom cost 6000/7000 dr. ***Studios Dionisia*** *(☎ 71 276/176)*, farther south near the Kamari fishing quay, has double studios for 7000 dr.

Around Kefalos

The southern peninsula has the island's most wild and rugged scenery. **Moni Agiou Theologou** is on the east coast, 4km away, just beyond a sand and pebble beach. Sunsets here are spectacular. **Moni Agiou Ioanni** is at the end of the road, 7km south of Kefalos.

Restaurant Agiou Theologou, near the beach, serves good main dishes and delicious home-made traditional cakes. The sea is quite rough here and the taverna rents out body boards for 2000 dr.

Limonas, 10km north of Kefalos, is a little fishing harbour. Its two small sandy beaches rarely get crowded. There are two tavernas.

Mountain Villages

Several attractive villages are scattered on the northern slopes of the green and wooded, alpine-like Dikeos mountain range. At **Zipari**, 10km from the capital, a road to the south-east leads to **Asfendion**. From Asfendion, a turn-off to the left leads to the pristine hamlets of **Agios Georgios** and **Agios Dimitrios**. The road straight ahead leads to the village of **Zia**, which is touristy but worth a visit for the surrounding countryside and some great sunsets. ***Taverna Olympia***, 70m uphill from the central square, is the best taverna.

Lagoudi is a small, unspoilt village to the west of Zia. From here you can continue to **Amaniou** (just before modern Pyli) where there is a left turn to the ruins of the medieval village of **Pyli**, overlooked by a ruined castle. Just off the central square at modern Pyli, the little ***Taverna Old Pygi***, overlooking a lion-headed fountain, serves tasty, low-priced fare.

Kalymnos Κάλυμνος

☎ 0243 • postcode 852 00 • pop 18,200

Kalymnos (**kah**-lim-nos), only 2.5km south of Leros, is a mountainous, arid island, speckled with fertile valleys. Kalymnos is renowned as the 'sponge-fishing island', but with the demise of this industry it has begun to exploit its tourist potential. However, out of high season its coast is still relatively uncrowded.

Kalymnos hit the Greek headlines in 1995 when local fisherman Antonis Hatziantoniou looked into his net on New Year's Eve and saw a beautiful 2m-high bronze statue of a woman. No, he hadn't been over-indulging in New Year celebrations. Archaeologists think his priceless 'catch' may be the work of the renowned 4th century BC sculptor Praxiteles. The statue is presently in Athens for evaluation. Theoretically a museum is to be built on Kalymnos to house it; needless to say it hasn't happened yet, but at least Antonis was suitably rewarded.

Getting There & Away

Air At the time of writing, Kalymnos' airport was due to open at the end of 1999 – but they've been saying that since 1995, so don't hold your breath.

Ferry The F/B *Nissos Kalymnos* is based on Kalymnos and runs an important service connecting most of the major islands in the chain, as well as the more outlying islands such as Astypalea and Kastellorizo, and Samos in the North-Eastern Aegean. It operates five different daytime routes six days a week, setting out each morning from either Kalymnos or Rhodes. You can check schedules at the company office (☎ 29 612) on 25 Martiou in Pothia.

The following table shows the F/B *Nissos Kalymnos* schedule from Kalymnos in high season.

Destination	Duration	Price	Frequency
Agathonisi	6½ hours	2700 dr	2 weekly
Arki	5¼ hours	2600 dr	2 weekly
Astypalea	3½ hours	2600 dr	2 weekly
Leros	2 hours	1800 dr	2 weekly
Lipsi	3 hours	1800 dr	2 weekly
Patmos	4 hours	2400 dr	2 weekly
Samos	7½ hours	3200 dr	2 weekly

Hydrofoil Kalymnos is served by both the Dodecanese Hydrofoil Company and Samos Hydrofoils. In high season there is a morning service daily to Kos (35 minutes, 2620 dr), with a connection to Rhodes, (three hours, 8055 dr), returning every evening. There are good connections to all the major islands in the group, as well as Samos, Ikaria and Fourni in the North-Eastern Aegean. From Samos you can easily connect with the Cyclades. Buy tickets for Samos hydrofoils at GA Ferries office. The Hydrofoil Agency (☎ 29 886, 28 502) is near the quay.

Excursion Boat In summer there are three excursion boats daily from Pothia to Mastihari on Kos, and one to Pserimos (2000 dr return). There are also weekly excursions to Turkey for 11,000 dr (including Turkish port tax).

There are daily excursions from Myrties to Xirokambos on Leros (3000 dr return).

Getting Around

Bus In summer there is a bus on the hour to Masouri (250 dr) via Myrties; to Emboreios (300 dr) at 9 am and 3.15 pm on Monday, Wednesday and Friday; to Vathy (300 dr) at 6.30 am, 1.30 and 5 pm from Monday to Saturday, and at 7.30 am, 1.30 and 5 pm on Sunday. Buy tickets from Themis Minimarket.

Motorcycle There are several motorcycle rental outlets along Pothia's waterfront.

Taxi Shared taxis are an unusual feature of Kalymnos that cost just a little more than buses. They go from Pothia to Masouri and leave from the taxi rank on Plateia Kyprou (☎ 50 300). These taxis can also be flagged down en route. A taxi to Emboreios costs 3000 dr and to Vathy 2000 dr.

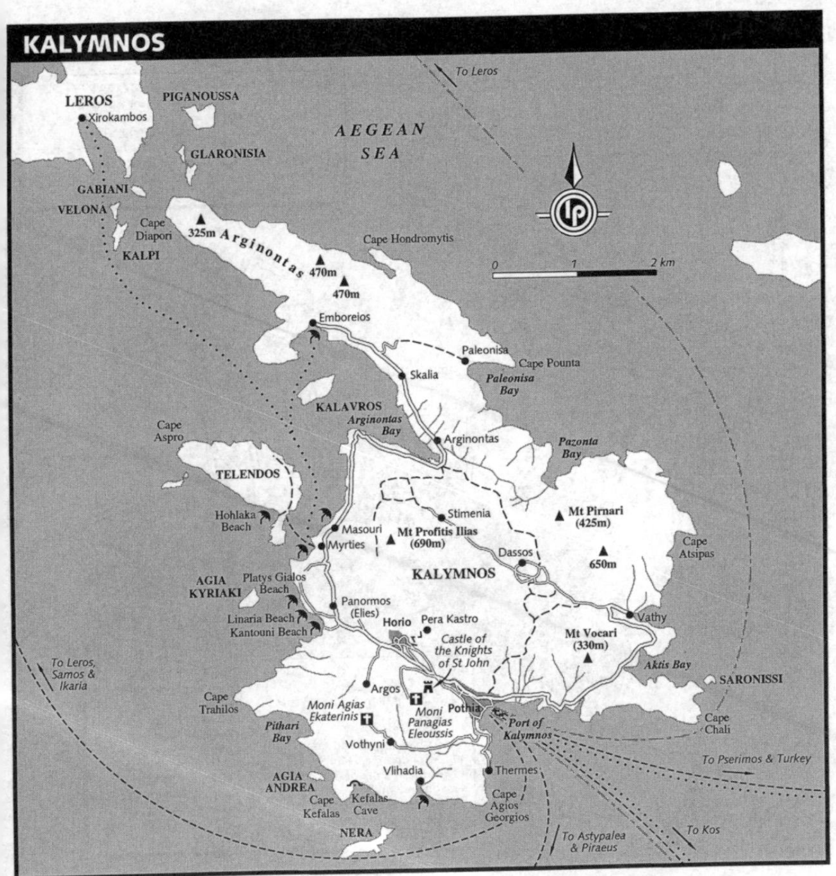

Excursion Boat From Myrties there are daily excursion boats to Emboreios (15,000 dr). Day trips to the Kefalas Cave (6000 dr), impressive for its stalactites and stalagmites, run from both Pothia and Myrties.

POTHIA Πόθια

Pothia, the port and capital of Kalymnos, is where the majority of the island's inhabitants live. Although it's considerably bigger and noisier than most island capitals, it's not without charm. However, a word of warning! Pothia is short in the pavement department and has more than its fair share of kamikaze motorcyclists – keep your wits about you.

Orientation & Information

Pothia's ferry quay is at the southern side of the bay. To reach the town centre, turn right at the end of the quay. Follow the waterfront around and you will pass a tourist information kiosk (☎ 23 140, open summer only) behind the statue of Poseidon, 100m north of the start of the quay.

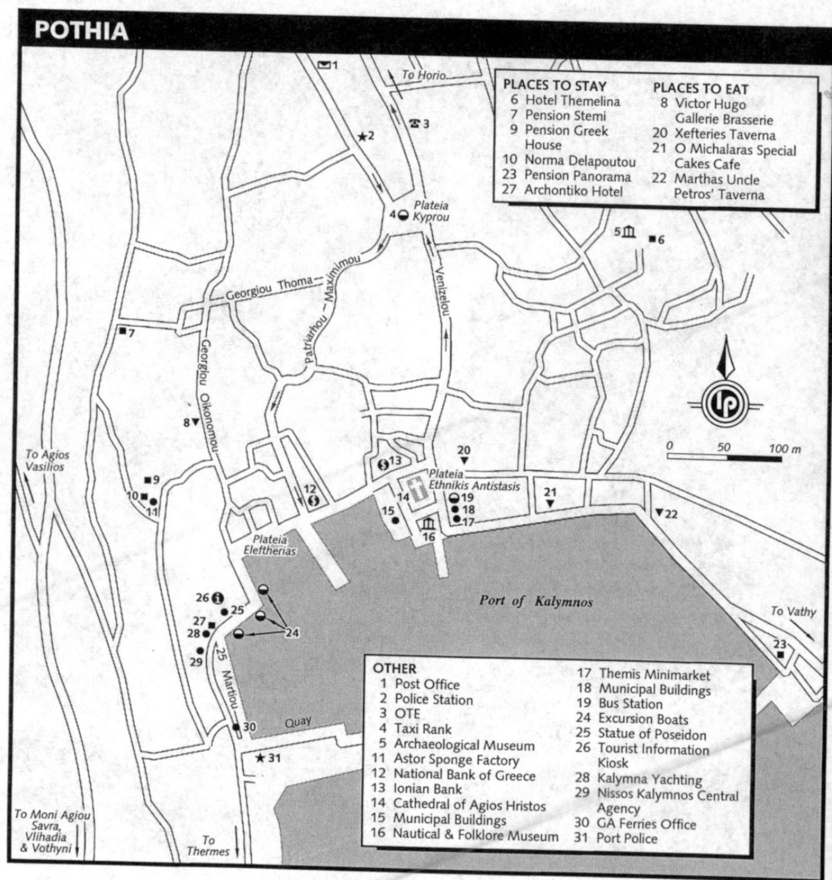

Continue around the waterfront and you will see the two matching municipal buildings flanking the Nautical & Folklore Museum. The Cathedral of Agios Hristos is behind, and the bus station is just to the east of the cathedral. The main thoroughfare of Venizelou runs north from here to Plateia Kyprou, the town's central square. Another busy street, Patriarhou Maximimou, also runs from the waterfront to this square. North of the square are the OTE, on Venizelou, and the post office and police (☎ 29 301), on Patriarhou Maximimou. The settlement of Horio, 3km inland, is the island's former capital.

The National Bank of Greece, at the bottom of Patriarhou Maximimou, and the Ionian Bank, 100m farther east along the waterfront, both have ATMs. The port police (☎ 29 304) are at the start of the quay.

Things to See & Do

The **Archaeological Museum** (☎ 23 113), housed in a neoclassical mansion which once belonged to a wealthy sponge merchant, Mr Vouvalis, is east of Plateia Kyprou. In one room there are some Neolithic and Bronze Age objects. Other rooms are reconstructed as they were when the Vouvalis family lived here. The museum is open 10 am to 2 pm Tuesday to Sunday. Admission is 500 dr. The **Nautical & Folklore Museum** is in the centre of the waterfront. It is open 8 am to 2 pm daily. Admission is 500 dr.

You can hire **yachts** from Kalymna Yachting (☎ 24 083/084, fax 29 125), 50m north of the quay.

Places to Stay

Domatia owners meet the ferries. A pleasant budget option is ***Pension Greek House*** *(☎ 29 559, 23 752)*, inland from the port near the Astor Sponge Factory. It has cosy wood-panelled singles/doubles/triples with bathroom and kitchen facilities for 4500/6000/7200 dr. Norma Delapoutou rents well kept ***domatia*** *(☎ 24 054, 48 145)* behind the Astor Sponge Factory, which is owned by her brother. Doubles with kitchen and verandah are 5000 dr.

Farther inland, ***Pension Stemi*** *(☎ 28 361)* has clean, modern rooms with balconies. Doubles/triples cost 6000/7000 dr. ***Pension Panorama*** *(☎ 29 249)*, 400m along the road to Vathy, has pleasant singles/doubles/triples for 5000/6500/8000 dr.

Archontiko Hotel *(☎/fax 24 149)*, at the top of the quay, is a new hotel in a renovated century-old mansion. Immaculate rooms go for a reasonable 7000/9000/ 10,000 dr.

Hotel Themelina *(☎ 22 682)*, by the well signposted archaeological museum, is a 19th century mansion with swimming pool. Spacious, traditionally furnished doubles/triples cost 16,000/19,500 dr with bathroom. In summer the mansion is booked by tour operators, but there are 30 modern rooms around the pool for the same price.

Places to Eat

The century-old ***Xefteries Taverna***, just off Venizelou, serves delicious, inexpensive food; you'll be taken into the kitchen to choose from the pots. Of the fish tavernas on the eastern waterfront, ***Marthas Uncle Petros' Taverna*** is the best; the crab salad is a delicious and filling starter. ***O Michalaras Special Cakes Cafe*** serves *galaktoboureko*, a speciality of Kalymnos. A generous slice of this gooey confection is 550 dr.

The owners of ***Victor Hugo Gallerie Brasserie***, on Georgiou Oikonomou, Soletatis Coulouritis, a professional photographer, and Vaughelis Kassos, a philosophy graduate, have travelled widely but returned to their island to 'do something for its young people'. Here, young locals are given the opportunity to exhibit their art work and stage live music performances. Coffees, soft and alcoholic drinks and snacks are served, and visitors are warmly welcomed.

AROUND POTHIA

The ruined **Castle of the Knights of St John** (or Castle Hrysoherias) looms to the left of the Pothia-Horio road.

Pera Kastro was a pirate-proof village inhabited until the 18th century. Within the crumbling walls are the ruins of stone houses and six tiny, well kept churches. Steps lead up to Pera Kastro from Horio. It's a strenuous climb but the splendid views make it worthwhile.

A tree-lined road continues from Horio to **Panormos** (also called Elies), a pretty village 5km from Pothia. Its pre-war name of Elies (olives) derived from its abundant olive groves, which were destroyed in WWII. An enterprising post-war mayor planted abundant trees and flowers to create beautiful panoramas wherever one looked – hence its present name, meaning 'panorama'. The sandy beaches of **Kantouni**, **Linaria** and **Platys Gialos** are all within walking distance.

Pension Graziella *(☎ 47 314/346)*, signposted from the main road in Panormos, has comfortable doubles for 5000 dr, double studios for 7000 dr and five-person apartments for 14,000 dr. The owner, the dynamic English-speaking Menelaos, enjoys informing guests of the delights of Kalymnos. Just outside Panormos, on the road to Myrties, ***Hotel Kamari*** *(☎ 47 278)* has great views and well kept singles/doubles/triples for 5000/6000/7000 dr.

The monastery **Moni Agiou Savra** is reached along a turn-off left from the Vothyni and Vlihadia road. You can enter the monastery but a strict dress code is enforced, so wear long sleeves and long trousers or skirts.

MYRTIES & TELENDOS ISLET

Μυρτιές & Νήσος Τέλενδος

From Panormos the road continues to the west coast with stunning views of Telendos

Sponge Fishing

Sponge fishing has occupied Kalymniots since ancient times and was, until recently, their major industry. Kalymnos is now the only Greek island with a sponge-diving fleet, comprising 300 divers.

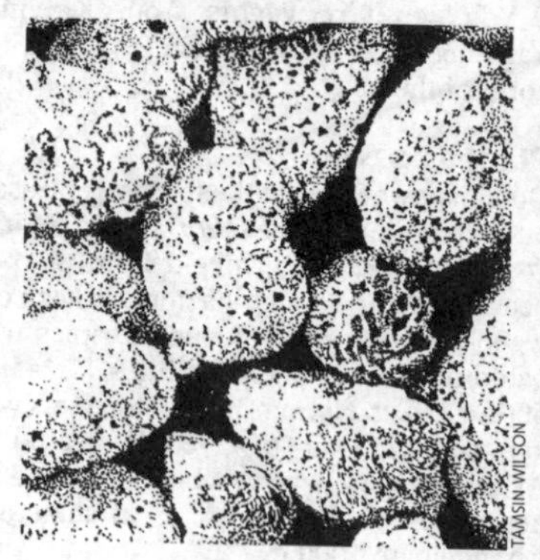
TAMSIN WILSON

As well as the obvious one, sponges have had many uses throughout history – everything from padding in armour to tampons. For hundreds of years the sponges were fished from the waters around Kalymnos, but as the industry grew, fishermen were forced to venture farther away. By the 19th century, divers sailed such great distances that they had to spend months at a time away from home, departing shortly after Easter and returning at the end of October. These two events were celebrated in religious and secular festivals.

Until the first diving suit was invented in the late 19th century, sponge divers were weighed down with stones and had to hold their breath under water. The early diving suits were made of rubber and canvas and were worn with a huge bronze helmet joined to an air pump by a long hose. This contraption enabled divers to stay under the water for much longer. Sponge diving was perilous work and those who didn't die young were often paralysed by the bends.

For many years fishing fleets dived for sponges off the Libyan coast, but Muammar Gadaffi proved an unwelcoming host, exacting an exorbitant tax from the divers. Nowadays, the few remaining sponge-gatherers wear oxygen tanks and work much closer to home, in the North-Eastern Aegean and around Crete. The demise of the sponge industry has been caused by overfishing in the Aegean and the availability of low-priced synthetic sponges.

Greeks are not ones to decline an excuse for feasting and celebration, even if the reasons for so doing have largely disappeared, so the festivals have been preserved. For the week following Easter, the Iprogros (Sponge Festival) occurs, with traditional dancing, music, feasting and drinking, ending with church bell ringing. The fleet then sails out of Pothia Harbour.

At the Astor Sponge Factory, behind Plateia Eleftherias in Pothia, you can watch the process which transforms a disgusting black object into a nice pale-yellow sponge. It goes without saying that Kalymnos is one of the best places in Greece to buy sponges, but if people realised what they were actually buying they might think again. The black objects retrieved from the sea are colonies of micro-organisms living in their fibrous waste products, which are then boiled alive and bleached in acid. Anyone for a bath?

Islet opposite the package resorts of Myrties. From Myrties there's a daily caïque to Xirokambos on Leros (3000 dr return) and frequent caïques for Telendos between 8 am and 11 pm (600 dr return).

The lovely, tranquil and traffic-free islet of Telendos, with a little quayside hamlet, was part of Kalymnos until separated by an earthquake in 554 AD.

If you turn right from the Telendos quay you will pass the ruins of a basilica. Farther on, beyond On the Rocks Cafe, there are several pebble and sand beaches. To reach **Hohlaka Beach**, turn left from the quay and then right at Zorba's Restaurant.

Places to Stay & Eat

Telendos has several domatia. All have pleasant, clean rooms with bathroom. Opposite the quay, ***Pension & Restaurant Uncle George*** *(☎ 47 502, 23 855)* has singles/doubles for 4000/6000 dr. Next door at ***Pension Rita*** *(☎ 47 914, fax 47 927)* the rates are the same, and there are also double studios for 7000 dr. To the right of the quay, ***Nicky Rooms*** *(☎ 47 584)* has doubles for 5000 dr and ***Galanommatis Fotini Rooms*** *(☎ 47 401)* has rooms for 7000 dr.

Port Potha Hotel *(☎ 47 321, fax 48 108)*, beyond On the Rocks Cafe, has well kept singles/doubles/triples for 6000/8000/9000 dr. The new ***apartments*** adjoining On the Rocks Cafe *(☎ 48 260, fax 48 261, email OTE@greece2000.freeserve.co.uk)* cost 10,000 dr for two people.

Restaurant Uncle George serves excellent seafood. ***On the Rocks Cafe*** serves well prepared meat and fish dishes. In the evening it's a lively music bar and if you can't drag yourself away from the fun to catch the last caïque back to Myrties, then George, the friendly Greek-Australian owner, will take you back in his boat free of charge.

EMBOREIOS Εμπορειός

The scenic west-coast road continues to Emboreios, where there's a pleasant tree-shaded pebble beach. One of the nicest places to stay is ***Harry's Apartments*** *(☎ 47 434/922)* where modern double/triple apartments cost 9000/10,800 dr. The adjoining ***Paradise Restaurant*** has a good reputation around the island. ***Taverna Kastril*** on the beach is also commendable.

VATHY Βαθύ

Vathy, 8km north-east of Pothia, is one of the most beautiful and peaceful parts of the island. Vathy means 'deep' in Greek and refers to the slender fjord which cuts through high cliffs into a fertile valley, where narrow roads wind between citrus orchards. There is no beach at Vathy's harbour, Rena, but excursion boats take tourists to quiet coves nearby.

Places to Stay & Eat

Vathy has two places to stay, both at Rena. The C class ***Hotel Galini*** has well kept doubles for 7000 dr with bathroom and balcony, breakfast included. ***Pension Manolis*** *(☎ 31 300)*, above the right side of the harbour, has beautiful singles/doubles/triples for 5000/6000/7200 dr with bathroom. There is a communal kitchen and terraces surrounded by an attractive garden. The English-speaking Manolis is a tour guide and very knowledgeable about the area.

Poppy's Taverna serves reasonably priced, well prepared food and, according to one customer, the best dolmades he's ever tasted.

Leros Λέρος

☎ 0247 • postcode 854 00 • pop 8059

An infamous psychiatric institution, shabby Mussolini-inspired public buildings, a heavy military presence and, during the junta years, a prison for political dissidents, have saddled Leros with an almighty image problem. However, offsetting these flaws is the island's gentle, hilly countryside dotted with small holdings and huge, impressive, almost-landlocked bays, which look more like lakes than open sea.

Lakki is the main port of Leros, but smaller ferries and some excursion boats

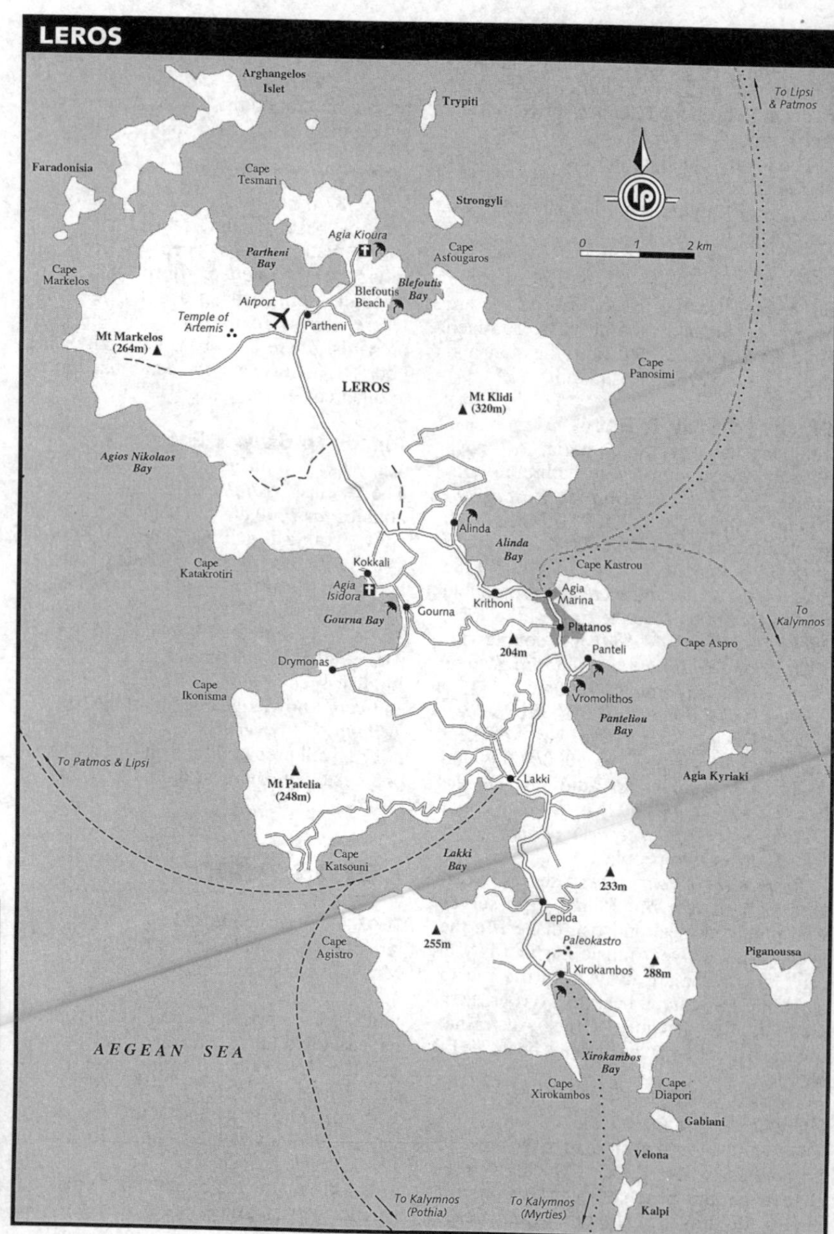
LEROS
Arghangelos
Islet
Trypiti
To Lipsi
& Patmos
Faradonisia
Cape
Tesmari
Strongyli
Agia Kioura
Partheni
Bay
Cape
Asfougaros
0
1
2 km
Cape
Markelos
Blefoutis
Beach
Blefoutis
Bay
Airport
Temple of
Artemis
Partheni
Mt Markelos
(264m)
Cape
Panosimi
LEROS
Mt Klidi
(320m)
Agios Nikolaos
Bay
Alinda
Alinda
Bay
Cape
Katakrotiri
Cape Kastrou
Kokkali
Agia
Isidora
Agia
Marina
Gourna
Krithoni
To
Kalymnos
Gourna Bay
Platanos
204m
Cape Aspro
Panteli
Drymonas
Cape
Ikonisma
Vromolithos
Panteliou
Bay
To Patmos & Lipsi
Agia Kyriaki
Mt Patelia
(248m)
Lakki
Cape
Katsouni
Lakki
Bay
233m
Lepida
Cape
Agistro
255m
Paleokastro
Piganoussa
Xirokambos
288m
AEGEAN SEA
Xirokambos
Bay
Cape
Xirokambos
Cape
Diapori
Gabiani
Velona
To Kalymnos
(Pothia)
To Kalymnos
(Myrties)
Kalpi

use the Agia Marina port, and the caïque from Myrties on Kalymnos docks at Xirokambos. Platanos is the capital of Leros. Lakki is one of the best natural harbours in the Aegean; during their occupation of the Dodecanese the Italians chose it as their principal naval base in the eastern Mediterranean.

Getting There & Away

Air There is one flight daily to Athens (21,200 dr). The Olympic Airways office (☎ 22 844, 24 144) is in Platanos, just before the turn-off for Panteli. The airport is in the north of the island at Partheni.

Ferry Leros has the same ferry connections as Kalymnos.

Hydrofoil In summer there are hydrofoils every day to Patmos (45 minutes, 3045 dr), Lipsi (30 minutes, 2650 dr), Samos (two hours, 5000 dr), Kos (one hour, 4100 dr) and Rhodes (3¼ hours, 9300 dr); and almost every day to Agathonisi (1½ hours, 4460 dr) via Patmos and Fourni (4600 dr). Hydrofoils leave from Agia Marina.

Excursion Boat The caïque leaves Xirokambos every day at 7.30 am for Myrties on Kalymnos (1500 dr one way). In summer the Lipsi-based *Anna Express* makes daily trips between Agia Marina and Lipsi, and the *Captain Makis* runs on Tuesday and Thursday. Both cost 5000 dr return.

Getting Around

The hub for Leros' buses is Platanos. There are four buses daily to Partheni via Alinda and six buses to Xirokambos via Lakki.

There is no shortage of car, motorcycle and bicycle rental outlets around the island.

LAKKI Λακκί

If you arrive on one of the large inter-island ferries, you'll disembark at Lakki. The grandiose buildings and wide tree-lined boulevards dotted around the Dodecanese reach their apogee here, for Lakki was built as a Fascist showpiece during the Italian occupation. But the buildings are now shabby and most visitors head straight for Platanos or one of the seaside resorts. Taxis meet all the boats.

PLATANOS Πλάτανος

Platanos, the capital of Leros, is 3km north of Lakki. It's a picturesque little place which spills over a narrow hill pouring down to the port of Agia Marina to the north, and Panteli to the south, both within walking distance. On the east side of Platanos, houses are stacked up a hillside topped by a massive castle. To reach the castle you can either climb up 370 steps, or walk or drive 2km along an asphalt road. It is usually – but not necessarily – open 8 am to noon; entry is 200 dr.

Orientation & Information

The focal point of Platanos is the lively central square, Plateia N Poussou. Xarami links this square with Agia Marina.

There is a tourist information kiosk at the quay. Laskarina Tours (☎ 24 550, fax 24 551), at the Elefteria Hotel, and Kastis Travel & Tourist Agency (☎ 22 140), near the quay in Agia Marina, are very helpful. Laskarina Tours organises trips around the island (3500 dr to 5500 dr).

The post office and OTE share premises on the right side of Xarami. The National Bank of Greece is on the central square. There is a freestanding Commercial Bank ATM on the quay in Agia Marina. The police station (☎ 22 222) is in Agia Marina; turn left from Xarami and it's on the right. The bus station and taxi rank are both on the Lakki-Platanos road, just before the central square.

Places to Stay & Eat

The C class ***Elefteria Hotel*** *(☎ 23 550/145)*, near the taxi rank, has pleasant, well kept rooms for 5000/6000/7500 dr with bathroom. The ***cafe*** on the main square does great coffee and sandwiches.

AROUND PLATANOS

The port of **Agia Marina** has a more authentic ambience than the resort of Alinda to the north. Walking in the other direction from Platanos, you'll arrive at **Panteli**, a little fishing village-cum-resort with a sand and shingle beach. Just outside of Platanos, beyond the turn-off for Panteli, a road winds steeply down to **Vromolithos** where there's a good shingle beach.

Places to Stay & Eat

In Panteli, the waterfront ***Pension Roza*** *(☎ 22 798)* has doubles/triples for 4000/6000 dr. A bit farther along, ***Rooms to Rent Kavos*** *(☎ 23 247, 25 020)* has rates of 8000/9000 dr. ***Pension Happiness*** *(☎ 23 498)*, on the left of the road down from Platanos, has modern, sunny rooms with bathroom for 9000/10,000 dr.

Dimitris Taverna is probably Leros' best taverna. Its delicious mezedes include cheese courgettes, stuffed calamari, and onion and cheese pies; main courses include chicken in retsina and pork in red sauce. Take the road to Vromolithos, a little way down turn left at a shop, and the taverna's on the right. There are also several tavernas at Agia Marina.

In Panteli, ***Zorbas*** and ***Psarapoula*** are popular tavernas, but the unpretentious little ***Taverna Drossia*** is just as good.

Entertainment

Agia Marina is the heart of the island's nightlife, with several late night music bars.

In Panteli, head for ***Savana Bar***, run by two English guys, Simon and Peter. It is open from mid-afternoon till late and has a great music policy: you can choose what you want.

KRITHONI & ALINDA

Κριθώνι & Αλινδα

Krithoni and Alinda are contiguous resorts on the wide Alinda Bay, 3km north-west of Agia Marina. On Krithoni's waterfront there is a poignant, well kept **war cemetery**. After the Italian surrender in WWII, Leros saw fierce fighting between German and British forces. The cemetery contains the graves of 179 British, two Canadian and two South African soldiers.

Alinda, the island's biggest resort, has a long, tree-shaded sand and gravel beach. If you walk beyond the development you'll find some quiet coves.

Places to Stay & Eat

Hotel Kostantinos *(☎ 22 337/904)*, on the right coming from Agia Marina, has comfortable doubles with bathrooms for 6000 dr. A bit farther along, the B class ***Crithoni Paradise Hotel*** *(☎ 25 120, fax 24 680)* complete with bars, restaurant and swimming pool, has singles/doubles/triples for 21,000/28,000/33,500 dr and suites for 45,000 dr. Just beyond the war cemetery, a road veers left to ***Hotel Gianna*** *(☎/fax 24 135)* which has nicely furnished rooms for 4000/8000/9600 dr. The sparkling, pine-furnished ***Studios & Apartments Diamantis*** *(☎ 22 378, 23 213)*, behind the cemetery, has rates of 7000/10,000/12,000 dr.

Alinda's waterfront ***Finikas Taverna*** has an extensive menu of well prepared Greek specialities; mezedes are 600 dr to 1200 dr and souvlaki is 1800 dr.

GOURNA Γούρνα

The wide bay of Gourna, on the west coast, has a similar beach to Alinda but is less developed. At the northern side, the chapel of **Agia Isidora** is on a tranquil islet reached by a causeway.

NORTHERN LEROS

Partheni is a scattered settlement north of the airport. Despite having a large army camp, it's an attractive area of hills, olive groves, fields of beehives and two large bays.

Artemis, the goddess of the hunt, was worshipped on Leros in ancient times. Just before the airport there's a signposted turn to the left that leads to the **Temple of Artemis**. A dirt track turns right 300m along it. Where the track peters out, clamber up to the left. You will see the little derelict **Chapel of Agia Irini**. There's little in the way of ancient ruins but it's a strangely evocative, slightly eerie place.

Farther along the main road there is a turn-off to the right to **Blefoutis Bay**, which has a shaded sand and pebble beach and a good taverna. Beyond this turn-off, the main road skirts **Partheni Bay** and its poor beach. But if you continue straight ahead, turn right at the T-junction, go through a gate to pass the **Chapel of Agia Kioura**, then through another gate and bear right, you'll come to a lovely secluded pebbled cove.

XIROKAMBOS Ξερόκαμπος

Xirokambos Bay, in the south of the island, is a low-key resort with a gravel and sand beach and some good spots for snorkelling. Just before the camp site, on the opposite side, a signposted path leads up to the ruined fortress of **Paleokastro**.

Leros' Diving Club (☎ 23 372) is based in Xirokambos. Seven-day diving courses cost around 85,000 dr (all-inclusive).

There are several ***domatia*** and the island's only camp site, ***Camping Leros*** *(☎ 23 372)*, on the right coming from Lakki. It's pleasant and shaded, with a restaurant and bar.

Patmos Πάτμος

☎ 0247 • postcode 855 00 • pop 2663

Patmos is a place of pilgrimage for both Orthodox and western Christians, for it was here that St John wrote his divinely inspired revelation (the Apocalypse). Once a favourite venue for the pious and hippies wishing to tune into its spiritual vibes, Patmos is now just as popular with sun and sea worshippers. The only remaining vestiges of the island's former isolation are the many signs (often ignored) that forbid topless and nude bathing.

History

In 95 AD, St John the Divine was banished to Patmos from Ephesus by the pagan Roman Emperor Domitian. While residing in a cave on the island, St John wrote the *Book of Revelations*. In 1088 the Blessed Christodoulos, an abbot who came from Asia Minor to Patmos, obtained permission from the Byzantine Emperor Alexis I Comnenus to build a monastery to commemorate St John. Pirate raids necessitated powerful fortifications, so the monastery looks like a mighty castle.

Under the Duke of Naxos, Patmos became a semiautonomous monastic state, and achieved such wealth and influence that it was able to resist Turkish oppression. In the early 18th century, a school of theology and philosophy was founded by Makarios Kalogheras and it flourished until the 19th century.

Gradually the island's wealth polarised into secular and monastic entities. The secular wealth was acquired through shipbuilding, an industry which diminished with the arrival of the steam ship.

Getting There & Away

Ferry Patmos has the same ferry connections as Kalymnos and Leros.

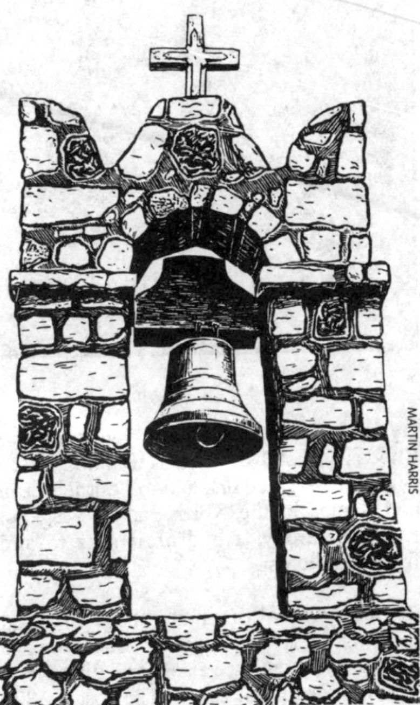

MARTIN HARRIS

Church belltower on Patmos

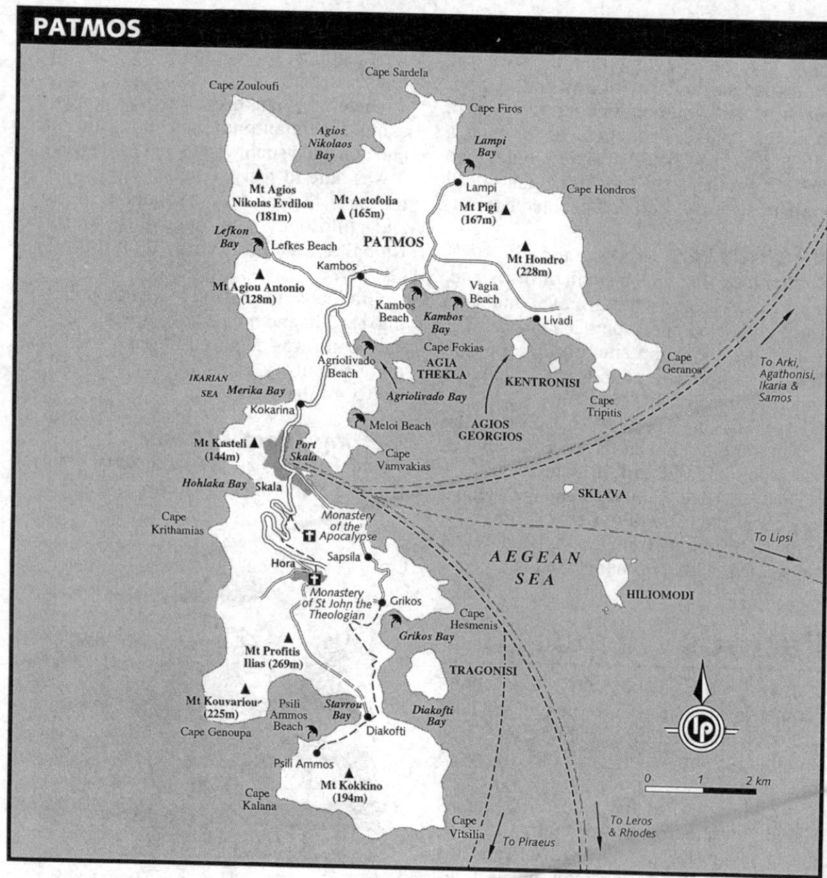

Hydrofoil There are daily hydrofoils to Rhodes (10,280 dr), via Kalymnos (4620 dr) and Kos (5560 dr), and to Fourni, Ikaria and Samos in the North-Eastern Aegean. Every Saturday, a hydrofoil runs to and from Agathonisi.

Excursion Boat In summer the Lipsi-based *Anna Express* and *Captain Makis* sail to Patmos every day (see also the Getting There & Away section for Lipsi). The cost is 3800 dr return.

Daily Patmos-based excursion boats go to Marathi, and the caïque *Delfini* goes to Arki almost every day in high season – Monday and Thursday at other times. If you can't see the *Delfini* at Skala's quay, call ☎ 31 995/371 for information.

Getting Around

Bus From Skala there are seven buses daily to Hora (210 dr), five to Grikos (230 dr) and four to Kambos (230 dr). There is no bus service to Lampi.

Motorcycle There are lots of motorcycle and car rental outlets in Skala. Competition is fierce, so shop around.

Taxi From Skala's taxi rank, examples of tariffs are: Meloi Beach (800 dr), Lampi (1500 dr), Grigos (1200 dr) and Hora (1000 dr).

Excursion Boat Boats go to all the island's beaches from Skala, leaving about 11 am and returning about 4 pm.

SKALA Σκάλα

All boats dock at the island's port and capital of Skala. The town sprawls around a large curving bay. It's quite a glitzy place, pandering to the passengers of the many visiting cruise ships.

Although it's very busy and not especially attractive, it's a convenient transport hub and has all the tourist facilities and plenty of accommodation. There are great views from the site of the island's ancient acropolis, behind Skala.

Orientation & Information

Facing inland from the quay, turn right to reach the main stretch of waterfront where excursion boats and yachts dock. The right side of the large, white Italianate building opposite the quay overlooks the central square. For the road to Hora, turn left at the quay and right at Taverna Grigoris.

The municipal tourist office (☎ 31 666), open summer only, shares the Italianate building with the post office and police station. Astoria Travel (☎ 31 205, fax 31 975), on the waterfront near the quay, and Travel Point (☎ 32 801, fax 32 802, email info@travelpoint.gr), just inland from the central square, are helpful. The latter has a room-finding service.

The National Bank of Greece on the central square has an ATM. Inland from the central square is another smaller square; the OTE is on the left side of the road heading inland from here. The hospital (☎ 31 211) is 2km along the road to Hora.

Just Like Home Laundry is at the western end of the waterfront.

Patmos' port police (☎ 31 231) are behind the large quay's passenger-transit building. The bus terminal and taxi rank (☎ 31 225) are at the large quay.

Places to Stay – Budget

Domatia owners meet the boat. If you are not scooped up by one, there are several budget places along the Hora road. ***Pension Sofia's*** *(☎ 31 876)*, 250m up on the left, has doubles/triples with bathroom and balcony for 6000/7000 dr. Farther up, ***Pension Maria Paskeledi*** *(☎ 32 152)* has singles/doubles/triples for 4000/7000/8500 dr.

The D class ***Hotel Rex*** *(☎ 31 242)* has rooms for 6000/7500/8500 dr with bathroom. It's on a narrow street opposite the cafeteria/passenger-transit building.

Pension Sydney *(☎ 32 118)* has rooms for 4000/7000/10,000 dr with bathroom. The nearby ***Pension Avgerinos*** *(☎ 32 118)*, run by the same family, has doubles with superb views and bathroom for 7000 dr. Turn left 100m past the cemetery to reach these places.

Villa Knossos *(☎ 32 189, fax 32 284)*, in a lovely garden, has immaculate rooms with bathroom and balcony. Doubles/triples are 10,000/12,000 dr. A sign points left 50m beyond the cemetery. Farther along the coast road, the C class ***Hotel Hellinos*** *(☎ 31 275)* has attractive rooms for 12,000/13,000 dr with bathroom. Co-owned with the hotel are some well kept ***domatia*** for 7500/8000 dr with shared bathroom.

Yvonne Studios *(☎ 32 466, 33 066)* has beautifully furnished apartments overlooking Hohlaka Bay for 10,000/12,000 dr. Inquire about them at Yvonne's Tourist Shop, near O Pantelis Taverna.

Places to Stay – Mid-Range

Hotel Chris *(☎ 31 403)* has singles/doubles/triples for 6600/11,000/13,200 dr. Turn right at the quay and it's on the waterfront.

The C class ***Hotel Delfina*** *(☎ 32 060, fax 32 061)*, to the left of the quay, has well kept rooms for 10,000/13,000/15,000 dr. Next door, ***Captain's House*** *(☎ 31 793, fax 34 077)* has rates of 7000/14,000/15,000 dr. Around the corner, ***Hotel Byzance*** *(☎ 31 052/663)* charges 11,000/16,000/19,000 dr.

Hotel Blue Bay *(☎ 31 165, fax 32 303)* has very clean, nicely furnished rooms for 13,500/17,000/20,000 dr. The owner lived in Australia for many years, and now offers Aussie guests Vegemite at breakfast. Turn left at the quay and the hotel is 150m along on the right.

Skala's best hotel is the B class ***Hotel Skala*** *(☎ 31 343, fax 31 747)*, on the waterfront. Rates are 18,000/25,000/30,500 dr, including breakfast, and there's a swimming pool. (For Patmos' most luxurious hotel see the North of Skala section.)

Places to Eat

For excellent seafood try ***Hiliomodi Ouzeri***, 50m up the Hora road on the left. The tasty 'variety of appetisers plate' is excellent value at 2000 dr. ***Grigoris Taverna***, on the corner of the Hora road, is also highly commendable. There are two excellent ***bakeries*** on the square. The waterfront ***Cafe Bar Arion*** is great for people-watching, and is a popular evening haunt for young locals.

Restaurant Benetou, a little way along the Grikou road, is Skala's best restaurant, favoured by Prince Michael of Greece during his annual sojourn on Patmos. The menu features a wide range of imaginative dishes.

Entertainment

For nightlife, try ***Music Club 2000***, just past the Argo petrol station on the far side of the bay. You can dance until 5 am and it has an outdoor swimming pool. Other 'in' places are ***Consolatos Dancing Bar*** and ***Aman***, next to one another left of the quay.

MONASTERIES & HORA

The immense **Monastery of St John the Theologian**, with its buttressed grey walls, crowns the island of Patmos. A 4km asphalt road leads in from Skala, but many people prefer to walk up the Byzantine path. To do this, walk up the Skala-Hora road and take the steps to the right 100m beyond the far side of the football field. The path begins opposite the top of these steps.

A little way along, a dirt path to the left leads through pine trees to the **Monastery of the Apocalypse**, built around the cave where St John received his divine revelation. In the cave you can see the rock which the saint used as a pillow, and the triple fissure in the roof, from which the voice of God issued, and which supposedly symbolises the Holy Trinity. Opening times are 8 am to 1 pm Monday to Saturday, 8 am to noon Sunday and 4 to 6 pm on Tuesday, Thursday and Sunday.

To rejoin the Byzantine path, walk across the monastery's car park and bear left onto the (uphill) asphalt road. After 60m, turn sharp left onto an asphalt road, and almost immediately the path veers off to the right. Soon you will reach the main road again. Cross straight over and continue ahead to reach Hora and the Monastery of St John the Theologian.

The finest frescoes of this monastery are those in the outer narthex. The priceless contents in the monastery's treasury include icons, ecclesiastical ornaments, embroideries and pendants made of precious stones. Opening times are the same as for the Monastery of the Apocalypse. Admission to the treasury is 1000 dr.

Huddled around the monastery are the immaculate whitewashed houses of **Hora**. The houses are a legacy of the island's great wealth of the 17th and 18th centuries. Some of them have been bought and renovated by wealthy Greeks and foreigners.

Places to Stay & Eat

There are no hotel or domatia signs in Hora. There is accommodation but it is expensive and the best places are pre-booked months in advance. If you wish to stay in Hora, contact Travel Point in Skala.

Vagelis Taverna, on the central square, with a garden at the back, is deservedly popular.

The elegant ***Patmian House*** *(☎ 31 180)* in a restored mansion, is the island's restaurant par excellence. There's a large choice of superb mezedes; the little spinach and cheese pies are especially good. The fillet steak is also commendable. Expect to pay around 10,000 dr for a three-course meal with wine. Reservations are recommended.

NORTH OF SKALA

The pleasant, tree-shaded **Meloi Beach** is just 2km north-east of Skala, along a turn-off from the main road.

Two kilometres farther along the main road there's a turn-off right to the relatively quiet **Agriolivado Beach**. The main road continues to the inland village of **Kambos** and then descends to the shingle beach from where you can walk to the secluded pebbled **Vagia Beach**. The main road ends at **Lampi**, 9km from Skala, where there is a beautiful beach of multicoloured stones.

Places to Stay & Eat

Stefanos Camping *(☎ 31 821)*, at Meloi, is a good camp site, with bamboo-shaded sites, a minimarket, cafe bar and motorcycle rental facilities. The rates are 1300 dr for an adult and 600 dr for a tent. The rainbow-coloured minibus meets most boats.

Next to the well signposted Taverna Meloi there is a basic ***domatia*** *(☎ 31 213, 31 247)* where doubles are 5000 dr. The family also owns some newer rooms nearby, where doubles with bathroom are 8000 dr.

At Kambos, the owners of George's Place Snack Bar (see Places to Eat) offer an unofficial room-letting service.

Patmos has two luxury hotels. ***Porto Scoutari*** *(☎ 33 124/125, fax 33 175)*, at Meloi, has double/triple studios for 26,000/30,000 dr. In Kambos, ***Patmos Paradise*** *(☎ 32 624)* has singles/doubles for 22,000/27,000.

The excellent ***Taverna Meloi*** serves traditional Greek dishes. ***Glaros Taverna*** on Agriolivado Beach is also commendable. ***George's Place Snack Bar***, on Kambos Beach, is a good place to hang out. It's home-made fare includes irresistible apple pie. ***Cafe Vagia***, overlooking Vagia Beach, has great food and views.

Lampi's ***Taverna Leonidas*** specialises in fish dishes but the *saganaki* is also very good.

SOUTH OF SKALA

Grikos, 4km south-east of Skala, is a rather lifeless resort with a sandy beach. Farther south, the long, sandy, tree-shaded **Psili Ammos**, reached by excursion boat, is the island's best beach. Most of the accommodation in Grikos is monopolised by tour groups. But try the ***Restaurant O Stamatis and Rooms*** *(☎ 31 302)*, by the beach, which has comfortable doubles with bathroom for 8000 dr. Psili Ammos has a seasonal ***taverna***, but no accommodation.

Lipsi Λειψοί

☎ 0247 • postcode 850 01 • pop 606

Lipsi (lip-**see**), 12km east of Patmos and 11km north of Leros, is an idyllic little island with good beaches. The cheery inhabitants busy themselves with fishing and farming and keeping happy the relatively small number of tourists who venture here. The picturesque port town of Lipsi is the only settlement. Lipsi produces a potent wine known as Lipsi Black.

Getting There & Away

Ferry The F/B *Nissos Kalymnos* calls at Lipsi on Wednesday and Saturday. It is also included in the route which links the Dodecanese to Mykonos and Syros.

Hydrofoil In summer, hydrofoils call at Lipsi at least twice daily (except Monday) on their routes north and south between Samos, in the North-Eastern Aegean, and Kos.

Excursion Boat The *Captain Makis* and *Anna Express* do daily trips in summer to Agia Marina on Leros and to Skala on Patmos (both 4200 dr return). *Black Beauty* and *Margarita* do excursion trips including Arki and Marathi for around 4000 dr return.

Getting Around

Lipsi has two minibuses which go to Platys Gialos (300 dr), Katsadia and Kohlakoura (both 250 dr). There are several motorcycle rental outlets.

LIPSI TOWN

Orientation & Information

All boats dock at Lipsi Town, where there are two quays. The Lipsi-based *Anna Express* and *Captain Makis* dock at the small quay opposite Hotel Calypso. All other boats and ferries dock at the large quay.

From the large quay, facing inland, turn right. Continue along the waterfront to the large Plateia Nikiforias, which is just beyond Hotel Calypso. Ascend the wide steps at the far side of Plateia Nikiforias and bear right to reach the central square. The left fork leads to a second, smaller square.

The municipal tourist office (☎ 41 288) is on the central square, but you may find Paradisos Travel (☎ 41 120, fax 41 110), at the base of the wide steps, more helpful. The post office and OTE are on the central square. There is a freestanding Commercial Bank ATM near the wide steps. Paradisos Travel changes money and cashes Eurocheques. The police (☎ 41 222) are in the large white building opposite Paradisos Travel. The port police (☎ 41 133) are in the long white building to the right of the wide steps.

Things to See & Do

Lipsi's **museum** is on the central square. Its underwhelming exhibits include pebbles and plastic bottles of holy water from around the world. Admission is free, but opening times are erratic. There is a **carpet factory** in the same building as the port police. The hand-woven carpets are not for sale here but you can see them being made.

The town beach of **Liendos** is a short walk from the waterfront.

Places to Stay

The D class ***Hotel Calypso*** *(☎ 41 242)* has comfortable doubles/triples for 8000/9000 dr

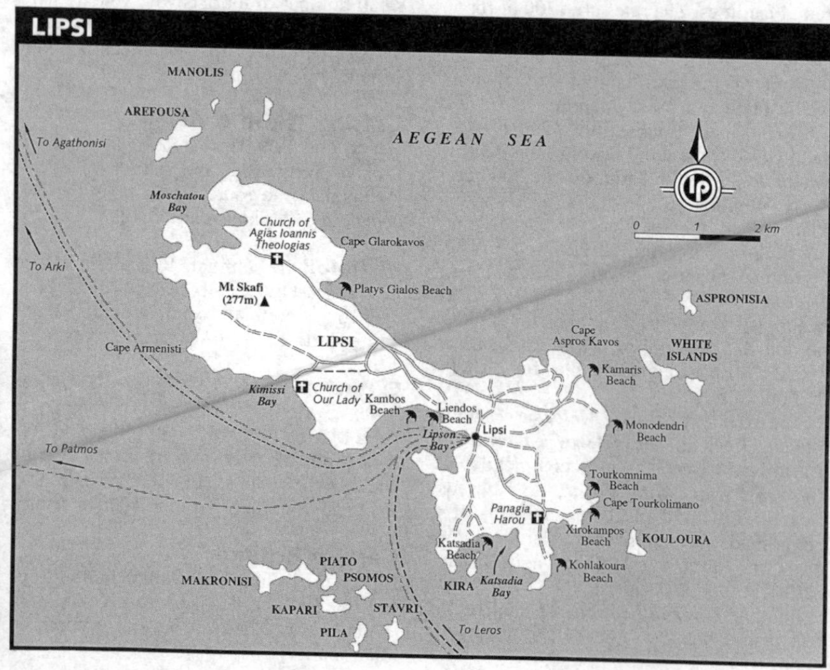

DODECANESE

with bathroom. ***Rena's Rooms*** *(☎ 41 363)*, owned by Greek-Americans John and Rena Paradisos (of Paradisos Travel), are spotless, beautifully furnished and spacious. Rooms are 9000/10,000 dr with bathroom. There is a communal refrigerator and electric hot plates, and a terrace overlooking Liendos Beach. Turn right from the large quay (left from the small quay) and take the signposted road to Liendos. The rooms are on the left.

Rooms Galini *(☎ 41 212)*, opposite the large quay, has lovely, light rooms with bathroom, refrigerator, gas ring and balcony for 9000/10,000 dr. Nearby, above Cafeteria Fotina, ***Panorama Studios*** *(☎ 41 235)* are equally agreeable and the rates are the same.

Flisvos Pension *(☎ 41 261)*, just beyond the carpet factory, has singles/doubles/triples for 5500/7500/9500 dr.

Barbarosa Studios *(☎ 41 092/312)*, near the central square, has spacious, well equipped studios from 12,500 dr.

The A class ***Aphrodite Hotel*** *(☎ 41 394)*, overlooking Liendos Beach, has luxurious double studios for 20,000 dr and four-person apartments for 28,000 dr.

Places to Eat

Restaurant Barbarosa, near Rena's Rooms, serves reasonably priced, decent food. There's a string of restaurants and cafes on the waterfront between the two quays. They include the highly recommended ***Giannis Restaurant***, ***Fish Restaurant***, which serves (surprise, surprise) only fish, ***Rock Coffee Bar & Ouzeri***, which offers some unusual mezedes, and ***Cafe Stratos*** which serves ice cream, pastries and good coffee. ***Calypso Restaurant***, adjoining the hotel, serves very tasty, low-priced food.

Lipsi's shady, traffic-free square, with two inexpensive ***kafeneia***, is a lovely spot for breakfast.

Entertainment

Lipsi's hot spots are ***Aphrodite Music Bar*** and ***Scorpion Night Club***. At the latter, evenings begin with international music but Greek music gradually takes over, with locals giving tourists impromptu lessons in Greek dancing.

BEACHES

Away from Lipsi Town the beaches are the island's main attractions. They make pleasant walks, passing through countryside dotted with small holdings, olive groves and cypresses but buses also go to most of them.

Beyond Liendos Beach the road forks; if you take the right fork, after about 40 minutes you will arrive at **Platys Gialos**, a lovely sandy beach with a decent taverna.

Another good beach is the sand and pebble **Katsadia**, shaded with tamarisk trees. Its small, rustic ***Gamricris Taverna***, above the beach, is owned by an elderly couple, who serve simple, low-priced meat and fish dishes. Nearer the beach, the modern ***Dilaila Cafe Restaurant*** is owned by their son, Christodoules, who has travelled widely and speaks good English. Good, reasonably priced food is served, and music from Christodoules' eclectic collection is played.

The pebble **Kohlakoura Beach**, to the east of Katsadia, is near the **Church of Panagia Harou** (The Virgin of Death), where, according to tradition, dried flowers are resurrected on 24 August, the church's festival day. Also nearby, is **Dimitris Makris' vineyard** where you can buy Lipsi Black wine (bring a container).

Farther north, **Monodendri** (One Tree) is the island's unofficial nudist beach. It stands on a rocky peninsula, the neck of which is pebbled. There are no facilities. It takes about one hour to walk there. To do so, turn left after Pension Flisvos and continue straight ahead passing the high school on the left. The road becomes a cobbled track, then climbs steadily and levels out to a dirt track. Continue ahead at the intersection by a church. Keep on this main track which eventually ends after curving sharply to the left. From here a network of paths lead down to Monodendri, recognisable by its one tree.

KIMISSI Κοίμηση

Kimissi is a little bay on the south-west coast. A hermit monk lives here beside the little **Church of Our Lady**. If you visit, behave appropriately with respect for his peace and holiness. In Ottoman times monks hid in a cave here, choosing death from starvation rather than capture by the Turks. A casket in the church contains their bones.

To walk there, take the Platys Gialos road, and veer left onto the uphill track by a stone wall, opposite the asphalt road to the right. Go through a gap in a stone wall, continue ahead and you will eventually come to the **Church of the Virgin of the Cross**, from where an asphalt road leads down to Kimissi.

Arki & Marathi

ARKI Αρκοί

☎ 0247 • 850 01 • pop 50

Tiny Arki, 5km north of Lipsi, is hilly, with shrubs but few trees. Its only settlement, the little port on the west coast, is also called Arki. Islanders make a meagre living from fishing.

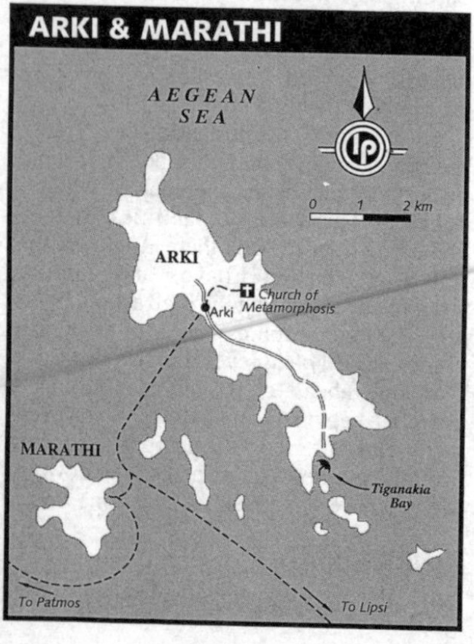

There is no post office, OTE or police on the island, but there is a cardphone. Away from its little settlement, the island seems almost mystical in its peace and stillness.

Getting There & Away

The F/B *Nissos Kalymnos* calls on Wednesday or Sunday. In summer the Lipsi-based excursion boats visit Arki and Marathi, and the Patmos-based caïque *Delfini* does frequent trips (4000 dr return) also.

Things to See & Do

The **Church of Metamorphosis** stands on a hill behind the settlement. From its terrace there are superb views of Arki and its surrounding islets. The cement road between Taverna Tripas and Taverna Nikolaos leads to the path up to the church. The church is kept locked but ask a local if it's possible to look inside.

Several secluded sandy coves can be reached along a path skirting the right side of the bay. To reach the path, walk around the last house at the far right of the bay, go through a little wooden gate in the stone wall, near the sea, and continue ahead.

Tiganakia Bay on the south-east coast has a good sandy beach. To walk there from Arki village, take the cement road which skirts the left side of the bay. Continue along the dirt track passing the blue-domed church. At the end of the track, take the path ahead and go through a gate at the seaward end of a stone wall. Tiganakia Bay, reached by a network of goat tracks, lies at the far side of the headland. You will recognise it by the incredibly bright turquoise water and the offshore islets.

Places to Stay & Eat

Arki has three tavernas, two of which have double rooms for 8000 dr with bathroom. ***O Tripas Taverna & Rooms*** *(☎ 32 230)* is to the right of the quay, as you face inland. The owner, Manolis, speaks good English. ***Taverna Nikolaos Rooms*** *(☎ 32 477)* is adjacent to it. Both tavernas are good. The black eye beans and onions served at O Tripas Taverna make a tasty starter.

The third taverna, ***Taverna Manolis***, opposite the quay, is also highly commendable. Nektaria, the delightful owner, doesn't speak English, but enjoys giving customers impromptu Greek lessons.

MARATHI Μαράθι

Marathi is the largest of Arki's satellite islets. Before WWII it had a dozen or so inhabitants, but now has only one family. The old settlement, with an immaculate little church, stands on a hill above the harbour. The island has a superb sandy beach.

Marathi has two tavernas, both of which rent rooms. ***Taverna Pantelis*** *(☎ 32 609/ 759)* and ***Taverna Mihalis*** *(☎ 31 580)*, owned by the island's only permanent inhabitants, have comfortable doubles for 8000 dr. Both owners speak English.

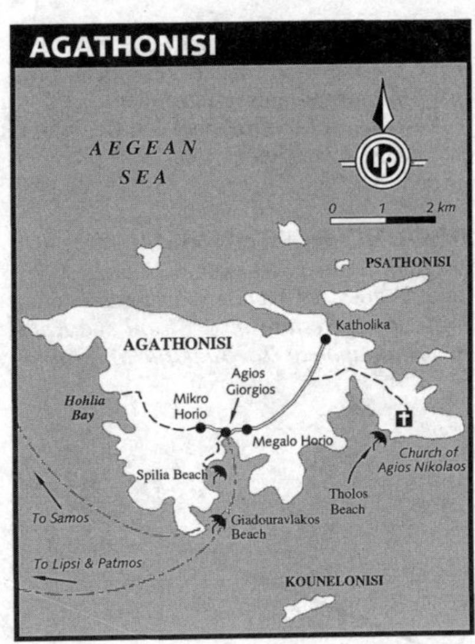

Agathonisi Αγαθονήσι

☎ 0247 • postcode 850 01 • pop 112

Agathonisi is the most northerly island of the archipelago. It's a little gem, still only visited by adventurous backpackers and yachties. There are three villages: the port of Agios Giorgios, Megalo Horio and Mikro Horio, all less than 1km apart. The island is hilly and covered with thorn bushes.

Getting There & Away

The F/B *Nissos Kalymnos* calls on Wednesday and Sunday. The twice-weekly supply boat from Samos also takes passengers, but its schedule is subject to change – check with the police officer or locals. A hydrofoil running to and from Samos, Patmos, Lipsi, Leros, Kalymnos and Kos calls in every day in summer except Sunday.

Getting Around

There is no public transport, but it takes less than 15 minutes to walk from Mikro Horio to Megalo Horio or Agios Giorgios.

AGIOS GIORGIOS Αγιος Γεώργιος

The village of Agios Giorgios is a delightful little place with just enough waterfront activity to stop you sinking into a state of inertia. It has a pebbled beach and **Spilia Beach**, also pebbled, is close by, reached along the track around the far side of the bay.

Orientation & Information

Boats dock at Agios Giorgios from where cement roads ascend right (facing inland) to Megalo Horio and left to Mikro Horio. There is no tourist information, post office, bank or OTE, but there are cardphones.

The one police officer, who is also the port police officer, has an office in the white building at the beginning of the Megalo Horio road.

Places to Stay & Eat

Agios Giorgios has three pensions: ***Pension Maria Commits*** *(☎ 29 003)*, ***Theologies Rooms*** *(☎ 29 005)* next door and ***George's Pension*** *(☎/fax 29 064)* behind them. All charge 7000 dr for doubles with bathroom.

There are three restaurants. ***George's Taverna*** is nearest the quay. George and his German wife speak English. ***Restaurant***

Seagull is farther around the bay. The owners, Ovule and Lianas, also speak English. Both restaurants are excellent.

Restaurant Lamina, between the two, is the locals' favourite, serving well prepared grilled fish.

AROUND AGATHONISI

Megalo Horio is Agathonisi's biggest village. It does not have any accommodation for tourists. ***Restaurant I Eireni*** and ***Kafeneio/Pantopoleio Ta Badelfia M Kanelli***, both on the central square, serve cheap meals.

Tholos Beach, and **Katholika**, an abandoned fishing hamlet, are reached by taking the cement road from Megalo Horio. At the T-junction turn left to reach Tholos Beach, near a fish farm. You can also visit the little **Church of Agios Nikolaos**; ask a local if it's possible to look inside.

Katholika is reached by turning left at the T-junction. There's not much to see but the walk is worth it for the views.

North-Eastern Aegean Islands
Τα Νησιά του Βορειοανατολικού Αιγαίου

The North-Eastern Aegean Islands are grouped together more for convenience than for any historical, geographical or administrative reason. Apart from Thasos and Samothraki, they are, like the Dodecanese, much closer to Turkey than to the Greek mainland, but, unlike the Dodecanese, they are not close to one another. This means island-hopping is not the easy matter it is within the Dodecanese and Cyclades, although, with the exception of Thasos and Samothraki, it is possible.

These islands are less visited than either the Dodecanese or the Cyclades. Scenically, they also differ from these groups. Mountainous, green and mantled with forests, they are ideal for hiking but most are also blessed with long stretches of delightful beaches.

Although historically diverse, a list of the islands' inhabitants from classical times reads like a who's who of the ancient world. Some of the North-Eastern Aegean Islands also boast important ancient sites. All of them became part of the Ottoman Empire and were then reunited with Greece after the Balkan Wars in 1912.

There are seven major islands in the group: Chios, Ikaria, Lesvos (Mytilini), Limnos, Samos, Samothraki and Thasos. Fourni near Ikaria, Psara and Inousses near Chios, and Agios Efstratios near Limnos are small, little-visited islands in the group.

Accommodation throughout the island chain tends to be a little more expensive than on some of the more touristed islands, but bear in mind that the high season (July to August) prices quoted in this chapter are 30 to 50% cheaper out of season.

HIGHLIGHTS

- Lush, sub-tropical Samos – a paradise for lovers of nature
- The abundant migratory bird life of Lesvos
- The mystical Sanctuary of the Great Gods on remote Samothraki
- Volcanic Limnos – offering space, solitude and sandy beaches
- Mesahti Beach near Armenistis, Ikaria, where you can believe you're in the Caribbean
- Ikaria's quirky and laid-back villages
- Medieval Mesta, the most atmospheric of Chios' mastic villages

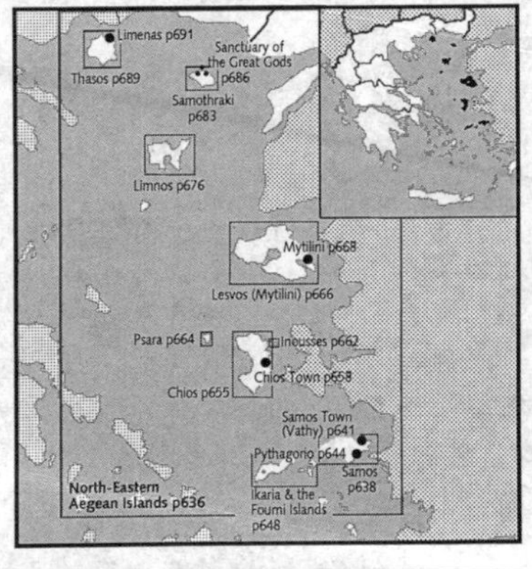

Getting There & Away

Air Samos, Chios, Lesvos, Limnos and Ikaria have air links with Athens. In addition, Samos, Chios, Lesvos and Limnos have flights to Thessaloniki.

Ferry – Domestic The following table gives an overview of scheduled domestic ferries to this island group from mainland ports during high season. Further details and inter-island links can be found under individual island entries.

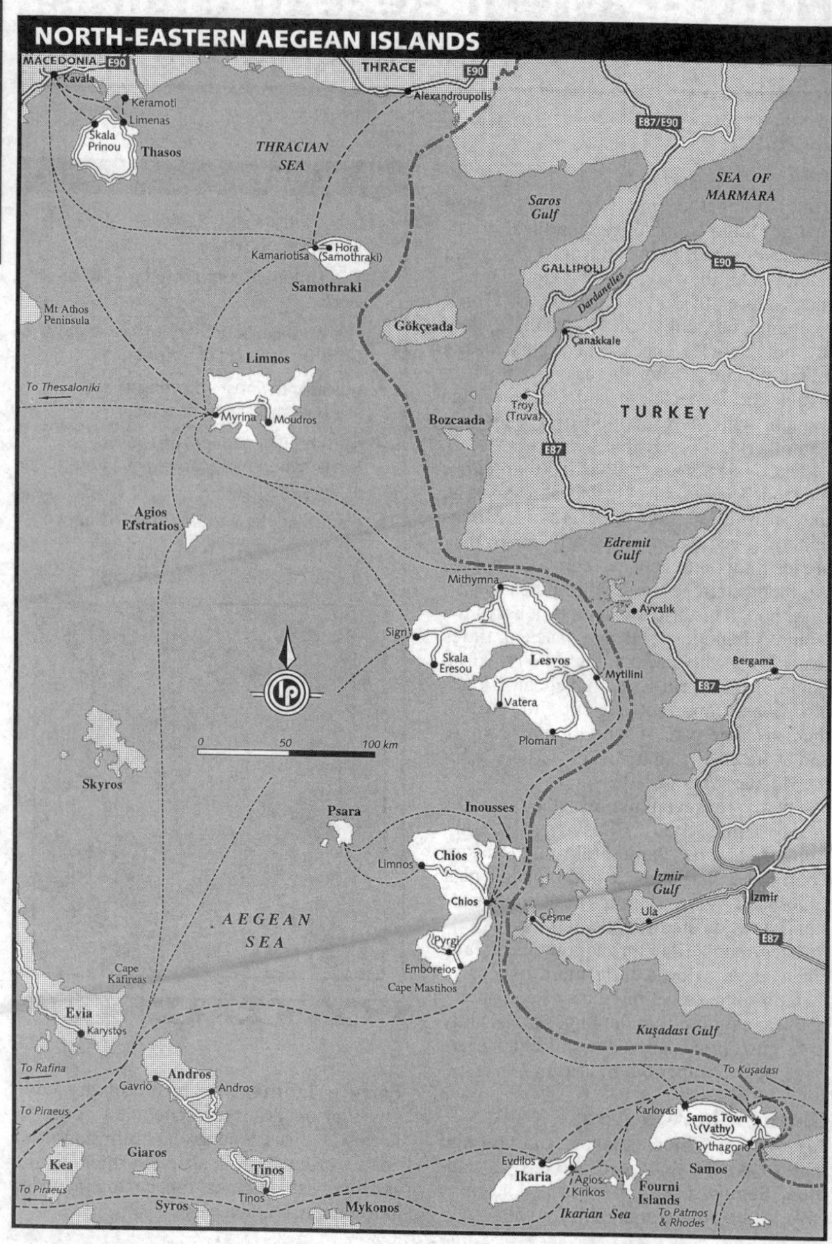
NORTH-EASTERN AEGEAN ISLANDS
MACEDONIA
E90
THRACE
Kavala
Keramoti
Limenas
Skala Prinou
Thasos
THRACIAN SEA
Alexandroupolis
E87/E90
SEA OF MARMARA
Saros Gulf
Hora (Samothraki)
Kamariotisa
Samothraki
GALLIPOLI
Dardanelles
Mt Athos Peninsula
Gökçeada
Çanakkale
Limnos
To Thessaloniki
Myrina
Moudros
Troy (Truva)
TURKEY
Bozcaada
E87
Agios Efstratios
Edremit Gulf
Mithymna
Ayvalık
Sigri
Skala Eresou
Lesvos
Mytilini
Bergama
Vatera
Plomari
0
50
100 km
Skyros
Psara
Inousses
Chios
Limnos
Chios
İzmir Gulf
İzmir
Çeşme
Ula
AEGEAN SEA
Pyrgi
Emboreios
Cape Mastihos
Cape Kafireas
Evia
Karystos
Kuşadası Gulf
To Rafina
Andros
Gavrio
Andros
To Kuşadası
To Piraeus
Karlovasi
Samos Town (Vathy)
Pythagorio
Samos
Kea
Giaros
Tinos
Evdilos
Ikaria
Agios Kirikos
Fourni Islands
To Piraeus
Tinos
Syros
Mykonos
Ikarian Sea
To Patmos & Rhodes

Ferry Connections to the North-Eastern Aegean Islands

Origin	Destination	Duration	Price	Frequency
Alexandroupolis	Agios Efstratios	7¼ hours	3790 dr	1 weekly
Alexandroupolis	Chios	16 hours	6800 dr	1 weekly
Alexandroupolis	Lesvos (Mytilini)	10 hours	5000 dr	1 weekly
Alexandroupolis	Limnos	5 hours	3300 dr	2 weekly
Alexandroupolis	Samothraki	2 hours	2300 dr	2 daily
Kavala	Agios Efstratios	6 hours	6700 dr	1 weekly
Kavala	Chios	16 hours	6800 dr	1 weekly
Kavala	Lesvos (Mytilini)	11 hours	5700 dr	3 weekly
Kavala	Limnos	5 hours	3700 dr	4 weekly
Kavala	Samothraki	4 hours	3000 dr	2 weekly
Kavala	Thasos (Skala Prinou)	1¼ hours	850 dr	hourly
Keramoti	Thasos (Limenas)	35 mins	330 dr	hourly
Piraeus	Chios	8 hours	5800 dr	1 daily
Piraeus	Ikaria	9 hours	5300 dr	1 daily
Piraeus	Lesvos (Mytilini)	12 hours	6700 dr	1 daily
Piraeus	Limnos	13 hours	7000 dr	1 weekly
Piraeus	Samos	13 hours	6700 dr	2 daily
Rafina	Agios Efstratios	8½ hours	4550 dr	1 weekly
Rafina	Lesvos (Sigri)	8½ hours	4460 dr	1 weekly
Rafina	Limnos	10 hours	5500 dr	4 weekly
Thessaloniki	Chios	18 hours	8400 dr	1 weekly
Thessaloniki	Lesvos	13 hours	8300 dr	2 weekly
Thessaloniki	Limnos	7 hours	3300 dr	2 weekly

Ferry – International In summer there are daily ferries from Samos to Kuşadası (for Ephesus) and from Chios to Çeşme. Ferries from Lesvos to Ayvalık run five times weekly.

Hydrofoil In summer there are regular hydrofoil links between Kavala and Thasos and some hydrofoils between Alexandroupolis, Samothraki and Limnos. Hydrofoils also operate out of Samos west towards Ikaria and south towards the Dodecanese.

Getting Around

Air Lesvos is connected to both Limnos and Chios by local flights. Samos is connected to Mykonos and Santorini by local flights.

Ferry There are ferries daily between Ikaria and Samos, Chios and Lesvos; three times weekly between Lesvos and Limnos; and twice weekly between Chios and Samos. See also the entries at the beginning of sections on individual islands.

Samos Σάμος

☎ 0273 • pop 32,000

Samos, the most southerly island of the group, is the closest of all the Greek islands to Turkey, from which it is separated by the 3km-wide Mykale Straits. The island is the most visited of the North-Eastern Aegean group. Charter flights of tourists descend on the island from many northern European countries. Samos is a popular transit point for travellers heading from the Cyclades to Turkey or vice versa. Most barely pause in Samos, which is a pity because the island has a lot to offer.

Despite the package tourists, Samos is still worth a visit. Forays into its hinterland are rewarded with unspoilt villages and mountain vistas. In summer the humid air is permeated with heavy floral scents, especially jasmine. This, and the prolific greenery of the landscape, lends Samos an exotic and tropical air. Orchids are grown here for export and an excellent table wine is made from the local muscat grapes.

Samos has three ports: Samos Town (Vathy) and Karlovasi on the north coast, and Pythagorio on the south coast.

History

The first inhabitants of Samos, the Pelasgian tribes, worshipped Hera, whose birthplace was Samos. Pythagoras was born on Samos in the 6th century BC. Unfortunately, his life coincided with that of the tyrant Polycrates, who in 550 BC deposed the Samian oligarchy. As the two did not see eye to eye, Pythagoras spent much of his time in exile in Italy. Despite this, Samos became a mighty naval power under Polycrates, and the arts and sciences also flourished. 'Big is beautiful' seems to have been Polycrates' maxim – almost every construction and artwork he commissioned appears to have been ancient Greece's biggest. The historian Herodotus wrote glowingly of the tyrant's achievements, stating that the Samians had accomplished the three greatest projects in Greece at that time: the Sanctuary of Hera (one of the Seven Wonders of the Ancient World), the Evpalinos Tunnel and a huge jetty.

After the decisive Battle of Plataea (479 BC), in which Athens had been aided by the Samians, Samos allied itself to Athens and returned to democracy. In the Battle of Mykale, which took place on the same day as the Battle of Plataea, the Greek navy (with many Samian sailors) defeated the Persian fleet. However, during the Peloponnesian Wars, Samos was taken by Sparta.

Under Roman rule Samos enjoyed many privileges, but after successive occupations by the Venetians and Genoese it was conquered by the Turks in 1453. Samos played a major role in the uprising against the Turks in the early 19th century, much to the

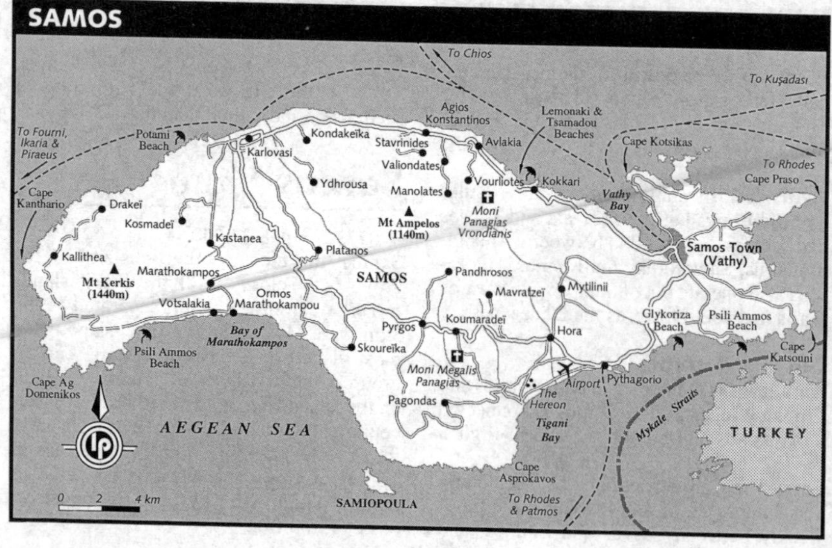

detriment of its neighbour, Chios (see the Chios section later in this chapter).

Trekking

Samos is a popular place for rambling, or more demanding mountain treks. Its natural fecundity and appealing combination of mountains and sea make it a popular destination for walkers from all over Europe. Should you be planning a hike on Samos, Brian and Eileen Anderson's *Landscapes of Samos*, a pocket guide to walks on the island, contains descriptions of over 20 walks. The book is available in most decent bookshops and can also be found in Samos.

Getting There & Away

Air There are at least four flights daily from Samos to Athens (17,400 dr) and two flights weekly to Thessaloniki (25,400 dr). The Olympic Airways office (☎ 27 237) is on the corner of Kanari and Smyrnis in Samos Town. There is also an Olympic Airways office (☎ 61 213) on Lykourgou Logotheti in Pythagorio.

Air Manos flies daily to Athens (12,000 dr) and twice weekly to Thessaloniki (18,400 dr), Mykonos (14,300 dr) and Santorini (16,400 dr). The airport is 4km west of Pythagorio.

Ferry – Domestic Samos is the transport hub of the North-Eastern Aegean, with ferries to the Dodecanese and Cyclades as well as to the other North-Eastern Aegean Islands. Schedules are subject to seasonal changes, so consult any of the ticket offices for the latest versions. ITSA Travel (☎ 23 605, fax 27 955, email itsa@gemini.diavlos.gr) is the closest agency to the ferry terminal in Samos Town and covers most destinations. Your luggage can also be stored for free whether you buy a ticket or not. Ask for Dimitris Sarlas. The following summary will give you some idea of the ferry options from Samos during summer.

Services to other North-Eastern Aegean Islands include two to three ferries daily to Ikaria (2½ hours, 2200 dr) and one to Fourni (two hours, 1800 dr); three weekly to Chios (four hours, 2690 dr); and one weekly to Lesvos (seven hours, 4000 dr), Limnos (11 hours, 6500 dr), Alexandroupolis (20 hours, 8300 dr) and Kavala (20 hours, 8400 dr).

To Piraeus there are one to two ferries daily (13 hours, 6700 dr) which usually call in at Ikaria and sometimes Fourni.

Cyclades services include daily ferries to Naxos and/or Paros (6½ hours, 4900 dr) with connections to Mykonos, Ios, Santorini (Thira) and Syros.

Dodecanese connections include about five ferries per week to Patmos (2½ hours, 2200 dr) and one per week to Leros (3½ hours, 2400 dr), Kalymnos (four hours, 3400 dr), Kos (5½ hours, 3800 dr) and Rhodes (nine hours, 6000 dr).

Ferry – International In summer two ferries go daily from Samos Town to Kuşadası (for Ephesus) in Turkey. From November to March there are one to two ferries weekly. Tickets cost around 8000/11,000 dr one way/return (plus 3000 dr Greek port tax and US$10 Turkish port tax, payable upon arrival). Daily excursions are also available from 1 April to 31 October and for an additional 6500 dr you can visit Ephesus. Tickets are available from many outlets but the main agent is ITSA Travel.

Bear in mind that the ticket office will require your passport in advance for port formalities. Turkish visas, where required, are issued upon arrival in Turkey for US$45. Check with the Turkish diplomatic mission in your home country for your own particular requirements since these change frequently.

Hydrofoil In summer hydrofoils link Pythagorio twice daily with Patmos (one hour, 5500 dr), Leros (two hours, 6600 dr) and Kos (3½ hours, 7800 dr). There are also two services weekly from Samos Town to Fourni (1¾ hours, 3450 dr) and Ikaria (2¼ hours, 4180 dr). Schedules are subject to frequent changes, so contact the tourist office in Pythagorio or the port police (☎ 61 225) for up-to-date information. Tickets are available from By Ship Travel (☎/fax 61 914) in Pythagorio or ITSA Travel in Samos Town.

Excursion Boat In summer there are excursion boats once weekly on Thursday between Pythagorio and Patmos (8000/11,000 dr one way/return) leaving at 8.30 am. Daily excursion boats also go to the little island of Samiopoula for 8000 dr, including lunch.

Getting Around

To/From the Airport There are no Olympic Airways buses to the airport. A taxi from Samos Town should cost about 2600 dr. Alternatively, you can take a local bus to Pythagorio and a taxi to the airport from there for about 1100 dr.

Bus Samos has an adequate bus service which continues till about 8 pm in summer. There are 13 buses daily from Samos Town bus station (☎ 27 262) to both Kokkari (20 minutes, 270 dr) and Pythagorio (25 minutes, 320 dr), eight to Agios Konstantinos (40 minutes, 450 dr), seven to Karlovasi (via the north coast, one hour, 750 dr), six to the Hereon (25 minutes, 450 dr), five to Mytilinii (20 minutes, 280 dr), three to Psili Ammos Beach on the east coast (20 minutes, 280 dr), and two to Ormos Marathokampou and Votsalakia (two hours, 1070 dr).

In addition to frequent buses to Samos Town there are six buses from Pythagorio to the Hereon and two to both Mytilinii and Karlovasi. Pay for your tickets on the bus.

Car & Motorcycle Samos has many car rental outlets, including Hertz (☎ 61 730), Lykourgou Logotheti 77, and Europcar (☎ 61 522), Lykourgou Logotheti 65, both in Pythagorio.

There are also many motorcycle rental outlets on Lykourgou Logotheti. Many of the larger hotels can arrange motorcycle or car rental for you.

Taxi From the taxi rank (☎ 28 404) on Plateia Pythagora in Samos Town, tariffs are: Kokkari 200 dr, Pythagorio 2200 dr, Psili Ammos 1900 dr, Avlakia 2300 dr, the airport 2600 dr, and the Hereon 2900 dr.

SAMOS TOWN (VATHY) Βαθύ

• postcode 831 00 • pop 5790

The island's capital is the large and bustling Samos Town, also called Vathy, on the north-east coast. The waterfront is crowded with tourists who rarely venture to the older and extremely attractive upper town of Ano Vathy where 19th century red-tiled houses perch on a hillside. The lower and newer town is strung out along Vathy Bay and it is quite a walk from one end to the other.

Orientation

From the ferry terminal (facing inland) turn right to reach the central square of Plateia Pythagora on the waterfront. It's recognisable by its four palm trees and statue of a lion. A little farther along and one block inland are the shady municipal gardens with a pleasant outdoor cafe. The waterfront road is called Themistokleous Sofouli.

Information

The municipal tourist office (☎ 28 530) is just north of Plateia Pythagora in a little side street, but it only operates during the summer season. The staff will assist in finding accommodation.

The tourist police (☎ 27 980) and the regular police are at Themistokleous Sofouli 129 on the south side of the waterfront.

The National Bank of Greece is on the waterfront just south of Plateia Pythagora and the Commercial Bank is on the east side of the square. Both sport ATMs.

The post office is on Smyrnis, four blocks from the waterfront. The OTE is on Plateia Iroön, behind the municipal gardens.

There is an Internet Cafe (☎ 28 521) at Emmanouil Sofouli 15, one block south-west of the museum. Access is fast and costs 1000 dr per hour.

The island's bus station (KTEL) is just back from the waterfront on Ioannou Lekati. The taxi rank (☎ 28 404) is on Plateia Pythagora. Samos' general hospital (☎ 27 407) is on the waterfront, north of the ferry quay.

The port police (☎ 27 318) are just north of the quay, one block back from the waterfront.

DIANA MAYFIELD

Church in Oia, Santorini, sited spectacularly on the caldera's precipitous sides (Cyclades)

STELLA HELLANDER

Rugged cliffs of west coast Kefallonia

LEANNE LOGAN

Cleaning octopus on the dock

JON DAVISON

Fishing net, Sitia, Crete

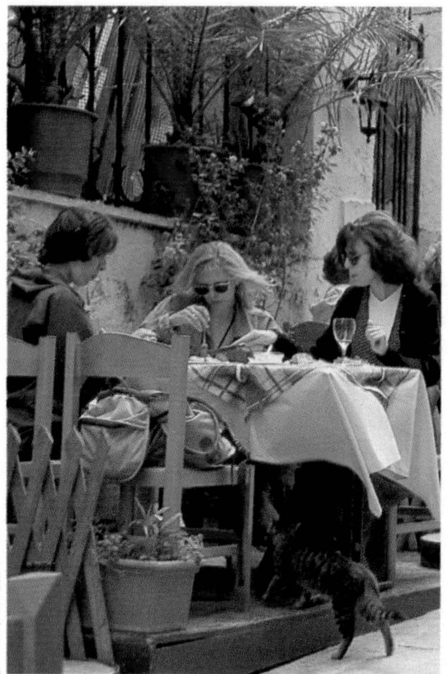
DIANA MAYFIELD

Atmospheric outdoor dining, Plaka, Athens

TONY FANKHAUSER

Lycian tomb, Kastellorizo (Dodecanese)

JULIET COOMBE

Living cheek by jowl with history: Athens sprawls out behind the Parthenon.

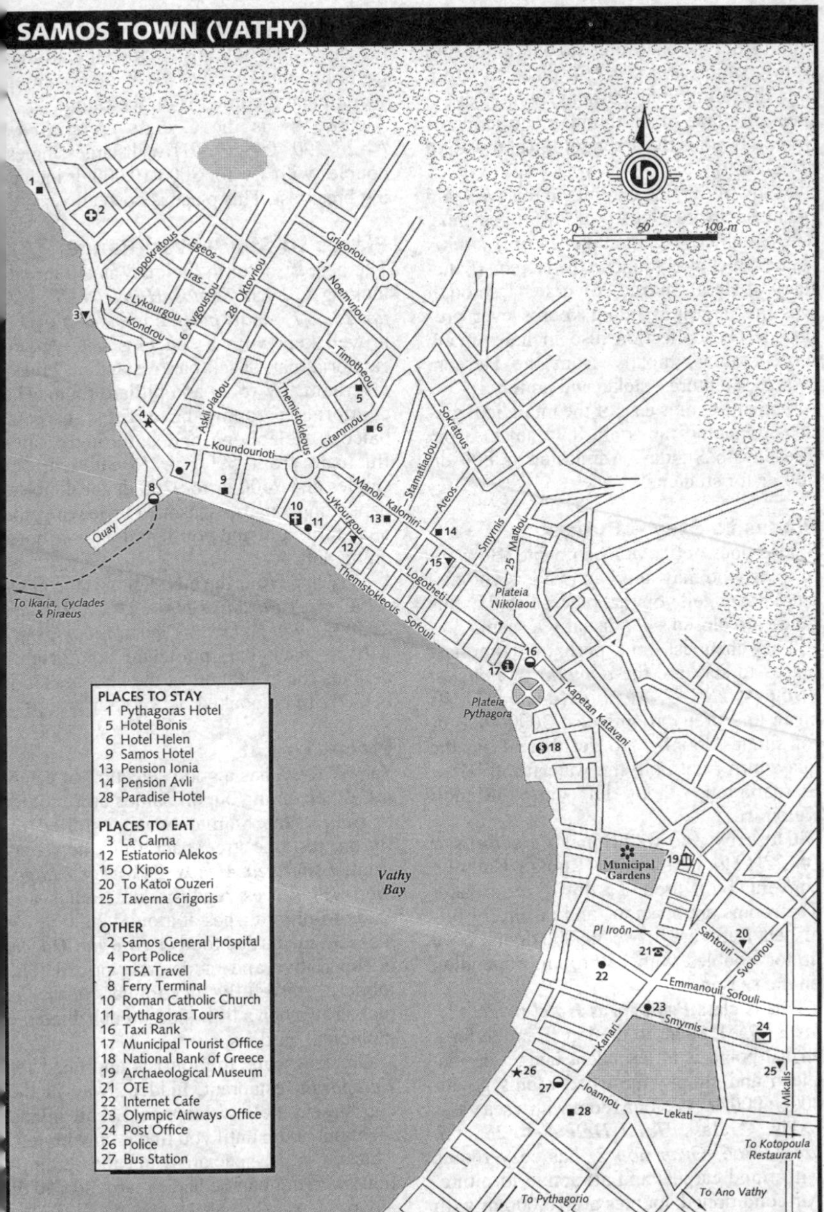
SAMOS TOWN (VATHY)
0
50
100 m
Ippokratous
Egeos
Iras
Lykourgou
Kondrou
6 Avgoustou
28 Oktovriou
Grigoriou
11 Noemvriou
Timotheou
Asklipiadou
Themistokleous
Grammou
Koundourioti
Manoli Kalomiri
Lykourgou
Stamatiadou
Sokratous
Areos
Smyrnis
25 Martiou
Logotheti
Themistokleous Sofouli
Plateia Nikolaou
Plateia Pythagora
Kapetan Katavani
Quay
To Ikaria, Cyclades & Piraeus
Vathy Bay
Municipal Gardens
Pl Iroön
Sahtouri
Svoronou
Emmanouil Sofouli
Smyrnis
Kanari
Ioannou
Lekati
Mikalis
To Kotopoula Restaurant
To Pythagorio
To Ano Vathy
PLACES TO STAY
1 Pythagoras Hotel
5 Hotel Bonis
6 Hotel Helen
9 Samos Hotel
13 Pension Ionia
14 Pension Avli
28 Paradise Hotel
PLACES TO EAT
3 La Calma
12 Estiatorio Alekos
15 O Kipos
20 To Katoï Ouzeri
25 Taverna Grigoris
OTHER
2 Samos General Hospital
4 Port Police
7 ITSA Travel
8 Ferry Terminal
10 Roman Catholic Church
11 Pythagoras Tours
16 Taxi Rank
17 Municipal Tourist Office
18 National Bank of Greece
19 Archaeological Museum
21 OTE
22 Internet Cafe
23 Olympic Airways Office
24 Post Office
26 Police
27 Bus Station

Things to See

Apart from the charming old quarter of Ano Vathy, which is a peaceful place to stroll, and the municipal gardens, which are a pleasant place to sit, the main attraction of Samos Town is the **archaeological museum** (☎ 27 469).

Many of the fine exhibits in this well laid out museum are a legacy of Polycrates' time. They include a gargantuan (4.5m) *kouros* statue which was found in the Hereon (Sanctuary of Hera). In true Polycrates fashion, it was the largest standing kouros ever produced. The collection also includes many more statues, mostly from the Hereon, bronze sculptures, stelae and pottery.

The museum is east of the municipal gardens. Opening times are 8.30 am to 3 pm Tuesday to Sunday. Admission is 800 dr, 400 dr for students.

Places to Stay – Budget

Samos does not have a camp site. Be wary of touts who may approach you as you disembark and tell you that places listed in this guide are closed – it's usually a scam.

The cheapest and perhaps homeliest places to stay are the *domatia* of ***Pension Ionia*** *(☎ 28 782, Manoli Kalomiri 5)*. Its clean and pretty rooms cost 3000/4000 dr for singles/doubles. To get there from the quay, turn right onto the waterfront, left at Stamatiadou, then left into Manoli Kalomiri.

Close by, the traditional ***Pension Avli*** *(☎ 22 939)* is a former Roman Catholic convent, built around a lovely courtyard. The rooms are spacious and tastefully furnished. Rates are between 5000 dr and 7000 dr for doubles with bathroom, depending on the season.

The C class ***Pythagoras Hotel*** *(☎ 28 422, fax 27 955)*, 800m to the left from the ferry arrival point, is an excellent budget option. Clean and simply furnished rooms go for 4000/6000 dr. Ask for a room with a sea view.

The C class ***Hotel Helen*** *(☎ 28 215, fax 22 866, Grammou 2)* has cosy rooms with fitted carpets and attractive furniture. Air-conditioned doubles are 10,000 dr with bathroom, fridge and TV. Turn right from the quay, and left just before the Roman Catholic church, veer right at the intersection and the hotel is on the right.

Close by is the C class ***Hotel Bonis*** *(☎ 28 790, fax 22 501)* with large singles/doubles with TV for 8000/10,000 dr including breakfast. This place is open all year.

Places to Stay – Mid-Range

The nearest hotel to the quay is the grand-looking C class ***Samos Hotel*** *(☎ 28 377, fax 23 771, email hotsamos@otenet.gr)*. It is well kept with a spacious and elegant cafeteria, bar, snack bar, restaurant, breakfast room, TV room and billiard room. The comfortable rooms have fitted carpets, balcony, telephone and bathroom. Rates fluctuate from 5900 dr to 8000 dr for singles and 7400 dr to 9200 dr for doubles, depending on the season. On leaving the quay turn right and you'll come to the hotel on the left.

Very handy for the bus station is the modern C class ***Paradise Hotel*** *(☎ 23 911, fax 28 754, email paradise@gemini.diavlos.gr)* with a snack bar, pool and comfortable doubles for 15,000 dr. In the high season it is likely to be booked out by tour groups.

Places to Eat

Samos Town has a good selection of eateries. When dining out on Samos don't forget to sample the Samian wine, extolled by Byron. Just one street back from the waterfront, ***Estiatorio Alekos*** *(Lykourgou Logotheti 49)* serves ready-made staples and made-to-order dishes at around 2000 dr for a decent meal. The food at ***To Katoï Ouzeri*** is superlative and moderately priced. The modern, tastefully decorated *ouzeri* is tucked away on a little side street behind the municipal gardens.

Greeks escape the tourists and head for ***Kotopoula*** restaurant, hidden away in the backstreets. Follow Ioannou Lekati inland for about 800m until you find it on your left. Chicken is the speciality, but the scrumptious *mezedes* can be had for around 750 dr a pop.

Another commendable place is ***Taverna Grigoris*** on Smyrnis, near the post office. If you are here between 8.30 and 9.30 pm your table number may be drawn out of a hat, in which case you'll eat free. This is a reasonably priced restaurant and is open all day.

For live *neo kyma* (1960s new wave) music and maybe some dancing, seek out ***O Kipos***, just off Lykourgou Logotheti (entry is from the next street up to the north) in a garden setting. The food is commendable; try a splendid Samena Golden white wine with it. For a romantic evening ambience, try ***La Calma*** which overlooks the sea. The seductive views and tasty food complement each other perfectly. Prices at these last two places are somewhat more upmarket.

PYTHAGORIO Πυθαγόρειο

• postcode 831 03 • pop 1400

Pythagorio, on the south east coast of the island, is 14km from Samos Town. Today, it's a crowded and rather twee tourist resort, but it's a convenient base from which to visit the ancient sites of Samos.

Pythagorio stands on the site of the ancient city of Samos. Although the settlement dates from the Neolithic era, most of the remains are from Polycrates' time (around 550 BC). The mighty jetty of Samos projected almost 450m into the sea, protecting the city and its powerful fleet from the vagaries of the Aegean. Remains of this jetty lie below and beyond the smaller modern jetty, which is on the opposite side of the harbour to the quay. The town beach begins just beyond the jetty. All boats coming from Patmos, and other points south of Samos, dock at Pythagorio.

Orientation

From the ferry quay, turn right and follow the waterfront to the main thoroughfare of Lykourgou Logotheti, a turn-off to the left. Here there are supermarkets, greengrocers, bakers, travel agents and numerous car, motorcycle and bicycle rental outlets. The central square of Plateia Irinis is farther along the waterfront.

Information

The tourist office (☎ 62 274, fax 61 022) is on the south side of Lykourgou Logetheti. The English-speaking staff are particularly friendly and helpful and give out a town map, bus timetable and information about ferry schedules. They also exchange currency, and are open 8 am to 10 pm daily.

The tourist police (☎ 61 100) are also on Lykourgou Logetheti, to the left of the tourist office.

The post office and the National Bank of Greece are both on Lykourgou Logotheti. The OTE is on the waterfront near the quay.

The bus station (actually a bus stop) is on the south side of Lykourgou Logotheti. There is a taxi rank (☎ 61 450) on the corner of the waterfront and Lykourgou Logotheti.

Things to See

Walking north-east on Polykratous from the town centre, a path off to the left passes traces of an ancient theatre. The **Evpalinos Tunnel** can also be reached along this path: take the left fork after the theatre. The right fork leads up to **Moni Panagias Spilianis** (Monastery of the Virgin of the Grotto). The ancient city walls extend from here to the Evpalinos Tunnel.

Back in town, the remains of the **Castle of Lykourgos Logothetis** are at the southern end of Metamorfosis. The castle was built in 1824 and became a stronghold of Greek resistance during the War of Independence.

The **Pythagorio Museum** (☎ 61 400) in the town hall at the back of Plateia Irinis has some finds from the Hereon. It is open 9 am to 2 pm Sunday, Tuesday, Wednesday and Thursday, and noon to 2 pm on Friday and Saturday. Admission is free.

Evpalinos Tunnel The 1034m-long Evpalinos Tunnel (Ευπαλίνειο Ορυγμα), completed in 524 BC, is named after its architect. It penetrated through a mountainside to channel gushing mountain water to the city. The tunnel is, in effect, two tunnels: a service tunnel and a lower water tunnel which you can see at various points along the narrow walkway. The diggers began at

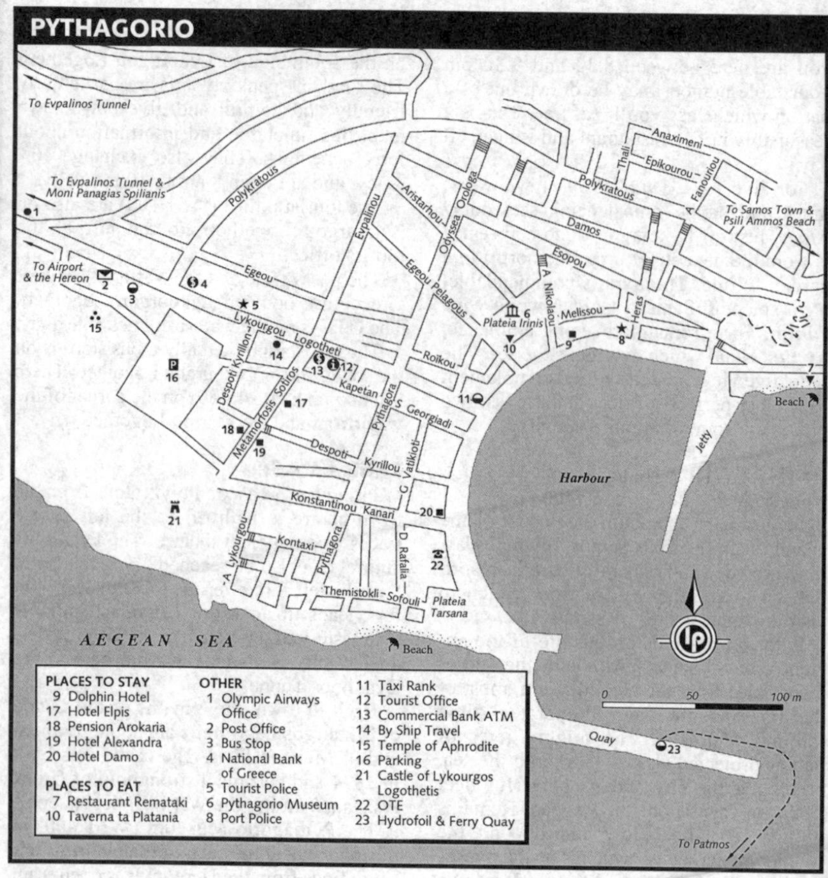

each end and managed to meet in the middle, an achievement of precision engineering that is still considered remarkable.

In the Middle Ages the inhabitants of Pythagorio used the tunnel as a hide-out during pirate raids. The tunnel is fun to explore, though access to it is via a very constricted stairway. If you are tall, portly, or suffer from claustrophobia, give it a miss!

The tunnel is most easily reached from the western end of Lykourgou Logotheti, from where it is signposted. If you arrive by road, a sign points you to the tunnel's southern mouth as you enter Pythagorio from Samos. Opening times are 8.15 am to 2 pm daily except Monday. Admission is 500 dr; 300 dr for students.

Places to Stay

Many of Pythagorio's places to stay are block-booked by tour companies. Two pleasant and quiet places for independent travellers are opposite one another on Metamorfosis. ***Pension Arokaria*** (☎ *61 287)* has a cool and leafy garden. The lovely owner charges 8000/10,500 dr for doubles/triples. The D class ***Hotel Alexandra*** *(☎ 61 429)*, just opposite, charges 8000 dr for a double with bathroom. In the same street is the neat and clean D class ***Hotel Elpis*** *(☎/fax 61 144)* with singles/doubles with a fridge for 7000/8000 dr.

At the northern end of the waterfront, beyond the main intersection, is the C class ***Dolphin Hotel*** *(☎ 61 205, fax 61 842)* with spotless and cosy wood-panelled rooms for 8650/11,350 dr with bathroom, fridge, TV, room safe and air-conditioning. At the other end of the waterfront is the C class ***Hotel Damo*** *(☎ 61 303, fax 61 745)*, which is near the OTE. The agreeable self-contained studios here are 16,000 dr for two or three people.

Places to Eat

The waterfront is packed with restaurants all offering much the same fare. Walk 100m east of Dolphin Hotel to find ***Restaurant Remataki*** at the beginning of the town beach. This place has an imaginative menu of carefully prepared, delicious food. Try a meal of various mezedes for a change: *revithokeftedes* (chickpea patties), *piperies Florinis* (Florina peppers) and *gigantes* (lima beans) make a good combination. Main courses start from around 1000 dr. A block inland is ***Taverna ta Platania*** on Plateia Irinis opposite the museum, and away from the more expensive waterfront eateries.

AROUND PYTHAGORIO

Hereon Ηραίον

The Sacred Way, once flanked by thousands of statues, led from the city to the Hereon. The Hereon was a sanctuary to Hera, built at the legendary place of her birth, on swampy land where the River Imbrasos enters the sea.

There had been a temple on the site since Mycenaean times, but the one built in the time of Polycrates was the most extraordinary: it was four times the size of the Parthenon. As a result of plunderings and earthquakes only one column remains standing, although the extent of the temple can be gleaned from the foundations. Other remains on the site include a *stoa*, more temples and a 5th century basilica.

The Hereon is now listed as a World Heritage Site. It is on the coast 8km west of Pythagorio. The site (☎ 95 277) is open 8.30 am to 2.30 pm Tuesday to Sunday. Admission is 800 dr; 400 dr for students. It's free on Sunday.

Mytilinii Μυτιληνιοί

The fascinating **paleontology museum** (☎ 52 055), on the main thoroughfare of the inland village of Mytilinii, between Pythagorio and Samos Town, houses bones and skeletons of prehistoric animals. Included in the collection are remains of animals that were the antecedents of the giraffe and elephant. The museum is open 9 am to 2 pm and 5 to 7 pm Monday to Saturday, and 10.30 am to 2.30 pm Sunday. Admission is 500 dr; free on Sunday.

Beaches

Back on the coast, sandy **Psili Ammos** (not to be confused with a beach of the same name near Votsalakia) is the finest beach near Pythagorio. This gently sloping beach is ideal for families and is popular, so be there early to grab your spot. The beach can be reached by car or scooter from the Vathy-Pythagorio road (signposted), or by excursion boat (3000 dr) from Pythagorio, leaving each morning at 9 am and returning at 4 pm. There are also buses from Samos Town. **Glykoriza Beach** nearer Pythagorio (also signposted) is dominated by a few hotels nearby, but is a clean, public beach of pebbles and sand and is a good alternative to the sometimes very busy Psili Ammos Beach. It's easily reached by scooter or car.

There are a couple of places to stay at Psili Ammos. ***Elena Apartments*** *(☎ 23 645, fax 28 959)*, right on the beach, has rather cramped self-contained double apartments for 10,000 dr for bookings of at least a few days. Nearby, ***Apartments Psili Ammos*** *(☎ 25 140)* has self-contained rooms for two to three people for between 9000 dr and 11,000 dr. There are four eating places, of which ***Restaurant Psili Ammos*** and the more intimate ***Sunrise*** – commendable for its classy choice of ambient music – are both favourably located overlooking the beach.

SOUTH-WEST SAMOS

The south west coast of Samos remained unspoilt for longer than the north coast, but in recent years a series of resorts have sprung up alongside the best beaches. **Ormos Marathokampou**, 50km from Samos Town, has a pebble beach. From here a road leads 6km to the inland village of **Marathokampos**, which is worth a visit for the stunning view down to the immense Bay of Marathokampos. **Votsalakia**, 4km west of Ormos Marathokampou and known officially as Kampos, and **Psili Ammos** (not to be confused with the Psili Ammos Beach near Pythagorio), 2km beyond, have long, sandy beaches. There are many domatia and tavernas on this stretch of coast though this stretch has a rather scrappy feel to it and lacks the intimacy of smaller coastal resorts. The best taverna of an otherwise uninspiring bunch is ***Ta Votsalakia***, with tables overlooking the beach.

With your own transport you may like to continue on the dirt road from Psili Ammos which skirts Mt Kerkis, above the totally undeveloped and isolated west coast. The road passes through the village of **Kallithea**, and continues to **Drakeï** where it terminates.

WEST OF SAMOS TOWN

The road which skirts the north coast passes many beaches and resorts. The fishing village of **Kokkari**, 10km from Samos Town, is also a holiday resort with a pebble beach. The place is fairly popular with tourists, but it is exposed to the frequent summer winds and for that reason is popular with windsurfers. Rooms, studios and tavernas abound, all offering much the same quality.

Beaches extend from here to **Avlakia**, with **Lemonaki** and **Tsamadou** beaches being the most accessible for walkers staying in Kokkari. Clothing is optional at these two pebbly, secluded beaches. Continuing west, beyond Avlakia, the road is flanked by trees, a foretaste of the alluring scenery encountered on the roads leading inland from the coast. A turn-off south along this stretch leads to the delightful mountain village of **Vourliotes**, from where you can walk another 3km to **Moni Panagias Vrondianis**. Built in the 1550s, it is the island's oldest extant monastery; a sign in the village points the way.

Continuing along the coast, a 5km road winds its way up the lower slopes of Mt Ampelos through thick, well watered woodlands of pine and deciduous trees, to the gorgeous village of **Manolates**. The area is rich in bird life, with a proliferation of nightingales, warblers and thrushes. There are no buses to Manolates so you'll have to find your own way (Agios Konstantinos is the nearest bus stop). In the village there are many old houses built of stone with projecting balconies. The surfaces of the narrow streets and idyllic little squares are decorated with whitewashed floral designs. There is also a sizable community of well fed and slightly aristocratic cats. The Samians say that if you have not visited either Vourliotes or Manolates, then you have not seen Samos.

Back on the coast, the road continues to the quiet resort of **Agios Konstantinos**. Beyond here it winds through rugged coastal and mountain scenery to the town of **Karlovasi**, Samos' second port. The town consists of three contiguous settlements: Paleo (old), Meson (middle) and Neo (new). It once boasted a thriving tanning industry, but now it's a lacklustre town with little of interest for visitors. The nearest beach is the sand and pebble **Potami**, 2km west of town.

Places to Stay

Despite the onset of package tourism, Kokkari still has many accommodation options for independent travellers. In the high season an EOT (☎ 92 217) operates in the village and will assist in finding accommodation. The bus stops on the main road at a large stone church, and the EOT is a little way down the street opposite the church.

Pension Eleni *(☎ 92 317, fax 92 620)* has immaculate, tastefully furnished rooms for 8000 dr a double with bathroom. From the large stone church in Kokkari, continue along the main road; at the T-junction veer left and, 50m along on the left, next to the Dionyssos Garden restaurant, you will see a sign pointing to the pension. There are many more domatia, apartments and small hotels along this stretch of road, which is just one block back from the waterfront.

Farther west along the coast road, close to a beach, are ***Calypso Rooms to Rent*** *(☎ 94 124)*, named after their friendly and kind owner. The rooms are well kept and surrounded by a gorgeous garden. Doubles are 7000 dr with bathroom and use of a communal kitchen. Coming from Kokkari, turn right opposite the turn-off for Manolates (signposted) and after 50m you will come to a sign pointing right to the rooms. There are quite a few more domatia in this area. The bus stop is just before the Manolates turn-off. In Manolates itself try ***Studio Angella*** *(☎ 94 478)* or call ☎ *94 331* for a little unnamed house to rent in the village.

If you get stuck in Karlovasi there are several budget hotels and ***domatia*** *(☎ 32 133)* with doubles for 7500 dr. This accommodation is signposted from the central square where the bus terminates.

Places to Eat

There are many reasonably priced restaurants in Kokkari all offering 'English menus' and the usual range of bland tourist fare. One reader recommends ***Brothers Restaurant***, the last restaurant at the eastern end of Kokkari, past the headland and the little harbour.

Paradisos Restaurant, at the turn-off to Manolates, serves delectable dishes; a full meal with wine or beer will cost around 2500 dr. In Manolates, head for ***Loukas Taverna*** for the best and cheapest food around and great views. Try the stuffed courgette flowers, or *bekri mezes* (tasty oven-cooked pork in sauce) and the special home-made *moschato* wines. Follow the prominent signs to the back end of the village to find this place.

Ikaria & the Fourni Islands

☎ 0275 • pop 9000

Ikaria (Ικαρία; ih-kah-**ree**-ah) is a rocky and mountainous island west of Samos. Like Samos it is also fertile, with an abundance of cypress trees, pine forests, olive and fruit trees – Ikarian apricots are especially luscious. At present the island's tourism is low-key, but Ikaria is slowly being 'discovered' by Germans and Austrians seeking a quiet alternative. Ikaria's beaches at Livadia and Mesahti, near Armenistis on the north coast, have to be rated as among the best in Greece.

Ailing Greeks have visited Ikaria since ancient times because of its therapeutic radioactive springs which they believe to be the most efficacious in Europe. One spring is so highly radioactive that it was deemed unsafe and forced to close.

The name Ikaria originates from the mythical Icarus (see 'The Myth of the Minotaur' boxed text in the Crete chapter). Another myth ascribes the island as the birthplace of Dionysos.

Ikaria has two ports, Agios Kirykos on the south coast, and Evdilos on the north coast. The island's best beaches are on the north coast, west of Evdilos.

Ikaria is a bit of an oddity as a tourist destination. Long neglected by mainland Greece and used as a dumping ground for left-wing political dissidents by various right-wing governments, Ikaria and Ikarians have a rather devil-may-care approach to things, including tourism. The islanders, while welcoming tourists, are taking a slow approach to cultivating the tourist dollar. The result is that Ikaria is an island that may take a bit of getting used to at first, but will surely remain long in your memory.

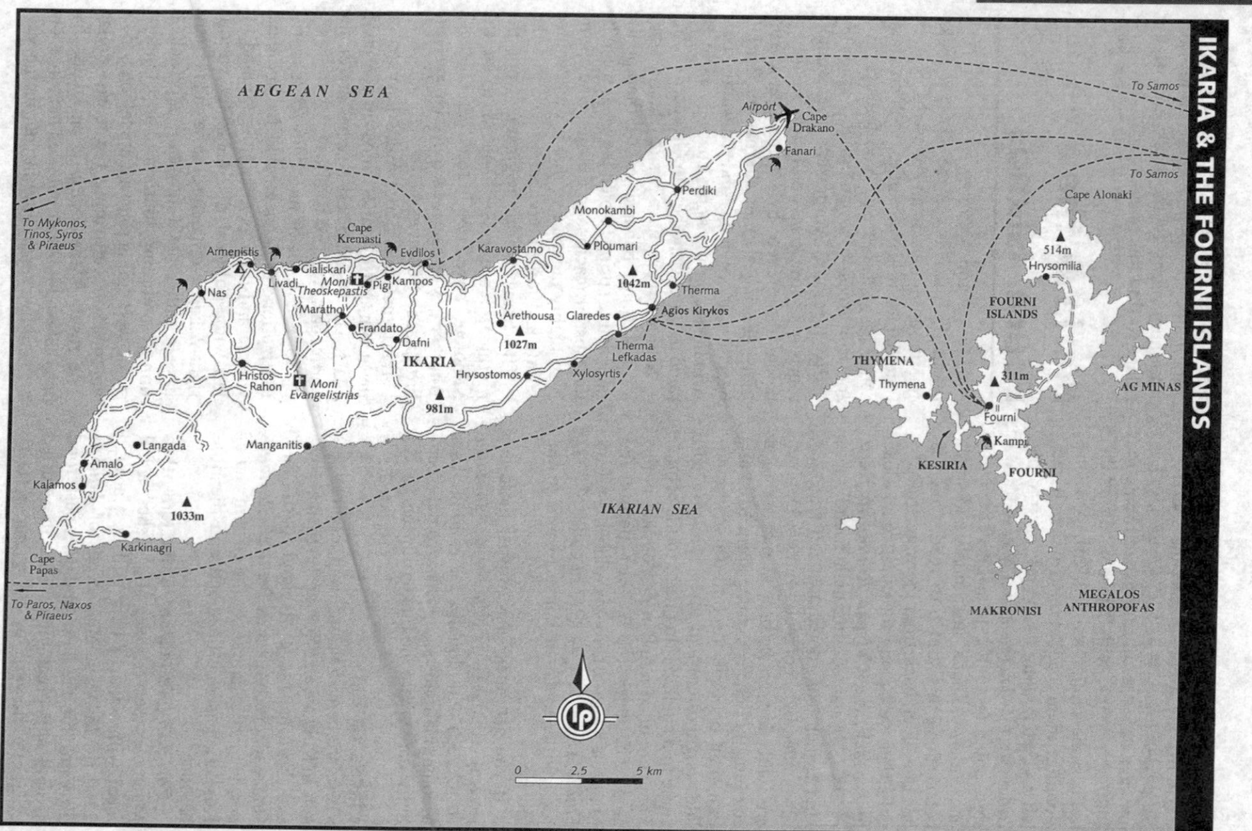
IKARIA & THE FOURNI ISLANDS
To Samos
To Samos
Cape Alonaki
AG MINAS
514m
Hrysomilia
FOURNI ISLANDS
311m
Fourni
Kampi
FOURNI
MEGALOS ANTHROPOFAS
MAKRONISI
KESIRIA
Thymena
THYMENA
Cape Drakano
Fanari
Airport
Perdiki
Therma
Agios Kirykos
1042m
Monokambi
Ploumari
Glaredes
Therma Lefkadas
Xylosyrtis
Karavostamo
Arethousa
1027m
Hrysostomos
IKARIAN SEA
981m
Evdilos
Kampos
Dafni
IKARIA
Cape Kremasti
Pigi
Moni Theoskepastis
Frandato
Maratho
Gialiskari
Livadi
Moni Evangelistrias
Armenistis
Hristos Rahon
Manganitis
Nas
1033m
Langada
Karkinagri
Amalo
Kalamos
Cape Papas
AEGEAN SEA
To Mykonos, Tinos, Syros & Piraeus
To Paros, Naxos & Piraeus
0
2.5
5 km

Getting There & Away

Air In summer there are four flights weekly to Athens (17,100 dr) which usually depart in the early afternoon. The Olympic Airways office (☎ 22 214) is in Agios Kirykos, though tickets can also be bought from Blue Nice Agency (☎ 31 990, fax 31 752) in Evdilos. There is no bus to the airport and a taxi will cost around 3000 dr.

Ferry Nearly all ferries which call at Ikaria's two ports of Evdilos and Agios Kirykos are on the Piraeus-Samos route. In general there are departures every day from Agios Kirykos and three to four times weekly from Evdilos. Sample fares are Piraeus (nine hours, 5300 dr), Samos (three hours, 2100 dr), Mykonos (three hours, 3100 dr) and Tinos (four hours, 3200 dr). Tickets can be bought at Roustas Travel (☎ 22 441, fax 31 428) in Agios Kirykos or from Roustas Travel (☎ 22 441, fax 31 428) and Blue Nice Agency in Evdilos.

Chios-based Miniotis Lines also runs a couple of small boats leaving twice weekly up to Chios (8½ hours, 4800 dr) from Agios Kirykos via Fourni and Samos.

Hydrofoil Ikaria and the Fourni Islands are linked with Samos by fairly frequent summer services and twice weekly connections to Patmos and further connections to Kos. Sample fares are Patmos (one hour, 3520 dr), Samos (2¼ hours, 4280 dr), Kos (2½ hours, 7230 dr). Check with Dolihi Tours (☎ 23 230, fax 22 346) for the latest information.

Caïque A caïque leaves Agios Kirykos on Monday, Wednesday and Friday at 1 pm for Fourni, the largest island in the miniature Fourni archipelago. The caïque calls at the main settlement, where there are domatia and tavernas. Tickets cost 1000 dr one way. Day excursion boats to Fourni from Agios Kirykos cost around 4000 dr and 6000 dr from Armenistis on the north coast.

Getting Around

Bus Ikaria's bus services are almost as mythical as Icarus, but they do occasionally exist. In summer a bus is supposed leave Evdilos for Agios Kirykos daily at 8 am and return to Evdilos at noon, or thereabouts. However, it is best not to count on there being a service since the buses (where they do operate) exist mainly to service the schools during term time.

Buses to the villages of Hristos Rahon (near Moni Evangelistrias), Xylosyrtis and Hrysostomos from Agios Kirykos are more elusive and depend mainly on the whims of the local drivers. It is usually preferable to share a taxi with locals or other travellers for long-distance runs.

Car & Motorcycle Cars can be rented from Dolihi Tours Travel Agency (☎ 23 230, fax 22 346), Rent Cars & Motorcycles DHM (☎ 22 426) in Agios Kirykos, Marabou Travel (☎ 71 460, fax 71 325) in Armenistis, and from Aventura Car Rental (☎ 31 140, fax 71 400) in Evdilos.

Taxi Boat In summer there are daily taxi boats from Agios Kirykos to Therma and to the sandy beach at Fanari on the northern tip of the island. A return trip costs 2000 dr.

AGIOS KIRYKOS Αγιος Κήρυκος

• postcode 833 00 • pop 1800

Agios Kirykos is Ikaria's capital and main port. It's a pleasant, relaxed little town with a tree-shaded waterfront flanked by several *kafeneia*. Beaches in Agios Kirykos are stony; the pebbled beach at Xylosyrtis, 7km to the south-west, is the best of a mediocre bunch of beaches near town.

Orientation & Information

To reach the central square from the quay, turn right and walk along the main road. As you walk away from the quay, turn left on the central square and you will come to the post office and OTE on the left. The bus stop is just west of the square.

Ikaria does not have an EOT or tourist police. A good unofficial source of information is Vasilis Dionysos, a charismatic fellow who owns the village store in the north coast village of Kampos (see the Kampos section).

At the bottom of the steps which lead to Agios Kirykos' police building you will find Dolihi Tours Travel Agency. The staff here have information about hydrofoil schedules and can also arrange accommodation.

The National Bank of Greece is on the central square, and the Ionian Bank is next to Dolihi Tours; both have ATMs. The police (☎ 22 222) and port police (☎ 22 207) share a building in the eastern part of town. Continue along the waterfront from the central square and go up the six steps; continue up the next flight of steps and at the top you will see the police building on the right.

Things to See & Do

The **radioactive springs** are between Hotel Akti and the police building. A dip costs 800 dr and supposedly cures a multitude of afflictions including arthritis, rheumatism, skin diseases and infertility. There are more hot springs at Therma, 3km north-east of Agios Kirykos. This thriving spa resort has many visitors in summer.

Agios Kirykos' small **archaeological museum** houses many local finds. Pride of place is given to a large, well preserved stele (500 BC) depicting in low relief a mother (seated) with her husband and four children. The stele was discovered some years ago during the building of a school in a nearby village. It took a court case to prize the stele from the clutches of the school.

The museum is west of the quay and is well signposted. Opening times are generally 10 am to 1 pm, but don't bet on it. Admission is free.

Places to Stay

One of the cheapest places to stay in Agios Kirykos is the E class ***Hotel Akti*** *(☎ 22 694, fax 22 346)*. The tidy rooms cost 6500/8500 dr for singles/doubles with bathroom. The pension has great sea views from its appealing garden. To reach it, turn right facing Dolihi Tours, go up the steps to the left and follow the signs.

Pension Maria-Elena *(☎ 22 835, fax 71 331)* has impeccable rooms. Rates are 12,000/14,000 dr for doubles/triples with bathroom. From the quay turn left at the main road, take the first right, and then first left into Artemidos – the pension is along here on the right.

Agios Kirykos' best-appointed hotel is the C class ***Hotel Kastro*** *(☎ 23 480, fax 23 700)*. The rooms are beautifully furnished and have a telephone, three-channel music system, bathroom and balcony. Rates are 12,650/15,950 dr for singles/doubles, including breakfast. On a clear day you can see the islands of Amorgos, Naxos, Fourni, Patmos, Samos, Arki and Lipsi from the communal terraces. The hotel is opposite the police building.

Places to Eat

Agios Kirykos has a number of restaurants, snack bars, ouzeria and kafeneia. ***Taverna Klimataria*** *(☎ 22 686)* serves good grilled meats in a neat little courtyard hidden away in the backstreets and is open all year. A decent-sized pork chop should be about 1300 dr and it will taste even better with a small bottle of Samaina Sec from Samos. On the main square is ***Restaurant Dedalos*** *(☎ 22 473)* which offers delicious fresh fish. Its draught wine is highly recommended.

Filoti Pizzeria Restaurant is one of the town's best regarded restaurants. Apart from excellent pizza and pasta, there are good souvlaki and chicken dishes. The restaurant can be found at the top of the cobbled street that leads from the butcher's shop.

If you feel like a brisk walk and fancy a change of scenery, try the nifty little taverna ***To Tzaki*** *(☎ 22 113)* in the village of Glares, about 4km west of Agios Kirykos.

AGIOS KIRYKOS TO THE NORTH COAST

The island's main north-south asphalt road begins a little west of Agios Kirykos and links the capital with the north coast. As the road climbs up to the island's mountainous spine there are dramatic mountain, coastal and sea vistas. The road winds through several villages, some with traditional stone houses topped with rough-hewn slate roofs. It then descends to the island's second port of Evdilos, 41km by road from Agios Kirykos. Look out for the island's only **cork tree** on the west side of the village of Monokambi. A returned migrant to America planted it many years ago. Look out for the white-painted steps leading up to it.

This journey is worth taking for the views, but if you are based in Agios Kirykos and want to travel by bus you will more than likely have to stay overnight in Evdilos or Armenistis. A taxi back to Agios Kirykos will cost 7000 dr. Hitching is usually OK, but there is not much traffic.

EVDILOS Εύδηλος

• postcode 833 00 • pop 440

Evdilos, the island's second port, is a small, dusty fishing village. Like Agios Kirykos it's a pleasant and relaxing place, but you may prefer to head further west to the island's best beaches. There is, nonetheless, a reasonable beach to the east of Evdilos. Walk 100m up the hill from the square and take the path down past the last house on the left. If you are heading to Ikaria by boat and intend to base yourself on the north coast, take a boat direct to Evdilos rather than Agios Kyrikos.

Places to Stay

For a quiet stay upon arrival in Evdilos you might consider making the 3km (40 minute) walk to Kampos (see West of Evdilos) where there are domatia, a couple of excellent beaches and a couple of restaurants. The nearest and cheapest accommodation option in Evdilos is the ***pension*** of Ioannis Spanos *(☎ 31 220)*. The rooms are centrally located just back from the main square. Reasonable singles/doubles are 6000/7000 dr. On the road to Kampos are the neat ***Stenos Domatia*** *(☎ 31 365)*, which go for around 7000 dr.

Facing the sea from the middle of the waterfront, the plush-looking building on the far right with black wrought-iron balconies is the ***domatia*** belonging to Spyros Rossos *(☎ 31 518)*. Rates are 7000 dr for a double with bathroom.

Evdilos has two good quality hotels. The B class ***Hotel Atheras*** *(☎ 31 434, fax 31 926)* is a breezy, friendly place with modern rooms with balconies. There is also a small pool and bar. Rooms go for 13,000/15,000 dr in high season. At the top of the hill is the small B class ***Hotel Evdoxia*** *(☎ 31 502, fax 31 571)* with doubles for 13,000 dr, if you don't mind the petty house rules. There is a minimarket with basic provisions, a laundry service, money exchange and restaurant (see Places to Eat), and it's open all year.

Places to Eat

In season, there are a number of eateries to choose from, including the fairly obvious ***Souvlarhio*** with its blue cane chairs. Try their tasty Ikarian specialities *soufiko* or *mayirio* – pan-simmered concoctions of the season's first vegetables. ***Kavos Restaurant*** on the east side of the little harbour is open all day for lunch and dinner.

Cuckoo Ouzeri, also on the harbour, serves tasty mezedes and has a comprehensive selection of bottled Ikarian wine. For home-cooked food with a view, ***Hotel Evdoxia Restaurant*** is a good meeting place for travellers. You can even order your favourite dish if you are staying at the hotel. Prices at all places are mid-range.

WEST OF EVDILOS

Kampos Κάμπος

• postcode 833 01 • pop 127

Kampos, 3km west of Evdilos, is an unspoilt little village with few concessions to tourism. Although it takes some believing, sleepy little Kampos was the island's ancient capital of Oinoe (etymologically derived from the Greek word for wine). The name comes from the myth that the Ikarians were the first people to make wine. In ancient times Ikarian wine was considered the best in Greece, but a phylloxera outbreak in the mid-60s put paid to many of the vines. Production is now low-key and mainly for local consumption. Ancient coins found in

Ancient coin depicting Dionysos, the god of wine and revelry

the vicinity of Kampos have a picture of Dionysos, the wine god, on them. Kampos' sandy beach is excellent and easily accessible.

Information The irrepressible Vasilis Dionysos, who speaks English, is a fount of information on Ikarian history and walking in the mountains. You will often find him in his gloomy but well stocked village store – on the right as you come from Evdilos. The village's post box is outside this shop and inside there is a metered telephone. There is also a cardphone nearby.

Things to See & Do As you enter Kampos from Evdilos, the ruins of a **Byzantine palace** (strictly speaking a *kyvernio*, or governor's house) can be seen up on the right. In the centre of the village there is a small **museum** housing Neolithic tools, geometric vases, fragments of classical sculpture, small figurines and a very fine 'horse head' knife sheath carved from ivory. The museum is open 8 am to 2 pm.

Next to the museum is the 12th century **Agia Irini**, the island's oldest church. It is built on the site of a 4th century basilica, and columns standing in the grounds are from this original church. Agia Irini's supposedly fine frescoes are currently covered with whitewash because of insufficient funds to pay for its removal. Vasilis Dionysos has the keys to both the museum and church.

The village is also a good base for mountain walking. A one day circular walk along dirt roads can be made, taking in the village of **Dafni**, the remains of the 10th century Byzantine **Castle of Koskinas**, and the villages of **Frandato** and **Maratho** and a cave at **Mikropouli** which can be difficult to find – ask Vasilis Dionysos if you get stuck. Take a torch if you plan to enter it. The trek up to the little granite-roofed Byzantine **Chapel of Theoskepasti** is worth the effort for this unusual and photogenic sight. Inside you will be shown the skulls of a couple of macabre internees. To get to the chapel and the neighbouring **Theoktisti Church** look for the signs at the village of Pigi on the road to Frandato.

Places to Stay & Eat There are a couple of ***domatia*** in Kampos, the best of which is owned by – you guessed it – Vasilis Dionysos *(☎ 31 300, fax 31 688)* and his brother Yiannis, who create a wonderful family atmosphere for their guests. The very pleasant rooms are between 5000 dr and 8000 dr for doubles with bathroom. The optional enormous breakfasts are something to be experienced and are accompanied by tasteful Greek music. From Evdilos, take the dirt road to the right from near the cardphone and follow it round to the blue and white building on your left. Alternatively, make your presence known at the village store.

Vasilis often cooks delicious fish or lobster dishes for his guests and his original pitta recipe is exquisite. Otherwise, there is a moderately priced taverna in the village, ***Klimataria***, and a summer taverna, ***Pashalia***, on Partheni Beach about 400m past Vasilis Dionysos' place.

Armenistis Αρμενιστής

• **postcode 833 01** • **pop 70**

Armenistis, 15km west of Evdilos, is the island's largest resort with two beautiful long beaches of pale golden sand, separated by a narrow headland. Places to stay are springing up quickly here, but it's still visited predominantly by independent travellers. Marabou Travel (☎ 71 460, fax 71 325), on the road which skirts the sea, organises walking tours and jeep safaris on the island. Just east of Armenistis a road leads inland to **Moni Evangelistrias**.

From Armenistis a 3.5km dirt road continues west to the small and secluded pebbled beach of **Nas** at the mouth of a stream. This is Ikaria's unofficial nudist beach. Behind the beach are some scant remains of a **temple of Artemis**. Nas has in recent times begun to witness a mini-boom with no less than 45 beds available and a choice of five tavernas to eat at.

Places to Stay – Budget Ikaria's only camp site is the rather scrawny ***Armenistis Camping*** *(☎ 71 250)*, on the beach at Armenistis. Facilities are fairly minimal though the owners are planning expansions and renovations. It opens about mid-June and costs 1600 dr for two persons with a tent.

One of the cheapest places to stay in Armenistis is ***Rooms Ikaros*** *(☎ 71 238)*. Doubles are 4000/5000 dr without/with bathroom. The elderly owner, Dimitris Hroussis, speaks a little English and is kind and friendly. The place is signposted as you enter the village. Above the Pashalia restaurant are the ***domatia*** *(☎ 71 302)* belonging to the restaurant. Clean and modern doubles with bathroom and most with sea-view balconies go for between 4000 dr and 7000 dr according to season.

At the approach to the village, before the road forks, you will see ***Rooms Fotinos*** *(☎ 71 235)* on the left. The rooms are light, airy and beautifully furnished. Rates are 7000/8400 dr for doubles/triples with bathroom.

Artemis Taverna *(☎ 71 485)* at Nas serves as a pension with small but neat double rooms with bathroom for 6000 dr. ***Pension Thea*** *(☎ 71 491)*, also at Nas, is newer, but the rooms are more exposed to the sun. Still, they have a fridge, a sea view and go for between 5000 dr and 8000 dr for two persons.

Places to Stay – Mid-Range One of Armenistis' better hotels is around to the west of the village. The C class ***Hotel Dedalos*** *(☎ 71 390, fax 71 393)* has a cool and inviting interior. The stucco-walled rooms open out onto a large private terrace overlooking a rocky seascape. The hotel has a large restaurant and bar and a sea water swimming pool built into the rocks. Singles/doubles cost 15,000/16,500 dr, breakfast included.

The most exquisite accommodation on the island, however, is the Cycladic-inspired ***pension*** *(☎/fax 71 310)* belonging to Dimitris Ioannidopoulos, known as *o yermanos* (the German) because of his many years of residence in that country. The individual studios and apartments, 800m west of Armenistis, spill down a hillside which overlooks the sea amid a riotous profusion of flowers and plants. A small studio for two people with private patio goes for 10,000 dr while a fully equipped two to three person apartment complete with music system and enormous patio goes for a very reasonable 12,000 dr. Bookings are absolutely essential and must be for a minimum of one week. Phone or fax ☎ 089-690 1097 in Germany during the winter months.

Places to Eat There are three restaurants along the Armenistis harbourside: ***To Symposio***, ***Kafestiatorio o Ilios*** and ***To Mouragio*** – take your pick, though the Symposio is probably more popular.

Farther up the hill, ***Pashalia Taverna*** offers prompt service and a variety of ready-made dishes. Try the filling pasta and veal in a clay pot for about 1400 dr.

Directly opposite and below the Pashalia Taverna is the folksy ***Delfini*** restaurant offering great grilled souvlaki to complement the view over the water. Wherever you eat, see if you can get to taste some of the locally made light but potent wine.

Handy for the camp site and the beach is ***Atsahas*** taverna, 2km east of Armenistis. The views are great and the food is pretty reasonable and moderately priced – though service is very slow.

Nas now has six tavernas of which ***Astra*** *(☎ 71 255)* is probably the best. All dishes are wood-oven cooked. Try the potato salad – almost a meal in itself – or ask to sample the oven-cooked kid and wash it down with the mean draught red wine.

FOURNI ISLANDS Οι Φούρνοι

• postcode 834 00 • pop 1030

The Fourni Islands are a miniature archipelago lying between Ikaria and Samos. Two of the islands are inhabited: Fourni and Thymena. The capital of the group is **Fourni Town** (also called Kampos), which is the port of Fourni Island. Fourni has one other village, tiny Hrysomilia, 10km north of the port; the island's only road connects the two. The islands are mountainous and a good number of beaches are dotted around the coast.

The telephone number of Fourni's port police is ☎ 51 207. The local police number is ☎ 51 222 and the local doctor's number is ☎ 51 202.

Fourni is the only island with accommodation for tourists and is ideal for those seeking a quiet retreat. Other than the settlement of Fourni itself and a beach over the headland to the south at **Kampi**, the island offers little else besides eating, sleeping and swimming. Most of the islanders make a living from fishing, sending their catch to the Athens fish market.

For accommodation try the rooms and studios of ***Nikolas Kondylas*** *(☎ 51 364, fax 51 209)* which range in price from 7000 dr to 12,000 dr depending on facilities. Some are in Fourni Town itself; others are on Kampi Beach, a 15 minute walk away. Alternatively, try the ***Pension*** *(☎ 51 148)* of Maria and Kostas Makrakis in Fourni Town.

For eating out ***Taverna Nikos*** *(☎ 51 253)* or ***Miltos*** *(☎ 51 407)* on the waterfront will keep you amply supplied with fresh fish and other grilled dishes.

Various services connect Fourni with Ikaria and other Aegean islands. See the Ikaria Getting There & Away section for information about how to get to Fourni.

Chios Χίος

☎ 0271 • pop 54,000

Chios (**hee**-os) does not feature prominently on the travel circuit. Situated rather awkwardly on the ferry routes and without a tangible international profile, the island attracts curious travellers and expat Greeks rather than hordes of package tourists, though those that do come find the island subtly rewarding in its own distinct way. Like its neighbours Samos and Lesvos, Chios is a large island covering 859 sq km. It is separated from the Turkish Karaburun Peninsula by the 8km-wide Chios Straits. It is a verdant island, although in recent years fires have destroyed many of its forests giving it a dry and scrawny appearance at first glance.

A large number of highly successful ship owners come from Chios and its dependencies, Inousses and Psara. This, and its mastic production, have meant that Chios has not needed to develop a large tourist industry. In recent years, however, package tourism has begun to make inroads, though it's limited to a fairly small coastal stretch south of Chios Town. The mastic villages of the south and its role as a stepping stone to Turkey is what primarily brings travellers to Chios.

History

In ancient times, Chios, like Samos, excelled in the arts, which reached their peak in the 7th century BC when the Chios school of sculpture produced some of Greece's most eminent sculptors of the time. The technique of soldering iron was invented in this school. During the Persian Wars, Chios was allied to Athens, but after the Battle of Plataea it became independent, and prospered because it didn't have to pay the annual tribute to Athens.

In Roman times Chios was invaded by Constantine, who helped himself to its fine sculptures. After the fall of Byzantium, the island fell prey to attacks by pirates, Venetians, Catalans and Turks. It revived somewhat under the Genoese, who took control in the 14th century. However, it was recaptured

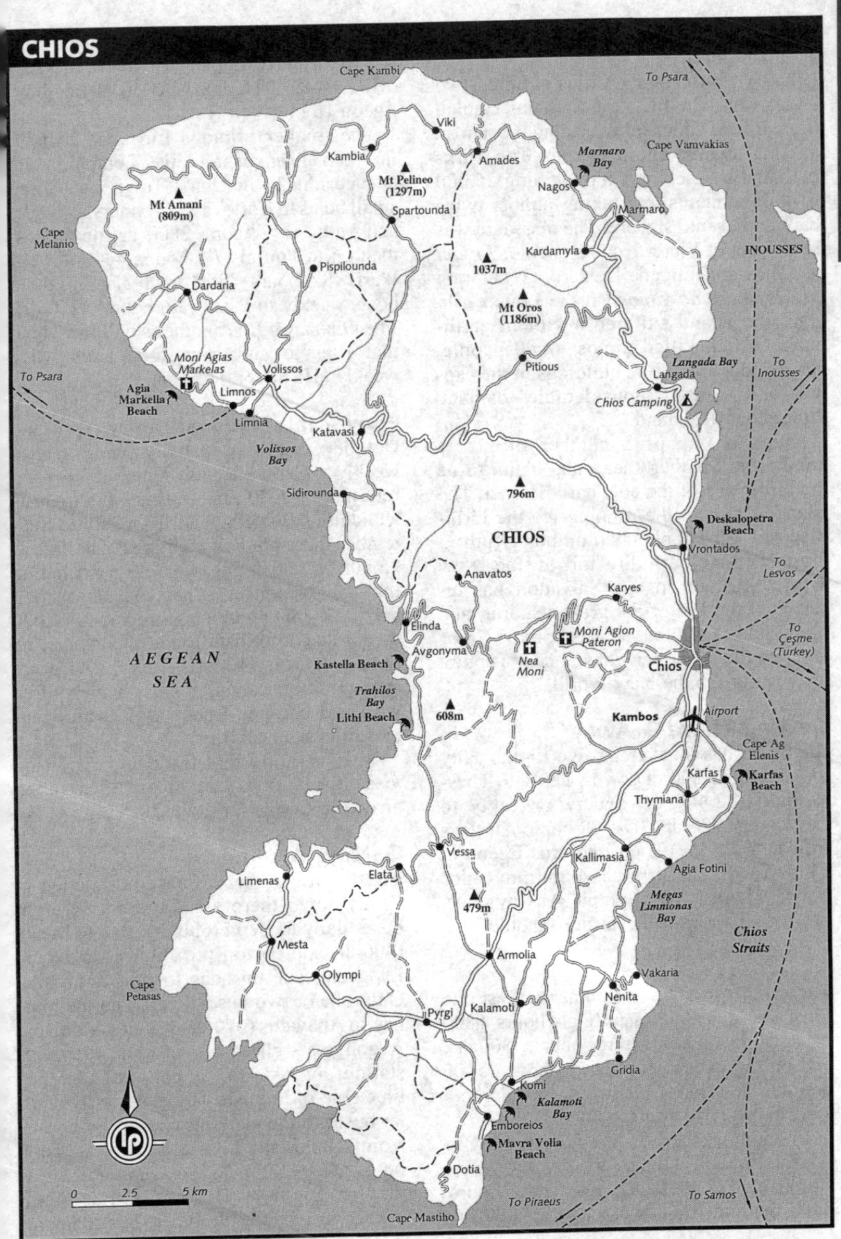
CHIOS
Cape Kambi
To Psara
Viki
Kambia
Amades
Marmaro Bay
Cape Vamvakias
Mt Pelineo (1297m)
Mt Amani (809m)
Nagos
Spartounda
Marmaro
Cape Melanio
INOUSSES
Kardamyla
Pispilounda
1037m
Dardaria
Mt Oros (1186m)
Moni Agias Markelas
Volissos
Pitious
Langada Bay
To Inousses
Langada
To Psara
Agia Markella Beach
Limnos
Chios Camping
Limnia
Katavasi
Volissos Bay
Sidirounda
796m
Deskalopetra Beach
CHIOS
Vrontados
Anavatos
To Lesvos
Karyes
Elinda
Moni Agion Pateron
To Çeşme (Turkey)
Avgonyma
Nea Moni
Chios
AEGEAN SEA
Kastella Beach
Trahilos Bay
Lithi Beach
608m
Kambos
Airport
Cape Ag Elenis
Karfas
Karfas Beach
Thymiana
Vessa
Kallimasia
Agia Fotini
Elata
Limenas
479m
Megas Limnionas Bay
Chios Straits
Mesta
Armolia
Olympi
Vakaria
Cape Petasas
Nenita
Kalamoti
Pyrgi
Gridia
Komi
Kalamoti Bay
Emboreios
Mavra Volia Beach
Dotia
0
2.5
5 km
To Piraeus
To Samos
Cape Mastiho

by the Turks in 1566 and became part of the Ottoman Empire.

In the 19th century, Chios suffered two devastations. In 1822 the Samians cajoled the people of Chios into assisting them in an uprising against Ottoman rule. The Turks retaliated by sacking Chios, killing 25,000 of its inhabitants and taking almost twice that number into slavery. The massacre was the subject of Victor Hugo's poem *L'Enfant de Chios* and Eugène Delacroix's painting *Le Massacre de Chios* (in the Louvre). In 1881 the island suffered a violent earthquake which killed almost 6000 people, destroyed many of the buildings in the capital and caused considerable damage throughout the island.

Chios is one of a number of places around the Mediterranean that claim to be the birthplace of the epic bard, Homer. The island is also in the running for the birthplace of Christopher Columbus. Ruth G Durlacher-Wolper, director of the New World Museum in San Salvador, has researched the life of the great seafarer, and has hypothesised that he was born on Chios and that the island may have been his point of departure to the New World.

Getting There & Away

Air Chios has on average five flights daily to Athens (15,800 dr), two weekly to Thessaloniki (22,400 dr) and two weekly to Lesvos (10,900 dr). The Olympic Airways office (☎ 20 359) is on Leoforos Egeou in Chios Town. The airport is 4km from Chios Town. There is no Olympic Airways bus, but a taxi to/from the airport should cost about 800 dr.

Ferry – Domestic In summer at least one ferry goes daily to Piraeus (eight hours, 5800 dr) and one to Lesvos (three hours, 3300 dr), and one weekly to Kavala (16 hours, 7400 dr) and Thessaloniki (18 hours, 8400 dr) both via Limnos (five hours, 5300 dr).

In addition, there is one ferry weekly to Alexandroupolis (16 hours, 6800 dr), Samos (three hours, 3000 dr), Kos (nine hours, 4900 dr) and Rhodes (15 hours, 7000 dr). Tickets for these routes can be bought from the Maritime Company of Lesvos (NEL) office (☎ 23 971, fax 41 319) at Leoforos Egeou 16 in Chios Town.

The smaller Miniotis Lines (☎ 24 670, fax 25 371, email miniotis@compulink.gr) at Neorion 23 in Chios Town runs three small boats to Karlovasi (3½ hours, 2400 dr) and Vathy (4½ hours, 2800 dr) on Samos, then on to Fourni (7½ hours, 4400 dr) and Ikaria (8½ hours, 4800 dr). It also has three boats weekly to Psara (3½ hours, 2250 dr). The *Oinoussai II* is another small local boat that runs to and from Oinousses twice weekly (1¼ hours, 1100 dr).

Ferry – International During April and October there are usually three ferries weekly to Çeşme, leaving Chios at 8 am and returning at 6.30 pm. During May there is an additional sailing and from July to September there are daily sailings. The fare is 15,000/20,000 dr one way/return (including the 3000 dr port tax). The cost for a small car is 23,000 dr and a motorcycle is 14,000 dr. Further information and tickets can be obtained from Miniotis Tours. There are special daily excursion rates which often work out cheaper. Check with local agencies offering such trips.

Bear in mind that travellers requiring visas for Turkey can obtain them upon arrival in Çeşme for around US$45.

Getting Around

Bus From the long-distance bus station in Chios Town there are, in summer, eight buses daily to Pyrgi (600 dr), five to Mesta (800 dr) and six to Kardamyla (700 dr) via Langada; take this bus for the camp site. Only one or two buses weekly do the journey to Anavatos (470 dr) via Nea Moni and Avgonyma – check the schedule at the bus station, or ask for a copy of the bus timetable in English. There are fairly regular buses to the main beaches of Emborios, Komi, Nagos and Lithi and extra excursion buses to Nea Moni and Anavatos are scheduled on Tuesdays. Buses to Karfas Beach are serviced by the blue (city) bus company.

Bus timetables are available from the municipal tourist office.

Car & Motorcycle The numerous car rental outlets in Chios Town include Budget (☎ 41 361), on Psyhari, near the post office and Europcar (☎ 41 031, mobile 094 517 141) on Leoforos Egeou 56. Chios' ELPA representative is K Mihalakis (☎ 22 445), Rodokanaki 19. There are many moped and motorcycle hire outlets on and near the waterfront.

CHIOS TOWN

• postcode 821 00 • pop 22,900

Chios Town, on the east coast, is the island's port and capital. It's a large town, home to almost half of the island's inhabitants. Its waterfront, flanked by concrete modern buildings and trendy coffee shops, is noisy in the extreme with an inordinate amount of cars and motorcycles careering up and down. However, things improve considerably once you begin exploring the backstreets. The atmospheric old quarter, with many Turkish houses built around a Genoese castle, and the lively market area, are both worth a stroll. Chios Town doesn't have a beach; the nearest is the sandy beach at Karfas, 6km south.

Orientation

Most ferries dock at the northern end of the waterfront at the western end of Neorion. Bear in mind that ferries from Piraeus (to Mytilini) arrive at the very inconvenient time of 4 am – worth remembering if you are planning to find a room. The old Turkish quarter (called Kastro) is to the north of the ferry quay. To reach the town centre from here, follow the waterfront round to the left and walk along Leoforos Egeou. Turn right onto Kanari to reach the central square of Plateia Vounakiou. To the north-west of the square are the public gardens, and to the south-east is the market area. As you face inland, the bus station for local buses (blue) is on the right side of the public gardens and the station for long-distance buses (green) is on the left.

Information

The municipal tourist office (☎ 44 389, fax 44 343, email tourismos@chi.forthnet.gr) is at Kanari 18. The helpful staff give information on accommodation, bus and boat schedules. The magazine *Chios Summertime* is available here. Opening hours are 7 am to 2.30 pm and 7.30 to 10 pm on weekdays, 10 am to 1 pm on Saturday and 7 to 10 pm on Sunday.

The post office and OTE are both one block back from the waterfront while most banks are between Kanari and Plateia Vounakiou. There is an ATM halfway along Aplotarias.

The Enter Internet Cafe (☎ 41 058) is at Egeou 48 (upstairs) on the southern waterfront and charges 1000 dr an hour.

The tourist police (☎ 44 427) and the port police (☎ 44 432) are at the eastern end of Neorion.

Museums

Chios Town's most interesting museum is the **Philip Argenti Museum** (☎ 23 463), in the same building as the **Koraïs Library**, one of the country's largest libraries. The museum, which is on Koraïs near the cathedral, contains exquisite embroideries, traditional costumes and portraits of the wealthy Argenti family. The museum and the library are open 8.30 am to 2 pm Monday to Thursday, 5 to 7 pm Friday and 8 am to 12.30 pm Saturday. Admission is free.

The town's other museums are not so compelling. The **archaeological museum** (☎ 44 239), on Polemidi, contains sculptures, pottery and coins and is open 10 am to 1 pm Tuesday to Sunday. No admission fee had been announced at the time of writing. The **Byzantine Museum** (☎ 26 866) is housed in a former mosque, the Medjitie Djami, on Plateia Vounakiou. Opening times are 10 am to 3 pm Tuesday to Sunday. Admission is 500 dr, 300 dr for students.

Places to Stay – Budget

With over 30 domatia to choose from, budget accommodation is fairly plentiful in Chios Town. Call into the municipal tourist office for a full listing. Be aware, though,

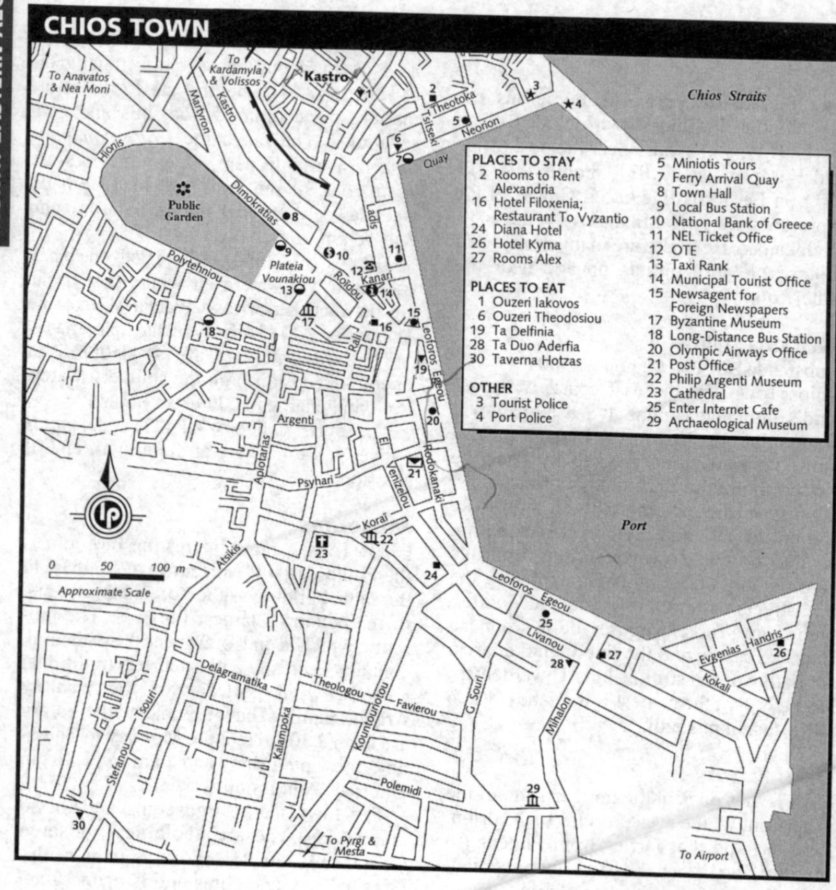

that accommodation in central Chios Town can be very noisy –choose carefully.

Chios has one camp site, ***Chios Camping*** *(☎ 74 111)*, on the beach at Agios Isidoros, between Sykiada and Langada, 14km north of Chios Town. The site has good facilities, a bar and restaurant. To reach it take a Kardamyla or Langada bus.

The most welcoming domatia option is ***Rooms Alex*** *(☎ 26 054, Livanou 29)*. Alex has six doubles which go for 7500/8000 dr without/with bathroom. There is a relaxing roof garden festooned with flags, and Alex will pick you up at your boat if you call him. He will also help with car or bike rentals and give general information on Chios.

The D class ***Hotel Filoxenia*** *(☎ 26 559)* is signposted from the waterfront and is above Restaurant To Vyzantio. The unadorned but clean singles/doubles cost 4500/6000 dr, or 6000/8500 dr with bathroom.

In the old quarter, ***Rooms to Rent Alexandria*** *(☎ 41 815)*, on Theotoka, has agreeable doubles for 6500 dr; a few rooms have private bathrooms.

Places to Stay – Mid-Range

The C class ***Diana Hotel*** *(☎ 44 180, fax 26 748, El Venizelou 92)* is a good hotel aimed primarily at the Greek business market. Single/double rates here are 10,500/15,000 dr including breakfast. The C class ***Hotel Kyma*** *(☎ 44 500, fax 44 600, email kyma@chi.forthnet.gr, Evgenias Handris 1)* occupies a century-old mansion and has lots of character. Rates for air-con rooms are 14,000/18,000 dr with breakfast.

Places to Eat

Restaurant To Vyzantio, on the corner of Ralli and Roïdou, is a bright, cheerful and unpretentious place which serves traditional Greek fare at low prices. Right opposite the ferry disembarkation point on Neorion is ***Ouzeri Theodosiou***, an old-style and very popular establishment. Tucked away in the old town is the relocated ***Ouzeri Iakovos*** *(Agiou Georgiou Frouriou 20)* specialising in tasty fish mezedes.

Ta Delfinia, on the waterfront, is a bit touristy (with photo menus), but the food and service are good and it's the best place to watch street life. Main dishes start at around 1300 dr. Opposite Rooms Alex is ***Ta Duo Aderfia*** *(Livanou 38)* with a pleasant walled garden. Try the special spare ribs in barbecue sauce for around 1500 dr.

Open evenings only, at the southern end of town is ***Taverna Hotzas*** *(☎ 42 787)* – a bit of an institution, with cats, hens and ducks wandering around the garden. To get there, walk up Aplotarias and turn right at the fork along Stefanou Tsouri; follow it until you come across the restaurant.

CENTRAL CHIOS

North of Chios Town is an elongated beach-side suburb leading to **Vrontados** where you can sit on the supposed stone chair of Homer, the Daskalopetra, though it is quietly accepted that it is unlikely to have been used by Homer himself. It is a serene spot though, and it would not be hard to imagine Homer and his acolytes reciting epic verses to their admiring followers.

Immediately south of Chios Town is a warren of walled mansions, some restored, others crumbling, called the **Kampos**. This was the preferred place of abode of wealthy Genoese and Greek merchant families from the 14th century onwards. It's easy to get lost here so keep your wits about you – the free Chios map from the EOT is helpful. You are also better off touring the area by bicycle or moped, since it is fairly extensive. Chios' main beach resort **Karfas** is here too, 7km south of Chios Town. The beach is sandy though comparatively small with some moderate development and some A class hotels; if you like your beaches quiet, look elsewhere.

In the centre of the island is the 11th century **Nea Moni**. This large monastery, now World Heritage-listed, stands in a beautiful mountain setting, 14km from Chios Town. Like many monasteries in Greece it was built to house an icon of the Virgin Mary before the eyes of three shepherds. In its heyday the monastery was one of the richest in Greece with the most pre-eminent artists of Byzantium commissioned to create the mosaics in its *katholikon*.

During the 1822 atrocities the buildings were set on fire and all the resident monks were massacred. There is a macabre display of their skulls in the ossuary at the monastery's little chapel. In the earthquake of 1881 the katholikon's dome caved in, causing quite a lot of damage to the mosaics. Nonetheless, the mosaics, esteemed for the striking contrasts of their vivid colours and the fluidity and juxtapositions of the figures, still rank among the most outstanding examples of Byzantine art in Greece. A few nuns live at the monastery. Opening times are 8 am until 1 pm and 4 to 8 pm daily. Admission is free. The bus service to the monastery is poor, but travel agents in Chios Town have excursions here and to the village of Anavatos.

Ten kilometres from Nea Moni, at the end of a road that leads to nowhere, stands the forlorn ghost village of **Anavatos**. Its abandoned grey-stone houses stand as lonely sentinels to one of Chios' great tragedies. Nearly all the inhabitants of the village perished in 1822 and today only a small number of elderly people live there, mostly in houses at the base of the village.

Anavatos is a striking village, built on a precipitous cliff which the villagers chose to hurl themselves over, rather than be taken captive by the Turks. Narrow, stepped pathways wind between the houses to the summit of the village. **Avgonyma**, farther back along the road, is only slightly more populated than Anavatos, but lacks the drama of its neighbour.

The beaches on the mid-west coast are not spectacular, but they are quiet and generally undeveloped. **Lithi Beach**, the southernmost, is popular with weekenders and can get busy.

SOUTHERN CHIOS

Southern Chios is dominated by medieval villages that look as though they were transplanted from the Levant rather than built by Genoese colonisers in the 14th century. The rolling, scrubby hills are covered in low mastic trees that for many years were the main source of income for these scattered settlements (see the boxed text 'Gum Mastic').

There are some 20 *Mastihohoria* (mastic villages); the two best preserved are Pyrgi and Mesta. As mastic was a highly lucrative commodity in the Middle Ages, many an invader cast an acquisitive eye upon the villages, necessitating sturdy fortifications. The archways spanning the streets were to prevent the houses from collapsing during earthquakes. However, because of the sultan's fondness for mastic chewing gum, the inhabitants of the Mastihohoria were spared in the 1822 massacre.

Pyrgi Πυργί

• pop 1300

The largest of the Mastihohoria, and one of the most extraordinary villages in the whole of Greece, is the fortified village of Pyrgi, 24km south-west of Chios Town. The vaulted streets of the fortified village are narrow and labyrinthine, but what makes Pyrgi unique are the building facades, decorated with intricate grey and white designs. Some of the patterns are geometric and others are based on flowers, leaves and animals. The technique used, called *xysta*, is achieved by coating the walls with a mixture of cement and black volcanic sand, painting over this with white lime, and then scraping off parts of the lime with the bent prong of a fork, to reveal the matt grey beneath.

From the main road, a fork to the right (coming from Chios Town) leads to the heart of the village and the central square. The little 12th century **Church of Agios Apostolos**, just off the square, is profusely decorated with well preserved 17th century frescoes. Ask at the taverna or kafeneio for the church's caretaker, who will open it up for you. The facade of the larger church, on the opposite side of the square, has the most impressive xysta of all the buildings here.

Places to Stay & Eat The ***Women's Agricultural Cooperative of Chios*** *(☎ 72 496)* rents a number of traditionally furnished rooms in private houses throughout Pyrgi. Rates are around 5000 dr to 7000 dr for doubles, depending on the season. The cooperative's office is near the central square of Pyrgi and is signposted. On the edge of the village are the very pleasant ***Rooms to Let Nikos*** *(☎ 72 425)*, with doubles for 7500 dr, including the use of a kitchen and fridge.

The little taverna ***I Manoula*** on the central square (on the left as you face the large church) is the main eating option, or the upstairs ***Snack Bar*** on the square can probably rustle up a few mezedes or a snack. Either way, the choice is sadly limited.

Emboreios Εμπορειός

Six kilometres to the south of Pyrgi, Emboreios was the port of Pyrgi in the days when mastic production was big business. These days Emboreios is a quiet holiday resort for people who like to relax. As you come from Chios Town, a signpost points left to Emboreios, just before you arrive at Pyrgi.

Gum Mastic

Gum mastic comes from the lentisk bush, and conditions in southern Chios are ideal for its growth. Many ancient Greeks, including Hippocrates, proclaimed the pharmaceutical benefits of mastic. Ailments it was claimed to cure included stomach upsets, chronic coughs and diseases of the liver, intestines and bladder. It was also used as an antidote for snake bites. During Turkish rule Chios received preferential treatment from the sultans who, along with the ladies of the harem, were hooked on chewing gum made from mastic – try the stuff and you will no doubt wonder why.

Until recently, mastic was widely used in the pharmaceutical industry, as well as in the manufacture of chewing gum and certain alcoholic drinks, particularly arak, a Middle Eastern liqueur. In most cases mastic has now been replaced by other products. But mastic production may yet have a future. Some adherents of alternative medicine claim that it stimulates the immune system and reduces blood pressure and cholesterol levels. Chewing gum made from mastic can be bought on Chios, under the brand name Elma.

There are three tavernas, ***Neptune*** with the most prominent position, and to the side ***Ifestio*** and ***Porto Emborios***, the former with a marginally better ambience. If you want to stay in Emboreios, call ***Studio Apartments Vasiliki*** (*☎ 71 422)*, or ***Themis Studios*** *(☎ 71 810)*.

Mavra Volia Beach is at the end of the road and has unusual black volcanic pebbles as its main attraction. There is another more secluded beach, just over the headland along a paved track.

Mesta Μεστά

Continuing on the main road from Pyrgi, after 5km you will reach the mastic village of **Olympi**. It's less immediately attractive than its two neighbours but still worth a brief stop.

Mesta, 5km farther on, has a very different atmosphere from that created by the striking visuals of Pyrgi and should be on any visitor's itinerary. The village is exquisite and is completely enclosed within massive fortified walls. Entrance to the maze of streets is via one of four gates. This method of limiting entry to the settlement and its disorienting maze of streets and tunnels is a prime example of 14th century defence architecture, as protection against pirates and marauders. The labyrinthine cobbled streets of bare stone houses and arches have a melancholy aura.

The village has two churches of the Taxiarhes (archangels). The older one dates from Byzantine times and has a magnificent 17th century iconostasis. The second one, built in the 19th century, has very fine frescoes.

Orientation Buses stop on Plateia Nikolaou Poumpaki, on the main road outside Mesta. To reach the central square of Plateia Taxiarhon, with your back to the bus shelter, turn right, and then immediately left, and you will see a sign pointing to the centre of the village.

Places to Stay & Eat Many of the rooms in Mesta belong to the Pyrgi Women's Cooperative, and prices are similar. One place to start is ***Anna Floradis Rooms*** *(☎ 28 891)* next to the church. Her five rooms are very comfortable and go for around 6500 dr a double. Otherwise look for the blue and yellow EOT signs on the walls and take pot luck.

Alternatively, Dionysios Karambelas, the affable owner of ***O Morias Sta Mesta*** *(☎ 76 400)* – one of the two restaurants on Plateia Taxiarhon in romantic courtyard settings – may be able to organise accommodation for you. Originally from the Peloponnese (hence the name of the restaurant: Morias is the old name for the Peloponnese), Dionysios will provide you with superb country cooking. Ask to try the *hortokeftedes* (vegetable patties) and an unusual wild green, *kritamos* (rock samphire), that grows by the sea. You may be given a glass of *souma*, an ouzo made from figs.

NORTHERN CHIOS

Northern Chios is characterised by its craggy peaks (Mt Pelineo, Mt Oros and Mt Amani), deserted villages and scrawny hill-sides once blanketed in rich pine forests. The area is mainly for the adventurous and those not fazed by tortuous roads. Public transport up here is poor; you will need a reasonably powered motorcycle to get around.

Volissos is the main focus for the villages of the north-western quarter. Reputedly Homer's place of birth, it is today a somewhat crumbling settlement, capped with an impressive Genoese fort. Volissos' port is **Limnia**, a workaday fishing harbour. It's not especially appealing, but has a welcoming ***taverna***. You can continue to **Limnos**, 1km away, where caïques sometimes leave for Psara. The road onwards round the north end is very winding and passes some isolated villages.

On the eastern side a picturesque road leads out of **Vrontados** through a landscape that is somewhat more visitor-friendly than the western side. Pretty **Langada** is the first village, wedged at the end of a bay looking out towards Inousses. Next are **Kardamyla** and **Marmaro**, the two main settlements, though coastal Marmaro is not geared for tourism and is mercilessly exposed to the summer *meltemi* wind that howls through its narrow bay. If you choose to stay up here, try the comfortable ***Hotel Kardamyla*** *(☎ 0272-23 353)* run by the same management as Hotel Kyma in Chios Town.

Most people go no further than the beach at **Nagos**, which is not bad, though still exposed to the vagaries of the winds – as is all the north coast. The road onwards winds upwards, skirting craggy Mt Pelineo. The scenery is green enough, but settlements are fewer and more remote. **Amades** and **Viki** are two villages you will traverse before hitting the last village, **Kambia**, perched high up on a ridge overlooking bare hillsides and the sea far below. From here a mostly sealed road leads you round Mt Pelineo, past a futuristic phalanx of 10 huge wind-driven generators on the opposite side of the valley, and back to the trans-island route near Volissos.

Inousses Οινούσσες

Off the north-eastern coast of Chios lie nine tiny islets, collectively called Inousses. Only one of these, also called Inousses, is inhabited. Those that live here permanently make their living from fishing and sheep farming. The island has three fish farms and exports small amounts of fish to Italy and France. Inousses is hilly and covered in scrub and has good beaches.

However, these facts apart, this is no ordinary Greek island. Inousses may be small, but it is the ancestral home of around 30% of Greece's ship owners. Most of these exceedingly wealthy maritime barons conduct their businesses from Athens, London and New York, but in summer return with their families to Inousses where they own luxurious mansions.

There is a rumour that these ship owners offer financial incentives to discourage people from opening tavernas or domatia on the island, because they don't want to attract foreign tourists. It may not be possible to vouch for the truth of this but certainly tourism is not encouraged on the island: no domatia owners come to meet the boat, there are no domatia signs and

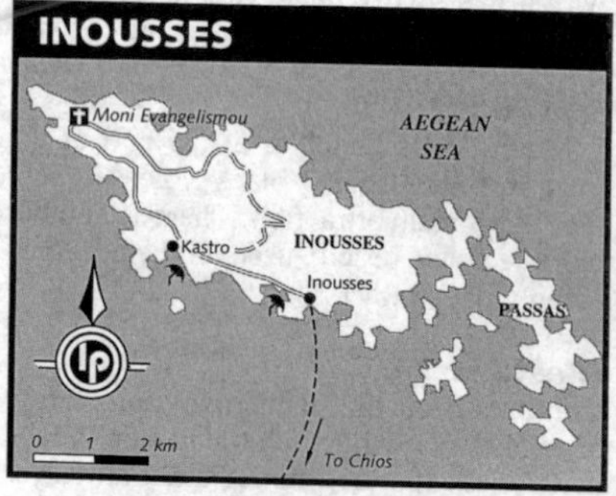

wandering around the streets fails to bring offers of accommodation. The place has a curiously barren and sterile air since there are few tourist facilities and even fewer visitors. Several islanders have stated that Inousses has a few domatia, but they are vague as to their whereabouts.

On a more positive note – and if these quirks have not discouraged you from going to Inousses – the island has a picturesque town of neoclassical mansions and abandoned houses; good beaches – **Kastro Beach** is the usual swimming stop for day-trippers; lots of opportunities for walking; stunning vistas and no package tourists. In Inousses Town there is a large naval boarding school. If you visit during term time you may well encounter the pupils parading around town to bellowed marching orders.

Getting There & Away

The island is served only by the local ferry boat *Oinoussai II*, which plies daily between the island and Chios Town. It leaves Chios Town at 2 pm and Inousses at 9 am, so is of no use for day trips. Purchase tickets on board for 1100 dr (one way). The trip takes about one hour. In summer there are sometimes excursion boats from Chios Town to the island. The little caïque *Smaragdi* does return excursions with a beach barbecue lunch thrown in for around 6000 dr. Call ☎ 0271-22 931 for details.

Getting Around

Inousses has no public transport, but there is one taxi.

INOUSSES TOWN

☎ 0271 • postcode 821 01 • pop 640

The island has one settlement, the little village called Inousses. To reach the centre of the village from the boat quay, facing inland turn left and follow the waterfront to Plateia Antoniou P Lemou; veer slightly right here, and you will immediately come to the tiny Plateia tis Naftisynis; veer right once again and you will see ahead Restaurant & Kafeneio Pateroniso. Facing this establishment turn right and ascend the steps.

There are no EOT or tourist police on the island. If you turn left at Restaurant Pateroniso and then take the first right into Konstantinou Antonopoulou you will come to the National Bank of Greece which, one can surmise, is kept very busy. Next door to the bank is a combined post office and OTE.

The police (☎ 55 222) are at the top of the steps which lead to the town centre.

Maritime Museum

This museum (☎ 55 182) is between the Restaurant Pateroniso and the National Bank of Greece. It opened in 1990 and the benefactors were wealthy ship owners from the island. Many island families donated nautical memorabilia, which includes *objets d'art*, photographs, models of early ships, cannons and nautical instruments.

The museum opens 10 am to 1.30 pm daily. Admission is 400 dr.

Places to Stay & Eat

There is no camp site on the island and camping freelance would definitely be frowned upon. For domatia, ask at one of the restaurants or kafeneia. Good luck!

Inousses' one hotel is the comfortable, but rather bland-looking C class ***Hotel Thalassoporos*** *(☎ 55 475)*, at the top of the steps which lead to the village centre. Rates are 7000/10,000 dr for singles/doubles with bathroom. These prices drop to 5500/8500 dr in low season. It's unlikely ever to be full, but just in case, phone ahead in July and August.

Of Inousses' two restaurants, ***Restaurant Pateroniso*** *(☎ 55 586)* has been established the longest. The food is reasonably priced and well prepared. Alternatively at the far western end of the harbour is the little ***Zepagas*** fish restaurant. ***Remezzo*** is a small bar on the waterfront while ***Trigono*** bar is up in the village and mainly patronised by the few local young people left on the island.

The town has three grocery stores: one is near Restaurant Pateroniso and the other two are in the centre of the village on the road which leads up to the prominent Agios Nikolaos church.

ISLAND WALK

Although most of this three hour circular walk is along a narrow cement road, you are unlikely to meet much traffic. Take plenty of water and a snack with you as there are no refreshments available along the way. Also take your swimming gear as you will pass many of the island's beaches and coves.

Just beyond the maritime museum you will see a signpost to **Moni Evangelismou**. This will take you along the cement road which skirts the west coast. Along the way you will pass several inviting beaches and coves. Only **Apiganos Beach** is signposted, but there are others which are easily accessible from the road. After about one hour the road loops inland, and a little farther along is the entrance to the palatial Moni Evangelismou, surrounded by extensive grounds.

Within the convent is the mummified body of Irini Pateras, daughter of the late Panagos Pateras, a multimillionaire ship owner. Irini became a nun in her late teens and died in the early 1960s when she was 20. Her distraught mother decided to build the convent in memory of her daughter. In the Greek Orthodox religion, three years after burial the body is exhumed and the bones cleaned and reburied in a casket. When Irini's body was exhumed it was found to have mummified rather than decomposed; this phenomenon is regarded in Greece as evidence of sainthood. Irini's mother is now abbess of the convent, which houses around 20 nuns. Only women may visit the convent and of course they must be appropriately (modestly) dressed.

Continuing along the cement road, beyond the entrance to the convent, you will come to two stone pillars on the left. The wide path between the pillars leads in 10 minutes to an enormous white cross which is a **memorial** to St Irini. This is the highest point of the island and commands stunning views over to northern Chios and the Karaburun Peninsula in Turkey. About 20 minutes farther along, the cement road gives way to a dirt track. Continue straight ahead to reach Inousses Town.

Psara Ψαρά

☎ 0274 • postcode 821 04 • pop 500

Psara (psah-**rah**) lies off the north-west coast of Chios. The island is 9km long and 5km wide and is rocky with little vegetation. During Ottoman times Greeks settled on the remote island to escape Turkish oppression. By the 19th century, many of these inhabitants, like those of Chios and Inousses, had become successful ship owners. When the rallying cry for self-determination reverberated through the country, the Psariots zealously took up arms and contributed a large number of ships to the Greek cause. In retaliation the Turks stormed the island and killed all but 3000 of the 20,000 inhabitants. The island never regained its former glory and today all of the inhabitants live in the island's one settlement, also called Psara.

Like Inousses, Psara sees few tourists. The old parliament building has been converted into an ***EOT Guesthouse*** (☎ *61 293).* Doubles without/with bathroom are 6500/7500 dr. Information may be obtained by either telephoning the guesthouse or ringing ☎ 0251-27 908 in Lesvos. There are also ***domatia*** in Psara.

There are a small number of eating places on the island.

Getting There & Away

Ferries leave Chios Town for Psara at 7 am three times weekly. Check with a local

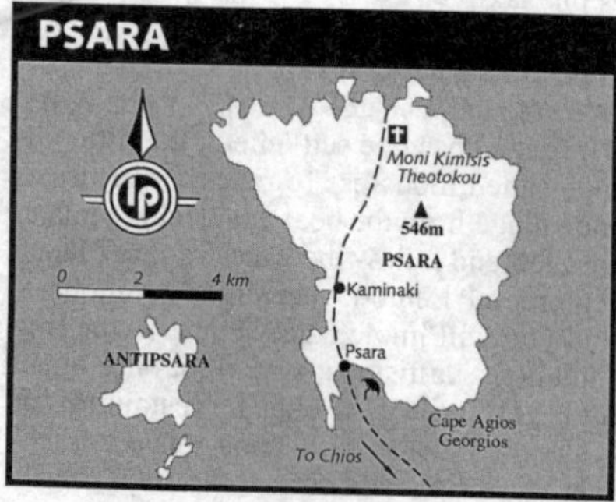

agent for current departure days since these may change from year to year. Local caïques also run from Limnos on the west coast, but departure times are unpredictable and often depend on the prevailing weather conditions.

Lesvos (Mytilini)
Λέσβος (Μυτιλήνη)

• **pop 88,800**

Lesvos is the third-largest island in Greece, after Crete and Evia. It lies north of Chios and south-east of Limnos. The island is mountainous with two bottleneck gulfs penetrating its south coast. The south and east of the island are fertile, with numerous olive groves. Lesvos produces the best olive oil in Greece and has many olive oil refineries. In contrast to the south and east, the west has rocky and barren mountains, creating a dramatic moonscape.

Lesvos is becoming a popular package-holiday destination, but is large enough to absorb tourists without seeming to be overrun. Most Greeks call the island Mytilini, which is also the name of the capital.

History

In the 6th century BC, Lesvos was unified under the rule of the tyrant Pittakos, one of ancient Greece's Seven Sages. Pittakos succeeded in resolving the long-standing animosity between the island's two cities of Mytilini and Mithymna. This new-found peace generated an atmosphere conducive to creativity, and Lesvos became a centre of artistic and philosophical achievement.

Terpander, the musical composer, and Arion, the poet, were both born on Lesvos in the 7th century BC. Arion's works influenced the tragedians of the 5th century BC such as Sophocles and Euripides. In the 4th century BC, Aristotle and Epicurus taught at an exceptional school of philosophy which flourished on Lesvos.

Sappho, one of the greatest poets of ancient Greece, was born on Lesvos around 630 BC. Unfortunately little of her poetry is extant, but what remains reveals a genius for combining passion with simplicity and detachment, in verses of great beauty and power.

On a more prosaic level, Lesvos suffered at the hands of invaders and occupiers to the same extent as all other Greek islands. In 527 BC the Persians conquered the island,

Sappho

Sappho is renowned chiefly for her poems that speak out in favour of lesbian relationships, though her range of lyric poetry extends beyond works of an erotic nature. She was born in 630 BC in the town of Eresos on the western side of Lesvos. Little is known about her private life other than that she was married, had a daughter and was exiled to Sicily in about 600 BC. Only fragments remain of her nine books of poems, the most famous of which are the marriage songs. Among her works were hymns, mythological poems and personal love songs. Most of these seem to have been addressed to a close inner-circle of female companions. Sappho uses sensuous images of nature to create her own special brand of erotic lyric poetry. It is a simple yet melodious style, later copied by the Roman poet Catullus.

Lesvos, and Eresos in particular, is today visited by many lesbians paying homage to Sappho.

MARTIN HARRIS

but in 479 BC it was captured by Athens and became a member of the Delian League. In the following centuries the island suffered numerous invasions, and in 88 BC it was conquered by Julius Caesar. Byzantines, Venetians, Genoese and Turks followed.

However, through all these vicissitudes the arts retained a high degree of importance. The primitive painter Theophilos (1866-1934) and the Nobel Prize-winning poet Odysseus Elytis were both born on Lesvos. The island is to this day a spawning ground for innovative ideas in the arts and politics, and is the headquarters of the University of the Aegean.

Trekking

Lesvos has an admirably well organised and well publicised set of trekking trails in the north and south of the island. These are marked with colour coded, easily spotted signs and cover a wide variety of landscapes. Get a copy of the booklet *Trekking Trails on Lesvos* from the Tourism Directorate of the North Aegean (☎ 0251-42 511), PO Box 37, Mytilini GR-811 00, or from any good EOT office. These walks can be taken in sections, or over a few days, stopping off along the way wherever appropriate. They are a mixture of dirt vehicle tracks and walking-only trails. The four trails are:

Vatera to Gera – This is a longish trail that leads from the beach enclave of Vatera over some of Lesvos' finest forest and mountain scenery to Gera on the gulf of the same name. This trail is marked by a sign with a yellow circle.

Petra to Lapsarna – This route takes you along the north coast of Lesvos from the resort of Petra to Lapsarna in the far west mainly along walking-only trails. This is a beautiful walk for beachcombers. The trail is marked by a sign with a yellow square.

Kapi to Sykamia – This route circles Mt Lepetymnos in northern Lesvos and traverses ravines covered with olive groves, poplar and oak trees and passes through a number of villages. This route is marked by a sign with a yellow triangle.

Sigri to Eresos – This route crosses the barren landscape of south western Lesvos between the two villages of Sigri and Eresos and follows the old road all the way, skirting the forest of petrified trees. This is an easy day trek. This route is marked by a sign with a yellow oblong.

Bird-Watching

Bird-watching – or 'birding', as the experts call it – is big business in Lesvos. The island is the transit point and home to over 279 species of birds ranging from raptors to waders. As a result, Lesvos is attracting an ever-increasing number of visitors – both human and feathered – particularly in spring. There are four main observation areas centred on Eresos, Petra, Skala Kallonis and Agiasos.

The major aim of birders seems to be spotting the elusive Cinereous bunting and Kruper's nuthatch. At any rate it is a growing and popular activity – birders seem to be more numerous than birds at times.

A folksy and detailed handbook to the hobby is Richard Brooks' *Birding in Lesbos*, which retails for a fairly steep 7500 dr on Lesvos, but is probably the most authoritative, and entertaining, book on the topic. Fax 44-1328-878 632 for further distribution details.

Getting There & Away

Air There are five flights daily from Lesvos to Athens (17,100 dr) and one daily to Thessaloniki (20,900 dr), as well as two flights weekly to Chios (10,900 dr) and weekly flights to Limnos (13,400 dr). Note that Lesvos is always referred to as Mytilini on air schedules. The Olympic Airways office (☎ 0251-28 659) in Mytilini is at Kavetsou 44 (Kavetsou is a southerly continuation of Ermou). The airport is 8km south of Mytilini. A taxi to/from the airport will cost about 1000 dr.

Ferry – Domestic In summer there is at least one ferry daily to Piraeus (12 hours, 6700 dr) via Chios and some direct services (10 hours), three weekly to Kavala (11 hours, 5700 dr) via Limnos, and two weekly to Thessaloniki (13 hours, 8300 dr) via Limnos. Ferry ticket offices line the eastern side of Pavlou Kountouriotou, in Mytilini. Get tickets for the above destinations from the Maritime Company of Lesvos (NEL) (☎ 0251-28 480, fax 28 601), Pavlou Kountouriotou 67.

The port police (☎ 0251-28 827) are next to Picolo Travel on the east side of Pavlou Kountouriotou.

Ferry – International Ferries to Ayvalık in Turkey run roughly five times weekly in season. There is a Turkish boat, *Yeni Istanbul,* plus two or three boats owned by Miniotis Lines from Chios. One-way tickets cost 16,000 dr (including port taxes) and return tickets cost 21,000 dr. A small car costs 18,000/23,000 dr one way/return. Tickets are available from Aeolic Cruises (☎ 0251-23 266, fax 34 694) at Kountouriotou 47.

Getting Around

Bus Lesvos' transport hub is the capital, Mytilini. In summer, from the long-distance bus station (☎ 0251-28 873) there are three buses daily to Skala Eresou (2½ hours, 1950 dr) via Eresos. There are five buses daily to Mithymna (1¾ hours, 1350 dr) via Petra, and two buses to Sigri (2½ hours, 2000 dr). There are no direct buses between Eresos, Sigri and Mithymna. If you wish to travel from one of these villages to another, change buses in the town of Kalloni, which is 48km from Eresos and 22km from Mithymna. There are five buses daily to the south coast resort of Plomari (1¼ hours, 900 dr).

Car & Motorcycle The many car hire outlets in Mytilini include Troho Kinisi (☎ 0251-41 160, mobile 0932-237 900), which operates from the Erato Hotel just south of the Olympic Airways office, and Lesvos Car (☎ 0251-28 242), Pavlou Kountouriotou 47.

Many motorcycle rental firms are located along the same stretch of waterfront. You will, however, be better off hiring a motorcycle or scooter in Mithymna or Skala Eresou, since Lesvos is a large island and an underpowered two-wheeler is not really a practical mode of transport for getting around.

MYTILINI Μυτιλήνη

☎ 0251 • postcode 811 00 • pop 23,970

Mytilini, the capital and port of Lesvos, is a large workaday town. If you are enthralled by pretty and sparkling towns like Mykonos and Paros then you won't necessarily find the same ambience in Mytilini. However, this town has its own attractions including a lively harbour and nightlife, its once-grand 19th century mansions (which are gradually being renovated), and its jumbled streets.

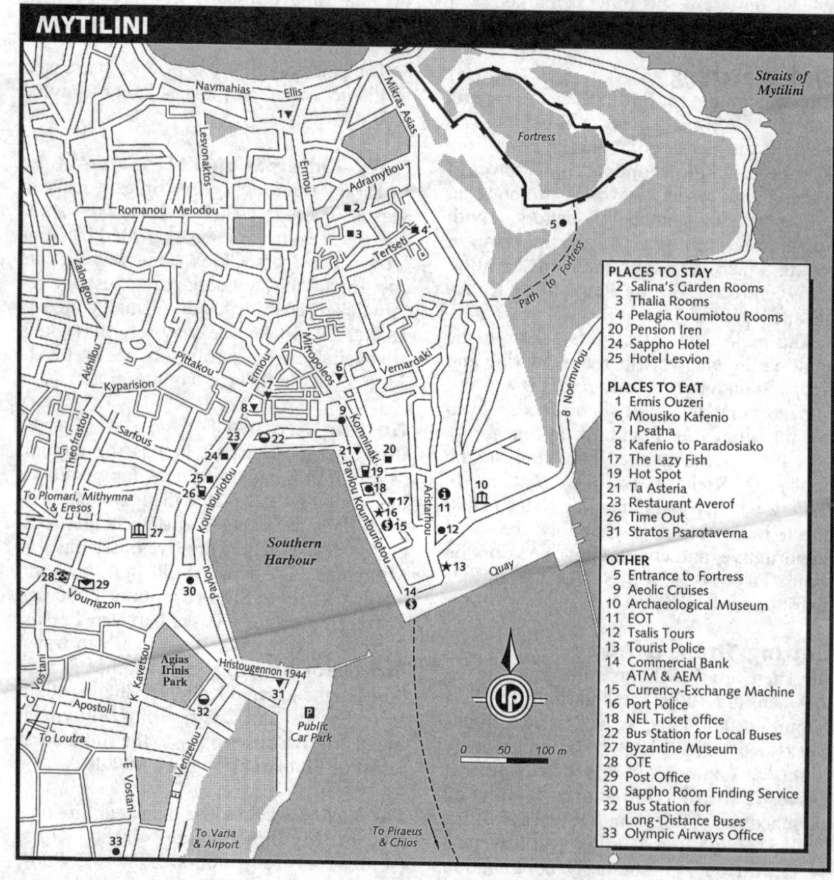

Mytilini won't enthral sun, sea and sand lovers. The town beach is mediocre, crowded and you have to pay to use it (adults 200 dr, children 100 dr). However, you will appreciate Mytilini if you enjoy seeking out traditional kafeneia and little backstreet ouzeria, or if you simply take pleasure in wandering through unfamiliar towns.

The northern end of Ermou, the town's main commercial thoroughfare, is a wonderful ramshackle street full of character. It has old-fashioned *zaharoplasteia*, grocers, fruit and vegetable stores, bakers, and antique, embroidery, ceramic and jewellery shops.

Orientation

Mytilini is built around two harbours (north and south) which occupy both sides of a promontory and are linked by the main thoroughfare of Ermou. East of the harbours is a large fortress surrounded by a pine forest. All passenger ferries dock at the southern harbour. The waterfront here is called Pavlou Kountouriotou and the ferry quay is at its southern end. The northern harbour's waterfront is called Navmahias Ellis.

Information

The EOT has an office close to the quay at Aristarhou 6. The tourist police (☎ 22 776) have an office at the entrance to the quay.

Tsalis Tours (☎ 42 174, fax 21 481, email tsalis@otenet.gr) is an independent travel agency which is very helpful to travellers seeking accommodation, car hire or tour bookings. It is a few doors away from the EOT at Aristarhou 2. Further information on Lesvos can be found on the Web at www.greeknet.com.

Banks, including the National Bank of Greece with an ATM, can be found on Pavlou Kountouriotou. There is also an ATM and an exchange machine at the Commercial Bank booth on this street, near the ferry terminal. The post office is on Vournazon, west of the southern harbour. The OTE is on the same street just west of the post office.

Things to See

Mytilini's imposing **castle** with its well preserved walls was built in early Byzantine times, renovated in the 14th century by Fragistco Gatelouzo, and subsequently enlarged by the Turks. The surrounding pine forest is a pleasant place for a picnic. The castle is open 8.30 am to 3 pm daily. Admission is 500 dr, 300 dr for students.

The **archaeological museum** (☎ 22 087) is housed in a neoclassical mansion one block north of the quay and has impressive finds from Neolithic to Roman times. Opening times are 8.30 am to 3 pm Tuesday to Sunday. Admission is 500 dr.

The dome of the **Church of Agios Therapon** can be spotted from almost anywhere on the southern waterfront. The church has a highly ornate interior with a huge chandelier, an intricately carved iconostasis and priest's throne, and a frescoed dome. The **Byzantine Museum** (☎ 28 916) in the church's courtyard houses some fine icons. The museum is open 10 am to 1 pm Monday to Saturday. Admission is 300 dr.

Whatever you do, don't miss the **Theophilos Museum** (☎ 41 644), which houses the works of the prolific primitive painter Theophilos, who was born on Lesvos. Several prestigious museums and galleries around the country now proudly display his works. However, he lived in abject poverty, painting the walls of kafeneia and tavernas in return for sustenance. The museum is open 8.30 am to 1.30 pm and 5.30 to 8 pm Tuesday to Sunday. Admission is 500 dr.

The **Teriade Museum** (☎ 23 372), next door, commemorates the artist and critic Stratis Eleftheriadis (he Gallicised his name to Teriade) who was born on Lesvos but lived and worked in Paris. It was largely due to Teriade's efforts that Theophilos' work gained international renown. On display are reproductions of Teriade's own illustrations and his collection of works by 20th century artists, including such greats as Picasso, Chagail and Matisse. The museum is open 8.30 am to 1.30 pm and 5.30 to 8 pm Tuesday to Sunday. Admission is 500 dr.

STELLA HELLANDER

The dome of the Church of Agios Therapon is a feature of Mytilini's charming waterfront

These museums are 4km from Mytilini in the village of **Varia** where Theophilos was born. Take a local bus from the bus station at the northernmost section of Pavlou Kountouriotou.

Places to Stay – Budget

In Mytilini, domatia owners belong to a cooperative called Sappho Room Finding Service. There are 28 establishments; if any of the ones recommended are full or don't suit, the owner will direct you to another. Most of these domatia are in little side streets off Ermou, near the northern harbour. The nearest to the quay is ***Iren*** *(☎ 22 787, Komninaki 41)*. The clean and simply furnished doubles/triples cost 8000/10,000 dr with breakfast. Komninaki is one block behind the eastern section of Pavlou Kountouriotou. ***Salina's Garden Rooms*** *(☎ 42 073, Fokeas 7)* are cosy and clean with a delightful garden. Doubles are 7000/7500 dr without/with bathroom. The rooms are signposted from the corner of Ermou and Adramytiou.

Coming from Ermou, if you turn right opposite Salina's rooms you will reach ***Thalia Rooms*** *(☎ 24 640, Kinikiou 1)*. The pleasant doubles/triples in this large family house are 7000/8000 dr with bathroom. ***Pelagia Koumiotou Rooms*** *(☎ 20 643, Tertseti 6)*, in an old family house near the castle, are lovely. Rates are 6500/8000 dr for doubles/triples. Walk along Mikras Asias and turn left into Tertseti; the rooms are on the right.

Places to Stay – Mid-Range

There are several hotels on the southern waterfront, but you will pay more at these than in the domatia. The C class ***Sappho Hotel*** *(☎ 22 888, fax 24 522, Kountouriotou 31)*, on the west side of the harbour, has singles/doubles for 9500/14,000 dr with bathroom. The more luxurious B class ***Hotel Lesvion*** *(☎ 22 037, fax 42 493,*

Kountouriotou 27a), just two doors away, has rooms for 10,000/17,500 dr which can usually be negotiated for a better deal.

Places to Eat

You will eat well on Lesvos whether you enjoy fish dishes, traditional Greek food, international cuisine or vegetarian meals. You might wish to avoid the restaurants on the western section of the southern waterfront where the waiters tout for customers. These restaurants are atypical of Mytilini as they pander to tourists and serve bland, overpriced food.

The small, mildly ramshackle but delightfully atmospheric ***Ermis Ouzeri*** *(☎ 26 232, Kornarou 2)* has yet to be discovered by the mass tourist crowd. It is at the north end of Ermou on the corner with Kornarou. Its interior is decorated with scattered antiques, old watercolour paintings and old black and white photos of previous clients. A mezedes style meal with beer will cost around 2300 dr. Closer to the main harbour, locals congregate at ***Kafenio to Paradosiako*** *(Thasou 3)*, a little ouzeri with tables that spill out into the street.

Restaurant Averof, in the middle of the southern waterfront, is a no-nonsense traditional restaurant serving hearty Greek staples like *patsas* (tripe soup), while ***Ta Asteria*** on the opposite side of the harbour is slightly more upmarket and serves similar food for slightly higher prices.

If you want some good value meat dishes, check out ***I Psatha*** (winter only) on Methodiou, off Ermou. There is an old jukebox that actually works. For top quality fish dishes, go to ***Stratos Psarotaverna*** *(☎ 21 739)*, on Hristougennon 1944, at the bottom end of the main harbour. It is more upmarket in price. Tables from all the surrounding restaurants take over the road in summer.

For a good beer and a decent meal try ***The Lazy Fish*** *(☎ 44 831, Imvrou 5)*. The restaurant is set back from the southern end of Komninaki and is a bit difficult to find – look for a stone building with black wrought-iron wall lamps at the entrance.

Entertainment

Mousiko Kafenio, on the corner of Mitropoleos and Vernardaki, is a hip place – arty without being pretentious. Drinks are in the mid-price range rather than cheap, but worth it for the terrific atmosphere. Tapes of jazz, blues and classical music are played, and there is live music on Wednesday evenings (winter only) – usually jazz. The cafe is open 7.30 am to 2 am. Another couple of 'in' places are ***Time Out*** on the west side of the harbour and ***Hot Spot*** on the east side. Both are popular with students and at the latter you can borrow board games.

Getting There & Away

Mytilini has two bus stations: the one for long-distance buses is just beyond the south-western end of Pavlou Kountouriotou; the bus station for buses to local villages is on the northernmost section of Pavlou Kountouriotou. For motorists, there is a large free parking area just south of the main harbour.

NORTHERN LESVOS

Northern Lesvos is dominated both economically and physically by the exquisitely preserved traditional town of Mithymna, a town of historical, and modern, importance in Lesvos' commercial life. The neighbouring beach resort of Petra, 6km south, receives low-key package tourism and the villages surrounding Mt Lepetymnos are authentic, picturesque and worth a day or two of exploration.

Mithymna Μήθυμνα

☎ 0253 • postcode 811 08 • pop 1333

Although this town has officially reverted to its ancient name of Mithymna (Methymna), most locals still refer to it as **Molyvos**. It is 62km from Mytilini and is the principal town of northern Lesvos. The one-time rival to Mytilini, picturesque Mithymna is nowadays the antithesis of the island capital. Its impeccable stone houses with brightly coloured shutters reach down to the harbour from a castle-crowned hill. Its two main thoroughfares of Kastrou and 17 Noemvriou are winding, cobbled and shaded by vines. In contrast to Mytilini, Mithymna's pretty streets are lined with souvenir shops.

Orientation & Information From the bus stop, walk straight ahead towards the town. Where the road forks, take the right fork into 17 Noemvriou. At the top of the hill, the road forks again; the right fork is Kastrou and the post office is along here on the left. The left fork is a continuation of 17 Noemvriou.

There is a small municipal tourist office (☎ 71 347) on the left, between the bus stop and the fork in the road. The National Bank of Greece is on the left, next to the tourist office and sports an ATM. There is also a Commercial Bank booth with an ATM directly opposite.

Things to See & Do One of the most pleasant things to do in Mithymna is to stroll along its gorgeous streets. If you have the energy, the ruined 14th century **Genoese castle** is worth clambering up to for fine views of the coastline and over the sea to Turkey. From this castle in the 15th century, Onetta d'Oria, wife of the Genoese governor, repulsed an onslaught by the Turks by putting on her husband's armour and leading the people of Mithymna into battle. In summer the castle is the venue for a drama festival; ask for details at the tourist office. The castle is open 8.30 am to 5 pm daily. Admission is 500 dr.

The beach at Mithymna is pebbled and crowded, but in summer excursion boats leave daily at 10 am for the superior beaches of Eftalou, Skala Sykaminias, Petra and Anaxos.

Places to Stay – Budget The excellent and refreshingly shady camp site, ***Camping Mithymna*** *(☎ 71 169)*, is 1.5km from town and signposted from near the tourist office. It opens in early June, though you can usually camp if you arrive a bit earlier than that. For one person with a tent it costs 1550 dr.

There are over 50 official domatia in Mithymna; most consist of only one or two rooms. All display domatia signs and most are of a high standard. The municipal tourist office will help you if you can't be bothered looking; otherwise, the best street to start at is 17 Noemvriou. Among the first signposted rooms you will come to are those of ***Nassos Guest House*** *(☎ 71 022)* on Arionos, which leads off to the right. The rooms are simply furnished and most have a panoramic view. The cost is 6000 dr.

A beautifully restored stone building on Myrasillou houses the ***domatia*** of Myrsina Baliaka *(☎ 71 414)*. From the bus stop walk towards the town and take the second right by the cardphone. The domatia are 50m on your right. Look out for the prominent green shutters. A double room will cost around 7500 dr.

Places to Stay – Mid-Range A pleasant C class hotel is ***Hotel Eftalou*** *(☎ 71 584, fax 71 669, email parmakel@otenet.gr)*, among the cluster of small, low-key resort hotels on the road out to Eftalou. A comfortable double goes for 12,000 dr in the low season and 17,000 dr in the high season. There's a swimming pool and restaurant to boot.

Nearby are the secluded ***Eftalou Villas*** *(☎ 22 662, fax 26 535, email dimopulu@otenet.gr)*, each with a different name and sleeping from four to eight people. A villa for four ranges in price from 16,000 dr to 20,000 dr, depending on the season.

An older but superior hotel is ***Hotel Delfinia*** (*☎ 71 315, fax 71 524, email delfinia@otenet.gr*). It caters mainly to packages, but is very accommodating to independent travellers. Single/double room rates in high season are 14,900/19,650 dr. It is 1km out of Mithymna on the road to Petra.

Places to Eat The streets 17 Noemvriou and Kastrou have a wide choice of restaurants serving typical Greek fare. Look out for ***Nassos***, ***Gatos***, ***Asteria tis Molyvou*** and ***To Hani***, most of which have fine views over the sea. For more of a fishing-village ambience, head down to the far end of the little harbour where there is a clutch of eating places, the best of which is the Australian-Greek ***Captain's Table*** *(☎ 71 241)*.

PAUL HELLANDER

embetika musician, Molyvos (Mithymna)

MARK DAFFEY

Grand Meteora Monastery, Meteora

CHRIS MELLOR

Colonnades, ancient Olympia, home of the games

MARK DAFFEY

Black sand beach at Kamari, Santorini (Cyclades)

DIANA MAYFIELD

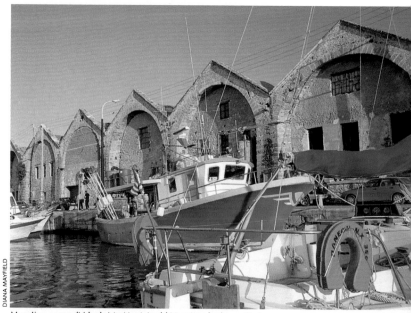

Venetian *arsenali* (docks) in Hania's old Venetian harbour, Crete

NEIL SETCHFIELD

Evzones (ceremonial guards) at parliament building, Athens

The mezedes are exquisite: try *adjuka* – a Ukrainian-inspired spicy aubergine dish – or the unique spinach salad. There is live bouzouki music once a week and Melinda and her husband Theodoros will make you more than welcome.

Petra Πέτρα

☎ 0253 • postcode 811 09 • pop 1150

Petra, 5km south of Mithymna, is a popular coastal resort with a long sandy beach shaded by tamarisk trees. Despite tourist development it remains an attractive village retaining some traditional houses. Petra means 'rock' and looming over the village is an enormous, almost perpendicular rock which looks as if it's been lifted from Meteora in Thessaly. The rock is crowned by the 18th century Panagia Glykophilousa (Church of the Sweet Kissing Virgin). You can reach it by climbing up the 114 rock-hewn steps – worth it for the view. Petra, like many settlements on Lesvos, is a 'preserved' village. It has not and will not make any concessions to the concrete monstrosities that characterise tourist development elsewhere in Greece.

Petra has a post office, OTE, bank, medical facilities and bus connections.

Places to Stay There are around 120 private rooms available in Petra, but your best bet for accommodation is to head straight for Greece's First Women's Agricultural Tourism Collective (☎ 41 238, fax 41 309). The women can arrange for you to stay with a family in the village where you will pay around 5000/7000 dr for a single/double room. The office is on the central square – signposted from the waterfront.

Of the cluster of small pensions at the western end of Petra's waterfront, ***Studio Niki*** *(☎ 41 601)* is a good bet. Neat double/triple rooms with kitchenette go for around 8500 dr. Bookings are recommended in peak season.

Places to Eat ***Syneterismos*** *(☎ 41 238)*, belonging to the Women's Agricultural Tourism Collective, has mouth-watering moussaka and Greek salad for about 2000 dr. There's a gamut of eateries along the waterfront, all pandering to the tourist and Greek palate alike.

The most outstanding restaurant both in service and food quality is ***Pittakos***, housed in an old building at the western end of the waterfront. Fresh fish, while always on the expensive side, is cooked to perfection here. Romantic tables for two are perched at the water's edge.

To Tyhero Petalo towards the eastern end, has attractive decor and sells ready-made food for around 1300 dr for a main course dish. For a change of scenery and a meal with a view, head up to ***Taverna tou Ilia*** *(☎ 71 536)* at Vafios, 8km inland from Mithymna. The food is top-notch.

WESTERN LESVOS

Western Lesvos is quite different from the rest of the island and this becomes apparent almost immediately as you wind westward out of Kalloni. The landscape becomes drier and barer and there are fewer settlements, though when they do appear they look very tidy and their red-tiled roofs add vital colour to an otherwise mottled green-brown landscape. The far western end is almost devoid of trees other than the petrified kind. Here you will find Lesvos' 'petrified forest' on a windswept and barren hillside. One resort, a remote fishing village, and the birthplace of Sappho are what attract people to western Lesvos.

Eresos & Skala Eresou

Ερεσός & Σκάλα Ερεσού

☎ 0253 • postcode 881 05 • pop 1560

Eresos, 90km from Mytilini, is a traditional inland village. It is reached via the road junction just after the hillside village of Andissa. The road leading down to Eresos, through what looks like a moonscape, belies what is ahead. Beyond the village of Eresos a riotously fertile agricultural plain leads to Eresos' beach annexe, Skala Eresou, which is 4km beyond on the west coast. It is a popular resort linked to Eresos by an attractive, very straight tree-lined road. A new sealed road links Eresos with Kalloni via Parakila and Agra.

Skala Eresou is built over ancient Eresos where Sappho (628-568 BC) was born. Although it gets crowded in summer it has a good, laid-back atmosphere. It is also a popular destination for lesbians who come on a kind of pilgrimage in honour of the poet. If you're a beach-lover you should certainly visit – there is almost 2km of coarse silvery-brown sand. Nudists congregate beyond the river, while lesbians tend to hang out near the river mouth.

Orientation & Information From the bus turnaround at Skala Eresou, walk towards the sea to reach the central square of Plateia Anthis & Evristhenous abutting the waterfront. The beach stretches to the left and right of this square. Turn right at the square onto Gyrinnis and just under 50m along you will come to a sign pointing left to the post office; the OTE is next door.

There is no EOT or tourist police, but Philippos at Krinellos Travel (☎ 53 246, 53 982, email krinellos@otenet.gr), close to the main square, is very helpful. He can arrange accommodation, car, motorcycle and bicycle hire and treks on foot or on horses and donkeys. Neither Skala Eresou nor Eresos has a bank but there is a prominent exchange machine and ATM.

Things to See Eresos' **archaeological museum** houses Archaic, classical Greek and Roman finds including statues, coins and grave stelae. The museum, in the centre of Skala Eresou, stands near the remains of the early Christian Basilica of Agios Andreas. Opening times are 8.30 am to 3 pm Tuesday to Sunday. Admission is free.

The **petrified forest**, as the EOT hyperbolically refers to this scattering of ancient tree stumps, is near the village of Sigri, on the west coast north of Skala Eresou. Experts reckon the petrified wood is at least 500,000, but possibly 20 million, years old. If you're intrigued, the forest is easiest reached as an excursion from Skala Eresou; inquire at Exeresis Travel. If you're making your own way, the turn-off to the forest is signposted 7km before the village of Sigri.

Places to Stay There are a few domatia in Eresos but most people head for Skala Eresou, where there are a number of domatia, pensions and hotels. ***Rooms to Let Katia*** *(☎ 53 148)*, at the eastern end of the waterfront, has comfortable singles/doubles with a view for 7000/10,000 dr.

The C class ***Sappho Hotel*** *(☎ 53 233, fax 53 174)* is a small women-only hotel on the waterfront with rooms for 7000/12,000 dr. It can be noisy here, though.

Skala Eresou's best hotel is the C class ***Hotel Galini*** *(☎ 53 137, fax 53 155)*. Its light and airy rooms cost 8000/10,000 dr for rooms with bathroom. The hotel has a comfortable TV room-cum-bar and an outside terrace under a bamboo shade. It is clearly signposted.

Places to Eat The shady promenade offers many eating options, most with beach and sea views across to Chios and Psara. ***Gorgona*** *(☎ 53 320)* with its stone-clad facade is as good a place to start as any. Sample its tasty, stuffed courgettes in lemon sauce. Excellent Greek home cooking can be found at ***Egeo*** *(☎ 53 608)* in the middle of the waterfront. Try its stuffed tomatoes or moussaka. Prices at both establishments are mid-range to budget.

Yamas *(☎ 53 693)* is a pancake and snack joint run by Canadians Nick and Linda. Here you can get home-made North American cooking and chocolate cake. You can also listen to 70s music, and the occasional jam takes place when the mood takes over. Chill out with a cold beer on their comfy, shaded sofas overlooking the beach.

Bennett's Restaurant *(☎ 53 624)* is an English-run establishment owned by Max and Jackie and offers a good menu selection, including vegetarian and Asian, at the eastern end of the waterfront. Prices are mid-range.

Tenth Muse on the square is the current favourite gay bar, though in practice it attracts a mixed clientele. ***Mariannas*** on the promenade is another popular watering hole.

SOUTHERN LESVOS

Southern Lesvos is dominated by Mt Olympus (968m). Pine forests decorate its flanks, though in recent years fires have ravaged large sections – particularly the steep slopes north of the resort town of Plomari.

The large village of **Agiasos** on the northern flank of Mt Olympus features prominently in most local tourist publications and is a popular day-trip destination. Agiasos is very picturesque but not tacky, with artisan workshops making anything from handcrafted furniture to pottery. Its winding, cobbled streets will eventually lead you to the church of the Panagia Vrefokratousa with its Byzantine Museum and Popular Museum in the courtyard.

A couple of restaurants near the bus stop are perhaps your best bet for eating in Agiasos. One of these is ***Anatoli*** and the other is a nameless ***psistaria*** owned by Grigoris Douladellis.

Plomari on the south coast is a cramped and crumbling resort. A large, traditional village, it also has a laid-back beach settlement. It is not too exciting, but is very popular with Scandinavian tourists who are lured by cheap accommodation, but end up paying for it with expensive food. Most people stay at **Agios Isidoros**, 3km to the east where there is a narrow, overcrowded beach.

A far superior option is the low-key family resort of **Vatera** over to the east and reached via the inland town of **Polyhnitos**. This relaxing oasis has a very good, clean 9km-long beach and widely scattered hotels, domatia and restaurants.

There is one camp site here: ***Camping Dionysos*** *(☎ 0252-61 151, fax 61 155)*. It's quite good, if somewhat small, but has a pool, minimarket, restaurant and cooking facilities. It is set back about 100m from the beach. Open 1 June to 30 September, it charges about 1700 dr per person with tent.

Your best eating and accommodation option by far is the modern C class ***Hotel Vatera Beach*** *(☎ 0252-61 212, fax 61 164,*

Fascinating Fossil Find

Lesvos is hardly the kind of place that you would associate with great excitement in the musty and dusty world of palaeontology. Nonetheless, the island has been thrust onto centre stage recently with the extraordinary discovery of fossils of animals, fish and plants at Vatera, a sleepy beach resort on the south coast of Lesvos, hitherto more associated with sun and sand than fossilised fish.

Among the fossils found in the Vatera region are elephants, mastodons, giraffes, bones of rhinoceros and hippopotamus, deer, tortoises, snails, fish, and pieces of a gigantic prehistoric horse. Dated up to 5.5 million years old, the fossils are being temporarily displayed at the newly established Museum of Natural History in the neighbouring village of Vrissa, just 2km from the excavation sites.

Dr Michael Dermitzakis, Athens University Professor of Palaeontology, formally announced his findings recently. He considers the collection of fossilised mammals found at Vatera to be unique to the entire Mediterranean area. During the continuing excavations, hundreds of important finds have been noted. Geological scientists maintain that the site was originally a large lake surrounded by forests in which many varieties of prehistoric animals lived.

The rarity and importance of these finds cannot be overemphasised. They have created enormous interest within the international scientific community, and for visitors who have the opportunity to view these unusual finds in their natural setting at Vatera.

email hovatera@otenet.gr). American-Greek owners George and Barbara Ballis provide a relaxed environment and offer chronic stress relief for burned-out members of the rat race. Excellent Greek home cooking tops it all off. A double room ranges in price from 11,200 dr to 15,500 dr depending on the season.

Limnos Λήμνος

☎ 0254 • pop 16,000

There is a saying on Limnos that when people come to the island they cry twice: once when they arrive and once when they leave. Limnos' appeal is not immediate; its charm slowly but surely captivates.

The deeply penetrating Moudros Bay almost severs the island in two. The landscape of Limnos lacks the imposing grandeur of the forested and mountainous islands and the stark beauty of the barren and rocky ones. Gently undulating, with little farms, Limnos has a unique and understated appeal. In spring vibrant wild flowers dot the landscape, and in autumn purple crocuses sprout forth in profusion. Large numbers of flamingoes grace the lakes of eastern Limnos and the coastline boasts some of the best beaches in the North-Eastern Aegean group. The island is sufficiently off the beaten track to have escaped the adverse effects of mass tourism.

History

Limnos' position near the Straits of the Dardanelles, midway between the Mt Athos Peninsula and Turkey, has given it a traumatic history. To this day it maintains a large garrison, and jets from the huge air base loudly punctuate the daily routine.

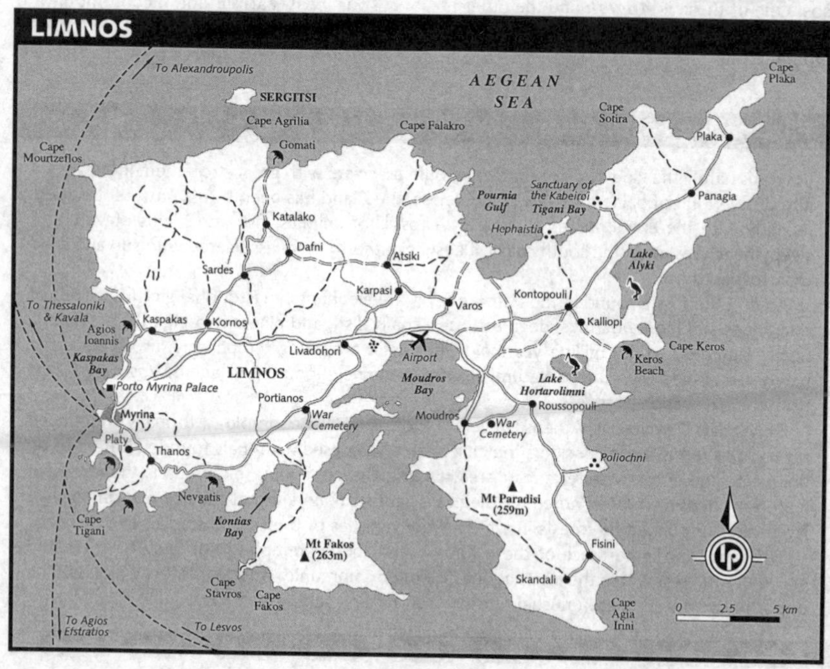

Limnos had advanced Neolithic and Bronze Age civilisations, and during these times had contact with peoples in western Anatolia, including the Trojans. In classical times the twin sea gods, the Kabeiroi, were worshipped at a sanctuary on the island, but later the Sanctuary of the Great Gods on Samothraki became the centre of this cult.

During the Peloponnesian Wars, Limnos sided with Athens and suffered many Persian attacks. After the split of the Roman Empire in 395 AD it became an important outpost of Byzantium. In 1462 it came under the domination of the Genoese who ruled Lesvos. The Turks succeeded in conquering the island in 1478 and Limnos remained under Turkish rule until 1912. Moudros Bay was the Allies' base for the disastrous Gallipoli campaign in WWI.

Getting There & Away

Air In summer there are two flights daily to Limnos from Athens (15,000 dr), five weekly from Thessaloniki (15,200 dr) and a weekly flight from Lesvos (13,400 dr). The Olympic Airways office (☎ 22 214) is on Nikolaou Garoufallidou, opposite Hotel Paris, in Myrina.

The airport is 22km east of Myrina. An Olympic Airways bus from Myrina to the airport (1000 dr) connects with all flights.

Ferry In summer four ferries go weekly from Limnos to Kavala (five hours, 3700 dr), and to Rafina (10 hours, 5500 dr) via Agios Efstratios (1½ hours, 1600 dr), and one via Sigri in Lesvos (six hours, 3200 dr). There are also three boats weekly to Chios (11 hours, 5300 dr), three to Piraeus via Lesvos and Chios, and one to Piraeus directly (13 hours, 7000 dr). There are two boats weekly to Thessaloniki (seven hours, 5300 dr) and Kavala (4½ hours, 3100 dr), and two to Alexandroupolis (five hours, 3300 dr) via Samothraki (three hours, 1600 dr).

Aiolis, a small local ferry, does the run to Agios Efstratios (2½ hours, 1600 dr) three times weekly on Monday, Wednesday and Friday. Tickets can be bought at Myrina Tourist & Travel Agency (☎ 22 460, fax 23 560, email root@mirina.lim.forthnet.gr) on the harbourfront in Myrina.

Hydrofoil In July and August there are two hydrofoils weekly to and from Alexandroupolis (three hours, 6600 dr) via Samothraki (1½ hours, 5000 dr). Purchase tickets from Myrina Tourist & Travel Agency.

Excursion Boat In July and August the *Aiolis* does a couple of extra day returns per week to the small island of Agios Efstratios (see Agios Efstratios, later in the chapter, for details). The boat usually leaves at about 8 am and returns from Agios Efstratios at 5 pm. The excursion fare is around 5000 dr.

Getting Around

Bus Bus services on Limnos are poor. In summer there are two buses daily from Myrina to most of the villages. Check the schedule (only in Greek) at the bus station (☎ 22 464) on Plateia Eleftheriou Venizelou.

Car & Motorcycle In Myrina, cars and jeeps can be rented from Myrina Rent a Car (☎ 24 476, fax 22 484) on Kyda near the waterfront. Prices range from 10,000 dr to 15,000 dr for a small car or jeep, depending on the season. There are several motorcycle hire outlets on Kyda.

MYRINA Μύρινα

• postcode 814 00 • pop 4340

Myrina is the capital and port of Limnos. Surrounded by massive hunks of volcanic rock, it is not immediately perceived as a picturesque town, but it is animated, full of character and unfettered by establishments pandering to tourism.

The main thoroughfare of Kyda is a charming paved street with clothing stores, traditional shops selling nuts and honey, old-fashioned kafeneia and barber shops – the latter are testimony to the island's military presence. Down the side streets you'll see (interspersed with modern buildings) little whitewashed stone dwellings, decaying neoclassical mansions and 19th century wattle-and-daub houses with overhanging wooden balconies. A Genoese castle looms dramatically over the town.

Orientation & Information

From the end of the quay turn right onto Plateia Ilia Iliou. Continue along the waterfront passing the Hotel Lemnos and the town hall. A little farther along you will see the Hotel Aktaion, set back from the waterfront. Turn left here, then immediately veer half-left onto Kyda. Proceeding up here you will reach the central square where the National Bank of Greece and the OTE are located. The taxi rank (☎ 23 033) is also on this square. Continue up Kyda and take the next turn right onto Nikolaou Garoufallidou. The post office is here on the right. Back on Kyda, continue for another 100m and you will come to Plateia Eleftheriou Venizelou where you will see the bus station.

There is a small tourist information kiosk on the quay. A laundrette (☎ 24 392) is on Nikolaou Garoufallidou, opposite the Olympic Airways office. The police station (☎ 22 201) is at the far end of Nikolaou Garoufallidou – on the right coming from Kyda. The port police (☎ 22 225) are on the waterfront near the quay.

Things to See & Do

As with any Greek island **castle**, the one towering over Myrina is worth climbing up to. From its vantage point there are magnificent views over the sea to Mt Athos. As you walk from the harbour, take the first side street to the left by an old Turkish fountain. An inconspicuous sign here points you to the castle.

Myrina has a lovely long sandy **beach** right in town. It stretches north from the castle and can be reached by walking along Kyda from the harbour, and taking any of the streets off to the left. The first part of the beach is known as Romeïkos Gialos, and the northern end, just before Akti Marina Hotel resort, is known as Riha Nera (shallow water), so named because of its gently shelving beach which is ideal for children.

The **archaeological museum** in Myrina, housed in a neoclassical mansion, is worth a visit. It contains finds from all the three sites on Limnos, and also from an unusual archaeological dig in the grounds of the Porto Myrina Palace. The museum overlooks the beach, next to the Hotel Castor. It's open 8 am to 2.30 pm Monday to Saturday and 9 am to 2.30 pm on Sunday and public holidays. Admission is 500 dr.

Organised Tours

In the absence of a decent bus service, daily bus excursions around the island can be organised with Theodoros Petridis Travel Agency (☎ 22 039, fax 22 129). These include a visit to ancient Poliochni, Hephaistia and the Sanctuary of the Kabeiroi. There is also a swimming stop and lunch break at Moudros. The cost is 6000 dr.

The agency also organises round-the-island boat trips which again include stops for swimming and lunch. The all-up cost is 10,000 dr.

Places to Stay – Budget

Limnos doesn't have any official camp sites. There is an information board with a map of the island and the names and telephone numbers of all domatia and hotels in Limnos on the harbourfront square. Budget accommodation is thin on the ground in Myrina.

On the harbourfront, ***Hotel Lemnos*** *(☎ 22 153, fax 23 329)* is about the cheapest hotel accommodation you will find, with singles/doubles for 8000/12,000 dr. But the staff are neither particularly friendly nor over-accommodating to backpackers.

The neoclassical ***Apollo Pavillion*** *(☎/fax 23 712, email apollo47@otenet.gr)* on Frynis, with friendly English-speaking owners, has spacious and clean rooms with a variety of accommodation options. Backpacker basement rooms cost 4500 dr per person. Studios with bathroom and kitchen cost 13,000/16,750 dr for doubles/triples. Walk along Nikolaou Garoufallidou from Kyda and you will see the sign 150m along on the right.

Places to Stay – Mid-Range

Blue Waters Hotel *(☎ 24 403, fax 25 004, email bwkon@otenet.gr)* on Romeïkos Gialos is a small discerning place on the beachfront, north of the Kastro, with tastefully decorated airy rooms with air-con and fridge. Singles/doubles go for a reasonable 12,000/14,000 dr.

Afroditi Apartments *(☎ 23 489, fax 25 031)*, set back 200m from Riha Nera Beach, provides tastefully furnished, self-contained doubles/triples, all with air-con, for 16,000/19,200 dr. The breezy, well appointed rooms of ***Poseidon Domatia*** *(☎ 23 982, fax 24 856)* are close to the beach near the museum. Each room has a TV and bathroom and there is a small bar and breakfast room for guests. Rooms go for 17,500/19,500 dr in high season.

One of the island's best is the A class ***Diamantidis Hotel*** *(☎ 22 397, fax 23 187)*. Spacious, airy single/doubles go for 18,000/20,000 dr. The hotel is located inland from Myrina town on the main road.

Places to Eat

Restaurants are of a high standard on Limnos. Several fish restaurants line the waterfront. Locals give top marks to ***Taverna Glaros***, which probably has the best harbourside location, but somewhat expensive prices. By the ferry quay is ***Avra*** restaurant; handy if you are waiting for a boat to leave.

Halfway along Kyda is the small, unassuming but very pleasant ***O Platanos Taverna***, on the left as you walk from the waterfront. It is on a small square under a couple of huge plane trees and makes an attractive alternative to the waterfront establishments. Moussaka, salad, chips and local retsina should cost around 2500 dr.

Finally, the posh ***Filoktetes*** restaurant, 200m inland from Riha Nera Beach has – unusually for Greece – an access ramp and toilet for disabled diners. The food is excellent and marginally cheaper than the harbourside joints. Open for lunch and dinner, it offers a range of ready-made dishes.

Given the large number of off-duty soldiers at any given moment, there are plenty of watering holes around town. ***Jolly Caffe***, overlooking the northern end of Romeïkos Gialos Beach, seemed to be the most popular spot among Greeks at the time of writing.

WESTERN LIMNOS

North of Myrina is the five-star mega resort ***Porto Myrina Palace*** on the south side of pristine Kaspakas Bay. Turn left just past the little village of **Kaspakas** and a narrow road will lead you down to **Agios Ioannis Beach**. The beach is pleasant enough, but Agios Ioannis consists of a few desultory fishing shacks, scattered beach houses and a couple of tavernas, one of which has its tables set out in the embrace of a large volcanic rock.

Inland from Kaspakas, the barren hilly landscape dotted with sheep and rocks (particularly on the road to Katalako via Sardes and Dafni) reminds you more of the English Peak District than an Aegean island. The villages themselves have little to cause you to pause and you will certainly be an object of curiosity if you do. There is a remote and completely undeveloped beach at Gomati on the north coast and it can be reached by a good dirt road from Katalako.

Heading 3km south from Myrina you will reach one of Limnos' best beaches, below the village of **Platy**. To get to Platy Beach follow the signs out of Myrina for Platy and Thanos, but turn right just before the cemetery. Look out for the signs to the resorts of Villa Afroditi and Lemnos Village.

As well as the clubby, exclusive and English-owned Lemnos Village Resort Hotel, Platy Beach has a few reasonably priced budget places to stay. In Platy village are ***Filoxenia Domatia*** *(☎ 24 211, fax 23 545)* owned by Greek-Australians Andreas and Konstantina Sarmonikas. The large, airy rooms with kitchenette have a great view and there is a guest common room downstairs. Doubles/triples go for 10,000/12,000 dr.

On the beach itself, the owner of Jimmy's Taverna has some somewhat cramped ***domatia*** *(☎ 24 142)* as well as some newer studios (with fridges) back on the road.

They go for between 8000 dr and 10,000 dr. There are also other unofficial domatia in the village.

Apart from ***Jimmy's Taverna*** on the beach which specialises in fish, the best food to be had is in Platy Village itself, where ***Zimbabwe*** restaurant and the striking blue and white ***Kalouditsa*** taverna vie for clientele by spilling out across two squares next to each other.

Back on the beach road, if you continue along the dirt road, past the Lemnos Village Resort Hotel, you will come to a sheltered sandy cove with an islet in the bay. The beach here will probably be less crowded than Platy. **Thanos Beach** is the next bay around from Platy; it is also less crowded, and long and sandy. To get there, continue on the main road from Platy Village to Thanos Village, where a sign points to the beach.

CENTRAL LIMNOS

Central Limnos is flat and agricultural with wheat fields, small vineyards, and cattle and sheep farms. The island's huge air-force base is ominously surrounded by endless barbed-wire fences. The muddy and bleak Moudros Bay cuts deep into the interior, with **Moudros**, the second-largest town, positioned on the eastern side of the bay. Moudros does not offer much for the tourist other than a couple of small hotels with tavernas on the waterfront. The harbour has none of Myrina's picturesque qualities.

One kilometre out of Moudros on the road to Roussopouli, you will come across the **East Moudros Military Cemetery** where Commonwealth soldiers from the Gallipoli campaign are buried. Limnos, with its large protected anchorage, was occupied by a force of Royal Marines on 23 February 1915 and became the principal base for this ill-fated campaign. A metal plaque, just inside the gates, gives a short history of the Gallipoli campaign. A second Commonwealth cemetery, the **Portianos Military Cemetery**, is at Portianos, about 6km south of the village of Livadohori on the trans-island highway. The cemetery is not as obvious as the Australian-style blue and white street sign sporting the name Anzac St. Follow Anzac St to the church and you will find the cemetery off a little lane behind the church.

EASTERN LIMNOS

Eastern Limnos has three archaeological sites. The Italian School of Archaeologists has uncovered four ancient settlements at **Poliochni**, on the island's east coast. The most interesting was a sophisticated pre-Mycenaean city, which predated Troy VI (1800-1275 BC). The site is well laid-out with colour-coded maps to show the so-called Blue, Green, Red and Yellow periods of settlement and there are good descriptions in Greek, Italian and English. However, there is nothing too exciting to be seen; the site is probably of greater interest to archaeological buffs than casual visitors.

The second site is that of the **Sanctuary of the Kabeiroi** (Ta Kaviria) in north-eastern Limnos on the shores of remote Tigani Bay. This was originally a site for the worship of Kabeiroi gods predating those of Samothraki (see Sanctuary of the Great Gods, under Samothraki, later in this chapter). There is little of the Sanctuary of Samothraki's splendour, but the layout of the site is obvious and excavations are still being carried out.

The major site, which has 11 columns, is that of a Hellenistic sanctuary. The older site is farther back and is still being excavated. Of additional interest is the cave of Philoctetes, the hero of the Trojan War, who was abandoned here while a gangrenous leg (a result of snakebite) healed. The sea cave can be reached by a path that leads down from the site. The cave can actually be entered by a hidden, narrow entrance (unmarked) to the left of the main entrance.

You can reach the sanctuary easily, if you have your own transport, via a fast new road that was built for the multimillion-drachma (and now white elephant) tourist enclave, Kaviria Palace. The turn-off is about 5km to the left, after the village of **Kontopouli**. From Kontopouli itself you can make a detour to the third site, along a rough dirt track to **Hephaistia** (Ta Ifestia), once the most important city on the island. Hephaestus was the god of fire and metallurgy and, according to mythology, was thrown here from Mt Olympus by Zeus. The site is widely scattered over a scrub-covered, but otherwise desolate, small peninsula. There is not much to see of the ancient city other than some low walls and a partially excavated theatre. Excavations are still under way. All three sites are open 8 am to 2.30 pm daily and admission is, so far, free.

The road to the northern tip of the island is worth exploring. There are some typical Limnian villages in the area and the often deserted beach at **Keros** is popular with windsurfers. From the cape at the north eastern tip of Limnos you can see the islands of Samothraki and Imvros (Gökçeada) in Turkey.

Agios Efstratios
Αγιος Ευστράτιος

☎ 0254 • postcode 815 00 • pop 290

The little-known island of Agios Efstratios, called locally Aï-Stratis, deservedly merits the title of perhaps the most isolated island in the Aegean. Stuck more or less plumb centre in the North Aegean some distance from its nearest neighbour Limnos, it has few cars and fewer roads, but a steady trickle of curious foreign island-hoppers seeking to find some peace and quiet.

Large numbers of political exiles were sent here for enforced peace and quiet before and after WWII. Among the exiled guests were such luminaries as composer Mikis Theodorakis and poets Kostas Varnalis and Giannis Ritsos.

The little village of Aï-Stratis was once picturesque, but in the early hours of the morning of 21 February 1968 a violent earthquake, with its epicentre in the seas between Limnos and Aï-Stratis, virtually destroyed the vibrant village in one fell swoop. Many people emigrated as a result and there are now large numbers of islanders living in Australia and elsewhere.

Ham-fisted intervention by the then ruling junta saw the demolition of most of the remaining traditional homes and in their place, cheaply built concrete boxes were erected to house the islanders. Needless to say, the islanders are still pretty miffed over 30 years after the event, and the remaining hillside ruins stand silent sentinel over a rather lacklustre village today.

Still, if you yearn for serenity and traffic-free bliss, and enjoy walking, Aï-Stratis is a great place to visit. It has some great beaches – though most are only accessible by caïque – ample accommodation, simple island food and a surprisingly busy nightlife.

There is a post office, one cardphone and one metered phone for the public.

Getting There & Away

Agios Efstratios is on the Kavala-Rafina ferry route, which includes Limnos. There are four services weekly to Rafina (8½ hours, 4500 dr) and another four in the other direction to Limnos (1½ hours, 1600 dr) and Kavala (6½ hours, 4500 dr).

In addition, the small local ferry *Aiolis* putters to and from Limnos three times weekly on Monday, Wednesday and Friday. On the off-days, during summer, *Aiolis* does a more or less daily excursion run from Limnos for around 5000 dr. But the harbour is exposed to the west winds, causing ferry services to often be cancelled or delayed.

Beaches

Apart from the reasonable village beach of dark volcanic sand, the nearest beach worth making the effort to visit is **Alonitsi Beach** on the north-east side of the island. It is a long, totally undeveloped, pristine strand and it can be all yours if you are prepared to walk the 90 minutes to reach it. To get there take the little track from the north-east side of the village, starting by a small bridge, and follow it up towards the power pylons. Halfway along the track splits; take the right track for Alonitsi, or the left track for the **military lookout** for great views. **Lidario Beach** on the west side can be reached – with difficulty – on foot, but is better approached by sea, if you can get someone to take you there.

Places to Stay & Eat

Accommodation options in Agios Efstratios are now pretty good. There is no hotel on the island but there are currently about 100 beds available and you will always find somewhere to stay unless you turn up at the height of the summer season without a reservation.

The spotless and airy ***Xenonas Aï-Strati*** *(☎ 93 329)*, run by Julia and Odysseas Galanakis, has doubles/triples ranging in price from 5000 dr to 10,000 dr, depending on facilities and the season. The rooms are in one of the few buildings that survived the earthquake on the north-eastern side of the village.

The ***domatia*** of Malama Panera *(☎ 93 209)*, on the south side of the village, are equally well appointed with similar prices. There are also other unofficial domatia available. Ask at the little convenience store, if you get stuck. You can fax the community fax machine (93 210) if you want to make a booking.

For eating you have the choice of the fairly obvious community-run ***Thanasis Taverna*** which overlooks the harbour, or ***Tasos Ouzeri*** diagonally opposite. At the far south end of the waterfront is ***Taverna tou Antoni*** which opens in the summer, when Antonis feels like it. All places are fairly inexpensive, though fish still tends to be a bit on the steep side.

Samothraki
Σαμοθράκη

☎ 0551 • pop 2800

The egg-shaped island of Samothraki is 32km south-west of Alexandroupolis. Scenically it is one of the most awe-inspiring of all Greek islands. It is a small island, but a great deal of diverse landscape is packed into its 176 sq km. Its natural attributes are dramatic, big and untamed, culminating in the mighty peak of Mt Fengari (1611m), the highest mountain in the Aegean. Homer related that Poseidon watched the Trojan War from Mt Fengari's summit.

The jagged, boulder-strewn Mt Fengari looms over valleys of massive gnarled oak and plane trees, thick forests of olive trees, dense shrubbery and damp, dark glades where waterfalls plunge into deep, icy pools. On the gentler, western slopes of the island there are corn fields studded with wild flowers. Samothraki is also rich in fauna Its springs are the habitat of a large number of frogs, toads and turtles; in its meadows you will see swarms of butterflies and may come across the occasional lumbering tortoise. On the mountain slopes there are an inordinate number of bell-clanking goats. The island's beaches, with one exception, are stony or pebbly.

Samothraki's ancient site, the Sanctuary of the Great Gods, at Paleopolis, is one of Greece's most evocative ancient sites. Historians are unable to ascertain the nature of the rites performed here, and its aura of potent mysticism prevails over the whole island.

Samothraki is relatively difficult to reach and does not have any package tourism. It does, however, attract a fair number of Greek holiday-makers in July and August, so you may have some difficulty finding a room then. With the exception of Xenia Hotel, all of Samothraki's hotels were built in the 1980s and were designed to a high standard with sensitive regard to the environment. All are very pleasant places to stay but none fall into the budget category. This doesn't mean budget travellers are not welcome or catered for as there are a fair number of domatia and two camp sites.

History

Samothraki was first settled around 1000 BC by Thracians who worshipped the Great Gods, a cult of Anatolian origin. In 700 BC the island was colonised by people from Lesvos, who absorbed the Thracian cult into the worship of the Olympian gods.

This marriage of two cults was highly successful and by the 5th century BC Samothraki had become one of Greece's major religious centres, attracting prospective initiates from far and wide to its Sanctuary of the Great Gods. Among the luminaries initiated into the cult were King Lysander of Sparta, Philip II of Macedon and Cornelius Piso, Julius Caesar's father-in-law. One famous visitor who did not come to be initiated was St Paul, who dropped in en route to Philippi.

The cult survived until paganism was outlawed in the 4th century AD. After this the island became insignificant. Falling to the Turks in 1457, it united with Greece, along with the other North-Eastern Aegean Islands, in 1912. During WWII Samothraki was occupied by the Bulgarians.

Getting There & Away

Ferry Samothraki has ferry connections with Alexandroupolis (two hours, 2300 dr), Kavala (four hours, 3000 dr), and Limnos (three hours, 1600 dr). The sailing times vary from year to year, but in summer there are usually five departures weekly to Kavala, two weekly to Limnos and two daily to Alexandroupolis. Tickets can be bought at Niki Tours (☎ 41 465, fax 41 304, mobile 093-534 648) or Saos Travel (☎ 41 505), in Kamariotissa.

Hydrofoil Hydrofoil services operate from Samothraki from 1 May to 31 October. Currently there are services linking Samothraki with Limnos, Thasos, Halkidiki (Stavros), Kavala, Maronia, Porto Lagos and Alexandroupolis. For departure details contact Niki Tours in Kamariotissa or the office for the *Thraki III* hydrofoil (☎ 41 100, fax 230 200) which is near Budget car rentals. Ticket prices are roughly twice as much as the equivalent ferry ticket.

Getting Around

Bus In summer there are at least nine buses daily from Kamariotissa to Hora and Loutra (Therma), via Paleopolis. Some of the Loutra buses continue to the nearby camp sites. There are four buses daily to Profitis Ilias (via Lakoma). A bus schedule is displayed in the window of Saos Travel, in Kamariotissa.

Car & Motorcycle Cars and small jeeps can be rented from Niki Tours (☎ 41 465,

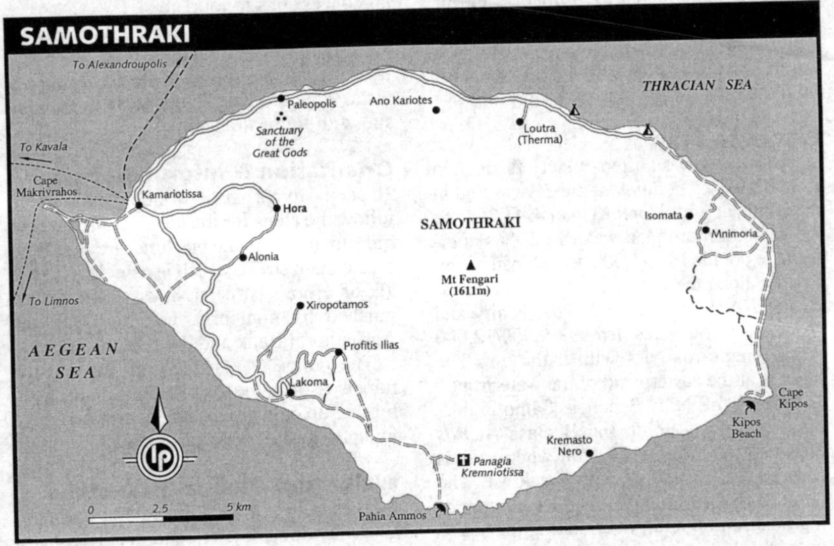

fax 41 304) and Budget (☎ 41 100). A 4WD jeep, recommended for Samothraki, costs about 18,000 dr per day, whereas a small car will cost about 12,000 dr. Motorcycles can be rented from Rent A Motor Bike, opposite the ferry quay

Excursion Boat Depending on demand, caïques do trips from the Kamariotissa jetty to Pahia Ammos and Kipos beaches.

KAMARIOTISSA Καμαριώτισσα

• postcode 680 02 • pop 826

Kamariotissa, on the north-west coast, is Samothraki's port. Hora (also called Samothraki), the island's capital, is 5km inland from here. Kamariotissa is the transport hub of the island, so you may wish to use it as a base. It has a fairly lively nightlife and a few decent restaurants.

Orientation & Information

The bus station is on the waterfront just east of the quay (turn left when you disembark). There is no EOT or tourist police and the regular police are in Hora. Opposite the bus station you will find Saos Travel and Niki Tours, both of which are reasonably helpful. There is a National Bank of Greece on the waterfront, but no post office or OTE; these are in Hora. The port police (☎ 41 305) are on the eastern waterfront at Kamariotissa.

Places to Stay

Domatia owners often meet ferries in Kamariotissa, but ***domatia*** are easy to find in the compact port. ***Hotel Kyma*** *(☎ 41 263)*, at the eastern end of the waterfront, has comfortable doubles for 11,000 dr with bathroom. Farther along the waterfront, the C class ***Niki Beach Hotel*** *(☎ 41 545, 41 461)* is airy and spacious. Room rates here are 9,000/12,000 dr for singles/doubles with bathroom. The hotel is at the eastern end of the waterfront.

Behind the Niki Beach is Samothraki's most luxurious hotel, the B class ***Aeolos Hotel*** *(☎ 41 595, fax 41 810)*, where rooms cost 10,000/15,000 dr with breakfast. The hotel has a swimming pool and a commanding position on a hill overlooking the sea.

Places to Eat

Samothraki's culinary offerings have improved considerably. ***Horizon*** is one of Kamariotissa's better restaurants. Main courses include chicken casserole for 1000 dr; meatballs, moussaka and souvlaki are all 1200 dr. The restaurant is just back from the waterfront on the left side of the road which leads up to Hora.

At the eastern end of the waterfront ***Klimitaria Restaurant*** *(☎ 41 535)* serves an unusual speciality called *gianiotiko* for 1800 dr. This is an oven-baked dish of diced pork, potatoes, egg and other goodies.

HORA Χώρα

Hora, concealed in a fold of the mountains above Kamariotissa, is one of the most striking of Greek-island villages. The crumbling red-tiled houses – some of grey stone, others whitewashed – are stacked up two steep adjacent mountainsides.

The twisting cobbled streets resound with cockerels crowing, dogs barking and donkeys braying, rather than the ubiquitous roar of motorcycles and honking of car horns. The village is totally authentic with no concessions to tourism.

The ruined castle at the top of the main thoroughfare is fascinating to explore and from its vantage point there are sweeping vistas down to Kamariotissa. It is an open site with free entrance.

Orientation & Information

To get to Hora's narrow winding main street, follow the signs for the kastro from the central square where the bus turns around. Here on the main street, which is nameless (as are all of Hora's streets; houses are distinguished by numbers), are the OTE, the Agricultural Bank and the post office.

The police (☎ 41 203) are next to the ruined castle at the top of Hora's main street. Further up on the main street, on the right, a fountain gushes refreshing mountain water.

Walk from Hora to Paleopolis

It takes between 45 minutes and one hour to walk along a dirt road from Hora to aleopolis (Sanctuary of the Great Gods). On this walk there are tremendous views of engari to the right and rolling hills, corn ields and the sea to the left. To get to the oad, walk up to the castle ruins in Hora and ake the dirt road which leads down to the ight. Alternatively, you can start the walk rom the road just below the bus stop.

Follow the main track all the way down nd around and look out for the Kastro Hotel o your left as you come over the rise. Bear ight along a smaller track as you come down the hill and you will eventually come across the museum and ancient site. You can negotiate this road in a car (4WD recommended, though). Keep going straight down the hill until you hit the main road.

Places to Stay & Eat

There are no hotels in Hora. There are two reasonably priced ***pensions*** just off the central square, but the best places to stay in Hora are ***domatia*** in private houses. Almost all of these are unofficial and do not display signs. If you ask in one of the kafeneia you will be put in touch with a room owner.

There is a ***psistaria*** on the square where the bus stops, and ***Taverna Kastro*** on the central square. Both places serve food catering for local tastes rather than for tourists. Ask for fish, if they have it. Bear in mind that these places may well be closed out of season.

SANCTUARY OF THE GREAT GODS

Το Ιερό των Μεγάλων Θεών

The Sanctuary of the Great Gods, next to the little village of Paleopolis, is 6km north-east of Kamariotissa. The extensive site, lying in a valley of luxuriant vegetation between Mt Fengari and the sea, is one of the most magical in the whole of Greece. The Great Gods were of greater antiquity than the Olympian gods worshipped in the official religion of ancient Greece. The principal deity, the Great Mother (Alceros Cybele), was worshipped as a fertility goddess.

When the original Thracian religion became integrated with the state religion, the Great Mother was merged with the Olympian female deities Demeter, Aphrodite and Hecate. The last of these was a mysterious goddess, associated with darkness, the underworld and witchcraft. Other deities worshipped here were the Great Mother's consort, the virile young Kadmilos (god of the phallus), who was later integrated with the Olympian god Hermes; as well as the demonic Kabeiroi twins, Dardanos and Aeton, who were integrated with Castor and Pollux (The Dioscuri), the twin sons of Zeus and Leda. These twins were invoked by mariners to protect them against the perils of the sea. The formidable deities of Samothraki were venerated for their immense power. In comparison, the Olympian gods were a frivolous and fickle lot.

Initiates were sworn on punishment of death not to reveal what went on at the sanctuary; so there is only very flimsy knowledge of what these initiations involved. All that the archaeological evidence reveals is that there were two initiations, a lower and a higher. In the first initiation, gods were invoked to bring about a spiritual rebirth within the candidate. In the second initiation the candidate was absolved of transgressions. There was no prerequisite for initiation – it was available to anyone.

The site's most celebrated relic, the Winged Victory of Samothrace (now in the Louvre in Paris), was found by Champoiseau, the French consul, at Adrianople (present-day Edirne in Turkey) in 1863. Sporadic excavations followed in the late 19th and early 20th centuries, but did not begin in earnest until just before WWII, when the Institute of Fine Arts, New York University, under the direction of Karl Lehmann and Phyllis Williams Lehmann, began digging.

The site is open 8.30 am to 3 pm Tuesday to Sunday. Admission is 500 dr, but is free on Sunday and public holidays.

Exploring the Site

The site is labelled in both Greek and English. If you take the path which leads south from the entrance you will arrive at the rectangular **anaktoron**, on the left. At the southern end was a **sacristy**, an antechamber where candidates put on white gowns ready for their first (lower) initiation. The initiation ceremony took place in the main body of the anaktoron. Then one at a time each initiate entered the holy of holies, a small inner temple at the northern end of the building, where a priest instructed them in the meanings of the symbols used in the ceremony. Afterwards the initiates returned to the sacristy to receive their initiation certificate.

The **arsinoein**, which was used for sacrifices, to the south-west of the anaktoron, was built in 289 BC and was then the large: cylindrical structure in Greece. It was a gi to the Great Gods from the Egyptian quee Arsinou. To the south-east of here you wi see the **sacred rock**, the site's earliest alta which was used by the Thracians.

The initiations were followed by a cele bratory feast which probably took place i the **temenos**, to the south of the arsinoein This building was a gift from Philip II. Th next building is the prominent Doric **hieron** which is the most photographed ruin on th

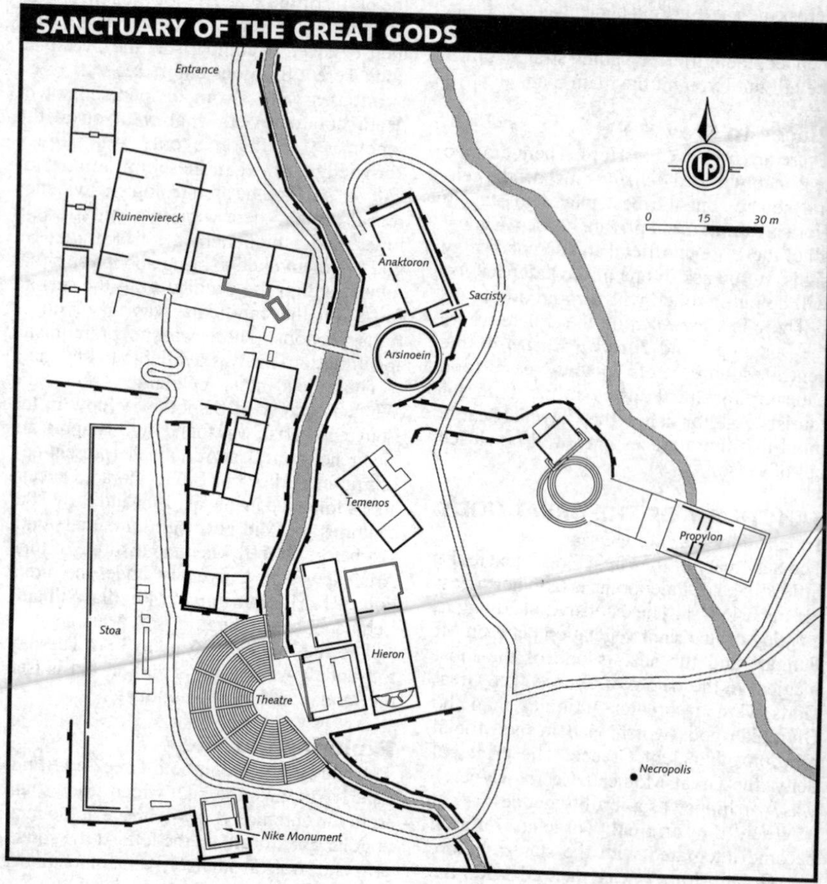

site; five of its columns have been reassembled. It was in this temple that candidates received the second initiation.

On the west side of the main path (opposite the hieron) are a few remnants of a **theatre**. Nearby, a path ascends to the **Nike monument** where the magnificent Winged Victory of Samothrace once stood. The statue was a gift from Demetrius Poliorketes (the 'besieger of cities') to the Kabeiroi for helping him defeat Ptolemy II in battle. To the north-west of here are the remains of a massive **stoa**, which was a two-aisled portico where pilgrims to the sanctuary sheltered. Names of initiates were recorded on its walls. North of the stoa are the ruins of the **ruinenviereck**, a medieval fortress.

Retrace your steps to the Nike monument and walk along the path leading east; on the left is a good plan of the site. The path continues to the southern **necropolis** which is the most important ancient cemetery so far found on the island. It was used from the Bronze Age to early Roman times. North of the cemetery was the **propylon**, an elaborate Ionic entrance to the sanctuary; it was a gift from Ptolemy II.

Museum The site's museum is well laid out, with English labels. Exhibits include terracotta figurines, vases, jewellery and a plaster cast of the Winged Victory. It's open 9 am to 3 pm Tuesday to Sunday. Admission is 500 dr, but is free on Sunday and public holidays.

Places to Stay & Eat

There are several ***domatia*** at Paleopolis, all of which are signposted from near the museum. The B class ***Xenia Hotel*** *(☎ 41 230, fax 41 166)* near the museum was built in 1952 to provide accommodation for archaeologists. Although clean, cool and comfortable, it lacks the sophistication of Samothraki's newer hotels. Doubles cost 10,800 dr with bathroom.

Just west of Paleopolis, above the coast road, is the C class ***Kastro Hotel*** *(☎ 41 001, fax 41 000)*, the island's newest hotel. The rooms are simply and tastefully furnished and rates are 13,000/17,000 dr for singles/doubles, including breakfast. The hotel has a swimming pool.

There is at least one taverna at Paleopolis but both hotels have a restaurant and bar. If you have your own transport there are some other eating places to choose from along the road towards Loutra (Therma).

AROUND SAMOTHRAKI

Loutra (Therma) Λουτρά (Θερμά)

Loutra, also called Therma, is 14km east of Kamariotissa and a short walk inland from the coast. It's in an attractive setting with a profusion of plane and horse-chestnut trees, dense greenery and gurgling creeks. While not an authentic village, it is the nearest Samothraki comes to having a holiday resort. Many of its buildings are purpose-built domatia, and most visitors to the island seem to stay here.

The village takes both its names from its therapeutic, sulphurous, mineral springs. Whether or not you are arthritic you may like to take a thermal bath here. The baths are in the large white building on the right as you walk to the central square from the bus stop. Opening times are 6 to 11 am, and 5 to 7 pm. Admission is 450 dr.

Places to Stay Samothraki has two official camp sites; both are near Loutra, and both are signposted 'Multilary Campings'. Rest assured, the authorities mean municipal camp sites and not military camp sites. The first ***Multilary Camping*** *(☎ 41 784)* is to the left of the main road, 2km beyond the turn-off for Loutra, coming from Kamariotissa. The site is very spartan, with toilets and cold showers but no other amenities. It charges 500 dr per person and 400 dr per tent. The second ***Multilary Camping*** *(☎ 41 491)* is 2km farther along the road. It has a minimarket, restaurant and hot showers, but is still a rather scrappy and dry camp site. It charges 800 dr per person, and 600 dr per tent. Both sites are open only from June through August.

Domatia owners meet the buses at Loutra. There are also two lovely hotels in Loutra.

The C class ***Mariva Bungalows*** *(☎ 98 230, fax 98 374)* are set on a hillside in a secluded part of the island, near a waterfall. The spacious doubles cost 12,000 dr with bathroom. To reach the hotel take the first turn left along the road which leads from the coast up to Loutra. Follow the signs to the hotel which is 600m along this road.

The B class ***Kaviros Hotel*** *(☎ 98 277, fax 98 278)* is bang in the middle of Loutra, just beyond the central square. It is a very pleasant family-run hotel with singles/doubles for 10,000/11,000 dr. The hotel is surrounded by a pretty garden.

Places to Eat In Loutra there are a number of restaurants and tavernas scattered throughout the upper and lower village. There is not a lot to choose between them, but chopping and changing may be part of the fun. In the upper village try ***Paradisos Restaurant*** which plies its trade under a huge plane tree with its welcome shade on a hot day. Take the road to the right from the bus stop to find it. ***Fengari Restaurant***, signposted from near the bus stop, cooks its food in traditional Samothraki ovens and is hidden away on a backstreet.

Fonias River

Visitors to the north coast should not miss the walk along the Fonias River to the **Vathres** rock pools. The walk starts at the bridge over the river 4.7km east of Loutra – the track being over-optimistically signposted as a vehicular road. After an easy 40 minute walk along a fairly well marked track you will come to a large rock pool fed by a dramatic 12m waterfall. The water is pretty cold but very welcome on a hot day. Locals call the river the 'Murderer' – winter rains can transform the waters into a raging torrent.

Beaches

The gods did not over-endow Samothraki with good beaches. However, its one sandy beach, **Pahia Ammos**, on the south coast, is superb. You can reach this 800m stretch of sand by walking along an 8km winding dirt road from Lakoma. In summer there are caïques from Kamariotissa to the beach. Around the headland is the equally superb **Vatos Beach**, used mainly by nudists.

Opposite Pahia Ammos, on a good day, you can see the mass of the former Greek island of Imvros (Gökçeada), ceded to the Turks under the Treaty of Lausanne in 1923.

There is now a restaurant, ***Taverna Pahia Ammos***, and ***domatia*** at Pahia Ammos, but bookings are recommended for July and August, since there are only six rooms, which go for 8000 dr each. Write to Nikolaos Kapelas, Profitis Ilias, Samothraki.

Samothraki's other decent beach is the pebbled **Kipos Beach** on the south-east coast. It can be reached on the unsealed road which is the easterly continuation of the road skirting the north coast. However, there are no facilities here other than a shower and a freshwater fountain, and there is no shade. It pales in comparison to Pahia Ammos Beach.

Kipos Beach can also be reached by caïque from Kamariotissa.

Other Villages

The small villages of **Profitis Ilias**, **Lakoma** and **Xiropotamos** in the south-west, and **Alonia** near Hora, are serene unspoilt villages all worth a visit. The hillside Profitis Ilias, with many trees and springs, is particularly delightful and has several tavernas of which ***Vrahos*** is famous for its delicious roast kid. Asphalt roads lead to all of these villages.

Thasos Θάσος

☎ 0593 • pop 13,300

Thasos lies 10km south-east of Kavala. It is almost circular in shape and although its scenery is not as awesome as Samothraki's it has some pleasing mountain vistas. The EOT brochures tout it as the 'emerald isle', but like so many other Greek islands it has suffered bad fires which have destroyed much of its forest. The main attractions of Thasos are its excellent beaches and the many archaeological remains in and around the capital of Limenas. A good asphalt road goes around the island so all the beaches are easily accessible.

There are still enough rooms for everyone even in the high season and Thasos has no less than six camp sites dotted around its coast. A notice opposite the bus station in Limenas lists the town's hotels, and also, very helpfully, indicates which hotels remain open in the winter.

History

Thasos has been continuously inhabited since the Stone Age. Its ancient city was founded in 700 BC by Parians, led there by a message from the Delphic oracle. The oracle told them to 'Find a city in the Isle of Mists'. From Thasos, the Parians established settlements in Thrace where they mined for gold in Mt Pangaion.

Gold was also mined on Thasos, and the islanders were able to develop a lucrative export trade based on ore, marble, timber and wine, as well as gold. As a result Thasos built a powerful navy, and culture flourished. Famous ancient Thassiots included the painters Polygnotos, Aglafon Aristofon and the sculptors Polyclitos and Sosicles. The merchants of Thasos traded with Asia Minor, Egypt and Italy.

After the Battle of Plataea, Thasos became an ally of Athens, but war broke out between the two cities when Athens attempted to curtail Thasos' trade with Egypt and Asia Minor. The islanders were defeated and forced into becoming part of the Delian League; the heavy tax imposed crippled its economy. Thasos' decline continued through Macedonian and Roman times. Heavy taxes were imposed by the Turks, many inhabitants left the island and during the 18th century the population dropped from 8000 to 2500.

Thasos was revived in the 19th century when Mohammed Ali Pasha of Egypt became governor of Kavala and Thasos. Ali allowed the islanders to govern themselves and exempted them from paying taxes. The revival was, however, short-lived. The Egyptian governors who superseded Ali Pasha usurped the island's natural resources and imposed heavy taxes. In 1912, along with the other islands of the group, Thasos was united with Greece. Like Samothraki, Thasos was occupied by Bulgaria in WWII.

In recent years Thasos has once again struck 'gold'. This time it's 'black gold', in the form of oil which has been found in the sea around the island. Oil derricks can now be spotted at sea at various locations around Thasos.

Getting There & Away

Ferry There are ferries every hour between Kavala, on the mainland, and Skala Prinou (1½ hours, 850 dr, 4400 dr for a car). There is only one ferry daily between Kavala and Limenas. Ferries direct to Limenas leave every hour or so in summer (40 minutes, 330 dr) from Keramoti, 46km south-east of Kavala.

Hydrofoil There are six hydrofoils every day between Limenas and Kavala (30 minutes, 1600 dr).

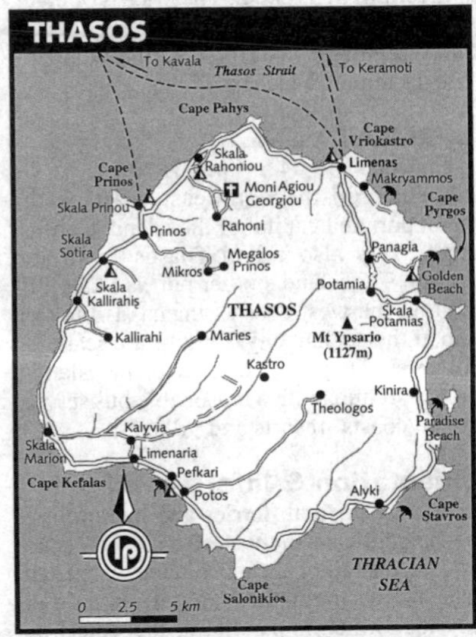

Getting Around

Bus Limenas is the transport hub of the island. There are many buses daily to Limenaria (via the west coast villages) and to Golden Beach via Panagia and Potamia. There are six buses to Theologos and three to Alyki. Six buses daily journey in a clockwise direction all the way around the island. The cost of a complete two hour circuit of the island by bus is 2000 dr.

Car & Motorcycle Cars can be hired from Avis Rent a Car (☎ 22 535) on the central square in Limenas or in Skala Prinou (☎ 71 202) and Potamia (☎ 61 506). You can hire motorcycles and mopeds from Billy's Bikes (☎ 22 490), opposite the foreign-language newspaper agency.

Bicycle Bicycles can be hired from Babi's Bikes (☎ 22 129), on a side street between 18 Oktovriou and the central square in Limenas.

Excursion Boat The *Eros 2* excursion boat makes daily trips around the island, with stops for swimming and a barbecue. The boat leaves from the old harbour at 9.30 am and returns at 5.30 pm. The price is 5000 dr. There are also a couple of water taxis running regularly to Hrysi Ammoudia and Makryammos beaches.

LIMENAS Λιμένας

• postcode 640 04 • pop 2600

Limenas, on the north-east coast, is the main port and capital of the island. Confusingly, it is also called Thasos Town and Limin. The island's other port is Skala Prinou on the west coast. Limenas is built on top of the ancient city, so ruins are scattered all over the place. It is also the island's transport hub, with a reasonable bus service to the coastal resorts and villages.

Orientation & Information

The quay for both ferries and hydrofoils is at the centre of the waterfront. The central square is straight ahead from the waterfront. The towns main thoroughfare is 18 Oktovriou, which is parallel to the waterfront and north of the central square. Turn left into 18 Oktovriou from the quay to reach the OTE on the right. Take the next turn right into Theogenous and the second turn right to reach the post office, which is on the left.

There is no EOT on Thasos, but the helpful tourist police (☎ 22 500) are on the waterfront near the bus station. They will assist in finding accommodation if necessary.

The National Bank of Greece is on the waterfront opposite the quay and has both an exchange machine and ATM. The newsagent on Theogenous sells English-language newspapers.

The bus station is on the waterfront; to reach it turn left from the quay. To reach the town's picturesque small harbour turn left from the quay and walk along the waterfront. The crowded town beach begins at the end of the western waterfront.

Street name signs are a bit of a novelty in Limenas, so don't be surprised if you can't find one.

Things to See

Thasos' **archaeological museum** is next to the ancient agora at the small harbour. The most striking exhibit is a very elongated 6th century BC *kouros* statue which stands in the foyer. It was found on the acropolis of the ancient city of Thasos. Other exhibits include pottery and terracotta figurines and a large well preserved head of a rather effeminate Dionysos. The ancient city of Thasos was excavated by the French School of Archaeology, so the museum's labelling is in French and Greek.

The **ancient agora** next to the museum was the bustling marketplace of ancient and Roman Thasos – the centre of its civic, social and business life. It's a pleasant, verdant site with the foundations of stoas, shops and dwellings. Entrance is free.

The **ancient theatre**, in a lovely wooded setting, has been fitted with wooden seats (now a bit dilapidated), and performances of ancient dramas are staged here annually, though the theatre is currently undergoing renovation. The theatre is signposted from the small harbour.

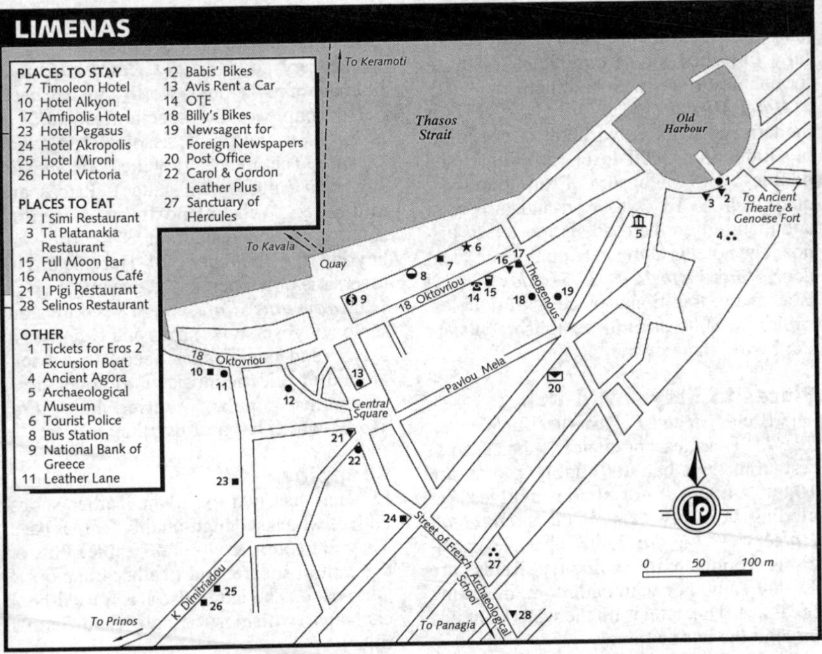

From the theatre a path leads up to the **acropolis** of ancient Thasos where there are substantial remains of a medieval fortress built on the foundations of the ancient walls which encompassed the entire city. From the topmost point of the acropolis there are magnificent views. From the far side of the acropolis, steps carved into the rock (with a dodgy-looking metal handrail) lead down to the foundations of the ancient wall. From here it's a short walk to the Limenas-Panagia road at the southern edge of town.

Special Events

In July and August, performances of ancient plays are held at Limenas' ancient theatre, as part of the Kavala Festival of Drama. Information and tickets can be obtained from the EOT in Kavala or the tourist police on Thasos. The theatre has been undergoing renovations; check whether performances have recommenced.

Places to Stay – Budget

The nearest camp site to Limenas is ***Nysteri Camping*** *(☎ 23 327)*, just west of the town. With the exception of the camp site on Golden Beach, all of Thasos' other camp sites are on the west and south-west coasts.

Limenas has many reasonably priced ***domatia***. If you are not offered anything when you arrive, then look for signs around the small harbour and the road to Prinos.

Close to the waterfront is the very pleasant and clean C class ***Hotel Alkyon*** *(☎ 22 148)*. Singles/doubles will cost about 7000/10,000 dr. Take a back room if you prefer less noise from street life. The hotel also has a snack bar where tea is the speciality; the co-owner is English. ***Hotel Akropolis*** *(☎ 22 488)*, one block south of the central square, is a very well maintained century-old mansion with a lovely garden. The beautifully furnished rooms cost 9000/11,800 dr for doubles/triples with bathroom.

Hotel Mironi *(☎ 23 256, fax 22 132)* is modern and spacious with lots of cool marble. Rates are 12,000 dr for both singles and doubles with bathroom. From the ferry quay walk to 18 Oktovriou and turn right and then left on the road signposted to Prinos. The hotel is along here on the left. Next door, ***Hotel Victoria*** *(☎ 22 556, fax 22 132)* is a lovely, traditional place with doubles/triples for 8000 dr. Both establishments are run by the same owner.

Places to Stay – Mid-Range

The B class ***Hotel Pegasus*** *(☎ 22 061, fax 22 373)* is a pleasant choice. It has a pool, restaurant and bar. Its quality rooms are 10,000/14,000 dr for singles/doubles, including breakfast. The B class ***Timoleon Hotel*** *(☎ 22 177, fax 23 277)* has clean spacious rooms with balcony. Rates are 12,000/15,000 dr with bathroom, including breakfast. The hotel is on the waterfront just beyond the bus station.

The A class ***Amfipolis Hotel*** *(☎ 23 101, fax 22 110)*, on the corner of 18 Oktovriou and Theogenous, is an attractive mock castle complete with turrets. Rates are 15,500/19,700 dr, including a buffet breakfast. The hotel has a swimming pool.

Places to Eat

Limenas has a good selection of restaurants serving well prepared food. ***I Pigi Restaurant***, on the central square, is an inviting, unpretentious restaurant next to a spring. The food is good and the service friendly and attentive. Try *stifado* (stew in tomato sauce), mussel *saganaki* or swordfish.

The old harbour, and the area just beyond it along the beach, boasts no less than eight restaurants. They all cater primarily to the tourist trade and feature multilingual menu cards. The first two, ***Ta Platanakia*** and ***I Simi***, are convenient and slightly more downmarket than the other establishments. The food is good at both restaurants and the prices aren't too bad. Reckon on about 2600 dr for a meal with beer or wine.

The very good ***Selinos Restaurant*** is a little out of town, but is worth a visit. Check out a couple of the specialities: *kolokythokeftedes* (zucchini rissoles), *ohtapodi krasato* (octopus in wine) or *mydia saganaki* (mussels in sauce). Prices are mid-range. Walk inland from the central square and the restaurant is a little way beyond the Sanctuary of Hercules. The taverna is only open in the evening.

Anonymous Cafe, on 18 Oktovriou, serves English-style snacks and Guinness in a can (and many other beers) to a background of eclectic music. Two doors along is another popular watering hole, ***Full Moon***, which has an Australian owner.

Shopping

Limenas has two excellent leather shops, both of which sell high-quality leather bags. They are Carol & Gordon Leather Plus on the central square, and Leather Lane on 18 Oktovriou. The latter also has a used-book exchange (with mostly English and German titles).

EAST COAST

The neighbouring hillside villages of **Panagia** and **Potamia** are quite touristy but picturesque. Both are 4km west of Golden Beach. The Greek-American artist Polygnotos Vagis was born in Potamia in 1894 and some of his work can be seen in the **Polygnotos Vagis Museum** in the village next to the main church. It is open 9 am to 1 pm and 6 to 9 pm Tuesday to Saturday and 10 am to 2 pm on Sunday and holidays. (The municipal museum in Kavala also has a collection of Vagis' work.)

The long and sandy **Golden Beach** is the island's best beach and roads from both Panagia and Potamia lead down to it. These roads are very pleasant to walk along, but if you prefer, the bus from Limenas calls at both villages before continuing to the southern end of the beach.

The next beach south is at the village of **Kinira**, and just south of here is the very pleasant **Paradise Beach**. The little islet just off the coast here is also called Kinira. **Alyki**, on the south-east coast, consists of two quiet beaches back to back on a headland. The southernmost beach is the better of the two. There is a small archaeological site near the beach and a marble quarry. The road linking the east side with the west side runs high across the cliffs, providing some great views of the bays at the bottom of the island. With only a few breaks, the island circuit (110km) can be completed by motorcycle in about 3½ hours.

Places to Stay & Eat

***Hrysi Ammoudia** (☎ 61 472)*, on Golden Beach, is the only camp site on this side of the island and is only a stone's throw from the inviting water. Facilities are good and include a minimarket. On Golden Beach, ***Hotel Emerald** (☎ 61 979, fax 61 451)* has self-contained studios for two to four people for around 15,000 dr.

In Panagia, ***Hotel Elvetia** (☎ 61 231, fax 61 451)* has pleasant doubles costing 12,000 dr. With your back to the fountain in the central square of Panagia (where the bus stops), turn left and take the first main road to the left and the hotel is on the left. Just beyond here on the right, ***Hotel Hrysafis** (☎/fax 61 451)* has singles and doubles for 11,000 dr with bathroom. There are ***domatia*** at both Kinira and Alyki.

There are reasonably priced restaurants in Panagia. ***Restaurant Vigli** (☎ 61 506)*, overlooking the northern end of Golden Beach, has superb views and food and offers live music on Thursday evenings. There are tavernas on the beach at Kinira and Alyki.

WEST COAST

The west coast consists of a series of seaside villages with Skala (literally 'step' or 'ladder', but in essence meaning 'by the sea') before their names. Roads lead from each of these to inland villages with the same name (minus the 'skala'). Beaches along the west coast are uniformly pebbly and exposed. Travelling from north to south the first village is **Skala Rahoniou**. This is Thasos' latest development, having recently been discovered by the package-tour companies. It has an excellent camp site and the inland village of Rahoni remains unspoilt. Just before Rahoni there is a turn-off left to Moni Agiou Georgiou.

Skala Prinou, the next coastal village, and Thasos' second port, is crowded and unattractive. **Skala Sotira** and **Skala Kallirahis** are more pleasant and both have small beaches. Kallirahi, 2km inland from Skala Kallirahis, is a peaceful village with steep narrow streets and old stone houses. It has a large population of skinny, anxious-looking cats and, judging by the graffiti and posters, a lot of communists.

Skala Marion is a delightful fishing village and one of the least touristy places around the coast. It was from here, early in the 20th century, that the German Speidel Metal Company exported iron ore from Thasos to Europe. There are beaches at both sides of the village, and between here and Limenaria there are stretches of uncrowded beach.

Limenaria (42km from Limenas) is Thasos' second-largest town and a very crowded resort with a narrow sandy beach. The town was built in 1903 by the Speidel Metal Company. There are slightly less crowded beaches around the coast at **Pefkari** and **Potos**.

From Potos a scenic 10km road leads inland to **Theologos**, which was the capital of the island in medieval and Turkish times. This is the island's most beautiful village and the only mountain settlement served by public transport. The village houses are of whitewashed stone with slate roofs. It's a serene place, still unblemished by mass tourism.

Places to Stay

Camping Perseus** (☎ 81 242)*, at Skala Rahoniou, is an excellent, grassy camp site in a pretty setting of flowers and olive and willow trees. The cook at the site's taverna will prepare any Greek dish you wish if you place your order a day in advance. The EOT-owned ***Camping Prinos *(☎ 71 171)*, at Skala Prinou, is well maintained with lots of greenery and shade and is about 1km or so south of the ferry quay.

The next camp site, ***Camping Daedalos*** *(☎ 71 365)*, is just north of Skala Sotira right on the beach. It has a minimarket, restaurant and bar. The next site, ***Pefkari Camping*** *(☎ 51 190)*, at Pefkari Beach, is a nifty site south of Limenaria but requires a minimum three night stay. Look carefully for the sign; it is not so obvious.

All sites charge around 850 dr per person and 650 dr per tent.

All of the seaside villages have hotels and domatia and the inland villages have rooms in private houses. For information about these inquire at kafeneia or look for signs.

Places to Eat

All of the coastal villages have tavernas. ***Taverna Drosia***, in Rahoni, features live bouzouki music on Friday and Saturday evenings. ***Taverna Orizontes*** *(☎ 31 389)*, first on the left as you enter Theologos, features *rembetika* nights. ***Taverna Kleoniki***, on the main street in Theologos, has an outdoor terrace with wonderful views of the surrounding mountains.

Ionian Islands Τα Επτάνησα

The Ionian group consists of seven main islands anchored in the Ionian Sea: Corfu, Paxi, Kefallonia, Zakynthos, Ithaki, Lefkada and Kythira. The last is more accessible from the Peloponnese. The islands differ from other island groups and, geographically, are less quintessentially Greek. More reminiscent of Corfu's neighbour Italy, not least in light, their colours are mellow and green compared with the stark, dazzling brightness of the Aegean.

These islands receive a great amount of rain and consequently, the vegetation, with the exception of the more exposed Kythira, is more luxuriant. Corfu has the nation's highest rainfall. Overall, vegetation combines elements of the tropical with forests that could be northern European: exotic orchids as well as wild flowers emerge below spring snowlines, and eucalypts and acacias share soil with plane, oak and maple trees. The islands do not experience the *meltemi*, and as a result they can be extremely hot in summer.

The culture and cuisine of each Ionian island is unique and differs from the Aegean islands and Crete. Influences from Mediterranean Europe and Britain have also been stronger yet have developed with special individuality on each island.

Accommodation prices in this chapter are for the high season (July and August).

HIGHLIGHTS

- The fine Venetian buildings and narrow streets of Corfu's old town
- The traditional, unspoilt villages and fine pebble beaches of Meganisi
- Cruising around Skorpios Islet near Lefkada, once home to Jackie and Aristotle Onassis
- Relaxing on the white sand beach of Myrtos with a bottle of the unique Robola white wine of Kefallonia
- The picturesque fishing villages of Frikes and Kioni on Ithaki, Odysseus' homeland
- The ancient olive groves of Paxi, and Antipaxi's exquisite wine
- The magically haunting inland villages of Kythira, and some of the Aegean's cleanest beaches

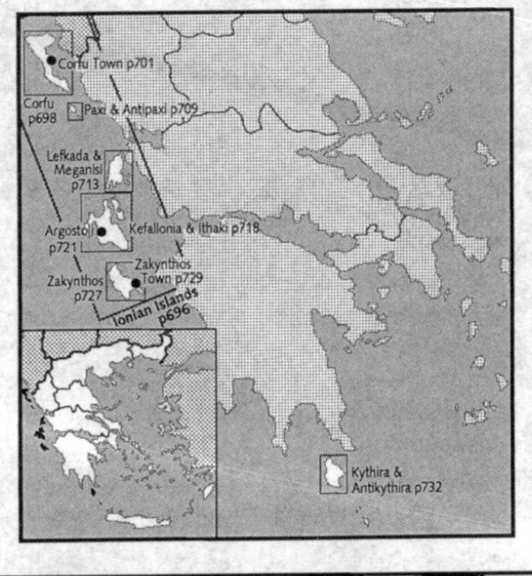

History & Mythology

The origin of the name Ionian is obscure but is thought to derive from the goddess Io. Yet another of Zeus' countless paramours, Io, while fleeing the wrath of a jealous Hera (in the shape of a heifer), happened to pass through the waters now known as the Ionian Sea.

If we are to believe Homer, the islands were important during Mycenaean times; however, no magnificent palaces or even modest villages from that period have been revealed, although Mycenaean tombs have been unearthed. Ancient history lies buried beneath tonnes of earthquake rubble – seismic activity has been constant on all Ionian Islands, including Kythira.

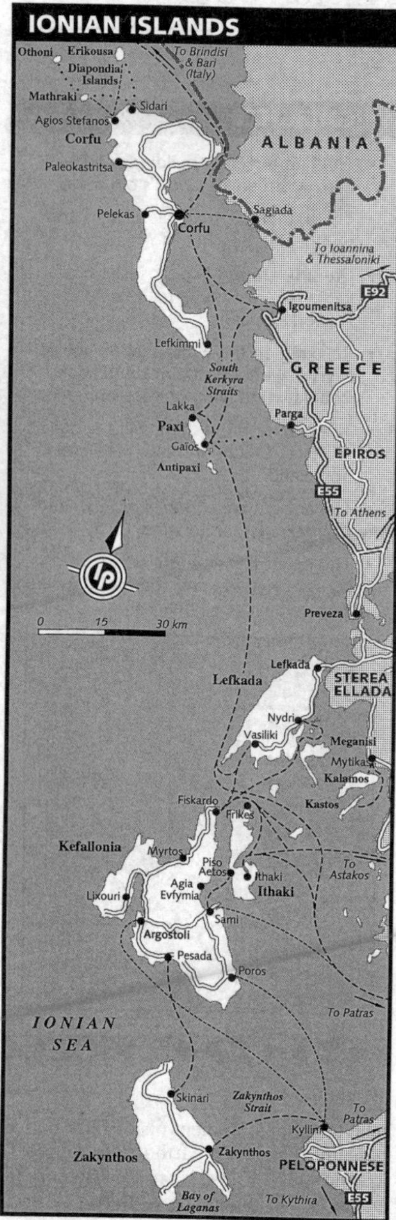

According to Homer, Odysseus' kingdom consisted not only of Ithaca (Ithaki) but also encompassed Kefallonia, Zakynthos and Lefkada. Ithaca has long been controversial. Classicists and archaeologists in the 19th century concluded that Homer's Ithaca was modern Ithaki, his Sami was Sami on Kefallonia, and his Zakynthos was today's Zakynthos, which sounded credible. But in the early 20th century German archaeologist Wilhelm Dorpfeld put a spanner in the works by claiming that Lefkada was ancient Ithaca, modern Ithaki was ancient Sami and Kefallonia was ancient Doulichion. His theories have now fallen from favour with everyone except the people of Lefkada.

By the 8th century BC, the Ionian Islands were in the clutches of the mighty city-state of Corinth, which regarded them of value as stepping stones on the route to Sicily and Italy. A century later, Corfu staged a successful revolt against Corinth, which was allied to Sparta, and became an ally of Sparta's archenemy, Athens. This alliance provoked Sparta into challenging Athens, thus precipitating the Peloponnesian Wars, which raged from 431 to 404 BC. The wars left Corfu depleted as they did all participants and Corfu became little more than a staging post for whoever happened to be holding sway in Greece. By the end of the 3rd century BC, Corfu, along with the other Ionian Islands, had become Roman. Following the decline of the Roman Empire, the islands saw the usual waves of invaders that Greece suffered. After the fall of Constantinople, the islands became Venetian.

Corfu was never part of the Ottoman Empire. Paxi, Kefallonia, Zakynthos, Ithaki and Kythira were variously occupied by the Turks, but the Venetians held them longest. The exception was Lefkada, which was Turkish for 200 years. The Ionian Islands fared better under the Venetians than their counterparts in the Cyclades.

Venice fell to Napoleon in 1797. Two years later, under the Treaty of Campo Formio, the Ionian Islands were allotted to France. In 1799 Russian forces wrested the islands from Napoleon, but by 1807 they were his again. By then, the all-powerful British couldn't resist meddling. As a result, in 1815, after Napoleon's downfall, the islands became a British protectorate under the jurisdiction of a series of Lord High Commissioners.

British rule was oppressive but, on a more positive note, the British constructed roads, bridges, schools and hospitals, established trade links and developed agriculture and industry. However, the nationalistic fervour in the rest of Greece soon reached the Ionian Islands.

A call for *enosis* (political union with Greece) was realised in 1862 when Britain relinquished the islands to Greece. In WWII the Italians invaded Corfu as part of Mussolini's plan to resurrect the mighty Roman Empire. Italy surrendered to the Allies in September 1943 and, in revenge, the Germans massacred thousands of Italians who had occupied the island. The Germans also sent some 5000 Corfiot Jews to Auschwitz.

A severe earthquake shook the Ionian Islands in 1953. It did considerable damage, particularly on Zakynthos and Kefallonia.

Getting There & Away

Air Corfu, Kefallonia, Zakynthos and Kythira have airports. Many charter flights to Corfu come from northern Europe and the UK. Kefallonia and Zakynthos also receive flights. These islands have frequent flights to Athens.

Bus Buses go from Athens and Thessaloniki to Corfu and from Athens to Kefallonia and Zakynthos. Lefkada is joined to the mainland by a causeway and can be reached by bus from Athens as well as Patras. There is a direct daily bus to Paxi from Athens.

Ferry – Domestic The Peloponnese has several ports of departure for the Ionian Islands: Patras for ferries to Kefallonia, Ithaki, Paxi and Corfu; Kyllini for ferries to Kefallonia and Zakynthos, and Piraeus, Monemvasia, Neapoli and Gythio for Kythira which is also served from Crete. Epiros has one port, Igoumenitsa, for Corfu and Paxi; and Sterea Ellada has one, Astakos, for Ithaki and Kefallonia.

The following table gives an overall view of the available scheduled domestic ferries to this island group from mainland ports in high season. Further details and inter-island links can be found under each island entry.

Ferry – International From Corfu, ferries depart for Brindisi, Bari, Ancona, Trieste and Venice in Italy. At least three times weekly, a ferry goes from Kefallonia to Brindisi via Igoumenitsa and Corfu. In July and August this ferry also calls at Zakynthos and Paxi.

Ferry Connections to the Ionian Islands

Origin	Destination	Duration	Price	Frequency
Astakos	Piso Aetos (Ithaki)	3 hours	1300 dr	1 daily
Gythio	Agia Pelagia (Kythira)	2½ hours	1700 dr	2 daily
Igoumenitsa	Corfu	1¼ hours	1400 dr	14 daily
Igoumenitsa	Paxi •	2 hours	1600 dr	3 weekly
Kyllini	Zakynthos	1½ hours	1160 dr	5 daily
Kyllini	Argostoli (Kefallonia)	2¼ hours	2310 dr	2 daily
Kyllini	Poros (Kefallonia)	1¼ hours	1620 dr	4 daily
Neapoli	Agia Pelagia (Kythira)	45 mins	1500 dr	2 daily
Patras	Sami (Kefallonia)	2½ hours	2630 dr	2 daily
Patras	Vathy (Ithaki)	3¾ hours	2900 dr	2 daily
Sagiada	Corfu	45 mins	1100 dr	1 weekly

Corfu & the Diapondia Islands

☎ 0661 (Corfu Town) • postcode 491 00

Corfu (Κέρκυρα) is the second-largest and greenest Ionian island. It is also the best known. In Greek, the island's name is Kerkyra (**ker**-kih-rah). It was Homer's 'beautiful and rich land', and Odysseus' last stop on his journey home to Ithaca. Shakespeare reputedly used it as a background for *The Tempest*. In the 20th century, the Durrell brothers, among others, have extolled its virtues.

With its beguiling landscape of vibrant wild flowers and slender cypress trees rising out of shimmering olive groves, Corfu is considered by many as Greece's most beautiful island. With the highest rainfall, it's also the nation's major vegetable garden and produces scores of herbs. The mountain air is heavily scented. In autumn, the night sky over the sea is a spectacular sight.

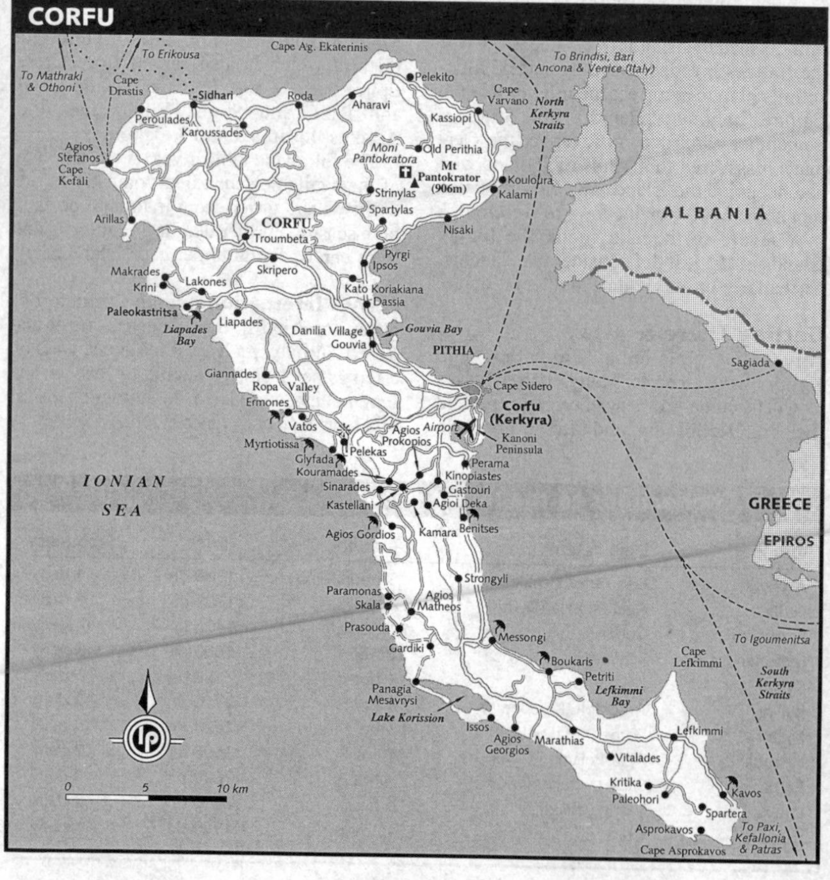

Getting There & Away

Air Corfu has at least three flights to Athens every day (20,700 dr). There are flights to Thessaloniki on Monday, Thursday and Saturday (20,900 dr). The Olympic Airways office (☎ 38 694, fax 36 634) is at Polyla 11, Corfu Town.

Bus There are two buses daily to Athens (11 hours, 8150 dr including ferry), at 9 am and 6.30 pm, and one to Thessaloniki (8000 dr), at 7 am. Tickets must be bought in advance.

Ferry – Domestic From Corfu, hourly ferries go to Igoumenitsa (1¼ hours, 1400 dr). Every Friday a ferry goes to Sagiada on the mainland (45 minutes, 1100 dr). Car ferries go to Paxi (four hours, 1900 dr) four times weekly, via Igoumenitsa. In summer, a fast passenger boat, the Pegasus, goes direct to Paxi (1½ hours, 3300 dr). This boat leaves from the old port. For details on ferries to Patras, see the following section. Corfu's port police can be contacted on ☎ 32 655.

Ferry – International Corfu is on the Patras-Igoumenitsa ferry route to Italy (Brindisi, Bari, Ancona, Trieste, Venice), though some ferries originate in Igoumenitsa. About six ferries daily go to Brindisi (9½ hours). At least one ferry daily goes to Bari and Ancona, and one goes to Venice daily (27 hours) in summer.

A fast daily catamaran service links Corfu with Brindisi from 1 July to 19 September with reduced services between April and June. The price of a one way ticket is 27,000 dr. The Corfu agents are Italian Ferries.

Brindisi-bound ferries tend to leave Corfu's new port between 8.30 and 9.30 am.

Prices to Italy from Corfu are the same as those from Igoumenitsa on the mainland. For comparative ticket prices see the Igoumenitsa Getting There & Away section in the Northern Greece chapter.

Agencies selling tickets are mostly on Xenofondos Stratigou. Shop around for the best deal. You can take one of the frequent international ferries to Patras (10 hours, 5800 dr), daily in summer.

The main ferry offices are:

Adriatica (☎ 38 089, fax 35 416)
Ilios Holidays Ltd, Xenofondos Stratigou 46
ANEK Lines (☎ 24 503, fax 36 935, email booking@anek.cha.forthnet.gr)
Mancan Travel, Eleftheriou Venizelou 38
Fragline (☎ 24 912, fax 37 967)
Ahilleas Avramidis, Eleftheriou Venizelou 46
Hellenic Mediterranean (☎ 39 747, fax 32 047, email hml@otenet.gr)
Eleftheriou Venizelou 46
Italian Ferries (☎ 36 439, fax 45 153)
3rd Parodos, Eleftheriou Venizelou 4
Minoan Lines (☎ 25 000, fax 46 555, email vergis@minoan.ker.forthnet.gr)
Ethnikis Antistasis 58a
Strintzis Lines (☎ 25 232, fax 46 945, email sales@strintzis.gr)
Ferry Travel, Ethnikis Antistasis 2
Ventouris Ferries (☎ 32 664, fax 36 935, email info@ventouris.gr)
Mancan Travel, Eleftheriou Venizelou 38

Getting Around

To/From the Airport There is no Olympic Airways shuttle bus between Corfu Town and the airport. Bus No 3 from Plateia San Rocco stops on the main road 500m from the airport.

Bus Destinations of KTEL buses (green-and-cream) from Corfu Town's long distance bus station (☎ 30 627) are as follows:

Destination	Duration	Frequency	Via
Agios Gordios	40 mins	4 daily	Sinarades
Agios Stefanos	1½ hours	5 daily	Sidari
Aharavi	1¼ hours	4 daily	Roda
Glyfada	45 mins	6 daily	Vatos
Kavos	1½ hours	10 daily	Lefkimmi
Loutses	1¼ hours	4 daily	Kassiopi
Messongi	45 mins	7 daily	
Paleokastritsa	45 mins	7 daily	
Pyrgi	30 mins	9 daily	Ypsos

Fares range from 300 dr to 800 dr. Sunday and holiday services are reduced considerably, often by as much as 70%.

The numbers and destinations of local buses (dark blue) from the bus station at Plateia San Rocco, Corfu Town, are:

Destination	Bus No	Duration	Frequency	Via
Afra	8	30 mins	8 daily	
Agios Ioannis	11	30 mins	9 daily	Pelekas
Ahillion	10	20 mins	6 daily	Gastouri
Kastellani	5	25 mins	14 daily	Kourmades
Kontokali	7	30 mins	hourly	Gouvia & Dassia
Perama	6	30 mins	12 daily	Benitses
Potamos	4	45 mins	12 daily	Evroupoli & Tembloni

The flat rate is 200 dr. Tickets can be bought on board or on Plateia San Rocco.

Car, Motorcycle & Bicycle Car hire companies in Corfu Town include Autorent (☎ 44 623/624/625), Xenofondos Stratigou 34; Avis (☎ 24 042), Ethnikis Antistasis 42; Budget (☎ 22 062), Donzelot 5; and Europcar (☎ 46 931/932/933), Xenofondos Stratigou 32.

Motorcycle hire outlets are on Xenofondos Stratigou and Avramiou. For mountain bikes try Charitos Travel Agency (☎ 44 611/620, fax 36 825), Arseniou 35.

CORFU TOWN

☎ 0661 • pop 36,000

The island's capital is Corfu Town (Kerkyra), built on a promontory. It's a gracious medley of numerous occupying influences, which never included the Turks. The Spianada (esplanade) is green, gardened and boasts Greece's only cricket ground, a legacy of the British. After a match, spectators may join players in drinking ginger beer made to an old Victorian recipe or, typically, tea or gin and tonic.

The Liston, a row of arcaded buildings flanking the north-western side of the Spianada, was built during the French occupation and modelled on Paris' Rue de Rivoli. The buildings function as upmarket cafes, lamplit by night. Georgian mansions and Byzantine churches complete the picture. The Venetian influence prevails, particularly in the enchanting old town, wedged between two fortresses. Narrow alleyways of 18th century shuttered tenements in muted ochres and pinks are more reminiscent of Venice or Naples than Greece.

Orientation

The town is separated into northern and southern sections. The old town is in the northern section between the Spianada and the New Fortress. The Palaio Frourio (Old Fortress) is east of here and projects out to sea, cut off from the town by a moat. The Neo Frourio (New Fortress) is west. The Spianada separates the Old Fortress from the town. The southern section is the new town.

The old port is north of the old town. The new port is west. Between them is the hulking New Fortress. The long distance bus station is on Avramiou, inland from the new port. The local bus station is on Plateia San Rocco. Local buses serve the town and nearby villages.

Information

Tourist Offices The EOT (☎ 37 520, fax 30 298) is on Rizospaston Voulefton. The tourist police (☎ 30 265) are at Samartzi 4, near Plateia Solomou.

Money The National Bank of Greece is at the junction of Voulgareos and G Theotoki. It has a 24 hour cash exchange machine as does the Commercial Bank opposite the new port, and many others. There is a handy Bureau de Change booth at the southern corner of the cricket ground. American Express is represented by Greek Skies Tours (☎ 32 469) at Kapodistria 20a.

Post & Communications The post office is on Alexandras. It is open 7.30 am to 8 pm Monday to Friday, 7.30 am to 2 pm Saturday, and 9 am to 1.30 pm Sunday. The OTE phone office at Mantzarou 9 is open 6 am to midnight daily.

Bookshops The Xenoglosso Bookshop, Markora 45, stocks English-language books

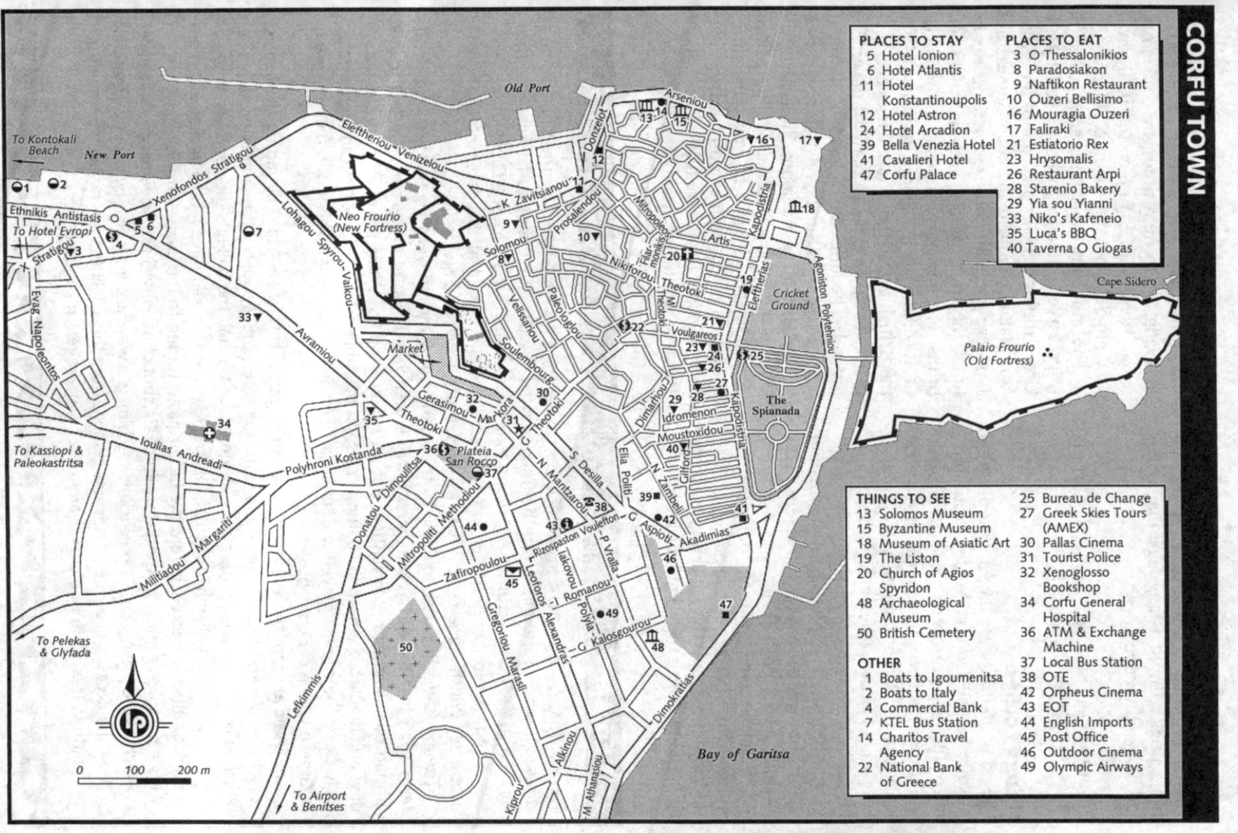
CORFU TOWN
PLACES TO STAY
5 Hotel Ionion
6 Hotel Atlantis
11 Hotel Konstantinoupolis
12 Hotel Astron
24 Hotel Arcadion
39 Bella Venezia Hotel
41 Cavalieri Hotel
47 Corfu Palace
PLACES TO EAT
3 O Thessalonikios
8 Paradosiakon
9 Naftikon Restaurant
10 Ouzeri Bellisimo
16 Mouragia Ouzeri
17 Faliraki
21 Estiatorio Rex
23 Hrysomalis
26 Restaurant Arpi
28 Starenio Bakery
29 Yia sou Yianni
33 Niko's Kafeneio
35 Luca's BBQ
40 Taverna O Giogas
THINGS TO SEE
13 Solomos Museum
15 Byzantine Museum
18 Museum of Asiatic Art
19 The Liston
20 Church of Agios Spyridon
48 Archaeological Museum
50 British Cemetery
25 Bureau de Change
27 Greek Skies Tours (AMEX)
30 Pallas Cinema
31 Tourist Police
32 Xenoglosso Bookshop
34 Corfu General Hospital
36 ATM & Exchange Machine
OTHER
1 Boats to Igoumenitsa
2 Boats to Italy
4 Commercial Bank
7 KTEL Bus Station
14 Charitos Travel Agency
22 National Bank of Greece
37 Local Bus Station
38 OTE
42 Orpheus Cinema
43 EOT
44 English Imports
45 Post Office
46 Outdoor Cinema
49 Olympic Airways
Old Port
New Port
To Kontokali Beach
To Hotel Evropi
To Kassiopi & Paleokastritsa
To Pelekas & Glyfada
To Airport & Benitses
Neo Frourio (New Fortress)
Palaio Frourio (Old Fortress)
Cape Sidero
Cricket Ground
The Spianada
Market
Plateia San Rocco
Bay of Garitsa
0 100 200 m

IONIAN ISLANDS

including novels and a few travel guides. English Imports, in a side street off Methodiou, stocks English-language magazines and daily newspapers.

Emergency The Corfu General Hospital (☎ 45 811) is on I Andreadi.

Things to See

The star exhibit of the **archaeological museum** is the Gorgon Medusa sculpture, one of the best-preserved pieces of Archaic sculpture in Greece. It was part of the west pediment of the 6th century Temple of Artemis at Corcyra (the ancient capital), on the peninsula south of the town. The petrifying Medusa is depicted in the instant before she was beheaded by Perseus. This precipitated the birth of her sons, Chrysaor and Pegasus (the winged horse), who emerged from her headless body.

Also impressive is the 7th century crouching lion, found near the Tomb of Menecrates. Archaeologists ascertained that it stood on top of the tomb. The museum (☎ 30 680) is at Vraïla 5. Opening times are 8.45 am to 3 pm Tuesday to Saturday and 9.30 am to 2.30 pm Sunday. Admission is 800 dr.

The **museum of Asiatic art** houses the impressive collection, bequeathed by the Greek diplomats Grigoris Manos and Nikolaos Hatzivasiliou. It includes Chinese and Japanese porcelain, bronzes, screens, sculptures, theatrical masks, armour, books and prints. The museum is housed in the Palace of St Michael & St George, built in 1819 as the British Lord High Commissioner's residence. The palace is just north of the cricket ground. The museum is open 8.30 am to 3 pm Tuesday to Sunday. Admission is free.

The **Byzantine museum**, housed in the Church of Our Lady of Antivouniotissa on Arseniou (☎ 38 313), has an outstanding collection of Byzantine and post-Byzantine icons. Opening times are 8.30 am to 2.30 pm Tuesday to Sunday. Admission is 500 dr.

Is it Cricket?

Newcomers to Corfu's Liston promenade cafe scene may be puzzled by the sight of men dressed in white surrounding another man dressed in white attempting to hit a hard leather ball out of the rather scruffy park with a long willow bat. This is cricket – Greek-style. Travellers from the former British Empire will recognise and delight at this eccentric and quintessentially British game replete with its sixes, fours, LBWs and owzats!

The game was imported to Corfu by the British during their 49 year hegemony of the island from 1815 to 1864. It has remained firmly entrenched in Corfu ever since. The few teams around the island gather to battle it out on sunny Sundays. While the pitch has seen better days and the distance from the batting crease to the tables of the Liston cafes can seem alarmingly close, the game is played with unusual verve and enthusiasm. This is also the only place in Greece where cricket is played.

The basic aim, for those unfamiliar with the game, is to score 'runs' by hitting the ball as far as possible and then running to and fro between the wooden wickets before the ball is returned by the fielders. Batters are considered 'out' when the ball hits their wickets, when a fielder catches the ball, when the ball hits the leg when it could have hit the wicket, or when the fielder hits the wickets before the batter has returned to the crease after running.

It's a complex game and spectators enjoy its subtleties as well as its seemingly slow pace as much as the players do. Good cricket watching is always accompanied by copious amounts of beer, the occasional shouts of encouragement from the sidelines and the odd comment on the weather. It wouldn't be cricket any other way – even in Greece.

The **Solomos museum** occupies the building that was once the home of the poet Dionysios Solomos who lived in Corfu for 30 years. Look for the sign at the western end of Arseniou. It is open 9.30 am to 2 pm Monday to Friday (200 dr).

Apart from the pleasure of wandering the narrow streets of the old town and the gardens of the Spianada, you can explore the two fortresses, Corfu Town's most dominant landmarks. The promontory on which the **Neo Frourio** stands was first fortified in the 12th century. The existing remains date from 1588. Entrance is 400 dr. The ruins of **Palaio Frourio** date from the mid-12th century. Entrance is 800 dr. Both are open all day.

In Corfu, many males are christened Spyros after the island's miracle-working patron St Spyridon. His mummified body lies in a silver glass-fronted coffin in the 16th century **Church of Agios Spyridon** on Agiou Spyridonos. It is paraded on Palm Sunday, Easter Sunday, 11 August and the first Sunday in November.

Activities

Go yachting with a crew or bareboat in fabled waters. Corfu's biggest charterer is Corfu Yachting Centre, Theotokou 120, near the new port. Or buy a copy of *Corfu Walks* by Hilary Whitton Piapeti, at Xenoglosso (see Bookshops earlier in this section), and take to the hills. The book also contains mountain bike tour details.

Cricket is played on Greece's only cricket ground on a rather scruffy pitch abutting the Liston. The actual wicket is made of artificial turf and resounds, during the summer months, to the rather incongruous sound of leather balls on willow bats as white-clad players of the few Corfu cricket clubs attempt to score sixes by dropping the balls into the coffee cups of the spectators watching from the Liston (see the 'Is it Cricket?' boxed text).

Organised Tours

Charitos Travel Agency (☎ 44 611, fax 36 825), Arseniou 35, has coach, mountain-bike and walking tours.

Places to Stay – Budget

Most of the D class hotels have closed, resulting in a shortage of low-priced accommodation. There are no EOT-approved ***domatia*** but locals who unofficially let rooms often meet the boats.

Hotel Evropi *(☎ 39 304)*, near the new harbour, is the town's only D class hotel. It has little to recommend it other than being near the new port. Singles/doubles cost 5500/6000 dr, and doubles with bathroom are 7000 dr. It's signposted from the western end of Xenofondos Stratigou.

Hotel Ionion *(☎ 30 628, fax 44 690, Xenofondos Stratigou 46)* is the cheapest C class, with reasonable rooms for 8500/10,600 dr.

Places to Stay – Mid-Range

Hotel Arcadion *(☎ 37 670, fax 45 087, Kapodistria 44)* has small, comfortable rooms for 13,000/17,000 dr, including breakfast. ***Hotel Atlantis*** *(☎ 35 560, fax 46 480, email atlanker@mail.otenet.gr, Xenofondos Stratigou 48)* has pleasant rooms for 13,750/16,500 dr.

The refurbished C class ***Hotel Konstantinoupolis*** *(☎ 48 716, fax 48 718, Zavitsianou 1)*, reincarnated from a shabby backpacker's favourite into a splendid art-nouveau hostelry, has rates of 14,000/19,000 dr with breakfast. Nearby, the B class ***Hotel Astron*** *(☎ 39 505, 33 708, Donzelot 15)* has a neoclassical ambience but somewhat timeworn room rates of 19,500/28,000 dr.

Places to Stay – Top End

The A class ***Cavelieri Hotel*** *(☎ 39 041, fax 39 283, Kapodistria 4)* occupies a 300-year-old building and has an interior of classical elegance. Rates are 30,000/35,000 dr and family suites cost 40,000 dr.

Corfu Palace *(☎ 39 485, fax 31 749, email cfupalace@hol.gr)* on Dimokratias is the town centre's only deluxe hotel, the choice of Prince Rainier and the late Princess Grace. It has two bars, two restaurants and pools. Rates are a healthy 54,000/74,000 dr.

Places to Eat – Budget

As it was not conquered by the Turks, Corfu maintains a distinctive cuisine influenced by other parts of Europe, including Russia.

There are several low-priced eateries near the new port. Both the tiny ***O Thessalonikios*** on Xenofondos Stratigou and ***Luca's BBQ*** on Avramiou serve low-priced, succulent spit-roast chicken.

There's a cluster of atmospheric restaurants at the southern end of the old town. ***Taverna O Giogas*** *(Guilford 16)* serves reasonably priced *mezedes* and main courses at outdoor tables under a grapevine. The cosy ***Yia sou Yianni*** *(Idromenon 19)* has similar food and prices.

Nearby, ***Restaurant Arpi*** *(Giotopoulou 20)* is a classy little place with *pastitsada* for 1900 dr and *sofrito* for 1700 dr.

One of Corfu's oldest restaurants is ***Hrysomalis*** *(Nik. Theotoki 6)*, just behind the expensive Liston cafe strip. Lawrence and Gerald Durrell used to dine here. The food is cheap and tasty and the local rosé wine is superb.

Farther north, most eateries are touristy and downmarket, but there are exceptions. ***Paradosiakon*** *(Solomou 20)* serves delicious food and ***Naftikon Restaurant*** *(Nik. Theotoki 150)* has fair prices and Corfiot food. At ***Ouzeri Bellisimo*** *(N Theotoki)*, a tasty mezedes plate costs 1900 dr.

Places to Eat – Mid-Range

Indulge in a little people-watching at one of the cafes on the Liston. You will pay around 1250 dr for coffee and croissant.

Mouragia Ouzeri *(Arseniou 15)* has a large range of mezedes. The small mixed fish plate (2250 dr) or the grilled beef patties *soudzoukakia* make an enjoyable meal overlooking the sea.

Behind the Liston is another established eatery which has operated since 1932, ***Estiatorio Rex*** *(Kapodistria 66)*. Claiming to be the oldest restaurant in town, it is now a quietly modern, tasteful eating place, with main courses averaging around 2200 dr.

Faliraki *(☎ 21 118)*, on the corner of Arseniou and Kapodistria, is a refurbishment of a popular Victorian bathing spot. It's a great waterside spot for a meal in the shadow of the old Kastro.

Entertainment

Having fun in Corfu is comprised mainly of strolling around, sitting at the cafes on the Liston or being cool at the multitude of little bars and pubs that dot the old and new town. Young and old have their spots and you can tell at a glance.

That said, perhaps the most entertaining spot to spend an idle hour or two is at one of the cafes bordering the cricket ground, watching cricket on a Sunday afternoon.

If it's visual entertainment you want, Corfu Town has two indoor cinemas: the ***Pallas*** *(Theotoki)* and the ***Orpheus*** *(Aspioti)*. A little farther south of the latter, there's an outdoor cinema that is supposed to operate in summer.

Corfu's disco strip lies 1 to 2km northwest of the new harbour. Here, high-tech palaces of hype jostle cheek by jowl for the tourist buck. The ***Hippodrome*** is the biggest and flashiest – it's even got a pool. ***Apokalypsis*** and ***Coco Club*** are garish and expensive and there's a pseudo ***Hard Rock Cafe*** to complete the scene.

The more sedate at heart may enjoy horse and carriage rides around the old town – great for taking photos or making a quick home video memento.

NORTH OF CORFU TOWN

Most of the coast of northern Corfu is package-tourist saturated, and thoroughly de-Greeked, though once you venture beyond the main package resorts ending at Pyrgi you enter some of Corfu's most privileged scenery. Writers Lawrence and Gerald Durrell knew this well too and spent much of their creative years along this coastline which, in parts, is little more than a short boat hop to the Albanian coastline opposite.

Ipsos is a brash tourist strip full of bars, restaurants and cafes. The beach is rather narrow and a very busy road separates the sea from the fun and entertainment. You will probably not want to linger long in Ipsos if you are seeking solitude.

More or less extending out of Ipsos is **Pyrgi**, 16km north of Corfu Town, where a road continues east around the base of **Mt Pantokrator** (906m), the island's highest peak. From Pyrgi, another road snakes north and inland over the western flank of the mountain to the north coast. A detour can be made to the picturesque village of **Strinylas** from where a now surfaced road leads through stark terrain to the summit, Moni Pantokratora and stupendous views. There is a small taverna near the summit.

Heading westwards around the winding coastal road you will first hit **Nisaki**, little more than a small cove with a pebble beach, a couple of tavernas and some domatia. Still, it's prettier than Ipsos.

The next village of interest is **Kalami** where the **White House** was the home of the Durrell brothers. The building is perched right on the water's edge and must have been idyllic during the writers' sojourn here. It is now a restaurant.

Just round the next headland west is the little harbour of **Kouloura**, where many daily excursion boats from farther north bring visitors. There is a pleasant restaurant overlooking the harbour here. From both Kalami and Kouloura the houses and buildings of Butrint in neighbouring Albania can be seen quite clearly.

Kassiopi is the next major port of call. It is a sizable little resort village around a circular harbour where its more sedate package-tour visitors opt for fishing and strolling. There is a reasonable beach just west of Kassiopi round the headland.

The coast road continues to the resort of **Roda**, a rather dull and uninspiring place after the arresting scenery of the east coast opposite Albania and the beach scene is not all that brilliant. Better to move on to **Sidhari**, where you can walk south along a footpath by the River Tyflos, a habitat for terrapins,

The Brothers Durrell

The name Durrell is synonymous with Corfu, though it is perhaps surprising that of the two brothers Lawrence (1912-90) and Gerald (1925-95) it is the naturalist Gerald rather than the poet and novelist Lawrence who has so inextricably linked the name of this famous duo with the island of Corfu and the little village of Kalami on Corfu's north-east coast.

Gerald Durrell was born in India and gained considerable repute among conservationists for his role in breeding endangered animal species for eventual release in the wild. He was also a prolific author, producing more than 35 informative yet amusing books about animals. Durrell's love of animals started when living in Corfu in the 1930s. His best-known books were *The Overloaded Ark* (1953), *Three Singles to Adventure* (1953), *My Family and other Animals* (1956), *A Zoo in my Luggage* (1960) and *Birds, Beasts and Relatives* (1969).

Brother Lawrence, also born in India, was the dedicated writer in the family. He was at once a novelist, poet, writer of topographical books, verse plays and farcical short stories. He is best known for the Alexandria Quartet, a series of four interconnected novels. His Greek trilogy included *Prospero's Cell* (1945) in which he describes his life in Corfu during 1937 and 1938, *Reflections on a Marine Venus* (1953) for which he spent two years in Rhodes in 1945-46 as press officer for the Allied government and *Bitter Lemons of Cyprus* (1957) where he spent the 1952-56 years as a teacher and government official – latterly during the Cypriot insurgency.

Both brothers were well known around Corfu and some of the older restaurant owners near Corfu Town's Liston still remember their illustrious literary patrons. Their former house overlooking the sea at the village of Kalami is now a quaint fish restaurant.

herons and egrets. Sidhari is still a rather tacky package resort, but its shallow sandy beach is ideal for children. **Peroulades**, 3km west of Sidhari, is less developed and there's a track to beautiful Cape Drastis.

Agios Stefanos, farther around the coast, is still quite pleasant out of high season. It has a long sandy beach extending under the lee of high sand cliffs and is a good spot for windsurfing. Regular boats to the Diapondia Islands (see the Diapondia Islands section following) leave from the little harbour of Agios Stefanos 1.5km from the village centre.

Places to Stay & Eat

Camp sites along the north-east coast include: ***Karda Beach*** *(☎ 0661-93 595)* and ***Kormarie*** *(☎ 0661-93 587)* at Dassia; ***Kerkira Camping*** *(☎ 0661-93 579)* and ***Ipsos Ideal*** *(☎ 0661-93 243)* at Ipsos; and ***Paradise Camping*** *(☎ 0661-93 557)* at Pyrgi. ***San Stefanos Golden Beach Hotel*** *(☎ 0663-51 053/154)*, by the bus stop in Agios Stefanos, has comfortable single/double rooms and studios for 7500/9000 dr.

Durrell fans can have a nostalgic meal at the ***White House*** in Kalami.

SOUTH OF CORFU TOWN

The Kanoni peninsula, 4km from Corfu Town, was the site of the ancient capital but little has been excavated. **Mon Repos Villa**, at its north-east tip was Prince Philip's birthplace. The beautiful wooded grounds are open 8 am to 8 pm daily. Opposite the entrance are two excavation sites, both closed to the public. One is the ruins of the 5th century **Basilica of Agia Kerkyra**, built on the site of a 5th century BC temple. You can walk to the **Kardaki Spring** from Analypsi nearby.

Just off the southern tip of Kanoni are two pretty islets. On one is **Moni Vlahernas**, reached by a causeway. On the other, **Mouse Island** (Poutikonisi), there is a 13th century church. Caïques ply back and forth from the top of the Kanoni peninsula.

The coast road continues south with a turn-off to the **Ahillion Palace** (☎ 0661-56 245), near the village of Gastouri. In the 1890s it was the summer palace of Austria's Empress Elizabeth (King Otho of Greece was her uncle). She dedicated the villa to Achilles. The beautifully landscaped garden is guarded by kitsch statues of the empress' other mythological heroes. The palace is open 9 am to 4 pm Monday to Sunday. Admission is 1000 dr.

The resort of **Benitses** used to be the playground of holiday hooligans, but in recent times has made strenuous efforts to get its act together. Still, the excesses of too much package tourism in the past have taken the sheen off the little fishing village, but the narrow winding streets of the old village still maintain an air of authenticity. If the beach scene is not to your liking, head inland for a splendid 30 minute walk along an almost tropical-looking valley to the scene of old waterworks, built during the time of the British protectorate.

The **Shell Museum** (☎ 0661-99 340) at Benitses reputedly contains the best private shell collection in Europe. It is open 9 am to 10 pm daily. Entrance is 500 dr.

Heading farther south from Corfu town you will next hit **Messonghi**, similar to Benitses but quieter. The beach scene while not ideal is certainly better than its neighbour farther north. The winding coastal road between Benitses and **Boukaris** is decidedly more appealing and is dotted with a few tavernas and small pebbly beaches.

Places to Stay & Eat

There is accommodation aplenty around Benitses and farther south along the coast. Try ***Potamaki Hotel*** *(☎ 0661-71 140, fax 72 451)* in Benitses itself if you can't decide. Singles/doubles are 10,500/12,500 dr.

It's touristy, kitsch and a bit over the top, but it's popular, it's been around a long time and the food is unusual. ***Tripa Tavern*** *(☎ 0661-56 333)* at the little village of Kinopiastes has hosted its fair share of illustrious patrons including Jane Fonda, Aristotle Onassis, Anthony Quinn and François Mitterand. For 6000 dr a head you get a sumptuous set banquet with a wide range of original Corfiot dishes.

THE WEST COAST

Corfu's best beaches are on the west coast. **Paleokastritsa**, 26km west of Corfu, is the coast's largest resort. Built around sandy and pebbled coves with a green mountain backdrop, it's incredibly beautiful. Once paradisal, it's been the victim of rampant development. While the water here looks enticing, it is generally considerably colder than on other parts of the island.

Moni Theotokou perches on the rocky promontory at Paleokastritsa, above the shimmering turquoise sea. The monastery was founded in the 13th century but the present building dates from the 18th century. A small museum contains icons. It is open 7 am to 1 pm and 3 to 8 pm daily. Admission is free, but a donation is expected.

From Paleokastritsa a path ascends to the unspoilt village of **Lakones**, 5km inland. Walk back along the approach road and you'll see a signposted footpath on the left.

There are superb views along the 6km road west to **Makrades** and **Krini**. The restaurants along the way extol the views from their terraces.

From Krini you can explore the ruins of the 13th century Byzantine fortress of **Angelokastro** where Paleokastritsa's inhabitants took refuge from attackers. A long distance bus goes twice daily to Krini from Corfu Town.

Farther south, the beach at **Ermones** is near **Corfu Golf Course**, the largest in Europe. Hilltop **Pelekas**, 4km away, is renowned for its spectacular sunsets. It's as busy as the coast, but with young independent travellers, rather than package tourists. Pelekas is close to three sandy beaches, **Glyfada**, **Pelekas** and **Myrtiotissa**, the last an unofficial nudist beach. There is a free bus from Pelekas to the first two. Don't miss the superb panoramic views over Corfu from the **Kaiser's Lookout** high up above Pelekas village. Just follow the main road upwards to the end.

Agios Gordios is a popular backpacker hang-out 8km south of Glyfada. The beach is reasonably pretty, but the village is rather overdeveloped with the usual conglomeration of shops, souvenir stalls, eateries and domatia accommodation. Overall it's a laid-back kind of place and will appeal to travellers interested primarily in the 'beach and bar' scene. There are three long distance buses daily from Corfu Town to Agios Gordios, via Sinarades.

At Sinarades, 4km from Agios Gordios, the **Folk Museum of Central Corfu** occupies a 19th century house. It is open 9.30 am to 3 pm Tuesday to Sunday. Admission is around 300 dr.

Freshwater **Lake Korission**, a little farther south, is a habitat for wading birds. The long stretch of inviting sand and dunes between the lake and sea continues to Issos. This is one of the least spoilt stretches of Corfu's coast, but it's back to rampant development at Agios Georgios.

Places to Stay

Paleokastritsa Camping *(☎ 0663-41 204, fax 41 104)* is on the main approach road to the resort, shortly after the signposted turn-off to the village of Lakones. It's a reasonably well organised camp site, with a restaurant and minimarket on site, but is a fair way back from the beach scene. The bus will drop you at the entrance. Paleokastritsa also has many hotels, studios and domatia. ***Vatos Camping*** *(☎ 0661-94 505)* near the village of Vatos is a quiet retreat but handier if you have some kind of transport of your own.

The Pink Palace *(☎ 0661-53 103)* at Agios Gordios is a brash backpacker hostel designed for the under 25s who want fun and sun without the hassles of having to look for it. You'll pay between 5000 dr and 10,000 dr per person for average accommodation and that includes breakfast and dinner.

Alexandros Pension *(☎ 0661-94 215, 94 833)*, at Pelekas, on the road signposted 'sunset', has pleasant doubles for 7000 dr with bathroom. A bit farther along, ***Rooms to Let Thomas*** *(☎ 0661-94 491, fax 94 190)* has clean, comfortable singles/doubles with private bathroom for 9000/11,000 dr, and doubles with shared bathroom for 6000 dr. Back near the central square, the bougainvillea-smothered ***Pension Tellis & Brigitte*** *(☎ 0661-94 326)* near the central square has pleasant doubles for 6500 dr with bathroom.

The stylish, neoclassical ***Levant Hotel*** *(☎ 0661-94 230, fax 94 115)*, higher up on the Pelekas road, has beautiful singles/doubles for 16,000/18,000 dr.

High up overlooking Paleokastritsa and just beyond Lakones village is ***Golden Fox Apartments*** *(☎/fax 0663-41 381)* with studios costing 13,000 dr. The swimming pool here must have the best view in the whole of Greece.

Places to Eat

Bella Vista perched high up above Paleokastritsa just past Lakones looks nothing special but the views are breathtaking. Reputedly the Kaiser, Tito and Nasser all dined here. Farther west from Lakones along the cliff-top road, ***Golden Fox Restaurant*** *(☎ 0663-41 381/409)* serves excellent charcoal-grilled dishes.

Alexandros Restaurant, of the pension of the same name in Pelekas, is as good as anywhere for an unfussy meal. In Paleokastritsa there is a fairly wide choice but little difference in quality between the eating places. Look out for ***Astakos Taverna*** or ***Corner Grill*** which serve up Greek and tourist favourites.

THE DIAPONDIA ISLANDS

Τα Διαπόντια Νησιά

☎ 0633

Scattered like forgotten stepping stones to Puglia in Italy, lie a cluster of little-known and even less visited satellite islands belonging administratively to Corfu. Of the five islands only Ereikousa, Mathraki and Othoni are inhabited, though many of their original residents have long since departed for the lure of New York city and only return in the summer months to renew their ties.

Often isolated by tricky seas, the islands are worth the extra effort to visit them and serious island collectors should place them high on their agenda. Development is proceeding slowly and cautiously and all offer places to stay. Most people visit on day trips from Sidhari, though regular ferries do link the islands with both Agios Stefanos on the north-west tip of Corfu and Corfu Town.

Getting There & Away

The most reliable link is the thrice-weekly service from Corfu Town (1500-1800 dr) with the *Alexandros II* which leaves shortly after dawn for the long haul round Corfu to bring supplies and the odd vehicle. From Agios Stefanos a small passenger boat services Ereikousa and then Othoni and Mathraki alternatively at least twice weekly (1000-1200 dr). Schedules vary without warning so check beforehand (☎ 094-999 771 or 0663-95 248).

The easiest solution may be to jump on a day excursion out of Sidhari Harbour. Excursions are advertised widely around Sidhari's hotels and travel agencies.

Ereikousa Ερείκουσα

Ereikousa (eh-**ree**-koo-sah; population 334) is perhaps the most visited and popular of the three islands and the closest of the three to Corfu Town and Sidhari. Touted as a desert island getaway, Ereikousa does in fact have some decent beaches and if you can only manage to visit one of the Diapondia Islands, then consider Ereikousa. Not surprisingly it attracts more than its share of visitors and can get busy in high season.

If you want to stay, contact the one hotel, ***Ereikousa Hotel*** *(☎ 71 555)*, for room availability. For eating you have ***Anemomylos Taverna*** *(☎ 71 647)*. It also has a few domatia.

Mathraki Μαθράκι

Wild and wooded Mathraki (population 143) is the least developed of the trio, but offers solitude, some fine walking, at least three seasonal tavernas and some domatia to stay at. There is a very long beach – which is also home to the loggerhead turtle, so discretion is necessary when beachcombing – a small scattered settlement inland and a tiny harbour with a cardphone. Excursion boats will inevitably drop you off at Piadini

Beach, which is a 30 minute walk east along a rough dirt track to the harbour.

Taverna o Yiannis *(☎ 72 108)* on Piadini beach will be open if you have come by excursion boat. By the harbour is the modern ***Port Center Restaurant*** owned by Spyridoula Kassimi and her husband and up in the village is the *kafeneio*/restaurant/store ***Taverna o Geis*** run by Spyros and his wife.

Accommodation is provided by the ***domatia*** of Christos Argyris *(☎ 71 652)* who has doubles for 6000 dr with breakfast, or newer ***apartments*** run by Anastasios Kassimis *(☎ 71 700)*.

Othoni Οθονοί

The largest of the group is also the farthest out. Othoni (o-tho-**nee**; population 98) is popular with Italian yachties. The interior is wooded and the 35 minute walk up to the inland village of Horio is worth the effort for the views. Beach bums will find little comfort in the island's two pebbly beaches near the port.

Gourmets will find one decent Italian restaurant here, ***La Locanda dei Sogni*** *(☎ 71 640)*, which also has rooms, but other eating options include ***New York*** and ***Mikros***. Rooms can also be found courtesy of the owner of New York; ring ☎ 71 581 for availability.

Paxi & Antipaxi

PAXI Παξοί

☎ 0662 • postcode 490 82 • pop 2200

Paxi (pahx-**ee**), 10km long and 4km wide, is the smallest main Ionian island. It has a captivating landscape of dense, centuries-old olive groves, snaking dry stone walls, derelict farmhouses and abandoned stone olive presses. The olive trees have amazingly twisted, gnarled and hollowed trunks, which gives them the look of sinister, ancient monsters. Walking through the olive groves at dusk is quite eerie.

Paxi has escaped the mass tourism of Corfu and caters for small, discriminating tour companies. People come here because they have fallen in love with Paxi's inimitable cosy feel, or have heard about its friendly islanders and its captivating scenery.

There are only three coastal settlements – Gaïos, Longos and Lakka – and a few inland villages. The whole island is walkable, though good roads do cover the length of the island. Paxi is an absolute must for any serious island-hopper and is worth the extra effort needed to get there.

Getting There & Away

Bus Buses go directly to Athens (eight hours, 8150 dr) three times weekly. Tickets are available at Bouas Tours (☎ 32 401). Buses from Athens to Paxi depart from the Hotel Marina (☎ 01-522 9109), Voulgari 13 in Athens, at midnight.

Ferry – Domestic At least one regular passenger ferry, the *Pegasus*, connects Paxi and Corfu daily in summer (1½ hours, 3300 dr). Twice weekly the *Pegasus* also calls in at Lakka on the north coast. Other larger car

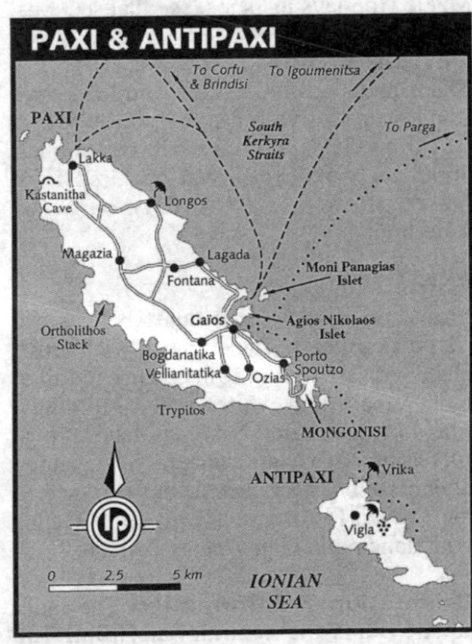

ferries also run throughout the year from Corfu and Igoumenitsa (two hours, 1600 dr) on the mainland. Daily excursion boats also come from Corfu and Parga on the mainland. Ferries dock at Gaïos' port 1km east of the central square, though the *Pegasus* departs from the Gaïos waterfront. Excursion boats dock by the central square and along the quay towards the new port. Hydrofoils between Corfu and Paxi started in 1999 and should hopefully be running each summer.

Tickets for Corfu and Igoumenitsa can be obtained from Zefi Travel (☎ 32 114, fax 32 253) on the waterfront. Tickets for the *Pegasus* can be obtained from Gaios Travel (☎ 32 033, fax 32 175). Paxi's port police can be contacted on ☎ 31 222.

Ferry – International In July and August a ferry goes two or three times weekly from Paxi to Brindisi in Italy, via Igoumenitsa and Corfu. Ticket prices are the same as from Corfu. A catamaran service to Brindisi via Corfu also runs from 8 July to 5 September, making the trip in 5¼ hours. A one way ticket costs 33,000 dr.

Tickets can be obtained from Paxos Magic Holidays in Gaïos (see that section).

Getting Around

The island's bus links Gaïos and Lakka via Longos up to five times daily (300 dr). A taxi from Gaïos to Lakka will cost around 3000 dr. Motorcycles can be hired from Makris Motorcycles (☎ 32 031), on Gaïos' waterfront.

Gaïos Γάιος

Gaïos, on a wide, east coast bay, is the island's capital. It's a delightfully attractive place with crumbling 19th century red-tiled pink, cream and whitewashed buildings. The fortified Agios Nikolaos Islet almost fills its harbour. Moni Panagias Islet, named after its monastery, lies at the entrance to the bay. On 15 August, a lively festival ends with dancing in Gaïos' central square.

Orientation & Information The main square abuts the central waterfront. The main street of Panagioti Kanga runs inland from here to another square where you'll find the bus stop. The post office is just beyond here and the OTE is next door.

There is no tourist office, but the staff at Paxos Magic Holidays (☎ 32 269, fax 32 122, email paxoshld@hol.gr), on Panagioti Kanga, are very helpful. They also sell the *Bleasdale Walking Map of Paxos* (3000 dr), which comes with an explanatory booklet. The Road Editions 'Corfu and Paxi' map is currently the best map available for the island.

Things to See & Do The excellent **Cultural Museum of Paxi**, on the waterfront, has a well displayed eclectic collection. Don't miss the mind-boggling stirrups hanging from a four-poster bed – a 19th century sex aid. The museum is open 11 am to 1.30 pm and 7 to 10 pm daily. Admission is 500 dr.

The best way to get to know Paxi is to walk the island along its many pathways lined with dry stone walls through the countless olive groves that blanket the island.

Paxos Magic Holidays also organises horseback picnic rides (13,900 dr), an island discovery cruise (5400 dr) or a History and Traditions Evening which takes in olive oil making, feta cheese making, cooking and finally dining to Greek music (8,500 dr, all inclusive).

Places to Stay Accommodation tends to mostly consist of prebooked studios and apartments, though you can always find somewhere private to stay. The large ***San Giorgio Rooms to Rent*** *(☎ 32 223)* above the waterfront, 150m north of the central square, has well kept doubles for 6000 dr, studios for 8000 dr and apartments for 14,000 dr.

Up the hill opposite the bus stop are a few domatia. ***Magda's Domatia*** *(☎ 32 573)* has a few clean and basic doubles/triples for 6000/8000 dr. Next door up the hill is ***Spiro's Domatia*** *(☎ 31 172)*. His somewhat better serviced rooms go for around 8000 dr for a double.

The B class ***Paxos Beach** (☎ 31 211, fax 31 166)* is a bungalow complex, overlooking the sea, 1.5km south-east of Gaïos. The tastefully furnished doubles cost 35,000 dr (half-board) in high season. The complex has a tennis court, beach, bar and restaurant.

Places to Eat Gaïos has a glut of generally good eating places. Cheap and popular is ***George's Place*** on the main square. Go there for his great gyros or chicken. Off the south side of the square is ***Taverna Andreas***. This cosy little eatery is the best place for fresh fish and home cooking. Close by is the homy ***Kirki***, offering among other tasty fare a chicken dish done in mustard sauce. Kirki is open all year round.

A great evening's eating can be had at the tastefully furbished ***Afthendiko*** at the inland end of Gaïos. This tavern does superb home-cooked dishes – try octopus in tomato sauce or rooster with pastitsada. Both dishes are around 2000 dr.

If you fancy a walk, head uphill along the signposted Vellianitatika road and look for the rather laid-back but still popular ***O Kakaletzos** (☎ 32 129)*, diagonally opposite the Paxos Club, just west of Gaïos. It serves a wide range of ready-cooked dishes and grilled food.

Around Paxi

Paxi's gentle east coast has small pebble beaches, while the west coast has awesome vistas of precipitous cliffs, punctuated by several grottoes only accessible by boat. You can walk to **Trypitos**, a high cliff from where there are stunning views of Antipaxi. From Gaïos, walk westwards along the Makratika road and turn right uphill at Villa Billy's, marked with a small sign on the wall. Stay on the main track and just before it ends turn left onto a narrow path which leads to Trypitos.

Longos A small fishing village-cum-resort, Longos is 5km north of Gaïos, and has several beaches nearby. It's much smaller than Gaïos and has a more intimate feel. The village consists of little more than a cramped square and a winding waterfront with a couple roads leading in and out. It's a great base if you want a quieter stay on Paxi.

Most of the accommodation is monopolised by tour companies, but ***Babis Dendias** (☎/fax 31 597)* rents four-person studios for between 22,000 dr and 28,000 dr. Inquire at his *pantopoleio* (general store), 20m beyond the bus stop.

For eating, try ***Kagarantzas*** or ***Taverna o Gios***. Coffees and cold drinks can be taken at ***Ores*** music cafe and wine bar in between the two. The best bread on the island can be found at the ramshackle ***Loukas Bakery***, up a little alley off the square.

Lakka This is another pretty harbour and feels more like Gaïos. It lies at the end of a deep, narrow bay on the north coast and is another popular yachtie call. It's an ideal alternative base to Gaïos since you can also take the twice-weekly ferry to Corfu from here. There are a couple of decent beaches, Vigla and Mesorahi, around either side of the bay's headland and there are some great walks from here.

If you would like to stay, contact Routsis Holidays (☎ 31 807, fax 31 161) on the waterfront. The helpful owners are the agents for many rooms in and around Lakka. They also organise various activities like day trips to Antipaxi and Parga, and rent out boats for 10,000 dr a day.

Lakka also has a glut of good and tasteful tavernas, though ***Souris*** on the square and ***Stasinos*** in a little side street off the square are worth looking at first

ANTIPAXI Αντίπαξοι

Diminutive Antipaxi, 2km south of Paxi, is covered with grape vines from which excellent wine is produced. Caïques and tourist boats run daily out of Gaïos and usually pull in at couple of beaches. Vrika Beach at the north-eastern tip is sandy and gently sloping. Two restaurants, ***Spiro's Taverna*** and ***Vrika Taverna***, serve the often busy tourist trade.

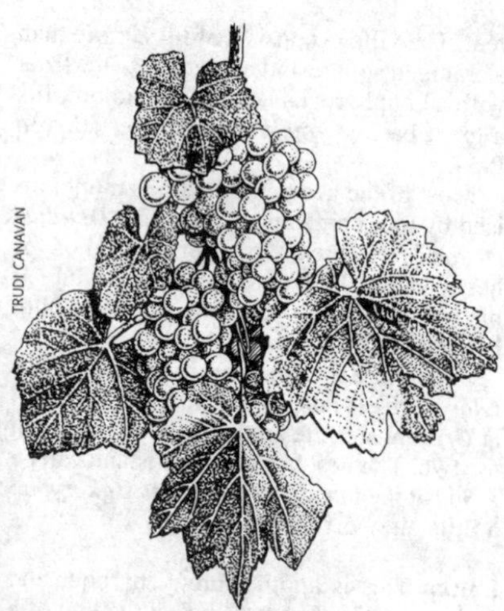

Vineyards are a common sight on the tiny island of Antipaxi

A coastal path links Vrika Beach with Voutoumi Beach, farther south round a couple of headlands. Voutoumi Beach is very pretty, but is made up of large pebbles. A ***taverna*** high up on the bluff serves hungry bathers.

If you don't fancy just beach bumming, take a walk up to the little scattered settlement of Vigla, stopping to admire the many little vineyards along the way and dotted throughout the village.

The cheapest way to get to Antipaxi is via the Antipaxos Lines boat (1300 dr return) from Gaïos that leaves at 10 am and returns from Vrika Beach at 5 pm.

Lefkada, Meganisi & Kalamos

LEFKADA Λευκάδα

☎ 0645 • postcode 311 00 • pop 21,100

Lefkada is the fourth largest island in the Ionian group. Joined to the mainland by a narrow isthmus until the occupying Corinthians dug a canal in the 8th century BC, its 25m strait is spanned from the mainland by a causeway.

Lefkada has 10 satellite islets: Meganisi, Kalamos, Kastos, Madouri, Skorpidi, Skorpios, Sparti, Thilia, Petalou and Kythros.

Lefkada is mountainous with two peaks over 1000m. It is also fertile, well watered by underground streams, with cotton fields, acres of dense olive groves, vineyards, fir and pine forests.

Once a very poor island, Lefkada's beauty is also in its people, who display intense pride in their island. Many of the older women wear traditional costume. An International Festival of Literature & Art is held in the last two weeks of August.

Getting There & Away

Air Lefkada has no airport but Aktion airport, near Preveza on the mainland, is a 30 minute bus journey away. It has four flights weekly to Athens (13,900 dr). Lefkada's Olympic Airways office (☎ 22 881) is at Dorpfeld 1; Preveza's (☎ 0682-28 343) is at Spiliadou 5.

Bus From Lefkada Town's bus station (☎ 22 364) there are buses to Athens (5½ hours, 6200 dr, four daily), Patra (three hours, 2900 dr, two weekly) and Aktion airport (30 minutes, 360 dr, five daily).

Ferry From Vasiliki, at least two ferries daily go to Fiskardo (1½ hours, 940 dr) on Kefallonia and Frikes (1½ hours, 940 dr) on Ithaki in high season. In summer one ferry leaves daily from Nydri for Frikes on Ithaki and then Fiskardo. Lefkada's port police can be contacted on ☎ 22 322.

Getting Around

From Lefkada Town, frequent buses go to Karya and Vlyho via Nydri. Four go daily to Vasiliki and two daily go to Poros. Other villages are served by one or two buses daily.

Cars are available for hire from Europcar (☎ 25 726), Stratigou Mela 7, among others,

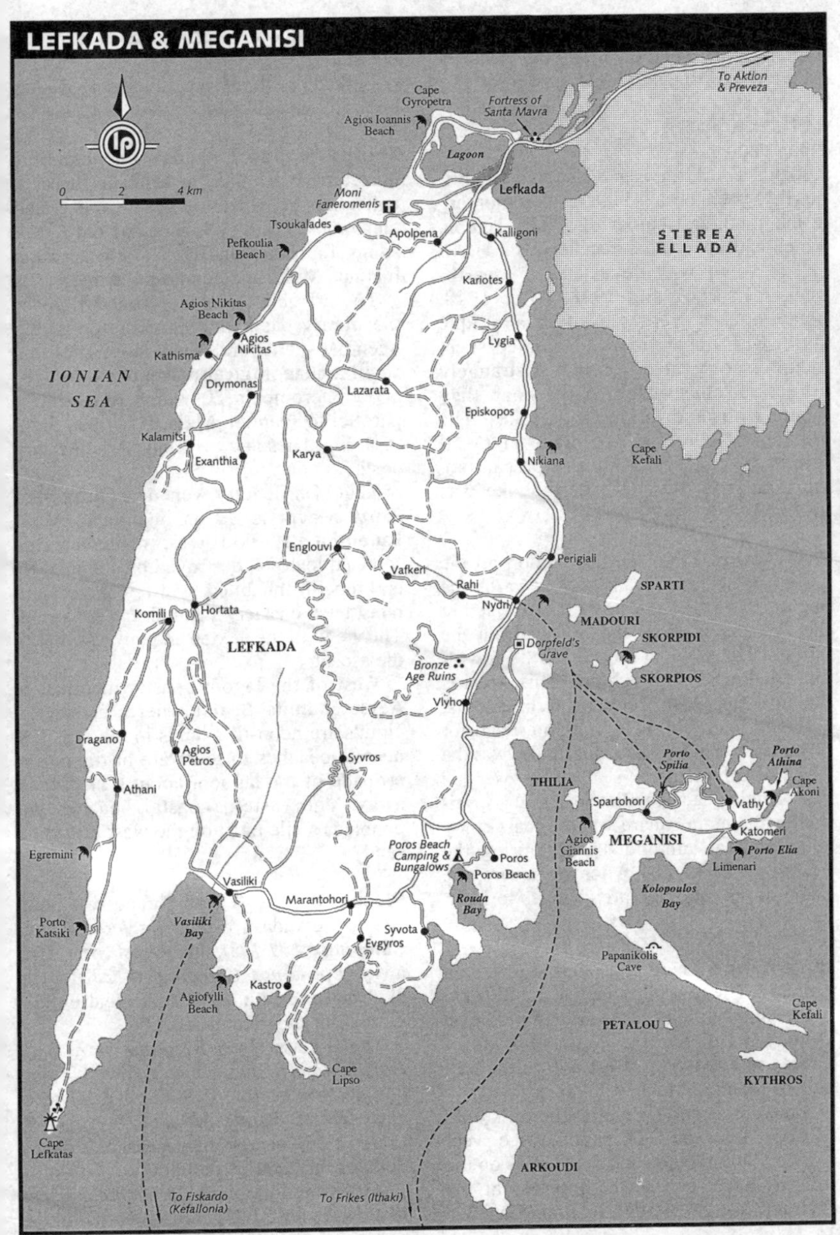
LEFKADA & MEGANISI
0
2
4 km
To Aktion & Preveza
Cape Gyropetra
Fortress of Santa Mavra
Agios Ioannis Beach
Lagoon
Lefkada
Moni Faneromenis
Tsoukalades
Apolpena
Kalligoni
STEREA ELLADA
Pefkoulia Beach
Kariotes
Agios Nikitas Beach
Agios Nikitas
Lygia
Kathisma
IONIAN SEA
Drymonas
Lazarata
Episkopos
Kalamitsi
Exanthia
Karya
Cape Kefali
Nikiana
Englouvi
Perigiali
Vafkeri
Rahi
SPARTI
Nydri
MADOURI
Komili
Hortata
SKORPIDI
Dorpfeld's Grave
LEFKADA
Bronze Age Ruins
SKORPIOS
Vlyho
Dragano
Agios Petros
Porto Spilia
Porto Athina
Syvros
THILIA
Cape Akoni
Athani
Spartohori
Vathy
Katomeri
MEGANISI
Egremini
Poros Beach Camping & Bungalows
Poros
Agios Giannis Beach
Porto Elia
Limenari
Vasiliki
Poros Beach
Marantohori
Rouda Bay
Kolopoulos Bay
Porto Katsiki
Vasiliki Bay
Syvota
Evgyros
Papanikolis Cave
Kastro
Agiofylli Beach
Cape Kefali
PETALOU
Cape Lipso
KYTHROS
Cape Lefkatas
ARKOUDI
To Fiskardo (Kefallonia)
To Frikes (Ithaki)

and motorcycles from Motorcycle Rental Santas (☎ 23 947), on Aristoteli Valaoriti. At the top of Ioannou Mela, turn right.

Lefkada Town

• pop 6800

Lefkada Town, the island's capital and primarily a yacht port, is built on a promontory at the south-east corner of a salty lagoon, which is used as a fish hatchery.

The town was devastated by earthquakes in 1867 and 1948. After 1948, many houses were rebuilt in a unique style, with upper floors of painted sheet metal or corrugated iron that is strangely attractive, constructed in the hope they would withstand future earthquakes. The belfries of churches are made of metal girders – another earthquake precaution. Damage from the 1953 earthquake was minimal.

Orientation From the bus station on the eastern waterfront, walk back towards the beginning of the causeway road, turn left at the first major road, and left again at the Nirikos Hotel on to Dorpfeld, the town's animated main thoroughfare. This street is named after 19th century archaeologist Wilhelm Dorpfeld, held in high esteem for postulating that Lefkada, not Ithaki, was the home of Odysseus.

Dorpfeld leads to Plateia Agiou Spyridonos, the main square where locals enjoy *soumadia* (an almond drink), during the evening *volta* (stroll). After the square, the name of the thoroughfare changes to Ioannou Mela.

Information There is no tourist office on Lefkada. The tourist police (☎ 26 450) are in the same building as the regular police on Dimitriou Golemi. The National Bank of Greece and the post office are on the east side of Ioannou Mela.

Take the second right after the bank onto Mitropolis for the OTE phone office. Veer right on to Zambelou and the OTE is on the left. You can access the Internet at the Internet Cafe (☎ 21 507), Ioannou Gazi 5, a five minute walk south (inland) from the bus station.

Lefkada's library, at Skiadaresis 1, has books about Lefkada in many languages.

Things to See Lefkada's **phonographic museum** (☎ 21 088) at Kalkani 10 has a collection of venerable gramophones and memorabilia and sells tapes of old Greek songs for 1000 dr. It's signposted from Ioannou Mela, and admission is free.

The art gallery in the ground floor of the library has changing exhibitions. It's open between 7 and 9 pm daily. There's a small **archaeological museum** (☎ 23 678) at Pefaneromenis 20 which runs almost parallel to Ioannou Mela. It is open 9 am to 1 pm Tuesday to Sunday; admission costs 300 dr.

The 14th century Venetian **Fortress of Santa Mavra** is on the mainland. **Moni Faneromenis**, 3km west of town, was founded in 1634, destroyed by fire in 1886 and rebuilt. Inhabited by a few monks and nuns, the monastery's church can be visited. The views of the lagoon and town are worth the ascent.

West of the lagoon, past windmills, is **Agios Ioannis Beach** where, at sunset, clouds are neon-lit islands in the sky. The nearest beaches to town are at the northern side of the lagoon, about a 2km walk away. The eastern coastal beaches are pebbled, while most on the west are white sand.

Places to Stay & Eat The nearest camp site to Lefkada Town is ***Kariotes Beach Camping*** *(☎ 71 103)*, on the east coast, 5km away. ***Episkopos Camping*** *(☎ 23 043)* is 3km farther south. See the Around Lefkda section for other camp sites.

The D class ***Hotel Byzantio*** *(☎ 21 315, Dorpfeld 4)* has clean, well kept doubles/triples for 5500/8800 dr. The C class ***Hotel Santa Maura*** *(☎ 21 308, fax 26 253)* nearby has pleasant singles/doubles for 9000/14,000 dr.

At the comfortable B class ***Hotel Niricos*** *(☎ 24 132, fax 23 756)*, on the corner of the waterfront and Dorpfeld, rooms cost 14,000 dr (half-board) for singles and doubles alike. Close by, facing the port, the palatial B class ***Hotel Lefkas*** *(☎ 23 916, fax 24 579, Panagou 2)* has rates of 17,000/26,000 dr with breakfast.

Karaboulias Restaurant on the eastern waterfront offers traditional fare with flair. The intimate ***Eftyhia Taverna*** *(Stambogli 2)* has hearty, inexpensive food. The walls are graced by watercolours by Panagos. Facing inland, turn left at the fountain on Dorpfeld to find the taverna.

Regantos Taverna *(Vergioti 17)* is another atmospheric little place with good food. A meal of stuffed eggplant, Greek salad and wine costs around 2200 dr. To reach the taverna, turn right at the central square off Dorpfeld.

Around Lefkada

Nydri A sleepy fishing village not so long ago, Nydri, 16km south of Lefkada Town, fell hook, line and sinker to the lure of the tourist trade. Now it's a busy, commercialised but fun town from where you can cruise around the islets of **Madouri**, **Sparti**, **Skorpidi** and **Skorpios** for 3000 dr, or 7000 dr if a barbecue and unlimited drinks are included.

The privately owned Madouri islet, where the Greek poet Aristotelis Valaoritis (1824-79) spent his last 10 years, is off limits. It's not officially possible to land on Skorpios, where Ari, sister Artemis and children Alexander and Christina Onassis are buried in a cemetery visible from the sea, but you can swim off a sandy beach on the north side of the island.

If you would rather explore the islets independently, boats can be hired from Trident Travel Agency (☎/fax 92 037) on the main street. Motorboats cost around 10,000 dr a day (excluding fuel) and sailing dinghies are 8000 dr. The agency also has motorcycle and car hire and a room-finding service.

Windsurfing, water-skiing, parasailing and sailing (bareboating with licence or crewed yachts) out of Nydri can be organised by Nikos Thermes' Sport Boat Charter (☎ 92 431), Perigiali. Englishman Andy Fenna runs the island's only PADI School of Diving (☎ 92 286) from Nydri.

The quiet village of Vlyho is 3km south of Nydri. Beyond here, a road leads to a peninsula where Wilhelm Dorpfeld is buried. Just west of the Nydra-Vlyho road are the Bronze Age ruins which he excavated, leading him to believe Lefkada was Homer's Ithaca.

Places to Stay & Eat ***Desimi Beach Camping*** *(☎ 95 223)* is south of Nydri. It is signposted after the village of Vlyho.

There are a large number of rooms and studios in Nydri though a fair few get block-booked by tour companies. Samba Tours (see the Vasiliki section following) also has an accommodation office in Nydri.

Onassis

The most famous of all shipping magnates is undoubtedly the Turkish-born Greek Aristotle Socrates Onassis, who was born in Smyrna (now İzmir) in 1906, the son of a tobacco merchant. At the age of 16 his family fled from Turkish hostility to Athens. The following year he arrived in Buenos Aires with a total of $60 and worked as a telephone operator by night while building up his own tobacco business during the day.

At the age of 25 he was already a millionaire and the following year he began what became the world's largest independent shipping line, investing in six Canadian freighters in the midst of a serious recession and putting them into service as the market recovered. Onassis was one of the pioneers of supertankers in the 1950s, and he was awarded the contract to operate the Greek national airline, Olympic Airways, which started in 1957. At 62 he married President Kennedy's widow, Jacqueline. He died in 1975.

Armeno Beach Hotel *(☎ 92 112, fax 92 018)*, at the quieter northern end of Nydri, has some wonderful rooms overlooking the beach and the island of Skorpios. Doubles go for 18,000 dr in high season and 10,000 dr in low season.

Forget the touristy waterfront restaurants and walk 1km north to Perigiali. ***Mangano*** *(☎ 93 188)* is easily the best restaurant in Nydri and is much better value for money. The moussaka served here is mouthwatering and you can dine on the beach. You'll find the restaurant close to Armeno Beach Hotel.

Poros This little village overlooks Poros Bay, and makes a great alternative base to the often raucous Nydri. The beach is good and there are boats for hire.

There is a camp site, ***Poros Beach Camping & Bungalows*** *(☎ 95 452)*, as well as the cosy and cool domatia of ***Yiannoula*** *(☎ 95 507)* at the eastern end of the bay. A double with kitchen will cost you 9000 dr. For meals, try the nearby ***Zolithros*** or ***Molos***, both quaint and friendly tavernas.

Vasiliki Purported to be *the* best windsurfing location in Europe, Vasiliki is a pretty fishing village with both sand and pebbled beaches. It attracts a sizable crowd each season and you can hop over to Kefallonia from here if you are heading south.

You can rent surf boards from Club Vas (☎ 31 588) and instruction for all levels is available. It's crowded in summer so prepare to commute.

Wild Wind (☎/fax 31 610) rents out catamarans and offers instruction. You can take a cruise on a *felucca* (☎ 93 116) for between 10,000 dr and 12,000 dr, including food and drink.

Caïques take visitors from Vasiliki to swim at the best sand beaches on the west coast, which include **Porto Katsiki**, **Egremini** and **Kathisma**. All are signposted on the west coast off the road leading to the island's south-west promontory. A boat will also take you to the unspoilt **Agiofylli Beach**. A sanctuary of Apollo once stood at **Cape Lefkatas**.

Places to Stay & Eat The best bet for accommodation is to drop in to Samba Tours (☎ 92 658, fax 92 659) and see what's available. Rooms go for between 8000 dr and 11,000 dr in season. Studios cost from 15,000 dr to 20,000 dr.

The waterfront restaurants are all pretty similar and of good quality. Instead, try ***To Steki ton Piraton***, set back from the waterfront on the main street. ***Alexandros***, on the west end of the waterfront, offers a wide range of Chinese dishes if you hanker after something other than Greek food.

MEGANISI Μεγανήσι

☎ 0645 • postcode 310 83 • pop 1250

Meganisi has the largest population of Lefkada's three inhabited satellite islets, but like many small Greek islands it has suffered population depletion. It's easily visited on a day trip.

It's a tranquil islet with a lovely, verdant landscape and deep bays of turquoise water, fringed by pebbled beaches. It's visited primarily by yachties and is untouched by package tour operators. It has three settlements: the capital of Spartohori, the port of Vathy and the village of Katomeri.

Getting There & Away

There are about four ferries daily between Nydri and Meganisi. They usually call in first at Porto Spilia and then into Vathy before heading back to Nydri. In the past there have been services from Meganisi to Kefallonia and Ithaki; check to see if they are running again.

A minibus meets boats at both ports and takes passengers to Spartohori and Katomeri.

Spartohori Σπαρτοχώρι

Spartohori, with narrow, winding lanes and pretty, flower-bedecked houses, perches on a plateau above Porto Spilia.

Boats dock at Porto Spilia. No-one lives here, but there are several tavernas. A road ascends steeply to Spartohori or you can walk the 1km there up steps. To reach Spartohori's main street and central square turn right at Tropicana Pizzeria. The island's only post office is at Vathy.

One of the island's best beaches is Agios Giannis, a long stretch of small pebbles, 3km south-west of Spartohori.

Other good beaches are on the island's tapering southern tail. In summer, the owner of Taverna Lakis (see Places to Stay & Eat) takes visitors there in his boat.

Places to Stay & Eat There are no official camp sites but wild camping is tolerated.

The owner of ***Chicken Billy's Psistaria*** *(☎ 51 442)* has some low-priced ***domatia***. Beyond the central square, just before the main street curves left, turn right, and Chicken Billy's is on the right.

Kostas Rooms *(☎ 51 372)* are clean and well kept with a communal kitchen. Double/triple rooms are 6000/8000 dr. Take the street signposted to Agios Giannis and the rooms are on the right.

The immaculate ***Studios For Rent Argyri*** *(☎ 51 502, fax 24 911)* has double/triple studios for 10,000/12,000 dr. Inquire at Oasi Bar, opposite Chicken Billy's.

Tropicana Pizzeria has pizzas for 1200 dr and stunning views of Skorpios.

Taverna Lakis offers tasty Greek fare and features Greek evenings. When things really get going, Mamma Lakis, who is no spring chicken, dances with a table on her head. ***Chicken Billy's*** serves delectably tender, low-priced chicken. In its heyday, it was visited by Christina Onassis – her photograph is on the wall to prove it.

Down on Agios Giannis Beach, ***Paradiso*** restaurant operates in season.

Vathy Βαθύ

This is the island's second port. The post office is on the waterfront near the quay. Farther round there's a children's playground. Beyond here, the road climbs to **Katomeri**, 700m away.

There are no EOT-approved domatia in Vathy or Katomeri, but locals let rooms unofficially – ask around. For dining try ***Taverna Porto Vathy***, a small fish tavern right next to the ferry quay, or ***Rose Garden***, a rose-covered restaurant-cum-cafe on the little square.

There are several beaches near Katomeri. At secluded Porto Elia beach, ***Porto Elia Rooms*** *(☎ 51 341)*, owned by English-speaking Fotis Katopodis, are lovely studios costing 12,000 dr. The well signposted ***Hotel Meganisi*** *(☎ 51 240)* has spotless, modern singles/doubles for 9000/13,000 dr with bathroom. Its restaurant serves tasty traditional dishes.

Restaurant Niagas, at Porto Athina Beach, serves well prepared, freshly caught fish.

KALAMOS Κάλαμος

☎ 0646 • postcode 311 00 • pop 400

Beautiful, mountainous and wooded, Kalamos is the second largest of Lefkada's satellite islets. It has two settlements, the port of Kalamos, on the south-east coast, where most of the inhabitants live, and the north coast village of Episkopi, 8km away. Most of the houses in Episkopi are derelict and only 20 inhabitants remain. Kefali, 8km south-west of Kalamos, was abandoned after the 1953 earthquake, but its church is well kept.

A few adventurous yachties sail into Kalamos port, but it is extremely unusual for any other type of tourist to turn up.

Kalamos village is built on a steep hillside. Its narrow lanes wind between well kept little houses with pretty gardens. There's a post office in the village and a cardphone on the waterfront. The beautiful long, pebbled **Agra Pedia Beach** is a short walk away; locals will direct you.

There is only one place to stay, ***Dionysis Lezentinos Rooms*** *(☎ 91 238)*, just back from the waterfront in Kalamos. Basic but clean doubles/triples are 5500/6500 dr. A reservation is essential in July and August. There are several restaurants on the waterfront. ***Restaurant O Zefyros*** is owned by a friendly couple. The food is delicious and reasonably priced.

Infrequent ferries serve Kalamos from Lefkada. A caïque leaves Mytikas on the mainland every morning around 11 am for Kalamos.

Kefallonia & Ithaki

KEFALLONIA Κεφαλλονιά

• pop 32,500

Kefallonia, the largest of the Ionian Islands, has rugged, towering mountains. The highest, Mt Enos (1520m), is the Mediterranean's only mountain with a unique fir forest species, *Abies kefallia*. While not as tropical as Corfu, Kefallonia has many species of wild flowers, including orchids and, when you approach it by sea on a windy summer's day, the scents of thyme, oregano, bay leaves and flowers will reach you before you land. The island receives package tourists, but not on the same scale as Corfu and Zakynthos. The island has received unprecedented publicity in recent times thanks to Louis de Bernières novel *Captain Corelli's Mandolin*, which is set in Kefallonia. Most beach bums will have a dog-eared copy of the novel.

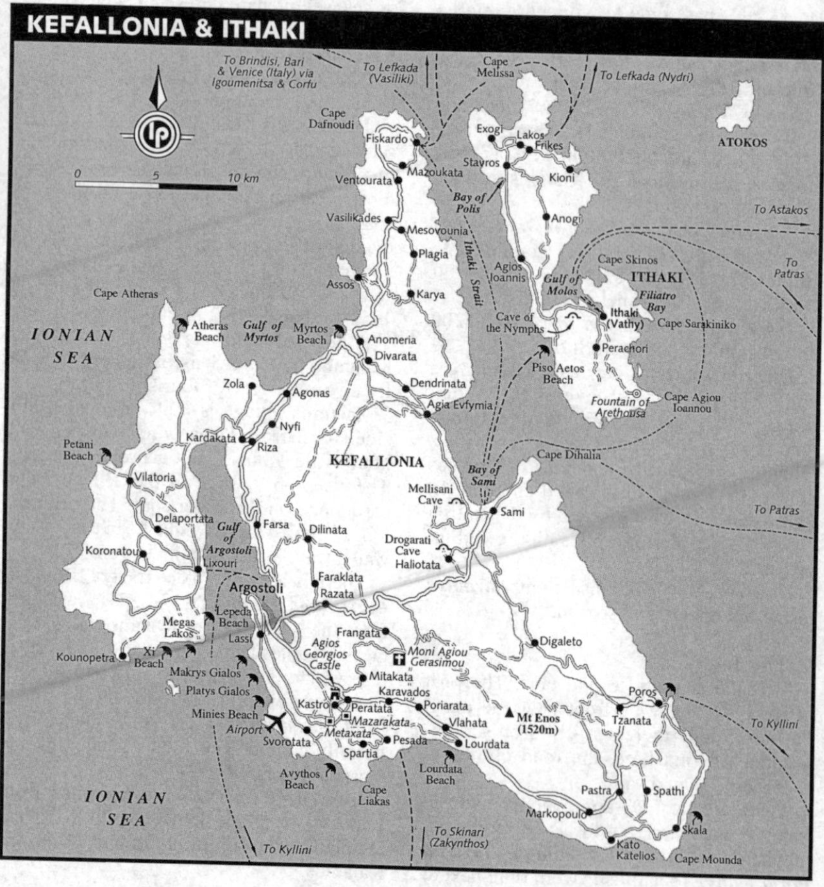

Monk seals may be seen on the north-west coasts of Kefallonia and Ithaki.

Kefallonia is also a nesting ground for loggerhead turtles, which lay their eggs on southern beaches in June. Turtle numbers ashore have remained stable, unlike on Zakynthos. See the boxed text 'Loggerhead Turtles' later in this chapter.

Kefallonia's capital is Argostoli but the main port is Sami. As the island is so big and mountainous, travelling between towns is time consuming. In summer there are art exhibitions in the major towns. In August and September an international choral festival is held in Argostoli and Lixouri.

Getting There & Away

Air There is at least one flight daily from Kefallonia to Athens (17,900 dr). The Olympic Airways office (☎ 0671-28 808) in Argostoli is at Rokou Vergoti 1.

Ferry Kefallonia has six ports – the telephone numbers of the port police are in

The Mediterranean Monk Seal

The Mediterranean monk seal is the rarest of all the seal species and one of the six most endangered mammals in the world. It belongs to the same genus as the Hawaiian and Caribbean monk seals. The latter is now believed to be extinct, since none has been sighted since the 1950s.

Monk seals *(Monachus monachus)* have been in existence for around 15 million years, and in ancient times were so abundant that Homer wrote of herds of them lying on beaches. There is also mention of them in the works of Plutarch, Pliny and Aristotle. It is estimated that in the 15th century around 5000 of the seals lived around the coasts of Spain, France, Portugal, Italy, Albania, Egypt, Israel, Turkey, Algeria and the Lebanon. Numbers have declined drastically in the last 100 years and the present population now stands at around 400 individuals, about half of which live in Greece. There are small numbers in Madeira and Italy, but the second-largest colony lives in the Atlantic, off the coast of north-west Africa, entirely cut off from the rest.

In the past the seals were hunted for their skin and oil, and were killed by fishers because they ate the fish caught in nets. Nowadays they are threatened by marine pollution, oil spills and the numerous pesticides that end up in the sea. But the greatest threat comes from disturbance by humans. Before the days of mass tourism the seals would haul themselves onto gently sloping sandy beaches to give birth, where they and their young were safe from rough waves. Then, as remote beaches became exploited by the tourist industry, the seals abandoned them and resorted to quiet coastal caves fronted by a patch of sand. However, these caves are now also becoming tourist attractions. Unfortunately, the births take place between May and November which coincides with the tourist season. A seal usually only has one pup at a time. The pup remains on land until it is weaned six to eight weeks later. If a female is frightened by the presence of tourists she may miscarry or abandon her helpless pup.

Tourism has driven the monk seal from Sardinia, Sicily and Corsica. To prevent the same happening in Greece it is imperative that tourists do not visit remote sea caves – the last safe refuge of the seal. If the necessary measures are not taken the species could become extinct within 25 years. If you are lucky enough to see a monk seal, keep a distance from it and keep quiet, to make your presence felt as little as possible.

The Hellenic Society for the Study & Protection of the Monk Seal (☎ 01-522 2888, fax 522 2450), Solomou 53, Athens 104 32, has a seal rescue centre on Alonnisos, and the WWF funds a seal watch led by Dimitris Panos (☎ 0671-31 114) at Fiskardo, Kefallonia.

brackets: Sami (☎ 0674-22 031), Argostoli (☎ 0671-22 224), Poros (☎ 0674-72 460), Lixouri (☎ 0671-94 100), Pesada, and Fiskardo (☎ 0674-41 400).

Domestic From Fiskardo, at least two ferries daily leave for Vasiliki (850 dr) on Lefkada. At least two daily go from Sami to Patras (2½ hours, 2630 dr). From Poros (90 minutes, 1620 dr), and Argostoli (2¾ hours, 2700 dr), at least two ferries ply daily to Kyllini in the Peloponnese. From Pesada, near Spartia, there are two high-season services daily (1¼ hours, 836 dr) to Skinari on Zakynthos. Daily ferries go from Fiskardo to Ithaki (Frikes) and Lefkada (Vasiliki).

In summer, small boats leave Sami at 6.30 am to go to Fiskardo via Piso Aetos on Ithaki. From Fiskardo they continue to Vasiliki to return to Kefallonia later in the day. Frequent ferries take 30 minutes to reach Lixouri from Argostoli. Tickets (350 dr) are sold on board.

International A daily ferry leaves Sami for Brindisi in Italy, via Igoumenitsa and Corfu. In high season two or three ferries weekly leave Sami for Ancona and Venice, via Igoumenitsa and Corfu.

Tickets can be obtained from either Vasilatos Shipping (☎ 0671-22 618, fax 24 992) on Metaxa 54, or Romanos Travel (☎ 0671-23 541, fax 25 451) at Antoni Tritsi 48, in Argostoli.

Getting Around

To/From the Airport The airport is 9km south of Argostoli. There is no airport bus. A taxi costs 2000 dr.

Bus From Argostoli (☎ 0671-22 276) frequent buses go to Platys Gialos and Sami (500 dr), three daily to Poros (850 dr), via Peratata, Vlahata and Markopoulo, two daily to Skala (800 dr) and two daily to Fiskardo (850 dr). In the off season, only one return service daily connects Fiskardo (1000 dr) with Argostoli. Four daily return buses leave Athens' A terminal for Argostoli (eight hours via ferry to Poros, 7500 dr).

Car & Motorcycle Cars can be hired from Ainos Travel (☎ 0671-22 333, fax 24 608), Georgiou Vergoti 14, and motorcycles from Sunbird Motor Rent (☎ 0671-23 723), on the waterfront in Argostoli. Vehicle hire is recommended during the off season because of the infrequency of buses.

Argostoli Αργοστόλι

☎ 0671 • postcode 281 00 • pop 7300

Argostoli, unlike Zakynthos Town, was not restored to its former Venetian splendour after the 1953 earthquake. It's a modern, lively port set on a peninsula. Its harbour is divided from Koutavos lagoon by a British-built causeway connecting it with the rest of Kefallonia. There is a colourful produce market on the waterfront on most mornings.

Orientation & Information The EOT (☎ 22 248) is on the waterfront, south of the quay. The post office is on Diad Konstantinou and the OTE phone office is on Georgiou Vergoti. Plateia Vallianou is the huge palm-treed central square up from the waterfront off 21 Maïou.

The modern and (for once) very user-friendly bus station is on the southern waterfront near the causeway. The ferry quay is at the waterfront's northern end.

The National Bank of Greece is one block back from the southern end of the waterfront. The National Mortgage Bank on the waterfront has a 24 hour cash exchange machine. There is also a Commercial Bank ATM on the corner of Vyronos and Vergoti.

The town's closest sandy beaches are **Makrys Gialos** and **Platys Gialos**, 5km south. The island's most expensive accommodation is here, although domatia can be found.

Things to See Argostoli's **archaeological museum** (☎ 28 300), on Rokou Vergoti, has a small collection of island relics including Mycenaean finds from tombs. Opening times are 8.30 am to 3 pm Tuesday to Sunday. Admission is 500 dr.

The **historical and cultural museum** (☎ 28 835), farther up Rokou Vergoti, has a collection of traditional costumes, furniture

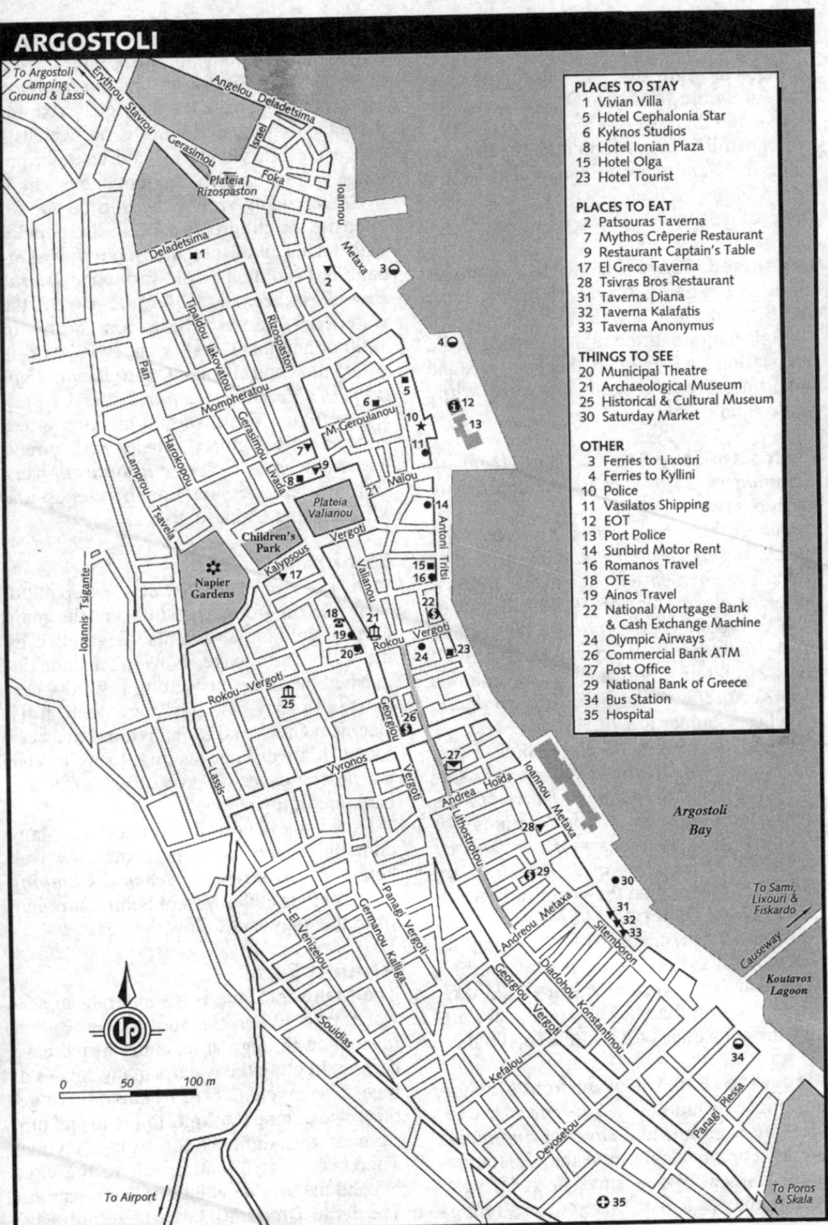
ARGOSTOLI
PLACES TO STAY
1 Vivian Villa
5 Hotel Cephalonia Star
6 Kyknos Studios
8 Hotel Ionian Plaza
15 Hotel Olga
23 Hotel Tourist
PLACES TO EAT
2 Patsouras Taverna
7 Mythos Crêperie Restaurant
9 Restaurant Captain's Table
17 El Greco Taverna
28 Tsivras Bros Restaurant
31 Taverna Diana
32 Taverna Kalafatis
33 Taverna Anonymus
THINGS TO SEE
20 Municipal Theatre
21 Archaeological Museum
25 Historical & Cultural Museum
30 Saturday Market
OTHER
3 Ferries to Lixouri
4 Ferries to Kyllini
10 Police
11 Vasilatos Shipping
12 EOT
13 Port Police
14 Sunbird Motor Rent
16 Romanos Travel
18 OTE
19 Ainos Travel
22 National Mortgage Bank & Cash Exchange Machine
24 Olympic Airways
26 Commercial Bank ATM
27 Post Office
29 National Bank of Greece
34 Bus Station
35 Hospital
To Argostoli Camping Ground & Lassi
Erythrou Stavrou
Angelou Deladetsima
Gerasimou
Israel
Foka
Plateia Rizospaston
Ioannou Metaxa
Deladetsima
Tipaldou Iakovatou
Rizospaston
Pan
Mompheratou
Gerasimou Livada
M Geroulanou
Harokopou
Lamprou Tsavela
21 Maïou
Plateia Valianou
Antoni Tritsi
Children's Park
Kalypsous
Vergoti
Valianou
Napier Gardens
Ioannis Tsigante
Rokou Vergoti
Georgiou Vergoti
Vyronos
Lassis
Andrea Hoïda
Lithostrotou
Argostoli Bay
To Sami, Lixouri & Fiskardo
Causeway
Koutavos Lagoon
El Venizelou
Germanou Kalliga
Panagi Vergoti
Andreou Metaxa
Sitemboron
Diadohou Konstantinou
Souidias
Kefalou
Devosetou
Panagi Plessa
0 50 100 m
To Airport
To Poros & Skala

and tools, items which belonged to British occupiers, and photographs of pre-earthquake Argostoli. The museum is open 9 am to 2 pm Monday to Saturday. Admission is 500 dr.

Argostoli's new **municipal theatre**, on Georgiou Vergoti, was inaugurated by the late Melina Merkouri. There's a ground-floor art gallery.

Organised Tours The KTEL organises tours to Drogarati Cave, Melissani Lake and Fiskardo for 5000 dr, and to Ithaki for 8000 dr. Inquire at the marked office at the bus station and pick up the handy island bus timetable and tour brochure while you're there.

Places to Stay The pleasant ***Argostoli Camping*** *(☎ 23 487)* is on the coast, 2km north of town.

One of the nicest places is ***Vivian Villa*** *(☎ 23 396, fax 28 670, Deladetsima 9)*. The friendly owners offers beautiful, spotless double/triple rooms for 10,000/12,000 dr with bathroom. Studios cost 13,000/15,800 dr and a large, well equipped apartment costs 21,000 dr. Another pleasant option is ***Kyknos Studios*** *(☎ 23 398, M Geroulanou 4)*, where doubles are 12,500 dr.

There's a string of C class hotels along the waterfront. ***Hotel Cephalonia Star*** *(☎ 23 181, 23 180, Ioannou Metaxa 60)* has comfortable air-con singles/doubles for 12,000/17,000 dr. Rates at ***Hotel Tourist*** *(☎/fax 22 510, Antoni Tritsi 109)* are 13,000/20,000 dr, and the beautifully refurbished ***Hotel Olga*** *(☎ 24 981, fax 24 985)*, on Antoni Tristi, charges 14,400/21,050 dr.

Argostoli's best hotel is the marble-decorated ***Hotel Ionian Plaza*** *(☎ 25 581, fax 25 585)* on Plateia Vallianou. Comfortable air-con suites cost 11,900/16,400 dr.

Places to Eat The waterfront's neighbouring restaurants ***Taverna Diana***, ***Taverna Kalafatis*** and ***Taverna Anonymus*** are all commendable, and the Kalafatis – around since 1945 – stays open all year. Kefallonia has a distinctive cuisine, represented by meat pies and *skordalia* (garlic dip) which accompanies fish. Greeks find these dishes at ***Patsouras Taverna*** *(Ioannou Metaxa 40)* opposite the ferry quay. Ask for the island's famed Robola wine, which is expensive but wonderful and comes from grapes grown in stony, mountainous soil.

El Greco Taverna *(Kalypsous Vergoti 3)*, opposite the children's park, is also popular with locals. Well prepared cod with skordalia is 1700 dr. The old-fashioned ***Tsivras Bros Restaurant*** *(☎ 24 259)*, just off the waterfront, serves filling goat broth for 1000 dr and many dishes under 1000 dr.

Off the central square, ***Restaurant Captain's Table*** *(Rizospaston 3)* serves pies, spaghetti and fish dishes at medium prices and has live guitar music each night. Nearby, ***Mythos Crêperie Restaurant*** has a similarly priced selection of crepes and Mexican and Chinese dishes.

Sami Σάμη

☎ 0674 • postcode 280 82 • pop 1000

Sami, 25km from Argostoli and the main port of Kefallonia, was also devastated by the 1953 earthquake. Now with undistinguished buildings, its setting is pretty, nestled in a bay, flanked by steep hills. Classical Greek and Roman ruins have been found. It's worth an overnight stay to visit the nearby caves. A post office, OTE and bank are in town.

Buses for Argostoli meet ferries. Many domatia owners meet the boats. The well kept ***Karavomylos Beach Camping*** *(☎ 22 480)* is 800m west of Sami. Turn right from the quay and follow the coast.

Around Sami

The **Mellisani Cave** is a subterranean sea-water lake. When the sun is overhead its rays shine through an opening in the cave ceiling, lighting the water's many shades of blue. The cave is 2.5km from Sami. To get there walk along the Argostoli road and turn right at the signpost for Agia Evfymia. There is a sign pointing left to the cave beyond the seaside village of Karavomylos. The large **Drogarati Cave** has impressive stalactites. It's signposted from the Argostoli road, 4km from Sami. Both caves are open all day and charge 1000 dr.

The picturesque fishing village of **Agia Evfymia** with its pebbled beach is 10km north of Sami. It is another popular yachting stop, and while the beach is rather narrow the water is very clear and the swimming is good. There are one or two hotels and some domatia for travellers wishing to stay.

Spiros Restaurant *(☎ 0674-61 739)* on the south waterfront is a good place to stop and eat. The food is great; aim for the roast suckling pig on Saturday night. Phone ahead to book your plate.

Fiskardo Φισκάρδο

☎ 0674 • postcode 280 84 • pop 300

Fiskardo, 50km north of Argostoli, was the only village not devastated by the 1953 earthquake. Framed by cypress-mantled hills, and with fine Venetian buildings, it's a delightful place. A Roman cemetery and Mycenaean pottery have been found here. It's a popular place, especially with yachties, but it's pleasant outside high season.

The bus will drop you off on the road which bypasses Fiskardo. Walk across the car park, descend the steps to the left of the church and continue ahead to Fiskardo's central square and waterfront.

You can get to Fiskardo by ferry from Lefkada and Ithaki or by bus from Argostoli.

Places to Stay & Eat You're unlikely to find accommodation in high season. At others times it's OK, but prices are high.

At ***Regina's Rooms*** *(☎ 41 125)* doubles/triples are 10,000/11,000 dr, and new studios are 12,000/15,000 dr. ***John Palikisianos Rooms*** *(☎ 41 304)*, opposite, has rates of 7000/8500 dr. To get to these from the bus stop, cross the car park, turn left at the church, turn left again, and look for the signs.

The tastefully furnished rooms at ***Tselenti Domatia*** *(☎ 41 204)*, just back from and west of the central square, are a pricey 15,000/18,000 dr. The ***Philoxenia Traditional Settlement*** *(☎ 41 410, fax 41 319)* occupies a lovely 19th century house near the square. Room rates are 20,700/22,000 dr. Farther around the waterfront, ***Nefeli Studios*** has immaculate self-contained units and great sea views. Rates are 25,000 dr.

Gaïta traditional grill house on the west harbourfront and ***Lagoudera*** just back from the harbourfront are both worth seeking out for a good traditional Kefallonian meal.

Around Fiskardo

Assos Village is a gem of white-washed and pastel houses, straddling the isthmus of a peninsula on which stands a Venetian fortress. Assos was damaged in the 1953 earthquake but sensitively restored with the help of a donation from the city of Paris.

There's an outstanding white sandy beach at **Myrtos**, 3km south of Assos. If you explore by boat, you'll find nearby hidden coves between tall limestone cliffs.

Southern Kefallonia

Kastro, above the village of **Peratata**, 9km south-east of **Argostoli**, was the island's capital in the Middle Ages. Ruined houses stand beneath the 13th century castle of **Agios Georgios**, which affords magnificent views.

Peratata has ***domatia***, as has **Vlahata**, a pleasant village east along the road which branches to **Lourdata Beach** where you can go horse riding. On a scenic 2½ hour circular walk from Lourdata, you pass thickets, orchards and olive groves with flowers and birds, and return along the coast. A free Lourdata trail walk guide is available from the EOT in Argostoli.

The superb two to four-person apartments of ***Ionian Star*** *(☎ 0671-31 419, fax 31 019)* at Lourdata Beach make a great base for this part of the island. Prices range between 10,000 dr and 20,000 dr depending on the season.

At **Markopoulo** an extraordinary event creeps up on 15 August (the Feast of the Assumption). The village church becomes infested with harmless snakes with crosses on their heads. They are said to bring good luck.

Poros is overdeveloped, but has a rather scruffy, pebbled beach. **Skala**, on the southern tip, is a preferable resort with a large, fine sand beach backed by a cooling pine wood. There are domatia and hotels at both locations.

ITHAKI Ιθάκη

☎ 0674 • postcode 283 00 • pop 3100

Ithaki (ancient Ithaca) was Odysseus' long-lost home, the island where the stoical Penelope sat patiently, weaving a shroud for her father-in-law. She told her suitors, who believed Odysseus was dead, that she would choose one of them once she had completed the shroud. Cunningly, she unravelled it every night in order to keep her suitors at bay, as she awaited Odysseus' return.

Ithaki is separated from Kefallonia by a strait, only 2 to 4km wide. The unspoilt island has a harsh, precipitous east coast and a soft, green west coast. The interior is mountainous and rocky with pockets of pine forest, stands of cypresses, olive groves and vineyards.

Because of its general lack of good beaches, Ithaki doesn't attract large crowds, but it's a great place to spend a quiet holiday, perhaps walking or just relaxing.

Odysseus & Ithaki

Ithaki (Ithaca) has long been the symbolic image for the end of a long journey. For mythical hero Odysseus (Ulysses), Ithaki was the home he left to fight in the Trojan Wars. According to the often wild tales recounted in Homer's *Iliad*, though more specifically in the *Odyssey*, it took the wily hero Odysseus 10 long years to return home to Ithaki from Troy on the Asia Minor coast.

Tossed by tempestuous seas, attacked by sea monsters, delayed by a cunning siren yet helped on his way by friendly Phaeacians, Odysseus finally made landfall on Ithaki. Here, disguised as a beggar, he teamed up with his son Telemachus and his old swineherd Eumaeus, and slayed a castleful of conniving suitors who had been eating him out of home and fortune while trying unsuccessfully to woo the ever-patient and faithful Penelope, Odysseus' long-suffering wife who had waited 20 years for him to return.

Despite Ithaki owing its fame to such illustrious classical connections, no mention of the island appears in writings of the Middle Ages. As late as 1504 AD Ithaki was almost uninhabited following repeated depredations by pirates. The Venetians were obliged to induce settlers from neighbouring islands to repopulate Ithaki. Yet the island is described in considerable detail in the *Odyssey*, which match in many respects the physical nature of the island today. 'The Fountain of Arethousa' has been identified with a spring rising at the foot of a sea cliff in the south of the island and the 'Cave of the Naiads' with a fairly nondescript cave up from the Bay of Phorkys. However, many Homerists have been hard-pressed to ascribe other locales described in the *Odyssey* – particularly Odysseus' castle – to actual places on the islands since scant archaeological remains assist the researcher. Other Homerists conclude that Ithaki may well have been Lefkada, a theory espoused by German archaeologist Willem Dorpfeld, though this idea seems to have fallen on rocky ground in more recent times.

Odysseus as a mythical man is everyone's hero, a pre-classical Robin Hood or John Wayne, both villain and king bundled into one well marketed package. Classical Greek writers presented him sometimes as an unscrupulous politician, and sometimes as a wise and honourable statesman. Philosophers usually admired his intelligence and wisdom. To listeners of yore he was the hero underdog that everyone wanted to see win. Whether he actually existed or not is almost irrelevant since the universal human qualities that he embodied are those that most of us, whether we want to or not, admire and aspire to.

Getting There & Away

From Ithaki there are daily ferries to Patras, to Vasiliki on Lefkada via Fiskardo on Kefallonia, and to Sami and Agia Efthymia on Kefallonia. In high season, a daily ferry sails from Frikes (Ithaki) to Fiskardo, Meganisi and Nydri. The telephone number of Ithaki's port police is ☎ 32 909.

Getting Around

The island's one bus runs two or three times daily to Kioni (via Stavros and Frikes) from Vathy (550 dr).

Ithaki Town Ιθάκη Χώρα

• pop 1800

Ithaki Town (or Vathy; Βαθύ) is small with a few twisting streets, a central square, nice cafes and restaurants, and a few tourist shops, grocers and hardware stores. Old mansions rise up from the seafront.

Orientation & Information The ferry quay is on the west side of the bay. To reach the central square of Plateia Efstathiou Drakouli, turn left and follow the waterfront. The main thoroughfare, Kallinikou, is parallel to, and one block inland from, the waterfront.

Ithaki has no tourist office. The tourist police (☎ 32 205) are on Evmeou, which runs south from the middle of the waterfront.

The National Bank of Greece is just south-west of the central square. The post office is on the central square and the OTE is farther east along the waterfront.

Things to See The town's **archaeological museum** is on Kallinikou. It is open 8.30 am to 3 pm Tuesday to Sunday. Entrance is free. The **nautical and folklore museum** is housed in an old generating station. Ithaki was the first place in Greece to have electricity, thanks to the generosity of George Drakoulis, a wealthy Ithakan shipowner. The museum, behind the Agricultural Bank, is open 9.30 am to 1.30 pm and 6 to 9 pm Monday to Friday; admission is 300 dr.

A summer music and theatre festival is held in Ithaki Town.

Places to Stay ***Andriana Kouloupi Domatia*** *(☎ 32 387)*, just south of the quay, has agreeable single/double rooms for 5000/6600 dr with shared bathroom, and doubles/triples with private bathroom for 8000/10,000 dr. At ***Vasiliki Vlasopoulou Domatia*** *(☎ 32 119)* pleasant doubles with bathroom cost 8000 dr. Turn left from the quay and right at the town hall, take the steps ahead, and you will see the sign.

Just off the eastern waterfront, ***Dimitrios Maroudas Rooms & Apartments*** *(☎/fax 32 751)*, signposted 180m beyond the OTE, has clean doubles/triples for 7000/10,000 dr and four-person apartments for 14,000 dr.

On the western waterfront, ***Hotel Odysseus*** *(☎ 32 381, fax 32 587)* has pleasant doubles for 9000 dr. The B class ***Hotel Mentor*** *(☎ 32 433, fax 32 293)* near the OTE has a bar, restaurant and roof garden. Attractive singles/doubles cost 12,500/17,000 dr.

Places to Eat ***Taverna Trehantiri***, a long-established place west of the central square, serves quality traditional Greek dishes. ***O Nikos***, one block back from the square, does great fish dishes which you can wash down with fine Ithakan wine. The classy ***Sirens Yacht Club Restaurant & Bar***, nearby, has old photos of Vathy on its walls. The imaginative menu includes shrimps with lemon and mushroom sauce. ***Restaurant Kantouni***, on the waterfront, excels in reasonably priced fish dishes.

Young locals meet at the stylish ***Drakoulis Cafe*** in a waterfront mansion, which was the home of George Drakoulis. Try the sweet, gooey *rovani*, the local speciality, at one of the waterfront's ***zaharoplasteia***.

Around Ithaki

Ithaki has a few sites associated with Homer's *Odyssey*. Though none is impressive, you may enjoy (or endure) the scenic walks to them. The most renowned is the **Fountain of Arethousa**, where Odysseus' swineherd, Eumaeus, brought his pigs to drink and where Odysseus, on his return to Ithaca, went to meet him disguised as a beggar after receiving directions from the goddess Athena. Lesser mortals have to deal with inadequate signposting. The walk takes 1½ to two hours. Take plenty of water as the spring shrinks in summer.

A shorter trek is to the **Cave of the Nymphs**, where Odysseus concealed the splendid gifts of gold, copper and fine fabrics that the Phaeacians had given him. The cave is signposted from the town. Below the cave is the **Bay of Dexa** (where there is decent swimming), thought to be ancient Phorkys where the Phaeacians disembarked and laid the sleeping Odysseus on the sand.

The location of Odysseus' palace has been much disputed and archaeologists have been unable to find conclusive evidence. Schliemann erroneously believed it was near Vathy, whereas present-day archaeologists speculate it was on a hill near Stavros.

Anogi Fourteen kilometres north of Vathy, Anogi was the old capital. Its church of Agia Panagia has beautiful frescoes. Ask for Gerasimos who has the key.

Stavros In this village, 17km north-west of Ithaki Town, there's a small **archaeological museum**. It's open 9.30 am to 2 pm Tuesday to Sunday. Admission is free. ***Villa St Ilias*** *(☎ 31 751)* near the museum has lovely rooms with bathroom for 12,500 dr. From Stavros it's 1km to the **Bay of Polis**, which has a stony beach.

Frikes This charming fishing village with wind-swept cliffs is 1.5km in the opposite direction. Kiki Travel Agency (☎ 31 726, fax 31 387), owned by helpful Angeliki Digaletou, has a range of services including moped hire.

Kiki Domatia *(☎ 31 726)* has tastefully furnished, spotless double rooms for 12,000 dr with bathroom. ***Raftopoulos Rooms*** *(☎ 31 733)*, 1km away in a quiet rural setting, has clean doubles/triples for 8000/9500 dr. Inquire about these at Restaurant Ulysses. The well kept C class ***Hotel Nostos*** *(☎ 31 644/716)*, in lovely verdant countryside behind the village, has spacious, modern singles/doubles for 13,000/17,000 dr and friendly, helpful owners.

Symposium Restaurant, owned by two friendly sisters, serves imaginative fare including local dishes from their grandmother's recipes. ***Restaurant Ulysses*** on the waterfront does fresh fish and lobster which you choose from a large tank.

Kioni Four kilometres south-east of Frikes, Kioni is perhaps one of Ithaki's better-kept secrets. It is a small village draped around a verdant hillside spilling down to a picturesque little harbour where yachties congregate. There are tavernas and a couple of bars, though it's not the best place to swim. Instead, seek out the little bays between Kioni and Frikes.

Kioni's cheapest accommodation is ***Maroudas Apartments*** *(☎ 31 691, fax 31 753)*, opposite the doctor's surgery. Immaculate double/triple studios are 12,000/16,000 dr. Farther back up the hill, the well maintained, beautifully furnished ***Dellaportas Apartments*** *(☎ 31 481, fax 31 090)* have spacious double studios with TV and phone for 12,000 dr and four-person apartments for 20,000 dr.

Zakynthos Ζάκυνθος

☎ 0695 • postcode 291 00 • pop 32,560

Zakynthos (**zahk**-in-thos) has inspired many superlatives. The Venetians called it Fior' di Levante (flower of the orient). The poet Dionysios Solomos wrote that 'Zakynthos could make one forget the Elysian Fields'. Indeed, it is an island of exceptional natural beauty and outstanding beaches.

Unfortunately, Zakynthos' coastline has been the victim of the most unacceptable manifestations of package tourism. The lack of general budget accommodation and a rapacious attitude to tourism on the part of islanders make Zakynthos the least attractive of the Ionian Islands as a destination for independent travellers. Even worse, tourism is endangering the loggerhead turtle,

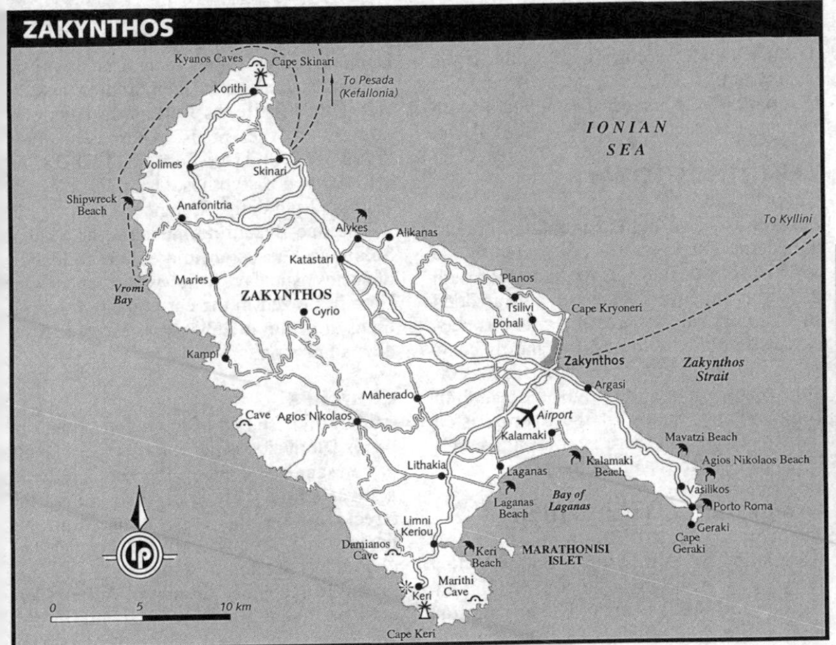

Caretta caretta (see the boxed text later in this section), and the Mediterranean monk seal, *Monachus monachus* (see the boxed text earlier in this chapter).

Getting There & Away

Air There is one daily flight from Zakynthos to Athens (17,400 dr). The Olympic Airways office (☎ 28 611) in Zakynthos Town is at Alexandrou Roma 16. You can call the airport on ☎ 28 322.

Bus There are five or more buses daily from Zakynthos Town to Patras (3½ hours, 2860 dr). The same bus continues on to Athens (seven hours, 6310 dr). Ticket price includes the ferry fare.

Ferry Depending on the season, between three and seven ferries daily operate from Zakynthos Town to Kyllini, in the Peloponnese (1½ hours, 1400 dr). Tickets can be obtained from the Zakynthos Shipping Cooperative (☎ 41 500, fax 48 301) at Lombardou 40 in Zakynthos Town.

From Skinari the F/B *Ionion Pelagos* shuttles across to Pesada on Kefallonia from May to October (two hours, 1025 dr). There is inexplicably no bus from Pesada to anywhere else on Kefallonia. Check with the port police (☎ 42 417) for the times of the Skinari-Pesada ferries, though in general there are two departures daily from Skinari at 9.15 am and 7 pm.

Getting Around

There is no shuttle service between Zakynthos Town and the airport, 6km to the southwest. A taxi costs 1400 dr.

Frequent buses go from Zakynthos Town's modern bus station (☎ 22 255) to Alykes (320 dr), Tsilivi (230 dr), Argasi

(230 dr) and Laganas (230 dr). Bus services to other villages are poor (one or two daily). Check the current schedule at the bus station.

A motorcycle and car hire outlet is Moto Stakis, at Dimokratias 3, Zakynthos Town.

ZAKYNTHOS TOWN

• pop 10,250

Zakynthos Town is the capital and port of the island. The town was devastated by the 1953 earthquake but was reconstructed with its former layout preserved in wide arcaded streets, imposing squares and gracious neoclassical public buildings. It is hardly cosy, given its strung-out feel, but it is a reasonable place for an overnight stop and in comparison to many of the overtouristed parts of the island there is at least a semblance of Greekness left in the town.

Orientation & Information

The central Plateia Solomou is on the waterfront of Lombardou, opposite the ferry quay. Another large square, Plateia Agiou Markou, is nearby. The bus station is on Filita, one block back from the waterfront and south of the quay. The main thoroughfare is Alexandrou Roma, parallel to the waterfront and several blocks inland.

Zakynthos Town has no tourist office. The helpful tourist police (☎ 27 367) are at Lombardou 62.

The National Bank of Greece is just west of Plateia Solomou, while directly opposite is a Commercial Bank with an ATM. The post office is at Tertseti 27, one block west of Alexandrou Roma. The OTE phone office is on Plateia Solomou. Zakynthos' hospital (☎ 22 514) is west of town.

The Top's Internet Cafe (☎ 26 650) is at Filita 34, near the bus station.

Museums

The **Museum of Solomos**, on Plateia Agiou Markou, is dedicated to Dionysios Solomos (1798-1857), who was born on Zakynthos. His work *Hymn to Liberty* became the stirring Greek national anthem. Solomos is regarded as the father of modern Greek poetry, because he was the first to use Demotic Greek rather than Katharevousa. This museum houses memorabilia associated with his life, as well as displays pertaining to the poets Andreas Kalvos (1792-1869) and Ugo Foskolo (1778-1827), also born on Zakynthos. Opening times are 9 am to 2 pm daily. Entrance is free.

The **neo-Byzantine museum**, on Plateia Solomou, houses an impressive collection of ecclesiastical art which was rescued from churches razed in the earthquake. Opening times are 8 am to 2.30 pm Tuesday to Sunday; admission is 500 dr.

Churches

At the southern end of town, the **Church of Agios Dionysios** is named after the island's patron saint and contains the saint's relics in a silver coffer. This is paraded around the streets during the festivals held in his honour on 24 August and 17 December. The church has notable frescoes.

The 16th century **Church of Agios Nikolaos**, on Plateia Solomou, was built in Italian Renaissance style. Partially destroyed in the earthquake, it has been carefully reconstructed.

Organised Tours

The KTEL has a 'round Zakynthos Island' tour which costs 3000 dr. Inquire at the bus station. There are many round-island boat tours operating from the northern end of the waterfront, but boat tours which visit Langadas and the blue cave should be avoided as they disturb the loggerhead turtles and monk seals.

Places to Stay

The nearest camp site to Zakynthos Town is ***Zante Camping*** *(☎ 61 710)* at Tsilivi, 5km away while 8km south-west of the port is ***Camping Laganas*** *(☎ 22 292)* at Agios Sostis.

The clean ***Rent Rooms*** *(☎ 26 012, Alexandrou Roma 40)* are 6000/8000 dr for singles/doubles. Enter from Spyrou Gouskou. ***Athina Rooms*** *(☎ 45 194, Tzoulati 29)* are simply furnished, costing 5000/10,000 dr.

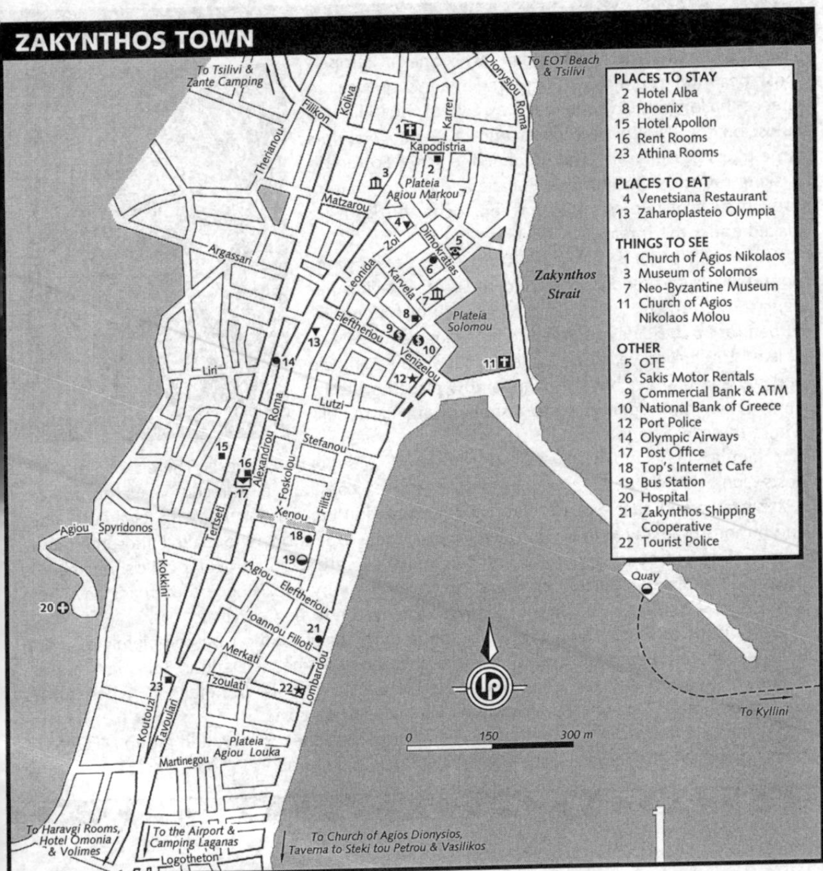

The pleasant ***Haravgi Rooms*** *(☎ 23 629, Xanthopoulou 4)* has doubles/triples with bathroom for 9000/10,000 dr. Opposite, ***Hotel Omonia*** *(☎ 22 113, Xanthopoulou 7)* has rates of 10,000/12,500 dr. Walk south along Alexandrou Roma, at the fork head right along Agiou Lazarou, and Xanthopoulou is 250m along on the left.

The small ***Hotel Apollon*** *(☎ 42 838, Tertseti 30)* with its unsmiling owner will do as an alternative resort. Its single/double rooms are 9000/13,000 dr.

The C class ***Phoenix*** *(☎ 23 514, 45 083, Plateia Solomou 2)*, close to the ferry quay, has standard rooms for 10,000/15,000 dr. Farther back and just off Plateia Agiou Markou is the B class ***Hotel Alba*** *(☎ 26 641, fax 26 642, 1 Ziva 38)*, which is good value with rates of 11,000/12,000 dr for small but adequate rooms.

Places to Eat

Cafes featuring *mandolato*, a local nougat sweet, are on Alexandrou Roma. Try the

Loggerhead Turtles

SARAH JOLLY

The loggerhead turtle *(Caretta caretta)* is one of Europe's most beautiful yet most endangered marine species. In Greece the loggerhead turtle nests on two of the Ionian Islands, on the Peloponnese coast and in Crete. It prefers large tracts of clean, flat and uninhabited sand. So too do basking tourists from northern Europe and it is this fateful convergence of interests that has led to the turtle being placed under the threat of extinction.

The female turtle lays about 120 eggs the size of ping-pong balls in the sand in preferred sites. After laying her eggs she returns to the sea and the eggs must lie undisturbed for up to 60 days before the hatchlings emerge. For at least 150 million years the turtle has survived geological and climatic changes but the change now placed on to its environment by modern mass tourism has rung alarm bells within the conservation world.

Zakynthos in the Ionian Islands hosts the largest congregation of nests. There are some 1300 nests along the Bay of Laganas on the island's south coast alone. In recent years this popular resort has come under repeated fire with conservation lobbies clashing with local authorities and businesses involved in the lucrative tourist trade. Operators who make handsome profits from renting out beach umbrellas and sun beds have attracted particular criticism. Umbrella poles indiscriminately destroy eggs and nests and the very coexistence of humans anywhere near the nesting sites is totally counterproductive to the turtles' survival.

As a visitor to Greece you can assist the deteriorating situation by completely avoiding beaches where loggerhead turtles nest. In Zakynthos this means Daphni, Sekania, Gerakas, Kalamaki and Laganas beaches as well as the islet of Marathonisi. In Kefallonia, where turtles are less common, Mounda Beach should be avoided at all costs.

For further information on the turtles get in touch with the conservation group MEDASSET (email medasset@hol.gr) at 24 Park Towers, 2 Brick St, London W1Y 7DF, UK.

traditional ***Zaharoplasteio Olympia*** for sheep's milk yogurt and rice pudding. ***Venetsiana Restaurant*** *(Plateia Agiou Markou 8)* is the best restaurant on the central square, with excellent pizzas featuring prominently. The untouristy ***Taverna To Steki tou Petrou***, 150m south of Agios Dionysios on Lombardou, serves delicious, reasonably priced food.

AROUND ZAKYNTHOS

Loggerhead turtles come ashore to lay their eggs on the golden sand beaches of the huge Bay of Laganas, on Zakynthos' south coast. Laganas is a highly developed, tacky resort and is a truly dreadful place to spend a holiday unless you like lager and loud discos and would rather be in the UK than Greece. Avoid it like the plague, or at least drop by to see how Mammon and mass tourism have met in the most abominable set of circumstances.

Kalamaki is not much quieter and even **Geraki**, where the highest number of turtles lay their eggs, has not been spared water sports. The turtles also nest on nearby **Marathonisi Islet**. You may decide to avoid these beaches for the turtles' sakes and to bypass the commercialism.

Vasilikos and **Porto Roma**, south of Zakynthos Town, both have crowded sand beaches but are less developed than those of Laganas. **Agios Nikolaos Beach** at the end of the peninsula has great (turtle-free) water sport facilities and a few domatia and studios, and is where the more discerning Greek youth hangs out in the summer.

The famous **Shipwreck Beach** (Navagio) is at the north-western tip of the island. It truly is a splendid beach with crystalline, aquamarine waters. But unless you have your own boat, it can only be visited by excursion boat, best undertaken from the little harbour of **Vromi Bay** which in turn is reachable by a decently powered motorbike or scooter from **Anafonitria**. Take a picnic since there are no facilities on the beach.

You can escape from the tourist hype by visiting inland farming villages. The village of **Maherado** has the impressive 14th century church of Agia Mavra. **Agios Nikolaos** is an attractive village. The drive north from here to **Maries** is through splendid hilly country. Make an effort to visit the little village of **Gyrio** in the centre of the island where there is a cosy ***taverna*** with live *arekia* (traditional Zakynthian ballads) music on weekends. It is patronised mainly by Greeks in the know.

Kythira & Antikythira

KYTHIRA Κύθηρα

☎ 0735 • pop 3100

The island of Kythira (**kee**-thih-rah) is to many Greeks the Holy Grail of island-hopping. The 'Road to Kythira', a well known 1973 song by Dimitris Mitropanos, epitomises what for most people is the end of the line that is never reached. Indeed Kythira can be a hard place to get to – mentally, if not physically – since you have to make a special effort just to get there.

Some 30km long and 18km wide, Kythira dangles off the Laconian Peninsula of the Peloponnese between the often turbulent Ionian and Aegean seas. It is a curiously barren island in parts, with misty moors, winding lanes backed by low stone walls and hidden valleys that rent the dreamy landscape. More than forty villages are scattered evenly across the island, and ghosts are said to roam the inland villages. Kythira was part of the British Ionian Protectorate for many years, evidenced by the sprinkling of arched stone bridges around the island.

Kythira is the least 'Ionian' of the Ionian island group. Physically separated from its nearest neighbour Zakynthos by a long stretch of sea, it is administered from Piraeus and mostly resembles the Cyclades in appearance and architecture.

Mythology suggests that it is in Kythira that Aphrodite was born. She is supposed to have risen from the foam where Zeus had thrown Cronos' sex organ after castrating him. The goddess of love then re-emerged near Paphos in Cyprus, so both islands haggle over her birthplace.

The EOT has begun encouraging tourists to visit Kythira but it's still unspoilt. Its attractions are its relatively undeveloped and excellent beaches, its enduring feel as a special island and the fact that it is 'the end of the line'.

Kythira's main port is Agia Pelagia, though hydrofoils depart from and arrive at the custom-built port of Diakofti. Public transport on Kythira ranges from abysmal to nonexistent, so bringing your own wheels or renting them locally is advisable.

Getting There & Away

Air There are flights to Athens (45 minutes, 14,400 dr) every day except Thursday. The Olympic Airways office (☎ 33 362) is on the central square in Potamos. Book also at Kythira Travel (☎ 31 390) in Hora. The airport is 10km east of Potamos.

Ferry The modern car ferry F/B *Maria* of Golden Ferries sails from Agia Pelagia to Gythio in the Peloponnese twice daily during summer (two hours, 1600 dr), with

KYTHIRA & ANTIKYTHIRA

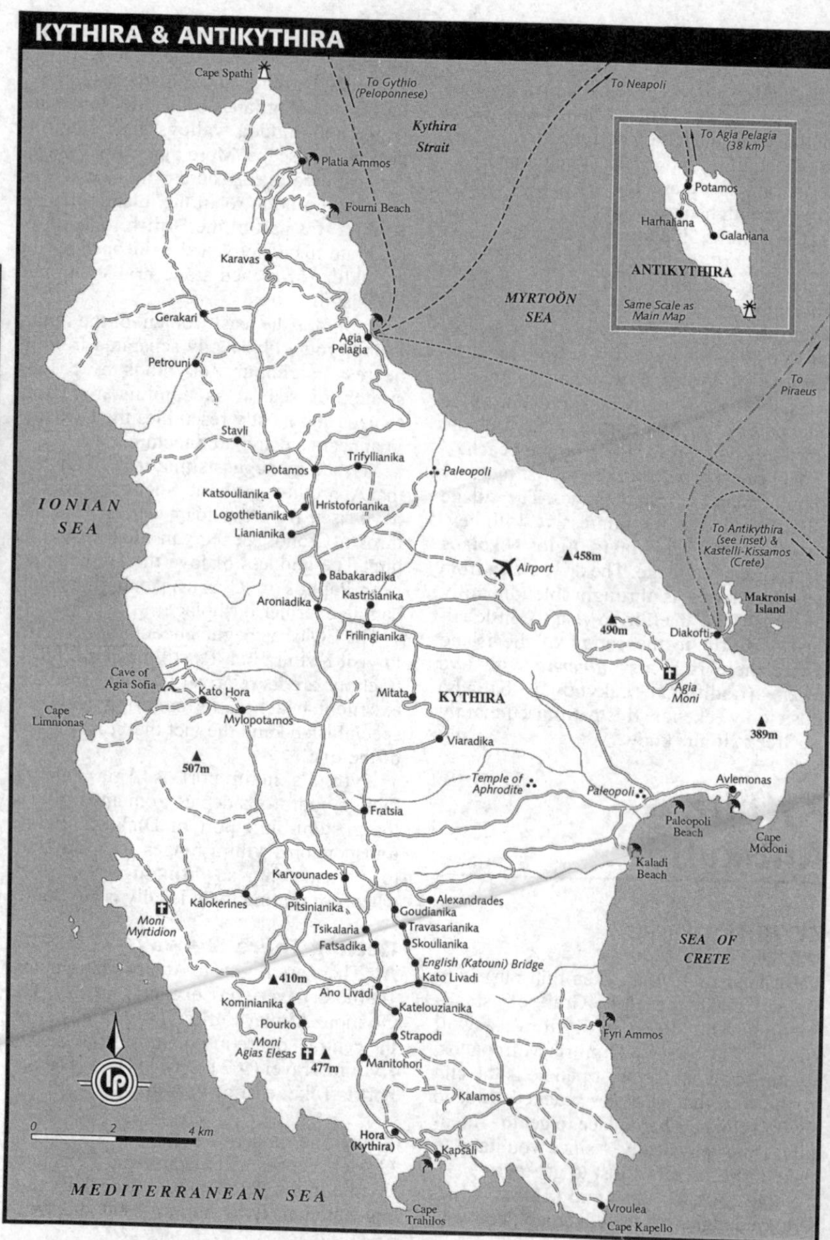
Cape Spathi
To Gythio (Peloponnese)
To Neapoli
Kythira Strait
Platia Ammos
Fourni Beach
Karavas
Gerakari
Agia Pelagia
Petrouni
MYRTOÖN SEA
To Agia Pelagia (38 km)
Potamos
Harhaliana
Galaniana
ANTIKYTHIRA
Same Scale as Main Map
To Piraeus
Stavli
Potamos
Trifyllianika
Paleopoli
Katsoulianika
Hristoforianika
Logothetianika
Lianianika
IONIAN SEA
To Antikythira (see inset) & Kastelli-Kissamos (Crete)
458m
Airport
Babakaradika
Aroniadika
Kastrisianika
Frilingianika
490m
Makronisi Island
Diakofti
Agia Moni
Cave of Agia Sofia
Kato Hora
Mitata
KYTHIRA
Cape Limnionas
Mylopotamos
Viaradika
389m
507m
Temple of Aphrodite
Paleopoli
Avlemonas
Fratsia
Paleopoli Beach
Cape Modoni
Kaladi Beach
Karvounades
Alexandrades
Kalokerines
Pitsinianika
Goudianika
Moni Myrtidion
Tsikalaria
Travasarianika
Skoulianika
Fatsadika
SEA OF CRETE
English (Katouni) Bridge
410m
Kato Livadi
Ano Livadi
Kominianika
Katelouzianika
Pourko
Fyri Ammos
Strapodi
Moni Agias Elesas
477m
Manitohori
Kalamos
0
2
4 km
Hora (Kythira)
Kapsali
MEDITERRANEAN SEA
Cape Trahilos
Vroulea
Cape Kapello

twice-weekly connections to Antikythira (two hours, 2000 dr) and Kasteli in Crete (4½ hours, 4000 dr). Schedules and times are often subject to delays so check at Agia Pelagia's Megalokonomou Shipping Agency (☎ 33 490, fax 33 890).

The older *Nisos Kythira* run by BOIAI Lines shuttles between Agia Pelagia, Neapoli (one hour, 1500 dr) and Gythio (two hours, 1600 dr). A newer ship may be in operation by the time you read this. Tickets are sold at the quay before departure, or at the BOIAI office in Potamos.

The port police (☎ 33 280) are at Agia Pelagia on the waterfront.

Hydrofoil In summer, there are five hydrofoils weekly from Diakofti on Kythira to Piraeus (five hours, 10,300 dr) via Monemvasia, Spetses and Hydra. Tickets are available from Kythira Travel in Hora, or Megalokonomou Shipping Agency in Agia Pelagia.

Getting Around

Bus Kythira's bus service is designed to ferry schoolchildren to and from school. Outside of term times it is nonexistent. During school terms a couple of services link Agia Pelagia with Kapsali twice daily – before school in the morning and in the early afternoon when school is out. There is no airport bus. Not surprisingly, Kythira has many taxis and a taxi from Agia Pelagia to Kapsali will cost around 4000 dr. Hitching is fairly easy.

Car & Motorcycle Panayiotis, at Moto Rent (☎ 31 600) on Kapsali's waterfront, rents cars, jeeps, mopeds and motorcycles. Easy Rider (☎ 33 486) rents motorbikes at Agia Pelagia.

Agia Pelagia Αγία Πελαγία

• pop 280

Kythira's northern port of Agia Pelagia is a simple, friendly waterfront village ideal for relaxing, swimming and finding peace of mind. A room-finding office (no telephone) is at the top of the quay, and operates in high season. Lia at Megalokonomou Shipping Agency, opposite the quay, happily assists newcomers.

Mixed sand and pebble beaches are to either side of the quay.

Places to Stay – Budget Prebooking in high season is almost essential in Agia Pelagia. One of the friendliest and most pleasant places to stay is the domatia of ***Georgos Kambouris*** *(☎ 33 480)*. His wife, Maria, maintains spotless, airy doubles/triples for 12,000/14,000 dr. The building is just in front of Hotel Romantica.

Opposite the quay above Faros Taverna, ***Alexandra Megalopoulou's Rooms*** *(☎ 33 282)* are tidy, simply furnished and with bathroom for 12,500 dr a double.

The welcoming D class ***Hotel Kytheria*** *(☎ 33 321, 33 825)*, owned by helpful Angelo from Australia, has very comfortable, tidy singles/doubles with bathroom for 13,000/17,000 dr. Considerable discounts to the above prices apply out of high season.

Places to Stay – Mid-Range & Top End ***Filoxenia Apartments*** *(☎ 33 100, fax 33 610)* each have a bedroom, lounge and kitchen. However, the interior layout is a little claustrophobic. An attached pool makes up for this. Rates for doubles/quads are 22,000/26,000 dr. Two-bedroom units for four/six people are 26,000 dr. Turn left then right from the quay.

Hotel Romantica *(☎ 33 834, fax 33 915)* has stunning, sparkling self-contained apartments for four (32,000 dr) and double air-con studios with TV and phone for 25,000 dr. There is also a swimming pool. Turn right from the quay and look for the sign after 600m.

Another good place is ***Venardos Hotel*** *(☎ 34 205, fax 33 850, email venardos@mail.otenet.gr)*, where airy singles/doubles are 18,000/22,000 dr. Australians get a special welcome and the hotel is open all year.

Kythira's sole A class hotel, ***Hotel Marou*** *(☎ 33 466, fax 33 497)*, with the island's only tennis court, a bar, snack bar and laundry, is above the north-west end of the village. Doubles are between 18,000 dr and 24,000 dr.

Places to Eat The blue and white ***Faros Taverna*** close to the quay serves good, economical Greek staples. To the far right, ***Ouzeri Moustakias***, next to the minimarket, offers food ranging from mezedes to seafood. ***Kaleris***, in between the two, is a tasteful little eatery with old photographs and painted wooden signs on the wall. The speciality is roast wild goat.

For breakfast ***Sempreviva Patisserie*** close by serves wickedly delicious Greek cakes and jugs of freshly brewed coffee.

Bar life revolves around ***En Plo***, ***Oionos*** and ***Mouragio***, all neat little bars slotted in between the eateries.

Potamos Ποταμός

• pop 680

Potamos, 10km from Agia Pelagia, is the island's commercial hub. On Sunday it attracts almost every islander to market. The National Bank of Greece is on the central square. The post office and police are south of the central square, and the OTE is 150m north.

The only domatia are those of ***Panayiotis Alevizopoulos*** *(☎ 33 245)* whose neat doubles are 13,000 dr. The one hotel is ***Hotel Porfyra*** *(☎ 33 329)*, where self-contained units surround an internal courtyard. Doubles/triples are 11,500/14,000 dr.

Taverna Panaretos *(☎ 34 290)* on the central square serves well prepared international and Greek dishes.

Mylopotamos Μυλοπόταμος

• pop 90

Mylopotamos is an alluring, verdant village. Its central square is flanked by a much-photographed church and kafeneio. Stroll to the **Neraïda** (water nymph) waterfall. From the square, continue along the road and take the right fork. After 100m, a path on the right leads to the waterfall. It's magical, with luxuriant greenery and mature, shady trees.

To reach the abandoned **kastro** of Mylopotamos, take the left fork after the church and follow the sign for Kato Hora (lower village). The road leads to the centre of Kato Hora, from where a portal with the insignia of St Mark leads into the spooky kastro, with derelict houses and well preserved little churches (locked).

The **Cave of Agia Sofia** was first explored by the famous speleologists Ioannis and Anna Patrohilos, who also discovered the Diros Cave in the Peloponnese. In the 12th century, the cave was converted into a chapel and dedicated to Agia Sophia. Legend says she visited the cave with her daughters Pistis, Elpis and Haris (Faith, Hope and Charity). The cave is reached by a precipitous 2km road or a steep path from Mylopotamos. Irregular opening times are pinned on a signpost to the cave beyond Mylopotamos' square. Admission is 500 dr and includes a guided tour.

Hora Χώρα

• postcode 801 00 • pop 550

Hora (or Kythira; Κύθηρα), the pretty capital, with white, blue-shuttered houses, perches on a long, slender ridge 2km uphill from Kapsali. The central square, planted with hibiscus, bougainvillea and palms, is Plateia Dimitriou Staï. The main street runs south of it. The post office is on the left, at its southern end. The OTE is up the steps beside Kythira Travel on the central square.

The National Bank of Greece is on the central square. Next to it is the Agricultural Bank which sports an ATM. The police station (☎ 31 206) is near the kastro.

Hora has no tourist office or tourist police but English-speaking Panayiotis offers information to tourists at his Moto Rent office (☎ 31 600) on Kapsali's waterfront.

Things to See Hora's Venetian **kastro** is at the southern end of town. If you walk to its southern extremity, passing the Church of Panagia, you will come to a sheer cliff. From here there is a stunning view of Kapsali and on a good day of Antikythira.

The **museum** is north of the central square. It features gravestones of British soldiers and their infants who died on the island in the 19th century. (Hora was part of the British Ionian Protectorate from 1815 to 1864.) A large stone lion is exhibited and a sweet terracotta figurine of a woman and child. The museum is open 8.45 am to 3 pm Tuesday to Saturday and 8.30 am to 2.30 pm Sunday. Admission is free.

Places to Stay Hora's cheapest accommodation is to be found at ***Georgiou Psi Rooms*** *(☎ 31 070)*, where doubles are 8,000 dr. Walk south along the main street and look for the sign on the left.

Castello Rooms *(☎/fax 31 069)* are spacious, and have kitchens, bathrooms and terraces with breathtaking views. Rates are 9000 dr a double. There's a sign at the southern end of the main street. ***Papadonicos Rooms*** *(☎ 31 129)*, a bit farther south, has pleasant double studios for 9000 dr. ***Belvedere Apartments*** *(☎/fax 31 761)*, just beyond the turn-off for Kapsali, features attractive apartments for 12,000 dr. It has terrific views of Kapsali.

The B class ***Hotel Margarita*** *(☎ 31 711, fax 31 325)*, on the main street, is a renovated 19th century mansion. Rates are 15,200/19,300 dr for singles/doubles with breakfast. Air-con rooms have TV and telephone.

Places to Eat There are not a lot of restaurant choices in Hora, but 100m south of the square is ***Zorba's Taverna*** *(Spyridonos Staï 34)* which offers tasty grilled food. On the square itself, ***La Frianderie*** on Plateia Staï is a hip place serving savoury and sweet crepes and snacks. Also on the square, ***Vengera Cafe*** serves evening snacks in summer.

Kapsali Καψάλι

• postcode 801 00 • pop 70

Kapsali is a picturesque village located down a winding road from Hora. It looks particularly captivating from Hora's castle, with its twin sandy bays and curving waterfront. Restaurants and cafes line the beach, and safe sheltered swimming in aquamarine waters is Kapsali's trademark. Not surprisingly, this is a very popular place so accommodation can be scarce unless you book well beforehand. It can also get pretty crowded so if you like your beach in solitude look elsewhere.

Offshore you can see the stark rock island known as the **Avgo** (Egg) rearing above the water. It is here that the Kytherians claim Aphrodite sprang from the sea.

Canoes, pedal boats, surf boards and water-skis can be hired from Panayiotis at Moto Rent, on the waterfront. Kapsali's port police (☎ 31 222) are next door.

Places to Stay & Eat Kythira's camp site, ***Camping Kapsali*** *(☎ 31 580)*, is pine-shaded and open in summer only. The site is 400m from Kapsali's quay and signposted from the inland road to Hora.

Irene Megaloudi's Rooms *(☎ 31 340)* has clean doubles/triples with bathroom for 10,000/12,000 dr. At ***Poulmendis Rooms*** *(☎ 31 451)* clean, pleasant rooms with bathroom cost 12,000/15,000 dr. Both are on the waterfront.

Rigas Apartments *(☎ 31 365, fax 31 265)* are more expensive. The accommodation, in a cluster of white terraced buildings back from the waterfront, ranges from beautifully furnished double studios for 22,000 dr to two-bedroom maisonettes for 38,000 dr.

There are three restaurants on the seafront road of Kytherias Afroditis. The first, heading towards Hora, is the ***Artena***, noticeable for its striking blue chairs and tables. In operation since 1935, it has a wide range of ready-made and to-order fish dishes at mid-range prices. The ***Venetsianiko*** farther along serves a wide range of Greek dishes, pasta and fish, and the lively ***Ydragogio*** at the far end by the rocks specialises in fish and mezedes.

Around Kythira

If you have transport, a tour round the island is rewarding. The monasteries of **Agia Moni** and **Agia Elesa** are mountain refuges with superb views. **Moni Myrtidion** is a beautiful monastery surrounded by trees. From Hora, drive north-east to the picturesque village of **Avlemonas** via **Paleopoli** with its wide, pebbled beach. Here, archaeologists spent years searching for evidence of a temple at Aphrodite's birthplace.

Just north of the village of Kato Livadi make a detour to see the remarkable, and seemingly out of place, British-made **Katouni Bridge**, a legacy of Kythira's time as part of the British Protectorate in the 19th century. In the far north of the island the village of **Karavas** is verdant and very attractive and close to both Agia Pelagia and the reasonable beach at **Platia Ammos**. Beachcombers should seek out **Kaladi Beach**, near Paleopoli. Another good beach is **Fyri Ammos**, closer to Hora.

While heading out across the island, stop in at ***Estiatorion Pierros*** *(☎ 31 014)* in **Ano Livadi**. Here you will find no-nonsense traditional Greek staples in a great little roadside establishment. The ***Karydies Taverna*** *(☎ 33 664)* in **Logothetianika**, near Potamos, attracts a good crowd to its weekend music evenings. Bookings are recommended. When the mist is up and sweeping across the island stop by the little ***Ouzeri-Kafeneio Grigoraki*** *(☎ 33 971)* on the main road in **Aroniadika** and partake of an ouzo and mezedes. It can get quite spooky in this little village around which ghosts are reported to roam on dark and windy winter's evenings.

ANTIKYTHIRA Αντικύθηρα

• pop 70

The tiny island of Antikythira, 38km southeast of Kythira, is the most remote island in the Ionian group. It has only one settlement, **Potamos**, one doctor, one police officer, one teacher (with five pupils), one metered telephone and a monastery. It has no post office or bank. The only accommodation for tourists is 10 basic ***rooms*** in two purpose-built blocks, open in summer only. Potamos has a ***kafeneio*** and ***taverna***.

The F/B *Maria* calls at least twice weekly in the early hours on the way to Crete, returning the same day to Kythira and Gythio. If the sea is choppy, the ferry does not stop, so this is not an island for tourists on a tight schedule. Check conditions in Piraeus if you intend to come direct, or with Megalokonomou Shipping Agency in Kythira's Agia Pelagia.

Evia & the Sporades

Evia (Εύβοια), Greece's second-largest island, is so close to the mainland historically, physically and topographically that one tends not to regard it as an island at all. Athenians regard Evia as a convenient destination for a weekend break, so consequently it gets packed. Except for the resort of Eretria, however, it is not frequently visited by foreign tourists.

The Sporades (Οι Σποράδες) lie to the north and east of Evia and to the east and south-east of the Pelion Peninsula, to which they were joined in prehistoric times. With their dense vegetation and mountainous terrain, they seem like a continuation of this peninsula. There are 11 islands in the archipelago, four of which are inhabited: Skiathos, Skopelos, Alonnisos and Skyros. The first two have a highly developed tourist industry, whereas Alonnisos and Skyros, although by no means remote, are far less visited and retain more local character.

Getting There & Away

Air Skiathos airport receives charter flights from northern Europe and there are also domestic flights to Athens. Skyros airport has domestic flights to Athens and occasional charter flights from the Netherlands.

Bus From Athens' Terminal B bus station there are buses every half-hour to Halkida from 5.45 am to 9.45 pm (one hour, 1350 dr), three daily to Kymi from 6 am to 7 pm (3¼ hours, 2950 dr), and three daily to Loutra Edipsou (3½ hours, 2800 dr). From the Mavromateon terminal in Athens, there are buses every 45 minutes to Rafina (for Karystos and Marmari; one hour, 460 dr).

Train There are hourly trains each day from Athens' Larisis station to Halkida (1½ hours, 700 dr).

HIGHLIGHTS

- The changing tides of the Evripous channel in Evia that so puzzled Aristotle
- Skiathos' golden beaches – among the best in Greece
- Getting delightfully lost in the labyrinthine streets of picturesque Skopelos Town
- Quirky Skyros and pretty Skyrian houses – Greece's hidden island treasure
- Nature walks, fine food and *rembetika* music on clean and green Skopelos
- Relaxing on Alonnisos, one of the Aegean's greenest and most underrated islands and mingling with artists and poets in restored Hora

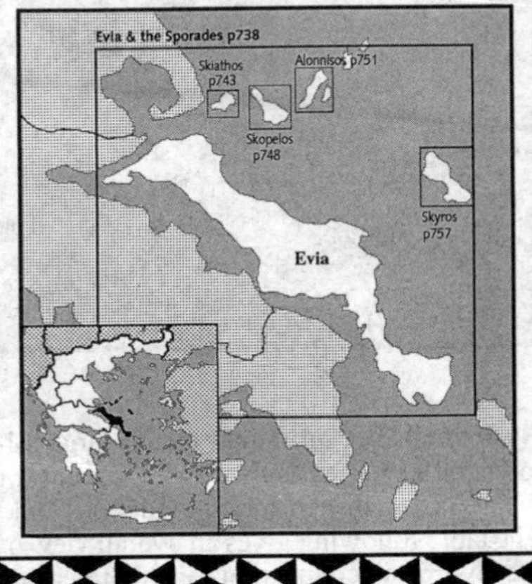

Ferry The table following gives an overall view of the available ferries to this island group from mainland ports in high season. Further details and inter-island links can be found under each island entry.

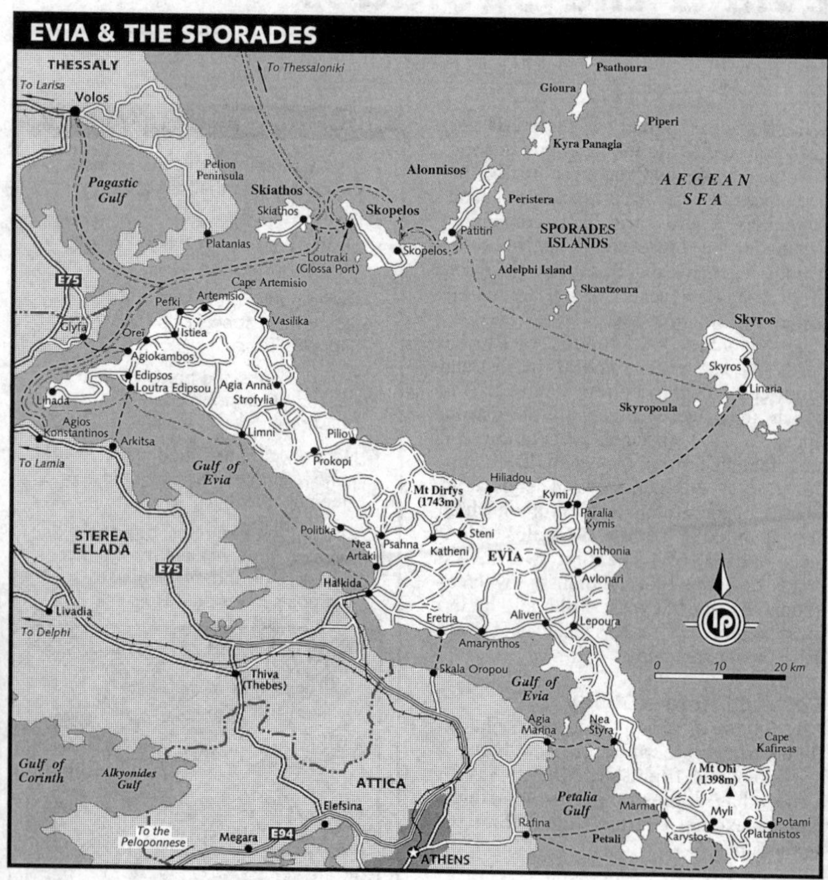

Hydrofoil Hydrofoil links by and large follow similar routes as the ferries, except for the Evia (Kymi) to Skyros (Linaria) link. The table following gives an overall view of the hydrofoil connections in high season. Further details and inter-island links can be found under each island entry. The summer hydrofoil timetable is usually available in late April from Minoan Flying Dolphin (☎ 01-428 0001, fax 428 3526), Akti Themistokleous 8, Piraeus GR-185 36. The Athens office (☎ 01-324 4600) is at Filellinon 3. The timetable is also available from local hydrofoil booking offices.

Getting Around

Halkida is the transport hub of Evia. There are buses to the port of Kymi (2½ hours, 1650 dr, nine daily) via Eretria and Kymi town; to Steni (45 minutes, 650 dr, six daily); and to Karystos (3½ hours, 2250 dr, three daily) via Eretria. There are also buses to Limni (2½ hours, 1500 dr, four daily). Timetables are outside the ticket office.

Ferry & Hydrofoil Connections to Evia & the Sporades

Ferries

Origin	Destination	Duration	Price	Frequency
Agia Marina	Evia (Nea Styra)	40 mins	650 dr	5 daily
Agios Konstantinos	Alonnisos	5½ hours	4400 dr	1 daily
Agios Konstantinos	Skiathos	3½ hours	3220 dr	2 daily
Agios Konstantinos	Skopelos	4½ hours	4100 dr	4 daily
Arkitsa	Evia (Edipsos)	1 hour	690 dr	12 daily
Kymi	Skyros	2¼ hours	2300 dr	2 daily
Rafina	Evia (Karystos)	1¾ hours	1768 dr	2 daily
Rafina	Evia (Marmari)	1¼ hours	1239 dr	4 daily
Skala Oropou	Evia (Eretria)	30 mins	310 dr	half-hourly
Thessaloniki	Skiathos	6½ hours	4500 dr	3 weekly
Thessaloniki	Skopelos	6 hours	4600 dr	3 weekly
Volos	Alonnisos	5 hours	3700 dr	3 daily
Volos	Skiathos	3½ hours	2750 dr	4 daily
Volos	Skopelos	4½ hours	3380 dr	4 daily

Hydrofoils

Origin	Destination	Duration	Price	Frequency
Agios Konstantinos	Alonnisos	2½ hours	8800 dr	3 daily
Agios Konstantinos	Skiathos	1½ hours	6600 dr	3 daily
Agios Konstantinos	Skopelos	2¼ hours	8200 dr	3 daily
Thessaloniki	Alonnisos	4½ hours	11,700 dr	1 daily
Thessaloniki	Skiathos	3½ hours	8500 dr	6 weekly
Thessaloniki	Skopelos	4¾ hours	9300 dr	1 daily
Thessaloniki	Skyros	6¼ hours	13,400 dr	4 weekly
Volos	Alonnisos	2½ hours	7500 dr	5 daily
Volos	Skiathos	1¼ hours	5500 dr	4 daily
Volos	Skopelos	2¼ hours	6800 dr	5 daily
Volos	Skyros	4¼ hours	14,100 dr	5 weekly

Evia Εύβοια

The island of Evia (**eh**-vih-ah) will probably never be a prime destination for foreign tourists, but if you're based in Athens with a few days to spare, and (preferably) your own transport, a foray into Evia is well worthwhile for its scenic mountain roads, pristine inland villages, and a look at some resorts which cater for Greeks (including one for ailing Greeks), rather than for foreign tourists.

A mountainous spine runs north-south; the east coast consists of precipitous cliffs, whereas the gentler west coast has a string of beaches and resorts. The island is reached overland by a bridge over the Evripous channel to the island's capital, Halkida. At the mention of Evia, most Greeks will eagerly tell you that the current in this narrow channel changes direction around seven times daily, which it does, if you are prepared to hang around to watch it. The next bit of the story, that Aristotle became so perplexed at not finding an explanation for this mystifying occurrence that he threw himself into the channel and drowned, can almost certainly be taken with a grain of salt.

HALKIDA Χαλκίδα

☎ 0221 • postcode 341 00 • pop 45,000

Halkida was an important city-state in ancient times, with several colonies dotted around the Mediterranean. The name derives from the bronze manufactured here in antiquity (*halkos* means 'bronze' in Greek). Today it's a lively industrial and agricultural town, but with nothing of sufficient note to warrant an overnight stay.

However, if you have an hour or two to spare between buses then have a look at the **archaeological museum**, Leoforos Venizelou 13; it's worth a mosey around. It houses finds from Evia's three ancient cities of Halkida, Eretria and Karystos, including a chunk from the pediment of the Temple of Dafniforos Apollo at Eretria. The museum (☎ 25 131) is open 8.30 am to 3 pm Tuesday to Sunday; admission is 500 dr.

The Halkida train station is on the mainland side of the bridge. To reach central Halkida, turn right outside the train station, walk over the bridge, turn left and you will find Leoforos Venizelou, Halkida's main drag, off to the right.

The phone number of the Halkida tourist police is ☎ 87 000.

CENTRAL EVIA

Steni Στενή

☎ 0228 • postcode 340 03 • pop 1300

From Halkida it's 31km to the lovely mountain village of Steni, with gurgling springs and plane trees. The village has two hotels, both C class. ***Hotel Dirfys** (☎ 51 217)* has singles/doubles for 5000/9500 dr. ***Hotel Steni** (☎ 51 221, fax 51 325)* has rooms for 7000/10,000 dr with bathroom.

For a meal, look for ***Sakaflias** (☎ 51 205)* restaurant on the main square. Try *tiganopsomo*, a kind of pan-fried cheese pie, and the house rosé. It shouldn't cost you more than 1900 dr.

Steni is the starting point for the climb up **Mt Dirfys** (1743m), which is Evia's highest mountain. The EOS-owned ***Dirfys Refuge** (☎ 51 285)*, at 1120m, can be reached along a 9km dirt road, or after a two hour walk along a forest footpath. From the refuge it's two hours to the summit. For further information contact the EOS (☎ 0221-25 230), Angeli Gyviou 22, Halkida.

A partially sealed road continues from Steni to **Hiliadou**, on the north coast, where there is a fine beach.

Kymi Κύμη

☎ 0222 • postcode 340 03 • pop 3850

Kymi is a picturesque town built on a cliff 250m above the sea. The port of Kymi (called Paralia Kymis), 4km downhill, is the only natural harbour on the precipitous east coast, and the departure point for ferries to Skyros.

The **folklore museum** (☎ 22 011), on the road to Paralia Kymis, has an impressive collection of local costumes and memorabilia, including a display commemorating Kymi-born Dr George Papanikolaou, who invented the Pap smear test. Opening times are 5 pm to 7.30 pm Wednesday and Saturday and 10 am to 1 pm Sunday.

Paralia Kymis has two hotels, both C class. ***Hotel Beis** (☎/fax 22 604)* has singles/doubles for 10,000/12,000 dr, and ***Hotel Corali** (☎ 22 212, fax 23 353)* has rooms for 8500/9900 dr. This hotel is set back from the main road up a steep hill on the south side of Paralia Kymis. There are some ***domatia** (☎ 23 896)* in Kymi itself, on the left along the main Halkida road. Neat, clean rooms with TV go for 8000 dr.

Back in Paralia Kymis, the best place to eat is ***To Egeo** (☎ 22 641)* where you can dine under an awning overlooking the sea. It specialises in lobsters and prawns and does tasty platters.

NORTHERN EVIA

From Halkida a road heads north to **Psahna**, the gateway to the highly scenic mountainous interior of northern Evia. The road climbs through pine forests to the beautiful agricultural village of **Prokopi**, 52km from Halkida. The inhabitants are descendants of refugees who, in 1923, came from Prokopion (present-day Ürgüp) in Turkey, bringing with them the relics of St John the Russian. On 27 May (St John's festival), hordes of pilgrims come to worship his relics in the Church of Agios Ioannis Rosses.

At Strofylia, 14km beyond Prokopi, a road heads south-west to **Limni**, a pretty (but crowded) fishing village with whitewashed houses and a beach. With your own transport or a penchant for walking, you can visit the 16th century **Convent of Galataki**, 8km south-east of Limni. Its *katholikon* (main church) has fine frescoes. Limni has two hotels and some domatia. There's one camp site, ***Rovies Camping*** *(☎ 71 120)*, on the coast, 13km north-west of Limni.

The road continues to the sedate spa resort of **Loutra Edipsou** (119km from Halkida) whose therapeutic sulphur waters have been celebrated since antiquity. Many luminaries, including Aristotle, Plutarch, Strabo and Plinius, sang the praises of these waters. The waters are reputed to cure many ills, mostly of a rheumatic, arthritic or gynaecological nature. Today the town has Greece's most up-to-date hydrotherapy-physiotherapy centre. If you're interested, contact any EOT or the EOT Hydrotherapy-Physiotherapy Centre (☎ 23 500), Loutra Edipsou. Even if you don't rank among the infirm you may enjoy a visit to this resort with its attractive setting, a beach, many domatia and hotels.

SOUTHERN EVIA

Eretria Ερέτρια

☎ 0211 • postcode 340 08 • pop 5000

As you head east from Halkida, Eretria is the first major place of interest. Ancient Eretria was a major maritime power and also had an eminent school of philosophy. The city was destroyed in 87 AD during the Mithridatic War, fought between Mithridates (king of Pontos) and the Roman commander Sulla. The modern town was founded in the 1820s by islanders from Psara fleeing the Turkish. Once Evia's major archaeological site, it has metamorphosed into a tacky resort patronised by British package tourists.

Things to See From the top of the **ancient acropolis**, at the northern end of town, there are splendid views over to the mainland. West of the acropolis are the remains of a palace, temple, and a theatre with a subterranean passage once used by actors. Close by, the **Museum of Eretria** (☎ 62 206) contains well displayed finds from ancient Eretria. Opening times are 8.30 am to 3 pm Tuesday to Sunday; admission is 500 dr. In the centre of town are the remains of the **Temple of Dafniforos Apollo** and a mosaic from an ancient bath.

Places to Stay Eretria has loads of ***hotels*** and ***domatia***, and ***Eva Camping*** *(☎ 61 081)* is at Malakonda, 5km west along the coast. ***Milos Camping*** *(☎ 60 360)* is 1km west of Eretria town.

Karystos Κάρυστος

☎ 0224 • postcode 340 01 • pop 4500

Continuing east from Eretria, the road branches at Lepoura: the left fork leads to Kymi, the right to Karystos (**kah**-ris-tos). Set on the wide Karystian Bay, below Mt Ohi (1398m), Karystos is the most attractive of southern Evia's resorts. The town was designed on a grid system by the Bavarian architect Bierbach, who was commissioned by King Otho. If you turn right from the quay you will come to the remains of a 14th century Venetian castle, the **Bourtzi**, which has marble from a temple dedicated to Apollo incorporated into its walls. Beyond this there is a sandy beach; there is another at the other end of the waterfront.

Places to Stay & Eat Look for ***domatia*** signs or the three easy-to-find hotels on the waterfront. Opposite the ferry quay, the C class ***Hotel Als*** *(☎ 22 202)* has single/double rooms for 5800/11,400 dr. The ageing ***Hotel Galaxy*** *(☎ 22 600, fax 22 463)* is at the west end of Kriezotou, on the corner with

Omirou, with rooms for 8500/12,300 dr including breakfast. The pleasant ***Hotel Karystion*** *(☎ 22 391, fax 22 727, Kriezotou 2)* is 200m south of the Bourtzi. It has rooms for 13,000/18,000 dr, including breakfast.

The best place to get a bite to eat is the ***Cavo d'Oro*** *(☎ 22 326)*, Parodos Sahtouri, in an alleyway just off the main square. It is a traditional restaurant serving cheap, oil-based dishes *(ladera)* from 700 dr, with meat dishes for 1350 dr. On the seafront opposite the harbour the pick of the bunch is ***Marinos Restaurant*** *(☎ 24 126)* with ladera from 1000 dr and tasty local fish at 2600 dr.

Around Karystos

The ruins of **Castello Rossa** (red castle), a 13th century Frankish fortress, are a short walk from **Myli**, a delightful, well watered village 4km inland from Karystos. The aqueduct behind the castle once carried water from the mountain springs and a tunnel led from this castle to the Bourtzi in Karystos. A little beyond Myli there is an **ancient quarry** scattered with fragments of the once-prized Karystian marble.

With your own transport you can explore the sleepy villages nestling in the southern foothills of Mt Ohi. The rough road winds through citrus groves and pine trees high above the south coast. From **Platanistos**, a charming village named for its plane trees, a 5km dirt road (driveable) leads to the coastal village of **Potami** with its sand and pebble beach.

Skiathos Σκιάθος

☎ 0427 • postcode 370 02 • pop 4100

The good news is that much of the pine-covered coast of Skiathos is blessed with exquisite beaches of golden sand. The bad news is that the island is overrun with package tourists – at least in August – and is very expensive. Despite the large presence of sun-starved northern Europeans, and the ensuing tourist excess, Skiathos is still a pretty island and not surprisingly one of Greece's premier resorts.

The island has only one settlement, the port and capital of Skiathos Town, on the south-east coast. The rest of the south coast is one long chain of holiday villas and hotels. The north coast is precipitous and less accessible. Most people come to the island for the beaches and nightlife, but the truly curious will discover some picturesque walks, hidden valleys and even quiet beaches.

Getting There & Away

Air As well as the numerous charter flights from northern Europe to Skiathos, during summer there are up to five flights daily to Athens (16,700 dr). The Olympic Airways office (☎ 22 200) is in Skiathos Town on the right side of Papadiamanti, the main thoroughfare, as you walk inland.

Ferry In summer, there are ferries from Skiathos to Volos (3½ hours, 2750 dr, three to four daily), to Agios Konstantinos (3½ hours, 3220 dr, two daily) and to Alonnisos (two hours, 1800 dr, four to six daily) via Glossa (Skopelos) and Skopelos Town (1½ hours, 1400 dr). There are also boats from Skiathos to Thessaloniki (5½ to seven hours, 4500 dr, three weekly) in July and August. Tickets can be most easily obtained from Alkyon Tourist Office (☎ 22 029). The port police can be contacted on ☎ 22 017.

Hydrofoil In summer, there is a bewildering array of hydrofoils from Skiathos and around the Sporades in general. Among the main services, there are hydrofoils from Skiathos to Volos (1¼ hours, 5500 dr, three or four daily), and to Alonnisos (one hour, 3600 dr, eight to 10 daily) via Glossa (Skopelos) and Skopelos Town (35 minutes, 2800 dr). There are also hydrofoils to Agios Konstantinos (1½ hours, 6600 dr, two or three daily). Three to five weekly go to Skyros (2¼ hours, 8400 dr) and Kymi (three hours, 10,055 dr), and five or six weekly go to Thessaloniki (3½ hours, 8500 dr). There are also services to the Pelion Peninsula, Halkidiki, various ports in northern Evia and to Stylida near Lamia. Hydrofoil tickets may be purchased from Skiathos Holidays

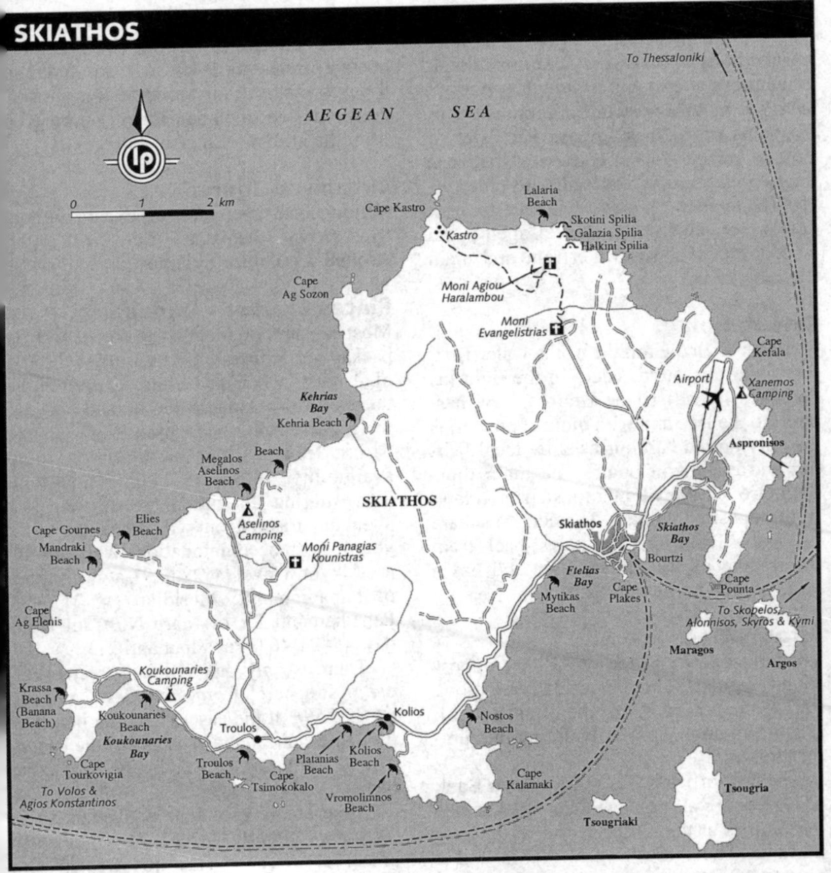

(☎ 22 018, fax 22 771) in the middle of Skiathos Town's new harbour waterfront.

Getting Around

Bus Crowded buses leave Skiathos Town for Koukounaries Beach (30 minutes, 350 dr) every half-hour between 7.30 am and 10.30 pm. The buses stop at all the access points to the beaches along the south coast. A couple of buses connect for passengers going to Megalos Aselinos Beach, on the north coast.

Car & Motorcycle Car hire outlets including Alamo (☎ 23 025) and Euronet (☎ 24 410), as well as heaps of motorcycle hire outlets, are along the town's waterfront.

Excursion Boat Excursion boats go to most of the south-coast beaches from the old harbour. Trips around the island cost about 3500 dr and include a visit to Kastro, Lalaria Beach, and the three caves of Halkini Spilia, Skotini Spilia and Galazia Spilia, which are only accessible by boat.

SKIATHOS TOWN

Skiathos Town, with its red-roofed, whitewashed houses, is built on two low hills. It is picturesque enough, although it doesn't have the picture postcard attractiveness of Skopelos or Skyros towns. The islet of Bourtzi (reached by a causeway) between the two harbours is covered with pine forest. The town is a major tourist centre, with hotels, souvenir shops, travel agents and bars dominating the waterfront and main thoroughfares.

Orientation

The quay is in the middle of the waterfront, just north of Bourtzi Islet. To the right (as you face inland) is the straight, new harbour; to the left, and with more character, is the curving old harbour used by local fishing and excursion boats. The main thoroughfare of Papadiamanti strikes inland from opposite the quay. The central square of Plateia Trion Ierarhon is just back from the middle of the old harbour and has a large church in the middle.

Information

The tourist police office (☎ 23 172), opposite the regular police about halfway along Papadiamanti, next to the high school, operates 8 am to 9 pm daily during the summer season.

The post office, OTE and National Bank of Greece are all on Papadiamanti. The bus terminus is at the northern end of the new harbour. There are several ATMs and a couple of automatic exchange machines around town. Mare Nostrum Holidays (☎ 21 463) at Papadiamanti 21 represents American Express. It will exchange travellers cheques without deducting a commission.

The Skiathos Internet Centre (☎ 22 021) is at Miaouli 12.

Museum

Skiathos was the birthplace of the Greek short-story writer and poet Alexandros Papadiamantis, as well as the novelist Alexandros Moraïtidis. Papadiamantis' house is now a museum with a small collection documenting his life. The museum's opening times are 9 am to 1 pm and 5 to 8 pm; it's closed on Monday. It is just off the right side of Papadiamanti coming up from the harbour. Entry is 250 dr.

Organised Tours

Various local operators run excursion boat trips around the island. See the Getting Around section for Skiathos Island.

Places to Stay – Budget

Most accommodation is booked solid by package-tour operators from July to the end of August, when prices are often double those of low season. Prices quoted here are for high season. There is a kiosk on the harbourfront with information on room availability. If you're brave enough to arrive during the summer rush, then just about any travel agent will endeavour to fix you up with accommodation. Worth trying are Alkyon Travel (☎ 22 029), at the bottom of Papadiamanti; Meridian (☎ 21 309, Papadiamanti 8); or Mare Nostrum Holidays (☎ 21 463, Papadiamanti 21).

There is only one officially recognised camp site here, ***Koukounaries Camping*** *(☎ 49 250)*, at the east end of the beach of the same name at the west end of the island. This is a well run setup and very close to the beach.

There are in principal two other sites: ***Aselinos Camping*** *(☎ 49 312)*, on the north coast, at Megalos Aselinos Beach; and ***Xanemos Camping***, close to the airport. In the first case, the site doesn't always open (it doesn't have a licence) and Xanemos Camping is far too close to the airport for comfort – hardly anyone uses it.

The E class ***Hotel Karafelas*** *(☎ 21 235, Papadiamanti 59)* is one of the town's best-value hotels. The comfortable singles/doubles are 8000/11,000 dr with bathroom. The hotel is at the far end of Papadiamanti, on the left. Also worth a try is the slightly more expensive E class ***Australia Hotel*** *(☎ 22 488)*, which has tidy rooms for 12,500/15,100 dr with bathroom. Walk up

EVIA & THE SPORADES

Papadiamanti to the post office, turn right and take the first left.

Kostis Hostel (☎ *23 982, fax 22 909, Evangelistrias 5)* has been given the thumbs up from some LP readers. Its neat rooms go for 12,000/14,000 dr.

Places to Stay – Mid-Range

The C class ***Hotel Morfo*** *(☎ 21 737, fax 23 222, Ananiou 23)* has smallish but quite adequate doubles for 13,000 dr with bathroom. From the waterfront take M Ananiou (parallel to, and to the right of, Papadiamanti), and the hotel is on the left.

For a very central location with a great waterfront view, try the C class ***Hotel Akti*** *(☎ 22 024)* overlooking the new harbour. Airy singles/doubles go for 14,000/18,000 dr. The roomy four-person penthouse apartment on the top floor goes for 30,000 dr. Book ahead if you can.

Places to Stay – Top End

Most of the island's top-end hotels are on the coast to the west of Skiathos Town. The A class ***Hotel Paradise*** *(☎/fax 21 939)*, 3km west of town, is one of the newest and smallest of these hotels. It has tastefully furnished air-con rooms and a restaurant and bar. Doubles are 25,500 dr.

At Nostos Beach, the A class ***Nostos Bungalows*** *(☎ 22 420, fax 22 525)* is a well designed complex 5km west of town. The complex has bars, a restaurant, taverna, pool and tennis court. Bungalows sleeping up to four cost 27,000 dr.

For solitude and a blissful rural ambience in a hidden valley look no further than ***Zorbades*** *(☎/fax 49 473, email info@skiathos.info.com)*. Proprietor Geof Baldry owns two fully equipped stone houses that accommodate up to five people. He rents them out to discerning clients for between 28,000 dr and 40,000 dr daily.

Places to Eat

The good news is that there is a wide choice of eateries in Skiathos; the downside is that most of them tend to gear their cuisine to the tourist trade and are somewhat more expensive than elsewhere. Finding some decent Greek cuisine can be a matter of trial and error. For a quick, cheap bite, the no-name ***souvladzidiko*** in the back streets off Papadiamanti seems to draw the Greek youth and is a clean, bright and cheery establishment.

There is a swathe of restaurants just down from Plateia Trion Ierarhon, overlooking the old harbour. Of these, ***Avra***, though seemingly not as popular as its more bustling neighbour, has a better reputation for grills and chicken dishes. Right opposite the hydrofoil terminal, is ***O Kavouras***. Service is surprisingly good for such a busy place and food is consistently tasty and reasonably priced.

Taverna Ouzeri Kambourelis on the waterfront of the old harbour also rates reasonably well and opens earlier in the season than other establishments. ***Psarotaverna to Aigaio*** has reasonable prices and ready-made dishes as well as fish, but is in a less attractive location on the new harbourfront. ***Psaradika Ouzeri*** at the far end of the old harbour near the fish market has, not surprisingly, fresh fish and also inventive *mezedes*. It's more expensive than other places. Reckon on around 5000 dr to 6000 dr for a meal for two with wine.

Two other restaurants close to each other and away from the main tourist traps are ***Mesogia*** and ***Alexandros***. Both are signposted from Polytehniou. Prices are still in the 2700 dr range for a meal from a varied menu, but the tables spill out onto the narrow streets, making a change from the rush of the waterfront.

Entertainment

Scan Papadiamanti and Polytehniou and check out which disco or bar takes your fancy. ***Banana Bar***, patronised by tourists from the UK, and ***Borzoï***, playing both Greek and non-Greek music, are both on Polytehniou. ***Admiral Benbow*** also on Polytehniou caters to the British crowd by playing favourites from the 1960s and 70s.

Kentavros Bar, one of Skiathos' more established joints, promises rock, funky soul, acid jazz and blues, and gets the thumbs up from local expats. It's in view of the Papadiamantis museum.

AROUND SKIATHOS

Beaches

With some 65 beaches to choose from, beach-hopping on Skiathos can become a full-time occupation. Many are only accessible by caïque and the ones that are more easily accessible tend to get crowded.

Buses ply the south coast stopping at the beach access points. The ones nearest town are extremely crowded; the first one worth getting off the bus for is the pine-fringed, long and sandy **Vromolimnos Beach**, which has been awarded an EU blue flag for cleanliness. Farther along, **Platanias** and **Troulos** beaches are also good but both, alas, are very popular. The bus continues to **Koukounaries Beach**, backed by pine trees and a lagoon and touted as the best beach in Greece. Nowadays it's best viewed at a distance from where the wide sweep of pale gold sand does indeed look beautiful.

Krassa Beach, at the other side of a narrow headland, is more commonly known as **Banana Beach**, because of its curving shape and soft yellow sand. It is nominally a nudist beach, though the skinny-dippers tend to abscond to **Little Banana Beach** around the corner if things get too crowded. It has two or three snack bars.

The north coast's beaches are less crowded but exposed to the strong summer *meltemi* winds. From Troulos a road heads north to the sandy, rather scruffy-looking **Megalos Aselinos Beach**. Turn left onto a dirt road to reach this beach. A right fork from this road leads to **Mikros Aselinos Beach** and farther on to **Kehria Beach**, also reachable by a dirt road from nearer Skiathos Town.

Lalaria, on the northern coast, is a striking beach of pale grey pebbles, much featured in tourist brochures. It is most easily reached by excursion boat from Skiathos Town.

Kastro Κάστρο

Kastro, perched dramatically on a rocky headland above the north coast, was the fortified pirate-proof capital of the island from 1540 to 1829. It consisted of some 300 houses and 20 churches and the only access was by a drawbridge. Except for two churches, it is now in ruins. Access is by steps, and the views from it are tremendous. Excursion boats come to the beach below Kastro, from where it's an easy clamber up to the ruins.

Moni Evangelistrias

Μονή Ευαγγελίστριας

The 18th century Moni Evangelistrias is the most appealing of the island's monasteries. It is in a delightful setting, poised above a gorge, 450m above sea level, and surrounded by pine and cypress trees. The monastery, like many in Greece, was a refuge for freedom fighters during the War of Independence, and the islanders claim the first Greek flag was raised here in 1807.

The monastery is an hour's walk from town or you can drive here. It's signposted off the Skiathos Town ring road, close to the turn-off to the airport.

Skopelos Σκόπελος

☎ 0424 • postcode 370 03 • pop 5000

Skopelos is less commercialised than Skiathos, but following hot on its trail. Like Skiathos, the north-west coast is exposed, with high cliffs. The sheltered south-east coast harbours many beaches but, unlike Skiathos, most are pebbled. The island is heavily pine-forested and has vineyards, olive groves and fruit orchards. There are two large settlements: the capital and main port of Skopelos Town on the east coast; and the lovely, unspoilt hill village of Glossa, the island's second port, 3km north of Loutraki on the west coast.

Skopelos has yielded an exciting archaeological find. In ancient times the island was an important Minoan outpost ruled by Staphylos, who, according to mythology, was the son of Ariadne and Dionysos. *Staphylos* means grape in Greek and the Minoan ruler is said to have introduced wine making to the island. In the 1930s a tomb containing gold treasures, and believed to be that of Staphylos, was unearthed at Staphylos, now a resort.

Getting There & Away

Ferry In summer there are three ferries daily to Alonnisos from Glossa (1¼ hours, 1300 dr) and Skopelos Town (30 minutes, 1100 dr). There are also ferries to Volos (4½ hours, 3380 dr, four daily), to Agios Konstantinos (4½ hours, 4100 dr, two daily) and to Skiathos (1½ hours, 1400 dr, four or five daily). In addition, there are boats to Thessaloniki (six hours, 4600 dr, three weekly). The times given are for Skopelos Town; Glossa is one hour less. Boats from Glossa actually depart from Loutraki, on the coast. Tickets are available from Lemonis Agents (☎ 23 055, fax 22 363). The telephone number of Skopelos' port police is ☎ 22 180.

Hydrofoil Like Skiathos, Skopelos is linked to a large number of destinations by hydrofoil. The main services during summer include: to Alonnisos (20 minutes, 2200 dr, eight or nine daily), to Skiathos (one hour, 2800 dr, 10 to 12 daily), to Volos (2¼ hours, 6800 dr, five daily), to Agios Konstantinos (2¼ hours, 8200 dr, three daily), to Skyros (2¼ hours, 8000 dr, four to six weekly) and to Thessaloniki (4¾ hours, 9300 dr, one daily). Cheaper return fares apply on most of these services. In addition, there are also services to the Pelion Peninsula, Halkidiki, to various ports in Evia and to Stylida, near Lamia. Tickets may be purchased from Madro Travel in Skopelos Town (☎ 22 145, fax 22 941).

Getting Around

Bus There are buses from Skopelos Town all the way to Glossa/Loutraki (one hour, 750 dr, eight daily), a further three that go only as far as Milia (35 minutes, 510 dr) and another two that go only as far as Agnontas (15 minutes, 225 dr).

Car & Motorcycle There are a fair number of car and motorcycle rental outlets, mostly at the eastern end of the waterfront. Among them is Motor Tours (☎ 22 986), on the waterfront near Hotel Eleni.

SKOPELOS TOWN

Skopelos Town is one of the most captivating of the island's towns. It skirts a semicircular bay and clambers in tiers up a hillside, culminating in a ruined fortress. Dozens of churches are interspersed among tall, dazzlingly white houses with brightly shuttered windows and flower-adorned balconies. Traditionally, roofs in Skopelos Town were tiled with beautiful rough-hewn bluestone, but these are gradually being replaced with mass-produced red tiles.

Orientation

Skopelos Town's quay is on the west side of the bay. From the ferry, turn left to reach the bustling waterfront lined with cafes, souvenir shops and travel agencies. The bus station is to the left of the new quay, at the end of the excursion boat moorings.

Information

There is no tourist office or tourist police on Skopelos. The regular police station (☎ 22 235) is above the National Bank. Go up the steps to the right of the bank, turn left and the entrance is on the left.

The post office lurks in an obscure alleyway: walk up the road opposite the bus station, take the first left, the first right and the first left and it's on the right. To reach the OTE follow the road inland next to the Armoloï craft shop and you'll come to it on the left at the first crossroad.

The National Bank of Greece is on the waterfront near the old quay. It has an ATM and an automatic exchange machine. To reach Skopelos' self-service laundrette go up the street opposite the bus station, turn right at Platanos Taverna and it's on the left.

Museum

Strolling around town and sitting at the waterside cafes will probably be your chief occupations in Skopelos Town, but there is also a small **folk art museum**. Located on

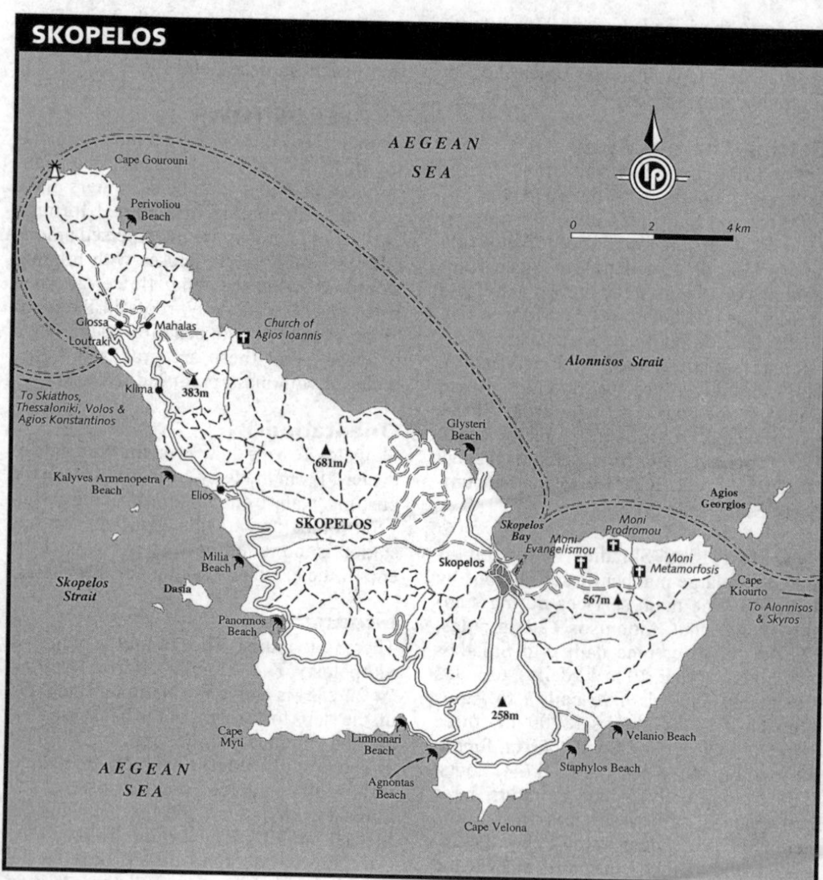

Hatzistamati, it is open 7 am to 10 pm daily and admission is free. Walk up the steps to the left of the pharmacy on the waterfront, take the first right, the first left, the first right and it's on the right.

Places to Stay – Budget

Skopelos Town is still a place where you have a good chance of renting a room in a family house, and people with rooms to offer meet the ferries and hydrofoils. The Rooms & Apartments Association of Skopelos (☎ 24 567) has an office on the waterfront and might be a better starting point.

There are a couple of places away from the town that are easy to find on your own. ***Pension Soula*** *(☎ 22 930)* is a lovely place owned by a hospitable elderly couple. Doubles/triples are 8000/10,000 dr with bathroom. Turn left at Hotel Amalia and, after about 200m, bear right. You will find the domatia on your right.

The domatia of ***Marigoula Abelakia*** *(☎ 22 662)* at Tria Platania are in a pleasant garden setting with a barbecue area, 10 minutes walk south from the waterfront. Rooms are 10,000/14,000 dr.

There are no official camp sites on Skopelos, though some people do camp rough on Velanio Beach near Staphylos.

Places to Stay – Mid-Range

The wooden-floored rooms of the pension ***Kyr Sotos*** *(☎ 22 549, fax 23 668)*, in a lovely old building in the middle of the waterfront, are delightful and very popular with visitors. There's a little courtyard, a communal kitchen and a fridge for guests' use, and each well appointed room is different. Doubles/triples are 8,800/14,600 dr respectively.

In a prime location overlooking all the waterfront action is the C class ***Hotel Adonis*** *(☎ 22 231)*. Its comfortable and homy rooms (a couple with large balconies overlooking the street) go for 15,000/20,000 dr.

Places to Stay – Top End

Ionia Hotel *(☎ 22 568, fax 23 30)* on Manolaki is an attractive hostelry located in the back streets. Comfy singles/doubles are 14,000/22,000 dr. The B class ***Dolphin Hotel*** *(☎ 23 015, fax 23 016)*, south of the bus station, is a striking pastel-coloured building with an ultramodern, luxurious interior. Rooms are 17,500/23,000 dr.

Places to Eat

For DIY diners there is a well stocked ***Alpha-Pi supermarket*** on Doulidi, just inland from the bus station. There are also a lot of restaurants in Skopelos Town and the quality is somewhat better than that on Skiathos. The following are among the better ones. ***O Platanos***, just back from the bus station, on a little open space known locally as Souvlaki Square, has tables beneath a large plane tree. It's cheap, basic and popular, and specialises in souvlaki (500 dr).

There are two reasonable Greek restaurants next to each other on the waterfront near the old ferry and hydrofoil quay. ***Klimataria*** and ***Molos*** serve a wide range of good food. A meal with retsina will cost around 2300 dr.

Two more expensive, but very pleasant restaurants are set back a little from the waterfront. ***Taverna Finikas*** *(☎ 23 247)*, on Drosopoulou, has a varied cuisine and is set round an enormous palm tree. ***Taverna Alexander*** *(☎ 22 324)*, on Anthypolohagou Hymou, has excellent local specialities including the local cheese pie, *tyropitta*. You dine in a cosy walled garden which also sports a very deep well that is floodlit at night. Look for the signs to both these places from the OTE.

For mezedes and live music, in summer only, head to ***Ouzeri Anatoli*** high up above the town in the Kastro. Here from 11 pm onwards, you will hear *rembetika* music sung by Skopelos' own exponent of the Greek blues, Georgos Xindaris. The easiest though most strenuous way there is to follow the path up past the church at the northern end of the quay.

Entertainment

Oionos Karaïskaki is a cool little bar offering tasteful jazz and ethnic music. Follow the street to the OTE and you will find it off to your right. For more lively entertainment there is a strip of clubs along Doulidi, just off Souvlaki Square. Still a favourite is ***Ano Kato*** for disco music, though ***Panselinos*** and ***Metro***, opposite, give it a run for its money. Each attracts its own age group; poke your nose in to see if you fit in.

GLOSSA Γλώσσα

Glossa, Skopelos' other major settlement, is another whitewashed delight and considerably quieter than the capital. It has managed to retain the feel of a pristine Greek village while having most of the amenities that visitors require.

The bus stops in front of a large church at a T-junction. As you face the church, the left road winds down to Loutraki and the right to the main thoroughfare of Agiou Riginou. Along here you'll find a bank and a few small stores.

Skopelos' beaches are just as accessible by bus from Glossa as they are from Skopelos Town; Milia, the island's best beach, is actually closer to Glossa. There are also places to stay and tavernas at Loutraki, but there's not a lot to do other than hang around, eat, sleep and drink since the narrow pebble beach is not so inviting.

Places to Stay & Eat

In summer, if accommodation gets tight in Skopelos Town, you can try ***Hotel Atlantes*** *(☎ 33 223)*, at the T-junction in Glossa. The clean, attractive single/double rooms are 7500/8500 dr. Just before you enter Glossa from Skopelos Town, you will see ***Rooms Kerasia*** *(☎ 33 373)* in a newish building set back from the road to the left. Rates here are around 8000 dr a double. Glossa also has a few other rooms in private houses – inquire at *kafeneia*.

Taverna Agnanti *(☎ 33 076)* serves well prepared, reasonably priced Greek fare. It's on the left side of Agiou Riginou as you walk from the T-junction. Just before you enter Glossa you'll find ***Kali Kardia*** *(☎ 33 716)* taverna, which has excellent views down to the sea.

AROUND SKOPELOS

Monasteries

Skopelos has many monasteries, several of which can be visited on a scenic, although quite strenuous, one day trek from Skopelos Town. Facing inland from the waterfront, turn left and follow the road which skirts the bay and then climbs inland (signposted 'Hotel Aegeon'). Continue beyond the hotel and you will come to a fork. Take the left fork for the 18th century **Moni Evangelismou** (now a convent). From here there are breathtaking views of Skopelos Town, 4km away. The monastery's prize piece is a beautiful and ornately carved and gilded iconostasis in which there is an 11th century icon of the Virgin Mary.

The right fork leads to the uninhabited 16th century **Moni Metamorfosis**, the island's oldest monastery. From here the track continues to the 18th century **Moni Prodromou** (now a nunnery), 8km from Skopelos Town.

Walking Tours

There is a useful English-language walking guide to Skopelos called *Sotos Walking Guide* by Heather Parsons. It lists 21 different walking itineraries around Skopelos Town and Glossa. The hand-drawn sketches and maps are a bit rough, but the suggestions for walking tours of the island are excellent. It costs 2500 dr and is available in waterfront stores selling books.

Heather also runs guided walking tours. Her evening walk to Panormos Beach is very popular as you finish off the four hour hike with a swim and a meal. The all-in cost is 3500 dr. Call ☎ 24 022 for bookings.

Beaches

Skopelos' beaches are almost all on the sheltered south-west and west coasts. All the buses stop at the beginning of paths which lead down to them. The first beach along is the crowded sand and pebble **Staphylos Beach** (site of Staphylos' tomb), 4km south-east from Skopelos Town. There is a welcoming taverna, ***Pefkos***, here with romantic views when there is a full moon.

From the eastern end of the beach a path leads over a small headland to the quieter **Velanio Beach**, the island's official nudist beach. **Agnontas**, 3km west of Staphylos, has a small pebble beach and from here caïques sail to the superior and sandy **Limnonari Beach**. There are three waterside tavernas at Agnontas; ***Pavlos*** is reputedly the best one and ***Fotini*** is next best. From Agnontas the road cuts inland through pine forests before re-emerging at sheltered **Panormos Beach**. The next beach along, **Milia**, is considered the island's best – a long swathe of tiny pebbles.

All of these beaches have tavernas or portable snack bars, and there are hotels and domatia at Staphylos, Limnonari, Panormos and Milia. However, the comfortable ***domatia*** at Limnonari *(☎ 23 046)* are a little more secluded and the beach is smaller and less likely to be crowded. Rooms here cost 14,000 dr for a double.

Alonnisos Αλόννησος

☎ 0424 • postcode 370 05 • pop 3000

Alonnisos is still a serene island despite having been ferreted out by 'high-quality' package-tour companies. Package tourism would no doubt have taken off in a bigger way had the airport (erroneously and optimistically shown on island maps) materialised. This project was begun in the mid-1980s, but the rocks of Alonnisos proved unyielding and the politics Byzantine, making the construction of a runway impossible.

Alonnisos once had a flourishing wine industry, but in 1950 the vines were struck with the disease phylloxera and, robbed of their livelihood, many islanders moved away. Fate struck another cruel blow in 1965 when a violent earthquake destroyed the hilltop capital of Alonnisos Town (now called Old Alonnisos, Hora or Palio Horio). The inhabitants abandoned their hilltop homes and were subsequently re-housed in

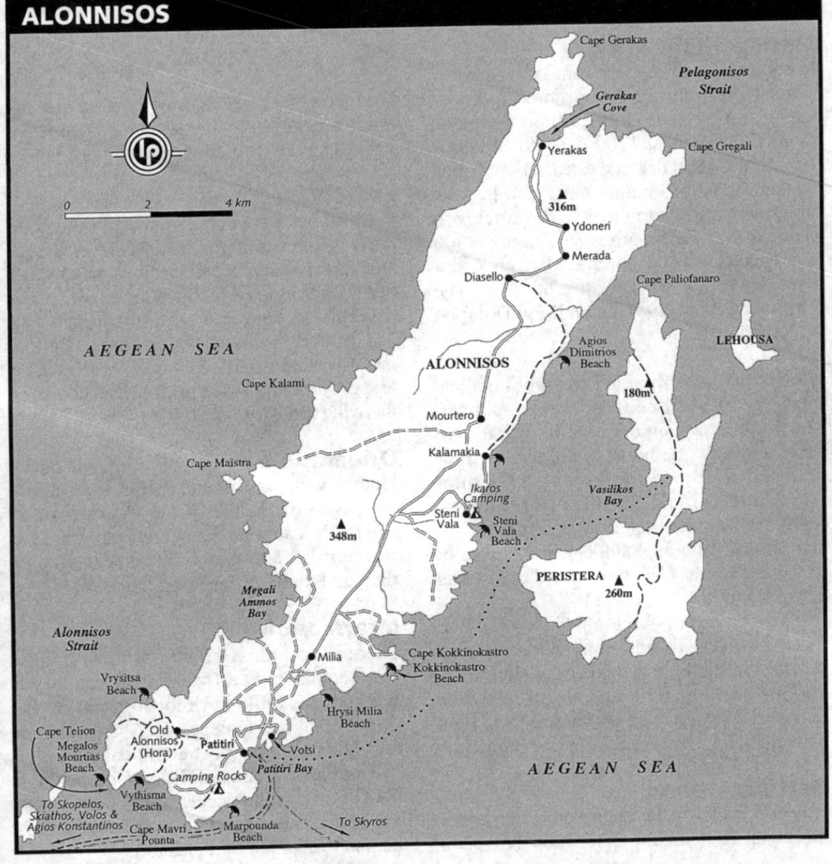

EVIA & THE SPORADES

hastily assembled concrete dwellings at Patitiri. In recent years many of the derelict houses in the capital have been bought for a song from the government and renovated by British and German settlers. There is now a flourishing expat artist community, several of whom reside here year-round.

Alonnisos is a green island with pine and oak trees, mastic and arbutus bushes, and fruit trees. The west coast is mostly precipitous cliffs but the east coast is speckled with pebbled beaches. The water around Alonnisos has been declared a marine park, and is the cleanest in the Aegean. Every house has a cesspit, so no sewage enters the sea.

Getting There & Away

Ferry There are ferries from Alonnisos to Volos (five hours, 3700 dr, two or three daily), four to five daily to both Skopelos Town (30 minutes, 1100 dr) and Skiathos (two hours, 1800 dr), and one daily to Agios Konstantinos (5½ hours, 4400 dr). In addition, there are one to three ferries weekly to Thessaloniki via Skiathos (6½ hours, 4500 dr). Tickets can be purchased from Alonnisos Travel (☎ 65 198, fax 65 511). The port police (☎ 65 595) are on Ikion Dolopon in Patitiri.

Hydrofoil As with Skiathos and Skopelos, there are a lot of connections in summer. The more important ones include up to five daily to Volos (2½ hours, 7500 dr), eight or nine daily to both Skopelos Town (20 minutes, 2200 dr) and Skiathos (40 minutes, 3600 dr), two or three daily to Agios Konstantinos (2½ hours, 8800 dr), and one daily to both Skyros (1¼ hours, 8000 dr) and Thessaloniki (4½ hours, 11,700 dr).

Cheaper return fares apply on most of these services. In addition, there are also services to the Pelion Peninsula, Halkidiki, various ports in Evia and to Stylida near Lamia. Tickets may be purchased from Ikos Travel (☎ 65 320, fax 65 321) in Patitiri.

Getting Around

If you'd prefer to leave the travel arrangements up to someone else, Ikos Travel in Patitiri operates various excursions. See Organised Tours under the Patitiri entry.

Bus In summer, Alonnisos' one bus plies more or less hourly between Patitiri (from opposite the quay) and Old Alonnisos (250 dr one way). There is also an additional service to Steni Vala from Old Alonnisos via Patitiri (300 dr one way).

Motorcycle There are several motorcycle hire outlets on Pelasgon, in Patitiri. I'M Bike Rentals (☎ 65 010) on Pelasgon is worth checking out. Be wary when taking the tracks off the main trans-island road down to the beaches since some of these tracks are steep and slippery.

Taxi Boat The easiest way to get to the east coast beaches is by the taxi boats that leave from the quay in Patitiri every morning.

PATITIRI Πατητήρι

Patitiri sits between two high sandstone cliffs at the southern end of the east coast. Not surprisingly, considering its origins, it's not a traditionally picturesque place, but it nevertheless makes a convenient base and has a very relaxed atmosphere. Patitiri means 'wine press' and is where, in fact, grapes were processed prior to the demise of the wine industry.

Orientation

Finding your way around Patitiri is easy. The quay is in the centre of the waterfront and two roads lead inland. Facing away from the sea, turn left and then right for Pelasgon or right and then left for Ikion Dolopon.

Information

There is no tourist office or tourist police. The regular police (☎ 65 205) are at the southern end of Ikion Dolopon, as is the National Bank of Greece. The bank has an ATM that accepts most credit cards.

The post office is on Ikion Dolopon and the OTE is on the waterfront to the right of the quay. There is a laundrette called Gardenia (☎ 65 831) on Pelasgon.

EVIA & THE SPORADES

Walk to Old Alonnisos

From Patitiri to Old Alonnisos a delightful path winds through shrubbery and orchards. Walk up Pelasgon and, 80m beyond Pension Galini, a now unmarked turn-off indicates the start of the path to Old Alonnisos. Take this path and after 10 minutes turn right at a water tap, which may not be functioning. After about 15 minutes the path is intersected by a dirt road. Continue straight ahead on the path and after about 25 minutes you will come to the main road. Walk straight along this road and you will see Old Alonnisos ahead.

If you are coming from Old Alonnisos the start of the track is fairly obvious though not yet marked with a sign. Walk down the main road to Patitiri for about 350m and look for a short, concrete OTE obelisk on the left. The stone-paved trail starts here on the opposite side of the road.

Organised Tours

Ikos Travel (☎ 65 320, fax 65 321), opposite the quay, offers several excursions. These include to Kyra Panagia, Psathoura and Peristera islets (10,000 dr, including a picnic on a beach, snacks and drinks), and a round-the-island excursion (6500 dr).

It also organises four guided walking tours along the back tracks of Alonnisos and then usually down to a beach for a picnic lunch and a swim. Stout walking shoes, trousers and a long-sleeved shirt are recommended. Ikos Travel, or your guides Chris and Julia, will provide you with a locally produced, but very detailed, walking map.

Places to Stay

Accommodation standards are good on Alonnisos (and cheaper than on Skiathos and Skopelos) and, except for the first two weeks of August, you shouldn't have any difficulty finding a room. The Rooms to Let service (☎ 65 577), opposite the quay, will help you find a room on any part of the island.

Places to Stay – Budget

The nearest camp site to the port is the semi-official ***Camping Rocks*** *(☎ 65 410)*. Don't be put off by the name; it doesn't refer to the site's surface but to the nearest rocky beach (a nudist beach). Camping is under cool and shady pine trees but can suffer from noise from the site's disco. The site is a 700m uphill slog from the quay (turn left at Enigma Disco on Pelasgon.

Eleni Athanasiou rents lovely ***domatia*** *(☎ 65 240, fax 65 598)* in a sparkling white, blue-shuttered building high above the harbour. Rates are 10,000 dr for a self-catering unit for two or three people with cooker and fridge, and 20,000 dr for five-person apartments. Take the first left off Ikion Dolopon and follow the path upwards until you see the rooms on your right.

The ***domatia*** of Eleni Alexiou *(☎ 65 149)* are a pleasant place to stay. If you call ahead, you will be met at the quay. Rates are 8000/9400 dr for doubles/triples. The rooms, equipped with kitchens, are a little higher up from Eleni Athanasiou and even have car parking. Along Pelasgon, on the left at No 27, are the prettily furnished ***Ilias Rent Rooms*** *(☎ 65 451)*. They cost 8000/9600 dr for rooms with bathroom.

Pension Galini *(☎ 65 573, fax 65 094)* is beautifully furnished and has a fine flower-festooned terrace. Rooms cost 8500/10,500 dr with bathroom, and well equipped apartments for five/six people are 15,000/17,500 dr. The pension can be found on the left, 400m up Pelasgon.

Places to Stay – Mid-Range

On the waterfront, the C class ***Alkyon Guest House*** *(☎ 65 220, fax 65 195)* has comfortable singles/doubles for 10,300/13,500 dr with bathroom. The entrance is from Ikion Dolopon.

The attractive rooms in the C class ***Liadromia Hotel*** *(☎ 65 521, fax 65 096)* have stucco walls, stone floors, balcony and traditional carved-wood furniture. Walk inland up Ikion Dolopon and take the first turn right up the steps, follow the path around and the hotel is on the left. Rooms are 12,000/15,000 dr.

Alonnisos' classiest hotel is the C class ***Galaxy Hotel*** *(☎ 65 251, fax 65 110)*, where luxurious rooms with balcony cost 12,500/16,500 dr. The hotel is built on a hill to the left of the bay as you face inland. Turn left at the port and beyond the waterfront tavernas take the steps up to the right; turn left at the top to reach the hotel.

Places to Eat

If you feel you can't stomach another moussaka, pastitsio or souvlaki, then Alonnisos will come as a revelation, for the island has some top-notch eateries. Most specialise in imaginatively prepared fish dishes. At ***To Kamaki Ouzeri***, on Ikion Dolopon, try mussels in cream sauce or other delicious *saganaki* ('cooked in a small frying pan') dishes. This place also opens out of season.

Farther up Ikion Dolopon on the opposite side is newcomer ***Kala Krassa***. It is yet another establishment specialising in tasty mezedes and manages to squeeze one or two tables onto its little streetside terrace.

Another superlative little ouzeri is ***Ouzeri Lefteris***, on Pelasgon, which offers stuffed cuttlefish as well as lobster with tomatoes and peppers. ***Argo Restaurant*** *(☎ 65 141)* has wonderful sea views from its terrace and the food is good, with main meals for about 2500 dr. The restaurant is on the headland on the north side of the harbour.

The waterfront restaurants are all much of a muchness: take your pick and hope for the best.

Entertainment

At the time of research, ***Symvolo Bar*** on Ikion Dolopon was the 'in' bar, though ***Ble Notes*** at the south end of the beach restaurant strip was offering live Greek music. ***Enigma Disco*** on Pelasgon rocks to teenybopper tunes when the tourist season kicks in.

OLD ALONNISOS

Nowadays, Old Alonnisos (Hora or Palio Horio) has a strange appearance. The narrow streets of the upper village have a haunted, deserted feel, but the lower village is coming alive with renovated houses and newer villas. These dwellings are owned mainly by Brits and Germans hankering after the simple life or artists seeking inspiration.

Old Alonnisos is a tranquil, picturesque place with lovely views. From the main road just outside Old Alonnisos a path leads down to Megalos Mourtias Beach and other paths lead south to Vythisma and Marpounda beaches.

Places to Stay

There are no hotels in Old Alonnisos, but there is a steadily growing number of domatia. One agreeable place is the ***Rooms & Studios*** of John Tsoukanas *(☎ 65 135)*, with rates of 6000/9000 dr for singles/doubles with bathroom. The triple rooms have a kitchen. It is on the central square of Plateia Hristou, which is named after its 17th century church. Nearby is the newer ***Fadasia House*** *(☎ 65 186)* with lovely rooms for 9000 dr and a studio with fridge and cooker for 13,000 dr. There is also a little snack bar and garden.

Places to Eat

Old Alonnisos has a couple of tavernas close to the bus stop. Both are good, but the one with the best view is ***Taverna Aloni***. Take the right fork at the bus stop to get to it. ***Bouboulina***, 50m towards the village, is also a decent eatery and farther up in the village itself, there are at least six tavernas open in season. ***Nappo*** does top-rate pizzas, ***Astrofengia*** *(☎ 65 182)*, to the left as you enter the village, gets high praise for its imaginative menus, and ***Paraport Taverna*** *(☎ 65 608)* up in the main village street has great views towards the south side of the island. Prices at all of them are much the same. A romantic meal for two will cost around 5000 dr including drinks.

AROUND ALONNISOS

Most of Alonnisos' beaches are on the east coast which also means they avoid the strong summer meltemi winds and the flotsam that gets dumped on the west coast beaches. Apart from the road from Patitiri to Old Alonnisos, the only road is one which goes north to the tip of the island. It is driveable and sealed all the way though the last settlement, Yerakas (19 km), is a bit of a let-down when you get there. Dirt tracks lead off to the beaches. Another sealed road leads to the yacht port of Steni Vala and a little farther as far as Kalamakia.

The first beach is the gently shelving **Hrysi Milia Beach**, which is the best beach for children. The next beach up is **Kokkinokastro**, the site of the ancient city of Ikos (once the capital); there are remains of city walls and a necropolis under the sea.

Steni Vala is a small fishing village with a permanent population of 30 and a good beach. There are three tavernas and 30-odd rooms in ***domatia***, as well as ***Ikaros Camping*** *(☎ 65 258)*. This is a small camp site, but it is right on the beach and has reasonable shade from olive trees. Try ***Taverna Steni Vala*** *(☎ 65 590)* for both food and lodgings. Mind you don't trip over the posing yachties; they're thick on the ground.

Kalamakia, 3km farther north, has a good beach, rooms and tavernas. **Agios Dimitrios Beach**, farther up still, is an unofficial nudist beach.

ISLETS AROUND ALONNISOS

Alonnisos is surrounded by eight uninhabited islets, all of which have rich flora and fauna. The largest remaining population of the monk seal *(Monachus monachus)*, a Mediterranean sea mammal faced with extinction, lives in the waters around the Sporades. These factors were the incentive behind the formation of the **marine park** in 1983, which encompasses the sea and islets around Alonnisos. Its research station is on Alonnisos, near Gerakas Cove. See the boxed text 'Alonnisos Marine Park'.

Piperi, to the north-east of Alonnisos, is a refuge for the monk seal and it is forbidden to set foot there without a licence to carry out research.

Alonnisos Marine Park

The National Marine Park of Alonnisos – Northern Sporades is an ambitious but belatedly conceived project begun in May 1992. Its prime aim was the protection of the endangered Mediterranean monk seal (see the boxed text under Kefallonia in the Ionian Islands chapter), but also the preservation of other rare plant and animal species threatened with extinction.

The park is divided into two zones. Zone B, west of Alonnisos, is the less accessible of the two areas and comprises the islets of Kyra Panagia, Gioura, Psathoura, Skantzoura and Piperi. Restrictions on activities apply on all islands and in the case of Piperi, visitors are banned, since the island is home to around 33 species of bird, including 350 to 400 pairs of Eleanora's falcon. Other threatened sea birds found on Piperi include the shag and Audouin's gull. Visitors may approach other islands with private vessels or on day trips organised from Alonnisos.

Zone A comprises Alonnisos Island itself and the island of Peristera off Alonnisos' east coast. Most nautical visitors base themselves here at the yacht port of Steni Vala, though in theory the little harbour of Yerakas in the north of the island could serve as a base, though there are no facilities whatsoever. Restrictions on activities here are less stringent.

For the casual visitor the Alonnisos Marine Park is somewhat inaccessible since tours to the various islands are fairly limited and run during summer only. Bear in mind also that the park exists for the protection of marine animals and not for the entertainment of human visitors, so do not be surprised if you see very few animals at all. In a country not noted in its recent history for long-sightedness in the protection of its fauna, the Alonnisos Marine Park is a welcome and long-overdue innovation.

Also north-east of Alonnisos, **Gioura** has many rare plants and a rare species of wild goat. **Kyra Panagia** has good beaches and two abandoned monasteries. **Psathoura** has the submerged remains of an ancient city and the brightest lighthouse in the Aegean.

Peristera, just off Alonnisos' east coast, has several sandy beaches and the remains of a castle. **Lehousa** sits immediately north-west of here.

Skantzoura, to the south-east of Alonnisos, is the habitat of falcons and the rare Aegean seagull. The eighth islet is tiny **Adelphi**, between Peristera and Skantzoura.

Skyros Σκύρος

☎ 0222 • postcode 340 07 • pop 2800

Skyros is some distance from the rest of the group and differs from them topographically. Almost bisected, its northern half has rolling, cultivated hills and pine forests, but the largely uninhabited south is barren and rocky.

There are only two settlements of any worth on the island: the small port of Linaria, and Skyros Town, the capital, 10km away on the east coast. Skyros is visited by poseurs rather than package tourists – and as many of these are wealthy young Athenians as foreigners. Skyros also has quite a different atmosphere from other islands in this region, reminding you more of the Cyclades than the Sporades, especially the stark, cubist architecture of Skyros Town.

Some visitors come to Skyros to attend courses at the Skyros Centre, a centre for holistic health and fitness. See the Skyros Town section for details. Solo women travellers are increasingly drawn to Skyros because of its reputation as a safe, hassle-free island.

Skyros' factual history was mundane in comparison to its mythological origins until Byzantine times, when rogues and criminals from the mainland were exiled on Skyros. Rather than driving away invading pirates, these opportunist exiles entered into a mutually lucrative collaboration with them.

The exiles became the elite of Skyrian society, furnishing and decorating their houses with elaborately hand-carved furniture, plates and copper ornaments from Europe, the Middle East and East Asia. Some of these items were brought by seafarers and some were simply looted by pirates from merchant ships.

Those people on the island before the mainland exiles arrived soon began to emulate the elite in their choice of decor, so local artisans cashed in by making copies of the furniture and plates, a tradition which continues to this day. Almost every Skyrian

Skyros Carnival

In this pre-Lenten festival, which takes place on the last two Sundays before *Kathara Deftera* (Clean Monday – the first Monday in Lent), young men don goat masks, hairy jackets and dozens of copper goat bells. They then proceed to clank and dance around town, each with a partner (another man), dressed up as a Skyrian bride but also wearing a goat mask. Women and children also wear fancy dress. During these revelries there is singing and dancing, performances of plays, recitations of satirical poems and drinking and feasting. These riotous goings-on are overtly pagan, with elements of Dionysian festivals, goat worship (in ancient times Skyros was renowned for its excellent goat meat and milk), and the cult of Achilles, the principal deity worshipped here. The transvestism evident in the carnival may derive from the fact that Achilles hid on Skyros dressed as a girl to escape the oracle's prophecy that he would die in battle at Troy.

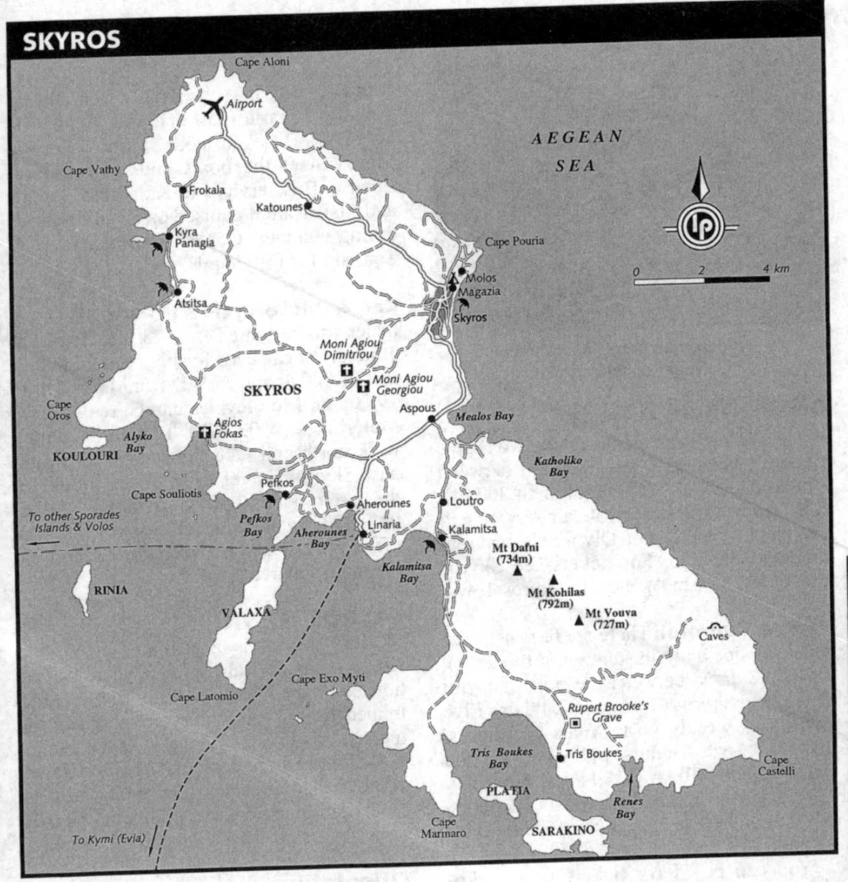

house is festooned with plates, copperware and hand-carved furniture.

Other traditions also endure. Many elderly Skyrian males still dress in the traditional baggy pantaloons and *trohadia* (multi-thonged footwear unique to the island). The Skyros Lenten Carnival is Greece's weirdest and most wonderful festival, and is the subject of Joy Koulentianou's book *The Goat Dance of Skyros*. See the 'Skyros Carnival' boxed text on the previous page.

Another special feature of Skyros which shouldn't go unmentioned, although it will probably go unseen, is the wild Skyrian pony, a breed unique to Skyros. The ponies used to roam freely but are now almost extinct. The only ones you are likely to see are tame ones kept as domestic pets.

Finally, Skyros was the last port of call for the English poet Rupert Brooke (1887-1915), who died of septicaemia at the age of 28 on a ship off the coast of Skyros in 1915, en route to Gallipoli.

GEORGE TSAFOS

The wild Skyrian pony population is in danger of extinction

Getting There & Away

Air In summer there are now only two flights weekly (Wednesday and Sunday) between Athens and Skyros (50 minutes, 14,200 dr). It is rumoured that a private air service will eventually supplement Olympic's severely reduced schedule. For tickets see Skyros Travel & Tourism Agency, in Skyros Town.

Ferry & Hydrofoil There are ferry services at least twice daily in summer, provided by F/B *Lykomidis,* between the port of Kymi (Evia) and Skyros (2¼ hours, 2300 dr). Five hydrofoils weekly go to Volos (4¼ hours, 14,100 dr) via Alonnisos (1¼ hours, 8000 dr), Skopelos Town (2¼ hours, 8000 dr), Glossa (Skopelos) and Skiathos (2¼ hours, 8400 dr). There are also hydrofoils to Thessaloniki (6¼ hours, 13,400 dr, four weekly).

You can buy ferry tickets from Lykomidis Ticket Office (☎ 91 789, fax 91 791), on Agoras in Skyros Town. Hydrofoil tickets can be bought at Skyros Travel & Tourism. There are also ferry and hydrofoil ticket offices at Linaria. The port police telephone number is ☎ 93 475.

Skyros Travel & Tourism also sells tickets for the Kymi-Athens bus (3¼ hours, 2950 dr) which meets the ferry on arrival at Kymi.

Getting Around

In addition to the options listed here, it is also possible to join a boat trip to sites around the island. See Organised Tours under the Skyros Town entry.

Bus There are five buses daily from Skyros Town to Linaria (250 dr), and Molos (via Magazia). Buses for both Skyros Town and Molos meet the boats and hydrofoils at Linaria. Bus services to Kalamitsa, Pefkos and Atsitsa are organised on an ad hoc basis during summer. Contact Skyros Travel & Tourism for full details.

Car & Motorcycle Cars and 4WD vehicles can be rented from Skyros Travel & Tourism. A car goes for between 12,000 dr and 14,000 dr and a 4WD from 17,000 dr to 19,000 dr. Motorcycles can be rented from Motorbikes (☎ 92 022). To find the outlet, walk north and take the second turn right past Skyros Travel & Tourism. Look for the prominent sign. Giannakakis Bikes (☎ 91 233) also rents out motorcycles. The office is on the left between the bus stop and the main square.

SKYROS TOWN

Skyros' capital is a striking, dazzlingly white town of flat-roofed Cycladic-style houses draped over a high rocky bluff, topped by a 13th century fortress and the monastery of Agios Georgios. It is a gem of a place and a wander around its labyrinthine, whitewashed streets will probably produce an invitation to admire a traditional Skyrian house by its proud and hospitable owner.

Orientation

The bus terminal is at the southern end of town on the main thoroughfare of Agoras, an animated street lined with tavernas, snack bars and grocery shops, and flanked by narrow winding alleyways. To reach the central square of Plateia Iroön walk straight ahead up the hill.

Beyond Plateia Iroön, Agoras forks, with the right fork leading up to the fortress and Moni Agiou Georgiou (with fine frescoes), from where there are breathtaking views. The left fork leads to Plateia Rupert Brooke, dominated by a disconcerting bronze statue of a nude Rupert Brooke. The frankness of the statue caused an outcry among the islanders when it was first installed in the 1930s. From this square a cobbled, stepped path leads in 15 minutes to Magazia Beach.

Information

Skyros does not have tourist police, but you can find most information from Skyros Travel & Tourism (☎ 91 600, fax 92 123) including room bookings. The regular police (☎ 91 274) are just beyond Motorbikes (see the previous Getting Around section).

The National Bank of Greece is on Agoras, a little way up from the bus terminal on the left, and sports an ATM. It is scheduled to move farther up into the village, so be alerted. Foreign-language newspapers and magazines can be bought at an agency just opposite the main square.

To get to the post office, take the first turn right after the bus terminal and it's on the left. The OTE is opposite the police station, a little way back towards Linaria, on the right as you walk from the bus terminal.

Museums

Skyros Town has three museums. The **archaeological museum** (☎ 91 327) features an impressive collection of artefacts from Mycenaean to Roman times, as well as a traditional Skyrian house interior, transported in its entirety from the home of the benefactor. It is open 8.30 am to 3 pm Tuesday to Sunday. Admission is 500 dr.

The **Faltaïts Museum** is a private museum housing the outstanding collection of a Skyrian ethnologist, Manos Faltaïts. The collection includes costumes, furniture, books, ceramics and photographs. Daily opening times are 10 am to 1 pm, and 5.30 to 8 pm. Admission is free. Both museums are just off Plateia Rupert Brooke.

The little-known **Traditional Skyrian House** (Skyriano Spiti) is just what its name implies. It's difficult to find, but worth the effort. Take the steps which lead up to the fortress. When you come to a crossroad with house No 992 on your right, turn left and the museum is a little way along on the left. It's open 11 am to noon and 6 to 8 pm Monday to Saturday. Admission is 400 dr.

Courses

The Skyros Centre runs courses on a whole range of subjects, from yoga and dancing, to massage and windsurfing. The emphasis is on developing a holistic approach to life. There is a branch in Skyros Town, but the main 'outdoor' complex is at Atsitsa Beach, on the west coast. For detailed information on their fortnightly programs contact the Skyros Centre (☎ 020-7267 4424, fax 7284 3063, email skyros@easynet.co.uk), 92 Prince of Wales Rd, London NW5 3NE, UK.

In the off season, Australian and long-term Skyros resident Kristin Brooks-Tsalapatani of Kristina's Restaurant (see Places to Eat) runs Kristina's Cooking School. Her Greek cookery course runs over five mornings, teaching a maximum of eight nascent gastronomes all about cooking Greek-style. The course costs A$600 (109,000 dr). Bookings are essential.

Organised Tours

Skyros Travel & Tourism (☎ 91 600, fax 92 123), on the left, north of the central square, runs a boat excursion (5500 dr) to Sarakino Islet and the Pendekali and Gerania sea caves. Ask for manager Lefteris Trakos.

Places to Stay – Budget

Accommodation in Skyros Town itself is usually in the form of traditional rooms often decorated with traditional plates. Since these can be hard to find yourself, you will often be met at the bus stop with offers of domatia from the women who run them. It's not a bad idea to take up one of these offers, at least for starters. Prices should be in the 8000 dr to 12,000 dr range, though as elsewhere there are seasonal fluctuations.

Failing that, head for Skyros Travel & Tourism (see Information) for references to suitable rooms. One of the better options is ***Elpida House*** where a room for two will work out at about 12,000 dr.

Pension Nikolas *(☎ 91 778, fax 93 400)* is a small complex of very comfortable, self-contained domatia at the back of Kristina's Restaurant. This is a better option for visitors wanting a quieter place to stay. Ask for the 'room with a view' if you can get it. Prices range from 13,000 dr to 18,000 dr for three people.

Places to Stay – Mid-Range

The C class ***Hotel Nefeli*** *(☎ 91 964, fax 92 061)* is the only decent hotel as such in Skyros Town. The lovely rooms have old photographs depicting traditional Skyrian life. It sports a large swimming pool. Rates are 17,500/21,500 dr for singles/doubles. The hotel is on the left just before you enter Skyros Town.

The same hotel can offer you an apartment in ***Skyriana Spitia***, an adjoining complex made up of self-contained units in traditional Skyrian style. An apartment for three people costs 36,850 dr but prices may be 50% lower out of season.

Places to Eat

Restaurants in Skyros have proliferated like mushrooms in a dark cellar in recent times and things are definitely looking up on the culinary front. For the best and cheapest coffee in town as well as breakfast, pizzas and sandwiches, seek out ***Trypa*** on the main street. It's only a small place – blink and you've missed it.

Skyriani Gonia is easy to spot (though the sign is only in Greek) just south of the main square. It opens at 9 am for breakfast and does lunch and dinner. Prices are generally lower than elsewhere. Along the main street is the very popular and tastefully decorated ***O Pappous kai Ego*** which serves traditional mezedes as well as dishes to order. It opens at 10 am and closes late. Prices are mid-range – around the 2200 dr mark for a good feed with local wine.

Margeris is the place to go for fresh fish. Other restaurants sell fish but Margeris specialises in it. It's only a small place, but easy enough to spot on the main street. Fish prices are somewhat higher, though still reasonable.

One of the more long-standing establishments is ***Kristina's Restaurant*** *(☎ 91 778)*, set in a delightful walled garden. Kristina conjures up delectable local and international dishes. The *kaseri* and *sac* cheeses (local specialities), chicken fricassee and cheesecake are recommended. Prices are very reasonable. The restaurant is closed on Sunday. Look for the sign on the south side of town.

Entertainment

The popularity enjoyed by particular bars in Skyros is ephemeral, but flavours of the month at the time of research were the stylish ***Kata Lathos***, ***Apokalypsis***, ***Ares*** and ***Iröon***, all on or just off Agoras. ***Borio***, just south of Skyros Town, was an 'in' disco. There is always some place open all year due to the large transient population of young soldiers.

At Linaria ***To Kastro*** is another 'in' disco club, as is ***O Kavos*** for drinks and evening gossip. Try to be at the Kavos when the Lykomidis ferry comes in and witness the impressive sound reception when Richard Strauss' *Also Sprach Zarathustra*, as used in the movie *2001: A Space Odyssey*, is blasted out over the bay from huge speakers. Better still, listen out for it while on the ferry – the sound is better. Sparklers are also handed out to Kavos customers in summer.

MAGAZIA & MOLOS

Μαγαζιά & Μώλος

The resort of Magazia is at the southern end of a splendid, long sandy beach, a short distance north of Skyros Town; quieter Molos is at the northern end of the beach, although there is not much to physically distinguish the two communities these days.

Places to Stay – Budget & Mid-Range

Skyros has one camp site, ***Skyros Camping*** *(☎ 92 458)*, at Magazia. It's a scruffy, rundown place with a few thirsty-looking olive trees offering shade.

Efrosyni Varsamou Rooms *(☎ 91 142)*, above the family ceramics shop in Magazia, are spacious and beautifully furnished. Rates are 12,000/14,800 dr for doubles/triples. If you're walking, go down the cobbled path from Skyros Town, turn right at the bottom, and then right at the camp site (signposted to Magazia and Xenia Hotel) and the rooms are on the left. If you take the bus, get off at the camp site.

If you turn left at Xenia Hotel, in just under 150m you will come to ***Alekos Domatia*** *(☎ 91 828)*, on the right overlooking the beach. Pleasant and comfortable rooms are 12,000/14,000 dr with bathroom.

To Perigiali *(☎ 91 889, fax 92 770)* is a newcomer to the scene. It offers very pleasant rooms surrounding a beautiful garden. It is set back and signposted from Magazia Beach. Rates are 15,500/18,000 dr for singles/doubles.

At Molos, ***Motel Hara*** *(☎ 91 601)* has clean, pine-furnished doubles/triples for 11,000/13,200 dr, and some newer self-contained apartments. If you arrive by bus look for it on the right. ***Angela's Bungalows*** *(☎ 91 764, fax 92 030)*, set in a lovely garden, has clean, spacious rooms with bathroom, balcony and telephone for 17,000/ 18,000 dr, including breakfast. The bungalows are signposted from the Molos bus terminal. The C class ***Hotel Paradise*** *(☎ 91 220, fax 91 441)*, next to the bus terminal, is an attractive hotel with cream marble floors and white walls. Rates here are 18,000 dr for doubles.

Places to Stay – Top End

The island's most luxurious hotel is the A class ***Skyros Palace*** *(☎ 91 994, fax 92 070)*, a complex of attractive apartments, which stand in splendid isolation just north of Molos. The apartments have air-con, verandas and music channels. The complex has a cafe, bar, restaurant, TV lounge and swimming pool, and is 50m from a good beach. Mosquitoes can be a problem here: ask for a mosquito zapper. Singles/doubles go for 19,000/22,900 dr in high season.

Places to Eat

Due the more compact nature of the layout of the village, Magazia is probably the better of the two settlements to dine in, with ***Stefanos*** restaurant first in the stakes for location overlooking the beach. ***Korfari*** farther along gets good press for its mezedes, while ***Tou Thoma to Magazi*** on the beach at Molos specialises in lobster. Prices at all three are mid-range, though lobster is quite expensive.

Shopping

A good selection of ceramics is on sale at Efrosyni Varsamou's shop below the domatia of the same name at Magazia. It's hard to imagine any non-Skyrian wanting to wear the multi-thonged trohadia, except maybe a foot fetishist who is into bondage. They can be bought at the Skyros Shop, on the street which leads to Plateia Rupert Brooke.

The Traditional Greek Products Shop (☎ 93 191), on the left at the north end of the main street, stocks all kinds of natural products from royal jelly to retsina, from olive oil to cheese. Woodcarvings are a classy buy, though they can be expensive. There are at least three workshops scattered round town and they're easy to spot.

AROUND SKYROS

Beaches

At **Atsitsa**, on the west coast, there's a tranquil pebble beach shaded by pines. The beach attracts freelance campers, and there's the main outdoor centre of the Skyros Centre and a ***taverna*** with domatia here. Just to the north is the even less crowded beach of **Kyra Panagia** (also with freelance campers). At **Pefkos**, 10km south-east of Atsitsa, there is another good but small beach and a taverna. If you don't have transport take a Skyros Town-Linaria bus and ask to be let off at the turn-off. It's a 3km walk from there to the beach. Farther east, the pebble and sand beach at **Kalamitsa** is reasonable but not really worth the extra effort to get there and there is not much shade.

Rupert Brooke's Grave

Rupert Brooke's well tended grave is in a quiet olive grove just inland from Tris Boukes Bay in the south of the island. The actual grave is poorly marked with a rough wooden sign in Greek on the roadside, but you can hardly miss it. The gravestone is inscribed with some verses of Brooke's among which is the following apt epitaph:

If I should die think only this of me:
That there's some corner of a foreign field
That is forever England.

No buses go to this corner of the island. However, you can take an excursion boat to Sarakino Islet, or drive or walk along a good, graded scenic road from Kalamitsa, built for the Greek navy, which now has a naval station on Tris Boukes Bay.

If you walk it will take about 1½ hours; take food and water. If you have come this far with the aim of getting to the sea, you will have to turn back since the area farther down the hill is restricted by the Greek navy and the road onwards is closed.

Language

The Greek language is probably the oldest European language, with an oral tradition of 4000 years and a written tradition of approximately 3000 years. Its evolution over the four millennia was characterised by its strength during the golden age of Athens and the Democracy (mid-5th century BC); its use as a lingua franca throughout the Middle Eastern world, spread by Alexander the Great and his successors as far as India during the Hellenistic period (330 BC to 100 AD); its adaptation as the language of the new religion, Christianity; its use as the official language of the Eastern Roman Empire; and its eventual proclamation as the language of the Byzantine Empire (380-1453).

Greek maintained its status and prestige during the rise of the European Renaissance and was employed as the linguistic perspective for all contemporary sciences and terminologies during the period of Enlightenment. Today, Greek constitutes a large part of the vocabulary of any Indo-European language, and much of the lexicon of any scientific repertoire.

The modern Greek language is a southern Greek dialect which is now used by most Greek speakers both in Greece and abroad. It is the result of an intralinguistic influence and synthesis of the ancient vocabulary combined with words from Greek regional dialects, namely Cretan, Cypriot and Macedonian.

Greek is spoken throughout Greece by a population of around 10 million, and by some five million Greeks who live abroad.

Pronunciation

All Greek words of two or more syllables have an acute accent which indicates where the stress falls. For instance, άγαλμα (statue) is pronounced ***a**ghalma*, and αγάπη (love) is pronounced *a**gha**pi*. In the following transliterations, bold lettering indicates where stress falls. Note also that **dh** is pronounced as 'th' in 'then'; **gh** is a softer, slightly guttural version of 'g'.

Greetings & Civilities

Hello.
***ya**sas* — Γειά σας.
***ya**su* (informal) — Γειά σου.

Goodbye.
*an**dio*** — Αντίο.

Good morning.
*kali**me**ra* — Καλημέρα.

Good afternoon.
***he**rete* — Χαίρετε.

Good evening.
*kalis**pe**ra* — Καλησπέρα.

Good night.
*kali**ni**hta* — Καληνύχτα.

Please.
*paraka**lo*** — Παρακαλώ.

Thank you.
*efharis**to*** — Ευχαριστώ.

Yes.
ne — Ναι.

No.
***o**hi* — Οχι.

Sorry. (excuse me, forgive me)
*sigh**no**mi* — Συγγνώμη.

How are you?
*ti **ka**nete?* — Τι κάνετε;
*ti **ka**nis?* (informal) — Τι κάνεις;

I'm well, thanks.
*ka**la** efharis**to*** — Καλά ευχαριστώ.

Essentials

Do you speak English?
*mi**la**te angli**ka**?* — Μιλάτε Αγγλικά;

I understand.
*katala**ve**no* — Καταλαβαίνω.

I don't understand.
*dhen katala**ve**no* — Δεν καταλαβαίνω.

Where is ...?
*pou **i**ne ...?* — Πού είναι ...;

How much?
***po**so **ka**ni?* — Πόσο κάνει;

When?
***po**te?* — Πότε;

The Greek Alphabet & Pronunciation

Greek	Pronunciation Guide		Example		
Α α	a	as in 'father'	αγάπη	a**gha**pi	love
Β β	v	as in 'vine'	βήμα	**vi**ma	step
Γ γ	gh	like a rough 'g'	γάτα	**gha**ta	cat
	y	as in 'yes'	για	ya	for
Δ δ	dh	as in 'there'	δέμα	**dhe**ma	parcel
Ε ε	e	as in 'egg'	ένας	**e**nas	one (m)
Ζ ζ	z	as in 'zoo'	ζώο	**zo**o	animal
Η η	i	as in 'feet'	ήταν	**i**tan	was
Θ θ	th	as in 'throw'	θέμα	**the**ma	theme
Ι ι	i	as in 'feet'	ίδιος	**i**dhyos	same
Κ κ	k	as in 'kite'	καλά	ka**la**	well
Λ λ	l	as in 'leg'	λάθος	**la**thos	mistake
Μ μ	m	as in 'man'	μαμά	ma**ma**	mother
Ν ν	n	as in 'net'	νερό	ne**ro**	water
Ξ ξ	x	as in 'ox'	ξύδι	**ksi**dhi	vinegar
Ο ο	o	as in 'hot'	όλα	**o**la	all
Π π	p	as in 'pup'	πάω	**pa**o	I go
Ρ ρ	r	as in 'road'	ρέμα	**re**ma	stream
		a slightly trilled *r*	ρόδα	**ro**dha	tyre
Σ σ, ς	s	as in 'sand'	σημάδι	si**ma**dhi	mark
Τ τ	t	as in 'tap'	τόπι	**to**pi	ball
Υ υ	i	as in 'feet'	ύστερα	**is**tera	after
Φ φ	f	as in 'find'	φύλλο	**fi**lo	leaf
Χ χ	h	as the *ch* in Scottish *loch*, or	χάνω	**ha**no	I lose
		like a rough *h*	χέρι	**he**ri	hand
Ψ ψ	ps	as in 'lapse'	ψωμί	pso**mi**	bread
Ω ω	o	as in 'hot'	ώρα	**o**ra	time

Combinations of Letters

The combinations of letters shown here are pronounced as follows:

Greek	Pronunciation Guide		Example		
ει	i	as in 'feet'	είδα	**i**dha	I saw
οι	i	as in 'feet'	οικόπεδο	i**ko**pedho	land
αι	e	as in 'bet'	αίμα	**e**ma	blood
ου	u	as in 'mood'	πού	pou	who/what
μπ	b	as in 'beer'	μπάλα	**ba**la	ball
	mb	as in 'amber'	κάμπος	**kam**bos	forest
ντ	d	as in 'dot'	ντουλάπα	dou**la**pa	wardrobe
	nd	as in 'bend'	πέντε	**pen**de	five
γκ	g	as in 'God'	γκάζι	**ga**zi	gas
γγ	ng	as in 'angle'	αγγελία	ange**li**a	classified
γξ	ks	as in 'minks'	σφιγξ	sfinks	sphynx
τζ	dz	as in 'hands'	τζάκι	**dza**ki	fireplace

The pairs of vowels shown above are pronounced separately if the first has an acute accent, or the second a dieresis, as in the examples below:

γαϊδουράκι	gaidhou**ra**ki	little donkey
Κάιρο	**kai**ro	Cairo

Some Greek consonant sounds have no English equivalent. The υ of the groups αυ, ευ and ηυ is generally pronounced 'v'. The Greek question mark is represented with the English equivalent of a semicolon ';'.

Small Talk

What's your name?
*pos sas **le**ne?* Πώς σας λένε;
My name is ...
*me **le**ne ...* Με λένε ...
Where are you from?
***a**po pou **is**te?* Από πού είστε;

I'm from ...
***i**me a**po** ...* Είμαι από ...
America
*tin ameri**ki*** την Αμερική
Australia
*tin afstra**li**a* την Αυστραλία
England
*tin ang**li**a* την Αγγλία
Ireland
*tin irlan**dhi**a* την Ιρλανδία
New Zealand
*ti **ne**a zilan**dhi**a* τη Νέα Ζηλανδία
Scotland
*ti sko**ti**a* τη Σκωτία

How old are you?
***po**son hro**non** **is**te?* Πόσων χρονών είστε;
I'm ... years old.
i**me ... hro**non Είμαι ... χρονών.

Getting Around

What time does the ... leave/arrive?
*ti **o**ra **fe**vyi/ **fta**ni to ...?* Τι ώρα φεύγει/ φτάνει το ...;

plane	*aero**pla**no*	αεροπλάνο
boat	*ka**ra**vi*	καράβι
bus (city)	*asti**ko***	αστικό
bus (intercity)	*leofo**ri**o*	λεωφορείο
train	***tre**no*	τραίνο

I'd like ...
*tha i**the**la ...* Θα ήθελα ...
a return ticket
*isi**ti**rio me episro**fi*** εισιτήριο με επιστροφή
two tickets
***dhi**o isi**ti**ria* δυο εισιτήρια
a student's fare
*fititi**ko** isi**ti**rio* φοιτητικό εισιτήριο

Signs

ΕΙΣΟΔΟΣ	ENTRY
ΕΞΟΔΟΣ	EXIT
ΩΘΗΣΑΤΕ	PUSH
ΣΥΡΑΤΕ	PULL
ΓΥΝΑΙΚΩΝ	WOMEN (toilets)
ΑΝΔΡΩΝ	MEN (toilets)
ΝΟΣΟΚΟΜΕΙΟ	HOSPITAL
ΑΣΤΥΝΟΜΙΑ	POLICE
ΑΠΑΓΟΡΕΥΕΤΑΙ	PROHIBITED
ΕΙΣΙΤΗΡΙΑ	TICKETS

first class
***pro**ti **the**si* πρώτη θέση
economy
*touristi**ki** **the**si* τουριστική θέση

train station
*sidhirodhro**mi**kos stath**mos*** σιδηροδρομικός σταθμός
timetable
*dhromo**lo**gio* δρομολόγιο
taxi
*ta**xi*** ταξί

Where can I hire a car?
*pou bo**ro** na ni**kya**so **e**na afto**ki**nito?*
Πού μπορώ να νοικιάσω ένα αυτοκίνητο;

Directions

How do I get to ...?
*pos tha **pa**o sto/ sti ...?* Πώς θα πάω στο/ στη ...;
Where is ...?
*pou **i**ne ...?* Πού είναι...;
Is it near?
***i**ne kon**da**?* Είναι κοντά;
Is it far?
***i**ne makri**a**?* Είναι μακριά;

straight ahead	*ef**thi**a*	ευθεία
left	*aris**te**ra*	αριστερά
right	*dex**i**a*	δεξιά
behind	***pi**so*	πίσω
far	*makri**a***	μακριά
near	*kon**da***	κοντά
opposite	***a**pe**nan**di*	απέναντι

Can you show me on the map?
borite na mou to dhixete sto harti?
Μπορείτε να μου το δείξετε στο χάρτη;

Around Town

I'm looking for (the) ...
psahno ya ...
Ψάχνω για ...

bank	*trapeza*	τράπεζα
beach	*paralia*	παραλία
castle	*kastro*	κάστρο
church	*ekklisia*	εκκλησία
... embassy	*tin ... presvia*	την ... πρεσβεία
market	*aghora*	αγορά
museum	*musio*	μουσείο
police	*astynomia*	αστυνομία
post office	*tahydhromio*	ταχυδρομείο
ruins	*arhea*	αρχαία

I want to exchange some money.
thelo na exaryiroso lefta
Θέλω να εξαργυρώσω λεφτά.

Accommodation

Where is ...?
pou ine ...? Πού είναι ...;
I'd like ...
thelo ena ... Θέλω ένα ...

a cheap hotel
ftino xenodohio φτηνό ξενοδοχείο
a clean room
katharo dhomatio καθαρό δωμάτιο
a good hotel
kalo xenodohio καλό ξενοδοχείο
a camp site
kamping κάμπιγκ

single	*mono*	μονό
double	*dhiplo*	διπλό
room	*dhomatio*	δωμάτιο
with bathroom	*me banio*	με μπάνιο
key	*klidhi*	κλειδί

How much is it ...?
poso kani ...? Πόσο κάνει ...;
per night
ti vradhya τη βραδυά

Emergencies

Help!
voithya! Βοήθεια!
Police!
astynomia! Αστυνομία!
There's been an accident.
eyine atihima Εγινε ατύχημα.
Call a doctor!
fonaxte ena yatro! Φωνάξτε ένα ιατρό!
Call an ambulance!
tilefoniste ya asthenoforo! Τηλεφωνήστε για ασθενοφόρο!
I'm ill.
ime arostos (m) Είμαι άρρωστος
ime arosti (f) Είμαι άρρωστη
I'm lost.
eho hathi Εχω χαθεί
Thief!
klefti! Κλέφτη!
Go away!
fiye! Φύγε!
I've been raped.
me viase kapyos Με βίασε κάποιος.
I've been robbed.
meklepse kapyos Μ'έκλεψε κάποιος.
Where are the toilets?
pou ine i toualetez? Πού είναι οι τουαλέτες;

for ... nights
ya ... vradhyez για ... βραδυές
Is breakfast included?
symberilamvani ke pro-ino? Συμπεριλαμβάνει και πρωϊνό;
May I see it?
boro na to dho? Μπορώ να το δω;
Where is the bathroom?
pou ine tobanio? Πού είναι το μπάνιο;
It's expensive.
ine akrivo Είναι ακριβό.
I'm leaving today.
fevgho simera Φεύγω σήμερα.

Food

breakfast	*pro-i**no***	πρωϊνό
lunch	*mesimvri**no***	μεσημβρινό
dinner	*vradhy**no***	βραδυνό
beef	*vodhi**no***	βοδινό
bread	*pso**mi***	ψωμί
beer	***by**ra*	μπύρα
cheese	*ty**ri***	τυρί
chicken	*ko**to**poulo*	κοτόπουλο
Greek coffee	*ellini**kos** ka**fes***	ελληνικός καφές
iced coffee	*fra**ppe***	φραππέ
lamb	*ar**ni***	αρνί
milk	***gha**la*	γάλα
mineral water	*metalli**ko** ne**ro***	μεταλλικό νερό
tea	***tsai***	τσάι
wine	*kra**si***	κρασί

I'm a vegetarian.
*ime horto**fa**ghos* Είμαι χορτοφάγος.

Shopping

How much is it?
*poso **ka**ni?*
Πόσο κάνει;
I'm just looking.
*ap**los** ki**ta**zo*
Απλώς κοιτάζω.
I'd like to buy ...
***the**lo n'agho**ra**so ...*
Θέλω ν΄αγοράσω ...
Do you accept credit cards?
***per**nete pistoti**ke**z **kar**tez?*
Παίρνετε πιστωτικές κάρτες;
Could you lower the price?
*bo**ri**te na mou **ka**nete mya kaliteri ti**mi**?*
Μπορείτε να μου κάνετε μια καλύτερη τιμή;

Time & Dates

What time is it?
*ti **o**ra **i**ne?* Τι ώρα είναι;

It's ...	***i**ne ...*	είναι ...
1 o'clock	***mi**a i **o**ra*	μία η ώρα
2 o'clock	***dhi**o i **o**ra*	δύο η ώρα
7.30	*ef**ta** ke mi**si***	εφτά και μισή
am	*to pro-**i***	το πρωί
pm	*to a**po**yevma*	το απόγευμα
today	***si**mera*	σήμερα
tonight	*a**po**pse*	απόψε
now	***to**ra*	τώρα
yesterday	*hthes*	χθες
tomorrow	***av**rio*	αύριο
Sunday	*kyria**ki***	Κυριακή
Monday	*dhef**te**ra*	Δευτέρα
Tuesday	***tri**ti*	Τρίτη
Wednesday	*te**tar**ti*	Τετάρτη
Thursday	***pem**pti*	Πέμπτη
Friday	*paraske**vi***	Παρασκευή
Saturday	***sa**vato*	Σάββατο
January	*ianou**a**rios*	Ιανουάριος
February	*fevrou**a**rios*	Φεβρουάριος
March	***mar**tios*	Μάρτιος
April	*a**pri**lios*	Απρίλιος
May	***ma**ïos*	Μάιος
June	*i**ou**nios*	Ιούνιος
July	*i**ou**lios*	Ιούλιος
August	***av**ghoustos*	Αύγουστος
September	*sep**tem**vrios*	Σεπτέμβριος
October	*ok**to**vrios*	Οκτώβριος
November	*no**em**vrios*	Νοέμβριος
December	*dhe**kem**vrios*	Δεκέμβριος

Health

I need a doctor.
*hri**a**zome ya**tro*** Χρειάζομαι ιατρό.
Can you take me to hospital?
*bo**ri**te na me **pa**te sto nosoko**mi**o?* Μπορείτε να με πάτε στο νοσοκομείο;
I want something for ...
***the**lo **ka**ti ya ...* Θέλω κάτι για ...

diarrhoea *dhi**a**ria*	διάρροια
insect bites *tsim**bi**mata a**po** **en**doma*	τσιμπήματα από έντομα
travel sickness *naf**ti**a taxidhi**ou***	ναυτία ταξιδιού
aspirin *aspi**ri**ni*	ασπιρίνη
condoms *profylakti**ka** (ka**po**tez)*	προφυλακτικά (καπότες)
contact lenses *fa**ki** epa**fis***	φακοί επαφής
medical insurance *yatri**ki** as**fa**lya*	ιατρική ασφάλεια

Numbers

0	*mi**dhen***	μηδέν
1	***en**as*	ένας (m)
	***mi**a*	μία (f)
	***en**a*	ένα (n)
2	***dhi**o*	δύο
3	*tris*	τρεις (m & f)
	tria	τρία (n)
4	***te**seris*	τέσσερεις (m & f)
	***te**sera*	τέσσερα (n)
5	***pe**nde*	πέντε
6	***ex**i*	έξη
7	*ep**ta***	επτά
8	*oh**to***	οχτώ
9	*en**e**a*	εννέα
10	***dhe**ka*	δέκα

20	***ik**osi*	είκοσι
30	*tri**an**da*	τριάντα
40	*sa**ran**da*	σαράντα
50	*pe**ni**nda*	πενήντα
60	*e**xi**nda*	εξήντα
70	*evdho**mi**nda*	εβδομήντα
80	*ogh**dho**nda*	ογδόντα
90	*ene**ni**nda*	ενενήντα
100	*eka**to***	εκατό
1000	***hi**lii*	χίλιοι (m)
	***hi**liez*	χίλιες (f)
	***hi**lia*	χίλια (n)

one million
*en**a** ekato**my**rio* ένα εκατομμύριο

Transliteration & Variant Spellings: An Explanation

The issue of correctly transliterating Greek into the Latin alphabet is a vexed one, fraught with inconsistencies and pitfalls. The Greeks themselves are not very consistent when it comes to providing transliterated names on their signs, though things are gradually improving. The word 'Piraeus', for example, has been variously represented by the following transliterations: Pireas, Piraievs and Pireefs; and when appearing as a street name (eg Piraeus Street) you will also find Pireos!

This is compounded by the linguistic minefield of diglossy, or the two forms of the Greek language. The purist form is called Katharevousa and the popular form is Dimotiki (Demotic). The Katharevousa form was never more than an artificiality and Dimotiki has always been spoken as the mainstream language, but this linguistic schizophrenia means there are often two Greek words for each English word. Thus, the word for 'baker' in everyday language is *fournos*, but the shop sign will more often than not say *artopoieion*. The baker's product will be known in the street as *psomi*, but in church as *artos*.

As if all that wasn't enough, there is also the issue of anglicised vs hellenised forms of place names: Athina vs Athens, Patra vs Patras, Thiva vs Thebes, Evia vs Euboia – the list goes on and on! Toponymic diglossy (the existence of both an official and everyday name for a place) is responsible for Kerkyra/Corfu, Zante/Zakynthos, and Santorini/Thira. In this guide we have usually provided modern Greek equivalents for town names, with one or two well known exceptions, eg Athens and Patras. For ancient sites, settlements or people from antiquity, we have attempted to stick to the more familiar classical names; so we have Thucydides instead of Thoukididis, Mycenae instead of Mykines.

Problems in transliteration have particular implications for vowels, especially given that Greek has six ways of rendering the vowel sound *ee*, two ways of rendering the *o* sound and two ways of rendering the *e* sound. In most instances in this book, *y* has been used for the *ee* sound when a Greek *upsilon* (υ, Y) has been used, and *i* for Greek *ita* (η, H) and *iota* (ι, I). In the case of the Greek vowel combinations that make the *ee* sound, that is οι, ει and υι, an *i* has been used. For the two Greek *e* sounds, αι and ε, an *e* has been employed.

As far as the transliteration of consonants is concerned, the Greek letter *gamma* (γ, Γ) appears as *g* rather than *y* throughout this book. This means that *agios* (Greek for male saint) is used rather than *ayios*, and *agia* (female saint) rather than *ayia*. The letter *delta* (δ, Δ) appears as *d* rather than *dh* throughout this book, so *domatia* (rooms), rather than *dhomatia*, is used. The letter *fi* (φ, Φ) can be transliterated as either *f* or *ph*. Here, a general rule of thumb is that classical names are spelt with a *ph* and modern names with an *f*. So Phaistos is used rather than Festos, and Folegandros is used rather than Pholegandros. The Greek *chi* (ξ, Ξ) has usually been repres-ented as *h* in order to approximate the Greek pronunciation as closely as possible. Thus, we have 'Haralambos' instead of 'Charalambos' and 'Polytehniou' instead of 'Polytechniou'. Bear in mind that the *h* is to be pronounced as an aspirated *h*, much like the *ch* in loch. The letter *kapa* (κ, K) has been used to represent that sound, except where well known names from antiquity have adopted by convention the letter *c*, eg Polycrates, Acropolis.

Wherever reference to a street name is made, we have omitted the Greek word *'odos'*, but words for avenue *(leoforos)* and square *(plateia)* have been included.

For a more detailed guide to the Greek language, check out Lonely Planet's comprehensive *Greek phrasebook*.

Glossary

Achaean civilisation – see *Mycenaean civilisation*
acropolis – highest point of an ancient city
AEK – Athens football club
agia (f), agios (m) – saint
agora – commercial area of an ancient city; shopping precinct in modern Greece
amphora – large two-handled vase in which wine or oil was kept
ANEK – Anonymi Naftiliaki Eteria Kritis; main shipping line to Crete
Archaic period (800-480 BC) – also known as the Middle Age; period in which the city-states emerged from the 'dark age' and traded their way to wealth and power; the city-states were unified by a Greek alphabet and common cultural pursuits, engendering a sense of national identity
architrave – part of the *entablature* which rests on the columns of a temple
arhontika – 17th and 18th century AD mansions which belonged to arhons, the leading citizens of a town
Arvanites – Albanian-speakers of north-western Greece
Asia Minor – the Aegean littoral of Turkey centred around İzmir but also including İstanbul; formerly populated by Greeks
askitiria – mini-chapels; places of solitary worship

baglamas – miniature *bouzouki* with a tinny sound
basilica – early Christian church
bouleuterion – council house
bouzouki – stringed lute-like instrument associated with rembetika music
bouzoukia – 'bouzoukis'; used to mean any nightclub where the bouzouki is played and low-grade blues songs are sung; see *skyladika*
buttress – support built against the outside of a wall
Byzantine Empire – characterised by the merging of Hellenistic culture and Christianity and named after Byzantium, the city on the Bosphorus which became the capital of the Roman Empire in 324 AD; when the Roman Empire was formally divided in 395 AD, Rome went into decline and the eastern capital, renamed Constantinople after Emperor Constantine I, flourished; the Byzantine Empire dissolved after the fall of Constantinople to the Turks in 1453

caïque – small, sturdy fishing boat often used to carry passengers
capital – top of a column
cella – room in a temple where the cult statue stood
choregos – wealthy citizen who financed choral and dramatic performances
city-states – states comprising a sovereign city and its dependencies; the city-states of Athens and Sparta were famous rivals
classical Greece – period in which the city-states reached the height of their wealth and power after the defeat of the Persians in the 5th century BC; ended with the decline of the city-states as a result of the Peloponnesian Wars, and the expansionist aspirations of Philip II, King of Macedon (ruled 359-336 BC), and his son, Alexander the Great (ruled 336-323 BC)
Corinthian – order of Greek architecture recognisable by columns with bell-shaped *capitals* with sculpted elaborate ornaments based on acanthus leaves
cornice – the upper part of the *entablature*, extending beyond the frieze
crypt – lowest part of a church, often a burial chamber
Cycladic civilisation (3000-1100 BC) – civilisation which emerged following the settlement of Phoenician colonists on the Cycladic islands
cyclopes – mythical one-eyed giants

dark age (1200-800 BC) – period in which Greece was under *Dorian* rule
delfini – dolphin; common name for hydrofoil

diglossy – the existence of two forms of one language within a country; has existed in Greece for most of its modern history
dimarhio – town hall
Dimotiki – Demotic Greek language; the official spoken language of Greece
domatio (s), domatia (pl) – room; a cheap accommodation option available in most tourist areas
Dorians – Hellenic warriors who invaded Greece around 1200 BC, demolishing the city-states and destroying the Mycenaean civilisation; heralded Greece's 'dark age', when the artistic and cultural advancements of the Mycenaeans and Minoans were abandoned; the Dorians later developed into land-holding aristocrats which encouraged the resurgence of independent city-states led by wealthy aristocrats
Doric – order of Greek architecture characterised by a column which has no base, a *fluted* shaft and a relatively plain capital, when compared with the flourishes evident on *Ionic* and *Corinthian* capitals

ELPA – Elliniki Leshi Periigiseon & Aftokinitou; Greek motoring and touring club
ELTA – Ellinika Tahydromia; Greek post office
entablature – part of a temple between the tops of the columns and the roof
EOS – Ellinikos Orivatikos Syllogos; Greek alpine club
EOT – Ellinikos Organismos Tourismou; national tourism organisation which has offices in most major towns
Epitaphios – picture on cloth of Christ on his bier
estiatorio – restaurant serving ready-made food as well as a la carte dishes
ET – Elliniki Tileorasi; state television company
evzones – famous border guards from the northern Greek village of Evzoni; they also guard the Parliament building

Filiki Eteria – friendly society; a group of Greeks in exile; formed during Ottoman rule to organise an uprising against the Turks
fluted – (of a column) having vertical indentations on the shaft
frappé – iced coffee
frieze – part of the *entablature* which is above the *architrave*

galaktopoleio (s), galaktopoleia (pl) – a shop which sells dairy products
Geometric period (1200-800 BC) – period characterised by pottery decorated with geometric designs; sometimes referred to as Greece's 'dark age'
GESEE – Greek trade union association
giouvetsi – casserole of meat and pasta

Hellas, Ellas or Ellada – the Greek name for Greece
Hellenistic period – prosperous, influential period of Greek civilisation ushered in by Alexander the Great's empire-building and lasting until the Roman sacking of Corinth in 146 BC
Helots – original inhabitants of Lakonia whom the Spartans used as slaves
hora – main town (usually on an island)

iconostasis – altar screen embellished with icons
Ionic – order of Greek architecture characterised by a column with truncated flutes and capitals with ornaments resembling scrolls

kafeneio (s), kafeneia (pl) – traditionally a male-only coffee house where cards and backgammon are played
kafeteria – upmarket *kafeneio*, mainly for younger people
kalderimi – cobbled footpath
kasseri – mild, slightly rubbery sheep's-milk cheese
kastro – walled-in town
Katharevousa – purist Greek language; very rarely used these days
katholikon – principal church of a monastic complex
kefi – an undefinable feeling of good spirit, without which no Greek can have a good time
KKE – Kommounistiko Komma Elladas; Greek communist party

Koine – Greek language used in pre-Byzantine times; the language of the church liturgy
kore – female statue of the Archaic period; see *kouros*
kouros – male statue of the Archaic period, characterised by a stiff body posture and enigmatic smile
KTEL – Kino Tamio Ispraxeon Leoforion; national bus cooperative; runs all long-distance bus services
Kypriako – the 'Cyprus issue'; politically sensitive and never forgotten by Greeks and Greek Cypriots

libation – in ancient Greece, wine or food which was offered to the gods
Linear A – Minoan script; so far undeciphered
Linear B – Mycenaean script; has been deciphered
lyra – small violin-like instrument, played on the knee; common in Cretan and Pontian music

malakas – literally 'wanker'; used as a familiar term of address, or as an insult, depending on context
mangas – 'wide boy' or 'dude'; originally a person of the underworld, now any streetwise person
mayiria – cook houses
megaron – central room of a Mycenaean palace
meltemi – north-easterly wind which blows throughout much of Greece during the summer
metope – the sculpted section of a *Doric frieze*
meze (s), mezedes (pl) – appetiser
Middle Age – see *Archaic period*
Minoan civilisation (3000-1100 BC) – Bronze Age culture of Crete named after the mythical king Minos and characterised by pottery and metalwork of great beauty and artisanship
moni – monastery or convent
Mycenaean civilisation (1900-1100 BC) – first great civilisation of the Greek mainland, characterised by powerful independent city-states ruled by kings; also known as the Achaean civilisation
myzithra – soft sheep's-milk cheese

narthex – porch of a church
nave – aisle of a church
Nea Dimokratia – New Democracy; conservative political party
necropolis – literally 'city of the dead'; ancient cemetery
nefos – cloud; usually used to refer to pollution in Athens
NEL – Naftiliaki Eteria Lesvou; Lesvos shipping company
neo kyma – 'new wave'; left-wing music of the boîtes and clubs of 1960s Athens
nomarhia – prefecture building
nomos – prefectures into which the regions and island groups of Greece are divided
nymphaeum – in ancient Greece, building containing a fountain and often dedicated to nymphs

OA – Olympiaki Aeroporia or Olympic Airways; Greece's national airline and major domestic air carrier
odeion – ancient Greek indoor theatre
odos – street
ohi – 'no'; what the Greeks said to Mussolini's ultimatum when he said surrender or be invaded; the Italians were subsequently repelled and the event is celebrated on October 28
omphalos – sacred stone at Delphi which the ancient Greeks believed marked the centre of the world
OSE – Organismos Sidirodromon Ellados; Greek railways organisation
OTE – Organismos Tilepikinonion Ellados; Greece's major telecommunications carrier
oud – a bulbous, stringed instrument with a sharply raked-back head
ouzeri (s), ouzeria (pl) – place which serves *ouzo* and light snacks
ouzo – a distilled spirit made from grapes and flavoured with aniseed

Panagia – Mother of God; name frequently used for churches

Pantokrator – painting or mosaic of Christ in the centre of the dome of a Byzantine church

pantopoleio – general store

PAO – Panathinaïkos football club

PAOK – main Thessaloniki football club

paralia – waterfront

PASOK – Panellinio Sosialistiko Komma; Greek socialist party

pediment – triangular section (often filled with sculpture) above the columns, found at the front and back of a classical Greek temple

periptero (s), periptera (pl) – street kiosk

peristyle – columns surrounding a building (usually a temple) or courtyard

pinakotheke – picture gallery

pithos (s), pithoi (pl) – large Minoan storage jar

plateia – square

Politiki Anixi – Political Spring; centrist political party

Pomaks – minority, non-Turkic Muslim people from northern Greece

Pontians – Greeks whose ancestral home was on the Black Sea coast of Turkey

PRO-PO – Prognostiko Podosferou; Greek football pools

propylon (s), propylaia (pl) – elaborately built main entrance to an ancient city or sanctuary; a propylon had one gateway and a propylaia more than one

psarotaverna – taverna specialising in seafood

psistaria – restaurant serving grilled food

rembetika – blues songs commonly associated with the underworld of the 1920s

retsina – resinated white wine

rhyton – another name for a libation vessel

rizitika – traditional, patriotic songs of Crete

sacristy – room attached to a church where sacred vessels etc are kept

sandouri – hammered dulcimer from Asia Minor

Sarakatsani – Greek-speaking nomadic shepherd community from northern Greece

SEO – Syllogos Ellinon Orivaton; Greek mountaineers' association

skites (s), skiti (pl) – hermit's dwelling

Skopia – what the Greeks call the Former Yugoslav Republic of Macedonia (FYROM)

skyladika – literally 'dog songs'; popular, but not lyrically challenging, blues songs often sung in *bouzoukia* nightclubs

spilia – cave

stele (s), stelae (pl) – grave stone which stands upright

stoa – long colonnaded building, usually in an *agora*; used as a meeting place and shelter in ancient Greece

taverna – traditional restaurant which serves food and wine

temblon – votive screen

tholos – Mycenaean tomb shaped like a beehive

toumberleki – small lap drum played with the fingers

triglyph – sections of a *Doric frieze* between the *metopes*

trireme – ancient Greek galley with three rows of oars on each side

tsikoudia – Cretan version of *tsipouro*

Tsingani – Gypsies or Roma

tsipouro – distilled spirit made from grapes

vaulted – having an arched roof, normally of brick or stone

velenza – flokati rug

Vlach – traditional, semi-nomadic shepherds from northern Greece who speak a Latin-based dialect

volta – promenade; evening stroll

volute – spiral decoration on *Ionic* capitals

xythomyzithra – soft sheep's-milk cheese

zaharoplasteio (s), zaharoplasteia (pl) – patisserie; shop selling cakes, chocolates, sweets and, sometimes, alcoholic drinks

Acknowledgments

THANKS

Many thanks to the travellers who used the last edition and wrote to us with helpful hints, useful advice and interesting anecdotes:

A Argyrou, Abigail Sandra, Ada Medak, Adrian Serafin, Adriane McFetridge, Alan Quinn, Alan Reece, Alex Bosser, Alison Campbell, Allan M Healy, Allen Chao, Amanda Cranmer, Ammanuel Lambert, Ana Steiner, Anders Allgulin, Andrea Williams, Andrew McIlwraith, Andrew Voutsis, Angel Villanveva, Angela Le Chen, Anita Bocquee, Anna Cantoni, Anna Hayward, Anna Ptaszynska, Armand Desroches, Audrey & John McLennan, Avrìl M Gater, Barbara Bagnell, Barbara Lutstorf, Barry Gavrich, Barry Hirtle, Barry Ward, Bas Jansen, Benedikt Lowe, Bert Cattoor, Bethany Parsons, Bill Lowe, Birgith Lange Nielsen, Blaguer, Blaz Krhin, Bob & Toos Hempenius, Bob Cromwell, Bob Lester, Brian & Sue Phillips, Brodie Woodland, Bruce Allen, Bruce Rogers, Burak Sadic, Carl Mackander, Carl Stein, Carley Aldridge, Carmen Montes Rico, Carol & Brian Little, Carol Ann Bernheim, Carol Iffland, Carol P Christ, Carole & Mark Shaughnessy, Carole Grimshaw, Carolyn Sequermank, Carolyn & Maree, Carolyn Spice, Carolyn Wingfield, Cathy S, Cato Kjaervik, Charles Hawkins, Charlotte Alcock, Charlotte Cross, Charlotte Larson, Chris & Peter Vasiliadis, Christian Ohly, Christina Sellis, Christina Soames, Christine Lea, Christopher M P Findlay, Claire Hill, Claire Smith, Clare Hogan, Claudia Schatz, Cliff Goulet, Colin & Gail Priest, D Dubbin, Dan Abbott, Dana Paniagua, Dave Ferguson, Dave Mountain, David Barnett, David Loukidelis, David Pindar, Deborah Lyons, Denis Tinsley Crewe, Denmin Moserman, Deryn Hardie, Diamantopoulos Kostas, Diamond D, Diana DePasquale, Didomizio Joel, Digger Dave, Dirk Drijbooms, Dirk Wahl, Dominic & Sam Guest, Donald D Binder, Douglas Mills, Dr Angela Zante, Dragan Simic, Dubravka Martinovic, Dwight & Linda Cassell, E A Greenway, E Budniak, E J D Swabey, E J Dagnell, Effie Antonara, Effie D Varitimidis, Eileen Noland, El Suttipong Aramkun, Elizabeth Ailue, Elizabeth Nead, Emma Dornan, Emmanuela Agatstein Erik Lobben, Eugenia Klopsis, Evan Grambas F Blackwood, Fatma Demirel, Flora Aaron Fokke Bokker, Francesco Randisi, Francine Belzile, Frank Hughes, Fred Bohrer, G Jones Gabrielle, Gary A White, Gary Budd, Gary Hockings, Gary Moss, Geff Binns, Gemma Ruijs, George Bangian, George Jackson Gerald Brisch, Gosta Koeck, Greg Arnold, Greg Lloyd Smith, Greg Vekar, H A Eiselt, Hanneke Faber, Harold & Jill Wicks, Harry Kaitis, Heather Burns, Heather Nielsen, Heikki Pauts Helen Durham, Helen Goss, Helen Leung Henrik Rasch, Henry Fan, Hugo Schurink, I C Davies, Ian & Sue Thompson, Ian Colford, Ian J Macdonald, Ida Strasser, Imogen Collins-Thomas, Ingrid Brink, Ira Kalb, Irina Simos, Irmi Schafer, Isobel Cunningham, J B Fairhall, J Herweg, J P Decker, J Schaper, Jaap Stavenuiter, James Gallantry, James Grant, James Howell, James Lea, James P Brown, Jan & Ian Scott, Jane & Blue Robinson, Jane Brodie, Jane Jenkins, Janine & Phillip Mills, Janine Georgder, Jaromir Javurek, Jay Jaggard, Jay Klein, Jay Kozak, Jay Russian, Jayne Verity, Jean & Michael Day, Jeff Bell, Jeff Lawrence, Jeffrey To, Jenny Barnes, Jenny Raisin, Jim Lotz, Jim Manion, Jo Reed, Jocelyn James, Jodie Stewart, Joe Bergen, Joel Hamm, Johan Thury, John Armarantides, John Blake More, John Dite, John Holden, John Kemp, John Knight, John Lennan, John Mantarakis, John McLennan, Johnny Huang, Jonathan Oakes, Juan Cories, Judd Millen, Judy Clarke, Justin Baty, Kara Cornish, Karen A Stafford, Karl O'Neill, Katerina Kostopoulou, Kathryn Freund, Kathryn Sharfman, Katie Buchanan, Kelly Keegan, Ken Cavender, Ken Shaw, Kenneth Austin, Kevin Mackenzie, Kim Frederic-Klein, Kim Ricci, Kirsten F, Kjetil Roe, L Middleton, L P Hennevanger, Laura Milsom, Leah Wilkes, Lefteris Trakos, Lena Liden, Lene Charlotte Tynes, Leon Macdonald, Lies

Hoekstra-Kan, Liliana Bosancic, Lillian Barstad, Line Lausted, Lisa Marie Gonzales, Lois Wickstrom, Louise & John Brekelmans, Louise Holman, Lucia Correia, Luke Hildmard, M B Kruyswyk, Malcolm Ward, Manuelle Prunier, Marco Wopkes, Margaret Hodgskin, Margrit Tuente, Maria Panousos, Maria Stadtmueller, Marianthe McLiesh, Marie Trimboli, Marika Poscic, Marion Reed, Mark & Frieda Van Scharem, Mark Ellison, Marleen Enschedé, Marvin Feldman, Mary Repucci, Matt Barrett, May Johnson, Meera Shah, Megan Cox, Melanie Dumont, Melissa Anderson, Melissa Michels, Melissa Schilling, Menno Dekker, Michael & Sarah Chaskes, Michael Bauer, Michael Body, Michael Richards, Michelle Kloet, Michelle Kunding, Mick Parker, Mike Vormittag, Mike Webber, Milly Morton, M'Leah Woodward, Morgan & Mela Handsaclarides, Morman Foot, Morten Wendt, Naomi Savva, Natalie Camara, Natalie Cleary, Neil & Delores Thistle, Nic Rone, Nick & Sue Howes, Nick Evangelinos, Nicola Harrison, Ninc Es Honan, Noel Kantaris, P McDonald, Pam Anders, Patrik Ferkl, Paul White, Paulien Wagemans, Penelope Krumm, Penny Rhodes, Peter Ceulemans, Peter Harrison, Peter Jern, Peter Malcolm, Peter Marks, Peter Mazis, Philippe Meyer, Pola Rapaport, Prof Benita Goldman, Prof U Luz, Prue Murray, R Burns, R J Conn, Randolf Nales, Raymond McFadgen, Reah Sutherland, Rebecca Davies, Rebekah Fowler, Richard & Sylvia Hutchinson, Richard F Deich, Richard Owen, Richard Safra, Rob Cook, Robert & Robyn Williams, Robert C McLaughlin, Robert Carpenter, Robin & Bob Dunn, Robyn St Clare, Rokos Frngus, Roland Vancappel, Rosalind Thoday, Ruth Chadney, Ruth Stanley, Sally Winterbon, Sam Goothouse, Samuel B Johnson, Sandra De Buck, Sanjay Kewlani, Sara & Bertrand Maltaverne, Sarah Hall, Sarah Silvester, Sarah Warne, Scott Eden, Scott Stoermer, Scott Tillman, Sebastian Schotte, Setz Benno, Shabnam Hussain, Shama Simms, Shawna Parks, Simon Stein, Sophia Shourounis, Stathis Mihos, Stathis Vassileiou, Stergios Kaprinis, Steve & Margy Baron, Steve Harper, Stuart Michael, Susan Daniels, Susan Davisson, Susan Schuren, Susan Spaulding, T G Dallas, Tasso Papadopoulos, Tatiana K Papas, Tatiana Mamula, Ted Bergman, Ted Theodore, Terry Teoh, Tessa Kirkpatrick, Theo Baak, Thomas Paschold, Tina Doukas, Tommy Johansson, Tony Weston, Toulla Panayiotou, Ursula Blum, Ursula Wynards, Valerie Panis, Valkan Farkas, Vanee Pang, Victor Amezwa, Vivienne & Trevor Williams, Walter van Munster, Wanda & Barry Syner, Warren Smythe, Wendy Tubbax, Werner Nouwen, Will Robert, William Bliss, Willy Duarte van Selm, Wolfgang Held, Wolfram Sparber, Yang-Un Eiman, Yvonne de Jong.

Lonely Planet Journeys

Journeys is a unique collection of travel writing – published by the company that understands travel better than anyone else. It is a series for anyone who has ever experienced – or dreamed of – the magical moment when they encountered a strange culture or saw a place for the first time. They are tales to read while you're planning a trip, while you're on the road or while you're in an armchair in front of a fire.

These outstanding titles explore our planet through the eyes of a diverse group of international writers. JOURNEYS books catch the spirit of a place, illuminate a culture, recount a crazy adventure or introduce a fascinating way of life. They always entertain, and always enrich the experience of travel.

MALI BLUES
Traveling to an African Beat
Lieve Joris (translated by Sam Garrett)

Drought, rebel uprisings, ethnic conflict: these are the predominant images of West Africa. But as Lieve Joris travels in Senegal, Mauritania and Mali, she meets survivors, fascinating individuals charting new ways of living between tradition and modernity. With her remarkable gift for drawing out people's stories, Joris brilliantly captures the rhythms of a world that refuses to give in.

THE GATES OF DAMASCUS
Lieve Joris (translated by Sam Garrett)

This best-selling book is a beautifully drawn portrait of day-to-day life in modern Syria. Through her intimate contact with local people, Lieve Joris draws us into the fascinating world that lies behind the gates of Damascus. Hala's husband is a political prisoner, jailed for his opposition to the Assad regime; through the author's friendship with Hala we see how Syrian politics impacts on the lives of ordinary people.

THE OLIVE GROVE
Travels in Greece
Katherine Kizilos

Katherine Kizilos travels to fabled islands, troubled border zones and her family's village deep in the mountains. She vividly evokes breathtaking landscapes, generous people and passionate politics, capturing the complexities of a country she loves.

'beautifully captures the real tensions of Greece' – *Sunday Times*

KINGDOM OF THE FILM STARS
Journey into Jordan
Annie Caulfield

Kingdom of the Film Stars is a travel book and a love story. With honesty and humour, Annie Caulfield writes of travelling in Jordan and falling in love with a Bedouin with film-star looks.

She offers fascinating insights into the country – from the tent life of traditional women to the hustle of downtown Amman – and unpicks tight-woven western myths about the Arab world.

LONELY PLANET

Lonely Planet Travel Atlases

Lonely Planet has long been famous for the number and quality of its guidebook maps. Now we've gone one step further and produced a handy companion series: Lonely Planet travel atlases – maps of a country produced in book form.

Unlike other maps, which look good but lead travellers astray, our travel atlases have been researched on the road by Lonely Planet's experienced team of writers. All details are carefully checked to ensure the atlas corresponds with the equivalent Lonely Planet guidebook.

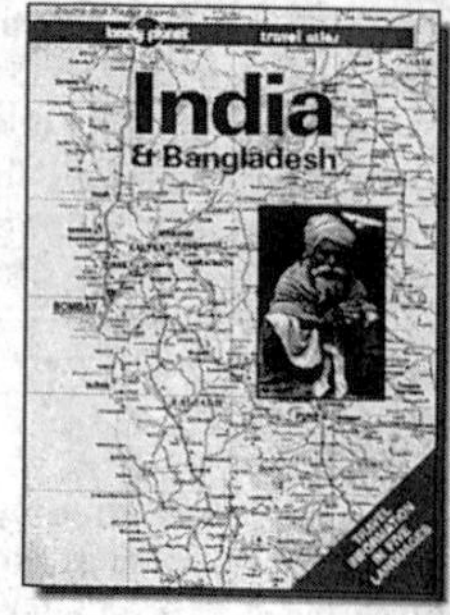

- full-colour throughout
- maps researched and checked by Lonely Planet authors
- place names correspond with Lonely Planet guidebooks
- no confusing spelling differences
- legend and travelling information in English, French, German, Japanese and Spanish
- size: 230 x 160 mm

Available now: Chile & Easter Island • Egypt • India & Bangladesh • Israel & the Palestinian Territories • Jordan, Syria & Lebanon • Kenya • Laos • Portugal • South Africa, Lesotho & Swaziland • Thailand • Turkey • Vietnam • Zimbabwe, Botswana & Namibia

---

Lonely Planet TV Series & Videos

Lonely Planet travel guides have been brought to life on television screens around the world. Like our guides, the programs are based on the joy of independent travel and look honestly at some of the most exciting, picturesque and frustrating places in the world. Each show is presented by one of three travellers from Australia, England or the USA and combines an innovative mixture of video, Super-8 film, atmospheric soundscapes and original music.

Videos of each episode – containing additional footage not shown on television – are available from good book and video shops, but the availability of individual videos varies with regional screening schedules.

Video destinations include: Alaska • American Rockies • Argentina • Australia – The South-East • Baja California & the Copper Canyon • Brazil • Central Asia • Chile & Easter Island • Corsica, Sicily & Sardinia – The Mediterranean Islands • East Africa (Tanzania & Zanzibar) • Cuba • Ecuador & the Galapagos Islands • Ethiopia • Greenland & Iceland • Hungary & Romania • Indonesia • Israel & the Sinai Desert • Jamaica • Japan • La Ruta Maya • London • The Middle East (Syria, Jordan & Lebanon • Morocco • New York City • Northern Spain • North India • Outback Australia • Pacific Islands (Fiji, Solomon Islands & Vanuatu) • Pakistan • Peru • The Philippines • South Africa & Lesotho • South India • South West China • South West USA • Trekking in Uganda & Congo • Turkey • Vietnam • West Africa • Zimbabwe, Botswana & Namibia

The Lonely Planet TV series is produced by: Pilot Productions
The Old Studio
18 Middle Row
London W10 5AT, UK

LONELY PLANET

Lonely Planet Online

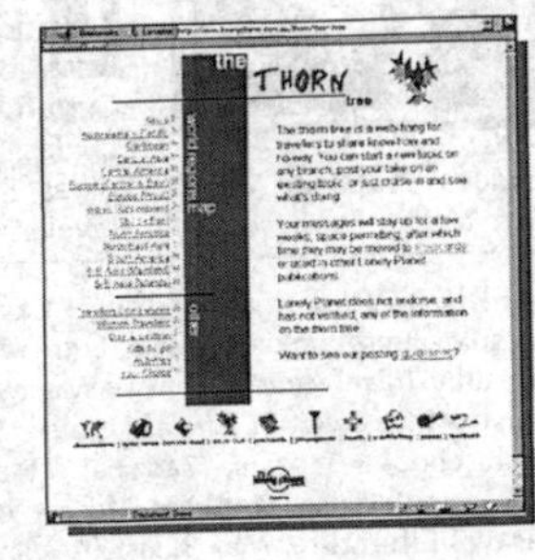

Whether you've just begun planning your next trip, or you're chasing down specific info on currency regulations or visa requirements, check out Lonely Planet Online for up-to-the-minute travel information.

As well as miniguides to more than 250 destinations, you'll find maps, photos, travel news, health and visa updates, travel advisories and discussion of the ecological and political issues you need to be aware of as you travel. You'll also find timely upgrades to popular guidebooks that you can print out and stick in the back of your book.

There's an online travellers' forum (The Thorn Tree) where you can share your experience of life on the road, meet travel companions and ask other travellers for their recommendations and advice.

There's also a complete and up-to-date list of all Lonely Planet travel products including travel guides, diving and snorkeling guides, phrasebooks, atlases, travel literature and videos, and a simple online ordering facility if you can't find the book you want elsewhere.

Lonely Planet Diving & Snorkeling Guides

Beautifully illustrated with full-colour photos throughout, Lonely Planet's Pisces books explore the world's best diving and snorkeling areas and prepare divers for what to expect when they get there, both topside and underwater.

Dive sites are described in detail with specifics on depths, visibility, level of difficulty, special conditions, underwater photography tips and common and unusual marine life present. You'll also find practical logistical information and coverage on topside activities and attractions, sections on diving health and safety, plus listings for diving services, live-aboards, dive resorts and tourist offices.

Guides by Region

Lonely Planet is known worldwide for publishing practical, reliable and no-nonsense travel information in our guides and on our Web site. The Lonely Planet list covers just about every accessible part of the world. Currently there are 16 series: Travel guides, Shoestring guides, Condensed guides, Phrasebooks, Read This First, Healthy Travel, Walking guides, Cycling guides, Watching Wildlife guides, Pisces Diving & Snorkeling guides, City Maps, Road Atlases, Out to Eat, World Food, Journeys travel literature and Pictorials.

AFRICA Africa on a shoestring • Cairo • Cape Town • Cape Town City Map • East Africa • Egypt • Egyptian Arabic phrasebook • Ethiopia, Eritrea & Djibouti • Ethiopian (Amharic) phrasebook • The Gambia & Senegal • Healthy Travel Africa • Kenya • Malawi • Morocco • Moroccan Arabic phrasebook • Mozambique • Read This First: Africa • South Africa, Lesotho & Swaziland • Southern Africa • Southern Africa Road Atlas • Swahili phrasebook • Tanzania, Zanzibar & Pemba • Trekking in East Africa • Tunisia • Watching Wildlife East Africa • Watching Wildlife Southern Africa • West Africa • World Food Morocco • Zimbabwe, Botswana & Namibia
Travel Literature: Mali Blues: Traveling to an African Beat • The Rainbird: A Central African Journey • Songs to an African Sunset: A Zimbabwean Story

AUSTRALIA & THE PACIFIC Auckland • Australia • Australian phrasebook • Australia Road Atlas • Bush-walking in Australia •Cycling New Zealand • Fiji • Fijian phrasebook • Healthy Travel Australia, NZ and the Pacific • Islands of Australia's Great Barrier Reef • Melbourne • Melbourne City Map • Micronesia • New Caledonia • New South Wales & the ACT • New Zealand • Northern Territory • Outback Australia • Out to Eat – Melbourne • Out to Eat – Sydney • Papua New Guinea • Pidgin phrasebook • Queensland • Rarotonga & the Cook Islands • Samoa • Solomon Islands • South Australia • South Pacific • South Pacific phrasebook • Sydney • Sydney City Map • Sydney Condensed • Tahiti & French Polynesia • Tasmania • Tonga • Tramping in New Zealand • Vanuatu • Victoria • Watching Wildlife Australia • Western Australia
Travel Literature: Islands in the Clouds: Travels in the Highlands of New Guinea • Kiwi Tracks: A New Zealand Journey • Sean & David's Long Drive

CENTRAL AMERICA & THE CARIBBEAN Bahamas, Turks & Caicos • Baja California • Bermuda • Central America on a shoestring • Costa Rica • Costa Rica Spanish phrasebook • Cuba • Dominican Republic & Haiti • Eastern Caribbean • Guatemala • Guatemala, Belize & Yucatán: La Ruta Maya • Healthy Travel Central & South America • Jamaica • Mexico • Mexico City • Panama • Puerto Rico • Read This First: Central & South America • World Food Mexico • Yucatán
Travel Literature: Green Dreams: Travels in Central America

EUROPE Amsterdam • Amsterdam City Map • Amsterdam Condensed • Andalucía • Austria • Baltic States phrasebook • Barcelona • Barcelona City Map • Berlin • Berlin City Map • Britain • British phrasebook • Brussels, Bruges & Antwerp • Budapest • Budapest City Map • Canary Islands • Central Europe • Central Europe phrasebook • Corfu & the Ionians • Corsica • Crete • Crete Condensed • Croatia • Cycling Britain • Cycling France • Cyprus • Czech & Slovak Republics • Denmark • Dublin • Dublin City Map • Eastern Europe • Eastern Europe phrasebook • Edinburgh • Estonia, Latvia & Lithuania • Europe on a shoestring • Finland • Florence • France • Frankfurt Condensed • French phrasebook • Georgia, Armenia & Azerbaijan • Germany • German phrasebook • Greece • Greek Islands • Greek phrasebook • Hungary • Iceland, Greenland & the Faroe Islands • Ireland • Istanbul • Italian phrasebook • Italy • Krakow • Lisbon • The Loire • London • London City Map • London Condensed • Madrid • Malta • Mediterranean Europe • Mediterranean Europe phrasebook • Moscow • Mozambique • Munich • Norway • Out to Eat – London • Paris • Paris City Map • Paris Condensed • Poland • Portugal • Portuguese phrasebook • Prague • Prague City Map • Provence & the Côte d'Azur • Read This First: Europe • Romania & Moldova • Rome • Russia, Ukraine & Belarus • Russian phrasebook • Scandinavian & Baltic Europe • Scandinavian Europe phrasebook • Scotland • Sicily • Slovenia • South-West France • Spain • Spanish phrasebook • St Petersburg • St Petersburg City Map • Sweden • Switzerland • Trekking in Spain • Tuscany • Ukrainian phrasebook • Venice • Vienna • Walking in Britain • Walking in France • Walking in Ireland • Walking in Italy • Walking in Spain • Walking in Switzerland • Western Europe • Western Europe phrasebook • World Food France • World Food Ireland • World Food Italy • World Food Spain
Travel Literature: Love and War in the Apennines • The Olive Grove: Travels in Greece • On the Shores of the Mediterranean • Round Ireland in Low Gear • A Small Place in Italy

INDIAN SUBCONTINENT Bangladesh • Bengali phrasebook • Bhutan • Delhi • Goa • Healthy Travel Asia & India • Hindi & Urdu phrasebook • India • Indian Himalaya • Karakoram Highway • Kerala • Mumbai

LONELY PLANET

Mail Order

Lonely Planet products are distributed worldwide. They are also available by mail order from Lonely Planet, so if you have difficulty finding a title please write to us. North and South American residents should write to 150 Linden St, Oakland, CA 94607, USA; European and African residents should write to 10a Spring Place, London NW5 3BH, UK; and residents of other countries to Locked Bag 1, Footscray, Victoria 3011, Australia.

(Bombay) • Nepal • Nepali phrasebook • Pakistan • Rajasthan • Read This First: Asia & India • South India • Sri Lanka • Sri Lanka phrasebook • Tibet • Tibetan phrasebook • Trekking in the Indian Himalaya • Trekking in the Karakoram & Hindukush • Trekking in the Nepal Himalaya
Travel Literature: The Age of Kali: Indian Travels and Encounters • Hello Goodnight: A Life of Goa • In Rajasthan • A Season in Heaven: True Tales from the Road to Kathmandu • Shopping for Buddhas • A Short Walk in the Hindu Kush • Slowly Down the Ganges

ISLANDS OF THE INDIAN OCEAN Madagascar & Comoros • Maldives • Mauritius, Réunion & Seychelles

MIDDLE EAST & CENTRAL ASIA Bahrain, Kuwait & Qatar • Central Asia • Central Asia phrasebook • Dubai • Hebrew phrasebook • Iran • Israel & the Palestinian Territories • Istanbul • Istanbul City Map • Istanbul to Cairo on a shoestring • Jerusalem • Jerusalem City Map • Jordan • Lebanon • Middle East • Oman & the United Arab Emirates • Syria • Turkey • Turkish phrasebook • World Food Turkey • Yemen
Travel Literature: Black on Black: Iran Revisited • The Gates of Damascus • Kingdom of the Film Stars: Journey into Jordan

NORTH AMERICA Alaska • Boston • Boston City Map • California & Nevada • California Condensed • Canada • Chicago • Chicago City Map • Deep South • Florida • Hawaii • Hiking in Alaska • Hiking in the USA • Honolulu • Las Vegas • Los Angeles • Miami • Miami City Map • New England • New Orleans • New York City • New York City City Map • New York City Condensed • New York, New Jersey & Pennsylvania • Oahu • Out to Eat – San Francisco • Pacific Northwest • Puerto Rico • Rocky Mountains • San Francisco • San Francisco City Map • Seattle • Southwest • Texas • USA • USA phrasebook • Vancouver • Virginia & the Capital Region • Washington, DC City Map • World Food Deep South, USA
Travel Literature: Caught Inside: A Surfer's Year on the California Coast • Drive Thru America

NORTH-EAST ASIA Beijing • Cantonese phrasebook • China • Hiking in Japan • Hong Kong • Hong Kong City Map • Hong Kong Condensed • Hong Kong, Macau & Guangzhou • Japan • Japanese phrasebook • Korea • Korean phrasebook • Kyoto • Mandarin phrasebook • Mongolia • Mongolian phrasebook • Seoul • South-West China • Taiwan • Tokyo
Travel Literature: In Xanadu: A Quest • Lost Japan

SOUTH AMERICA Argentina, Uruguay & Paraguay • Bolivia • Brazil • Brazilian phrasebook • Buenos Aires • Chile & Easter Island • Colombia • Ecuador & the Galapagos Islands • Healthy Travel Central & South America • Latin American Spanish phrasebook • Peru • Quechua phrasebook • Read This First: Central & South America • Rio de Janeiro • Rio de Janeiro City Map • Santiago • South America on a shoestring • Santiago • Trekking in the Patagonian Andes • Venezuela
Travel Literature: Full Circle: A South American Journey

SOUTH-EAST ASIA Bali & Lombok • Bangkok • Bangkok City Map • Burmese phrasebook • Cambodia • Hanoi • Healthy Travel Asia & India • Hill Tribes phrasebook • Ho Chi Minh City • Indonesia • Indonesian phrasebook • Indonesia's Eastern Islands • Jakarta • Java • Lao phrasebook • Laos • Malay phrasebook • Malaysia, Singapore & Brunei • Myanmar (Burma) • Philippines • Pilipino (Tagalog) phrasebook • Read This First: Asia & India • Singapore • Singapore City Map • South-East Asia on a shoestring • South-East Asia phrasebook • Thailand • Thailand's Islands & Beaches • Thailand, Vietnam, Laos & Cambodia Road Atlas • Thai phrasebook • Vietnam • Vietnamese phrasebook • World Food Thailand • World Food Vietnam

ALSO AVAILABLE: Antarctica • The Arctic • The Blue Man: Tales of Travel, Love and Coffee • Brief Encounters: Stories of Love, Sex & Travel • Chasing Rickshaws • The Last Grain Race • Lonely Planet Unpacked • Not the Only Planet: Science Fiction Travel Stories • Lonely Planet On the Edge • Sacred India • Travel with Children • Travel Photography: A Guide to Taking Better Pictures

FREE Lonely Planet Newsletters

We love hearing from you and think you'd like to hear from us.

Planet Talk

Our FREE quarterly printed newsletter is full of tips from travellers and anecdotes from Lonely Planet guidebook authors. Every issue is packed with up-to-date travel news and advice, and includes:

- a postcard from Lonely Planet co-founder Tony Wheeler
- a swag of mail from travellers
- a look at life on the road through the eyes of a Lonely Planet author
- topical health advice
- prizes for the best travel yarn
- news about forthcoming Lonely Planet events
- a complete list of Lonely Planet books and other titles

To join our mailing list, residents of the UK, Europe and Africa can email us at go@lonelyplanet.co.uk; residents of North and South America can email us at info@lonelyplanet.com; the rest of the world can email us at talk2us@lonelyplanet.com.au, or contact any Lonely Planet office.

Comet

Our FREE monthly email newsletter brings you all the latest travel news, features, interviews, competitions, destination ideas, travellers' tips & tales, Q&As, raging debates and related links. Find out what's new on the Lonely Planet Web site and which books are about to hit the shelves.

Subscribe from your desktop: www.lonelyplanet.com/comet

~~Athens~~

Argos p. 239 ✓

~~Epidavros p. 252~~

~~Tripolis p. 252~~

~~Koroni p. 278~~

~~Larisa p. 308~~

~~Meteora p. 324~~

~~[illegible]~~

Andros p. 423

Syros p. 442

Santorini p. 486

Nafi p. 488

Sikinos p. 490

~~[illegible]~~ p. 506

Crete Chania, Sitia, Hania

Mirtos, Sougia

Tilos

Astypalea

Anne

~~School~~ 7242460

home 7236313

Crouching Tiger

Requiem for a dream

Mansfield Park

Sweet November - Themistokleos 5

Titania 5:30, 8, 10:30

check email

sell books

check ferry length / placement

mail letter

reserve room?

get money

enjoy day

Index

Abbreviations

Ath – Athens
Att – Attica
Cen – Central Greece
Cre – Crete
Cyc – Cyclades
Dod – Dodecanese
Evi – Evia
Ion – Ionian Islands
NEA – North-Eastern Aegean Islands
NG – Northern Greece
Pel – Peloponnese
SG – Saronic Gulf Islands
Spo – Sporades

Text

A

Bold indicates maps.

B

Bold indicates maps.

Bold indicates maps.

Bold indicates maps.

Bold indicates maps.

R

S

Boxed Text

MAP LEGEND

HYDROGRAPHY

- Coastline
- River, Creek
- Lake
- Canal
- Spring, Rapids
- Waterfalls

AREA FEATURES

- Building
- Park, Gardens
- Cemetery
- Market
- Pedestrian Mall
- Urban Area

ROUTES & LAND TRANSPORT

- Freeway
- Highway
- Major Road
- Minor Road
- Unsealed Road
- City Highway
- Road
- City Street
- Lane
- Pedestrian Mall
- Tunnel
- Train Route & Station
- Metro & Station
- Tramway
- Cable Car or Chairlift
- Walking Track

WATER TRANSPORT

- Daily Ferries
- Low Frequency Ferries
- Hydrofoil
- Excursion Boats

BOUNDARIES

- International
- State

MAP SYMBOLS

- CAPITAL ... National Capital
- CAPITAL ... State Capital
- CITY ... City
- Town ... Town
- Village ... Village
- Place to Stay
- Camping Ground
- Caravan Park
- Hut or Chalet
- Place to Eat
- Pub or Bar
- Airport
- Ancient or City Wall
- Archaeological Site
- Bank
- Beach, Surf Beach
- Border Crossing
- Castle or Fort
- Church
- Cliff or Escarpment
- Embassy
- Hospital
- Lookout
- Mosque
- Monument
- Mountain or Hill
- Museum
- Pass
- Police Station
- Post Office
- Shopping Centre
- Ski field
- Building of Interest
- Swimming Pool
- Synagogue
- Telephone
- Tomb
- Tourist Information
- Transport

Note: not all symbols displayed above appear in this book

LONELY PLANET OFFICES

Australia
PO Box 617, Hawthorn, Victoria 3122
☎ 03 9819 1877 fax 03 9819 6459
email: talk2us@lonelyplanet.com.au

USA
150 Linden St, Oakland, CA 94607
☎ 510 893 8555 TOLL FREE: 800 275 8555
fax 510 893 8572
email: info@lonelyplanet.com

UK
10a Spring Place, London NW5 3BH
☎ 020 7428 4800 fax 020 7428 4828
email: go@lonelyplanet.co.uk

France
1 rue du Dahomey, 75011 Paris
☎ 01 55 25 33 00 fax 01 55 25 33 01
email: bip@lonelyplanet.fr
www.lonelyplanet.fr

World Wide Web: www.lonelyplanet.com *or* AOL keyword: lp
Lonely Planet Images: lpi@lonelyplanet.com.au

METRIC CONVERSION

TEMPERATURE

To convert °C to °F multiply by 1.8 and add 32

To convert °F to °C subtract 32 and multiply by .55

LENGTH, DISTANCE & AREA	multiply by
inches to centimetres	2.54
centimetres to inches	0.39
feet to metres	0.30
metres to feet	3.28
yards to metres	0.91
metres to yards	1.09
miles to kilometres	1.61
kilometres to miles	0.62
acres to hectares	0.40
hectares to acres	2.47

WEIGHT	multiply by
ounces to grams	28.35
grams to ounces	0.035
pounds to kilograms	0.45
kilograms to pounds	2.21
British tons to kilograms	1016
US tons to kilograms	907

A British ton is 2240 lbs, a US ton is 2000 lbs

VOLUME	multiply by
imperial gallons to litres	4.55
litres to imperial gallons	0.22
US gallons to litres	3.79
litres to US gallons	0.26

5 imperial gallons equals 6 US gallons

a litre is slightly more than a US quart, slightly less than a British one

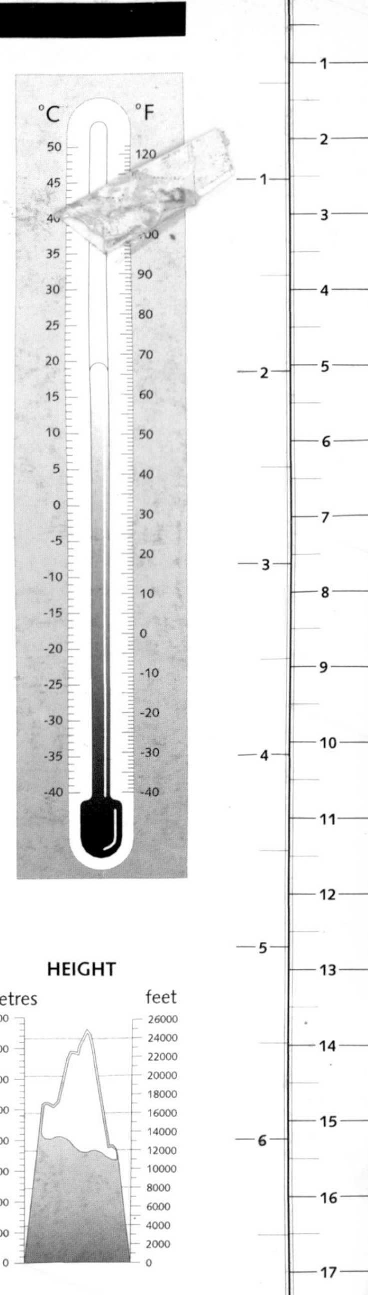

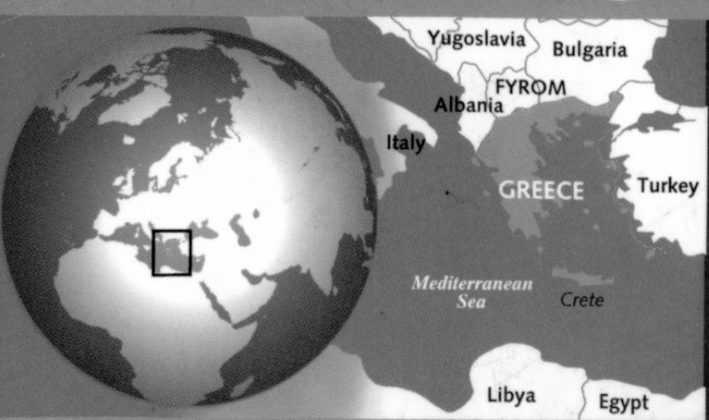

For reliable and authoritative travel information reach for your Lonely Planet guide
– The Time[s]

As usual the guide-book standard is set by Lonely Planet
– Outside

Whether you want to escape to a quiet island beach, trek through the mountains of mainland Greece or live it up in Athens, all the information you need is right here at your fingertips.

- 140 easy-to-read maps, including plans of ancient sites
- new, expanded coverage of the Cyclades
- the latest information on inter-island ferries, catamarans and hydrofoils
- hundreds of places to stay, from cosy *domatia* to centuries-old monasteries
- comprehensive coverage of major sites and museums

Also available from Lonely Planet:

Greek phrasebook, Greek Island[s], Crete, Corfu & the Ionians, Mediterranean Europe, Mediterranean Europe phrasebo[ok], Western Europe, Western Europ[e] phrasebook

ISBN 0 - 86442 - 682 - 8

9 780864 426826

USA	$19.95
UK	£12.99
France	160,00 FF

4th Edition

Cover photograph by Neil Setchfield, Lonely Planet Images

News, views & updates: *www.lonelyplanet.com*